The Law of
Tax-Exempt Organizations

NONPROFIT LAW, FINANCE, AND MANAGEMENT SERIES

The Art of Planned Giving: Understanding Donors and the Culture of Giving by
  Douglas E. White

Charity, Advocacy, and the Law by Bruce R. Hopkins

The Complete Guide to Nonprofit Management by Smith, Bucklin & Associates

Developing Affordable Housing: A Practical Guide for Nonprofit Organizations by
  Bennett L. Hecht

Financial and Accounting Guide for Not-for-Profit Organizations, Fifth Edition by
  Malvern J. Gross, Jr., Richard F. Larkin, Roger S. Bruttomesso, John J. McNally,
  Price Waterhouse LLP

Financial Management for Nonprofit Organizations by Jo Ann Hankin, Alan Seidner, and
  John Zeitlow

Financial Planning for Nonprofit Organizations by Jody Blazek

*Fund-Raising Regulation: A State-by-State Handbook of Registration Forms, Requirements, and
  Procedures* by Seth Perlman and Betsy Hills Bush

Intermediate Sanctions: Curbing Nonprofit Abuse by Bruce R. Hopkins and
  D. Benson Tesdahl

International Guide to Nonprofit Law by Lester A. Salamon and Stefan Toeplar & Associates

The Law of Fund-Raising, Second Edition by Bruce R. Hopkins

The Law of Tax-Exempt Healthcare Organizations by Thomas K. Hyatt and Bruce R. Hopkins

The Law of Tax-Exempt Organizations, Seventh Edition by Bruce R. Hopkins

The Legal Answer Book for Nonprofit Organizations by Bruce R. Hopkins

A Legal Guide to Starting and Managing a Nonprofit Organization, Second Edition by
  Bruce R. Hopkins

Managing Affordable Housing: A Practical Guide to Creating Stable Communities by
  Bennett L. Hecht, Local Initiatives Support Corporation, and James Stockard

Nonprofit Boards: Roles, Responsibilities, and Performance by Diane J. Duca

The Nonprofit Counsel by Bruce R. Hopkins

The Nonprofit Guide to the Internet by Robbin Zeff

The Nonprofit Law Dictionary by Bruce R. Hopkins

Nonprofit Litigation: A Practical Guide with Forms and Checklists by Steve Bachmann

The Nonprofit Handbook, Second Edition: Volume I—Management by Tracy Daniel Connors

The Nonprofit Manager's Resource Dictionary by Ronald A. Landskroner

Nonprofit Organizations' Business Forms: Disk Edition by John Wiley & Sons, Inc.

Partnerships and Joint Ventures Involving Tax-Exempt Organizations by Michael I. Sanders

Planned Giving: Management, Marketing, and Law by Ronald R. Jordan and
  Katelyn L. Quynn

Private Foundations: Tax Law and Compliance by Bruce R. Hopkins and Jody Blazek

Program Related Investments: A Technical Manual for Foundations by Christie I. Baxter

Reinventing the University: Managing and Financing Institutions of Higher Education by
  Sandra L. Johnson and Sean C. Rush, Coopers & Lybrand, LLP

Strategic Planning for Nonprofit Organizations: A Practical Guide and Workbook by
  Michael Allison and Jude Kaye, Support Center for Nonprofit Management

Streetsmart Financial Basics for Nonprofit Managers by Thomas A. McLaughlin

A Streetsmart Guide to Nonprofit Mergers and Networks by Thomas A. McLaughlin

The Tax Law of Charitable Giving by Bruce R. Hopkins

The Tax Law of Colleges and Universities by Bertrand M. Harding

*Tax Planning and Compliance for Tax-Exempt Organizations: Forms, Checklists, Procedures,
  Second Edition* by Jody Blazek

*The Universal Benefits of Volunteering: A Practical Workbook for Nonprofit Organizations,
  Volunteers, and Corporations* by Walter P. Pidgeon, Jr.

TheLaw of
Tax-Exempt Organizations

SEVENTH EDITION

BRUCE R. HOPKINS

John Wiley & Sons, Inc.
New York • Chichester • Weinheim • Brisbane • Singapore • Toronto

This publication is designed to provide accurate and authoritative information in regard to the subject matter covered. It is sold with the understanding that the publisher is not engaged in rendering legal, accounting, or other professional services. If legal advice or other expert assistance is required, the services of a competent professional person should be sought.

Library of Congress Cataloging-in-Publication Data:
Hopkins, Bruce R.
　　The law of tax-exempt organizations / Bruce R. Hopkins. — 7th ed.
　　　　p.　cm. — (Nonprofit law, finance, and management series)
　　Includes bibliographical references and index.
　　ISBN 0-471-19629-0 (cloth : alk. paper)
　　1. Nonprofit organizations—Taxation—Law and legislation—United
States.　2. Charitable uses, trusts, and foundations—Taxation—
United States.　I. Title.　II. Series.
　KF6449.H6　1998
　343.7306'68—dc21　　　　　　　　　　　　　　　　　97-28975

Printed in the United States of America.

10 9 8 7 6 5 4 3 2

This book is dedicated to my son,
Christopher B. Hopkins, Esq.,
with love.

SUBSCRIPTION NOTICE

This Wiley product is updated on a periodic basis with supplements to reflect important changes in the subject matter. If you purchased this product directly from John Wiley & Sons, Inc., we have already recorded your subscription for this update service.

If, however, you purchased this product from a bookstore and wish to receive future updates and revised or related volumes billed separately with a 30-day examination review, please send your name, company name (if applicable), address, and the title of the product to:

Supplement Department
John Wiley & Sons, Inc.
One Wiley Drive
Somerset, NJ 08875
1-800-225-5945

For customers outside the United States, please contact the Wiley office nearest you:

Professional & Reference Division
John Wiley & Sons Canada, Ltd.
22 Worcester Road
Rexdale, Ontario M9W 1L1
CANADA
(416) 675-3580
1-800-567-4797
FAX (416) 675-6599

Jacaranda Wiley Ltd.
PRT Division
P.O. Box 174
North Ryde, NSW 2113
AUSTRALIA
(02) 805-1100
FAX (02) 805-1597

John Wiley & Sons, Ltd.
Baffins Lane
Chichester
West Sussex, PO19 1UD
UNITED KINGDOM
(44) (243) 779777

John Wiley & Sons (SEA) Pte. Ltd.
37 Jalan Pemimpin
Block B # 05-04
Union Industrial Building
SINGAPORE 2057
(65) 258-1157

About the Author

Bruce R. Hopkins is a lawyer in Kansas City, Missouri, with the firm of Polsinelli, White, Vardeman & Shalton, having practiced law in Washington, D.C., for 26 years. He specializes in the representation of nonprofit organizations. His practice ranges over the entirety of tax matters involving nonprofit organizations, including representation of many different types of tax-exempt organizations, starting and qualifying organizations for tax exemption, legislative and political campaign activities issues, public charity and private foundation status, review of annual information returns, disclosure matters, audits, litigation, applications of the commerciality doctrine, unrelated business issues, involvement of exempt organizations in partnerships and joint ventures, and the use of exempt and for-profit subsidiaries.

Mr. Hopkins served as Chair of the Committee on Exempt Organizations, Tax Section, American Bar Association; Chair, Section of Taxation, National Association of College and University Attorneys; and President, Planned Giving Study Group of Greater Washington, D.C. He was accorded the Assistant Commissioner's (IRS) Award in 1984. He also teaches a course on nonprofit organizations at the University of Missouri–Kansas City School of Law.

Mr. Hopkins is the series editor of Wiley's Nonprofit Law, Finance, and Management Series. In addition to *The Law of Tax-Exempt Organizations*, he is the author of *The Legal Answer Book for Nonprofit Organizations; The Law of Fund-Raising, Second Edition; Charity, Advocacy, and the Law; The Nonprofit Law Dictionary; The Tax Law of Charitable Giving;* and *A Legal Guide to Starting and Managing a Nonprofit Organization, Second Edition;* and is co-author, with Jody Blazek, of *Private Foundations: Tax Law and Compliance,* with Thomas K. Hyatt, of *The Law of Tax-Exempt Healthcare Organizations,* and with D. Benson Tesdahl, of *Intermediate Sanctions: Curbing Nonprofit Abuse.* He also writes *The Nonprofit Counsel,* a monthly newsletter, published by John Wiley & Sons.

Mr. Hopkins earned his J.D. and LL.M. degrees at the George Washington University and his B.A. at the University of Michigan.

Preface

One highlight of my life is writing books about nonprofit organizations. This started in the mid 1970s and I haven't been able to stop. Ten books have been authored or co-authored by me over the years, and more await their turn. *The Law of Tax-Exempt Organizations*, however, was the first book I wrote. I find it extraordinary that it is now in its seventh edition.

By the time this edition is available, it will be over 23 years of age (1975–1998). My law partners and I prefer not to think of the thousands of hours that underly this project. Certainly the field of tax-exempt organizations has been dynamic, volatile at times, and the fact that this book is now in its seventh edition is testament to the complexity of the subject matter and its astounding growth. In fact, the number of books in the Wiley Nonprofit Law, Finance, and Management Series, and the wonderful range of that material, evidences the explosiveness of the nonprofit sector in recent years.

Most of the law reflected in this book did not exist 30 years ago. Tax exemption was provided for in the first revenue act in 1913 and the unrelated business income rules came in 1950, but that was about all. A considerable portion of the statutory law of tax-exempt organizations is the product of enactment of the Tax Reform Act of 1969. (I am often asked how I found myself practicing in the realm of tax-exempt organizations. My law practice started in 1969, I got caught up in the writing and interpreting of the law Congress passed that year, and I just kept on going.) This body of statutory law has been significantly expanded by over a dozen major tax acts. In recent months alone, the field has been enlarged by reason of enactment of the Taxpayer Bill of Rights 2 (1996), the Small Business Job Protection Act of 1996, the Health Insurance Portability and Accountability Act of 1996, and the Taxpayer Relief Act of 1997. The IRS restructuring legislation is imminent.

But the tax law affecting exempt organizations is by no means confined to statutes. Like other areas of tax law, the field is heavily informed by Treasury Department regulations, Internal Revenue Service revenue rulings and revenue procedures, and opinions from various federal courts. More so than in other aspects of the tax law, the world of tax-exempt organizations is dramatically affected daily by IRS "private" determinations, in the form of private letter rulings, technical advice memoranda, and general counsel memoranda. All of this has resulted in a mammoth body of law.

The last decade or so alone bears witness to an immense augmentation of the law of tax-exempt organizations. Developments in the health care, higher education, private foundations, and associations fields, just to name a few, have been awesome to watch and challenging to chronicle. Other notable expansions of this law have occurred and are occurring in the realms of private inurement and private benefit, legislative and political activities, the applications for recognition of exemption and the annual information returns, the use of partnerships and subsidiaries, the commerciality doctrine, and the unrelated business rules.

New bodies of law have also emerged. While perhaps the most notable are the intermediate sanctions rules, others include disclosure and document distribution requirements, exempt organizations and insurance, mergers and other reorganizations, and fund-raising regulation.

This book evolved out of materials developed for the course on tax-exempt organizations that I taught for 19 years at the George Washington University National Law Center, in Washington, D.C., beginning in 1973. I continue to use it in the course I currently teach at the University of Missouri-Kansas City School of Law.

The book reflects hundreds of questions asked by law students over the years. It also has been shaped by the inquiries of clients and colleagues. At the same time, the task has been to capture all of the law and developments across the entire field.

I have tried to provide a summary of the law of tax-exempt organizations, one that is sufficiently general to present the subject in all of its wonderful expanse, yet with enough particularity to give the reader the specifics when needed. Thus, the book has been written in as nontechnical a way as I can muster, yet with footnotes and other sources that lead to more detailed information. The latter includes references to Internal Revenue Code provisions, tax regulations, court opinions, and public and private rulings from the Internal Revenue Service.

Lawyers, managers, accountants, directors and officers, fund-raising executives, and students of the field hopefully can use this book to learn particular aspects of the subject matter or to refresh their minds about one rule or another. The book is designed for the newcomer as well as for the expert practitioner.

One aspect of this book that has been a problem over the years has been its size. Each edition has been larger than the previous one. The cumulative supplements end up being books in their own right. While I admit to some overwriting, the core difficulty has been the sheer number of ways in which this area of the law has broadened.

This edition is smaller than the previous one. This was accomplished in part by tightening the writing and jettisoning various sections. However, the single-most important reason for this shrinkage is that nearly 200 pages of the law concerning private foundations was removed and incorporated into a separate book (i.e., *Private Foundations: Tax Law and Compliance*, John Wiley & Sons, Inc., 1997, co-authored with Jody Blazek). Private foundation law is still covered in this book (see Chapter 11) but the details in this area are now in this companion volume.

There have been other instances of this nature. I have authored or co-authored books on charitable giving, fund-raising regulation, intermediate sanctions, and health law. These efforts, too, have helped to trim the size of the book.

PREFACE

There isn't enough space in the book for a detailed analysis of cases, rulings, and the like. I try to do this, however, in my monthly newsletter, *The Nonprofit Counsel*, which is now in its fifteenth year. The format of the newsletter was recently revised to include references to this book for additional reading and background information. Thus, the newsletter will continue as a stand-alone publication; at the same time, for those with the book, it will also serve as a monthly update.

The flow of this edition has been substantially revised. Subjects like private inurement, legislative and political activities, and insurance activities have been newly placed and discussed from the standpoint of several types of exempt organizations. Some chapters have been consolidated. There are 33 chapters in this edition compared to 46 in the previous one. It is hoped that the new format will make the book more useful.

It was observed earlier that the law of tax-exempt organizations is mammoth. All indications are that more, perhaps much more, is in the offing. For example, the IRS will be testing its authority to levy penalties in instances of excess benefit transactions, there will be litigation over charities in politics, the annual return will be revised and expanded, and more creativity and ensuing regulation will evolve as the result of reorganizations, mergers, affiliations, use of subsidiaries, conversions, and liquidations.

Essays like this, it seems, cannot be written these days without using the word *millenium*. Where will the law of tax-exempt organizations be in the year 2000? We may be at a major point in the development of this law. It will either continue to expand—or it will suddenly come to an end. The latter is a possibility if there is a radical reworking of the nation's tax system. What would be the role of tax exemption (and deductible charitable giving) in the absence of an income tax? Depending on the elections this fall and in the year 2000, we just might find out.

Clichés about a book like this can abound. "Labor of love" and "work in progress" come to mind. The most important one of all, however, has to be said: There have been a lot of people along the way who have helped enormously, doing so much to nurture the book over the years, particularly my friends and colleagues at John Wiley & Sons, Inc. Most notable in the past are Marla Bobowick and Jeffrey Brown. Those who deserve current thanks are Martha Cooley and Robin Goldstein. Thanks also go to Kimberley Knipp for her work in editing the manuscript.

Revising and updating a book of this nature is a time-consuming project, requiring much intense focus. In reflection of these facts, I also extend my gratitude to my dear wife, Bonnie Buchele, for her patience, understanding, and support.

BRUCE R. HOPKINS
April, 1998

Contents

CONTENTS

CONTENTS

CONTENTS

PART FOUR: GENERAL EXEMPT ORGANIZATION LAWS

19   Private Inurement, Private Benefit, and Excess Benefit Transactions — 427

20   Legislative Activities by Exempt Organizations — 473

21   Political Campaign Activities by Tax-Exempt Organizations — 503

22   Insurance and Fund-Raising Activities — 523

CONTENTS

CONTENTS

■   xxi   ■

CONTENTS

Introduction to the Law
of Tax-Exempt Organizations

CHAPTER ONE

Philosophy Underlying and Rationales for Tax-Exempt Organizations

Nearly all of federal and state law pertains, directly or indirectly, to tax-exempt organizations, and there are few areas of law that have no bearing whatsoever on these entities. The fields of federal law that directly apply to tax-exempt organizations include tax exemption and charitable giving requirements, and the laws concerning antitrust, contracts, employee benefits, the environment, estate planning, health care, labor, the postal system, securities, and fund-raising for charitable and political purposes. The aspects of state law concerning exempt organizations are much the same as the federal ones, along with laws pertaining to the formation and operation of corporations and trusts, and charitable solicitation acts. Both levels of government have much constitutional and administrative law directly applicable to tax-exempt organizations. A vast array of other civil and criminal laws likewise apply. The principal focus of this book is the federal tax law as it applies to nonprofit organizations, although other laws applicable to exempt organizations are referenced throughout.

§ 1.1 *NONPROFIT* ORGANIZATIONS

A tax-exempt organization is a unique entity; among its features is the fact that it is a nonprofit organization. Most of the laws that pertain to the concept and creation of a nonprofit organization originate at the state level, while most laws concerning tax exemption are federally generated. Although almost every nonprofit entity is incorporated or otherwise formed under state law, a few nonprofit organizations are chartered by federal statute. The nonprofit organizations that are the chief focus from a federal tax standpoint are corporations, trusts, and unincorporated associations.

A nonprofit organization is not necessarily a tax-exempt organization. To be tax-exempt, a nonprofit organization must meet certain criteria. As noted, most of these criteria are established under federal law. However, state law may have additional criteria; those rules can differ in relation to the tax from which exemption is sought (such as taxes on income, sales of goods or services, use of property, tangible personal property, intangible personal property, or real property).[1] Thus, there are nonprofit organizations that are taxable entities, under both federal and state law.

(a) Definition of *Nonprofit Organization*

The term *nonprofit organization* does not refer to an organization that is prohibited by law from earning a *profit* (that is, an excess of earnings over expenses). In fact, it is quite common for nonprofit organizations to generate profits. Rather, the definition of nonprofit organization essentially relates to requirements as to what must be done with the profits earned. This fundamental element is found in the doctrine of *private inurement*.[2]

The legal concept of a nonprofit organization is best understood through a comparison with a *for-profit* organization. The essential difference between nonprofit and for-profit organizations is reflected in the private inurement doctrine.[3] Nonetheless, the characteristics of the two categories of organizations are often identical, in that both mandate a legal form,[4] one or more directors or trustees, and usually officers, and both of these types of entities can have employees (and thus pay compensation), face essentially the same expenses, make investments, may enter into contracts, can sue and be sued, produce goods and/or services, and, as noted, generate profits.

A fundamental distinction between the two entities is that the for-profit organization has owners that hold the equity in the enterprise, such as stockholders of a corporation. The for-profit organization is operated for the benefit of its owners; the profits of the business undertaking are passed through to them, such as by the payment of dividends on shares of stock. That is what is meant by the term *for-profit* organization: It is one that is designed to generate a profit for its owners. The transfer of the profits from the organization to its owners is the inurement of net earnings to them in their private capacity.

---

[1] However, in establishing its criteria for tax exemption, a state may not develop rules that are discriminatory to the extent that they unconstitutionally burden interstate commerce (Camps Newfound/Owatonna, Inc. v. Town of Harrison, Maine, et al., 117•S. Ct. 1590 (1997)).

[2] The doctrine states that the entity be organized and operated so that "no part of . . . [its] net earnings . . . inures to the benefit of any private shareholder or individual" (e.g., Internal Revenue Code of 1986, as amended, section (IRC §) 501(c)(3)). The technical aspects of the private inurement doctrine are the subject of Chapter 19.

[3] The word *nonprofit* should not be confused with the term *not-for-profit* (although it often is). The former describes a type of organization; the latter describes a type of activity. For example, in the federal tax setting, expenses associated with a not-for-profit activity (namely, one conducted without the requisite profit motive) are not deductible as business expenses (IRC § 183).

[4] See § 4.1.

By contrast, the nonprofit organization generally is not permitted to distribute its profits (net earnings) to those who control it (such as directors and officers).[5] (A nonprofit organization usually does not have owners.[6]) That is, a nonprofit organization is one that cannot engage in private inurement. Consequently, the private inurement doctrine is the substantive defining characteristic that distinguishes nonprofit organizations from for-profit organizations for purposes of the tax law.

To reiterate: Both nonprofit and for-profit organizations are legally able to generate a profit. Yet, as the comparison between the two types of organizations indicates, there are two categories of profit: one at the *entity level* and one at the *ownership level*. Both can yield the former type of profit; the distinction between the two types of entities pivots on the latter category of profit.[7] The for-profit organization endeavors to produce a profit for its owners—what one commentator called its "residual claimants."[8] For-profit organizations are supposed to engage in private inurement; nonprofit entities may not do so. Indeed, the nonprofit organization often seeks to devote its profit to ends that are beneficial to society.

(b) The Nonprofit Sector

Critical to an understanding of the nonprofit organization is appreciation of the concept of the *nonprofit sector* of society. This sector of society has been termed, among other titles, the *independent sector*, the *third sector*, the *voluntary sector*, and the *philanthropic sector*. The English language has yet to capture the precise nature of this sector; in a sense, none of these appellations is appropriate.[9]

A tenet of political philosophy is that a democratic state—or, as it is sometimes termed, a civil society—has three sectors. These sectors contain institutions and organizations that are governmental, for-profit, and nonprofit in nature. Thus, in the United States, the governmental sector includes the branches, departments, agencies, and bureaus of the federal, state, and local governments; the class of for-profit entities comprises the business, trade, professional, and commercial segment of society; and nonprofit entities constitute the balance of this society. The nonprofit sector is seen as being essential to the maintenance of freedom for individuals and a bulwark against the excesses of the other two sectors, particularly the governmental sector.

---

[5] The U.S. Supreme Court wrote that a "nonprofit entity is ordinarily understood to differ from a for-profit corporation principally because it 'is barred from distributing its net earnings, if any, to individuals who exercise control over it, such as members, officers, directors, or trustees'" (Camps Newfound/Owatonna, Inc. v. Town of Harrison, Maine, et al., *supra* note 1 at 1603, quoting from Hansmann, "The Role of Nonprofit Enterprise," 89 *Yale L. J. 835*, 838 (1980)).

[6] A few states allow nonprofit organizations to issue stock. This is done as an ownership (and control) mechanism only; this type of stock does not carry with it any rights to earnings (such as dividends).

[7] One commentator stated that charitable and other nonprofit organizations "are not restricted in the amount of profit they may make; restrictions apply only to what they may do with the profits" (Weisbrod, "The Complexities of Income Generation for Nonprofits," Chapter 7, Hodgkinson, Lyman, and Assocs., *The Future of the Nonprofit Sector* (San Francisco: Jossey-Bass, 1989).

[8] Norwitz, " 'The Metaphysics of Time': A Radical Corporate Vision," 46 *Bus. Law.* (No. 2) 377 (Feb. 1991).

[9] A discussion of these sectors appears in Ferris & Graddy, "Fading Distinctions among the Nonprofit, Government, and For-Profit Sectors," Chapter 8, Hodgkinson, Lyman, and Assocs., *supra* note 7. An argument that the sector should be called the "first sector" is advanced in Young, "Beyond Tax Exemption: A Focus on Organizational Performance Versus Legal Status," id. at Chapter 11.

PHILOSOPHY AND RATIONALES FOR TAX-EXEMPT ORGANIZATIONS

There are, as indicated earlier, subsets within the nonprofit sector. Tax-exempt organizations represent a subset of nonprofit organizations. Organizations that are eligible to attract deductible charitable gifts, charitable organizations (using the broad definition[10]), and other types of exempt organizations are subsets of tax-exempt organizations. Charitable organizations (in the narrow, technical sense of that term) are subsets of charitable organizations (as defined in the broader sense).[11] These elements of the nonprofit sector may be visualized as a series of concentric circles.

[10] This broad definition carries with it the connotation of *philanthropy* (e.g., Van Til, "Defining Philanthropy," Chapter 2, Van Til & Assocs., *Critical Issues in American Philanthropy* (San Francisco: Jossey-Bass, 1990). Also Payton, *Philanthropy: Voluntary Action for the Public Good* (New York: Macmillan Pub. Co., 1988); O'Connell, *Philanthropy in Action* (New York: The Foundation Center, 1987).

[11] The complexity of the federal tax law is such that the charitable sector (using the term in its broadest sense) is also divided into two segments: charitable organizations that are considered *private* (private foundations) and charitable organizations that are considered *public* (all charitable organizations other than those that are considered private); these nonprivate charities are frequently referred to as *public charities*. See Chapter 11.

§ 1.2   *TAX-EXEMPT* ORGANIZATIONS

For the most part, in this book, the term *tax-exempt organization* refers to a nonprofit organization that is exempt from (excused from paying) the federal income tax. There are, of course, other federal taxes (such as excise and employment taxes) and there are categories of exemptions from them. At the state level, there are exemptions associated with income, sales, use, excise, and property taxes.

Nonetheless, there is no category of nonprofit organization that is not subject to some form of federal tax. The income tax that is potentially applicable to nearly all tax-exempt organizations is the tax on unrelated business income.[12] Tax-exempt entities can be taxed for engaging in political activities;[13] public charities are subject to tax in the case of efforts to influence legislation[14] or participation in political campaign activities;[15] and some exempt organizations, such as social clubs, are taxable on their investment income.[16] Associations and like organizations can be subject to a proxy tax when engaged in attempts to influence legislation or engage in political activities.[17] Private foundations can be caught up in a variety of excise taxes.[18]

There is no entitlement in a nonprofit organization to tax exemption; there is no entity that has some inherent right to tax-exempt status. The existence of tax exemption, and the determination of the entities that have it, are essentially the whim of the legislature involved. There is no constitutional law principle mandating tax exemption.[19]

An illustration of this point is the grant by Congress of tax-exempt status to certain mutual organizations—albeit with the stricture that to qualify for the exemption, an organization must be organized before September 1, 1957.[20] (Prior to that date, tax exemption was available for all savings and loan associations. This exemption was repealed because Congress determined that the purpose of the exemption, which was to afford savings institutions that did not have capital stock the benefit of tax exemption so that a surplus could be accumulated to provide the depositors with greater security, was no longer appropriate, because the savings and loan industry had developed to the point where the ratio of capital account to total deposits was comparable to non-exempt commercial banks.) A challenge to this law by an otherwise qualified organization formed in 1962 failed, with the U.S. Supreme Court holding that Congress did not act in an arbi-

---

[12] See Part VI.
[13] See § 17.5.
[14] See § 20.5.
[15] See § 21.4.
[16] See § 14.3.
[17] See §§ 20.7, 21.7.
[18] See § 11.3.
[19] Nonetheless, see *supra* note 1.
[20] IRC § 501(c)(14)(B).

trary and unconstitutional manner in declining to extend the tax exemption be-yond the particular year.[21]

There are other illustrations of this point. For years, organizations like Blue Cross and Blue Shield entities were tax-exempt[22]; however, Congress deter-mined that these organizations had evolved to be little different from commer-cial health insurance providers and thus generally legislated this tax exemption out of existence.[23] (Later, Congress realized that it had gone too far in this regard and restored tax exemption for some providers of insurance that function as charitable risk pools.[24]) Congress allowed the tax-exempt status for group legal service organizations[25] to expire without ceremony in 1992; it also created a cate-gory of tax exemption for state-sponsored worker's compensation reinsurance organizations, with the stipulation that they be established before June 1, 1996.[26] Indeed, in 1982, Congress established tax exemption for a certain type of veter-ans' organizations, with one of the criteria being that the entity be established before 1880.[27]

There is a main list of tax-exempt organizations,[28] to or from which Con-gress periodically adds or deletes categories of organizations. Occasionally, Con-gress extends the list of organizations that are exempt as charitable entities.[29] Otherwise, it may create a new provision describing the particular exemption criteria.[30]

A compendium of tax law containing an analysis of the law of tax-exempt organizations proclaims that exempt status is the "most prized of all tax conces-sions sanctioned by Congress."[31] That bit of hyperbole, intending to confer mo-mentum and stature to the exempt organizations field, is in fact a considerable overstatement. For example, in the case of some charitable organizations, the eli-gibility to receive tax-deductible contributions is a far more prized attribute than tax exemption. From an economic viewpoint, there are several tax expendi-tures that are "worth more" (in terms of revenue "losses" to the federal fisc) than the charitable contribution deduction or the federal tax exemption for nonprofit organizations.[32]

---

[21] Maryland Sav.-Share Ins. Corp. v. United States, 400 U.S. 4 (1970).

[22] By reason of IRC § 501(c)(4).

[23] See § 22.1.

[24] See § 10.6.

[25] See § 16.6.

[26] See § 18.5.

[27] See § 18.10(b).

[28] IRC § 501(c).

[29] IRC §§ 501(e), 501(f), 501(k), 501(m), 501(n).

[30] IRC §§ 521, 526–529.

[31] 8 Stand. Fed. Tax Rep. (CCH) ¶ 22,604.01 (1996).

[32] The congressional budget committees and the Department of the Treasury measure the economic value (revenue "losses") of various tax preferences, such as tax deductions, credits, and exclusions (termed *tax expenditures*). While the income tax charitable contribution deduction tends to be the sixth largest tax expenditure, the ones that are greater than it include the exclusion from gross income of employer contributions for medical insurance premiums and medical care, the exclusion for pension contributions and earnings, the deductibility of mortgage interest on personal residences, and the step-up of capital gains at death.

§ 1.3   PRINCIPLES OF EXEMPT ORGANIZATIONS LAW PHILOSOPHY

The definition in the law of the term *nonprofit organization* and the concept of the nonprofit sector as critical to the creation and functioning of a civil society do not distinguish nonprofit organizations that are tax-exempt from those that are not. This is because the tax aspect of nonprofit organizations is not relevant to either subject. Indeed, rather than defining either the term *nonprofit organization* or its societal role, the federal tax law principles respecting tax exemption of these entities reflect and flow out of the essence of these subjects.

This is somewhat unusual; most tax laws are based on some form of rationale that is inherent in tax policy. However, the law of tax-exempt organizations has very little to do with any underlying tax policy. Rather, this aspect of the tax law is grounded in a body of thought far distant from tax policy: political philosophy as to the proper construct of a democratic society.

This raises, then, the matter of the rationale for tax-exemption eligibility of nonprofit organizations. That is, what is the fundamental characteristic—or characteristics—that enable a nonprofit organization to qualify as a tax-exempt organization? In fact, there is no single qualifying feature. This circumstance mirrors the fact that the present-day statutory tax exemption rules are not the product of a carefully formulated plan. Rather, they are a hodgepodge of statutory law that has evolved over more than 80 years, as various Congresses have deleted from (infrequently) and added to (frequently) the roster of exempt entities, causing it to grow substantially over the decades. One observer wrote that the various categories of tax-exempt organizations "are not the result of any planned legislative scheme" but were enacted over the decades "by a variety of legislators for a variety of reasons."[33]

There are six basic rationales underlying qualification for tax-exempt status for nonprofit organizations. On a simplistic plane, a nonprofit entity is tax-exempt because Congress wrote a provision in the Internal Revenue Code according tax exemption to it. Thus, some organizations are tax-exempt for no more engaging reason than that Congress said so. Certainly, as to this type of exemption, there is no grand philosophical construct buttressing the exemption.

Some of the federal income tax exemptions were enacted in the spirit of being merely declaratory of, or furthering, then-existing law. The House Committee on Ways and Means, in legislating a forerunner to the provision that exempts certain voluntary employees' beneficiary associations,[34] commented that "these associations are common today [1928] and it appears desirable to provide specifically for their exemption from ordinary corporation tax."[35] The exemption for nonprofit cemetery companies[36] was enacted to parallel then-existing state and local property tax exemptions.[37] The exemption for

---

[33] McGovern, "The Exemption Provisions of Subchapter F," 29 *Tax Law.* 523 (1976). Other overviews of the various tax exemption provisions are in Hansmann, "The Rationale for Exempting Nonprofit Organizations from Corporate Income Taxation," 91 *Yale L.J.* 69 (1981); Bittker & Rahdert, "The Exemption of Nonprofit Organizations from Federal Income Taxation," 85 *Yale L.J.* 299 (1976).

[34] See § 16.3.

[35] H. Rep. No. 72, 78th Cong., 1st Sess. 17 (1928).

[36] See § 18.6.

[37] Lapin, "The Golden Hills and Meadows of the Tax-Exempt Cemetery," 44 *Taxes* 744 (1966).

farmers' cooperatives[38] has been characterized as part of the federal government's posture of supporting agriculture.[39] The provision exempting certain U.S. corporate instrumentalities from tax[40] was deemed declaratory of the exemption simultaneously provided by the particular enabling statute.[41] The provision according tax exemption to multiparent title-holding corporations was derived from the IRS's refusal to recognize exempt status for title-holding corporations serving more than one unrelated parent entity.[42]

Tax exemption for categories of nonprofit organizations can arise as a byproduct of enactment of other legislation. In these instances, tax exemption is granted to facilitate accomplishment of the purpose of another legislative end. Thus, tax-exempt status has been approved for funds underlying employee benefit programs.[43] Other examples include tax exemption for professional football leagues that emanated out of the merger of the National Football League and the American Football League,[44] and for state-sponsored providers of health care to the needy, which was required to accommodate the goals of Congress in creating health care delivery legislation.[45]

There is a pure tax rationale for some tax-exempt organizations. Social clubs stand out as an illustration of this category.[46]

The fourth rationale for tax-exempt status is a policy one—not tax policy, but policy with regard to less essential elements of the structure of a civil society. This is why, for example, tax-exempt status has been granted to fraternal organizations,[47] title-holding companies,[48] and state-sponsored prepaid tuition programs.[49]

The fifth rationale for tax-exempt status is one that rests solidly on a philosophical principle. Yet, there are degrees of scale here; some principles are less grand than others. Thus, there are nonprofit organizations that are tax-exempt because their objectives are of direct importance to a significant segment of society and indirectly of consequence to all of society. Within this frame lies the rationale for tax exemption for entities such as labor organizations,[50] trade and business associations,[51] and veterans' organizations.[52]

The sixth rationale for tax-exempt status for nonprofit organizations is predicated on the view that exemption is required to facilitate achievement of an end of significance to the entirety of society. Most organizations that are generally

---

[38] See § 18.11.
[39] Comment, 27 *Iowa L. Rev.* 128, 151–155 (1941).
[40] See § 18.1.
[41] H. Rep. No. 704, 73d Cong., 2d Sess. 21–25 (1934). This policy has changed, however (see § 18.1, text accompanying note 1.
[42] See § 18.2(b).
[43] See Chapter 16.
[44] See § 13.5.
[45] See § 18.14.
[46] See *infra* § 5.
[47] See § 18.4.
[48] See § 18.2.
[49] See § 18.6.
[50] See § 15.1.
[51] See Chapter 13.
[52] See § 18.10.

thought of as *charitable* in nature[53] are entities that are meaningful to the structure and functioning of society in the United States.[54] At least to some degree, this rationale embraces social welfare organizations.[55] This rationale may be termed the *public policy* rationale.

§ 1.4   PUBLIC POLICY RATIONALE

The public policy rationale is one involving political philosophy rather than tax policy. The key concept underlying this philosophy is *pluralism*; more accurately, the pluralism of institutions, which is a function of competition between various institutions within the three sectors of society. In this context, the competition is between the nonprofit and governmental sectors. This element is particularly critical in the United States, whose history originates in distrust of government. (Where the issue is unrelated business income taxation, the matter is one of competition between the nonprofit and for-profit sectors.) Here, the nonprofit sector serves as an alternative to the governmental sector as a means for addressing society's problems.

One of the greatest exponents of pluralism was John Stuart Mill. He wrote in *On Liberty*, published in 1859:

> In many cases, though individuals may not do the particular thing so well, on the average, as officers of government, it is nevertheless desirable that it should be done by them, rather than by the government, as a means to their own mental education—a mode of strengthening their active faculties, exercising their judgment, and giving them a familiar knowledge of the subjects with which they are thus left to deal. This is a principal, though not the sole, recommendation of . . . the conduct of industrial and philanthropic enterprises by voluntary associations.

Following a discussion of the importance of "individuality of development, and diversity of modes of action," Mill wrote:

> Government operations tend to be everywhere alike. With individuals and voluntary associations, on the contrary, there are varied experiments, and endless diversity of experience. What the State can usefully do is to make itself a central depository, and active circulator and diffuser, of the experience resulting from many trials. Its business is to enable each experimentalist to benefit by the experiments of others; instead of tolerating no experiments but its own.

This conflict among the sectors—a sorting out of the appropriate role of governments and nonprofit organizations—is, in a healthy society, a never-ending process, ebbing and flowing with the politics of the day. A Congress may work to

---

[53] These are the charitable, educational, religious, scientific, and like organizations referenced in IRC § 501(c)(3).

[54] This book is written from the perspective of United States law. However, the philosophical principles are applicable with respect to any society. In general, Hopkins & Moore, "Using the lessons learned from US and English law to create a regulatory framework for charities in evolving democracies," 3 *Voluntas* 194 (1992).

[55] See Chapter 12. Tax exemption for social welfare organizations also originated in 1913; the promotion of social welfare is one of the definitions of the term *charitable* for federal tax purposes (see § 6.6).

reduce the scope of the federal government and a President may proclaim that the "era of big government is over," while a preceding and/or succeeding generation may celebrate strong central government.

One of the greatest commentators on the impulse and tendency in the United States to utilize nonprofit organizations was Alexis de Tocqueville. Writing in 1835, as expressed in *Democracy in America*, he observed:

> Feelings and opinions are recruited, the heart is enlarged, and the human mind is developed only by the reciprocal influence of men upon one another. I have shown that these influences are almost null in democratic countries; they must therefore be artificially created, and this can only be accomplished by associations.

De Tocqueville's classic formulation on this subject came in his portrayal of the use by Americans of "public associations" as a critical element of the societal structure:

> Americans of all ages, all conditions, and all dispositions constantly form associations. They have not only commercial and manufacturing companies, in which all take part, but associations of a thousand other kinds, religious, moral, serious, futile, general or restricted, enormous or diminutive. The Americans make associations to give entertainments, to found seminaries, to build inns, to construct churches, to diffuse books, to send missionaries to the antipodes; in this manner they found hospitals, prisons, and schools. If it is proposed to inculcate some truth or to foster some feeling by the encouragement of a great example, they form a society. Wherever at the head of some new undertaking you see the government in France, or a man of rank in England, in the United States you will be sure to find an association.

This was the political philosophical climate concerning nonprofit organizations in place when Congress, toward the close of the 19th century, began considering enactment of an income tax. Although courts would subsequently articulate policy rationales for tax exemption, one of the failures of American jurisprudence is that the Supreme Court and the lower courts have never adequately articulated the public policy doctrine.

Contemporary Congresses legislate by writing far more intricate statutes than their forebears, and in doing so usually leave in their wake rich deposits in the form of extensive legislative histories. Thus, it is far easier to ascertain what a recent Congress meant when creating law than is the case with respect to an enactment of decades ago.

At the time a constitutional income tax was coming into existence (the first enacted in 1913[56]), Congress legislated in spare language and rarely embellished

---

[56] In 1894, Congress imposed a tax on corporate income. This was the first time Congress was required to define the appropriate subjects of tax exemption (inasmuch as prior tax schemes specified the entities subject to taxation). The Tariff Act of 1894 provided exemption for nonprofit charitable, religious, and educational organizations, fraternal beneficiary societies, certain mutual savings banks, and certain mutual insurance companies. The 1894 legislation succumbed to a constitutional law challenge (Pollock v. Farmers' Loan & Trust Co., 157 U.S. 429 (1895), overruled on other grounds, State of South Carolina v. Baker, 485 U.S. 505 (1988)), the Sixteenth Amendment was subsequently ratified, and the Revenue Act of 1913 was enacted.

upon its statutory handiwork with legislative histories. Therefore, there is no contemporary record, in the form of legislative history of what members of Congress had in mind when they first started creating categories of tax-exempt organizations. Congress, it is generally assumed, saw itself doing what other legislative bodies have done over the centuries. One observer stated that the "history of mankind reflects that our early legislators were not setting precedent by exempting religious or charitable organizations" from income tax.[57] That is, the political philosophical policy considerations pertaining to nonprofit organizations were such that taxation of these entities—considering their contributions to the well-being and functioning of society—was unthinkable.

Thus, in the process of writing the Revenue Act of 1913, Congress viewed tax exemption for charitable organizations as the only way to consistently correlate tax policy to political theory on the point, and saw the exemption of charities in the federal tax statutes as an extension of comparable practice throughout the whole of history. No legislative history enlarges upon the point. Presumably, Congress simply believed that these organizations ought not be taxed and found the proposition sufficiently obvious that extensive explanation of its actions was not required.

Some clues are found in the definition of *charitable activities* in the income tax regulations,[58] which are thought to be reflective of congressional intent. The regulations refer to purposes such as relief of the poor, advancement of education and science, erection and maintenance of public buildings, and lessening of the burdens of government. These definitions of charitable undertakings have an obvious derivation in the Preamble to the Statute of Charitable Uses,[59] written in England in 1601. Reference is there made to certain "charitable" purposes:

> . . . some for relief of aged, impotent and poor people, some for maintenance of sick and maimed soldiers and mariners, schools of learning, free schools, and scholars in universities, some for repair of bridges, ports, havens, causeways, churches, seabanks and highways, some for education and preferment of orphans, some for or towards relief, stock or maintenance for houses of correction, some for marriages of poor maids, some for supportation, aid and help of young tradesmen, handicraftsmen and persons decayed, and others for relief of redemption of prisoners or captives . . .

(As this indicates, a subset of the public policy doctrine implies that tax exemption for charitable organizations derives from the concept that they perform functions that, in the absence of these organizations, government would have to perform. This view leads to the conclusion that government is willing to forgo the tax revenues it would otherwise receive in return for the public interest services rendered by charitable organizations.)

Since the founding of the United States and beforehand in the colonial period, tax exemption—particularly with respect to religious organizations—was common.[60] Churches were uniformly spared taxation.[61] This practice has been

---

[57] McGovern, *supra* note 33, at 524.
[58] Income Tax Regulations ("Reg.") § 1.501(c)(3)–1(d)(2).
[59] Stat. 43 Eliz. i, ch. 4.
[60] Cobb, *The Rise of Religious Liberty in America* 482–528 (1902).
[61] Torpey, *Judicial Doctrines of Religious Rights in America* 171 (1948).

sustained throughout the history of the nation—not only at the federal level but also at the state and local levels of government, which grant property tax exemptions, as an example.

The U.S. Supreme Court concluded, soon after enactment of the income tax, that the foregoing rationalization was the basis for the federal tax exemption for charitable entities (although in doing so it reflected a degree of uncertainty in the strength of its reasoning, undoubtedly based on the paucity of legislative history). In 1924, the Court stated that "[e]vidently the exemption is made in recognition of the benefit which the public derives from corporate activities of the class named, and is intended to aid them when [they are] not conducted for private gain."[62] Nearly 50 years later, in upholding the constitutionality of income tax exemption for religious organizations, the Court observed that the "State has an affirmative policy that considers these groups as beneficial and stabilizing influences in community life and finds this classification [tax exemption] useful, desirable, and in the public interest."[63] Subsequently, the Court wrote that, for most categories of nonprofit organizations, "exemption from federal income tax is intended to encourage the provision of services that are deemed socially beneficial."[64]

A few other courts have taken up this theme. One federal court of appeals wrote that the "reason underlying the exemption granted" to charitable organizations "is that the exempted taxpayer performs a public service."[65] This court continued:

> The common element of charitable purposes within the meaning of the . . . [federal tax law] is the relief of the public of a burden which otherwise belongs to it. Charitable purposes are those which benefit the community by relieving it pro tanto from an obligation which it owes to the objects of the charity as members of the community.[66]

This federal appellate court subsequently observed, as respects the exemption for charitable organizations, that "[o]ne stated reason for a deduction or exemption of this kind is that the favored entity performs a public service and benefits the public or relieves it of a burden which otherwise belongs to it."[67] Another federal court opined that the justification of the charitable contribution deduction was "historically . . . that by doing so, the Government relieves itself of the burden of meeting public needs which in the absence of charitable activity would fall on the shoulders of the Government."[68]

Only one federal court has fully articulated the public policy doctrine, even there noting that the "very purpose" of the charitable contribution deduction "is

---

[62] Trinidad v. Sagrada Orden de Predicadores de la Provincia del Santisimo Rosario de Filipinas, 263 U.S. 578, 581 (1924).

[63] Walz v. Tax Comm'n, 397 U.S. 664, 673 (1970).

[64] Portland Golf Club v. Comm., 497 U.S. 154, 161 (1990).

[65] Duffy v. Birmingham, 190 F.2d 738, 740 (8th Cir. 1951).

[66] Id.

[67] St. Louis Union Trust Co. v. United States, 374 F.2d 427, 432 (8th Cir. 1967).

[68] McGlotten v. Connally, 338 F. Supp. 448, 456 (D.D.C. 1972).

rooted in helping institutions because they serve the public good."[69] The doctrine was explained as follows:

> [A]s to private philanthropy, the promotion of a healthy pluralism is often viewed as a prime social benefit of general significance. In other words, society can be seen as benefiting not only from the application of private wealth to specific purposes in the public interest but also from the variety of choices made by individual philanthropists as to which activities to subsidize. This decentralized choice-making is arguably more efficient and responsive to public needs than the cumbersome and less flexible allocation process of government administration.[70]

Occasionally, Congress issues a pronouncement on this subject. One of these rare instances occurred in 1939, when the report of the House Committee on Ways and Means, part of the legislative history of the Revenue Act of 1938, stated:

> The exemption from taxation of money or property devoted to charitable and other purposes is based upon the theory that the government is compensated for the loss of revenue by its relief from financial burden which would otherwise have to be met by appropriations from public funds, and by the benefits resulting from the promotion of the general welfare.[71]

The doctrine also is referenced from time to time in testimony before a congressional committee. For example, the Secretary of the Treasury testified before the House Committee on Ways and Means in 1973, observing:

> These organizations [which he termed "voluntary charities, which depend heavily on gifts and bequests"] are an important influence for diversity and a bulwark against over-reliance on big government. The tax privileges extended to these institutions were purged of abuse in 1969 and we believe the existing deductions for charitable gifts and bequests are an appropriate way to encourage those institutions. We believe the public accepts them as fair.[72]

The literature on this subject is extensive. The contemporary versions of it are traceable to 1975, when the public policy rationale was reexamined and reaffirmed by the Commission on Private Philanthropy and Public Needs. The Commission observed:

> Few aspects of American society are more characteristically, more famously American than the nation's array of voluntary organizations, and the support in both time and money that is given to them by its citizens. Our country has been decisively different in this regard, historian Daniel Boorstin observes, "from the beginning." As the country was settled, "communities existed before governments were there to care for public needs." The result, Boorstin

---

[69] Green v. Connally, 330 F. Supp. 1150, 1162 (D.D.C. 1971), *aff'd sub nom.* Coit v. Green, 404 U.S. 997 (1971).

[70] *Id.*, 330 F. Supp. at 1162.

[71] H. Rep. No. 1860, 75th Cong., 3d Sess. 19 (1939).

[72] Department of the Treasury, "Proposals for Tax Change," Apr. 30, 1973.

says, was that "voluntary collaborative activities" were set up to provide basic social services. Government followed later.

The practice of attending to community needs outside of government has profoundly shaped American society and its institutional framework. While in most other countries, major social institutions such as universities, hospitals, schools, libraries, museums and social welfare agencies are state-run and state-funded, in the United States many of the same organizations are privately controlled and voluntarily supported. The institutional landscape of America is, in fact, teeming with nongovernmental, noncommercial organizations, all the way from some of the world's leading educational and cultural institutions to local garden clubs, from politically powerful national associations to block associations—literally millions of groups in all. This vast and varied array is, and has long been widely recognized as part of the very fabric of American life. It reflects a national belief in the philosophy of pluralism and in the profound importance to society of individual initiative.

Underpinning the virtual omnipresence of voluntary organizations, and a form of individual initiative in its own right, is the practice—in the case of many Americans, the deeply ingrained habit—of philanthropy, of private giving, which provides the resource base for voluntary organizations.

These two interrelated elements, then, are sizable forces in American society, far larger than in any other country. And they have contributed immeasurably to this country's social and scientific progress. On the ledger of recent contributions are such diverse advances as the creation of noncommercial "public" television, the development of environmental, consumerist and demographic consciousness, community-oriented museum programs, the protecting of land and landmarks from the often heedless rush of "progress." The list is endless and still growing; both the number and deeds of voluntary organizations are increasing. "Americans are forever forming associations," wrote de Tocqueville. They still are: tens of thousands of environmental organizations have sprung up in the last few years alone. Private giving is growing, too, at least in current dollar amounts.[73]

Here the concept of *philanthropy* enters, with the view that charitable organizations, maintained by tax exemption and nurtured by the ability to attract deductible contributions, reflect the American philosophy that not all policy-making and problem-solving should be reposed in the governmental sector. Earlier, a jurist wrote, in a frequently cited article, that philanthropy

> is the very possibility of doing something different than government can do, of creating an institution free to make choices government cannot— even seemingly arbitrary ones—without having to provide a justification that will be examined in a court of law, which stimulates much private giving and interest.[74]

---

[73] Id. at 9–10.

[74] Friendly, "The Dartmouth College Case and the Public-Private Penumbra," 12 *Tex. Q.* (2d Supp.) 141, 171 (1969). Two other sources of prominence are Rabin, "Charitable Trusts and Charitable Deductions," 41 *N.Y.U. L. Rev.* 912 (1966); Saks, "The Role of Philanthropy: An Institutional View," 46 *Va. L. Rev.* 516 (1960).

A component part of the public policy doctrine is its emphasis on *voluntarism*. This principle was expressed as follows:

> Voluntarism has been responsible for the creation and maintenance of churches, schools, colleges, universities, laboratories, hospitals, libraries, museums, and the performing arts; voluntarism has given rise to the public and private health and welfare systems and many other functions and services that are now an integral part of the American civilization. In no other country has private philanthropy become so vital a part of the national culture or so effective an instrument in prodding government to closer attention to social needs.[75]

One of the modern-day exponents of the role and value of the independent sector in the United States is John W. Gardner, former Secretary of Health, Education, and Welfare, founder of Common Cause, and one of the founders of Independent Sector. Mr. Gardner has written extensively on the subject of the necessity for and significance of the nation's nonprofit sector. He wrote that "[t]he area of our national life encompassed by the deduction for religious, scientific, educational, and charitable organizations lies at the very heart of our intellectual and spiritual strivings as a people, at the very heart of our feeling about one another and about our joint life."[76] He added that "[t]he private pursuit of public purpose is an honored tradition in American life"[77] and believed that "[a]ll elements in the private sector should unite to maintain a tax policy that preserves our pluralism."[78] Likewise, Robert J. Henle, formerly president of Georgetown University, wrote of how "[t]he not-for-profit, private sector promotes the free initiative of citizens and gives them an opportunity on a nonpolitical basis to join together to promote the welfare of their fellow citizens or the public purpose to which they are attracted."[79]

It is not possible, in a book of this nature, to fully capture the philosophical underpinnings of the nonprofit sector. Yet, this task has been accomplished by Brian O'Connell, while President of Independent Sector.[80] In a foreword to Mr. O'Connell's work, John W. Gardner stated this basic truth: "All Americans interact with voluntary or nonprofit agencies and activities regularly, although they are often unaware of this fact."[81] Still, the educational process must continue, for as Mr. Gardner wrote: "The sector enhances our creativity, enlivens our communities, nurtures individual responsibility, stirs life at the grassroots, and reminds us that we were born free."[82] Mr. O'Connell's collection includes thoughts from sources as diverse as Max Lerner (". . . the associative impulse is strong in American life; no other civilization can show as many secret fraternal orders, businessmen's 'service clubs,' trade and occupational associations, social clubs, garden clubs, women's

---

[75] Fink, "Taxation and Philanthropy—A 1976 Perspective," 3 *J. Coll. & Univ. L.* 1, 6–7 (1975).

[76] Gardner, "Bureaucracy vs. The Private Sector," 212 *Current* 17–18 (May 1979).

[77] *Id.* at 17.

[78] *Id.* at 18.

[79] Henle, "The Survival of Not-For-Profit, Private Institutions," *America* 252 (Oct. 23, 1976).

[80] O'Connell, *America's Voluntary Spirit* (New York: The Foundation Center, 1983).

[81] *Id.* at xi.

[82] *Id.* at xv.

clubs, church clubs, theater groups, political and reform associations, veterans' groups, ethnic societies, and other clusterings of trivial or substantial importance"[83]), Daniel J. Boorstin (". . . in America, even in modern times, communities existed before governments were here to care for public needs"[84]), Merle Curti (". . . voluntary association with others in common causes has been thought to be strikingly characteristic of American life"[85]), John W. Gardner ("For many countries . . . monolithic central support of all educational, scientific, and charitable activities would be regarded as normal . . . [b]ut for the United States it would mean the end of a great tradition"[86]), Richard C. Cornuelle ("We have been unique because another sector, clearly distinct from the other two, has, in the past, borne a heavy load of public responsibility"[87]), John D. Rockefeller 3rd ("The third sector is . . . the seedbed for organized efforts to deal with social problems"[88]), Waldemar A. Neilsen (". . . the ultimate contribution of the Third Sector to our national life—namely what it does to ensure the continuing responsiveness, creativity and self-renewal of our democratic society"[89]), Richard W. Lyman (". . . an array of its [the independent sector's] virtues that is by now fairly familiar: its contributions to pluralism and diversity, its tendency to enable individuals to participate in civic life in ways that make sense to them and help to combat that corrosive feeling of powerlessness that is among the dread social diseases of our era, its encouragement of innovation and its capacity to act as a check on the inadequacies of government"[90]), and himself ("The problems of contemporary society are more complex, the solutions more involved and the satisfactions more obscure, but the basic ingredients are still the caring and the resolve to make things better").[91]

Consequently, it is erroneous to regard tax exemption (or, where appropriate, the charitable contribution deduction) as anything other than a reflection of this larger doctrine. Congress is not merely "giving" eligible non-profit organizations any "benefits"; the exemption from taxation (or charitable deduction) is not a "loophole," a "preference," or a "subsidy"—it is not really an "indirect appropriation."[92] Rather, the various Internal Revenue Code provisions comprised in the tax exemption system exist as a reflection of the affirmative policy of American government to refrain from inhibiting by taxation the beneficial activities of qualified tax-exempt organizations acting in community and other public interests.[93]

---

[83] *Id.* at 81.

[84] *Id.* at 131.

[85] *Id.* at 162.

[86] *Id.* at 256.

[87] *Id.* at 278.

[88] *Id.* at 356.

[89] *Id.* at 368.

[90] *Id.* at 371.

[91] *Id.* at 408. A companion book by the author addresses this point in additional detail, and traces the origins and development of a hypothetical charitable organization to illustrate the applicability of various federal and state laws concerning nonprofit organizations (*A Legal Guide to Starting and Managing a Nonprofit Organization* (New York: John Wiley & Sons, Inc., 2d ed. 1993)). This hypothetical organization is also treated in Blazek, *Tax Planning and Compliance for Tax-Exempt Organizations* (New York: John Wiley & Sons, Inc., 2d ed. 1993).

[92] Cf. *supra* note 32.

[93] In general, Pappas, "The Independent Sector and the Tax Law: Defining Charity in an Ideal Democracy," 64 *S. Cal. L. Rev.* 461 (Jan. 1991).

§ 1.5 INHERENT TAX RATIONALE

Aside from considerations of public policy, there exists an inherent tax theory for tax exemption. The essence of this rationale is that the receipt of what otherwise might be deemed income by a tax-exempt organization is not a taxable event, in that the organization is merely a convenience or means to an end, a vehicle whereby each of those participating in the enterprise may receive and expend money in much the same way as they would if the money was expended by them individually.

This rationale chiefly underlies the exemption for certain social clubs, which enable individuals to pool their resources for the purpose of provision of recreation and pleasure more effectively than can be done on an individual basis.[94] This tax rationale was summarized by one federal court as follows:

> Congress has determined that in a situation where individuals have banded together to provide recreational facilities on a mutual basis, it would be conceptually erroneous to impose a tax on the organization as a separate entity. The funds exempted are received only from the members and any "profit" which results from overcharging for the use of the facilities still belongs to the same members. No income of the sort usually taxed has been generated; the money has simply been shifted from one pocket to another, both within the same pair of pants.[95]

This rationale has also been reflected in congressional committee reports.[96] It was most recently invoked by Congress when enacting the specific tax exemption for homeowners' associations.[97] Thus the Senate Finance Committee observed:

> Since homeowners' associations generally allow individual homeowners to act together in order to maintain and improve the area in which they live, the committee believes it is not appropriate to tax the revenues of an association of homeowners who act together if an individual homeowner acting alone would not be taxed on the same activity.[98]

This rationale, however, operates only where "public" money is not unduly utilized for private gain.[99]

The inherent tax theory also serves as the rationale for the tax exemption for political organizations.[100] Thus, the legislative history underlying this tax exemp-

---

[94] See Chapter 14.

[95] *McGlotten v. Connally, supra* note 67 at 458.

[96] H. Rep. No. 91-413, 91st Cong., 1st Sess. 48 (1969); S. Rep. No. 91-552, 91st Cong., 1st Sess. 71 (1969). A similar rationale for the income tax exemption of churches (see Chapter 8) has been advanced. (Bittker, "Churches, Taxes, and the Constitution," 78 *Yale L. J.* 1285 (1969)).

[97] See § 18.13.

[98] S. Rep. No. 938, 94th Cong., 2d Sess. 394 (1976).

[99] West Side Tennis Club v. Comm'r, 111 F.2d 6 (2d Cir. 1940), *cert. den.*, 311 U.S. 674 (1940).

[100] See Chapter 17.

tion states that these organizations should be treated as tax-exempt organizations, "since political activity (including the financing of political activity) as such is not a trade or business which is appropriately subject to tax."[101]

§ 1.6 OTHER RATIONALES AND REASONS FOR TAX-EXEMPT ORGANIZATIONS

There are, as noted,[102] rationales for tax exemption other than the public policy rationale and the inherent tax rationale. One of these, somewhat less lofty than that accorded charitable and social welfare organizations, is extended as justification for the exemption of trade associations and other forms of business leagues.[103] These entities function to promote the welfare of a segment of society: the business, industrial, and professional community. An element of the philosophy supporting this type of tax exemption is that a healthy business climate advances the public welfare. The tax exemption for labor unions and other labor organizations rests upon a similar rationale.

The tax exemption for fraternal beneficiary organizations also depends, at least in part, on this defense. A study of the insurance practices of large societies by the Department of the Treasury[104] concluded that this rationale is inapplicable with respect to the insurance programs of these entities because "the provision of life insurance and other benefits is generally not considered a good or service with significant external benefits" to society generally. However, the report stated that "tax exemption for these goods and services [insurance and like benefits] may be justified in order to encourage" the charitable activities conducted by these organizations. The inherent tax rationale[105] "may" provide a basis for tax exemption for "certain" of these societies' services, according to the report. Further, the report observed that "[i]nsurance is not a type of product for which consumers may lack access to information on the appropriate quantity or quality that they need." Therefore, the market failure rationale[106] "may not be applicable" in this instance.

Other federal tax exemption provisions may be traced to an effort to achieve a particular objective. These provisions tend to be of more recent vintage, testimony to the fact of a more complex Internal Revenue Code. For example, specific tax exemption for veterans' organizations[107] was enacted to create a category of organizations entitled to use a particular exemption from the unrelated business income tax,[108] and exemption for homeowners' associations[109] came about because of a shift in the policy of the Internal Revenue Service[110] regarding the scope

---

[101] S. Rep. No. 1357, 93d Cong., 2d Sess. 26 (1974).

[102] See *supra* § 3.

[103] See Chapter 13.

[104] "Report to the Congress on Fraternal Benefit Societies," U.S. Department of the Treasury, January 15, 1993. See § 18.4(a), note 93.

[105] See *supra* § 3.

[106] See *infra*, text accompanied by notes 116–121.

[107] See § 18.10(a).

[108] See § 28.3, text accompanied by note 26.

[109] See § 18.13.

[110] Hereinafter IRS.

of tax exemption provided for social welfare organizations. The tax exemption for college and university investment vehicles was the result of Congress's effort to preserve the exempt status of a specific common investment fund in the face of a determination by the IRS to the contrary.[111] As is so often the case with respect to the tax law generally, a particular tax exemption provision can arise as the result of case law, or to clarify it; this was the origin of statutes granting tax exemption to cooperative hospital service organizations,[112] charitable risk pools,[113] child care organizations,[114] public safety testing entities,[115] and state prepaid tuition programs.[116]

All of the foregoing rationales for tax-exempt organizations have been described in philosophical, historical, political, policy, or technical tax terms. Yet another approach to an understanding of exempt organizations can be found in economic theory.

Principles of economics are founded on the laws of supply (production) and demand (consumption). Using the foregoing analyses, exempt organizations appear to have arisen in response to the pressures of the supply side, namely, the need for the goods and services provided, and the force of pluralistic institutions and organizations in society. However, others view tax-exempt organizations as responses to sets of social needs that can be described in demand-side economic terms, a "positive theory of consumer demand."[117]

According to the demand-side analysis, consumers in many contexts prefer to deal with nonprofit, tax-exempt organizations in purchasing goods and services, because the consumer knows that a nonprofit organization has a "legal commitment to devote its entire earnings to the production of services,"[118] while for-profit organizations have a great incentive to raise prices and cut quality. Generally, it is too difficult for consumers to monitor these forces. This means that consumers have a greater basis for trusting tax-exempt organizations to provide the services—a restatement, in a way, of the fiduciary concept. Thus, the consumer, pursuant to this analysis, "needs an organization that he can trust, and the non-profit, because of the legal constraints under which it must operate, is likely to serve that function better than its for-profit counterpart."[119]

This phenomenon has been described as "market failure" as far as for-profit organizations are concerned, in that, in certain circumstances, the market is unable to police the producers by means of ordinary contractual devices.[120] This, in turn, has been described as "contract failure," which occurs where "consumers may be incapable of accurately evaluating the goods promised or delivered" and "market competition may well provide insufficient discipline for a profit-seeking producer."[121] Hence, according to this theory, the consum-

---

[111] See § 10.5.
[112] See § 10.4.
[113] See § 10.6.
[114] See § 7.7.
[115] See § 10.3.
[116] See § 18.16.
[117] Hansmann, "The Role of Nonprofit Enterprise," *supra* note 5 at 896.
[118] *Id*. at 844.
[119] *Id*. at 847.
[120] *Id*. at 845.
[121] *Id*. at 843.

ing public selects the nonprofit organization, which operates without the profit motive[122] and offers the consumer the "trust element" that the for-profit organizations cannot always provide.

However, although the economic demand-side theory is fascinating and undoubtedly contains much truth, it probably overstates the aspect of consumer demand and downplays historical realities, tax considerations, and human frailties. The nonprofit organization antedates the for-profit corporation, and many of today's tax-exempt organizations may be nonprofit because their forebears started out as such. In addition, the forces of pluralism of institutions and organizations continue to shape much of the contemporary independent sector.

§ 1.7 FREEDOM OF ASSOCIATION

Tax exemption for nonprofit membership organizations may be viewed as a manifestation of the constitutionally protected right of association accorded the members of these organizations. There are two types of "freedoms of association." One type—termed the "freedom of intimate association"—is the traditional type of protected association derived from the right of personal liberty. The other type—the "freedom of expressive association"—is a function of the right of free speech protected by the First Amendment to the U.S. Constitution.

By application of the doctrine of freedom of intimate association, the formation and preservation of certain types of highly personal relationships are afforded a substantial measure of sanctuary from unjustified interference by government.[123] These personal bonds are considered to foster diversity and advance personal liberty.[124] In assessing the extent of constraints on the authority of government to interfere with this freedom, a court must make a determination of where the objective characteristics of the relationship, which is created where an individual enters into a particular association, are located on a spectrum from the most intimate to the most attenuated of personal relationships.[125] Relevant factors will include size, purpose, policies, selectivity, and congeniality.[126]

The freedom to engage in group effort is guaranteed under the doctrine of freedom of expressive association[127] and is viewed as a way of advancing political, social, economic, educational, religious, and cultural ends.[128] Government, however, has the ability to infringe on this right where compelling state interests,

---

[122] See § 4.9.

[123] Pierce v. Society of Sisters, 268 U.S. 510 (1925); Meyer v. Nebraska, 262 U.S. 390 (1923).

[124] Zablocki v. Redhail, 434 U.S. 374 (1978); Quilloin v. Walcott, 434 U.S. 246 (1978); Smith v. Organization of Foster Families, 431 U.S. 816 (1977); Carey v. Population Serv. Int'l, 431 U.S. 678 (1977); Moore v. East Cleveland, 431 U.S. 494 (1977); Cleveland Bd. of Educ. v. LaFleur, 414 U.S. 632 (1974); Wisconsin v. Yoder, 406 U.S. 205 (1973); Stanley v. Illinois, 405 U.S. 645 (1972); Stanley v. Georgia, 394 U.S. 557 (1969); Griswold v. Connecticut, 381 U.S. 479 (1965); Olmstead v. United States, 277 U.S. 438 (1928).

[125] Runyon v. McCrary, 427 U.S. 160 (1976).

[126] Roberts v. United States Jaycees, 468 U.S. 609 (1984).

[127] Rent Control Coalition for Fair Housing v. Berkeley, 454 U.S. 290 (1981).

[128] NAACP v. Claiborne Hardware Co., 458 U.S. 886 (1982); Larson v. Valente, 456 U.S. 228 (1982); In re Primus, 436 U.S. 412 (1978); Abood v. Detroit Bd. of Educ. 431 U.S. 209 (1977).

unrelated to the suppression of ideas and that cannot be achieved through means significantly less restrictive of associational freedoms, are served.[129]

These two associational freedoms have recently been the subject of a U.S. Supreme Court analysis concerning an organization's right to exclude women from its voting membership.[130] The Court found that the organization involved and its chapters were too large and unselective to find shelter under the doctrine of freedom of intimate association. While the Court also conceded that the "[f]reedom of association therefore plainly presupposes a freedom not to associate," it concluded that the governmental interest in eradicating gender-based discrimination is superior to the associational rights of the organization's male members.[131] In general, the Court held that to tolerate this form of discrimination would be to deny "society the benefits of wide participation in political, economic, and cultural life."[132]

---

[129] Brown v. Socialist Workers '74 Campaign Comm., 459 U.S. 87 (1982); Democratic Party v. Wisconsin, 450 U.S. 107 (1981); Buckley v. Valeo, 424 U.S. 1 (1976), Cousins v. Wigoda, 419 U.S. 477 (1975); American Party v. White, 415 U.S. 767 (1974); NAACP v. Button, 371 U.S. 415 (1963); Shelton v. Tucker, 364 U.S. 486 (1960), NAACP v. Alabama, 347 U.S. 449 (1958).

[130] Roberts v. United States Jaycees, *supra* note 125.

[131] *Id.* at 622–629.

[132] *Id.* at 625. In general, Linder, "Freedom of Association After *Roberts v. United States Jaycees*," 82 *Mich. L. Rev.* (No. 8) 1878 (1984).

CHAPTER TWO

Overview of Nonprofit Sector and Exempt Organizations

The nonprofit sector and the federal tax law with respect to it have had in recent years—and continue to have—a common feature: enormous growth. As to the sector itself, this expansion can be seen in all aspects, including the number of organizations, the sector's asset base, its annual expenditures, its share of the gross national product, the size of its workforce, and the extent of charitable giving. There is a direct correlation: As the sector enlarges, so too does the body of federal and state law regulating it.

Over the years, there have been many efforts to analyze and portray the nonprofit sector by means of statistics. One of the first and significant of these contemporary undertakings, conducted jointly by the Survey Research Center at the University of Michigan and the U.S. Census Bureau, was published in 1975 as part of the findings of the Commission on Private Philanthropy and Public Needs (also known as the Filer Commission).[1] The data compiled for the Commission's use were for 1973. Charitable giving statistics are explored below, but one striking basis of comparison cannot be resisted at this point: Charitable giving by individuals in 1973 added up to about $26 billion, while for 1996 the amount was about $150 billion.[2]

Research of the nature developed for the Filer Commission has spawned subsequent and recurring statistical portraits of the sector. The most comprehensive of these analyses is that provided in the *Nonprofit Almanac: Dimensions of the Independent Sector.*[3] Others include the annual survey of charitable giving published by the American Association of Fund Raising Counsel Trust for Philan-

---

[1] *Giving in America—Toward a Stronger Voluntary Sector* (1975).

[2] See the text accompanied by *infra* note 28.

[3] Hodgkinson & Weitzman, *Nonprofit Almanac: Dimensions of the Independent Sector* (San Francisco: Jossey-Bass Publishers, various editions). The edition referenced here (the fifth) was published in 1996 (*Nonprofit Almanac*).

thropy.[4] The IRS collects data on tax-exempt organizations in its Statistics of Income Division.[5] Various subsets of the nonprofit sector are the subject of more specific portrayals.[6]

§ 2.1 STATISTICAL PROFILE OF NONPROFIT SECTOR

In an understatement, it has been observed that "[c]ounting the number of institutions in the independent sector is a challenge."[7] There are several reasons for this: Most religious organizations (of which there are well in excess of 300,000) are not required to file annual information returns with the IRS,[8] so that data concerning them is difficult to amass; hundreds of organizations are under a group exemption[9] and thus not separately identified; and smaller nonprofit organizations need not report to the IRS,[10] to name a few.

Certainly, there are in excess of one million nonprofit organizations. The number of them in 1992 was estimated in the *Nonprofit Almanac* to be approximately 1.4 million.[11] However, this number was principally based on entities reporting to the IRS. Within this grouping of organizations, there were 546,000 reporting charitable organizations,[12] 341,000 religious organizations, 143,000 social welfare organizations,[13] and 396,000 other nonprofit, tax-exempt organizations.[14]

In 1992, tax-exempt organizations represented 5.8 percent of total United States organizations. (Business organizations constituted 93.8 percent of total entities.) The number of reporting charitable and social welfare organizations (689,000) increased by 70 percent since 1977 (406,000 in that year).[15] The IRS data on this subject are discussed below.[16]

In 1994, the total national income was $5.59 trillion. The tax-exempt organization's sector's share of this was 6.9 percent ($387.4 billion). The value of volun-

---

[4] These annual publications of this organization (*Trust for Philanthropy*) are titled *Giving USA*.

[5] The IRS publishes various editions of the "Statistics of Income Bulletins."

[6] E.g., *Yearbook of American and Canadian Churches* (Nashville, Tenn.: National Council of the Churches of Christ in the United States of America, various editions); *Foundation Giving: Yearbook of Facts and Figures on Private, Corporate and Community Foundations* (New York: The Foundation Center, various editions); *Foundation Management Report* (Washington, D.C.: Council on Foundations, various editions). The American Hospital Association publishes statistics concerning hospitals, the National Center for Education Statistics publishes data on independent colleges and universities, and the American Society of Association Executives publishes information concerning the nation's trade, business, and professional associations.

[7] *Nonprofit Almanac* at 25.

[8] See § 24.3.

[9] See § 23.6.

[10] These are organizations that normally do not generate more than $25,000 annually in revenues. See § 24.3.

[11] *Nonprofit Almanac* at 25.

[12] That is, organizations described in IRC § 501(c)(3).

[13] That is, organizations described in IRC § 501(c)(4).

[14] *Nonprofit Almanac* at 25.

[15] *Id.* at 25–26.

[16] See the text accompanied by *infra* notes 26–27.

teer time for that year was $116 billion. There has been a decline in volunteering, particularly since 1992; the value of volunteer time as a share of national income has declined from 2.4 percent in 1982 to 2 percent in 1994.[17] In 1994, an estimated 134.1 million individuals received compensation for work. Charitable and social welfare organizations increased their share of total employment from 5.3 percent in 1977 to 6.7 percent in 1994. With volunteer time taken into account, the 1994 percentage was 10.6 percent.[18] In 1994, the annual earnings from paid work totaled $3.75 trillion. In that year, reporting tax-exempt organizations accounted for $336.6 billion of total earnings.[19]

In 1993, current operating expenditures for all nonprofit organizations were said to be $499.1 billion. (In a telling statistic, the comparable outlays in 1960 were $18.4 billion.) In constant (1987) dollars, these expenditures increased from $126 billion to $376 billion (an increase of 198 percent). In constant dollars, nonprofit organizations expended in 1993—for every individual in the country—$1,454. If the assigned value of volunteer time were included in this estimate of operating expenditures, the per capita expenditure in constant dollars would be $1,817.[20]

Also in 1993, the current operating expenditures by nonprofit organizations were 20 percent of total services. In that year, these expenditures were 11.4 percent of personal consumption expenditures and 7.9 percent of the gross domestic product. Current operating expenditures as a percentage of gross domestic product have more than doubled over three decades from 3.6 percent in 1960 to 7.9 percent in 1993.[21]

In 1994, there were nearly 10.3 million paid employees in the nonprofit sector. Employment in the nonprofit sector grew at an annual rate of 3.3 percent from 1977 to 1994. In 1994, the nonprofit sector's share of total wages and salaries was 7 percent ($222.3 billion). Within the framework of charitable and social welfare organizations, the health services subsector's share of total wages and salaries in 1994 was 57.1 percent ($117 billion), up from 49 percent ($23 billion) in 1977. Yet the education and research subsector's share of total wages and salaries was 19.8 percent, down from over 28 percent in 1977.[22]

In 1994, total revenues for charitable and social welfare organizations were estimated to be $568.4 billion. In 1992, the major sources of funds for these organizations were forms of exempt function revenue (dues, fees, and other charges) (39.1 percent), government grants and contracts (31.3 percent), contributions (18.4 percent), and other forms of revenue (11.2 percent). In 1994, total current operating expenditures by these organizations totaled $487 billion. Current operating expenditures accounted for 86 percent of these revenues; wages and salaries consumed 42 percent of operating expenditures.[23] In 1992, total revenues in the health services subsector were $261 billion, in the education and research subsector were $95 billion, in the religion subsector were $58.3 billion, in the social and

---

[17] *Id.* at 27–28.
[18] *Id.* at 28–30.
[19] *Id.* at 30–31.
[20] *Id.* at 32–33.
[21] *Id.* at 34–35.
[22] *Id.* at 129–130.
[23] *Id.* at 156–163.

legal services subsector were $56 billion, and in the arts and cultural subsector were $8.2 billion.[24]

As has been observed, the "IRS collects the only data files encompassing the universe of tax-exempt organizations."[25] Some of these data are in the IRS Business Master File of Exempt Organizations and some in the agency's annual return files. On the basis of these sources, it was estimated that there were 582,082 charitable organizations, other than religious ones, in 1995. In 1992, out of 540,040 charitable entities, there were 493,984 public charities and 46,056 private foundations. About two thirds of these organizations are very small. In 1992, 164,247 charitable organizations filed annual information returns with the IRS. (Of these entities, 34 percent were founded between 1985 and 1992.) Over 70 percent of these organizations had total expenses under $500,000; only 3.5 percent of these entities (5,722) had total expenses exceeding $10 million (yet this group represented 79 percent of total expenses, 73 percent of total assets, and 51 percent of public support for all of the filing institutions).[26]

Of these 5,722 charitable organizations, 58 percent (3,321) were in the health field and 18 percent (1,056) were in education. Thus, 76 percent of these major institutions were in the arenas of health and education. In 1992, the major categories with the highest percentage of total institutions were human services (34 percent), health (18 percent), education (15 percent), and arts and culture (11 percent). Out of the $84.3 billion in total public support reported by institutions in 1992, a total of 75 percent went to the major categories of organizations: human services (27 percent), education (26 percent), and health (22 percent). Within this category of health institutions, hospitals received 33 percent of total public support; within the category of educational institutions, higher education institutions received 66 percent of public support; and within the category of human services, multi-purpose human services organizations received 64 percent of public support. Other major categories with a significant percentage of total public support were arts, culture, and humanities (7 percent), and public, societal benefit (7 percent).

The major category of health dominated total expenses for the sector. In 1992, 62 percent of total expenses was in this subsector. By major purpose, 59 percent of these total expenses was in general health—predominantly, hospitals. The category of education comprised 18 percent of these expenses and human services 11 percent. Total expenses for the sector were $458 billion in 1992.

Two major categories, health (49 percent) and education (30 percent), accounted for over three quarters of the assets of filing institutions. By major purpose, hospitals accounted for 81 percent of the total assets in health; higher education institutions accounted for 71 percent of the total assets in education. Other major categories with a significant percentage of total sector assets were human services (10 percent) and arts, culture, and humanities (4 percent). In 1992, total assets reported by filing institutions were $685 billion.[27]

According to the Trust for Philanthropy, charitable giving in the United

[24] *Id.* at 165, 170, 175, 180, 183.
[25] *Id.* at 215.
[26] *Id.* at 218–221.
[27] *Id.* at 222–225.

States in 1996 totaled $150.7 billion.[28] The sources of these contributions were living individuals in the amount of $119.9 billion (79.6 percent), private foundations $11.8 billion (7.8 percent), bequests $10.5 billion (6.9 percent), and corporations $8.5 billion (5.6 percent). The overwhelming single purpose of these contributions was, as always, religion ($69.4 billion). The other fields of allocation were education ($18.8 billion); health ($13.9 billion); human services ($12.2 billion); arts, culture, and humanities ($10.9 billion); non-corporate foundations ($8.3 billion); public/society benefit ($7.6 billion); environment and wildlife ($4.04 billion); and international affairs ($1.97 billion). Giving in the amount of $3.6 billion was unallocated.

As the Commission on Private Philanthropy and Public Needs observed, the "arithmetic of the nonprofit sector finds much of its significance in less quantifiable and even less precise dimensions—in the human measurements of who is served, who is affected by nonprofit groups and activities." The Commission added:

> In some sense, everybody is: the contributions of voluntary organizations to broadscale social and scientific advances have been widely and frequently extolled. Charitable groups were in the forefront of ridding society of child labor, abolitionist groups in tearing down the institution of slavery, civic-minded groups in purging the spoils system from public office. The benefits of nonprofit scientific and technological research include the great reduction of scourges such as tuberculosis and polio, malaria, typhus, influenza, rabies, yaws, bilharziasis, syphilis and amoebic dysentery. These are among the myriad products of the nonprofit sector that have at least indirectly affected all Americans and much of the rest of the world besides.
>
> Perhaps the nonprofit activity that most directly touches the lives of most Americans today is noncommercial "public" television. A bare concept twenty-five years ago, its development was underwritten mainly by foundations. Today it comprises a network of some 240 stations valued at billions of dollars, is increasingly supported by small, "subscriber" contributions and has broadened and enriched a medium that occupies hours of the average American's day.
>
> More particularly benefited by voluntary organizations are the one quarter of all college and university students who attend private institutions of higher education. For hundreds of millions of Americans, private community hospitals, accounting for half of all hospitals in the United States, have been, as one Commission study puts it, "the primary site for handling the most dramatic of human experiences—birth, death, and the alleviation of personal suffering." In this secular age, too, it is worth noting that the largest category in the nonprofit sector is still very large indeed, that nearly two out of three Americans belong to and evidently find comfort and inspiration in the nation's hundreds of thousands of religious organizations. All told, it would be hard to imagine American life without voluntary nonprofit organizations and associations, so entwined are they in the very fabric of our society, from massive national organizations to the local Girl Scouts, the parent-teachers association or the bottle recycling group.[29]

---

[28] *Giving USA* (1997).
[29] *Giving in America—Toward a Stronger Voluntary Sector, supra,* note 40, at 34–38.

§ 2.2 CATEGORIES OF TAX-EXEMPT ORGANIZATIONS

Data compiled by the IRS, through 1994, indicates that there were 1,138,598 organizations in its Master File of Tax-Exempt Organizations.[30] This compilation, of course, does not include nonprofit organizations that are not required to file applications for recognition of tax exemption with the IRS, including churches, integrated auxiliaries of churches, conventions and associations of churches, and certain subordinate units of churches;[31] as noted above, however, it has been estimated that there were, in 1992, 341,000 churches.[32] Also taking into account small organizations and those covered by a group exemption (such as scout troops and fraternal lodges), there undoubtedly are at least nearly 1.5 million tax-exempt organizations in the United States.

The breakdown as to these tax-exempt organizations is as follows: 9 instrumentalities of the United States,[33] 6,967 single-parent title-holding companies,[34] 599,745 charitable organizations,[35] 140,143 social welfare organizations,[36] 68,144 labor and agricultural organizations,[37] 74,273 business leagues,[38] 65,273 social clubs,[39] 92,284 fraternal beneficiary societies,[40] 14,835 voluntary employees' beneficiary societies,[41] 21,215 domestic fraternal beneficiary societies,[42] 11 teachers' retirement funds,[43] 6,221 benevolent life insurance associations,[44] 9,294 cemetery companies,[45] 5,391 credit unions,[46] 1,161 mutual insurance companies,[47] 23 crop operations finance corporations,[48] 601 supplemental unemployment benefit trusts,[49] 4 employee-funded pension trusts,[50] 30,282 war veterans' organizations,[51] 181 group legal services organizations,[52] 25 black lung benefit trusts,[53] two veterans' organizations founded prior to 1880,[54] one trust de-

---

[30] *Nonprofit Almanac* at 38.
[31] See § 24.3.
[32] See the text accompanied by *supra* note 8.
[33] Organizations described in IRC § 501(c)(1) (see § 18.1).
[34] Organizations described in IRC § 501(c)(2) (see § 18.2(a)).
[35] Organizations described in IRC § 501(c)(3) (see Part Two). The entities referenced *infra* notes 58–59 are also charitable organizations.
[36] Organizations described in IRC § 501(c)(4) (see Chapter 12).
[37] Organizations described in IRC § 501(c)(5) (see Chapter 15).
[38] Organizations described in IRC § 501(c)(6) (see Chapter 13).
[39] Organizations described in IRC § 501(c)(7) (see Chapter 14).
[40] Organizations described in IRC § 501(c)(8) (see § 18.4(a)).
[41] Organizations described in IRC § 501(c)(9) (see § 16.3).
[42] Organizations described in IRC § 501(c)(10) (see § 18.4(b)).
[43] Organizations described in IRC § 501(c)(11) (see § 16.6).
[44] Organizations described in IRC § 501(c)(12) (see § 18.5).
[45] Organizations described in IRC § 501(c)(13) (see § 18.6).
[46] Organizations described in IRC § 501(c)(14) (see § 18.7).
[47] Organizations described in IRC § 501(c)(15) (see § 18.8).
[48] Organizations described in IRC § 501(c)(16) (see § 18.9).
[49] Organizations described in IRC § 501(c)(17) (see § 16.4).
[50] Organizations described in IRC § 501(c)(18) (see § 16.6).
[51] Organizations described in IRC § 501(c)(19) (see § 18.10(a)).
[52] Organizations described in IRC § 501(c)(20) (see § 16.6).
[53] Organizations described in IRC § 501(c)(21) (see § 16.5).
[54] Organizations described in IRC § 501(c)(23) (see § 18.10(b)).

scribed in section 4049 of the Employee Retirement Income Security Act,[55] 479 title-holding companies for multiple beneficiaries,[56] 99 religious and apostolic organizations,[57] 68 cooperative hospital service organizations,[58] one cooperative service organization of educational institutions,[59] and 1,866 farmers' cooperatives.[60]

This enumeration of tax-exempt organizations by the IRS does not include references to multiemployer pension trusts,[61] day care centers,[62] shipowners' protection and indemnity organizations,[63] political organizations,[64] or homeowners' associations.[65] Because there are no data yet compiled as to them, there is no listing of charitable risk pools[66] or prepaid tuition plan trusts.[67]

The federal tax law recognizes 63 categories of tax-exempt organizations.[68]

§ 2.3   ORGANIZATION OF THE IRS

The Internal Revenue Service is a component of the U.S. Department of the Treasury. One of the functions of the Treasury Department is to formulate national tax policy, including that pertaining to tax-exempt organizations. This policy formulation is the responsibility of the Assistant Treasury Secretary for Tax Policy.

The IRS is administered at the national level by its office in Washington, D.C. (the National Office),[69] headed by a Commissioner of Internal Revenue, who generally superintends the assessment and collection of all taxes imposed by any law providing for federal (internal) revenue.[70] There are seven Assistant Commissioners, one of whom is the Assistant Commissioner (Employee Plans and Exempt Organizations).[71] One of the functions of this Assistant Commissioner is to establish and oversee policy for the IRS in the field of tax-exempt organizations.

---

[55] Organizations described in IRC § 501(c)(24) (see § 16.6).
[56] Organizations described in IRC § 501(c)(25) (see § 18.2(b)).
[57] Organizations described in IRC § 501(d) (see § 8.7).
[58] Organizations described in IRC § 501(e) (see § 10.4).
[59] Organizations described in IRC § 501(f) (see § 10.5).
[60] Organizations described in IRC § 521 (see § 18.11).
[61] Organizations described in IRC § 501(c)(22) (see § 16.6).
[62] Organizations described in IRC § 501(k) (see § 7.7).
[63] Organizations described in IRC § 526 (see § 18.12).
[64] Organizations described in IRC § 527 (see Chapter 17).
[65] Organizations described in IRC § 528 (see § 18.13).
[66] Organizations described in IRC § 501(n) (see § 10.6).
[67] Organizations described in IRC § 529 (see § 18.16). As the preceding footnotes indicate, the many categories of tax-exempt organizations are discussed in various chapters throughout the book. Nonetheless, as the following observation by the U.S. Tax Court affirms, "[t]rying to understand the various exempt organization provisions of the Internal Revenue Code is as difficult as capturing a drop of mercury under your thumb" (Weingarden v. Comm'r, 86 T.C. 669, 675 (1986), rev'd, 825 F.2d 1027 (6th Cir. 1987)).
[68] See Appendix C.
[69] Reg. § 601.101(a).
[70] IRC § 7802(a).
[71] IRC § 7802(b).

Within this Assistant Commissioner's structure is the Exempt Organizations Division, which functions to develop policy and administer the law in the realm of tax-exempt organizations. This Division includes five technical branches, two projects branches, and one review branch.

Another component of the IRS at the national level is the Office of the IRS Chief Counsel, which is part of the Legal Division of the Treasury Department. The Chief Counsel is the principal legal adviser on federal tax matters to the Commissioner. There are eight Associate Chief Counsels, one of whom is the Associate Chief Counsel (Employee Benefits and Exempt Organizations). One of the functions of this Associate Chief Counsel's office, which includes an Assistant Chief Counsel with direct responsibility in the exempt organizations area and seven branches, is to develop legal policy and strategy in the fields of tax-exempt organizations.

§ 2.4 EVOLUTION OF THE STATUTORY SCHEME

The statutory law of tax-exempt organizations was initiated in 1913, and given major boosts in 1950 and 1969. Indeed, the statutory structure of today (along with the charitable giving rule[72]) was shaped substantially by the 1969 legislation. Nearly every tax act of any consequence since then (particularly in 1974, 1976, 1982, 1984, 1986, 1987, 1993, 1996, and 1997) has added to this body of law. (Additional legislation that would have augmented this collection of law, passed in 1992 and 1995, was vetoed.)

The original statutory tax exemption for nonprofit organizations in United States law—for charitable organizations—was contained in the Tariff Act of 1894.[73] The provision stated that "nothing herein contained shall apply to . . . corporations, companies, or associations organized and conducted solely for charitable, religious, or educational purposes."[74]

After ratification of the Sixteenth Amendment, Congress enacted the Tariff Act of 1913, exempting from the federal income tax "any corporation or association organized and operated exclusively for religious, charitable, scientific, or educational purposes, no part of the net income of which inures to the benefit of any private shareholder or individual."[75]

In the Revenue Act of 1918, the enumeration of tax-exempt organizations was expanded to include those organized "for the prevention of cruelty to children or animals."[76] The Revenue Act of 1921 expanded the statute to exempt "any community chest, fund, or foundation" and added "literary" groups to

---

[72] See *infra* § 5.
[73] 28 Stat. 556 (Act ch. 349).
[74] The income tax enacted in 1894 was declared unconstitutional by the Supreme Court in Pollock v. Farmer's Loan & Trust Co., 158 U.S. 601 (1895), overruled on other grounds in State of South Carolina v. Baker, 485 U.S. 505 (1988).
[75] 38 Stat. 114, 166.
[76] 40 Stat. 1076.

the list of exempt entities.[77] The Revenue Acts of 1924,[78] 1926,[79] 1928,[80] and 1932[81] did not provide for any changes in the law of tax-exempt organizations.

The Revenue Act of 1934 carried forward the exemption requirements as stated in the prior revenue measures and added the rule that "no substantial part" of the activities of an exempt organization can involve the carrying on of "propaganda" or "attempting to influence legislation."[82] The Revenue Acts of 1936[83] and 1938[84] brought forward these same rules, as did the Internal Revenue Code of 1939.[85]

The unrelated business income rules were enacted in 1950.[86] This was a radical addition to the law, in part because it introduced the concept that some or all nonprofit organizations could be taxed. This would lead to many more federal taxes on or in connection with "tax-exempt" organizations.

IRC § 501(c)(3) came into being upon enactment of the Internal Revenue Code in 1954.[87] The previous rules were retained and two additions to the statute were made: the listing of tax-exempt organizations was amplified to include entities that are organized and operated for the purpose of "testing for public safety"[88] and organizations otherwise described in IRC § 501(c)(3) became expressly forbidden to "participate in, or intervene in (including the publishing or distributing of statements), any political campaign on behalf of any candidate for public office."[89]

Enactment of the Revenue and Expenditure Control Act of 1968 brought rules concerning cooperative hospital service organizations.[90] These rules would be amended by provisions of the Revenue Act of 1988, the Tax Reform Act of 1976, and the Tax Payer Relief Act of 1997. The rules pertaining to cooperative service organizations of operating educational organizations were enacted in 1974,[91] as was statutory law concerning political organizations.[92]

The Tax Reform Act of 1969[93] brought an array of exempt organizations provisions, including rules differentiating public charities from private foundations, imposing taxes on various aspects of the operations of private foundations, and revising the unrelated debt-financed property rules and the tax treatment of social clubs.

---

[77] 42 Stat. 253.
[78] 43 Stat. 282.
[79] 44 Stat. 40.
[80] 45 Stat. 813.
[81] 47 Stat. 193.
[82] 48 Stat. 700.
[83] 49 Stat. 1674.
[84] 52 Stat. 481.
[85] 53 Stat. 1.
[86] See Part Five.
[87] 68A Stat. 163.
[88] See § 10.3.
[89] See § 21.1.
[90] 82 Stat. 269.
[91] 88 Stat. 235.
[92] 88 Stat. 2108.
[93] 83 Stat. 487.

The Tax Reform Act of 1976 also brought law concerning declaratory judgment rules for charitable organizations, lobbying by public charities (the expenditure test), amateur sports organizations, social clubs, homeowners' associations, definition of the term *agricultural,* and tax exemption for group legal services plans (the latter of which expired in 1992).[94] The next year saw enactment of the Black Lung Benefits Revenue Act of 1977.[95]

The Tax Equity and Fiscal Responsibility Act of 1982 revised the rules pertaining to veterans' organizations and amended the law concerning amateur sports organizations.[96] The Tax Reform Act of 1984 caused the church audit rules, changes in the United States instrumentalities rules, and the child care organizations rules to become law.[97] The Deficit Reduction Act of 1984 brought the tax-exempt entity leasing rules.[98]

The Tax Reform Act of 1986 changed the Internal Revenue Code formal reference to the Code of 1986 (which, as amended, is its status today).[99] This act also introduced the law concerning provision of commercial-type insurance, liquidations of for-profit entities into tax-exempt organizations, and multiparent title-holding corporations; also, it revised the exempt entity leasing rules.

The Revenue Act of 1987 brought taxes on public charities for engaging in excessive lobbying and political campaign activities, as well as fund-raising disclosure requirements for noncharitable organizations.[100] Enactment of the Omnibus Budget Reconciliation Act of 1993 introduced rules concerning the deductibility of expenses for lobbying and political campaign activities, and disclosure rules as to these activities for associations.[101]

Legislation known as the Taxpayer Bill of Rights 2, enacted in 1996, added the intermediate sanctions rules, expanded the penalties for failure to timely file complete annual information returns, expanded the contents of these returns, revised disclosure rules, and added the private inurement language to the law pertaining to social welfare organizations.[102] The Small Business Job Protection Act of 1996 added revisions to the unrelated business rules, exemption opportunities for charitable risk pools and state tuition programs, and the ability of charitable organizations to own stock in small business corporations.[103] The Health Insurance Portability and Accountability Act of 1996 brought two new categories of tax-exempt organizations.[104] The enactment of the Taxpayer Relief Act of 1997 caused several changes and additions to the law of tax-exempt organizations, including various modifications of the unrelated business income rules and treatment of associations of holders of timeshare interests as homeowners' associations.[105]

---

[94] 90 Stat. 1520.
[95] 92 Stat. 11.
[96] 96 Stat. 324.
[97] 98 Stat. 494.
[98] *Id.*
[99] 100 Stat. 1951.
[100] 101 Stat. 1330.
[101] 107 Stat. 312.
[102] 110 Stat. 1452.
[103] 110 Stat. 1755.
[104] 110 Stat. 1936.
[105] 111 Stat. 788.

§ 2.5 CHARITABLE CONTRIBUTION DEDUCTION RULES

The tax laws pertaining to tax-exempt charitable organizations and deductible charitable giving are closely intertwined.[106] Not only are the two subject matters intimately related conceptually, but the Internal Revenue Code also frequently cross-references one to the other. For example, many of the organizations that are considered public charities are described in the income tax charitable contribution deduction rules.[107]

The basic concept of the federal income tax charitable contribution deduction is that individual taxpayers who itemize deductions and corporate taxpayers can deduct, subject to varying limitations, an amount equivalent to the value of a contribution made to a qualified donee. A *charitable contribution* for income tax purposes is a gift to or for the use of one or more qualified donees.[108]

Aside from the nature of the donee, the other basic element in determining whether a charitable contribution is deductible is the nature of the property contributed. Basically, the distinctions are between current giving and planned (or deferred) giving, between gifts of cash and of property, and between outright gifts and those of partial interests or in trust. The value of a qualified charitable contribution of an item of property generally is its fair market value.[109]

The tax treatment of gifts of property is dependent upon whether the property is *capital gain property*, that is, a capital asset that has appreciated in value, which if sold would result in long-term capital gain.[110] (To be capital gain property, the property must be held for the long-term capital gain holding period, which is twelve months.[111]) Other property is *ordinary-income property* (including short-term capital gain property).

The deductibility of charitable contributions for a tax year is confined by certain percentage limitations, which in the case of individuals are a function of the donor's *contribution base*, which is essentially the same as adjusted gross income.[112] These percentage limitations are (1) 50 percent of the donor's contribution base for contributions of cash and ordinary-income property to public charities and private operating foundations;[113] (2) 20 percent of contribution base for contributions of capital gain property to organizations other than public charities and operating foundations, including private foundations;[114] (3) 30 percent of contribution base for contributions of capital-gain property to public charities;[115] (4) 30 percent of contribution base for contributions of cash and ordinary-income property to private foundations and certain other recipients;[116] and (5) 50 percent

---

[106] The federal tax laws pertaining to charitable giving are the subject of Hopkins, *The Tax Law of Charitable Giving* (New York: John Wiley & Sons, Inc., 1993).

[107] See § 11.3.

[108] IRC § 170(c).

[109] Reg. § 1.170A-1(c).

[110] IRC § 170(b)(1)(C)(iv).

[111] IRC § 1222(1), (2).

[112] IRC § 170(b)(1)(E).

[113] IRC § 170(b)(1)(A). See Chapter 11.

[114] IRC § 170(b)(1)(B).

[115] IRC § 170(b)(1)(C)(i).

[116] IRC § 170(b)(1)(B)(i).

of contribution base for contributions of capital-gain property to public charities where the amount of the contribution is reduced by all of the unrealized appreciation in the value of the property.[117]

Where an individual makes a contribution to a public charity or certain other recipients to the extent that a percentage limitation is exceeded, the excess generally may be carried forward and deducted in subsequent years, up to five.[118] In the case of gifts of cash and ordinary-income property to private foundations in excess of the 30 percent limitation, the five-year carryforward rule also is applicable.[119]

Deductible charitable contributions by corporations in any tax year may not exceed 10 percent of taxable income, as adjusted.[120] A corporation on the accrual method of accounting can elect to treat a contribution as having been paid in a tax year if it is actually paid during the first two and one-half months of the following year.[121] While corporate gifts of property are generally subject to the rules discussed below, special rules apply to the deductibility of gifts of inventory.[122] The making of a charitable gift by a business corporation is not an *ultra vires* act and may be deductible where the general interests of the corporation and its shareholders are advanced.[123]

A donor (individual or corporate) who makes a gift of ordinary income property to any charity (public or private) must reduce the deduction by the full amount of any gain.[124] Any donor who makes a gift of capital gain property to a public charity generally can compute the deduction at the property's fair market value at the time of the gift, regardless of basis and with no taxation of the appreciation.[125] An individual donor who makes a gift of capital gain tangible personal property to a public charity must reduce the deduction by all of the long-term capital gain that would have been recognized had the donor sold the property at its fair market value as of the date of contribution, where the use by the donee is unrelated to its exempt purposes.[126] Generally, an individual donor who makes a gift of capital gain property to a private foundation must reduce the amount of the otherwise allowable deduction by all of the appreciation element.[127]

Most itemized deductions, including the charitable contribution deduction, are subject to a floor of three percent of adjusted gross income in excess of

---

[117] IRC § 170(b)(1)(C)(iii).

[118] IRC §§ 170(b)(1)(C)(ii), 170(d)(1)(A).

[119] IRC § 170(b)(1)(B), last sentence.

[120] IRC § 170(b)(2).

[121] IRC § 170(a)(2).

[122] IRC § 170(e)(3).

[123] E.g., A. P. Smith Mfg. Co. v. Barlow, 98 A.2d 581 (N.J. 1953), *app. dis.*, 346 U.S. 861 (1953).

[124] IRC § 170(e)(1)(A). E.g., IRC § 1221(3).

[125] IRC § 170(e).

[126] IRC § 170(e)(1)(B)(i).

[127] IRC § 170(e)(1)(B)(ii). There is a special rule in this regard: A donor is allowed to base the charitable deduction, for a gift of certain publicly traded stock to a private foundation, on the full fair market value of the property (in the case of gifts made after July 18, 1984, in years ending after that date, and before 1995, and during the period July 1, 1996, through June 30, 1998) (IRC § 170(e)(5)).

$100,000 (with this amount adjusted for inflation).[128] However, total otherwise allowable deductions need not be reduced by more than 80 percent. Also, this floor is inapplicable to medical expenses, casualty and theft losses, and investment interest.

The tax preferences in the alternative minimum income tax rules include an "appreciated property charitable deduction," which is an amount equal to the appreciation element inherent in the contributed capital gain property, to the extent it is included in the allowable charitable deduction for regular income tax purposes.[129] However, this tax preference rule is inapplicable where the contributed appreciated property is the subject of the 50 percent election.[130] While this tax preference rule also applies to amounts carried forward and deducted in subsequent years,[131] it does not apply to any deduction attributable to contributions made before August 16, 1986.

A deduction for a contribution of less than the donor's entire interest in property (that is, a partial interest), including the right to use property, is generally denied.[132] The exceptions are gifts of interests in trust,[133] gifts of an outright remainder interest in a personal residence or farm,[134] gifts of an undivided portion of one's entire interest in property,[135] gifts of a lease on, option to purchase, or easement with respect to real property granted in perpetuity to a public charity exclusively for conservation purposes,[136] and a remainder interest in real property that is granted to a public charity exclusively for conservation purposes.[137]

Contributions of income interests in property in trust are basically confined to the use of charitable lead trusts.[138] Aside from the charitable gift annuity and gifts of remainder interests in personal residences or farms, there is no deduction for a contribution of a remainder interest in property unless it is in trust and the trust is one of three types:[139] a charitable remainder annuity trust or unitrust[140] or a pooled income fund.[141] Defective charitable split-interest trusts may be reformed to preserve the charitable deduction where certain requirements are satisfied.[142]

Other notable features of the income tax charitable contribution deduction

---

[128] IRC § 68.

[129] IRC § 57(a)(6).

[130] See *supra* note 14. Also, this tax preference rule is inapplicable where the gift property is (1) tangible personal property, (2) used in connection with the donee's tax-exempt purposes, (3) not inventory, other than ordinary income property, and (4) contributed during tax years beginning in 1991 (Omnibus Budget Reconciliation Act of 1990 § 11344).

[131] See *supra* note 115.

[132] IRC § 170(f)(3).

[133] IRC § 170(f)(3)(A).

[134] IRC § 170(f)(3)(B)(i).

[135] IRC § 170(f)(3)(B)(ii).

[136] IRC § 170(f)(3)(B)(iii).

[137] IRC § 170(f)(3)(B)(iv).

[138] IRC § 170(f)(2)(B).

[139] IRC § 170(f)(2)(A).

[140] IRC § 664(d).

[141] IRC § 642(c)(5).

[142] IRC §§ 170(f)(7), 664(f), 2055(e)(3), 2522(c)(4).

are the carryover rules,[143] the lack of deduction for contributions of services,[144] and the requirement of the filing of an information return with respect to certain transfers of income-producing property to charity.[145]

Charitable gifts are not subject to the gift tax[146] nor to the estate tax.[147] There is no percentage ceiling on the amount of an estate that may be subject to the estate tax charitable deduction and appreciated property may pass to charity from estates without any taxation on the appreciation element.

---

[143] IRC § 170(d).
[144] Reg. § 1.170A-1(g).
[145] IRC § 6050.
[146] IRC § 2522.
[147] IRC § 2055.

CHAPTER THREE

Sources, Advantages, and Disadvantages of Tax Exemption

As subsequent chapters indicate, there are many categories of tax-exempt organizations and, accordingly, the advantages and disadvantages of tax exemption will differ, depending upon the particular category.

§ 3.1 SOURCE OF TAX EXEMPTION

Section 61(a) of the Internal Revenue Code provides that "[e]xcept as otherwise provided in this subtitle [Subtitle A—income taxes], gross income means all income from whatever source derived . . .," including items such as interest, dividends, compensation for services, and receipts derived from business. The Code provides for a variety of deductions, exclusions, and exemptions in computing taxable income. Many of these are contained in Internal Revenue Code Subtitle A, Subchapter B, entitled "Computation of taxable income." However, of pertinence in the tax-exempt organizations context is the body of exemption provisions contained in Subtitle A, Subchapter F, captioned "Exempt organizations."

Exemption from federal income taxation is derived from a specific provision to that end in the Internal Revenue Code. *Derivation* of exemption is here used in the sense of *recognition* of exemption by the appropriate administrative agency (the IRS) or as a matter of law, as opposed to exemption that is a by-product (albeit a resolutely sought one) of some other tax status (such as a cooperative or a state instrumentality).

A federal tax exemption is a privilege (a matter of legislative grace), not an entitlement,[1] and—being an exception to the norm of taxation—is often

---

[1] As discussed, however, the federal tax exemption for many nonprofit organizations (such as charitable ones) is a reflection of the heritage and societal structure of the United States (see § 1.3).

■ 39 ■

strictly construed.[2] This type of exemption must be by enactment of Congress and will not be granted by implication.[3] At the same time, provisions giving tax exemption for charitable organizations are usually liberally construed.[4] Similarly, the exemption of income devoted to charity by means of the charitable contribution deductions has been held not to be narrowly construed,[5] as are most other deductions.[6] These provisions respecting income destined for charity are accorded favorable construction, since they are "begotten from motives of public policy"[7] and any ambiguity therein has been traditionally resolved against taxation.[8]

The provision in the Internal Revenue Code that is the general source of the federal income tax exemption is IRC § 501(a),[9] which states, "[a]n organization described in subsection (c) or (d) or section 401(a) shall be exempt from taxation under this subtitle [Subtitle A—income taxes] unless such exemption is denied under section 501 or 503."

The U.S. Supreme Court characterized IRC § 501(a) as "the linchpin of the statutory benefit [exemption] system."[10] The Court summarized the exemption provided by IRC § 501(a) as according "advantageous treatment to several types of nonprofit corporations [and trusts and unincorporated associations], including exemption of their income from taxation and [for those that are also eligible charitable donees] deductibility by benefactors of the amounts of their donations."[11]

Thus, to be recognized as exempt under IRC § 501(a), an organization must conform to the appropriate descriptive provisions of IRC § 501(c), IRC § 501(d), or IRC § 401(a). The exemption, however, does not extend to an organization's unrelated business taxable income.[12] Thus, the term *tax-exempt organization* is often not literally accurate, inasmuch as this type of nonprofit organization may be subject to the tax on unrelated income, as well as other taxes, such as those imposed on private foundations,[13] on organizations that engage in excessive lobby-

---

[2] E.g., Knights of Columbus Ass'n of Stamford, Conn., Inc. v. United States, 88-1 U.S.T.C. ¶ 9336 (D. Conn. 1988); Granznow v. Comm'r, 739 F.2d 265 (7th Cir. 1984); Estate of Levine v. Comm'r, 526 F.2d 717 (2d Cir. 1975); Alfred I. duPont Testamentary Trust v. Comm'r, 514 F.2d 917 (5th Cir. 1975); Conference of Major Religious Superiors of Women, Inc. v. District of Columbia, 348 F.2d 783 (D.C. Cir. 1965); Mercantile Bank & Trust Co. v. United States, 441 F.2d 364 (8th Cir. 1971); American Automobile Ass'n v. Comm'r, 19 T.C. 1146 (1953); Associated Indus. of Cleveland v. Comm'r, 7 T.C. 1449 (1946); Deputy v. DuPont, 308 U.S. 488 (1940); Bingler v. Johnson, 394 U.S. 741 (1969) and authorities cited therein. In general, Murtagh, "The Role of the Courts in the Interpretation of the Internal Revenue Code," 24 *Tax Law.* 523 (1971).

[3] E.g., Mescalero Apache Tribe v. Jones, 411 U.S. 145 (1973).

[4] American Inst. for Economic Research v. United States, 302 F.2d 934 (Ct. Cl. 1962), *cert. den.*, 372 U.S. 976 (1963), reh'g den., 373 U.S. 954 (1963); Harrison v. Barker Annuity Fund, 90 F.2d 286 (7th Cir. 1937).

[5] Sico Found. v. United States, 295 F.2d 924, 930, note 19 (Ct. Cl. 1962), and cases cited therein.

[6] White v. United States, 305 U.S. 281, 292 (1938).

[7] Helvering v. Bliss, 293 U.S. 144, 151 (1934).

[8] C. F. Mueller Co. v. Comm'r, 190 F.2d 210 (3d Cir. 1951).

[9] Also IRC §§ 521, 526, 527, 528, 529.

[10] Simon v. Eastern Ky. Welfare Rights Org., 426 U.S. 26, 29, note 1 (1976).

[11] *Id.*, at 28.

[12] IRC § 501(b); Reg. § 1.501(a)-1(a)(1). See Part Five.

[13] See § 11.4.

ing,[14] on organizations that engage in certain political activities,[15] or on the investment income of certain nonprofit organizations.[16]

As will be discussed,[17] an organization that seeks to obtain tax-exempt status, therefore, bears the burden of proving that it satisfies all the requirements of the exemption statute involved.[18]

§ 3.2   ADVANTAGES OF TAX-EXEMPT STATUS

(a) Tax Relief

Of course, the one advantage shared by all categories of tax-exempt organizations is that, barring loss of exemption or imposition of the tax on income other than exempt function income, the unrelated business income tax, the tax on excessive legislative activities, the tax on certain political activities, or (if private foundations) a variety of excise taxes and the tax on net investment income,[19] they are spared federal income taxation. In some instances, tax-exempt status under federal law will mean comparable status under state and local law; in other cases, additional requirements must be satisfied.[20]

Federal income tax exemption may also involve exemption from certain federal excise and employment taxes. However, if an exempt organization is deemed to be a private foundation, it will be subject to a special excise tax on investment income[21] and, if it chooses to dissolve, perhaps a termination tax.[22] Generally, the private foundation rules carry sanctions in the form of taxes.[23]

Many organizations that are tax-exempt under federal law also qualify for exemption from state and local taxes on purchases of items of property, use of property, tangible personal property, intangible personal property, real property, and other activities.[24]

(b) Deductibility of Contributions

Tax-exempt organizations that qualify as entities described in IRC § 170(c) are eligible to attract deductible charitable contributions from individual and corpo-

---

[14] See §§ 20.2, 20.3.

[15] See § 21.2.

[16] See Chapters 14, 17, § 18.13.

[17] See Chapter 21.

[18] Harding Hosp. v. United States, 505 F.2d 1068, 1071 (6th Cir. 1974); Haswell v. United States, 500 F.2d 1133, 1140 (Ct. Cl. 1974).

[19] See *supra* notes 13–16.

[20] E.g., in the District of Columbia, franchise (income) tax exemption is available to charitable (IRC § 501(c)(3)) organizations only if they are "organized and operated to a substantial extent" within the District of Columbia (9 D.C., Code, Title 47 § 47-1802.1(4)).

[21] See § 11.4(f).

[22] *Id.*

[23] See § 11.4.

[24] E.g., University v. People, 99 U.S. 309 (1878); Ladies Literary Club v. City of Grand Rapids, 298 N.W.2d 422 (Mich. 1980). As respects the local property tax exemption, see Balk (ed.), The Free List (1971).

rate donors. In large part, this advantage is extended only to organizations described in IRC § 501(c)(3).[25] Occasionally, an organization the exemption of which is based on a section of the Internal Revenue Code other than § 501(c)(3) can achieve the same results with respect to deductibility of contributions, even if not classified as charitable donees. The most common example of this is the ability of trade associations to be exempt under IRC § 501(c)(6)[26] and yet have payments to them deductible as business expenses under IRC § 162. Some organizations that are not inherently charitable ones can establish a related "foundation" and utilize the charitable contribution deduction through that subsidiary.[27]

(c) Grants

Many tax-exempt organizations are the likely subject of grants from private foundations. This is especially the case with charitable organizations, which have achieved public charity status, since a foundation generally may distribute funds to a public charity in satisfaction of the mandatory payout requirements[28] without having to assume expenditure responsibility for the grant.[29] In some instances, federal and state governmental agencies only make grants to or enter into contracts with nonprofit, tax-exempt organizations, oftentimes only those organizations determined to be charitable entities.

(d) Reduced Postal Rates

Many types of tax-exempt organizations are eligible for the preferential second- and third-class postal rates.[30] This body of law, however, excludes from the qualification for reduced mailing rates mailings that are not in furtherance of the organizations' exempt purposes.

(e) Employee Benefits

The employees of a charitable organization may take advantage of special rules providing favorable tax treatment for contributions for certain annuity benefit programs.[31] There are unique rules concerning a variety of deferred compensation arrangements that exist for the benefit of employees of tax-exempt organiza-

---

[25] IRC § 170(c)(2). Cf. IRC §§ 170(c)(1), 170(c)(3)–170(c)(5), 170(h).

[26] See Chapter 13.

[27] See Chapter § 30.2(a),(b).

[28] See § 11.4(b).

[29] See § 11.4(e).

[30] 39 U.S.C. §§ 4355(a), 4452(d). The organizations entitled to the preferential postal rates (essentially charitable entities) are defined in the Domestic Mail Manual §§ 423.13, 623.2. This body of law is summarized in Hopkins, *The Law of Fund-Raising* 2d ed. (New York: John Wiley & Sons, Inc., 1996) Chapter 6 § 20.

[31] IRC § 403(b). This body of law is summarized in Hyatt & Hopkins, *The Law of Tax-Exempt Healthcare Organizations* (New York: John Wiley & Sons, Inc., 1995) Chapter 28 § 5(b).

tions.[32] Services performed for a tax-exempt organization may be exempt from federal unemployment taxation.[33]

(f) Antitrust Laws

In general, tax-exempt organizations—including charitable ones—can be subject to the antitrust laws, including (at the federal level) the Clayton Act[34] and the Sherman Act.[35] As the U.S. Supreme Court observed, "[t]here is no doubt that the sweeping language of section 1 [of the Sherman Act] applies to nonprofit entities."[36] This fact is based on the proposition that the absence of a profit motive by those who operate a nonprofit entity is no guarantee that the organization will act in the best interest of consumers. Thus, although "pure charity" is beyond the reach of antitrust law, "commercial transactions with a 'public service aspect' " are not.[37] This distinction is not always easy to make, as illustrated by the finding that increasing the percentage of minority-group students at a group of schools through a "need-blind" admissions program is too commercial because even reduced tuition is a commercial payment for educational services.[38] However, the solicitation of contributions by a charitable organization is not engaging in trade or commerce and is not covered by the Sherman Act.[39]

There is, nonetheless, an advantage for tax-exempt charitable organizations in this context in that they may agree to use, or use, the same annuity rate for the purpose of issuing one or more charitable gift annuities[40] without violation of federal or state antitrust laws.[41] This protection is not confined to charities: it extends to lawyers, accountants, actuaries, consultants, and others retained or employed by a charitable organization when assisting in the issuance of a charitable gift annuity or the setting of charitable annuity rates.[42] Moreover, this antitrust exemption also sweeps within its ambit the act of publishing suggested annuity rates. Thus, organizations—most notably, the American Council on Gift Annuities—cannot be in violation of the antitrust laws as a result of publication of actuarial tables or annuity rates for use in issuing gift annuities.[43]

---

[32] IRC § 457.

[33] IRC § 3306(c).

[34] 15 U.S.C. § 12.

[35] 15 U.S.C. § 9.

[36] NCAA v. University of Okla., 468 U.S. 85, 100, note 22 (1984).

[37] United States v. Brown Univ., 5 F.3d 658, 666 (3d Cir. 1993).

[38] Id.

[39] DELTA v. Humane Soc'y, 50 F.3d 710 (9th Cir. 1995).

[40] This term has the same meaning as in IRC § 501(m)(5). See § 22.1, text accompanied by notes 14–16.

[41] 15 U.S.C. § 37, 109 Stat. 687. This law was created upon enactment of the Charitable Gift Annuity Antitrust Relief Act of 1995 (Pub. L. No. 104-63). A state may override this legislation with regard to its antitrust laws; to do this, the state must (by December 7, 1998) enact a law that expressly provides that the antitrust exemption does not apply with respect to the otherwise protected conduct.

[42] H.R. Rep. 336, 104th Cong., 1st Sess. 6 (1995).

[43] Id. This legislation was enacted to shield charitable organizations from litigation based on the use of agreed-upon annuity rates, as well as to provide a complete defense to then-pending litigation (Richie v. American Council on Gift Annuities (Civ. No. 7:94-CV-128-X)). The scope of this legislation was clarified and tightened by the enactment of Pub. L. No. 105-26.

(g) Securities Laws

The federal securities laws consist principally of the Securities Act of 1933,[44] the Securities Exchange Act of 1934,[45] the Investment Company Act of 1940,[46] and the Investment Advisers Act of 1940.[47] There are also securities laws at the state level.

Exempt from the provisions of the Securities Act (other than the anti-fraud provisions) are securities issued by a person organized and operated exclusively for religious, educational, benevolent, fraternal, charitable, or reformatory purposes, and not for pecuniary profit, as long as there is no private inurement.[48] A comparable exemption is available with respect to the Securities Exchange Act.[49] Likewise, an organization of this type is excluded from the definition of an investment company under the Investment Company Act.[50]

Another advantage of classification as a charitable or similar organization is the limitation on the applicability of federal and state securities laws to the activities of charitable organizations in connection with the maintenance of certain "charitable income funds."[51] This limitation provides certain exemptions under the federal securities laws for charitable organizations that maintain these funds.

A charitable income fund is a fund maintained by a charitable organization exclusively for the collective investment and reinvestment of one or more assets of a charitable remainder or similar trust, of a pooled income fund, contributed in exchange for the issuance of charitable gift annuities, of a charitable lead trust, of the general endowment fund or other funds of one or more charitable organizations, or of certain other trusts the remainder interests of which are revocably dedicated to or for the benefit of one or more charitable organizations.[52] The Securities and Exchange Commission (SEC) has the authority to expand the scope of the exemptive provisions of the legislation to include funds that may include assets not expressly defined.[53]

A fund that is excluded from the definition of *investment company* under the Investment Company Act must provide, to each donor to a charity by means of the fund, at the later of the time of donation or within 90 days after the date of enactment of the legislation,[54] written information describing the material terms of operation of the fund.[55] However, this disclosure requirement is not a condition of exemption from the Investment Company Act.[56] Thus, a charitable income

---

[44] 15 U.S.C. § 77b.

[45] 15 U.S.C. § 78c.

[46] 15 U.S.C. § 80a.

[47] 15 U.S.C. § 80b.

[48] 15 U.S.C. § 77c-3(a)(4).

[49] 15 U.S.C. § 78l-12(g)(2)(D).

[50] 15 U.S.C. § 80b-3(c)(10).

[51] 15 U.S.C. § 80a, 109 Stat. 682. This body of law was created upon enactment of the Philanthropy Protection Act of 1995 (Pub. L. No. 104-62). There is an opt-out provision similar to that written into the Charitable Gift Annuity Antitrust Relief Act (see *supra* note 41). That is, a state can enact a statute that specifically states that this law does not prospectively preempt the laws of the state. This statute can be enacted at any time during the three-year period ending on December 7, 1998.

[52] 15 U.S.C. §§ 80a-3(c)(10)(B)(i)–80a-3(c)(10)(B)(vii).

[53] 15 U.S.C. § 80a-3(c)(10)(B)(viii).

[54] As noted, this was December 8, 1995 (see *supra* note 51).

[55] 15 U.S.C. § 80a-7(e).

[56] H.R. Rep. 333, 104th Cong., 1st Sess. 13 (1995).

fund that fails to provide the requisite information is not subject to the securities laws, although the fund may be subject to an enforcement or other action by the SEC. Charitable organizations have flexibility in determining the contents of the required disclosure.

This exemption in the Investment Company Act is also engrafted onto the Securities Act, although charitable income funds are not exempted from that law's anti-fraud provisions.[57] A similar rule operates with respect to the Securities Exchange Act.[58]

A charitable organization is not subject to the Securities Exchange Act's broker-dealer regulation solely because the organization trades in securities on its behalf, or on behalf of a charitable income fund, or the settlors, potential settlors, or beneficiaries of either.[59] This protection is also extended to trustees, directors, officers, employees, or volunteers of a charitable organization, acting within the scope of their employment or duties with the organization. Similar exemptions are provided for charitable organizations, and certain persons associated with them, in connection with the provision of advice, analyses, or reports, from the reach of the Investment Advisors Act of 1940 (other than its anti-fraud elements).[60]

Interests in charitable income funds excluded from the definition of *investment company*, and any offer or sale of these interests, are exempt from any state law that requires registration or qualification of securities.[61] No charitable organization or trustee, director, officer, employee, or volunteer of a charity (acting within the scope of his or her employment or duties) is subject to regulation as a dealer, broker, agent, or investment adviser under any state securities law because the organization or person trades in securities on behalf of a charity, charitable income fund, or the settlors, potential settlors, or beneficiaries of either.[62] These rules do not alter the reach or scope of state anti-fraud laws.[63]

---

[57] 15 U.S.C. § 77c(a)(4).

[58] 15 U.S.C. § 78c(a)(12)(A)(v).

[59] 15 U.S.C. § 78c(e).

[60] 15 U.S.C. § 80b-3(b)(4).

[61] 15 U.S.C. § 80a-3a(a).

[62] 15 U.S.C. § 80a-3a(b).

[63] Prior to the enactment of this legislation, the applicability of the Securities Act, the Securities Exchange Act, and the Investment Company Act to charitable income funds had been addressed by the staff of the SEC. This administrative approach can be traced back to 1972, when the American Council on Education received a no-action letter as to pooled income funds, which was predicated on the fact that these entities are the subject of federal tax law and are subject to the oversight of the IRS. One of the principal conditions of this no-action assurance was that each prospective donor receive written disclosures fully and fairly describing the fund's operations. (Also, the SEC staff has consistently maintained that the anti-fraud provisions of the securities laws apply to the activities of these funds and their associated persons.) This no-action position has always been rationalized by the view that (1) the primary purpose of those who transfer money and property to these funds is to make a charitable gift, rather than to make an investment, and (2) this field has historically been regulated by the IRS.

Until this legislation ensued, the oversight by the IRS and the no-action position of the SEC worked in tandem rather nicely. However, as a lawsuit (see *supra* note 43) illustrated, a favorable letter from the SEC staff does not insulate the recipient of it from liability asserted by a private litigant who alleges that the same transaction violates the securities laws. For the most part, the Philanthropy Protection Act of 1995 codifies the approach taken over the past 23 years by the staff of the SEC.

The scope of this legislation was clarified and tightened by the enactment of Pub. L. No. 105-26.

(h) Other

Numerous other advantages to be derived from tax exemption exist. The other advantages may be more important to an organization than tax exemption. In one instance, an organization (unsuccessfully) sought categorization as a charitable entity so that its child day-care centers would qualify for the food reimbursement program administered by the U.S. Department of Agriculture.[64]

One advantage of tax exemption for charitable organizations[65] once was exemption of services performed for them from taxation under the Federal Insurance Contributions Act (Social Security).[66] However, this general exemption was repealed as of January 1, 1984.[67] Nonetheless, a one-time irrevocable election by a church[68] or a "qualified church-controlled organization" to exclude from the FICA tax base remuneration for all services performed for it (other than in an unrelated trade or business) is available, with the employees of electing organizations liable for self-employment taxes with respect to the excluded services.[69] This election may be made only where the employer organization states that it is opposed for religious reasons to the payment of the FICA tax.[70] A *qualified church-controlled organization* is any charitable organization controlled by a church, other than an organization that (1) offers goods, services, or facilities for sale, other than on an incidental basis, to the general public, other than goods, services, or facilities that are sold at a nominal charge that is substantially less than the cost of providing the goods, services, or facilities; and (2) normally receives more than 25 percent of its support from either governmental sources or receipts from admissions, sales of merchandise, performance of services, or furnishing of facilities, in activities that are not unrelated trades or businesses, or both.[71]

Although obviously relatively minor in scope, another advantage to the exemption for charitable organizations is that it provides exemption from the Organized Crime Control Act,[72] which prohibits certain gambling businesses. Specifically, this law exempts from its application

> any bingo game, lottery, or similar game of chance conducted by an organization exempt from tax under paragraph (3) of subsection (c) of section 501 of the Internal Revenue Code of 1954, as amended, if no part of the gross receipts derived from such activity inures to the benefit of any private shareholder,

---

[64] Baltimore Regional Joint Bd. Health & Welfare Fund, Amalgamated Clothing & Textile Workers Union v. Comm'r, 69 T.C. 554 (1978).

[65] That is, those described in IRC § 501(c)(3).

[66] IRC § 3121(b).

[67] Social Security Amendments of 1983 (Pub. L. No. 98-21), 97 Stat. 65 § 102.

[68] For this purpose, the term *church* means a church, a convention or association of churches, or an elementary or secondary school that is controlled, operated, or principally supported by a church or by a convention or association of churches (IRC § 3121(w)(3)(A)).

[69] IRC §§ 3121(b)(8)(B), 3121(w)(1), (2).

[70] IRC § 3121(w)(1). This election is made by means of Form 8274 (Ann. 84-95, 1984 40 I.R.B. 16).

[71] IRC § 3121(w)(3)(B). A federal district court upheld these rules against a challenge to the constitutionality of them in Bethel Baptist Church v. United States, 629 F. Supp. 1073 (M.D. Pa. 1986), *aff'd*, 822 F.2d 1334 (3d Cir. 1987), *cert. den.*, 485 U.S. 959 (1988).

[72] 18 U.S.C. § 1955.

member, or employee of such organization except as compensation for actual expenses incurred by him in the conduct of such activity.[73]

Still another advantage of income tax exemption is the exemption that a nonprofit organization may have from the federal price discrimination law, known as the Robinson-Patman Act. This law, in essence, makes it "unlawful for any person engaged in commerce, in the course of such commerce, either directly or indirectly, to discriminate in price between different purchasers of commodities of like grade and quality, where either or any of the purchasers involved in such discrimination are in commerce, or such commodities are sold for use, consumption, or resale within the United States . . ., and where the effect of such discrimination may be substantially to lessen competition or tend to create a monopoly in any line of commerce. . . ."[74] Exempted from coverage of this law are certain nonprofit institutions that purchase supplies for their own use at lower prices than can be obtained by other purchasers. This exemption is accorded to "schools, colleges, universities, public libraries, churches, hospitals, and charitable institutions not operated for profit."[75] The purpose of the exemption is to enable nonprofit institutions to operate as inexpensively as possible.[76]

Another advantage that flows from income tax exemption relates to the federal excise tax on wagers.[77] A lottery, raffle, drawing, or other form of *wagering* conducted by a tax-exempt organization[78] is excluded from the tax as long as no part of the net proceeds from the wagering inures to the benefit of any individual in his or her private capacity.[79]

Another federal tax advantage for certain tax-exempt organizations is an exemption from user fees on permits for industrial use of specially denatured distilled spirits. This exemption is available for any "scientific university, college of learning, or institution of scientific research," where the entity is issued a permit and, as to any year in which the permit is in effect, procures less than 25 gallons of the spirits for "experimental or research use but not for consumption (other than organoleptic tests) or sale."[80]

Still another federal tax advantage for tax-exempt organizations is the exemption from the harbor maintenance tax. This exemption is applicable to any nonprofit organization or cooperative for cargo that is owned or financed by the entity and that is certified by the U.S. Customs Service as intended for use in "humanitarian or developmental assistance overseas."[81]

It is clear, nonetheless, that an organization is not exempt from a statutory requirement merely because it is a nonprofit entity. That is, in the absence of an

---

[73] See, e.g., United States v. Hawes, 529 F.2d 472, 481 (5th Cir. 1976).
[74] 15 U.S.C. § 13(a).
[75] 15 U.S.C. § 13(c).
[76] Logan Lanes, Inc. v. Brunswick Corp., 378 F.2d 212 (9th Cir. 1967).
[77] IRC §§ 4401(a), 4411, 4421.
[78] That is, an organization described in IRC § 501 or IRC § 521.
[79] IRC § 4421; Reg. § 44.4421-1(b)(2)(ii).
[80] IRC § 5276(c).
[81] IRC § 4462(h).

express or implied exception in a statute, a nonprofit organization (irrespective of tax exemption) is required to comply with the statute in the same manner as a for-profit organization.[82]

§ 3.3 DISADVANTAGES OF TAX-EXEMPT STATUS

In general, it may seem that an ability to avoid income taxation affords little opportunity for a disadvantage. While often this is the case, the government usually imposes one or more operational limitations on a nonprofit organization in exchange for tax-exempt status. The most common of these limitations is the rule that the exempt organization may not engage in forms of private inurement.[83]

Qualification as a tax-exempt organization may impose certain disadvantages. Thus, certain categories of exempt organizations are prohibited from engaging in substantial legislative activities[84] and in campaign or similar political activities.[85] In other instances, most notably in the field of private foundations, qualification as an exempt organization brings with it a host of limitations that must be adhered to if exempt status is to be maintained.[86] Exempt status also will likely entail extensive annual reporting requirements, including the filing of an annual information return with the IRS and a tax return for each year in which there is unrelated business income.[87] Tax-exempt noncharitable organizations must disclose the nondeductibility of contributions to them[88] and exempt organizations are subject to a penalty if they fail to disclose that information or services being offered are available without charge from the federal government.[89]

In some instances, these limitations and forms of regulation may be more extensive than those imposed on for-profit organizations. In occasional instances, the requirement of adherence to these limitations will not be worth qualification as a tax-exempt organization, such as where a more preferable alternative is available.

§ 3.4 ALTERNATIVES TO TAX-EXEMPT STATUS

An organization may elect or be required to operate without formal recognition as a tax-exempt entity and yet achieve the same basic objective: the nonpayment of income tax. However, the legitimate alternatives to tax-exempt status are few.

---

[82] Tony & Susan Alamo Found. v. Secretary of Labor, 471 U.S. 290 (1985).
[83] See Chapter 19.
[84] See Chapter 20.
[85] See Chapter 21.
[86] See, e.g., Chapter 11.
[87] See § 24.3.
[88] IRC § 6113. See § 22.2.
[89] IRC § 6711. See § 24.6.

Perhaps the simplest illustration of this principle is the organization (non-profit or not) that is operated so that its deductions equal or exceed income in any taxable year. In essence, this is the basis upon which cooperatives function without having to pay tax.

The tax treatment of nonexempt cooperatives is the subject of IRC §§ 1381 through 1383. These sections apply to any "corporation operating on a cooperative basis" (with exceptions) and to farmers' cooperatives exempt under IRC § 521.[90] Basically, a qualified cooperative escapes taxation because, in computing taxable income, a deduction is available for "patronage dividends" and qualified and nonqualified "per-unit retain allocations."[91] Moreover, a farmers' cooperative is entitled to certain deductions for nonpatronage dividends.[92] Generally, amounts received as patronage dividends and qualified per-unit retain certificates are includable in the patrons' gross income.

An organization that loses its tax-exempt status may continue to operate without taxation by conversion to operation as a cooperative.[93] Similarly, an organization that cannot qualify as a tax-exempt entity may choose to function as a cooperative.[94]

If a nonexempt organization that does not operate on a cooperative basis seeks to avoid taxation by matching deductions and income, federal tax law may foil the scheme if the organization is a social club or other membership organization operated to furnish goods or services to its members.[95] In this situation, the expenses of furnishing services, goods, or other items of value (e.g., insurance) to members are deductible only to the extent of income from members (including income from institutes or trade shows primarily for members' education). This means that any expenses attributable to membership activities in excess of membership income may not be deducted against membership income (although the increment may be carried forward). Prior to enactment of these rules, the courts had upheld contrary treatment.[96]

There is a line of law that permits nontaxability of an organization where it is merely a conduit for the expenditure of a fund established for a specific purpose. Thus, a soft drink manufacturer that received funds from bottlers for a national advertising fund was held not taxable on these funds, since they were earmarked for advertising purposes; the manufacturer was considered only an administrator of a trust fund.[97] Initially, the IRS took the position that this precept would be followed only where the recipient of the funds received

---

[90] See § 18.11.

[91] IRC §§ 1382(b), 1388.

[92] IRC § 1382(c).

[93] E.g., A. Duda & Sons Coop. Ass'n v. United States, 495 F.2d 193 (5th Cir. 1974). This decision was subsequently withdrawn and superseded by the decision reported at 504 F.2d 970 (5th Cir. 1975).

[94] E.g., Rev. Rul. 69-633, 1969-2 C.B. 121.

[95] IRC § 277.

[96] E.g., Anaheim Union Water Co. v. Comm'r, 321 F.2d 253 (9th Cir. 1963). An application of IRC § 277 appears in Boating Trade Ass'n of Metro. Houston v. United States, 75-1 U.S.T.C. ¶ 9398 (S.D. Tex. 1975).

[97] The Seven-Up Co. v. Comm'r, 14 T.C. 965 (1950). Also Rev. Rul. 69-96, 1969-1 C.B. 32; Ford Dealers Advertising Fund, Inc. v. Comm'r, 55 T.C. 761 (1971), aff'd, 456 F.2d 255 (5th Cir. 1972); Park Place, Inc. v. Comm'r, 57 T.C. 767 (1972); Greater Pittsburgh Chrysler Dealers Ass'n of W. Pa. v. United States, 77-1 U.S.T.C. ¶ 9293 (W.D. Pa. 1977); Insty-Prints, Inc. Nat'l Advertising Fund Trust v. Comm'r, 44 T.C.M. 556 (1982); Broadcast Measurement Bureau v. Comm'r, 16 T.C. 988 (1951).

them with the obligation to expend them solely for a particular purpose.[98] However, this position was subsequently superseded by a ruling that taxes to the recipient organization the amounts received and permits related deductions, subject to the previously discussed expense allocation rules.[99] Also, the IRS distinguished the above-described factual setting involving a soft drink manufacturer from one in which the participants (dealers, bottlers, and the like) form an unincorporated organization to conduct a national advertising program; the IRS ruled that the organization is separately taxable as a corporation.[100]

If tax-exempt status is unavailable, lost, or not desired, and if deductions do not or cannot equal income, and cooperative status is either unavailable or unwanted, and if the organization is not formally incorporated, perhaps the entity can escape taxation by contending it is nonexistent for tax purposes. This is generally unlikely, in view of the authority of the IRS to treat an unincorporated entity as a taxable corporation.[101] Yet this is what political campaign committees did for many years, as the IRS failed or refused to assert tax liability. However, early in 1974, the IRS ruled that campaign committees are to be treated as taxable corporations (although contributions remain nontaxable).[102] This ruling was in turn superseded by the enactment of IRC § 527 and related sections[103] late in 1974.[104] Nonetheless, even after its 1974 ruling, the IRS continued to uphold the per-donee gift tax exclusion for separate fund-raising campaign committees,[105] despite opposition in the courts.[106] However, in 1974, Congress exempted contributions to political parties or committees from the gift tax.[107]

Thus, to be exempt from federal income taxation, an organization generally must formally qualify as a tax-exempt organization (by means of recognition or otherwise), operate as a cooperative, legally marshall deductions against income, or seek a change in the law. Otherwise, it is nearly certain that the entity will be liable for tax as a taxable corporation (even if it is organized as a nonprofit organization).

---

[98] Rev. Rul. 58-209, 1958-1 C.B. 19.

[99] Rev. Rul. 74-318, 1974-2 C.B. 14.

[100] Rev. Rul. 74-319, 1974-2 C.B. 15. Also Michigan Retailers Ass'n v. United States, 676 F. Supp. 151 (W.D. Mich. 1988)); Dri-Power Distribrs. Ass'n Trust v. Comm'r, 54 T.C. 460 (1970); N.Y. State Ass'n Real Est. Bd. Group Ins. Fund v. Comm'r, 54 T.C. 1325 (1970); Angelus Funeral Home v. Comm'r, 47 T.C. 391 (1967), aff'd, 407 F.2d 210 (9th Cir. 1969), cert. den., 396 U.S. 824 (1969).

[101] E.g., Rev. Rul. 75-258, 1975-2 C.B. 503, where the IRS ruled that the "Family Estate" trust is an association taxable as a corporation under IRC § 7701, and Rev. Rul. 77-214, 1977-1 C.B. 408, where the IRS determined that a certain type of German unincorporated business organization ("Gesellschaft mit beschrankter Haftung" or "GmbH") is taxable as a corporation. Also, the U.S. Tax Court concluded that real estate syndicates organized under the California limited partnership act are associations taxable as corporations with the meaning of IRC § 7701(a)(3) (Larson v. Comm'r, 65 T.C. No. 10 (1975) (withdrawn), 66 T.C. 159 (1976)). In general, Morrissey v. Comm'r, 296 U.S. 344 (1935); Reg. § 301.7701-2(a)(1).

[102] Rev. Rul. 74-21, 1974-1 C.B. 14.

[103] IRC §§ 41 (as amended), 84, 2501(a)(5).

[104] See Chapter 17.

[105] Rev. Rul. 72-355, 1972-2 C.B. 532; Rev. Rul. 74-199, 1974-1 C.B. 285.

[106] Tax Analysts & Advocates v. Schultz, 376 F. Supp. 889 (D.D.C. 1974), aff'd, 75-1 U.S.T.C. ¶ 13,052 (D.C. Cir. 1975).

[107] IRC § 2501(a)(5).

CHAPTER FOUR

Organizational, Operational, and Similar Tests

In addition to other rules underlying tax-exempt status, the federal tax law mandates adherence to certain general organizational and operational requirements as a condition of tax exemption. These requirements are the most pronounced as respects charitable organizations.

§ 4.1 CONSIDERATIONS OF FORM

Generally, the Internal Revenue Code does not prescribe a specific organizational form for entities to qualify for tax exemption. Basically, the choices are nonprofit corporation, trust (*inter vivos* or testamentary), or unincorporated association.[1] However, some provisions of the Code expressly mandate, in whole or in part, the corporate form,[2] and other Code provisions (particularly in the employee plan context[3]) mandate the trust form.[4] Throughout the categories of tax-exempt organizations are additional terms such as *clubs, associations, societies, leagues, companies, boards, orders, posts,* and *units,* which are not terms referencing legal forms. For tax purposes, an organization may be deemed a corporation even though it is not formally incorporated.[5]

    The federal tax provision which describes charitable organizations[6] pro-

---

[1] Rev. Proc. 82-2, 1982-1 C.B 367.
[2] IRC §§ 501(c)(1), 501(c)(2), 501(c)(3), 501(c)(14), 501(c)(16).
[3] See Chapter 16.
[4] IRC §§ 501(c)(17), 501(c)(18), 501(c)(19), 501(c)(20), 401(a).
[5] IRC § 7701(a)(3).
[6] IRC § 501(c)(3).

vides that an organization described in that provision must be a corporation, community chest, fund, or foundation. An unincorporated association or trust can qualify under this provision, presumably as a fund or foundation or perhaps, as noted, as a corporation.[7] However, a partnership cannot be tax-exempt as a charitable organization.[8]

An organization already exempt from federal taxation may establish a separate fund or like entity that is itself an exempt organization.[9] The attributes of this type of a fund include a separate category of tax exemption (for example, an educational research and scholarship fund established by a bar association[10]), a separate governing body, and separate books and accounts.[11] However, a mere bank deposit cannot amount to a requisite fund; thus, a contribution to it would be considered a nondeductible gift to an individual rather than a possibly deductible gift to a qualified organization.[12]

For purposes of the rules concerning charitable organizations,[13] an organization tax-exempt by reason of those rules may be a unit of government[14] or a foreign organization,[15] or may conduct all or part of its activities in foreign countries.[16]

The formalities of organization of an entity may have a bearing on the tax exemption. This is the case not only in connection with the sufficiency of the governing instruments,[17] but also, and more fundamentally, with regard to whether there is a separate organization in the first instance. An individual may perform worthwhile activities, such as providing financial assistance to needy students, but will receive no tax benefits from his or her beneficence, unless he or she establishes and funds a qualified organization that in turn renders the charitable works, such as scholarship grants. One court observed, in the process of denying a charitable contribution deduction, that the federal tax law makes no provision for a charitable deduction in the context of personal ventures, however praiseworthy in character. The court noted that "[t]here is no evidence of such enterprise being a corporation, community chest, fund, or foundation and little information, if any, as to its organization or activities."[18] However, assum-

---

[7] Fifth-Third Union Trust Co. v. Comm'r, 56 F.2d 767 (6th Cir. 1932).

[8] IRS Exempt Organizations Handbook (IRM 7751) § 315.1. Also Emerson Inst. v. United States, 356 F.2d 824 (D.C. Cir. 1966), *cert. den.*, 385 U.S. 822 (1966). In one opinion, a court, in deciding that an organization could not qualify for tax-exempt status because of its role as a general partner in a limited partnership (see § 32.2), placed emphasis on the fact that the partnerships involved "are admittedly for-profit entities" and that none of these partnerships is "intended to be nonprofit" (Housing Pioneers, Inc. v. Comm'r, 65 T.C.M. 2191, 2195 (1993)); however, the law does not make provision for an entity such as a nonprofit partnership.

[9] E.g., IRC § 509(a), last sentence.

[10] American Bar Ass'n v. United States, 84-1 U.S.T.C. ¶ 9179 (N.D. Ill. 1984); Rev. Rul. 58-293, 1958-1 C.B. 146.

[11] Rev. Rul. 54-243, 1954-1 C.B. 92.

[12] E.g., Pusch v. Comm'r, 39 T.C.M. 838 (1980).

[13] IRC § 501(c)(3).

[14] Rev. Rul. 60-384, 1960-2 C.B. 172.

[15] Rev. Rul. 66-177, 1966-1 C.B. 132.

[16] Rev. Rul. 71-460, 1971-2 C.B. 231.

[17] Cone v. McGinnes, 63-2 U.S.T.C. ¶ 9551 (E.D. Pa. 1963). Also *infra* § 2.

[18] Hewitt v. Comm'r, 16 T.C.M. 468, 471 (1957). Also Doty, Jr. v. Comm'r, 6 T.C. 587 (1974); Walker v. Comm'r, 37 T.C.M. 1851 (1978).

ing the organization is not operated to benefit private interests, its tax exemption will not be endangered because its creator serves as the sole trustee and exercises complete control,[19] although state law may limit or preclude close control.

It is the position of the IRS that a "formless aggregation of individuals" cannot be tax-exempt as a charitable entity.[20] At a minimum, the entity—to be exempt—must have an organizing instrument, some governing rules, and regularly chosen officers.[21] These rules have been amply illustrated in the cases concerning so-called personal churches.[22]

As of January 1, 1997, a tax-exempt organization generally is treated for tax purposes as a corporation. This is a consequence of adoption by the IRS of entity classification regulations largely pertaining to business corporations, by which they elect to be regarded for tax purposes as corporations or partnerships. Under these regulations, an exempt organization is treated as having made an election to be classified as an *association*.[23] This classification, in turn, causes the entity to be regarded as a corporation.[24]

Among the nontax factors to be considered in selecting an organizational form are legal liabilities in relation to the individuals involved (the corporate form can limit certain personal liabilities), local law requirements, necessities of governing instruments, local annual reporting requirements, organizational expenses, and any membership requirements.[25] Federal law, other than the tax laws, may also have a bearing on the choice, such as the organization's comparable status under the postal laws.[26]

A change in form may require a tax-exempt organization to reapply for recognition of tax-exempt status. For example, an unincorporated organization that has been recognized by the IRS as a tax-exempt charitable entity must commence the application anew if it incorporates.[27]

---

[19] Rev. Rul. 66-219, 1966-2 C.B. 208.

[20] IRS Exempt Organizations Handbook (IRM 7751) §§ 315.1, 315.2(3), 315.4(2).

[21] Kessler v. Comm'r, 87 T.C. 1285 (1986); Trippe v. Comm'r, 9 T.C.M. 622 (1950). Cf. Morey v. Riddell, 205 F. Supp. 918 (S.D. Cal. 1962).

[22] E.g., United States v. Jeffries, 88-2 U.S.T.C. ¶ 9,459 (7th Cir. 1988). In general, Chapter 8, text accompanying notes 96–99.

[23] Reg. § 301.7701-3(c)(1)(v)(A).

[24] Reg. §§ 301.7701-2(b)(2), 301.7701-3(a).

[25] However, a separate form (even the corporate form) is not always respected. For example, courts find charitable organizations to be the "alter ego" of their founders or others in close control and operating proximity, so that IRS levies against the organizations for their income and assets to satisfy the individuals' tax obligations are upheld (e.g., Towe Antique Ford Found. v. Internal Revenue Serv., 999 F.2d 1387 (9th Cir. 1993); United States v. Kitsos, 770 F. Supp. 1230 (N.D. Ill. 1991), *aff'd*, 968 F.2d 1219 (7th Cir. 1992); Zahra Spiritual Trust v. United States, 910 F.2d 240 (5th Cir. 1990); Loving Savior Church v. United States, 556 F. Supp. 688 (D.S.D. 1983), *aff'd*, 728 F.2d 1085 (8th Cir. 1984); Faith Missionary Baptist Church v. Internal Revenue Serv., 174 ¶ 454 (U.S. Bankr. Ct. E.D. Tex. 1994); Church of Hakeem v. United States, 79-2 U.S.T.C. ¶ 9651 (N.D. Cal. 1979)). In general, Henn & Pfeifer, "Nonprofit Groups: Factors Influencing Choice of Form," 11 *Wake Forest L. Rev.* 181 (1975).

[26] 39 C.F.R. Part 132 (second class), Part 134 (third class).

[27] See § 24.1(6).

§ 4.2 GOVERNING INSTRUMENTS

An organization must have governing instruments to qualify for tax exemption, if only to satisfy the appropriate organizational test. This is particularly the case for charitable organizations, as to which the federal tax law imposes specific organizational requirements.[28] These rules are more stringent if the charitable organization is a private foundation.[29]

If the corporate form is used, the governing instruments will be articles of incorporation and bylaws. An unincorporated organization will have articles of organization, perhaps in the form of a constitution, and, undoubtedly, also bylaws. If a trust, the basic document will be a declaration of trust or trust agreement.

The articles of organization should contain provisions stating the organization's purposes; whether there will be members and, if so, their qualifications and classes; the initial board of directors or trustee(s); the registered agent and incorporators (if a corporation); the dissolution or liquidation procedure; and the required language referencing the appropriate tax law (federal and state) requirements and prohibitions. If the organization is a corporation, particular attention should be given to the appropriate state nonprofit corporation statute, which will contain requirements that may supersede the provisions of the articles of incorporation and bylaws or may apply where the governing instruments are silent.

The bylaws may also contain the provisions of the articles of organization and, in addition, should contain provisions amplifying or stating the purposes of the organization; the terms and conditions of membership (if any); the manner of selection and duties of the directors or trustees, and officers; the voting requirements; the procedure for forming committees; the accounting period; any indemnification provisions; the appropriate tax provisions; and the procedure for amendment of the bylaws.[30]

§ 4.3 ORGANIZATIONAL TEST

An organization, to be exempt as a charitable entity, must be both organized and operated exclusively for one or more of the permissible exempt purposes. This requirement has given rise to an *organizational test* and an *operational test* for charitable organizations. If an organization fails to meet either the organizational test or the operational test, it cannot qualify for exemption from federal income taxation as a charitable entity.[31] (The organizational and operational tests of other categories of tax-exempt organizations are discussed in the respective chapters.)

---

[28] See *infra* § 4.

[29] See § 11.1(g).

[30] In general, see Oleck, *Non-Profit Corporations, Organizations, and Associations* (6th ed. 1996); Webster, *The Law of Associations* (Matthew Bender); Chaffe, "The Internal Affairs of Associations Not For Profit," 43 *Harv. L. Rev.* 993 (1930).

[31] Reg. § 1.501(c)(3)-1(a); Levy Family Tribe Found. v. Comm'r, 69 T.C. 615, 618 (1978).

§ 4.3   ORGANIZATIONAL TEST

The income tax regulations contemplate two types of governing instruments for a charitable organization: the instrument by which the organization is created (*articles of organization*) and the instrument stating the rules pursuant to which the organization is operated (*bylaws*).[32] For the incorporated organization, the articles of organization are *articles of incorporation*. For the unincorporated entity, the articles of organization may be so termed or may be termed otherwise, such as a *constitution, agreement of trust*, or *declaration of trust*. Occasionally, an unincorporated organization will combine these two types of instruments in one document; while this is technically inappropriate, the IRS is unlikely to find the practice a violation of the organizational test.

An organization is organized exclusively for one or more tax-exempt, charitable purposes only if its articles of organization limit its purposes to one or more exempt purposes[33] and do not expressly empower it to engage, otherwise than as an insubstantial part of its activities, in activities that in themselves are not in furtherance of one or more exempt purposes.[34] Additional requirements are imposed for the governing instruments of private foundations.[35]

(a) Statement of Purposes

In meeting the organizational test, the charitable organization's purposes, as stated in its articles of organization, may be as broad as, or more specific than, the particular exempt purposes, such as religious, charitable, or educational ends. Therefore, an organization that, by the terms of its articles of organization, is formed "for literary and scientific purposes within the meaning of section 501(c)(3) of the Internal Revenue Code" shall, if it otherwise meets the requirements of the organizational test, be considered to have met the test. Similarly, articles of organization stating that the organization is created solely "to receive contributions and pay them over to organizations which are described in section 501(c)(3) and exempt from taxation under section 501(a) of the Internal Revenue Code" are sufficient for purposes of the organizational test. If the articles of organization state that the organization is formed for "charitable purposes," the articles ordinarily will be adequate for purposes of the organizational test.[36]

Articles of organization of charitable entities may not authorize the carrying on of nonexempt activities (unless they are insubstantial), even though the organization is, by the terms of its articles, created for a purpose that is no broader than the specified charitable purposes.[37] Thus, an organization that is empowered by its articles "to engage in a manufacturing business" or "to engage in the operation of a social club" does not meet the organizational test, regardless of the fact that its articles of organization may state that the organization is created "for

---

[32] Reg. § 1.501(c)(3)-1(b)(2).
[33] See Reg. § 1.501(c)(3)-1(d).
[34] Reg. § 1.501(c)(3)-1(b)(1)(i).
[35] IRC § 508(e). See § 11.1(g).
[36] Reg. § 1.501(c)(3)-1(b)(1)(ii).
[37] Rev. Rul. 69-279, 1969-1 C. B. 152; Rev. Rul. 69-256, 1969-1 C.B. 151.

charitable purposes within the meaning of section 501(c)(3) of the Internal Revenue Code."[38]

In no case will an organization be considered to be organized exclusively for one or more exempt charitable purposes if, by the terms of its articles of organization, the purposes for which the organization is created are broader than the specified charitable purposes. The fact that the actual operations of the organization have been exclusively in furtherance of one or more exempt purposes is not sufficient to permit the organization to meet the organizational test. An organization wishing to qualify as a charitable entity should not provide in its articles of organization that it has all of the powers accorded under the particular state's nonprofit corporation act, since those powers are likely to be broader than those allowable under federal tax law.[39] Similarly, an organization will not meet the organizational test as a result of statements or other evidence that its members intend to operate only in furtherance of one or more exempt purposes.[40]

An organization is not considered organized exclusively for one or more exempt charitable purposes if its articles of organization expressly authorize it to (1) devote more than an insubstantial part of its activities to attempting to influence legislation by propaganda or otherwise;[41] (2) directly or indirectly participate in, or intervene in (including the publishing or distributing of statements), any political campaign on behalf of or in opposition to any candidate for public office;[42] or (3) have objectives and engage in activities that characterize it as an *action* organization.[43] However, the organizational test is not violated where an organization's articles empower it to make the expenditure test election (relating to expenditures for legislative activities)[44] and, only if it so elects, to make direct lobbying or grass roots lobbying expenditures that are not in excess of the ceiling amounts prescribed by that test.[45]

It is the position of the IRS that only a *creating document* may be looked to in meeting the organizational test:

> Accordingly, the organizational test cannot be met by reference to any document that is not the creating document. In the case of a corporation, the bylaws cannot remedy a defect in the corporate charter. A charter can be amended only in accordance with state law, which generally requires filing of the amendments with the chartering authority. In the case of a trust, operating rules cannot substitute for the trust indenture. In the case of an unincorporated association, the test must be met by the basic creating document and the amendments thereto, whatever that instrument may be called. Subsidiary documents that are not amendments to the creating document may not be called on.[46]

---

[38] Reg. § 1.501(c)(3)-1(b)(iii). Also Interneighborhood Housing Corp. v. Comm'r., 45 T.C.M. 115 (1982); Santa Cruz Bldg. Ass'n v. United States, 411 F. Supp. 871 (E. D. Mo. 1976).

[39] E.g., Gen. Couns. Mem. 39633.

[40] Reg. § 1.501(c)(3)-1(b)(1)(iv).

[41] See Chapter 20.

[42] See Chapter 21.

[43] Reg. § 1.501(c)(3)-1(b)(3). See *infra* § 4.5(b).

[44] See § 20.5(a).

[45] Reg. § 1.501(c)(3)-1(b)(3).

[46] IRS Exempt Organizations Handbook (IRM 7751) § 332(2).

However, it is the view of one court that the organizational test entails a "purely
. . . factual inquiry" and that it is not required to "myopically consider *only*" articles of incorporation or another creating document; in the case, an organization
was found to qualify as a charitable organization meeting the organizational test
because of suitable language in its bylaws.[47]

The law of the state in which an organization is created is controlling in construing the terms of its articles of organization.[48] However, an organization that
contends that the terms have, under state law, a different meaning from their generally accepted meaning must establish the special meaning by clear and convincing reference to relevant court decisions, opinions of the state attorney
general, or other evidence of applicable state law.[49]

An organization that would be classified as a private foundation[50] if it were
recognized as a charitable entity does not satisfy the organizational test by virtue
of having complied with the special governing instrument provisions applicable
only to private foundations.[51] In so ruling, the IRS considered a case where an organization's articles of incorporation lacked the requisite provision requiring the
distribution of its assets for charitable purposes upon dissolution. The state law
under which the organization operates had not been construed to assure dedication of assets to charitable purposes,[52] although the state had a statute that mandates reference to the various private foundation rules in the foundation's articles
of incorporation on all private foundations formed in the state.[53] The IRS reasoned that a private foundation is a charitable organization, yet an organization
cannot be so classified where its governing instrument fails to include a dissolution clause, and the special governing instrument provisions only apply to private foundations. Also, the IRS reviewed the legislative history of the private
foundation rules, which makes it clear that these rules comprise requirements
that are in addition to the general tax exemption requirements.[54]

(b) Dissolution Requirements

An organization is not organized exclusively for one or more exempt charitable
purposes unless its assets are dedicated to an exempt purpose. An organization's
assets will be considered dedicated to an exempt purpose, for example, if, upon
dissolution, the assets would, by reason of a provision in the organization's articles of organization or by operation of law, be distributed for one or more exempt
purposes, or to the federal government, or to a state or local government, for a
public purpose or would be distributed by a court to another organization to be
used in a manner as in the judgment of the court will best accomplish the general

---

[47] Colorado State Chiropractic Soc'y v. Comm'r, 93 T.C. 487, 495 (1989). Emphasis in the original.
[48] Estate of Sharf v. Comm'r, 38 T.C. 15 (1962), *aff'd* 316 F.2d 625 (7th Cir. 1963); Holden Hosp. Corp. v.
Southern Ill. Hosp. Corp., 174 N.E. 2d 793 (Ill. 1961).
[49] Reg. § 1.501(c)(3)-1(b)(5).
[50] See Chapter 11.
[51] IRC § 508(e). See § 11.1(g).
[52] See text accompanying *supra* note 49.
[53] Rev. Rul. 75-38, 1975-1 C.B. 161.
[54] Rev. Rul. 85-160, 1985-2 C.B. 162.

purposes for which the dissolved organization was organized. However, a charitable organization does not meet the organizational test if its articles of organization or the law of the state in which it was created provide that its assets would, upon dissolution, be distributed to its members or shareholders.[55] Consequently, federal income tax exemption as a charitable organization will be denied where, upon dissolution of the organization, its assets would revert to the individual founders rather than to one or more qualifying charities.[56] However, a charitable organization's assets may, upon dissolution, be transferred for charitable purposes without necessarily being transferred to a charitable organization.[57]

The dedication-of-assets requirement contemplates that, notwithstanding the dissolution of a charitable entity, the assets will continue to be devoted to a charitable purpose (albeit a substituted one). Under the *cy pres* rule, a state court, in the exercise of its equity power, may modify the purpose of a charitable trust or place the funds of a charitable corporation in a new entity.[58] Organizations that are organized for both exempt and nonexempt purposes fail to satisfy the organizational test.[59]

The IRS published guidelines for identification of states and circumstances where an express dissolution clause for charitable organizations is not required. Basically, these guidelines are a function of the type of organization that is involved. For example, the IRS has determined that the *cy pres* doctrine in any jurisdiction is insufficient to prevent an *inter vivos* charitable trust or an unincorporated association from failing, and thus that an adequate dissolution clause is essential for satisfaction of the organizational test. By contrast, the law of several states applies the *cy pres* doctrine to testamentary charitable trusts and the law of a few states applies the doctrine to nonprofit charitable corporations.[60] Consequently, from the standpoint of the IRS, an organization in a jurisdiction where the *cy pres* doctrine is inapplicable must have an express, qualifying distribution or liquidation clause to satisfy the organizational test.[61]

---

[55] Reg. § 1.501(c)(3)-1(b)(4). E.g., Chief Steward of the Ecumenical Temples and the Worldwide Peace Movement and His Successors v. Comm'r, 49 T.C.M. 640 (1985). Cf. Bethel Conservative Mennonite Church v. Comm'r, 746 F.2d 388 (7th Cir. 1984).

[56] Church of Nature in Man v. Comm'r, 49 T.C.M. 1393 (1985); Stephenson v. Comm'r, 79 T.C. 995 (1982); Truth Tabernacle v. Comm'r, 41 T.C.M. 1405 (1981); Calvin K. of Oakknoll v. Comm'r, 69 T.C. 770 (1978), *aff'd*, 603 F.2d 211 (2d Cir. 1979); General Conference of the Free Church of Am. v. Comm'r, 71 T.C. 920 (1979).

[57] Gen. Couns. Mem. 37126, clarifying Gen. Couns. Mem. 33207. Moreover, the absence of a dissolution clause has been held to not be fatal to IRC § 501(c)(3) status, in Universal Church of Scientific Truth, Inc. v. United States, 74-1 U.S.T.C. ¶ 9360 (N.D. Ala. 1973).

[58] Scott, *The Law of Trusts* (2d ed. 1956) §§ 397, 339.3; IRS Exempt Organizations Handbook (IRM 7751) § 335(4), (6). Also Davis v. United States, 201 F. Supp. 92 (S.D. Ohio 1961).

[59] Rev. Rul. 69-256, *supra* note 37; Rev. Rul. 69-279, *supra* note 37.

[60] Rev. Proc. 82-2, 1982-1 C.B. 367. The statute enacted by the state of North Carolina in 1981 failed the necessary requirements, according to the Chief Counsel of the IRS (Gen. Couns. Mem. 39377).

[61] The IRS will accept the following phraseology of a dissolution clause: "Upon the dissolution of [this organization], assets shall be distributed for one or more exempt purposes within the meaning of section 501(c)(3) of the Internal Revenue Code, or corresponding section of any future Federal tax code, or shall be distributed to the Federal government, or to a state or local government, for a public purpose" (Rev. Proc. 82-2, *supra* note 60 § 3.05).

(c) Prototype Provisions

The articles of organization or bylaws of a charitable organization *may but need not* contain provisions such as the following:

> No part of the net earnings, gains or assets of the corporation [or organization] shall inure to the benefit of or be distributable to its directors [or trustees], officers, other private individuals, or organizations organized and operated for a profit (except that the corporation [or organization] shall be authorized and empowered to pay reasonable compensation for services rendered and to make payments and distributions in furtherance of the purposes as hereinabove stated). No substantial part of the activities of the corporation [or organization] shall be the carrying on of propaganda or otherwise attempting to influence legislation, and the corporation [or organization] shall be empowered to make the election authorized under section 501(h) of the Internal Revenue Code of 1986. The corporation [or organization] shall not participate in or intervene in (including the publishing or distribution of statements) any political campaign on behalf of or in opposition to any candidate for public office. Notwithstanding any other provision herein, the corporation [or organization] shall not carry on any activities not permitted to be carried on—
> (a) by an organization exempt from federal income taxation under section 501(a) of the Internal Revenue Code of 1986 as an organization described in section 501(c)(3) of such Code, or
> (b) by an organization, contributions to which are deductible under sections 170(c)(2), 2055(a)(2), or 2522(a)(2) of such Code.

> References herein to sections of the Internal Revenue Code of 1986 are to provisions of the Internal Revenue Code of 1986, as amended, as those provisions are now enacted or to corresponding provisions of any future United States revenue law.

An organization must, if it is to satisfy the federal tax law organizational requirements for charitable entities, have in its articles of organization provisions substantially equivalent to the following:

> The corporation [or organization] is organized and operated exclusively for [charitable, educational, etc.] purposes within the meaning of section 501(c)(3) of the Internal Revenue Code of 1986.

> In the event of dissolution or final liquidation of the corporation [or organization], the board of directors [or trustees] shall, after paying or making provision for the payment of all the lawful debts and liabilities of the corporation [or organization], distribute all the assets of the corporation [or organization] to one or more of the following categories of recipients as the board of directors [or trustees] of the corporation [or organization] shall determine:
> (a) a nonprofit organization or organization which may have been created to succeed the corporation [or organization], as long as such organization or each of such organizations shall then qualify as a governmental unit under section 170(c) of the Internal Revenue Code of 1986 or as an organization exempt from federal income taxation under section 501(a) of such Code as an organization described in section 501(c)(3) of such Code; and/or
> (b) a nonprofit organization or organizations having similar aims and objects as the corporation [or organization] and which may be selected as an

appropriate recipient of such assets, as long as such organization or each of such organizations shall then qualify as a governmental unit under section 170(c) of such Code or as an organization exempt from federal income taxation under section 501(a) of such Code as an organization described in section 501(c)(3) of such Code.

(d) Judicial Gloss on Test

In most respects, the courts have adhered to these specific requirements of the organizational test. However, prior to the effective date of the organizational test requirements in the income tax regulations (July 27, 1959),[62] there was a tendency to read into the term *organized* in the federal tax law rules for charitable organizations a greater flexibility than is contemplated by the regulations.[63] That is, the courts tended to blur the technical distinction between the organizational test and the operational test by viewing the former in the light of the predominant purpose for forming the organization and its manner of operations.[64] In one case,[65] for example, a court concluded that the word organized does not state a "narrowly limited formal requirement" and that the term largely requires only the requisite inurement:

> Our conclusion is that a corporation satisfies the requirement of being "organized" for a charitable purpose if, at the time in question, its setup or organization of ownership, directors, and officers is such that its earnings must inure to a charity.[66]

The organization in this case remained organized as a for-profit corporation with stockholders. However, once all of its stock became held by a tax-exempt hospital and the hospital's trustees assumed control over it, the organization was deemed qualified as a charitable entity even though the corporate charter was never amended—with the court finding that it was properly organized "for all practical purposes."[67]

By contrast, another court had elected to follow the "reasonable interpretation" of the word *organized*.[68] The organization involved was organized as a for-profit corporation and the fact that it was a holding company for a tax-exempt art museum was considered insufficient for passage of the organizational test. The court held that the term " 'organized' means 'incorporated' and not 'operated' " and that, in line with the IRS requirements, the "right of the corporation to an exemption is to be determined by the powers given it in its charter."[69]

---

[62] Reg. § 1.501(c)(3)-1(b)(6).

[63] Rev. Rul. 60-193, 1969-1 C.B. 195.

[64] Passaic United Hebrew Burial Ass'n v. United States, 216 F. Supp. 500 (D. N.J. 1963).

[65] Dillingham Transp. Bldg. v. United States, 146 F. Supp. 953 (Ct. Cl. 1957).

[66] *Id*. at 955.

[67] Also Roche's Beach, Inc. v. Comm'r, 96 F.2d 776 (2d Cir. 1938).

[68] Sun-Herald Corp. v. Duggan, 73 F.2d 298 (2d Cir. 1934), *cert. den.*, 294 U.S. 719 (1934). Also Sun-Herald Corp. v. Duggan, 160 F.2d 475 (2d Cir. 1947). Cf. Universal Oil Prods. Co. v. Campbell, 181 F.2d 451 (7th Cir. 1950).

[69] Sun-Herald Corp. v. Duggan, *supra* note 68, 73 F.2d at 300.

Some courts sought a middle ground. In one case, the court wrote:

> The better view, based in part upon the doctrine of liberality of construction respecting charitable exemptions which resolves ambiguities in favor of the taxpayer and in part upon a refusal to allow form to control over substance, is that "organized" means "created to perform" or "established to promote" charitable purposes rather than meaning merely "incorporated" with powers limited solely to charitable activities.[70]

Thus, this court dismissed the approach that focuses only on "recitations in a charter or certificate" and held that the analysis must extend to the "actual objects motivating the organization and the subsequent conduct of the organization" and the "manner in which the corporation has been operated."[71]

Since promulgation of the regulations containing the organizational test, the courts have been somewhat silent on the subject. However, one court hinted that a provision in an organization's articles of organization that is contrary to the requirements of the organizational test (i.e., permitting substantial lobbying activities) may not be a bar to tax exemption where that aspect of the organization's activities is "dormant."[72] Another court has observed that the "mere existence of power to engage in activities other than those set out in section 501(c)(3) does not in itself prevent . . . [an organization] from meeting the organizational test."[73]

In the final analysis, however, prudence dictates compliance with the organizational test whenever possible. There are many barriers to tax-exempt status and the organizational test is one of the easiest to clear. This point is underscored by the approach of the IRS that, since articles of organization that fail to meet the organizational test are ordinarily amendable and since after amendment the exemption may be retroactive to the period before amendment, the "resolution of an organizational test question is only the first step in determining whether an organization is exempt."[74] Even if doing battle with the IRS over the tax-exempt status of an organization appears inevitable, presumably the struggle can be joined over matters of greater substance.

§ 4.4 PRIMARY PURPOSE TEST

Section 501(c)(3) of the Internal Revenue Code provides that an organization must, to qualify as a tax-exempt organization by reason of that provision, be organized and operated *exclusively* for an exempt purpose. It is clear that the term *exclusively* as employed in this context does not mean *solely* but rather *primarily*.[75]

Although the term *exclusively* is not used with respect to categories of tax-

---

[70] Samuel Friedland Found. v. United States, 144 F. Supp. 74, 84 (D. N.J. 1956).
[71] *Id.* at 85. Also Comm'r v. Battle Creek, Inc., 126 F.2d 405 (5th Cir. 1942); Forest Press, Inc. v. Comm'r, 22 T.C. 265 (1954); Lewis v. United States, 189 F. Supp. 950 (D. Wyo. 1961).
[72] Center on Corporate Responsibility v. Shultz, 368 F. Supp. 863, 878, note 31 (D. D.C. 1973).
[73] Peoples Translation Service/Newsfront Int'l v. Comm'r, 72 T.C. 42, 48 (1979).
[74] IRS Exempt Organizations Handbook (IRM 7751) § 338(2).
[75] Reg. § 1.501(c)(3)-1(c)(1). Also Reg. § 1.501(c)(3)-1(a)(1).

exempt organizations other than charitable ones, its presence may be presumed. That is, as a general precept, any type of tax-exempt organization must operate primarily for its exempt purpose to remain exempt.[76] This is the *primary purpose* test.

The law could not reasonably be interpreted in any other way. That is, if *exclusively* truly meant *exclusively*, there would not be an opportunity for the conduct of unrelated business activity. Since that interpretation would render the entire law of unrelated business income taxation[77] meaningless, the interpretation would not be reasonable. Consequently, by treating the word *exclusively* as if it meant *primarily*, the law accommodates the co-existence of some unrelated activities with related ones.

The general rule, as stated by the U.S. Supreme Court, is that the "presence of a single . . . [nonexempt] purpose, if substantial in nature, will destroy the exemption regardless of the number or importance of truly . . . [exempt] purposes."[78] A federal court of appeals held that nonexempt activity will not result in loss or denial of exemption where it is "only incidental and less than substantial" and that a "slight and comparatively unimportant deviation from the narrow furrow of tax approved activity is not fatal."[79] In the words of the IRS, the rules applicable to charitable organizations in general have "been construed as requiring all the resources of the organization [other than an insubstantial part] to be applied to the pursuit of one or more of the exempt purposes therein specified."[80] So, the existence of one or more truly exempt purposes of an organization will not be productive of tax exemption as a charitable entity if there is present in its operations a substantial nonexempt purpose.[81]

There is no definition of the term *insubstantial* in this context. Thus, application of these rules is an issue of fact to be determined under the facts and circumstances of each case.[82] However, a court opinion in one case suggested that, where a function represents less than 10 percent of total efforts, the primary purpose test will not be contravened.[83] By contrast, another court opinion stated that an organization that received approximately one third of its revenue from an unrelated business could not qualify for tax-exempt status.[84]

It is essential to observe at the outset that the primary purpose test looks—

---

[76] E.g., Orange County Agric. Soc'y, Inc. v. Comm'r, 55 T.C.M. 1602 (1988), *aff'd*, 893 F.2d 647 (2d Cir. 1990).

[77] See Part Five.

[78] Better Business Bureau of Washington, D.C. v. United States, 326 U.S. 279, 283 (1945). E.g., Universal Church of Jesus Christ, Inc. v. Comm'r, 55 T.C.M. 143 (1988).

[79] St. Louis Union Trust Co. v. United States, 374 F.2d 427, 431–432 (8th Cir. 1967). Also Seasongood v. Comm'r, 227 F.2d 907, 910 (6th Cir. 1955).

[80] Rev. Rul. 77-366, 1977-2 C.B. 192.

[81] Stevens Bros. Found. v. Comm'r, 324 F.2d 633 (8th Cir. 1963), *cert. den.*, 376 U.S. 969 (1964); Scripture Press Found. v. United States, 285 F.2d 800, 806 (Ct. Cl. 1961), *cert. den.*, 368 U.S. 985 (1962); Fides Publishers Ass'n v. United States, 263 F. Supp. 924, 935 (N.D. Ind. 1967); Edgar v. Comm'r, 56 T.C. 717, 755 (1971); The Media Sports League, Inc. v. Comm'r, 52 T.C.M. 1093 (1986).

[82] E.g., Kentucky Bar Found. v. Comm'r, 78 T.C. 921 (1982).

[83] World Family Corp. v. Comm'r, 81 T.C. 958 (1983).

[84] Orange County Agric. Soc'y, Inc. v. Comm'r, *supra* note 76 (where the unrelated business was held to have "exceeded the benchmark of insubstantiality" (55 T.C.M., at 1604)). This view of the law may be changing, in the aftermath of increasing emphasis on the *commensurate test* (see *infra* § 7).

in a rule frequently honored in its breach—to an organization's purposes rather than its activities.[85] The focus should not be on an organization's primary activities as the test of tax exemption but on whether the activities accomplish one or more tax-exempt purposes.[86] This is why, for example, an organization may engage in nonexempt or profit-making activities and nonetheless qualify for tax exemption.[87]

The proper approach to be taken, therefore, when determining whether an organization qualifies as a tax-exempt entity, is to assume *arguendo* one or more tax-exempt purposes and endeavor to ascertain whether the organization has a commercial or other nonexempt purpose. Upon finding a nonexempt purpose, an inquiry should then be made as to whether it is primary or incidental to the exempt purposes.[88] Then, if there is a nonexempt purpose that is substantial in nature, the exemption would be precluded. This approach was adhered to by a court, in concluding that a policemen's benevolent association could not qualify for tax exemption as a charitable organization because the payment of retirement benefits to its members was a substantial nonexempt activity.[89] This approach was again followed by the court in a case holding that a religious organization was ineligible for tax exemption because a substantial portion of its receipts was expended for the nonexempt function of medical care of its members.[90] However, the second of these two holdings was reversed on appeal, with the appellate court holding that the medical aid plan was carried out in furtherance of the church's religious doctrines and therefore was an exempt purpose.[91]

This approach is not always followed, however, as illustrated by a case involving a would-be religious organization that was denied tax exemption on the basis of the primary purpose test.[92] The disqualifying aspect of its activities was that the organization made grants that "carried with them no legal obligation to repay any interest or principal" and as to which the organization was "unable to furnish any documented criteria which would demonstrate the selection process of a deserving recipient, the reason for specific amounts given, or the purpose of

---

[85] Reg. § 1.501(c)(3)-1(c)(1).

[86] Aid to Artisans, Inc. v. Comm'r, 71 T.C. 202 (1978).

[87] Nonetheless, the courts occasionally stretch this criterion, as illustrated by the decision denying tax-exempt status to a scholarship fund, for violation of the primary purpose test, because its fund-raising activities were conducted in a cocktail lounge and attracted customers to the lounge (P.L.L. Scholarship Fund v. Comm'r, 82 T.C. 196 (1984); also *KJ's* Fund Raisers, Inc. v. Comm'r., 74 T.C.M. 669 (1997)). Cf. Hope Charitable Found. v. Ridell, 61-1 U.S.T.C. ¶ 9437 (S.D. Cal. 1961).

[88] American Inst. for Economic Research v. United States, 302 F.2d 934 (Ct. Cl. 1962); Edward Orton, Jr., Ceramic Found. v. Comm'r, 56 T.C. 147 (1971); Pulpit Resource v. Comm'r, 70 T.C. 594 (1978); Aid to Artisans, Inc. v. Comm'r, *supra* note 86.

[89] Policemen's Benevolent Ass'n of Westchester County, Inc. v. Comm'r, 42 T.C.M. 1750 (1981). Also Police Benevolent Ass'n of Richmond, Va. v. United States, 87-1 U.S.T.C. ¶ 9238 (E.D. Va. 1987).

[90] Bethel Conservative Mennonite Church v. Comm'r, 80 T.C. 352 (1983).

[91] Bethel Conservative Mennonite Church v. Comm'r, 746 F.2d 388 (7th Cir. 1984). The court wrote that "[r]eligions by their very nature provide many services that benefit only the members of the individual congregation, and to say that any church which so provides these benefits must be denied tax exemption would disrupt many organized churches as we know them," citing, *inter alia*, O'Leary v. Social Security Bd., 153 F.2d 704 (3d Cir. 1946); Passaic Hebrew Burial Ass'n v. United States, 216 F. Supp. 500 (D.N.J.).

[92] Church in Boston v. Comm'r, 71 T.C. 102 (1978).

the grant."[93] However, the statutory and regulatory law contains no criteria by which public charities are to consider and award grants.[94]

The difficulties inherent in applying the primary purpose test were amply illustrated by a court opinion, where the opinion initially prepared as the majority holding was converted by the full court into a dissenting opinion. At issue was the tax status of an organization that operated a pharmacy that sold prescription drugs at cost to the elderly and handicapped. The court held that the organization did not constitute a charitable entity, inasmuch as it did not use its surplus receipts to provide drugs to these persons below cost and it was in competition with profit-making drug stores. Contrary arguments that the organization operated to promote health and relieve the financial distress of a charitable class were unavailing. The dissenting opinion took the position that an organization's activities are not to be evaluated in a vacuum but in the context of accomplishment of tax-exempt purposes, that generation of a profit is not a *per se* bar to tax exemption, and that the organization was not being operated for commercial ends but rather to promote health.[95]

The primary purpose test was subsequently applied in an opinion denying tax-exempt status as a religious entity to an organization that operated a mountain lodge as a retreat facility.[96] While the organization contended that "its primary purpose is to provide a religious retreat facility for Christian families where they may come to reflect upon and worship the Lord in a setting free from the outside interferences of everyday life," the government asserted that its "substantial, if not sole, purpose is to provide a facility where guests can relax, socialize and engage in recreational activities, or, in other words, to operate a vacation resort."[97] The court held that the organization was not operated exclusively for religious (or other tax-exempt) purposes largely because of the organization's inability to demonstrate that "the recreational facilities were not used extensively and were not used in more than an insubstantial manner."[98] The court also appeared concerned with the fact that a guest at the lodge was not required to participate in any type of religious activity and that the organization was governed and was initially funded by members of the same family.[99]

By contrast, an organization formed to construct, and sell or lease, housing at a religious retreat facility owned and operated by a church was held to be tax-exempt as a charitable entity because the predominant use of the housing units was inextricably tied to the religious activities of the church.[100] While housing construction is not inherently an exempt function, in this instance the organiza-

---

[93] *Id.* at 106–107.

[94] Cf. IRC § 4945(d), applicable only to private foundations (see § 11.4 (e)).

[95] Federation Pharmacy Servs., Inc. v. Comm'r, 72 T.C. 687 (1979), *aff'd*, 625 F.2d 804 (8th Cir. 1980).

[96] The Schoger Found. v. Comm'r, 76 T.C. 380 (1981).

[97] *Id.* at 386.

[98] *Id.* at 388.

[99] At the same time, in a showing as to how the exclusivity doctrine can dictate the outcome of a case, the court observed that "[i]n a proper factual case, the operation of a lodge as a religious retreat facility would no doubt constitute an exempt religious purpose under [IRC] section 501(c)(3), and the presence of some incidental recreational or social activities might even be found to be activities to further or accomplish that exempt purpose" (*id.* at 389).

[100] Junaluska Assembly Housing, Inc. v. Comm'r, 86 T.C. 1114 (1986).

tion was found to be organized and operated exclusively for exempt purposes because of the manner of the development of the project, in that the organization had not advertised, it confined sale of the units to those who would take an active part in the religious activities, restrictions were placed on the properties as to resale, and otherwise was not operating for commercial purposes or private benefit. In general, the organization's function of providing additional housing was held essential to its continuing ability to carry out the purposes of the church.

The primary purpose test was also invoked to deny tax exemption to an organization formed to provide a service through which public and private libraries, commercial organizations, and others centrally pay license fees for the photocopying of certain copyrighted publications. In this capacity, the organization functioned as a clearinghouse for licensing photocopying and as a conduit for the transfer of license fees to copyright holders. The organization sought tax-exempt status as a charitable organization because it operated channels of communication necessary to implement the copyright clause of the U.S. Constitution and the federal copyright law as revised in 1976. To this end, it showed that it promoted social welfare, lessened the burdens of government, and promoted education and science.[101] The court involved conceded that the organization served tax-exempt purposes and did so to a substantial degree. Nonetheless, the court found a substantial nonqualifying purpose, precluding the organization from tax exemption. The organization was founded by a division of the American Association of Publishers and was funded almost entirely by commercial publishers. The court wrote that "there is little persuasive evidence that . . . [the organization's] founders had interests of any substance beyond the creation of a device to protect their copyright ownership and collect license fees."[102] Finding that "the potential for a substantial private profit was the driving force behind the organization and operation" of the entity, the court concluded that the nonexempt purpose was not incidental but represented the "dominant and overriding concern of those who organized, sponsored, and promoted" the organization.[103] Consequently, the court determined that the organization could not qualify for tax exemption as a charitable entity.

Thereafter, in application of the primary purpose test, the same court analyzed the tax status of a scholarship fund. While normally a scholarship fund is a charitable entity because it advances education,[104] in this case the court was moved to decide to the contrary by reason of the fact that the fund was established pursuant to a collective bargaining agreement between a labor union and an employers' association. The only recipients of the scholarships were children of the employees. The court concluded that the class of persons served was "too restricted" to confer the requisite "public benefit."[105] The court also held that the benefits were compensation in the form of a "negotiated fringe benefit,"[106] so that

---

[101] See §§ 6.3, 6.5, 6.6.

[102] Copyright Clearance Center, Inc. v. Comm'r, 79 T.C. 793, 805 (1982).

[103] Id. at 807, 808.

[104] See § 6.5.

[105] Local Union 712, I.B.E.W. Scholarship Trust Fund v. Comm'r, 45 T.C.M. 675, 678 (1983).

[106] Id.

the fund was not operated exclusively for an exempt purpose and therefore did not qualify as a charitable organization.

The primary purpose test was applied by a federal district court to deny tax-exempt status as charitable entities to two cemetery associations.[107] The court found that the cemetery associations generally conducted charitable activities, on two grounds. First, the "fundamental responsibility" of the associations for "the proper disposal of human remains is critical to society and would otherwise have to be assumed by the government." This was in recognition of the fact that an organization can be charitable where it lessens the burdens of government.[108] Second, the associations had a long-standing policy in providing free burial to indigents. This practice, said the court, served to "historically infuse" the cemetery associations with "a charitable concept." However, the court applied the primary purpose test to preclude the associations from being eligible recipients of deductible charitable bequests. In so doing, the court concluded that two of the cemetery associations' activities were the sale of burial plots and maintenance of the cemeteries. Since the court found these two activities to be substantial in nature, the associations were found to not be charitable entities.

§ 4.5 OPERATIONAL TEST

(a) In General

An organization, to qualify as a charitable entity, is regarded as operated exclusively for one or more tax-exempt purposes only if it engages primarily in activities that accomplish one or more of its exempt purposes.[109] The IRS observed that, to satisfy this *operational test*, the "organization's resources must be devoted to purposes that qualify as exclusively charitable within the meaning of section 501(c)(3) of the Code and the applicable regulations."[110] An organization will not be so regarded if more than an insubstantial part of its activities is not in furtherance of an exempt purpose.[111] An organization is not considered as operated exclusively for one or more exempt purposes if its net earnings inure in whole or in part to the benefit of private shareholders or individuals.[112] An organization can be substantially dominated by its founder without, for that reason alone, failing to satisfy the operational test.[113] However, one court concluded that an organiza-

---

[107] Smith v. United States, 84-2 U.S.T.C. ¶ 13,595 (W.D. Mo. 1984).

[108] See § 6.3.

[109] Reg. § 1.501(c)(3)-1(a)(1).

[110] Rev. Rul. 72-369, 1972-2 C.B. 245.

[111] Reg. § 1.501(c)(3)-1(c)(1). In one instance, the operational test was found to be unmet because the organization involved, which was organized for the study and promotion of the philately of the Central American republics, operated a mail bid stamps sales service for its members as a substantial activity (Society of Costa Rica Collectors v. Comm'r, 49 T.C.M. 304 (1984)).

[112] Reg. §§ 1.501(c)(3)-1(c)(2), 1.501(a)-1(c). Also Wildt's Motorsport Advancement Crusade, Bill v. Comm'r, 56 T.C.M. 1401 (1989); Athenagoras I Christian Union of the World, Inc. v. Comm'r, 55 T.C.M. 781 (1988); Levy Family Tribe Found. v. Comm'r, *supra* note 31. See Chapter 19.

[113] E.g., The Church of the Visible Intelligence That Governs the Universe v. United States, 83-2 U.S.T.C. ¶ 9726 (Cl. Ct. 1983).

tion cannot qualify for tax exemption where one individual controls all aspects of the organization's operations and "is not checked" by any governing body.[114]

A deficiency in an organization's operations that causes failure of the operational test cannot be cured by language in its governing instruments. Thus, the IRS has stated that "[a]n organization whose activities are not within the statute cannot be exempt by virtue of a well-written charter."[115]

An organization may meet the federal tax law requirements for charitable entities even though it operates a trade or business as a substantial part of its activities.[116] However, if the organization has as its primary purpose the carrying on of a trade or business, it may not be tax-exempt.[117] (The existence of an operating profit is not conclusive as to a business purpose.[118]) Even though the operation of a business does not deprive an organization of classification as a charitable entity, there may be unrelated trade or business tax consequences.[119]

In one instance, the operational test was said to look more toward an organization's purposes rather than its activities, in recognition of the fact that an organization may conduct a business in furtherance of a tax-exempt purpose and qualify as a charitable entity:

> Under the operational test, the purpose towards which an organization's activities are directed, and not the nature of the activities themselves, is ultimately dispositive of the organization's right to be classified as a section 501(c)(3) organization exempt from tax under section 501(a). . . . [I]t is possible for . . . an activity to be carried on for more than one purpose. . . . The fact that . . . [an] activity may constitute a trade or business does not, of course, disqualify it from classification under section 501(c)(3), provided the activity furthers or accomplishes an exempt purpose. . . . Rather, the critical inquiry is whether . . . [an organization's] primary purpose for engaging in its . . . activity is an exempt purpose, or whether its primary purpose is the nonexempt one of operating a commercial business producing net profits for . . . [the organization] . . . Factors such as the particular manner in which an organization's activities are conducted, the commercial hue of those activities and the existence and amount of annual or accumulated profits are relevant evidence of a forbidden predominant purpose.[120]

This important distinction between activities and purpose is frequently overlooked by the IRS and the courts. For example, in one case the court concluded that the operational test was not satisfied because the organization failed to de-

---

[114] Chief Steward of the Ecumenical Temples and the Worldwide Peace Movement and His Successors v. Comm'r, *supra* note 55, at 643.

[115] IRS Exempt Organizations Handbook (IRM 7751) § 320(2).

[116] E.g., Rev. Rul. 64-182, 1964-1 (Part 1) C.B. 186.

[117] Reg. § 1.501(c)(3)-1(e)(1).

[118] Rev. Rul. 68-26, 1968-1 C.B. 272; Elisian Guild, Inc. v. United States, 412 F.2d 121 (1st Cir. 1969). Cf. Fides Publishers Assn. v. United States, 263 F. Supp. 924 (N.D. Ind. 1967).

[119] See Part Five.

[120] B.S.W. Group, Inc. v. Comm'r, 70 T.C. 352, 356–357 (1978). Also Ohio Teamsters Educ. & Safety Training Fund v. Comm'r, 77 T.C. 189 (1981), *aff'd*, 692 F.2d 432 (6th Cir. 1982).

scribe its activities in sufficient detail in its application for recognition of tax exemption.[121]

An illustration of the application of the operational test rules was provided by a case concerning the tax-exempt status of an organization established to provide a fund for the purpose of giving scholarships to contestants in a state pageant.[122] As a condition for qualifying for the scholarships, the organization required the participants to enter into a contract obligating them, in the event they are selected to participate in the pageant, to abide by its rules and regulations. A court ruled that the "scholarships" were compensatory in nature, being payment for the contestants' agreement to perform the requirements of the contract, thus not constituting tax-excludable[123] scholarships. Because the grant of the scholarships was the organization's sole activity, and because the primary purpose of the payments was to provide compensation, the court concluded that the organization did not qualify for tax exemption as a charitable organization.

Another illustration of the application of these rules is inherent in a court decision concluding that an organization that principally administered projects funded and recommended by donors, for a commission, qualified as a charitable entity.[124] Interested persons submit a project proposal application, that if accepted leads to the formation of an account for the project; the donor does not retain any ownership of or discretion with respect to the funds, although the donor may request that the funds be used for particular activities. The government unsuccessfully contended in court that the organization lacked tax-exempt purposes, being instead an association of individuals for which it performs commercial services for fees. Rejecting the thought that the organization is a mere conduit for its donors, the court—conceding that the entity's "methods of operating may be somewhat unique and innovative"—found that its "goal is to create an effective national network to respond to many worthy charitable needs at the local level which in many cases might go unmet" and that its activities "promote public policy and represent the very essence of charitable benevolence as envisioned by Congress in enacting" tax-exempt status for charitable organizations.

Still another example illustrating application of the operational test rules involved a court opinion that invoked the concept of private benefit, holding that when an organization operates to confer a private benefit, where the benefit is more than incidental, it cannot satisfy the test. The case concerned an otherwise qualifying school, that trained individuals for careers as political campaign professionals, because of the benefit accruing to entities of a political party and its candidates, since nearly all of the school's graduates became employed by or con-

---

[121] General Conference of the Free Church of Am. v. Comm'r, 71 T.C. 920 (1979).

[122] Miss Georgia Scholarship Fund, Inc. v. Comm'r, 72 T.C. 267 (1979).

[123] IRC § 117.

[124] National Found., Inc. v. United States, 87-2 U.S.T.C. ¶ 9602 (Cl. Ct. 1987). Subsequently, the U.S. Claims Court determined that the organization cannot recover attorney's fees under the Equal Access to Justice Act in connection with its successful litigation (National Found., Inc. v. United States, 15 Cl. Ct. 209 (1988)). By contrast, an organization that pooled charitable gifts and allowed the donors to control the investment decisions was ruled to have substantial non-charitable purposes (The Fund for Anonymous Gifts v. Internal Revenue Service, 97-2 U.S.T.C. ¶ 50, 710 (D.D.C. 1997)).

sultants to these entities or candidates.[125] The court was not concerned with the "primary" private benefit accruing to the students but with the "secondary" private benefit accruing to the party's organizations and candidates.[126]

The operational test is used to apply the tests of *commerciality* and *competition* to charitable and other categories of tax-exempt organizations. Previously, the test has been used in conjunction with the *exclusivity* requirement[127] and the rules defining *business* for unrelated income taxation purposes.[128] This application of the commerciality doctrine has largely been by the U.S. Tax Court, where, for example, it denied tax-exempt status, as a charitable and religious entity, to an organization associated with the Seventh-day Adventist Church that, in advancement of Church doctrine, operated vegetarian restaurants and health food stores; the court wrote that the organization's "activity was conducted as a business and was in direct competition with other restaurants and health food stores" and that "[c]ompetition with commercial firms is strong evidence of a substantial nonexempt commercial purpose."[129] Likewise, the Tax Court held that an organization that supported religious missionary work properly had its exemption revoked because it conducted a mail order business in tape and electronic equipment, as a substantial part of its activities and purposes,[130] and that an organization cannot be tax-exempt because it functioned the same as a purchasing, brokering, or consulting organization in the private sector.[131] The only prior opinion from the Tax Court that invoked the commerciality standard is one that looked at the issue from a somewhat different slant, in that the court wrote that the operational test is violated where the organization's "primary purpose is the nonexempt one of operating a commercial business producing net profits for" the organization.[132]

(b) Action Organizations

An organization is not operated exclusively for one or more exempt purposes if it is an *action organization*.[133]

An organization is an action organization if a substantial part of its activities is attempting to influence legislation by propaganda or otherwise. For this purpose, an organization is regarded as attempting to influence legislation if the organization contacts, or urges the public to contact, members of a legislative body for the purpose of proposing, supporting, or opposing legislation or if it advocates the adoption or rejection of legislation. The term *legislation* includes action by the U.S. Congress, a state legislature, a local council or similar governing body, or the public in a referendum, initiative, constitutional amendment, or similar

[125] American Campaign Academy v. Comm'r, 92 T.C. 1053 (1989).
[126] See § 19.10.
[127] See *infra* § 6.
[128] See § 26.2.
[129] Living Faith, Inc. v. Comm'r, 60 T.C.M. 710, 713 (1990), *aff'd*, 950 F.2d 365 (7th Cir. 1991).
[130] United Missionary Aviation, Inc. v. Comm'r, 60 T.C.M. 1152 (1990), *rev'd and rem'd*, 89-2 U.S.T.C. ¶ 9595 (8th Cir. 1989), *cert. den.*, 506 U.S. 816.
[131] Public Indus., Inc. v. Comm'r, 61 T.C.M. 1626 (1991).
[132] B.S.W. Group, Inc. v. Comm'r, *supra* note 120 at 356.
[133] Reg. § 1.501(c)(3)-1(c)(i).

procedure. An organization will not fail to meet the operational test merely because it advocates, as an insubstantial part of its activities, the adoption or rejection of legislation.[134] Also, an organization for which the expenditure test election (relating to expenditures for legislative activities)[135] is in effect for a tax year is not considered an action organization for the year if it avoids loss of tax exemption by reason of that test.[136]

An organization is an action organization if it participates or intervenes, directly or indirectly, in any political campaign on behalf of or in opposition to any candidate for public office. The phrase *candidate for public office* means an individual who offers himself or herself, or is proposed by others, as a contestant for an elective public office, whether the office is national, state, or local. Activities that constitute participation or intervention in a political campaign on behalf of or in opposition to a candidate include, but are not limited to, the publication or distribution of written or printed statements or the making of oral statements on behalf of or in opposition to the candidate.[137]

An organization is an action organization if it has the following two characteristics: (1) Its main or primary objective or objectives (as distinguished from its incidental or secondary objectives) may be attained only by legislation or a defeat of proposed legislation, and (2) it advocates or campaigns for the attainment of this main or primary objective or objectives as distinguished from engaging in nonpartisan analysis, study, or research, and making the results thereof available to the public. In determining whether an organization has these characteristics, all the surrounding facts and circumstances, including the articles of organization (see above) and all activities of the organization, are considered.[138]

The IRS is aware that the regulations' terms *exclusively, primarily*, and *insubstantial* present "difficult conceptual problems."[139] The IRS concluded that "[q]uestions involving the application of these terms can more readily be resolved on the basis of the facts of a particular case."[140]

Application of the operational test is, therefore, intertwined with the proscriptions on private inurement, and legislative and political activities.[141] In essence, however, to meet the operational test, an organization must be engaged in activities that further public rather than private purposes.[142]

The entwining of the operational test with the other requirements of the federal tax rules governing charitable organizations was explicitly recognized by a court in a decision refusing to reclassify a health and welfare fund, which was tax-exempt as an employee beneficiary association,[143] as a charitable organiza-

---

[134] Reg. § 1.501(c)(3)-(c)(3)(ii).
[135] See § 20.5(a).
[136] Reg. § 1.501(c)(3)-1(c)(3)(ii).
[137] Reg. § 1.501(c)(3)-1(c)(3)(iii).
[138] Reg. § 1.501(c)(3)-1(c)(3)(iv).
[139] IRS Exempt Organizations Handbook (IRM 7751) § 341.1(2).
[140] *Id.*
[141] See Chapters 19–21.
[142] Reg. § 1.501(c)(3)-1(d)(1)(ii). E.g., American Campaign Academy v. Comm'r., *supra* note 125.
[143] See § 16.3.

tion.[144] The court ruled against the organization on the ground that it was not operated exclusively for charitable purposes[145] and that its activities were furthering private interests[146] but cloaked its opinion in the mantle of the operational test. (The organization's activities consisted of operating child day-care centers—which the court seemed to imply is not a charitable activity[147]—and providing services to members, and the organization charged the employees less tuition for the day-care services than it charged other parents.)

An organization deemed to be an action organization, other than because of more than merely incidental political campaign activities, though it cannot for that reason qualify as a charitable organization, may nonetheless qualify as a social welfare organization.[148]

§ 4.6   THE EXCLUSIVELY STANDARD

To be tax-exempt as a charitable organization, an entity must be organized and operated *exclusively* for exempt purposes. As noted,[149] this rule is reflected in the primary purpose test. However, there is additional law pertaining to the *exclusivity* rule.

One of the more controversial opinions in this regard was authored by a federal court of appeals, which accorded tax exemption to a public parking facility as a charitable organization.[150] The organization was formed by several private businesses and professional persons to construct and operate the facility, utilizing a validation stamp system in an effort to attract shoppers to a center city. The government contended that the operation of a commercial parking facility is not an exempt activity[151] and that a substantial objective of the organization was to encourage the general public to patronize the businesses that participate in the validation stamp system, which constituted private inurement and only incidental public benefit.[152] Concluding that the city involved was the primary beneficiary of the organization's activities, the district court had held that the "business activity itself is similar to that which others engage in for profit, but it is not carried on in the same manner; it is carried on only because it is necessary for the attainment of an undeniably public end."[153] On appeal, the appellate court observed that the lower court "made a quantitative comparison of the private versus the public benefits derived from the organization and operation of the

---

[144] Baltimore Regional Joint Bd. Health & Welfare Fund, Amalgamated Clothing & Textile Workers Union v. Comm'r, 69 T.C. 554 (1978).

[145] See *infra* § 6.

[146] See Chapter 19.

[147] Cf. Rev. Rul. 70-533, 1970-2 C.B. 112; San Francisco Infant School, Inc. v. Comm'r, 69 T.C. 957 (1978); Michigan Early Childhood Cent., Inc. v. Comm'r, 37 T.C.M. 808 (1978). See § 7.7.

[148] Reg. § 1.501(c)(3)-1(c)(3)(v). See Chapter 12.

[149] See § 4.4.

[150] Monterey Pub. Parking Corp. v. United States, 481 F.2d 175 (9th Cir. 1973), *aff'd.* 321 F. Supp. 972 (N.D. Cal. 1970).

[151] See Chapter 25.

[152] See Chapter 19.

[153] Monterey Pub. Parking Corp. v. United States, *supra* note 150, 321 F. Supp., at 977.

plaintiff corporation" and determined that the requirements for exemption were "adequately fulfilled."[154] The opinion is not illustrative of blind adherence to the *exclusively* doctrine.

The IRS does not subscribe to the principles of the public parking corporation case and announced that it does not follow the decision.[155] The IRS asserts that this type of a public parking corporation does not operate exclusively for charitable purposes and carries on a business with the general public in a manner similar to organizations that are operated for profit. This position was made clear earlier when the IRS ruled that an organization formed to revive retail sales in an area suffering from continued economic decline by constructing a shopping center that would complement the area's existing retail facilities could not qualify for tax exemption as a charitable entity. The IRS, then taking no notice of the appellate court decision, said that the activities of the organization "result in major benefits accruing to the stores that will locate within the shopping center," thereby precluding the exemption.[156] (However, an organization that provided free parking to persons visiting a downtown area can qualify as a social welfare organization.[157])

Application of the concept of *exclusively* may require even more flexibility than has been previously displayed. This may be particularly unavoidable as respects organizations performing services that are considered necessary in today's society, even where the services are parallel with those rendered in commercial settings. For example, the provision of medical services can obviously be an enterprise for profit, yet the IRS was able to rule that an organization formed to attract a physician to a medically underserved rural area, by providing the doctor with a building and facilities at a reasonable rent, qualified as a charitable organization.[158] "In these circumstances," said the IRS, "any personal benefit derived by the physician (the use of the building in which to practice medicine) does not detract from the public purpose of the organization nor lessen the public benefit flowing from its activities."[159] Similarly, an organization formed to provide legal services for residents of economically depressed communities was ruled to be engaged in charitable activities.[160] Even though those providing the services were subsidized by the organization, the IRS minimized this personal gain by the rationale that they were merely the instruments by which the charitable purposes were accomplished.[161]

A court considered the tax status of an organization, the primary purpose of which was to promote, improve, and expand the handicraft output of disadvan-

---

[154] Monterey Public Parking Corp. v. United States, *supra* note 150, 481 F. 2d at 177. Cf. Rev. Rul. 73-411, 1973-2 C.B. 180.

[155] Rev. Rul. 78-86, 1978-1 C.B. 151.

[156] Rev. Rul. 77-111, 1977-1 C.B. 144. Also Rev. Rul. 64-108, 1964-1 (Part I) C.B. 189.

[157] Rev. Rul. 81-116, 1981-1 C.B. 333. Social welfare organizations are the subject of Chapter 12.

[158] Rev. Rul. 73-313, 1973-2 C.B. 174.

[159] *Id*. at 176 citing In re Estate of Carlson, 358 P.2d 669 (Kan. 1961). Cf. Rev. Rul. 69-266, 1969-1 C.B. 151.

[160] Rev. Rul. 72-559, 1972-2 C.B. 247. Also Rev. Rul. 70-640, 1970-2 C.B. 117; Golf Life World Entertainment Golf Championship, Inc. v. United States, 65-1 U.S.T.C. ¶ 9174 (S. D. Cal. 1964). Cf. Rev. Rul. 72-369, 1972-2 C.B. 245.

[161] See § 5.5(d).

taged artisans in developing societies of the world.[162] The organization's primary activities were the purchase, import, and sale of handicrafts—taken alone, clearly commercial activities—undertaken to alleviate economic deficiencies in communities of disadvantaged artisans, educate the American public in the artistry, history, and cultural significance of handicrafts from these communities, preserve the production of authentic handicrafts, and achieve economic stabilization in disadvantaged communities where handicrafts are central to the economy. The court found that these activities advanced charitable and educational objectives[163] and that the furtherance of nonexempt purposes (benefit to nondisadvantaged artisans) was an insubstantial part of the organization's activities. The essence of the case is captured in the following excerpt: "Thus, the sale of handicrafts to exempt organizations [museums] is neither an exempt purpose as argued by . . . [the organization] nor a non-exempt purpose as argued by . . . [the IRS]. Rather, such sale is merely an activity carried on by . . . [the organization] in furtherance of its exempt purposes."[164]

By contrast, the same court refused to find a scholarship fund established pursuant to a collective bargaining agreement to be a charitable entity, holding it to be a voluntary employees' beneficiary association[165] instead.[166] The court concluded that the fund failed the exclusively test because one of the substantial purposes of the entity was the provision of compensation for services rendered by employees pursuant to the agreement. The court also found that an organization failed the exclusively test because its primary purpose was to operate bingo games for other tax-exempt organizations.[167]

The IRS revoked the tax-exempt status of a charitable organization which had as its purpose the promotion of understanding among the people of the world through learning of nations' sports activities, because of its extensive golf and tennis tours. Those on the tours were regarded as "sports ambassadors"; they (and their families and friends) were the beneficiaries of "good parties" and enjoyable accommodations, meals, and transportation. These facts were aggravated by the fact that two for-profit travel agencies had exclusive accounts for planning and operation of the tours. The operation of the golf and tennis programs in this fashion was found to be a substantial nonexempt purpose of the organization.[168]

In another instance, a nonprofit organization was created, by three restaurant owners in a city in Vermont, for the purpose of making "travel grants" to indigent and antisocial persons. The court found that the true purposes of the organization were to rid the downtown area (where the restaurants are located) of disruptive homeless persons and to protect the commercial interests of the

---

[162] Aid to Artisans, Inc. v. Comm'r, *supra* note 86.

[163] The court held that the first of these activities relieved the poor and distressed or the underprivileged (see, § 6.1) and that the fourth of these activities promoted social welfare (see § 6.6).

[164] Aid to Artisans, Inc. v. Comm'r, *supra* note 86 at 214.

[165] See § 16.3.

[166] The Newspaper Guild of New York, Times Unit–The New York Times College Scholarship Fund v. Comm'r, 57 T.C.M. 812 (1989).

[167] Make a Joyful Noise, Inc. v. Comm'r, 56 T.C.M. 1003 (1989).

[168] Tech. Adv. Mem. 9540002.

restaurateurs (who were the organization's officers). The organization was found to not be "genuinely concerned with the fate of the homeless persons it was relocating, but rather with relocating such persons out of" the city, and thus not be operating exclusively for the advancement of charitable purposes.[169]

In another case, tax-exempt status was denied pursuant to the exclusively doctrine to an organization that is part of the Scientology hierarchy of churches and other organizations.[170] The court found that the organization was established for the primary purpose of obtaining tax-exempt status to serve the financing interests of other, nonexempt entities. In reaching its decision, the court took into account the overall structure and financing of the Scientology organization. The court observed that the organization was linked by "a cat's cradle of connections" to a range of Scientology organizations; the court wrote of the "commercial character" of the organization, its "scripturally-based hostility to taxation," and its role as a "shelter from taxation."[171] Its ostensible tax-exempt purpose was to create an archive of Scientology scriptures but the court concluded that that purpose was secondary to its principal (nonexempt) purposes.

§ 4.7   THE COMMENSURATE TEST

Somewhat related to the operational test is another test that the IRS has developed but, until recently, had rarely used. This test is termed the *commensurate test*, which was first articulated in 1964.[172] Under this test, the IRS is empowered to assess whether a charitable organization is maintaining program activities that are commensurate in scope with its financial resources.

In the particular facts underlying the 1964 ruling, the organization derived most of its income from rents, yet was successful in preserving its tax-exempt status because it satisfied the test, in that it was engaging in an adequate amount of charitable functions notwithstanding the extent of its rental activities.

The commensurate test lay dormant for years, then surfaced again in 1990, when the IRS began a close review of the fund-raising practices of charitable organizations. In that connection, the IRS developed an 82-question "checksheet" for use by its auditing agents; its full title is "Exempt Organizations Charitable Solicitations Compliance Improvement Program Study Checksheet." One question asks the reviewing agent to determine whether the charitable organization being examined is meeting the *commensurate* test.[173] In this context, the agent is to ascertain whether the charitable organization is engaging in sufficient charitable activity in relation to its available resources, including gifts received through fund-raising campaigns, as measured against the time and expense of fund-raising.

---

[169] Westward Ho v. Comm'r, 63 T.C.M. 2617 (1992).

[170] Church of Spiritual Technology v. United States, 92-1 U.S.T.C. § 50,305 (Cl. Ct. 1992), *aff'd*, 991 F.2d 812 (Fed. Cir. 1993), *cert. den.*, 114 S. Ct. 197 (1993). See § 8.2, note 95.

[171] *Id.*, 92-1 U.S.T.C. ¶ 50,305, at 84,217.

[172] Rev. Rul. 64-182, 1964-1 C.B. (Part 1) 186.

[173] This checksheet is discussed in detail in Hopkins, *The Law of Fund-Raising, Second Edition* (New York: John Wiley & Sons, Inc., 1996), Chapter 6 § 1.

§ 4.7 THE COMMENSURATE TEST

Later in 1990, the IRS revoked the tax-exempt status of a charitable organization on a variety of rationales, including the ground that its fund-raising costs were too high and thus violated the *commensurate* test. In a technical advice memorandum, unpublished by the IRS,[174] the IRS concluded that the test was transgressed because of its finding that the charity involved expended, during the two years examined, only about 4 percent of its revenue for charitable purposes; the rest was allegedly spent for fund-raising and administration. (The matter of the organization's tax-exempt status was ultimately resolved in court, albeit without application of the commensurate test; the case turned out to be one involving private inurement.[175])

Wrote the IRS:

> The "commensurate test" does not lend itself to a rigid numerical distribution formula—there is no fixed percentage of income that an organization must pay out for charitable purposes. The financial resources of any organization may be affected by such factors as startup costs, overhead, scale of operations, whether labor is voluntary or salaried, phone or postal costs, etc. In each case, therefore, the particular facts and circumstances of the organization must be considered. Accordingly, a specific payout percentage does not automatically mandate the conclusion that the organization under consideration has a primary purpose that is not charitable. In each case, it should be ascertained whether the failure to make real and substantial contributions for charitable purposes is due to reasonable cause.

The IRS added:

> While there is no specified payout percentage, and while special facts and circumstances may control the conclusion, distribution levels that are low invite close scrutiny. The "commensurate" test requires that organizations have a charitable program that is both real and, taking the organization's circumstances and financial resources into account, substantial. Therefore, an organization that raises funds for charitable purposes but consistently uses virtually all its income for administrative and promotional expenses with little or no direct charitable accomplishments cannot reasonably argue that its charitable program is commensurate with its financial resources and capabilities.

The commensurate test and the primary purpose test have an awkward coexistence; the former may, at least in some contexts, be replacing the latter. For example, a charitable organization was allowed to retain its tax-exempt status while receiving 98 percent of its support from unrelated business income, since 41 percent of the organization's activities were charitable programs.[176]

---

[174] This technical advice memorandum is reproduced at 4 *Exempt Org. Tax Rev.* (No. 5) 726 (July 1991), and is discussed in detail in Hopkins, *supra* note 173, at Chapter 6 § 15, text accompanied by notes 564–576.

[175] United Cancer Council, Inc. v. Comm'r, 109 T.C. No. 17 (1997). (U.S. Tax Ct., Docket No. 2008-91X.) This case is discussed in §§ 19.3, 19.4, and in Hopkins, note 173, at Chapter 6 § 15 text accompanied by notes 577–584, and at Chapter 8 § 12.

[176] IRS Tech. Adv. Mem. 9711003.

§ 4.8 BOARDS OF DIRECTORS

There is nothing in the federal statutory law, the federal tax regulations, or the rulings from the IRS that, as a general rule, dictates the composition of the board of directors (or other governing body) of a tax-exempt organization.[177]

Nonetheless, the courts are building up some presumptions in this area. For example, it is the view of the U.S. Tax Court that "where the creators [of an organization] control the affairs of the organization, there is an obvious opportunity for abuse, which necessitates an open and candid disclosure of all facts bearing upon the organization, operation, and finances so that the Court can be assured that by granting the claimed exemption it is not sanctioning an abuse of the revenue laws."[178] The court added that, where this disclosure is not made, "the logical inference is that the facts, if disclosed, would show that the taxpayer [organization] fails to meet the requirements" for tax-exempt status.[179]

In another case, the Tax Court found that all of the directors and officers of an organization were related and it could not find the "necessary delineation" between the organization and these persons acting in their personal and private capacity.[180] Earlier, a court found the fact that a husband and wife were two of three members of an organization's board of directors required a special justification of certain payments by the organization to them.[181] Before that, an appellate court concluded that one individual who had "complete and unfettered control" over an organization had a special burden to explain certain withdrawals from the organization's bank account.[182]

In still another setting, a court considered an organization with three directors, namely, the founder, his wife, and their daughter; these three individuals were among the membership base of five. The small size of the organization was held to be "relevant," with the court finding private inurement and private benefit because of the "amount of control" the founder exercised over the organization's operations and the "blurring of the lines of demarcation between the activities and interests" of the organization.[183] The court observed that "[t]his is not to say that an organization of such small dimensions cannot qualify for tax-exempt status."[184]

Thus, while there is nothing specific in the operational test concerning the size or composition of the governing board of a charitable organization, the

---

[177] A charitable organization that wishes to avoid private foundation status as a donative publicly supported organization by means of the *facts-and-circumstances test* (see § 11.3(6)(ii)) may have to meet certain criteria as to the composition of its governing board.

[178] United Libertarian Fellowship, Inc. v. Comm'r, 65 T.C.M. 2175, 2181 (1993).

[179] *Id*. Identical language was used by the court in a prior opinion (Bubbling Well Church of Universal Love, Inc. v. Comm'r, 74 T.C. 531, 535 (1980), *aff'd*, 670 F.2d 104 (9th Cir. 1981)).

[180] Levy Family Tribe Found., Inc. v. Comm'r, 69 T.C. 615, 619 (1978).

[181] Founding Church of Scientology v. United States, 412 F.2d 1197, 1201 (Ct. Cl. 1969), *cert. den.*, 397 U.S. 1009 (1970).

[182] Parker v. Comm'r, 365 F.2d 792, 799 (8th Cir. 1966), *cert. den.*, 385 U.S. 1026 (1967).

[183] Western Catholic Church v. Comm'r, 73 T.C. 196, 213 (1979).

[184] *Id*. In Blake v. Comm'r, 29 T.C.M. 513 (1970), an organization of similar dimensions was ruled to be tax-exempt, although private inurement or private benefit was not at issue in the case.

courts are engrafting onto the test greater burdens of proof when the organization has a small board of directors, dominated by an individual.

§ 4.9   OPERATIONS FOR PROFIT

The IRS, when alleging that an organization is not operated exclusively for an exempt purpose, frequently bases its contention on a finding that the organization's operation is similar to a commercial enterprise operated for profit. However, as one court observed, "the presence of profitmaking activities is not *per se* a bar to qualification of an organization as exempt if the activities further or accomplish an exempt purpose."[185] Similarly, the IRS expressly acknowledged that a charitable organization can have a qualified[186] profit-sharing plan for its employees without endangering its tax exemption.[187]

In one instance, a plan was designed by a hospital as an employee incentive plan, with "profits" defined in the general accounting sense of excess of receipts over expenses.[188] Plan distributions must be reasonable; the distributions were held to not be "dividends" and to not constitute private inurement.[189]

The question as to whether, and if so to what extent, a tax-exempt organization (particularly one that is classified as a charitable entity) can earn a profit is at once difficult and easy to answer. The question is easy to answer in the sense that it is clear that the mere showing of a profit (excess of revenue over expenses) for one or more tax years will not bar tax exemption. However, if the profit is from what is perceived as a business activity and the fact of a profit is used to show the commercial hue of the activity, the answer to the question will depend upon the facts and circumstances of the particular case. That is, the decisive factor is likely to be the nature of the activities that give rise to the profits.[190]

An illustrative body of law is that concerning organizations that prepare and sell publications at a profit.[191] In one case, an organization sold religious publications to students attending classes it sponsored and to members of its religious following, for a relatively small profit.[192] In rejecting the government's argument that the receipt of the income indicated that the organization was not operated exclusively for religious purposes, a court held that the sale of religious literature was an activity "closely associated with, and incidental to" the organization's tax-exempt purposes and bore "an intimate relationship to the proper functioning" of it, and thus that the receipt of the income did not prevent the or-

---

[185] Aid to Artisans, Inc. v. Comm'r, *supra* note 86, at 211.

[186] IRC § 401(a).

[187] See § 19.4(i)

[188] Gen. Couns. Mem. 38283.

[189] Priv. Ltr. Rul. 8442064. In general, Note, "The Semantic Anomaly: Maintenance of Qualified Profit-Sharing Plans by Non-Profit Organizations—A Concept Whose Time Has Come," 59 *Notre Dame L. Rev.* (No. 3) 754 (1984).

[190] See the discussion of the *commerciality doctrine* in Chapter 25.

[191] See Chapter 8 § 4.

[192] Saint Germain Found. v. Comm'r, 26 T.C. 648 (1956).

ganization from being an organization organized and operated exclusively for religious purposes.[193]

By contrast, a court denied status as a charitable entity to an organization that prepared and sold religious literature on a nondenominational basis. Because the organization's materials were competitively priced and the sales over a seven-year period yielded substantial accumulated profits that greatly exceeded the amount expended for its activities, the court concluded that the sales activities were the organization's primary concern and that it was engaging in the conduct of a trade or business for profit.[194] Another organization was denied tax exemption for publishing on a for-profit basis, with the court observing that, were the law otherwise, "every publishing house would be entitled to an exemption on the ground that it furthers the education of the public."[195] Likewise, an organization could not achieve tax exemption because its primary activity—the publication and sale of books that are religiously inspired and oriented and written by its founder—was conducted in a commercial manner, at a profit.[196]

Each case on this point, therefore, must reflect one of these two analyses. In one case, a court accepted the contention by an organization that its publishing activities furthered its religious purpose of improving the preaching skills and sermons of the clergy of the Protestant, Roman Catholic, and Jewish faiths. Subscriptions for the publications were obtained by advertising and direct mail solicitation, and the publications were sold at a modest profit. The court found that the organization was not in competition with any commercial enterprise and that the sale of religious literature was an integral part of the organization's religious purposes. Said the court: "The fact that . . . [the organization] intended to make a profit, alone, does not negate [the fact] that . . . [it] was operated exclusively for charitable purposes."[197]

By contrast, an organization was denied tax exemption as a charitable entity because it was directly engaged in the conduct of a commercial leasing enterprise for the principal purpose of realizing profits. The enterprise was regarded as its principal activity (measured by total gross income), in which it was an active participant, and not related to an exempt purpose. Further, its charitable activities were deemed to be of relatively minimal consequence.[198] Similarly, a court reflected upon a nonprofit organization's accumulated profits and decided that this was evidence that the primary function of the organization was commercial in nature.[199]

One court determined that "[c]ases where a tax-exempt organization conducts only one activity present particular difficulty" in this area and singled out

---

[193] *Id.* at 658. Also Elisian Guild, Inc. v. United States, 412 F.2d 121 (1st Cir. 1969), *rev'g* 292 F. Supp. 219 (D. Mass. 1968).

[194] Scripture Press Found. v. United States, *supra* note 81.

[195] Fides Publishers Ass'n v. United States, *supra* note 81, at 936.

[196] Christian Manner Int'l, Inc. v. Comm'r, 71 T.C. 661 (1979).

[197] Pulpit Resource v. Comm'r, *supra* note 88, at 611. Also Junaluska Assembly Housing, Inc. v. Comm'r, *supra* note 100; Industrial Aid for the Blind v. Comm'r, 73 T.C. 96 (1979).

[198] Greater United Navajo Dev. Enters., Inc v. Comm'r, 74 T.C. 69 (1980).

[199] Elisian Guild, Inc. v. United States, *supra* note 193, at 412 F. 2d 124.

for uniquely stringent review "religious publishing companies."[200] In the leading case on the subject, an organization had as its sole function the publication of literature in furtherance of a religious doctrine, although it was not affiliated with any particular church. This the organization had done since 1931, and over the years it achieved what the court characterized as "substantial profits" and "consistent and comfortable net profit margins."[201] The issue thus became whether the publishing activities were tax-exempt functions because they were primarily carried on in advancement of charitable, educational, and religious purposes or whether the organization was engaged in a business activity that was carried out in a manner similar to a commercial enterprise. In the case, the court concluded that, due to a "gradual growth and eventual engulfing," a "commercial purpose assumed such significance that we cannot conclude that it was merely incidental to its religious mission."[202]

In arriving at its conclusions, the court first set forth its preliminary premise: "If . . . an organization's management decisions replicate those of commercial enterprises, it is a fair inference that at least one purpose is commercial, and hence nonexempt," and "if this nonexempt goal is substantial, tax exempt status must be denied."[203] Having found that the organization's "conduct of a growing and very profitable publishing business must imbue it with some commercial hue," the court articulated the factors to determine "[h]ow deep a tint these activities impart."[204] Four of the factors were deemed to be the principal ones: the presence of substantial profits, the method of pricing the books sold, consistent and comfortable net profit margins, and competition with commercial publishers.[205] Other factors were considered that showed, to the court, that the organization "consciously attempted to transform itself into a more mainline commercial enterprise"[206]: it searched out additional readers, employed paid workers, dropped money-losing plans, paid substantial royalties, made formal contracts with some authors, expanded into a new facility "from which it could continue to reap profits," and was not affiliated or controlled by any particular church.[207]

The criteria recognized by the court as indicating "a nonprofit-oriented approach" were: reliance on volunteers, payment of "modest amounts" to those that are paid, publication of books even if they would not sell well, and the making of interest-free loans and contributions to tax-exempt organizations.[208] The court hastened to state that it "reject[ed] the notion . . . that efficiency and success automatically negate tax-exempt status."[209] Nevertheless, this opinion went a long way toward establishing the principle that efforts to be efficient, productive, and successful will be equated with substantial commercialism, and that tax ex-

---

[200] Presbyterian & Reformed Publishing Co. v. Comm'r, 70 T.C. 1070, 1083, 1087 (1982).
[201] *Id.* at 1085.
[202] *Id.* at 1087.
[203] *Id.* at 1083.
[204] *Id.*
[205] *Id.* at 1083–1086.
[206] *Id.* at 1086.
[207] *Id.*
[208] *Id.* at 1086–1087.
[209] *Id.* at 1087.

emption is fostered by volunteers struggling to keep an organization afloat in a sea of red ink. Some of these criteria simply reflected a misunderstanding of the reality of operation of a nonprofit organization today. Others—such as employing workers and entering into contracts—would produce nonsensical results if applied to "mainline" tax-exempt institutions that conduct many activities, such as colleges, universities, hospitals, and large, national charities.

However, a federal court of appeals rejected these views, as it was "troubled by the inflexibility" of the approach of the lower court.[210] The appellate court wrote that the federal tax law does not "define the purpose of an organization claiming tax-exempt status as a direct derivative of the volume of business of that organization"; instead, said the court, "the inquiry must remain that of determining the purpose to which the increased business activity is directed."[211] Thus, the court of appeals concluded that financial expansion and success experienced by a nonprofit organization does not, in and of itself, lead to revocation of tax-exempt status.

An aspect of the facts that generated much attention from the appellate court was the accumulation by the organization of capital for the purchase of land and the construction of buildings. While the court of appeals observed that "[t]here is no doubt that unexplained accumulations of cash may properly be considered as evidence of commercial purpose,"[212] it refused to endorse the thought that aggregations of funds automatically constitute a form of undue commerciality. Instead, it initiated a precept in the law of tax-exempt organizations by analogizing to the accumulated earnings tax, which is imposed on businesses that accumulate earnings beyond their reasonable needs.[213] In the case, the higher court found no evidence of improper motives for the accumulation.

The court of appeals stated that "success in terms of audience reached and influence exerted, in and of itself, should not jeopardize the tax-exempt status of organizations that remain true to their stated goals."[214] The appellate court expressed concern that, under the lower court's approach, organizations seeking charitable status "may be forced to choose between expanding their audience and influence on the one hand, and maintaining their tax-exempt status on the other"—a concern that would "evaporate," wrote the court, "[i]f this were a stagnant society in which various ideas and creeds preserve a hold on a fixed proportion of the population."[215] But, said the appellate court, the view of the lower court "does not reflect either the dynamic quality of our society or the goals that generated the grant of tax-exempt status to religious publishers."[216] The approach of the lower court would, said the appellate court, allow a large institution to engage in an activity such as publishing without loss of tax exemption, yet deny tax exemption to an entity where that activity is its only function; the court of ap-

---

[210] Presbyterian & Reformed Publishing Co. v. Comm'r, 743 F.2d 148 (3d Cir. 1984).
[211] *Id.* at 156.
[212] *Id.* at 157.
[213] IRC § 531 *et seq.*
[214] Presbyterian & Reformed Publishing Co. v. Comm'r, *supra* note 209, at 158.
[215] *Id.* at 159.
[216] *Id.*

peals refused to uphold this "inequitable disparity in treatment,"[217] thereby voiding the determination of the lower court that single-purpose organizations are to be subject to more stringent review than multipurpose organizations.

Moreover, one federal court of appeals held that the unrelated income rules are not triggered solely by virtue of the "commercial character" of the activity in question.[218] The appellate court reversed the lower court, which had found unrelated activity, and commented that the lower court "was apparently distracted by the commercial character" of the activity and thus "place[d] too great an emphasis on the similarity of the activity to commercial" undertakings.[219] The court reiterated the fact that the essential test is the relationship between the activity under examination and the tax-exempt purposes of the organization.[220]

Nonetheless, one court revoked the tax-exempt status of an organization, using the commerciality rationale, before it became aware of either of these appellate court decisions.[221] The court adhered to its earlier tests, utilizing the same language, relying on the "commercial hue" of the activities, the existence and amount of accumulated profits, the charging of fees for services, the organization's pricing policies, its promotional efforts, the presence of cash reserves, and the fact of contractual arrangements.[222] Likewise, another court refused to grant tax-exempt status to an adoption agency, on the ground that it operated in a manner indistinguishable from, and in competition with, commercial entities.[223]

---

[217] *Id.*

[218] American College of Physicians v. United States, 743 F.2d 1570, 1576 (Fed. Cir. 1984), *rev'd*, 475 U.S. 834 (1986).

[219] *Id.*, 743 F.2d at 1576.

[220] See *supra* § 1, Cf. Petersen v. Comm'r, 53 T.C.M. 235 (1987).

[221] Church of Scientology of Calif. v. Comm'r, 83 T.C. 381 (1984), *aff'd*, 823 F.2d 1310 (9th Cir. 1987), *cert. den.*, 486 U.S. 1015 (1988).

[222] *Id.* at 473–490. The Tax Court subsequently held that payments to the Church of Scientology for "auditing and training" services are not deductible as charitable contributions, in part because the Church was found to be "commercial" in nature (Graham v. Comm'r, 83 T.C. 575 (1984), *aff'd*, 822 F.2d 844 (9th Cir. 1987)). Likewise, Hernandez v. Comm'r, 819 F.2d 1212 (1st Cir. 1987); Miller v. Internal Revenue Service, 829 F.2d 500 (4th Cir. 1987); Christiansen v. Comm'r, 843 F.2d 418 (10th Cir. 1988). Cf. Staples v. Comm'r, 821 F.2d 1324 (8th Cir. 1987); Foley v. Comm'r, 844 F.2d 94 (2d Cir. 1988); Neher v. Comm'r, 852 F.2d 848 (6th Cir. 1988). This matter seemingly was resolved by the U.S. Supreme Court, when it held that payments to the Church of Scientology are not deductible as charitable contributions (Hernandez v. Comm'r, 490 U.S. 680 (1989)). See § 8.2, note 95. In general, Shaller, "Tax Exemption of Charitable Organizations and Deductibility of Charitable Contributions: Dangerous New Tests," 8 *Bridgeport L. Rev.* 77 (1987); Colliton, "The Meaning of 'Contribution or Gift' for Charitable Contribution Deduction Purposes," 41 *Ohio St. L. J.* 973 (1980).

Also, the Tax Court found that the performance of the sacrament of "spinology" is not a religious function, in that a substantial purpose of the activity is the "training and practicing of an art akin to chiropractic" (Triune of Life Church, Inc. v. Comm'r, 85 T.C. 45 (1985), *aff'd*. 791 F.2d 922 (3d Cir. 1986)). Likewise, the Tax Court found that an organization, formed to facilitate the transfer of technology from the laboratories of tax-exempt research institutions to public use and generate royalty income for the institutions, was not qualified for tax exemption as a charitable entity because its activities of developing patentable products and licensing them to private industry were commercial in nature (Washington Research Found. v. Comm'r, 50 T.C.M. 1457 (1985)). However, this latter case was "overruled" by Congress when it enacted § 1605 of the Tax Reform Act of 1986 (see H. Rep. 841, 99th Cong., 2d Sess. II-827 (1986)).

[223] Easter House v. United States, 87-2 U.S.T.C. ¶ 9359, *aff'd*, 846 F.2d 78 (Fed. Cir. 1988), *cert. den.*, 488 U.S. 907 (1988).

Yet, given an appropriate set of circumstances, the greater the extent of profits, the greater the likelihood that the revenue-producing activity may be considered to be in furtherance of tax-exempt purposes. In one case, an activity—which the organization regarded as fund-raising and the IRS considered a business—was held to not be a *business* because the activity generated a "staggering amount of money" and "astounding profitability" in a manner that could not be replicated in a commercial context.[224] Also, the organization was much more candid with its supporters than would be the case in a commercial setting, leading the court to note that, "[b]y any standard, an enterprise that depends on the consent of its customers for its profits is not operating in a commercial manner and is not a trade or business."[225]

A federal court of appeals, in considering this latter case, took that occasion to strongly state that "[u]nlike what some other courts may do, this court does not find 'profits,' or the maximization of revenue, to be the controlling basis for a determination" as to whether the activity involved is a "business."[226]

Thus, the mere fact of profit-making activities should not, as a matter of law, adversely affect an organization's tax-exempt status. As another federal court of appeals has noted, the "pertinent inquiry" is "whether the [organization's] exempt purpose transcends the profit motive rather than the other way around."[227] However, the IRS may use the existence of a profit to characterize the activity as being commercial in nature, thus placing at issue the question as to whether the organization's activities are devoted exclusively to tax-exempt purposes. This approach is sometimes also taken by the courts, such as in a case where the publications of an organization were held to produce an unwarranted profit, thereby depriving it of qualification as an educational organization.[228]

---

[224] American Bar Endowment v. United States, 84-1 U.S.T.C. ¶ 9204 (Cl. Ct. 1984).

[225] *Id.* at 83, 353.

[226] American Bar Endowment v. United States, 761 F.2d 1573 (Fed. Cir. 1985). (This case was resolved by the U.S. Supreme Court, in favor of the government (see § 26.2(a), text accompanied by notes 43–44)). The reference to the "other courts" is to the U.S. Courts of Appeal for the Fourth Circuit (e.g., Carolinas Farm & Power Equip. Dealers v. United States, 699 F.2d 167 (1983)); Fifth Circuit (e.g., Louisiana Credit Union League v. United States, 693 F.2d 525 (1982)); and Sixth Circuit (e.g., Professional Ins. Agents of Mich. v. Comm'r, 726 F.2d 1097 (1984)).

[227] The Incorporated Trustees of the Gospel Worker Soc'y v. United States, 510 F. Supp. 374 (D.D.C. 1981), *aff'd*, 672 F.2d 894 (D.C. Cir. 1981), *cert. den.*, 456 U.S. 944 (1982).

[228] American Institute for Economic Research v. United States, 302 F.2d 934 (Ct. Cl. 1962). See § 7.6.

Tax-Exempt Charitable Organizations

CHAPTER FIVE

Scope of Term *Charitable*

Organizations that are exempt from federal income tax by reason of IRC § 501(c)(3) are often simply referred to as *charitable* organizations. The pertinent portion of this provision is the basis of tax exemption for

> [C]orporations, and any community chest, fund or foundation, organized and operated exclusively for religious, charitable, scientific, testing for public safety, literary, or educational purposes, or to foster national or international amateur sports competition (but only if no part of its activities involve the provision of athletic facilities or equipment), or for the prevention of cruelty to children or animals . . .

The term *charitable* is often used in this broader context notwithstanding the fact that *charitable* is only one of the eight descriptive words and phrases used in the federal tax law to describe the various organizations embraced by this provision. That is, the term *charitable* is considered a generic term and, in its expansive sense, includes *religious, scientific, educational,* and the other entities.[1]

The use of the term *charitable* to describe all IRC § 501(c)(3) organizations has arisen in part because, with one exception, all of these organizations are also qualified charitable donees[2] and thus are eligible to attract charitable contributions that are deductible for federal tax purposes. (The exception is public safety

---

[1] E.g., United States v. Proprietors of Social Law Library, 102 F.2d 481 (1st Cir. 1939). Indeed, the U.S. Supreme Court, in *Bob Jones University* v. *United States,* 461 U.S. 574 (1983), *aff'g* 639 F.2d 147 (4th Cir. 1980), *rev'g* 468 F. Supp. 890 (D.S.C. 1978), held that all organizations described in IRC § 501(c)(3) and tax-exempt under IRC § 501(a) are charitable entities for purposes of exempt organizations and charitable gift deductibility law analysis. Frequently, therefore, throughout the text of this book, the term *charitable* is used to reference any category of organization described in IRC § 501(c)(3).

[2] IRC §§ 170(c)(2) (income tax deduction), 2055(a)(2) (estate tax deduction), 2522(b)(2) (gift tax deduction).

testing organizations.[3]) Thus, the focus of this chapter is on the parameters of the term *charitable* as it is used to portray all of the organizations described in IRC § 501(c)(3).

§ 5.1 DEFINITION OF *CHARITABLE* IN LAW

The term *charitable* is usually thought to mean assistance to the poor, the indigent, the destitute. For many, this seems to be the only definition of charity. Thus, often churches, synagogues, mosques, universities, colleges, schools, hospitals, and similar institutions are not understood to be *charitable* entities—even though contributors to them receive a *charitable* deduction for their support.

This concept of *charity* is known in the law as the "popular and ordinary" or ("vulgar"[4]) usage of the term. In this setting, the word *charity* means *relief of the poor*.

The term *charitable* has been given formal recognition in the law for centuries, inasmuch as the term emanates from the common law of charitable trusts.[5] This definition is rather broad, meaning essentially that a function promoting the general welfare is charitable. The general rule is that the word *charitable* at common law encompassed "trusts for the relief of poverty; trusts for the advancement of education, trusts for the advancement of religion; and trusts for other purposes beneficial to the community, not falling under any of the preceding heads."[6]

The term *charitable*, under the English common law, had a broadly inclusive scope, yet it remained a definable legal concept. The definition of the term *charitable* dates back to the definition of *charitable purposes* in the Preamble to the Statute of Charitable Uses of 1601.[7] The Statute itself is based upon holdings of the English Court of Chancery before 1601 and upon earlier experiences (such as the Codes of Justinian) of previous civilizations including those of Rome and Greece and in early Judaism, as well as in many other early cultures and religions. The Statute enumerates certain charitable purposes, as follows:

> . . . some for relief of aged, impotent and poor people, some for maintenance of sick and maimed soldiers and mariners, schools of learning, free schools, and scholars in universities, some for repair of bridges, ports, havens, causeways, churches, seabanks and highways, some for education and preferment of orphans, some for or towards relief, stock or maintenance for houses of correction, some for marriages of poor maids, some for supportation, aid and help of young tradesmen, handicraftsmen and persons decayed, and others for relief or redemption of prisoners or captives, and for aid or ease of any

---

[3] See § 10.3.

[4] See *infra* note 7.

[5] Of course, the definition of the term *charitable* is independent of and predates tax systems. Thus, for example, in the Bible, it is stated that "also we certify you, that, touching any of the priests and Levites, singers, porters, Nethinim, or Ministers of this House of God, it shall not be lawful to impose toll, tribute, or customs upon them" (Ezra 7:24).

[6] Commissioners for Special Purposes of Income Tax v. Pemsel, A.C. 531, 583 (1891).

[7] Stat. 43 Eliz., c.4.

poor inhabitants concerning payments of fifteens, setting out of soldiers and other taxes.

These and other classifications of the concept of charity were discussed by Lord Macnaghten in 1891, who said:

> Of all words in the English language bearing a popular as well as a legal significance I am not sure that there is one which more unmistakably has a technical meaning in the strictest sense of the term, that is a meaning clear and distinct, peculiar to the law as understood and administered in this country, and not depending upon or coterminous with the popular or vulgar use of the word.[8]

Lord Macnaghten's discussion was cited with approval by the U.S. Supreme Court.[9]

The English common law concept of *philanthropy* is considerably broader than that of *charity*. The basic opinion on this point was authored in 1896, wherein Lindley, L.J., wrote: "Philanthropy and benevolence both include charity; but they go further, and include more than mere charitable purposes. 'Philanthropic' is a very wide word, and includes many things which are only for the pleasure of the world, and cannot be called 'charitable.' "[10] In the case, Sterling, J., wrote that the word *philanthropic*, in meaning "goodwill to mankind at large," is "wide enough to comprise purposes which are not charitable in the technical sense."[11] This approach is traceable into the common law of the United States.[12]

Consequently, the categories of organizations described in IRC § 501(c)(3) may be referred to on occasion as *philanthropic* or also as *benevolent* or *eleemosynary*.[13] These terms, however, are generally regarded, from a federal tax law standpoint, as overbroad in relation to IRC § 501(c)(3) organizations, as being less descriptive, or invoking peculiarities of local law.[14] The term *charitable*, then, has a legal meaning and is regarded as a term of art, while terms such as *philanthropy* remain popularized words lacking in legal significance.[15]

---

[8] Commissioners for Special Purposes of Income Tax v. Pemsel, *supra* note 6.

[9] Evans v. Newton, 382 U.S. 296, 303 (1966). In general, Bogart, *Trusts and Trustees* (2d ed. 1959) § 369.

[10] 2 Ch. 451, 459 (1896).

[11] *Id.* at 457.

[12] E.g., Drury v. Inhabitants of Natick, 10 Allen 169 (Mass. 1865). A minority view evident in English common law and reflected in U.S. cases was that the terms *philanthropic* and *charitable* are synonymous (e.g., Commissioners for Special Purposes of Income Tax v. Pemsel, *supra* note 6; Jackson v. Phillips, 14 Allen 539 (Mass. 1867); Rotch v. Emerson, 105 Mass. 431 (1870)).

[13] In general, Clark, "Charitable Trusts, the Fourteenth Amendment and the Will of Stephen Girard," 66 *Yale L. J.* 979 (1957).

[14] Westchester County Society for Prevention of Cruelty to Animals v. Mengel, 54 N.E. 329, 330 (N.Y. 1944); Schall v. Comm'r, 174 F.2d 893, 894 (5th Cir. 1949); Allebach v. City of Friend, 226 N.W. 440, 441 (Neb. 1929); In re Downer's Estate, 142 A. 78 (Sup. Ct. Ver. 1938); Thorp v. Lund, 116 N.E. 946 (Mass. 1917). Several state charitable solicitation (charitable fund-raising regulation) statutes, however, use terms such as *philanthropic* and *eleemosynary* to define charitable organizations (see Hopkins, *The Law of Fund-Raising, Second Edition* (New York: John Wiley & Sons, Inc., 1996), Chapter 4 § 1).

[15] Bogart, *Trusts and Trustees* (2d ed. 1959) § 370.

§ 5.2 FEDERAL TAX LAW DEFINITION OF *CHARITABLE*

Congress, in enacting and perpetuating federal income tax exemption for organizations described in IRC § 501(c)(3), did not and has not clearly indicated whether it was influenced by the common law definition of the term *charitable* or by the use of that term in its "popular and ordinary" sense. This fact has two ramifications: the meaning to be ascribed to the term *charitable* as used in IRC § 501(c)(3) and whether the entirety of that section is intended to describe organizations that are in some sense *charitable*.

The latter point can be regarded as an exercise in construing the statute itself. That is, pursuant to the canons of statutory construction, the search for congressional intent is to begin with the express words of the statute.[16]

The provision—IRC § 501(c)(3)—describes as organizations that are eligible for federal income tax exemption those that are "organized and operated exclusively for" eight specifically enumerated purposes or functions. These purposes or functions include those that are considered *charitable, educational, religious*, and *scientific*. However—and this is absolutely fundamental to those who in these regards place heavy emphasis on the statutory construction argument—the enumeration of the exempt functions or purposes is framed in the disjunctive: The law describes "religious, charitable, scientific . . . or educational purposes . . ." This use of the disjunctive can be regarded as evidence of congressional intent to accord tax exemption to any organization organized and operated for any *one* of the designated purposes or functions. As the U.S. Supreme Court has noted: "Canons of construction ordinarily suggest that terms connected by a disjunctive be given separate meanings, unless the context dictates otherwise."[17] Thus, the distinct references in IRC § 501(c)(3) to charitable *or* educational *or* scientific *or* like organizations can be read as confirming "Congress' intent that [for example] not all educational institutions must also be charitable institutions (as that term was used in the common law) in order to receive tax-exempt status."[18]

There is another applicable canon of statutory construction, which is that related statutory provisions should be interpreted together.[19] This has considerable relevance in this context, inasmuch as sister provisions of IRC § 501(c)(3) (both those in existence and those since repealed) reiterate the separate and disjunctive purposes or functions described in IRC § 501(c)(3).[20] The principal one of these sister provisions is IRC § 170(c)(2)(B), which defines the term *charitable contribu-*

---

[16] E.g., Northwest Airlines, Inc. v. Transport Workers Union, 451 U.S. 77 (1981); United States v. Oregon, 366 U.S. 643 (1961).

[17] Reiter v. Sonotone Corp., 442 U.S. 330, 339 (1979).

[18] Prince Edward School Found. v. United States, 450 U.S. 944, 947 (1981) (dissent from denial of certiorari).

[19] E.g., Kokoska v. Belford, 417 U.S. 642 (1974); United States v. Cooper Corp., 312 U.S. 600 (1941).

[20] For example, phraseology in the disjunctive similar to that in IRC § 501(c)(3) can be found in IRC §§ 170(c)(2) (income tax charitable contribution deduction), 503(b)(3) (references to IRC § 501(c)(3) organizations repealed in 1969), 504(a)(1) and 504(a)(3) (repealed in 1969), 513(a) (defining the phrase *unrelated trade or business*), 2055(a)(2) (estate tax charitable contribution deduction), and 2522(a)(2) (gift tax charitable contribution deduction).

tion for purposes of the federal income tax charitable contribution deduction.[21] This provision also recites the eight separate and independent categories of exempt functions, thereby providing further support for the proposition that Congress intended to recognize each category of purpose or function enumerated in IRC § 501(c)(3) as a distinct basis for tax exemption.[22]

Thus, it can be argued that, in IRC § 501(c)(3) and its sister provisions, Congress "has spoken in the plainest of words"[23] in intending to accord federal income tax exemption to any organization organized and operated exclusively for any one of the purposes or functions enumerated in IRC § 501(c)(3).

For example, it can be readily asserted that if Congress had intended that all organizations embraced by IRC § 501(c)(3) must qualify as charitable entities in the common law sense of the term, it would not have made reference in 1894 to "charitable, religious, or educational purposes," since the references to *religious* and *educational* purposes would have been subsumed within the references to the term *charitable*. Likewise, the subsequent additions of the references to *scientific* purposes (in 1913), the *prevention of cruelty to children or animals* (in 1918), *literary* purposes (in 1921), testing for public safety (in 1934), and for certain amateur sports organizations (in 1976) arguably would have been unnecessary if the term *charitable* were used in its common law sense. Similarly, it can be contended that if Congress had intended to condition tax exemption on satisfaction of the requirements of a common law charity, there would have been no need to add to the statutory law (as was done in 1913) the prohibition concerning the inurement of net earnings to private persons,[24] inasmuch as, under the common law, the income of a charitable organization cannot inure to the benefit of private persons.[25]

Therefore, one can regard the overall structure of the federal tax law regarding tax exemption and charitable giving as evidence that each of the eight purposes enumerated in IRC § 501(c)(3) are not overlain with a requirement that all organizations, to be exempt under that section, must qualify as entities that are *charitable* in the common law sense.[26]

Aside from the matter of whether the entirety of IRC §§ 170(c)(2)(B) and 501(c)(3) is subject to overarching requirements imposed by the common law of charitable trusts, there is the ambiguity of Congress's intent when it employed the term *charitable* in those two, and related, provisions. That is, did Congress have in mind the common law definition of the term *charitable* or did it intend to

---

[21] See § 2.5.

[22] A contrasting argument (ultimately adopted by the U.S. Supreme Court) is stated in Bob Jones University v. United States, 639 F.2d 147 (4th Cir. 1980), where, in part because contributions to all organizations described in IRC § 170(c)(2)(B) are referred to as *charitable contributions*, the court concluded that each of the separately enumerated purposes are to be considered as within a broad classification of *charitable*.

[23] TVA v. Hill, 437 U.S. 153, 194 (1978).

[24] See Chapter 19.

[25] 4 Scott, *The Law of Trusts* (2d ed. 1956) § 376.

[26] This reading of the law is in conformance with still another axiom of statutory construction, which is that statutes are to be construed to give effect to each word and that no one part of a statute should be interpreted so as to render another part of the statute redundant (Jarecki v. G.D. Searle & Co., 367 U.S. 303 (1961); United States v. Menasche, 348 U.S. 528 (1955)).

apply the word in its "popular and ordinary" sense? There is little concrete evidence to support a proposition that Congress intended the application of either definition.

The strongest argument that Congress did not intend the use of the common law definition of the term *charitable* is the statutory construction argument, discussed above, which is that application of the broad, common law definition of the word would render other words and phrases in the provisions redundant.[27] There is no legislative history, however, that gives much (if any) support for the proposition that Congress intended use of the narrower, "popular" meaning of the term.

In fact, the scarce legislative history that exists is usually cited in support of the view that the common law public policy definition is the one to be applied. The chief component of this legislative history is a portion of a report of the House of Representatives issued in 1939, explaining the theory that inspired Congress to exempt from taxation organizations devoted to charitable and other purposes, which is as follows:

> The exemption from taxation of money or property devoted to charitable and other purposes is based upon the theory that the Government is compensated for the loss of revenue by its relief from financial burdens which would otherwise have to be met by appropriations from other public funds, and by the benefits resulting from the promotion of the general welfare.[28]

This phraseology, which includes words such as "public" and "general welfare," can thus be read as evidencing the need to follow the dictates of the common law meaning of *charitable*, including the public policy doctrine. (At the same time, this legislative history speaks of "charitable and other purposes," which can be read as evidence of an intent to invoke a narrower meaning of the term *charitable*.) Another element of legislative history that suggests a broader use of the term *charitable* is a statement by the sponsor of the 1909 tax exemption statute that the provision was designed to relieve from the income tax (then imposed only on corporations) those organizations "devoted exclusively to the relief of suffering, to the alleviation of our people, and to all things which commend themselves to every charitable and just impulse."[29]

As noted below, the courts will occasionally look to contemporaneous administrative agency interpretation of a statute in an attempt to divine the statute's true meaning.[30] It is, therefore, instructive to note that, as early as 1923, in reviewing the law that is now IRC § 501(c)(3), the IRS interpreted the word *charitable* in its "popular and ordinary sense" and not in its common law sense.[31]

---

[27] *Id.*

[28] H.R. Rep. No. 1860, 75th Cong., 3d Sess. 19 (1938).

[29] 44 *Cong. Rec.* 4150 (1909).

[30] See *infra* text accompanying notes 39–41.

[31] I.T. 1800, II-2 C.B. 152, 153 (1923), which discussed the intended meaning of the word *charitable* in section 231(6) of the Revenue Acts of 1918 and 1921. As the U.S. Supreme Court observed, "a consistent and contemporaneous construction of a statute by the agency charged with its enforcement is entitled to great deference" (NLRB v. Boeing Co., 412 U.S. 67, 75 (1973); Power Reactor Dev. Co. v. Electricians, 367 U.S. 396 (1961)).

As revenue acts were subsequently enacted, the accompanying regulations stated: "Corporations organized and operated exclusively for charitable purposes comprise, in general, organizations for the relief of the poor"[32]—clearly the "popular and ordinary" meaning of the term *charitable*. During the 15 years that the Internal Revenue Code of 1939[33] was in effect, three sets of regulations were issued, each of which defined the term *charitable* in its popular and ordinary sense.[34] When the Internal Revenue Code of 1954 was enacted, IRC § 501 was derived from the 1939 Code.[35] As to IRC § 501, a report of the House Committee on Ways and Means stated that "[n]o change in substance has been made . . ."[36] Consequently, it appears rather apparent that, as of the adoption of the Internal Revenue Code of 1954, the "popular and ordinary" meaning of the term *charitable* governed the definition of that word for federal tax purposes.

Nonetheless, in 1959, new regulations were promulgated that vastly expanded the federal tax definition of the term *charitable*. This regulation (which is presently in effect) reads as follows:

> The term 'charitable' is used in section 501(c)(3) in its generally accepted legal sense and is, therefore, not to be construed as limited by the separate enumeration in section 501(c)(3) of other tax-exempt purposes which may fall within the broad outlines of 'charity' as developed by judicial decisions. Such term includes: Relief of the poor and distressed or of the underprivileged; advancement of religion; advancement of education or science; erection or maintenance of public buildings, monuments, or works; lessening of the burdens of Government; and promotion of social welfare by organizations designed to accomplish any of the above purposes, or (i) to lessen neighborhood tensions; (ii) to eliminate prejudice and discrimination; (iii) to defend human and civil rights secured by law; or (iv) to combat community deterioration and juvenile delinquency.[37]

This regulation has several striking features. One of these is its claim that the definition of the term *charitable* in IRC § 501(c)(3) is used in its "generally accepted legal sense," which is at least somewhat akin to its common law meaning. Another is that "[r]elief of the poor"[38] is now only one of several ways in which an organization can qualify as a charitable entity.

Thus, the above-quoted tax law definition of the term *charitable*, as supplemented and amplified by subsequent court cases and IRS rulings, is the existing

---

[32] Reg. 65, Art. 517 (Revenue Act of 1924, 43 Stat. 282); Reg. 69, Art. 517 (Revenue Act of 1926, 44 Stat. 40); Reg. 74, Art. 527 (Revenue Act of 1928, 45 Stat. 813); Reg. 77, Art. 527 (Revenue Act of 1932, 47 Stat. 193); Reg. 86, Art. 101(6)-1 (Revenue Act of 1934, 48 Stat. 700); Reg. 94, Art. 101(6)-1 (Revenue Act of 1936, 49 Stat. 1674); Reg. 101, Art. 101(6)-1 (Revenue Act of 1938, 52 Stat. 481).

[33] See *infra* note 183.

[34] Reg. 103, § 19.101(6)-1; Treas. Reg. 111, § 29.101(6)-1; Reg. 118, § 39.101(6)-1(b).

[35] Specifically, 1939 Code §§ 101, 421.

[36] H.R. Rep. No. 1337, 83d Cong., 2d Sess. A165 (1954).

[37] Reg. § 1.501(c)(3)-1(d)(2).

[38] See § 6.1.

law on the subject. To that extent, any concern as to the original intended meaning of the term charitable for federal tax purposes may (or seems to) be academic. Thus, there is almost no likelihood that an argument that the 1959 regulations are of suspect validity because they are so inconsistent with the intent of Congress at the time would be successful.[39] The sheer passage of time since promulgation of the 1959 regulations gives these regulations ongoing validity simply because Congress has—despite many opportunities to do so—refrained from enacting a statutory definition of the term *charitable* and thus has tacitly accepted the broader meaning of the word as articulated by the Department of the Treasury and the IRS.

These regulations clearly reflect an interpretation of IRC § 501(c)(3) that affords tax-exempt status to any organization qualifying under *one* of the eight categories enumerated in the statute, without regard to whether it also accords with the characteristics of a common law charity. Under the regulations, an organization may be exempt "if it is organized and operated exclusively for *one or more of the following purposes*: (a) Religious, (b) Charitable, (c) Scientific, (d) Testing for public safety, (e) Literary, (f) Educational, or (g) Prevention of cruelty to children or animals."[40] As if this regulation was not adequately clear as to the independence of the separate exempt purposes, the regulations continue with the observations that "*each* of the[se] purposes . . . is an exempt purpose in itself" and that "an organization may be exempt if it is organized and operated exclusively for any one or more of such purposes."[41]

Therefore, the pertinent regulations take the position that each purpose or function stated in IRC §§ 170(c)(2)(B) and 501(c)(3) is an independent basis for qualification as a tax-exempt charitable donee. However, as noted, these regulations were adopted in 1959 and thus cannot be reflective of congressional intent in, for example, 1894 or 1913.[42]

This background notwithstanding, the position taken by various courts since the inception of the income tax exemption for charitable entities emphasized the breadth of the meaning of the term *charitable*.

For example, the Supreme Court seemingly emphasized the overarching application of the term *charitable* when it observed that "Congress, in order to encourage gifts to religious, educational *and other charitable objects*, granted the privilege of deducting such gifts from gross income."[43] Earlier, the Court wrote that "[e]vidently the exemption [was] made in recognition of the benefit which the public derives from corporate activities of the class named, and [was] intended to aid them when not conducted for private gain."[44]

---

[39] As the U.S. Supreme Court observed, an administrative agency has the authority only "to adopt regulations to carry into effect the will of Congress as expressed by the statute" and that a regulation "which does not do this, but operates to create a rule out of harmony with the statute, is a mere nullity" (Manhattan Gen. Equip. Co. v. Comm'r, 297 U.S. 129, 134 (1936)).

[40] Reg. § 1.501(c)(3)-1(d)(1)(i) (emphasis supplied).

[41] Reg. § 1.501(c)(3)-1(d)(1)(iii) (emphasis supplied).

[42] Cf. National Muffler Dealers Ass'n v. United States, 440 U.S. 472, 477 (1979), where the Supreme Court wrote of "a substantially contemporaneous construction of the statute by those presumed to have been aware of congressional intent."

[43] Helvering v. Bliss, 293 U.S. 144, 147 (1934) (emphasis supplied).

[44] Trinidad v. Sagrada Orden de Predicadores de la Provincia del Santisimo Rosario de Filipinas, 263 U.S. 578, 581 (1924). Likewise, St. Louis Union Trust Co. v. United States, 374 F.2d 427, 432 (8th Cir. 1967).

This approach is also reflected in a variety of appellate court opinions. Thus, a federal court of appeals determined that "[t]he term 'charitable' is a generic term and includes literary, religious, scientific and educational institutions."[45] Likewise, another federal court of appeals stated: "That Congress had in mind these broader definitions is confirmed by the words used in the [District of Columbia Code] for by its terms it embraces religious, charitable, scientific, literary or educational corporations, thus including within the exemption clause every nonprofit organization designed and operating for the benefit and enlightenment of the community, the State, or the Nation."[46] Similarly, still another federal court of appeals (and later the U.S. Supreme Court) held that the structure of the statutory framework (IRC §§ 170 and 501(c)) demonstrates that an organization seeking tax exemption under IRC § 501(c)(3) must show that it is charitable, irrespective of the particular nature of its activities (e.g., religious, educational, or scientific).[47]

A federal court of appeals observed that "we must look to established [trust] law to determine the meaning of the word 'charitable' "[48] Subsequently, the same appellate court stated that Congress intended to apply these tax rules "to those organizations commonly designated charitable in the law of trusts."[49]

This approach thus makes certain fundamental criteria applicable to all IRC §§ 501(c)(3) and 170(c)(2) organizations. As the Supreme Court observed over 100 years ago, "[a] charitable use, where neither law nor public policy forbids, may be applied to almost any thing that tends to promote the well-doing and well-being of social man."[50] A federal district court later held, in application of the broader definitional approach to educational entities, that this "doctrine operates as a necessary exception to or qualifier of the precept that in general trusts for education are considered to be for the benefit of the community."[51]

Thus, it is clear today that all of the organizations described in IRC § 501(c)(3) share certain common characteristics of *charitable* organizations. This clarity has come about by reason of application of the *public policy doctrine*.

§ 5.3   THE PUBLIC POLICY DOCTRINE

The U.S. Supreme Court ruled that tax exemption for charitable organizations may be granted only where the organizations are operating in conformance with a public policy doctrine.[52]

---

[45] United States v. Proprietors of Social Law Library, *supra* note 1, at 483.
[46] International Reform Fed. v. District Unemployment Brd., 131 F.2d 337, 339 (D.C. Cir. 1942).
[47] *Bob Jones Univ. v. United States, supra* note 22.
[48] Pennsylvania Co. for Ins. on Lives v. Helvering, 66 F.2d 284, 285 (D.C. Cir. 1933).
[49] International Reform Fed. v. District Unemployment Bd., *supra* note 46, at 339.
[50] Ould v. Washington Hosp. for Foundlings, 95 U.S. 303, 311 (1877).
[51] Green v. Connally, 330 F. Supp. 1150, 1160 (D.D.C. 1971), *aff'd sub nom.* Coit v. Green, 404 U.S. 997 (1971).
[52] Bob James Univ. v. United States, *supra* note 1.

Authority for this proposition is traceable to a 1958 U.S. Supreme Court opinion, holding that tax benefits such as deductions and exclusions generally are subject to limitation on public policy grounds.[53] At issue in that case was the deductibility of fines paid for violation of state maximum weight laws applicable to motor vehicles (enacted to protect state highways from damage and to ensure the safety of highway users) as "ordinary and necessary" business expenses.[54] The Supreme Court held that an expense is not "necessary" to the operation of a business "if allowance of the deduction would frustrate sharply defined national or state policies proscribing particular types of conduct, evidenced by some governmental declaration thereof."[55] Observing that "[d]eduction of fines and penalties uniformly has been held to frustrate state policy in severe and direct fashion by reducing the 'sting' of the penalty prescribed by the state legislature," the Court concluded that Congress did not intend to allow income tax deductions for fines incurred to punish violations of state penal laws.[56]

The U.S. Supreme Court in 1983 generally resolved the issues as to the scope of the term *charitable* in favor of those who asserted that all organizations described in IRC §§ 501(c)(3) and 170(c)(2) must satisfy the common law test as to what is charitable—finding specifically that private schools must (to be tax-exempt) meet "certain common law standards of charity."[57] In so doing, the Court relied heavily on the classification of deductible gifts to nearly all IRC § 501(c)(3) entities as *charitable* contributions, concluding that IRC § 170 "reveals that Congress' intention was to provide tax benefits to organizations serving charitable purposes."[58] This reliance led the Court to decide that "[t]he form and history of the charitable exemption and deduction sections of the various income tax acts reveal that Congress was guided by the common law of charitable trusts."[59]

---

[53] Tank Truck Rentals, Inc. v. Comm'r, 356 U.S. 30 (1958).

[54] The deduction there at issue was that available pursuant to the predecessor of IRC § 162(a).

[55] Tank Truck Rentals, Inc. v. Comm'r, *supra* note 53, at 33.

[56] *Id*. at 35–36. After this opinion, Congress (in 1969 and 1971) enacted rules explicitly limiting the public policy doctrine of nondeductibility of expenses of this nature to fines paid for violations of law and to illegal bribes, kickbacks, and similar payments (IRC §§ 162(c), 162(f)). The statutory law addition in 1969 involved an item of legislative history, stating: "Public policy, in other circumstances, generally is not sufficiently clearly defined to justify the disallowance of deductions" (S. Rep. No. 552, 91st Cong., 1st Sess. (1969), at 2 *U.S. Code Cong. & Admin. News* 2311 (1969)). This was presaged by a Supreme Court admonishment that the public policy exception to the general rule of deductibility is "sharply limited and carefully defined" (Comm'r v. Tellier, 383 U.S. 687, 691, 693–694 (1966)). In *Tellier*, the Court added: "[T]he federal income tax is a tax on net income, not a sanction against wrongdoing. That principle has been firmly imbedded in the tax statute from the beginning. One familiar facet of the principle is the truism that the statute does not concern itself with the lawfulness of the income it taxes" (*id*. at 691). However, these words of restraint did not prevent the Supreme Court from applying the public policy doctrine in the context of tax exemption for charitable entities.

[57] Bob Jones Univ. v. United States, *supra* note 1, at 586.

[58] *Id*. at 587.

[59] *Id*. at 587–588. However, the Court added that "[w]e need not consider whether Congress intended to incorporate into the Internal Revenue Code any aspects of charitable trust law other than the requirements of public benefit and a valid public purpose." *Id*. An unexpected application of the *Bob Jones University* opinion materialized when a court ruled that these concepts cause at least some nonprofit cemetery organizations to be charitable (Mellon Bank v. United States, 590 F. Supp. 160 (W.D. Pa. 1984)). However, this decision was reversed on appeal (Mellon Bank v. United States, 762 F.2d 283 (3d Cir. 1985)). See §§ 6.10(f), 18.6.

Having formulated this breadth of the federal tax doctrine of *charity*, the Court consequently adopted the view that, based upon the common law of charitable trusts, the purpose of a charitable entity "may not be illegal or violate established public policy."[60] The Court thus concluded as follows:

> History buttresses logic to make clear that, to warrant [tax] exemption under [IRC] § 501(c)(3), an institution must fall within a category specified in that section and must demonstrably serve and be in harmony with the public interest. [footnote omitted] The institution's purpose must not be so at odds with the common community conscience as to undermine any public benefit that might otherwise be conferred.[61]

(In the setting of the case, the Supreme Court found that racial discrimination in education is contrary to public policy and that the IRS is vested with the authority to determine what is public policy. The Court concluded that "[c]learly an educational institution engaging in practices affirmatively at odds with [the] declared position of the whole government cannot be seen as exercising a 'beneficial and stabilizing influenc[e] in community life,' . . . and is not 'charitable,' within the meaning of [IRC] § 170 and [IRC] § 501(c)(3)."[62]

The Court majority took notice of the fact that "determinations of public benefit and public policy are sensitive matters with serious implications for the institutions affected" and wrote that "a declaration that a given institution is not 'charitable' should be made only where there can be no doubt that the activity involved is contrary to a fundamental public policy."[63] Yet, in a concurring opinion, one justice stated that he was "troubled by the broader implications of the Court's opinion,"[64] "find[ing] it impossible to believe that all or even most of . . . [the IRC § 501(c)(3)] organizations could prove that they 'demonstrably serve and [are] in harmony with the public interest' or that they are 'beneficial and stabilizing influences in community life'."[65] Quoting other passages of the majority's opinion that impart "the element of conformity that appears to inform the Court's analysis," this justice wrote that "these passages suggest that the primary function of a tax-exempt organization is to act on behalf of the Government in carrying out governmentally approved policies."[66] Moreover, he disassociated himself from the majority by being "unwilling to join any suggestion that the Internal Revenue Service is invested with authority to decide which public policies are sufficiently 'fundamental' to require denial of tax exemptions."[67]

In dissent, another justice viewed the matter as largely one of statutory construction; he summarized the statutory scheme and traced its history, and

---

[60] *Id*. at 591.
[61] *Id*. at 591–592.
[62] *Id*. at 598–599.
[63] *Id*. at 592.
[64] *Id*. at 606.
[65] *Id*. at 609.
[66] *Id*. at 609.
[67] *Id*. at 611.

concluded that the Court majority's public policy standard reflects an unconstitutional attempt by the Court to act where Congress has failed to legislate. He also expressed his view that Congress has legislated the requirements for achieving tax-exempt status and that, therefore, the IRS is powerless to enforce the application of other criteria, such as satisfaction of a public policy test.[68]

Although the reach of this Supreme Court decision has not been extensive, certainly the public policy doctrine will be applied far beyond the scope of racial discrimination in private schools. In one case, the government contended that an organization was ineligible for tax exemption because it engaged in violent and illegal activities. The case was dismissed but the Court nonetheless concluded that the requirements articulated by the Supreme Court could have been applied in the case had the court decided the matter on its merits.[69]

Subsequently, a court revoked the tax exemption of an organization on the ground that it violated fundamental notions of public policy. The court found a violation of the public policy requirement in the organization's "conspir[acy] to impede the IRS in performing its duty to determine and collect taxes" from the organization, in contravention of federal criminal laws.[70]

It is clear that the IRS will continue to apply the rule that an organization must satisfy the public policy test to qualify under IRC § 501(c)(3).[71] For example, in determining whether activities such as demonstrations, economic boycotts, strikes, and picketing are permissible means for furthering charitable ends,[72] the IRS adheres to the public policy doctrine.[73]

§ 5.4 PUBLIC POLICY DOCTRINE AND DISCRIMINATION

(a) Racial Discrimination

A private educational institution that has racially discriminatory policies cannot qualify for tax-exempt status under federal law as a charitable organization.

---

[68] *Id.* at 612–623.
[69] Synanon Church v. United States, 579 F. Supp. 967, 978–979 (D.D.C. 1984), *aff'd*, 820 F.2d 421 (D.C. Cir. 1987).
[70] Church of Scientology of Calif. v. Comm'r, 83 T. C. 381 (1984), *aff'd*, 823 F.2d 1310 (9th Cir. 1987).
[71] Congress is not evidencing any interest in legislating on this subject.
[72] See Hopkins, *Charity, Advocacy, and The Law* (New York: John Wiley & Sons, Inc., 1992), Chapter 19; Bachmann, *Nonprofit Litigation* (New York: John Wiley & Sons, Inc., 1991), Chapter 4.
[73] IRS Gen. Coun. Mem. 37858. In general, Thompson, "Public Policy Limitations on the Tax Exemption for Charitable Organizations," 2 *Tax L. J.* (No. 1) 1 (1984); Galston, "Public Policy Constraints on Charitable Organizations," 3 *Va. Tax Rev.* (No. 2) 291 (Winter 1984); McNulty, "Public Policy and Private Charity: A Tax Policy Perspective," 3 *Va. Tax Rev.* 229 (Winter 1984); Bender, "Has the Supreme Court Laid Fertile Ground for Invalidating the Regulatory Interpretation of Code Section 501(c)(3)?," 58 *Notre Dame L.R.* (No. 3) 564 (1983); Dye & Webster, "Sup. Ct. in Bob Jones holds that exempt organizations are bound by law of charity," 59 *J. Tax.* (No. 2) 70 (1983).

The rationale in the federal tax law for this principle was articulated by the Supreme Court in 1983, when it held that private schools may not racially discriminate and at the same time be tax-exempt and eligible for deductible charitable contributions.[74] This conclusion was expressly made applicable to all nonprofit private schools, including those that engage in racial discrimination on the basis of sincerely held religious beliefs. As to the religious schools, the Court found that the "governmental interest at stake here is compelling" and that this interest substantially outweighs the burden the denial of the tax benefits places on the schools' exercise of their religious beliefs.[75] The application of its holding to religious schools was played down by the Court as follows: "Denial of tax benefits will inevitably have a substantial impact on the operation of private religious schools, but will not prevent those schools from observing their religious tenets."[76]

The Court majority unabashedly adopted a public policy argument. The Court found in the "Congressional purposes" underlying this tax exemption "unmistakable evidence" of an "intent that entitlement to tax exemption depends on meeting certain common law standards of charity—namely, that an institution seeking tax-exempt status must serve a public purpose and not be contrary to established public policy."[77]

Persuaded that the use by Congress of the term *charitable* in the charitable contribution deduction context meant that the common law of charitable trusts fully applies, the Court concluded that "a corollary principle" also is applicable, which is "that the purpose of a charitable trust may not be illegal or violate established public policy."[78] Therefore, wrote the Court, an institution that is to be tax-exempt because it is a charitable entity "must demonstrably serve and be in harmony with the public interest" and its "purpose must not be so at odds with the common community conscience as to undermine any public benefit that might otherwise be conferred."[79]

As to the requisite public policy involved in this context, the Court concluded that "there can no longer be any doubt that racial discrimination in education violates deeply and widely accepted views of elementary justice."[80] "It would be wholly incompatible with the concepts underlying tax exemption," held the Court, "to grant the benefit of tax-exempt status to racially discriminatory educational entities. . . ."[81] The Court added: "Whatever may be the rationale for such private schools' policies, and however sincere the rationale may be, racial discrimination in education is contrary to public policy."[82]

---

[74] Bob Jones Univ. v. United States, *supra* note 1. See § 5.3.

[75] *Id.* at 604.

[76] *Id.* at 603–504.

[77] *Id.* at 586.

[78] *Id.* at 591–592.

[79] *Id.* at 592.

[80] *Id.*

[81] *Id.* at 595.

[82] *Id.* Also Clarksdale Baptist Church v. Green (Green v. Regan), 731 F.2d 995 (D.C. Cir. 1984), *cert. den.*, 469 U.S. 834 (1984).

The Court confronted the fact that Congress, while it clearly has the authority to revise the statutory law on this subject, has not done so. Congress, held the Court, had known about the posture of the IRS in these regards for a dozen years and thus had acquiesced in and had impliedly ratified IRS rulings in 1970 and 1971.[83] In fact, the Court cited the failure by Congress to enact bills that would statutorily override the IRS position as providing "added support for concluding that Congress acquiesced in" the IRS determinations.[84] Moreover, the Court concluded that the enactment by Congress of antidiscrimination rules in 1976, applicable to tax-exempt social clubs,[85] represented that "Congress affirmatively manifested its acquiescence in the IRS policy" pertaining to private schools.[86]

Prior to the Supreme Court's forceful pronouncement, the law was not so clear. The IRS had taken the position since 1967 that private educational institutions may not, to be tax-exempt, have racially discriminatory policies. In a 1971

---

[83] *Id*. at 598–602.

[84] *Id*. at 601.

[85] See § 14.5.

[86] Bob Jones Univ. v. United States, *supra* note 1, at 601–602. In general, Shaviro, "From *Big Mama Rag to National Geographic:* The Controversy Regarding Exemptions for Educational Publications," 41 *Tax L. Rev.* (No. 4) 693 (1986); Schweizer, "Federal Taxation—Exempt Organizations—Constitutional Law—First Amendment—Right to Free Exercise of Religion," 30 *N. Y. Law Sch. L. Rev.* (No. 4) 825 (1986); "*Bob Jones University v. United States*: For Whom Will the Bell Toll?," 29 *St. Louis U. L. J.* (No. 2) 561 (1985); Simon, "Applying the *Bob Jones* public-policy test in light of *TWR* and *U.S. Jaycees*," 62 *J. Tax.* (No. 3) 166 (1985); Thompson, "The Availability of the Federal Educational Tax Exemption for Propaganda Organizations," 18 *U.C. Davis L. Rev.* (No. 2) 487 (1985); Thornton, "Taxation in Black and White: The Disallowance of Tax-Exempt Status to Discriminatory Private Schools," 27 *Howard L. J.* (No. 4) 1769 (1984); Miller, "Applying a Public Benefit Requirement to Tax-Exempt Organizations," 49 *Mo. L. Rev.* (No. 2) 353 (1984); Johnston, Jr., "Federal Taxation—*Bob Jones University v. United States*: Segregated Sectarian Education and IRC Section 501(c)(3)," 62 *N. C. L. Rev.* (No. 5) 1038 (1984); Note, "IRS Acted Within Its Authority in Determining that Racially Discriminatory Non-Profit Schools Are Not 'Charitable' Institutions Entitled to Tax-Exempt Status," 15 *St. Mary's L. J.* (No. 2) 461 (1984); Kee, "The I.R.S. Fights Racial Discrimination in Higher Education: No Tax Exemption for Religious Institutions That Discriminate Because of Race," 10 *S. U. L. Rev.* (No. 2) 291 (1984); Galvin & Devine, "A Tax Policy Analysis of *Bob Jones University v. United States*," 36 *Vand. L. Rev.* (No. 6) 1353 (1983); Asaki, Jacobs, & Scott, "Racial Segregation and the Tax-Exempt Status of Private Educational and Religious Institutions," 25 *Howard L. J.* (No. 3) 545 (1982); Note, "Federal Income Taxation—Tax-Exempt Status for Educational Organizations in Treasury Regulation § 1.501(c)(3)-1(d)(3) is Unconstitutionally Vague in Violation of the First Amendment," 49 *Geo. Wash. L. Rev.* (No. 3) 623 (1981); Winslow & Ash, "Effects of *Big Mama Rag* on exempt educational organizations," 55 *J. Tax.* 20 (1981); Note, "*Big Mama Rag*: An Inquiry Into Vagueness," 67 *Va L. Rev.* (No. 8) 1543 (1981); Laycock, "Observation: Tax Exemptions for Racially Discriminatory Religious Schools," 60 *Tex. L. Rev.* (No. 2) 259 (1982); Milich, "Racially Discriminatory Schools and the IRS," 33 *Tax Law.* 571 (1980); Comment, "Tax Exemptions for Educational Institutions: Discretion and Discrimination," 128 *U. Pa. L. Rev.* 849 (1980); Anderson, "Tax-Exempt Private Schools Which Discriminate on the Basis of Race: A Proposed Revenue Procedure," 55 *Notre Dame Law.* 356 (1980); Christians, "The IRS, Discrimination, and Religious Schools: Does the Revised Proposed Revenue Procedure Exact Too High a Price?," 56 *Notre Dame Law.* 141 (1980); Neuberger & Crumplar, "Tax Exempt Religious Schools Under Attack: Conflicting Goals of Religious Freedom and Racial Integration," 48 *Fordham L. Rev.* 229 (1979); Note, "The Judicial Role in Attacking Racial Discrimination in Tax-Exempt Private Schools," 93 *Harv. L. Rev.* 378 (1979); Connell, "The Tax-Exempt Status of Sectarian Educational Institutions That Discriminate on the Basis of Race," 65 *Iowa L. Rev.* 258 (1979); Drake, "Tax Status of Private Segregated Schools: The New Revenue

case,[87] the Secretary of the Treasury and the Commissioner of Internal Revenue were enjoined from approving any application for recognition of tax exemption, continuing any current exemption, or approving charitable contribution deductions for any private school in Mississippi that failed to show that it has a publicized policy of nondiscrimination. The court found a "Federal public policy against support for racial segregation of schools, public or private" and held that the law "does not contemplate the granting of special Federal tax benefits to trusts or organizations . . . whose organization or operation contravene Federal public policy."[88] Thus, this decision was essentially founded on the principle that the statutes providing tax deductions and exemptions are not construed to be applicable to actions that are either illegal or contrary to public policy.[89] The court in this case concluded: "Under the conditions of today they [the federal tax law rules allowing tax exemption for and deductibility of gifts to charitable organizations] can no longer be construed so as to provide to private schools operating on a racially discriminatory premise the support of the exemptions and deductions which Federal tax law affords to charitable organizations and their sponsors."[90]

The IRS in 1971 stated that it would deny recognition of tax-exempt status to any private school that otherwise meets the requirements for tax exemption and charitable donee status but that "does not have a racially nondiscriminatory policy as to students."[91] The IRS initially announced its position on the exempt status of private nonprofit schools in 1967, stating that exemption and deductibility of contributions would be denied if a school was operated on a segregated basis.[92] This position was basically reaffirmed early in 1970 and the IRS

Procedure," 20 *W. & Mary L. Rev.* 463 (1979); Bagni, "Discrimination in the Name of the Lord: A Critical Evaluation of Discrimination by Religious Organizations," 79 *Columbia L. Rev.* 1514 (1979); Myers, "The Internal Revenue Service's Treatment of Religiously Motivated Racial Discrimination by Tax Exempt Organizations," 54 *Notre Dame Law.* 925 (1979); Kurtz, "Difficult Definitional Problems in Tax Administration: Religion and Race," 23 *Cath. Law.* 301 (1978); Colvin, "Contesting Loss of Exemption Under I.R.C. Section 501(c)(3) After *Bob Jones University* and *'Americans United' Inc.*, 34 *Fed. Bar J.* 182 (1975).

The reach of the decision by the U.S. Supreme Court in the *Bob Jones University* case may have been significantly augmented by its opinions in Shaare Tefila Congregation v. Cobb, 481 U.S. 615 (1987), and Saint Francis College v. Al-Khazraji, 481 U.S. 604 (1987), holding that the term "race," as used in the Civil Rights Act of 1866 and the voting rights act of 1870 (now reflected in 42 U.S.C. §§ 1981–1983) is to be interpreted in accordance with its usage in the nineteenth century, rather than in the context of modern scientific theory, so that the term embraces intentional discrimination on the basis of ancestry or ethnicity.

[87] Green v. Connally, 330 F. Supp. 1150 (D.D.C. 1971), *aff'd sub nom.* Coit v. Green, 404 U.S. 997 (1971).

[88] *Id.,* 330 F. Supp. at 1162, 1163.

[89] In general, Note, "Charities, Exempt Status and Public Policy," 50 *Tex. L. Rev.* 544 (1972); also Notes at 100 *Harv. L. Rev.* 1606 (1987); 19 *Wayne L. Rev.* 1629 (1973); 72 *Col. L. Rev.* 1215 (1972); 23 *Syr. L. Rev.* 1189 (1972); 68 *Mich. L. Rev.* 1410 (1970); 23 *Tax L. Rev.* 399 (1968); 68 *Col. L. Rev.* 992 (1968); 21 *Vand. L. Rev.* 406 (1968).

[90] Green v. Connally, *supra* note 86, 330 F. Supp. 1164. Also Note, "Constitutionality of Federal Tax Benefits to Private Segregated Schools," 11 *Wake Forest L. Rev.* 289 (1975).

[91] Rev. Rul. 71-447, 1971-2 C.B. 230.

[92] Rev. Rul. 67-325, 1967- 2 C.B. 113. In general, Spratt, "Federal Tax Exemption for Private Segregated Schools: The Crumbling Foundation," 12 *Wm. & Mary L. Rev.* 1 (1970).

began announcing denials of exemption later that year. However, a clamor began for stricter guidelines when the recognition of exemptions resumed to allegedly segregated schools.[93]

In 1972, the IRS issued guidelines and record-keeping requirements for determining whether private schools that have tax exemption rulings or are applying for recognition of tax exemption have racially nondiscriminatory policies as to students.[94] In 1975, the IRS promulgated new guidelines on the subject, which superseded the 1972 rules.[95] Under the 1975 guidelines, the racially nondiscriminatory policy of every private school must be stated in its governing instruments or governing body resolution, and in its brochures, catalogs, and similar publications. This policy must be publicized to all segments of the general community served by the school, either by notice in a newspaper or by use of broadcast media. All programs and facilities must be operated in a racially nondiscriminatory manner and all scholarships or comparable benefits must be offered on this basis. Each school must annually certify its racial nondiscrimination policy.[96]

The 1975 guidelines describe the information that must be provided by every school filing an application for recognition of tax-exempt status. Also included are an assortment of record-keeping requirements, mandating the retention for at least three years of records indicating the racial composition of the school's student body, faculty, and administrative staff; records documenting the award of financial assistance, copies of all brochures, catalogs, and advertising dealing with student admissions, programs, and scholarships; and copies of all materials used by or on behalf of the school to solicit contributions. Failure to maintain or to produce the required reports and information ostensibly creates a presumption that the school has failed to comply with the guidelines and thus has a racially discriminatory policy as to students.

In general, a private school must be able to affirmatively demonstrate (for example, as upon audit) that it has adopted a racially nondiscriminatory policy as to students that is made known to the general public, and that since the adoption of that policy it has operated in a bona fide manner in accordance with that policy.

It is the position of the IRS that church-related schools that teach secular subjects and generally comply with state law requirements for public education for the grades for which instruction is provided may not rely on the First Amendment to avoid the bar on tax exemption to those educational institutions that practice racial discrimination.[97] It is therefore the view of the IRS that a church-

---

[93] E.g., "Equal Educational Opportunity," Hearings Before the Senate Select Committee on Equal Educational Opportunity, at 1991–2038, 91st Cong., 2d Sess. (1970).

[94] Rev. Proc. 72-54, 1972-2 C.B. 834.

[95] Rev. Proc. 75-50, 1975-2 C.B. 587. These guidelines are applicable only to organizations that are classified as schools under IRC § 170(b)(1)(A)(ii) (see §§ 7.3, 11.3(a), although the doctrine of the *Bob Jones University* opinion (see text accompanying *supra* notes 74-86) may nonetheless be applicable (Gen. Coun. Mem. 39757).

[96] TIR-1449 (Mar. 19, 1976); also Ann. 76-57, 1976-16 I.R.B. 24.

[97] Rev. Rul. 75-231, 1975-1 C.B. 158. In general, Brown v. Dade Christian Schools, Inc., 556 F.2d 310 (5th Cir. 1977); Goldsboro Christian Schools, Inc. v. United States, 436 F. Supp. 1314 (E.D.N.C. 1977), *aff'd in unpub. op.* (4th Cir. Feb. 24, 1981).

sponsored school (that is not an entity separate from the church) that has racially discriminatory policies (in violation of IRS guidelines[98]) causes the sponsoring church to fail to qualify for tax exemption.[99]

The Supreme Court held that private schools are barred by federal law from denying admission to children solely for the reason of race.[100] The Court held that a statute that grants equal rights to make and enforce contracts is contravened where a minority applicant is denied a contractual right that would have been granted to him or her if he or she were a member of the racial majority. This statute has been characterized as a limitation on private discrimination and, by virtue of the Court's decision, applies to private schools irrespective of state action or tax exemption.[101]

The IRS ruled that an organization that was formed to conduct an apprentice training program offering instruction in a skilled trade is a charitable entity, even though it confined its instruction to native Americans. Admissions were so limited in accordance with the Adult Vocational Training Act (which authorizes programs of vocational and on-the-job training to help adult native American living on or near reservations obtain gainful employment) and with a Bureau of Indian Affairs funding contract. The IRS concluded that the organization's "admission policy is designed to implement certain statutorily defined Federal policy goals that are not in conflict with Federal public policy against racial discrimination in education" and that "[i]t is not a type of racial restriction that is contrary to Federal public policy."[102]

In an effort to further regulate in this field, the IRS proposed guidelines, on August 21, 1978,[103] and again in revised form on February 13, 1979,[104] for ascertaining whether private schools have racially discriminatory policies toward students. These rules would have established certain presumptions as to discriminatory practices by a private school, such as the nature of its minority enrollment and the relationship between formation or expansion of the school and local public school desegregation.

While these guidelines were pending, Congress, in enacting the fiscal year 1980 appropriations act for the Department of the Treasury,[105] prohibited the IRS from using funds appropriated under that law to implement the guidelines. In addition to specifically precluding the use of these appropriations to carry out the proposed guidelines, the legislation stated that none of the appropria-

---

[98] Rev. Proc. 75-50, *supra* note 95.

[99] Gen. Couns. Mem. 39574.

[100] This position is based upon 42 U.S.C. § 1981.

[101] Runyon v. McCrary, 424 U.S. 941 (1976), as limited by Patterson v. McLean Credit Union, 491 U.S. 164 (1989).

[102] Rev. Rul. 77-272, 1977-2 C.B. 191.

[103] 43 Fed. Reg. 37296.

[104] 44 Fed. Reg. 9451. In general, Sanders, "Exemptions for private schools threatened by Service's latest controversial guidelines," 50 *J. Tax.* 234 (1979); Wilson "An Overview of the IRS's Revised Proposed Revenue Procedure on Private Schools as Tax-Exempt Organizations," 57 *Taxes* 515 (1979).

[105] Pub. L. No. 96-74, 93 Stat. 559 (1979).

tions "shall be used to formulate or carry out any rule, policy, procedure, guideline, regulation, standard, or measure which would cause the loss of tax-exempt status to private, religious, or church-operated schools under section 501(c)(3) of the Internal Revenue Code of 1954 unless in effect prior to August 22, 1978."[106]

The position of the IRS in this regard became particularly aggravated when, notwithstanding the prohibition on the use of appropriated funds, a court ordered the IRS to refrain from according or continuing tax-exempt status for racially discriminatory private schools in the state of Mississippi.[107] This court order likewise used certain criteria concerning the timing of establishment of the school to raise an inference of discrimination, to be overcome only by clear and convincing evidence to the contrary. This prohibition was dropped from the House of Representatives' version of the measure to provide the fiscal year 1981 appropriations for the Department of the Treasury.[108]

A federal court subsequently gave considerable impetus to the philosophy underlying the proposed IRS guidelines, when it upheld the IRS's revocation of tax-exempt status of a private school on the ground that the institution maintained a racially discriminatory admissions policy. In so holding, the court noted that the school did not directly prove a nondiscriminatory admissions policy and that the government did not directly prove that the policy was discriminatory. Nonetheless, the court inferred from the circumstances surrounding the establishment of the school that it administered a racially discriminatory policy. The court also upheld the revocation of tax exemption retroactive to 1970.[109]

Although this area of law had seemed relatively settled as of 1981, in early 1982, the Reagan Administration announced that it had decided to abandon the 12-year-old effort to deny tax exemption and the eligibility to receive deductible contributions to private schools that have racially discriminatory practices, essentially on the ground that the IRS lacked the authority to develop this type of law and that only Congress, by statute, could cause racially discriminatory practices to be a prohibition on tax exemption. As part of this announcement, the Reagan Administration stated that it was going to accord tax-exempt and charitable donee status to Bob Jones University and Goldsboro Christian Schools, and claimed that cases then before the Supreme Court concerning these institutions were thereby rendered moot. Ten days later, the Administration submitted legislation on the subject, intended to place regulation

---

[106] Congress, in this legislation, also barred the IRS from carrying out any ruling to the effect "that a taxpayer is not entitled to a charitable deduction for general purpose contributions which are not used for educational purposes by [an exempt] religious organization," thereby prohibiting enforcement of Rev. Rul. 79-99, 1979-1 C.B. 108, during fiscal year 1980. Rev. Rul. 79-99 was subsequently revoked by Rev. Rul. 83-104, 1983-2 C.B. 46, which stated guidelines as to when payments to private schools are deductible charitable contributions or nondeductible tuition payments.

[107] Green v. Miller, 80-1 U.S.T.C. ¶ 9401 (D.D.C. 1980).

[108] H.R. 7583, 96th Cong., 2d Sess. (1980).

[109] Prince Edward School Found. v. United States, 80-1 U.S.T.C. ¶ 9295 (D.D.C. 1980), *aff'd in unpub. op.* (1981), *cert. den.*, 450 U.S. 944 (1981).

in this field on a statutory basis, rather than on the foundation of "federal public policy."

Five weeks later, a federal court of appeals ordered the Reagan Administration not to grant recognition of tax exemption to any private schools with racially discriminatory practices.[110] The order, which applied to Bob Jones University and Goldsboro Christian Schools, appeared to erase any basis the Administration may have had for contending that the cases before the Supreme Court were mooted by its earlier announcement. Much speculation arose thereafter as to what the Reagan Administration would do next. Many believed that the President would not reverse his mootness claim, and wait for Congress or the courts to act. One week later, however, the Reagan Administration asked the Supreme Court to consider the private school issue. The court did so, responding with its historic decision in mid-1983.[111]

With the issue as to the appropriate tax policy for private schools with racially discriminatory policies now generally resolved, the ramifications of this policy are beginning to have an impact on the tax status of other types of racially discriminatory organizations. This development is amply illustrated by litigation involving an organization known as the National Alliance, which disseminates several publications including the monthly newsletter *Attack!* A lawsuit concerning the tax-exempt status of the National Alliance was instituted in federal district court, which remanded the case to the IRS for further review.[112]

The National Alliance was formed as a nonprofit organization in 1974 to, according to its articles of incorporation, develop "in those with whom communication is established" an "understanding of and a pride in their racial and cultural heritage and an awareness of the present dangers to that heritage," with a view to establishing an "effective force for building a new order in American life." According to court records, its membership is confined to "persons of the European race." Its primary activities are the publication and distribution of a newspaper, a bulletin, and books and pamphlets. In the words of an amici curiae brief filed by the American Jewish Congress, the Anti-Defamation League, and the National Association for the Advancement of Colored People, the organization is engaged in the "propagation of racial hatred and advocacy of the extermination of Jews and Blacks (as well as other 'non-European' peoples)."

The IRS determined that the National Alliance could not qualify for tax exemption because it is neither charitable nor educational. In return, the organization took the matter to court, contending that denial of the tax exemption was an infringement of its constitutional rights. This argument was largely based on the fact that a federal court of appeals had concluded that the tax regulations defining the term *educational* were unconstitutionally vague.[113]

---

[110] Wright v. Regan, 49 A.F.T.R. 2d 82-757 (D.C. Cir. 1982).
[111] See text accompanying *supra* notes 74–76.
[112] National Alliance v. United States, 81-1 U.S.T.C. ¶ 9464 (D.D.C. 1981).
[113] Big Mama Rag, Inc. v. United States, 631 F.2d 1030 (D.C. Cir. 1980).

The correlation with this case and the private school issue is the reach of the doctrine that an organization cannot be charitable where it engages in an activity that is contrary to public policy.[114] In the school context, the position reflected in court decisions is that racially discriminatory policies are contrary to public policy. The counterargument was that schools are *educational*, not *charitable*, so that the public policy doctrine is inapplicable. The National Alliance case presented this issue in a somewhat larger context. Neither the district court[115] nor the appellate court[116] directly faced the issue of whether the propagation of racial hatred and violence can be considered charitable or educational. Moreover, the two courts did not resort to applicability of the public policy doctrine (or something approximating it) in reaching their decisions, although the appellate court twice found the occasion to favorably cite the private school case.[117]

The appellate court in the National Alliance case declined to address the issue directly from the standpoint of whether or not the organization is educational.[118] Indeed, the court concluded that "[e]ven under the most minimal requirement of a rational development of a point of view, National Alliance's materials fall short."[119] As the court's opinion made starkly clear, there was no direct precedent for resolving this issue. There is caselaw holding that organizations that engage in political agitation or in propagandizing cannot be educational.[120] However, the political agitation cases may not be on point, and the court elected to avoid becoming ensnarled in the "propaganda" issue by concluding that the material fell short of being educational to begin with. Thus, the National Alliance case did not resolve the controversy of whether an organization can advocate racial discrimination and simultaneously be educational where the advocacy is preceded by reasoned development of the viewpoint—something akin to compliance with the *full and fair exposition* standard.[121]

There are also First Amendment considerations. The appellate court had "no doubt that publication of the National Alliance material is protected by the First Amendment from abridgment by law."[122] However, the court rejected the idea that a denial of tax exemption is a contravention of free speech rights,[123] stating that "it does not follow [from free speech protection of material] that the First Amendment requires a construction of the term 'educational' which embraces every continuing dissemination of views."[124] Thus, apparently racially discriminatory activity that is protected by the free speech doctrine is

---

[114] See *supra* § 3.
[115] *Supra* note 112.
[116] National Alliance v. United States, 710 F.2d 868 (D.C. Cir. 1983).
[117] *Id*. at notes 4, 15.
[118] See § 7.1.
[119] National Alliance v. United States, *supra* note 116, at 873.
[120] See Chapters 20 and 21.
[121] See § 7.2.
[122] National Alliance v. United States, *supra* note 116, at 875.
[123] Citing Regan v. Taxation With Representation of Washington, 461 U.S. 54 (1983). See § 20.9.
[124] National Alliance v. United States, *supra* note 116, at 875.

not automatically educational simply because it is not merely propagandizing.[125]

The U.S. Supreme Court subsequently ruled that parents of black schoolchildren lack standing to challenge the process being utilized by the IRS in denying recognition of tax exemption to racially discriminatory private schools.[126] Another court ruled that an organization that made grants to private schools is not entitled to tax exemption, because a substantial portion of its funds was granted to schools that have failed to adopt racially nondiscriminatory policies with respect to students.[127]

In application of its guidelines, the IRS adheres to a judicially recognized position that, under certain circumstances, rebuttable inferences of discriminatory policies as to students can arise.[128] Thus, for example, where a school has a history of racial discrimination, efforts by the school to attract minority group applicants will be regarded as ineffective in relation to the guidelines unless they are "reasonably calculated to succeed," such as active and vigorous recruitment of minority students and teachers, financial assistance to minority students, and effective communication of the nondiscriminatory policy to the minority population.[129] "[A]ctual enrollment of minority students," the IRS's lawyers observed, "while not determinative of the issue, is generally the most convincing evidence of the existence of a non-discriminatory policy as to students."[130] These principles have been applied by a court, that, holding that a private school seeking tax exemption must prove racial nondiscrimination by a preponderance of the evidence, concluded that a school failed to meet this burden of proof because it was founded at a time when courts were forcing desegregation in public schools, had never enrolled a black student, and did not adequately publicize a policy of racial nondiscrimination.[131]

The IRS applies the rule denying recognition of tax-exempt status as a char-

---

[125] *Id.* In general, Morris and White, "Beware a Forgotten Trap for Tax-Exempt Schools," 3 *J. Tax. Exempt Orgs.* 13 (Spring 1991); Note, "Granting Charitable Tax Exemptions to Racially Discriminatory Schools," 70 *Ky. L. J.* 807–829 (1981–1982); Nevin & Bills, *The Schools That Fear Built* (1977); Comment, "The Tax Exempt Status of Sectarian Educational Institutions That Discriminate on the Basis of Race," 65 *Iowa L. Rev.* 258 (1979); Note, "Racial Exclusion by Religious Schools, Brown v. Dade Christian Schools, Inc.," 91 *Harv. L. Rev.* 879 (1978); Adams, "Racial and Religious Discrimination in Charitable Trusts: A Current Analysis of Constitutional and Trust Law Solutions," 25 *Clev. St. L. Rev.* 1 (1976); Note, "Constitutionality of Federal Tax Benefits to Private Segregated Schools," 11 *Wake Forest L. Rev.* 289 (1975); Horvitz, "Tax Subsidies to Promote Affirmative Action in Admission Procedures for Institutions of Higher Learning—Their Inherent Danger," 52 *Taxes* 452 (1974); Comment, "Denial of Tax Exempt Status to Southern Segregation Academies," 6 *Harvard Civil Rights—Civil Liberties L. Rev.* 179 (1970); Note, "Federal Tax Exempt Status of Private Segregated Schools," 7 *Wake Forest L. Rev.* 121 (1970).

[126] Allen v. Wright, 468 U.S. 737 (1984); Regan v. Wright, 468 U.S. 737 (1984).

[127] Virginia Educ. Fund v. Comm'r, 85 T.C. 743 (1985), *aff'd*, 799 F.2d 903 (4th Cir. 1986). Also Estate of Clopton v. Comm'r, 93 T.C. 275 (1989).

[128] Norwood v. Harrison, 382 F. Supp. 921, 924–926 (N.D. Miss. 1984).

[129] Gen. Couns. Mem. 39525.

[130] Gen. Couns. Mem. 39524.

[131] Calhoun Academy v. Comm'r, 94 T.C. 284 (1990).

itable organization because of racially discriminatory policies to all entities seeking that classification, not just private educational institutions.[132]

(b) Gender-Based Discrimination

While there is a recognized federal public policy against support for racial segregation in private schools (and, presumably, other varieties of racial discrimination[133]), a somewhat comparable federal public policy against support for institutions that engage in gender-based discrimination may be developing.[134] The question is whether this is a sufficiently established federal policy so that its contravention would have an impact on the tax status of these institutions and other charitable organizations.[135] The issue has been raised, with the courts concluding that sex discrimination does not bar federal tax exemption.[136] However, at least one court, having concluded that the charitable contribution deduction is equivalent to a federal matching grant, found that by allowing the deduction of charitable contributions, the federal government has conferred a "benefit" on the recipient organization and that the Fifth Amendment is applicable.[137]

Nonetheless, the U.S. Supreme Court determined that a national nonprofit membership organization is compelled to accept women as regular members, by direction of a state human rights act, notwithstanding the organization's free speech and associational rights.[138] The organization's chapters were found to be "place[s] of public accommodations," the skills it develops were held to be "goods," and business contacts and employment promotions were ruled to be "privileges" and "advantages"—all so that the state's law banning gender-based discriminatory practices in access to places of public accommodation could be made applicable.

This opinion broadly exposes the Court's interest in eradicating gender-based discrimination in all feasible quarters, including the nonprofit organization context. In some respects, it is strongly analogous to the Court's efforts to elimi-

---

[132] Priv. Ltr. Rul. 8910001.

[133] Bob Jones Univ. v. Simon, 416 U.S. 725 (1974); Crenshaw County Private School Found. v. Connally, 474 F.2d 1185 (3d Cir. 1973), *cert. den.*, 417 U.S. 908 (1973).

[134] E.g., McGlotten v. Connally, 388 F. Supp. 448 (D.D.C. 1972). Also Bittker & Kaufman, "Taxes and Civil Rights: 'Constitutionalizing' the Internal Revenue Code," 82 *Yale L. J.* 51 (1972).

[135] E.g., Executive Order 11246, as amended, 30 Fed. Reg. 12319 (1965); Title VII of the Civil Rights Act of 1964, as amended, 42 U.S.C. § 2000e *et seq.*; Equal Employment Opportunity Commission regulations, 29 C.F.R. § 1604 *et seq.*; Title IX of the Education Amendments of 1972, 20 U.S.C. § 1681 *et seq.*; the Equal Pay Act of 1963, 29 U.S.C. § 206 *et seq.*; Califano v. Webster, 430 U.S. 313 (1977); Alexander v. Louisiana, 405 U.S. 625 (1972); Reed v. Reed, 404 U.S. 71 (1971).

[136] McCoy v. Shultz, 73-1 U.S.T.C. ¶ 9233 (D.D.C. 1973); Junior Chamber of Commerce of Rochester, Inc., Rochester, New York v. U.S. Jaycees, Tulsa, Okla. 495 F.2d 883 (10th Cir. 1974), *cert den.*, 419 U.S. 1026 (1974); New York City Jaycees, Inc. v. United States Jaycees, Inc., 512 F.2d 856 (2d Cir. 1975).

[137] McGlotten v. Connally, *supra* note 134, at 456–457, note 37. Also Stearns v. Veterans of Foreign Wars, 500 F.2d 788 (D.C. Cir. 1974) (remand).

[138] Roberts, Acting Commissioner, Minn. Dep't of Human Rights v. United States Jaycees, 468 U.S. 609 (1984).

nate race discrimination in private education.[139] Indeed, the Court, recalling its upholding of Title II of the Civil Rights Act of 1964, which forbids race discrimination in public accommodations, wrote that injuries caused by discrimination are "surely felt as strongly by persons suffering discrimination on the basis of their sex as by those treated differently because of their race."[140] The Court wrote that "discrimination based on archaic and overbroad assumptions about the relative needs and capacities of the sexes forces individuals to labor under stereotypical notions that often bear no relationship to their actual abilities."[141] This discrimination, added the Court, "both deprives persons of their individual dignity and denies society the benefits of wide participation in political, economic, and cultural life."[142]

(c) Other Forms of Discrimination

It may also be quite validly asserted that there is a federal public policy, either presently in existence or in the process of development, against other forms of discrimination, such as discrimination on the basis of marital status, national origin, religion, handicap, sexual preference, and age.[143] Thus, the law may develop to the point where a charitable organization will jeopardize its tax status where it engages in one or more of these forms of discrimination. The IRS itself has displayed some sensitivity to these matters, such as by including discrimination on the ground of national origin as being within the scope of racial discrimination for purposes of the nondiscrimination rules applicable to private educational in-

---

[139] See this chapter, *supra* text accompanying notes 73–131.

[140] Roberts, Acting Commissioner, Minn. Dep't of Human Rights v. United States Jaycees, *supra* note 138, at 625.

[141] *Id.*

[142] *Id.* Also New York State Club Ass'n. v. New York City, 487 U.S. 1 (1987); Board of Directors of Rotary Int'l v. Rotary Club of Duarte, 481 U.S. 537 (1987). Cf. Trustees of Smith College v. Board of Assessors of Whately, 434 N.E.2d 182 (Mass. 1982) (successful defense of single-sex admissions policy at private college). In general, Comment, "Taxing Sex Discrimination: Revoking Tax Benefits of Organizations Which Discriminate on the Basis of Sex," 1976 *Ariz. State L. J.* 641 (1976); Note, "Sex Restricted Scholarships and the Charitable Trust," 59 *Iowa L. Rev.* 1000 (1974).

Where the educational institution is operated by a government, the maintenance of it exclusively for the members of one gender is likely to be a violation of the equal protection doctrine (e.g., the operation by the Commonwealth of Virginia of the military college, Virginia Military Institute, exclusively for males) (United States v. Virginia, 116 S. Ct. 2264 (1996)).

[143] E.g., Title VII of the Civil Rights Act of 1964, as amended, 42 U.S.C. § 2000e *et seq.*; Executive Order 11246, as amended, 30 Fed. Reg. 12319 (1965); Title IX of the Education Amendments of 1972, 20 U.S.C. § 1681 *et seq.*; the Rehabilitation Act Amendments of 1974, 29 U.S.C. §§ 793, 794; the Age Discrimination in Employment Act, 29 U.S.C. § 621 *et seq.*; and the Age Discrimination Act of 1975, 89 Stat. 713.

For example, where a university was held by a court to be in violation of the District of Columbia human rights act, which prohibits an educational institution from discriminating against any individual on the basis of his or her sexual orientation (D.C. Code, Title 1 § 1-2520), the court wrote that the "eradication of sexual orientation discrimination is a compelling governmental interest" (Gay Rights Coalition of Georgetown Univ. Law Cent. D.C. v. Georgetown Univ.; 536 A.2d 1 (D.C. Ct. App. 1987)). In general, Duttle, "God and Gays at Georgetown: Observations on Gay Rights Coalition of Georgetown University Law Center v. Georgetown University," 15 *J.C.U.L.* (No. 1) 1 (1988).

stitutions[144] and by evincing concern that a 1965 ruling carries overtones of a condonation of age discrimination.[145]

§ 5.5 SOME COLLATERAL CONCEPTS

Conceptually, the term *charitable* has a broad, wide-ranging, multifaceted meaning. While specific applications of the concept are continually generating new illustrations of charitable organizations, the basic categories of charity are encompassed by the common law definition of the term[146] as opposed to terms such as *philanthropy, eleemosynary,* or *benevolent.*[147] The IRS observed that the provisions in the federal tax statutory law relating to charitable organizations "do not reflect any novel or specialized tax concept of charitable purposes, and that . . . [those provisions] should be interpreted as favoring only those purposes which are recognized as charitable in the generally accepted legal sense."[148] The concept of *charitable* thus includes relief of poverty by assisting the poor, distressed, and underprivileged, advancement of religion, advancement of education and science, performance of government functions and lessening of the burdens of government, promotion of health, and promotion of social welfare for the benefit of the community. Viewing the foregoing categories as substantially the totality of the concept of *charitable*, there is a striking similarity between the Preamble to the Statute of Charitable Uses enacted in 1601 and the Department of the Treasury regulation under IRC § 501(c)(3).[149]

The scope of these six categories in relation to tax law requirements is discussed in Chapter 6. However, there are some collateral principles derived from the law of charitable trusts with respect to the concept of charity as applied for federal income tax purposes that should be distilled at this point.[150]

(a) Requirement of *Charitable Class*

The persons who are to benefit from the purported charitable activity must constitute a sufficiently large or indefinite class. Thus, it is inadequate if the beneficiaries of the alleged charitable works are specifically named, are solely relatives of the donor or donors, or are organizations such as social clubs and fraternal organizations.[151] Conversely, an adequate class may be present even where the beneficiaries are confined to the inhabitants of a particular town or are employees of a particular company. Thus, a foundation established to award scholarships solely to members of a designated fraternity was ruled exempt as an educational

---

[144] Rev. Proc. 75-50, *supra* note 95.
[145] Rev. Rul. 77-365, 1977-2 C.B. 192.
[146] Reg. § 1.501(c)(3)-1(d)(2). See *supra* note 37.
[147] E.g., People v. Thomas Walters Chapter of Daughters of Am. Revolution, 142 N.E. 566 (Ill. 1924); In re Dol's Estate, 187 P. 428 (Cal. 1920); Hamburger v. Cornell Univ., 166 N.Y.S. 46 (Sara. Cty. 1917).
[148] Rev. Rul. 67-325, 1967-2 C.B. 113.
[149] Also *Restatement of Trusts* 2d §§ 368–374.
[150] It is commonplace for the law of charitable trusts to be analogized to in exploring the meaning of terms used in IRC § 501(c)(3). E.g., Green v. Connally, *supra* note 51, 330 F. Supp. at 1157–1159.
[151] Rev. Rul. 56-403, 1956-2 C.B. 307.

organization.[152] However, another foundation lost its tax-exempt status because it expended a considerable portion of its funds on a scholarship grant to the son of a trustee of the foundation.[153] Basically, where a class of persons is involved as beneficiaries, the sufficiency of the class for purposes of ascertaining whether charitable activities are being engaged in becomes a question of degree.[154]

A case in point is the regard of the IRS for the elderly. Until the 1970s, the IRS's position was that the aged were not a charitable class per se, even the unemployed aged.[155] There was some support for this stance from the courts.[156] When an organization operated to assist the elderly, any exemption as a charitable entity was tied to the concept that they were also impoverished, as illustrated by the charitable and educational status accorded an organization to aid elderly unemployed persons of limited means in obtaining employment by providing these persons with free counseling and placement services and by educating the general public in the employment capabilities of the elderly.[157]

This position of the IRS began to soften in the early 1970s, as evidenced by its change of heart with respect to homes for the aged, when the IRS first articulated the thought that the elderly face forms of distress other than financial distress and have special needs for housing, health care, and economic security in general.[158] Thereafter, the IRS held that charitable status could be extended to an organization that established a service center providing information, referrals, counseling services relating to health, housing, finances, education, employment, and recreational facilities for a particular community's senior citizens,[159] that operated a rural rest home to provide, at a nominal charge, two-week vacations for elderly poor people,[160] and that provided home delivery of meals to elderly and handicapped people by volunteers.[161]

In 1977, the IRS first recognized that the elderly can constitute a charitable class *per se*. In so doing, the IRS continued to impose as a touchstone the corollary requirement that the elderly also be distressed, but the facts reveal that the presence of this element was minimal. The circumstances involved an organization that provided low-cost bus transportation to senior citizens and the handicapped in a community where public transportation was unavailable or inadequate. The IRS observed: "Providing the elderly and the handicapped with necessary transportation within the community is an activity directed toward meeting the spe-

---

[152] *Id.*

[153] Charleston Chair Co. v. United States, 203 F. Supp. 126 (E.D.S.C. 1962). Also Rev. Rul. 67-367, 1967-2 C.B. 188.

[154] E.g., *Restatement of Trusts* (2d ed. 1959) § 375; Bogert, *Trusts and Trustees* (2d ed. 1959) § 365; Rev. Rul. 57-449, 1957-2 C.B. 622. Also Rev. Rul. 67-325, *supra* note 147, where the IRS discussed this concept in the context of ruling, following the decision in Peters v. Comm'r, 21 T.C. 55 (1953), that community recreational facilities may be classified as charitable if they are provided for the use of the general public in the community. Cf. Rev. Rul. 59-310, 1959-2 C.B. 146.

[155] Rev. Rul. 68-422, 1968-2 C.B. 207. Rev. Rul. 56-138, 1956-1 C.B. 202.

[156] Watson v. United States, 355 F.2d 269 (3d Cir. 1965).

[157] Rev. Rul. 66-257, 1966-2 C.B. 212.

[158] Rev. Rul. 72-124, 1972-1 C.B. 145.

[159] Rev. Rul. 75-198, 1975-1 C.B. 157.

[160] Rev. Rul. 75-385, 1975-2 C.B. 205.

[161] Rev. Rul. 76-244, 1976-1 C.B. 155.

cial needs of these charitable classes of individuals."[162] Subsequently, the IRS ruled that an organization that provided specially designed housing "that is within the financial reach of a significant segment of the community's elderly persons" qualified as a charitable entity.[163]

The IRS ruled that a law library qualified as an exempt educational organization, even though the organization's rules limit "access to and use of the library facilities . . . to a designated class of persons . . ."[164] The IRS, on this point, said that "[w]hat is of importance is that the class benefited be broad enough to warrant a conclusion that the educational facility or activity is serving a broad public interest rather than a private interest." The rationale for the favorable ruling was that the library facilities are available to a "significant number" of people and that the restrictions were placed on use of the library because of the limited size and scope of the facilities.[165]

Therefore, the requirements as to what is *charitable* generally contemplate the presence of a sufficient class or community. On occasion, however, the IRS will attempt to use this requirement as a basis for denial of exemption, by characterizing the beneficiaries as being too small in number or too limited in interests, such as where benefits are confined to an organization's membership. However, there are reasonable limitations on the reach by the IRS in applying this doctrine. As one court has observed: "To our knowledge, no charity has ever succeeded in benefiting *every* member of the community. If to fail to so benefit *everyone* renders an organization noncharitable, then dire times must lie ahead for this nation's charities."[166]

A charitable purpose may be served regardless of whether corpus is immediately distributed or is continued indefinitely, or whether the number of persons actually relieved is small as long as they are selected from a valid charitable class. Nor is the economic status of the individuals benefited necessarily a factor, except where relief of poverty is the basis for designation of the purpose as charitable. That is, it is not necessary that the beneficiaries of a charitable organization's program be members of a charitable class in the colloquial sense of that term (such as the poor or the distressed). Rather, the essential requirement for achieving charitable status is that benefits be accorded the general public or the community, or some sufficiently general subgroup thereof, such as students, patients, or the aged.[167] For example, the IRS determined that community recreational facilities are classifiable as charitable if they are provided for the use of the general public of a community.[168] As one court stated, "[r]elief of poverty is not a condition of

---

[162] Rev. Rul. 77-246, 1977-2 C.B. 190.

[163] Rev. Rul. 79-18, 1979-1 C.B. 194.

[164] Rev. Rul. 75-196, 1975-2 C.B. 155.

[165] Rev. Rul. 68-504, 1968-2 C.B. 211, and Rev. Rul. 65-298, 1965-2 C.B. 163, held that an organization formed to conduct educational programs for a specific group is entitled to IRC § 501(c)(3) classification.

[166] Sound Health Ass'n v. Comm'r, 71 T.C. 158, 185 (1978) (emphasis in the original). A contemporary application of the charitable class requirement was provided by the IRS, when it held that a bequest for scholarships at two universities failed to qualify for the estate tax charitable deduction inasmuch as the only other criterion for the grants was that the recipients have the same surname as the decedent; the IRS determined that only 603 families have that name (Priv. Ltr. Rul. 9631004).

[167] E.g., Rev. Rul. 68-422, *supra* note 154.

[168] Rev. Rul. 67-325, *supra* note 147.

charitable assistance. If the benefit conferred is of sufficiently widespread social value, a charitable purpose exists."[169] Likewise, another court accorded tax exemption to an organization that functioned primarily as a crop seed certification entity, despite the government's contention that its activities only incidentally benefit the public, with the court observing that "[t]he fact that the majority of persons interested in seed technology may well come from the agricultural community does not mean that farmers and gardeners are not an important part of the general public. . . ."[170]

(b) Community Benefit

A limited number of persons may be benefited as the result of an organization's activities and the assistance considered charitable in nature as long as the effect is to benefit the community rather than merely individual recipients. Thus, the funding of a chair at a university will benefit individual professors although the actual effect is to promote education, and is therefore an exempt activity. In these instances, the individuals benefited are frequently regarded as "means" or "instruments" to a charitable end. As an illustration, an organization was ruled exempt as a charitable entity for providing substantially free legal services to low-income residents of economically depressed communities by providing financial and other assistance to legal interns; the IRS recognized that the interns themselves are not members of a charitable class but that they are "merely the instruments by which the charitable purposes are accomplished."[171] Likewise, proxy contests when conducted in the public interest are charitable activities, in that there is a "community benefit" (i.e., the "beneficiary of this activity and educational process to promote socially responsible corporations will be the public"), even though the exempt organization's resources are being devoted to direct participation in the processes of corporate management.[172] Similarly, a member of an organization may properly obtain financial benefit from the organization where the members are the means by which public purposes are served.[173] The same principle obtains as respects the operation of public interest law firms.[174] The IRS has accepted the view that a charitable organization may provide services or make distributions to nonexempt organizations where done in furtherance of its exempt purpose.[175]

Thus, the IRS ruled that an organization did not fail to qualify as a charitable and educational entity because its tax-exempt function (the training of unem-

---

[169] In re Estate of Henderson, 112 P.2d 605, 607 (Sup. Ct. Cal. 1941).

[170] Indiana Crop Improvement Ass'n, Inc. v. Comm'r, 76 T.C. 394, 400 (1981).

[171] Rev. Rul. 72-559, 1972-2 C.B. 247.

[172] Center on Corporate Responsibility, Inc. v. Shultz, 368 F. Supp. 863, 874, note 21 (D.D.C. 1973).

[173] Gen. Couns. Mem. 38459.

[174] Rev. Proc. 71-39, 1971-2 C.B. 575. See § 6.10(d).

[175] Rev. Rul. 81-29, 1981-1 C.B. 329; Rev. Rul. 68-489, 1968-2 C.B. 210. However, where a grant is for the improvement of a study room, the room must be used primarily for educational purposes, according to the IRS Chief Counsel, analogizing to IRC § 280A(c)(1)(A) (concerning the business deduction for a home office), in Gen. Couns. Mem. 39288, as mod. by Gen. Couns. Mem. 39612.

ployed and underemployed individuals) was carried out through the manufacturing and selling of toy products.[176] The IRS observed:

> The question in this case is whether the organization is conducting its manufacturing and merchandising operation as an end in itself or as the means by which it accomplished a charitable purpose other than through the production of income. Here, the facts clearly support the conclusion that the manufacturing and merchandising operation is the means of accomplishing the organization's declared charitable objectives. Thus, there is a clear and distinct causal relationship between the manufacturing activity and the training of individuals for the purpose of improving their individual capabilities. There is likewise no evidence that the scale of the endeavor is such as to suggest that it is being conducted on a larger scale than is reasonably necessary to accomplish the organization's charitable purpose.

Similarly, the IRS stated that:

> The performance of a particular activity that is not inherently charitable may nonetheless further a charitable purpose. The overall result in any given case is dependent on why and how that activity is actually being conducted.[177]

(c) *Charity* as Evolutionary Concept

The concept of what is *charitable* is continually changing and evolving. This principle may be illustrated by the abandonment by the IRS of its prior rule that homes for the aged may be exempt only where services are provided free or below cost, to be replaced by the requirement that housing, health care, and financial security needs be met.[178] Thus, the old law that focused solely upon relief of financial distress of the aged has been supplanted by a recognition of other forms of "distress": need for housing, health care services, and financial security. Changes in the concept are expounded in constitutions, statutes, and, for the most part, court decisions. In the latter instance, the changes "are wrought by changes in moral and ethical precepts generally held, or by changes in relative values assigned to different and sometimes competing and even conflicting interests of society."[179]

A particular charitable activity may partake of more than one of the basic six categories, such as a scholarship program for impoverished youths, which constitutes both the relief of poverty and the advancement of education.

---

[176] Rev. Rul. 73-128, 1973-1 C.B. 222.
[177] Rev. Rul. 69-572, 1969-2 C.B. 119. Also Rev. Rul. 80-279, 1980-2 C.B. 176; Rev. Rul. 80-278, 1980-2 C.B. 175; Rev. Rul. 67-4, 1967-1 C.B. 121. Cf. Senior Citizens Stores, Inc. v. United States, 602 F.2d 711 (5th Cir. 1979).
[178] Rev. Rul. 72-124, *supra* note 158, superseding Rev. Rul. 57-467, 1957-2 C.B. 313.
[179] Green v. Connally, *supra* note 51, 330 F. Supp. at 1159; Bogert, *Trusts and Trustees* (2d ed. 1959) § 369 and Scott, *The Law of Trusts* (2d ed. 1956) §§ 368, 374.2.

(d) Motive

The motive of the founder in initiating the alleged charitable activity is immaterial in terms of ascertaining whether the activity is in fact charitable in nature.[180] This principle was illustrated by the case of a decedent's bequest to a cemetery association formed to maintain a cemetery and sell burial plots. In the absence of proof that the cemetery was operated exclusively for charitable purposes or that the bequest was to be used exclusively for such purposes, a court held that the bequest was not a charitable bequest for federal estate tax purposes.[181] The court stated that "[i]t is the use to which a bequest is to be applied that determines its deductibility and not the motive prompting the bequest."[182]

(e) Private Use

A charitable purpose cannot be served where the property involved or the income therefrom is directed to a private use.[183] Thus, a charitable organization cannot be one organized and operated for a profit or for other private ends. For example, a book publishing venture was denied exemption as a charitable and/or educational organization because a substantial purpose of the organization was found to be the derivation of substantial profits by the organization and the authors to which it made grants.[184] Other illustrations include an organization that was denied exemption because its principal activity was the making of research grants for the development of new machinery to be used in a commercial operation[185] and an association that was denied exemption as a business league because its "research program" benefited its members rather than the public.[186]

It was for this reason that the IRS refused to recognize an organization as being charitable where its primary purpose was to encourage individuals to contribute funds to charity and its primary activity was the offering of free legal services for personal tax and estate planning to individuals who wish to make current and planned gifts to charity as part of their overall tax and estate planning. Stating that "[a]iding individuals in their tax and estate planning is not a charitable activity in the generally accepted legal sense," the IRS ruled that "the benefits to the public are tenuous in view of the predominantly private purpose served by arranging individuals' tax and estate plans."[187]

However, the fact that private individuals or organizations incidentally derive a benefit from a charitable undertaking does not destroy the charitable nature of the endeavor. For example, an organization of educational institutions

---

[180] Bogert, *Trusts and Trustees* (2d ed. 1959) §§ 366.

[181] Estate of Amick v. Comm'r, 67 T.C. 924 (1977).

[182] *Id.* at 928. Also Wilbur Nat'l Bank v. Comm'r, 17 B.T.A. 654 (1929); Estate of Wood v. Comm'r, 39 T.C. 1 (1962); Rev. Rul. 67-170, 1967-1 C.B. 272. Cf. Estate of Audenried v. Comm'r, 26 T.C. 120 (1956).

[183] *Restatement of Trusts* (2d ed. 1959) § 376.

[184] Rev. Rul. 66-104, 1966-1 C.B. 135; Christian Manner Int'l, Inc. v. Comm'r, 71 T.C. 661 (1979).

[185] Rev. Rul. 65-1, 1965-1 C.B. 226.

[186] Rev. Rul. 69-632, 1969-2 C.B. 120.

[187] Rev. Rul. 76-442, 1976-2 C.B. 148. In general, Note, "The Twilight Zone of Charity: The IRS Denies Exemption for a Free Tax Planning Service under Section 501(c)(3)," 55 *N.C.L. Rev.* 721 (1977).

that accredited schools and colleges was found to foster excellence in education and to qualify as a charitable and educational entity even though its membership contained a small number of proprietary schools, since "[a]ny private benefit that may accrue to the few proprietary members because of accreditation is incidental to the purpose of improving the quality of education."[188] Thus, the IRS, which accorded status as a charitable entity to an organization formed and supported by residents of an isolated rural community to provide a medical building and facilities at reasonable rent to attract a physician who would provide medical services to the community, stated:

> In these circumstances, any personal benefit derived by the doctor (the use of the building in which to practice his profession) does not detract from the public purpose of the organization nor lessen the public benefit flowing from its activities and is not considered to be the type of private interest prohibited by the regulations.[189]

Likewise, the IRS ruled that the fact that lawyers use a tax-exempt library to derive personal benefit in the practice of their profession is incidental to the exempt purpose of the library and is, in most instances, a "logical by-product" of an educational process.[190] Similarly, a court held that a day care center qualified as an educational organization and that the provision of custodial care was "merely a vehicle for or incidental to achieving petitioner's only substantial purpose, education of the children, and is not ground for disqualification from exemption."[191] The same court subsequently reiterated this position, holding that an early childhood center is a tax-exempt educational organization, "with custodial care being incidental only because of the needs of the children for such care if they are to receive the education offered."[192] Likewise, this court held that an organization may sell artworks without jeopardizing its tax exemption because the sales activities "are but a means to the end of increasing public appreciation of the arts."[193] Still another illustration is the ability of an exempt organization to provide services (such as research) in furtherance of an exempt function where nonexempt entities are among the recipients of the services.[194] In still another illustration of this point, the IRS determined that a professional standards review organization can qualify as a charitable entity, as promoting health and lessening the burdens of government, because the benefits accorded by it to members of the medical profession were incidental to the charitable benefits it provided.[195]

---

[188] Rev. Rul. 74-146, 1974-1 C.B. 129. One IRS private letter ruling suggested that an association of this nature may receive up to 15 percent of its resources from for-profit members without endangering its tax-exempt status (Priv. Ltr. Rul. 9237034).

[189] Rev. Rul. 73-313, 1973-2 C.B. 174.

[190] Rev. Rul. 75-196, *supra* note 164. Also Rev. Rul. 75-471, 1975-2 C.B. 207; Rev. Rul. 78-85, 1978-1 C.B. 150.

[191] San Francisco Infant School, Inc. v. Comm'r, 69 T.C. 957, 966 (1978). See § 7.7.

[192] Michigan Early Childhood Cent., Inc. v. Comm'r, 37 T.C.M. 808, 810 (1978).

[193] Cleveland Creative Arts Guild v. Comm'r, 50 T.C.M. 272 (1985).

[194] Rev. Rul. 81-29, *supra* note 175.

[195] Rev. Rul. 81-276, 1981-2 C.B. 128. Also Fraternal Medical Specialist Servs., Inc. v. Comm'r, 49 T.C.M. 289 (1984).

(f) Illegal Activities

A charitable purpose cannot be one that is illegal or contrary to public policy.[196] The IRS determined that an organization formed to promote world peace and disarmament could not qualify as either a charitable or social welfare organization, because its primary activity was the sponsoring of antiwar protest demonstrations, where it urged its participants to commit violations of local ordinances and breaches of public order.[197] The IRS held:

> In this case the organization induces or encourages the commission of criminal acts by planning and sponsoring such events. The intentional nature of this encouragement precludes the possibility that the organization might unfairly fail to qualify for exemption due to an isolated or inadvertent violation of a regulatory statute. Its activities demonstrate an illegal purpose which is inconsistent with charitable ends. Moreover, the generation of criminal acts increases the burdens of government, thus frustrating a well recognized charitable goal, i.e., relief of the burdens of government. Accordingly, the organization is not operated exclusively for charitable purposes and does not qualify for exemption from Federal income tax under section 501(c)(3) of the Code.
>
> Illegal activities, which violate the minimum standards of acceptable conduct necessary to the preservation of an orderly society, are contrary to the common good and the general welfare of the people in a community and thus are not permissible means of promoting the social welfare for purposes of section 501(c)(4) of the Code. Accordingly, the organization in this case is not operated exclusively for the promotion of social welfare and does not qualify for exemption from Federal income tax under section 501(c)(4).

However, the fact that a particular purpose requires efforts to bring about a change in the statutory law does not preclude the purpose from being charitable. Thus, the proscription on substantive legislative activities by charitable organizations is a statutory constraint on otherwise permissible charitable activities rather than a declaration of a feature of the term charitable in the common law.[198]

In conclusion, the "common element of all charitable purposes is that they are designed to accomplish objects which are beneficial to the community."[199] A frequently cited case on this point is an 1877 U.S. Supreme Court pronouncement, where the Court stated: "A charitable use, where neither law nor public policy forbids, may be applied to almost any thing that tends to promote the well-doing and well-being of social man."[200]

---

[196] *Restatement of Trusts* (2d ed. 1959) § 377; Tank Truck Rentals, Inc. v. Comm'r, *supra* note 53.

[197] Rev. Rul. 75-384, 1975-2 C.B. 204.

[198] See § 20.2.

[199] *Restatement of Trusts* (2d ed. 1959) § 368, cmt. a.

[200] Ould v. Washington Hosp. for Foundlings, *supra* n. 50, at 311. In general, Reiling, "What is a Charitable Organization," 44 *A.B.A.J.* 528 (1958); Annot. 12 A.L.R. 2d 849, 855 (1950). Also Peters v. Comm'r, *supra* note 154, at 59.

CHAPTER SIX

Charitable Organizations

Section 501(a) of the Internal Revenue Code provides federal income tax exemption for organizations described in IRC § 501(c)(3), namely, entities that are organized and operated exclusively for charitable purposes.

The term *charitable*, which has the most extensive history and the broadest meaning of any of the terms in IRC § 501(c)(3), is used in the section in its "generally accepted legal sense" and is, therefore, not to be construed as limited by the other purposes stated in the section that may fall within the broad outlines of *charity* as developed by judicial decisions.[1] These uses of the word *charitable* involve the definitions of the term as used in its technical sense (rather than in its broader, more encompassing sense[2]). The various categories of purposes comprehended by the term *charitable* in the federal tax law are discussed in this chapter.

---

[1] Reg. § 1.501(c)(3)-1(d)(2). Also Reg. § 1.501(c)(3)-1(d)(1)(i)(b).
[2] See § 5.2.

§ 6.1 RELIEF OF THE POOR

The regulations accompanying the federal tax law concerning charitable organizations define the term *charitable* as including "[r]elief of the poor and distressed or of the underprivileged."[3]

The relief of poverty is the most basic and historically founded form of charitable activity. Assistance to the poor encompasses aid in the form of "the distribution of money or goods among the poor, by letting land to them at low rent, by making loans to them, by assisting them to secure employment, by the establishment of a home or other institution, by providing soup kitchens and the like."[4] Thus, relieving poverty can entail direct financial assistance or, more likely in contemporary society, the provision of services.

Organizations deemed tax-exempt because they relieve the poor, distressed, or underprivileged may be categorized on the basis of the types of services they provide. Some organizations provide assistance to enable the impoverished to secure employment, such as vocational training,[5] establishment of a market for products of the needy,[6] or employment assistance for the elderly,[7] while others provide assistance to maintain employment, such as operation of a day care center,[8] promote the rights and welfare of public housing tenants,[9] provide technical and material assistance under foreign self-help programs,[10] provide financial assistance in securing a private hospital room,[11] or operate a service center providing information, referral, and counseling services relating to health, housing, finances, education, and employment, as well as a facility for specialized recreation, for a particular community's senior citizens.[12]

Others of these organizations provide services more personal in nature, such as provision of low-income housing,[13] legal services,[14] money management advice,[15] vacations for the elderly poor at a rural rest home,[16] home delivery of meals to the elderly,[17] and transportation services for the elderly and handicapped.[18] Still others of these organizations seek to render assistance to the poor and distressed by helping them at a time when they are particularly

---

[3] Reg. § 1.501(c)(3)-1(d)(2).
[4] *Restatement of Trusts* (2d ed. 1959) § 369, cmt. a.
[5] Rev. Rul. 73-128, 1973-1 C.B. 222.
[6] Rev. Rul. 68-167, 1968-1 C.B. 255; Industrial Aid for the Blind v. Comm'r, 75 T.C. 96 (1979).
[7] Rev. Rul. 66-257, 1966-2 C.B. 212.
[8] Rev. Rul. 70-533, 1970-2 C.B. 112; Rev. Rul. 68-166, 1968-1 C.B. 255.
[9] Rev. Rul. 75-283, 1975-2 C.B. 201.
[10] Rev. Rul. 68-117, 1968-1 C.B. 251; Rev. Rul. 68-165, 1968-1 C.B. 253.
[11] Rev. Rul. 79-358, 1979-2 C.B. 225.
[12] Rev. Rul. 75-198, 1975-1 C.B. 157. Also Rev. Rul 77-42, 1977-1 C.B. 142.
[13] Rev. Rul. 70-585, 1970-2 C.B. 115; Rev. Rul. 68-17, 1968-1 C.B. 247; Rev. Rul. 67-250, 1967-2 C.B. 182; Rev. Rul. 67-138, 1967-1 C.B. 129.
[14] Rev. Rul. 78-428, 1978-2 C.B. 177; Rev. Rul. 72-559, 1972-2 C.B. 247; Rev. Rul. 69-161, 1969-1 C.B. 149.
[15] Rev. Rul. 69-441, 1969-2 C.B. 115.
[16] Rev. Rul. 75-385, 1975-2 C.B. 205.
[17] Rev. Rul. 76-244, 1976-1 C.B. 155.
[18] Rev. Rul. 77-246, 1977-2 C.B. 190.

needy, such as prisoners requiring rehabilitation,[19] the elderly requiring specially designed housing,[20] the physically handicapped requiring specially designed housing,[21] hospital patients needing the visitation and comfort provided by their relatives and friends,[22] and widow(er)s and orphans of police officers and firefighters killed in the line of duty.[23] Similarly, exemption on this basis was accorded to an organization that posted bail for individuals who were otherwise incapable of paying for bail, as part of its integrated program for their release and rehabilitation;[24] to a legal aid society that provided free legal services and funds to pay fees of commercial bondsmen for indigent persons who were otherwise financially unable to obtain these services,[25] and to an organization that provided rescue and emergency services to persons suffering because of a disaster.[26] Under appropriate circumstances,[27] an organization can qualify as a charitable one where the impoverished being assisted are in countries other than the United States.[28]

As noted, the provision of low-income housing can be a charitable purpose.[29] The IRS held that an organization formed to develop a program to provide housing not otherwise affordable to low-income families is a form of relief to the poor and thus is a charitable activity.[30] Providing affordable housing to persons who are not poor or otherwise members of a charitable class is not a charitable undertaking; thus, the IRS ruled that a nonprofit housing organization created to aid moderate-income families did not qualify for tax exemption because its program is not designed to carry out a charitable purpose.[31] Nevertheless, inclusion of some individuals who are not poor and distressed or underprivileged in a housing project for the poor may indirectly advance charitable purposes by providing some degree of stability, resource, and role model function. The IRS developed safe-harbor guidelines for determining whether organizations that provide low-income housing will be considered charitable entities on the ground that they relieve the poor and distressed, as well as a facts-and-circumstances test for these organizations that are outside the safe harbor.[32] In general, the organization must demonstrate, for each project, that at least 75 percent of the units are occupied by low-income residents; either at least 20 percent of the units are occupied by residents that also meet a very-low-income limit for the area or 40 percent of the units are occupied by

---

[19] Rev. Rul. 70-583, 1970-2 C.B. 114; Rev. Rul 67-150, 1967-1 C.B. 133.

[20] Rev. Rul. 79-18, 1979-1 C.B. 194.

[21] Rev. Rul. 79-19, 1979-1 C.B. 195.

[22] Rev. Rul. 81-28, 1981-1 C.B. 328.

[23] Rev. Rul. 55-406, 1955-1 C.B. 73.

[24] Rev. Rul. 76-21, 1976-1 C.B. 147.

[25] Rev. Rul. 76-22, 1976-1 C.B. 148. Also Rev. Rul. 69-161, *supra* note 14.

[26] Rev. Rul. 69-174, 1969-1 C.B. 149. Cf. Rev. Rul. 77-3, 1977-1 C.B. 140.

[27] See § 30.2(d).

[28] E.g., Rev. Rul. 68-165, *supra* note 10, Rev. Rul. 68-117, *supra* note 10.

[29] See *supra* note 13.

[30] Rev. Rul. 70-585, *supra* note 13, Situation 1.

[31] *Id.* , Situation 4.

[32] Rev. Proc. 96-32, 1996-1 C.B. 717, superseding guidelines issued in 1993 (Notice 93-1, 1993-1 C.B. 290).

residents that also do not exceed 120 percent of the area's very-low-income limit; up to 25 percent of the units may be provided at market rates to individuals who have incomes in excess of the low-income limit; the project is actually occupied by poor and distressed residents; the housing is affordable to the charitable beneficiaries; and, if the project consists of multiple buildings, they share the same grounds.[33]

This view of the meaning of *charity* was dramatically illustrated in the litigation that followed the pronouncement by the IRS in 1969 of new criteria for defining a charitable hospital.[34] In that year, the IRS issued a ruling that the promotion of health was itself a charitable purpose as long as the requisite charitable class was present; specifically, the ruling enables a hospital to qualify for exemption where it provides emergency room services to all individuals requiring health care irrespective of their ability to pay.[35] A lawsuit ensued, with a federal district court holding that a hospital, to be exempt, must significantly serve the poor for a reduced or forgone charge. The court concluded that "Congress and the judiciary have consistently insisted that the application of sections 501 and 170 to hospitals be conditioned upon a demonstration that ameliorative consideration be given poor people in need of hospitalization."[36] To find otherwise, said the court, would be "to disregard what has been held to be the underlying rationale for allowing charitable deductions."[37] On appeal, however, this construction of the term *charitable* was reversed. Upon finding that the law of charitable trusts has promotion of health as a charitable purpose and noting the IRS citation of the appropriate authority, the appeals court held that the term *charitable* is "capable of a definition far broader than merely relief of the poor."[38] After reviewing the changes in the financing of health care in the United States over past decades (including the advent of Medicare and Medicaid), the court found that the rationale by which hospitals' charitable status is confined to the extent they provide for the poor "has largely disappeared."[39] Indeed, the court noted, "[t]oday, hospitals are the primary community health facility for both rich and poor."[40]

On occasion, a view is expressed that assistance to the poor is the only basis on which an organization can achieve tax-exempt status as a charity under the federal tax law. However, there is no requirement, in the federal statutory law or in the tax regulations, that an organization must provide services only to

---

[33] An organization that is engaged in housing activities but cannot qualify for exemption on the basis of relieving the poor and distressed may nonetheless be exempt because it combats community deterioration (see *infra* § 6) or lessens a burden of government (see *infra* § 3) (e.g., IRS Priv. Ltr. Rul. 9731038). In general, Wexler, "IRS Proposes Useful New Safe Harbor for Nonprofits That Provide Low-Income Housing," 83 *J. Tax.* (No. 2) 100 (Aug. 1995); Roady, "New Guideline Sets Standards for Low-Income Housing Organizations," 6 *J. Tax. Exempt Orgs.* (No. 3) 99 (Nov./Dec. 1994); Harlan, "Housing for the Elderly: Federal Income Tax Concerns," 5 *Exempt Org. Tax Rev.* (No. 1) 39 (1992).

[34] See *infra* § 2.

[35] Rev. Rul. 69-545, 1969-2 C.B. 117.

[36] Eastern Ky. Welfare Rights Org. v. Shultz, 370 F. Supp. 325, 332 (D.D.C. 1973).

[37] *Id*. at 333.

[38] Eastern Ky. Welfare Rights Org. v. Simon, 506 F.2d 1278, 1287 (D.C. Cir. 1974).

[39] *Id*. at 1288.

[40] *Id*. The *Eastern Kentucky* case was heard by the U.S. Supreme Court, which did not address the merits of the case but held that the plaintiffs lacked standing to bring the action (426 U.S. 26 (1976)).

the poor and distressed or the underprivileged to qualify as a charitable organization. As one writer stated, "[i]t is a general rule in the construction of exemptions from taxation that the word 'charity' is not to be restricted to the relief of the sick or the poor, but extends to any form of philanthropic endeavor or public benefit."[41] Thus, as discussed throughout, an organization may achieve status as a charitable entity if it functions, for example, to promote health, to advance education, or to lessen the burden of a government. These are independent grounds for acquiring classification as a charitable organization and do not require proof that the organization is also operated to relieve the poor and distressed. This principle was noted by the IRS in 1975 when it observed, when considering tax exemption for public interest law firms, that these organizations are regarded as "charities because they provide a service which is of benefit to the community as a whole."[42]

Another case in point involved consumer credit counseling agencies that offer their services to the general public. That is, the definition of eligibility for assistance is not limited to a low-income classification that indicates a need for credit counseling assistance. It was the initial view of the IRS that these agencies cannot qualify as charitable organizations, because they do not confine the provision of their services to low-income individuals. The issue of the tax-exempt status of these agencies was resolved in court, where it was held that the IRS cannot condition a nonprofit organization's tax status solely on the extent to which it provides assistance to the indigent.[43] The court said that the status of consumer credit counseling agencies as charitable entities cannot be regarded by the IRS as dependent on whether they confine their assistance to low-income individuals (or provide their services without charge). These agencies were found to be entitled to classification as charitable organizations as long as they can demonstrate that they satisfy at least one of the definitions of the term *charitable* (or qualify as *educational* organizations).[44]

As noted,[45] a charitable undertaking may be present where the beneficiaries of the program are the "poor and distressed." Yet, the IRS based a finding of charitable status for an organization solely on the ground that it relieves the "distressed" irrespective of whether they are also poor. The occasion was the IRS's consideration of the tax treatment of a nonprofit hospice that operated on both inpatient and outpatient bases, to assist persons of all ages who have been advised

---

[41] Black, *A Treatise in the Law of Income Taxation* 40 (2d ed. 1950). Another commentator stated: "Although the relief of the poor, or benefit to them is, in its popular sense a necessary ingredient in the charity, this is not so in the view of the law" (Zollman, *American Law of Charity* 135–136 (1924)).

[42] Rev. Rul. 75-74, 1975-1 C.B. 152.

[43] Consumer Credit Counseling Serv. of Ala., Inc. v. United States, 78-2 U.S.T.C. ¶ 9660 (D.D.C. 1978). Also Credit Counseling Cents. of Okla., Inc. v. United States, 79-2 U.S.T.C. ¶ 9468 (D.D.C. 1979).

[44] Subsequently, the Department of Justice elected to not pursue any appeals of these cases and the IRS decided that any "further litigation of this issue would be futile" (Gen. Couns. Mem. 38881). This conclusion was also reached by the Sixth Circuit Court of Appeals in Lugo v. Miller, 640 F.2d 823 (6th Cir. 1981), *rev'g* (on the issue) Lugo v. Simon, 453 F. Supp. 677 (N.D. Ohio). It is because of this expansion of the patient base of contemporary tax-exempt health care providers that the principle that promotion of health is a separate basis for exemption (see *infra* § 2) is of such significance.

[45] See the text accompanied by *supra* note 3.

by a physician that they are terminally ill in coping with the distress arising from their condition.[46] Thus, the classification of the organization as a charitable entity was predicated on the fact that the hospice "alleviat[ed] the mental and physical distress of persons terminally ill."

Thus, it is clear that a charitable purpose is not necessarily dependent on a showing that the poor are being relieved. Functions such as promotion of social welfare, advancement of religion, and promotion of the arts are, therefore, charitable enterprises that need not involve any nexus with relief of the poor. At the same time, the belief persists in some quarters that a charitable activity must involve free or reduced-cost services to indigents, and that a charitable purpose cannot be present where "the rich, the poor and the in-between are treated alike."[47]

§ 6.2 PROMOTION OF HEALTH

The promotion of health as a charitable purpose includes the establishment or maintenance of hospitals, clinics, homes for the aged, and other providers of health care; advancement of medical and similar knowledge through research; and the maintenance of conditions conducive to health. Health, for this purpose, includes mental health and would include, were it not for a separate enumeration in the federal tax law description of charitable organizations, the prevention of cruelty to children.[48] The tax regulations defining the types of charitable entities do not contain any specific reference to the promotion of health as a charitable purpose, but this aspect of charitable activity has been reaffirmed by the courts and the IRS on several occasions.[49]

(a) Hospitals

The most common example of an organization established and operated for the promotion of health is a hospital.[50] To qualify for exemption as a charitable organization, however, a hospital must demonstrate that it serves a public rather than a private interest.[51] The Supreme Court observed that "[n]onprofit hospitals have never received these benefits [tax exemption and eligibility to receive deductible contributions] as a favored general category, but an individual nonprofit hospital has been able to claim them if it could qualify" as a charitable en-

---

[46] Rev. Rul. 79-17, 1979-1 C.B. 193. A similar discussion, concerning similar forms of distress facing the elderly, appears in the IRS ruling concerning homes for the aged (see *infra* § 6.2(d)). Also Rev. Rul. 79-19, *supra* note 21, which discussed the distress confronting the physically disabled.

[47] Child v. United States, 540 F.2d 579, 582 (2d Cir. 1976); Bank of Carthage v. United States, 304 F. Supp. 77, 80 (W.D. Mo. 1969).

[48] *Restatement of Trusts* (2d ed. 1959) § 372, cmt. b.

[49] E.g., Rev. Rul. 69-545, *supra* note 35, also *Restatement of Trusts* (2d ed. 1959) §§ 368, 372 (1959); IV *Scott on Trusts* (3d ed. 1967) §§ 368, 372. Yet, despite this clarity, a federal court of appeals in 1993 seemed to adhere to the IRS view in a case that the law "require[s] more than mere promotion of health in order to qualify for tax exemption" (Geisinger Health Plan v. Comm'r, 985 F.2d 1210, 1216 (3d Cir. 1993)).

[50] IRC § 170(b)(1)(A)(iii); Bogert, *Trusts and Trustees* (rev. 2d ed. 1977) § 374.

[51] Reg. § 1.501(c)(3)-1(d)(1)(ii); *Restatement of Trusts* (2d ed. 1959) § 372, cmt. b.

tity.[52] The Court added: "As the Code does not define the term *charitable*, the status of each nonprofit hospital is determined on a case-by-case basis by the IRS."[53]

The initial position of the IRS in this regard was published in 1956, in which the IRS set forth requirements for tax exemption, including a rule requiring patient care without charge or at below cost.[54] At that time, the IRS stated that a hospital, to be charitable, "must be operated to the extent of its financial ability for those not able to pay for the services rendered and not exclusively for those who are able and expected to pay."[55] This approach (the *charity care* standard) was a reflection of the charitable hospital as it once was—a health care provider emphasizing care more for the poor than for the sick.

Today's tax-exempt hospital provides health services for the entire community, with a commensurate increase in patient care revenue (especially in relation to private contributions) and health care costs. Prepayment plans cover hospital expenses for much of the citizenry, and reimbursement programs under Medicare and Medicaid have reduced the number of patients who lack an ability to "pay" for health care services. Because of these changes in society, in 1969, the IRS modified its 1956 position by recognizing that the promotion of health is inherently a charitable purpose and is not obviated by the fact that the cost of services is borne by patients or third-party payors.[56] Under the 1969 ruling, to be exempt, a hospital must promote the health of a class broad enough to benefit the community and must be operated to serve a public rather than a private interest. (This is the *community benefit* standard.) In practical terms, this means that the emergency room must be open to all and that hospital care is provided to all who can pay, directly or indirectly. The hospital may generate a surplus of receipts over disbursements and nonetheless be exempt. The requirement that health care must be provided free or at reduced costs was abandoned.

---

[52] Simon v. Eastern Ky. Welfare Rights Org., *supra* note 34 at 29.

[53] *Id.* at 29 (emphasis in original). In general, Schaffer & Fox, "Tax Administration as Health Policy: The Tax Exemption of Hospitals, 1969–1990," 4 *Exempt Org. Tax Rev.* (No. 9) 1185 (1991); Simpson & Strum, "How Good a Samaritan? Federal Income Tax Exemption for Charitable Hospitals Reconsidered," 4 *Exempt Org. Tax Rev.* (No. 8) 1084 (1991); Peregrine & McNulty, "Emerging Standards: The Impact of Medicare Law on Hospital Tax-Exempt Status," 4 *Exempt Org. Tax Rev.* (No. 7) 941 (1991). Also Comment, "Income Taxation—A Pauper a Day Keeps the Taxman Away: Qualification of Hospitals as Charitable Institutions under Section 501(c)(3)," 54 *N.C. L. Rev.* 1195 (1976); Note, "Federal Income Tax Exemptions for Private Hospitals," 36 *Fordham L. Rev.* 747 (1968). Cf. Congdon, "With Charity for All: Did the I.R.S. Comply With the Administrative Procedure Act in Changing the Requirements for Charitable Exemptions of Hospitals?," 1 *ISL L. Rev.* (No. 1) 41 (1976); Barker, "Re-Examining the 501(c)(3) Exemption of Hospitals as Charitable Organizations," 3 *Exempt Org. Tax. Rev.* (No. 5) 539 (1990).

The various types of nonprofit health care entities that qualify for tax-exempt status are discussed more fully in Hyatt & Hopkins, *The Law of Tax-Exempt Healthcare Organizations* (New York: John Wiley & Sons, Inc., 1995), particularly Chapters 8–13.

[54] Rev. Rul. 56-185, 1956-1 C.B. 202.

[55] *Id.* at 203.

[56] Rev. Rul. 69-545, *supra* note 35. Also *Restatement of Trusts* (2d ed. 1959) § 372, cmt. b. This ruling was upheld in Eastern Ky. Welfare Rights Org. v. Simon, *supra* note 38. Also Recent Decision, 9 *Ga. L. Rev.* 729 (1975).

Other factors that may indicate that a hospital is operating for the benefit of the public include control of the institution in a board of trustees composed of individuals who do not have any direct economic interest in the hospital; maintenance by the hospital of an open medical staff, with privileges available to all qualified physicians, consistent with the size and nature of the facilities; a hospital policy enabling any member of the medical staff to rent available office space; hospital programs of medical training, research, and education; and involvement by the hospital in various projects and programs to improve the health of the community.[57] These and similar factors are of particular help in the qualification for tax exemption of hospitals that do not operate an emergency room, either because other institutions provide emergency care sufficient to the size of the served community or because the hospital is a specialized institution (e.g., an eye hospital or cancer center) that offers medical care under conditions unlikely to necessitate emergency care.[58]

For tax purposes, the term *hospital* includes federal government hospitals, state, county, and municipal hospitals that are instrumentalities of governmental units, rehabilitation institutions, outpatient clinics, extended care facilities, or community mental health or drug treatment centers, and cooperative hospital service organizations,[59] if they otherwise qualify. However, the term does not include convalescent homes, homes for children or the aged, or institutions the principal purpose or function of which is to train handicapped individuals to pursue a vocation,[60] nor does it include free clinics for animals.[61]

The term *medical care* includes the treatment of any physical or mental disability or condition, whether on an inpatient or outpatient basis, as long as the cost of the treatment is eligible for deductibility[62] by the person treated.[63]

The state of the law of tax-exempt organizations today regarding tax-exempt charitable hospitals is nearly overshadowed by the emergence, to a far greater extent than ever before, of the for-profit hospital. The principal reason for this is the acquisition of charitable health care institutions by for-profit (investor-owned) chains of proprietary health care providers. Another reason is the advent of the large hospital systems or networks, involving many institutions and organizations (often a mix of for-profit and nonprofit entities). These facts, accompanied by the greater reliance by hospitals on patient fees rather than charitable gifts and the change in the demographics of patients, have convinced some that there is now no material difference between nonprofit and for-profit hospitals.[64] Although as a matter of law, there remains a fundamental

---

[57] IRS Exempt Organizations Handbook (IRM 7751) § 343.5(2).

[58] Rev. Rul. 83-157, 1983-2 C.B. 94.

[59] As to the latter, see § 10.4. Cf. Rev. Rul. 76-452, 1976-2 C.B. 60.

[60] Reg. § 1.170A-9(c)(1).

[61] Rev. Rul. 74-572, 1974-2 C.B. 82.

[62] IRC § 213.

[63] Reg. § 1.170A-9(c)(1).

[64] One of the most well-known court opinions reflecting this viewpoint lamented the "gradual disappearance of the traditional charitable hospital for the poor" and concluded that it has been replaced by a "medical-industrial complex" (County Board of Utilization of Utah County v. Intermountain Health Care, Inc., 709 P.2d 265, 270, 271 (Utah 1985)). This court wrote that "[i]t is precisely because such a vast system of third-party payers has developed to meet the expense of modern hospital care

difference between the two types of entities,[65] this superficial likeness between the two types of hospitals is bringing calls for abandonment of the *community benefit* standard and a return to some form of a *charity care* standard.[66]

(b) Hospital Clinical Departments

Application of the concept that the term *charitable* embraces the function of promoting health continues to trouble the IRS as the courts persist in allowing various forms of the practice of medicine (generally, a for-profit endeavor) to lodge

---

that the historical distinction between for-profit and nonprofit hospitals has eroded" (*id.* at 274). The court noted that, in its view, the primary care services of both types of hospitals are largely the same, the rates are similar, both types accumulate capital, and both types have comparable operations; the nonprofit hospital was criticized for using its "profits" to acquire "capital improvements and new, updated equipment" (*id.* at 275). Also Hospital Utilization Project v. Commonwealth, 487 A.2d 1306 (Sup. Ct. Pa. 1985)).

[65] See § 6.2(a).

[66] The overlap of charitable health care activities and the private practice of medicine was illustrated by the IRS's approval of the transfer of components of a physicians' group's medical practice to an exempt charitable organization (Priv. Ltr. Rul. 9710030).

An organization will not fail to be treated as organized and operated exclusively for a charitable purpose solely because a hospital, which is owned and operated by it, participates in a provider-sponsored organization (as defined in § 1853(e) of the Social Security Act), irrespective of whether the provider-sponsored organization is tax-exempt (IRC § 501(o)). For purposes of private inurement (see Chapter 19), a person with a material financial interest in one of these provider-sponsored organizations is regarded as an insider with respect to the hospital (*id.*). In general, Copeland, "Nonprofit Versus For-Profit Hospitals," 18 *Exempt Org. Tax Rev.* (No. 1) 35 (1997); Columbo, "Health Care Reform and Federal Tax Exemption: Rethinking the Issues," 10 *Exempt Org. Tax Rev.* (No. 2) 335 (1994); Gourevitch, "CRS Report: Tax Aspects of Health Care Reform: The Tax Treatment of Health Care Providers," 9 *Exempt Org. Tax Rev.* (No. 6) 1317 (1994); Flynn, "Hospital Charity Care Standards: Reexamining the Grounds for Exempt Status," 3 *J. Tax. Exempt Orgs.* 13 (Winter 1992); Bove, "When Should a Hospital Be Treated as a Charity?," 3 *J. Tax. Exempt Orgs.* 10 (Spring 1991); Sullivan, "Tax Issues in the Delivery of Health Care (Part 1)," 15 *ALI-ABA Course Materials J.* (No. 4) 65 (1991); Sullivan & Moore, "A Critical Look at Recent Developments in Tax-Exempt Hospitals," 23 *J. Health & Hosp. Law* (No. 3) 65 (1990); Copeland & Rudney, "Federal Tax Subsidies for Not-for-Profit Hospitals," 46 *Tax Notes* (No. 13) 1559 (1990); Barker, "Reexamining the 501(c)(3) Exemption of Hospitals as Charitable Organizations," 48 *Tax Notes* (No. 3) 339 (1990); Hall, "The Charitable Status of Nonprofit Hospitals: Toward a Donative Theory of Tax Exemption," 66 *Wash. L. Rev.* 307 (Apr. 1991); Simpson & Strum, "How Good a Samaritan? Federal Income Tax Exemption for Charitable Hospitals Reconsidered," 14 *U. Puget Sound L. Rev.* 633 (Spring 1991); Note, "Nonprofit Hospitals and the State Tax Exemption: An Analysis of the Issues Since *Utah County v. Intermountain Healthcare, Inc.* ," 9 *Va. Tax Rev.* (No. 3) 599 (Winter 1990); Roska, "Nonprofit Hospitals: The Relationship Between Charitable Tax Exemptions and Medical Care for Indigents," 43 *Sw. L. J.* (No. 2) 759 (1989); Milligan, Jr., "Provision of Uncompensated Care in American Hospitals: The Role of the Tax Code, the Federal Courts, Catholic Health Care Facilities, and Local Governments in Defining the Problem of Access for the Poor," 31 *Cath. Law.* (No. 1) 7 (1987); McGovern, "Restructured Nonprofit Hospitals," 33 *Tax Notes* (No. 4) 405 (1987); McCoy, "Health Care and the Tax Law: Reorganizations, Structural Changes, and Other Contemporary Problems of Tax-Exempt Hospitals," 44. *N.Y.U. Inst. on Fed. Tax.* 58-1 (1986); Hopkins & Beckwith, "The Federal Tax Law of Hospitals: Basic Principles and Current Developments," 24 *Duq. L. Rev.* (No. 2) 691 (Winter 1985); Richeda, "Comment—Hospitals, Tax Exemption, and the Poor," 10 *Harv. Civil Rights-Civil Liberties L. Rev.* 653 (1975); Dwyer, "Income Tax—Section 501(c)(3)—Qualification of Hospitals for Tax Exempt Status as Charitable Organizations," 7 *U. Tol. L. Rev.* 278 (1975); Bromberg, "The Charitable Hospital," 20 *Cath. U. L. Rev.* 237 (1970); Rose, "The IRS Contribution to the Health Problems of the Poor," 21 *Cath. U. L. Rev.* 35 (1971).

within its ambit. Of course, the practice of medicine occurs in hospitals but, as noted, the law has rationalized the classification of most nonprofit hospitals as charitable. Thereafter, also as noted, charitable entities have been determined to include a variety of clinics, centers, research agencies, plans, and health maintenance organizations. The IRS has been confronted with another type of noncommercial health provider: the incorporation of clinical departments of teaching hospitals associated with medical schools.

In one instance, at issue was the tax-exempt status of a professional corporation, all of the stockholders (who were also its employees) of which were physicians on the clinical staff of a teaching hospital operated by a state university and full-time members of the faculty of the university's school of medicine. The corporation consisted of four departments of the medical school and, in addition to the provision of medical care, was empowered to provide academic and clinical instruction of medical students, medical research, and ancillary administrative services solely for the benefit of the medical school and the teaching hospital. The financial support of the organization was derived from the receipt of fees for medical care performed by its employees at the teaching hospital; approximately 25 percent of the billable value of the services performed by the employees was rendered to patients who were unable to pay and were not required to pay for the services.

Rejecting the position of the IRS, a court found that the corporation was organized and operated for charitable, educational, and scientific purposes, in that it, in part, "delivers health care to the general public."[67] The fact that the organization was authorized to engage in the general practice of medicine did not deter the court, in that the organization's activities were limited to serving the interests of the medical school and hospital involved; thus, it was not authorized to practice medicine for profit. The court also excused the form of the professional corporation, rationalizing it as necessary because that is the only corporate entity permitted to practice medicine in the state. Further, the court tolerated the existence of stockholders and dismissed the fact that each shareholder was entitled to receive the par value of his or her single share ($1.00) in the event of dissolution as being insubstantial and thus not a violation of the rule requiring dedication of assets for a charitable purpose.[68]

Consequently, on the basis of this and prior court decisions,[69] it appears that this type of corporate collective of physicians is tax-exempt, even though it generates fees for the performance of medical care services and pays the resulting earnings to individuals who are its stockholders. In these instances, of course, it is the

---

[67] University of Md. Physicians, P.A. v. Comm'r, 41 T.C.M. 732, 735 (1981). Other exempt activities were held to be the rendering of services without charge to the indigent (§ 1 hereof), provision of clinical training to the students, interns, and residents of the medical school (§ 3 hereof; Chapter 8 § 2), and medical research for the advancement of the healing arts (§ 3 hereof; Chapter 10).
[68] See Chapter 6 § 1.
[69] University of Mass. Medical School Group Practice v. Comm'r, 74 T.C. 1299 (1980); B.H.W. Anesthesia Found. v. Comm'r, 72 T.C. 681 (1979). In general, Columbo, "Are Associations of Doctors Tax-Exempt? Analyzing Inconsistencies in the Tax-Exemption of Health Care Providers," 9 *Va. Tax Rev.* (No. 3) 469 (1990).

close nexus with a medical school and teaching hospital that provides the under-lying basis for the tax exemption.[70]

Occasionally, the IRS will rule that an organization is a charitable entity because it is carrying out an integral part of the activities of another charitable organization.[71] The IRS used this rationale to find that a trust created by a tax-exempt hospital to accumulate and hold funds for the settlement of malprac-tice claims against the hospital, and from which the hospital directs the trustee to make payments to claimants, is a charitable organization for federal tax pur-poses.[72]

(c) Medical Research Organizations

Charitable organizations that promote health include certain *medical research organizations* that are "directly engaged in the continuous active conduct of medical research in conjunction with a hospital."[73] The term *medical research* means the conduct of investigations, experiments, and studies to discover, de-velop, or verify knowledge relating to the causes, diagnosis, treatment, pre-vention, or control of physical or mental diseases and impairments of man. To qualify, the organization must have the appropriate equipment and profes-sional personnel necessary to carry out its principal function.[74] Medical re-search encompasses the associated disciplines spanning the biological, social, and behavioral sciences.

This type of organization must have the conduct of medical research as its principal purpose or function[75] and be primarily engaged in the continuous ac-tive conduct of medical research in conjunction with a hospital, which itself is a public charity. The organization need not be formally affiliated with a hospital to be considered primarily engaged in the active conduct of medical research in conjunction with a hospital. However, there must be a joint effort on the part of the research organization and the hospital pursuant to an understanding that the two organizations will maintain continuing close cooperation in the active conduct of medical research.[76] An organization will not be considered to be "primarily engaged directly in the continuous active conduct of medical re-search" unless it, during the applicable computation period,[77] devoted more than one half of its assets to the continuous active conduct of medical research or it expended funds equaling at least 3.5 percent of the fair market value of its endowment for the continuous active conduct of medical research.[78] If the orga-nization's primary purpose is to disburse funds to other organizations for the conduct of research by them or to extend research grants or scholarships to oth-

---

[70] E.g., Priv. Ltr. Rul. 9434041, superseded by Priv. Ltr. Rul. 9442025.
[71] Rev. Rul. 75-282, 1975-2 C.B. 201.
[72] Rev. Rul. 78-41, 1978-1 C.B. 148.
[73] IRC § 170(b)(1)(A)(iii).
[74] Reg. § 1.170A-9(c)(2)(iii).
[75] Reg. § 1.170A-9(c)(2)(iv).
[76] Reg. § 1.170A-9(c)(2)(vii).
[77] Reg. § 1.170A-9(c)(2)(vi)(a).
[78] Reg. § 1.170A-9(c)(2)(v)(b).

ers, it is not considered directly engaged in the active conduct of medical research.[79]

(d) Homes for the Aged

Another well-recognized health care provider is the home for the aged. Until 1972, the chief basis for tax exemption of a home for the aged as a charitable entity was that free or below-cost services must be provided, in conformance with the early IRS view of hospitals.[80] This approach was abandoned in that year and replaced with a requirement that the charitable home for the aged be operated so as to satisfy the primary needs of the aged: housing, health care, and financial security.[81] The need for housing is generally satisfied if the home "provides residential facilities that are specifically designed to meet some combination of the physical, emotional, recreational, social, religious, and similar needs" of the aged. As for health care, that need is generally satisfied where the home "either directly provides some form of health care, or in the alternative, maintains some continuing arrangement with other organizations, facilities, or health personnel, designed to maintain the physical, and if necessary, mental well-being of its residents." Satisfaction of the financial security need has two aspects: The home must (1) maintain in the residence "any persons who become unable to pay their regular charges" and (2) provide its services "at the lowest feasible cost." A home for the aged will qualify for tax-exempt status as a charitable organization, assuming it otherwise qualifies, if it operates in a manner designed to meet these primary needs of the aged. However, a home for the aged may, in the alternative, qualify under prior IRS rulings for tax-exempt status, if the home is primarily concerned with providing care and housing for financially distressed aged persons.[82]

(e) Health Maintenance Organizations

One of the most controversial of the health provider institutions—from the standpoint of federal tax categorization—is the health maintenance organization (HMO).[83] The HMO provides health care services by means of facilities and pro-

---

[79] Reg. § 1.170A-9(c)(2)(v)(c). For purposes of the charitable contribution deduction, the organization must be committed, during the calendar year in which the contribution is made, to expend the contribution for medical research before January 1 of the fifth calendar year that begins after the date the contribution is made (Reg. § 1.170A-9(c)(2)(ii), 1.170A-9(c)(2)(viii)).

[80] Rev. Rul. 56-185, *supra* note 54. Also Rev. Rul. 57-467, 1957-2 C.B. 313.

[81] Rev. Rul. 72-124, 1972-1 C.B. 145. Also Rev. Rul. 75-198, 1975-1 C.B. 157.

[82] Rev. Rul. 64-231, 1964-2 C.B. 139; Rev. Rul. 61-72, 1961-1 C.B. 188. In general, Note, "The Property Tax Exemption and Non-Profit Homes for the Aged," 53 *Marq. L. Rev.* 140 (Spring 1970); Bromberg, "Non-Profit Homes for the Aged: An Analysis of Their Current Tax Exempt Status," 38 *J. Tax.* 54, 120 (1973); Bromberg, "Tax Exemption of Homes for the Aged," 46 *Taxes* 68 (1968).

[83] HMOs are authorized under federal law pursuant to Title XIII of the Public Health Service Act, 42 U.S.C. § 300e.

grams, in a manner comparable to that of a tax-exempt hospital. It is a membership organization; its services are provided to members on a prepaid basis and to nonmembers on a fee-for-service basis. In most instances, the HMO handles emergency cases without regard to whether the patient is a member and annually provides care either free or at reduced rates to a limited number of indigent patients. Frequently, HMOs sponsor education programs and research efforts to study ways to deliver better health care services. The HMO governing board is usually elected by and from its membership.

The position of the IRS originally was that an HMO may qualify for tax exemption as a social welfare organization[84] but cannot qualify for exemption as a charitable organization, because the preferential treatment accorded its member-subscribers constitutes the serving of private interests and because the prepayment feature constitutes a form of insurance that is not a charitable activity. However, this position was rejected in court, in connection with the one model of an HMO, where it was held that (1) the persons benefited by an HMO represent a class large enough to constitute a requisite community,[85] (2) the HMO meets all of the IRS criteria applied to determine charitable status for nonprofit hospitals,[86] and (3) while the risk of illness is spread throughout its entire membership, the HMO does operate not for commercial purposes but for charitable purposes, and thus the risk-spreading feature[87] is not a bar to designation of an HMO as a charitable organization.[88]

Following the issuance of this court opinion, the IRS relented somewhat, agreeing in 1981 that where an HMO possesses certain characteristics, it qualifies as a charitable entity.[89] Essentially, an HMO will qualify for charitable status, in the eyes of the IRS, when it operates primarily to benefit the community, rather than private interests. Nearly a decade later, however, the IRS determined that certain HMOs cannot qualify as charitable organizations, because they are not operating for the benefit of the community. A 1990 IRS pronouncement distilled the key factors that, in the view of the IRS, differentiate an exempt HMO from a nonexempt HMO.[90] These factors include the following: actual provision of services to nonmembers on a fee-for-service basis; care and reduced rates for the indigent; care for those covered by Medicare, Medicaid, or similar assistance programs; emergency room facilities available to the community without regard to ability to pay (and communication of this fact to the community); a meaningful subsidized membership program; a board of directors broadly representative of the community; health education programs open to the community; health research programs; health care providers who are paid on a fixed fee basis; and the

---

[84] See, in general, Chapter 12.

[85] See § 5.5(b). The court, in dismissing the IRS's private inurement rationale, held that the concept of private inurement is limited to situations where an organization's *insiders* are benefited. See § 19.3.

[86] Rev. Rul. 69-545, *supra* note 35.

[87] The IRS ruled that prepaid group practice plans are not insurance companies for federal tax law purposes (IRC Subchapter L) (Rev. Rul. 68-27, 1968-1 C.B. 315).

[88] Sound Health Ass'n v. Comm'r, 71 T.C. 158 (1978).

[89] Gen. Couns. Mem. 38735.

[90] Gen. Couns. Mem. 39828.

application of any surplus to improving facilities, equipment, patient care, or to any of the above programs.

This 1990 pronouncement by the IRS stated additional factors that must be considered where the HMO is a membership organization. The relevant factors in this determination include the following: a membership composed of both groups and individuals, where the individuals compose a substantial portion of the membership; an overt program to attract individuals to become members; a community rating system that provides uniform rates for prepaid care; similar rates charged to individuals and groups (with a possible modest initiation fee for individuals); and no substantive age or health barriers to eligibility for either individuals or groups.

The two plans that are the subject of this 1990 IRS pronouncement were found to not qualify as charitable organizations, because there are "substantial discrepancies" between their operations and the operations of the tax-exempt HMO described in the 1981 IRS pronouncement and the 1978 court opinion. The disqualifying features of the HMOs concerned included denial of health care services to nonmembers; failure to make emergency care available to the community; a non-comprehensive, cost-based scope of care; absence of need-based cost reduction or a subsidized dues program; absence of health education or research programs; and failure to show an "overt attempt" to increase membership.[91]

A federal court of appeals held that a nonprovider HMO does not qualify as a tax-exempt charitable organization.[92] The government won this case by distinguishing the facts from those in the prior litigation.[93] In the previous case, the HMO provided health care services itself, rather than arranging for others to provide that care. It employed physicians and other health care providers who were not affiliated with the HMO to provide health care services. It provided services to both subscribers and members of the general public through an outpatient clinic that it operated and through which it treated emergency patients, subscribers or not, regardless of ability to pay. It adjusted rates for and provided some free care to patients who were not subscribers. It offered public educational programs regarding health.

The court in that litigation concluded that, as noted, the criteria to be applied in this context are those that are used to determine the tax-exempt status of non-profit hospitals. It thus applied the community benefit standard to find that the HMO in that case was tax-exempt. The appellate court in the subsequent case agreed that the community benefit standard could be used. However, it went on to find that the HMO did not provide any health care services itself, it did not ensure that people who are not its subscribers have access to health care or information about health care, it did not conduct research, and it did not offer educational

---

[91] In general, Neal & Papiewski, "Taxation of HMOs Now and Under Health Care Reform—Separating Fact From Fiction," 9 *Exempt Org. Tax Rev.* (No. 3) 577 (1994).

[92] Geisinger Health Plan v. Comm'r, *supra* note 49 *rev'g* 62 T.C.M. 1656 (1991).

[93] Sound Health Ass'n v. Comm'r, *supra* note 88.

programs open to the public. In short, wrote the court, "it benefits no one but its subscribers."[94]

(f) Integrated Delivery Systems

Another of the organizations eligible for tax exemption as charitable organizations because they promote health is the *integrated delivery system* (IDS). Private determination letters (from the National Office of the IRS), recognizing the tax-exempt and public charity status of these entities, first appeared in early 1993.[95]

An IDS is a health care provider (or a component entity of an affiliated network of providers) created to integrate the provision of hospital services with medical services provided by physicians. Previously, these services were provided (and paid for, by patients, their insurers, or government programs) separately; the hospital provided its services and facilities (such as diagnostic services, surgery, nursing, emergency care, room, and board), while physicians provided medical services to patients by means of private medical practices, admitting and treating patients in hospital facilities. In an IDS, an entity provides and bills for both hospital and physician services, either itself or by contract with another organization.

There are several models of an IDS. In one, a charitable organization obtains (by purchase, lease, license, stock transfer, or contribution) all of the assets needed to operate one or more hospitals, clinics, and physician offices. (There is concern on this point about the potential for forms of private inurement or private benefit (see below), particularly in connection with leasing and licensing arrangements; the IRS prefers arrangements where the system's assets are purchased (for fair market value) and the IDS clearly controls them.) It acquires the services of physicians, through direct employment or independent contract (the latter known as a professional services agreement). The organization is the provider of health care services—hospital and medical, inpatient and outpatient. It enters into all payer contracts, provides all nonprofessional personnel for the system, maintains all assets, and collects all rev-

---

[94] Geisinger Health Plan v. Comm'r, *supra* note 49, at 1219. This opinion contains some odd statements. The court seemed to endorse this view: "The IRS argues that the relevant precedents require at least some 'indicia of charity' in the form of serving the public and providing some services free of charge" (*id.*); that is not the law (see § 26.2(c). Another is that this organization could not be charitable because it does not provide health care services itself—it "simply arrang[es] for others to provide them" (*id.* , 1217; this is not the law—if it were, PROs and HSAs (see infra §§ (g), (h)) could not qualify for tax exemption).

The appellate court remanded the case for a decision as to whether the HMO could be tax-exempt because it is an integral part of a health care system. However, that approach also failed (see § 23.7(a), text accompanied by notes 188-192).

In general, Rasman, "Third Circuit's "Boost' Test Denies Section 501(c)(3) Status to HMO," 6 *J. Tax. Exempt Orgs.* (No. 4) 147 (Jan./Feb. 1995); Gerhart & Rasman, "HMO Denied Section 501(c)(3) Status by Third Circuit," 4 *J. Tax. Exempt Orgs.* (No. 6) 17 (May/June 1993).

[95] The first two of these rulings were issued to Friendly Hills HealthCare Network and Facey Medical Foundation (BNA) (*Daily Tax Report*, April 7, 1993, p. G-6).

enues for services provided. Other models have the tax-exempt IDS as a subsidiary of a hospital, hospital system, or clinic. (Another type of IDS, which is jointly controlled by a health care provider and physicians, cannot qualify for tax exemption as a charitable entity because of the ownership and control by physicians.[96])

The tax exemption for an IDS is tested against the community benefit standard. In this connection, the exempt IDS can (1) minimize or eliminate duplication of tests, procedures, and treatments, resulting in greater efficiency and reduced costs to the public, (2) provide increased accessibility to Medicare, Medicaid, and charity care patients, (3) undertake research in primary care or areas of specialization that benefit the public, and (4) conduct health education programs open to the public. The IRS expects (as it does in the hospital setting) the governing board, and most committees and subcommittees, of an IDS to be independent (that is, not controlled by the physicians) and reflective of the community. Generally, the IRS has been allowing no more than 20 percent of board members to be representative of physicians' interests, although that position is in the process of changing.[97]

(g) Peer Review Organizations

Another category of organization posing problems with regard to eligibility for tax exemption is the *utilization and quality control peer review organization* (PRO), which was given statutory authorization in 1972.[98] PROs are qualified groups of physicians that establish mandatory cost and quality controls for medical treatment rendered in hospitals and financed under Medicare and Medicaid and that monitor this care. PROs were conceived as part of a larger effort to curb the rising costs of health care, in this instance by minimizing or

---

[96] Somewhat similar to an IDS is a *medical service organization* (MSO). Typically, with the MSO structure, a hospital or affiliate, in return for a share of revenues, provides to an independent physician or group of physicians all real and personal property, support staff, and management and billing services required to manage an otherwise private medical practice. An MSO is not an IDS because there is no one entity with responsibility for providing both types of services.

The IRS ruled that hospitals may form a health care delivery system, using a supporting organization (see § 11.3(c)) as the coordinating mechanism, pursuant to a *joint operating agreement* ("JOA") (Priv. Ltr. Rul. 9651047). These hospitals ceded authority under the JOA to the governing body of the supporting organization to establish their budgets, including major expenditures, debts, contracts, managed care agreements, and capital expenditures; to direct their provision of health care services; and to monitor and audit their compliance with its directives. In addition, the governing body and its committees meet regularly to exercise overall responsibility for operational decisions involving the day-to-day and long-range strategic management decisions that have been delegated by the participating entities. The IRS concluded that this arrangement is analogous to circumstances where the hospitals are subsidiaries of the coordinating entity.

[97] In general, Jedrey, "Standards Evolve for Hospital-Affiliated Group Practice Exemption, 6 *J. Tax. Exempt Orgs.* (No. 1) 3 (July/Aug. 1994); Peregrine & Broccolo, "IRS Releases Detailed Position on Exempt Status of Integrated Delivery Systems", 8 *Exempt Org. Tax Rev.* (No. 5) 903 (Nov. 1993); Bromberg, "Tax Considerations in Forming MSOs and Clinics without Walls," 8 *Exempt Org. Tax Rev.* (No. 5) 887 (Nov. 1993).

[98] Social Security Amendments of 1972 (Pub. L. No. 603) § 249F, 86 Stat. 1429 (adding new Title XI to the Social Security Act); 42 U.S.C. § 1320c *et seq.* These organizations were formerly known as professional standards review organizations (PSROs).

eliminating unnecessary services (the services being termed *overutilization)* by assuring that payments under these governmental health care programs are made only when and to the extent that the health care services provided are medically necessary.

Congress views PROs as entities that act in the public interest, their chief purpose being to generally improve the quality of medical care in the United States and to obtain maximum value for every federal health dollar expended.[99] Assuming that the tax law requirements for charitable organizations are otherwise satisfied, this purpose would seem to clearly constitute a charitable activity: the promotion of health, lessening of the burdens of government, and promotion of social welfare. However, there may also be a private purpose being served by PROs, namely, enhancement of and establishment of confidence in the medical profession (even though much of the medical community initially was bitterly opposed to the PRO concept).

The law requires PROs to be nonprofit organizations, and they are reimbursed by the federal government for administrative costs. Members of a PRO must be licensed practitioners of medicine or osteopathy. The remaining question with respect to tax-exempt charitable status is whether a PRO functions primarily to benefit the general public or to serve the interests of the medical profession. The inclination of the IRS is to treat certain health care organizations as business leagues rather than as charitable organizations.[100] The IRS recognized that incidental benefit to physicians will not defeat exemption as a charitable organization,[101] but also made it clear that, when it concludes a profession is itself receiving substantial benefit from an organization's activities, status as a business league is the likely result.[102] Prior to the ensuing litigation, it was the position of the IRS that the public benefits flowing from physician peer review activities are overshadowed by the benefits ostensibly accorded physicians in their professional capacities, and thus that these organizations could not qualify as tax-exempt charitable entities.[103]

By contrast, the IRS has recognized a health systems agency (HSA), an organization established by federal law[104] to establish and maintain a system of health planning and resources development aimed at providing adequate health care

---

[99] The law states that the purpose of these organizations is to perform medicine and osteopathy peer reviews of the "pattern of quality of care in an area of medical practice where actual performance is measured against objective criteria which define acceptable and adequate practice" (42 U.S.C. § 1320c-1(2)). In general, Gosfield, *PSROs: The Law and the Health Consumer* (1975); Welch, "Professional Standards Review Organizations—Problems and Prospects," *New Eng. J. Med.* 289 (Aug. 1973).

[100] See Chapter 13.

[101] Rev. Rul. 73-313, 1973-2 C.B. 174.

[102] Rev. Rul. 74-553, 1974-2 C.B. 168; Rev. Rul. 73-567, 1973-2 C.B. 178; Rev. Rul. 70-641, 1970-2 C.B. 119. Cf. Kentucky Bar Found., Inc. v. Comm'r, 78 T.C. 921 (1982). This posture of the IRS may be contrasted with the fact that the medical profession instituted an (unsuccessful) action to enjoin implementation of the PSRO law and to declare the 1972 act unconstitutional (Association of Am. Physicians & Surgeons v. Weinberger, 395 F. Supp. 125 (N.D. Ill. 1975)). Cf. American Ass'n of Councils of Medical Staffs v. Mathews, 421 F. Supp. 848 (E.D. La. 1976)).

[103] Bromberg, "The Effect of Tax Policy on the Delivery and Cost of Health Care," 53 *Taxes* 452, 475–478 (1975); Somers, "PSRO: Friend or Foe?," *New Eng. J. Med.* 289 (Aug. 1973).

[104] National Health Planning and Resources Development Act of 1974, 42 U.S.C. § 300k *et seq.*

for a specified geographic area, to be a charitable organization.[105] Among the functions of the agency is the establishment of a health systems plan after appropriate consideration of the recommended national guidelines for health planning policy issued by the Department of Health and Human Services. The agency receives planning and matching grants from the federal government. Finding the basis of the designation of the agency as a charitable entity to be the promotion of health, the IRS observed that, "[b]y establishing and maintaining a system of health planning and resources development aimed at providing adequate health care, the HSA is promoting the health of the residents of the area in which it functions."[106]

Nonetheless, the adverse position of the IRS regarding PROs was rejected in court, in a case involving PRO support centers.[107] The court held that Congress's principal purpose in establishing PROs was to ensure the economical and effective delivery of health care services under Medicare and Medicaid, and that any benefits that physicians and others may derive (including reimbursement for services, limitation on tort liability, or promotion of esteem for the medical profession) have only a "tenuous, incidental, and non-substantial connection with the PSRO scheme."[108] On this latter point, the court added that the PRO support centers do not engage "in financial transactions designed to benefit the members of the organizations or the organizations themselves, activities in the nature of a patient referral service, or other potential money-making activities designed to benefit members or participants."[109]

As a sidelight of this PRO decision, the court found it "difficult to reconcile" the position of the IRS against PROs and the ruling granting classification as charitable entities to HSAs. Said the court: "The similarity between HSAs and PROs and PSRO support centers is obvious. PSROs collect and analyze data, establish regional norms and criteria of care, and coordinate activities with HSAs and other federal and state health planning entities."[110]

As the result of these two court decisions,[111] the IRS revised its position concerning physician peer review organizations and concluded that, in certain circumstances, this type of entity is a charitable organization because it "is promoting the health of the beneficiaries of governmental health care programs by preventing unnecessary hospitalization and surgery."[112] However, the IRS regards these factors as essential for exemption of a PRO as a charitable entity: (1) Membership in it is open by law to all physicians without charge; (2) it is an organization mandated by federal statute as the exclusive method of assuring appropriate quality and utilization of care provided to Medicare and Medicaid patients; (3) the composition of the board of directors of the PRO is not tied to

---

[105] Rev. Rul. 77-69, 1977-1 C.B. 143.

[106] *Id.* at 144.

[107] Virginia Professional Standards Review Found. v. Blumenthal, 466 F. Supp. 1164 (D.D.C. 1979).

[108] *Id.* at 1170.

[109] *Id.* at 1173.

[110] *Id.* at 1172. Also Professional Standards Review Org. of Queens County, Inc. v. Comm'r, 74 T.C. 240 (1980).

[111] See *supra* notes 108, 110.

[112] Rev. Rul. 81-276, 1981-2 C.B. 128.

any membership or association with any medical society; and (4) the PRO has the authority to make final decisions regarding quality and utilization of medical care for purposes of payment under the Medicare and Medicaid programs. The fact that the activities of the PRO "may indirectly further the interests of the medical profession by promoting public esteem for the medical profession, and by allowing physicians to set their own standards for the review of Medicare and Medicaid claims and thus prevent outside regulation" was dismissed as being "incidental" to the charitable benefits provided by the organization.[113]

(h) Other Health Care Organizations

There are various other types of health provider institutions that qualify as charitable organizations for federal tax purposes. These include entities such as preferred provider organizations, drug rescue centers,[114] blood banks,[115] halfway houses,[116] organizations that minister to the nonmedical needs of patients in a proprietary hospital,[117] nursing bureaus,[118] senior citizens centers,[119] organizations that provide private hospital rooms when medically necessary,[120] Christian Science medical care facilities,[121] and medical research organizations.[122] Moreover, tax-exempt status has been accorded several types of organizations providing specialized health care services. Thus, for example, the home health agency, an organization that provides low-cost health care to patients in their homes, is a charitable entity.[123] Similarly, an organization created to attract a physician to a medically underserved community by providing a medical building and facilities was ruled to be tax-exempt, notwithstanding the fact that the physician would generally charge for services provided and receive some personal benefit (use of building) under the arrangement.[124] Also, an organization was determined to be furthering the charitable purpose of promoting the health of the community where it built and leased a public hospital and related facilities to an exempt charitable association that operated the facilities for an amount sufficient only to retire indebtedness and meet necessary operating expenses.[125] Likewise, organizations

---

[113] *Id.* at 129.

[114] Rev. Rul. 70-590, 1970-2 C.B. 116.

[115] Rev. Rul. 66-323, 1966-2 C.B. 216, as modified by Rev. Rul. 78-145, 1978-1 C.B. 169.

[116] Rev. Rul. 72-16, 1972-1 C.B. 143. Also Rev. Rul. 75-472, 1975-2 C.B. 208.

[117] Rev. Rul. 68-73, 1968-1 C.B. 251.

[118] Rev. Rul. 55-656, 1955-2 C.B. 262.

[119] Rev. Rul. 75-198, *supra* note 81.

[120] Rev. Rul. 79-358, *supra* note 11.

[121] Rev. Rul. 80-114, 1980-1 C.B. 115, superseding Rev. Rul. 78-427, 1978-2 C.B. 176. This determination is consistent with the IRS's position that payments to Christian Science practitioners for services rendered are deductible medical expenses (Rev. Rul. 55-261, 1955-1 C.B. 307).

[122] IRC § 170(b)(1)(A)(iii).

[123] Rev. Rul. 72-209, 1972-1 C.B. 148.

[124] Rev. Rul. 73-313, *supra* note 101; also In re Carlson's Estate, 358 P.2d 669 (Kan. 1961); cf. Rev. Rul. 69-266, 1969-2 C.B. 151.

[125] Rev. Rul. 80-309, 1980-2 C.B. 183.

that conduct medical research are frequently ruled to be tax-exempt as charitable organizations, although these organizations may instead be considered as engaged in scientific research.[126] As another illustration, an organization that operated a free computerized donor authorization retrieval system to facilitate transplantation of body organs upon a donor's death qualified as a charitable organization as engaged in the promotion of health.[127] Still another example is an organization that provided services (e.g., housing, transportation, and counseling) for relatives and friends who have traveled to the organization's community to visit and comfort patients at local health care facilities.[128]

In 1977, the IRS stated that the term *charitable* includes the promotion of *public health*, in ruling that an organization formed to provide individual psychological and educational evaluations, as well as tutoring and therapy, for children and adolescents with learning disabilities qualifies as a charitable organization for federal income tax purposes.[129] The organization's psychologists and other professionals administered tests designed to determine intellectual capacity, academic achievement, psychological adjustment, speech and language difficulties, and perceptual-motor abilities. Therapy was available through staff professionals specially trained in the various areas of learning disabilities.

Despite the efforts of the IRS to deny tax-exempt status to nearly all forms of referral services,[130] a court held that an organization that operated a medical and dental referral service is a charitable entity because it promotes health.[131] Users of the service (subscribers) paid the organization an annual fee and were provided an array of information concerning the availability of health-related supplies, equipment, and services at a discount. The service providers did not pay any fees to be listed with the referral service, although many made contributions to the organization. Other program activities of the organization were the publication of a health care newsletter, sponsorship of a community health fair, the provision of speakers, and the presentation of an annual conference for physicians and dentists. The court said that the referral service "serves its charitable purpose by providing a resource whereby subscribers can be made aware of and referred to medical specialists who can serve their health care needs" and that any financial benefit inuring to the referral service is merely incidental to the overall charitable purposes being served.[132]

Thus, there is a variety of types of nonprofit organizations that promote health. Many of these entities, including hospitals, operate as members of a health care provider system. Generally, an aggregation of organizations, even

---

[126] E.g., Rev. Rul. 69-526, 1969-2 C.B. 115. See Chapter 9.
[127] Rev. Rul. 75-197, 1975-1 C.B. 156.
[128] Rev. Rul. 81-28, *supra* note 22.
[129] Rev. Rul. 77-68, 1977-1 C.B. 142.
[130] Kentucky Bar Found., Inc. v. Comm'r, *supra* note 102.
[131] Fraternal Med. Specialist Servs., Inc. v. Comm'r, 49 T.C.M. 289 (1984).
[132] *Id.* at 292.

where they have a common purpose (sometimes termed *system*), cannot itself qualify for tax exemption as a charitable entity.[133] Usually, each organization must separately establish (if it can) a basis in law for its claim to tax exemption.[134] In this context, at least, the IRS resists the concept of "exemption by attachment" or "derivative exemption."[135]

§ 6.3 LESSENING THE BURDENS OF GOVERNMENT

The regulations accompanying the federal tax law concerning charitable organizations define the term *charitable* as including "lessening of the burdens of Government" and also the "erection or maintenance of public buildings, monuments, or works."[136] This first concept relates more to the provision of governmental or municipal services rather than facilities, because of inclusion in the regulations of the exempt activity of erection or maintenance of public facilities.

According to the IRS, a determination as to whether an organization is lessening the burdens of government requires consideration of whether the organization's activities are activities that a governmental unit considers to be its burdens and whether the activities actually lessen a governmental burden.[137] For an activity to be a burden of government, there must be an "objective manifestation" by a governmental unit that it considers the activity to be part of its burden. It is insufficient that an organization engages in an activity that is sometimes undertaken by a government or that a government or a governmental official expresses approval of an organization and its activities. The interrelationship between a governmental unit and an organization may provide evidence that the governmental unit considers the activity to be its burden. All relevant facts and circumstances are to be considered in determining whether an organization is actually lessening the burdens of government. A favorable working relationship between a government and an organization is "strong evidence" that the organization is actually lessening the burdens of the government. For example, an organization that provided funds to a county's law enforcement agencies to police illegal narcotic traffic was held to lessen the burdens of government and thus be charitable, in that governmental funds were not available to purchase the drugs used to apprehend drug traffickers.[138] Likewise, an organization that provided legal advice and training to guardians *ad litem* representing neglected or abused children before a juvenile court was found to lessen governmental burdens, because otherwise the

---

[133] Cf. § 6.2(d).
[134] Gen. Couns. Mem. 39508. In general, see Chapter 23.
[135] Gen. Couns. Mem. 31433.
[136] Reg. § 1.501(c)(3)-1(d)(2).
[137] Rev. Rul. 85-2, 1985-1 C.B. 178.
[138] Rev. Rul. 85-1, 1985-1 C.B. 177.

government would have to train the lay volunteers or appointed lawyers as guardians.[139]

Some organizations that are tax-exempt under this category of *charitable* provide services directly in the context of governmental activity, such as assisting in the preservation of a public lake,[140] beautifying a city,[141] operating a prisoner correctional center,[142] assisting in the operation of a mass transportation system,[143] maintaining a volunteer fire company,[144] conserving natural resources,[145] or encouraging plantings of public lands.[146] In the latter case, the IRS observed that "[p]roviding fire and rescue service for the general community has been held to be a charitable purpose because it lessens the burden of government."

Other organizations that are charitable because they reduce a governmental burden, provide services in tandem with existing governmental agencies. As examples, an organization that made funds available to a police department for use as reward money is tax-exempt as being charitable,[147] as is an organization that assisted firefighters, police, and other personnel to perform their duties more efficiently during emergency conditions,[148] an organization that provided bus transportation to isolated areas of a community not served by the existing city bus system as a Model Cities demonstration project performed under the authority of the federal and local governments,[149] a community foundation that participated in an investment plan to retain a for-profit baseball team in a city (when the governmental units involved demonstrated an "intense and unique interest" in professional sports franchises),[150] and an organization that provided expert opinions to local government officials concerning traffic safety.[151] A government internship program may likewise come within this category of charitable activities,[152] as would a program of awards to citizens for outstanding civic achievements.[153] Likewise, physician peer review organizations[154] can qualify as charitable entities because they enable the med-

---

[139] Rev. Rul. 85-2, *supra* note 137. In one instance, claims for tax exemption on this basis failed because the organization did not show that the entities ostensibly assisted were government agencies, that activities they undertook were those that a government considers its burden, and that the activities lessened any burdens (University Med. Resident Servs., P.C. v. Comm'r, 71 T.C.M. 3130, 3131–3134 (1996)).

[140] Rev. Rul. 70-186, 1970-1 C.B. 128.

[141] Rev. Rul. 68-14, 1968-1 C.B. 243. Cf. Rev. Rul. 75-286, 1975-2 C.B. 210.

[142] Rev. Rul. 70-583, *supra* note 19.

[143] Rev. Rul. 71-29, 1971-1 C.B. 150.

[144] Rev. Rul. 74-361, 1974-2 C.B. 159.

[145] Rev. Rul. 67-292, 1967-2 C.B. 184.

[146] Rev. Rul. 66-179, 1966-1 C.B. 139.

[147] Rev. Rul. 74-246, 1974-1 C.B. 130.

[148] Rev. Rul. 71-99, 1971-1 C.B. 151.

[149] Rev. Rul. 78-68, 1978-1 C.B. 149. Cf. Rev. Rul. 78-69, 1978-1 C.B. 156.

[150] Priv. Ltr. Rul. 9530024.

[151] Rev. Rul. 76-418, 1976-2 C.B. 145. Cf. Rev. Rul. 70-79, 1970-1 C.B. 127.

[152] Rev. Rul. 70-584, 1970-2 C.B. 114.

[153] Rev. Rul. 66-146, 1966-1 C.B. 136.

[154] See *supra* § 2(g).

ical profession to assume the government's responsibility for reviewing the appropriateness and quality of services provided under the Medicare and Medicaid programs.[155]

In one application of these rules, an organization that certified crop seed within a state was found to be performing a service required by federal and state law—a service performed in other states by a governmental agency—and thus to be charitable because it was lessening the burdens of government. The organization, functioning in conjunction with one of the state's universities, was held to be protecting the "purchasing public—generally farmers and gardeners—from perceived abuses in the sale of agricultural and vegetable seed which is impure, mislabeled or adulterated" and therefore to be undertaking a "public service" and a "recognized governmental function."[156]

Organizations that qualify for *charitable* status as performing functions for the benefit of a government also include those that supply a community with facilities ordinarily provided at the taxpayers' expense or maintain the facilities, such as town halls, bridges, streets, parks, trees, and monuments.[157] Examples of organizations in this category include those that engage in activities such as solid waste recycling,[158] community improvement,[159] and community land-use analysis,[160] as well as those that provide public parks,[161] other recreational facilities,[162] and public parking lots.[163]

A corollary of the foregoing law is that an organization that frustrates attempts to relieve the burdens of government and thereby increases these burdens cannot qualify as a charitable organization.[164] Likewise, where an organization engages in activities that are specifically proscribed under federal and applicable state law, it will be denied charitable organization status on the ground that it is lessening the burdens of government.[165]

§ 6.4   ADVANCEMENT OF RELIGION

The regulations accompanying the federal tax law concerning charitable organizations provide that the term *charitable* includes the "advancement of religion."[166]

---

[155] Rev. Rul. 81-276, *supra* note 112.
[156] Indiana Crop Improvement Ass'n, Inc. v. Comm'r, 76 T.C. 394, 398, 399 (1981).
[157] *Restatement of Trusts* (2d ed. 1959) § 373, cmt. a.
[158] Rev. Rul. 72-560, 1972-2 C.B. 248.
[159] Rev. Rul. 68-15, 1968-1 C.B. 244.
[160] Rev. Rul. 67-391, 1967-2 C.B. 190.
[161] Rev. Rul. 66-358, 1966-2 C.B. 218.
[162] Rev. Rul. 70-186, *supra* note 140; Rev. Rul. 59-310, 1959-2 C.B. 332.
[163] Monterey Pub. Parking Corp. v. United States, 481 F.2d 175 (9th Cir. 1973).
[164] Rev. Rul. 75-384, 1975-2 C.B. 204.
[165] Public Indus., Inc. v. Comm'r, 61 T.C.M. 1626 (1991).
[166] Reg. § 1.501(c)(3)-1(d)(2).

The advancement of religion has long been considered a charitable purpose, although the scope of this category of charitable endeavors is imprecise because of the separate enumeration in federal tax law of other charitable purposes (in this case, *religious*). The concept of *advancement of religion* includes the construction or maintenance of a church building, monument, memorial window, or burial ground, and collateral services such as the provision of music, payment of salaries, dissemination of religious doctrines, maintenance of missions, or distribution of religious literature.[167] This category of tax exemption includes organizations the works of which extend to the advancement of particular religions, religious sects, or religious doctrines, as well as religion in general.[168]

Organizations deemed exempt as charitable entities because they advance religion include those maintaining a church newspaper,[169] providing material for a parochial school system,[170] affording young adults counseling,[171] and undertaking genealogical research.[172] The IRS ruled that an organization that supervised the preparation and inspection of food products prepared commercially in a particular locality to ensure that they satisfy the dietary rules of a particular religion was tax-exempt as advancing religion.[173] An organization that provided funds for the defense of members of a religious sect in legal actions involving a state's abridgement of religious freedom was ruled tax-exempt as a charitable organization by virtue of "promoting social welfare by defending human and civil rights secured by law," although it would seem that it was also advancing religion.[174] An organization formed and controlled by an exempt conference of churches, that borrowed funds from individuals and made mortgage loans at less than the commercial rate of interest to affiliated churches to finance the construction of church buildings, qualified as a charitable organization because it advances religion.[175] An organization that provided a continuing educational program in an atmosphere conducive to spiritual renewal for ministers, members of churches, and their families may qualify as a tax-exempt organization because it advanced religion.[176] An organization that provided traditional religious burial services, which directly support and maintain basic tenets and beliefs of a religion regarding burial of its members, was ruled to advance religion.[177] Likewise, an organization that conducted weekend religious retreats, open to individuals of diverse religious denominations, at a rural lakeshore site at which the participants may enjoy recreational facilities in

---

[167] *Restatement of Trusts* (2d ed. 1959) § 371, cmt. a.

[168] *Id.*, cmts. b, d.

[169] Rev. Rul. 68-306, 1968-1 C.B. 257. Cf. Foundation for Divine Meditation, Inc. v. Comm'r, 24 T.C.M. 411 (1965), *aff'd sub nom.* Parker v. Comm'r, 365 F.2d 792 (8th Cir. 1966), *cert. den.*, 385 U.S. 1026 (1967).

[170] Rev. Rul. 68-26, 1968-1 C.B. 272.

[171] Rev. Rul. 68-72, 1968-1 C.B. 250.

[172] Rev. Rul. 71-580, 1971-2 C.B. 235.

[173] Rev. Rul. 74-575, 1974-2 C.B. 161.

[174] Rev. Rul. 73-285, 1973-2 C.B. 174.

[175] Rev. Rul. 75-282, *supra* note 71.

[176] Rev. Rul. 77-366, 1977-2 C.B. 192.

[177] Rev. Rul. 79-359, 1979-2 C.B. 226.

their limited amount of free time, qualified as an organization that advances religion.[178]

Religion may be advanced by an organization that operates a noncommercial broadcasting station presenting programming on religious subjects.[179] Similarly, a nonprofit religious broadcasting station may acquire classification as a charitable organization even though it operates on a commercial license, as long as it does not sell commercial or advertising time[180] or, if it does so, sells the time as an incidental part of its activities.[181]

The IRS determined that an organization established to provide temporary low-cost housing and related services for missionary families on furlough for recuperation or training in the United States from their assignments abroad qualified as a charitable organization acting to advance religion because the assistance to the missionaries was provided them in their official capacities for use in furtherance of and as part of the organized religious program with which they were associated.[182] The IRS cautioned, however, that "the providing of assistance to individuals in their individual capacities solely by reason of their identification with some form of religious endeavor, such as missionary work, is not a charitable use."

§ 6.5   ADVANCEMENT OF EDUCATION OR SCIENCE

The regulations accompanying the federal tax law concerning charitable organizations include among the definitions of the term *charitable* the "advancement of education or science."[183]

The *advancement of education* includes the establishment or maintenance of nonprofit educational institutions, financing of scholarships and other forms of student assistance, establishment or maintenance of institutions such as public libraries and museums, advancement of knowledge through research, and dissemination of knowledge by publications, seminars, lectures, and similar activities. The *advancement of science* includes comparable activities devoted to the furtherance or promotion of science and the dissemination of scientific knowledge. However, inasmuch as the federal tax law exemption for charitable organizations also contains the terms *educational* and *scientific*, organizations coming within one or both of these two terms are likely to also qualify as charitable in nature.

For federal income tax purposes, the more traditional forms of advancement of education, such as the establishment or maintenance of educational institutions, libraries, museums, and the like, will fall within the scope of the term

---

[178] Rev. Rul. 77-430, 1977-2 C.B. 194.
[179] Rev. Rul. 66-220, 1966-2 C.B. 209.
[180] Rev. Rul. 68-563, 1968-2 C.B. 212.
[181] Rev. Rul. 78-385, 1978-2 C.B. 174.
[182] Rev. Rul. 75-434, 1975-2 C.B. 205. Also World Family Corp. v. Comm'r, 81 T.C. 958 (1983). The IRS also ruled that an organization formed to aid immigrants in the United States qualified under IRC § 501(c)(3) (Rev. Rul. 76-205, 1976-1 C.B. 154).
[183] Reg. § 1.501(c)(3)-1(d)(2).

educational, leaving to the broader term *charitable* related concepts of advancement of education in the collateral sense. Nonetheless, the IRS, in ruling that an organization is *educational*, frequently also finds it to be charitable.[184]

For example, while the operation of a college or university is an educational undertaking, many satellite endeavors are regarded as charitable in nature. Thus, the provision of scholarships is a charitable activity,[185] as is the making of low-interest college loans,[186] and the provision of free housing, books, or supplies.[187] Other charitable activities that constitute the advancement of education include publication of student journals such as law reviews,[188] maintenance of a training table for athletes,[189] provision of assistance to law students to obtain experience with public interest law firms and legal aid societies,[190] operation of a foreign student center,[191] selection of students for enrollment at foreign universities,[192] operation of an alumni association,[193] provision of work experience in selected trades and professions to high school graduates and college students,[194] the operation of interscholastic athletic programs,[195] and the provision of housing for students of a college.[196] Still other activities that are charitable because they advance education are more institutionally oriented, such as bookstores,[197] organizations that accredit schools and colleges,[198] or provide financial and investment assistance[199] or computer services[200] to educational organizations. However, one type of organization operated closely with colleges and universities—fraternities and sororities—generally is not regarded as being charitable or educational in nature.[201]

With regard to college, university, or school bookstores, it is clear that the sale to students and faculty of books, supplies, materials, athletic wear necessary for participation in the institution's athletic and physical education programs, and other items that are required by or are otherwise necessary for courses at the institution (including computer hardware and software) is an activity that is

---

[184] E.g., Rev. Rul. 77-272, 1977-2 C.B. 191.

[185] Rev. Rul. 69-257, 1969-1 C.B. 151; Rev. Rul. 66-103, 1966-1 C.B. 134.

[186] Rev. Rul. 63-220, 1963-2 C.B. 208; Rev. Rul. 61-87, 1961-1 C.B. 191.

[187] Rev. Rul. 64-274, 1964-2 C.B. 141.

[188] Rev. Rul. 63-235, 1963-2 C.B. 610.

[189] Rev. Rul. 67-291, 1967-2 C.B. 184.

[190] Rev. Rul. 78-310, 1978-2 C.B. 173.

[191] Rev. Rul. 65-191, 1965-2 C.B. 157.

[192] Rev. Rul. 69-400, 1969-2 C.B. 114.

[193] Rev. Rul. 60-143, 1960-1 C.B. 192; Rev. Rul. 56-486, 1956-2 C.B. 309; Estate of Thayer v. Comm'r, 24 T.C. 384 (1955).

[194] Rev. Rul. 75-284, 1975-2 C.B. 202; Rev. Rul. 70-584, *supra* note 152.

[195] Rev. Rul. 55-587, 1955-2 C.B. 261.

[196] Rev. Rul. 76-336, 1976-2 C.B. 143.

[197] Squire v. Students Book Corp., 191 F.2d 1018 (9th Cir. 1951).

[198] Rev. Rul. 74-146, 1974-1 C.B. 129.

[199] Rev. Rul. 71-529, 1971-2 C.B. 234; Rev. Rul. 67-149, 1967-1 C.B. 133.

[200] Rev. Rul. 74-614, 1974-2 C.B. 164, *amp; by* Rev. Rul. 81-29, 1981-1 C.B. 329.

[201] Rev. Rul. 69-573, 1969-2 C.B. 125; Phinney v. Dougherty, 307 F.2d 357 (5th Cir. 1962); Davison v. Comm'r, 60 F.2d 50 (2d Cir. 1932); Alumnae Chapter Beta of Clovia v. Comm'r, 46 T.C.M. 297 (1983); Johnson v. Southern Greek Hous. Corp., 307 S.E.2d 491 (Ga. 1983); Alford v. Emory Univ., 116 S.E.2d 596 (Ga. 1960). Also Rev. Rul. 64-117, 1964-1 (Part 1) C.B. 180 (student clubs), Rev. Rul. 64-118, 1964-1 (Part 1) C.B. 182 (fraternity housing corporations).

charitable in nature.[202] However, some bookstores associated with educational institutions sell items that are not related to the education of the students; the sale of these items is likely to be an unrelated business activity,[203] unless the sales are within the scope of the *convenience doctrine*.[204]

Colleges and universities frequently utilize affiliated nonprofit organizations in connection with the carrying out of their charitable and educational activities. These related organizations can be charitable in character. As illustrations, the IRS has ruled to be tax-exempt an organization that operated a book and supply store that sold items only to students and faculty of the college,[205] that operated a cafeteria and restaurant on the campus of a university primarily for the convenience of its students and faculty,[206] and that provided housing and food service exclusively for students and faculty of a university.[207]

For this category of tax exemption to be available, the organization must in fact engage in advancement activities. In one instance, a court rejected two organizations' claim for tax exemption based on this ground, because they provided "minimal, if any" assistance to educational and other entities.[208]

The nature of the law regarding organizations whose functions represent assistance to other organizations that are tax-exempt can shift radically where the assistance is directed to two or more exempt entities. Tax-exempt organizations, such as colleges and universities, often turn to cooperative ventures to reduce costs and improve the quality of performance. Universities often find it productive and more efficient to share, for example, data processing or library resources.[209]

Organizations not affiliated with any formal institution of learning but that provide instruction may also be deemed to advance education, such as those that teach industrial skills,[210] conduct work experience programs,[211] provide apprentice training,[212] act as a clearinghouse and course coordinator for instructors and students,[213] instruct in the field of business,[214] evaluate the public service obligations of broadcasters,[215] and provide services to relieve psychological tensions and improve the mental health of children and adolescents.[216]

---

[202] College and university examination guidelines (see § 24.8(d)) § 342.(13) (availability announced by Ann. 94-112, 1994-37 I.R.B. 36).

[203] See § 26.5(a)(i).

[204] See § 27.2(b).

[205] Rev. Rul. 69-538, 1969-2 C.B. 116.

[206] Rev. Rul. 58-194, 1958-1 C.B. 240.

[207] Rev. Rul. 67-217, 1967-2 C.B. 181.

[208] University Med. Resident Servs., P.C. v. Comm'r, *supra* note 139.

[209] See Patterson, *Colleges in Consort* (1974). See § 6.8.

[210] Rev. Rul. 72-101, 1972-1 C.B. 144. Cf. Rev. Rul. 78-42, 1978-1 C.B. 158.

[211] Rev. Rul. 78-310, *supra* note 190 Rev. Rul. 76-37, 1976-1 C.B. 146; Rev. Rul. 75-284, *supra* note 194; Rev. Rul. 70-584, *supra* note 152.

[212] Rev. Rul. 67-72, 1967-1 C.B. 125.

[213] Rev. Rul. 71-413, 1971-2 C.B. 228.

[214] Rev. Rul. 68-16, 1968-1 C.B. 246.

[215] Rev. Rul. 79-26, 1979-1 C.B. 196.

[216] Rev. Rul. 77-68, *supra* note 129.

The advancement of education can consist of making a grant to a tax-exempt fraternity or sorority[217] for the purpose of constructing or maintaining educational facilities, such as financing of allocable construction costs of the fraternity or sorority house, maintaining a library, and funding study facilities.[218] Where the grantor is a private foundation,[219] it should be certain that the grant is a qualifying distribution[220] and not a taxable expenditure.[221]

Education may be advanced through such modes as the publication and dissemination of research,[222] maintenance of collections,[223] the provision of anthropological specimens,[224] the operation of a foreign exchange program,[225] and the operation of an honor society.[226] Likewise, the IRS determined that the provision of bibliographic information by means of a computer network to researchers at both exempt and nonexempt libraries constituted the advancement of education.[227] Similarly, the IRS held that an organization formed to preserve the natural environment by acquiring ecologically significant underdeveloped land and to maintain the land or to transfer it to a government conservation agency qualified for exemption at least in part for the reason that it was advancing education and science.[228]

Although an organization that is deemed to be a scientific entity is usually engaged in scientific research,[229] an organization may be classified as one that advances education and/or science where it publishes or otherwise distributes scientific information without having performed the supporting research.[230]

§ 6.6 PROMOTION OF SOCIAL WELFARE

The "promotion of social welfare" is one of the most indefinite categories of charitable purposes. In the general law of charitable trusts, the concept includes a broad spectrum of activities, such as the promotion of temperance, prevention or alleviation of suffering of animals, promotion of national security, inculcation of patriotism, promotion of the happiness or well-being of the members of the community, promotion of the happiness or well-being of persons who have few opportunities for recreation and enjoyment, and (perhaps) the erection or maintenance of a tomb or monument.[231] As was observed, "[n]o attempt . . . can

---

[217] These entities are tax-exempt by reason of IRC § 501(c)(7). See Chapter 14.
[218] E.g., Priv. Ltr. Rul. 9014061.
[219] See Chapter 11.
[220] See § 11.4(b). E.g., Priv. Ltr. Rul. 9002036.
[221] See § 11.4(e). E.g., Priv. Ltr. Rul. 9002036.
[222] Rev. Rul. 67-4, 1967-1 C.B. 121.
[223] Rev. Rul. 70-321, 1970-1 C.B. 129.
[224] Rev. Rul. 70-129, 1970-1 C.B. 128.
[225] Rev. Rul. 80-286, 1980-2 C.B. 179.
[226] Rev. Rul. 71-97, 1971-1 C.B. 150.
[227] Rev. Rul. 81-29, *supra* note 200.
[228] Rev. Rul. 76-204, 1976-1 C.B. 152. Cf. Rev. Rul. 78-384, 1978-2 C.B. 174.
[229] See Chapter 9.
[230] E.g., Gen. Couns. Mem. 38459.
[231] *Restatement of Trusts* (2d ed. 1959) § 374, cmts. b–h.

successfully be made to enumerate all of the purposes which fall within the scope" of this category of charitable purpose, and the question in each case is whether "the purpose is one the accomplishment of which might reasonably be held to be for the social interest of the community."[232]

The federal tax regulations defining *charitable purpose* state five types of endeavors that constitute the promotion of social welfare: activities "designed to accomplish any of the above [charitable] purposes," "lessen neighborhood tensions," "eliminate prejudice and discrimination," "defend human and civil rights secured by law," and "combat community deterioration and juvenile delinquency."[233]

The types of organizations that are tax-exempt as charitable organizations because they are operated to eliminate prejudice and discrimination are illustrated by three rulings issued by the IRS in 1968. One of these organizations worked to educate the public about integrated housing and conducted programs to prevent panic selling when neighborhoods were integrated.[234] Another entity conducted investigations and research to obtain information regarding discrimination against minority groups in housing and public accommodations.[235] The third operated to advance equal job opportunities in a particular community for qualified workers discriminated against because of race or creed.[236] An organization qualified as a charitable organization where it was formed because it acted to eliminate discrimination against members of minorities seeking employment in the construction trades by recruiting, educating, and counseling workers, providing technical assistance to lawyers involved in suits to enforce workers' rights, and acting as a court-appointed monitor after successful suits.[237] Combating community deterioration in the charitable sense involves remedial action leading to the elimination of the physical, economic, and social causes of the deterioration,[238] such as by purchasing and renovating deteriorating residences and selling or leasing them to low-income families on a nonprofit basis,[239] and by operating a self-help home building program.[240] The charitable activity of combating community deterioration can be present "whether or not the community is in a state of decline."[241]

Discrimination in this context is not confined to racial discrimination. Thus, an organization formed to promote equal rights for women in employment and other economic contexts was ruled to be tax-exempt as promoting social welfare by eliminating prejudice and discrimination.[242] Also, an organization created to aid immigrants to the United States in overcoming social, cultural, and economic

---

[232] *Id.*, comt. a.

[233] Reg. § 1.501(c)(3)-1(d)(2).

[234] Rev. Rul. 68-655, 1968-2 C.B. 613.

[235] Rev. Rul. 68-438, 1968-2 C.B. 609.

[236] Rev. Rul. 68-70, 1968-1 C.B. 248.

[237] Rev. Rul. 75-285, 1975-2 C.B. 203.

[238] Rev. Rul. 67-6, 1967-1 C.B. 135.

[239] Rev. Rul. 68-17, *supra* note 13; also Rev. Rul. 76-408, 1976-2 C.B. 145; Rev. Rul. 70-585, *supra* note 13.

[240] Rev. Rul. 67-138, *supra* note 13.

[241] Rev. Rul. 76-147, 1976-1 C.B. 151.

[242] Rev. Rul. 72-228, 1972-1 C.B. 148.

problems by personal counseling or referral to appropriate agencies was granted federal income tax exemption on this basis.[243]

The position of the IRS once was that the phrase "human and civil rights secured by law" refers only to those individual liberties, freedoms, and privileges involving human dignity that are either specifically guaranteed by the U.S. Constitution or by a special statutory provision coming directly within the scope of the Thirteenth or Fourteenth Amendment or some other comparable constitutional provision, or that otherwise fall within the protection of the Constitution by reason of their long-established recognition in the common law as rights that are essential to the orderly pursuit of happiness by free people. Consequently, tax exemption as a charitable organization was denied to an organization whose primary activity was the provision of legal assistance to employees the rights of whom were violated under compulsory unionization arrangements, on the theory that its criterion for intervention in a case is whether there is a grievance arising out of a compulsory union membership requirement, and that the right to work is not a protected constitutional right. Upon review, a court disagreed, holding that the right to work is an individual liberty involving a human dignity that is guaranteed by the Constitution, and is therefore a human and civil right secured by law. The organization was thus ruled to be tax-exempt as a charitable entity.[244]

One of the ways in which an organization can qualify for tax exemption as a charitable entity is by preserving the historic or architectural character of a community, which promotes social welfare by combating community deterioration. This can be accomplished, for example, with a program of acquiring historic structures, restoring them, and selling them subject to restrictive covenants.[245]

With regard to the promotion of social welfare by combating juvenile delinquency, the IRS upheld the activity of an organization that promoted sports for children. The organization involved in the case developed, promoted, and regulated a sport for individuals under 18 years of age, and generally provided a recreational outlet for young people.[246] Similarly, an organization that provided teaching of a particular sport to children, by holding clinics conducted by qualified instructors and by providing free instruction, equipment, and facilities, was found to be combating juvenile delinquency and thus charitable in nature.[247]

Obviously, these five categories of social welfare activities tend to overlap. Thus, one organization that was ruled to be engaged in the elimination of prejudice and discrimination was also found to operate to "lessen neighborhood ten-

---

[243] Rev. Rul. 76-205, *supra* note 182.
[244] National Right to Work Legal Defense & Educ. Found., Inc. v. United States, 487 F. Supp. 801 (E.D.N.C. 1979).
[245] Rev. Rul. 86-49, 1986-1 C.B. 243; Rev. Rul. 75-470, 1975-2 C.B. 207.
[246] Rev. Rul. 80-215, 1980-2 C.B. 174.
[247] Rev. Rul. 65-2, 1965-1 C.B. 227. Cf. Rev. Rul. 70-4, 1970-1 C.B. 126, holding that an organization promoting and regulating a sport for amateurs qualifies under IRC § 501(c)(4) (see Chapter 12) but not under IRC § 501(c)(3) because it directs its activities to all members of the general public regardless of age.

sions" and "prevent deterioration of neighborhoods,"[248] while another was ruled to also act to lessen neighborhood tensions and to defend "human and civil rights secured by law."[249] An organization that counseled residents of a community and city officials in the best use of vacant lots in order to eliminate potential gathering places for "unruly elements" was held to be engaged in combating juvenile delinquency, as well as, because of other activities, the elimination of prejudice and discrimination, the lessening of neighborhood tensions, and the combating of community deterioration.[250]

There can also be an overlap of categories of charitable organizations where they operate to eliminate prejudice and discrimination and to educate the public. Thus, an organization educating the public as to how to invest in housing made available to the public on a nondiscriminatory basis was ruled to be tax-exempt.[251] Similar illustrations include an organization that informed the public, through lectures and discussions, of the advantages of nondiscriminatory hiring[252] and an organization that operated programs to prevent panic selling from resulting integration of a neighborhood.[253]

As noted, the regulation defining *charitable* endeavors states that the promotion of social welfare includes activities that seek to accomplish otherwise charitable ends. By nature, these activities tend to be characterized as lessening the burdens of government. Thus, an organization created to assist local governments of a metropolitan region by studying and recommending regional policies directed at the solution of mutual problems was held to be involved in both the combating of community deterioration and lessening of the burdens of government.[254] Yet, social welfare activities of this nature may traverse the gamut of charitable works, as in the case of an organization that made awards to individuals who have made outstanding contributions and achievements in the field of commerce, communications, creative arts and crafts, education, finance, government, law, medicine and health, performing arts, religion, science, social services, sports and athletics, technology, and transportation.[255]

§ 6.7   PROMOTION OF THE ARTS

Organizations devoted to promotion of the arts may qualify for exemption as tax-exempt charitable entities. For example, an organization that functioned to arouse and give direction to local interest in a given community for the establishment of a repertory theater qualified as a charitable entity.[256] The repertory the-

---

[248] Rev. Rul. 68-655, *supra* note 234.
[249] Rev. Rul. 68-438, *supra* note 235. Also see Rev. Rul. 73-285, *supra* note 174.
[250] Rev. Rul. 68-15, *supra* note 159. Also Rev. Rul. 81-284, 1981-2 C.B. 130; Rev. Rul. 76-419, 1976-2 C.B. 146; Rev. Rul. 74-587, 1974-2 C.B. 162. Cf. Rev. Rul. 77-111, 1977-1 C.B. 144.
[251] Rev. Rul. 67-250, *supra* note 13.
[252] Rev. Rul. 68-70, *supra* note 236.
[253] Rev. Rul. 68-655, *supra* note 234.
[254] Rev. Rul. 70-79, *supra* note 151.
[255] Rev. Rul. 66-146, *supra* note 153; also Bok v. McCaughn, 42 F.2d 616 (3d Cir. 1930).
[256] Rev. Rul. 64-174, 1964-1 (Part I) C.B. 183.

ater company itself can be charitable in nature.[257] This type of charitable activity was initially recognized by the IRS as being "cultural," with emphasis on the musical arts.[258]

One feature of this aspect of charitable endeavor is the effort akin to advancement of education, that is, to promote public appreciation of one of the arts. Thus, an organization formed to perpetuate group harmony singing and to educate the general public as to this type of music was ruled to be tax-exempt.[259] Similarly, an organization formed to promote an appreciation of jazz music as an American art form was held to be an exempt organization,[260] as was a nonprofit school of contemporary dancing.[261] The tax exemption for charitable groups may likewise extend to an organization that seeks to encourage the creative arts and scholarship by making grants to needy artists,[262] by promoting interest in and appreciation of contemporary symphonic and chamber music,[263] or by sponsoring public exhibits of art works by unknown but promising artists.[264]

Other organizations are tax-exempt because they function to promote and encourage the talent and ability of young artists. The scope of types of these activities include the training of young musical artists in concert technique,[265] the promotion of filmmaking by conducting festivals to provide unknown independent filmmakers with opportunities to display their films,[266] and the encouragement of musicians and composers through commissions and scholarships and the opportunity for students to play with accomplished professional musicians.[267] Organizations in this category frequently promote (and finance) their charitable function through the sponsorship of public festivals, concerts, exhibits, and other productions.[268] In nearly all of these instances, the artists are amateurs, performing solely for the onstage experience or to enable the charitable organization to meet expenses.

Organizations operated to promote the arts, which otherwise qualify as charitable entities, may easily find themselves engaging in an activity the IRS regards as serving a private interest. Thus, while the preservation of classical music programming can be a charitable purpose,[269] an organization that undertook a variety of activities to enable a for-profit radio station to continue broadcasting classical music was denied tax exemption.[270] Likewise, although the displaying of

---

[257] Rev. Rul. 64-175, 1964-1 (Part I) C.B. 185.
[258] S.M. 176, 1 C.B. 147 (1919); I.T. 1475, 1-2 C.B. 184 (1922).
[259] Rev. Rul. 66-46, 1966-1 C.B. 133.
[260] Rev. Rul. 65-271, 1965-2 C.B. 161.
[261] Rev. Rul. 65-270, 1965-2 C.B. 160.
[262] Rev. Rul. 66-103, *supra* note 185.
[263] Rev. Rul. 79-369, 1979-2 C.B. 226.
[264] Rev. Rul. 66-178, 1966-1 C.B. 138.
[265] Rev. Rul. 67-392, 1967-2 C.B. 191.
[266] Rev. Rul. 75-471, 1975-2 C.B. 207.
[267] Rev. Rul. 65-271, *supra* note 260.
[268] E.g., Priv. Ltr. Rul. 9217001.
[269] Rev. Rul. 64-175, *supra* note 257.
[270] Rev. Rul. 76-206, 1976-1 C.B. 154.

art works may be a charitable activity,[271] an organization will not achieve exemption as a charitable entity where it sells the art works it exhibits and remits the proceeds to the artists.[272] (However, the fact that exhibited art works are available for sale will not necessarily deprive the organization sponsoring the show of tax exemption as a charitable group.[273])

Status as tax-exempt charitable organizations has been accorded organizations that sponsor professional presentations, such as plays, musicals, and concerts. The chief rationale for extending the exemption to these organizations is that they operate to foster the development in a community of an appreciation for the dramatic and musical arts, such as by staging theatrical productions that are not otherwise available in the community.[274] At the same time, these tax-exempt theaters may be perceived as placing the commercial theaters in the same locale at a competitive disadvantage. Defenders of the exempt cultural centers claim that they champion theatrical presentations that otherwise would never be produced, while their critics insist that they are frequently presenting popular entertainment in unfair competition with privately owned theaters.

One court discussed the distinctions between tax-exempt performing arts organizations and commercial theaters as follows:

> Admittedly, the line between commercial enterprises which produce and present theatrical performances and nonprofit, tax-exempt organizations that do the same is not always easy to draw. Indeed, the theater is the most prominent area of the performing arts in which commercial enterprises co-exist, often in the same city, with nonprofit, tax-exempt charitable organizations that also sponsor professional presentations. . . .
>
> However, there are differences. Commercial theaters are operated to make a profit. Thus, they choose plays having the greatest mass audience appeal. Generally, they run the plays so long as they can attract a crowd. They set ticket prices to pay the total costs of production and to return a profit. Since their focus is perennially on the box office, they do not generally organize other activities to educate the public and they do not encourage and instruct relatively unknown playwrights and actors.
>
> Tax-exempt organizations are not operated to make a profit. They fulfill their artistic and community obligations by focusing on the highest possible stan-

---

[271] Goldsboro Art League, Inc. v. Comm'r, 75 T.C. 337 (1980) (where artworks displayed were selected by jury procedures and the organization maintained the only art gallery in the geographic area); Rev. Rul. 66-178, *supra* note 264.

[272] St. Louis Science Fiction Ltd. v. Comm'r, 49 T.C.M. 1126 (1985) (where the organization did not apply any controls to ensure the quality of artworks sold and the "tone" of its annual convention was found to be predominantly social and recreational); Rev. Rul. 76-152, 1976-1 C.B. 151. Also Rev. Rul. 71-395, 1971-2 C.B. 228.

[273] Cleveland Creative Arts Guild v. Comm'r, 50 T.C.M. 272 (1985) (where the organization's art sales activity was found to be a means to the end of increasing public appreciation of the arts); Rev. Rul. 78-131, 1978-2 C.B. 156.

[274] Rev. Rul. 73-45, 1973-1 C.B. 220.

dards of performance; by serving the community broadly; by developing new and original works; and by providing educational programs and opportunities for new talent. Thus, they keep the great classics of the theater alive and are willing to experiment with new forms of dramatic writing, acting, and staging. Usually nonprofit theatrical organizations present a number of plays over a season for a relatively short specified time period. Because of a desired quality in acoustics and intimacy with the audience, many present their performances in halls of limited capacity. The combination of the shortness of the season, the limited seating capacity, the enormous costs of producing quality performances of new or experimental works coupled with the desire to keep ticket prices at a level which is affordable to most of the community means that except in rare cases, box office receipts will never cover the cost of producing plays for nonprofit performing arts organizations. . . . We feel that . . . [the arts organization involved] has shown that it is organized and operated similar to other nonprofit theater organizations, rather than as a commercial theatre.[275]

§ 6.8 CONSORTIA

Tax-exempt organizations frequently utilize cooperative ventures to further their purposes. The early position of the IRS toward cooperative venturing by or for charitable (including educational) organizations was relatively favorable. This may be seen in a 1969 IRS ruling concerning an organization that was created to construct and maintain a building to house member agencies of a community chest.[276] The purpose of this organization was to facilitate coordination among the agencies and to make more efficient use of the available voluntary labor force. The rental rate charged the agencies was substantially lower than commercial rates for comparable facilities (the organization leased the land from a city and itself paid only a nominal rental) and the organization's annual rental income was approximately equal to its total annual operating costs. Citing the concept that the "performance of a particular activity that is not inherently charitable may nonetheless further a charitable purpose,"[277] the IRS ruled that the organization was exempt as a charitable entity, emphasizing the low rental rates and the close relationship between its purposes and functions and those of the tenant organizations.[278]

However, the state of the law in this regard is that these cooperative ventures are likely to be nonexempt entities, even where the venture is controlled by and performs a function for its members that each exempt institution would otherwise have to undertake for itself, without incidence of tax. The IRS has two narrow exceptions to this policy, in that exemption as a charitable organization will be granted where the consortium conducts substantive programs that are inher-

---

[275] Plumstead Theatre Soc'y, Inc. v. Comm'r, 74 T.C. 1324, 1332–1333 (1980), *aff'd* 675 F.2d 244 (9th Cir. 1982).
[276] Rev. Rul. 69-572, 1969-2 C.B. 119.
[277] Rev. Rul. 67-4, *supra* note 222.
[278] Also Rev. Rul. 64-182, 1964-1 C.B. (Part 1) 186; Rev. Rul. 58-147, 1958-2 C.B. 275.

ently exempt in nature[279] or where at least 85 percent of the organization's revenue is derived from outside sources (the *donative element* test).[280] The IRS also bases its position on a passage in the regulations accompanying the federal tax rules pertaining to feeder organizations.[281] The IRS policy toward cooperative ventures had, for many years, been rejected in the courts on nearly every occasion when it was considered[282] and Congress has legislated in this area, contravening the IRS's policy three times.[283]

The direction of the law regarding tax exemption for consortia began to shift as a result of consideration of the issue by the U.S. Tax Court. The case involved a cooperative hospital laundry service owned and operated by tax-exempt hospitals. Finding the regulations under the feeder organization rules[284] to have the force of law because of long-standing congressional awareness of them, and concluding that the legislative history of related statutes evidenced congressional intent to not allow tax exemption for hospital-controlled laundries, the court found that the hospital laundry service organization was a feeder organization and thus not exempt from taxation.[285] Because of the emphasis placed on this legislative history, however, it was not clear whether consortia other than hospital laundry enterprises would receive like treatment by the Tax Court. Shortly after the Tax Court reached this decision, the Third,[286] Ninth,[287] and Sixth Circuit courts of appeal arrived at the same conclusion.[288]

Despite this policy, the IRS recognized the necessity and utility of cooperative endeavors in the field of higher education. Thus, the IRS stated:

---

[279] Rev. Rul. 74-614, *supra* note 200, *amp. by* Rev. Rul. 81-29, *supra* note 200.

[280] Rev. Rul. 72-369, 1972-2 C.B. 245; Rev. Rul. 71-529, *supra* note 199. A corollary policy of the IRS is that, where neither of the exceptions is present, the provision of services by one exempt organization to one or more other exempt (or nonexempt) organizations may be the conduct of an unrelated trade or business (see Part VI) (Rev. Rul. 69-528, 1969-2 C.B. 127).

[281] Rev. Rul. 69-528, *supra* note 280. See § 28.6.

[282] Hospital Bur. of Standards & Supplies v. United States, 158 F. Supp. 560 (Ct. Cl. 1958); United Hosp. Serv., Inc. v. United States, 384 F. Supp. 766 (S.D. Ind. 1974); Hospital Cent. Serv. Ass'n v. United States, 77-2 U.S.T.C. ¶ 9601 (W.D. Wash. 1977); Metropolitan Detroit Area Hosp. Serv., Inc. v. United States, 445 F. Supp. 857 (E.D. Mich. 1978); Northern Calif. Cent. Serv. Inc. v. United States, 591 F.2d 620 (Ct. Cl. 1979); Community Hosp. Services, Inc. v. United States, 79-1 U.S.T.C. ¶ 9301 (E.D. Mich. 1979); HCSC-Laundry v. United States, 473 F. Supp. 250 (E.D. Pa. 1979). In general, Gailey, "Tax-Exempt Auxiliary Corporations and Major Public Institutions," 14 *Bus. Off.* (No. 5) 24 (1980); Hopkins, "Cooperative Ventures of Colleges and Universities: The Current Tax Law Developments," 4 *Coll. & Univ. Bus. Off.* (No. 5) (1975); Whaley, "Interinstitutional Cooperation Among Educational Organizations," 1 *J. Coll. & Univ. Law* (No. 2) 93 (1973).

[283] IRC §§ 501(e), 501(f), 513(e).

[284] See § 28.6.

[285] Associated Hosp. Serv., Inc. v. Comm'r, 74 T.C. 213 (1980), *aff'd, unrep. dec.* (5th Cir. 1981).

[286] HCSC-Laundry v. United States, 624 F.2d 428 (3d Cir. 1980), *rev'g* 473 F. Supp. 250 (E.D. Pa. 1979), *aff'd*, 450 U.S. 1 (1981).

[287] Hospital Cent. Servs. Ass'n v. United States, 623 F.2d 611 (9th Cir. 1980), *cert. den.*, 450 U.S. 911 (1980), *rev'g* 77-2 U.S.T.C. ¶ 9601 (W.D. Wash. 1977). Also Community Hosp. Serv., Inc. v. United States, 81-1 U.S.T.C. ¶ 9198 (6th Cir. 1981), *rev'g* 79-1 U.S.T.C. ¶ 9301 (E.D. Mich. 1979).

[288] Metropolitan Detroit Area Hosp. Serv. v. United States, 634 F.2d 330 (6th Cir. 1980), *cert. den.*, 450 U.S. 1031 (1980), *rev'g* 445 F. Supp. 857 (E.D. Mich. 1978). Also Community Hosp. Serv., Inc. v. United States, 81-1 U.S.T.C. ¶ 9198 (6th Cir. 1981), *rev'g* 79-1 U.S.T.C. ¶ 9301 (E.D. Mich. 1979).

> Many activities normally carried on by colleges and universities can be more effectively accomplished through the combined efforts of a group of such institutions. . . . Associations composed entirely of privately supported nonprofit colleges and universities have been created and are operated exclusively to carry out these activities.

> [These associations] aid and promote the educational endeavors of their members and interpret to the public the aims, functions, and needs of the institutions, with a view to better understanding and cooperation.[289]

The IRS subscribed to this view in the intervening years.[290]

Some IRS rulings are contradictory to its announced position on college, university, and similar consortia. For example, the IRS ruled that an organization whose members are educational (including some proprietary) institutions qualified as a charitable organization because it accredits these institutions.[291] The rationale for the exemption was that the organization advanced education and thus was charitable in nature; it engaged in activities that "support and advance education by providing significant incentive for maintaining a high quality educational program." The act of accreditation is not inherently a charitable activity; the fact that service was rendered for educational institutions gave rise to the exemption.

Similarly, the IRS accorded charitable entity status to an organization controlled by a tax-exempt conference of churches, where its purpose was to make mortgage loans to the churches to enable them to finance the construction of church buildings.[292] The rationale for the exemption was that the organization was advancing religion. Obviously, the making of mortgage loans is not an inherently religious activity. Rather, the exemption was derived from the fact that the loans were made at lower than commercial interest rates to churches of the conference to enable them to construct buildings at reduced cost for religious purposes.

Also, the IRS granted tax-exempt charitable status to a consortium of counties all located in the same state.[293] This exemption was accorded on the ground that the organization's activities contribute to the "more efficient operation of county government." Efficiency of operation is, as noted, one of the principal reasons for establishment of consortia.

Further, it has long been the position of the IRS that an organization formed

---

[289] Rev. Rul. 63-15, 1963-1 C.B. 189.
[290] E.g., Rev. Rul. 63-208, 1963-2 C.B. 468, and Rev. Rul. 63-209, 1963-2 C.B. 469 (offices formed by an exempt religious entity to administer its statewide parochial school system and a convent to house teachers in parochial schools organized by the religious institution functioned as integral parts of the educational activities of the schools); Rev. Rul. 64-286, 1964-2 C.B. 401 (general board of a church that made purchases for the exclusive use of parochial schools and missions shared the exempt status of the primary educational organization); Rev. Rul. 71-553, 1971-2 C.B. 404 (student government association was an integral part of a university).
[291] Rev. Rul. 74-146, *supra* note 198.
[292] Rev. Rul. 75-282, *supra* note 71.
[293] Rev. Rul. 75-359, 1975-2 C.B. 79.

and operated for the purpose of providing financial assistance to organizations that are regarded as charitable is itself qualified for tax exemption as a charitable entity.[294]

One federal court had occasion to reaffirm its original position (in 1958) concerning consortia.[295] In a 1975 case,[296] the court stated:

> This court has held in the past that where one organization provides a service which is necessary and indispensable to the operations of another, the first will take on the tax status of the second.[297]

Invoking an *adjunct theory*, the court added:

> These cases clearly indicate that where one organization serves as a mere adjunct for a primary organization by providing services which are essential to the functioning of the primary organization and which would be normally performed by it, the adjunct will acquire the tax status of the primary company.[298]

The adjunct theory was initially invoked by a federal court of appeals in 1934.[299] The first application of this theory to adjuncts of charitable organizations occurred in 1951. In that year, another federal appellate court reviewed the tax status of a corporation organized to operate a bookstore and restaurant on the campus of a state college. Despite the fact that these operations were not inherently charitable or educational activities, the court of appeals invoked the rationale of the adjunct theory as follows: "[T]he business enterprise in which taxpayer is engaged obviously bears a close and intimate relationship to the functioning of the [c]ollege itself."[300] The appellate court concluded that this corporation was entitled to exemption as an educational organization.

The adjunct theory was again espoused by a court in 1970, which concluded that a museum was a tax-exempt educational organization because it was an integral part of and a valuable adjunct to a public school system.[301] At issue in this case was the availability of the pre-1969 additional charitable contribution deduction of 10 percent of a taxpayer's adjusted gross income for contributions to operating educational institutions that engage in the presentation of formal instruction.[302] The court concluded that gifts to the museum qualified for the bonus charitable contribution deduction, even though the museum itself did not satisfy the statutory requirements, because it was an integral part

---

[294] Rev. Rul. 67-149, *supra* note 199. E.g., Rev. Rul. 78-310, *supra* note 190.

[295] See *supra* note 282.

[296] Trustees of Graceland Cemetery Improvement Fund v. United States, 515 F.2d 763 (Ct. Cl. 1975).

[297] *Id*. at 770.

[298] *Id*. at 771.

[299] Produce Exch. Stock Clearing Ass'n. v. Helvering, 71 F.2d 142 (2d Cir. 1934).

[300] Squire v. Students Book Corp., 191 F.2d 1018, 1020 (9th Cir. 1951). Also Rev. Rul. 78-41, *supra* note 72.

[301] Brundage v. Comm'r, 54 T.C. 1468 (1970). Cf. Miller v. United States, 527 F.2d 231 (8th Cir. 1975).

[302] See IRC § 170(b)(1)(A)(ii).

of the school system and thus was clothed with the educational status of the system.[303]

The adjunct theory, however, does not have broad application. That is, it cannot be used to sidestep the prerequisites for tax exemption that an organization must meet under the statutory rules. As one court stated, the "adjunct doctrine has developed in unique factual settings which when reconciled do not stand for a general principle capable of eroding the statutory limitations on exemptions" as provided in the Internal Revenue Code.[304]

One of the principal reasons that the Treasury Department and the IRS have opposed tax-exempt status for a consortium arrangement is their fear that an organization that is not formed and controlled by charitable entities will by its own choice confine its services to charitable entities and thereby itself acquire charitable status, even where the provision of its services is in competition with commercial enterprises. Of course, this factual situation is easily distinguishable from the normal consortium arrangement, but the government's concern persisted nonetheless.

The government's concerns in this regard were presumably largely alleviated by a court decision in 1978, holding that an organization that planned to offer consulting services for a fee to a class of nonprofit (but not all tax-exempt) organizations did not qualify as a charitable entity but was taxable as a business.[305] The court's opinion might have come out the other way, however, had the organization confined its clientele to charitable organizations (even though not controlled by them), not set its fees to return an 11 percent net profit, and been able to include within the evidentiary base some demonstration that its services would not be in competition with commercial businesses.

A private letter ruling issued by the IRS in 1979 is at odds with its public pronouncements and positions on this point. The matter concerned an organization whose members were nonprofit universities and municipal libraries and that operated a computer network to enable its members to exchange information concerning the availability of books and other research materials in the libraries throughout a particular state. The IRS had previously determined that the organization was exempt as a charitable entity, apparently for the reason that its programs are inherently exempt in nature.[306] The issue was whether the organization could, without jeopardy to its tax-exempt status or incurrence of unrelated income, extend its resource services to various private businesses (such as banks, utilities, and automotive, chemical, and pharmaceutical industries). The IRS held that "in making your information dissemination services available to private institutions on the same basis, and for the same fee, as services are provided to your

---

[303] Also Rosehill Cemetery Co. v. United States, 285 F. Supp. 21 (N.D. Ill. 1968); Industrial Aid for the Blind v. Comm'r, 73 T.C. 96 (1979).

[304] Knights of Columbus Bldg. Ass'n of Stamford, Conn., Inc. v. United States, 88-1 U.S.T.C. ¶ 9336 (D. Conn. 1988). The court held that an organization, while closely affiliated with and principally holding title to property for a tax-exempt organization, could not qualify for tax-exempt status under the adjunct theory because it failed to meet the requirements for tax-exempt title-holding corporations under IRC § 501(c)(2)) (see § 18.2).

[305] B.S.W. Group, Inc. v. Comm'r, 70 T.C. 352 (1978).

[306] Rev. Rul. 74-614, *supra* note 200.

members you are serving your exempt purpose of disseminating useful bibliographic information to researchers."[307]

Among the most well-known of the consortia is The Common Fund, a cooperative arrangement formed by a group of colleges and universities for the collective investment of their funds, which in 1970 was ruled to be a charitable
organization. During its formative years, the management and administrative expenses of the Fund were largely met by start-up grants from a private foundation.
However, as the Fund became more reliant upon payments from its member institutions, it became unqualified for status as a charitable entity, according to the
IRS, because of the donative element test, in that the Fund's services were no
longer being provided to members at a charge of no more than 15 percent of
costs. In the face of loss of the Fund's exemption, Congress legislated the rule that
cooperative arrangements such as The Common Fund are exempt charitable organizations.[308]

The legislative history of The Common Fund provision stated that it applies
only to cooperative organizations formed and controlled by the participating institutions themselves, rather than to private organizations furnishing the same
services even where those services might be made available only to educational
organizations. Congress stated that, in enacting this statute, "it is not intended
that any inference be drawn as to the exempt status of other organizations
formed by educational institutions or by other charities on their behalf to carry
out their normal functions in a cooperative manner."[309]

Congress changed the law in this area in one respect in 1976.[310] It had been
the position of the IRS that income derived by an exempt hospital from providing
services to other exempt hospitals constitutes unrelated business income to the
hospital providing the services, on the rationale that the provision of services to
other hospitals is not an activity that is substantially related to the tax-exempt
purposes of the hospital providing the services.[311] Congress acted to override this
position in the case of small hospitals where a tax-exempt hospital[312] provides
services only to other tax-exempt hospitals, as long as each of the recipient hospitals has facilities to serve not more than 100 inpatients and the services would be
consistent with the recipient hospitals' exempt purposes if performed by them on
their own behalf.[313]

This law change was implemented to enable a number of small hospitals to
receive services from a single institution instead of providing them directly or
creating a tax-exempt organization to provide the services. However, language
in the legislative history is somewhat broader than the specifics of this rule,

---

[307] Priv. Ltr. Rul. 7951134.

[308] IRC § 501(f).

[309] S. Rep. No. 93-888, 93d Cong., 2d Sess. 3 (1974).

[310] IRC § 513(e). See § 27.2(g).

[311] Rev. Rul. 69-633, 1969-2 C.B. 121. However, in 1980, the IRS issued a technical advice memorandum
that held that the provision by an exempt organization of administrative services for other unrelated
exempt organizations constitutes the performance of an unrelated business (8032039), which holds
open the possibility that services to related organizations may, for that reason, be considered related
activities.

[312] IRC § 170(b)(1)(A)(iii). See §§ 6.2(a), 11.3(a).

[313] The services provided must be confined to those described in IRC § 501(e)(1)(A). See § 10.4.

inasmuch as the Senate Finance Committee explanation stated that "a hospital is not engaged in an unrelated trade or business simply because it provides services to other hospitals if those services could have been provided, on a tax-free basis, by a cooperative organization consisting of several tax-exempt hospitals."[314]

The U.S. Supreme Court in 1981 held that a cooperative hospital laundry organization does not qualify for tax exemption as a charitable entity.[315] Such an organization is, of course, a type of consortium. However, the Court ruled in opposition to tax exemption in this context because the facts necessitated application of the rules concerning cooperative hospital organizations—a unique and narrow set of circumstances[316]—and not because the tax law is generally in opposition to tax exemption for consortia. Thus, for example, a court held that an organization, operated on a cooperative basis, was entitled to tax-exempt status as a charitable organization because it was controlled by its member tax-exempt organizations (libraries) and provided indispensable program and administrative services to them.[317] The court stated that "where a group of tax exempt organizations form a cooperative to provide services exclusively to those tax exempt organizations, and the services provided are necessary and indispensable to the operations of the tax exempt organizations, the cooperative is a tax exempt organization."[318]

§ 6.9 INSTRUMENTALITIES OF GOVERNMENT

A wholly owned state or municipal instrumentality that is a separate entity may qualify for exemption as a charitable entity if it is a *clear counterpart* of a charitable, educational, religious, or like organization.[319] The test set by the IRS is the scope of the organization's purposes and powers, that is, whether the purposes and powers are beyond those of a charitable organization. For example, a state or municipality itself cannot qualify as a charitable organization, since its purposes are not exclusively those inherent in charities, nor can an integral component of the state or municipality.[320]

---

[314] S. Rep. No. 94-938 (Part 2), 94th Cong., 2d Sess. 76 (1976).

[315] HCSC-Laundry v. United States, 450 U.S. 1 (1981).

[316] See § 10.4.

[317] The Council for Bibliographic & Information Technologies v. Comm'r, 63 T.C.M. 3186 (1992).

[318] Id. at 3188. This court expressly concluded that the Supreme Court decision in 1981 is confined to cooperative hospital organizations, citing Chart, Inc. v. United States, 491 F. Supp. 10 (D.D.C. 1979), *rev'd*, 652 F.2d 195 (D.C. Cir. 1981).

This "necessary and indispensable" analysis was applied in a case involving an organization providing insurance services to its member charitable organizations; in denying tax exemption on this ground, the court wrote that "providing insurance to 487 unrelated exempt organizations is not an activity that is vital to each member's exempt purpose" and that "[s]uch a service neither goes to the essence of running each of . . . [the] member organizations nor constitutes an activity which would normally be performed by the member organizations" (Nonprofits' Ins. Alliance of Calif. v. United States, 94-2 U.S.T.C. ¶ 50,593 (Cl. Ct. 1994)). However, see § 10.6.

[319] Rev. Rul. 60-384, 1960-2 C.B. 172; Rev. Rul. 55-319, 1955-1 C.B. 119; Estate of Slayton v. Comm'r, 3 B.T.A. 1343 (1926).

[320] Cf. IRC § 115(a).

An otherwise qualified instrumentality meeting the *counterpart* require-ment, such as a school, college, university, or hospital, can be deemed a chari-table organization.[321] However, if an instrumentality is clothed with powers other than those described in the federal tax rules for charitable groups, such as enforcement or regulatory powers in the public interest (for example, health, welfare, safety), it would not be a clear counterpart organization. Two 1974 rulings draw the contrast. In one ruling,[322] a public housing authority was denied tax exemption as a charitable organization, even though its purpose was to provide safe and sanitary dwelling accommodations for low-income families in a particular municipality. The state statute under which it was in-corporated conferred upon it the power to conduct examinations and investi-gations, administer oaths, issue subpoenas, and make its findings and recommendations available to appropriate agencies; these powers were ruled to be regulatory or enforcement powers. By contrast, in the other ruling,[323] a public library organized under a state statute was ruled to be a counterpart to a charitable organization and hence tax-exempt. The organization had the power to determine the tax rate necessary to support its operations within specified maximum and minimum rates; since the organization lacked the power to impose or levy taxes, the power was deemed not regulatory or en-forcement in nature.

Thus, the clear counterpart type of state instrumentality may qualify for ex-emption as a charitable organization, while the type of instrumentality having enforcement or regulatory powers (presumably a *political subdivision*[324]) will not so qualify. While both instrumentalities and political subdivisions constitute qualified charitable donees,[325] the non–clear counterpart instrumentality appar-ently does not.

Until 1975, the IRS had not specifically distinguished between state instru-mentalities and state political subdivisions. In that year, the IRS made the distinc-tion, ruling that an association of counties in a state constituted an instrumentality of the state or the counties (themselves political subdivisions) but not a political subdivision of the state.[326]

In 1957,[327] the IRS promulgated criteria for identifying both state instrumen-talities and political subdivisions:

> In cases involving the status of an organization as an instrumentality of one or more states or political subdivisions, the following factors are taken into consideration: (1) whether it is used for a governmental purpose and per-forms a governmental function; (2) whether performance of its function is on behalf of one or more states or political subdivisions; (3) whether there are any private interests involved, or whether the states or political subdivisions involved have the powers and interests of an owner; (4) whether control and

---

[321] E.g., Estate of Ethel P. Green v. Comm'r, 82 T.C. 843 (1984); Rev. Rul. 67-290, 1967-2 C.B. 183.
[322] Rev. Rul. 74-14, 1974-1 C.B. 125.
[323] Rev. Rul. 74-15, 1974-1 C.B. 126.
[324] IRC §§ 103(a)(1), 115(a)(1), 170(c)(1).
[325] IRC §§ 170(c)(2), 170(c)(1), respectively.
[326] Rev. Rul. 75-359, *supra* note 293.
[327] Rev. Rul. 57-128, 1957-1 C.B. 311.

supervision of the organization is vested in public authority or authorities; (5) if express or implied statutory or other authority is necessary for the creation and/or use of such an instrumentality and whether such authority exists; and (6) the degree of financial autonomy and the source of its operating expenses.

According to the government, however, an additional characteristic separates a political subdivision from a state instrumentality: the former has been delegated the right to exercise part of the sovereign power of the governmental unit of which it is a division (or is a municipal corporation).[328] Thus, the association of counties discussed above was denied status as a political subdivision of the state because it was not delegated any of the counties' or state's sovereign powers. However, the IRS ruled that the association was nonetheless a qualified donee for charitable contribution purposes, with contributions deductible as being "for the use of" political subdivisions (that is, the counties), subject to the annual limitation of 20 percent of the donor's contribution base.[329]

Presumably, a state law characterization of an entity's status as a type of governmental unit is overridden for federal tax purposes by the criteria established in 1957. For example, the University of Illinois has been determined by the supreme court of that state to be a "public corporation."[330] However, because the University of Illinois met the criteria promulgated in 1957 and has been delegated the right to exercise part of the sovereign power of the State of Illinois, it constitutes a political subdivision of the state. (Both the IRS and the courts have recognized that the education of its citizens is an essential governmental function of a state.[331]) Thus it is that a state college or university (and comparable entities such as state hospitals) may qualify as both a clear counterpart state instrumentality (and thus have tax exemption as a charitable entity) and a political subdivision because its activities, in addition to those described in the 1957 criteria, are neither regulatory nor enforcement powers.[332] However, it is the position of the IRS that most state universities cannot qualify as political subdivisions.[333]

The foregoing analysis by the IRS did not take into account the consequence of operation of the adjunct theory.[334] By this theory, the association of counties should have been regarded as a political subdivision of the state rather than an instrumentality of the state, inasmuch as the characteristics of the counties are attributable to the association.[335]

---

[328] Reg. § 1.103(b).

[329] IRC § 170(b)(1)(B).

[330] The People ex rel. The Board of Trustees of the Univ. of Ill. v. George F. Barrett, Att'y Gen., 46 N.E.2d 951 (Ill. 1943).

[331] Rev. Rul. 75-436, 1975-2 C.B. 217; Gilliam v. Adams, 171 S.W.2d 813 (Tenn. 1943).

[332] Cf. Rev. Rul. 74-14, *supra* note 322.

[333] Rev. Rul. 77-165, 1977-1 C.B. 21. See the discussion in § 18.17.

[334] See text accompanying *supra* notes 294–304.

[335] E.g., Brundage v. Comm'r, *supra* note 301; cf. Miller v. United States, *supra* note 301; Puerto Rico Marine Mgt., Inc. v. International Longshoremen's Ass'n, AFL-CIO, 398 F. Supp. 118 (D.P.R. 1975).

The IRS ruled on several occasions as to whether an entity is a political subdivision or a state instrumentality. The IRS characterized a county board of education as an instrumentality of a state in the fact statement of a 1970 ruling, but then concluded that the board qualified as a political subdivision.[336] Similarly, the IRS ruled a governor's conference to be a political subdivision of a state.[337] Also, an organization created by the governors of 11 states to foster interstate cooperation and to otherwise coordinate action among these states was ruled to be an instrumentality of the states.[338] Likewise, the IRS held that an industrial commission established by a state legislature to study the problems of industrial life in a geographic area qualified as a charitable donee.[339]

Reversing an earlier position, the IRS ruled that an incorporated integrated state bar, which engaged in a variety of activities with respect to lawyers, did not qualify as an instrumentality or political subdivision of a state.[340] The IRS reasoned that the state bar was a "dual purpose" organization, in that it had public purposes (such as admission, suspension, disbarment, and reprimand of licensed attorneys) and private purposes (such as the protection of professional interests of its members), and thus that it was "not an arm of the state because it is a separate entity and has private as well as public purposes." The IRS also held that the state bar was "not a political subdivision because it has no meaningful sovereign powers."

A committee, created by joint resolution of a state legislature, established to receive and expend contributions to provide state units for a parade incident to a presidential inauguration, was ruled to be a political subdivision.[341] A committee that was created by a governor's executive order to educate the public about the activities of the United Nations was considered a political subdivision of the state.[342] Under appropriate circumstances, a nonprofit corporation may qualify as a political subdivision of a state.[343]

In other illustrations, the Supreme Court has held that the concept of a *federal instrumentality* includes army post exchanges[344] and the American National Red Cross.[345] While neither is directly controlled by the United States, they have an "unusual relationship" with the federal government, such as operation pursuant to a federal charter, federal government audit, involvement of a presidential appointee or government employees, and government funding or provision of services. Applying these criteria, one federal court found

---

[336] Rev. Rul. 70-562, 1970-2 C.B. 63.
[337] Rev. Rul. 69-459, 1969-2 C.B. 35.
[338] Priv. Ltr. Rul. 7935043.
[339] Rev. Rul. 79-323, 1979-2 C.B. 106.
[340] Rev. Rul. 77-232, 1977-2 C.B. 71, revoking Rev. Rul. 59-152, 1959-1 C.B. 54. This change in classification also means that contributions to these state bars are not deductible under IRC §§ 170(c)(1), 2055(a)(1), and 2522(a)(1). However, Rev. Rul. 77-232 is inapplicable to contributions made prior to July 5, 1977 (Rev. Rul. 78-129, 1978-1 C.B. 67).
[341] Rev. Rul. 58-265, 1958-1 C.B. 127.
[342] Rev. Rul. 62-66, 1962-1 C.B. 83.
[343] Rev. Rul. 59-41, 1959-1 C.B. 13; Rev. Rul. 54-296, 1954-2 C.B. 59.
[344] Standard Oil Co. v. Johnson, 316 U.S. 481 (1942).
[345] Department of Employment v. United States, 85 U.S. 355 (1966). Also United States v. Livingston, 179 F. Supp. 9 (E.D.S.C. 1959), *aff'd* , 364 U.S. 281 (1960).

the U.S. Capital Historical Society to be a federal instrumentality, also finding that it performs an essential function for the federal government (with the result that the District of Columbia was held to lack the power to tax sales by the historical society).[346]

In 1963, the IRS considered the question of whether a nonprofit membership corporation qualified as a political subdivision.[347] The members of the corporation consisted of representatives of the local chambers of commerce and other private business groups in a particular county, the county commissioners, and officials of participating municipalities. There was no private inurement and the corporation's articles provided that upon any dissolution of the corporation the beneficial interest in any property owned by the corporation would pass to the county.

The IRS held that obligations of such a corporation would be considered issued *on behalf of* the state or a political subdivision of the state, provided each of the following requirements is met: the corporation must engage in activities that are essentially public in nature; the corporation must be one that is not organized for profit (except to the extent of retiring indebtedness); the corporate income must not inure to any private person; the state or a political subdivision thereof must have a beneficial interest in the corporation while the indebtedness remains outstanding and it must obtain full legal title to the property of the corporation with respect to which the indebtedness was incurred upon the retirement of such indebtedness; and the corporation must have been approved by the state or a political subdivision of the state.[348]

State liquor stores are generally considered political subdivisions, as being part of the states' effort to regulate the use of alcohol.[349] Lawyers' trust accounts, created and supervised by a state's supreme court, are exempt from federal income tax as an integral part of the state.[350]

A federal court of appeals held that a *political subdivision* is any division of any state that has been delegated the right to exercise part of the sovereign power of the unit.[351] The appellate court stated:

> The term "political subdivision" is broad and comprehensive and denotes any division of the State made by the proper authorities thereof, acting within their constitutional powers, for the purpose of those functions of the State which by long usage and the inherent necessities of government have always been regarded as public.[352]

---

[346] United States v. District of Columbia, 558 F. Supp. 213 (D.D.C. 1982).

[347] Rev. Rul. 63-20, 1963-1 C.B. 24.

[348] Also Rev. Rul. 60-243, 1960-2 C.B. 35; Rev. Rul. 57-187, 1957-1 C.B. 65.

[349] Rev. Rul. 71-132, 1971-1 C.B. 29; Rev. Rul. 71-131, 1971-1 C.B. 28.

[350] Rev. Rul. 87-2, 1987-1 C.B. 18. Also Rev. Rul. 81-209, 1981-2 C.B. 16.

[351] Commissioner v. Estate of Alexander J. Shamberg, 3 T.C. 131 (1944), *aff'd* , 144 F.2d 998, (particularly 1004–1006) (2d Cir. 1944), *cert. den.* , 323 U.S. 792 (1944).

[352] *Id.* , 144 F. 2d at 1004.

Similarly, a state supreme court observed that:

> ... [i]mportant factors, among others, which must be considered in determining that ... [a]n agency is an instrument of government are: [whether] (1) It was created by the government; (2) it is wholly owned by the government; (3) it is not operated for profit; (4) it is primarily engaged in the performance of some essential governmental function; [and] (5) the proposed tax will impose an economic burden upon the government, or it serves to materially impair the usefulness or efficiency of the agency, or to materially restrict it in the performance of its duties.[353]

An organization may seek instrumentality status rather than tax exemption as a charitable entity to avoid the annual reporting requirements, the private foundation rules, other federal tax limitations on charitable groups, or because it cannot qualify as charitable in nature. Contributions to instrumentalities are deductible as long as they qualify as a *governmental unit* and the gift is made for exclusively public purposes;[354] the interest they pay on their borrowings generally is exempt from the lender's gross income.[355]

§ 6.10 OTHER CATEGORIES OF CHARITABLE ORGANIZATIONS

There are several other categories of tax-exempt charitable organizations. Many of these do not fit within any of the traditional definitions of *charitable* function.

(a) Environmental Protection

An organization established to promote environmental conservancy is a charitable entity.[356] The IRS ruled that "[i]t is generally recognized that efforts to preserve and protect the natural environment for the benefit of the public serve a charitable purpose."[357] The IRS concluded that the organization involved was "enhancing the accomplishment of the express national policy of conserving the nation's unique natural resources."[358] However, the IRS refused to classify an organization as a charitable entity where it merely restricted land to uses that did not change the environment, where the land lacked any "distinctive ecological significance" and where any public benefit was "too indirect and insignificant."[359]

---

[353] Unemployment Compensation Comm'n of N.C. v. Wachovia Bank & Trust Co., 2 S.E.2d 592, 596 (N.C. 1939). Also City of Cincinnati v. Gamble, 34 N.E.2d 226, 231 (Ohio 1941); City of Bay Minette v. Quinly, 82 So.2d 192, 194 (Ala. 1955); War Memorial Hosp. of District No. 1, Park County v. Board of County Comm'rs of County of Park, 279 P.2d 472, 475 (Wyo. 1955); Gebhardt v. Village of La Grange Park, 188 N.E. 372, 374 (Ill. 1933).

[354] IRC §§ 170(c)(1), 170(b)(1)(A)(v).

[355] IRC § 103(a)(1). Cf. State of S.C. v. Baker , 485 U.S. 505 (1988).

[356] Rev. Rul. 76-204, *supra* note 228; Rev. Rul. 80-279, 1980-2 C.B. 176; Rev. Rul. 80-278, 1980-2 C.B. 175. Also Rev. Rul. 75-207, 1975-1 C.B. 361; Rev. Rul. 70-186, *supra* note 140; Rev. Rul. 67-292, *supra* note 145.

[357] Rev. Rul. 76-204, *supra* note 228, at 153.

[358] *Id* .

[359] Rev. Rul. 78-384, *supra* note 228.

Nonetheless, the position of the IRS that only land of "distinctive ecological significance" can qualify as an exempt function holding of an environmental conservation organization was implicitly rejected by a court when it accorded classification as a charitable organization to a model farm operated as a conservation project.[360] The facts of the case were that the organization's land "is generally representative of the surrounding farmland in the county" and that the organization "readily admits its land does not have special environmental attributes, nor is the land part of an ecologically significant undeveloped area such as a swamp, marsh, forest, or other wilderness tract."[361] Instead, the organization's "goal is to test and demonstrate the restoration of over-cultivated, exhausted land to a working ecological balance."[362] The organization simply "encourages more local practice of the farming and conservation techniques it is developing."[363] Rather than focus on the nature of the land as such, the court emphasized the use of the land: The organization's "agricultural program seeks to demonstrate the commercial viability of ecologically sound farming techniques not yet practiced in the surrounding community."[364]

(b) Promotion of Patriotism

The IRS concluded that the promotion of patriotism is a charitable objective. The ruling came in the case of a membership organization, formed by citizens of a community to promote "civic pride in the community, the state, and the country," by providing a color guard and conducting flag raising and other ceremonies at patriotic and community functions.[365] As authority for this position, the IRS stated that "[t]rusts created for the purpose of inculcating patriotic emotions have been upheld as charitable, as have trusts for the purchase and display of a flag, and for the celebration of a patriotic holiday."[366]

(c) Promotion of Sports

A court held that the promotion, advancement, and sponsoring of recreational and amateur sports is a charitable activity.[367] The organization involved owned

---

[360] Dumaine Farms v. Comm'r, 73 T.C. 650 (1980).

[361] *Id*. at 653.

[362] *Id*.

[363] *Id*.

[364] *Id*. at 656.

[365] Rev. Rul. 78-84, 1978-1 C.B. 150.

[366] Citing IV *Scott on Trusts* (3d ed. 1967) § 374.3; Bogert, *Trusts and Trustees* (2d ed. 1964) § 378. Also Buder v. United States, 7 F.3d 1382 (8th Cir. 1993) (where a trust, established to foster and promote the cause of patriotism, loyalty, and fundamental constitutional government (and to combat subversive activities, socialism, and communism), was held to qualify as a tax-exempt charitable entity).

[367] Hutchinson Baseball Enters., Inc. v. Comm'r, 73 T.C. 144 (1979), *aff'd*, 696 F.2d 757 (10th Cir. 1982). However, where the sports organization is primarily established to further the recreational interests of its creators, tax exemption as a charitable organization will not be available (North Am. Sequential Sweepstakes v. Comm'r, 77 T.C. 1087 (1981)). Although the IRS continues to disagree with this decision, the government did not request Supreme Court review (AOD 1984-016).

and operated an amateur baseball team that played in a semiprofessional league, leased and maintained a baseball field used by its team and other teams, furnished instructors and coaches for a baseball camp, and provided coaches for Little League teams. The players were not paid for their participation on the team, although they received free lodging and were guaranteed employment in local industries during the season. The government's contention that the team was semiprofessional, and thus that the operation of it was a nonexempt activity, was rejected.[368]

(d) Public Interest Law

Organizations structured as *public interest law firms*—entities that provide legal representation for important citizen interests that are unrepresented because the cases are not economically feasible for private law firms—can qualify as charitable organizations where they provide a "service which is of benefit to the community as a whole," with "[c]haritability . . . also dependent upon the fact that the service provided by public interest law firms is distinguishable from that which is commercially available."[369] The recognition by the IRS that public interest law firms can be charitable in nature was significant, in that beforehand it would not find tax-exempt an organization operating in support of interests of a majority of the public since that segment of society does not constitute a charitable class.[370]

In guidelines containing criteria for these firms, the IRS acknowledged that legal representation for disadvantaged minorities, victims of racial discrimination, and those denied human and civil rights has long been recognized as a charitable activity.[371]

These guidelines state that the "engagement of the organization in litigation can reasonably be said to be in representation of a broad public interest rather than a private interest." In addition to generally complying with the requirements of the federal tax law rules concerning charitable organizations, the IRS guidelines for the public interest law firm require the following: (1) It may accept fees for services rendered but only in accordance with specific IRS procedures; (2) it may not have a program of "disruption of the judicial system, illegal activity, or violation of the applicable canons of ethics"; (3) it files with its annual information return (Form 990) a description of cases litigated and the "rationale for the determination that they would benefit the public generally"[372]; (4) its policies and programs are the responsibility of a "board or

---

[368] This case did not involve the IRC § 501(c)(3) provision for certain amateur sports organizations. See § 10.2.

[369] Rev. Rul. 75-74, *supra* note 42.

[370] See § 5.5(a).

[371] Rev. Proc. 71-39, 1971-2 C.B. 575. In general, see § 6.6.

[372] Failure, absent reasonable cause, by a public interest law firm to comply with this filing requirement constitutes a failure to file a return under IRC § 6652(d)(1) (see § 24.3, (vii)) and revocation of tax exemption is a valid sanction, according to the IRS (Gen. Couns. Mem. 37159).

committee representative of the public interest," not controlled by its employees or those who litigate on its behalf nor by noncharitable organizations; (5) it is not operated so as to create "identification or confusion with a particular private law firm"; and (6) "[t]here is no arrangement to provide, directly or indirectly, a deduction for the cost of litigation which is for the private benefit of the donor."

Subsequently, the IRS promulgated procedures for the acceptance of fees by these firms.[373] In essence, these procedures forbid a firm from seeking fees from clients; allow the acceptance of fees where paid by opposing parties under court or agency award; require the firm to use awarded fees solely to defray normal operating expenses, with no more than one half of such costs (calculated over five years) so defrayed; and require the firm to file with its annual information return a report of all fees sought and recovered.

The IRS recognized that the awarding of lawyers' fees serves to effectuate a legislative or judicial policy in deterring or encouraging certain actions.[374] Thus, concluded the IRS, the "award or acceptance of attorneys' fees by public interest law firms in these situations is consistent with and tends to support the statutory and public policy objectives in awarding such fees," and such a firm constitutes a charitable organization as long as it is "clear that neither the expectation nor the possibility, however remote, of an award of fees is a substantial motivating factor in the selection of cases."[375] By contrast, where the firm "has an established policy of charging or accepting attorneys' fees from its clients, the representation provided cannot be distinguished from that available through traditional private law firms" and the exemption as a charitable entity will be denied or revoked.[376] Similarly, a public interest law firm will lose its tax exemption if it enters into a fee-sharing arrangement with a private lawyer who will keep a portion of a court-awarded fee that exceeds the amount paid by the firm to the lawyer for services rendered.[377]

(e) Local Economic Development

A form of charitable organization is the *local economic development corporation* (LEDC). LEDCs engage in a variety of activities, including investment in local businesses; direct operation of job-training, housing, and other programs; business counseling; and encouragement to established national businesses to open plants or offices in economically depressed areas. A prime purpose of an LEDC is to alleviate poverty—clearly a charitable purpose. However, by necessity, LEDCs

---

[373] Rev. Proc. 75-13, 1975-1 C.B. 662.
[374] Citing Mills v. Electric Auto-Lite Co., 396 U.S. 375 (1970); Newman v. Piggie Park Enter., Inc., 309 U.S. 400 (1968).
[375] Rev. Rul. 75-76, 1975-1 C.B. 154.
[376] Rev. Rul. 75-75, 1975-1 C.B. 154.
[377] Rev. Rul. 76-5, 1976-1 C.B. 146. In general, Houck, "With Charity for All," 93 *Yale L.J.* 1415 (1984); Note, "Public Interest Law Firms and Client-Paid Fees," 33 *Tax Law* . 915 (1980); Hobbet, "Public Interest Law Firms—To Fee or Not to Fee," 27 *Nat'l Tax J.* 45 (1974); Chomsky, "Tax-Exempt Status of Public Interest Law Firms," 45 *S. Cal. L. Rev.* 228 (1972); Note, "IRS Man Cometh: Public Interest Law Firms Meet the Tax Collector," 13 *Ariz. L. Rev.* 857 (1971); Goldberg & Cohen, "Does higher authority than IRS guidelines exist for public interest law firms?," 34 *J. Tax* . 77 (1971).

render assistance to commercial business enterprises and make investments in businesses as part of their principal function. While these activities are not normally regarded as charitable in nature, there is authority for a determination that these LEDCs engage in charitable endeavors.

The IRS ruled that an organization is tax-exempt as a charitable entity (as promoting social welfare) where it maintained a program of providing low-cost financial assistance and other aid designed to improve economic conditions and economic opportunities in economically depressed areas.[378] The organization undertook to combat these conditions by providing funds and working capital to business corporations or individual proprietors who were unable to obtain funds from conventional commercial sources because of the poor financial risks involved. The IRS noted that "these loans and purchases of equity interest are not undertaken for purpose of profit or gain but for the purpose of advancing the charitable goals of the organization and are not investments for profit in any conventional business sense."[379]

It is possible for an LEDC to qualify for tax exemption as a charitable entity even though it is licensed as a nonprofit small business investment company (SBIC) under the Small Business Investment Act.[380] A SBIC licensee is required to comply with certain regulations promulgated by the Small Business Administration (SBA) that set requirements as to the level of interest rates charged by a licensee and impose various restrictions on the degree of financial support that may be offered to a prospective recipient. The difficulty is that an SBA-regulated SBIC may be prevented from engaging in certain loan transactions in which it would otherwise be able to engage in furtherance of charitable purposes. However, even though "a narrower range of permissible transactions" is available to an SBIC than to non-SBA-regulated LEDCs, the IRS concluded that the SBIC "may still provide loans to businesses that cannot secure financing through conventional commercial sources, the operation of which businesses will achieve charitable purposes. . . ."[381] Thus, although this ruling does not mean that all SBA-regulated SBICs are automatically tax-exempt LEDCs, it does mean that the mere fact that the organization is subject to the SBA regulations does not preclude it from tax exemption.

Subsequently, the IRS distinguished the situation involved in its prior ruling from that where the primary purpose of the organization is to promote business in general rather than to provide assistance only to businesses owned by minority groups or to businesses experiencing difficulty because of their location in a deteriorated section of the community. Thus, the IRS denied classification as a charitable entity to an organization formed to increase business patronage in a deteriorated area mainly inhabited by minority groups by providing information on the area's shopping opportunities, local transportation, and accommodations, and to an organization the purpose of which was to re-

---

[378] Rev. Rul. 74-587, *supra* note 250.

[379] *Id*. at 163.

[380] 15 U.S.C. § 681(d).

[381] Rev. Rul. 81-284, *supra* note 250. The IRS likewise recognized that an IRC § 501(c)(3) organization can provide funding for a minority enterprise small business investment company (Gen. Couns. Mem. 38497).

vive retail sales in an area suffering from continued economic decline by constructing a shopping center in the area to arrest the flow of business to competing centers in outlying areas.[382]

(f) Other Charitable Organizations

The IRS ruled that the term *charitable* includes the "care of orphans."[383] The occasion was consideration of the tax status of an organization that arranged for the placement of orphan children living in foreign countries with adoptive parents in the United States. The IRS also determined that "facilitating student and cultural exchanges" is a charitable activity.[384]

While one federal court allowed an estate tax charitable deduction for a bequest to a "public" cemetery because of the "important social function" it performed and the "concurrent lessening of the burden of the public fisc,"[385] the decision was overturned on appeal on the grounds that Congress has not enacted an estate tax counterpart to the income tax exemption provision for cemetery companies[386] and that the common-law definition of the term *charity* in the income tax context cannot be imported into the estate tax field.[387] The appellate court was unable to discern why Congress elected to treat contributions to cemetery organizations differently for income and estate tax deduction purposes, regarding the matter as an "anomaly" that must be left to "congressional wisdom."[388] The attempt by the lower court to categorize public cemeteries as charities because the "maintenance of cemetery facilities by cemetery associations benefits the community both through its aesthetic effects and by the performance of a necessary social task"[389] thus failed.[390]

---

[382] Rev. Rul. 77-111, *supra* note 250. In general, Buehler, "Community Development and Tax-Exempt Business Incubators," 2 *J. Tax. Exempt Orgs.* 16 (Spring 1990).

[383] Rev. Rul. 80-200, 1980-2 C.B. 173.

[384] Rev. Rul. 80-286, *supra* note 225. The U.S. Tax Court concluded that the purpose of "maintain[ing] public confidence in the legal system" through "various means of improving the administration of justice" is charitable (Kentucky Bar Found., Inc. v. Comm'r, *supra* note 102).

[385] Mellon Bank v. United States, 509 F. Supp. 160 (W.D. Pa. 1984).

[386] IRC § 501(c)(13). See § 18.6.

[387] Mellon Bank v. United States, 762 F.2d 283 (3d Cir. 1985), *cert. den.*, 475 U.S. 1031 (1986).

[388] *Id.* at 286. Also Child v. United States, 540 F.2d 579, 584 (2d Cir. 1976), *cert. den.*, 429 U.S. 1092 (1977).

[389] Mellon Bank v. United States, *supra* note 385, at 164.

[390] In general, Note, "Estate Tax—Charitable Deduction: Cemetery Not a Charitable Organization," 18 *B.C. Ind. & Comm. L. Rev.* 955 (1977).

CHAPTER SEVEN

Educational Organizations

Section 501(c)(3) of the Internal Revenue Code provides that an organization may be exempt from federal income tax if it is organized and operated exclusively for an *educational* purpose.[1] There is some overlap in this area with the classification of organizations as being charitable entities, inasmuch as the term *charitable* includes the *advancement of education*.[2]

§ 7.1 FEDERAL TAX LAW DEFINITION OF *EDUCATIONAL*

The federal tax law defines the term *educational* as encompassing far more than formal schooling. Basically, the concept of *educational* as used for federal tax purposes is defined as relating to the "instruction or training of the individual for the purpose of improving or developing his capabilities" or the "instruction of the public on subjects useful to the individual and beneficial to the community."[3]

For many years, the definition accorded the term *educational* by the Department of the Treasury and the IRS was routinely followed. However, in 1980, a federal court of appeals found portions of the regulation defining the term unconstitutionally vague.[4] That segment of the regulation—pertaining to a *full and fair exposition test*[5]—permits materials that advocate a viewpoint to qualify as being educational in nature but only if the advocacy is preceded by an objective discussion of the issue or subject involved. Subsequently, this appellate court—albeit recognizing "the inherently general nature of the term 'educational' and the wide range of meanings Congress may have intended to convey," and stating that

---

[1] Also Reg. § 1.501(c)(3)-1(d)(1)(i)(f).

[2] See § 6.5.

[3] Reg. § 1.501(c)(3)-1(d)(3)(i).

[4] Big Mama Rag, Inc. v. United States, 631 F.2d 1030 (D.C. Cir. 1980).

[5] See *infra* § 2.

"[w]e do not attempt a definition" of the term—set forth some general criteria as to what material may qualify as educational.[6]

In the subsequent case, this federal appellate court decided that the materials there at issue "fall short" of being educational, "[e]ven under the most minimal requirement of a rational development of a point of view."[7] Said the court: "It is the fact that there is no reasoned development of the conclusions which removes it [the material at issue] from any definition of 'educational' conceivably intended by Congress."[8] Moreover, the court ruled, "in order to be deemed 'educational' and enjoy tax exemption some degree of intellectually appealing development of or foundation for the views advocated would be required."[9] The court wrote:

> The exposition of propositions the correctness of which is readily demonstrable is doubtless educational. As the truth of the view asserted becomes less and less demonstrable, however, 'instruction' or 'education' must, we think, require more than mere assertion and repetition.[10]

Thereafter, the court observed that, "[i]n attempting a definition suitable for all comers, IRS, or any legislature, court, or other administrator is beset with difficulties which are obvious."[11]

Thus, the federal tax law does not contain a threshold, generic definition of the term *educational*, but rests on the concept that subjects spoken or written about be appropriately developed or founded.

§ 7.2 *EDUCATION* VERSUS *PROPAGANDA*

Inherent in the concept of *educational* is the principle that an organization is not educational in nature where it zealously propagates particular ideas or doctrines without presentation of them in any reasonably objective or balanced manner. The point was reflected in the income tax regulations that define the term *educational*, where it is stated that

> [a]n organization may be educational even though it advocates a particular position or viewpoint so long as it presents a sufficiently full and fair exposition of the pertinent facts as to permit an individual or the public to form an independent opinion or conclusion. On the other hand, an organization is not educational if its principal function is the mere presentation of unsupported opinion.[12]

---

[6] National Alliance v. United States, 710 F.2d 868, 873 (D.C. Cir. 1983).
[7] *Id.*
[8] *Id.*
[9] *Id.*
[10] *Id.*
[11] *Id.*
[12] Reg. § 1.501(c)(3)-1(d)(3)(i).

This requirement is designed to exclude from the concept of *educational* the technique of the dissemination of *propaganda*, a term that also is considered in the context of the rules governing legislative activities by charitable organizations.[13] In this context, it can be said that the term *educational* does not extend to "public address with selfish or ulterior purpose and characterized by the coloring or distortion of facts."[14]

An organization may avoid the charge that its principal function is the mere presentation of unsupported opinion either by presenting a sufficiently full and fair exposition of the pertinent facts in the materials it prepares and disseminates or by circulating copies of materials that contain this type of an exposition.[15] As discussed below, this precept is now embodied in the IRS's *methodology* test. The test bears that name in reflection of the point that the method used by an organization in advocating its position, rather than the position itself, is the standard for determining whether the organization has educational purposes.

These regulations were applied by the IRS in a case involving an organization that endeavored to educate the public concerning the obligations of the broadcast media to serve the public interest. Periodically, the organization prepared evaluations of the performance of local broadcasters and made the evaluations available to the general public and governmental agencies. The IRS ruled that these evaluations were "objective" (members of the organization with a personal, professional, or business interest in a particular evaluation did not participate in the consideration) and that the organization qualified as a tax-exempt educational entity.[16]

Also, an educational organization, for federal tax purposes, may not so carry on its work as to become an *action organization*.[17] Thus the income tax regulations provide as follows:

> The fact that an organization, in carrying out its primary purpose, advocates social or civic changes or presents opinion on controversial issues with the intention of molding public opinion or creating public sentiment to an acceptance of its views does not preclude such organization from qualifying under section 501(c)(3) so long as it is not an "action" organization of any one of the types described in paragraph (c)(3) of this section.[18]

The foregoing points were illustrated by a ruling from the IRS holding that an organization operated to educate the public about homosexuality in order to foster an understanding and tolerance of homosexuals and their problems qualified as an educational entity.[19] The IRS noted that the information disseminated by the organization was "factual" and "independently compiled," and that the

---

[13] See Chapter 20.
[14] Seasongood v. Comm'r, 227 F.2d 907, 911 (6th Cir. 1955).
[15] National Ass'n. for the Legal Support of Alternative Schools v. Comm'r, 71 T.C. 118 (1978).
[16] Rev. Rul. 79-26, 1979-1 C.B. 196, 197.
[17] See Chapters 20 and 21.
[18] Reg. § 1.501(c)(3)-1(d)(2).
[19] Rev. Rul. 78-305, 1978-2 C.B. 172.

materials distributed "contain a full documentation of the facts relied upon to support conclusions contained therein."[20] Further, the IRS observed that the organization "does not advocate or seek to convince individuals that they should or should not be homosexuals."[21]

By contrast, an organization, the principal activity of which was publication of a feminist monthly newspaper, was found by a federal district court to not qualify as a tax-exempt educational entity because it failed to meet the *full and fair exposition* standard.[22] The newspaper contained material designed to advance the cause of the women's movement; the organization refused to publish items it considered damaging to that cause. The court, characterizing the organization as an "advocate" that had eschewed a policy of offering any balancing facts, said that its holding "is not to say that a publication may not advocate a particular point of view and still be educational, or that it must necessarily present views inimical to its philosophy, only that in doing so it must be sufficiently dispassionate as to provide its readers with the factual basis from which they may draw independent conclusions."[23] The court rejected the assertion that the standard is a *per se* violation of the First Amendment,[24] although it did observe that the regulation does not allow the IRS to censor views with which it does not agree.

On appeal, in an upset of the tax regulations concerning educational organizations, a federal court of appeals concluded that the *full and fair exposition* requirement is so vague as to violate the First Amendment.[25] The appellate court conceded that the terms in the tax-exempt organizations field, such as "religious," "charitable," and "educational," easily "lend themselves to subjective definitions at odds with the constitutional limitations."[26] However, the court said that the full and fair exposition test lacks the "requisite clarity, both in explaining which applicant organizations are subject to the standard and in articulating its substantive requirements."[27]

The regulations state that only an organization that "advocates a particular position or viewpoint" must pass the test. The rules looked to by the IRS classify this type of an organization as one that is "controversial."[28] That, held the court, was too vague to pass First Amendment muster, because the IRS lacked any "objective standard by which to judge which applicant organizations are advocacy groups," in that the determination is made solely on the basis of a subjective evaluation of what is "controversial."[29]

---

[20] *Id.* at 173.

[21] *Id.*

[22] Big Mama Rag, Inc. v. United States, 494 F. Supp. 473 (D.D.C. 1979).

[23] *Id.* at 479.

[24] In so doing, the court relied largely upon Cammarano v. United States, 358 U.S. 498 (1959), and Hannegan v. Esquire, 327 U.S. 146 (1946).

[25] Big Mama Rag, Inc. v. United States, *supra* note 4.

[26] *Id.* at 1035.

[27] *Id.* at 1036.

[28] E.g., IRS Exempt Organizations Handbook § 345 (12); Rev. Rul. 78-305, *supra* note 19.

[29] Big Mama Rag, Inc. v. United States, *supra* note 25, at 1036.

Also, the court found wanting the requirements of the full and fair exposition standard. The court posed these questions: What is a "full and fair" exposition? Can an exposition be "fair" but not "full"? What is a "pertinent" fact? When is the exposition "sufficient" to permit persons to form an independent opinion? and who makes these determinations?[30] Noting the "futility of attempting to draw lines between fact and unsupported opinion," the appeals court observed that the district court did not actually apply the test but instead found the organization too "doctrinaire."[31] This approach was severely criticized, with the higher court writing that it "can conceive of no value-free measurement of the extent to which material is doctrinaire, and the district court's reliance on that evaluative concept corroborates for us the impossibility of principled and objective application of the fact/opinion distinction."[32]

Summarizing its findings (in words with implications reaching far beyond the specific case), the court said: "Applications for tax exemption must be evaluated, however, on the basis of criteria capable of neutral application. The standards may not be so imprecise that they afford latitude to individual IRS officials to pass judgment on the content and quality of an applicant's views and goals and therefore to discriminate against those engaged in protected First Amendment activities."[33]

In the aftermath of the voiding of the full and fair exposition test, the IRS advanced the *methodology test,* pursuant to which a presentation is evaluated by that agency to determine whether it may be *educational,* as opposed to *propaganda.* Pursuant to the methodology test, initially unveiled in litigation, the federal government endeavors (because of the free speech considerations) to avoid being the "arbiter of 'truth' " and accordingly "test[s] the method by which the advocate proceeds from the premises he furnishes to the conclusion he advocates . . ."[34]

Although a federal district court found the methodology test itself unconstitutionally vague,[35] on appeal, the appellate court did not reach the question of the constitutionality of the test, having concluded that the material at issue was not, in the first instance, educational in nature.[36] Nonetheless, the appellate court implicitly endorsed the methodology test by observing that "starting from the breadth of terms in the regulation, application by IRS of the methodology test would move in the direction of more specifically requiring, in advocacy material, an intellectually appealing development of the views advocated," that the "four criteria tend toward ensuring that the educational exemption be restricted to material which substantially helps a reader or listener in a learning process," and

---

[30] *Id.* at 1037.
[31] *Id.* at 1038.
[32] *Id.*
[33] *Id.* at 1040. In general, Comment, "Tax Exemptions for Educational Institutions: Discretion and Discrimination," 128 *U. Pa. L. Rev.* 849 (1980).
[34] National Alliance v. United States, *supra* note 6, at 874.
[35] National Alliance v. United States, 81-1 U.S.T.C. ¶ 9464 (D.D.C. 1981).
[36] National Alliance v. United States, *supra* note 6.

that the "test reduces the vagueness found" to be present in the full and fair exposition standard.[37] Indeed, the appellate court noted—without contradiction—that the "government does argue that the Methodology Test goes as far as humanly possible in verbalizing a line separating education from noneducational expression."[38]

The criteria of the methodology test as developed by the IRS were enunciated in a court opinion[39] and subsequently by the IRS administratively.[40] This test rests on the predicate that the IRS "renders no judgment as to the viewpoint or position of the organization." Under this test, "[t]he method used by the organization will not be considered educational if it fails to provide a factual foundation for the viewpoint or position being advocated, or if it fails to provide a development from the relevant facts that would materially aid a listener or reader in a learning process."[41]

The "presence of any of the following factors in the presentations made by an organization is indicative that the method used by the organization to advocate its viewpoints or positions is not educational": the "presentation of viewpoints or positions unsupported by facts is a significant portion of the organization's communications," the "facts that purport to support the viewpoints or positions are distorted," the "organization's presentations make substantial use of inflammatory and disparaging terms and express conclusions more on the basis of strong emotional feelings than of objective evaluations," and the "approach used in the organization's presentations is not aimed at developing an understanding on the part of the intended audience or readership because it does not consider their background or training in the subject matter."[42] The criteria state that "[t]here may be exceptional circumstances, however, where an organization's advocacy may be educational even if one or more of the factors listed" above are present.[43] The IRS states that it "will look to all the facts and circumstances to determine whether an organization may be considered educational despite the presence of one or more of such factors."[44] The IRS observed that, in applying these rules, it "has attempted to eliminate or minimize the potential for any public official to impose his or her preconceptions or beliefs in determining whether the particular viewpoint or position is educational."[45] "It has been, and it remains," read the guidelines, "the policy of the Service to maintain a position of disinterested neutrality with respect to the beliefs advocated by an organization."[46]

Thus, the IRS "recognizes that the advocacy of particular viewpoints or po-

---

[37] National Alliance v. United States, *supra* note 6, at 875.
[38] *Id.*
[39] *Id.*
[40] Rev. Proc. 86-43, 1986-2 C.B. 729.
[41] *Id.* § 3.02.
[42] *Id.* § 3.03.
[43] *Id.* at § 3.04.
[44] *Id.* at § 3.04.
[45] *Id.* § 2.02.
[46] *Id.* § 2.02.

sitions may serve an educational purpose even if the viewpoints or positions being advocated are unpopular or are not generally accepted."[47]

A court applied the methodology test and concluded that an organization's publication and other activities violated three of the four standards of the test and thus were not educational, including a finding that a significant portion of the activities "consists of the presentation of viewpoints unsupported by facts."[48] As to *substantiality*, it was written that "[w]hether an activity is substantial is a facts-and-circumstances inquiry not always dependent upon time or expenditure percentages"[49]; on the basis of the record showing the activities in question to be one of two sets of programs, the court found the non-educational activity to be substantial. The court held that the test "is not unconstitutionally vague or overbroad on its face, nor is it unconstitutional as applied."[50] It added: "Its provisions are sufficiently understandable, specific, and objective both to preclude chilling of expression protected under the First Amendment and to minimize arbitrary or discriminatory application by the IRS," because it "focuses on the method rather than the content of the presentation."[51]

§ 7.3   FORMAL EDUCATIONAL INSTITUTIONS

Nonprofit educational institutions, such as primary, secondary, and postsecondary schools, colleges and universities, early childhood centers,[52] and trade schools, are educational organizations for federal tax law purposes.[53] These organizations all have, as required, "a regularly scheduled curriculum, a regular faculty, and a regularly enrolled body of students in attendance at the place where the educational activities are regularly carried on."[54] To be tax-exempt, however, the schools must, like all charitable organizations (as the term is used in its broadest sense), meet all of the tax law requirements pertaining to these entities, including a showing that they are operated for public, rather than private, interests.

---

[47] Rev. Proc. 86-43, *supra* note 40, § 3.01. In general, Shaviro, "From *Big Mama Rag* to *National Geographic*: The Controversy Regarding Exemptions for Educational Publications," 41 *Tax L. Rev.* (No. 4) 693 (1986); Thompson, "The Availability of the Federal Educational Tax Exemption for Propaganda Organizations," 18 *U.C. Davis L. Rev.* (No. 2) 487 (1985); Note, "Federal Income Taxation—Tax-Exempt Status for Educational Organizations in Treasury Regulation § 1.501(c)(3)-1(d)(3) is Unconstitutionally Vague in Violation of the First Amendment," 49 *Geo. Wash. L. Rev.* (No. 3) 623 (1981); Winslow & Ash, "Effects of *Big Mama Rag* on exempt educational organizations," 55 *J. Tax.* 20 (1981); Note, "*Big Mama Rag*: An Inquiry Into Vagueness," 67 *Va. L. Rev.* (No. 8) 1543 (1981).

[48] The Nationalist Movement v. Comm'r, 102 T.C. 558, 592 (1994), *aff'd*, 37 F.3d 216 (5th Cir. 1994).

[49] *Id.* 102 T.C. at 589.

[50] *Id.* at 588–589.

[51] *Id.* at 589.

[52] Michigan Early Childhood Cent., Inc. v. Comm'r, 37 T.C.M. 808 (1978); San Francisco Infant School, Inc. v. Comm'r, 69 T.C. 957 (1978); Rev. Rul. 70-533, 1970-2 C.B. 112. See *infra* § 7.

[53] Reg. § 1.501(c)(3)-1(d)(3)(ii)(1).

[54] *Id.* Also IRC § 170(b)(1)(A)(ii).

This type of institution must have as its primary function the presentation of formal instruction.[55] Thus, an organization that has as its primary function the presentation of formal instruction, has courses that are interrelated and given in a regular and continuous manner (thereby constituting a regular curriculum), normally maintains a regular faculty, and has a regularly enrolled student body in attendance at the place where its educational activities are regularly carried on, qualifies as an educational institution.[56]

An organization may not achieve status as an operating educational institution where it is engaged in both educational and noneducational activities, unless the latter activities are merely incidental to the former.[57] Thus, the IRS denied status as an operating educational institution to an organization the primary function of which was not the presentation of formal instruction but the maintenance and operation of a museum.[58]

An organization may be regarded as presenting formal instruction even though it lacks a formal course program or formal classroom instruction. Thus, an organization that provided elementary education on a full-time basis to children at a facility maintained exclusively for that purpose, with a faculty and enrolled student body, was held to be an educational institution despite the absence of a formal course program.[59] Similarly, an organization that conducted a survival course was granted classification as an educational institution, although its course periods were only 26 days and it used outdoor facilities more than classrooms, since it had a regular curriculum, faculty, and student body.[60] By contrast, a tax-exempt organization, the primary activity of which was providing specialized instruction by correspondence and a five-to-ten-day seminar program of personal instruction for students who have completed the correspondence course, was ruled to not be an operating educational organization "[s]ince the organization's primary activity consists of providing instruction by correspondence."[61] In another instance, tutoring on a one-to-one basis in the students' homes was ruled insufficient to make the tutoring organization an operating educational entity.[62]

The fact that an otherwise qualifying organization offers a variety of lectures, workshops, and short courses concerning a general subject area, open to the general public and to its members, is not sufficient for it to acquire nonprivate foundation status as an educational institution.[63] This is because this type of an

---

[55] Reg. § 1.170A-9(b). In one instance, an organization was held to not lose its classification as an operating educational institution where it made a grant of over one half of its annual income to another organization, because the grant did not affect its instructional activities and involved almost none of its employees' time and effort (Gen. Couns. Mem. 38437).

[56] Rev. Rul. 78-309, 1978-2 C.B. 123.

[57] Reg. § 1.170A-9(b).

[58] Rev. Rul. 76-167, 1976-1 C.B. 329.

[59] Rev. Rul. 72-430, 1972-2 C.B. 105.

[60] Rev. Rul. 73-434, 1973-2 C.B. 71. Also Rev. Rul. 79-130, 1979-1 C.B. 332; Rev. Rul. 73-543, 1973-2 C.B. 343, *clar. by* Ann. 74-115, 1974-52 I.R.B. 29; Rev. Rul. 75-215, 1975-1 C.B. 335; Rev. Rul. 72-101, 1972-1 C.B. 144; Rev. Rul. 69-492, 1969-2 C.B. 36; Rev. Rul. 68-175, 1968-1 C.B. 83.

[61] Rev. Rul. 75-492, 1975-2 C.B. 80.

[62] Rev. Rul. 76-384, 1976-2 C.B. 57. Also Rev. Rul. 76-417, 1976-2 C.B. 58.

[63] Rev. Rul. 78-82, 1978-1 C.B. 70.

"optional, heterogeneous collection of courses is not formal instruction" and does not constitute a "curriculum."[64] Where the attendees are members of the general public and can attend the functions on an optional basis, there is no "regularly enrolled body of pupils or students."[65] Further, where the functions are led by various invited authorities and personalities in the field, there is no "regular faculty."[66]

Even if an organization qualifies as a school or other type of formal educational institution, it will not be able to achieve tax-exempt status if it maintains racially discriminatory admissions policies[67] or if it benefits private interests to more than an insubstantial extent.[68] As an illustration of the latter point, an otherwise qualifying school, which trained individuals for careers as political campaign professionals, was denied tax-exempt status because of the secondary benefit accruing to entities of a political party and its candidates, since nearly all of the school's graduates became employed by or consultants to these entities or candidates.[69]

One federal court rejected the contention of the IRS that a board of education cannot qualify as an operating educational organization. While this type of entity does not actually present formal instruction, it employs all of the teachers in a school system and maintains control over a community's school districts. The court viewed the board as an entity that merely delegated the conduct of the formal educational process to the schools administered by the school districts.[70]

Museums, zoos, planetariums, symphony orchestras, and other similar organizations may also be considered institutions providing formal instruction and training and therefore are educational in nature.[71] In this regard, tax-exempt status was accorded entities such as a sports museum,[72] a bird and animal sanctuary,[73] an international exposition,[74] and a bar association library.[75] The IRS noted that an organization established to maintain and operate a museum facility, which offers, in sponsorship with a university, a degree program in museology, is an educational organization.[76]

An illustration of what the IRS regards as an institution "similar" to a museum was provided when the IRS categorized as a museum an organization formed to create and operate a replica of an early American village.[77] The orga-

---

[64] Rev. Rul. 62-23, 1962-1 C.B. 200.

[65] Rev. Rul. 64-128, 1964-1 (Part I) C.B. 191.

[66] Rev. Rul. 78-82, *supra* note 63.

[67] Bob Jones Univ. v. United States, 461 U.S. 574 (1983). See § 5.4(a).

[68] See § 19.10.

[69] American Campaign Academy v. Comm'r, 92 T.C. 1053 (1989).

[70] Estate of Ethel P. Green v. Comm'r, 82 T.C. 843 (1984).

[71] Reg. § 1.501(c)(3)-1(d)(3)(ii)(4).

[72] Rev. Rul. 68-372, 1968-2 C.B. 205.

[73] Rev. Rul. 67-292, 1967-2 C.B. 184.

[74] Rev. Rul. 71-545, 1971-2 C.B. 235.

[75] Rev. Rul. 75-196, 1975-1 C.B. 155.

[76] Rev. Rul. 76-167, 1976-1 C.B. 329. Also, e.g., Rev. Rul. 83-140, 1983-2 C.B. 185, *rev'g* Rev. Rul. 80-21, 1980-1 C.B. 233.

[77] Rev. Rul. 77-367, 1977-2 C.B. 193.

nization, which made the village open to the public, was determined by the IRS to be "engaging in activities similar to those of a museum" and thus to be educational in nature. In so finding, the IRS relied upon one of its prior determinations in which an organization was found to be educational because it promoted an appreciation of history through the acquisition, restoration, and preservation of homes, churches, and public buildings having special historical or architectural significance and opened the structures for viewing by the general public.[78]

§ 7.4 INSTRUCTION OF INDIVIDUALS

As noted, the term *educational* for federal tax law purposes relates to the instruction or training of the individual for the purpose of improving or developing his or her capabilities.[79]

Within this category of educational organizations are those entities the primary function of which is to provide instruction or training for a general purpose or on a particular subject, although they may not have a regular curriculum, faculty, or student body. Thus, an organization that provided educational and vocational training and guidance to nonskilled persons to improve employment opportunity was ruled to be an educational organization,[80] as was an organization that conducted an industrywide apprentice training program,[81] operated community correctional centers for the rehabilitation of prisoners,[82] provided a facility and program for the rehabilitation of individuals recently released from a mental institution,[83] provided apprentice training in a skilled trade to native Americans,[84] offered instruction in basic academic subjects, speech, perceptual motor coordination, and psychological adjustment for children and adolescents with learning disabilities,[85] and provided room, board, therapy, and counseling for persons discharged from alcoholic treatment centers.[86] Similarly, the IRS ruled tax-exempt as educational in nature an organization that maintained a government internship program for college students,[87] that provided assistance to law students to obtain experience with public interest law firms and legal aid societies,[88] and that promoted student and cultural exchanges.[89] As for instruction on a particular subject, organiza-

---

[78] Rev. Rul. 75-470, 1975-2 C.B. 207. In general, Yang, "Collaboration Between Nonprofit Universities and Commercial Enterprises: The Rationale for Exempting Nonprofit Universities from Taxation," 95 *Yale L. J.* (No. 8) 1857 (1986).

[79] See the text accompanied by *supra* note 3.

[80] Rev. Rul. 73-128, 1973-1 C.B. 222.

[81] Rev. Rul. 67-72, 1967-1 C.B. 125. Cf. Rev. Rul. 59-6, 1959-1 C.B. 121.

[82] Rev. Rul. 70-583, 1970-2 C.B. 114; Rev. Rul. 67-150, 1967-1 C.B. 133.

[83] Rev. Rul. 72-16, 1972-1 C.B. 143.

[84] Rev. Rul. 77-272, 1977-2 C.B. 191.

[85] Rev. Rul. 77-68, 1977-1 C.B. 142.

[86] Rev. Rul. 75-472, 1975-2 C.B. 208.

[87] Rev. Rul. 70-584, 1970-2 C.B. 114. Also Rev. Rul. 75-284, 1975-2 C.B. 204.

[88] Rev. Rul. 78-310, 1978-2 C.B. 173.

[89] Rev. Rul. 68-165, 1968-1 C.B. 253; Rev. Rul. 80-286, 1980-2 C.B. 179.

tions that provided instruction in securities management,[90] dancing,[91] sailboat racing,[92] drag car racing,[93] and the promotion of sportsmanship[94] were ruled to be tax-exempt as educational entities. However, the training of animals is not an educational activity, even where the animals' owners also receive some instruction.[95]

Another category of educational organizations that relate to the instruction or training of individuals are those that conduct discussion groups, panels, forums, lectures, and the like.[96] For example, the operation of a coffee house by a number of churches, where church leaders, educators, businesspersons, and young people discuss a variety of topics, was held to be an educational endeavor.[97] Comparable organizations include those that instruct individuals as to how to improve their business or professional capabilities, such as the conduct of seminars and training programs on the subject of managing credit unions (for individuals in developing nations),[98] the practice of medicine (for physicians),[99] and banking (for bank employees).[100] Other tax-exempt organizations in this category include an organization that conducted discussion groups and panels in order to acquaint the public with the problems of ex-convicts and parolees,[101] an organization that sponsored public workshops for training artists in concert technique,[102] and an organization that conducted clinics for the purpose of teaching a particular sport.[103] Organizations that present courses of instruction by means of correspondence or through the utilization of television or radio may qualify as educational in nature.[104]

However, if the functions of a discussion group are to a significant extent fraternal or social in nature, and where the speeches and discussions are deemed subjective and more akin to the exchanges of personal opinions and experiences in the informal atmosphere of a social group or club, the organization will not qualify as organized and operated exclusively for educational purposes.[105] Likewise, an organization that does not employ any faculty and does not provide any classes, lectures, or instructional material may be regarded, for federal tax

---

[90] Rev. Rul. 68-16, 1968-1 C.B. 246.

[91] Rev. Rul. 65-270, 1965-2 C.B. 160.

[92] Rev. Rul. 64-275, 1964-2 C.B. 142.

[93] Lions Assoc. Drag Strip v. United States, 64-1 U.S.T.C. ¶ 9283 (S.D. Cal. 1963).

[94] Rev. Rul. 55-587, 1955-2 C.B. 261.

[95] Ann Arbor Dog Training Club, Inc. v. Comm'r, 74 T.C. 207 (1980); Rev. Rul. 71-421, 1971-2 C.B. 229.

[96] Reg. § 1.501(c)(3)-1(d)(3)(ii), Example (2).

[97] Rev. Rul. 68-72, 1968-1 C.B. 250.

[98] Rev. Rul. 74-16, 1974-1 C.B. 126.

[99] Rev. Rul. 65-298, 1965-2 C.B. 163

[100] Rev. Rul. 68-504, 1968-2 C.B. 211.

[101] Rev. Rul. 67-150, *supra* note 82.

[102] Rev. Rul. 67-392, 1967-2 C.B. 191.

[103] Rev. Rul. 65-2, 1965-1 C.B. 227, as amplified by Rev. Rul. 77-365, 1977-2 C.B. 192. Also Hutchinson Baseball Enters., Inc. v. Comm'r, 73 T.C. 144 (1979), *aff'd*, 696 F.2d 757 (10th Cir. 1982).

[104] Reg. § 1.501(c)(3)-1(d)(3)(ii)(3).

[105] North Am. Sequential Sweepstakes v. Comm'r, 77 T.C. 1087 (1981).

purposes, as a social or recreational group rather than an educational organization, as was the case with a flying club that merely provided its members with an opportunity for unsupervised flight time.[106] This conclusion was also reached in a case involving an organization that arranged chess tournaments for its members, provided chess magazines and books to libraries, and offered instruction in and sponsored exhibitions of the game of chess, yet was denied classification as an educational organization because a substantial activity of the organization was the promotion and conduct of the tournaments, which were found to serve "recreational interests."[107] In still another instance, an organization that was originally classified as a social club was denied reclassification as a charitable or educational organization because of the "substantial social and personal aspects" of the organization.[108] Still another application of this principle occurred when an organization, the principal function of which was an annual science fiction convention, was denied classification as an educational organization because of its substantial "social and recreational purposes."[109] Another application of this principle took place when it was held that an association of descendants of a settler from England in the United States in the 1600s did not qualify for tax exemption as an educational organization, in part because its annual meeings and other activities were held to be "family-focused" and "social and recreational."[110]

A third category of educational organizations that instruct individuals are those that primarily engage in study and research. As an illustration, educational status was accorded an organization that undertook a program of study, research, and assembly of materials relating to court reform in a particular state.[111] Other organizations ruled to be tax-exempt under this category of *educational* include an organization that researched and studied Civil War battles[112] and one that conducted and published research in the area of career planning and vocational counseling.[113]

A subject of considerable controversy in this context is the tax-exempt status of organizations that conduct "study tours," with the IRS concerned that exemption not be attached to activities amounting to sightseeing or other forms of vacation travel. An organization that conducted study tours for the purpose of educating individuals about the culture of the United States and other countries was ruled to be tax-exempt,[114] although the commercial travel industry challenged the policy of the IRS in granting tax-exempt status to organizations that substantially provided commercial travel services, claiming a competitive disadvantage.[115] Of course, where a tax-exempt educational pro-

---

[106] Syrang Aero Club, Inc. v. Comm'r, 73 T.C. 717 (1980).

[107] Minnesota Kingsmen Chess Ass'n, Inc. v. Comm'r, 46 T.C.M. 1133, 1135 (1983). Also Spanish Am. Cultural Ass'n of Bergenfield v. Comm'r, 68 T.C.M. 931 (1994).

[108] Alumnae Chapter Beta of Clovia v. Comm'r, 46 T.C.M. 297, 298 (1983).

[109] St. Louis Science Fiction Ltd. v. Comm'r, 49 T.C.M. 1126, 1129 (1985).

[110] Manning Ass'n v. Comm'r, 93 T.C. 596, 606 (1989).

[111] Rev. Rul. 64-195, 1964-2 C.B. 138.

[112] Rev. Rul. 67-148, 1967-1 C.B. 132.

[113] Rev. Rul. 68-71, 1968-1 C.B. 249.

[114] Rev. Rul. 70-534, 1970-2 C.B. 113; Rev. Rul. 69-400, 1969-2 C.B. 114.

[115] American Soc'y of Travel Agents, Inc. v. Simon, 36 A.F.T.R. 2d 75-5142 (D.D.C. May 23, 1975) (complaint dismissed), *aff'd*, 566 F.2d 145 (D.C. Cir. 1977) (finding of no standing to sue), *cert. den.*, 435 U.S. 947 (1978).

gram involving travel (such as wintertime ocean cruises) is intermixed with substantial social and recreational activities, tax-exempt status will not be forthcoming.[116] Thus, an organization, the sole purpose and activity of which was to arrange group tours for students and faculty members of a university, was ruled to not be educational for federal tax purposes,[117] while an organization that arranged for and participated in the temporary exchange of children between families of a foreign country and the United States was found to be tax-exempt because it was fostering the cultural and educational development of children.[118]

According to the IRS, the tax status of travel tours is dependent on how they are structured, what they consist of, and what they accomplish. This amounts to a facts and circumstances test, which examines the "nature, scope and motivation for a tour in making a determination as to whether there is a connection between a particular tour and the accomplishment of an exempt purpose." A "critical factor" is the methods used, such as organized study, reports, lectures, library access, and reading lists. To be an exempt function, each tour must have the achievement of exempt ends as its primary purpose. Another factor the IRS evaluates is other relevant facts that demonstrate the advancement of exempt objectives, such as mandated classroom and other structured activities and "choice of destination." An exempt function tour is likely to consist of "an intensive learning experience," rather than tours and visits that are essentially social and recreational experiences.[119]

Although it appears obvious, the IRS was constrained to rule that the definition of the term *educational* relating to the instruction of individuals (and, presumably, also as respects instruction of the public) "contains no limitation with regard to age in defining that term."[120] The issue arose when the IRS, in ruling that an organization organized and operated for the purpose of teaching a particular sport qualified as a tax-exempt educational entity,[121] observed in the facts that the program of instruction was offered only to children. This earlier ruling was amplified to make it clear that the concept of *educational* extends to the instruction of individuals "of all ages."[122]

The instruction of individuals is thus inherently an exempt function, and tax exemption is not dependent upon the subjects under instruction or the number or motives of those being instructed (unless the facts demonstrate the presence of some private benefit[123]). There is, then, no requirement that the "general public" be directly instructed; in this context, there is nothing akin to any requirement that a charitable class be served.[124] For example, an organization may con-

---

[116] Rev. Rul. 77-366, 1977-2 C.B. 192. Also International Postgraduate Med. Found. v. Comm'r, 56 T.C.M. 1140 (1989).

[117] Rev. Rul. 67-327, 1967-2 C.B. 187.

[118] Rev. Rul. 80-286, *supra* note 89.

[119] Tech. Adv. Mem. 9702004. These criteria are refinements of the IRS position articulated in 1990 (Tech. Adv. Mem. 9027003).

[120] Rev. Rul. 77-365, *supra* note 103, at 192.

[121] Rev. Rul. 65-2, *supra* note 103.

[122] Rev. Rul. 77-365, *supra* note 103, at 192.

[123] See § 19.10.

[124] Cf. § 5.5(a).

duct a seminar for lawyers on some aspect of the law and the lawyers may attend solely for the purpose of augmenting their law practices, yet the seminar is clearly an educational undertaking. The fact is that, generally, tax-exempt educational activities provide direct benefits to parties in their private capacity. However, the dissemination of information and the training of individuals is seen as serving public purposes (and thus as being educational) in that the increased capabilities of those receiving the instruction serves to improve the public welfare. In one instance, the IRS advised that "an educational activity may be performed in the public interest even if members of the public have no access to the activity whatsoever."[125]

§ 7.5 INSTRUCTION OF THE PUBLIC

As noted, the income tax regulations state that the term *educational* as used for federal tax purposes relates, in part, to the "instruction of the public on subjects useful to the individual and beneficial to the community."[126] In many instances, an organization is considered educational, because it is regarded as instructing the public as well as the individual. Nonetheless, even though it is difficult (and usually unnecessary) to formulate rigid distinctions between the two types of educational purposes, various categories of the former purpose have emerged.

One category of this type of educational organization is the one that provides certain personal services deemed beneficial to the general public. The IRS, under this rationale, ruled to be tax-exempt organizations that disseminated information concerning hallucinatory drugs,[127] conducted personal money management instruction,[128] and educated expectant mothers and the public in a method of painless childbirth.[129] Similarly, an organization that functioned primarily as a crop seed certification entity was held to be educational because of its adult education classes, seminars, newsletter, and lending library.[130]

Another way an organization can be educational in this regard is by providing instruction by means of counseling. For example, an organization that provided free counseling to men concerning methods of voluntary sterilization was held to be an educational entity.[131] Other exempt personal counseling organizations include those that offered group counseling to widows and widowers to assist them in legal, financial, and emotional problems caused by the death of their spouses;[132] counseling to women on methods of resolving unwanted pregnan-

---

[125] Gen. Couns. Mem. 38459. In general, Rev. Rul. 75-196, *supra* note 75. Cf. American Campaign Academy v. Comm'r, *supra* note 69.

[126] See the text accompanied by *supra* note 3.

[127] Rev. Rul. 70-590, 1970-2 C.B. 116.

[128] Rev. Rul. 69-441, 1969-2 C.B. 115.

[129] Rev. Rul. 66-255, 1966-2 C.B. 210. Also Rev. Rul. 76-205, 1976-1 C.B. 178.

[130] Indiana Crop Improvement Ass'n, Inc. v. Comm'r, 76 T.C. 394 (1981).

[131] Rev. Rul. 74-595, 1974-2 C.B. 164.

[132] Rev. Rul. 78-99, 1978-1 C.B. 152.

cies;[133] marriage counseling;[134] vocational counseling;[135] and counseling as to personal health and fitness.[136]

Another category of educational organization is those that endeavor to instruct the public in the field of civic betterment. In this regard, this type of organization frequently also qualifies under one or more varieties of the concept of *charitable* or *social welfare*. Thus, an organization that disseminated information, in the nature of results of its investigations, in an effort to lessen racial and religious prejudice in the fields of housing and public accommodations was ruled to be tax-exempt.[137] Other organizations in this category include ones that distributed information about the results of a model demonstration housing program for low-income families conducted by it,[138] disseminated information on the need for international cooperation,[139] educated the public as to the means of correcting conditions such as community tension and juvenile delinquency,[140] enlightened the public in a particular city as to the advantages of street planning,[141] developed and distributed a community land-use plan,[142] and educated the public regarding environmental deterioration due to solid waste pollution,[143] radio and television programming,[144] and accuracy of news coverage by newspapers.[145]

The fourth category of educational organization that exists to instruct the public is those that conduct study and research. The variety of efforts encompassed by these organizations is nearly limitless. As illustrations, these organizations include those that conducted analyses, studies, and research into the problems of a particular region (pollution, transportation, water resources, waste disposal) and published the results,[146] instructed the public on agricultural matters by conducting fairs and exhibitions,[147] and published a journal to disseminate information about specific types of physical and mental disorders.[148]

The publication of printed material can be an educational activity in a variety of other contexts. For example, an organization that surveyed scientific and medical literature and prepared, published, and distributed abstracts of it was recognized as tax-exempt.[149] Similarly, an organization was ruled tax-

---

[133] Rev. Rul. 73-569, 1973-2 C.B. 178. Also Rev. Rul. 76-205, 1976-1 C.B. 178.
[134] Rev. Rul. 70-640, 1970-2 C.B. 117.
[135] Rev. Rul. 68-71, *supra* note 113.
[136] Priv. Ltr. Rul. 9732032.
[137] Rev. Rul. 68-438, 1968-2 C.B. 209. Also Rev. Rul. 75-285, 1975-2 C.B. 203; Rev. Rul. 68-70, 1968-1 C.B. 248; Rev. Rul. 67-250, 1967-2 C.B. 182.
[138] Rev. Rul. 68-17, 1968-1, C.B. 247; Rev. Rul. 67-138, 1967-1 C.B. 129.
[139] Rev. Rul. 67-342, 1967-2 C.B. 187.
[140] Rev. Rul. 68-15, 1968-1 C.B. 244.
[141] Rev. Rul. 68-14, 1968-1 C.B. 243.
[142] Rev. Rul. 67-391, 1967-2 C.B. 190.
[143] Rev. Rul. 72-560, 1972-2 C.B. 248.
[144] Rev. Rul. 64-192, 1964-2 C.B. 136.
[145] Rev. Rul. 74-615, 1974-2 C.B. 165.
[146] Rev. Rul. 70-79, 1970-1 C.B. 127.
[147] Rev. Rul. 67-216, 1967-2 C.B. 180.
[148] Rev. Rul. 67-4, 1967-1 C.B. 121.
[149] Rev. Rul. 66-147, 1966-1 C.B. 137.

exempt for assisting the National Park Service by preparing, publishing, and distributing literature concerning a particular park.[150] Likewise, a nonprofit corporation that compiled and published a manual on the standard library cataloguing system was ruled to be engaged in educational activities.[151] Of course, where a publication effort is operated by an entity akin to normal commercial practices, tax exemption as an educational organization will be denied.[152] Thus, the IRS held that an organization, the only activities of which were the preparation and publication of a newspaper of local, national, and international news articles with an ethnic emphasis, soliciting advertising and selling subscriptions to the newspaper in a manner indistinguishable from ordinary commercial publishing practices, was not operated exclusively for educational purposes.[153]

In general, an organization engaged in publishing can qualify as a tax-exempt educational entity where the content of the publication is educational; the preparation of the material follows methods generally accepted as educational in character; the distribution of the materials is necessary or valuable in achieving the organization's tax-exempt purposes; and the manner in which the distribution is accomplished is distinguishable from ordinary commercial publishing practices.[154] The IRS relied on these criteria in concluding that the recording and sale of musical compositions that were not generally produced by the commercial recording industry was educational because it was a means for presenting new works of unrecognized composers and the neglected works of more recognized composers.[155] By contrast, a publication of a tax-exempt organization was held to not be educational because its contents were found to be primarily news concerning the organization's members and current events affecting the organization, with the information provided of limited interest to the general public.[156]

The educational activities of organizations may be carried on through a club, such as a gem and mineral club[157] or a garden club,[158] or by means of public lectures and debates.[159] These organizations may function as broad-based membership organizations,[160] as organizations formed to promote a specific cause,[161] or as a transitory organization, such as one to collect and collate campaign materials of a particular candidate for ultimate donation to a university or public library.[162]

A somewhat controversial ruling from the IRS concerning this category of

---

[150] Rev. Rul. 68-307, 1968-1 C.B. 258.
[151] Forest Press, Inc. v. Comm'r, 22 T.C. 265 (1954).
[152] Rev. Rul. 60-351, 1960-2 C.B. 169.
[153] Rev. Rul. 77-4, 1977-1 C.B. 141. Also Christian Manner Int'l, Inc. v. Comm'r, 71 T.C. 661 (1979).
[154] Rev. Rul. 67-4, *supra* note 148.
[155] Rev. Rul. 79-369, 1979-2 C.B. 226.
[156] Phi Delta Theta Fraternity v. Comm'r, 90 T.C. 1033 (1988), *aff'd*, 887 F.2d 1302 (6th Cir. 1989).
[157] Rev. Rul. 67-139, 1967-1 C.B. 129.
[158] Rev. Rul. 66-179, 1966-1 C.B. 139.
[159] Rev. Rul. 66-256, 1966-2 C.B. 210.
[160] Rev. Rul. 68-164, 1968-1 C.B. 252.
[161] Rev. Rul. 72-228, 1972-1 C.B. 148.
[162] Rev. Rul. 70-321, 1970-1 C.B. 129.

educational organization is one involving a society of heating and air conditioning engineers and others having a professional interest in this field that was held to be educational in nature.[163] Its educational purposes were deemed to be the operation of a library, dissemination of the results of its scientific research, and the making available of model codes of minimum standards for heating, ventilating, and air conditioning. The IRS went to considerable lengths to distinguish this type of professional society from a business league.[164]

Organizations that are charitable, educational, or scientific societies have been recognized by the IRS as being charitable organizations. Frequently, their membership base is composed of individuals (rather than organizations); these persons share common professional and/or disciplinary interests. In most instances, these organizations satisfy the criteria for classification as charitable, educational, or like entities, but, because they provide services to individual members, the tendency of the IRS may be to categorize or reclassify them as business leagues, on the ground that they serve to enhance the professional development of the members rather than advance a charitable purpose.[165]

An otherwise tax-exempt organization that produced and distributed free, or for small, cost-defraying fees, educational, cultural, and public interest programs for public viewing via public educational channels of commercial cable television companies was held to be operated for educational purposes and thus qualified for tax exemption because an organization may achieve its educational purposes through the production of television programs where it does so in a noncommercial manner.[166] Similarly, a nonprofit organization established to operate a noncommercial educational broadcasting station presenting educational, cultural, and public interest programs qualified as an exempt educational entity,[167] as did an organization that produced educational films concerning a particular subject and that disseminated its educational material to the public by means of commercial television, where the films were presented in a noncommercial manner.[168]

With these three rulings as precedent, the IRS considered the case of an organization that made facilities and equipment available to the general public for the production of noncommercial educational or cultural television programs intended for communication to the public via the public and educational access channels of a commercial cable television company. The programs did not support or oppose specific legislation and, where a particular viewpoint was advocated, the organization ensured that the program presented a full and fair exposition of the pertinent facts. The organization was informally affiliated with, but did not control and was not controlled by, the commercial cable television company. The IRS ruled that, "[b]y providing members of the general public with the opportunity to produce television programs of an educational or a cultural

[163] Rev. Rul. 71-506, 1971-2 C.B. 233.
[164] Cf. Rev. Rul. 70-641, 1970-2 C.B. 119.
[165] See § 13.3.
[166] Rev. Rul. 76-4, 1976-1 C.B. 145.
[167] Rev. Rul. 66-220, 1966-2 C.B. 209.
[168] Rev. Rul. 67-342, *supra* note 139.

nature for viewing on the public access channels of a commercial cable television company," the organization was operating exclusively for educational purposes.[169]

In this ruling, the IRS characterized the prior three rulings as "clearly indicat[ing] that an organization may achieve its educational purposes through the production of television programs, regardless of whether the programs are to be broadcast over the airwaves or over a cable system, so long as the programs are presented in a noncommercial manner."[170] The IRS added: "The absence of commercial advertising is a key factor in determining the noncommercial nature of the programming activity."[171] However, where an organization engages in educational programming by means of television to a substantial extent, it can be accorded designation as an educational entity, even though the organization owns and operates the station under a commercial broadcasting license.[172]

§ 7.6 EDUCATIONAL ACTIVITY AS COMMERCIAL BUSINESS

One of the most troublesome aspects of the law of tax-exempt organizations is differentiation between tax-exempt and commercial functions.[173] While this aspect of the law is by no means confined to educational organizations,[174] much of the clashing of principles occurs in this context because what may be an exempt educational activity in one context may be a commercial business in another. Certainly, for example, in the general world of commerce, operation of a restaurant, bookstore, broadcasting station, portfolio management service, publishing company, and the like is a trade or business. However, this type of an operation may qualify as a tax-exempt educational organization, as, for example, has a university restaurant,[175] a university store,[176] a broadcasting station,[177] an endowment fund management service,[178] a retail sales enterprise,[179] a money lending operation,[180] and an organization publishing a law school journal.[181]

---

[169] Rev. Rul. 76-443, 1976-2 C.B. 149, 150.

[170] *Id*. at 149.

[171] *Id*. With regard to programs prepared for cable television, Federal Communications Commission regulations prohibit cable operators from advertising commercially on their educational or "public access" channels.

[172] Rev. Rul. 78-385, 1978-2 C.B. 174.

[173] The *commerciality doctrine* is the subject of Chapter 25.

[174] Indeed, many of the difficulties in this area occur in the health care field. See § 6.2.

[175] Rev. Rul. 67-217, 1967-2 C.B. 181.

[176] Rev. Rul. 68-538, 1968-2 C.B. 116; Rev. Rul. 58-194, 1958-1 C.B. 240; Squire v. Students Book Corp., 191 F.2d 1018 (9th Cir. 1951).

[177] Rev. Rul. 66-220, *supra* note 167.

[178] Rev. Rul. 71-529, 1971-2 C.B. 234.

[179] Rev. Rul. 68-167, 1968-1 C.B. 255.

[180] Rev. Rul. 63-220, 1963-2 C.B. 208; Rev. Rul. 61-87, 1961-1 C.B. 191. Cf. Rev. Rul. 69-177, 1969-1 C.B. 150.

[181] Rev. Rul. 63-234, 1963-2 C.B. 210. Cf. Rev. Rul. 66-104, 1966-1 C.B. 135; Rev. Rul. 60-351, *supra* note 152.

It is difficult to formulate guidelines to determine when a given purpose or activity is *educational* or a commercial business. Of course, an exempt purpose or activity must be one that benefits the public, or an appropriate segment of the public, rather than any private individual or individuals and the organization must not be operated for the benefit of private shareholders or individuals.[182] Nevertheless, even these rules, aside from the essential questions as to what constitutes an educational activity, require some subjective judgments.

The task of making these judgments befell one federal court, in a case involving an organization created to disseminate knowledge of economics with a view to advancing the welfare of the American people. The court concluded that the primary purpose of the organization was not educational but was a commercial one.[183] The organization published periodicals containing analyses of securities and industries and of general economic conditions; no forecasting of stock market trends was made, although the publications did contain recommendations as to the purchase and sale of securities. These publications were sold at subscription at a cost above production expenses, as was a separate service providing advice for sales and purchases of securities in a particular portfolio; the organization also published special studies prepared by its research staff and maintained fellowship and scholarship programs.

In this case, the court developed an instructive process of reasoning. First, it noted that "education" is an "extremely broad concept."[184] Second, recognizing that the tax exemption provision is to be liberally construed, the court "first assume[d] *arguendo* an educational purpose without giving definitive meaning to that concept."[185] Third, the court then "ascertain[ed] whether or not the taxpayer has an additional commercial purpose."[186] Fourth, upon finding a commercial purpose, the court had to decide "whether the commercial purpose is primary or incidental to the exempt purpose."[187] The court found the commercial purpose to be primary and not incidental to any tax-exempt purpose, and thus held the organization to not be tax-exempt as an educational organization.

This court held that the required element of *exclusivity* was absent and that the tax exemption was thus unavailable, citing the Supreme Court that "the presence of a single [nonexempt] . . . purpose, if substantial in nature, will destroy the exemption regardless of the number or importance of truly [exempt] . . . purposes."[188] The court, in concluding that the publications of the organization merely provided investment advice to subscribers for a fee, noted that the existence of profits, while not conclusive, is some evidence that the business purpose

---

[182] Reg. §§ 1.501(c)(3)-1(c)(ii), 1.501(c)(3)-1(c)(2).

[183] American Inst. for Economic Research v. United States, 302 F.2d 934 (Ct. Cl. 1962).

[184] *Id.* at 937.

[185] *Id.* at 938. Also Griess v. United States, 146 F. Supp. 505 (N.D. Ill. 1956).

[186] *Id.* 302 F.2d at 938.

[187] *Id.* This line of reasoning was followed in, for example, Pulpit Resource v. Comm'r, 70 T.C. 594 (1978).

[188] *Id.* at 937. The quote is from Better Business Bureau v. United States, 326 U.S. 279, 283 (1945). See § 4.6.

is primary[189] and that the services of the organization are those "commonly associated with a commercial enterprise."[190] Of course, the argument of the organization that any profits gained from the sale of its publications were used for exempt purposes was unavailing.[191]

Subsequently, the IRS determined that an association of investment clubs, formed for the mutual exchange of investment information among its members and prospective investors to enable them to make sound investments, was not an educational organization, inasmuch as the association was serving private economic interests.[192] Likewise, an organization operated to protect the financial stability of a teachers' retirement system, and the contributions and pensions of retiree members of the system, was held to not be educational and to serve its members' private interests, notwithstanding its publication of a newsletter.[193]

The same result occurred with respect to a nonprofit organization that clearly engaged in educational activities, namely, the sponsorship of programs involving training, seminars, lectures, and the like in areas of intrapersonal awareness and communication.[194] However, the educational activities were conducted pursuant to licensing arrangements with for-profit corporations that amounted to substantial control over the functioning of the nonprofit organization. In rejecting tax-exempt status for the nonprofit organization, the court held that it "is part of a franchise system which is operated for private benefit and that its affiliation with this system taints it with a substantial commercial purpose."[195] Thus, the organization's entanglements with for-profit corporations were such that commercial ends were imputed to it, notwithstanding the nature of its activities when viewed alone.

Likewise, an organization, originally exempted from federal income tax as an educational and religious entity, had its tax exemption revoked as a result of evolving into a commercial publishing entity.[196] Both the IRS and a court concluded that the publishing activities had taken on a "commercial hue" and the organization had "become a highly efficient business venture."[197] In reaching this conclusion, the court noted that the organization followed publishing and sales practices used by comparable nonexempt commercial publishers, had generated increasing profits in recent years,[198] was experiencing a growth in accumulated surplus, and had been paying substantially increased salaries to its top employees.[199]

---

[189] Scripture Press Found. v. United States, 285 F.2d 800 (Ct. Cl. 1961), *cert. den.*, 368 U.S. 985 (1962).

[190] American Inst. for Economic Research v. United States, *supra* note 183, at 938.

[191] IRC § 502; § 28.6.

[192] Rev. Rul. 76-366, 1976-2 C.B. 144.

[193] Retired Teachers Legal Defense Fund, Inc. v. Comm'r, 78 T.C. 280 (1982).

[194] Est of Hawaii v. Comm'r, 71 T.C. 1067 (1979), *aff'd*, 647 F.2d 170 (9th Cir. 1981).

[195] *Id.* at 1080.

[196] The Incorporated Trustees of the Gospel Worker Soc'ty. v. United States, 510 F. Supp. 374 (D.D.C. 1981), *aff'd* , 672 F.2d 894 (D.C. Cir. 1981), *cert. den.*, 456 U.S. 944 (1982).

[197] *Id.* at 381.

[198] See § 4.9.

[199] See 19.4(a).

This line of law is troublesome for tax-exempt organizations. Nonprofit organizations (particularly charitable ones) are often criticized for not operating more efficiently and prudently (for not functioning "like a business"). For example, the IRS considered the status of an organization that operated a retail grocery store to sell food to residents in a poverty area at substantially lower-than-usual prices, that maintained a free delivery service for the needy, and that allocated about 4 percent of its earnings for use in a training program for the hard-core unemployed. The IRS held that the operation of the grocery store was a substantial nonexempt activity, since it was conducted on a scale larger than reasonably necessary for the training program (an exempt activity)[200] and since the operation could not be characterized as an investment or business undertaking for the production of income for use in carrying on qualified charitable purposes, and denied the tax exemption.[201] Similarly, the IRS ruled nonexempt an organization, wholly owned by a tax-exempt college, that manufactured and sold wood products primarily to employ students of the college to enable them to continue their education, on the ground that the enterprise itself was not an instructional or training activity.[202] Conversely, the IRS recognized that a tax-exempt organization may engage in a commercial activity without endangering its tax status where the business is not an end in itself but is a means by which charitable purposes are accomplished and where the endeavor is not conducted on a scale larger than is reasonably necessary to accomplish the organization's tax-exempt purpose.[203] Likewise, an organization that provided training of procurement officials for countries receiving United States aid was found to be educational in nature, despite an IRS contention that procurement activity is not inherently exempt, since the procurement activity furthered the organization's educational and training program.[204]

A case involving an organization's tax-exempt status, where the IRS is claiming that the organization is operated for a substantial commercial purpose, may be dependent upon the organization's charges for services or products in relation to its costs.[205] Where the fees are set at a level less than costs, the courts and sometimes the IRS will be spurred on to the conclusion that the organization is not operated in an ordinary commercial manner.[206] Other considerations govern where a nonprofit organization is experiencing net receipts.[207]

This aspect of the law is being greatly influenced by developments in the field of unrelated income taxation.[208] In recent years, the courts have developed law concerning the scope of the phrase *trade or business* that ranges considerably beyond the criteria set forth in the statutory definition of the phrase.[209] As this as-

---

[200] See *supra* § 4.
[201] Rev. Rul. 73-127, 1973-1 C.B. 221.
[202] Rev. Rul. 69-177, *supra* note 180.
[203] Rev. Rul. 73-128, *supra* note 80.
[204] Afro-American Purchasing Cent., Inc. v. Comm'r, 37 T.C.M. 184 (1978).
[205] See § 26.2(c).
[206] Peoples Translation Service/Newsfront Int'l v. Comm'r, 72 T.C. 42 (1979).
[207] See § 4.9.
[208] See Part Six.
[209] See § 26.2.

pect of the law is evolving, great consideration is being given to the concepts of *unfair competition* and *profit motive*.[210] More contemporaneously, the courts are focusing on the question as to whether or not a particular activity is being operated in a *commercial* manner.[211]

Thus, some courts will, in characterizing an activity as a trade or business, place emphasis on the conclusion that the undertaking was conducted with a profit motive.[212] This conclusion is usually buttressed by a finding that the particular activity was in fact profitable. This approach is a reflection of the test for business expense deduction purposes,[213] which looks to determine whether the activity was entered into with the dominant hope and intent of realizing a profit.[214] One appellate court commented that where an activity is not substantially related to exempt purposes (the principal statutory test), is "conducted in a competitive profit seeking manner, and regularly earns significant profits, a heavy burden must be placed on the organization to prove profit is not its motive" for engaging in the activity.[215]

Other courts place more emphasis on the question as to whether the activity constitutes unfair competition with taxable business.[216] This is understandable, given the legislative history of the unrelated income rules, which clearly reflects the intent of Congress to eliminate unfair competitive advantages that tax-exempt organizations may otherwise have over for-profit business entities.[217]

The U.S. Supreme Court indicated a tendency to favor both of these lines of cases, noting the rationale for the profit motive approach[218] and that a focus should be on whether the activity under examination is the kind of activity that is "provided by private commercial entities in order to make a profit."[219] Lower courts are now reflecting a willingness to utilize both of these lines of cases.[220]

§ 7.7 CHILD CARE ORGANIZATIONS

The term *educational* purposes includes the "providing care of children away from their homes if—(1) substantially all of the care provided by the organization

---

[210] See § 26.2(a), (b).

[211] See Chapter 25.

[212] E.g., Professional Ins. Agents of Mich. v. Comm'r, 726 F.2d 1097 (6th Cir. 1984); Carolinas Farm & Power Equip. Dealers Ass'n, Inc. v. United States, 699 F.2d 167 (4th Cir. 1983); Louisiana Credit Union League v. United States, 693 F.2d 525 (5th Cir. 1982); Professional Ins. Agents of Wash. v. Comm'r, 53 T.C.M. 9 (1987).

[213] IRC § 162.

[214] E.g., United States v. American Bar Endowment, 477 U.S. 105, 110, note 1 (1986).

[215] Carolinas Farm & Power Equip. Dealers Ass'n, Inc. v. United States, *supra* note 208, at 171.

[216] E.g., Disabled Am. Veterans v. United States, 650 F.2d 1178 (Ct. Cl. 1981); Hope School v. United States, 612 F.2d 298 (7th Cir. 1980); Carle Found. v. United States, 611 F.2d 1192 (7th Cir. 1979).

[217] See § 26.1.

[218] United States v. American Bar Endowment, *supra* note 214, at 112–114.

[219] *Id.* at 111.

[220] E.g., Illinois Ass'n of Professional Ins. Agents, Inc. v. Comm'r, 86-2 U.S.T.C. ¶ 9702 (7th Cir. 1986), *aff'g* 49 T.C.M. 925 (1985).

is for purposes of enabling individuals [their parents] to be gainfully employed, and (2) the services provided by the organization are available to the general public."[221] It is the view of the IRS that a child care facility will not qualify under these rules if it provides preference in enrollment for the children of employees of a specific employer.[222]

The Office of the Chief Counsel of the IRS issued an opinion that the provision of day care referrals and assistance information to the general public is not a charitable or educational activity but, rather, a commercial one.[223] In so doing, the IRS modified an earlier opinion from that office which indicated that these activities were considered to not be unrelated business when undertaken by an organization the primary purpose of which was the operation of day care centers.[224] In the earlier opinion, the IRS also took the position that the provision of specialized child care assistance to employers in the organization's locale is not an exempt activity because of the substantial benefit provided the employers in connection with the operation of their qualified dependent care assistance programs.[225]

This statutory definition was enacted because of the reach of the ruling policy by the IRS in this area. This policy has been described as follows: "The IRS has recognized that nonprofit day care centers may be eligible for tax exemption and tax-deductible contributions where enrollment is based on the financial need of the family and the need of the child for the program, or where the center provides preschool-age children of working parents with an educational program through a professional staff of qualified teachers."[226]

This definition of *educational* purposes is "not intended to affect the meaning of terms 'educational' or 'charitable' for any purpose other than considering the child care organizations described in the provision as having educational purposes."[227]

---

[221] IRC § 501(k). The reference to the words *general public* means that the IRC § 501(k) organization cannot be racially discriminatory (see § 5.4(a)), although it does not have to satisfy the IRS guidelines on the subject (*id.*, text accompanied by notes 94–98), unless it is also classified under IRC § 170(b)(1)(A)(ii) (see § 11.3(a)) (Gen. Couns. Mem. 39757).

[222] Gen. Couns. Mem. 39613.

[223] Gen. Couns. Mem. 39872.

[224] Gen. Couns. Mem. 39622.

[225] *Id.* These specialized child care assistance plans are operated pursuant to IRC § 129, which provides that the gross income of an employee does not include amounts paid or incurred by the employer for eligible dependent care assistance.

[226] H. Rep. No. 98-861, 98th Cong., 2d Sess. 1100 (1984). See *supra* note 52.

[227] *Id.*

Religious Organizations

Section 501(c)(3) of the Internal Revenue Code provides that an organization may be exempt from federal income tax under IRC § 501(a) if it is organized and operated exclusively for a *religious* purpose.[1] Because of policy and constitutional law constraints, the IRS and the courts are usually reluctant to define, at least for tax purposes, what is or is not a *religious* activity or organization. The income tax regulations do not contain any definition of the term *religious*.

§ 8.1 CONSTITUTIONAL LAW FRAMEWORK

For the most part, governmental agencies and the courts have either refused to, or been quite cautious in attempting to, define a religious activity or organization. This reticence at the federal level stems largely from First Amendment considerations, as articulated in judicial opinions in tax, labor, and other cases.

The First Amendment provides, in the religion clauses, that "Congress shall make no law respecting an establishment of religion, or prohibiting the free exercise thereof . . ." While most First Amendment cases in this context involve either the *establishment clause* or the *free exercise clause*, both of these religious clauses are directed toward the same goal: the maintenance of government neutrality with regard to affairs of religion. Thus, the U.S. Supreme Court observed that the First Amendment "rests upon the premise that both religion and government can best work to achieve their lofty aims if each is left free from the other within its respective sphere."[2]

Free exercise clause cases generally arise out of conflict between secular laws and individual religious beliefs. The free exercise clause was characterized by the Supreme Court as follows:

---

[1] Reg. § 1.501(c)(3)–1(d)(1)(i)(a).
[2] Illinois ex rel. McCollum v. Board of Educ., 333 U.S. 203, 212 (1948).

> The door of the Free Exercise Clause stands tightly closed against any governmental regulation of religious beliefs as such. [citations omitted] Government may neither compel affirmation of a repugnant belief, [citation omitted] nor penalize or discriminate against individuals or groups because they hold religious views abhorrent to the authorities. . . . On the other hand, the Court has rejected the challenges under the Free Exercise Clause to governmental regulations of certain overt acts prompted by religious beliefs or principles, for "even when the action is in accord with one's religious convictions, [it] is not totally free from legislative restrictions."[3]

The Court added that "in this highly sensitive constitutional area, '[o]nly the gravest abuses, endangering paramount interest, give occasion for permissible limitation.' "[4]

The more significant free exercise cases include the clash between the secular law prohibiting polygamy and the precepts of the Mormon religion,[5] military service requirements and conscientious objectors' principles,[6] state unemployment compensation law requiring Saturday work and the dictates of the Seventh-day Adventists' religion,[7] compulsory school attendance laws and the doctrines of the Amish religion,[8] and a license tax on canvassing and the missionary evangelism objectives of Jehovah's Witnesses.[9] Where there is to be government regulation, notwithstanding free exercise claims, there must be a showing by the government of "some substantial threat to public safety, place or order."[10] Thus, courts upheld a compulsory vaccination requirement,[11] prosecution of faith healers practicing medicine without a license,[12] and a prohibition on snake handling as part of religious ceremonies.[13] By contrast, the courts have voided sales and use tax exemptions that are solely for the sale of religious publications.[14]

Short of such a "substantial threat," however, the government may not investigate or review matters of ecclesiastical cognizance. This principle frequently manifests itself in the realm of alleged employment discrimination in violation of the Civil Rights Act of 1964.[15] Thus, there must be a compelling governmental interest in regulation before free exercise rights may be infringed.[16]

---

[3] Sherbert v. Verner, 374 U.S. 398, 402–403 (1963).

[4] *Id.* at 406, quoting from Thomas v. Collins, 323 U.S. 516, 530 (1937).

[5] Reynolds v. United States, 98 U.S. 145 (1878).

[6] Gillette v. United States, 401 U.S. 437 (1971).

[7] Sherbert v. Verner, *supra* note 3.

[8] Wisconsin v. Yoder, 406 U.S. 205 (1972).

[9] Murdock v. Pennsylvania, 319 U.S. 105 (1943).

[10] Sherbert v. Verner, *supra* note 3, at 403.

[11] Jacobson v. Massachusetts, 197 U.S. 11 (1905).

[12] People v. Handzik, 102 N.E.2d 340 (Ill. 1964).

[13] Kirk v. Commonwealth, 44 S.E.3d 409 (Va. 1947).

[14] Finlator v. Secretary of Revenue of N.C., 902 F.2d 1158 (4th Cir. 1990); Texas Monthly, Inc. v. Bullock, 489 U.S. 1 (1989); Arkansas Writers' Project, Inc. v. Ragland, 481 U.S. 221 (1987).

[15] E.g., McClure v. Salvation Army, 460 F.2d 553 (5th Cir. 1972).

[16] The Supreme Court held that a city ordinance prohibiting animal sacrifice for religious purposes is a violation of the constitutional right to the free exercise of religion (Church of the Lukumi Babalu Aye, Inc. v. City of Hialeah, 113 S. Ct. 2217 (1993)). In general, Clark, "Guidelines for the Free Exercise Clause," 83 *Harv. L. Rev.* 327 (1969).

While the free exercise clause cases usually involve alleged unwarranted intrusions of government into the sphere of individuals' religious beliefs, the establishment clause cases usually involve governmental regulation of religious institutions. These cases frequently arise as attacks on the propriety of state aid (often to religious schools) or special treatment (such as tax exemption) to religious organizations.[17] This clause is designed to prohibit the government from establishing a religion, or aiding a religion, or preferring one religion over another. Thus, the Supreme Court observed that the establishment clause is intended to avoid "sponsorship, financial support, and active involvement of the sovereign in religious activity."[18]

The Supreme Court has repeatedly held that the First Amendment is intended to avoid substantial entangling church–state relationships. In one case, where state aid to religious schools, conditioned on pervasive restrictions, was held to be excessive entanglement, the Court stated:

> . . . [a] comprehensive, discriminating, and continuing state surveillance will inevitably be required to ensure that these restrictions are obeyed and the First Amendment otherwise respected. . . . This kind of state inspection and evaluation of religious content of a religious organization is fraught with the sort of entanglement that the Constitution forbids. It is a relationship pregnant with dangers of excessive government direction of church schools and hence of churches . . . and we cannot ignore here the danger that pervasive modern governmental power will ultimately intrude on religion and thus conflict with the Religion Clauses.[19]

Thus, where there is significant government investigation and/or surveillance, particularly analysis of the sincerity or application of religious beliefs, of a religious institution, there is likely to be a violation of the establishment clause.[20]

In a posture of particular significance to the law of tax-exempt organizations, the Supreme Court articulated the possibility of permissible government involvement with religious organizations, but in a manner that furthers neutrality. Thus, the Court, in a case concerning an attack on tax exemption for religious properties as being violative of the establishment clause, said that the government may become involved in matters relating to religious organizations so as "to mark boundaries to avoid excessive entanglement" and to adhere to the "policy of neutrality that derives from an accommodation of the Establishment and Free Exercise Clauses that has prevented that kind of involvement that would tip the balance toward government control of Church or governmental restraint on religious practice. . . ."[21] Consequently, the current stance of the law as articulated

---

[17] E.g., Committee for Public Educ. v. Nyquist, 413 U.S. 756 (1973); Lemon v. Kurtzman, 403 U.S. 602 (1971); Walz v. Tax Comm'n, 397 U.S. 664 (1970); Engle v. Vitale, 370 U.S. 421 (1962); Abington School Dist. v. Schempp, 374 U.S. 203 (1953); Zorach v. Clausen, 343 U.S. 306 (1952); Illinois ex rel. McCollum v. Board of Education, *supra* note 2; and Everson v. Board of Educ., 330 U.S. 1 (1946).

[18] Lemon v. Kurtzman, *supra* note 17, at 612.

[19] *Id.* at 619–620.

[20] E.g., Presbyterian Church v. Hull Church, 393 U.S. 440 (1969); Caulfield v. Hirsh, 95 L.R.R.M. 3164 (E.D. Pa. 1977).

[21] Walz v. Tax Comm'n, *supra* note 17, at 669–670.

by the Supreme Court is that tax exemption for religious organizations is not violative of the First Amendment, since it promotes neutrality, inasmuch as the alternative of nonexemption would necessarily lead to prohibited excessive entanglements (such as valuation of property, imposition of tax liens, and foreclosures).

As regards nonprofit organizations seeking tax exemption as religious entities, it is difficult to mark the boundary between proper government regulation and unconstitutional entanglement. Not infrequently, for example, a religious organization will claim a violation of its constitutional rights when the IRS probes too extensively in seeking information about it in the context of evaluation of an application for recognition of exemption. However, the courts appear to agree that the IRS is obligated, when processing an exemption application, to make inquiries and gather information to determine whether the organization's purposes and activities are in conformance with the statutory requirements, and that this type of an investigation is not precluded by the First Amendment's guarantee of freedom of religion.[22]

It is against this constitutional law backdrop that the regulatory agencies' and courts' difficulties in defining and regulating religious entities may be viewed.

§ 8.2 FEDERAL TAX LAW DEFINITION OF *RELIGION*

Although the federal income tax law provides tax exemption for religious organizations, there is no statutory or regulatory definition of the terms *religious* or *religion* for this purpose. Indeed, by reason of the religion clauses of the First Amendment, it would be unconstitutional for the federal government to adopt and apply a strict definition of these terms. Nonetheless, in specific cases, government officials, judges, and justices have grappled with the meaning of the term *religious*. The Supreme Court ventured the observation, authored decades ago, that the term *religion* has "reference to one's views of his relations to his Creator, and to the obligations they impose of reverence for his being and character, and of obedience to his will."[23] Subsequently, the Court wrote that the "essence of religion is belief in a relation to God involving duties superior to those arising from any human relation."[24] In other than the constitutional law and federal tax law

---

[22] Church of Scientology of Calif. v. Comm, 83 T.C. 381 (1984), *aff'd*, 823 F.2d 1310 (9th Cir. 1987); United States v. Toy Natl. Bank, 79-1 U.S.T.C. ¶ 9344 (N.D. Iowa 1979); General Conference of the Free Church of Am. v. Comm'r, 71 T.C. 920, 930–932 (1979); Coomes v. Comm'r, 572 F.2d 554 (6th Cir. 1978); United States v. Holmes, 614 F.2d 985 (5th Cir. 1980); United States v. Freedom Church, 613 F.2d 316 (1st Cir. 1980); Bronner v. Comm'r, 72 T.C. 368 (1979). Cf. United States v. Dykema, 80-2 U.S.T.C. ¶ 9735 (E.D. Wis. 1980). It is the position of the IRS that the tax-exempt status of a church is to be revoked where the church fails to produce its books and records following a proper request for them (Gen. Couns. Mem. 38248). Churches and certain other types of religious organizations are exempted from the requirement of filing an application for recognition of tax exemption (see § 23.3(b)) and filing an annual information return (see § 24.3(b)), and churches are the subject of special IRS audit rules (see § 24.8(b)).

[23] Davis v. Beason, 133 U.S. 333, 342 (1890).

[24] United States v. Macintosh, 283 U.S. 605, 633 (1931).

contexts, these instances have arisen in cases concerning, for example, conscientious objector status,[25] employment discrimination,[26] state and local real property tax exemptions,[27] and zoning restrictions.[28]

Over the years, state courts have ventured into this area. One court stated that the term *religion* has "reference to man's relation to Divinity; to reverence, worship, obedience, and submission to the mandates and precepts of supernatural or superior beings" and in its broadest sense "includes all forms of belief in the existence of superior beings, exercising power over human beings by volition, imposing rules of conduct with future rewards and punishments."[29] Many courts have advanced definitions, including the following: "Religion as generally accepted may be defined as a bond uniting man to God and a virtue whose purpose is to render God the worship due to him as the source of all being and the principle of all government of things;"[30] and "the Christian religion, in its most important ultimate aspect, recognizes, has faith in and worships a Divine Being or Spirit—one Father of all mankind—who has the power to and will forgive the transgressions of repentants and care for the immortal souls of the believers, and which belief brings earthly solace and comfort to and tends to induce right living in such believers."[31] One summary definition of the term is: "Religion is squaring human life with superhuman life. . . . What is common to all religions is belief in a superhuman power and an adjustment of human activities to the requirements of that power, such adjustment as may enable the individual believer to exist more happily."[32]

The literature contains many definitions of the term *religious*.[33] For example, one author posits six "dimensions of religion." These are:

> The doctrinal dimension. "A religion typically has a system of doctrines."
> The mythic dimension. "Typically a religion has a story or stories to tell. . . .
>   In the field of religion such stories are called myths."
> The ethical dimension. "A religion has an ethical dimension. Believers are
>   enjoined to observe certain rules and precepts."

---

[25] Welsh v. United States, 398 U.S. 333 (1970); United States v. Seeger, 380 U.S. 163 (1965); Berman v. United States, 156 F.2d 377 (9th Cir. 1946), *cert. den.*, 329 U.S. 795 (1946); United States ex rel. Phillips v. Downer, 135 F.2d 521 (2d Cir. 1943); United States v. Kauten, 133 F.2d 703 (2d Cir. 1943).

[26] Braunfield v. Brown, 366 U.S. 599 (1961); Johnson v. U.S. Postal Serv., 364 F. Supp. 37 (N.D. Fla. 1973); Powers v. State Dept. of Social Welfare, 493 P.2d 590 (Kan. 1972); Martin v. Industrial Accident Comm'n, 304 P.2d 828 (D.C. Cal. 1956).

[27] Walz v. Tax Comm'n, *supra* note 17; Washington Ethical Soc'y v. District of Columbia, 249 F.2d 127 (D.C. Cir. 1957); American Bible Soc'y v. Lewisohn, 351 N.E.2d 697 (Ct. App. N.Y. 1976); Watchtower Bible & Tract Soc'y, Inc. v. Lewisohn, 315 N.E.2d 801 (N.Y. 1974); People ex rel. Watchtower Bible & Tract Soc'y, Inc. v. Haring, 170 N.E.2d 677 (Ct. App. N.Y. 1960); Fellowship of Humanity v. County of Alameda, 315 P.2d 394 (N.Y. 1957).

[28] In re Community Synagogue v. Bates, 136 N.E.2d 488 (N.Y. 1956).

[29] McMasters v. State of Okla., 29 A.L.R. 292, 294 (Okla. Crim. App. 1922).

[30] Nikulnikoff v. Archbishop & Consistory of Russian Orthodox Greek Catholic Church, 255 N.Y.S. 653, 663 (Sup. Ct. N.Y. Cty. 1932).

[31] Taylor v. State, 11 So.2d 663, 673 (Miss. 1943).

[32] Hopkins, *The History of Religions*, 2 (New York: Macmillan 1918), quoted in Minersville School Dist. v. Gobitis, 108 F.2d 683, 685 (3d Cir. 1939).

[33] The author thanks Christopher B. Hopkins, Esq., for his contribution to this portion of the text.

The ritual dimension. ". . . [T]ypically a religion has a ritual dimension" such as "acts of worship, praying, singing . . . and . . . sacraments."

The experiential dimension. "Ritual helps to express feelings—awe and wonder, for instance—and can itself provide a context of dramatic experience . . ."

The social dimension. "Any tradition needs some kind of organization in order to perpetuate itself. It thus embeds itself in society."[34]

One student of the subject believes that religion comprises a set of beliefs that assists human beings in giving meaning to otherwise unanswerable questions. Religion is a way that human beings orient themselves to the reality of the world. Religion often involves a ritual (tradition), prayer, ethics, a figurehead, a center of worship, a text (for example, the Bible or the Koran), one or more practices (for example, in Christianity, baptism), symbols (for example, in Christianity, the cross), and a goal (an ideal state of existence). Religion usually entails a belief in a realm of existence that lies beyond humans' planetary existence, efforts to progress toward a goal, and the achievement of personal benefits through techniques such as prayer, offerings, rituals, and pilgrimages.[35]

The federal government and the courts have generally been reluctant to take the position that a particular activity, function, or purpose is not religious in nature. One court succinctly stated the reason why:

> Neither this Court, nor any branch of this Government, will consider the merits or fallacies of a religion. Nor will the Court compare the beliefs, dogmas, and practices of a newly organized religion with those of an older, more established religion. Nor will the Court praise or condemn a religion, however excellent or fanatical or preposterous it may seem. Were the Courts to do so, it would impinge upon the guarantees of the First Amendment.[36]

Similarly, a federal court of appeals observed that "[i]t is not the province of government officials or courts to determine religious orthodoxy."[37] Another court evidenced a like attitude, when it wrote that, "[a]s a judicial body, we are loathe to evaluate and judge ecclesiastical authority and duties in the various religious disciplines."[38]

This approach has been sanctioned by the Supreme Court, which has repeatedly held[39] that freedom of thought and religious belief "embraces the right

---

[34] Smart, *Worldviews: Crosscultural Explorations of Human Beliefs* 7–8 (New York: Charles Scribner's Sons, 1983). Also Elide, *The Sacred & The Profane: The Nature of Religion* (New York: Harcourt Brace Jovanovich 1959).

[35] *Supra* note 33.

[36] Universal Life Church, Inc. v. United States, 372 F. Supp. 770, 776 (E.D. Cal. 1974). This decision has not estopped subsequent federal court actions adverse to the Universal Life Church and to those who establish "congregations" with respect to it (see *infra* note 95) (Universal Life Church, Inc. v. United States, 86-1 U.S.T.C. ¶ 9271 (Ct. Cl. 1986); Universal Life Church v. United States, 76-2 U.S.T.C. ¶ 9548 (E.D. Cal. 1976).

[37] Teterud v. Burns, 522 F.2d 357 (8th Cir. 1975).

[38] Colbert v. Comm'r, 61 T.C. 449, 455 (1974).

[39] See *supra* notes 2–22.

to maintain theories of life and of death and of the hereafter which are rank heresy to followers of the orthodox faiths," and that, if triers of fact undertake to examine the truth or falsity of the religious beliefs of a sect, "they enter a forbidden domain."[40] Subsequently, the Supreme Court observed that "[i]t is not within the judicial ken to question the centrality of particular beliefs or practices to a faith, or the validity of particular litigants' interpretations of those creeds."[41] Yet some courts are not reluctant to attempt to separate secular beliefs from religious ones, as illustrated by a court opinion involving an organization that, in addition to lacking "external manifestations analogous to other religions," had as its major doctrine a "single-faceted doctrine of sexual preference and secular lifestyle."[42]

An illustration of the courts' policy to abstain from a determination of what is and is not religious is an opinion of a federal court concerning an organization, the founder of which received "revelations" from "Ascended Masters," principally Saint Germain.[43] The founder's spouse continued to receive the revelations after his death. The entity was organized and operated to propagate the teachings of the "I AM Religious Activity." In this case, the IRS did not allege that the organization was not religious but principally sought to convince the court that net income of the organization inured to the benefit of private individuals. The court devoted little effort to finding the organization religious in nature but largely relied on its statement in a prior case:

> Religion is not confined to a sect or a ritual. The symbols of religion to one are anathema to another. What one may regard as charity another may scorn as foolish waste. And even education is today not free from divergence of view as to its validity. Congress left open the door of tax exemption to all corporations meeting the test, the restriction being not as to the species of religion, charity, science or education under which they might operate, but as to the use of its profits and the exclusive purpose of its existence.[44]

The court, noting that it was not "compelled to decide whether the objectives of the . . . [organization] are worthy or desirable," concluded that the organization was established exclusively for religious purposes.[45]

Another federal court reflected the same degree of caution when deciding a case involving an organization formed as the parent church of scientology.[46] The

---

[40] United States v. Ballard, 322 U.S. 78, 86, 87 (1943). Also United States v. Seeger, *supra* note 25, at 174–176.

[41] Hernandez v. Comm'r, 490 U.S. 680 (1989).

[42] Church of the Chosen People (North Am. Panarchate) v. United States, 548 F. Supp. 1247, 1252, 1253 (D. Minn. 1982).

[43] Saint Germain Found. v. Comm'r, 26 T.C. 648 (1956).

[44] Unity School of Christianity v. Comm'r, 4 B.T.A. 61, 70 (1926).

[45] Saint Germain Found. v. Comm'r, *supra* note 43, at 657. Also Rev. Rul. 68-563, 1968-2 C.B. 212, *amp. by* Rev. Rul. 78-385, 1978-2 C.B. 174; Rev. Rul. 68-26, 1968-1 C.B. 272.

[46] Founding Church of Scientology v. United States, 412 F.2d 1197 (Ct. Cl. 1969), *cert. den.*, 397 U.S. 1009 (1970). Cf. Church of Scientology of Haw. v. United States, 485 F.2d 313 (9th Cir. 1973); Church of Scientology of Calif. v. United States, 75-2 U.S.T.C. ¶ 9584 (9th Cir. 1975); Founding Church of Scientology of Washington, D.C. v. United States, 409 F.2d 1146 (D.C. Cir. 1968), *cert. den.*, 396 U.S. 963 (1969).

court concluded that the organization was not exempt from tax—not because it was not religious (that issue was not even considered)—but because the net income of the entity inured to the founders in their private capacity.[47]

In one instance, an organization attempted to become recognized as a religious organization by virtue of its operation of a retreat facility.[48] The facility was a mountain lodge; the activities available at the lodge—being religious, recreational, and social—were not regularly scheduled nor required. The religious activities revolved around individual prayer and contemplation, with optional daily devotions and occasional Sunday services available. The IRS asserted that the organization's "substantial, if not sole, purpose is to provide a facility where guests can relax, socialize and engage in recreational activities, or, in other words, to operate a vacation resort."[49] Conversely, the organization contended that "its primary purpose is to provide a religious retreat facility for Christian families where they may come to reflect upon and worship the Lord in a setting free from the outside interferences of everyday life."[50] The court involved, holding that the organization failed to sustain its burden of proof that the facilities were not used in more than an insubstantial manner for recreational purposes, concluded that tax exemption as a religious organization could not be found, in that "[w]holesome family recreation or just sitting on a rock contemplating nature may well provide a family or an individual with a religious, or at least a spiritually uplifting experience, but it is difficult to see how that experience differs, if it does, from the same experience one can have at any quiet inn or lodge located in the beautiful mountains of Colorado."[51]

Nonetheless, retreat facilities can be regarded as religious organizations, particularly where the IRS or a court is not burdened with the thought that something other than authentic religious pursuits dominate the establishment and operation of the entity. For example, an organization, controlled by an auxiliary of a major church denomination, formed to contract for the construction of housing at a conference and retreat center owned and operated by the church, was held to be a religious organization, in that the housing it was to provide was predominantly to aid and enhance the religious purposes of the auxiliary and ultimately the church.[52] The court observed that the auxiliary had served the church since 1910 and the facilities had been used "as a gathering place of missionaries on leave, retired clergy, active laymen and pastors for reli-

---

[47] The U.S. Tax Court held that the expenses of scientology processing and auditing are not deductible medical expenses in Brown v. Comm'r, 62 T.C. 551 (1974), aff'd, 523 F.2d 365 (8th Cir. 1975). Cf. Handeland v. United States, 75-2 U.S.T.C. ¶ 9586 (9th Cir. 1975); Rev. Rul. 78-188, 1978-1 C.B. 40; Rev. Rul. 78-190, 1978-1 C.B. 74. The Supreme Court held that payments to the Church of Scientology for auditing sessions are not deductible as charitable contributions, in Hernandez v. Comm'r, *supra* note 41. The IRS adopted the same position in 1978 (Rev. Rul. 78-189, 1978-1 C.B. 68), although it rendered that ruling obsolete in 1993 (Rev. Rul. 93-73, 1993-2 C.B. 75). See *infra* note 95. In general, United States v. Moon, 718 F.2d 1210 (2d Cir. 1983), *cert. den.*, 466 U.S. 971 (1984).

[48] The Schoger Found. v. Comm'r, 76 T.C. 380 (1981).

[49] *Id.* at 386.

[50] *Id.* at 387.

[51] *Id.* at 388. Also Petersen v. Comm'r, 53 T.C.M. 235 (1987).

[52] Junaluska Assembly Hous., Inc. v. Comm'r, 86 T.C. 1114 (1986).

gious services, religious seminars, and religious training."[53] The court cautioned, however, that if the "housing units are in fact utilized substantially for vacation or recreational purposes, or otherwise by individuals who do not have active roles in the planning, organization, operation of or participation in the [auxiliary's] . . . programs and religious activities, then a substantial nonexempt purpose would be served" and the organization would not qualify for tax exemption.[54] Nonetheless, despite the government's assertion that the housing to be constructed at the "beautiful surroundings" of the retreat grounds is "primarily to provide an enviable vacation spot not unlike others situated in the neighboring Smokey Mountains," the court wrote that "the tax law, however, does not require churches to hold their retreats or other gatherings for religious purposes in the wilderness or to eschew recreation incident to gatherings held primarily for religious activity."[55]

In another instance, a federal court held that an organization was a religious entity because it held regular prayer meetings and weekly services, and published a newsletter.[56]

The U.S. Postal Service has not been as reticent as the IRS and the Department of the Treasury about promulgating some general definition of a *religious* organization in the nonprofit organization context. Thus, for purposes of preferred mailing privileges for qualified nonprofit organizations, the Domestic Mail Manual states that a religious organization is an organization the primary purpose of which is one of the following: (1) to conduct religious worship, for example, churches, synagogues, temples, or mosques, (2) to support the religious activities of nonprofit organizations the primary purpose of which is to conduct religious worship, or (3) to perform instruction in, to disseminate information about, or otherwise to further the teaching of particular religious faiths or tenets.[57]

Typically, when a court finds an alleged religious organization to not be tax-exempt, it generally does so not on the ground that the organization's purpose is not religious but rather on a finding that the activity smacks too much of a commercial enterprise operated for private gain or that the organization engages in an inappropriate amount of lobbying.[58] In one case, a restaurant was operated as a private business for profit with the net profits going to a church, which itself was engaged in commercial activities; contributions to the church were held to not be deductible because the organization's business activities defeated the requisite tax status.[59] Another purported religious organization's tax-exempt status

---

[53] *Id.* at 1122

[54] *Id.* at 1123.

[55] *Id.* at 1122–1123. Previously, the Tax Court upheld the tax-exempt status of an organization that operated religious facilities in an idyllic setting, finding the social and recreational aspects of its program insubstantial (Alive Fellowship of Harmonious Living v. Comm'r, 47 T.C.M. 1134 (1984)).

[56] The Church of the Visible Intelligence That Governs the Universe v. United States, 83-2 U.S.T.C. ¶ 9726 (Cl. Ct. 1983).

[57] Chapter 1, Part 134.5.

[58] See Chapters 25 and 20, respectively.

[59] Riker v. Comm'r, 244 F.2d 220 (9th Cir. 1957), *cert. den.*, 355 U.S. 839 (1957). Also Parker v. Comm'r, 365 F.2d 792 (8th Cir. 1966), *cert. den.*, 385 U.S. 1026 (1967).

was precluded because its primary activity was the operation of a (religious) publishing house.[60]

In still another variant of this same approach, a court found that an organization's social aspects were so predominant as to relegate any religious activities to secondary status.[61] The organization, formed to further the doctrine of "ethical egoism," was found to have as its principal purpose the social functions of sponsoring dinner meetings and publishing a newsletter. While "church meetings" were also held, the court believed they were in reality merely an extension of the social meetings. In general, the court concluded that the "religious aspects of such conclaves seems . . . indistinct."[62] Likewise, an organization was determined to not qualify as a religious organization because its primary activity was the investment and accumulation of funds, albeit for the purpose of eventually building a church.[63]

The IRS invokes the private inurement doctrine in still another context involving religious organizations: the tax treatment of communal groups. The IRS position is that, generally, where individuals reside in a communal setting in the context of professing religious beliefs, with room, board, and other costs provided by the organization, the result is unwarranted private benefit to the individuals which precludes tax exemption. This position has been upheld by the courts on three occasions.[64]

These and similar cases have enormous implications. Certainly, the "traditional" church, for example, may provide lodging, food, and the like to its ministers and family,[65] or operate a school, and not attract any difficulties with the IRS. Parsonages and parochial schools are not likely to be the basis for IRS revocation of a church's tax-exempt status. Perhaps the publicity given to "cults" and the uncovering of immense property holdings of and substantial government infiltration by controversial "churches" have influenced the IRS to shy away from any aid and comfort to burgeoning "nontraditional" churches by merely denying them tax exemption.

Regardless of individual attitudes toward new religions or new religious structures, the full consequences of the government's position are yet to unfold. As respects the tax status of monasteries, nunneries, and religious orders, the IRS has recognized that support of monks, nuns, and other clerics (in the form of

---

[60] Scripture Press Found. v. United States, 285 F.2d 800 (Ct. Cl. 1961), *cert. den.*, 368 U.S. 985 (1962). Also Christian Manner Int'l, Inc. v. Comm'r, 71 T.C. 661 (1979); Fides Publishers Ass'n v. United States, 263 F. Supp. 924 (N.D. Ind. 1967); Unitary Mission Church of Long Island v. Comm'r, 74 T.C. 507 (1980), *aff'd*, 647 F.2d 163 (2d Cir. 1981); Bubbling Well Church of Universal Love, Inc. v. Comm'r, 74 T.C. 531 (1980), *aff'd*, 670 F.2d 104 (9th Cir. 1981); Loiler v. Comm'r, 53 T.C.M. 785 (1987). Cf. Elisian Guild, Inc. v. United States, 412 F.2d 121 (1st Cir. 1969); Rev. Rul. 68-26, *supra* note 45.

[61] First Libertarian Church v. Comm'r, 74 T.C. 396 (1980).

[62] *Id.* at 405.

[63] Western Catholic Church v. Comm'r, 73 T.C. 196 (1979), *aff'd*, 631 F.2d 736 (7th Cir. 1980), *cert. den.*, 450 U.S. 981 (1981).

[64] Canada v. Comm'r, 82 T.C. 973 (1984); Beth-El Ministries, Inc. v. United States, 79-2 U.S.T.C. ¶ 9412 (D.D.C. 1979); Martinsville Ministries, Inc. v. United States, 80-2 U.S.T.C. ¶ 9710 (D.D.C. 1979).

[65] E.g., IRC § 107.

shelter, food, clothing, medical care, and other necessities) is an exempt religious function.[66]

Repercussions of this attitude toward communal groups were felt soon after these court decisions, as the IRS quickly recognized the extremity of its position (notwithstanding the court approval) and moved to confine the scope of the above-noted three court decisions. Now, the IRS position—as manifested in a 1981 general counsel memorandum (overruling the IRS rulings division[67])—is that communal groups can qualify as religious organizations where the facilities and benefits provided by the organization to its membership "do not exceed those strictly necessary to exist in a communal religious organization . . ."; references such as "primitive," "stark," and "deprivation in material terms of life" are used in the memorandum. Also, the IRS found a distinguishing feature in the fact that, in the case of the organization that achieved tax exemption, "few" of its members worked outside the community. (However, these allegedly "distinguishing" factors were not discussed in the court opinions, where the very fact of a communal existence was found to be the barrier to classification as a religious organization.)

In describing the activities of this (religious) organization, the IRS observed that the members believe that their religious beliefs (noted as being "Christian in origin") require them to "live together and in relative isolation . . . under primitive living conditions." Said the IRS: "They eat, work, and worship together in a tightly ordered Christian environment in which work and prayer are viewed as worship." The IRS added that the "community's minimum food and shelter needs are met by the mutual efforts of all. . . ." Finding, as noted, the organization to be religious, the IRS concluded that the members of the organization "have a sincere and meaningful belief in a set of doctrines," that the "provision of minimum food and lodging to the members primarily furthers its religious purposes," that the members "may be viewed as proper participants in an exempt activity acting in the public interest rather than in their private capacities as members" of the organization, and that the provision of food and lodging in this context "constitutes an indirect benefit which is qualitatively incidental because it is a necessary concomitant to . . . operation [of the organization] as a communal religious organization with its particular religious tenets."

One of the difficulties with the original IRS position is that it would have precluded federal tax exemption for monasteries, nunneries, and religious orders. For these entities, the IRS previously recognized the support of monks, nuns, and other clerics (in the form of shelter, food, clothing, medical care, and other necessities) as a tax-exempt function. However, this general counsel memorandum states that "many religious orders that practice communal living in furtherance of their religious goals, or churches that have such religious orders" are recognized as tax-exempt entities. Added the IRS: "It is implicit to the recog-

---

[66] The IRS held that a monastery of the Order of Cistercians of the Strict Observance, a Roman Catholic order, engages in an exempt function when it provides the monks "with food, shelter, clothing, and the other necessities of life" (Priv. Ltr. Ruls. 7838028–7838036).

[67] Gen. Couns. Mem. 38827.

nition of these organizations' exempt status, that communal living with the inherent provision of support in the nature of food and lodging to its members can, depending on all the facts and circumstances, be primarily in furtherance of a religious purpose.[68]

An illustration of the application of the legislative activities rules[69] in this context is the government's successful revocation of the tax-exempt status of a national ministry organization. The organization maintained religious radio and television broadcasts, authored publications, engaged in evangelistic campaigns and meetings, operated the Summer Anti-Communist University, and conducted other activities. All parties (the IRS and courts) recognized this organization as being a religious entity; its tax exemption was lost on the grounds that a substantial part of its activities consisted of carrying on propaganda, attempting to influence legislation, and intervening in political campaigns.[70] Similarly, the IRS successfully revoked the tax-exempt status of an organization the purpose of which is to defend and maintain religious liberty in the United States by the dissemination of knowledge concerning the constitutional principle of the separation of church and state, on the ground that the organization engaged in a substantial amount of lobbying.[71]

The U.S. Supreme Court concluded that tax exemption (specifically, for state property tax purposes) for religious organizations does not constitute excessive entanglement by the state with religion as proscribed by the First Amendment.[72] Recognizing that either taxation or tax exemption of churches "occasions some degree of involvement with religion," the Court held that "[g]ranting tax exemptions to churches necessarily operates to afford an indirect economic benefit and also gives rise to some, but yet a lesser, involvement than taxing them."[73] This argument was presaged in the literature[74] and in state court cases.[75] An unavoidable aspect of this process is that a government is placed in the position of deciding which organizations qualify as being religious in nature—a difficult decision to make, particularly where unorthodox beliefs are involved.

The difficulties confronting the IRS in deciding whether organizations can

---

[68] Also New Life Tabernacle v. Comm'r, 44 T.C.M 309 (1982); Rev. Rul. 76-323, 1976-2 C.B. 18; Rev. Rul. 68-123, 1968-1 C.B. 35. In general, Emory & Zelenak, "The Tax Exempt Status of Communitarian Religious Organizations: An Unnecessary Controversy?," 50 *Fordham L. Rev.* 1085 (1982).

[69] See Chapter 20.

[70] Christian Echoes Nat'l Ministry, Inc. v. United States, 470 F.2d 849 (10th Cir. 1972), *cert. den.*, 414 U.S. 864 (1973).

[71] Alexander v. "Americans United," Inc., 416 U.S. 752 (1974).

[72] Walz v. Tax Comm'n, *supra* note 17. In general, Note, 16 *Vill. L. Rev.* 374 (1970).

[73] *Id.* at 674. E.g., Committee for Public Educ. v. Nyguist, 413 U.S. 756 (1973).

[74] E.g., Harpster, "Religion, Education, and the Law," 36 *Marq. L. Rev.* 24, 66 (1952); Note, "Exemption of Property Owned and Used by Religious Organizations," 11 *Minn. L. Rev.* 541, 550 (1927).

[75] E.g., Murray v. Comptroller of Treas., 216 A.2d 897 (Md. 1966), *cert. den.*, 385 U.S. 816 (1966); General Fin. Corp. v. Archetto, 176 A.2d 73 (R.I. 1961), *app. dis.*, 369 U.S. 424 (1962); Fellowship of Humanity v. County of Alameda, *supra* note 24, Lundberg v. County of Alameda, 298 P.2d 1 (Cal. 1956), *app. dis. sub nom.*, Heisey v. County of Alameda, 352 U.S. 921 (1956); Franklin St. Soc'ty. v. Manchester, 60 N.H. 342 (1880). Cf. Sostre v. McGinnes, 334 F.2d 906 (2d Cir. 1964); Washington Ethical Soc'ty. v. District of Columbia, *supra* note 24, Cooke v. Tramburg, 205 A.2d 889 (Sup. Ct. N.J. 1964).

qualify for tax exemption as religious organizations, and in some cases as churches, have become nearly overwhelming. Instances involving blatant abuses are generating numerous court opinions and thus are forming the evolving law.[76] The concerns of the IRS about mail-order ministries, real estate tax exemption frauds, and questionable tax deductions are leading the IRS to many adverse decisions, which, in turn, are causing like decisions by the courts, so that the law is shaping up as being appropriately tough as regards the sham situations but it is formulating some legal principles that are highly questionable when applied outside the areas of abuse.[77]

As one court stated, "[t]he lack of a precise definition [of the term *religious*] is not surprising in light of the fact that a constitutional provision is involved."[78] Most of what caselaw there is on the subject finds the courts' rejection of a narrow definition, rather than an affirmative statement of an encompassing definition. Thus, a court observed that, "[i]n implementing the establishment clause, the Supreme Court has made clear that an activity may be religious even though it is neither part of nor derives from a societally recognized religious sect."[79] Occasional attempts made in the literature to define *religion*[80] usually become criticized for being incomplete or outdated.[81]

There are, nonetheless, some explicit discussions of what may constitute *religion* or *religious belief*. In one case, it was said that "[r]eligious belief . . . is a belief finding expression in a conscience which categorically requires the believer to disregard elementary self-interest and to accept martyrdom in preference to transgressing its tenets."[82] Another court found an activity religious because it was centered around belief in a higher being "which in its various forms is given the name 'god' in common usage" and because a form of prayer was involved.[83] Still another court formulated a three-part test for determining the religious nature of an organization's goals: whether the beliefs address fundamental and ultimate questions concerning the human condition, are comprehensive in nature and constitute an entire system of belief instead of merely an isolated teaching, and are manifested in external forms.[84] The Supreme Court placed emphasis on belief in a "supreme being," and looked to see whether "a given belief that is sincere and meaningful occupies a place in the life of its possessor parallel to that filled by the orthodox belief in God"[85] and whether the belief occupies in the life of the individual involved " 'a place parallel to that filled by . . . God' in traditional religious persons."[86] However,

---

[76] E.g., The Southern Church of Universal Bhd. Assembled, Inc. v. Comm'r, 74 T.C. 1223 (1980).

[77] Basic Bible Church v. Comm'r, 74 T.C. 846 (1980); Truth Tabernacle v. Comm'r, 41 T.C.M. 1405 (1981). Cf. McGahen v. Comm'r, 76 T.C. 468 (1981), aff'd, 720 F.2d 664 (3d Cir. 1983).

[78] Malnak v. Yogi, 440 F. Supp. 1284 (D.N.J. 1977), aff'd, 592 F.2d 197 (3d Cir. 1979).

[79] Id., 440 F. Supp. at 1313.

[80] E.g., Note, "Toward a Constitutional Definition of Religion," 91 Harv. L. Rev. 1056 (1978).

[81] E.g., Worthing, " 'Religion' and 'Religious Institutions' Under the First Amendment," 7 Pepp. L. Rev. 313, 320–321 (1980).

[82] United States v. Kauten, supra note 25 at 708.

[83] Malnak v. Yogi, supra note 78, 440 F. Supp. at 1320, 1323.

[84] Africa v. Commonwealth of Pa., 662 F.2d 1025, 1032 (3d Cir. 1981), cert. den., 456 U.S. 908 (1982).

[85] United States v. Seeger, supra note 25, 380 U.S. at 165–166.

[86] Welsh v. United States, supra note 25, 398 U.S. at 340.

some courts have been reluctant to confine the concept of *religious belief* to theistic beliefs.

For example, one court held that the permissible inquiry on this subject is "whether or not the belief occupies the same place in the lives of its holders that the orthodox beliefs occupy in the lives of believing majorities, and whether a given group that claims the exemption conducts itself the way groups conceded to be religious conduct themselves."[87] This court added that the appropriate test is whether the activities of the organization in question "serve the same place in the lives of its members, and occupy the same place in society, as the activities of the theistic churches."[88] Indeed, this court developed what is apparently the most expansive, yet definitional statement as to the general characteristics of the concept of *religion*:

> Religion simply includes: (1) a belief, not necessarily referring to supernatural powers; (2) a cult, involving a gregarious association openly expressing the beliefs; (3) a system of moral practice directly resulting from an adherence to the belief; and (4) an organization within the cult designed to observe the tenets of belief.[89]

Indeed, the difficulties contemporary courts are having in grappling with a definition of the term *religion* can be seen in court holdings that the use of basic reader textbooks, offensive to the religious beliefs of some, in public schools does not advance "secular humanism" or inhibit theistic religion.[90]

Consequently, federal tax law lacks a crisp and workable definition of the term *religious*. There is, nonetheless, an approach to application of the term that adheres to the admonition offered concerning the meaning of the term *obscenity*, that one "knows it when one sees it."[91] As the foregoing citations reflect, there are unabashed references in the court opinions to "traditional," "orthodox," and "majority" religious beliefs, and at least one opinion differentiates between groups "conceded to be religious" and others. Also, as noted, it is relatively clear that religious belief is not confined to theistic belief. Indeed, the most pertinent one-sentence summary on this point is that the term *religion* as employed in federal and state statutes "has been held to encompass nontheistic beliefs which occupy a place in the lives of their possessors parallel to that occupied by belief in God in persons with traditional religious faith."[92]

---

[87] Fellowship of Humanity v. County of Alameda, *supra* note 27, 315 P.2d at 406.

[88] *Id.*, 315 P.2d at 409–410.

[89] *Id.*, 315 P.2d at 406.

[90] Smith v. Board of School Comm'rs of Mobile County, 827 F.2d 684, 688–689 (11th Cir. 1987), *rev'g* 655 F. Supp. 939 (S.D. Ala. 1987); also Mozert v. Hawkins County Board of Educ., 827 F.2d 1058 (6th Cir. 1987), *rev'g* 647 F. Supp. 1194 (E.D. Tenn. 1986), where it was observed that "[a]lthough the Supreme Court has shied away from attempting to define religion, the past forty years has witnessed an expansion of the court's understanding of religious belief," so that the "concept of religion has shifted from a fairly narrow religious theism . . . to a broader concept providing protection for the views of unorthodox and nontheistic faiths" (concurring opinion, 827 F.2d at 1078).

[91] In Jacobellis v. Ohio, 378 U.S. 184 (1964), Justice Potter Stewart, conceptualizing as to the meaning of the word "obscene," observed that one may not succeed in intelligibly defining the term but would "know it when I see it" (at 197).

[92] Worthing, " 'Religion' and 'Religious Institutions' Under the First Amendment," *supra* note 81 at 332.

An organization that is deemed to be a religious entity may well engage in activities that by themselves may not be regarded as religious, such as charitable, educational, social welfare, and community activities. It appears generally recognized that the conduct of these activities will not deprive an otherwise religious organization of its classification as a religious group. For example, one court held that "[s]trictly religious uses and activities are more than prayer and sacrifice" and include social activities, study, and community service.[93] A commentator observed that "[r]eligious activities or uses have been held to include incidental social, charitable, and maintenance activities (for both persons and property) as well as religious worship."[94]

There is no question but that the current state of the law on this subject poses perplexing and probably unresolvable burdens on regulatory officials and judges. These difficulties are exacerbated as new religions emerge (for example, the Unification Church and Scientology movements)[95] and as new forms of approach to the practice of religion emerge (for example, the "electronic churches" and the "mail-order ministries"[96]). In some instances, such as with respect to

---

[93] In re Community Synagogue v. Bates, *supra* note 28, 136 N.E.2d at 493.

[94] Worthing, " 'Religion' and 'Religious Institutions' Under the First Amendment," *supra* note 81 at 332.

[95] On Oct. 1, 1993, the IRS, without explanation, recognized the tax-exempt status of twenty-five Church of Scientology organizations in rulings issued by the National Office of the IRS (61 *Tax Notes* 279 (Oct. 18, 1993)). The terms of the settlement with the IRS, that gave rise to these rulings, were published in *The Wall Street Journal* on December 30, 1997.

[96] The IRS has been particularly concerned with the tax status of mail-order ministries, such as those chartered by the Universal Life Church (ULC). In 1977, the IRS commenced a study of illegal tax protestor activities, which culminated in a report published in 1979. One finding of this report was that illegal protest schemes are increasingly employing the technique of establishing "bogus churches," where "a secularly employed individual places all of his or her wages in an organization created through the use of a mail order charter whereby the organization pays for his or her living expense." To date, the courts have uniformly rejected claims for tax exemption for, or the deductibility of gifts to, these "organizations." E.g., Davis v. Comm'r, 81 T.C. 806 (1983), *aff'd*, 767 F.2d 931 (9th Cir. 1985), holding that the payment of personal expenses from a ULC congregation bank account constitutes private inurement (see Chapter 13) and that the transfer of funds to the account was not a bona fide gift; also Richardson v. Comm'r, 70 T.C.M. 14 (1995); Page v. Comm'r, 66 T.C.M. 571 (1993); Bruce Goldberg, Inc. v. Comm'r, 58 T.C.M. 519 (1989); Gookin v. United States, 707 (N.D. Cal. 1988); Bullock v. Comm'r, 56 T.C.M. 636 (1988); Johnston v. Comm'r, 56 T.C.M. 520 (1988); Bray v. Comm'r, 56 T.C.M. 430 (1988); Mulvaney v. Comm'r, 55 T.C.M. 998 (1988); Boharski v. Comm'r, 55 T.C.M. 604 (1988); Jackson v. Comm'r, 55 T.C.M. 537 (1988); Webb v. Comm'r, 55 T.C.M. 245 (1988), *aff'd*, 872 F.2d 380 (11th Cir. 1989); Dunn v. Comm'r, 55 T.C.M. 66 (1988); Burwell v. Comm'r, 89 T.C.M. 590 (1987), *app. dis.* (9th Cir., May 4, 1988); Ruberto v. Comm'r, 54 T.C.M. 1388 (1987); Goodnight v. Comm'r, 54 T.C.M. 1272 (1987); Roughen v. Comm'r, 54 T.C.M. 510 (1987); Randolph v. Comm'r, 54 T.C.M. 339 (1987); Bobbit v. Comm'r, 53 T.C.M. 1285 (1987); Graboske v. Comm'r, 53 T.C.M. 896 (1987); Krause v. Comm'r, 53 T.C.M. 589 (1987); Fowler v. Comm'r, 53 T.C.M. 377 (1987); Fowler v. Comm'r, 53 T.C.M. 373 (1987); Petersen v. Comm'r, 53 T.C.M. 235 (1987); Adamson v. Comm'r, 52 T.C.M. 699 (1987); McMains v. Comm'r, 51 T.C.M. 1297 (1986); Mathis v. Comm'r, 51 T.C.M. 1067 (1986); Starks v. Comm'r, 51 T.C.M. 500 (1986); Zollo v. Comm'r, 51 T.C.M. 443 (1986); Roben v. Comm'r, 51 T.C.M. 407 (1986); Grew v. Comm'r 51 T.C.M. 405 (1986); Martin v. Comm'r, 51 T.C.M. 403 (1986); Van Cleve v. Comm'r, 50 T.C.M. 1353 (1985), Rager v. Comm'r, 775 F.2d 1081 (9th Cir. 1985); Bell v. Comm'r, 85 T.C. 436 (1985); Gambardella v. Comm'r, 50 T.C.M. 1331 (1985); Neil v. Comm'r, 50 T.C.M. 1254 (1985); Gookin v. Comm'r, 50 T.C.M. 1163 (1985); Botwinick v. Comm'r, 50 T.C.M. 1161 (1985); Woo v. Comm'r, 50 T.C.M. 1115 (1985); Elliott v. Comm'r, 50 T.C.M. 1111 (1985); Pryor v. Comm'r, 50 T.C.M. 1093 (1985); Weaver v. Comm'r, 50 T.C.M. 1020 (1985); Sensing v. Comm'r, 50 T.C.M. 973 (1985); Cox v. Comm'r, 50 T.C.M. 971 (1985); Eutsler v. Comm'r, 50 T.C.M. 872 (1985);

"personal churches,"[97] the matter is evolving away from the law of tax-exempt organizations and into the realm of criminal tax fraud.[98] Indeed, personal churches have been added to the concept of tax shelters, so that special penalties for substantial understatements of federal income tax[99] are applicable.[100] Yet policymakers are to tread carefully even when confronting the nontraditional, minority, and/or unorthodox religious groups. The First Amendment applies to them as well. As one court noted, "[n]ew religions appear in this country frequently and they cannot stand outside the first amendment merely because they did not exist when the Bill of Rights was drafted."[101]

Nonetheless, church abuse cases abound, with tax avoidance clearly taking precedence over religion.[102] The U.S. Tax Court is being inundated with these

Marinovich v. Comm'r, 50 T.C.M. 839 (1985); Conlow v. Comm'r, 50 T.C.M. 832 (1985); Layden v. Comm'r, 50 T.C.M. 527 (1985); Rutter v. Comm'r, 50 T.C.M. 506 (1985); Taylor v. Comm'r, 50 T.C.M. 313 (1985); Morgan v. Comm'r, 50 T.C.M. 114 (1985); Ebner v. Comm'r, 49 T.C.M. 1541 (1985); Brown v. Comm'r, 49 T.C.M. 1531 (1985); Wilcox v. Comm'r, 49 T.C.M. 1525 (1985); Lufkin v. Comm'r, 49 T.C.M. 1462 (1985); Dummler v. Comm'r, 49 T.C.M. 1460 (1985); Witherow v. Comm'r, 49 T.C.M. 1458 (1985); Uhrig v. Comm'r, 49 T.C.M. 1355 (1985); Beauvais v. Comm'r, 49 T.C.M. 1346 (1985); Howard v. Comm'r, 49 T.C.M. 1344 (1985); Green v. Comm'r, 49 T.C.M. 1320 (1985); Estate of Sweeney v. Comm'r, 49 T.C.M. 1249 (1985); Porter v. Comm'r, 49 T.C.M. 1015 (1985); Williamson v. Comm'r, 49 T.C.M. 928 (1985); Booker v. Comm'r, 49 T.C.M. 854 (1985); Lane v. Comm'r, 49 T.C.M. 837 (1985); Nelson v. Comm'r, 49 T.C.M. 799 (1985); Schmidel v. Comm'r, 49 T.C.M. 351 (1984); Abercrombie v. Comm'r, 49 T.C.M. 347 (1984); Shade v. Comm'r, 49 T.C.M. 212 (1984); Moriarty v. Comm'r, 48 T.C.M. 1345 (1984) Hoskinson v. Comm'r, 48 T.C.M. 678 (1984); Hodges v. Comm'r, 48 T.C.M. 617 (1984); Hawbaker v. Comm'r, 47 T.C.M. 231 (1983); Universal Life Church, Inc. (Full Circle) v. Comm'r, 83 T.C. 292 (1984); Lee v. Comm'r, 48 T.C.M. 1454 (1984); Ruberto v. Comm'r, 48 T.C.M. 1438 (1984), rev'd, 774 F.2d 61 (2d Cir. 1985), on remand, 54 T.C.M. 1388 (1988); Beck v. Comm'r, 48 T.C.M. 1425 (1984); Pollard v. Comm'r, 48 T.C.M. 1303 (1984), aff'd, 786 F.2d 1063 (11th Cir. 1986); Martinez v. Comm'r, 48 T.C.M. 1271 (1984); Swanson v. Comm'r, 48 T.C.M. 1267 (1984); Ford v. Comm'r, 48 T.C.M. 1173 (1984); Brennan v. Comm'r, 48 T.C.M. 1165 (1984); Wert v. Comm'r, 48 T.C.M. 1158 (1984); Di Pierri v. Comm'r, 48 T.C.M. 1156 (1984); Addeo v. Comm'r, 48 T.C.M. 1126 (1984); Bradfield v. Comm'r, 48 T.C.M. 1071 (1984); Kent v. Comm'r, 48 T.C.M. 952 (1984); Snodgrass v. Comm'r, 48 T.C.M. 883 (1984); Makkay v. Comm'r, 47 T.C.M. 869 (1984); Poldrugovaz v. Comm'r, 47 T.C.M. 860 (1984); Hoskinson v. Comm'r, 48 T.C.M. 678 (1984); Hodges v. Comm'r, 48 T.C.M. 617 (1984); Clark v. Comm'r, 48 T.C.M. 371 (1984); Fowler v. Comm'r, 48 T.C.M. 309 (1984); Johnson v. Comm'r, 48 T.C.M. 289 (1984); Beasley v. Comm'r, 48 T.C.M. 287 (1984); Hawbaker v. Comm'r, 47 T.C.M. 231 (1983); Kalgaard v. Comm'r, 48 T.C.M. 106 (1984); aff'd, 764 F.2d 1322 (9th Cir. 1985); Winston v. Comm'r, 48 T.C.M. 55 (1984); Odd v. Comm'r, 47 T.C.M. 1483 (1984); Chicone v. Comm'r, 47 T.C.M. 980 (1984); Schreiber v. Comm'r, 47 T.C.M. 680 (1984); Stephenson v. Comm'r, 79 T.C. 995 (1982); Mendenhall v. Comm'r, 46 T.C.M. 1120 (1983); Bronner v. Comm'r, 45 T.C.M. 738 (1983); Solanne v. Comm'r, 45 T.C.M. 657 (1983); Owens v. Comm'r, 45 T.C.M. 157 (1982); Mustain v. Comm'r, 45 T.C.M. 153 (1982); Harcourt v. Comm'r, 44 T.C.M. 1506 (1982); Neil v. Comm'r, 44 T.C.M. 1237 (1982); Magin v. Comm'r, 44 T.C.M. 397 (1982); Murphy v. Comm'r, 45 T.C.M. 621 (1983); Hall v. Comm'r, 44 T.C.M. 151 (1982), aff'd, 729 F.2d 632 (9th Cir. 1984); Schilberg v. Comm'r, 44 T.C.M. 148 (1982); Kellman v. Comm'r, 42 T.C.M. 1508 (1981); Riemers v. Comm'r, 42 T.C.M. 838 (1981); Brown v. Comm'r, 41 T.C.M. 542 (1980). A ULC congregation seems doomed to noncharitable status in the U.S. Tax Court, due to the "cynical abuse of the church concept for tax purposes in recent years" (Church of Ethereal Joy v. Comm'r, 83 T.C. 20, 27 (1984)). Likewise, a federal court of appeals has referenced the "patently frivolous appeals filed by abusers of the tax system [who create unqualified religious groups] merely to delay and harass the collection of public revenues" (Granzow v. Comm'r, 739 F.2d 265, 267 (7th Cir. 1984), aff'g 46 T.C.M. 223 (1983)). In general, those who establish a Life Science Church congregation fare no better (e.g., Troyer v. Comm'r, 57 T.C.M. 334 (1989)). See also Woods v. Comm'r, 58 T.C.M. 673 (1989), aff'd without op. (6th Cir. 1991).

In one instance, an appeal of a ULC congregation case was deemed by the court to be so frivolous

cases; in 1983, the court wrote that "our tolerance for taxpayers who establish churches solely for tax avoidance purposes is reaching a breaking point."[103] The court added: "Not only do these taxpayers use the pretext of a church to avoid paying their fair share of taxes, even when their brazen schemes are uncovered many of them resort to the courts in a shameless attempt to vindicate themselves."[104] Consequently, the court gave notice that it will impose damages in these cases for using the court for purposes of delay.[105]

The Tax Court imposes the penalty for fraudulently intending to evade and defeat the payment of taxes legally due[106] in a situation where an individual established a bogus church. In one of these cases, a correctional officer, while attending a "tax strike convention," obtained information on how to form an "independent church." The church was formed with the assistance of materials acquired from the "Church of the Golden Rule." Banking accounts

that double costs and lawyers' fees were awarded the government (Larsen v. Comm'r, 765 F.2d 939 (9th Cir. 1985)). In another instance, the deduction for alleged gifts to a ULC congregation was denied on the ground that the receipts offered as evidence were hearsay (McMains v. Comm'r, 53 T.C.M. 118 (1987)). Further, charitable contribution deductions were denied by the U.S. Tax Court for payments made by ULC charter holders to other ULC congregations, where the payments were repaid by means of a check-swapping arrangement, with the court noting that the claimants "present[ed] more tiresome claims to deductions for alleged contributions" to the ULC (Wedvik v. Comm'r, 87 T.C. 1458, 1465 (1986)). Also Dew v. Comm'r, 91 T.C. 615 (1988) (where the court found a "daisy chain" sequence of payments to be a "perfidious twist to the usual Universal Life Church" case, a "brazen scheme," and "as blatant an example of [private] inurement as this Court has encountered in the innumerable ULC scams and check-swapping schemes it has been called upon to rule on" (id., at 623, 624); Svedahl v. Comm'r, 89 T.C. 245 (1987), app. dis. (9th Cir., June 24, 1988). Yet these cases are not automatically won by the government on appeal; in one case, the appellate court refused to find private inurement for purposes of a summary judgment request, and the case was remanded for trial on the point (Carter v. United States, 973 F.2d 1479 (9th Cir. 1992)).

The courts are upholding summonses served on banks in connection with investigations into the legitimacy of deductions for contributions made to ULC congregations (e.g., LaMura v. Comm'r, 765 F.2d 974 (11th Cir. 1985)). On September 4, 1984, the IRS announced that it will no longer recognize the tax-exempt status of the "parent" Universal Life Church (Ann. 84-90, 1984-36 I.R.B. 32). This revocation was subsequently upheld by the U.S. Claims Court in Universal Life Church, Inc. v. United States, 87-2 U.S.T.C. ¶ 9617 (Cl. Ct. 1987), aff'd, 862 F.2d 321 (Fed. Cir. 1988). The practices represented by these cases can amount to tax fraud (e.g., Braswell v. Comm'r, 66 T.C.M. 627 (1993); Mobley v. Comm'r, 65 T.C.M. 1939 (1993), aff'd in unpub. op. (11th Cir. 1994)).

In general, Petkanics & Petkanics, "Mail Order Ministries, the Religious Purpose Exemption, and the Constitution," 33 Tax Law. 959 (1980).

[97] E.g., Rev. Rul. 81-94, 1981-1 C.B. 330; Rev. Rul. 78-232, 1978-1 C.B. 69.

[98] E.g., United States v. Daly, 756 F.2d 1076 (5th Cir. 1985).

[99] IRC § 6661.

[100] Rev. Rul. 89-74, 1989-1 C.B. 311; Tweeddale v. Comm'r, 92 T.C. 501 (1989).

[101] Malnak v. Yogi, supra note 78, 440 F. Supp. at 1315.

[102] E.g., Self-Realization Bhd., Inc. v. Comm'r, 48 T.C.M. 344 (1984); The Ecclesiastical Order of the Ism of Am v. Comm'r, 80 T.C. 833 (1983), aff'd, 740 F.2d 967 (6th Cir. 1984), cert. den., 471 U.S. 1015 (1985). Also King Shipping Consum, Inc. v. Comm'r, 58 T.C.M. 574 (1989) (alleged church operated for the purpose of selling illegal drugs held not tax-exempt); Baustert v. Comm'r, 54 T.C.M. 673 (1987).

[103] Miedaner v. Comm'r, 81 T.C. 272, 282 (1983).

[104] Id.

[105] IRC § 6673. Also Sommer v. Comm'r, 45 T.C.M. 1271 (1983); Van Dyke v. Comm'r, 45 T.C.M. 1233 (1983); Noberini v. Comm'r, 45 T.C.M. 587 (1983).

[106] IRC § 6653(b).

were opened in the name of the "church." The minister, his wife, and his daughter were signatories on the accounts, and personal expenses were paid from these accounts. The minister executed an ostensible vow of poverty but did not change his lifestyle in any way. A delinquent tax return included a sizable gift deduction for a transfer made to the "church." Reviewing all of the facts, the court concluded that the "minister" "fraudulently intended to evade and defeat the payment of taxes legally due from him." Thus, the court upheld the imposition of the addition to tax. The "deliberate willful nature" of his intent was devined from the establishment of "his purported church," the claiming of unsubstantiated contributions to it, the submission of a false letter to his employer concerning tax withholdings, and his failure to timely file a tax return.[107]

There are several categories of institutions that are regarded, for federal tax purposes, as *religious* organizations. These include churches, conventions and associations of churches, integrated auxiliaries of churches, religious orders, and apostolic organizations. There are a variety of church-administered organizations (usually tax-exempt but not necessarily religious in nature), such as schools, hospitals, orphanages, nursing homes, broadcasting and publishing entities, and cemeteries.

§ 8.3 CHURCHES AND SIMILAR INSTITUTIONS

A bona fide *church* (including institutions such as synagogues and mosques) clearly is a religious entity. Yet, just as is the case with respect to the term *religious*, there is no definition in the Internal Revenue Code or in a currently applicable tax regulation of the term *church*. Again, a rigid regulatory definition of the term church would undoubtedly be unconstitutional. As one court observed: "We can only approach this question with care for all of us are burdened with the baggage of our own unique beliefs and perspectives."[108]

The concept of a tax-exempt church is recognized in the Internal Revenue Code.[109] Federal tax law applies the term *church* in a variety of contexts. One of

---

[107] Butler v. Comm'r, 50 T.C.M. 218 (1985). Another approach used by the courts to deny tax-exempt status to a mail-order church is that it failed to keep adequate financial records to demonstrate entitlement to tax exemption as required by IRC § 6001 (Church of Gospel Ministry, Inc. v. United States (D.D.C. 1986)). In general, Flynn, "Witchcraft and Tax Exempt Status Under Section 501(c)(3) of the Internal Revenue Code," 21 *U. San Fran. L. Rev.* (No. 4) 763 (1987); Slye, "Rendering Unto Caesar: Defining 'Religion' for Purposes of Administering Religion-Based Tax Exemptions," 6 *Harv. J. Law Public Policy* 219 (1983); Peacock, "Emerging Criteria for Tax-Exempt Classification for Religious Organizations," 60 *Taxes* (No. 1) 61 (1982).

[108] Foundation of Human Understanding v. Comm'r, 88 T.C. 1341, 1356–1357 (1987).

[109] IRC § 170(b)(1)(A)(i). The term *church* has been defined for state law purposes in a variety of ways. One of the most straightforward definitions is that a church is "an organization for religious purposes, for the public worship of God" (Bennett v. City of La Grange, 112 S.E. 482, 485 (Ga. 1922)). Other definitions of the term *church* include the following: "A body or community of Christians,

---

the oldest of these instances is reflected in tax regulations issued in 1958 and applicable for tax years before 1970, which defined the term *church* (in the unrelated business and charitable contribution deduction settings).[110] Those regulations focused on the "duties" of a church, which were said to include the "ministration of sacerdotal [priestly] functions and the conduct of religious worship." The existence of these elements was said to depend on the "tenets and practices of a particular religious body."

The IRS has since formulated the criteria that it uses to ascertain whether or not an organization qualifies as a church.[111] The IRS position is that, to be a church for tax purposes, an organization must satisfy at least some of the following criteria: a distinct legal existence, a recognized creed and form of worship, a definite and distinct ecclesiastical government, a formal code of doctrine and discipline, a distinct religious history, a membership not associated with any other church or denomination, a complete organization of ordained ministers ministering to their congregations and selected after completing prescribed courses of study, a literature of its own, established places of worship, regular congregations, regular religious services, Sunday schools for the religious instruction of the young, and schools for the preparation of its ministers.[112]

The Commissioner of Internal Revenue first made these criteria public in

united under one form of government by the same profession of the same faith, and the observance of the same ritual and ceremonies" (McNeilly v. First Presbyterian Church in Brookline, 137 N.E. 691 (Mass. 1923)); "The term may denote either a society of persons who, professing Christianity, hold certain doctrines or observances which differentiate them from other like groups, and who use a common discipline, or the building in which such persons habitually assemble for public worship" (Baker v. Fales, 16 Mass. 488, 498, quoted in First Indep. Missionary Baptist Church of Chosen v. McMillan, 153 So.2d 337, 342 (Fla. 1963)); and "A church society is a voluntary organization whose members are associated together, not only for religious exercises, but also for the purpose of maintaining and supporting its ministry and providing the conveniences of a church home and promoting the growth and efficiency of the work of the general church of which it forms a co-ordinate part" (First Presbyterian Church of Mt. Vernon v. Dennis, 161 N.W. 183, 187 (Iowa 1917)). Thus, the term *church* carries many meanings, including the congregation and the physical facilities themselves. As one court observed, the term "may refer only to the church building or house of worship; it may mean in a more consecrated way the great body of persons holding the Christian belief, or in a restricted sense confined to those adhering to one of the several denominations of the Christian faith, at large or in a definite territory; and it may mean the collective membership of persons constituting the congregation of a single permanent place of worship" (Forsberg v. Zehm, 143 S.E. 284, 286 (Va. 1928)).

[110] Reg. §§ 1.170-2 (b)(2), 1.511-2 (a)(3)(ii) (inapplicable with respect to tax years after 1969).

[111] Guam Power Auth. v. Bishop of Guam, 383 F. Supp. 476 (D. Guam 1974).

[112] Internal Revenue Manual § 321.3. Also Rev. Rul. 59-129, 1959-1 C.B. 58. The Chief Counsel of the IRS advised against formal publication of the church criteria on the theory that the publication would prejudice criminal cases under review by the Department of Justice (e.g., Gen. Couns. Mem. 38699). One federal court of appeals reversed the U.S. Tax Court in one of these cases, holding that the lower court abused its discretion in refusing to give the individuals involved a reasonable opportunity to produce evidence to substantiate their alleged contributions to the Universal Life Church (Roberto v. Comm'r, *supra* note 95).

1977.[113] He observed that "few, if any, religious organizations—conventional or unconventional—could satisfy all of these criteria" and that the IRS does "not give controlling weight to any single factor." Further, he asserted that "[t]his is obviously the place in the decisional process requiring the most sensitive and discriminating judgment." He concluded by noting that the IRS has "been criticized for the scope and breadth of the criteria we use and it has been implied that the Service has been trying in recent years to discourage new religions and new churches"; he offered the assurance "that this is not the case with the IRS."

Although the IRS continues to utilize these criteria,[114] it—upon advice of its chief counsel[115]—made it clear that the criteria are not exclusive and are not to be mechanically applied, and added another criterion that embraces "any other facts and circumstances which may bear upon the organization's claim to church status."[116] The IRS has resisted suggestions to publish these criteria in a revenue ruling because of concern for potential prejudice to various church cases under review by the government and concern that the criteria could be interpreted as providing a "safe harbor" for certain alleged churches.[117] The most public pronouncement of these criteria is a tax guide for churches published by the IRS in 1994.[118]

As has been discussed, the courts have been reluctant to pass on the question as to what is a religious organization, let alone what is a church. Still, an extreme factual setting may embolden a court to make a distinction between religious activities and personal codes of conduct that lack spiritual import. This was the case with the Neo-American Church, the chief precept of which was that psychedelic substances, such as LSD and marijuana, are the "true Host of the Church," thereby specifying that it is "the Religious *duty* of all members to partake of the sacraments on regular occasions." The Church had the equivalent of bishops (known as "Boo Hoos"), a symbol (a three-eyed toad), official songs (e.g., "Puff, the Magic Dragon"), a Church key (a bottle opener), a Catechism and Handbook (excerpt: "we have the *right* to practice our religion, even if we are a bunch of filthy, drunken bums"), and a motto ("Victory over Horseshit"). Recognizing that judges "must be ever careful not to permit their own moral and ethical standards to determine the religious im-

---

[113] "Difficult Definitional Problems in Tax Administration: Religion and Race," remarks by then Commissioner Jerome Kurtz before the Practicing Law Institute Seventh Biennial Conference on Tax Planning for Foundations, Tax-Exempt Status and Charitable Contributions, on Jan. 9, 1977, reproduced at Bureau of National Affairs, *Daily Executive Report*, Jan. 11, 1977, at page J8.

[114] The Chief Counsel of the IRS invoked another criterion, which is whether the organization involved characterized itself as a church from its inception (Gen. Couns. Mem. 38982).

[115] Gen. Couns. Mem. 38699.

[116] Internal Revenue Manual—Administration § 321.3.

[117] Gen. Couns. Mem. 38699. The IRS criteria are not without their critics. One commentator stated that they "tend to require an organization to be a developed denomination according to the pattern reflected in the most accepted mainline churches"; they "tend to . . . limit the religious scene to the denominations already in existence, in violation of the establishment clause"; and "Christ and His band of disciples certainly did not meet these criteria" (Worthing, " 'Religion' and 'Religious Institutions' Under the First Amendment," *supra* note 81, at 344–345).

[118] "Tax Guide for Churches and Other Religious Organizations" (Pub. 1828).

plications of beliefs and practices of others," a court nonetheless concluded that the Neo-American Church was not a religious entity, in the absence of any "solid evidence of a belief in a supreme being, a religious discipline, a ritual, or tenets to guide one's daily existence."[119]

Nonetheless, some courts are becoming more willing to enunciate criteria for a church. Thus, in the view of the U.S. Tax Court, a church is an organization that, in addition to having a "religious-type function," holds services or meetings on a regular basis, has ministers or other "representatives," has a record of performance of "marriages, other ceremonies or sacraments," has a place of worship, ordains ministers, requires some financial support by its members, has a form of "formal operation," and satisfies all other requirements of the federal tax law rules for religious organizations.[120]

In the first instance of a court's utilization of the IRS criteria as to the definition of the term *church*, the Tax Court concluded that an organization, albeit religious, could not qualify as a church because there was no "congregation," nor requisite "religious instruction" nor "conduct of religious worship."[121] Laying down a "minimum" definition of a church as including "a body of believers or communicants that assembles regularly in order to worship," the court said that of "central importance" is "the existence of an established congregation served by an organized ministry, the provision of regular religious services and religious education for the young, and the dissemination of a doctrinal code."[122] In the case, no "congregation" was found present, in that the only communicants were the founder of the church and his wife who "pray together in the physical solitude of their home" the organization's "religious instruction" consisted of "a father preaching to his son"; and its "organized ministry" was a "single self-appointed clergyman."[123] Because the organization "does not employ recognized, accessible channels of instruction and worship" and was merely a "quintessentially private religious enterprise," the court concluded that it was not a church.[124] The U.S. Claims Court also endorsed these criteria, concluding that, while a "new religious organization should not be held to a

---

[119] United States v. Kuch, 288 F. Supp. 439, 443–444 (D.D.C. 1968). Also Puritan Church of Am. v. Comm'r, 10 T.C.M. 485 (1951), aff'd, 209 F.2d 306 (D.C. Cir. 1953), cert. den., 347 U.S. 975 (1954), 350 U.S. 810 (1955). Cf. Malnak v. Yogi, *supra* note 78; People v. Woody, 394 P.2d 813 (Cal. 1964); Heller v. Comm'r, 37 T.C.M. 643 (1978); Baker v. Comm'r, 40 T.C.M. 983 (1980); Clippinger v. Comm'r, 37 T.C.M. 484 (1978).

[120] Pusch v. Comm'r, 39 T.C.M. 838 (1980), aff'd, 628 F.2d 1353 (5th Cir. 1980). Also Pusch v. Comm'r, 44 T.C.M. 961 (1982); Abney v. Comm'r, 39 T.C.M. 965 (1980); Manson v. Comm'r, 40 T.C.M. 972 (1980); Lynch v. Comm'r, 41 T.C.M. 204 (1980). Cf. Morey v. Riddell, 205 F. Supp. 918 (S.D. Cal. 1962); Peek v. Comm'r, 73 T.C. 912 (1980); Chapman v. Comm'r, 48 T.C. 358 (1967).

[121] American Guidance Found. Inc. v. United States, 490 F. Supp. 304, 306 (D.D.C. 1980), aff'd (without opinion) (D.C. Cir. 1981).

[122] *Id*. at 306.

[123] *Id*. at 307.

[124] *Id*. Likewise The Church of Eternal Life & Liberty, Inc. v. Comm'r, 86 T.C. 916 (1986); Universal Bible Church, Inc. v. Comm'r, 51 T.C.M. 936 (1986).

In a subsequent case, the Tax Court wrote that the court does not adopt the IRS criteria as to the definition of the term church "as a test," then went on to explicitly find the organization at issue to be a church because it "possess[es] most of the criteria to some degree" and because "most of the factors considered to be of critical importance are satisfied" (Foundation of Human Understanding v. Comm'r, *supra* note 108, at 1360).

standard only an established church can satisfy," "one man's publication of a newsletter and extemporaneous discussion of his beliefs, even when advertised, is not sufficient to constitute a church within the common understanding of that word."[125]

Courts are evidencing acceptance of the IRS criteria. Thus, one federal court of appeals concluded that a social service agency, substantially connected with a particular faith, was not a church because it did not hold regular worship services, and because it provided services to individuals irrespective of their religious beliefs and counseling without any particular religious orientation.[126] Another appellate court held that an organization that did not meet enough of the IRS criteria could not qualify as a church.[127]

The U.S. Supreme Court offered a partial definition of the term *church* in the tax context, in an opinion construing an exemption from unemployment compensation taxes imposed by the Federal Unemployment Tax Act and complementary state law. The issue was the eligibility for the exemption for services performed for church-related schools that do not have a separate legal existence, pursuant to provision of exemption for employees "of a church or convention or association of churches."[128] The Court rejected the view that the term *church* means no more than "the actual house of worship used by a congregation" and held that the word "must be construed, instead, to refer to the congregation or the hierarchy itself, that is, the church authorities who conduct the business of hiring, discharging, and directing church employees."[129] Thus, in one instance, a church-operated day school, financed by the church's congregation and controlled by a board of directors elected from that congregation, was considered part of the church, and a secondary school owned, supported, and controlled by a Synod was considered part of a convention or association of churches; neither school was separately incorporated. Although the Court recognized that the issue carries with it potential constitutional law questions,[130] it also expressly "disavow[ed] any intimations in this case defining or limiting what constitutes a church under FUTA or under any other provision of the Internal Revenue Code."[131]

Traditionally, courts have enunciated only two guides as to what constitutes

---

[125] The Church of the Visible Intelligence That Governs the Universe v. United States, *supra* note 56, at 88, 597.

[126] Lutheran Social Servs. of Minn. v. United States, 758 F.2d 1283 (8th Cir. 1985). A court concluded that a "church is a coherent group of individuals and families that join together to accomplish the religious purposes of mutually held beliefs" and that a "church's principal means of accomplishing its religious purposes must be to assemble regularly a group of individuals related by common worship and faith." (The Church of Eternal Life & Liberty, Inc. v. Comm'r, *supra* note 124, at 924.) An organization unsuccessfully contested an IRS finding that it was not a church; a motion for summary judgment on the point, relying on dicta in a bankruptcy court opinion, failed (Gates Community Chapel of Rochester, Inc. d/b/a Freedom Village USA v. United States, 96-1 U.S.T.C. ¶ 50,093 (Cl. Ct. 1996)).

[127] Spiritual Outreach Soc'y v. Comm'r, 91-1 U.S.T.C. ¶ 50,111 (8th Cir. 1991)).

[128] IRC § 3309(b)(1)(A).

[129] St. Martin Evangelical Lutheran Church v. South Dakota, 451 U.S. 772, 784 (1981).

[130] *Id*. at 780.

[131] *Id*. at 784, note 15.

a church in the federal tax context: it must be a religious organization and it must be the equivalent of a "denomination" or a "sect." For example, in 1967, a court held that "though every church may be a religious organization, every religious organization is not per se a church" and that the "concept of 'church' appears to be synonymous with the concept of 'denomination.' "[132] However, then the court hastened to add that its holding "is not to imply, however, that in order to be constituted a church, a group must have an organizational hierarchy or maintain church buildings."[133]

If the definition stated in the now-withdrawn unrelated income tax regulation is employed, the conclusion becomes that the primary function of a church is "sacerdotal" activities, while a religious organization may permissibly engage in a broader range of activities, and a charitable and educational organization may engage in a still wider range of activities that may nonetheless have a nexus with religious undertakings (for example, the charitable purpose of advancement of religion).[134]

From this standpoint, a church is, in the absence of a statutory definition, an organization that is a church under the "common meaning and usage of the word."[135] Pursuant to this approach, "[a]n organization established to carry out 'church' functions, under the general understanding of the term, is a 'church.' "[136] These functions, according to this view, principally are forms of conduct of religious worship (such as a mass or communion) but are not activities such as the operation of schools, religious orders, wineries, and missions, even where these "religious organizations . . . [or functions are] formed [or conducted] under church auspices."[137] If the latter categories of activities predominate, the organization cannot be a church, inasmuch as the "tail cannot be permitted to wag the dog" and the conduct of such "incidental activities" cannot make an organization a church.[138] Some subsequent cases follow this approach, such as the court finding that an organization is not a church because "there is no showing in the record of any marriages, other ceremonies or sacraments performed by any 'minister' or representative of the Church."[139] Other cases reject this narrow reading of the term and embrace within the ambit of church functions activities such as "mission or evangelistic program[s]" and efforts for "the care of the needy, the sick, or the imprisoned, traditionally the beneficiaries of the ministration of churches."[140]

Thus, just as the law cannot formulate a tax definition of the term *religion*, it seems unable to formulate a formal definition of the term *church*. This is not sur-

---

[132] Chapman v. Comm'r, *supra* note 120, at 363. As to the latter element, the court observed that the organization involved is "merely a religious organization comprised of individual members who are already affiliated with various churches" (*id.* at 364).

[133] *Id.* at 363.

[134] See § 6.4.

[135] De La Salle Inst. v. United States, 195 F. Supp. 891, 903 (N.D. Cal. 1961).

[136] *Id.* at 903.

[137] *Id.* at 902.

[138] *Id.* at 901.

[139] Pusch v. Comm'r, *supra* note 120, 39 T.C.M., at 841. An organization formed to promote "wellness" among its members, through education in exercise, nutrition, and stress management, was held to not qualify as a church (VIA v. Comm'r, 68 T.C.M. 212 (1994)).

[140] Bubbling Well Church of Universal Love, Inc. v. Comm'r, *supra* note 60, 74 T.C. at 536.

prising, in that the religion clauses preclude the strict application of definitions of this nature.[141]

§ 8.4. CONVENTIONS OR ASSOCIATIONS OF CHURCHES

Another type of religious organization is the convention or association of churches.[142] The IRS recognizes that the phrase has a historical meaning generally referring to a cooperative undertaking by a church of the same denomination.[143] However, the IRS ruled that the term also applies to a cooperative undertaking by churches of differing denominations, assuming that the convention or association otherwise qualifies as a religious organization.[144]

The phrase "convention or association of churches" was used by Congress to refer to the organizational structures of congregational churches. The term was employed to accord them the comparable tax treatment granted to hierarchical churches.[145]

§ 8.5 INTEGRATED AUXILIARIES OF CHURCHES

An integrated auxiliary of a church is a religious organization.[146]

The phrase "integrated auxiliary of a church" means an organization that is a tax-exempt charitable entity,[147] a public charity,[148] affiliated with a church or a convention or association of churches, and internally supported.[149]

---

[141] In general, Shaller, "Churches and Their Enviable Tax Status," 51 *U. of Pittsburgh L. Rev.* (No. 2) 345 (1990); Lashbrooke, Jr., "An Economic and Constitutional Case for Repeal of the I.R.C. Section 170 Deduction for Charitable Contributions to Religious Organizations," 27 *Duq. L. Rev.* (No. 4) 695 (1989); Scialabba, Kurzman, & Steinhart, "Mail-Order Ministries Under the Section 170 Charitable Contribution Deduction: The First Amendment Restrictions, the Minister's Burden of Proof, and the Effect of TRA '86," 11 *Campbell L. Rev.* (No. 1) 1 (1988); Whelan, " 'Church' in the Internal Revenue Code: The Definitional Problems," 45 *Fordham L. Rev.* 885 (1977); Worthing, "The Internal Revenue Service as a Monitor of Church Institutions: The Excessive Entanglement Problem," 45 *Fordham L. Rev.* 929 (1977); Schwarz, "Limiting Religious Tax Exemptions: When Should the Church Render Unto Caesar," 29 *U. Fl. L. Rev.* 50 (1976); Burns, "Constitutional Aspects of Church Taxation," 9 *Col. J. Law & Social Problems* 646 (1973).

[142] IRC § 170(b)(1)(A)(i). A discussion of the legislative history of this phrase appears in De La Salle Inst. v. United States, *supra* note 135 at 897-910. See Reg. § 1.170A-9(a).

The IRS, on October 5, 1994, issued a "Tax Guide for Churches and Other Religious Organizations," *supra* note 118. This publication addressed matters such as the definition of a church, the private inurement prohibition (see Chapter 19), the rules as to legislative activities (see Chapter 20) and political campaign activities (see Chapter 21), the procedure for acquiring recognition of tax exemption (see Chapter 23), the annual reporting rules (see § 24.3), the church audit rules (see § 24.8), the unrelated business income rules (see Part IV), and special rules applicable to the compensation of clergy.

[143] Rev. Rul. 74-224, 1974-1 C.B. 61. Cf. Chapman v. Comm'r, *supra* note 120.

[144] *Id.*

[145] Lutheran Social Servs. of Minn. v. United States, *supra* note 126, at 1288.

[146] IRC § 170(b)(1)(A)(i).

[147] That is, an organization described in IRC § 501(c)(3).

[148] That is, an organization described in IRC § 509(a)(1), 509(a)(2), or 509(a)(3). See § 11.3.

[149] Reg. § 1.6033-2(h)(1).

An organization is *affiliated* with a church or a convention or association of churches, for this purpose, if the organization is covered by a group exemption letter issued to a church or a convention or association of churches;[150] the organization is operated, supervised, or controlled by or in connection with[151] a church or a convention or association of churches; or relevant facts and circumstances show that it has the requisite affiliation.[152]

The following factors are among those used to determine whether an organization is affiliated with a church or a convention or association of churches (although the absence of one or more of them does not necessarily preclude a finding of affiliation): the organization's enabling instrument[153] or bylaws affirm that the organization shares common religious doctrines, principles, disciplines, or practices with a church or a convention or association of churches; a church or a convention or association of churches has the authority to appoint or remove, or to control the appointment or removal of, at least one of the organization's officers or directors; the corporate name of the organization indicates an institutional relationship with a church or a convention or association of churches; the organization reports at least annually on its financial and general operations to a church or a convention or association of churches; an institutional relationship between the organization and a church or a convention or association of churches is affirmed by the church, or convention or association of churches, or a designee of one or more of them; and, in the event of dissolution, the organization's assets are required to be distributed to a church or a convention or association of churches, or to an affiliate (as defined by these rules) of one or more of them.[154]

An organization is *internally supported*, for these purposes, unless it both offers admissions, goods, services, or facilities for sale, other than on an incidental basis, to the general public (except goods, services, or facilities sold at a nominal charge or for an insubstantial portion of the cost) and normally receives more than 50 percent of its support from a combination of government sources, public solicitation of contributions, and receipts from the sale of admissions, goods, performance of services, or furnishing of facilities in activities that are not unrelated trades or businesses.[155]

Men's and women's organizations, seminaries, mission societies, and youth groups that meet all of the criteria for qualification of an integrated auxiliary of a church or a convention or association of churches are such integrated auxiliaries irrespective of whether these entities satisfy the internal support requirement.[156]

Under rules previously in existence, the term integrated auxiliary of a church meant an organization that is a tax-exempt charitable organization, affili-

---

[150] See § 23.6.
[151] This phraseology is the same as that used in connection with the supporting organization rules (see § 11.3(c), text accompanied by note 189).
[152] Reg. § 1.6033-2(h)(2).
[153] That is, its corporate charter, trust instrument, articles of association, constitution, or similar document. This is what the IRS refers to in other contexts as the *articles of organization* (see, e.g., § 4.2).
[154] Reg. § 1.6033-2(h)(3).
[155] Reg. § 1.6033-2(h)(4).
[156] Reg. § 1.6033-2(h)(5).

ated with a church, and engaged in a principal activity that is "exclusively religious."[157] However, an organization's principal activity was not considered to be exclusively religious if that activity was of a nature other than religious that would serve as a basis for tax exemption (such as charitable, educational, or scientific activity).[158]

Litigation ensued as the consequence of issuance of these previous rules. A federal court of appeals invalidated the requirement that an organization must be exclusively religious to qualify as an integrated auxiliary of a church.[159] This court held that that portion of the regulation was inconsistent with clear congressional policy,[160] thus ruling that the organization involved—a social service agency that was affiliated with various synods of a church—was an integrated auxiliary of the church because "it performs functions of the church bodies to which it is related by satisfying the tenet of the . . . faith [of the church] which requires the stimulation of works of mercy through social action ministries developed to promote human welfare."[161] By contrast, a federal district court found these regulations to be valid, but only after finding an organization to be an integrated auxiliary of a church because the entity was exclusively religious.[162]

§ 8.6 RELIGIOUS ORDERS

Another type of religious organization is the *religious order*, a term that is not defined in the Internal Revenue Code or the tax regulations. However, the IRS promulgated guidelines for determining whether an organization qualifies as

---

[157] Former Reg. § 1.6033-2(g)(5)(i).

[158] Former Reg. § 1.6033-2(g)(5)(ii).

[159] Lutheran Social Serv. of Minn. v. United States, 758 F.2d 1283 (8th Cir. 1985), *rev'g* 583 F. Supp. 1298 (D. Minn. 1984). Also Lutheran Children & Family Serv. of Eastern Pa. v. United States, 86-2 U.S.T.C. ¶ 9593 (E.D. Pa. 1986).

[160] The appellate court was particularly influenced by the fact that Congress specifically imposed the "exclusively religious" standard upon religious orders (IRC § 6033(a)(2)(A)(iii)) but did not do so with respect to integrated auxiliaries of churches (IRC § 6033(a)(2)(A)(i)).

[161] Lutheran Social Serv. of Minn. v. United States, *supra* note 159, 758 F.2d at 1291.

[162] Tennessee Baptist Children's Homes, Inc. v. United States, 604 F. Supp. 210 (M.D. Tenn. 1984), *aff'd*, 790 F.2d 534 (6th Cir. 1986). Under prior law, for example, schools that were operated, supported, and controlled by a church or a convention or association of churches were integrated auxiliaries (St. Martin Evangelical Lutheran Church v. South Dakota, *supra* note 129), an organization was held to not qualify as an integrated auxiliary because the church involved lacked any control over the assets or income of the organization (Parshall Christian Order v. Comm'r, 45 T.C.M. 488 (1983), and a church-affiliated college that trained ministers and lay workers to serve religious functions in the church qualified as an integrated auxiliary (Rev. Rul. 77-381, 1977-2 C.B. 462). Private letter rulings issued by the IRS provided illustrations of organizations that were integrated auxiliaries of a church under prior law (e.g., Priv. Ltr. Rul. 8416065) and of those that did not qualify as an integrated auxiliary of a church (e.g., Priv. Ltr. Rul. 8402014).

In general, Blaine, "The Unfortunate Church-State Dispute Over the I.R.C. Section 6033 'Exclusively Religious' Test," 23 *New Eng. L. Rev.* (No. 1) 1 (1988); Reed, "Integrated Auxiliaries, Regulations and Implications," 23 *Cath. Law.* 211 (Summer 1978).

a religious order, utilizing a variety of characteristics drawn from the caselaw.[163] These characteristics are as follows: the organization is a charitable one;[164] the members of the organization vow to live under a strict set of rules requiring moral and spiritual self-sacrifice and dedication to the goals of the organization at the expense of their material well-being; the members of the organization, after successful completion of the organization's training program and probationary period, make a long-term commitment to the organization (normally more than two years); the organization is, directly or indirectly, under the control and supervision of a church or convention or association of churches, or is significantly funded by a church or convention or association of churches; the members of the organization normally live together as part of a community and are held to a significantly stricter level of moral and religious discipline than that required by lay church members; the members of the organization work or serve full-time on behalf of the religious, educational, or charitable goals of the organization; and the members of the organization participate regularly in activities such as public or private prayer, religious study, teaching, care of the aging, missionary work, or church reform or renewal.[165]

In determining whether an organization is a religious order, all of the facts and circumstances must be considered. Generally, the presence of all of these characteristics is determinative that the organization is a religious order; however, the absence of the first of these characteristics is determinative that the organization is not a religious order. The absence of one or more of the other enumerated characteristics is not necessarily determinative in a particular case. Generally, if application of these characteristics to the facts of a particular case does not clearly indicate whether the organization is a religious order, the IRS's procedures call for it to contact the particular authorities affiliated with the organization for their views concerning the characterization of the organization, which views are to be "carefully considered."[166]

§ 8.7 APOSTOLIC ORGANIZATIONS

Certain *religious or apostolic* organizations are exempt from federal income taxation, even though they are not embraced by the general reference to religious organizations. These are "religious or apostolic associations or corporations, if such associations or corporations have a common treasury or community treasury, even if such associations or corporations engage in business for the com-

---

[163] Rev. Proc. 91-20, 1991-1 C.B. 524. The cases cited by the IRS in this regard are St. Joseph Farms of Indiana Bros. of the Congregation of Holy Cross, Southwest Province, Inc. v. Comm'r, 85 T.C. 9 (1985), *app. dis.* (7th Cir. 1986); De La Salle Inst. v. United States, *supra* note 110; Eighth Street Baptist Church, Inc. v. United States, 295 F. Supp. 1400 (D. Kan. 1969), *aff'd*, 431 F.2d 1193 (10th Cir. 1970); Kelley v. Comm'r, 62 T.C. 131 (1974); Estate of Margaret Callaghan v. Comm'r, 33 T.C. 870 (1960).
[164] That is, it is described in IRC § 501(c)(3).
[165] Rev. Proc. 91-20, *supra* note 163, § 3.
[166] *Id.*

mon benefit of the members, but only if the members thereof include (at the time of filing their returns) in their gross income their entire pro rata shares, whether distributed or not, of the taxable income of the association or corporation for such year."[167] Any amount so included in the gross income of a member is treated as a dividend received.[168] It is the position of the IRS that a member of a religious or apostolic organization may not claim his or her minor children as dependents for tax purposes because the organization provides their food, clothing, medical care, and the like, the members cannot claim the investment tax credit on their proportionate shares of property purchased by the organization,[169] the members cannot claim the fuel tax credit on fuels purchased by the organization, the costs of personal goods and services provided by such an organization for its members are not deductible business expenses, and the amounts distributed to the members of the organization do not constitute self-employment income.[170]

The requirement that there be a "common treasury or community treasury" does not mean that the members of the apostolic organization must take a vow of poverty and irrevocably contribute all of their property to the organization upon becoming members and not be entitled to any part of that property upon leaving the organization.[171] The concept of this type of treasury "connotes that the property of such organizations not be held by members individually but rather held in a 'community capacity' with all members having equal interests in the community property" and does not mean "that members are necessarily prohibited from owning property outside and apart from the organization."[172] This requirement is satisfied "when all of the income generated internally by community-operated business and any income generated from property owned by the organization is placed into a common fund that is maintained by such organization and is used for the maintenance and support of its members, with all members having equal, undivided interests in this common fund, but no right to claim title to any part thereof."[173]

For purposes of determining the pro rata shares of the taxable income of an apostolic organization (to be included in the members' gross income), the membership in the organization is to be determined in accordance with the rules of the organization itself and applicable state law. Individuals qualified to be members of this type of an organization must consent to this membership status; parents may consent to the membership on behalf of their minor children to the extent allowed under applicable state law.[174]

---

[167] IRC § 501(d).
[168] Reg. § 1.501(d)-1(a); Rev. Rul. 58-328, 1958-1 C.B. 327; Rev. Rul. 57-574, 1957-2 C.B. 161; Riker v. Comm'r, *supra* note 59.
[169] Kleinsasser v. United States, 707 F.2d 1024 (9th Cir. 1983), *aff'g* 522 F. Supp. (D. Mont. 1981).
[170] Priv. Ltr. Rul. 7740009.
[171] Twin Oaks Community, Inc. v. Comm'r, 87 T.C. 1233 (1986).
[172] *Id.* at 1248.
[173] *Id.* at 1254.
[174] Rev. Rul. 77-295, 1977-2 C.B. 196.

The origins of these rules (in 1936) are reflected in the following excerpt from its legislative history:

> It has been brought to the attention of the committee that certain religious and apostolic associations and corporations, such as the House of David and the Shakers, have been taxed as corporations, and that since their rules prevent their members from being holders of property in an individual capacity the corporations would be subject to the undistributed-profits tax. These organizations have a small agricultural or other business. The effect of the proposed amendment is to exempt these corporations from the normal corporations tax and the undistributed-profits tax, if their members take up their shares of the corporations' income on their own individual returns. It is believed that this provision will give them relief, and their members will be subject to a fair tax.[175]

Subsequently, a federal court of appeals, in commenting on the type of organization contemplated by these rules, said: "One might assume, then, that Congress intended an association somewhat akin to the ordinary association or partnership in which each member has a definite, though undivided, interest in the business conducted for the common benefit of the members, as well as a common interest in the community treasury and property."[176]

Also, the statute's beginnings are traceable to the fact that apostolic organizations were early found to not qualify for tax exemption under the general rules for religious organizations because of the presence of commercial activities and private inurement, as discussed in the cases concerning the tax status of the Hutterische Church.[177] Few exemptions under this provision have been granted; the most notable example may be the 1939 determination of exemption thereunder accorded the Israelite House of David.[178] The courts appear to prefer to cope with organizations of this nature in the context of the law applicable to religious groups generally.[179]

Organizations contemplated by these rules are those that are supported by internally operated businesses in which all the members have an individual interest. In one instance, a communal religious organization did not conduct any business activities and instead was supported by the wages of some of its members who were engaged in outside employment and thus was ruled to not qualify as an apostolic organization.[180]

---

[175] 80 *Cong. Rec.* 9074 (1936).

[176] Riker v. Comm'r, *supra* note 59 at 230.

[177] Hofer v. United States, 64 Ct. Cl. 672 (1928); Hutterische Bruder Gemeinde v. Comm'r, 1 B. T. A. 1208 (1925).

[178] Blume v. Gardner, 262 F. Supp. 405, 408 (W.D. Mich. 1966), *aff'd*, 397 F.2d 809 (6th Cir. 1968). Also Israelite House of David v. United States, 58 F. Supp. 862 (W.D. Mich. 1945); People v. Israelite House of David, 225 N.W. 638 (Mich. 1929).

[179] Golden Rule Church Ass'n v. Comm'r, 41 T.C. 719 (1964), State v. King Colony Ranch, 350 P.2d 841 (Mont. 1960).

[180] Rev. Rul. 78-100, 1978-1 C.B. 162.

It is the position of the IRS (general counsel) that failure to qualify as an apostolic organization under these rules does not preclude the possibility that an organization may qualify as a communal religious organization.[181] In other words, the IRS does not believe that Congress occupied the field with respect to tax exemption of all communal religious organizations in enacting the rules for apostolic organizations.

---

[181] Gen. Couns. Mem. 38827. In general, Wylie & Pfeifer, "Distinguishing Among Churches, Religious Orders, and Other Religious Organizations," 7 *J. Tax. Exempt Orgs.* (No. 2) 6557 (Sept./Oct. 1995); Spirtos, "Draft IRS Publication Details Tax Constraints for Churches and Religious Organizations," 6 *J. Tax. Exempt Orgs.* (No. 5) 213 (Mar./Apr. 1995). Marshall & Blomgren, "Regulating Organizations Under the Establishment Clause," 47 *Ohio St. L. J.* 316 (1986); Mangrum, "Naming Religion (and Eligible Cognates) in Tax Exemption Cases," 19 *Creighton L. Rev.* (No. 4) 821 (1985); Sciarrino, "United States v. Sun Myung Moon: Precedent For Tax Fraud Prosecution of Local Pastors?," 1984 *S. Ill. L. J.* (No. 2) 237 (1985); Nomady, "Mail Order Ministries: Application of the Religious Purpose Exemption Under the First Amendment," 17 *J. Mar. L. Rev.* 895 (1984); Hageman, "An Examination of Religious Tax Exemption Policy Under Section 501(c)(3) of the Internal Revenue Code," 17 *Val. Law Rev.* 405 (1983); Comment, "Real Property Tax Exemptions for Religious Organizations: The Dilemma of *Holy Spirit Association v. Tax Commissioner*," 47 *Albany L. Rev.* 1117 (1983); Note, "The Forbidden Fruit of Church-State Contacts: The Role of the Entanglement Theory in Its Ripening," 16 *Suffock U. L. Rev.* 725 (1982); Peacock, "Emerging Criteria for Tax-Exempt Classification for Religious Organizations," 61 *Taxes* 61 (Sept. 1982); Choper, "Defining 'Religion' in the First Amendment," 1982 *U. Ill. L. Rev.* 579 (Summer 1982); Moore, "Piercing the Religious Veil of the So Called Cults," 7 *Pepp. L. Rev.* 655 (1980); Note, "Mail Order Ministries, the Religious Purpose Exemption, and the Constitution," 33 *Tax Law.* 959 (1980); Kelley, "Why Churches Do Not Pay Taxes," XIII *The Philanthropy Monthly* 20 (Nov. 1980); Jackson, "Are Churches Charitable or Public Trusts?," XIII *The Philanthropy Monthly* 21 (Nov. 1980); Brancato, "Characterization in Religious Property Tax-Exemption: What is Religious? A Survey and a Proposed Definition and Approach," 44 *Notre Dame Law.* 60 (1968); Consedine & Whelan, "Church Tax Exemptions," 15 *Cath. Law.* 93 (1969); Hurvich, Religion and the Taxing Power," 35 *U. Cinn. L. Rev.* 531 (1966); Katz, "Radiations from Church Tax Exemption," 1970 *Sup. Ct. Rev.* 93 (1970); Korbel, "Do the Federal Income Tax Laws Involve an 'Establishment of Religion'?," 53 *A. B. A. J.* 1018 (1967); Note, "Aid to Religion Through Taxation," 43 *Notre Dame Law.* 756 (1968); Boyan, "Defining Religion in Operational and Institutional Terms," 116 *U. Pa. L. Rev.* 479 (1967–1968); Note, "Constitutionality of Tax Exemptions Accorded American Church Property," 30 *Albany L. Rev.* 58 (1966); Van Alstyne, "Tax Exemption of Church Property," *Ohio State L. J.* 461 (1959); Stimson, "The Exemption of Churches from Taxation," 18 *Taxes* 361 (1940); Paulsen, "Preferment of Religious Institutions in Tax and Labor Legislation," 14 *Law & Contemp. Prob.* 144 (1949); Zollman, "Tax Exemption of American Church Property," 14 *Mich. L. Rev.* 646 (1916); Zollman, *American Church Law* 328–329 (1933).

CHAPTER NINE

Scientific Organizations

Section 501(c)(3) of the Internal Revenue Code provides that an organization may be exempt from federal income tax under IRC § 501(a) if it is organized and operated exclusively for *scientific* purposes.[1]

§ 9.1 FEDERAL TAX LAW DEFINITION OF *SCIENCE*

Neither the Internal Revenue Code, nor any income tax regulation, nor IRS ruling defines the term *scientific* as used in the tax-exempt organizations context. A dictionary definition states that *science* is "a branch of study that is concerned with observation and classification of facts and especially with the establishment ... of verifiable general laws chiefly by induction and hypotheses."[2] Another dictionary defines *science* as "[k]nowledge, as of facts and principles, gained by systemic study."[3] A more technical definition of the term is that science is a "branch of study in which facts are observed, classified, and, usually, quantitative laws are formulated and verified; [or] involves the application of mathematical reasoning and data analysis to natural phenomena."[4]

One federal district court, however, offered the view that, "while projects may vary in terms of degree of sophistication, if professional skill is involved in the design and supervision of a project intended to solve a problem through a search for a demonstrable truth, the project would appear to be scientific research."[5] Another federal court was of the view that the term *science* means "the

---

[1] Reg. § 1.501(c)(3)-1(d)(1)(i)(c).

[2] *Webster's Third New International Dictionary*.

[3] *Random House Dictionary of the English Language* (Stein, ed., 1967).

[4] *McGraw-Hill Dictionary of Scientific and Technical Terms* (Lapedes, ed., 2d ed. 1978).

[5] Midwest Research Inst. v. United States, 554 F. Supp. 1379, 1386 (W.D. Mo. 1983), *aff'd* 744 F.2d 635 (8th Cir. 1984). Also Oglesby v. Chandler, 288 P. 1034 (1930); In re Massachusetts General Hosp., 95 F. 973 (C.C. Mass. 1899).

process by which knowledge is systematized or classified through the use of observation, experimentation, or reasoning."[6]

In one instance, concerning an organization the exempt purpose of which was to provide multidisciplinary scientific research for government and industry, the court found all of the contractual arrangements challenged by the government to consist of scientific research. The contracts, said the court, involved "work performed by, and capable of being performed only by, qualified engineers and scientists with expertise in particular technological fields."[7] The court observed that the organization was not involved in the commercialization of the products or processes developed as a result of its research, nor did it conduct consumer or market research, social science research, or ordinary testing of the type carried on incident to commercial operations (see below). Said the court: "The fact that research is directed towards solving a particular industrial problem does not necessarily indicate that the research is not scientific."[8]

Basically, then, a *scientific* organization is one engaged in scientific research or otherwise operated for the dissemination of scientific knowledge. A fundamental requirement underlying this form of tax exemption is that the organization must serve a public rather than a private interest.[9] Thus, the tax-exempt scientific organization must, among the other criteria for the exemption, be organized and operated in the public interest.[10]

An organization composed of members of an industry to develop new and improved uses for products of the industry was ruled to not be a tax-exempt scientific organization on the ground that it was serving the private interests of its creators.[11] By contrast, an organization formed by a group of physicians specializing in heart disease to research the cause and publish treatments of heart defects was found to be an exempt scientific organization.[12] In the latter instance, any personal benefit (in the form of increased prestige and enhanced reputation) derived by the physician-creators was deemed not to lessen the public benefits flowing from the organization's operations.

§ 9.2   CONCEPT OF *RESEARCH*

In this area, the focus is largely on the concept of *research*. *Research*, when taken alone, is a word with various meanings—it is not synonymous with *science*. Inasmuch as the nature of particular research depends upon the purpose that it serves, for research to be scientific, it must be carried on in furtherance of a scien-

---

[6] IIT Research Inst. v. United States, 85-2 U.S.T.C. ¶9734 (Cl. Ct. 1985).

[7] *Id.*

[8] *Id.* While the IRS disagrees with this opinion, the case was not appealed (AOD 1986-034). In general, Simpson & Powell, "Does Income of Exempt Scientific Research Organizations Come from Unrelated Business?," 64 *J. Tax* (No. 4) 210 (1986).

[9] Reg. §§ 1.501(a)-1(c), 1.501(c)(3)–1(c)(2).

[10] Reg. § 1.501(c)(3)-1(d)(5)(i).

[11] Rev. Rul. 69-632, 1969-2 C.B. 120. Also Medical Diagnostic Ass'n v. Comm'r, 42 B.T.A. 610 (1940).

[12] Rev. Rul. 69-526, 1969-2 C.B. 115.

tific purpose. Thus, the term *scientific* includes the carrying on of scientific research in the public interest.

The determination of whether research is scientific can depend on whether the research is classified as *fundamental* or *basic* as contrasted with *applied* or *practical*. However, federal tax law excludes from unrelated business taxable income, in the case of an organization operated primarily for purposes of carrying on fundamental research the results of which are freely available to the general public, all income derived from research performed for any person and all deductions directly connected with the activity.[13] For purposes of the unrelated income rules, therefore, it is necessary to determine whether the organization is operated primarily for purposes of carrying on fundamental, as contrasted with applied, research.[14]

Consequently, scientific research does not include activities ordinarily carried on incident to commercial operations, as, for example, the testing or inspection of materials or products or the designing or construction of equipment or buildings.[15] For example, an organization that fostered the development of machinery in connection with a commercial operation, and was empowered to sell, assign, and grant licenses with respect to its copyrights, trademarks, trade names, or patent rights, was held by the IRS to not be engaged in scientific research.[16] Similarly, an organization that tested drugs for commercial pharmaceutical companies was held by the IRS to not qualify for tax exemption as a scientific organization because the testing was regarded as principally serving the private interests of the manufacturers.[17] Likewise, an organization that inspected, tested, and certified for safety shipping containers used in the transport of cargo, and engaged in related research activities, was determined by the IRS to not be undertaking scientific research because these activities were incidental to commercial or industrial operations.[18]

Scientific research is regarded as carried on in the public interest if the results of the research (including any patents, copyrights, processes, or formulas) are made available to the public on a nondiscriminatory basis, if the research is performed for the United States, or any of its agencies or instrumentalities, or for a state or political subdivision thereof, or if the research is directed toward benefiting the public.[19] Examples of scientific research that is considered as meeting this last criterion include scientific research carried on for the purpose of aiding in the scientific education of college or university students, obtaining scientific information that is published in a form that is available to the interested public, dis-

---

[13] IRC § 512(b)(9).
[14] Reg. § 1.501(c)(3)-1(d)(5)(i).
[15] Reg. § 1.501(c)(3)-1(d)(5)(ii). Also Rev. Rul. 68-373, 1968-2 C.B. 206. In one case, this type of activity was described as "generally repetitive work done by scientifically unsophisticated employees for the purpose of determining whether the item tested met certain specifications, as distinguished from testing done to validate a scientific hypothesis" (Midwest Research Inst. v. United States, *supra* note 5, at 1386).
[16] Rev. Rul. 65-1, 1965-1 C.B. 226.
[17] Rev. Rul. 68-373, *supra* note 15.
[18] Rev. Rul. 78-426, 1978-2 C.B. 175.
[19] Reg. § 1.501(c)(3)-1(d)(5)(iii).

covering a cure for a disease, or aiding a community or geographical area by attracting new industry thereto or by encouraging the development of, or retention of, an industry in the community or area.[20] Publication of research results, consequently, is not the only means by which scientific research can be in the public interest.[21] Scientific research is regarded as carried on in the public interest even though research is performed pursuant to a contract or agreement under which the sponsor of the research has the right to obtain ownership or control of any patents, copyrights, processes, or formulas resulting from research.[22] Thus, an organization formed by physicians to research heart disease was ruled to be tax-exempt as a scientific organization.[23] An organization engaged in conducting research programs in the social sciences may qualify as a scientific organization.[24]

The IRS unsuccessfully asserted that an organization that conducted a crop seed certification program and scientific research in seed technology was engaged in activities of a type ordinarily conducted incident to commercial operations and served the private interests of commercial seed producers and commercial farmers. A court concluded that the scientific research involved qualified the organization for tax exemption because the research was being conducted either pursuant to its delegated authority as the official seed certification agency for a state or in conjunction with the state's designated agency for agricultural research and experimentation. Also, the research was considered carried on for public rather than private interests because the research was performed for a state or political subdivision thereof, because the results of the research were made available to the public on a nondiscriminatory basis, and because the research was directed toward benefiting the public. While conceding that "the majority of persons interested in seed technology may well come from the agricultural community," the court stated that that "does not mean that farmers and gardeners are not an important part of the general public."[25]

It is often very difficult to ascertain whether a particular activity constitutes *scientific research* or *commercial testing*. This is particularly the case where the activity is conducted in the public interest.[26]

The IRS accorded categorization as a tax-exempt scientific organization to a membership organization formed to encourage and assist in the establishment of nonprofit regional health data systems, conduct scientific studies and propose improvements with regard to quality, utilization, and effectiveness of health care

---

[20] In one case, an organization that engaged in research projects for nongovernmental sponsors on a contract basis, in the fields of physics, chemistry, economic development, engineering, and biological sciences, was held to be a scientific entity (as defined; see *supra* note 7), rather than engaged in commercial testing; it satisfied the public benefit test because the research was intended to attract and develop industry in a particular geographic area (the Midwest) (Midwest Research Inst. v. United States, *supra* note 7).

[21] IIT Research Inst. v. United States, *supra* note 7.

[22] *Id.*

[23] Rev. Rul. 69-526, *supra* note 12. Also Comm'r v. Orton, 173 F.2d 483 (6th Cir. 1949).

[24] Rev. Rul. 65-60, 1965-1 C.B. 231.

[25] Indiana Crop Improvement Ass'n, Inc. v. Comm'r, 76 T.C. 394, 400 (1981).

[26] See *infra* § 3.

and health care agencies, and to educate those involved in furnishing, administering, and financing health care.[27] The IRS observed that "[b]y improving and enlarging the body of knowledge concerning current usage of health facilities and methods of treatment, the organization seeks to create a more efficient use of the nation's health facilities, and to aid in the planning of better care for future health needs."[28] The IRS also ruled that an organization formed to develop scientific methods for the diagnosis, prevention, and treatment of diseases, and to disseminate the results of its developmental work to members of the medical profession and the general public, qualified for tax exemption as a scientific entity.[29]

§ 9.3   REQUIREMENT OF *PUBLIC INTEREST*

An organization is regarded as not organized or operated for the purpose of carrying on scientific research in the public interest and, consequently, will not qualify as a scientific organization for federal tax exemption purposes if (1) it performs research only for persons that are (directly or indirectly) its creators and that are not charitable organizations, or (2) it retains (directly or indirectly) the ownership or control of more than an insubstantial portion of the patents, copyrights, processes, or formulas resulting from its research and does not make the items available to the public on a nondiscriminatory basis.[30] In addition, although one person may be granted the exclusive right to the use of a patent, copyright, process, or formula, it is considered as made available to the public if the granting of the exclusive right is the only practicable manner in which the patent, copyright, process, or formula can be utilized to benefit the public.[31] In this case, however, the research from which the patent, copyright, process, or formula resulted will be regarded as carried on in the public interest only if it is carried on for the United States (or instrumentality thereof) or a state (or political subdivision thereof) or if it is scientific research that is directed toward benefiting the public.[32]

These distinctions were the subject of an IRS ruling discussing the federal tax treatment, in the exempt organizations context, of commercially sponsored scientific research, which is scientific research undertaken pursuant to contracts with private industries.[33] Under these contracts, the sponsor pays for the research

---

[27] Rev. Rul. 76-455, 1976-2 C.B. 150.

[28] *Id.* at 150–151.

[29] Rev. Rul. 65-298, 1965-2 C.B. 163. Cf. Rev. Rul. 74-553, 1974-2 C.B. 168. When Congress enacted the Economic Recovery Tax Act of 1981 (95 Stat. 172), it created a 25 percent tax credit for certain research and experimental expenditures paid in carrying on a trade or business (IRC § 41). This credit is available for, *inter alia,* "basic research" expenses. That term is defined to mean "any original investigation for the advancement of scientific knowledge not having a specific commercial objective, except that such term shall not include (i) basic research conducted outside of the United States, and (ii) basic research in the social sciences, arts, or humanities" (IRC § 41(e)(7)(A)).

[30] Reg. § 1.501(c)(3)-1(d)(5)(iv).

[31] *Id.*

[32] *Id.*

[33] Rev. Rul. 76-296, 1976-2 C.B. 141.

and receives the right to the results of the research and all ownership rights in any patents resulting from work on the project.

Where the results and other relevant information of the commercially sponsored projects are "generally published in such form as to be available to the interested public either currently, as developments in the project warrant, or within a reasonably short time after completion of the project," the organization is considered to be engaging in scientific research in the public interest.[34] Publication of the research is not required "in advance of the time at which it can be made public without jeopardy to the sponsor's right by reasonably diligent action to secure any patents or copyrights resulting from the research."[35] By contrast, the carrying on of sponsored research is considered the conduct of an unrelated trade or business[36] where the organization agrees, at the sponsor's request, to "forego publication of the results of a particular project in order to protect against disclosure of processes or technical data which the sponsor desires to keep secret for various business reasons" or where the research results are withheld beyond the time reasonably necessary to obtain patents or copyrights.[37]

§ 9.4 *SCIENTIFIC* AS *CHARITABLE* OR *EDUCATIONAL*

Organizations qualifying as tax-exempt scientific entities may also be tax-exempt as charitable and/or educational entities.[38]

For example, an organization formed to survey scientific and medical literature published throughout the world and to prepare and distribute free abstracts of the literature was ruled to be both charitable and scientific in nature for federal tax purposes.[39] This is because the federal tax definition of the term *charitable* embraces the concept of *advancement of science*.[40]

An organization engaged in research on human diseases, developing scientific methods for treatment, and disseminating its results through physicians' seminars was determined to be a tax-exempt educational organization.[41] Also, an engineering society created to engage in scientific research in the areas of heating, ventilating, and air conditioning for the benefit of the general public was deemed to qualify as an educational and scientific organization.[42]

---

[34] *Id*. at 142.

[35] *Id*. at 143.

[36] See Part VI.

[37] Rev. Rul. 76-296, *supra* note 33, at 142. In general, see *infra* § 5.

[38] See Chapters 6, 7.

[39] Rev. Rul. 66-147, 1966-1 C.B. 137. Also Science & Research Found. Inc. v. United States, 181 F. Supp. 526 (S.D. Ill. 1960); Forest Press, Inc. v. Comm'r, 22 T.C. 265 (1954).

[40] See § 6.5.

[41] Rev. Rul. 65-298, *supra* note 29.

[42] Rev. Rul. 71-506, 1971-2 C.B. 233. Also American Kennel Club, Inc. v. Hoey, 148 F.2d 920 (2d Cir. 1945).

§ 9.5 TECHNOLOGY TRANSFERS

The IRS is struggling to determine the criteria by which an organization that has the primary purpose of transferring technology can qualify for tax exemption as a scientific or other charitable organization. The difficulty lies in the essence of *technology transfer*: the conduct of scientific or other research by and within the organization and the subsequent transfer of the results of that research to others for development commercially and for the marketing and sale of the resulting products or services to the general public. The technology transfer function can place a nonprofit organization in a position where it is, or appears to be, engaging in commercial activities that are not related to its tax-exempt functions (and/or is receiving income that may be taxed as unrelated business income).[43]

Part of the problem is that the other areas of federal law, which are being developed to facilitate technology transfer, involve concepts that the authors of the federal tax law are finding awkward to assimilate. Contemporary "public/private partnerships" and other ventures that blend the efforts of charitable organizations and commercial businesses are not easily accommodated by the existing tax law. Colleges and universities are leading the way in this regard, because of the immense volume of research being funded by private firms and governments. Indeed, one recent federal law encourages universities and businesses to collaborate and "commercialize," and to license federally funded technology to U.S. businesses.[44] The relationships among these institutions of higher education (or other types of tax-exempt organizations), their faculty, and the licensees or other for-profit users of the technology raise issues of private inurement,[45] private benefit,[46] and unrelated income taxation.

The initial reaction of the IRS to technology transfer organizations was to resist granting them tax exemption as charitable entities.[47] In the one court case on the point, the IRS prevailed on the issue.[48] However, as technology transfer became more commonplace in the large colleges, universities, and scientific research institutions (and with much of the research activity protected from taxation[49]), the views of the IRS began to change. The first indication of this alteration in policy came in the fall of 1982. The IRS ruled that, when a foundation, as its primary activity, assisted colleges and universities in bringing their scientific inventions into public use under the patent system, the foundation qualified for tax exemption as a charitable organization. Twelve years earlier,

---

[43] See Part Four.

[44] Patent and Trademark Amendments of 1980, 35 U.S.C. § 200 *et seq.*

[45] See Chapter 19.

[46] See § 19.10.

[47] An IRS technical advice memorandum issued in 1970, discussed in Tech. Adv. Mem. 8306006, concluded that a technology transfer program constituted a business activity ordinarily carried on in a commercial manner for profit (and thus an unrelated trade or business).

[48] Washington Research Found. v. Comm'r, 50 T.C.M. 1457 (1985). See § 4.9, note 222, second paragraph.

[49] See § 27.1(l).

the activity, then much smaller in scope, was ruled to be an unrelated business.[50]

Subsequent rulings have involved organizations that were created in implementation of a state program; the basis for their exemption is the lessening of the burdens of a government.[51] Other organizations have transferred the technology they created through research to for-profit subsidiaries, which thereafter develop and manufacture the resulting products.[52] Still other organizations simply contract with unrelated commercial entities for the transfer of technology, often by means of a license agreement for a patent and technical information that results in tax-free royalties—the type of practice that the IRS found to be private inurement at the outset.[53]

The IRS seems particularly concerned about the financing associated with technology transfers. Thus, in late 1984, the IRS grudgingly ruled that a scientific technology transfer organization would not lose its tax exemption by taking title and copyright to software developed at universities, introducing the software into public use by means of licenses, and paying the universities royalties from consumer use of the software. The IRS went out of its way to note that the software transfer program was incidental to the organization.[54]

A recent IRS ruling on technology transfer organizations is one of its most extensive rulings on the point.[55] The organization involved was a scientific research organization that concentrated its efforts in biotechnology (the use of biological materials to create and facilitate useful processes and products) with the objective of economic development and job creation in a particular region of states. The IRS wrote that the organization "conducts research and development to the stage where the technical risk is reduced and the technology is acceptable to the private sector for commercialization." The organization sought a ruling because of its shift away from basic research and toward applied research, its focus on the maximization of the potential for creating marketable technologies (such as by entering into research agreements with industry businesses), and its establishment of a for-profit subsidiary to seek commercial application of resultant products. Although the IRS ruled that these new facts would not alter the organization's tax exemption, it did not do so by directly addressing the technology transfer issue. Instead, the organization's continuing exemption was predicated on the fact that it "is operated for the purpose of aiding a geographical area by attracting new industry to the area or by encouraging the development of, or retention of, an industry in the area"; the use of a subsidiary or of licensees was cast as the "only practicable manner" in which the organization's technology can be used to benefit the public.

In its examination guidelines developed for use in the audits of colleges and universities,[56] the IRS observed that these and other institutions are being encour-

[50] Tech. Adv. Mem. 8306006 (see *supra* note 47).

[51] E.g., Priv. Ltr. Rul. 9243008 (see § 6.3, particularly the text accompanied by note 149).

[52] E.g., Priv. Ltr. Rul. 8606056.

[53] E.g., IRS Priv. Ltr. Rul. 9527031.

[54] Priv. Ltr. Rul. 8512084.

[55] Priv. Ltr. Rul. 9316052.

[56] See § 24.8(d).

aged to "collaborate with business and to 'commercialize' and license federally-funded technology to U.S. businesses," and that, as a result, the "relationship between institutions and these licensees is growing more complex."[57] These guidelines add, "To gain access to research and/or faculty and students, industry may fund university research through many forms, such as research contracts, joint ventures, venture capital funds, industry liaison programs, spin-off companies, consortia, jointly-owned research facilities, material transfers, commercial licenses, consultations and clinical trial agreements."[58] The auditing agent is to examine research activities for private inurement or impermissible private benefit and for unrelated business activities.[59]

---

[57]*Id.*, § 342(10)(1).

[58]*Id.*

[59]*Id.* In general, Monroe, "Collaboration Between Tax-Exempt Research Organizations and Commercial Enterprises—Federal Income Tax Limitations," 62 *Taxes* 297 (1984); Sugarman & Mancino, "Tax Aspects of University & Patent Policy," 3 *J. Coll. U.L.* (No. 1) 41 (1976); Wolfman, "Federal Tax Policy and the Support of Science," 114 *U. Pa. L. Rev.* 171 (1965); Gray, "What Is 'Research' for the Purpose of Exemption?," 5th *Biennial N.Y.U. Conf. on Char. Fdns.* 233 (1961).

CHAPTER TEN

Other *Charitable* Organizations

Aside from the organizations discussed in the previous four chapters, Section 501(c)(3) of the Internal Revenue Code provides the basis for tax exemption for certain other organizations. These are entities that are organized and operated to prevent cruelty to children and animals, amateur sports organizations, public safety testing organizations, certain cooperative service organizations, charitable risk pools, and literary organizations.

§ 10.1 PREVENTION-OF-CRUELTY ORGANIZATIONS

Charitable organizations include those that are organized and operated exclusively for the "prevention of cruelty to children or animals."[1]

An organization that prevented the birth of unwanted animals and their eventual suffering by providing funds for pet owners who cannot afford the spaying or neutering operation was ruled tax-exempt under this provision,[2] as was an organization that sought to secure humane treatment of laboratory animals.[3]

An organization to protect children from working at hazardous occupations in violation of state laws and in unfavorable work conditions was held by the IRS to be an organization established to prevent cruelty to children.[4]

§ 10.2 AMATEUR SPORTS ORGANIZATIONS

Another category of charitable organization is the amateur athletic organization. This exemption was established in 1976 by adding to the tax-exempt organiza-

[1] Reg. § 1.501(c)(3)-1(d)(1)(i)(g).
[2] Rev. Rul. 74-194, 1974-1 C.B. 129.
[3] Rev. Rul. 66-359, 1966-2 C.B. 219.
[4] Rev. Rul. 67-151, 1967-1 C.B. 134.

tions rules[5] and the charitable contribution deduction rules[6] the following phraseology: "... or to foster national or international amateur sports competition (but only if no part of its activities involve the provision of athletic facilities or equipment)."[7]

The legislative history of this provision contains the observation that, under prior law, organizations that "teach youth or which are affiliated with charitable organizations" may qualify as charitable entities and may receive charitable contributions but that organizations that foster national or international sports competition may be granted tax exemption as social welfare organizations[8] or business leagues[9] and be ineligible to receive deductible contributions. This history also stated, as respects the parenthetical limitation, that "[t]his restriction . . . is intended to prevent the allowance of these benefits for organizations which, like social clubs, provide facilities and equipment for their members."[10]

At issue in the first court case to interpret this parenthetical restriction was the federal tax status of an organization that promoted the building and use of a particular class of racing sailboats by, in part, maintaining the design character of the class of boat (the "International E22 Class"). Its activities included the supervision of the conduct of builders of the E22 class of sailboats through the measurement of hulls, spars, and sails, and the formulation and enforcement of measurement rules relating to the shape of, and equipment and materials used in, E22 Class sailboats to ensure that all of these boats conform to a standard design. The organization maintained a precisely measured, full-size shape of the hull of an E22 Class sailboat (the "master plug") and precisely measured pieces of aluminum or mylar that represent the required shapes of different parts of an E22 Class sailboat, such as the rudder, keel, mast, and boom (the "measurement templates"). The IRS contended that the organization's use of the master plug and measurement templates for enforcing measurement rules and for providing measurement control services at the time of construction and in connection with races constituted the proscribed provision of athletic facilities or equipment. However, the U.S. Tax Court declined to support that interpretation, ruling instead that the items are "tools" that are necessary to standardize competitive categories in the amateur competition that the organization fosters.[11] The court wrote that the term "athletic facilities" refers to physical structures such as clubhouses, swimming pools, and gymnasiums, and that the term "athletic equipment" means "property used directly in athletic endeavors."[12] The court concluded that "[w]e know of no athletic exercise, game, competition, or other endeavor in which those items [the

---

[5] IRC § 501(c)(3).

[6] IRC §§ 170(c)(2)(B), 2055(a)(2), 2522(a)(2).

[7] In general, Hutchinson Baseball Enters. v. Comm'r, 73 T.C. 144 (1979), *aff'd* 696 F.2d 757 (10th Cir. 1982). Cf. The Media Sports League, Inc. v. Comm'r, 52 T.C.M. 1093 (1986).

[8] IRC § 501(c)(4). See Chapter 12.

[9] IRC § 501(c)(6). See Chapter 13.

[10] Joint Committee on Taxation, "General Explanation of the Tax Reform Act of 1976," 94th Cong., 2d Sess. 423–424 (1976).

[11] International E22 Class Ass'n v. Comm'r, 78 T.C. 93 (1982).

[12] *Id.* at 99.

master plug and the measurement templates] may be used," and thus held that the items were not "athletic facilities or equipment."[13]

The parenthetical prohibition is a limitation only upon the purpose added in 1976; that is, it is not a limitation on the tax exemption and charitable contribution provisions generally. Thus, a private foundation was advised by the IRS that it could make a grant to a state university-related foundation for the purpose of constructing an aquatic complex as an integral part of the university's educational program, with the grant constituting a qualifying distribution,[14] because it would be made to accomplish educational and charitable purposes.[15]

This aspect of the law of tax-exempt organizations was modified again in 1982.[16] Thus, in the case of a *qualified amateur sports organization*, the requirement in the law that no part of the organization's activities may involve the provision of athletic facilities or equipment does not apply.[17] Also, it is now clear that a qualified amateur sports organization will not fail to qualify as a charitable entity merely because its membership is local or regional in nature.[18] A qualified amateur sports organization is any organization organized and operated exclusively to foster national or international amateur sports competition if the organization is also organized and operated primarily to conduct national or international competition in sports or to support and develop amateur athletes for national or international competition in sports.[19]

§ 10.3   PUBLIC SAFETY TESTING ORGANIZATIONS

A federal appellate court held that an organization that conducted tests, experiments, and investigations into the causes of losses against which insurance companies provided coverage was neither charitable, scientific, nor educational.[20] Congress responded by providing tax-exempt status for organizations that engage in "testing for public safety."[21] This term includes "the testing of consumer products, such as electrical products, to determine whether they are safe for use by the general public."[22]

This provision was the basis for tax exemption for an organization that tested boating equipment and established safety standards for products used

---

[13] *Id.* at 98.

[14] See § 11.4(b).

[15] Priv. Ltr. Rul. 8037103.

[16] IRC § 501(j).

[17] IRC § 501(j)(1)(A).

[18] IRC § 501(j)(1)(B).

[19] IRC § 501(j)(2). The legislative history of this provision is discussed in Gen. Couns. Mem. 39775, which held that an organization that assists in securing and conducting state, regional, national, and international sports competitions in a particular geographic area and an organization that sponsors a postseason college football game are qualified amateur sports organizations. In general, Moot, Jr., "Tax-Exempt Status of Amateur Sports Organizations," 40 *Wash. & Lee L. Rev.* (No. 4) 1705 (1983).

[20] Underwriters' Laboratory, Inc. v. Comm'r, 135 F.2d 371 (7th Cir. 1943), *cert. den.*, 320 U.S. 756 (1943).

[21] IRC § 501(c)(3).

[22] Reg. § 1.501(c)(3)-1(d)(4). Also Reg. § 1.501(c)(3)-1(d)(1)(i)(d).

aboard pleasure craft by the boating public.[23] However, an organization that clinically tested drugs for commercial pharmaceutical companies was denied tax exemption under this provision, on the ground that the testing principally served the private interests of the manufacturer and that a drug is not a "consumer product" until it is approved for marketing by the Food and Drug Administration.[24] Similarly, an organization whose activities included the inspection, testing, and safety certification of cargo shipping containers and research, development, and reporting of information in the field of containerization was denied tax exemption under this provision because these activities served the private interests of manufacturers and shippers by facilitating their operations in international commerce.[25]

An organization that performed flammability tests and evaluations for manufacturers of building materials qualified under this category of tax exemption.[26] By contrast, an organization that had as its principal activity preservice and in-service examinations and evaluations of nuclear reactor power plants, to ensure their safe operation, did not qualify for this exemption because the examinations did not involve the testing of consumer products.[27] Likewise, an organization that tested various hydraulic and mechanical devices designed for the protection of a public water supply from contamination and pollution did not qualify because the devices were not consumer products.[28] This approach was also reflected in a ruling holding that testing performed for commercial entities, of either products for pre-market clearance or air samples or like substances for compliance with environmental laws, is unrelated business activity.[29]

These organizations are expressly exempted from classification as private foundations.[30] However, contributions, bequests, or gifts to public safety testing organizations (as such) are not deductible, inasmuch as provision has not been made for them in the charitable contribution deduction rules.[31]

§ 10.4 COOPERATIVE HOSPITAL SERVICE ORGANIZATIONS

Qualifying "cooperative hospital service organizations" are tax-exempt entities by virtue of being charitable organizations.[32] These organizations must be organized and operated solely for two or more tax-exempt member hospitals and

---

[23] Rev. Rul. 65-61, 1965-1 C.B. 234.

[24] Rev. Rul. 68-373, 1968-2 C.B. 206.

[25] Rev. Rul. 78-426, 1978-2 C.B. 175.

[26] Priv. Ltr. Rul. 7930005.

[27] *Id.*

[28] Priv. Ltr. Rul. 7820007.

[29] Priv. Ltr. Rul. 8409055. An organization that developed and administered a program setting safety and other standards in a field of engineering qualified as a charitable organization because its quality control program lessened the burdens of a local government (see § 6.3) (Gen. Couns. Mem. 38577).

[30] IRC § 509(a)(4). See § 11.3(d).

[31] IRC §§ 170, 2055, 2106, 2522.

[32] IRC § 501(e).

must be organized and operated on a cooperative basis. They must perform certain specified services[33] on a centralized basis for their members, namely, data processing, purchasing (including the purchasing of insurance on a group basis),[34] warehousing, billing and collection (including the purchase of patron accounts receivable on a recourse basis), food, clinical, industrial engineering,[35] laboratory, printing, communications, records center, and personnel (including selection, testing, training, and education of personnel) services. To qualify, these services must constitute exempt activities if performed on its own behalf by a participating hospital.[36] Although this type of cooperative must have hospitals as members (patrons), its membership may include comparable entities, such as the outpatient component of a county health department.[37]

The IRS takes the position that, to qualify as a cooperative hospital service organization, the organization may provide only the services specified in the specific authorizing legislation.[38] This position is based upon the legislative history of the provision.[39] Thus, the IRS ruled that a cooperative hospital laundry service cannot be tax-exempt as a charitable organization by reason of these rules, and observed that this type of an entity may qualify as a tax-exempt cooperative.[40] (As discussed below, the IRS prevailed on this point. Thus, although it had been expressly held by a court that an organization that qualifies under the cooperative hospital service organization rules may nonetheless also qualify as a charitable organization generally,[41] this opinion was reversed on appeal, with the appellate court holding that these cooperatives can qualify (if at all) only under the cooperative hospital service organization rules.[42])

A court, in a case involving a centralized laundry service operated for tax-exempt hospitals, held that the organization qualified for status as a charitable entity, notwithstanding these specific rules.[43] The court maintained that the "question of whether it [the plaintiff organization] is organized and operated for an exempt purpose is a question of fact for this Court to decide."[44] Commenting on the rules for certain hospital cooperatives, the court said: "The clearly expressed Congressional purpose behind the enactment of Section

---

[33] IRC § 501(e)(1)(A).

[34] An organization performs the service of *purchasing* when it buys equipment for one of its patron hospitals, even though it holds legal title to the equipment, where that arrangement is used merely as a convenience to the hospital, which remains the beneficial owner of and solely responsible for paying for the equipment (Rev. Rul. 80-316, 1980-2 C.B. 172).

[35] Rev. Rul. 74-443, 1974-2 C.B. 159.

[36] Rev. Rul. 69-633, 1969-2 C.B. 121.

[37] Gen. Couns. Mem. 39692.

[38] Rev. Rul. 69-160, 1969-1 C.B. 147.

[39] H. Rep. No. 1533, 90th Cong., 2d Sess. 1, 20 (1968). Also S. Rep. No. 744, 90th Cong., 1st Sess. 200–201 (1967); H. Rep. No. 1030, 90th Cong., 1st Sess. 73 (1967).

[40] Rev. Rul. 69-633, *supra* note 36. (The rules concerning cooperative organizations are at IRC §§ 1381–1383.) Services performed in the employ of a cooperative hospital service organization described in IRC § 501(e) are exempted from "employment" for purposes of the F.U.T.A. (Rev. Rul. 74-493, 1974-2 C.B. 327).

[41] Chart, Inc. v. United States, 491 F. Supp. 10 (D.D.C. 1979).

[42] Chart, Inc. v. United States, 652 F.2d 195 (D.C. Cir. 1981).

[43] United Hosp. Servs., Inc. v. United States, 384 F. Supp. 776 (S.D. Ind. 1974).

[44] *Id*. at 780.

501(e) was to enlarge the category of charitable organizations under Section 501(c)(3) to include certain cooperative hospital service organizations, and not to narrow or restrict the reach of Section 501(c)(3)."[45] Since the organization was operational prior to the enactment of these rules, the court, having concluded that it was charitable in nature, found the specific rules irrelevant to the case.[46]

The Senate Finance Committee's version of the Tax Reform Act of 1976 contained a provision[47] that would have inserted "laundry" services in the statutory enumeration of permissible services. The Finance Committee observed that "it is appropriate to encourage the creation and operation of cooperative service organizations by exempt hospitals because of the cost savings to the hospitals and their patients that result from providing certain services, such as laundry and clinical services, on a cooperative basis."[48] However, this provision was defeated on the floor of the Senate.[49]

Following the enactment of these rules in 1968,[50] there was controversy as to the meaning and scope of the provision in relation to the general rules defining charitable entities.[51] There were two competing views: the hospital cooperative rules were enacted to (1) provide the exclusive and controlling means by which a cooperative hospital service organization can achieve tax exemption, so that this type of an organization that fails to satisfy the requirements of the rules thereby fails to qualify as a charitable organization,[52] or (2) enlarge the category of charitable organizations to include certain types of cooperative hospital service organizations, so that it does not narrow or restrict the reach of the rules defining charitable organizations generally.[53]

In a 1981 decision, the U.S. Supreme Court ruled that the first of these two views is the correct one.[54] In reaching this conclusion, the Court utilized a statutory construction rationale (namely, the rule that a specific statute controls over a general provision, particularly where the two are interrelated and closely positioned[55]), but principally relied on the legislative history underlying the rules for hospital cooperatives. The case involved a cooperative laundry organization serving tax-exempt entities and, as noted, laundry service is not specifically refer-

---

[45] *Id*. at 781.
[46] *Id*. Also Northern Calif. Cent. Servs., Inc. v. United States, 591 F.2d 620 (Ct. Cl. 1979).
[47] H.R. 10612 (1976) (as reported by the Senate Committee on Finance) § 2509.
[48] S. Rep. No. 94-938 (Part 2), 94th Cong., 2d Sess. 76 (1976).
[49] Amendment No. 315, 122 *Cong. Rec.* 25915 (1976).
[50] Pub. L. No. 374, 90th Cong. 2d Sess. (1968), § 109(a), 82 Stat. 269.
[51] IRC § 501(c)(3).
[52] E.g., HCSC-Laundry v. United States, 624 F.2d 428 (3d Cir. 1980), *rev'g* 473 F. Supp. 250 (E.D. Pa. 1979); Metropolitan Detroit Area Hosp. Servs., Inc. v. United States, 634 F.2d 330 (6th Cir. 1980), *rev'g* 445 F. Supp. 857 (E.D. Mich. 1978); Community Hosp. Servs., Inc. v. United States. 47 AFTR 2d 81-999 (6th Cir. 1981), *rev'g* 43 AFTR 2d 79-934 (E.D. Mich. 1979): Hospital Cent. Servs. Ass'n v. United States, 623 F.2d 611 (9th Cir. 1980), *rev'g* 40 AFTR 2d 77-5646 (W.D. Wash. 1977).
[53] E.g., Northern Calif. Cent. Servs., Inc. v. United States, 591 F.2d 620 (Ct. Cl. 1979); United Hosp. Servs., Inc. v. United States, *supra* note 43; Chart, Inc. v. United States, *supra* note 41.
[54] HCSC-Laundry v. United States, 450 U.S. 1 (1981), *aff'g* 624 F.2d 428 (3d Cir. 1980).
[55] Citing Bulova Watch Co. v. United States, 365 U.S. 753, 761 (1961).

enced in the rules despite efforts in 1978 and 1976 to include such a reference.[56] The Court thus determined that:

> In view of all this, it seems to us beyond dispute that subsection (e)(1)(A) of § 501, despite the seemingly broad general language of subsection (c)(3), specifies the types of hospital service organizations that are encompassed within the scope of § 501 as charitable organizations. Inasmuch as laundry service was deliberately omitted from the statutory list and, indeed, specifically was refused inclusion in that list, it inevitably follows that petitioner is not entitled to tax-exempt status. The Congress easily can change the statute whenever it is so inclined.[57]

A public charity, formed to provide and maintain a variety of cooperatively planned hospital and health-related programs and facilities, performed services on a centralized basis for tax-exempt hospitals. The IRS reviewed these services to test them against the statutory requirements for cooperative hospital service organizations. Some of the services clearly qualified because they were expressly referenced in the statute, such as printing, warehousing of records, and purchasing. Some qualified because of interpretation of the law; thus, courier services and alarm installation and maintenance services were held to fall within the meaning of "communications," while maintenance of biomedical equipment, environmental monitoring, and infectious waste disposal were found to be within the ambit of "clinical" or "laboratory" services. However, the IRS rejected as non-qualifying services those for security, parking, and housekeeping and grounds maintenance; it also held that the organization could not subcontract for impermissible services. Consequently, the organization was found not to be operating solely as a cooperative hospital entity and its tax-exempt status was revoked.[58]

§ 10.5   COOPERATIVE EDUCATIONAL SERVICE ORGANIZATIONS

"Cooperative service organizations of operating educational organizations" are regarded as charitable organizations.[59]

These organizations must be organized and controlled by and composed solely of members that are private or public educational institutions.[60] They must

---

[56] *Supra* notes 39; 47–49;

[57] HCSC-Laundry v. United States, *supra* note 54, at 8. The decision in HCSC-Laundry v. United States, may be contrasted with another 1981 Supreme Court decision, where the Court went out of its way to ignore directly pertinent legislative history and to interpret a statute in a manner wholly inconsistent with congressional intent, so as to avoid constitutional law difficulties, finding that approach "simpler and more reasonable" (St. Martin Evangelical Lutheran Church v. South Dakota, 451 U.S. 772, 782 (1981)). The IRS has, in reliance upon the *HCSC-Laundry* decision, ruled that, if an organization fails to qualify under a specific category of tax exemption, it is therefore precluded from qualifying under a more general category of tax exemption (Rev. Rul. 83-166, 1983-2 C.B. 96).

[58] Tech. Adv. Mem. 9542002. In general, Tuthill, "Qualifying as a Tax Exempt Cooperative Hospital Service Organization," 50 *Notre Dame Law.* 448 (1975).

[59] IRC § 501(f).

[60] That is, organizations defined in IRC § 170(b)(1)(A)(ii) or § 170(b)(1)(A)(iv). See § 11.3(a).

be organized and operated solely to hold, commingle, and collectively invest and reinvest (including arranging for and supervising the performance by independent contractors of investment services), in stocks and securities, the monies contributed to it by each of the members of the organization, and to collect income from the investments and turn over the entire amount, less expenses, to its members. While this type of organization may not invest in assets other than stocks and other securities, it may use a taxable subsidiary to make these investments.[61]

These rules were enacted to forestall the contemplated revocation by the IRS of the tax-exempt status of The Common Fund, a cooperative arrangement formed by a large group of colleges and universities for the collective investment of their funds. During its formative years, the management and administrative expenses of the Fund were largely met by start-up grants from a private foundation. However, as the Fund became more reliant upon payments from its member institutions, the IRS decided that this factor alone disqualified the Fund for tax-exempt status.[62] In the face of loss of the Fund's tax exemption, Congress made it clear that cooperative arrangements for investments of the type typified by The Common Fund are eligible for tax exemption as charitable entities.

§ 10.6 CHARITABLE RISK POOLS

Still another category of charitable organization is the "qualified charitable risk pool," added to the federal tax statutory law in 1996.[63] This body of statutory law overrides otherwise applicable caselaw denying tax-exempt status to eligible charitable risk pools.[64]

A qualified charitable risk pool is an entity that is organized and operated solely to pool insurable risks of its members (other than medical malpractice risks) and to provide information to its members with respect to loss control and risk management.[65] No profit or other benefit may be accorded to any member of the organization other than through the provision of members with insurance coverage below the cost of comparable commercial coverage (and loss control and risk management information).[66] Only charitable organizations can be members of these pools.[67]

This type of pool is required to be organized as a nonprofit organization under state law authorizing risk pooling for charitable organizations, to be exempt from state income tax, to obtain at least $1 million in start-up capital[68] from non-

---

[61] Gen. Couns. Mem. 39776.

[62] See S. Rep. No. 888, 93d Cong. 2d Sess. 2–3 (1974). See § 6.8.

[63] IRC § 501(n)(1)(A).

[64] See § 22.1.

[65] IRC § 501(n)(2)(A).

[66] H.R. Rep. No. 737, 104th Cong., 2d Sess. 189 (1996).

[67] IRC § 501(n)(2)(B).

[68] This term means any capital contributed to, and any program-related investments (see § 11.4(d)) made in, the risk pool before the pool commences operations (IRC § 501(n)(4)(A)).

member charitable organizations,[69] to be controlled by a board of directors elected by its members, and to provide three elements in its organizational documents, namely, that members must be tax-exempt charitable organizations at all times, that if a member loses that status it must immediately notify the organization, and that no insurance coverage applies to a member after the date of any final determination that the member no longer qualifies as a tax-exempt charitable organization.[70]

The rule that a charitable organization cannot be exempt from tax if a substantial part of its activities consists of providing commercial-type insurance[71] is not applicable to charitable risk pools.[72] Because this category of tax exemption is based on qualification as a charitable organization, a risk pool must satisfy all of the other requirements for achievement of this tax-exempt status.[73]

§ 10.7   LITERARY ORGANIZATIONS

Although there is a statutory basis for tax exemption as a "literary" organization,[74] there is no law on the subject. The concept is encompassed by the terms "charitable" and "educational."[75]

There is, in a sense, a variety of charitable organizations other than those surveyed in this chapter. Most of these entities are (or will be) derived from interpretations of the term *charitable* in its more technical sense.[76] As discussed, the term *charitable* has an ongoing, dynamic meaning.[77] There is, of course, always the possibility that Congress will legislate into existence one or more types of charitable organizations (using that term in the largest sense) that are not presently recognized as such.

---

[69] A *nonmember charitable organization* is a tax-exempt organization described in IRC § 501(c)(3), which is not a member of the risk pool and does not benefit, directly or indirectly, from the insurance coverage provided by the pool to its members (IRC § 501(n)(4)(B)).

[70] IRC §§ 501(n)(2)(C), 501(n)(C)(3).

[71] See § 22.1.

[72] IRC § 501(n)(1)(B).

[73] See Part Two. In general, Larue, Jr., "Small Business Act Grants Exempt Status to Charitable Risk Pools," 8 *J. Tax. Exempt Orgs.* 103 (Nov./Dec. 1996).

[74] IRC § 501(c)(3); Reg. § 1.501(c)(3)-1(d)(1)(i)(e). In general, Trenberry, "A Literary Pilgrim's Progress Along Section 501(c)(3)," 51 *A.B.A.J.* 252 (1965).

[75] See Chapters 6, 7.

[76] See Chapter 6.

[77] See § 5.1.

Public Charities and Private Foundations

The federal tax law relating to charitable organizations[1] differentiates between *public charities* and *private foundations*. This is done for a variety of reasons, including the fact that the charitable giving rules make this distinction[2] and because special regulatory requirements specifically target private foundations.[3] Despite

---

[1] That is, organizations described in IRC § 501(c)(3) and tax-exempt by reason of IRC § 501(a). See Part Two.

[2] See § 2.5.

[3] See *infra* § 4.

the relative scarcity of private foundations,[4] the extent and growth of the law governing them is extraordinary.[5]

§ 11.1   FEDERAL TAX LAW DEFINITION OF *PRIVATE FOUNDATION*

(a) Standard Definition of *Private Foundation*

The federal tax law does not define the term *private foundation*. Rather, it enumerates the types of charitable organizations that are not private foundations.[6] From a statutory law perspective, a private foundation is a charitable organization, domestic or foreign, that does not qualify as a public charity; to clarify, a public charity is an institution (such as a university or a hospital), an organization that has broad public support, or an organization that functions in a supporting relationship to one or more institutions or publicly supported entities.[7] However, there is a general presumption that a charitable entity is a private foundation; this presumption is rebutted by a showing that the entity is a public charity.[8]

A standard private foundation is a type of tax-exempt organization that has four characteristics: It is a charitable organization; it is funded from one source (usually, an individual, married couple, family, or corporation); its ongoing funding is in the form of investment income (rather than from a flow of investment income); and it makes grants for charitable purposes to other persons (rather than conducting its own programs). (In many respects, then, a private foundation is much like an endowment fund.) The *private* aspect of a private foundation thus relates principally to the nature of its financial support.

(b) Private Operating Foundations

The *private operating foundation* is a private foundation that operates its own programs, in contrast to the standard private foundation which is a grantmaking en-

---

[4] There are about 50,000 private foundations, compared to nearly 1 million charitable organizations (see § 2.1).

[5] The law in this area originated with the Tax Reform Act of 1969; it was written at a time when Congress was in an anti-private foundation mood. One of the principal stimuli for this legislation was a report prepared by the Department of the Treasury in 1965 ("Treasury Report on Private Foundations," Committee on Finance, United States Senate, 89th Cong., 1st Sess. (1969)). In the intervening years, however, the general perception has been that private foundations are being properly operated and are in conformity with the tax law requirements. One court stated that Congress enacted these rules "to put an end, so far as it reasonably could, to the abuses and potential abuses associated with private foundations" (Hans S. Mannheimer Charitable Trust v. Comm'r, 93 T.C. 35, 39 (1989)). This objective of Congress seems to have been successfully reached. In general, Hopkins & Blazek, *Private Foundations: Tax Law and Compliance* (New York: John Wiley & Sons, Inc., 1998).

[6] IRC § 509(a), the misleading heading of which is "Private Foundation Defined."

[7] Reg. § 1.509(a)-1. The term *public charity* is the subject of *infra* § 3.

[8] IRC § 508(b); Reg. § 1.508-1(b).

tity. This type of foundation devotes most of its earnings and much of its assets directly to the conduct of its charitable programs.[9]

A private operating foundation must meet an *income test*.[10] To satisfy this test, a private foundation must expend an amount equal to substantially all[11] of the lesser of its adjusted net income or its minimum investment return,[12] in the form of qualifying distributions,[13] directly for the active conduct of its exempt charitable activities.[14]

The term *adjusted net income* means any excess of a private foundation's gross income for a year over the sum of deductions allowed to a taxable corporation.[15] This amount of gross income is determined using certain *income modifications*[16] and the allowable deductions are determined using certain *deduction modifications*.[17]

The funds expended must be applied by the private foundation itself; these outlays are termed *direct expenditures*, while grants to other organizations are *indirect expenditures*.[18] Amounts paid to acquire or maintain assets that are used directly in the conduct of exempt activities are direct expenditures, as are administrative expenses and other operating costs necessary to conduct exempt activities. An amount set aside[19] by a foundation for a specific project involving the active conduct of exempt activities may qualify as a direct expenditure.[20] The making or awarding of grants or similar payments to individuals to support active tax-exempt programs constitutes direct expenditures only if the foundation maintains some significant involvement in the programs.[21]

To qualify as a private operating foundation, an organization must also satisfy an *assets test*,[22] an *endowment test*,[23] or a *support test*.[24]

A private foundation will satisfy the assets test where substantially more than one half[25] of its assets is (1) devoted directly to the active conduct of its tax-exempt activities, to functionally related businesses,[26] or to a combination of these functions; (2) stock of a corporation that is controlled by the foundation and substantially all of the assets of which are devoted to charitable activities; or (3) in

---

[9] IRC § 4942(j)(3).
[10] IRC § 4942(j)(3)(A); Reg. § 53.4942(b)-1(a).
[11] Namely, at least 85 percent (Reg. § 53.4942(b)-1(c)).
[12] See *infra* § 4(b), text accompanied by note 243.
[13] *Id.*, text accompanied by note 241.
[14] Reg. § 53.4942(b)-1(a)(1).
[15] IRC § 4942(f)(1); Reg. § 53.4942(a)-2(d)(1).
[16] IRC § 4942(f)(2); Reg. § 53.4942 (a)-2(d)(2).
[17] IRC § 4942(f)(3); Reg. § 53.4942(a)-2(d)(4).
[18] Reg. § 53.4942(b)-1(b)(1).
[19] See *infra* § 4(b).
[20] Reg. § 53.4942(b)-1(b)(1). E.g, Rev. Rul. 74-450, 1974-2 C.B. 388.
[21] Reg. § 53.4942(b)-1(b)(2). E.g., The "Miss Elizabeth" D. Leckie Scholarship Fund v. Comm'r, 87 T.C. 251 (1986); Rev. Rul. 78-315, 1978-2 C.B. 271.
[22] IRC § 4942(j)(3)(B)(i).
[23] IRC § 4942(j)(3)(B)(ii).
[24] IRC § 4942(j)(3)(B)(iii).
[25] Namely, at least 65 percent (Reg. § 53.4942(b)-2(a)(5)).
[26] See *infra* § 4(c).

part assets described in the first category and in part stock described in the second category.[27]

An asset, to qualify under this test, must actually be used by the foundation directly for the active conduct of its tax-exempt purpose. It can consist of real estate, physical facilities or objects, and intangible assets, but it cannot include assets held for the production of income, investment, or other similar use. Property used for both exempt and other purposes will meet the assets test (assuming it otherwise qualifies) as long as the exempt use represents at least 95 percent of total use.[28]

A private foundation will satisfy the endowment test where it normally expends its funds, in the form of qualifying distributions, directly for the active conduct of exempt activities, in an amount equal to at least two thirds of its minimum investment return.[29] The concept of expenditures directly for the active conduct of exempt activities under the endowment test is the same as that under the income test.[30]

A private foundation will satisfy the support test if (1) substantially all of its support (other than gross investment income[31]) is normally received from the general public and from at least five tax-exempt organizations that are not disqualified persons[32] with respect to each other or the foundation involved; (2) not more than 25 percent of its support (other than gross investment income) is normally received from any one of these exempt organizations; and (3) not more than one half of its support is normally received from gross investment income.[33]

An organization may satisfy the income test and either the assets, endowment, or support test by one of two methods: meeting the requirements for any three years during a four-year period consisting of the year involved and the three immediately preceding tax years, or on the basis of an aggregation of all pertinent amounts of income or assets held, received, or distributed during the four-year period. The same method must be used for satisfying the tests.[34] A foundation, to be regarded as a private operating foundation, generally must satisfy the income test and one of the other tests for its first year.[35]

Contributions to a private operating foundation are treated as if made to a public charity.[36]

(c) Exempt Operating Foundations

Another variant of private foundation is the *exempt operating foundation*.[37] This type of private foundation is termed an *exempt* one because it does not have to

---

[27] Reg. § 53.4942(b)-2(a)(1).
[28] Reg. § 53.4942(b)-2(a)(2).
[29] Reg. § 53.4942(b)-2(b)(1).
[30] Reg. § 53.4942(b)-2(b)(2).
[31] IRC § 509(e).
[32] See *infra* § 2.
[33] Reg. § 53.4942(b)-2(c)(1).
[34] Reg. § 53.4942(b)-3(a).
[35] Reg. § 53.4942(b)-3(b)(1).
[36] IRC §§ 170(b)(1)(A)(vii), 170(b)(1)(E)(i); Reg. § 1.170A-9(f).
[37] IRC § 4940(d).

pay the private foundation excise tax on investment income[38] nor are grants to it subject to the expenditure responsibility requirement.[39] The reason this category of foundation was established is to provide organizations that are not, in a generic sense, private foundations (such as many museums and libraries) some of the attributes of public charities.[40]

To be an exempt operating foundation for a year, a private foundation is required to have these characteristics: It qualifies as a private operating foundation; it has been publicly supported[41] for at least 10 years; its governing body consists of individuals at least 75 percent of whom are not *disqualified individuals*[42] and is broadly representative of the general public; and at no time during the year did it have an officer who is a disqualified individual.[43]

(d) Conduit Foundations

A *conduit private foundation* is not a separate category of private foundation but is a standard private foundation that, under certain circumstances, is regarded as a public charity for charitable contribution deduction purposes.[44]

This type of foundation makes qualifying distributions that are treated as distributions from its corpus[45] in an amount equal in value to 100 percent of all contributions received in the year involved, whether as money or property.[46] The distributions must be made not later than the fifteenth day of the third month after the close of the private foundation's year in which the contributions were received, and the foundation must not have any remaining undistributed income for the year.

The qualifying distribution may be of the contributed property or of the proceeds from its sale. In making the calculation in satisfaction of the 100 percent requirement, the amount distributed generally must be equal to the fair market value of the contributed property on the date of its distribution. However, the amount of this fair market value may be reduced by any reasonable selling expenses incurred by the foundation in disposing of the contributed property. At the option of the private foundation, if the contributed property is sold or distributed within 30 days of its receipt by the foundation, the amount of the fair market value is either the gross amount received from the sale of the property (less reasonable selling expenses) or an amount equal to the fair market value of the property on the date of its distribution to a public charity.[47]

These distributions are treated as made first out of contributions of property and then out of contributions of money received by the private foundation in the

---

[38] IRC § 4940(d)(1). See *infra* § 4(f).
[39] IRC § 4945(d)(4)(A). See *infra* § 4(e).
[40] H. Rep. No. 98-861, 98th Cong., 2d Sess. 1084 (1984).
[41] IRC § 4940(d)(3)(A).
[42] Namely, substantial contributors (see *infra* § 2(a)) and certain related persons (IRC §§ 4940(d)(3)(B)–4940(d)(3)(E)).
[43] IRC § 4940(d)(2).
[44] IRC §§ 170(b)(1)(A)(vii), 170(b)(1)(E)(ii). See § 2.5.
[45] IRC § 4942(h).
[46] IRC § 170(b)(1)(E)(ii); Reg. § 1.170A-9(g)(1).
[47] Reg. § 1.170A-9(g)(2)(iv).

year involved. The distributions cannot be made to an organization controlled directly or indirectly by the private foundation or by one or more disqualified persons[48] with respect to the private foundation or to a private foundation that is not a private operating foundation.[49]

(e) Common Fund Foundations

A special type of standard private foundation (that is, it is not a private operating foundation) is one that pools contributions received in a common fund but allows the donor or his or her spouse (including substantial contributors[50]) to retain the right to designate annually the organizations to which the income attributable to the contributions is given (as long as the organizations qualify as certain types of entities that are not private foundations[51]) and to direct (by deed or will) the organizations to which the corpus of the contributions is eventually to be given. Moreover, this type of private foundation must pay out its adjusted net income to public charities by the fifteenth day of the third month after the close of the tax year in which the income is realized by the fund and the corpus must be distributed to these charities within one year after the death of the donor or his or her spouse.[52]

Contributions to this type of private foundation are treated as if made to a public charity.[53]

(f) Other Types of *Foundations*

There are various types of tax-exempt charitable organizations that are termed *foundations* although they are not private foundations. For example, a form of publicly supported charity is the *community foundation*, which is a fund established to support charitable organizations in an identified geographical area.[54] Various *supporting organizations* are termed foundations, although they are public charities.[55] Public colleges and universities often have related "foundations," that are in fact public charities.[56]

One of the types of organizations eligible to receive funding, that qualifies for the scientific research tax credit,[57] is a fund organized and operated exclusively to make basic research grants to qualified institutions of higher education.[58] This type of fund must be a charitable organization that is not a private foundation and must make its grants pursuant to written research con-

---

[48] See *infra* § 2.
[49] Reg. § 1.170A-9(g).
[50] See *infra* § 2.
[51] IRC § 509(a)(1). See *infra* § 3(a), (b).
[52] Reg. § 170A-9(h).
[53] IRC §§ 170(b)(i)(A)(vii), 170(b)(i)(E)(iii). See *infra* §§ 2-5.
[54] This entity is a publicly supported charity by reason of IRC §§ 170(b)(1)(A)(vi) and 509(a)(1). See *infra* § 3.
[55] See *infra* § 3(c).
[56] See *infra* § 3(b)(v).
[57] IRC § 41.
[58] IRC § 41(e)(6)(D).

tracts. A fund must elect this status; by doing so, it becomes treated as a private foundation, although the tax on net investment income[59] is not applicable.[60]

(g) Organizational Rules

An organization must satisfy the applicable organizational test in order to achieve tax-exempt status.[61] There are specific organizational rules for private foundations, which must be met in addition to the organizational test applicable for charitable organizations generally.[62]

A private foundation cannot be exempt from tax (nor will contributions to it be deductible as charitable gifts) unless its governing instrument includes provisions the effects of which are to require distributions at such time and in such manner as to comply with the payout rules and prohibit the foundation from engaging in any act of self-dealing, retaining any excess business holdings, making any jeopardizing investments, and making any taxable expenditures.[63] Generally, these elements must be in the foundation's articles of organization and not solely in its bylaws.[64]

The provisions of a foundation's governing instrument must require or prohibit, as the case may be, the foundation to act or refrain from acting so that the foundation, and any foundation managers or other disqualified persons with respect to it, will not be liable for any of the private foundation excise taxes.[65] The governing instrument of a nonexempt split-interest trust[66] must make comparable provision as respects any of the applicable private foundation excise taxes.[67] Specific reference in the governing instrument to the appropriate sections of the Internal Revenue Code is generally required, unless equivalent language is used that is deemed by the IRS to have the same full force and effect. However, a governing instrument that contains only language sufficient to satisfy the requirements of the organizational test for charitable entities generally does not meet the specific requirements applicable with respect to private foundations, regardless of the interpretation placed on the language as a matter of law by a state court, and a governing instrument does not meet the organizational requirements if it expressly prohibits the distribution of capital or corpus.[68]

---

[59] See *infra* § 4(f).

[60] IRC § 41(e)(6)(D)(iv).

[61] The law contains an express organizational test for charitable organizations; there is an implied test of this nature for other categories of exempt organizations. For the latter, the requirement essentially is that the organizational document be reflective of the organization's primary exempt purposes (see § 4.4).

[62] See § 4.3.

[63] IRC § 508(e)(1).

[64] Reg. § 1.508-3(c).

[65] Rev. Rul. 70-270, 1970-1 C.B. 135, contains sample governing instrument provisions.

[66] That is, entities described in IRC § 4947(a)(1).

[67] Reg. § 1.508-3(e). Rev. Rul. 74-368, 1974-2 C.B. 390, contains sample governing instrument provisions.

[68] Reg. § 1.508-3(b).

A foundation's governing instrument is deemed to conform with the organizational requirements if valid provisions of state law have been enacted that require the foundation to act or refrain from acting so as to not subject it to any of the private foundation excise taxes or that treat the required provisions as contained in the foundation's governing instrument.[69] The IRS ruled as to which state statutes contain sufficient provisions in this regard.[70]

Any provision of state law is presumed valid as enacted, and in the absence of state law provisions to the contrary, applies with respect to any foundation that does not specifically disclaim coverage under state law (either by notification to the appropriate state official or by commencement of judicial proceedings).[71] If a state law provision is declared invalid or inapplicable with respect to a class of foundations by the highest appellate court of the state or by the U.S. Supreme Court, the foundations covered by the determination must meet certain requirements[72] within one year from the date on which the time for perfecting an application for review by the Supreme Court expires. If such an application is filed, these requirements must be met within a year from the date on which the Supreme Court disposes of the case, whether by denial of the application for review or decision on the merits. In addition, if a provision of state law is declared invalid or inapplicable with respect to a class of foundations by any court of competent jurisdiction, and the decision is not reviewed by the highest state appellate court of the Supreme Court, and the IRS notifies the general public that the provision has been so declared invalid or inapplicable, then all foundations in the state must meet these requirements, without reliance upon the statute to the extent declared invalid or inapplicable by the decision, within one year from the date such notice is made public. These rules do not apply to any foundation that is subject to a final judgment entered by a court of competent jurisdiction, holding the law invalid or inapplicable with respect to the foundation.[73]

§ 11.2 DISQUALIFIED PERSONS

A basic concept of the tax laws relating to private foundations is that of the *disqualified person*. Essentially, a disqualified person is a person (including an individual, corporation, partnership, trust, or estate) that has a particular, usually intimate, relationship with respect to a private foundation.[74]

---

[69] Reg. § 1.508-3(d)(1).
[70] Rev. Rul. 75-38, 1975-1 C.B. 161.
[71] Reg. § 1.508-3(b)(6).
[72] IRC § 508(e).
[73] Reg. § 1.508-3(d)(2).
[74] The term *disqualified person* is defined, for these purposes, in IRC § 4946(a). The term is defined somewhat differently in the setting of excess benefit transactions involving public charities and social welfare organizations (see § 19.11(c)).

§ 11.2   DISQUALIFIED PERSONS

(a) Substantial Contributor

One category of disqualified person[75] is a *substantial contributor* to a private foundation.[76] A substantial contributor generally is any person who contributed or bequeathed an aggregate amount of more than $5,000 to the private foundation involved, where the amount is more than 2 percent of the total contributions and bequests received by the foundation before the close of its year in which the contribution or bequest is received by the foundation from that person.[77] In making this computation, all contributions and bequests to the private foundation, made since its establishment, are taken into account.[78]

In the case of a trust, the term *substantial contributor* also means the creator of the trust.[79] The term *person* includes tax-exempt organizations[80] (except as discussed below) but does not include governmental units.[81] The term *person* also includes a decedent, even at the point in time preceding the transfer of any property from the estate to the private foundation.[82] With one exception, once a person becomes a substantial contributor to a private foundation, it can never escape that status,[83] even though it might not be so classified if the determination were first made at a later date.[84]

Only one exception enables a person's status as a substantial contributor to terminate in certain circumstances after 10 years with no connection with the private foundation.[85] This requires that, during the 10-year period, (1) the person (and any related persons) did not make any contributions to the private foundation, (2) neither the person (nor any related person) was a foundation manager of the private foundation, and (3) the aggregate contributions made by the person (and any related person) are determined by the IRS "to be insignificant when compared to the aggregate amount of contributions to such foundation by one other person,"[86] taking into account appreciation on contributions while held by the private foundation. For these purposes, the term *related person* means related disqualified persons, and in the case of a corporate donor includes the officers and directors of the corporation.[87]

For certain purposes,[88] the term *substantial contributor* does not include most organizations that are not private foundations[89] or an organization

---

[75] IRC § 4946(a)(1)(A); Reg. § 53.4946-1(a)(1)(i).
[76] IRC §§ 4946(a)(2), 507(d)(2).
[77] IRC § 507(d)(2)(A).
[78] Reg. § 1.507-6(a)(1).
[79] *Id.*
[80] That is, organizations encompassed by IRC § 501(a).
[81] That is, entities described in IRC § 170(c)(1).
[82] *Rockefeller v. United States*, 572 F. Supp. 9 (E.D. Ark. 1982), *aff'd*, 718 F.2d 290 (8th Cir. 1983), *cert. den.*, 466 U.S. 962 (1984).
[83] IRC § 507(d)(2)(B)(iv).
[84] Reg. § 1.507-6(b)(1).
[85] IRC § 507(d)(2)(C).
[86] IRC § 507(d)(2)(C)(i)(III).
[87] IRC § 507(d)(2)(C)(ii).
[88] IRC §§ 170(b)(1)(D)(iii), 507(d)(1), 508(d), 509(a)(1), 509(a)(3), and IRC Chapter 42.
[89] That is, organizations described in IRC §§ 509(a)(1), 509(a)(2), or 509(a)(3).

wholly owned by a public charity. Moreover, for purposes of the self-dealing rules,[90] the term does not include any charitable organization,[91] since to require inclusion of charitable organizations for this purpose would preclude private foundations from making large grants to or otherwise interacting with other private foundations.[92] However, in computing the support fraction for purposes of one category of publicly supported organization,[93] the term *substantial contributor* includes public charities where the $5,000/2 percent test is exceeded, although the support may qualify as a material change in support or an unusual grant.

In determining whether a contributor is a substantial contributor, the total of the amounts received from the contributor and the total contributions and bequests received by the private foundation must be ascertained as of the last day of each tax year commencing with the first year ending after October 9, 1969.[94] Generally, all contributions and bequests made before October 9, 1969, are deemed to have been made on that date, and each contribution or bequest made after that is valued at its fair market value on the date received, with an individual treated as making all contributions and bequests made by his or her spouse.[95]

(b) Foundation Manager

Another category of disqualified person[96] is the *foundation manager*. A foundation manager is an officer, director, or trustee of a private foundation, or an individual having powers or responsibilities similar to one or more of these three positions.[97] An individual is considered an *officer* of a private foundation if he or she is specifically designated as such under the documents by which the foundation was formed or if he or she regularly exercises general authority to make administrative or policy decisions on behalf of the foundation.[98] Independent contractors acting in that capacity—such as lawyers, accountants, and investment managers and advisers—are not officers.[99]

An organization can be a foundation manager, such as a bank, a similar financial institution, or an investment adviser.[100]

---

[90] See *infra* § 4(a).

[91] For these purposes, an organization described in IRC § 501(c)(3), other than an organization that tests for public safety (IRC § 509(a)(4)). See *infra* § 3(a)-(c).

[92] Reg. § 1.507-6(a)(2). This exception also applies to IRC § 4947(a)(1) trusts (Rev. Rul. 73-455, 1973-2 C.B. 187).

[93] IRC § 509(a)(2)(A). See *infra* § 3(b)(iv).

[94] Reg. § 1.507-6(b)(i).

[95] IRC § 507(d)(2)(B)(i)–507(d)(2)(B)(iii).

[96] IRC § 4946(a)(1)(B); Reg. § 53.4946-1(f)(1).

[97] IRC § 4946(b)(1).

[98] Reg. § 53.4946-1(f)(1). An example of the latter is in Rev. Rul. 74-287, 1974-1 C.B. 327.

[99] Reg. § 53.4946-1(f)(2).

[100] E.g., Priv. Ltr. Rul. 9535043.

(c) Twenty Percent Owner

An owner of more than 20 percent of the total *combined voting power* of a corporation, the *profits interest* of a partnership, or the *beneficial interest* of a trust or unincorporated enterprise, any of which is (during the ownership) a substantial contributor to a private foundation, is a disqualified person.[101]

The term combined voting power[102] includes voting power represented by holdings of voting stock, actual or constructive,[103] but does not include voting rights held only as a director or trustee.[104]

The term *voting power* includes outstanding voting power and does not include voting power obtainable but not obtained, such as voting power obtainable by converting securities or nonvoting stock into voting stock, by exercising warrants or options to obtain voting stock, and voting power that will vest in preferred stockholders only if and when the corporation has failed to pay preferred dividends for a specified period or has otherwise failed to meet specified requirements.[105]

The profits interest[106] of a partner is that equal to his or her distributive share of income of the partnership as determined under special federal tax rules.[107] The term *profits interest* includes any interest that is outstanding but not any interest that is obtainable but has not been obtained.[108]

The beneficial interest in an unincorporated enterprise (other than a trust or estate) includes any right to receive a portion of distributions from profits of the enterprise or, in the absence of a profit-sharing agreement, any right to receive a portion of the assets (if any) upon liquidation of the enterprise, except as a creditor or employee.[109] A right to receive distribution of profits includes a right to receive any amount from the profits other than as a creditor or employee, whether as a sum certain or as a portion of profits realized by the enterprise. Where there is no agreement fixing the rights of the participants in an enterprise, the fraction of the respective interests of each participant therein is determined by dividing the amount of all investments or contributions to the capital of the enterprise made or obligated to be made by the participant by the amount of all investments or contributions to capital made or obligated to be made by all of them.[110]

A person's beneficial interest in a trust is determined in proportion to the actuarial interest of the person in the trust.[111]

---

[101] IRC § 4946(a)(1)(C).
[102] IRC § 4946(a)(1)(C)(i).
[103] See IRC § 4946(a)(3).
[104] Reg. § 53.4946-1(a)(5).
[105] Reg. § 53.4946-1(a)(6).
[106] IRC § 4946(a)(1)(C)(ii).
[107] IRC §§ 707(b)(3), 4946(a)(4); Reg. § 53.4946-1(a)(2).
[108] Reg. § 53.4946-1(a)(6).
[109] IRC § 4946(a)(1)(C)(iii).
[110] Reg. § 53.4946-1(a)(3).
[111] Reg. § 53.4946-1(a)(4).

The term *beneficial interest* includes any interest that is outstanding but not any interest that is obtainable but has not been obtained.[112]

(d) Family Member

Another category of disqualified person is a member of the family of an individual who is a substantial contributor, a foundation manager, or one of the previously discussed 20 percent owners.[113] The term *member of the family* is defined to include only an individual's spouse, ancestors, children, grandchildren, great-grandchildren, and the spouses of children, grandchildren, and great-grandchildren.[114] Thus, these family members are themselves disqualified persons.

A legally adopted child of an individual is treated for these purposes as a child of the individual by blood.[115] A brother or sister of an individual is not, for these purposes, a member of the family.[116] However, for example, the spouse of a grandchild of an individual is a member of his or her family for these purposes.[117]

(e) Corporation

A corporation is a disqualified person if more than 35 percent of the total combined voting power in the corporation (including constructive holdings[118]) is owned by substantial contributors, foundation managers, 20 percent owners, or members of the family of any of these individuals.[119]

(f) Partnership

A partnership is a disqualified person if more than 35 percent of the profits interest in the partnership (including constructive holdings[120]) is owned by substantial contributors, foundation managers, 20 percent owners, or members of the family of any of these individuals.[121]

(g) Trust or Estate

A trust or estate is a disqualified person if more than 35 percent of the beneficial interest in the trust or estate (including constructive holdings[122]) is owned by sub-

---

[112] Reg. § 53.4946-1(a)(6).
[113] IRC § 4946(a)(1)(D).
[114] IRC § 4946(d).
[115] Reg. § 53.4946-1(h).
[116] *Id.*
[117] *Id.*
[118] IRC § 4946(a)(3).
[119] IRC § 4946(a)(1)(E).
[120] IRC § 4946(a)(4).
[121] IRC § 4946(a)(1)(F).
[122] IRC § 4946(a)(4).

stantial contributors, foundation managers, 20 percent owners, or members of the family of any of these individuals.[123]

(h) Private Foundation

A private foundation may be a disqualified person with respect to another private foundation but only for purposes of the excess business holdings rules.[124] The disqualified person private foundation must be effectively controlled,[125] directly or indirectly, by the same person or persons (other than a bank, trust company, or similar organization acting only as a foundation manager) who control the private foundation in question, or must be the recipient of contributions substantially all of which were made, directly or indirectly, by substantial contributors, foundation managers, 20 percent owners, and members of their families who made, directly or indirectly, substantially all of the contributions to the private foundation in question.[126] One or more persons are considered to have made *substantially all* of the contributions to a private foundation for these purposes if the persons have contributed or bequeathed at least 85 percent of the total contributions and bequests that have been received by the private foundation during its entire existence, where each person has contributed or bequeathed at least two percent of the total.[127]

(i) Governmental Official

A governmental official may be a disqualified person with respect to a private foundation but only for purposes of the self-dealing rules.[128] The term *governmental official* means (1) an elected public official in the U.S. Congress or executive branch, (2) presidential appointees to the U.S. executive or judicial branches, (3) certain higher compensated or ranking employees in one of these three branches, (4) House of Representatives or Senate employees earning at least $15,000 annually, (5) elected or appointed public officials in the U.S. or D.C. governments (including governments of U.S. possessions or political subdivisions or areas of the United States) earning at least $15,000 annually, or, as regards compensation received after December 31, 1985, $20,000 annually, or (6) the personal or executive assistant or secretary to any of the foregoing.[129]

In defining the term *public office* for purposes of the fifth category of governmental officials, this term must be distinguished from mere public employment. Although holding a public office is one form of public employment, not every position in the employ of a state or other governmental subdivision[130] constitutes a public office. Although a determination as to whether a public

---

[123] IRC § 4946(a)(1)(G).
[124] IRC § 4946(a)(1)(H). See *infra* § 4(c).
[125] Reg. § 1.482-1(a)(3).
[126] Reg. § 53.4946-1(b)(1).
[127] Reg. § 53.4946-1(b)(2).
[128] IRC § 4946(a)(1)(I).
[129] IRC § 4946(c).
[130] IRC § 4946(c)(5).

employee holds a public office depends on the facts and circumstances of the case, the essential element is whether a significant part of the activities of a public employee is the independent performance of policy-making functions. Several factors may be considered as indications that a position in the executive, legislative, or judicial branch of the government of a state, possession of the United States, or political subdivision or other area of any of the foregoing, or of the District of Columbia, constitutes a public office. Among the factors to be considered, in addition to that set forth above, are that the office is created by Congress, a state constitution, or the state legislature, or by a municipality or other governmental body pursuant to authority conferred by Congress, state constitution, or state legislature, and the powers conferred on the office and the duties to be discharged by the official are defined either directly or indirectly by Congress, a state constitution, or a state legislature, or through legislative authority.[131]

§ 11.3 CATEGORIES OF PUBLIC CHARITIES

A *public charity* is a charitable organization[132] that does not constitute a private foundation. There are, in essence, four categories of charitable organizations that are not private foundations: *public institutions, publicly supported charities, supporting organizations*, and *organizations that test for public safety.*

(a) Public Institutions

There are types of charitable organizations that generally are recognized as entities that are not private foundations, under any reasonable definition of that term, by virtue of the nature of their programs, how they are structured, and their relationship with the general public. These are the *public institutions.*

The category of public institutions comprises churches, and conventions and associations of churches;[133] educational organizations that normally maintain a regular faculty and curriculum, and normally have a regularly enrolled body of pupils or students in attendance at the place where the educational activities are regularly carried on, that is, schools, colleges, and universities;[134] hospitals and medical research organizations;[135] and governmental units,[136] including a state, a possession of the United States, a political subdivision of either of the foregoing, the United States, or the District of Columbia.[137]

---

[131] Reg. § 53.4946-1(g)(2).
[132] That is, an entity described *supra* note 1.
[133] IRC §§ 170(b)(1)(A)(i), 509(a)(1). See §§ 8.3, 8.4.
[134] IRC §§ 170(b)(1)(A)(ii), 509(a)(1). See § 7.3.
[135] IRC §§ 170(b)(1)(A)(iii), 509(a)(1). See § 6.2.
[136] IRC §§ 170(b)(1)(A)(v), 509(a)(1). See § 6.9.
[137] IRC § 170(c)(1).

(b) Publicly Supported Charities

(i) Donative Publicly Supported Charities—In General. An organization qualifies as a *donative* type of publicly supported charity if it normally receives a substantial part of its support (other than exempt function revenue) from a governmental unit[138] or from direct or indirect contributions from the general public.[139]

The principal requirement for a charitable organization to qualify as a donative publicly supported organization is that it normally derive at least one third of its financial support from qualifying contributions and grants.[140] This type of entity must maintain a *support fraction* (using the cash basis method of accounting), the denominator of which is total eligible support received during the computation period and the numerator of which is the amount of eligible public support for the period.

The term *support* means amounts received as contributions, grants, net income from unrelated business activities,[141] gross investment income,[142] tax revenues levied for the benefit of the organization and either paid to or expended on behalf of it, and the value of services or facilities (exclusive of services or facilities generally furnished to the public without charge) furnished by a governmental unit to the organization without charge.[143] All of these items are amounts that, if received by the organization, represent the denominator of the support fraction.

Support does not include any gain from the disposition of property that would be considered gain from the sale or exchange of a capital asset, or the value of exemption from any federal, state, or local tax or any similar benefit.[144] A loan is not a form of support; however, should the lender forgive the debt, the amount becomes support in the year of the forgiveness.[145]

In general, contributions and grants constitute public support to the extent that the total amount of gifts or grants from a source during the computation period does not exceed an amount equal to 2 percent of the organization's total includible support for the period.[146] (Where a contributor or grantor provides an amount that is in excess of the 2 percent threshold, the portion that does not exceed the threshold qualifies as public support.) Therefore, the total amount of support from a donor or grantor is included in full in the denominator of the support fraction, while the amount determined by application of the 2 percent threshold is included in the numerator of the support fraction. Persons who have a defined relationship with one another (such as spouses) are consid-

---

[138] *Id.*
[139] IRC §§ 170(b)(1)(A)(vi), 509(a)(1).
[140] Reg. § 1.170A-9(e)(2).
[141] See Part Five.
[142] IRC § 509(e).
[143] IRC § 509(d).
[144] *Id.*
[145] Priv. Ltr. Rul. 9608039.
[146] Reg. § 1.170A-9(e)(6)(i).

ered as one source for purposes of computing the two percent threshold amount.

Qualifying gifts and grants constitute support in the form of *direct* contributions from the general public. Support received from governmental units and other donative publicly supported organizations, in the form of grants, are forms of *indirect* contributions from the general public (in that these grantors are considered conduits of direct public support).

This 2 percent threshold does not generally apply to support received by a donative publicly supported charity from other donative publicly supported charities nor to support from governmental units. That is, this type of support is, in its entirety, public support.[147] This is also the case concerning grants from a public institution, the support of which satisfies the rules for donative publicly supported charities.[148]

In constructing the support fraction, an organization must exclude from the numerator and denominator of it amounts that constitute *exempt function revenue*, which are amounts received from the exercise or performance of its exempt purpose or function and contributions of services for which a deduction is not allowable.[149] However, the organization is not treated as meeting the support test if it receives almost all of its support in the form of exempt function revenue and an insignificant amount of its support from governmental units and the general public.[150] The organization also may exclude from the support fraction an amount equal to one or more qualifying *unusual grants*.[151]

The determination of whether a payment is a contribution rather than exempt function revenue, or whether a payment is a grant rather than an amount paid pursuant to a contract (the latter being a form of exempt function revenue) can be controversial. As to the former, a membership fee is not a contribution.[152] As to the latter, an amount paid by a governmental unit to an organization is not regarded as received from the exercise or performance of its exempt functions, and thus is a grant, if the purpose of the payment is primarily to enable the organization to provide a service to the direct benefit of the public rather than to serve the direct and immediate needs of the payor.[153]

---

[147] *Id.*

[148] E.g., Rev. Rul. 78-95, 1978-1 C.B. 71 (grants by a church).

[149] Reg. § 1.170A-9(e)(7)(i).

[150] Reg. § 1.170A-9(e)(7)(ii).

[151] Reg. §§ 1.170A-9(e)(6)(ii), 1.170A-9(e)(6)(iii). E.g., Rev. Rul. 76-440, 1976-2 C.B. 58.

[152] Reg. § 1.170A-9(e)(7)(iii). E.g., Williams Home, Inc. v. United States, 540 F. Supp. 310 (W.D. Va. 1982) (monies paid to a home for the aged by incoming residents as a condition of admission are not contributions but are a form of exempt function revenue).

[153] Reg. § 1.170A-9(e)(8)(ii). E.g., payments by the federal government to a professional standards review organization were held to not be excludable gross receipts but instead includable public support because the payments compensated the organization for a function that promoted the health of the beneficiaries of government health care programs in the areas in which the organization operated (Rev. Rul. 81-276, 1981-2 C.B. 128). By contrast, Medicare and Medicaid payments to tax-exempt health care organizations constitute gross receipts derived from the performance of exempt functions and thus are not forms of public support, inasmuch as the patients control the ultimate recipients of the payments by their choice of a health care provider, so that they, not the governmental units, are the payors (Rev. Rul. 83-153, 1983-2 C.B. 48).

Calculation of the support fraction entails an assessment of the organization's support that is *normally* received. This means that the organization must meet the one-third support test for a period encompassing the four years immediately preceding the year involved, on an aggregate basis. Where this is done, the organization is considered as meeting the one-third support test for its current year and the year immediately succeeding it.[154] (A five-year computational period for meeting the support test is used for organizations in the initial years of their existence.)[155]

(ii) Facts-and-Circumstances Test. There are some charitable organizations that are not private foundations in the generic sense, yet are not publicly supported under the general rules. Organizations in this position include entities such as museums and libraries that rely principally on endowments for their financial support. The *facts-and-circumstances test* offers a way for an organization of this type to qualify as a donative publicly supported charity, even though it does not receive at least one third of its support from the public.

An organization may qualify as a publicly supported donative organization—where it cannot satisfy the one-third public support requirement—as long as the amount normally received from governmental and/or public sources is *substantial*.[156] To meet this test, the organization must demonstrate the existence of three elements: (1) The total amount of governmental and public support normally received by the organization is at least 10 percent of its total support normally received; (2) the organization has a continuous and bona fide program for solicitation of funds from the general public, governmental units, or public charities; and (3) all other pertinent facts and circumstances, including the percentage of its support from governmental and public sources, the public nature of the organization's governing board, the extent to which its facilities or programs are publicly available, its membership dues rates, and whether its activities are likely to appeal to persons having some broad common interest or purpose.[157]

Concerning the governing board factor, the organization's nonprivate foundation status will be enhanced where it has a governing body that represents the interests of the public, rather than the personal or private interests of a limited number of donors. This can be accomplished by the election of board members by a broadly based membership or otherwise by having the board composed of public officials, persons having particular expertise in the field or discipline involved, community leaders, and the like.

---

[154] Reg. § 1.170A-9(e)(4)(i).

[155] See § 23.4.

[156] Reg. § 1.170A-9(e)(3). An illustration of an organization that failed both the general rules and the facts and circumstances test appears in Collins v. Comm'r, 61 T.C. 693 (1974).

[157] Reg. § 1.170A-9(e)(3). In a case concerning the public charity status of a home for the elderly, a court held that the practice of the home to encourage lawyers to mention to their clients the possibility of bequests to the home was inadequate compliance with the requirement of an ongoing development program (Trustees for the Home for the Aged Women v. United States, 86-1 U.S.T.C. ¶ 9290 (D. Mass. 1986)).

(iii) Community Foundations. A community trust (or community foundation) may qualify as a donative publicly supported charity if it attracts, receives, and depends on financial support from members of the general public on a regular, recurring basis. Community foundations are designed primarily to attract large contributions of a capital or endowment nature from a small number of donors, with the gifts often received and maintained in the form of separate trusts or funds. They are generally identified with a particular community or area and are controlled by a representative group of persons from that community or area. Individual donors relinquish control over the investment and distribution of their contributions and the income generated from them, although donors may designate the purposes for which the assets are to be used, subject to change by the governing body of the community trust.[158]

A community foundation, to qualify as a publicly supported organization, must meet the support requirements for a donative publicly supported charity[159] or meet the facts-and-circumstances test for donative charities.[160] As to the latter, the requirement of attraction of public support will generally be satisfied if a community foundation seeks gifts and bequests from a wide range of potential donors in the community or area served, through banks or trust companies, through lawyers or other professional individuals, or in other appropriate ways that call attention to the community foundation as a potential recipient of gifts and bequests made for the benefit of the community or area served. A community foundation is not required to engage in periodic, community-wide, fund-raising campaigns directed toward attracting a large number of small contributions in a manner similar to campaigns conducted by a community chest or united fund.

A community foundation wants to be treated as a single entity, rather than as an aggregation of funds. To be regarded as a component part of a community foundation, a trust or fund must be created by gift or like transfer to a community foundation that is treated as a separate entity and may not be subjected by the transferor to any material restriction[161] with respect to the transferred assets.[162] To be treated as a separate entity, a community foundation must be appropriately named, be so structured as to subject its funds to a common governing instrument, have a common governing body, and prepare periodic financial reports that treat all funds held by the community foundation as its funds.[163] The governing body of a community foundation must have the power to modify any restriction on the distribution of funds where it is inconsistent with the charitable needs of the community, must commit itself to the exercise of its powers in the best interests of the community foundation, and must commit itself to seeing that the funds are invested pursuant to accepted standards of fiduciary conduct.[164]

---

[158] Reg. § 1.170A-9(e)(10).
[159] See *supra* § 3(b)(i).
[160] See *supra* § 3(b)(ii).
[161] See Reg. §§ 1.507-2(a)(7), (8).
[162] Reg. § 1.170A-9(e)(11)(ii).
[163] Reg. §§ 1.170A-9(e)(11)(iii)–1.170A-9(e)(11)(vi).
[164] Reg. § 1.170A-9(e)(11)(v).

Grantors, contributors, and distributors to community trusts may rely on the publicly supported charity status of these trusts under circumstances that are the same as those applicable to reliance in the case of other categories of public charities[165] or of private operating foundations.[166]

(iv) Service Provider Publicly Supported Organizations.   An organization qualifies as a *service provider* type of publicly supported charity[167] if it satisfies two tests.[168] One test requires that the charity normally receive more than one third of its support from any combination of (1) contributions, grants, or membership fees, and (2) gross receipts from admissions, sales of merchandise, performance of services, or furnishing of facilities in activities related to exempt purposes, as long as the support is from *permitted sources.*[169] (As discussed below, there is an additional limitation on the qualification of exempt function revenue as public support.) Thus, an organization seeking to qualify under this set of rules must construct a *support fraction* (using the cash basis method of accounting), with the amount of qualified support received from these two sources constituting the numerator of the fraction and the total amount of support received being the denominator.[170]

Permitted sources are public institutions, donative publicly supported organizations, and persons other than disqualified persons with respect to the organization.[171] The term *support* means the two types of public support, along with net income from unrelated business activities,[172] gross investment income,[173] tax revenues levied for the benefit of the organization and either paid to or expended on behalf of it, and the value of services or facilities (exclusive of services or facilities generally furnished to the public without charge) furnished by a governmental unit to the organization without charge.[174] All of these items are amounts that, if received by the organization, comprise the denominator of the support fraction.

Support does not include any gain from the disposition of property that would be considered gain from the sale or exchange of a capital asset, or the value of exemption from any federal, state, or local tax or any similar benefit.[175] A loan is not a form of support; however, should the lender forgive the debt, the amount becomes support in the year of the forgiveness.[176]

The second test requires that an organization, to qualify as a service provider publicly supported charity, normally receive not more than one third of

---

[165] Reg. § 1.509(a)-7.

[166] See *supra* § 1(b). The reliance rule for community trusts appears at Reg. § 1.508 1(b)(4)(i).

[167] This term was adopted by the U.S. Supreme Court in Camps Newfound/Owatonna, Inc. v. Town of Harrison, Maine, 117 S. Ct. 1590, 1596 (1997).

[168] IRC § 509(a)(2).

[169] IRC § 509(a)(2)(A).

[170] Reg. § 1.509(a)-3(a)(2).

[171] IRC § 509(a)(2)(A).

[172] See Part Five.

[173] IRC § 509(e).

[174] IRC § 509(d).

[175] *Id.*

[176] Priv. Ltr. Rul. 9608039.

its support from the sum of gross investment income[177] and any excess of the amount of unrelated business taxable income over the amount of the tax imposed on that income.[178] This entails the construction of a *gross investment income fraction*, with the amount of gross investment income and any unrelated income (less the tax paid on it) received constituting the numerator of the fraction and the total amount of support received being the denominator.[179]

These support and investment income tests are computed on the basis of the organization's *normal* sources of support. Generally, an organization is considered as *normally* receiving one-third of its support from permitted sources and not more than one-third of its support from gross investment income for its current year and immediately succeeding year if, for the four years immediately preceding its current year, the aggregate amount of support received over the four-year period from permitted sources is more than one-third of its total support and the aggregate amount of support over the four-year period from gross investment income is not more than one-third of its total support.[180] Substantial contributions and bequests that are unusual or unexpected in terms of the amount—termed *unusual grants*—may be excluded from these calculations.[181]

In computing the amount of support received from gross receipts that is allowable toward the one-third support requirement, gross receipts from related activities (other than from membership fees) received from any person or from any bureau or similar agency of a governmental unit are includable in a year to the extent that the receipts do not exceed the greater of $5,000 or one percent of the organization's support for the year.[182]

(v) Foundations Supporting Public Colleges and Universities. Public charity status is provided for certain organizations providing support for public colleges and universities.[183] The organization must normally receive a substantial part of its support (exclusive of income received in the exercise or performance of its tax-exempt activities) from the United States or from direct or indirect contributions from the general public. It must be organized and operated exclusively to receive, hold, invest, and administer property and to make expenditures to or for the benefit of a college or university (including a land grant college or university) that is a public charity and that is an agency or instrumentality of a state or political subdivision thereof, or that is owned or operated by a state or political subdivision thereof or by an agency or instrumentality of one or more states or political subdivisions.

---

[177] IRC § 509(e).
[178] IRC § 509(a)(2)(B).
[179] Reg. § 1.509(a)-3(a)(3).
[180] Reg. § 1.509(a)-3(c)(1)(i).
[181] Reg. § 1.509(a)-3(c)(3). E.g., Rev. Rul. 76-440, *supra* note 151. The IRS has promulgated "safe haven" criteria that automatically cause a contribution or a grant to be considered *unusual* (Rev. Proc. 81-7, 1981-1 C.B. 621).
[182] IRC § 509(a)(2)(A)(ii); Reg. § 1.509(a)-3(b)(1). E.g., Rev. Rul. 83-153, 1983-2 C.B. 48; Rev. Rul. 75-387, 1975-2 C.B. 216.
[183] IRC § 170(b)(1)(A)(iv).

These expenditures include those made for any one or more of the regular functions of colleges and universities, such as the acquisition and maintenance of real property representing part of the campus area; the construction of college or university buildings; the acquisition and maintenance of equipment and furnishings used for, or in conjunction with, regular functions of colleges and universities; or expenditures for scholarships, libraries, and student loans.[184]

Another frequently important feature of the state college or university related foundation is its ability to borrow money for or on behalf of the supported institution, with the indebtedness bearing tax-excludable interest.[185]

(c) Supporting Organizations

A category of organization that is a public charity is the *supporting organization*.[186] This type of entity must be sufficiently related to one or more qualified organizations, which include public institutions and publicly supported organizations.[187]

A supporting organization must be organized and operated exclusively for the benefit of, to perform the functions of, or to carry out the purposes of one or more specified qualified supported organizations.[188] A supporting organization must be operated, supervised, or controlled by or in connection with one or more supported organizations.[189] A supporting organization may not be controlled directly or indirectly by one or more disqualified persons (other than foundation managers).[190]

A supporting organization must engage solely in activities that support or benefit one or more supported organizations.[191] These activities may include making payments to or for the use of, or providing services or facilities for, individual members of the charitable class benefited by one or more supported public charities. A supporting organization may, but need not, pay over its income to a supported organization. It may carry on an independent program that supports or benefits one or more supported organizations.[192]

The relationship between a supporting organization and a supported organization must be one of three types: *operated, supervised or controlled by, supervised or controlled in connection with*, or *operated in connection with*.[193] The first of these types of relationships requires a relationship comparable to that of a parent and a subsidiary.[194] The third of these relationships entails a programmatic interlock,

---

[184] Reg. § 1.170A-9(b)(2).
[185] IRC § 103.
[186] IRC § 509(a)(3).
[187] Reg. § 1.509(a)-4(a)(5).
[188] IRC § 509(a)(3)(A); Reg. § 1.509(a)-4(a)(2).
[189] IRC § 509(a)(3)(B).
[190] IRC § 509(a)(3)(C); Reg. § 1.509(a)-4(a)(4).
[191] Reg. §§ 1.509(a)-4(e)(1), 1.509(a)-4(e)(2).
[192] Reg. § 1.509(a)-4(e)(2).
[193] Reg. §§ 1.509(a)-4(a)(3), 1.509(a)-4(f)(2).
[194] Reg. §§ 1.509(a)-4(f)(4), 1.509(a)-4(g)(1)(i).

where the supporting organization is responsive to and significantly involved in the operations of the supported organization.[195]

As noted, a supporting organization must be organized and operated to support or benefit one or more *specified* supported organizations. This specification must be in the articles of organization of the supporting organization, with the manner of the specification dependent on which of the three types of relationships is involved.[196]

A supporting organization may operate to support and benefit a social welfare organization,[197] a labor or agricultural organization,[198] or a business league.[199] The principal requirement in this regard is that the beneficiary organization meet the one-third public support test of the rules concerning the service provider publicly supported charitable organization.[200]

(d) Public Safety Testing Organizations

Another category of organization that is deemed to not be a private foundation is an organization that is organized and operated exclusively for testing for public safety.[201] These entities are described in the analysis of charitable organizations.

§ 11.4 PRIVATE FOUNDATION RULES

The federal tax law governing the operations of private foundations is a composite of rules pertaining to self-dealing, mandatory payout requirements, business holdings, investment practices, various types of expenditures, and more. The sanctions for violation of these rules are five sets of excise taxes, with each set entailing three tiers of taxation. The three tiers are known as the *initial tax*,[202] the *additional tax*,[203] and the *involuntary termination tax*.[204] In general, when there is a violation, the initial tax must be paid; the additional tax is levied only when the initial tax is not timely paid and the matter not timely corrected; the termination tax is levied when the other two taxes have been imposed and there continues to be willful, flagrant, or repeated acts or failures to act giving rise to one or more of the initial or additional taxes.

The IRS generally has the authority to abate these initial taxes, where the taxable event was due to reasonable cause and not to willful neglect, and the event was timely corrected.[205] However, this abatement authority does not extend

---

[195] Reg. § 1.509(a)-4(f)(4).
[196] Reg. § 1.509(a)-4(c)(1).
[197] See Chapter 12.
[198] See Chapter 15.
[199] See Chapter 13.
[200] IRC § 509(a), last sentence Reg. § 1.509(a)-4(k).
[201] IRC § 509(a)(4). See § 10.3.
[202] IRC § 4941(a), 4942(a), 4943(a), 4944(a), 4945(a).
[203] IRC § 4941(b), 4942(b), 4943(b), 4944(b), 4945(b).
[204] IRC § 507(a)(2).
[205] IRC § 4962(a).

to initial taxes imposed in the context of self-dealing.[206] Where a taxable event is timely corrected, any additional taxes that may have been assessed or paid are abated.[207]

Because of the stringency of these rules, the sanctions are far more than merely taxes, being rather a system of absolute prohibitions.

(a) Self-Dealing

In general, the federal tax law prohibits acts of self-dealing between a private foundation and a disqualified person.[208] An act of self-dealing may be direct or indirect. The latter generally is a self-dealing transaction between a disqualified person and an organization controlled by a private foundation.[209]

The sale or exchange of property between a private foundation and a disqualified person generally constitutes an act of self-dealing.[210] The transfer of real or personal property by a disqualified person to a private foundation is treated as a sale or exchange if the property is subject to a mortgage or similar lien that the foundation assumes or if it is subject to a mortgage or similar lien that a disqualified person placed on the property within the 10-year period ending on the date of transfer.[211]

The leasing of property between a private foundation and a disqualified person generally constitutes self-dealing.[212] However, the leasing of property by a disqualified person to a private foundation without charge is not an act of self-dealing.[213]

The lending of money or other extension of credit between a private foundation and a disqualified person generally constitutes an act of self-dealing.[214] This rule does not apply to an extension of credit by a disqualified person to a private foundation if the transaction is without interest or other charge and the proceeds of the loan are used exclusively for charitable purposes.[215]

The furnishing of goods, services, or facilities between a private foundation and a disqualified person generally constitutes an act of self-dealing.[216] However, the furnishing of goods, services, or facilities by a disqualified person to a private foundation is not an act of self-dealing if they are furnished without charge and used exclusively for charitable purposes.[217] The furnishing of goods, services, or facilities by a private foundation to a disqualified person is not self-dealing if the furnishing is made on a basis no more favorable than

---

[206] IRC § 4962(b).
[207] IRC § 4961.
[208] IRC § 4941.
[209] Reg. § 53.4941(d)-1(b).
[210] IRC § 4941(d)(1)(A); Reg. § 53.4941(d)-2(a)(1). E.g., Rev. Rul. 76-18, 1976-1 C.B. 355.
[211] IRC § 4941(d)(2)(A); Reg. § 53.4941(d)-2(a)(2).
[212] IRC § 4941(d)(1)(A); Reg. § 53.4941(d)-2(b)(1).
[213] Reg. § 53.4941(d)-2(b)(2).
[214] IRC § 4941(d)(1)(B): Reg. § 53.4941(d)-2(c)(1).
[215] IRC § 4941(d)(2)(B); Reg. § 53.4941(d)-2(c)(2).
[216] IRC § 4941(d)(1)(C); Reg. § 53.4941(d)-2(d)(1).
[217] IRC § 4941(d)(2)(C); Reg. § 53.4941(d)-2(d)(3).

that on which the goods, services, or facilities are made available to the general public.[218]

The payment of compensation (or payment or reimbursement of expenses) by a private foundation to a disqualified person generally constitutes an act of self-dealing.[219] However, except in the case of a governmental official, the payment of compensation (or payment or reimbursement of expenses) by a private foundation to a disqualified person for the performance of personal services that are reasonable and necessary to carrying out the charitable purpose of the foundation is not self-dealing if the compensation (or payment or reimbursement) is not excessive.[220]

The transfer to, or use by or for the benefit of, a disqualified person of the income or assets of a private foundation generally constitutes self-dealing.[221] Unlike the other sets of rules describing specific categories of acts of self-dealing, this one is a catch-all provision designed to sweep into the ambit of self-dealing a variety of transactions that might otherwise technically escape the discrete transactions defined to be self-dealing ones. However, the fact that a disqualified person receives an incidental or tenuous benefit from the use by a private foundation of its income or assets will not, by itself, make the use an act of self-dealing.[222]

An agreement by a private foundation to make a payment of money or other property to a government official generally constitutes self-dealing, unless the agreement is to employ the individual for a period after termination of his or her government service if he or she is terminating service within a 90-day period.[223] In the case of a government official, the self-dealing rules do not apply to the receipt of certain prizes and awards, scholarship and fellowship grants, annuities, gifts, and traveling expenses.[224]

There are several other exceptions to the self-dealing rules, one of which holds that a transaction between a private foundation and a corporation that is a disqualified person with respect to the foundation is not an act of self-dealing if the transaction is engaged in pursuant to a liquidation, merger, redemption, recapitalization, or other corporate adjustment, organization, or reorganization.[225] For this exception to apply, all the securities of the same class as that held by the foundation prior to the transfer must be subject to the same terms and these terms must provide for receipt by the foundation of no less than fair market value.[226]

---

[218] IRC § 4941(d)(2)(D); Reg. § 53.4941(d)-3(b).
[219] IRC § 4941(d)(1)(D); Reg. § 53.4941(d)-2(e).
[220] IRC § 4941(d)(2)(E); Reg. § 53.4941(d)-3(c).
[221] IRC § 4941(d)(1)(E); Reg. § 53.4941(d)-2(f)(1). There are special rules concerning indemnification and the purchase of insurance by private foundations for the benefit of foundation managers (Reg. § 53.4941(d)-2(f)(3)–53.4941(d)-2(8)(9)).
[222] Reg. § 53.4941(d)-2(f)(2).
[223] IRC § 4941(d)(1)(F); Reg. § 53.4941(d)-2(g).
[224] IRC § 4941(d)(2)(G); Reg. § 53.4941(d)-3(e).
[225] IRC § 4941(d)(2)(F); Reg. § 53.4941(d)-3(d).
[226] Reg. § 53.4941(d)-3(d)(1).

An act of self-dealing *occurs* on the date on which all of the terms and conditions of the transaction and the liabilities of the parties have been fixed.[227] The *amount involved* generally is the greater of the amount of money and the fair market value of the other property given or the amount of money and the fair market value of the other property received.[228] *Correction* of an act of self-dealing means undoing the transaction that constituted the act to the extent possible, but in no case may the resulting financial position of the private foundation be worse than would be the case if the disqualified person was dealing under the highest fiduciary standards.[229]

An initial tax is imposed on each act of self-dealing between a disqualified person and a private foundation; the tax is imposed on the self-dealer at a rate of 5 percent of the amount involved with respect to the act for each year in the taxable period or part of a period.[230] Where this initial tax is imposed, a tax of $2\frac{1}{2}$ percent of the amount involved is imposed on the participation of any foundation manager in the act of self-dealing, where the manager knowingly participated in the act.[231] However, this tax is not imposed where the participation is not willful and is due to reasonable cause.[232] This tax, which must be paid by the foundation manager, may not exceed $10,000.[233]

Where an initial tax is imposed and the self-dealing act is not timely corrected, an additional tax is imposed in an amount equal to 200 percent of the amount involved; this tax must be paid by the disqualified person (other than a foundation manager) who participated in the act of self-dealing.[234] An additional tax equal to 50 percent of the amount involved, up to $10,000,[235] is imposed on a foundation manager (where the additional tax is imposed on the self-dealer) who refuses to agree to all or part of the correction.[236]

In a case where more than one person is liable for any initial or additional tax with respect to any one act of self-dealing, all of the persons are jointly and severally liable for the tax or taxes.[237]

Willful repeated violations of these rules will result in involuntary termination of the private foundation's status and the imposition of additional taxes.[238] The termination tax thus serves as a third-tier tax.

---

[227] Reg. § 53.4941(e)-1(a)(2).

[228] IRC § 4941(e)(2); Reg. § 53.4941(e)-1(b)(1).

[229] IRC § 4941 (e) (3); Reg. § 53.4941(e)-1(c).

[230] IRC § 4941(a)(1); Reg. § 53.4941(a)-1(a)(1). The *taxable period* is the period beginning with the date on which the transaction occurred and ending on the earliest of the date of mailing of a notice of deficiency with respect to the initial tax, the date on which the initial tax is assessed, or the date on which correction of the transaction is completed (IRC § 4941(e)(1); Reg. § 53.4941(e)-1(a)).

[231] IRC § 4941(a)(2); Reg. § 53.4941(a)-1(b).

[232] *Id.*

[233] IRC § 4941(c)(2); Reg. § 53.4941(c)-1(b).

[234] IRC § 4941(b)(1); Reg. § 53.4941(b)-1(a).

[235] IRC § 4941(c)(2); Reg. § 53.4941(c)-1(b).

[236] IRC § 4941(b)(2); Reg. § 53.4941(b)-1(b).

[237] IRC § 4941(c)(1); Reg. § 53.4941(c)-1(a).

[238] IRC § 507(a)(2).

(b) Mandatory Distributions

A private foundation is required to distribute, for each year, at least a minimum amount of money and/or property for charitable purposes.[239] The amount that must annually be distributed by a private foundation is the *distributable amount*.[240] That amount must be in the form of *qualifying distributions*, which essentially are grants, outlays for administration, and payments made to acquire charitable assets.[241] Generally, the distributable amount for a private foundation is an amount equal to 5 percent of the value of the noncharitable assets of the foundation;[242] this is the *minimum investment return*.[243] The distributable amount also includes amounts equal to repayments to a foundation of items previously treated as qualifying distributions (such as scholarship loans), amounts received on disposition of assets previously treated as qualifying distributions, and amounts previously set aside for a charitable project but not so used.[244]

The charitable assets of a private foundation are those actually used by the foundation in carrying out its charitable objectives or assets owned by the foundation where it has convinced the IRS that its immediate use for exempt purposes is not practical and that definite plans exist to commence a related use within a reasonable period.[245] Thus, the assets that are in the minimum investment return base are those held for the production of income or for investment (such as stocks, bonds, interest-bearing notes, endowment funds, and leased real estate).[246] Where property is used for both exempt and other purposes, it is considered to be used exclusively for tax-exempt purposes where the exempt use represents at least 95 percent of the total use; otherwise, a reasonable allocation between the two uses is required.[247]

An exception to the timing of distributions by a private foundation for mandatory payout purposes is the *set-aside*, where funds are credited for a charitable purpose, rather than immediately granted; where the requirements are met, the set aside is regarded as a qualifying distribution.[248] One type of set aside is that referenced in the *suitability test*; this requires a specific project, a payment period not to exceed 60 months, and a ruling from the IRS.[249] The other type of set aside is that of the *cash distribution test*; this test entails set per-

---

[239] IRC § 4942.

[240] IRC § 4942(d).

[241] IRC § 4942(g)(1); Reg. §§ 53.4942(a)-3(a), 53.4942(a)-3(c).

[242] Reg. §§ 53.4942(a)-2(c)(1), 53.4942(a)-2(c)(5). A private foundation is required to ascertain the aggregate fair market value of its assets, although those used or held for use for charitable purposes are not considered when determining its minimum investment return (IRC § 4942(e)(1)(A)).

[243] IRC §§ 4942(d)(1), 4942(e)(1)(A); Reg. § 53.4942(a)-2(b)(1). The minimum investment return is reduced by any acquisition indebtedness (see § 29.3) with respect to the assets (IRC § 4942(e)(1)(B)).

[244] IRC §§ 4942(d)(1), 4942(f)(2)(C).

[245] Reg. § 53.4942(a)-2(c)(3). These assets include interests in a functionally related business (see the text accompanied by *infra* notes 262–263) and in a program-related investment (see the text accompanied by *infra* notes 277–278).

[246] IRC § 4942(e)(1)(A).

[247] Reg. § 53.4942(a)-2(c)(3).

[248] Reg. § 53.4942(a)-3(b)(1).

[249] Reg. §§ 53.4942(a)-3(b)(2), 53.4942(a)-3(b)(7)(i).

centages of distributions over a multi-year period and does not require an IRS ruling.[250]

An initial tax of 15 percent is imposed on the undistributed income of a private foundation for any year that has not been distributed on a timely basis in the form of qualifying distributions.[251] In a case in which an initial tax is imposed on the undistributed income of a private foundation for a year, an additional tax is imposed on any portion of the income remaining undistributed at the close of the taxable period.[252] This tax is equal to 100 percent of the amount remaining undistributed at the close of the period.[253]

Payment of these taxes is required in addition to, rather than in lieu of, making the required distributions.[254]

The termination taxes[255] serve as third-tier taxes.

(c) Excess Business Holdings

Private foundations are limited as to the extent to which they can own interests in commercial business enterprises.[256] A private foundation and all disqualified persons with respect to it generally are permitted to hold no more than 20 percent of a corporation's voting stock or other interest in a business enterprise; these are *permitted holdings*.[257] If effective control of the business can be shown to be elsewhere, a 35-percent limit may be substituted for the 20 percent limit.[258] A private foundation must hold, directly or indirectly, more than 2 percent of the value of a business enterprise before these limitations become applicable.[259]

There are three principal exceptions to these rules. One is for a business at least 95 percent of the gross income of which is derived from passive sources.[260] These sources generally include dividends, interest, annuities, royalties, and capital gain.[261] The second exception is for holdings in a *functionally related business*.[262] This is a business that is substantially related to the achievement of the foundation's exempt purposes (other than merely providing funds for the foundation's programs); in which substantially all the work is performed for the private foundation without compensation; that is carried on by

---

[250] IRC § 4942(g)(2); Reg. § 53.4942(a)-3(b)(3)–53.4942(a)-3(b)(6)(7)(ii).

[251] IRC § 4942(a); Reg. § 53.4942(a)-1(a)(1).

[252] IRC § 4942(b); Reg. § 53.4942(a)-1(a)(2). The *taxable period* is the period beginning with the first day of the year involved and ending on the date of mailing of a notice of deficiency with respect to the initial tax or the date on which the initial tax is assessed (IRC § 4942(j)(1); Reg. § 53.4942(a)-1(c)(1)).

[253] IRC § 4942(b); Reg. § 53.4942(a)-1(a)(2).

[254] Reg. § 53.4942(a)-1(a)(3).

[255] IRC § 507(a)(2).

[256] IRC § 4943.

[257] IRC §§ 4943(c)(2)(A), 4943(c)(3); Reg. §§ 53.4943-1, 53.4943-3(b)(1), 53.4943-3(b)(2), 53.4943-3(b)(3)(c).

[258] IRC § 4943(c)(2)(B); Reg. § 53.4943-3(b)(3).

[259] IRC § 4943(c)(2)(C); Reg. § 53.4943-3(b)(4).

[260] IRC § 4943(d)(3)(B).

[261] Reg. § 53.4943-10(c).

[262] IRC §§ 4943(d)(3)(A).

a private foundation primarily for the convenience of its employees; that consists of the selling of merchandise, substantially all of which was received by the foundation as contributions; or that is carried on within a larger aggregate of similar activities or within a larger complex of other endeavors that is related to the exempt purposes of the foundation.[263] The third exception is for program-related investments.[264]

If a private foundation obtains holdings in a business enterprise, in a transaction that is not a purchase by the foundation or by disqualified persons with respect to it, and the additional holdings would result in the foundation having an excess business holding, the foundation has five years to reduce the holdings to a permissible level without penalty.[265] The IRS has the authority to allow an additional five-year period for the disposition of excess business holdings in the case of an unusually large gift or bequest of diverse business holdings or holdings with complex corporate structures.[266] This latter rule entails several requirements, including a showing that diligent efforts were made to dispose of the holdings within the initial five-year period and that disposition within that five-year period was not possible (except at a price substantially below fair market value) by reason of the size and complexity or diversity of the holdings.

An initial excise tax is imposed on the excess business holdings of a private foundation in a business enterprise for each tax year that ends during the taxable period.[267] The amount of this tax is 5 percent of the total value of all of the private foundation's excess business holdings in each of its business enterprises.[268]

If the excess business holdings are not disposed of during the period, an additional tax is imposed on the private foundation; the amount of this tax is 200 percent of the value of the excess business holdings.[269]

The termination taxes[270] serve as third-tier taxes.

(d) Jeopardizing Investments

There are rules governing the type of investments that a private foundation is allowed to make.[271] In general, a private foundation cannot invest any amount—income or principal—in a manner that would jeopardize the carrying

---

[263] IRC § 4942(j)(4), Reg. § 53.4943-10 (b).

[264] Reg. § 53.4943-10(b) (see the text accompanied by *infra* notes 277–278).

[265] IRC § 4943(c)(6); Reg. § 53.4943-6(a).

[266] IRC § 4943(c)(7).

[267] IRC §§ 4943(a)(1); Reg. § 53.4943-2(a)(1). The *taxable period* is the period beginning on the first day on which there are excess business holdings and ending on the earlier of the date of mailing of a notice of deficiency with respect to the initial tax or the date on which the initial tax is assessed (IRC § 4943(d)(2); Reg. § 53.4943-9(a)(1)).

[268] IRC § 4943(a)(1); Reg. § 53.4943-2(a)(1).

[269] IRC § 4943 (b); Reg. § 53.4943-2(b).

[270] IRC § 507(a)(2).

[271] IRC § 4944.

out of any of its tax-exempt purposes.[272] An investment is considered to jeopardize the carrying out of the exempt purposes of a private foundation if it is determined that the foundation managers, in making the investment, failed to exercise ordinary business care and prudence, under the facts and circumstances prevailing at the time of the investment, in providing for the long-term and short-term financial needs of the foundation in carrying out its charitable activities.[273]

A determination as to whether the making of a particular investment jeopardizes the exempt purposes of a private foundation is made on an investment-by-investment basis, in each case taking into account the private foundation's portfolio as a whole.[274] Although the IRS will not rule as to an investment procedure governing investments to be made in the future, it will rule as to a currently proposed investment.[275]

No category of investments is treated as a per se violation of these rules. However, the types or methods of investment that are closely scrutinized to determine whether the foundation managers have met the requisite standard of care and prudence include trading in securities on margin, trading in commodity futures, investments in oil and gas syndications, the purchase of puts and calls (and straddles), the purchase of warrants, and selling short.[276]

A *program-related investment* is not a jeopardizing investment. This is an investment the primary purpose of which is to accomplish one or more charitable purposes and no significant purpose of which is the production of income or the appreciation of property.[277] No purpose of the investment may be the furthering of substantial legislative or political campaign activities.[278]

If a private foundation invests an amount in a manner as to jeopardize the carrying out of any of its charitable purposes, an initial tax is imposed on the foundation on the making of the investment, at the rate of 5 percent of the amount so invested for each year or part of a year in the taxable period.[279]

In any case in which this initial tax is imposed, a tax is imposed on the participation of any foundation manager making an investment in the knowledge that it jeopardizes the carrying out of any of the foundation's exempt purposes; the tax is equal to 5 percent of the amount so invested for each year of the foundation (or part of the year) in the period.[280] With respect to any one investment,

---

[272] IRC § 4944(a)(1).

[273] Reg. § 53.4944-1(a)(2)(i).

[274] *Id.*

[275] E.g., Priv. Ltr. Rul. 9451067.

[276] Reg. § 53.4944-1(a)(2)(i).

[277] IRC § 4944(c); Reg. § 53.4944-3(a).

[278] Reg. § 53.4944-3(a)(1)(iii).

[279] IRC § 4944(a)(1); Reg. § 53.4944-1(a)(1). The *taxable period* is the period beginning with the date of the jeopardizing investment and ending on the earliest of the date of mailing of a notice of deficiency with respect to the initial tax, the date on which the initial tax is assessed, or the date on which the amount invested is removed from jeopardy (as defined in IRC § 4944(e)(2); Reg. § 53.4944-5(b)) (IRC § 4944(e)(1); Reg. § 53.4944-5(a)).

[280] IRC § 4944(a)(2); Reg. § 53.4944-1(b)(1).

the maximum amount of this tax is $5,000.[281] This tax, which must be paid by any participating foundation manager, is not imposed where the participation was not willful and was due to reasonable cause.[282]

An additional tax is imposed in any case in which this initial tax is imposed and the investment is not removed from jeopardy within the period; this tax, which is to be paid by the private foundation, is at the rate of 25 percent of the amount of the investment.[283] In any case in which this additional tax is imposed and a foundation manager has refused to agree to all or part of the removal of the investment from jeopardy, a tax is imposed at the rate of 5 percent of the amount of the investment.[284] With respect to any one investment, the maximum amount of this tax is $10,000.[285]

Where more than one foundation manager is liable for an initial tax or an additional tax with respect to a jeopardizing investment, all of the managers are jointly and severally liable for the taxes.[286]

The termination taxes[287] serve as third-tier taxes.

(e) Taxable Expenditures

The federal tax law provides restrictions, in addition to those discussed above, on the activities and purposes for which private foundations may expend their funds.[288] These rules pertain to matters such as legislative activities, electioneering, grants to individuals, and grants to noncharitable organizations. Improper and, in effect, prohibited expenditures are termed *taxable expenditures*.

One form of taxable expenditure is an amount paid or incurred by a private foundation to carry on propaganda or otherwise attempt to influence legislation.[289] Thus, the general rule, by which charitable organizations can engage in a certain amount of legislative activity,[290] is inapplicable to private foundations.

Attempts to influence legislation generally include certain communications with a member or employee of a legislative body or with an official or employee of an executive department of a government who may participate in formulating legislation or efforts to affect the opinion of the general public or a segment of it.[291] An expenditure is an attempt to influence legislation if it is for a *direct lobbying communication* or a *grass roots lobbying communication*.[292]

---

[281] IRC § 4944(d)(2); Reg. § 53.4944-4(b).
[282] IRC § 4944(a)(2); Reg. § 53.4944-1(b)(1).
[283] IRC § 4944(b)(1); Reg. § 53.4944-2(a).
[284] IRC § 4944(b)(2); Reg. § 53.4944-2(b).
[285] IRC § 4944(d)(2); Reg. § 53.4944-4(b).
[286] IRC § 4944(d)(1); Reg. § 53.4944-4(a).
[287] IRC § 507(a)(2).
[288] IRC § 4945.
[289] IRC § 4945(d)(1).
[290] See Chapter 20.
[291] IRC § 4945(e).
[292] Reg. § 53.4945-2(a)(1).

Engaging in nonpartisan analysis, study, or research and making the results of this type of an undertaking available to the general public (or a segment of it) or to governmental bodies or officials is not a prohibited form of legislative activity.[293] Likewise, amounts paid or incurred in connection with the provision of technical advice or assistance to a governmental body or committee (or other subdivision of it) in response to a written request from the entity do not constitute taxable expenditures.[294] Another exception is that the taxable expenditures rules do not apply to any amount paid or incurred in connection with an appearance before or communication to a legislative body with respect to a possible decision of that body which might affect the existence of the private foundation, its powers and duties, its tax-exempt status, or the deductibility of contributions to the foundation.[295] Expenditures for examinations and discussions of broad social, economic, and similar issues are not taxable even if the problems are of the types with which government would be expected to deal ultimately.[296]

The term *taxable expenditure* includes an amount paid or incurred by a private foundation to influence the outcome of a specific public election or to conduct, directly or indirectly, a voter registration drive.[297] The first of these prohibitions generally parallels the prohibition on political campaign activities by all charitable organizations.[298] However, a private foundation may engage in electioneering activities (including voter registration drives) without making a taxable expenditure, where a variety of criteria are satisfied, such as not confining the activity to one election period and carrying it on in at least five states.[299]

The term *taxable expenditure* includes an amount paid or incurred by a private foundation as a grant to an individual for travel, study, or other similar purposes.[300] However, this type of grant is not prohibited if it is awarded on an objective and nondiscriminatory basis pursuant to a procedure approved in advance by the IRS and the IRS is satisfied that the grant is one of three specified types: (1) a scholarship or fellowship grant that is excludable from the recipient's gross income and used for study at an educational institution; (2) a prize or award that is excludable from the recipient's gross income, where the recipient is selected from the general public; or (3) a grant the purpose of which is to achieve a specific objective, produce a report or similar product, or improve or enhance a literary, artistic, musical, scientific, teaching, or other similar capacity, skill, or talent of the grantee.[301]

The requirement as to objectivity and nondiscrimination generally requires

---

[293] IRC § 4945(e); Reg. § 53.4945-2(d)(1).
[294] IRC § 4945(e)(2); Reg. § 53.4945-2(d)(2).
[295] IRC § 4945(e) (last sentence); Reg. § 53.4945-2(d)(3).
[296] Reg. § 53.4945-2(d)(4).
[297] IRC § 4945(d)(2); Reg. § 53.4945-3(a)(1).
[298] Reg. § 53.4945-3(a)(2). See Chapter 21.
[299] IRC § 4945(f); Reg. § 53.4945-3(b).
[300] IRC § 4945(d)(3); Reg. § 53.4945-4(a)(1), 53.4945-4(a)(2).
[301] IRC § 4945 (g); Reg. § 53.4945-4(a)(3)(ii).

that the group from which grantees are selected be chosen on the basis of criteria reasonably related to the purposes of the grant. The group must be sufficiently broad so that the making of grants to members of the group would be considered to fulfill a charitable purpose.[302] The individual or group of individuals who select grant recipients should not be in a position to derive a private benefit as the result of the selection process.[303]

These rules as to individual grants generally require (1) the receipt by a private foundation of an annual report from the beneficiary of a scholarship or fellowship;[304] (2) that a foundation investigate situations indicating that all or a part of a grant is not being used in furtherance of its purposes;[305] and (3) recovery or restoration of any diverted funds, and withholding of further payments to a grantee in an instance of improper diversion of grant funds.[306] A private foundation must maintain certain records pertaining to grants to individuals.[307]

A private foundation may make grants to an organization that is not a public charity;[308] however, when it does so it must exercise *expenditure responsibility* with respect to the grant.[309] A private foundation is considered to be exercising expenditure responsibility in connection with a grant as long as it exerts all reasonable efforts and establishes adequate procedures to see that the grant is spent solely for the purpose for which it was made, obtain full and complete reports from the grantee on how the funds are spent, and make full and detailed reports with respect to the expenditures to the IRS.[310]

The term *taxable expenditure* includes an amount paid or incurred by a private foundation for a *noncharitable* purpose.[311] Ordinarily, only an expenditure for an activity that, if it were a substantial part of the organization's total activities, would cause loss of tax exemption is a taxable expenditure.[312]

Expenditures ordinarily not treated as taxable expenditures under these rules are (1) expenditures to acquire investments entered into for the purpose of obtaining income or funds to be used in furtherance of charitable purposes, (2) reasonable expenses with respect to investments, (3) payment of taxes, (4) any expenses that qualify as deductions in the computation of unrelated business income tax,[313] (5) any payment that constitutes a qualifying distribution[314]

---

[302] Reg. § 53.4945-4(b)(2).
[303] Reg. § 53.4945-4(b)(4).
[304] Reg. §§ 53.4945-4(c)(2), 53.4945-4(c)(3).
[305] Reg. § 53.4945-4(c)(4).
[306] Reg. § 53.4945-4(c)(5).
[307] Reg. § 53.4945-4(c)(6).
[308] See *supra* § 3.
[309] IRC § 4945(d)(4); Reg. § 53.4945-5(a). For this purpose, exempt operating foundations (see *supra* § 1(c)) are regarded the same as public charities.
[310] IRC § 4945(h); Reg. §§ 53.4945-5(b)–53.4945-5(d).
[311] IRC § 4945(d)(5).
[312] Reg. § 53.4945-6(a).
[313] See § 28.2.
[314] IRC § 4942(g). See *supra* § 4(b).

or an allowable deduction pursuant to the investment income tax rules,[315] (6) reasonable expenditures to evaluate, acquire, modify, and dispose of program-related investments,[316] or (7) business expenditures by the recipient of a program-related investment. Conversely, expenditures for unreasonable administrative expenses, including compensation, consultants' fees, and other fees for services rendered, are ordinarily taxable expenditures, unless the private foundation can demonstrate that the expenses were paid or incurred in the good faith belief that they were reasonable and that the payment or incurrence of the expenses in amounts was consistent with ordinary business care and prudence.[317]

An excise tax is imposed on each taxable expenditure of a private foundation, which is to be paid by the private foundation at the rate of 10 percent of the amount on each taxable expenditure.[318] An excise tax is imposed on the agreement of any foundation manager to the making of a taxable expenditure by a private foundation.[319] This latter initial tax is imposed only where the private foundation initial tax is imposed, the manager knows that the expenditure to which he or she agreed was a taxable one, and the agreement is not willful and not due to reasonable cause. This initial tax, which is at the rate of $2\frac{1}{2}$ percent of each taxable expenditure, must be paid by the foundation manager.[320]

An excise tax is imposed in any case in which an initial tax is imposed on a private foundation because of a taxable expenditure and the expenditure is not corrected within the taxable period; this additional tax is to be paid by the private foundation and is at the rate of 100 percent of the amount of each taxable expenditure.[321] An excise tax in any case in which an initial tax has been levied is imposed on a foundation manager because of a taxable expenditure and the foundation manager has refused to agree to part or all of the correction of the expenditure; this additional tax, which is at the rate of 50 percent of the amount of the taxable expenditure, is to be paid by the foundation manager.[322]

Where more than one foundation manager is liable for an excise tax with respect to the making of a taxable expenditure, all the foundation managers are jointly and severally liable for the tax.[323] The maximum aggregate amount collectible as an initial tax from all foundation managers with respect to any one taxable expenditure is $5,000 and the maximum aggregate amount so collectible as an additional tax is $10,000.[324]

---

[315] IRC § 4940.
[316] See *supra* § 4(d).
[317] Reg. § 53.4945-6(b).
[318] IRC § 4945(a)(1); Reg. § 53.4945-1(a)(1).
[319] IRC § 4945(a)(2).
[320] Reg. § 53.4945-1(a)(2).
[321] IRC §§ 4945(b)(1), 4945(i); Reg. 53.4945-1(b)(1). The *taxable period* begins with the event giving rise to the expenditure tax and ends on the earlier of the date a notice of deficiency with respect to the first-tier tax is mailed or the date the first-tier tax is assessed if there has not been a mailing of a deficiency notice (IRC § 4945(i)(2); Reg. § 53.4945-1(e)(1)).
[322] IRC § 4945(b)(2); Reg. § 53.4945-1(b)(2).
[323] IRC § 4545(c)(1); Reg. § 53.4945-1(c)(1).
[324] IRC § 4545(c)(2); Reg. § 53.4945-1(c)(2).

The second-tier excise taxes will be imposed at the end of the *taxable period*, which begins with the event giving rise to the expenditure tax and ends on the earlier of (1) the date a notice of deficiency with respect to the first-tier tax is mailed or (2) the date the first-tier tax is assessed if no deficiency notice is mailed.[325]

The termination taxes[326] serve as third-tier taxes.

(f) Other Provisions

An excise tax of 2 percent is generally imposed on the net investment income of private foundations for each tax year.[327] This tax must be estimated and paid quarterly, generally following the estimated tax rules for corporations.[328] Under certain circumstances, this tax rate is reduced to one percent in a year where the foundation's payout for charitable purposes is increased by an equivalent amount.[329] Exempt operating foundations[330] are exempt from this tax on investment income.[331]

As to certain of the private foundation rules, non-exempt charitable trusts[332] and split-interest trusts[333] are treated as private foundations.[334] A 4 percent tax is imposed on the gross investment income derived from sources within the United States by foreign organizations that constitute private foundations.[335]

§ 11.5 CONSEQUENCES OF PRIVATE FOUNDATION STATUS

Because there are no advantages to a charitable organization in classification of it as a private foundation, these organizations almost always attempt (when they can) to become characterized as a public charity.[336] The disadvantages are several, and the importance of any of them largely depends upon the circumstances of the particular charitable organization.

The disadvantages to private foundation status include (1) the obligation of payment of a tax on net investment income;[337] (2) probable inability of the organization to be funded by private foundations, because of the requirement that such grants be the subject of expenditure responsibility;[338] (3) a lesser degree of de-

---

[325] IRC § 4945(i)(2); Reg. § 53.4945-1(e)(1).

[326] IRC § 507(a)(2).

[327] IRC § 4940(a), Reg. § 53.4940-1(a).

[328] IRC § 6655.

[329] IRC § 4940(e)(1).

[330] See *supra* § 1(c).

[331] IRC § 4940(d)(1).

[332] That is, entities described in IRC § 4947(a)(1).

[333] That is, entities described in IRC § 4947(a)(2), including charitable remainder trusts (IRC § 664) and pooled income funds (IRC § 642(c)(5)).

[334] IRC § 4947.

[335] IRC § 4948.

[336] The various ways in which public charity status can be achieved are described in *supra* § 3.

[337] IRC § 4940.

[338] *Supra* § 4(e).

ductibility of charitable contributions to the organization;[339] (4) the fact that the charitable deduction for a gift of appreciated property to a private foundation generally is confined to its basis rather than the full fair market value of the property;[340] (5) requirement of compliance with a broad range of onerous rules and limitations as to programs and investment policy;[341] and (6) more extensive record-keeping and annual reporting requirements.[342]

It may be asserted that the ability of a small number of individuals to preside over an aggregation of investment assets and "privately" determine how to apply the income from the assets for charitable purposes is an "advantage." However, the same opportunities can be available for a charitable entity that is regarded by the federal tax law as a public charity.

---

[339] See § 2.5.
[340] *Id.,*
[341] See *supra* § 4.
[342] See § 24.3.

PART THREE

Noncharitable Tax-Exempt Organizations

CHAPTER TWELVE

Social Welfare Organizations

The federal tax law provides tax exemption for "[c]ivic leagues or organizations not organized for profit but operated exclusively for the promotion of social welfare . . ."[1]

The reference to organizations operated for the promotion of *social welfare* is both somewhat confusing and outdated. It is confusing because of the considerable similarity between these entities and those that are *charitable* in nature; *promotion of social welfare* is one of the definitions of a tax-exempt charitable organization.[2] It is outmoded in the sense that the principal type of organization that is tax-exempt by reason of this category of exemption is one that is advocacy-oriented—in the sense of focus on community, state, and/or national policymaking, including lobbying—rather than one that is generally functioning to promote some vague form of social betterment.

§ 12.1 CONCEPT OF *SOCIAL WELFARE*

(a) General Rules

There is no precise definition of the term *social welfare* for federal law tax exemption purposes. The regulations amplifying the law concerning this category of tax-exempt organization offer two basic precepts: (1) "Social welfare" is commensurate with the "common good and general welfare" and "civic betterments and social improvements,"[3] and (2) the promotion of social welfare does not include activities that primarily constitute "carrying on a business with the general public in a manner similar to organizations which are operated for profit."[4] The regula-

---

[1] IRC § 501(c)(4); Reg. § 1.501(c)(4)-1(a)(1).

[2] See §§ 6.6, 12.4.

[3] Reg. § 1.501(c)(4)-1(a)(2)(i).

[4] Reg. § 1.501(c)(4)-1(a)(2)(ii). E.g., *Industrial Addition Ass'n v. Comm'r*, 149 F.2d 294 (6th Cir. 1945); *Club Gaona, Inc. v. United States*, 167 F. Supp. 741 (S.D. Cal. 1958); *Harvey v. Campbell*, 107 F. Supp. 757 (N.D. Tex. 1952); *Interneighborhood Hous. Corp. v. Comm'r*, 45 T.C.M. 115 (1982).

tions also contain a prohibition on political campaign activity[5] and state that an organization is not operated primarily for the promotion of social welfare "if its primary activity is operating a social club for the benefit, pleasure, or recreation of its members."[6] However, the conduct of social functions for the benefit of its members will not defeat social welfare status for an organization, where these activities are something less than primary,[7] or are otherwise incidental to a primary function.[8]

Like all tax-exempt organizations, the social welfare organization, to be operated *exclusively* for the promotion of social welfare, must be operated *primarily* for that purpose.[9] The key principle in this area is that, to qualify as a tax-exempt social welfare organization, the activities of the organization must be those that will benefit the community as a whole, rather than merely benefit the organization's membership or other select group of individuals or organizations.[10] Thus, an organization that restricted its membership to individuals of good moral character and health belonging to a particular ethnic group residing in a geographical area and that provided sick benefits to members and death benefits to their beneficiaries was ruled to not be tax-exempt as a social welfare organization, as it was essentially a mutual, self-interest type of organization.[11] Likewise, an individual practice association was denied categorization as a tax-exempt social welfare organization because its primary beneficiaries were its member-physicians, in that it provided an available pool of physicians who abided by its fee schedule when rendering medical services to the subscribers of a health maintenance organization and provided its members with access to a large group of patients (the subscribers) who generally may not be referred to nonmember-physicians.[12]

As an additional example, a nonprofit organization, incorporated for the purpose of furnishing television reception to its members on a cooperative basis in an area not adaptable to ordinary reception, where the members contracted for services and the payment of installment fees, was deemed to not be a tax-exempt social welfare organization because it was "operate[d] for the benefit of its members rather than for the promotion of the welfare of mankind."[13] Yet, a similar organization, which obtained memberships and contributions on a voluntary basis, was found to be a tax-social welfare organization, since it "operate[d] its system for the benefit of all television owners in the community."[14]

---

[5] See § 21.4.

[6] Reg. § 1.501(c)(4)-1(a)(2)(ii). There is a separate category of tax exemption for social clubs (see Chapter 14), which can encompass entities that do not qualify as social welfare organizations (e.g., Ye Mystic Krewe of Gasparilla v. Comm'r, 80 T.C. 755 (1983); Polish Am. Club v. Comm'r, 33 T.C.M. 925 (1974)).

[7] Rev. Rul. 66-179, 1966-1 C.B. 139; Rev. Rul. 63-190, 1963-2 C.B. 212.

[8] Rev. Rul. 74-361, 1974-2 C.B. 159. Also Rev. Rul. 68-224, 1968-1 C.B. 262 (annual festival); Priv. Ltr. Rul. 9220010 (recreational activities).

[9] See § 4.4.

[10] Reg. § 1.501(c)(4)-1(a)(2)(i).

[11] Rev. Rul. 75-199, 1975-1 C.B. 160, *mod'g* Rev. Rul. 55-495, 1955-2 C.B. 259.

[12] Rev. Rul. 86-98, 1986-2 C.B. 74.

[13] Rev. Rul. 54-394, 1954-2 C.B. 131. Also Rev. Rul. 55-716, 1955-2 C.B. 263, *mod. by* Rev. Rul. 83-170, 1983-2 C.B. 97.

[14] Rev. Rul. 62-167, 1962-2 C.B. 142.

Similarly, because of the lack of sufficient benefit to the entire community, a trust to provide group life insurance only for members of an association was not considered a tax-exempt social welfare organization.[15] Likewise, a resort operated for a school's faculty and students was held to not be an exempt social welfare organization.[16] In the latter instance, a federal court of appeals wrote that the "exemption granted to social welfare . . . organizations is made in recognition of the benefit which the public derives from their social welfare activities."[17] Conversely, a consumer credit counseling service that assisted families and individuals with financial problems was ruled to qualify as a tax-exempt social welfare organization because its objectives and activities "contribute to the betterment of the community as a whole" by checking the rising incidence of personal bankruptcy in the community.[18] Also, exempt social welfare status was accorded an organization that processed consumer complaints concerning products and services provided by businesses, met with the parties involved to encourage resolution of the problem, and recommended an appropriate solution, and (where the solution was not accepted) informed the parties about the administrative or judicial remedies available to resolve the dispute.[19] Likewise, an organization created to maintain a system for the storage and distribution of water to raise the underground water level in a community was ruled a tax-exempt social welfare organization because of the benefits to those whose wells were thereby supplied.[20]

Organizations that operate in a manner inimical to principles of what constitutes the common good and the general welfare of the people in a community will not, of course, qualify as a tax-exempt social welfare organization. In part for that reason, the IRS denied tax exemption to an antiwar protest organization that urged demonstrators to commit violations of local ordinances and breaches of public order.[21] Said the IRS: "Illegal activities, which violate the minimum standards of acceptable conduct necessary to the preservation of an orderly society, . . . are not a permissible means of promoting social welfare . . ."[22]

Other examples of tax-exempt social welfare organizations include an organization that provided a community with supervised facilities for the teaching of the safe handling and proper care of firearms,[23] encouraged industrial development to relieve unemployment in an economically depressed area,[24] helped to secure accident insurance for the students and employees in a school district,[25] provided bus transportation between a community and the major employment centers in a metropolitan area during rush hours when the regular bus service

---

[15] New York State Ass'n of Real Estate Boards Group Ins. Fund v. Comm'r, 54 T.C. 1325 (1970).

[16] People's Educ. Camp Soc'y, Inc. v. Comm'r, 331 F.2d 923 (2d Cir. 1964), *aff'g* 39 T.C. 756 (1963), *cert. den.*, 379 U.S. 839 (1964).

[17] *Id*. at 932.

[18] Rev. Rul. 65-299, 1965-2 C.B. 165.

[19] Rev. Rul. 78-50, 1978-1 C.B. 155.

[20] Rev. Rul. 66-148, 1966-1 C.B. 143.

[21] Rev. Rul. 75-384, 1975-2 C.B. 204.

[22] *Id*. at 205.

[23] Rev. Rul. 66-273, 1966-2 C.B. 222.

[24] Rev. Rul. 67-294, 1967-2 C.B. 193.

[25] Rev. Rul. 61-153, 1961-2 C.B. 114. Cf. Rev. Rul. 66-354, 1966-2 C.B. 207.

was inadequate,[26] conducted a community art show for the purpose of encouraging interest in painting, sculpture, and other art forms,[27] provided assistance to low-income farm families in a particular state,[28] conducted a free public radio forum for the dissemination of progressive social views,[29] maintained parking for visitors to a downtown business district,[30] provided low-cost rural electrification,[31] and established and maintained a roller-skating rink for residents of a particular county.[32] Junior chambers of commerce usually qualify as tax-exempt social welfare organizations.[33]

Organizations formed to promote sports frequently are a type of nonprofit organization likely to gain status as tax-exempt social welfare organizations. A corporation formed to initiate programs designed to stimulate the interest of youth in organized sports, by furnishing youths virtually free admission and encouraging their attendance at sporting events, was considered a tax-exempt social welfare organization because it provided "wholesome entertainment for the social improvement and welfare of the youths of the community."[34] Sports organizations can fall short of the requisite criteria in this regard, however, as illustrated by the fate of a nonprofit corporation that was organized to provide facilities for training men and horses for use in emergencies, and obtained qualification as a tax-exempt social welfare organization, only to subsequently lose its tax exemption because it evolved into a commercial riding stable.[35] Said the court: "[T]he few persons eligible to use . . . [the organization's] facilities as members or on any basis other than by paying a regular commercial fee for such use causes . . . [the] operation (no matter how laudable) to be such as not to come within the meaning of 'social welfare.' "[36]

In one instance, a corporation maintained a vacation home for "working girls and women of proper character."[37] All of the trustees were required to be employees of a particular business corporation; the use of the farm's facilities was by invitation only to a select and limited number of women who were predominantly (80 percent) employees of the same business corporation. The government unsuccessfully asserted that the vacation home did not benefit the community as a whole, by virtue of the predominance of the employees of a single business or the invitational process. Indeed, the court concluded that the organization "is an institution which has served a broad community need in the sense that Congress intended, that is, that when one segment or slice of the community, in this case

---

[26] Rev. Rul. 78-69, 1978-1 C.B. 156. Cf. Rev. Rul. 78-68, 1978-1 C.B. 149; Rev. Rul. 55-311, 1955-1 C.B. 72.
[27] Rev. Rul. 78-131, 1978-1 C.B. 156. Cf. § 6.7.
[28] Scofield v. Rio Farms, Inc., 205 F.2d 68 (5th Cir. 1953).
[29] Debs Memorial Radio Fund, Inc. v. Comm'r, 148 F.2d 948 (2d Cir. 1945).
[30] Rev. Rul. 81-116, 1981-1 C.B. 333. Cf. Rev. Rul. 78-86, 1978-1 C.B. 151.
[31] United States v. Pickwick Elec. Membership Corp., 158 F.2d 272 (6th Cir. 1946).
[32] Rev. Rul. 67-109, 1967-1 C.B. 136.
[33] Rev. Rul. 65-195, 1965-2 C.B. 164.
[34] Rev. Rul. 68-118, 1968-1 C.B. 261. Also Rev. Rul. 70-4, 1970-1 C.B. 126; Rev. Rul. 69-384, 1969-2 C.B. 122. As discussed in § 10.2, Congress amended IRC § 501(c)(3) in 1976 to provide tax exemption for organizations the primary purpose of which is to foster national or international sports competition.
[35] Los Angeles County Remount Ass'n v. Comm'r, 27 T.C.M. 1035 (1968).
[36] Id. at 1044. Also Rev. Rul. 55-516, 1955-2 C.B. 260.
[37] Eden Hall Farm v. United States, 389 F. Supp. 858 (W.D. Penn. 1975).

thousands of working women . . ., are [sic] served, then the community as a whole benefits."[38]

(b) Benefits to Members

A related criterion of the tax-exempt social welfare organization is that it must not be operated primarily for the economic benefit or convenience of its members.

Thus, a corporation that purchased and sold unimproved land, invested proceeds received from the sales, and distributed profits to members, was deemed to not be a tax-exempt social welfare organization.[39] Similarly, as noted, an organization formed to manage low- and moderate-income housing property for a fee was ruled to not qualify for tax-exempt social welfare status.[40] Likewise, a federal court of appeals held that a consumer and producer membership cooperative that rebated a percentage of net income to members as patronage dividends made the disbursements "primarily to benefit the taxpayer's membership economically" and not exclusively for promotion of social welfare,[41] and that a membership corporation composed of buyers of ready-to-wear apparel and accessories was not a tax-exempt social welfare organization, since its functions were largely social and many of its activities were designed to enable presently employed members to earn more money.[42] Subsequently, another federal court of appeals denied tax-exempt social welfare status to a mutual assistance association established by a church in furtherance of its "mutual aid" practices, because its practices and policies were found to benefit only its members, rather than the requisite community.[43] Similarly, an association of police officers primarily engaged in providing retirement benefits to members and death benefits to beneficiaries of members was held to not qualify for tax exemption as a social welfare organization because the primary benefits from the organization were limited to its members,[44] although the exemption may be available where this type of an association is established and is maintained by, and where the benefits provided are funded primarily by, a government.[45] Likewise, an individual practice association providing health services through written agreements with health maintenance organizations was ruled to not qualify as a social welare or-

---

[38] *Id.* at 866. The IRS does not follow the *Eden Hall Farm* decision, *supra* note 37, on the ground that an organization providing recreational facilities to the employees of selected corporations cannot qualify as a tax-exempt social welfare organization (Rev. Rul. 80-205, 1980-2 C.B. 184).

[39] Rev. Rul. 69-385, 1969-2 C.B. 123.

[40] Rev. Rul. 70-535, 1970-2 C.B. 117.

[41] Consumer-Farmer Milk Coop. v. Comm'r, 186 F.2d 68, 71 (2d Cir. 1950), *aff'g* 13 T.C. 150 (1949), *cert. den.*, 341 U.S. 931 (1951).

[42] American Women Buyers Club, Inc. v. United States, 338 F.2d 526 (2d Cir. 1964).

[43] Mutual Aid Ass'n of the Church of the Brethren v. United States, 759 F.2d 792 (10th Cir. 1985), *aff'g* 578 F. Supp. 1451 (D. Kan. 1983). Also American Ass'n of Christian Schools Voluntary Employees Beneficiary Ass'n Welfare Plan Trust v. United States, 850 F.2d 1510 (11th Cir. 1988), *aff'g* 663 F. Supp. 275 (M.D. Ala. 1987); El Paso Del Aguila Elderly v. Comm'r, 64 T.C.M. 376 (1992).

[44] Rev. Rul. 81-58, 1981-1 C.B. 331. Also Police Benevolent Ass'n of Richmond, Va. v. United States, 661 F. Supp. 765 (E.D. Va. 1987).

[45] Rev. Rul. 87-126, 1987-2 C.B. 150.

ganization because the primary beneficiaries were its member physicians,[46] and an organization carrying on a business with the general public was found to not qualify as a social welfare entity because it was operated primarily for the benefit of its members.[47]

Many other types of membership service groups have been denied categorization as tax-exempt social welfare organizations, such as an automobile club,[48] an organization that operated a dining room and bar for the exclusive use of its members,[49] and a national sorority controlled by a business corporation that furnished the member chapters with supplies and services.[50] In another instance, an organization formed to purchase groceries for its membership at the lowest possible prices on a cooperative basis was denied tax-exempt social welfare status.[51] The rationale: "The organization . . . is a private cooperative enterprise [operated primarily] for the economic benefit or convenience of the members."[52] Similarly, the IRS denied classification as a tax-exempt social welfare entity to a cooperative organization providing home maintenance services to its members, even though payments for the services were made in kind.[53] In another instance, an organization, the membership of which was limited to persons who owned shares of public utility companies, was ruled to not qualify as an exempt social welfare entity because it was operated to serve private interests, in that it promoted the interests of the public utility industry and its stockholders by preparing and filing statements concerning public utility matters pending before state and federal agencies and legislative bodies, and by publishing a newsletter about matters affecting the stockholders.[54]

However, the rendering of services to members does not necessarily work a denial or loss of tax-exempt social welfare status. For example, a memorial association formed to develop methods of achieving simplicity and dignity in funeral services and to maintain a registry for the wishes of its members in regard to funeral arrangements qualified for tax exemption as a social welfare organization,[55] as did an organization engaged in rehabilitation and job placement of its members.[56] Likewise, an organization that promoted the legal rights of all tenants in a particular community and occasionally initiated litigation to contest the validity of legislation adversely affecting tenants was held to qualify as a tax-exempt social welfare organization because its activities were directed toward benefiting all tenants in the community.[57] By contrast, a tenants' rights group was denied tax-

---

[46] Rev. Rul. 86-98, 1986-2 C.B. 74.
[47] Santa Cruz Bldg. Ass'n v. United States, 411 F. Supp. 871 (D. Mo. 1976).
[48] Smyth v. California State Automobile Ass'n, 175 F.2d 752 (9th Cir. 1949), *cert. den.*, 338 U.S. 905 (1949). Also Automobile Club of St. Paul v. Comm'r, 12 T.C. 1152 (1949).
[49] Rev. Rul. 61-158, 1961-2 C.B. 115.
[50] Rev. Rul. 66-360, 1966-2 C.B. 228.
[51] Rev. Rul. 73-349, 1973-2 C.B. 179.
[52] *Id.* at 180.
[53] Rev. Rul. 78-132, 1978-1 C.B. 157.
[54] Rev. Rul. 80-107, 1980-1 C.B. 117.
[55] Rev. Rul. 64-313, 1964-2 C.B. 146.
[56] Rev. Rul. 57-297, 1957-2 C.B. 307.
[57] Rev. Rul. 80-206, 1980-2 C.B. 185.

exempt social welfare organization status because its activities were directed primarily toward benefiting only tenants who were its members.[58]

Also, qualification as a tax-exempt social welfare entity will not be precluded where an organization's services are equally available to members and non-members. As an illustration of this point, the IRS accorded tax-exempt social welfare classification to an organization formed to prevent oil and other liquid spills in a city port area, and to contain and clean up any spills that occur.[59] The organization's membership included business firms, primarily oil and chemical companies, that stored or shipped liquids in the port area. Because the organization cleaned up spills of both members and nonmembers, the IRS found that it was acting to prevent deterioration of the port community and not merely to prevent damage to the facilities of its members, so that any benefits to its members were incidental. Had the organization confined its repairs to property damaged by its members, the tax exemption would not have been available.[60]

Veterans' organizations frequently qualify as tax-exempt social welfare organizations;[61] however, the IRS has ruled to the contrary.[62] Organizations that have a membership of veterans may qualify as tax-exempt social welfare groups,[63] although tax exemption may also be available under a separate category of tax exemption enacted for the benefit of veterans' groups.[64] A subsidiary organization must establish tax-exempt status on its own rather than on the basis of the functions of the parent veterans' organization.[65]

§ 12.2 THE REQUISITE *COMMUNITY*

As discussed, a social welfare organization may not—if it is to qualify for tax exemption—operate for the benefit of a select group of individuals but must be engaged in the promotion of the common good and general welfare of those in a *community*.[66] It has proved difficult to quantify the meaning of the term *community*, as can be seen, for example, as respects the question of the appropriate tax status of community associations, principally, homeowners' associations. The typical homeowners' association is a nonprofit membership corporation composed of landowners and tenants in a housing development. The association may have been created by the real estate developer or subsequently by the homeown-

---

[58] Rev. Rul. 73-306, 1973-2 C.B. 179.

[59] Rev. Rul. 79-316, 1979-2 C.B. 228.

[60] Contracting Plumbers Coop. Restoration Corp. v. United States, 488 F.2d 684 (2d Cir. 1973), *cert. den.*, 419 U.S. 827 (1974).

[61] Rev. Rul. 66-150, 1966-1 C.B. 147. Cf. Rev. Rul. 58-117, 1958-2 C.B. 196.

[62] Rev. Rul. 68-46, 1968-1 C.B. 260. Also see Veterans Found. v. United States, 281 F.2d 912 (10th Cir. 1960).

[63] Rev. Rul. 68-455, 1968-2 C.B. 215; Rev. Rul. 68-45, 1968-1 C.B. 259; Rev. Rul. 55-156, 1955-1 C.B. 292; Polish Army Veterans Post 147 v. Comm'r, 236 F.2d 509 (3d Cir. 1956), *vac'g and rem'g* 24 T.C. 891 (1956).

[64] IRC § 501(c)(19). See § 18.10.

[65] Rev. Rul. 66-150, *supra* note 61.

[66] Reg. § 1.501(c)(4)-1(a)(2)(i). Also Rev. Rul. 76-147, 1976-1 C.B. 151; Erie Endowment v. United States, 316 F.2d 151 (3d Cir. 1963).

ers themselves. These associations are normally supported by annual assessments or membership dues; membership in these organizations may be voluntary or involuntary. A homeowners' association typically engages in one or more of the following functions: It owns and/or maintains common green areas, streets, and sidewalks for the use of all residents; it administers and enforces covenants for preserving the architecture and general appearance of the development; and/or it participates in the formulation of public policies having an impact on the development, such as the expansion of nearby principal roads, development of nearby lands, or encroachment of commercial enterprises. In this latter capacity, the association is functioning much as a conventional civic league.[67]

The IRS ruled, in relation to an association performing the first two of the above functions, that the association is exempt from federal income tax as a social welfare organization.[68] The association was found to be "serving the common good and the general welfare of the people of the entire development," with the IRS noting that a "neighborhood, precinct, subdivision, or housing development" may constitute the requisite "community."[69] Thus, even though the association was established by the developer and its existence may have aided the developer in selling housing units, any benefits to the developer were dismissed as incidental. Also deemed incidental were the benefits that accrued to the individual members, such as the preservation and protection of property values.[70]

Following issuance of this ruling in 1972, the IRS quickly concluded that its "increasing experience" with homeowners' associations demonstrated that the ruling was being misconstrued as to its scope. Consequently, in 1974, the IRS issued a "clarifying" ruling.[71] The IRS said that homeowners' associations, as described in the 1972 ruling, are *prima facie* presumed to be essentially and primarily formed and operated for the benefit of the individual members and, accordingly, not tax-exempt—a position wholly absent from the 1972 ruling. Subsequently, however, the IRS ruled that an organization with membership limited to the residents and business operators within a city block and formed to preserve and beautify the public areas in the block, thereby benefiting the community as a whole as well as enhancing the members' property rights, may qualify as a tax-exempt social welfare entity.[72] Moreover, a membership organization formed to help preserve, beautify, and maintain a public park was ruled to qualify as a tax-exempt charitable organization.[73]

The position of the IRS as to the definition of the word *community*, as stated in this 1974 ruling, is that the term "has traditionally been construed as having reference to a geographical unit bearing a reasonably recognizable relationship to an area ordinarily identified as a governmental subdivision or a unit or district thereof."[74] Thus, the IRS held

---

[67] Rev. Rul. 67-6, 1967-1 C.B. 135, *mod. by* Rev. Rul. 76-147. *supra* note 66.

[68] Rev. Rul. 72-102, 1972-1 C.B. 149, *mod. by* Rev. Rul. 74-99, 1974-1 C.B. 131.

[69] Rev. Rul. 72-102, *supra* note 68 at 149.

[70] Cf. Rev. Rul. 69-280, 1969-1 C.B. 152.

[71] Rev. Rul. 74-99, *supra* note 68.

[72] Rev. Rul. 75-286, 1975-2 C.B. 210. Cf. Rev. Rul. 68-14, 1968-1 C.B. 243.

[73] Rev. Rul. 78-85, 1978-1 C.B. 150.

[74] Rev. Rul. 74-99, *supra* note 68, at 132.

that a community is "not simply an aggregation of homeowners bound together in a structured unit formed as an integral part of a plan for the development of a real estate subdivision and the sale and purchase of homes therein."[75]

The IRS, in this 1974 ruling, also held that, where the association's activities include those directed to exterior maintenance of private residences, the above *prima facie* presumption is reinforced. Moreover, the 1974 ruling stated that, as far as ownership and maintenance of common areas is concerned, the IRS's approval is only extended to those areas "traditionally recognized and accepted as being of direct governmental concern in the exercise of the powers and duties entrusted to governments to regulate community health, safety, and welfare."[76] That is, the IRS's "approval" was extended only to ownership and maintenance by a homeowners' association of areas such as "roadways and parklands, sidewalks and street lights, access to, or the use and enjoyment of which is extended to members of the general public, as distinguished from controlled use or access restricted to the members of the homeowners' association."[77]

Subsequent pronouncements by the IRS in this area illustrate that the IRS has continued to issue a variety of determinations as to the meaning of the term *community*. In 1975, the IRS issued a ruling that, assuming the presence of a community, accorded tax-exempt social welfare status to an organization formed to provide the community with security protection, improved public services, recreational and holiday activities, and a community newspaper.[78] Because these services clearly redounded to the benefit of the individual residents in the community, it is difficult to reconcile this ruling with the foregoing 1974 ruling. This is particularly the case in view of still another ruling, this one denying classification as a tax-exempt social welfare entity to an organization formed to promote the common interest of tenants in an apartment complex, by negotiating with the apartment management and engaging in litigation activities.[79]

The IRS granted tax-exempt social welfare classification to an organization that operated an airport that was used by the public.[80] In the face of the prohibition in the income tax regulations on according tax-exempt social welfare classification to an organization carrying on a business with the general public,[81] the IRS decided that the rule was not contravened because the organization used volunteer services and received government grants. The requirement of a benefited community was held met because the airport served a rural area that had no other airport facilities; at the same time, most of the airplanes berthed at the airport were owned by key local businesses that were essential to the area's economy and the airport was used predominantly by executives, employees, and clients of the companies. The organization was deemed responsive to the com-

---

[75] Comm'r v. Lake Forest, Inc., 305 F.2d 814, 820 (4th Cir. 1962), *rev'g and rem'g* 36 T.C. 510 (1962); Rev. Rul. 56-225, 1956-1 C.B. 58.

[76] Rev. Rul. 74-99, *supra* note 68, at 133.

[77] *Id.*

[78] Rev. Rul. 75-386, 1975-2 C.B. 211.

[79] Rev. Rul. 73-307, 1973-2 C.B. 186.

[80] Rev. Rul. 78-429, 1978-2 C.B. 178.

[81] See text accompanied by *supra* note 4.

munity because it was supervised by a city council, inasmuch as the airport was located on land owned by a municipality.[82]

Thereafter, the IRS moderated its position in these regards somewhat, by stating that whether a particular homeowners' association meets the requirements of conferring benefit on a community must be determined according to the facts and circumstances of each case. The IRS also indicated that, although an area represented by an association may not be a community, the association may nonetheless still qualify for tax exemption if its activities benefit a community (such as owning and maintaining common areas and facilities for the use and enjoyment of the general public). However, the government continues to insist that tax exemption as a social welfare organization is not available to a homeowners' association (that does not represent a community) if it restricts the use of its facilities (such as parking and recreational facilities) to its members.[83] However, this position of the IRS is generally being accepted by the courts.[84]

Nonetheless, a federal district court rejected some of the positions of the IRS concerning the eligibility of homeowners' associations for tax-exempt status as social welfare organizations, holding that the association in the case represented a development that is an "independent community" (with 3,000 members and 6,100 acres of land), so that its benefits were provided to persons within the requisite community.[85] "There is no requirement," wrote the court, "that if the work of the association benefits the entire community, that it must also benefit the general public in terms of the world-at-large."[86] The court also stated: "Thus, only where an association represents less than the entire community is it a concern whether the benefits of the association are made available to the general public, because in that situation the benefits which are restricted to association members are not benefiting the community as a whole."[87] Therefore, held the court, the association was not required to give unlimited access to its golf course and tennis courts "beyond the community it serves to the world-at-large" to be tax-exempt.[88]

As noted, another court was in agreement with the IRS position in these regards, holding that an association of homeowners, which owned, controlled, leased, and sold real estate and built, maintained, and operated recreational facilities for the pleasure and convenience of its members, did not qualify as a tax-exempt social welfare organization.[89] The court noted that membership in the association was mandatory and was restricted to lot owners in the development, the association prohibited certain structures and uses of property, it provided road maintenance for the common roadways, and the facilities of the association were strictly limited to members and their guests. Holding that "a private association of homeowners which restricts its facilities to the exclusive use of its mem-

---

[82] Cf. § 6.3.

[83] Rev. Rul. 80-63, 1980-1 C.B. 116, *clar.* Rev. Rul. 74-99, *supra* note 68.

[84] E.g., Flat Top Lake Ass'n, Inc. v. United States, 86-2 U.S.T.C. ¶ 9756 (S.D. W. Va. 1986), *rev'd*, 89-1 U.S.T.C. ¶ 9180 (4th Cir. 1989); Lake Petersburg Ass'n v. Comm'r, 33 T.C.M. 259 (1974).

[85] Rancho Santa Fe Ass'n v. United States, 84-2 U.S.T.C. ¶ 9536 (S.D. Cal. 1984).

[86] *Id.* at 84, 530.

[87] *Id.*

[88] *Id.*

[89] Flat Top Lake Ass'n, Inc. v. United States, *supra* note 84.

bers" cannot be tax-exempt, the court observed that in other court holdings to the contrary there was "availability of taxpayer's facilities to the general public."[90]

The tax status of homeowners' associations has become even more important with the popularity of condominiums and the condominium management corporation. Basically, a condominium involves an ownership arrangement whereby individuals own a unit in a building and—with the other owners—the underlying land and commonly used improvements. The condominium management corporation, formed and supported by the unit owners, performs the maintenance and repair activities of the commonly owned properties.[91]

The position of the IRS is that condominium management corporations do not qualify as tax-exempt social welfare organizations inasmuch as the organizations' activities are for the private benefit of the members.[92] The IRS's rationale underlying this position is of two parts. First, the IRS ruled that, because of the essential nature and structure of the condominium system of ownership, the rights, duties, privileges, and immunities of the members are "inextricably and compulsorily tied to the owner's acquisition and enjoyment of his property in the condominium."[93] Second, the IRS noted that "condominium ownership necessarily involves ownership in common by all condominium unit owners of a great many so-called common areas, the maintenance and care of which necessarily constitutes the provision of private benefits for the unit owners."[94]

The IRS traces its position as to condominium management organizations to a 1962 federal court of appeals opinion.[95] There, the court held that a cooperative housing corporation was not a tax-exempt social welfare organization, since its activities were in the nature of an economic and private cooperative undertaking. In 1965, the IRS ruled that a cooperative organization operating and maintaining a housing development and providing housing facilities did not qualify as a tax-exempt social welfare organization.[96] Again, in 1969, the IRS ruled that a nonprofit organization formed to provide maintenance of exterior walls and roofs of members' homes in a development was not tax-exempt as a social welfare entity.[97]

The homeowners' association and condominium management organization may, if attempts to qualify as a tax-exempt social welfare organization fail, qualify as a tax-exempt social club.[98] That is, an organization may have as its primary

---

[90] *Id*. at 85, 865. Cf. Columbia Park & Recreation Assn, Inc. v. Comm'r, 88 T.C. 1 (1987).

[91] E.g., Garrett, "The Taxability of Condominium Owners' Associations," 12 *San Diego L. Rev.* 778 (1975); Curry, "Tax Considerations of Condominiums," 19 *Tul. Tax Inst.* 347 (1970); Anderson, "Tax Aspects of Cooperative and Condominium Housing," 25 *N.Y.U. Inst. on Fed. Tax.* 79 (1967).

[92] Rev. Rul. 74-17, 1974-1 C.B. 130. Cf. Rev. Rul. 70-604, 1970-2 C.B. 9.

[93] Rev. Rul. 74-17, *supra* note 92, at 131.

[94] *Id*.

[95] See *supra* note 75.

[96] Rev. Rul. 65-201, 1965-2 C.B. 170.

[97] Rev. Rul. 69-280, *supra* note 70. Cf. Rev. Rul. 74-563, 1974-2 C.B. 38. Also Eckstein v. United States, 452 F.2d 1036 (Ct. Cl. 1971).

[98] See Chapter 14.

purpose the establishment and operation of social facilities, such as a swimming pool, for the benefit of the homeowners in a community.[99]

Also, a tax-exempt homeowners' association may establish a separate but affiliated organization, to own and maintain recreational facilities and restrict their use to members of the association, as long as the organization is operated totally separate from the association.[100]

Congress, in 1976, brought some clarification of the tax law concerning homeowners' associations.[101] This provision provides an elective tax exemption for condominium management and residential real estate management associations.[102]

§ 12.3 ADVOCACY ORGANIZATIONS

As noted at the outset, the contemporary tax-exempt social organization often is an advocacy organization. The term *advocacy* is used to embrace attempts to influence legislation and involvement in political campaign activities. Thus, a social welfare organization can be what a charitable organization may not be—an *action organization*.[103]

Thus, a tax-exempt social welfare organization may draft legislation, present petitions for the purpose of having legislation introduced, and circulate speeches, reprints, and other material concerning legislation.[104] This type of organization may appear before a federal or state legislative body, or a local council, administrative board, or commission, and may encourage members of the community to contact legislative representatives in support of its programs.[105]

The IRS ruled that a tax-exempt social welfare organization can operate to inform the public on controversial subjects, "even though the organization advocates a particular viewpoint."[106] The IRS noted that "seeking of legislation germane to the organization's program is recognized by the regulations ... as permissible means of attaining social welfare purposes."[107] Offering a rationale for allowing a tax-exempt social welfare organization to engage in legislative activities, the IRS stated: "The education of the public on [controversial subjects] is deemed beneficial to the community because society benefits from an informed citizenry."[108] Likewise, the IRS extended tax-exempt status as a social welfare organization to an organization formed to educate the public on the subject of abor-

---

[99] Rev. Rul. 69-281, 1969-1 C.B. 155. Cf. Rev. Rul. 75-494, 1975-2 C.B. 214. In general, Frank, "IRS Takes Harsh Position on Exempting Condominium and Homeowners' Association," 44 *J. Tax*. 306 (1976); Snowling. "Federal Taxation of Homeowners' Associations," 28 *Tax Law*. 117 (1974).

[100] Rev. Rul. 80-63, *supra* note 83.

[101] IRC § 528.

[102] See § 18.13.

[103] See § 20.2.

[104] Rev. Rul. 68-656, 1968-2 C.B. 216.

[105] Rev. Rul. 67-6, 1967-1 C.B. 135.

[106] Rev. Rul. 68-656, *supra* note 104 at 216.

[107] *Id*. at 216–217.

[108] *Id*. at 216.

tions, promote the rights of the unborn, and support legislative and constitutional changes to restrict women's access to abortions, recognizing that the organization "advocates objectives that are controversial."[109]

Similarly, an organization that engaged in attempts to influence legislation intended to benefit animals, animal owners, persons interested in the welfare of animals, and the community at large was considered a tax-exempt social welfare organization, although it was denied tax-exempt status as a charitable entity (as an organization operated for the prevention of cruelty to animals) because it was deemed to be an action organization.[110]

Like tax-exempt charitable organizations, exempt social welfare organizations generally are forbidden from participating or intervening in any political campaign on behalf of or in opposition to any candidate for public office.[111] The IRS has traditionally been particularly strict in applying this restriction, as illustrated by the denial of classification as a tax-exempt social welfare organization to a group that rated candidates for public office on a nonpartisan basis and disseminated its ratings to the general public, on the theory that its rating process was intervention or participation on behalf of those candidates favorably rated and in opposition to those less favorably rated.[112]

Nor will objectivity necessarily ward off an unfavorable determination, as evidenced by the nonprofit group that selected slates of candidates for school board elections and engaged in campaigns on their behalf, and that was accordingly denied tax exemption as a charitable organization (and thus presumably as a social welfare organization) because of these political campaign activities, "even though its process of selection may have been completely objective and unbiased and was intended primarily to educate and inform the public about the candidates."[113]

The foregoing does not mean, however, that a tax-exempt social welfare organization is completely foreclosed from participation in governmental and political affairs. An organization the activities of which were primarily directed, on a nonprofit and nonpartisan basis, toward encouraging individuals in business to become more active in politics and government and toward promoting business, social, or civic action was held to qualify for tax exemption as a social welfare organization.[114] Likewise, a group that engaged in nonpartisan analysis, study, and research, made the results available to the public, and publicized the need for a code of fair campaign practices, was ruled to be a tax-exempt educational organization.[115] Also, an organization that recruited college students for an internship program providing employment with local municipal agencies qualified as a tax-exempt educational and charitable organization.[116] Thus, a tax-exempt social welfare organization could similarly undertake these activities.

---

[109] Rev. Rul. 76-81, 1976-1 C.B. 156.
[110] Rev. Rul. 67-293, 1967-2 C.B. 185.
[111] Reg. § 1.501(c)(4)-1(a)(2)(ii). See Chapter 21.
[112] Rev. Rul. 67-368, 1967-2 C.B. 194.
[113] Rev. Rul. 67-71, 1967-1 C.B. 125.
[114] Rev. Rul. 60-193, 1960-1 C.B. 145.
[115] Rev. Rul. 66-258, 1966-2 C.B. 213.
[116] Rev. Rul. 70-584, 1970-2 C.B. 114.

The IRS, therefore, in determining an organization's tax-exempt status in light of the requirements for a social welfare entity, carefully adheres to the distinction between those groups that actively participate or intervene in a political campaign for or against candidates for public office and those that more passively seek to stimulate public interest in improved government, better campaign practices, and the like.

However, this prohibition on political campaign activities by tax-exempt social welfare organizations is not absolute, in that the requirement is that these organizations must be *primarily* engaged in activities that promote social welfare. Thus, a tax-exempt organization primarily engaged in social welfare functions may also carry on activities (such as financial assistance and in-kind services) involving participation and intervention in political campaigns on behalf of or in opposition to candidates for nomination or election to public office.[117]

An organization that was tax-exempt as a charitable entity and lost that status as the result of excessive legislative activities may be precluded from thereafter converting to a tax-exempt social welfare organization.[118]

§ 12.4 COMPARISON WITH CHARITABLE ORGANIZATIONS

In several ways, the tax-exempt charitable organization and the tax-exempt social welfare organization are identical. Neither may be organized nor operated for private gain.[119] Neither may, to any appreciable degree, participate or intervene in any political campaign on behalf of or in opposition to any candidate for public office.[120] Both are liable for taxation on unrelated business income.[121] Moreover, of greatest importance, the concepts of what is charitable and what constitutes social welfare can be very much alike. Thus, the same organization may simultaneously qualify under both categories of tax exemption.[122]

As noted,[123] the promotion of social welfare is one of the definitions of *charitable activity* for purposes of tax exemption.[124] Thus, a variety of activities and programs may be characterized as tax-exempt functions for purposes of either charitable entities or social welfare entities. For example, the following charitable efforts have been treated as promoting social welfare: furnishing of housing to low-income groups,[125] relieving unemployment by area development,[126] and rehabilitating the elderly unemployed.[127]

---

[117] Rev. Rul. 81-95, 1981-1 C.B. 332. However, these political campaign activities will cause the organization to be subject to the tax imposed by IRC § 527(f) on the expenditures for political activities that are within the meaning of IRC § 527(e)(2) (see § 17.3(b)).

[118] IRC § 504. See § 20.7.

[119] Rev. Rul. 69-385, 1969-2 C.B. 123; Amalgamated Hous. Corp. v. Comm'r, 37 B.T.A. 817 (1938), *aff'd*, 108 F.2d 1010 (2d Cir. 1940).

[120] See § 21.4.

[121] See Part Five.

[122] E.g., Rev. Rul. 74-361, 1974-2 C.B. 159. In general, Reg. § 1.501(c)(4)-1(a)(2)(i).

[123] See § 6.6.

[124] Reg. § 1.501(c)(3)-1(d)(2).

[125] Rev. Rul. 55-439, 1955-2 C.B. 257; Garden Homes Co. v. Comm'r, 64 F.2d 593 (7th Cir. 1932).

[126] Rev. Rul. 64-187, 1964-1 (Part 1) C.B. 187.

[127] Rev. Rul. 57-297, 1957-2 C.B. 307.

The principal distinction, as regards its federal tax status, between a charitable and social welfare organization is that the former is prohibited from "carrying or propaganda, or otherwise attempting to influence legislation" as a "substantial part" of its activities.[128] Conversely, a social welfare organization, while not so circumscribed as to permissible legislative activities,[129] cannot attract charitable contributions that are deductible for income, gift, and estate tax purposes. However, federal tax law provides that a *charitable contribution* includes a gift to a "state, a possession of the United States, or any political subdivision of the foregoing, or the United States or the District of Columbia, but only if the contribution or gift is made for exclusively public purposes."[130] Thus, contributions to a social welfare organization that was organized to build a stadium and lease it to a school district, which would eventually get title, were ruled deductible as charitable contributions;[131] but deductible charitable contributions in this context are infrequent.

Thus, the basic trade-off between these two types of tax-exempt organizations is a greater scope of permissible legislative activities as opposed to deductible contributions as a source of revenue.

The basic operational difference between tax-exempt charitable and social welfare organizations, then, is embodied in the regulations accompanying both sections by the concept of the *action organization*. A tax-exempt charitable organization must not have any of the characteristics of an action organization,[132] while a tax-exempt social welfare organization may be a certain type of action organization.[133] A social welfare organization that is not exempt from taxation as a charitable organization may qualify as a tax-exempt social welfare entity even though it is an action organization because of its legislative activities.[134] Stated another way, a social welfare organization may qualify for tax exemption as a charitable organization, as long as it is not deemed an action organization.[135]

Action organization is defined as being any one of three types of organizations.[136] In contrast to the tax-exempt charitable organization, the tax-exempt social welfare organization may be an action organization, as long as it is not the type of action organization that is substantively involved in political campaigns.[137] A tax-exempt social welfare organization can undertake legislative activities within the general framework established by the regulations describing the two types of action organizations that may engage in activities involving legislation.

---

[128] See § 20.7.
[129] However, tax-exempt social welfare organizations that engage in lobbying activities are ineligible for the receipt of federal funds by means of a grant, contract, loan, award, or the like (Lobbying Disclosure Act of 1995 (2 U.S.C. 1601) § 1611.
[130] IRC § 170(c)(1).
[131] Rev. Rul. 57-493, 1957-2 C.B. 314.
[132] Reg. § 1.501(c)(3)-1(c)(3).
[133] Reg. § 1.501(c)(4)-1(a)(2)(ii).
[134] *Id.*
[135] Reg. § 1.501(c)(4)-1(a)(2)(i).
[136] See § 4.3.
[137] Reg. §§ 1.501(c)(3)-1(c)(3)(v), 1.501(c)(4)-1(a)(2)(ii).

CHAPTER 13

Associations and Other Business Leagues

§ 13.1 Business Leagues in General
§ 13.2 Business and Trade Associations
§ 13.3 Professional Organizations
§ 13.4 Nonqualifying Business Leagues

§ 13.5 Chambers of Commerce, Boards of Trade, and the Like
§ 13.6 Consequences of Abandonment of Tax-Exempt Status

The federal tax law provides tax exemption for "[b]usiness leagues . . . not organized for profit and no part of the net earnings of which inures to the benefit of any private shareholder or individual."[1] This exemption also extends to chambers of commerce, real estate boards, boards of trade, and professional football leagues (whether or not administering a pension fund for football players).

§ 13.1 BUSINESS LEAGUES IN GENERAL

A business league is an association of persons having some common business interest, the purpose of which is to promote that common interest and not to engage in a regular business of a kind ordinarily carried on for profit. Its activities are directed to the improvement of business conditions of one or more lines of business, as distinguished from the performance of particular services for individual persons. An organization whose purpose is to engage in a regular business of a kind ordinarily carried on for profit, even though the business is conducted on a cooperative basis or produces only sufficient income to be self-sustaining, cannot be a tax-exempt business league.[2] An exempt business league is not required to promote the general commercial welfare.[3]

---

[1] IRC § 501(c)(6).
[2] Reg. § 1.501(c)(6)-1; Engineers Club of San Francisco v. United States, 791 F.2d 686 (9th Cir. 1986) (where this definition was said to have been given the "imprimatur of Congress and is thus entitled to the effect of law" (at 689)); United States v. Oklahoma City Retailers Ass'n, 331 F.2d 328 (10th Cir. 1964); Retailers Credit Ass'n of Alameda County v. Comm'r, 90 F.2d 47 (9th Cir. 1937); Credit Union Ins. Corp. v. United States, 95-1 U.S.T.C. ¶ 50,286 (D. Md. 1995), aff'd, 96-2 U.S.T.C. ¶ 50,323 (4th Cir. 1996). A discussion of the legislative history of this exemption appears in National Muffler Dealers Ass'n, Inc. v. United States, 440 U.S. 472, 477–479 (1979).
[3] Rev. Rul. 59-391, 1959-2 C.B. 151; Comm'r v. Chicago Graphic Arts Fed'n, Inc., 128 F.2d 424 (7th Cir. 1942).

The term *business* is broadly construed and includes nearly any activity carried on for the production of income,[4] including the professions[5] and consumer cooperatives.[6] Tax exemption has been denied for lack of a sufficient common business interest in situations involving an organization of individuals engaged in different trades or professions not in competition who exchanged business information,[7] an association of motorists,[8] and an association of dog owners, most of whom were not in the business of raising dogs.[9] At a minimum, to qualify as a tax-exempt business league, an organization must have some program directed to the improvement of business conditions; for example, the mere provision of bar and luncheon facilities is insufficient.[10] Organizations that promote the common interests of hobbyists do not qualify as business leagues, although tax exemption may be found within some other category of tax-exempt organization.[11]

In this context, a *line of business* is a "trade or occupation, entry into which is not restricted by a patent, trademark, or similar device which would allow private parties to restrict the right to engage in the business."[12]

The line-of-business requirement was upheld by the U.S. Supreme Court in 1979 as being consistent with the intent of Congress in granting tax exemption to business leagues. The occasion for the Court's review of the pertinent regulations was a case involving the tax-exempt status of a trade organization of muffler dealers that confined its membership to dealers franchised by Midas International Corporation and that had as its principal activity the bargaining with the corporation on behalf of its members. The Court held that Midas Muffler franchisees do not constitute a line of business, in that their efforts do not benefit a sufficiently broad segment of the business community, as would the efforts of the entire muffler industry.[13] Thus, concluded the Court, tax exemption as a business league "is not available to aid one group in competition with another within an industry."[14]

Consequently, the line-of-business rule generally requires that a tax-exempt trade group represent an entire industry.[15] Thus, in one instance, an organization

---

[4] See § 26.2.

[5] Rev. Rul. 70-641, 1970-2 C.B. 119; I.T. 3182, 1938-1 C.B. 168.

[6] Rev. Rul. 67-264, 1967-2 C.B. 196.

[7] Rev. Rul. 59-391, *supra* note 3.

[8] American Automobile Ass'n v. Comm'r, 19 T.C. 1146 (1953).

[9] American Kennel Club v. Hoey, 148 F.2d 920 (2d Cir. 1945).

[10] Rev. Rul. 70-244, 1970-1 C.B. 132.

[11] Rev. Rul. 66-179, 1966-1 C.B. 144.

[12] IRS Exempt Organizations Handbook (IRM 7751) § 652(1).

[13] National Muffler Dealers Ass'n, Inc. v. United States, *supra* note 2, aff'g 565 F.2d 845 (2d Cir. 1977). The Supreme Court thus rejected the contrary view of the U.S. Court of Appeals for the Seventh Circuit, which had held that an association composed solely of bottlers of a single brand of soft drink was an exempt business league (Pepsi-Cola Bottlers' Ass'n, Inc. v. United States, 369 F.2d 250 (7th Cir. 1966)).

[14] National Muffler Dealers Ass'n, Inc. v. United States, *supra* note 2 at 488. Three justices dissented from the majority view, in part because the pertinent regulation originally promulgated (in force from 1919 to 1929) embodied a position opposite to the one contained in the present regulation and they believed that was "strong evidence of the understanding of the meaning of the law at the time it was enacted" in 1913. *Id.* at 489. However, the Court majority deferred to the revised regulation, which has been the administrative law on the point since 1929 and which reflects the view of those who originally advocated tax exemption for business leagues. *Id.* at 472–484.

[15] E.g., American Plywood Ass'n v. United States, 267 F. Supp. 830 (W.D. Wash. 1967); National Leather & Shoe Finders Ass'n v. Comm'r, 9 T.C. 121 (1947).

was held to not be entitled to tax exemption as a business league because "[n]othing is done to advance the interests of the community or to improve the standards or conditions of a particular trade."[16] However, the courts (including the U.S. Supreme Court) have recognized as tax-exempt a business league that represents all components of an industry within a geographic area.[17]

Where business groups have a narrower range of purposes and/or membership base, classification as a tax-exempt business league will not be forthcoming. For example, the IRS denied tax exemption to groups composed of businesses that market a single brand of automobile[18] or bottle one type of soft drink.[19] In these and similar cases, the IRS reasoned that groups of this nature are not designed to better conditions in an entire industrial "line" but rather are devoted to the promotion of a particular product at the expense of others in the industry.[20] That is, tax exemption as a business league is not available for organizations that endeavor to improve business conditions in only "segments" of lines of business.[21]

Thus, tax exemption was denied an association composed of the licensees of a patent on a particular product, since its activities did not benefit those who manufactured competing products of the same type as that covered by the patent.[22] Likewise, an organization of users of a manufacturer's computers, formed to discuss computer use operational and technical problems, was ruled by the IRS to not qualify as a tax-exempt business league, in part because the organization helped to provide a competitive advantage to the manufacturer and its customers.[23] This position of the IRS was endorsed by a federal district court, holding that a computer users' group did not qualify as a tax-exempt business league, because it promoted a single manufacturer's computers, in that the group's "activities advance the interests of . . . [the vendor] and fail to bestow a benefit upon either an entire industry or all components of an industry within a geographic area" as the federal tax law requires.[24] By contrast, an organization formed by members of an industry that contracted with research organizations to develop new and improved uses for existing products was recognized as a tax-exempt business league, in part because none of the organization's patents and trademarks was licensed to any member on an exclusive basis.[25] As one federal court of appeals observed, the line-of-business requirement "is well suited to assuring that an organization's efforts do indeed benefit a sufficiently broad segment of the business community."[26]

---

[16] Produce Exch. Stock Clearing Ass'n v. Helvering, 71 F.2d 142, 144 (2d Cir. 1934).
[17] E.g., Comm'r v. Chicago Graphic Arts Fed'n, Inc., *supra* note 3; Crooks v. Kansas City Hay Dealers Ass'n, 37 F.2d 83 (8th Cir. 1929); Washington State Apples, Inc. v. Comm'r, 46 B.T.A. 64 (1942).
[18] Rev. Rul. 67-77, 1967-1 C.B. 138.
[19] Rev. Rul. 68-182, 1968-1 C.B. 263 (wherein the IRS announced its nonacquiescence in Pepsi-Cola Bottlers' Association, Inc. v. United States, *supra* note 13).
[20] Rev. Rul. 76-400, 1976-2 C.B. 153.
[21] Rev. Rul. 83-164, 1983-2 C.B. 95.
[22] Rev. Rul. 58-294, 1958-1 C.B. 244.
[23] Rev. Rul. 83-164, *supra* note 21.
[24] National Prime Users Group, Inc. v. United States, 667 F. Supp. 250 (D. Md. 1987)). Also Guide Int'l Corp. v. United States, 948 F.2d 360 (7th Cir. 1991).
[25] Rev. Rul. 69-632, 1969-2 C.B. 120.
[26] National Muffler Dealers Ass'n v. United States, *supra* note 13, at 565 F.2d 847.

Activities that promote a common business interest include the development and distribution of publications of pertinence to the common business interests of the members (such as journals and newsletters), the conduct of annual conventions and educational seminars, other means by which information pertaining to the field is disseminated, presentation of information and opinions to government agencies,[27] promotion of improved business standards and methods and uniform business practices,[28] advocacy of the open shop principle,[29] attempts to influence legislation germane to the members' common business interests,[30] other annual events (such as sports tournaments, forums, and holiday parties),[31] and the holding of luncheon meetings for the purpose of discussing the problems of a particular industry.[32] In other instances, the IRS ruled that an organization formed to promote the acceptance of women in business and the professions was a tax-exempt business league because it attempted to seek to improve conditions in one or more lines of business,[33] as was an organization formed to attract conventions to a city for the benefit of the economic interest of business throughout the community.[34]

Even though it is essential to qualification as a tax-exempt business league that the organization be an association of persons having a common business interest, the persons do not necessarily have to be engaged in a business at the time they are acting in association. As an illustration, an organization of persons studying for a degree in a particular profession can qualify as a tax-exempt business league if the purpose of the organization is to promote their common interests as future members of that profession and if it otherwise qualifies.[35] Also, a tax-exempt association will not jeopardize its business league status if it characterizes as nonvoting "associate members" persons who are merely sponsors of the organization and lack a common business interest with the regular members.[36]

The typical business league has as its membership—in conformity with the requirement that it be an "association of persons"—business corporations or individuals. However, a tax-exempt business league may have tax-exempt organizations as its membership, even where there are only two entities as members. For example, the IRS held that a trust created by a labor union and a business league qualified as a tax-exempt business league.[37] Likewise, a trust created pursuant to

---

[27] American Refractories Inst. v. Comm'r, 6 T.C.M. 1302 (1947); Atlanta Master Printers Club v. Comm'r, 1 T.C.M. 107 (1942).

[28] Rev. Rul. 68-657, 1968-2 C.B. 218.

[29] Associated Indus. of Cleveland v. Comm'r, 7 T.C. 1449 (1946).

[30] Rev. Rul. 61-177, 1961-2 C.B. 117, *mod'g* Rev. Rul. 54-442, 1954-2 C.B. 131.

[31] Priv. Ltr. Rul. 9550001.

[32] Rev. Rul. 67-295, 1967-2 C.B. 197.

[33] Rev. Rul. 76-400, *supra* note 20.

[34] Rev. Rul. 76-207, 1976-1 C.B. 158.

[35] Rev. Rul. 77-112, 1977-1 C.B. 149.

[36] In one case, the requirement that there be an "association of persons" was deemed met solely because the organization was created by three incorporators and has a board of directors (North Carolina Ass'n of Ins. Agents, Inc. v. United States, 83-2 U.S.T.C. ¶ 9445 (E.D.N.C. 1983)). However, the government secured a reversal of this opinion (739 F.2d 949 (4th Cir. 1984)).

[37] Rev. Rul. 70-31, 1970-1 C.B. 130.

collective bargaining agreements between a labor union and several business leagues was ruled to be tax-exempt as a business league.[38]

The requirement that a tax-exempt business league not engage in business for profit had more significance before enactment of the unrelated business income rules in 1950.[39] Before that date, business activities could preclude tax exemption, as occurred with respect to an organization selling credit information and collection services,[40] operating an employment agency,[41] and testing the safety of electrical products.[42] Today, tax exemption will not be threatened where a business is not an organization's principal activity, such as a chamber of commerce operating a credit bureau as one of 15 departments,[43] a chamber of commerce developing an industrial park to attract new industry to the community,[44] and an association of insurance agents collecting (as an insubstantial activity) commissions on municipal insurance placed through its members.[45] However, even where its principal purpose is not the operation of a business, an association may nonetheless be subject to liability for the unrelated business income tax, notwithstanding the fact that the business is conducted with its members.[46] It is the view of the Chief Counsel of the IRS that a business league must have meaningful support in the form of members' dues and revenue from related activities, and cannot—to be tax-exempt—receive its principal support from unrelated business activities.[47]

Varieties of tax-exempt business leagues abound, in part because the term lacks a well-defined meaning or common usage outside the parameters of the federal tax law rules concerning business leagues.[48]

For example, an organization created under state statute to pay claims against (that is, act as guarantor for) insolvent insurance companies, where the companies were mandatory members of the organization, was ruled to be a tax-exempt business league, with the IRS holding that the "organization is serving a quasi-public function imposed by law which is directed at relieving a common cause of hardship and distress of broad public concern in the field of insurance protection."[49] Likewise, an association of insurance companies created pursuant to a state's no-fault insurance statute to provide personal injury protection for residents of the state who sustain injury and are not covered by any insurance was ruled to qualify as a tax-exempt business league because its activities "promote the common busi-

---

[38] Rev. Rul. 82-138, 1982-2 C.B. 106.

[39] See Part Five.

[40] Credit Bur. of Greater N.Y. Inc. v. Comm'r, 162 F.2d 7 (2d Cir. 1947), aff'g 5 T.C.M. 826 (1947).

[41] American Ass'n of Eng'rs Employment, Inc. v. Comm'r, 11 T.C.M. 207 (1952), aff'd, 204 F.2d 19 (7th Cir. 1953).

[42] Underwriters Laboratories, Inc. v. Comm'r, 135 F.2d 371 (7th Cir. 1943), cert. den., 320 U.S. 756 (1943). Cf. § 10.3.

[43] Milwaukee Ass'n of Commerce v. United States, 72 F. Supp. 310 (E.D. Wis. 1947).

[44] Rev. Rul. 70-81, 1970-1 C.B. 131, amp., Rev. Rul. 81-138, 1981-1 C.B. 358.

[45] King County Ins. Ass'n v. Comm'r, 37 B.T.A. 288 (1938).

[46] Rev. Rul. 66-151, 1966-1 C.B. 152.

[47] E.g., Gen. Couns. Mem. 39108. The IRS ruled, however, that an organization can qualify as a tax-exempt business league, notwithstanding the fact that the organization does not have a membership.

[48] Helvering v. Reynolds Co., 306 U.S. 110, 114 (1939).

[49] Rev. Rul. 73-452, 1973-2 C.B. 183.

ness interests of its members by fulfilling an obligation that the state has imposed upon the insurance industry as a prerequisite for doing business within the state and by enhancing the image of the industry."[50] Tax-exempt business league status was accorded an organization of representatives of diversified businesses that own or lease one or more digital computers produced by various manufacturers; the IRS found that the "primary objective of the organization is to provide a forum for the exchange of information which will lead to the more efficient utilization of computers by its members and other interested users, and thus improve the overall efficiency of the business operations of each."[51] Similarly, an organization that operated a "plan room" and published a news bulletin that contained information about plans available at the plan room, bid results and activities of concern to persons in the industry, was ruled to be a tax-exempt business league.[52]

Other tax-exempt business leagues include an organization composed of members of a particular industry formed to develop new and improved uses for existing products of the industry,[53] an organization composed of advertising agencies that verified the advertising claims of publications selling advertising space and made reports available to members of the advertising industry generally,[54] an organization that collected contributions to further an industry's programs,[55] an organization that promoted convention and tourism business in a particular town,[56] an organization that effected improvement in public awareness of thoroughbred racing,[57] an organization that made recommendations concerning the establishment and revision of regulations and rates for its members who were regulated by the Interstate Commerce Commission,[58] an organization of packaging manufacturers with an industry advertising program,[59] an organization that provided its member small loan companies with information concerning borrowers,[60] an organization of individuals who advanced their spouses' profession,[61] and an organization formed to improve the business conditions of financial institutions by offering rewards for information leading to the arrest and conviction of individuals committing crimes against its members.[62] Also, an organization, the members of which were involved in the commercial fishing industry in a state, that published a monthly newspaper of commercial fishing technical information and news, and that derived its income primarily from membership dues and sales of advertising, may qualify as a tax-exempt business

---

[50] Rev. Rul. 76-410, 1976-2 C.B. 155.
[51] Rev. Rul. 74-147, 1974-1 C.B. 136. Cf. Rev. Rul. 83-164, *supra* note 21; Rev. Rul. 74-116, 1974-1 C.B. 127.
[52] Rev. Rul. 72-211, 1972-1 C.B. 150, clarifying Rev. Rul. 56-65, 1956-1 C.B. 199. Also Builder's Exch. of Tex., Inc. v. Comm'r, 31 T.C.M. 844 (1972).
[53] Rev. Rul. 69-632, *supra* note 25.
[54] Rev. Rul. 69-387, 1969-2 C.B. 124.
[55] Priv. Ltr. Rul. 8422170.
[56] Priv. Ltr. Rul. 9032005.
[57] Priv. Ltr. Rul. 9050002.
[58] Rev. Rul. 67-393, 1967-2 C.B. 200.
[59] Rev. Rul. 67-344, 1967-2 C.B. 199.
[60] Rev. Rul. 67-394, 1967-2 C.B. 201.
[61] Rev. Rul. 67-343, 1967-2 C.B. 198.
[62] Rev. Rul. 69-634, 1969-2 C.B. 124.

league.[63] A merger, consolidation, or other reorganization of business leagues can result in one or more tax-exempt business leagues.[64]

The IRS recognized that programs of testing and certification of an industry's products is a tax-exempt function for a business league.[65] In a speech in 1973, the Commissioner of Internal Revenue, analogizing to organizations that accredit television repairers and automobile mechanics, commented that organizations that accredit physicians in their fields of specialization will be treated as tax-exempt business leagues and not as tax-exempt charitable organizations.[66] Thus, in the view of the IRS, enhancement of the medical profession, not delivery of adequate health care, is the primary objective of these organizations. The Commissioner's observations are memorialized in a ruling published in 1973.[67]

Similarly, the IRS ruled that an organization formed by physicians of a state medical society to operate peer review boards for the purpose of establishing and maintaining standards for quality, quantity, and reasonableness of the costs of medical services qualified as a tax-exempt business league.[68] The IRS recognized that these organizations are being established in response to concern over the rising costs of medical care, in an effort to curb these expenses by reviewing medical procedures and utilization of medical facilities. Nonetheless, ruled the IRS, "[al]though this activity may result in a measurable public benefit, its primary objective is to maintain the professional standards, prestige, and independence of the organized medical profession and thereby further the common business interest of the organization's members."[69] However, the promotion of health is a charitable purpose,[70] and some courts are of the view that improvements in the delivery of health care is a charitable function, even if the profession is somewhat benefited.[71]

As discussed below,[72] the performance of particular services for individuals can preclude an otherwise qualified business league from tax-exempt status. However, an activity may be found to benefit a common business interest even though services are being rendered to members, as long as a member's benefit is incidental. Examples of this include organizations that conduct negotiations for members and nonmembers in an industry,[73] mediate and settle disputes affecting an industry,[74] operate a bid registry,[75] investigate criminal aspects of claims

---

[63] Rev. Rul. 75-287, 1975-2 C.B. 211.

[64] E.g., Priv. Ltr. Rul. 9003045.

[65] Rev. Rul. 70-187, 1970-1 C.B. 131; Rev. Rul. 81-127, 1981-1 C.B. 357.

[66] Remarks of then-Commissioner of Internal Revenue Donald C. Alexander, August 29, 1973, before the American Society of Association Executives (IR-1326).

[67] Rev. Rul. 73-567, 1973-2 C.B. 178. Cf. Kentucky Bar Found., Inc. v. Comm'r, 78 T.C. 921 (1982).

[68] Rev. Rul. 74-553, 1974-2 C.B. 168.

[69] Id. at 169.

[70] See § 6.2.

[71] San Antonio District Dental Soc'y v. United States, 340 F. Supp. 11 (W.D. Tex. 1972); Huron Clinic Found. v. United States, 212 F. Supp. 847 (S.D. 1962).

[72] See infra § 4.

[73] American Fishermen's Tuna Boat Ass'n v. Rogan, 51 F. Supp. 933 (S.D. Cal. 1943).

[74] Rev. Rul. 65-164, 1965-1 C.B. 238.

[75] Rev. Rul. 66-223, 1966-2 C.B. 224.

against members,[76] subsidize litigation,[77] operate an insurance rating bureau,[78] negotiate the sale of broadcast rights,[79] conduct fire patrols and salvage operations for insurance companies,[80] provide for equitable distribution of high-risk insurance policies among member insurance companies,[81] and publish a magazine containing information of interest to an entire industry.[82]

§ 13.2 BUSINESS AND TRADE ASSOCIATIONS

The most common form of tax-exempt business league is the business or trade association. This type of association has as its membership companies or other persons engaged in the same line of business or operating within the same industry. Its purpose is to promote and improve the conditions of the business or industry. One non–tax law definition of *business or trade association* characterized it as "a nonprofit, cooperative, voluntarily-joined, organization of business competitors designed to assist its members and its industry in dealing with mutual business problems."[83]

The criteria in the tax regulations for the tax-exempt business or trade association are generally followed by the courts, but there has been disagreement, such as over the scope of the proscription in the regulations that a tax-exempt association's activities should not be the "performance of particular services for individual persons."[84] However, in one case, a court did not deny an association tax exemption even though it maintained laboratories for quality control testing and promoted the association's trademark through television advertising, because these activities were incidental.[85] Nonetheless, the IRS ruled that an association of manufacturers, the principal activity of which was the promotion of its members' products under its required trademark, did not qualify for tax exemption.[86] Further, the regulations maintain that a tax-exempt association's activities must be directed to the "improvement of business conditions of one or more lines of business" and not just for a limited group (such as a single brand or product)[87] within a line of business. Nonetheless, an association of bottlers of a particular brand of soft drink was held to be a tax-exempt trade association (although this holding is now inconsistent with the law).[88]

An organization may fail to qualify as a tax-exempt business league because it disseminates advertising carrying the name of its members. Illustrations of this include an association created to attract tourism to a particular area, the principal

---

[76] Rev. Rul. 66-260, 1966-2 C.B. 225.
[77] Rev. Rul. 67-175, 1967-1 C.B. 139.
[78] Oregon Cas. Ass'n v. Comm'r, 37 B.T.A. 340 (1938).
[79] Priv. Ltr. Rul. 7922001.
[80] Minneapolis Bd. of Fire Underwriters v. Comm'r, 38 B.T.A. 1532 (1938).
[81] Rev. Rul. 71-155, 1971-1 C.B. 152.
[82] National Leather & Shoe Finders Ass'n v. Comm'r, *supra* note 15.
[83] Judkins, *National Associations of the United States*, vii (1949).
[84] See *infra* § 4.
[85] American Plywood Ass'n v. United States, *supra* note 15. Cf. Rev. Rul. 56-65, *supra* note 52.
[86] Rev. Rul. 70-80, 1970-1 C.B. 130.
[87] Rev. Rul. 68-182, 1968-1 C.B. 263; Rev. Rul. 58-294, *supra* note 22.
[88] Pepsi-Cola Bottlers' Ass'n, Inc. v. United States, *supra* note 13.

activity of which was publication of a yearbook consisting primarily of paid advertisements by its members[89] and an association that published catalogs that listed only products manufactured by the members.[90] Conversely, if the organization advertises the products and services of an entire industry, tax exemption will not be denied,[91] even if the advertising incidentally results in the performance of services by occasionally mentioning the names of its members.[92] Often, however, the advertising function is treated as an unrelated business,[93] so that the tax-exempt status of the association is not affected.

Other areas of controversy as respects the tax status of trade associations include the requisite availability of association research,[94] operation of trade shows,[95] provision of credit information,[96] and provision of group insurance for the employees of employer-members.[97]

§ 13.3   PROFESSIONAL ORGANIZATIONS

Some nonprofit membership organizations operate for the benefit of a profession, rather than a trade or business. These entities are often known as *professional societies*. This can cause tax exemption classification controversies, in that the likelihood is greater than these entities engage in at least some charitable, educational, scientific, or like activities.

In many instances, the rules concerning business leagues serve as the basis of tax exemption for professional societies. For example, the IRS presumes that bar associations, medical societies, and similar organizations are business leagues, even though some of these organizations' activities are clearly charitable and educational.[98] That is, the IRS applies the primary purpose test and presumes

---

[89] Rev. Rul. 65-14, 1965-1 C.B. 236.
[90] Automotive Elec. Ass'n v. Comm'r, 168 F.2d 366 (6th Cir. 1948), *aff'g* 8 T.C. 894 (1947). Also Rev. Rul. 56-84, 1956-1 C.B. 201.
[91] Washington State Apples, Inc. v. Comm'r, *supra* note 17.
[92] Rev. Rul. 55-444, 1955-2 C.B. 258.
[93] E.g., Priv. Ltr. Rul. 9440001.
[94] Rev. Rul. 69-106, 1969-1 C.B. 153; Glass Container Indus. Research Corp. v. United States, 70-1 U.S.T.C. ¶ 9214 (W.D. Pa. 1970).
[95] E.g., Rev. Rul. 58-224, 1958-1 C.B. 242; Rev. Rul. 67-219, 1967-2 C.B. 212; Orange County Builders Ass'n, Inc. v. United States, 65-2 U.S.T.C. ¶ 9679 (S.D. Cal. 1956); Texas Mobile Home Ass'n v. Comm'r, 324 F.2d 691 (5th Cir. 1963); American Inst. of Interior Designers v. United States, 204 F. Supp. 201 (N.D. Cal. 1962); American Woodworking Mach. & Equip. Show, v. United States, 249 F. Supp. 392 (M.D.N.C. 1966); Men's & Boys' Apparel Club of Fla. v. United States, 64-2 U.S.T.C. ¶ 9840 (Ct. Cl. 1964); National Ass'n of Display Indus. v. United States, 64-1 U.S.T.C. ¶ 9285 (S.D.N.Y. 1964).
[96] E.g., Rev. Rul. 70-591, 1970-2 C.B. 118; Rev. Rul. 68-265, 1968-1 C.B. 265; Oklahoma City Retailers Ass'n v. United States, 331 F.2d 328 (10th Cir. 1964).
[97] Rev. Rul. 70-95, 1970-1 C.B. 137; Rev. Rul. 67-176, 1967-1 C.B. 140; Rev. Rul. 66-151, *supra* note 46; Oklahoma Cattlemen's Ass'n v. United States, 310 F. Supp. 320 (W.D. Okla. 1969). Also United States v. Omaha Live Stock Traders Exch., 366 F.2d 749 (8th Cir. 1966); Retail Credit Ass'n of Minneapolis v. United States, 30 F. Supp. 855 (D. Minn. 1938); Little Rock Grain Exch. v. Thompson, 30 F. Supp. 571 (E.D. Ark. 1950); Leaf Tobacco Exporters Ass'n, Inc. v. Comm'r, 10 T.C.M. 706 (1951), *appeal dis.* (4th Cir. 1952); National Retail Credit Ass'n v. Comm'r, 45 B.T.A. 1160 (1941); Waynesboro Mfg. Ass'n v. Comm'r, 1 B.T.A. 911 (1925); Priv. Ltr. Rul. 8623006.
[98] See Chapters 6, 7.

that these organizations' activities are directed primarily at the promotion of the particular profession and that they are operated to further the common business purpose of their members.

A tax-exempt medical society may engage in the following charitable and educational activities: meetings where technical papers are presented, maintenance of a library, publication of a journal, provision of lecturers and counseling services at medical schools, and the support of public health programs. This type of a society may also undertake the following activities: provision of a patient referral service, maintenance of a grievance committee, meetings concerned with the promotion and protection of the practice of medicine, operation of a legislative committee, and conduct of a public relations program. Where the latter category of activities is primary, charitable status is denied, and tax-exempt status as a business league is accorded.[99] A bar association may likewise engage in charitable and educational activities, such as law institutes, law review journal, moot court program, speakers' panels, and legal assistance to indigents. However, the bar association will be a tax-exempt business league where the following activities predominate: preparation of studies on the economics of law office administration, programs directed toward making the practice of law more profitable, enforcement of standards of conduct, and sponsorship of social events (for example, holiday parties, golf tournaments, and travel plans).[100] Some court opinions have implied that bar associations may qualify as tax-exempt charitable organizations.[101] In fact, one court decision held that the maintenance of "public confidence in the legal system" is a "goal of unquestionable importance in a civil and complex society" and that activities such as the operation of a client security fund, an inquiry tribunal, a fee arbitration plan, and a lawyer referral service "are devoted to that goal through various means of improving the administration of justice."[102]

If a professional society's dominant activities are noncommercial research, maintenance of a library, publication of a journal, and the like, it will qualify for tax exemption as being charitable, educational, or perhaps scientific, as long as no substantial activities are directed at or are concerned with the protection or promotion of the professional practice or business interests of any of the professions represented by its membership.[103] A professional society, then, may fail to qualify as a tax-exempt charitable organization and will be deemed a tax-exempt business league where it, other than incidentally, engages in public relations activities, polices a profession, seeks to improve the condition of its members, seeks to develop good will or fellowship among its members, engages in social and recreational activities, maintains facilities (for example, restaurant, lounge, or club house) for its members, or engages in legislative or political campaign activi-

---

[99] Rev. Rul. 71-504, 1971-2 C.B. 231. Also Rev. Rul. 77-232, 1977-2 C.B. 71.
[100] Rev. Rul. 71-505, 1971-2 C.B. 232. Also Hammerstein v. Kelly, 349 F.2d 928 (8th Cir. 1965); Colonial Trust Co. v. Comm'r, 19 B.T.A. 174 (1930).
[101] St. Louis Union Trust Co. v. United States, 374 F.2d 427 (8th Cir. 1967); Dulles v. Johnson, 273 F.2d 362 (2d Cir. 1959); Rhode Island Hosp. Trust Co. v. United States, 159 F. Supp. 204 (D.R.I. 1958).
[102] Kentucky Bar Found., Inc. v. Comm'r, *supra* note 67, at 930 (1982). Also Fraternal Medical Specialist Serv., Inc. v. Comm'r, 49 T.C.M. 289 (1984).
[103] Rev. Rul. 71-506, 1971-2 C.B. 233.

ties.[104] In one instance, an organization of individuals from various public health and welfare professions (seemingly charitable undertakings) was ruled to be a tax-exempt business league, for the reasons that its "activities promote the business and professional interests of the members by increasing the effectiveness of the interaction among the various professions, by developing greater efficiency in the professions, and by solving problems common to the professions."[105] It is the position of the IRS that activities such as the operation of certification programs and the maintenance of codes of ethics are suitable programs for professional organizations that are business leagues but not for professional organizations that are charitable, educational, and/or scientific organizations, because these programs are designed and operated to achieve professional standing for the line of business represented and to enhance the respectability of those who are certified.[106]

§ 13.4   NONQUALIFYING BUSINESS LEAGUES

There are several bases on which tax-exempt status may be denied to an otherwise qualifying business league. One is the prohibition on business activities for profit. Thus, an organization that issued shares of stock carrying the right to dividends was denied tax exemption as a business league.[107] Also, an association of insurance companies that provided medical malpractice insurance to doctors, nurses, hospitals, and other health care providers in a particular state, where that type of insurance was not available from for-profit insurers in the state, was denied classification as a tax-exempt business league on the ground that the provision of medical malpractice insurance is a business of a kind ordinarily carried on for profit.[108] Similarly, an association of insurance companies that accepted for reinsurance high-risk customers who would ordinarily be turned down by the member companies was ruled to not qualify as a tax-exempt business league, because reinsurance is a business ordinarily carried on by commercial insurance

---

[104] As to the latter, see Chapters 20, 21.

[105] Rev. Rul. 70-641, *supra* note 5, at 119. Also I.T. 3182, *supra* note 5.

[106] Gen. Couns. Mem. 39721. There can be interplay between the rules describing a qualifying business league and those defining a tax-exempt social club (see Chapter 14). In one instance, the IRS attempted to classify an engineering society as a social club, claiming that it was regularly engaged in substantial restaurant, beverage, and other social operations. However, this approach was rejected in litigation, inasmuch the court concluded that the primary purpose of the organization was the promotion of the profession of engineering (through the conduct of professional education, training, and information dissemination activities) with the food, beverage, and social activities deemed either incidental or related to the professional activities (The Engineers Club of San Francisco v. United States, 609 F. Supp. 519 (N.D. Cal. 1985)). Also United States v. Engineers Club of San Francisco, 325 F.2d 204 (9th Cir. 1963).) Nonetheless, on appeal, the government prevailed, albeit on another argument, namely, that the society could not qualify as a tax-exempt business league because the food and beverage service constituted a service performed for individual persons rather than the engineering profession as a whole (Engineers Club of San Francisco v. United States, *supra* note 2. For a discussion of this principle, see *infra* § 4.).

[107] Northwestern Jobbers Credit Bur. v. Comm'r, 37 F.2d 880 (8th Cir. 1930). Cf. Crooks v. Kansas City Hay Dealers Ass'n, 37 F.2d 83 (8th Cir. 1929).

[108] Rev. Rul. 81-174, 1981-1 C.B. 335.

companies for a profit.[109] Another basis for nonqualification as a tax-exempt business league is a finding that the organization is not structured along particular business or industry lines.[110] Still another basis for failure to qualify as a business league is violation of the private inurement doctrine.[111]

The chief basis on which tax exemption as a business league may be denied is a finding that the organization is performing particular services for its members, as distinguished from the improvement of business conditions in the particular business or industry.[112] Thus, the IRS denied tax-exempt business league status to a telephone answering service for tow truck operators, on the ground that it provided its members with economy and convenience in the conduct of their individual businesses.[113] A nurses' registry was denied categorization as a tax-exempt business league on a finding that it was no more than an employment service for the benefit of its members.[114] Similarly, an independent practice association was ruled to not qualify as a tax-exempt business league, with the IRS portraying it as akin to a billing and collection service that provided an economy or convenience to its members relating to the operation of their private medical practices.[115] By contrast, a lawyer referral service was ruled to be a tax-exempt business league, since (because of the manner in which it was operated) it was more than a mere business referral service and served to improve the image and functioning of the legal profession in general.[116]

Under limited circumstances, a tax-exempt business league can operate a "warranty or guarantee" program, which is a program designed to assure purchasers of a product that it meets acceptable standards and to provide insurance and arbitration services, without deprivation of its tax-exempt status on the ground that it is providing services to its membership. These circumstances are as follows: The program must primarily benefit the industry in its entirety rather than the private interests of its members, the advertisements do not have the purpose of giving members a competitive edge over nonmembers (where the membership does not encompass an industry), and the activity is not ordinarily carried on for profit; also, the IRS favors an enforced policy of a business league of obtaining reimbursement from the members responsible for defects.[117] The IRS, however, is likely to conclude that unwarranted private interests are being conferred on an organization's members in this setting where only a small portion of the eligible sellers participate in the program.[118]

Other organizations providing services to individual persons and denied

---

[109] Rev. Rul. 81-175, 1981-1 C.B. 337.

[110] See *supra* § 1.

[111] See Chapter 19.

[112] Southern Hardware Traffic Ass'n v. United States, 283 F. Supp. 1013 (W.D. Tenn. 1968), *aff'd*, 411 F.2d 563 (6th Cir. 1969).

[113] Rev. Rul. 74-308, 1974-2 C.B. 168.

[114] Rev. Rul. 61-170, 1961-2 C.B. 112. Also Rev. Rul. 71-175, 1971-1 C.B. 153 (concerning a telephone-answering service for physicians). Cf. Rev. Rul. 55-656, 1955-2 C.B. 262.

[115] Rev. Rul. 86-98, 1986-2 C.B. 74.

[116] Rev. Rul. 80-287, 1980-2 C.B. 185. Also Kentucky Bar Found., Inc. v. Comm'r, *supra* note 67.

[117] Gen. Couns. Mem. 34608.

[118] Gen. Couns. Mem. 39105.

tax exemption as business leagues include entities promoting and selling national advertising in members' publications,[119] providing insurance,[120] operating a traffic bureau,[121] appointing travel agents to sell passages on members' ships,[122] making interest-free loans to member credit unions,[123] operating commodity and stock exchanges,[124] promoting its members' writings,[125] supplying management services and supplies and equipment,[126] operating a multiple listing service,[127] conducting a trading stamp plan,[128] operating a laundry and dry cleaning plant,[129] operation of a warehouse,[130] promoting the exchange of orders by wire,[131] acting as a receiver and trustee for a fee,[132] appraising properties,[133] performing services in connection with bond investments,[134] estimating quantities of building materials for its members' projects,[135] ensuring the discharge of its members' obligations to pay taxes,[136] publishing and distributing a directory of its members to businesses likely to require the members' services,[137] administration of a welfare benefit plan pursuant to a collective bargaining agreement,[138] and maintaining a library for its members' use.[139]

In one case, a court held that an organization did not qualify as a tax-exempt business league, because it both engaged in a regular business of a kind ordinarily carried on for profit and its activities were directed to the performance of particular services for individual members.[140] As respects the business activity, the court found that the organization was engaging in an insurance business to a substantial extent (measured in terms of time and finances), as its officers and employees were involved on a daily basis with record keeping, processing claims for benefits, paying claims, and performing other administrative duties in connection with the insurance activities. The court distinguished this insurance activity from that conducted by associations only on a passive basis (that is, mere

---

[119] Rev. Rul. 56-84, 1956-1 C.B. 201.

[120] Rev. Rul. 74-81, 1974-1 C.B. 135.

[121] Rev. Rul. 68-264, 1968-1 C.B. 264.

[122] Rev. Rul. 74-228, 1974-1 C.B. 136.

[123] Rev. Rul. 76-38, 1976-1 C.B. 157.

[124] Reg. § 1.501(c)(6)-1. Cf. Rev. Rul. 55-715, 1955-2 C.B. 263.

[125] Rev. Rul. 57-453, 1957-2 C.B. 310.

[126] Rev. Rul. 66-338, 1966-2 C.B. 226; Indiana Retail Hardware Ass'n v. United States, 366 F.2d 998 (Ct. Cl. 1966); Apartment Operators Ass'n v. Comm'r, 136 F.2d 435 (9th Cir. 1943); Uniform Printing & Supply Co. v. Comm'r, 33 F.2d 445 (7th Cir. 1929), cert. den., 280 U.S. 69 (1929).

[127] Rev. Rul. 59-234, 1959-2 C.B. 149. Also Evanston-North Shore Bd. of Realtors v. United States, 320 F.2d 375 (Ct. Cl. 1963).

[128] Rev. Rul. 65-244, 1965-2 C.B. 167.

[129] A-1 Cleaners & Dyers Co. v. Comm'r, 14 B.T.A. 1314 (1929).

[130] Growers Cold Storage Whse. Co. v. Comm'r, 17 B.T.A. 1279 (1929).

[131] Florists' Telegraph Delivery Ass'n, Inc. v. Comm'r, 47 B.T.A. 1044 (1942).

[132] O.D. 786, 4 C.B. 269 (1921).

[133] Central Appraisal Bur. v. Comm'r, 46 B.T.A. 1281 (1942).

[134] Northwestern Mun. Ass'n, Inc. v. United States, 99 F.2d 460 (8th Cir. 1938).

[135] General Contractors Ass'n v. United States, 202 F.2d 633 (7th Cir. 1953).

[136] Rev. Rul. 66-354, 1966-2 C.B. 207.

[137] Rev. Rul. 76-409, 1976-2 C.B. 154.

[138] Gen. Couns. Mem. 39411, revoking Gen. Couns. Mem. 38458.

[139] Rev. Rul. 67-182, 1967-1 C.B. 141.

[140] Associated Master Barbers & Beauticians of Am., Inc. v. Comm'r, 69 T.C. 53 (1977).

sponsorship of the insurance program) and where a self-insurance program was not involved.[141] With respect to the provision of services, the court observed that the organization offered its members, in addition to the many insurance programs, an eyeglass and prescription lens replacement service, and sold its local chapters and members various supplies, charts, books, shop emblems, and association jewelry. The court concluded that the organization was undertaking activities that "serve as a convenience or economy to ... [its] members in the operation of their businesses" and was not promoting a common business interest or otherwise conducting itself like a qualified business league.[142]

In reliance upon this case, the IRS denied tax exemption as a business league to two types of associations of insurance companies because they engaged in a business of a kind ordinarily carried on for profit and were performing particular services for their members. In one instance, an association of insurance companies in a state that provided medical malpractice insurance to health care providers where the insurance was not available from for-profit insurers in the state was held to be "performing particular services for its member companies and policyholders" because its "method of operation involves it in its member companies' insurance business, and since the organization's insurance activities serve as an economy or convenience in providing necessary protection to its policyholders engaged in providing health care."[143] The same rationale was applied to the activities of an association of insurance companies that accepted for reinsurance high-risk customers who would ordinarily be turned down by its member companies.[144] However, the rule remains that an association of insurance companies that assigns applications for insurance to member companies that perform the actual insurance functions can qualify as a tax-exempt business league because it does not assume the risk on the policies.[145]

Likewise, an engineering society that provided food and beverage service to its individual members was found to be providing a service for individual persons, and thus was deprived of qualification for tax-exempt status as a business league.[146]

Also, an association of life insurance companies that operated an insurance underwriting information exchange among its members was ruled to not qualify as a business league, despite the contention that its primary purpose was to benefit the entire life insurance industry by deterring fraud in the application process and that any benefits to its members were incidental. In the latter instance, the court agreed that the organization's activities advanced the members' interests generally but concluded that the member companies were also provided "particular services."[147] The court held that a major factor in determining whether ser-

---

[141] Oklahoma Cattlemen's Ass'n, Inc. v. United States, *supra* note 97, San Antonio District Dental Soc'y v. United States, 340 F. Supp. 11 (W.D. Tex. 1972). See § 26.5(d).
[142] Associated Master Barbers & Beauticians of Am., Inc. v. Comm'r, *supra* note 140, at 70.
[143] Rev. Rul. 81-174, *supra* note 108, at 336.
[144] Rev. Rul. 81-175, *supra* note 109.
[145] Rev. Rul. 71-155, *supra* note 81.
[146] Engineers Club of San Francisco v. United States, *supra* note 2.
[147] MIB, Inc. v. Comm'r, 734 F.2d 71, 78–81 (1st Cir. 1984).

vices are *particular* is whether they are supported by fees and assessments in approximate proportion to the benefits received.

One court concluded that a nonprofit organization that itself functioned as an insurance agent was a tax-exempt business league. The organization's sole client was a state, which it served in the purchase of all insurance and bonding coverage required by the state and its agencies. The court held that the organization functioned on behalf of agents in the state in that its competent handling of the state's insurance needs enhanced the image of the insurance industry in the eyes of the public.[148] However, on appeal, it was held that the organization was not a tax-exempt business league because it conducted a business of a kind ordinarily carried on for profit and did so more than incidentally.[149]

Despite the express prohibition as stated in the regulations, it is the position of the IRS that a tax-exempt business league will lose its exemption because it performs particular services for individual members only where the services are a principal or sole undertaking of the organization.[150] Where these services are less than a primary function of a business league, the IRS will characterize them as a business of a kind ordinarily carried on for profit and treat the business as an unrelated activity.[151] For example, the IRS concluded that an executive referral service conducted by a tax-exempt association constituted the performance of particular services for individual persons but, because other activities were the association's primary ones, the IRS ruled that the service was an unrelated, taxable business.[152] Similarly, a compensation consulting service, while a particular service, did not jeopardize an association's tax exemption because it was not a primary activity of the organization.[153]

It is frequently difficult in a specific instance to distinguish between the performance of particular services and activities directed to the improvement of business conditions. Perhaps the best illustration of this difficulty is the case of organizations that maintain a "plan room." In one case, an organization of contractors operated a plan room, containing information about plans available, bid results, and activities of concern to persons in the industry. The IRS ruled that the organization was a tax-exempt business league because its activities improved the business conditions of the line of business served inasmuch as it made the information on construction projects freely available to the construction industry as a whole. Clearly, the existence of this type of a plan room is a significant convenience or economy for the member contractors. However, the IRS dismissed this aspect of the facts on the ground that the information on file at the plan room generally duplicated the information already available to its members.[154]

One court, in addressing this issue, concluded that an activity of a business league was a tax-exempt function where the activity benefited its membership as

---

[148] North Carolina Ass'n of Ins. Agents, Inc. v. United States, *supra* note 36.

[149] North Carolina Ass'n of Ins. Agents, Inc. v. United States, 739 F.2d 949 (4th Cir. 1984).

[150] E.g., Rev. Rul. 68-265, *supra* n. 96; Rev. Rul. 68-264, *supra* note 120. In general, Retailers Credit Ass'n of Alameda County v. Comm'r, *supra* note 2.

[151] See Part Five.

[152] Priv. Ltr. Rul. 8524006.

[153] Priv. Ltr. Rul. 9128003.

[154] Rev. Rul. 72-211, *supra* note 52. Also Rev. Rul. 56-65, *supra* note 52.

a group, rather than in their individual capacities.[155] The benefit to the group occurred where the business league provided a product or service to its members for a fee, with the benefit not directly proportional to the fees (for example, seminars, legislative activities). This court wrote that "[s]ervices which render benefits according to the fee that is paid for them are taxable business activities, not tax exempt services."[156] The court added: "Therefore, the activities that serve the interests of individual . . . [members] according to what they pay produce individual benefits insufficient to fulfill the substantial relationship test, since those activities generally do not generate inherent group benefits that inure to the advantage of its members as members."[157]

Subsequently, the IRS grappled with these distinctions, differing between "an industry-wide benefit or a particular service to members." The IRS held that activities that provide an industry-wide benefit "usually possess certain characteristics," such as being an "activity for which individual members could not be expected to bear the expense and thus lends itself to cooperative effort" and the fact that the "benefits are intangible and only indirectly related to the individual business." Activities constituting particular services "can usually be characterized as either a 'means of bringing buyers and sellers together' or a 'convenience or economy' to members in conducting their business," wrote the IRS, which also cautioned that "[f]ull participation by industry components does not guarantee that the activity provides an industry-wide benefit."[158] Thus, for example, the IRS held that the operation, by an exempt association of members in the trucking industry, of an alcohol and drug testing program for members and nonmembers was a particular service (as opposed to an incident of membership), notwithstanding the fact that the prevention of alcohol and drug abuse is a "legitimate goal" of trucking companies.[159]

---

[155] Professional Ins. Agents of Mich. v. Comm'r, 726 F.2d 1097 (6th Cir. 1984).

[156] Id. at 1104.

[157] Id.

[158] Priv. Ltr. Rul. 8524006.

[159] Tech. Adv. Mem. 9550001. Business leagues should be contrasted with organizations operating to better the conditions of persons engaged in agriculture or to improve the grade of their products. These organizations may qualify for tax exemption as labor, agricultural, or horticultural organizations (see Chapter 15) rather than as business leagues. However, if the organization is promoting the common business interests of persons in an industry related to agricultural pursuits, tax-exempt business league designation would be appropriate assuming the organization otherwise qualifies. (Rev. Rul. 70-31, *supra* note 37; Rev. Rul. 67-252, 1967-2 C.B. 195).

Other illustrations of organizations denied classification as business leagues are in Contracting Plumbers Coop. Restoration Corp. v. United States, 488 F.2d 684 (2d Cir. 1974); Credit Managers Ass'n of N. & Cent. Calif. v. United States, 148 F.2d 41 (9th Cir. 1945); Clay Sewer Pipe Ass'n v. United States, 139 F.2d 130 (3d Cir. 1943); Park West-Riverside Assocs., Inc. v. United States, 110 F.2d 1023 (2d Cir. 1940); Motor & Equip. Mfrs. Ass'n v. United States, 57-1 U.S.T.C. ¶ 9253 (D. Ill. 1957); Jockey Club v. United States, 137 F. Supp. 419 (Ct. Cl. 1956), *cert. den.*, 352 U.S. 834 (1956); Cook County Loss Adjustment Bur. v. United States, 42-2 U.S.T.C. ¶ 9638 (D. Ill. 1942); Durham Merchants Ass'n v. United States, 34 F. Supp. 71 (M.D.N.C. 1940); Louisville Credit Men's Ass'n v. United States, 39-2 U.S.T.C. ¶ 9649 (D. Ky. 1939); Louisville Credit Men's Adjustment Bur. v. United States, 6 F. Supp. 196 (W.D. Ky. 1934); Lake Petersburg Ass'n v. Comm'r, 33 T.C.M. 259 (1974); National Automobile Dealers Ass'n v. Comm'r, 2 T.C.M. 291 (1943); Adjustment Bur. of St. Louis Ass'n of Credit Men v. Comm'r, 21 B.T.A. 232 (1930); Rev. Rul. 64-108, 1964-1 C.B. (Part 1) 189; Priv. Ltr. Rul. 7902006.

§ 13.5   CHAMBERS OF COMMERCE, BOARDS OF TRADE, AND THE LIKE

A chamber of commerce or a board of trade that is tax-exempt is an organization the "common business interest" of which is the general economic welfare of a community.[160] That is, it is an organization whose efforts are directed at promoting the common economic interests of all the commercial enterprises in a given trade community. For example, the attraction of business to a particular community is an appropriate tax-exempt activity in this context, even where it necessitates the development of an industrial park.[161] Similarly, an organization formed for the purpose of encouraging national organizations to hold their conventions in a city was recognized by the IRS as being a tax-exempt chamber of commerce.[162]

One court observed that the terms *chamber of commerce* and *board of trade* are "nearly synonymous," although there is a "slight distinction" between their meanings. The court explained: "The former relates to all businesses in a particular geographic location, while the latter may relate to only one or more lines of business in a particular geographic location, but need not relate to all."[163]

By contrast, a business league serves only the common business interests of the members of a single line of business or of closely related lines of business within a single industry. Also, as respects a chamber of commerce or a board of trade, membership is voluntary and generally open to all business and professional persons in the community.[164]

The IRS ruled that a tenants' association (specifically, an association of shopping center merchants) did not qualify as a tax-exempt chamber of commerce or a board of trade.[165] The IRS noted that membership in the association was compulsory, imposed by the landlord owner of the shopping center, and that the requisite "community" was not being served, as the "community represented by the membership of the present organization is a closed, non-public aggregation of commercial enterprises having none of the common characteristics of a community in the usual geographical or political sense."[166] Finally, the IRS invoked a private inurement rationale, holding that the organization was designed to serve the tenants' business interests in the center. (Tax-exempt status as a business league was denied because the association was not structured along particular industry or business lines.[167]) Similarly, a board of trade was denied tax exemption because its principal activity was the provision of services to individuals (grain analysis laboratory services to both members and

---

[160] IRC § 501(c)(b).
[161] Rev. Rul. 70-81, *supra* note 44; Rev. Rul. 81-138, *supra* note 44.
[162] Rev. Rul. 76-207, *supra* note 34.
[163] Retailers Credit Ass'n v. Comm'r, *supra* note 2, at 51.
[164] A self-insurer guaranty trust fund was ruled tax-exempt by reason of IRC § 501(c)(6) because it was "of the same general class" as a chamber of commerce or board of trade (Georgia Self-Insurers Guar. Trust Fund v. United States, 78 A.F.T.R. 2d 6552 (N.D. Ga. 1996)).
[165] Rev. Rul. 73-411, 1973-2 C.B. 180.
[166] *Id.* at 182. Also Rev. Rul. 59-391, *supra* note 3.
[167] Rev. Rul. 64-315, 1964-2 C.B. 147, *clar. by* Rev. Rul. 73-411, *supra* note 165.

nonmembers) and because the board was supported almost entirely from the substantial profits of the laboratory.[168] Likewise, a board of trade does not encompass "organizations which provide conveniences or facilities to certain persons in connection with buying, selling, and exchanging goods."[169] By contrast, an organization regulating the sale of an agricultural commodity to assure equal treatment of producers, warehousers, and purchasers was ruled to be a board of trade.[170]

However, a "neighborhood community association" may qualify for tax exemption in this context where the following criteria are satisfied: The organization has a voluntary membership, it is not concerned with tenants' matters, and the organization is operated to improve the business conditions of a community (rather than a single one-owner shopping mall).[171] This may be the case even though a majority of the association's member businesses is located in one shopping center.

Tax exemption for real estate boards, added in 1928, came into being as an overturning of a court decision. A court, in 1927, denied tax exemption as a business league to a corporation organized by associations of insurance companies to provide printing services for member companies.[172] Thereafter, the statute was revised so as to specifically exempt real estate boards from taxation.

Tax exemption for professional football leagues was added in 1966.[173] This was done to forestall any claim that a football league's pension plan would be considered inurement of benefits to a private individual. The amendment was part of a larger legislative package that paved the way for a merger that created an "industry-wide" professional football league. It is not clear as to why this provision is confined to one professional sport.

§ 13.6 CONSEQUENCES OF ABANDONMENT OF TAX-EXEMPT STATUS

The advantages and benefits of the classification of tax exemption are many: (1) exemption from federal income taxation (thereby sheltering from tax the receipt of dues and other items of income, except with respect to any tax on unrelated income); (2) exemption from taxation (such as income, sales, excise, franchise, and property taxes) at state and local levels; (3) access to contract and grant funds under programs where contractees and grantees must be nonprofit organizations; (4) enhancement of the public's perception and acceptance of the organization and its programs as the result of being designated tax-exempt; (5) much greater flexibility as respects accumulation of funds

---

[168] Rev. Rul. 78-70, 1978-1 C.B. 159. Also Fort Worth Grain & Cotton Exch. v. Comm'r, 27 B.T.A. 983 (1933).
[169] L.O. 1123, III-1 C.B. 275 (1924).
[170] Rev. Rul. 55-715, 1955-2 C.B. 263.
[171] Rev. Rul. 78-225, 1978-1 C.B. 159.
[172] Uniform Printing & Supply Co. v. Comm'r, *supra* note 126.
[173] Pub. L. No. 89-800, 80 Stat. 1515, Sess. (1966) § 6(a).

without adverse tax consequences; and (6) a deduction of $1,000[174] in computing taxable income.[175]

Nonetheless, a business league with a membership base may contemplate abandonment of its tax exemption, in the hope that it can achieve the equivalent of exemption by using the expenses of some related activities and those associated with investments to offset the net income from other related activities. The thought is that, by converting to a taxable organization, the entity can escape the various forms of regulation with which it is burdened as an exempt organization.

Prior to 1969, this stratagem would have worked, because the income of the organization from business activities (including services to nonmembers) and investments could have been offset by deductions in the form of expenses of providing services to members (as related activities), thereby generating little if any overall net income. This approach was tolerated by a federal court of appeals, which held that the investment income of a nonexempt water company could be offset by its losses in supplying water to its members.[176] However, other courts were not permitting this result.[177]

In 1969, Congress created special rules in an attempt to resolve the matter.[178] These rules are applicable with respect to any membership organization that is not exempt from taxation and is operated primarily to furnish services or goods to its members. This provision allows deductions for a tax year attributable to the furnishing of services, insurance, goods, or other items of value to the organization's membership only to the extent of income derived during the year from members or transactions with members (including income derived during the year from institutes and trade shows that are primarily for the education of members).

The intent of these rules is to preclude the result previously sanctioned by the above-referenced appellate court, that is, to prevent a taxable membership organization from offsetting its business and investment income with deductions created by the provision of related services to members. Stated another way, these rules are designed to make taxable membership organizations allocate and confine their deductions to the corresponding sources of income.[179] As a result, an organization that operated in a particular year at an overall loss may still have to pay tax if its unrelated business and investment activities produced net income.

---

[174] See § 28.2.

[175] Classification of an organization under IRC § 501(c)(3) brings the same advantages and benefits as classification under IRC § 501(c)(6), except for the limitation on legislative activities, along with the preferences of charitable donee status and various postal privileges. See § 3.2.

[176] Anaheim Union Water Co. v. Comm'r, 321 F.2d 253 (9th Cir. 1963), rev'g 35 T.C. 1972 (1961). Also Bear Valley Mut. Water Co. v. Riddell, 283 F. Supp. 949 (C.D. Cal. 1968), aff'd, 427 F.2d 713 (9th Cir. 1970); San Antonio Water Co. v. Riddell, 285 F. Supp. 297 (C.D. Cal. 1968), aff'd, 427 F.2d 713 (9th Cir. 1970).

[177] Adirondack League Club v. Comm'r, 55 T.C. 796 (1971), aff'd, 458 F.2d 506 (2d Cir. 1972); Five Lakes Outing Club v. United States, 468 F.2d 443 (8th Cir. 1972); Iowa State Univ. of Science & Technology v. United States, 500 F.2d 508 (Ct. Cl. 1974).

[178] IRC § 277.

[179] E.g., Concord Consumers Hous. Coop. v. Comm'r, 89 T.C. 105 (1987); Armour-Dial Men's Club, Inc. v. Comm'r, 77 T.C. 1 (1981). Also Rev. Rul. 90-36, 1990-1 C.B. 59.

In this fashion, these rules are intended to serve as a deterrent to the abandonment of tax-exempt status by membership organizations, particularly those that are serving their members at less than cost.[180]

Where, for a tax year, a taxable membership organization's deductions attributable to the furnishing of items of value to members exceed income from its members, the excess may be carried forward and used as a deduction against income from its members in the succeeding tax year.[181]

---

[180] H. Rep. No. 91-413 (Part 1), 91st Cong., 1st Sess. 49 (1969); S. Rep. No. 91-552, 91st Cong., 1st Sess. 74 (1969).

[181] Certain nonprofit membership organizations that receive prepaid dues income (such as the American Automobile Association) are not subject to the IRC § 277 restrictions on deductions. See IRC §§ 277(b)(2), 456(c). IRC § 277 is applicable to any nonexempt membership organization that otherwise meets the requirements of the section and was previously tax-exempt under any provision of IRC § 501(c), including IRC §§ 501(c)(3), 501(c)(4), 501(c)(5), 501(c)(6), or 501(c)(7). In general, Brittain & Crotty, "Creation of Tax-Exempt Business Leagues: For the Section 501(c)(6) 'First Timer'," 16 *Washburn L.J.* 628 (1977); Crawford, "The Money Side: Associations," XXX *Golf J.* (No. 2) 24 (1977); Denny, "Professional and Social Organizations," 25 *Tul. Tax Inst.* 2200 (1975); Combs, "Tax Implications of Association Efforts for Members," 69 *The Brief* 155 (1974); Fox & Jackson, "Trade Associations: Present and Future Problems," 26 *Tax L. Rev.* 781 (1971); Bodner, "Antitrust Restrictions on Trade Association Membership and Participation," 54 *A.B.A.J.* 37 (1968); Cooper, "The Tax Treatment of Business Grassroots Lobbying: Defining and Attaining the Public Policy Objectives," 68 *Columbia L. Rev.* 801 (1968); Orrick, "Risks Inherent in Trade Associations," *Nat'l Oil Jobber* 11 (May 1967); Note, "Tax-Exempt Business League and Its Functions," 8 *B.C. Ind. & Com. L. Rev.* 953 (1967); Note, "Taxation—Business Leagues—Noncompetitive Membership Does Not Preclude Exempt Status," 13 *Wayne L. Rev.* 611 (1967); Van De Linder, "Trade Associations: Retaining Exemption, Unrelated Business Income Problems," 24 *J. Tax.* 250 (1966); Webster, "Current Federal Tax Aspects of Association Activities," 27 *A.B.A. Sec. Antitust Law* 150 (1965); Webster, "Should a Trade Association Give Up Its Tax Exemption? The Pros and Cons," 23 *J. Tax.* 358 (1962); Teschner, "Business Leagues, Tax Exemption v. Service to Members," 37 *Taxes* 669 (1959).

As to the IRC § 277 rules, see Crimm, "Should Internal Revenue Code Section 277 Be Applied to Cooperative Housing Organizations," 7 *Akron Tax J.* (No. 2) 87 (1990); Miller, "Condominiums and Cooperatives: IRS Tiers Section 277 Allowances So As to Minimize Reduction of Tenant-Stockholder Deductions," 18 *J. Real Estate Tax.* (No. 2) 167 (1991); Fleck, "Cooperatives—Accounting and Tax Developments: Section 277 Issues in Private Letter Rulings," 11 *J. Agric. Tax. & Law* (No. 1) 86 (1989).

CHAPTER FOURTEEN

Social Clubs

The tax-exempt social club has as the essential prerequisite of its exemption the provision of pleasure and recreation to its members. By contrast, many other tax-exempt organizations find their classification as such rationalized by a concept of public service (charitable works, promotion of social welfare, economic betterment, or the like).

§ 14.1 SOCIAL CLUBS IN GENERAL

The federal tax law provides tax exemption for qualified social clubs, which are "organized for pleasure, recreation, and other nonprofitable purposes, substantially all of the activities of which are for such purposes and no part of the net earnings of which inures to the benefit of any private shareholder."[1] Generally, this tax exemption extends to social and recreation clubs that are supported primarily by membership fees, dues, and assessments.[2] However, an organization that otherwise qualifies as a tax-exempt social club will not be denied tax exemption solely because it adopts a method of raising revenue from members by means other than fees, dues, and assessments.[3]

Social clubs are tax-exempt in part because Congress recognized that these organizations are generally not appropriate subjects of taxation, that is, that the operation of a social club does not involve the requisite shifting of income.[4] One court summarized the rationale as follows:

> Congress has determined that in a situation where individuals have banded together to provide recreational facilities on a mutual basis, it would be conceptually erroneous to impose a tax on the organization as a separate entity. The funds exempted are received only from the members and any "profit" which results from overcharging for the use of the facilities still belongs to the

---

[1] IRC § 501(c)(7).

[2] Reg. § 1.501(c)(7)-1(a); Maryland Country Club, Inc. v. United States, 539 F.2d 345 (4th Cir. 1976).

[3] Rev. Rul. 44, 1953-1 C.B. 109.

[4] See § 1.5.

same members. No income of the sort usually taxed has been generated; the money has simply been shifted from one pocket to another, both within the same pair of pants.[5]

The Department of the Treasury acknowledged the legitimacy of the tax exemption for social clubs for essentially the same reason:

> [T]he tax exemption for social clubs is designed to allow individuals to join together to provide recreational or social facilities on a mutual basis, without further tax consequences . . . [where] the sources of income of the organization are limited to receipts from the membership . . . the individual is in substantially the same position as if he had spent his income on pleasure or recreation without the intervening separate organization.[6]

This theme was echoed in the legislative history accompanying the extension, in 1969, of the tax on unrelated business income to social clubs.[7] Thus, one committee report explained:

> Since the tax exemption for social clubs and other groups is designed to allow individuals to join together to provide recreational or social facilities or other benefits on a mutual basis, without tax consequences, the tax exemption operates properly only when the sources of income of the organization are limited to receipts from the membership. Under such circumstances, the individual is in substantially the same position as if he had spent his income on pleasure or recreation (or other benefits) without the intervening separate organization. However, where the organization receives income from sources outside the membership, such as income from investments . . . upon which no tax is paid, the membership receives a benefit not contemplated by the exemption in that untaxed dollars can be used by the organization to provide pleasure or recreation (or other benefits) to its membership . . . In such a case, the exemption is no longer simply allowing individuals to join together for recreation or pleasure without tax consequences. Rather, it is bestowing a substantial additional advantage to the members of the club by allowing tax-free dollars to be used for their personal recreational or pleasure purposes. The extension of the exemption to such investment income is, therefore, a distortion of its purpose.[8]

Reflecting on this rationale, the U.S. Supreme Court concluded that the federal tax exemption for social clubs "has a justification fundamentally different from that which underlies the grant of tax exemption to other nonprofit entities."[9] That is, while for most nonprofit organizations "exemption from federal income tax is intended to encourage the provision of services that are deemed socially beneficial," "[s]ocial clubs are exempted from tax not as a means of conferring tax *advantages*, but as a means of ensuring that the members are not subject to tax *disadvantages* as a consequence of their decision to pool their resources for the pur-

[5] McGlotten v. Connally, 338 F. Supp. 448, 458 (D.D.C. 1972).
[6] Treasury Department, *Tax Reform Studies and Proposals* (Comm. Prt.), 91st Cong., 1st Sess. 317 (1969).
[7] See § 26.1, text accompanied by notes 25–26.
[8] S. Rep. No. 91-552, 91st Cong., 1st Sess. 71 (1969).
[9] Portland Golf Club v. Comm'r., 497 U.S. 154, 161 (1990).

pose of social or recreational services."[10] The Court restated this rationale by observing that the "statutory scheme for the taxation of social clubs was intended to achieve tax *neutrality*, not to provide these clubs a tax advantage: even the exemption for income derived from members' payments was designed to ensure that members are not disadvantaged as compared with persons who pursue recreation through private purchases rather than through the medium of an organization."[11]

To qualify as a tax-exempt social club, an organization not only must be a nonprofit entity[12] but must meet both an organizational test and an operational test.[13] To satisfy the requirement of a pleasure, recreation, or other permissible purpose,[14] the club must have an established membership of individuals, personal contacts and fellowship.[15] A commingling of the members must play a material part in the life of the organization.[16]

Where the requisite degree of fellowship is absent, tax exemption may be denied, as occurred with respect to an organization formed to furnish television antenna service to its members[17] and associations composed primarily of "artificial" persons or other clubs.[18] Thus, a club operated to assist its members in their business endeavors through study and discussion of problems and similar activities at weekly luncheon meetings was denied tax exemption as a social club on the ground that any social activities at the meetings were merely incidental to the business purpose of the organization.[19] A related concept is that a club, to be tax-exempt, must have members actively sharing interests or goals, as evidenced, for example, by appropriate prerequisite conditions or limitations upon members.[20] It is insufficient, for purposes of this tax exemption, for an organization to be able to demonstrate a common objective or interest of the members. Consequently, for example, most nonprofit automobile clubs are denied tax exemption as social clubs.[21]

---

[10] *Id.* at 161–162 (emphasis in original).

[11] *Id.* at 163 (emphasis in original).

[12] West Side Tennis Club v. Comm'r, 111 F.2d 6 (2d Cir. 1940), *cert. den.*, 311 U.S. 674 (1940).

[13] E.g., Rev. Rul. 70-32, 1970-1 C.B. 140.

[14] Discussions of the scope of the phrase "other nonprofitable purposes" appear in Allgemeiner Arbeiter Verein v. Comm'r, 237 F.2d 605 (3d Cir. 1956); Allied Trades Club v. Comm'r, 228 F.2d 906 (3d Cir. 1956); The Associates v. Comm'r, 28 B.T.A. 521 (1933). Clubs providing sickness and death benefits to their members do not qualify as exempt social clubs (e.g., Polish Army Veterans Post 147 v. Comm'r, 24 T.C. 891 (1955), *rev'd on another issue*, 236 F.2d 509 (3d Cir. 1956); St. Albert's American-Polish Citizens & Social Club v. Comm'r, 14 T.C.M. 196 (1955); Spokane Commercial Travelers v. United States, 126 F. Supp. 424 (W. D. Wash. 1954); Rev. Rul. 63-190, 1963-2 C.B. 212).

[15] Kanawha-Roane Lands, Inc. v. United States, 136 F. Supp. 631 (D. W. Va. 1956); Barstow Rodeo & Riding Club v. Comm'r, 12 T.C.M. 1351 (1953).

[16] Rev. Rul. 58-589, 1958-2 C.B. 266.

[17] Rev. Rul. 55-716, 1955-2 C.B. 263, *mod. by* Rev. Rul. 83-170, 1983-2 C.B. 97; also Gen. Couns. Mem. 39063. (Cf. Rev. Rul. 62-167, 1962-2 C.B. 142.)

[18] Rev. Rul. 67-428, 1967-2 C.B. 204.

[19] Rev. Rul. 69-527, 1969-2 C.B. 125.

[20] Arner v. Rogan, 40-2 U.S.T.C. ¶ 9567 (S.D. Cal. 1940).

[21] Warren Automobile Club v. Comm'r, 182 F.2d *551* (6th Cir. 1950); Keystone Automobile Club v. Comm'r, 181 F.2d 402 (3d Cir. 1950); Chattanooga Automobile Club v. Comm'r, 182 F.2d 551 (6th Cir. 1950); Smyth v. California State Automobile Ass'n, 175 F.2d 752 (9th Cir. 1949), *cert. den.*, 338 U.S. 905 (1949); Automobile Club of St. Paul v. Comm'r, 12 T.C. 1152 (1949); Rev. Rul. 69-635, 1969-2 C.B. 126; Rev. Rul. 67-249, 1967-2 C.B. 179.

To the IRS, the criterion of providing pleasure or recreation by a tax-exempt social club to its members is paramount to the qualification of the club for tax exemption. Thus, gambling can be a tax-exempt purpose for a social club, even where substantial income is derived from the practice, as long as the source of the revenue is the club's members and their guests. The IRS will refrain from denying or revoking an organization's tax exemption on this basis, notwithstanding the fact that the gambling activities are illegal under state or local law.[22]

While country clubs, dinner clubs, variety clubs, swim, golf, and tennis clubs, and the like set the norm for the tax-exempt social club,[23] the concept of an exempt social club is considerably broader. Thus, a flying club was ruled to qualify for tax exemption, where the members were interested in flying as a hobby, commingled in informal meetings, maintained and repaired aircraft owned by the club, and flew together in small groups,[24] as opposed to a club that was operated primarily to provide flying facilities suitable for members' individual business or personal use.[25] Social club status was accorded an organization composed solely of persons who were members of a political party and those interested in party affairs,[26] and of members of a specific family to bring them into closer communication through social, family history, and newsletter activities.[27] Gem and mineral clubs or a federation of these clubs may qualify as tax-exempt social clubs.[28] Other illustrations of tax-exempt social clubs include pet clubs,[29] garden clubs,[30] fraternities and sororities,[31] a sponsor of bowling tournaments,[32] a promoter of golf,[33] a horse-riding club,[34] and clubs affiliated with tax-exempt lodges.[35]

A tax-exempt social club may provide social and recreational facilities to its members who are limited to homeowners of a housing development and nonetheless qualify for tax exemption. However, the exemption will be precluded where any of the following services are provided by the club: owning and maintaining residential streets, administering and enforcing covenants for the preservation of the architecture and appearance of the housing development, or providing police and fire protection and a trash collection service to residential areas.[36]

---

[22] Rev. Rul. 69-68, 1969-1 C.B. 153.

[23] Hillcrest Country Club, Inc. v. United States, 152 F. Supp. 896 (D. Mo. 1957); Slovene Workers Home v. Dallman, 56-1 U.S.T.C. ¶ 9205 (S.D. Ill. 1956); Coeur D'Alene Athletic Round Table, Inc. v. Comm'r, 21 T.C.M. 1430 (1962); Rev. Rul. 69-281, 1969-1 C.B. 155.

[24] Rev. Rul. 74-30, 1974-1 C.B. 137. Also Syrang Aero Club, Inc. v. Comm'r, 73 T.C. 717 (1980).

[25] Rev. Rul. 70-32, *supra* note 13. Also Rev. Rul. 56-475, 1956-2 C.B. 308.

[26] Rev. Rul. 68-266, 1968-1 C.B. 270. Cf. Thomas J. McGee Regular Democratic Club, Inc. v. Comm'r, 1 T.C.M. 18 (1942) (where public use was too extensive).

[27] Rev. Rul. 67-8, 1967-1 C.B. 142.

[28] Rev. Rul. 67-139, 1967-1 C.B. 129.

[29] Rev. Rul. 73-520, 1973-2 C.B. 180; Rev. Rul. 71-421, 1971-2 C.B. 229.

[30] Rev. Rul. 66-179, 1966-1 C.B. 139.

[31] Rev. Rul. 69-573, 1969-2 C.B. 125; Rev. Rul. 64-118, 1964-1 C.B. (Part 1) 182; Phinney v. Dougherty, 307 F.2d 357 (5th Cir. 1962); Alumnae Chapter Beta of Clovia v. Comm'r, 46 T.C. 297 (1983).

[32] Rev. Rul. 74-148, 1974-1 C.B. 138.

[33] Augusta Golf Ass'n v. United States, 338 F. Supp. 272 (S.D. Ga. 1971).

[34] Clements Buckaroos v. Comm'r, 21 T.C.M. 83 (1962).

[35] Rev. Rul. 66-150, 1966-1 C.B. 164; Rev. Rul. 56-305, 1956-2 C.B. 307.

[36] Rev. Rul. 75-494, 1975-2 C.B. 214.

A social club constitutes a *welfare benefit fund*[37] and therefore a *disqualified benefit*[38] provided by the organization will give rise to tax liability.[39]

There is no business expense or other tax deduction for amounts paid or incurred for membership in a social club, whether or not tax-exempt.[40] This rule is effective for taxable years beginning after December 31, 1993.[41]

§ 14.2 PUBLIC USE OF FACILITIES

Under the income tax regulations (which antedate the 1976 statutory revision, discussed below), a "club which engages in business, such as making its social and recreational facilities available to the general public . . ., is not organized and operated exclusively for pleasure, recreation, and other nonprofitable purposes, and is not exempt" from federal income tax.[42] Solicitation of the general public to utilize club facilities will disqualify the social club for tax exemption.[43]

The IRS promulgated guidelines for determining the effect on a social club's tax exemption of gross receipts derived from nonmember use of the club's facilities.[44] The concern in this regard is not with the situation where a club member entertains a few guests at his or her club, but where a club's facilities are made available to the general public on a regular and recurring basis, thereby removing that segment of the public from the marketplace of competing commercial operations.[45] Of course, infrequent use of a tax-exempt social club by the general public is permissible, since it is an incidental use.[46] Thus, for example, a club cannot be tax-

---

[37] IRC § 419(e)(3)(A).

[38] IRC § 4976(b).

[39] IRC § 4976(a).

[40] IRC § 274(a)(3).

[41] For this purpose, a *club* organized for business, pleasure, recreation, or other social purpose includes any membership organization "if a principal purpose of the organization is to conduct entertainment activities for members of the organization or their guests or to provide members or their guests with access to entertainment facilities" (Reg. § 1.274-2(a)(2)(iii)(a)). These clubs include country clubs, golf and athletic clubs, airline clubs, and clubs operated to provide meals under circumstances generally considered to be conducive to business discussion (*id.*). Unless a principal purpose of the organization is to conduct or provide entertainment, this rule is inapplicable to (1) trade associations, professional organizations (such as bar and medical associations), other business leagues, chambers of commerce, boards of trade, or real estate boards (see Chapter 13); or (2) civic or public service organizations (including those described in Chapter 12) (Reg. § 1.274-2(a)(2)(iii)(b)).

[42] Reg. § 1.501(c)(7)-1(b).

[43] Keystone Automobile Club v. Comm'r, *supra* note 21; United States v. Fort Worth Club of Fort Worth, Texas, 345 F.2d 52 (5th Cir. 1965), *mod. and reaff'd*, 348 F.2d 891 (5th Cir. 1965); Polish Am. Club, Inc. v. Comm'r, 33 T.C.M. 925 (1974).

[44] Rev. Proc. 71-17, 1971-1 C.B. 683. Also The Minnequa Univ. Club v. Comm'r, 30 T.C.M. 1305 (1971).

[45] Rev. Rul. 60-324, 1960-2 C.B. 173. Also Rev. Rul. 69-220, 1969-1 C.B. 154; Rev. Rul. 69-217, 1969-1 C.B. 115; Rev. Rul. 68-638, 1968-2 C.B. 220; Rev. Rul. 65-63, 1965-1 C.B. 240; United States v. Fort Worth Club of Fort Worth, Texas, *supra* n. 43; Spokane Motorcycle Club v. United States, 222 F. Supp. 151 (E.D. Wash. 1963); Sabers of Denver, Inc. v. United States, 65-2 U.S.T.C. ¶ 9670 (D. Col. 1965); Matter of The Breakfast Club, Ltd., 35-1 U.S.T.C. ¶ 9265 (D. Cal. 1935).

[46] Rev. Rul. 60-323, 1960-2 C.B. 173; Rev. Rul. 66-149, 1966-1 C.B. 146; Town & Country Club v. Comm'r, 1 T.C.M. 334 (1942).

exempt when a significant portion of its revenue is derived from greens fees charged to the general public,[47] yet can be exempt where fees of this nature are incidental.[48]

The IRS guidelines make it clear that use of a tax-exempt social club's facilities by the general public may indicate the existence of a nonexempt purpose, which if substantial would cause loss of tax exemption, or may make the club liable for the unrelated business income tax.[49] These guidelines establish a basic set of assumptions (which are also utilized for audit purposes) regarding member-sponsored income and a complex record-keeping system to substantiate them. Detailed records are also required to determine under what circumstances and to what extent the social club makes its facilities available to nonmembers.

Essentially, the guideline assumptions are as follows:

1. Where a group of no more than eight individuals, at least one of whom is a member, uses club facilities, it is assumed that the nonmembers are the guests of the member, provided payment for the use is received by the club directly from the member or his or her employer.

2. Where at least 75 percent of a group using club facilities are members, a similar assumption will be made. The validity of this test was rejected by a federal district court as being "unreasonable," with the court opining that "revenue from member-sponsored occasions involving attendance of nonmembers should not be considered as outsider transactions with respect to their impact on exempt status if it would be reasonable and normal, in the ordinary course of the activities usually pursued by social clubs, to utilize club premises or services for such occasions."[50]

3. Payment by a member's employer is assumed to be for a use that serves a direct business objective of the employee-member. A corporation may pay for individual club memberships without jeopardizing the club's tax exemption,[51] although an organization the membership of which was entirely in corporations' names would not qualify for tax exemption.[52] However, to the extent a tax-exempt social club has corporate members, the individuals who use the club's facilities under the memberships are treated as the general public for purpose of the guidelines.[53]

4. In all other situations, a host-guest relationship is not assumed but must be substantiated. As to these occasions, the social club must maintain books and records containing specific information (as stated in the guidelines) about each use and the income derived from the uses. However,

---

[47] Rev. Rul. 69-219, 1969-1 C.B. 153.
[48] Coeur d'Alene Country Club v. Viley, 64 F. Supp. 540 (D. Idaho 1946).
[49] See Part Five.
[50] Pittsburgh Press Club v. United States, 388 F. Supp. 1269, 1276 (W.D. Pa. 1975), *rev. and rem.*, 536 F.2d 572 (3d Cir. 1976), 426 F. Supp. 553 (W.D. Pa. 1977), *rem.*, 579 F.2d 751 (3d Cir. 1978), 462 F. Supp. 322 (W.D. Pa. 1978), *rev'd*, 615 F.2d 600 (3d Cir. 1980).
[51] Rev. Rul. 74-168, 1974-1 C.B. 139.
[52] Rev. Rul. 67-428, *supra* note 18.
[53] Rev. Rul. 74-489, 1974-2 C.B. 169.

even as to the first and second of these items, adequate records must be maintained.[54]

As well as stating the above assumptions, these IRS guidelines detail the bookkeeping requirements that tax-exempt social clubs must follow.

Where the group includes eight or fewer individuals, the tax-exempt social club must maintain records that substantiate that the group included no more than eight individuals, at least one of whom was a member, and that payment was received from the member or his or her employer. Where 75 percent or more of the group are members of the club, records must be maintained that substantiate that at least 75 percent of the group were club members and that payment was received directly from members or members' employers.

On all other occasions involving nonmembers, the tax-exempt social club must maintain records showing each use and the income derived from the use, even though a member pays initially for the use. The club's records must also include the following: the date, the total number in the party, the number of nonmembers in the party, the total charges, the charges attributable to nonmembers, and the charges paid by nonmembers. If a member pays all or part of the charges, there must be a statement signed by the member as to whether he or she has been or will be reimbursed and to what extent by the nonmembers.

Further, where a member's employer reimburses the member, or pays the social club directly for nonmember charges, there must be a statement indicating the name of the employer, the amount attributable to nonmember use, the nonmember's name and business or other relationship to the member, and the business, personal, or social purpose of the member served by the nonmember use. If a nonmember (other than a member's employer) makes payment to the club or reimburses a member and claims the amount was paid gratuitously, the member must sign a statement indicating the donor's name, relationship to the member, and information demonstrating the gratuitous nature of the payment.

The requirements for record keeping under these IRS guidelines are extensive, and the penalty for failing to maintain adequate records is severe. If these records are not maintained, the IRS will not apply the minimum gross receipts standard or the audit assumptions and all income will be treated as unrelated business income. Therefore, tax-exempt social clubs must maintain adequate records for the purpose of labeling income from members as *exempt function income*.

Excessive use of tax-exempt social club facilities by the general public is not the only way in which a club may be considered as engaging in business. In one instance, a swim club was held to be operated as a commercial venture for the financial benefit of its manager and thus was denied tax exemption.[55] (However, a club may, without jeopardizing its tax exemption, enter into a management and lease agreement for the operation of its facilities.[56]) In another case, a club had

---

[54] It is the position of the IRS that amounts paid to a tax-exempt social club by visiting members of another tax-exempt social club are forms of nonmember income even though paid pursuant to a reciprocal arrangement (Gen. Couns. Mem. 39343).

[55] Rev. Rul. 65-219, 1965-2 C.B. 168.

[56] Rev. Rul. 67-302, 1967-2 C.B. 203.

such a large number of "associate members" that the IRS treated it as selling services for profit to these individuals.[57]

As referenced, one of the statutory requirements for tax exemption of social clubs was that they must be organized and operated *exclusively* for pleasure, recreation, and other nonprofitable purposes.[58] Congress in 1976 changed this rule so that now *substantially all* of a club's activities must be for these purposes.[59] This allows a tax-exempt social club to receive some outside income (including investment income) and a higher level of income from nonmembers using its facilities or services than the IRS previously allowed without losing its tax-exempt status. The intent of Congress in this regard was that a tax-exempt social club can receive up to 35 percent of its gross receipts (other than unusual amounts) from investment income and receipts from nonmembers, as long as the latter do not exceed 15 percent of total receipts.[60]

In computing this percentage, a tax-exempt social club need not take into consideration "unusual amounts of income." This rule was generally intended to cover receipts from the sale of a clubhouse or similar facility. Presumably, the rule is also applicable to receipts from a major sporting event (such as a golf or tennis tournament) that is open to the public but is held by the club on an irregular basis. This interpretation would be in conformance with prior caselaw.[61]

However, some clubs hold tournaments on a regularly recurring basis (for example, annually). In this situation, the exclusion for unusual amounts is presumably unavailable. Thus, the tax exemption of a social club in this circumstance would be adversely affected if the 15 percent limitation was exceeded[62] but, even if the level of receipts did not trigger revocation of tax exemption, the return from the tournament would nonetheless be subject to taxation as non-exempt function income.[63]

A tax-exempt social club that makes its facilities available to the general public in hosting an athletic tournament generates receipts from nonmember use of the facilities, with these receipts subject to the 15 percent test. For example, the IRS ruled that an association of professional tournament golfers that maintained a championship course may make the course available to the general public when the tournament is not being held, without disturbing its tax-exempt status but with the income from the use subject to taxation as unrelated business income.[64]

It is the view of the Chief Counsel of the IRS, however, that the revision of the law in 1976 did not modify the preexisting rule that revenue derived by an activity that does not advance exempt purposes, whether engaged in for the benefit of members or nonmembers, will lead to revocation of a social club's tax-exempt

---

[57] Rev. Rul. 58-588, 1958-2 C.B. 265.
[58] See text accompanying *supra* note 42.
[59] Pub. L. No. 94-568, 94th Cong., 2d Sess. (1976).
[60] H. Rep. No. 94-1353, 94th Cong., 2d Sess. 4 (1976); S. Rep. No. 94-1318, 94th Cong., 2d Sess. 4 (1976). Also I.R. 1731 (Jan. 11, 1977).
[61] E.g., Santee Club v. White, 87 F.2d 5 (1st Cir. 1936).
[62] West Side Tennis Club v. United States, 111 F.2d 6 (2d Cir. 1940); Rev. Rul. 68-638, *supra* note 45.
[63] See *infra* § 3.
[64] Priv. Ltr. Rul. 7838108.

status.[65] These activities, known as *nontraditional* activities, may not cause loss of tax-exempt status if the income from them represents only *de minimis* amounts of income. In one instance, the IRS's lawyers considered the tax status of a social club that rented rooms as temporary principal residences, rented offices, operated a barber shop, provided a take-out service, operated a service station and parking garage, and maintained in its lobby a commercial ticket agency, a flower and gift shop, and a liquor store. The sale of petroleum products and services, and of take-out food, were found to be nontraditional activities; the rental of rooms, operation of the barber shop and parking garage, and maintenance of the ticket agency were termed "questionable."[66]

§ 14.3 TAXATION OF SOCIAL CLUBS

The income tax regulations deprive tax exemption for a social club that "engages in business, such as by selling real estate, timber or other products," unless a sale of property is incidental.[67] Nonetheless, abuses were prevalent, perhaps fostered by the courts' willingness to salvage a social club's tax exemption. For example, a federal court of appeals held that two golf clubs did not lose tax exemption because of the execution of oil leases on their properties that generated substantial income, on the theory that the leases were "incidental" to club operations.[68] Of course, the profits from the oil leases went untaxed.[69]

In 1969, Congress adhered to the Department of the Treasury's recommendation for reform in this area. The Treasury Department had, in effect, relied on the basic rationale for the tax exemption of social clubs[70] and ran the rationale in reverse, contending that the investment income of social clubs was equivalent to income earned by the club members in their individual capacity. Thus, the Senate Finance Committee stated:

> Since the tax exemption for social clubs and other groups is designed to allow individuals to join together to provide recreational and social facilities or other benefits on a mutual basis, without tax consequences, the exemption operates properly only when the sources of income of the organization are limited to the receipts from the membership.... However where the organization receives income from sources outside the membership, such as income from investments ... upon which no tax is paid, the membership receives a benefit not contemplated by the exemption in that untaxed dollars can be used by the

---

[65] See *supra* § 2.

[66] Gen. Couns. Mem. 39115.

[67] Reg. § 1.501(c)(7)-1(b); Rev. Rul. 69-232, 1969-1 C.B. 154.

[68] Scofield v. Corpus Christi Golf & Country Club, 127 F.2d 452 (5th Cir. 1942); Koon Kreek Klub v. United States, 108 F.2d 616 (5th Cir. 1940). Cf. The Coastal Club, Inc. v. Comm'r, 43 T.C. 783 (1965), aff'd, 368 F.2d 231 (5th Cir. 1966), cert. den., 386 U.S. 1032 (1967).

[69] Other cases involving social clubs that were nonexempt businesses are Aviation Club of Utah v. Comm'r, 162 F.2d 984 (10th Cir. 1947), cert. den., 332 U.S. 837 (1947). However, where the business activity was incidental, tax exemption was permitted (e.g., Town & Country Club v. Comm'r, *supra* note 46; Aviation Country Club, Inc. v. Comm'r, 21 T.C. 807 (1954)).

[70] See text accompanying *supra* notes 5–11.

organization to provide pleasure or recreation (or other benefits) to its membership.[71]

In that year, Congress subjected income unrelated to the normal operation of a social club to the tax on unrelated business income.

For most types of tax-exempt organizations, revenue is nontaxable other than net income from unrelated business activities.[72] Thus, for nearly all tax-exempt organizations, nontaxable revenue embraces gifts, grants, income from the performance of exempt functions, and passive (investment) income. However, the income of a qualified social club is taxed in a significantly different manner: rather than isolate and tax unrelated business taxable income (the general rule), the law isolates the exempt function income of social clubs and subjects the balance of its revenue (including investment income) to taxation. (Thus, one of the principal disadvantages of classification as a "tax-exempt" social club is that all of its investment income—including passive income—generally is taxable.[73])

Specifically, a tax-exempt social club's *unrelated business taxable income* is defined as "gross income (excluding any exempt function income), less the deductions allowed . . . [for business expenses] which are directly connected with the production of the gross income (excluding exempt function income) . . ."[74] This income is computed for tax purposes by deducting all expenses directly connected with production of the income and by applying certain of the modifications generally used in determining unrelated business taxable income.[75]

In recent years, there has been a substantial dispute (eventually resolved by the U.S. Supreme Court, as discussed below) as to the extent to which deductions may be taken in determining a tax-exempt social club's taxable income, leading to differing positions by federal appellate courts. This dispute was stimulated by

---

[71] S. Rep. No. 91-552, *supra* note 8; also H. Rep. No. 91-413, 91st Cong., 1st Sess. 47 (1969) (Part 1); Rev. Rul. 69-220, *supra* note 45. Applying this doctrine, a federal court of appeals held that the regular drawings with the public by a Knights of Columbus council (an IRC § 501(c)(8) fraternal society (see § 18.4(a))) were subject to the wagering excise and occupational taxes (IRC § 4421), in that the exception from the taxes for activities where there is no inurement of net earnings was ruled to not apply, on the theory that the revenues derived from the gaming are used to preclude dues increases, so that the "subsidization" constitutes a form of private inurement to the council's members (Knights of Columbus Council No. 3660 v. United States, 83-2 U.S.T.C. ¶ 16,410 (S.D. Ind. 1983), *aff'd*, 783 F.2d 69 (7th Cir. 1986).

[72] See Part Five.

[73] E.g., Carlson, "The Little Known Repeal of the Income Tax Exemption of Social Clubs," 26 *Tax L. Rev.* 45 (1970).

[74] IRC § 512(a)(3)(A); Prop. Reg. § 1.512(a)-3(a), (b). Thus, in one case, the interest earned by a tax-exempt social club on deposits required for its charter flights was held taxable as unrelated income (Council of British Socies in S. Calif. v. United States, 78-2 U.S.T.C. ¶ 9744 (C.D. Cal. 1978), *aff'd*, 587 F.2d 931 (9th Cir. 1978)). Also Deer Park Country Club v. Comm'r, 70 T.C.M. 1445 (1995); Confrerie De La Chaine Des Rotisseurs v. Comm'r, 66 T.C.M. 1845 (1993); Inter-Com Club, Inc. v. United States, 89-2 U.S.T.C. ¶ 9497 (D. Neb. 1989).

[75] IRC § 162, 512(b). The foregoing rules are also applicable to organizations described in IRC §§ 501(c)(9), 501(c)(17), and 501(c)(20). See Chapter 16.

IRC § 513(a)(3) was amended in 1976 to make it clear that the dividends received deduction (of IRC § 243) is treated as not directly connected with the production of gross income for these purposes. This, however, was the intent of Congress since 1969 (Rolling Rock Club v. United States, 85-1 U.S.T.C. ¶ 9374 (W.D. Pa. 1985), *aff'd*, 785 F.2d 93 (3d Cir. 1986)).

the practice of social clubs of deducting from investment income losses incurred in connection with the sale of meals and beverages to nonmembers. Thus, an effort commenced to develop a theory to preclude a tax-exempt social club from generating losses from the performance of nonexempt functions that could be offset against gross investment income.

The IRS announced in 1981 that, when a social club operates a food and beverage concession catering to nonmembers and has consistently sold the food and beverages at prices insufficient to recover the cost of sales, the club "may not, in determining its unrelated business taxable income . . . , deduct from its net investment income its losses from such sales to nonmembers."[76] The concept underlying this position was that, where a tax-exempt social club does not endeavor to realize a profit from the sales to nonmembers, the expenses cannot be deductible as business expenses under the general rules for that deduction.[77]

This position was tested in the U.S. Tax Court and was upheld, albeit on a different theory. The Tax Court, relying on the statutory language that states that a social club's taxable income is gross nonexempt income less the deductions that are "directly connected" with the production of gross income, held that a social club's expense may only be offset against income it directly helped to generate, thereby precluding a club from deducting the expenses of service to nonmembers against investment income.[78] However, on appeal, the U.S. Court of Appeals for the Second Circuit held that the Tax Court's interpretation of the statute was incorrect and that federal tax law "authorizes deductions to be taken from the sum total of a club's non-exempt gross income, not merely from the portion of the income connected to the particular deduction."[79] This appellate court returned to the IRS position and concluded that tax-exempt social clubs can only deduct the expenses of activities engaged in with the intention of making a profit, thereby precluding the club in the case from reducing its taxable investment income with nonmember service expenses.

The stance of the IRS in this regard was initially upheld in another case,[80] but was rejected on appeal by the U.S. Court of Appeals for the Sixth Circuit. This appellate court's position, which is founded on the difference in tax treatment, in the unrelated income context, of social clubs,[81] was that a social club has a business expense deduction for outlays associated with activities engaged in with "a basic purpose of economic gain."[82] Under this principle, with which the Second Circuit expressly disagreed, a club could deduct, as business expenses, all expenses of providing food and beverages to nonmembers against investment income.

The U.S. Court of Appeals for the Ninth Circuit sided with the Second Circuit on this point, holding that a tax-exempt social club must pursue a nonmem-

---

[76] Rev. Rul. 81-69, 1981-1 C.B. 351, 352.

[77] IRC § 162. Thus, a tax-exempt social club was permitted to deduct the donations of the net proceeds of beano games it conducted, where the payments were a condition of its license for the games (South End Italian Independent Club, Inc. v. Comm'r, 87 T.C. 168 (1986)).

[78] The Brook, Inc. v. Comm'r, 50 T.C.M. 959, 51 T.C.M. 133 (1985).

[79] The Brook, Inc. v. Comm'r, 799 F.2d 833 (2d Cir. 1986).

[80] The Cleveland Athletic Club, Inc. v. United States, 588 F. Supp. 1305 (N.D. Ohio 1984).

[81] See text accompanied by *supra* notes 72–75.

[82] The Cleveland Athletic Club, Inc. v. United States, 779 F.2d 1160, 1165 (6th Cir. 1985).

ber activity with a profit motive before it can properly deduct its losses.[83] The appellate court agreed with the IRS that the omission of the term *trade or business* from the definition of *unrelated business taxable income* as applied to tax-exempt social clubs[84] (see below) does not allow social clubs to deduct losses in nonmember activities that are not businesses, writing that it is "well-established" that, to qualify as a trade or business, "an activity must be regular and profit-seeking."[85] In the case, the club's nonmember food and bar activity was held to not be profit-seeking, because of consistent losses for six years.[86]

As noted, this matter was resolved by the U.S. Supreme Court in 1990, when it held that a tax-exempt social club may use losses incurred in connection with sales to nonmembers to offset investment income only if the sales were motivated by an intent to generate a profit.[87] The Court held that the requisite "profit motive" means "an intent to generate receipts in excess of costs" and concluded that there is "no basis for dispensing with the profit-motive requirement" in these circumstances.[88] The Court explained that elimination of the profit motive standard would create "considerable tension" with the overall statutory scheme of tax treatment of social clubs, in that "Congress intended that the investment income of social clubs (unlike the investment income of most other exempt organizations) should be subject to the same tax consequences as the investment income of any other taxpayer," so that the allowance of the offset for social clubs "would run counter to the principle of tax neutrality which underlies the statutory scheme."[89]

Under the general rules of unrelated income taxation,[90] unrelated business taxable income is defined as the "gross income derived by any organization from any unrelated trade or business . . . regularly carried on by it, less the deductions . . . which are directly connected with the carrying on of such trade or business."[91]

---

[83] North Ridge Country Club v. Comm'r, 877 F.2d 750 (9th Cir. 1989), *rev'g* 89 T.C. 563 (1987).

[84] IRC § 512(a)(3)(A).

[85] North Ridge Country Club v. Comm'r, *supra* note 83, at 753, citing Comm'r v. Groetzinger, 480 U.S. 23 (1987) (see § 26.2(a)).

[86] Cf. Portland Golf Club v. Comm'r, 55 T.C.M. 212 (1988); West Va. State Med. Ass'n v. Comm'r, 91 T.C. 651 (1988), *aff'd*, 882 F.2d 123 (4th Cir. 1989), *cert. den.*, 493 U.S. 1044 (1990). In general, Chiechi & Munk, "When Can Social Clubs Offset Investment Income With Losses From Nonmember Activities?," 73 *J. Tax.* (No. 3) 184 (1990).

[87] Portland Golf Club v. Comm'r, *supra* note 9.

[88] *Id.* at 165, 166.

[89] *Id.* at 165. There is confusion resulting from this Supreme Court opinion concerning the manner in which social clubs demonstrate the necessary profit motive; the Court majority held that the same method of determining "costs" (both direct and indirect) used to ascertain intent to profit must be used in computing actual profit or loss. This holding was criticized in a partial concurring opinion, on the ground that economic reality and statements of income and expenses for tax purposes may be different. Miller, "U.S. Supreme Court in *Portland Golf Club* Reserves on a Key Profit-Intent Question and Adopts a Pervasive Estoppel-by-Reporting Rule," 15 *Rev. of Tax. of Indivs.* 108 (1991); Falk, "Portland Golf Club—Uncertain Direction from the Supreme Court," 2 *J. Tax. Exempt Orgs.* 11 (Fall 1990).

Thereafter, the U.S. Tax Court ruled that a tax-exempt social club was not entitled to offset losses from its nonmember activities against investment income because it did not undertake the activities with the requisite profit motive (Atlanta Athletic Club v. Comm'r, 61 T.C.M. 2011 (1991), overruled on another issue, 980 F.2d 1409 (11th Cir. 1993)).

[90] See Part Five.

[91] IRC § 512(a)(1).

However, the "trade or business" requirement is not in the definition of unrelated business taxable income applicable to social clubs, thereby, as noted, subjecting these organizations to, in the words of the Second Circuit Court of Appeals, "a much more far-reaching tax than" most other categories of tax-exempt organizations.[92]

Exempt function income is gross income from dues, fees, charges, or similar amounts paid by members of the tax-exempt organization in connection with the purposes constituting the basis for the tax exemption of the club.[93] Also, the passive income of a tax-exempt social club is generally not taxed if it is set aside to be used for charitable and similar purposes.[94] In one instance, an attempted set-aside failed to immunize net investment income from taxation because the activity funded by the investment income, which was publication of a magazine, was found to not be educational.[95]

In an illustration of these rules, the U.S. Tax Court ruled that a tax-exempt social club, the principal activity of which was to annually stage a mock pirate invasion and a parade, incurred taxable income from the sale of refreshments along the parade route, souvenirs, and advertising, inasmuch as the concession and other income was derived from dealings with nonmembers. The court also held that the expenses of staging the invasion and parade could not be used to offset

---

[92] The Brook, Inc. v. Comm'r, *supra* note 79, at 841.

[93] IRC § 512(a)(3)(B); Prop. Reg. §§ 1.512(a)-3(c)(1), 1.512(a)-3(c)(2).

[94] IRC § 170(c)(4); Prop. Reg. §§ 1.512(a)-3(c)(3), 1.512(a)-3(c)(4). In 1926, the U.S. District Court for the Southern District of New York had occasion to review a set-aside provision contained in the Revenue Act of 1918, in Slocum v. Bowers, 15 F.2d 400 (S.D. N.Y. 1926), the classic opinion on the subject of set-asides. Noting that the "policy of exempting" charitable and similar organizations "is firmly established," the court wrote that the set-aside rule should be read "in such a way as to carry out this policy and not to make the result turn on accidental circumstances or legal technicalities" (at 403). The tax consequences depend, said the court, "upon who is ultimately entitled to the property constituting [the] income" (at 404). Consequently, the court interpreted the set-aside rule to exempt from taxation the income of an estate that was destined for charitable purposes even though the representative of the estate still held legal title to the underlying property during the period of administration and even though there was no entry made on the books of the representative crediting the charitable organizations with the income. This decision was affirmed on appeal, with the U.S. Court of Appeals for the Second Circuit holding that it was the intent of Congress to not tax income going to charitable entities and that the designation made by the decedent in the will was the "most effective method" of setting the income aside (Bowers v. Slocum, 20 F.2d 350, 352, 353 (2d Cir. 1927)). Comparable caselaw invokes the law of trusts, where the courts have concluded that the segregated funds are housed in a constructive trust, an implied trust, or a resulting trust. For example, the U.S. Tax Court, having found in the facts a "reasonable certainty as to the property, the objects and the beneficiaries," held that funds transferred to an organization for the purpose of carrying out the objects "were impresed with a trust upon their receipt" (Broadcast Measurement Bur., Inc. v. Comm'r, 16 T.C. 988, 997 (1951)). "No express words of trust were used, but none are necessary," wrote the court in concluding that the recipient organization "was merely a designated fiduciary" (at 997, 1000). In finding that the funds did not constitute gross income to the organization, this court singled out the essential criteria for what is also known as the set-aside: The organization's "books showed the total amount of such fees it received and the unexpended balance thereof at all times" (at 1001). A commingling of the funds with other receipts was expressly held to "not destroy their identity as a trust fund" (*id.*; also The Seven-Up Co. v. Comm'r, 14 T.C. 965 (1950)). Further, Reg. § 1.512(a)-4(b)(5); Phi Delta Theta Fraternity v. Comm'r, 887 F.2d 1302 (6th Cir. 1989), *aff'g*, 90 T.C. 1033 (1988) (set aside not found); Alpha Tau Omega Fraternity, Inc. v. Comm'r (U.S. Tax Court Dkt. No. 2810-84 (settled)).

[95] Phi Delta Theta Fraternity v. Comm'r, *supra* note 94.

concession revenue, because the expenses did not have the requisite "direct" relationship with the income.[96]

It is the view of the Department of the Treasury that the dividends received deduction is not allowed in computing the taxable income of these organizations.[97] Believing that the reason for this deduction is inapplicable in the context of these organizations, Congress clarified this point by agreeing to the Treasury Department's position.[98] (A similar law change was made for nonexempt membership organizations.[99]) Although the statutory revision took effect in 1976, it has been held that tax-exempt social clubs are not entitled to the dividends-paid deduction for prior years (back to 1970) because the deduction is not for an expense incurred in the production of income but comes into being as a consequence of the existence of the income.[100]

§ 14.4 SALE OF CLUB ASSETS

Congress, in 1969, relegated to statute the law governing nonrecurring sales of club assets. A common example of this is a country club that sells land that has become encroached upon by developers to buy land further out in the countryside for new facilities.[101] Where the purpose of this type of a sale is not profit but to facilitate relocation or a comparable purpose, the law provides a carryover of basis, that is, nonrecognition of gain.[102] Specifically, where property used directly in the performance of the club's tax-exempt function is sold and the proceeds reinvested in exempt function property, within a period beginning one year before the sale date and ending three years thereafter, any gain from the sale is recognized only to the extent that the sale price of the old property exceeds the purchase price of the new property.[103]

There can be controversy over the meaning of the term *used directly*. In one case, the government argued that there must be "actual, direct, continuous, and regular usage," and that the property involved must form "an integral part of the exempt functions of a social club"; it lamented the club's "desultory activities" on the property, which it regarded as essentially investment property. But the court involved held that these requirements are not in the statute and, if they should be, Congress should expand the statute.[104]

---

[96] Ye Mystic Krewe of Gasparilla v. Comm'r, 80 T.C. 755 (1983).

[97] Prop. Reg. § 1.512(a)-3(b)(2) (withdrawn).

[98] IRC § 512(a)(3)(A), last sentence. Pub. L. No. 94-568, *supra* note 59; H. Rep. No. 1353, 94th Cong. 2d Sess. 6 (1976).

[99] IRC § 277. See § 13.6.

[100] Rolling Rock Club v. United States, *supra* note 75.

[101] Rev. Rul. 69-232, *supra* note 67; Rev. Rul. 65-64, 1965-1 C.B. 241; Rev. Rul. 58-501, 1958-2 C.B. 262; Santee Club v. White, *supra* note 61; Mill Lane Club v. Comm'r, 23 T.C. 433 (1954); Anderson Country Club, Inc. v. Comm'r, 2 T.C. 1238 (1943); Juniper Hunting Club, Inc. v. Comm'r, 28 B.T.A. 525 (1933).

[102] IRC § 512(a)(3)(D).

[103] Cf. IRC § 1034. E.g., Tamarisk Country Club v. Comm'r, 84 T.C. 756 (1985).

[104] Atlanta Athletic Club v. Comm'r, *supra* note 89; 980 F.2d at 1414. By contrast, in another instance, the government prevailed in a case involving the "used directly" requirement (Deer Park Country Club v. Comm'r, *supra*, note 74).

By contrast, where the sale of tax-exempt social club assets occurs more than once, the IRS is likely to resist application of this special rule, particularly in any case where the sale transactions substantially deplete the club of its assets and the club has not evidenced an intention to replace the property that is being sold.[105] Also, where a club derives revenue as the result of a grant of an option on the sale of the property, rather than from the sale of the property itself, this non-recognition rule is inapplicable, so that the option income is taxable as unrelated income.[106]

§ 14.5 DISCRIMINATION POLICIES

The U.S. Constitution, in the Fifth and Fourteenth Amendments, prohibits racial discrimination by government and government-supported private institutions. In general, private organizations may lawfully discriminate, absent applicability of the *state action* doctrine by which government is deemed to have sufficiently supported or encouraged the private discrimination as to amount to a constitutional law violation.[107]

The relationship between the state action doctrine and tax exemptions for social clubs and other nonprofit organizations has been the focus of several cases. This relationship as regards social clubs was the subject of a case in which a black individual, allegedly denied membership in a lodge of a fraternal organization solely because of his race, brought a class action to enjoin the granting of tax benefits to nonprofit fraternal organizations that exclude nonwhite individuals from membership.[108] The issue thus became whether tax exemptions and deductions cause the benefited private organizations to have the requisite imprimatur of government, that is, whether exemptions and deductions amount to a grant of federal funds to them. Where such a "grant" is involved, the state action doctrine will bring the protections of the Constitution to the otherwise "private" acts.

In this case, the court concluded that a tax-exempt social club's policy of

---

[105] E.g., Priv. Ltr. Rul. 8337092.
[106] Framingham Country Club v. United States, 659 F. Supp. 650 (D. Mass. 1987).
[107] Cases discussing the state action doctrine (in areas other than but including the private club context) have flourished over the years (e.g., Burton v. Wilmington Parking Auth., 356 U.S. 715 (1961); United States v. Texas Educ. Agency, 532 F.2d 380 (5th Cir. (1976); Golden v. Biscayne Bay Yacht Club, 530 F.2d 16 (5th Cir. 1976); Doe v. Charleston Area Med. Cent., Inc., 529 F.2d 638 (4th Cir. 1975); New York City Jaycees, Inc. v. United States Jaycees, Inc., 512 F.2d 856 (2d Cir. 1975); Greenya v. George Washington Univ., 512 F.2d 556 (D.C. Cir. 1975); Barrett v. United Hosp., 375 F. Supp. 791 (S.D.N.Y. 1974), aff'd, 506 F.2d 1395 (2d Cir. 1974); Coleman v. Wagner College, 429 F.2d 1120 (2d Cir. 1970); Taylor v. Maryland School for the Blind, 409 F. Supp. 148 (D. Md. 1976); Hollenbaugh v. Board of Trustees of Carnegie Free Library of Connellsville, Pa., 405 F. Supp. 629 (W.D. Pa. 1975); McMenamin v. Philadelphia County Democratic Executive Committee of Philadelphia, 405 F. Supp. 998 (E.D. Pa. 1975); Berrios v. Inter American Univ., 409 F. Supp. 769 (D. P. R. 1975); Falkenstein v. Department of Revenue, 350 F. Supp. 887 (D. Ore. 1972), *app. dis.*, 409 U.S. 1099 (1973)). Also Note, "State Action and the United States Junior Chamber of Commerce," 43 *Geo. Wash. L. Rev.* 1407 (1975). Further, Reitman v. Mulkey, 387 U.S. 369 (1967); Evans v. Newton, 382 U.S. 296 (1966); Pennsylvania v. Board of City Trusts, 353 U.S. 230 (1957); Shelley v. Kraemer, 334 U.S. 1 (1948); Steele v. Louisville & Nashville R.R., 323 U.S. 192 (1944); Civil Rights Cases, 109 U.S. 3 (1883).
[108] McGlotten v. Connally, *supra* note 6.

racial discrimination would not preclude tax exemption, although the exemption given to fraternal organizations[109] requires the absence of discriminatory practices. The rationale underlying this distinction in treatment turned on the peculiar manner in which social clubs are taxed; since they are taxed on all receipts other than exempt function income, there is no state action-type "benefit" but only a matter of defining appropriate subjects of taxation, whereas fraternal organizations, being taxed only on unrelated business taxable income, do receive a government benefit in that investment income goes untaxed.[110]

Congress, in 1976, concluded that it is "inappropriate" for a tax-exempt social club to have a "written policy" of discrimination on account of race, color, or religion. Accordingly, Congress enacted a rule that bars tax exemption for social clubs maintaining any of these types of discriminatory policies.[111] It is the position of the IRS that this proscription on discriminatory practices does not extend to tax-exempt social clubs that limit membership on the basis of ethnic or national origin.[112]

In 1980, Congress refined this requirement to allow tax-exempt social clubs that are affiliated with fraternal beneficiary societies[113] to retain tax exemption even though membership in the clubs is limited to members of a particular religion. Also, this law change allows certain alumni clubs, which are limited to members of a particular religion in order to further the religion's teachings or principles, to retain their tax exemption as social clubs.[114]

---

[109] IRC § 501(c)(8). See § 18.4(a).

[110] Golden v. Biscayne Bay Yacht Club, *supra* note 107; Olzman v. Lake Hills Swim Club, Inc., 495 F.2d 1331 (2d Cir. 1974); Cornelius v. Benevolent Protective Order of Elks, 382 F. Supp. 1182 (D. Conn. 1974); Moose Lodge v. Irvis, 407 U.S. 163 (1972). Cf. Pitts v. Department of Revenue, 333 F. Supp. 662 (E.D. Wis. 1971).

[111] IRC § 501(i).

[112] Priv. Ltr. Rul. 8317004.

[113] See § 18.4(a).

[114] IRC § 501(i), last sentence. In general, Chiechi & Munk, "When Can Social Clubs Offset Investment Income With Losses From Nonmember Activities?," 73 *J. Tax.* (No. 3) 184 (1990); Banspach, "Social Clubs and the Profit Motive Test: Allowability of Excess Deductions Against Investment Income," 27 *San Diego L. Rev.* (No. 1) 81 (1990); Graham, "Social Clubs: Establishing the Right to Exemption Under Section 501(c)(7) and a Proposal for Expanding the Scope of Exemption," 33 *Tax Law.* 881 (1980); Crawford, "New Laws Indicate Scope of Exempt Clubs' Revenues from Investments, Nonmembers," 47 *J. Tax.* 48 (1977); Crawford, "Country Clubs: The Money Side," XXIX *Golf J.* (No. 2) 28 (1976); Moffet, "The Problems of Section 501(c)(7) Organizations," 54 *Taxes* 4 (1976); Denny, "Professional and Social Organizations," 25 *Tul. Tax Inst.* 2200 (1975); Horn, "Unrelated Business Income of Social Clubs," 49 *Taxes* 738 (1971); Ginstling, "Social Clubs Coming Under Closer IRS Scrutiny; Nonmember Use Can Kill Exemption," 23 *J. Tax.* 162 (1966); Gasperow, "Tax Problems of Country Clubs," *J. Acct.* 60 (Oct. 1964).

CHAPTER FIFTEEN

Labor, Agricultural, and Horticultural Organizations

§ 15.1 Labor Organizations
§ 15.2 Agricultural Organizations

§ 15.3 Horticultural Organizations

The federal tax law provides tax exemption for qualified labor, agricultural, or horticultural organizations. No part of the net earnings of this type of an organization may inure to the benefit of any member.[1] Moreover, this category of organization must have as its principal object the betterment of the conditions of those engaged in the tax-exempt pursuits, the improvement of the grade of their products, and the development of a higher degree of efficiency in the particular occupation.[2]

§ 15.1 LABOR ORGANIZATIONS

The principal purpose of a tax-exempt labor organization is to engage in collective action to better the working conditions of individuals engaged in a common pursuit.[3] The most common example of the exempt labor entity is labor unions that negotiate with employers on behalf of workers for improved wages, fringe benefits, and hours and similar working conditions. Nonetheless, the exempt labor organization category encompasses a broader range of entities, including union-controlled organizations that provide benefits to workers that enhance the union's ability to bargain effectively. This classification includes, for example, an organization of tax-exempt labor unions representing public employees,[4] an organization to provide strike and lockout benefits (strike funds),[5] the "labor temple"

---

[1] Reg. § 1.501(c)(5)-1(a)(1). The pro rata refund of excess dues to members by an exempt agricultural organization does not constitute private inurement and thus does not disqualify the organization from continuing tax exemption (Rev. Rul. 81-60, 1981-1 C.B. 335).

[2] Reg. § 1.501(c)(5)-1(a)(2).

[3] The income tax exemption for labor organizations was created by enactment of the Corporation Excise Tax Act of 1909 (Pub. L. No. 61-5), 36 Stat. 11, 112–118.

[4] Rev. Rul. 74-596, 1974-2 C.B. 167.

[5] Rev. Rul. 67-7, 1967-1 C.B. 137.

(offices, meeting rooms, auditoriums, and the like for labor union members),[6] and an organization publishing a labor newspaper.[7]

According to the IRS, "[g]eneral usage defines a labor organization as an association of workmen who have combined to protect or promote the interests of the members by bargaining collectively with their employers to secure better working conditions, wages, and similar benefits."[8] One court characterized the term *labor organization* as "bespeak[ing] a liberal construction to embrace the common acceptation of the term, including labor unions and councils and groups which are ordinarily unions and councils and the groups which are ordinarily organized to protect and promote the interests of labor."[9] Subsequently, another court observed that a labor organization is "a voluntary association of workers which is organized to pursue common economic and social interests."[10]

Thus, a tax-exempt labor organization must have authority to represent or speak for its members in matters relating to their employment, such as wages, hours of labor, conditions, or economic benefits. An organization that does not function, or directly support the efforts of any labor organization, to better employment conditions cannot qualify as a tax-exempt labor organization. For example, an organization (controlled by individuals in their private capacity) that provided weekly income to its members in the event of a lawful strike by the member's labor union by reason of its contractual agreements with and payments from the workers was ruled to not qualify as a tax-exempt labor organization.[11]

A tax-exempt labor organization is generally composed of employees or representatives of the employees (such as collective bargaining agents) and similar groups. However, an organization whose membership is composed principally of laborers will not, for that reason alone, qualify as a tax-exempt labor organization.[12] An exempt labor organization's membership must be composed of those who are employees. For example, an organization the members of which were independent contractors and entrepreneurs (persons engaged in harness racing in a specific geographical area as drivers, trainers, and horse owners) was held to not qualify as a tax-exempt labor organization because the members were not employees.[13]

One case concerned the appropriateness of the membership of a tax-exempt labor organization, a union, with the government asserting that certain associate members were not bona fide members. The court disagreed, holding that the "membership of a union is a matter of self-definition, found in the organization's constitution or other governing documents."[14] This court observed that "neither

---

[6] Portland Co-Operative Labor Temple Ass'n v. Comm'r, 39 B.T.A. 450 (1939).

[7] Rev. Rul. 68-534, 1968-2 C.B. 217.

[8] IRS Exempt Organizations Handbook (IRM 7751) § 521.

[9] Portland Co-Operative Labor Temple Ass'n v. Comm'r, *supra* note 6, at 455.

[10] American Postal Workers Union, AFL-CIO v. United States, 90-1 U.S.T.C. ¶ 50,013 (D.D.C. 1989).

[11] Rev. Rul. 76-420, 1976-2 C.B. 153.

[12] Workingmen's Co-Op. Ass'n of the United States Ins. League of N.Y. v. Comm'r, 3 B.T.A. 1352 (1978). Cf. Rev. Rul. 78-287, 1978-2 C.B. 146.

[13] Rev. Rul. 78-288, 1978-2 C.B. 179. On this point, the IRS will look to see whether the members are self-employed for purposes of IRC § 1402.

[14] American Postal Workers Union, AFL-CIO v. United States, *supra* note 10, at 83,055.

the Congress, the Treasury, the Internal Revenue Service nor the courts have made tax exemption for labor organizations dependent on the identity of the particular group or groups of employees represented or the types of economic benefits provided" and that "[t]here is no authority for limiting a labor union's exempt purposes to representing a particular classification of employees or providing particular kinds of benefits to its members."[15] The court added that "[t]here is no requirement in the Internal Revenue Code that a union member receive any particular quantum of benefit in order to be considered a bona fide member," so that a union or other type of labor organization can have different classes of membership.[16] The consequence of these findings was that the dues revenue from the associate members was held nontaxable.

By contrast, another case, on essentially the same facts, produced the opposite conclusion of law. The court involved found taxable the income paid to the organization by its "limited benefit members" for the opportunity to obtain insurance under its health plan.[17] The organization operated for the economic well-being of its regular and associate members, the court found, but these operations were held to benefit the limited benefit members only incidentally and indirectly. The court held that the provision of the insurance to limited benefit members, who could not vote or hold office in the organization, was not related to the organization's tax-exempt purposes (which were to serve the regular and associate members) and thus was taxable as income from the performance of unrelated services.

Labor organizations may also meet the requirements of exemption by providing benefits that directly improve working conditions or compensate for unpredictable hazards that interrupt work. Thus, the IRS recognized as a tax-exempt labor organization a committee formed pursuant to a collective bargaining agreement to improve working conditions for apprentices in various skilled crafts and to aid in the settlement of disputes between employers and apprentices.[18] The IRS so held, even though the committee's membership consisted of an equal number of employer and employee representatives, and the committee was financed primarily by employer and union contributions. Another example was an organization that operated a dispatch hall to match union members with work assignments.[19] Tax-exempt labor organization classification was also recognized in the case of a trust organized pursuant to a collective bargaining agreement, funded and administered solely by the employers in an industry, because the purpose of the trust was to compensate a multiemployer steward who was under a union's direct control with responsibility to settle disputes, investigate complaints, and otherwise encourage compliance with the agreement throughout the entire industry.[20] Similarly, the IRS determined that a nurses' association,

[15] *Id.*

[16] *Id.* This opinion was reversed on appeal, on the issue of unrelated income taxation (925 F.2d 480 (D.C. Cir. 1991)) (see § 26.5(e)).

[17] National Ass'n of Postal Supervisors v. United States, 90-2 U.S.T.C. ¶ 50,445 (Cl. Ct. 1990). See *supra* note 16.

[18] Rev. Rul. 59-6, 1959-1 C.B. 121. Also Rev. Rul. 78-42, 1978-1 C.B. 158.

[19] Rev. Rul. 75-473, 1975-2 C.B. 213.

[20] Rev. Rul. 77-5, 1977-1 C.B. 148.

which had as its primary purposes the acting as a collective bargaining agent for its members in contract negotiations between various institutions and the nurses employed by them and the operation of a health and welfare fund for its membership, constituted a tax-exempt labor organization.[21]

In another illustration, the IRS ruled that a city school teachers' association was a tax-exempt labor organization.[22] The organization was formed to improve the professional abilities of its members and to secure for them better salaries and working conditions. It sponsored seminars and courses for its members, participated in teacher conventions, bargained collectively and processed grievances, and kept its members informed of its activities through regular meetings and a newsletter.

Generally, a tax-exempt labor organization is one that operates to better the conditions of those (frequently its members) engaged in a particular trade, such as by striking for better wages and working conditions. Where the labor organization has members, they will mostly be employees, although the inclusion of some self-employed persons in the membership will not deprive the organization of its classification as a tax-exempt labor group if it otherwise qualifies.[23] Similarly, the payment by a labor organization of death, sick, accident, and similar benefits to its members generally will not preclude the tax exemption, even in circumstances in which a majority of the organization's members are retired.[24] Likewise, the payment by an organization of law enforcement officers for its members' legal defense in actions brought against them in connection with the performance of their official duties did not adversely affect the organization's tax-exempt status as a labor organization.[25]

The IRS had occasion to consider the tax status of a nonprofit organization that was established pursuant to a collective bargaining agreement between a union and an employers' association to enable members of the union to save money under a plan by which a fixed amount was withheld from their pay and deposited in a bank account. The funds were paid to the union's members annually, along with any interest remaining after payment of administrative expenses. In determining that this organization did not qualify as a tax-exempt labor organization, the IRS noted that, to so qualify, the activities of this type of an organization must "be those commonly or historically recognized as characteristic of labor organizations, or be closely related and necessary to accomplishing the principal purposes of exempt labor organizations."[26] Thus, the IRS concluded that "savings plans that disburse money on an annual basis are not closely related to the labor organization's principal activities of negotiating wages, hours, and working conditions nor are such savings plans closely related

---

[21] Rev. Rul. 77-154, 1977-1 C.B. 148.

[22] Rev. Rul. 76-31, 1976-1 C.B. 157.

[23] Rev. Rul. 77-154, *supra* note 21; Rev. Rul. 74-167, 1974-1 C.B. 134.

[24] Rev. Rul. 62-17, 1962-1 C.B. 87. This position represents a reversal of the IRS's prior stance, as stated in Rev. Rul. 58-143, 1958-1 C.B. 239. Also American Postal Workers Union, AFL-CIO v. United States, *supra* note 10.

[25] Rev. Rul. 75-288, 1975-2 C.B. 212.

[26] Rev. Rul. 77-46, 1977-1 C.B. 147.

and necessary to providing the mutual benefits characteristically associated with labor organizations."[27]

As noted, one of the purposes of a tax-exempt labor organization may be the development among its members of a higher degree of efficiency in their occupations. To this end, a labor organization may administer bona fide skill-improvement or self-improvement programs as part of its tax-exempt activity, as long as the programs are administered by the organization specifically for, and involve substantial participation by, its members. Thus, this doctrine does not embrace programs substantially developed and administered by other organizations (even though they improve the skills of the labor organization's membership) or that require only insubstantial participation by a labor organization's members in educational activities. For example, a labor organization was advised that its conduct of travel tours for nonmembers and members who do not substantially participate in educational programs administered by it was not a tax-exempt activity.[28]

According to the tax regulations, an organization cannot qualify as an exempt labor organization if its principal activity is to receive, hold, invest, disburse, or otherwise manage funds associated with savings or investment plans or programs, including pension or other retirement savings plans or programs.[29] For example, a trust organized pursuant to a collective bargaining agreement between a labor union and multiple employers, that as most of its activities (1) receives funds from the employers who are subject to the agreement, (2) invests the funds and uses them and accumulated earnings to pay retirement benefits to union members as specified in the agreement, (3) provides information to union members about their retirement benefits and assists them with administrative tasks associated with the benefits, and (4) participates in the renegotiation of the agreement, cannot qualify as an exempt labor organization.[30] This regulation is a reflection of the view of the IRS that, a decision of an appellate court[31] notwithstanding, managing saving and investment plans for workers, including retirement plans, does not bear directly on working conditions.[32] Nonetheless, the IRS continues to recognize that negotiation of the terms of a retirement plan and other postretirement benefits, and designation of one or more representatives to the board of a multiemployer pension trust, are appropriate activities for an exempt labor organization.[33]

A labor union owned-and-controlled company organized to provide em-

---

[27] *Id.*

[28] Priv. Ltr. Rul. 7944018.

[29] Reg. § 1.501(c)(5)-1(b)(1). There is an exception for certain dues-financed pension plans that do not have any employer involvement (Reg. § 1.501(c)(5)-1(b)(2)).

[30] Reg. § 1.501(c)(5)-1(b)(2).

[31] Morganbesser v. United States, 984 F.2d 560 (2d Cir. 1993). The court relied heavily on IRS general counsel memoranda (37942, 37726, and 35862) in its decision. The IRS Office of Chief Counsel recommended nonacquiescence in this case (AOD 1995-016); 33–36.

[32] Rev. Rul. 77-46, *supra* note 24. A federal district court subsequently refused to follow the *Morganbesser* rationale, holding that the term *labor organization* does not encompass a pension fund that exists only to provide retirement benefits for its members (Stichting Pensioenfonds Voor de Gezondheid v. United States, 950 F. Supp. 373 (D.D.C. 1996), *aff'd*, 97-2 U.S.T.C. ¶ 50, 917 (D.C. Cir. 1997)). Also Tupper v. United States, 1998 WL 5848 (1st Cir. 1998).

[33] In general, Note, "Can a Pension Plan be a Labor Organization?, 47 *Tax Law.* (No. 2) 501 (Winter 1994).

ployment to the union's members did not qualify for tax exemption, even though its net profits were turned in to the union's treasury.[34] Tax exemption was also denied an organization established by an employer and a union under a collective bargaining agreement to ensure the efficient discharge of the employer's obligation to pay withheld employment taxes to federal and state authorities.[35] An organization of farmers formed to furnish farm laborers for individual farmers also did not qualify for tax exemption as a labor organization.[36] With the advent of the unrelated business income taxation scheme,[37] labor organizations may engage in some nonexempt activities, in the nature of "business" functions or services, and nonetheless continue to remain exempt from federal income taxation.[38]

The effectiveness of labor organizations, particularly unions, on the legislative and political fronts continually generates controversy. The matter came before the courts in a case brought by aerospace workers covered by compulsory union-shop contracts and thus required to pay union dues, to enjoin the government from continuing to recognize tax exemption in the case of any labor organization that expended membership dues for partisan political campaigns.[39] The court rejected the idea that the tax exemption of unions should be terminated where union dues are used in political campaigns, stating that Congress has considered and not adopted that result.[40] The court also rejected the argument that the tax exemption amounts to a federal subsidy and consequently that general political activity of labor organizations should be proscribed, finding that the exemption is "benevolent neutrality" and that there is not the requisite "nexus" between the exemption and any government "involvement" in union activities.[41]

§ 15.2 AGRICULTURAL ORGANIZATIONS

As respects agricultural organizations, the principal tax issue is likely to be the scope of the term *agricultural*. For many years, the IRS relied on the narrow dictionary definition of the term *agriculture* as meaning "the science or art of cultivating the soil, harvesting crops and raising livestock."[42]

Prior to 1976, neither the federal statutory tax law nor the income tax regulations defined the term *agricultural*. There was a body of law holding that this

---

[34] Rev. Rul. 69-386, 1969-2 C.B. 123.

[35] Rev. Rul. 66-354, 1966-2 C.B. 207.

[36] Rev. Rul. 72-391, 1972-2 C.B. 249.

[37] See Part Five.

[38] E.g., Rev. Rul. 62-191, 1962-2 C.B. 146; Rev. Rul. 59-330, 1959-2 C.B. 153.

[39] Marker v. Schultz, 485 F.2d 1003 (D.C. Cir. 1973), *aff'g* 337 F. Supp. 1301 (D.D.C. 1972).

[40] E.g., 18 U.S.C. § 610.

[41] Marker v. Schultz, *supra* note 43, at 1006, citing Waltz v Tax Comm'n, 397 U.S. 664 (1970). However, this characterization of tax exemption was expressly rejected in Regan v. Taxation with Representation of Washington, 461 U.S. 540 (1983). In general, Graves, "When Will Political Activities of Unions and Associations Cost Them Their Exemption?," 35 *J. Tax* 254 (1971); Albert & Hansell, "The Tax Status of the Modern Labor Union," 111 *U. Pa. L. Rev.* 137 (1962).

[42] Citing *Webster's Third New International Dictionary*. Also Dorrell v. Norida Land & Timber Co., 27 P.2d 960 (Id. 1933).

term must, for tax purposes, be given its normal and customary meaning.[43] This approach did not entail mere reference to dictionary definitions, inasmuch as statutes are to be interpreted in effectuation of intended congressional policy, which may not be identical to the meaning of certain words in lay terms. Certainly, the principal dictionary meaning of *agriculture* is the cultivation of land, as in the raising of crops. However, *agriculture* also means *husbandry* which connotes *farming* as well as *agriculture*. *Agriculture* means "farming (in a broad sense, including . . . stock raising, etc.)."[44] Certainly, *stock* raising can be interpreted as broader than the raising of *livestock*.[45] Thus, it was contended that the meaning reflected in the statutory scheme should be relied upon, rather than dictionary definitions.[46]

An illustration of the foregoing was the IRS's refusal to accord tax-exempt status to organizations engaged in the harvesting of aquatic resources (often termed *aquaculture*). Yet it appeared that, in the face of contemporary food, health, and related needs, any distinction in this context between land farming and sea resource gathering was artificial. In other statutory and regulatory contexts, this distinction has disappeared. For example, the Farm Credit Act, as amended, provided that those engaging in commercial fishing may qualify for the benefits of the Act as "producers or harvesters of aquatic products." The Rural Development Act of 1972 authorized individuals involved in producing fish and fishery products to obtain loans in the same manner as farmers. Additionally, the Federal Energy Office's Petroleum Allocation and Price Regulations included fishing under the definition of *agricultural production*. In other contexts, the IRS has readily turned, in the process of assessing organizations' claims to tax exemption, to nontax statutes to divine congressional intent or the basis for federal public policy bearing on the organizations' activities.[47]

Unlike the term *farmer*,[48] it is clear that the term *agriculture*, for federal tax purposes, is to be liberally construed. Thus, for example, an organization that annually hosted a rodeo was recognized as being a tax-exempt agricultural organization.[49] An organization that was concerned with methods of raising fur-bearing animals and marketing pelts was ruled to be a tax-exempt agricultural organization,[50] as was an organization that tested soil for farmers and nonfarmers and furnished test results for educational purposes.[51] It is not mandatory that the membership of the organization desiring tax categorization as an agricultural entity be engaged in agricultural pursuits.[52] For example, an organization

---

[43] United States v. Byrum, 408 U.S. 125, 136 (1972). Also Comm'r v. Caulkins, 144 F.2d 482, 484 (6th Cir. 1944), *aff'g* 1 T.C. 656 (1944).

[44] *The American College Dictionary*.

[45] Fromm Bros. Inc. v. United States, 35 F. Supp. 145 (W.D. Wis. 1940); Rev. Rul. 57-588, 1957-2 C.B. 305.

[46] Mitchell v. Cohn, 333 U.S. 411 (1948).

[47] E.g., Rev. Rul. 76-204, 1976-1 C.B. 152.

[48] IRC § 521; § 18.11.

[49] Campbell v. Big Spring Cowboy Reunion, 210 F.2d 143 (5th Cir. 1954).

[50] Rev. Rul. 56-245, 1956-1 C.B. 204.

[51] Rev. Rul. 54-282, 1954-2 C.B. 126.

[52] Rev. Rul. 60-86, 1960-1 C.B. 198.

of women who had no relationship to agriculture other than the fact that their husbands were farmers in a particular state, was ruled to be a tax-exempt agricultural organization.[53]

Efforts were made to invest the law in this area with a broader interpretation of the term agriculture. A federal court of appeals provided precedent for this undertaking:

> According to the lexicographers, agriculture is defined as the art or science of cultivating the ground including the harvesting of crops and *in a broader sense the science or art of the production of plants and animals useful to man*, including in a variable degree the preparation of these products for man's use.[54]

However, the IRS did not accept this broader view, conceding only that an organization formed for the purpose of encouraging better and more economical methods of fish farming was an agricultural organization.[55] Also, the IRS determined that an organization, the members of which were involved in the commercial fishing industry in a state, that published a monthly newspaper of commercial fishing technical information and news, and that derived its income primarily from membership dues and sale of advertising, did not qualify as a tax-exempt agricultural organization but instead as a business league.[56]

In an attempt to settle this controversy, Congress, in enacting the Tax Reform Act of 1976, authored a rule[57] providing that, for purposes of tax exemption as an agricultural organization, the term *agriculture* includes (but is not limited to) the art or science of cultivating land, harvesting crops or aquatic resources, or raising livestock. The insertion of the phrase "harvesting . . . aquatic resources" was designed to encompass fishing and related pursuits (such as the taking of lobsters and shrimp), the cultivation of underwater vegetation, and the cultivation or growth of any edible organism. This change resulted from Congress's realization that there is no tax policy to be served under the provision for tax-exempt agricultural groups for differentiating between occupations devoted to the production of foodstuffs and other items from the earth and from the waters. The statutory definition became effective for tax years beginning after 1975, although inasmuch as the statute may be declaratory of what Congress perceived the law should have been beforehand,[58] it can be contended that the definition is of utility with respect to pre-1976 tax years.

Another dimension of this dilemma for organizations engaged in or associated with aquatic harvesting is that the Postal Service followed the position of the IRS and categorized them as business leagues rather than agriculture organizations, thereby depriving them of the preferential postal rates under the second and third classes. Congress also remedied this aspect of the problem in 1976,

---

[53] Rev. Rul. 74-118, 1974-1 C.B. 134.

[54] Sancho v. Bowie, 93 F.2d 323, 324 (1st Cir. 1937) (emphasis added).

[55] Rev. Rul. 74-488, 1974-2 C.B. 166. Cf. Rev. Rul. 76-241, 1976-1 C.B. 131.

[56] Rev. Rul. 75-287, 1975-2 C.B. 211. See Chapter 13.

[57] IRC § 501(g).

[58] 121 *Cong. Rec.* 34442 (1975).

when it enacted the Postal Reorganization Act Amendments of 1976.[59] This law added a definition of the term agriculture to the postal laws, as including "the art or science of cultivating land, harvesting crops or marine resources, or raising of livestock," thereby removing these organizations from business league status under the postal laws as well.[60] For postal law purposes, this definition also extends to "any organization or association which collects and disseminates information or materials relating to agricultural pursuits."

Other tax-exempt agricultural organizations include an organization engaged in ways to improve the breed of cattle,[61] an association engaged in the promotion of the artificial insemination of cattle,[62] an association formed to guard the purity of Welsh ponies,[63] an organization established to advance agriculture, that purchased supplies and equipment for resale to its members,[64] a local association of dairy farmers that participated in the U.S. Department of Agriculture's National Cooperative Dairy Herd Improvement Program,[65] a local association of farmers formed to promote more effective agricultural pest control,[66] an organization that produced and distributed certified seed to a state's corn producers,[67] an organization of agricultural growers and producers formed principally to negotiate with processors for crop prices,[68] and an organization that participated in furthering research, sales, and distribution of seed stock.[69]

An exempt agricultural organization usually has a membership; those served by the entity must represent a significant portion of the interested agricultural community.[70] However, the performance of services directly on behalf of an individual member is not improving the grade of the person's product or developing a higher degree of efficiency in the person's agricultural-related pursuits.[71] Yet, where an activity benefits agriculture as a whole and only incidentally benefits individual members, tax exemption is available.[72]

The IRS will not recognize, as an exempt agricultural entity, an organiza-

---

[59] P.L. 94-421, 94th Cong., 2d Sess. (1976).

[60] 39 U.S.C. § 3626(d). While the tax law definition of the term *agricultural* encompasses the "harvesting . . . [of] aquatic resources," the postal law definition of the term includes the "harvesting . . . [of] marine resources." The dictionary definition of *aquatic* is "of or pertaining to water," whereas the dictionary definition of *marine* is "of or pertaining to the sea," thereby holding open the possibility that an organization engaged in or associated with the harvesting of fresh waters will acquire classification as an agricultural organization for federal tax purposes but as a business league for postal law purposes.

[61] Minnesota Holstein-Friesian Breeders Ass'n v. Comm'r, 64 T.C.M. 1319 (1992). Also California Thoroughbred Breeders Ass'n v. Comm'r, 57 T.C.M. 962 (1989).

[62] East Tenn. Artificial Breeders Ass'n v. United States, 63-2 U.S.T.C. ¶ 9748 (E.D. Tenn. 1963).

[63] Rev. Rul. 55-230, 1955-1 C.B. 71.

[64] Rev. Rul. 57-466, 1957-2 C.B. 311. Cf. Rev. Rul. 67-252, 1967-2 C.B. 195.

[65] Rev. Rul. 74-518, 1974-2 C.B. 166, clarifying Rev. Rul. 70-372, 1970-2 C.B. 118.

[66] Rev. Rul. 81-59, 1981-1 C.B. 334.

[67] Priv. Ltr. Rul. 8429010.

[68] Rev. Rul. 76-399, 1976-2 C.B. 152.

[69] Priv. Ltr. Rul. 9732022.

[70] *Id.*

[71] Rev. Rul. 70-372, *supra* note 65; Rev. Rul. 66-105, 1966-1 C.B. 145; Rev. Rul. 57-466, *supra* note 64.

[72] Rev. Rul. 81-59, *supra* note 66; Rev. Rul. 74-518, *supra* note 65.

tion the principal purpose of which is to provide a direct business service for its members' economic benefit. Thus, an organization engaged in the management, grazing, and sale of its members' cattle was denied tax-exempt status as an agricultural entity.[73] The same fate befell an organization composed of agricultural producers the principal activity of which was marketing livestock for its members.[74] Similarly, the IRS denied an organization classification as a tax-exempt agricultural entity where it furnished farm laborers for individual farmers, ruling that the organization was "merely providing services to individual farmers that they would have to provide for themselves or get someone else to provide for them."[75] In another illustration of this rule, the IRS denied agricultural status to an organization that owned and operated a livestock facility and leased it to local members of a nonexempt national association of farmers for use in implementing the association's collective bargaining program with processors. The facility was used to collect, weigh, sort, grade, and ship livestock marketed through the program. The IRS determined that the operation and leasing of the facility "is the providing of a business service to those members who make use of the national association's collective bargaining program" and that this service "merely relieves the members of the organization of work they would either have to perform themselves or have performed for them."[76]

As noted, to be tax-exempt as an agricultural organization, the organization must have as its objective the betterment of the conditions of those *engaged in* agricultural pursuits. The IRS on one occasion used this rule as the rationale for denying tax-exempt agricultural status to an institute of butter and cheese manufacturers, concluding that those who benefit directly from its activities were not engaged in agricultural pursuits (allowing, however, that it may qualify as a business league).[77] Similarly, the IRS was successful, using the rationale that activities only remotely promoting the interests of those engaged in agricultural pursuits cannot qualify an organization for this tax exemption, in refusing an organization tax exemption where it was organized to hold agricultural fairs, stock shows, and horse race meets but actually devoted itself solely to horse racing.[78]

As has been pointed out, the IRS may conclude that an organization is being operated in the furtherance of interests other than agriculture and that, consequently, it is more properly classifiable as a business league rather than as an agricultural organization.[79] The tax exemptions for agricultural and charitable organizations may also overlap, such as where an organization conducts a state or county fair or otherwise presents expositions and exhibitions in an educational manner.[80]

---

[73] Rev. Rul. 74-195, 1974-1 C.B. 135.
[74] Rev. Rul. 66-105, *supra* note 71. Also Rev. Rul. 70-372, *supra* note 65.
[75] Rev. Rul. 72-391, *supra* note 36, at 249.
[76] Rev. Rul. 77-153, 1977-1 C.B. 147, 148.
[77] Rev. Rul. 67-252, *supra* note 64.
[78] Forest City Live Stock & Fair Co. v. Comm'r, 26 B.T.A. 1494 (1932).
[79] E.g., Rev. Rul. 67-252, *supra* note 64; Rev. Rul. 56-245, *supra* note 50.
[80] Rev. Rul. 67-216, 1967-2 C.B. 180. Also Indiana Crop Improvement Ass'n, Inc. v. Comm'r, 76 T.C. 394 (1981).

§ 15.3   HORTICULTURAL ORGANIZATIONS

Horticulture is the art or science of cultivating fruits, flowers, and vegetables.[81]

Tax exemption as a horticultural organization was determined by the IRS to be appropriate for a garden club formed for the purpose of bettering the conditions of persons engaged in horticultural pursuits and improving their products, by publishing a monthly journal, reporting new developments in horticultural products to its members, and encouraging the development of such products through a system of awards.[82]

---

[81] Guerrero v. United States Fidelity & Guar. Co., 98 S.W.2d 796 (Tex. 1936).
[82] Rev. Rul. 66-179, 1966-1 C.B. 139.

CHAPTER SIXTEEN

Employee Benefit Funds

The law of tax-exempt organizations and the law of employee benefits are inextricably intertwined. This is because the funding underlying the various forms of employee benefits plans is derived from assets contributed to and held in a trust or fund, and the law provides for federal income tax exemption for these funds, so as to maximize the resources available to provide the benefits.

This interrelationship is reflected in the organization of the IRS. The Commissioner of Internal Revenue is supported by assistant commissioners, one of whom is the Assistant Commissioner (Employee Plans and Exempt Organizations). This Assistant Commissioner position is the only one that is the subject of specific authorization in the Internal Revenue Code.[1]

The same dichotomy is reflected in the organization of the IRS Chief Counsel's office. In that office is an Associate Chief Counsel (Technical), within which is the position of Assistant Chief Counsel (Employee Benefits and Exempt Organizations). Under the auspices of this Assistant Chief Counsel are various Branches, with one branch having responsibility for tax-exempt organizations matters.

The tax-exempt organizations aspect of the law of employee benefits is reflected in the opening passage of the statutory law of tax-exempt organizations, where it is provided that organizations referenced in the rules concerning retire-

---

[1] IRC § 7802(b).

ment, profit-sharing, and similar plans[2] are exempt from federal income taxation.[3] That section makes reference to trusts that are part of qualified stock bonus, pension, or profit-sharing plans.

The law of employee benefits as such is outside the scope of this book.[4] However, as a prelude to a summary of the law concerning various employee benefit funds that are tax-exempt, a brief overview of this aspect of the law is appropriate to provide a context.

§ 16.1   OVERVIEW OF EMPLOYEE BENEFITS LAW

Basically, employees—whether of nonprofit, for-profit, or governmental employers—are individuals who provide services to an employer. That is, these individuals are provided compensation in exchange for their services. There are employees of nonprofit, tax-exempt organizations who choose to earn less than what they would receive were they working in the for-profit sector, but for the most part those who work for nonprofit organizations (other than volunteers) expect and must have remuneration for their services. Indeed, the law is clear that an individual need not necessarily accept reduced compensation merely because he or she renders services to a tax-exempt, as opposed to a taxable, organization.[5] Thus, a 1987 analysis concluded that those who work for nonprofit organizations "display few characteristics that set them off from other service workers."[6]

Compensation in general is provided in three forms: current, deferred, and retirement. Each of these forms of compensation is available to employees of nonprofit organizations. However, whatever the mode of compensation—be it wages, salaries, bonuses, commissions, fringe benefits, deferred compensation, and/or retirement benefits—most tax-exempt organizations are constrained by the private inurement doctrine.[7] This essentially means that all compensation, no matter how determined or whatever the form, must, for the employer to be or remain tax-exempt, be *reasonable*.

(a) Current Compensation in General

A nonprofit organization may pay a salary or wage. This is a form of *current*, as opposed to *deferred* (see below), compensation. Generally speaking, the payments must be reasonable, largely using the community's standard, taking into account factors such as the value of the services being rendered and pertinent experience. (The same rule essentially applies with respect to for-profit employers, in that, to be

---

[2] IRC § 401(a).

[3] IRC § 501(a).

[4] See, however, Pianko & Samuels, *Nonprofit Employment Law: Compensation, Benefits and Regulation* (New York: John Wiley & Sons, Inc., 1998).

[5] H. Rep. 104-506, 104th Cong., 2d Sess. 56, note 5 (1996).

[6] Johnston and Rudney, "Characteristics of Workers in Nonprofit Organizations," 110 *Monthly Labor Rev.* (No. 7) 28, 29 (July 1987).

[7] See Chapter 19. In this regard, public charities and social welfare organizations must also take into account the rules concerning excess benefit transactions (see § 19.11) and private foundations must also take into account the self-dealing rules (see § 11.4(a)).

deductible as a business expense, a payment of compensation must be ordinary and necessary.[8]) For this purpose, reasonable current compensation includes appropriate salary increases based on merit and appropriate cost-of-living adjustments.

Nonprofit organizations may pay bonuses. Again, a bonus is also subject to the standard of reasonableness. However, a bonus is likely to be more closely scrutinized than regular current compensation, because of the fact that it is additional compensation and thus more susceptible than regular compensation to the allegation that it is excessive compensation or otherwise is a form of inurement of net earnings. The sensitivity is increased where a bonus is paid to one who is a director, officer, key employee, or similar insider with respect to the nonprofit organization.[9]

In many respects, commissions are subject to the same rules as bonuses, in that both are forms of incentive compensation. However, commissions and other forms of percentage-based compensation can result in heightened inquiry because, by nature, they are computed using percentages and thus tend to approximate, if not constitute, private inurement. Consequently, the IRS will carefully scrutinize compensation programs of nonprofit organizations that are predicated on an incentive feature where compensation is a function of revenues received, is guaranteed, or is otherwise outside the boundaries of conventional compensation arrangements.

(b) Fringe Benefits

Federal tax and other law does not prohibit the payment of fringe benefits by nonprofit organizations. A *fringe benefit* usually is a form of noncash compensation to an employee, although it may well entail a cash outlay by the employer. Once again, a fringe benefit (or a package of them), paid by a tax-exempt employer to an employee, usually must be reasonable to preserve the tax exemption of the employer.

Typically, an employer that is a tax-exempt organization will pay for fringe benefits such as health insurance, major medical insurance, disability insurance, and perhaps travel insurance. For the most part, nonprofit organizations can pay for one or more of these benefits without tax law difficulties.

Other common forms of fringe benefits paid (either directly or by reimbursement) by employers in general are entertainment costs, costs of an automobile, moving expenses, costs of attending conventions and/or educational seminars, costs of parking, club memberships, and costs of certain professional fees (such as physicians' charges for physicals, financial planning fees, and stress management expenses).

These latter types of fringe benefits are likely to cause problems for the tax-exempt organizations that pay them. Some entities may be able to pay moving expenses, continuing education expenses, and perhaps automobile and parking expenses, without attracting too much investigation by the IRS. However, generally, a tax-exempt organization will be suspect, in the eyes of legislators and regu-

---

[8] IRC § 162(a)(1).
[9] In the case of public charities, social welfare organizations, and private foundations, these persons are known as *disqualified persons* (see §§ 11.2, 19.11 (c)).

lators (and perhaps the general public), if its employees are granted fringe benefits such as country club memberships, financial planning services, or substantial entertainment allowances.

(c) Deferred Compensation

It is becoming more common for tax-exempt organizations to provide *deferred compensation* to their employees, and many tax and other issues are resulting from this practice. As with current compensation, deferred compensation is subject to the rule of reasonableness.

Deferred compensation embraces retirement plans and profit-sharing plans. (A nonprofit organization can maintain a profit-sharing plan; the words "excess of revenue over expenses" are used instead of "profit.") These plans are usually subject to the law laid down by the Employee Retirement Income Security Act of 1974,[10] as well as subsequent enactments, such as those extending rules of nondiscrimination.

Deferred compensation plans are basically divided into qualified and nonqualified plans.

(d) Qualified Plans

A *qualified plan* is a plan that satisfies a variety of tax law requirements, as to coverage, contributions, other funding, vesting, nondiscrimination, and distributions.

For for-profit organizations, it is desirable for a plan to be a qualified one, to enable employer contributions to the plan to be deductible as business expenses. This, of course, is not of relevance to tax-exempt organizations. Other considerations of a qualified plan are that the income and capital gains from the assets underlying the plan are not subject to the federal income tax, in that they are held in a tax-exempt trust, and that employees are usually not taxed until the benefits of the plans are actually received.

Qualified plans are either *defined benefit* plans or *defined contribution* plans, the latter also referred to as individual account plans. A pension plan may fall into either category.

(i) Defined Benefit Plans. A defined benefit plan is a plan established and maintained by an employer primarily to systematically provide for the payment of definitely determinable benefits to the employees over a period of years, usually life, following retirement. Retirement benefits under a defined benefit plan are measured by and based on various factors, such as years of service rendered by the employee and compensation earned by the employee. The determination of the amount of benefits and the contributions made to the plan are not dependent upon the profits of the employer. Under a defined benefit plan, the benefits are established in advance by a formula and the employer contributions are treated as the variable factor.

Any plan that is not a defined contribution plan is a defined benefit plan.

---

[10] Pub. L. No. 406, 93d Cong., 2d Sess. (1974).

(ii) Defined Contribution Plans.   A defined contribution plan is a plan that provides an individual account for each participant and bases benefits solely upon the amount contributed to the participant's account and any expense, investment return, and forfeitures allocated to the account.

This type of plan defines the amount of contribution to be added to each participant's account. This may be done in one of two ways: by directly defining the amount the employer will contribute on behalf of each employee or by leaving to the employer's discretion the amount of contribution but defining the method of allocation. The individual accounts must receive, at least annually, their share of the total investment return, including investment income received and realized, and unrealized gain.

Ordinarily, the total plan assets are completely allocated to the individual accounts. If a participant terminates his or her employment before becoming vested, the account balance is forfeited and is applied either to reduce future employer contributions or to increase the accounts of other participants. When a participant becomes eligible to receive a benefit, his or her benefit equals the amount that can be provided by the account balance. The benefit may be paid in the form of a lump-sum distribution, a series of installments, or an annuity for the lifetime of the participant or for the joint lifetimes of the participant and other beneficiary.

Where the undertaking is to set aside periodic contributions according to a predetermined formula, the plan is referred to as a *money purchase pension plan.* Contributions are generally expressed as a percentage of covered payroll, with the rate sometimes varying with the employee's age at entry into the plan. A *target benefit plan* is a money purchase plan that sets a targeted benefit to be met by actuarily determined contributions. Special antidiscrimination rules apply to target benefit plans.

Another type of defined contribution plan is a *profit-sharing* plan. A profit-sharing plan is one established and maintained by an employer to provide for participation in profits by employees or their beneficiaries. The plan must have a definite, predetermined formula for allocating contributions made under the plan among the participants and for distributing the funds accumulated under the plan after a fixed number of years, the attainment of a stated age, or upon the prior occurrence of some event, such as layoff, illness, disability, retirement, death, or severance of employment. A plan cannot qualify as a profit-sharing plan unless the employer's contributions are contingent upon the existence of the necessary profits. A profit-sharing plan may, but is not required to, have a definite, predetermined formula for computing the amount of annual employer contributions.

Other defined contribution plans (some of which are profit-sharing plans) include stock bonus plans, employee stock ownership plans, thrift plans, simplified employee pension plans (which can be a form of individual retirement accounts), and so-called cash or deferred arrangements.

(iii) The Funding Mechanism.   The usual method of funding a pension or profit-sharing plan is through a tax-exempt trust. A trusteed plan uses a trust to receive and invest the funds contributed under the plan and to distribute the benefits to participants and/or their beneficiaries. In order for a trust forming part of a pension, profit-sharing, or like plan to constitute a qualified trust, (1) the trust

must be created or organized in the United States and must be maintained at all times as a U.S. domestic trust; (2) the trust must be part of a pension, profit-sharing, or like plan established by the employer for the exclusive benefit of the employees and/or their beneficiaries; (3) the trust must be formed or availed of for the purpose of distributing to employees and/or their beneficiaries the corpus and income of the fund accumulated by the trust in accordance with the plan; (4) it must be impossible under the trust instrument at any time before all liabilities, with respect to employees and their beneficiaries, are satisfied for any part of the trust's corpus or income to be used for, or diverted to, purposes other than for the exclusive benefit of employees and/or their beneficiaries; (5) the trust must be part of a plan that benefits a nondiscriminatory classification of employees under IRS guidelines and provides nondiscriminatory benefits; and (6) if the trust is part of a pension plan, the plan must provide that forfeitures cannot be applied to increase the benefit of any participant.

The tax advantages of a qualified plan can be obtained without the use of a trust through an *annuity plan*, under which contributions are used to purchase retirement annuities directly from an insurance company. An annuity contract is treated as a qualified trust if it would, except for the fact that it is not a trust, satisfy all the requirements for qualification. In that case, the annuitant is treated as if he or she were the trustee.

A segregated asset account of a life insurance company can be used as an investment medium for assets of a qualified pension, profit-sharing, or annuity plan. Assets of a qualified plan may be held in this type of account without the use of a trust.

Another form of a nontrusteed plan is the use of a custodial account. Under this approach, the employer arranges with a bank or other qualified institution to act as custodian of the plan funds placed in the account. Although a custodial account is not a trust, a qualifying custodial account is treated for tax purposes as a qualified trust.

(e) Nonqualified Plans

Nonqualified plans are used as means to provide supplemental benefits and/or to avoid the technical requirements imposed upon qualified plans. However, the advantages of nonqualified plans for many employers (particularly for-profit ones) have been substantially eroded in recent years. Also, the employer's deduction is deferred until the amount attributable to the contribution is includable in the employee's income. Yet, nonqualified plans are of great importance to tax-exempt employers.

The federal tax consequences of nonqualified plans vary, depending upon whether the plan is funded or unfunded. Where the plan is funded, contributions by an employer to a nonexempt employees' trust are includable in an employee's gross income in the first tax year in which the rights of the individual having the beneficial interest in the trust are transferable and are not subject to a substantial risk of forfeiture. Unfunded plans are those plans that do not constitute qualified employees' trusts nor as certain nonqualified annuity contracts. The tax consequences to an employee under an unfunded arrangement are determined by application of the doctrines of constructive receipt or economic benefit.

Funds in these plans can be deemed constructively received by employees and accessible by creditors of the employer.

(f) 457 Plans

Congress, in 1986, extended rules for the provision of nonqualified unfunded deferred compensation to employees of nonprofit organizations. This type of compensation is provided by means of *457 plans*.[11] Prior to 1986, these plans were available only to employees of state and local governments.

A 457 plan is one that is available to employees of tax-exempt organizations (and, still, governmental agencies). Compliance with the rules for these plans enables employees to defer the taxation of income; otherwise, the deferred amount is immediately taxable. Also, these plans are unfunded, so that the deferred amounts (and the resulting earnings) remain the property of the employer and thus are subject to the creditors of the employer.

In this type of plan, the maximum amount of compensation that can be deferred in a year is the lesser of $7,500 or one-third of the employee's (or other participant's) gross income. Under certain circumstances, catch-up deferrals are permitted, up to $15,000 annually. Distributions cannot be made before the earlier of the discontinuance of employment or the occurrence of an unforeseeable emergency. Distributions payable upon death must be paid within 15 years or within the life expectancy of a surviving spouse.

The law requires, as to distributions, that these plans satisfy certain minimum distribution requirements and imposes a penalty excise tax equal to 50 percent of the amount that should have been distributed; for lifetime distributions, at least two-thirds of the total amount payable must be paid during the life expectancy of the participant and any amount not distributed during the life of the participant must be distributed at death at least as rapidly as required by the method that was used during the participant's life; and in the case of distributions that do not begin until after the participant's death, the entire amount payable must be paid during a period that does not exceed 15 years or, if the beneficiary is the surviving spouse, the life expectancy of that spouse.

Amounts in this type of plan cannot be rolled over (that is, transferred without taxation) to a qualified plan or to an individual retirement account. However, a transfer from one of these plans to another will not trigger a tax.

(g) 403(b) Plans

Another form of deferred compensation in the tax-exempt organizations context is the tax-sheltered (or tax-deferred) annuity. This is an annuity paid out of a *403(b) plan*.[12] A tax-sheltered annuity is treated as a defined contribution plan.

Tax-sheltered annuity programs are available only to employees of charitable

---

[11] These plans are authorized by IRC § 457.
[12] These plans are authorized by IRC § 403(b).

(including educational, scientific, and religious) organizations, as well as employees of public educational institutions. Essentially, the rule is that if amounts are contributed by an employer toward the purchase of an annuity contract for an employee, then, to the extent that the amounts do not exceed the exclusion allowance (see below) for the tax year of the employees, the employee is not required to include the amounts in gross income for the tax year. These plans are usually represented by an individual annuity contract purchased by the employee or a group annuity contract with the employer where a separate account is maintained for each participant. As an alternative, funding may be through a custodial account.

Contributions to a tax-sheltered annuity plan—usually made on a salary reduction basis—are excluded from the employees' taxable income, with certain limitations. Generally, elective (employee) contributions may not exceed $9,500 annually. The funds involved accumulate without taxation, except for contributions by the employer that are substantially vested in the employee.

Amounts contributed by an employee to a tax-sheltered annuity plan are not required to be included in the gross income of the employee to the extent that the amounts do not exceed the employee's *exclusion allowance* for the year. The exclusion allowance for a year is (1) the product of (a) 20 percent of an employee's includable compensation times (b) his or her years of service with the employer as of the close of the taxable year over (2) the aggregate of the amount contributed by the employer for annuity contracts and excludable from the gross income of the employee for any prior year. The minimum exclusion allowance is the lesser of $3,000 or the employee's includable compensation. Thus, all of an eligible employee's includable compensation may be contributed to a tax-sheltered annuity plan on an excludable basis, up to $3,000.

Tax-sheltered annuity plans are generally subject to less federal law regulation. However, various provisions of the Employee Retirement Income Security Act are applicable, as are many of the nondiscrimination, distribution, and other limitations (including restrictions on loans) of qualified plans.

Distributions from a tax-sheltered annuity plan are taxed in the same way as are periodic distributions from qualified plans.

(h) Perspective

The law in this field has become quite complex, with Congress repeatedly visiting the subject in recent years. The enactment of the Employee Retirement Income Security Act in 1974 brought a vast amount of new statutory law on the subject, for nonprofit and for-profit employers alike. In 1986, Congress, as noted above, extended these deferred compensation plan rules to nonprofit employees and made it clear that tax-exempt organizations can maintain qualified profit-sharing plans.[13] In 1996, Congress decided that, for plan years beginning after December 31, 1996, tax-exempt organizations may maintain the qualified cash or deferred

---

[13] IRC § 401(a)(27).

arrangements known as *401(k) plans*.[14] Congress, Treasury, and the IRS will assuredly add more law in this field in the coming years—much of it of direct applicability in the tax-exempt organizations context.[15]

There are eight categories of tax-exempt organizations, other than those entities that are tax-exempt as retirement or profit-sharing plans, that are funds underlying employee benefit plans or are otherwise principally concerned with employee compensation.[16] Three of these are termed *welfare benefit funds*;[17] they are the voluntary employees' beneficiary associations (VEBA), supplemental unemployment benefit trusts (SUB), and group legal services organizations (GLSO).

§ 16.2   SPECIAL RULES FOR WELFARE BENEFIT FUNDS

(a)   Nondiscrimination Requirements

A VEBA or a GLSO, which is part of a plan, cannot be tax-exempt unless it meets certain nondiscrimination requirements.[18] That is, in general, the plan meets these requirements only if (1) each class of benefits under the plan is provided under a classification of employees that is set forth in the plan and that is found by the IRS not to be discriminatory in favor of employees who are highly compensated individuals, and (2) in the case of each class of benefits, the benefits do not discriminate in favor of employees who are highly compensated individuals.[19]

The following categories of employees may be excluded from consideration in this regard: employees who have not completed three years of service, employees who have not attained age 21, seasonal employees or less than half-time employees, employees covered by a collective bargaining agreement that was the subject of good faith bargaining, and employees who are nonresident aliens and who do not receive earned income from United States sources.[20]

---

[14] IRC § 401(k)(4)(B)(i).

[15] In general, Walsh Skelly, "Getting More for Less: Tax-Advantaged Compensation Packages for Employees of Tax-Exempt Organizations," 3 *Exempt Org. Tax Rev.* (No. 10) 1135 (1990); Altieri, "Nonqualified Deferred Compensation and the Tax-Exempt Employer," 16 *J. Pension Planning & Compliance* (No. 3) 229 (1990).

[16] See *infra* § 2–4.

[17] IRC § 505.

[18] IRC § 505(a)(1). This rule does not apply to any organization that is part of a plan maintained pursuant to an agreement between employee representatives and one or more employers if the IRS finds that the agreement is a collective bargaining agreement and that the plan was the subject of good faith bargaining between the employee representatives and the employer or employers (IRC § 505(b)).

[19] IRC § 505(b)(1). A life insurance, disability, severance pay, or supplemental unemployment compensation benefit will not fail the second of these requirements merely because the benefits available bear a uniform relationship to the total compensation, or the basic or regular rate of compensation, of employees covered by the plan (*id.*, last sentence).

The term *compensation* is defined in IRC § 414(s) and the term *highly compensated individual* is defined in IRC § 414(q).

[20] IRC § 505(b)(2).

(b) Tax-Exempt Status

A VEBA, SUB, or GLSO is not an organization that is tax-exempt for federal income purposes unless it has made timely application to the IRS for recognition of tax-exempt status.[21]

§ 16.3 VOLUNTARY EMPLOYEES' BENEFICIARY ASSOCIATIONS

The federal tax law accords tax-exempt status to voluntary employees' beneficiary associations "providing for the payment of life, sick, accident or other benefits to the members of such association or their dependents or designated beneficiaries," absent private inurement.[22]

One of the basic requirements for achievement of tax exemption as a voluntary employees' beneficiary association (as noted, a VEBA[23]) is that the organization be an association of employees.[24] Thus, a trust that provides benefits to only one employee cannot qualify as a tax-exempt VEBA.[25] Typically, those eligible for membership in a VEBA are defined by reference to a common employer (or affiliated employers), to coverage under one or more collective bargaining agreements (with respect to benefits provided by reason of the agreement(s)), to membership in a labor union, or to membership in one or more locals of a national or international labor union. Employees of one or more employers engaged in the same line of business in the same geographic locale are considered to share an employment-related bond for purposes of an organization through which their employers provide benefits. Employees of a labor union are considered to share an employment-related common bond with members of the union, and employees of a VEBA are considered to share an employment-related common bond with members of the VEBA. Whether a group of individuals is defined by reference to a permissible standard or standards is a question to be determined with regard to all the pertinent facts and circumstances.[26]

Despite the foregoing criteria, contained in the tax regulations, one federal court of appeals has declared the regulation invalid to the extent of the "same geographic locale" requirement. The court reviewed the legislative history of the statute and the phraseology of other tax exemption provisions, and concluded that Congress intentionally elected to not place a geographic restriction on tax-exempt VEBAs. Noting that the "quintessential element" of a tax-exempt VEBA is the "commonality of interests among its employee members," the court wrote that "the relatedness among a group of employees is neither

---

[21] IRC § 505(c). The concept of recognition of tax-exempt status by the IRS is the subject of § 23.1.

[22] IRC § 501(c)(9); Reg. § 1.501(c)(9)-1.

[23] See text accompanied by *supra* note 17.

[24] Reg. § 1.501(c)(9)-2(b).

[25] Rev. Rul. 85-199, 1985-2 C.B. 163.

[26] Reg. § 1.501(c)(9)-2(a)(1).

established nor dissipated upon the geographic locale of the group's members."[27]

Eligibility for membership in a VEBA may be restricted by geographic proximity, or by objective conditions or limitations reasonably related to employment, such as a limitation as to a reasonable classification of workers, a limitation based on a reasonable minimum period of service, a limitation based on maximum compensation, or a requirement that members be employed on a full-time basis. Also, eligibility for benefits may be restricted by objective conditions relating to the type or amount of benefits offered. Any objective criteria used to restrict eligibility for membership or benefits may not, however, be selected or administered in a manner that limits membership or benefits to officers, shareholders, or highly compensated employees of an employer contributing to or otherwise funding a VEBA. Similarly, eligibility for benefits may not be subject to conditions or limitations that have the effect of entitling officers, shareholders, or highly compensated employees of an employer contributing to or otherwise funding the VEBA to benefits that are disproportionate in relation to benefits to which other members of the VEBA are entitled.[28] Whether the selection or administration of objective conditions has the effect of providing disproportionate benefits to officers, shareholders, or highly compensated employees generally is to be determined on the basis of all the facts and circumstances.[29] The tax exemption does not apply to pension funds distributing benefits to partners.[30]

Membership in a VEBA must be voluntary. Membership is *voluntary* if an affirmative act is required on the part of an employee to become a member rather than the designation as a member due to employee status. However, a VEBA is considered voluntary even though membership is required of all employees, as long as the employees do not incur a detriment (such as deductions from compensation) as the result of membership in the VEBA. An employer is not deemed to have imposed involuntary membership on the employee if membership is required as the result of a collective bargaining agreement or as an incident of membership in a labor organization.[31]

A tax-exempt VEBA must be controlled either by its membership, an inde-

---

[27] Water Quality Ass'n Employees' Benefit Corp. v. United States, 795 F.2d 1303, 1310–1311 (7th Cir. 1986), *rev'g* 609 F. Supp. 91 (N.D. Ill. 1985).

The IRS, on August 6, 1992, proposed regulations that would supplement the existing regulations with rules for determining whether the membership of a VEBA consists of employees of employers engaged in the same line of business in the same geographic locale (EE-23-92). The regulations will provide guidance necessary to comply with the law in the case of an organization that does not consist exclusively of the employees of a single employer or the members of a single labor union. They will affect entities seeking to sponsor VEBAs covering the employees of more than one unrelated employer, as well as those employees. (Prop. Reg. § 1.501(c)(9)-2(a)(d)).

[28] E.g., Lima Surgical Assocs., Inc. Voluntary Employees' Beneficiary Ass'n Plan Trust v. United States, 90-1 U.S.T.C. ¶ 50,329 (Cl. Ct. 1990), *aff'd*, 944 F.2d 885 (Fed. Cir. 1991).

[29] Reg. § 1.501(c)(9)-2(a)(2)(i). The income tax regulations enumerate certain generally permissible restrictions or conditions (Reg. § 1.501(c)(9)-2(a)(2)(ii); also Reg. § 1.501(c)(9)-4(b)).

[30] Nelson v. Joyce, 404 F. Supp. 489 (N.D. Ill. 1975); Rev. Rul. 70-411, 1970-2 C.B. 91; Rev. Rul. 69-144, 1969-1 C.B. 115.

[31] Reg. § 1.501(c)(9)-2(c)(2).

pendent trustee (such as a bank), or trustees, at least some of whom are designated by or on behalf of the membership.[32] Loose forms of affiliation are inadequate.[33]

The life, sick, accident, or other benefits provided by a VEBA must be payable to its members, their dependents, or their designated beneficiaries.[34] Life, sick, accident, or other benefits may take the form of cash or noncash benefits. To be tax-exempt, the VEBA must function so that substantially all of its operations are in furtherance of the provision of the requisite benefits.[35] The income tax regulations define the terms *life benefit*[36] and *sick and accident benefit*,[37] and provide that the term *other benefits* includes only benefits that are similar to life, sick, or accident benefits, namely, a benefit that is intended to safeguard or improve the health of a member or a member's dependents, or that protects against a contingency that interrupts or impairs a member's earning power.[38] Other benefits include paying vacation benefits, providing vacation facilities, reimbursing vacation expenses, subsidizing recreational activities, the provision of child-care facilities for preschool and school-age dependents, and personal legal service benefits.[39] Other benefits do not include the payment of commuting expenses, the provision of accident or homeowner's insurance benefits for damage to property, the provision of malpractice insurance,[40] the provision of loans to members (except in times of distress), the provision of pension and annuity benefits payable at the time of mandatory or voluntary retirement, or the provision of savings facilities for members.[41]

An illustration of VEBAs, under the law prior to the promulgation of the pertinent income tax regulations, was an organization that reimbursed its members for premiums paid under the Medicare program.[42] An association that merely ensured the discharge of an obligation imposed by law upon an employer corporation (for example, worker's compensation benefits) was held to not qualify for tax exemption as a VEBA because the employees did not receive any additional benefits.[43]

The private inurement doctrine as applied to VEBAs means not only a prohibition on matters such as unreasonable compensation or self-dealing, but also the payment to any member of disproportionate benefits.[44] Thus, one plan was held to merely be a separate fund controlled by a company's sole share-

---

[32] Reg. § 1.501(c)(9)-2(c)(3)(iii). E.g., Lima Surgical Assocs., Inc. Voluntary Employees' Beneficiary Ass'n Plan Trust v. United States, *supra* note 28.

[33] E.g., American Ass'n of Christian Schools Voluntary Employees Beneficiary Ass'n Welfare Plan Trust v. United States, 663 F. Supp. (M.D. Ala. 1987), aff'd, 850 F.2d 1510 (11th Cir. 1988).

[34] E.g., Milwaukee Sign Painters Welfare Fund v. United States, 66-1 U.S.T.C. ¶ 9170 (E.D. Wis. 1965).

[35] Reg. § 1.501(c)(9)-3(a).

[36] Reg. § 1.501(c)(9)-3(b).

[37] Reg. § 1.501(c)(9)-3(c).

[38] Reg. § 1.501(c)(9)-3(d).

[39] Reg. § 1.501(c)(9)-3(e).

[40] E.g., Anesthesia Serv. Med. Group, Inc., Employee Protective Trust, San Diego Trust & Sav. Bank, Trustee v. Comm'r, 85 T.C. 1031 (1985).

[41] Reg. § 1.501(c)(9)-3(f). This regulation was upheld in Canton Police Benevolent Ass'n of Canton, Ohio v. United States, 658 F. Supp. 411 (N.D. Ohio 1987), aff'd, 88-1 U.S.T.C. ¶ 9285 (6th Cir. 1988); Bricklayers Benefit Plans of Delaware Valley, Inc. v. Comm'r, 81 T.C. 735 (1983).

[42] Rev. Rul. 66-212, 1966-2 C.B. 230.

[43] Rev. Rul. 74-18, 1974-1 C.B. 139. Also Rev. Rul. 66-354, 1966-2 C.B. 207. Cf. § 18.15.

[44] Reg. § 1.501(c)(9)-4(a), (b). E.g., Lima Surgical Assocs, Inc. Voluntary Employees' Beneficiary Ass'n Plan Trust v. United States, *supra* note 28.

holder for his own benefit, with coverage of other employees incidental, in part because deducted contributions were found to be excessive in relation to amounts paid out for insurance premiums and costs, and because funds of the plan were invested in a speculative manner.[45] The rebate of excess insurance premiums, based on the mortality or morbidity experience of the insurer to which the premiums were paid, to the person or persons whose contributions were applied to the premiums, is not prohibited inurement.[46] Also, the termination of a VEBA, with the remaining assets used to provide permissible benefits (such as a transfer of assets from one VEBA to another[47]), or certain distributions to members upon dissolution of a VEBA, are not forms of prohibited inurement.[48]

Congress, in 1969, removed a limitation that no more than 15 percent of a VEBA's annual receipts could be in the form of investment income, thereby enabling VEBAs to accumulate reserves at reasonable levels. (VEBAs must conform to the requirements of the Employee Retirement Income Security Act, however, including those governing investment practices.) With this restriction eliminated, business corporations are utilizing VEBAs to provide employee benefits on the self-insurance basis, because the benefits program can be fashioned to meet the employers' desires and because it is less expensive than insurance premium costs.[49]

---

[45] Sunrise Constr. Co., Inc. v. Comm'r, 52 T.C.M. 1358 (1987).

[46] Reg. § 1.501(c)(9)-4(c).

[47] E.g., Priv. Ltr. Rul. 9414011.

[48] Reg. § 1.501(c)(9)-4(d). In general, see Chapter 19.

[49] In general, Hoffman & Lerner, "Pension Funds and Exempt Organizations: Prefunding Welfare Benefits with VEBAs," 8 *J. Tax. Inv.* (No. 1) 66 (1990); Paxton, "26 U.S.C. Sec. 501(c)(9): Tax-Exempt Status of Voluntary Employees' Benefit Associations," 5 *Akron Tax J.* 253 (1988); Ryan, "DEFRA Requires a Current Look at VEBAs," 15 *Col. Law.* (No. 7) 1184 (1986); Sollee, "Analyzing the New Temporary Regulations for Welfare Benefit Plans: Part II," 64 *J. Tax.* (No. 6) 322 (1986); Sollee, "Analyzing the New Temporary Regulations for Welfare Benefit Plans," 64 *J. Tax.* (No. 5) 258 (1986); Hira & Perry, "IRS Provides Much Guidance on Welfare Benefit Funds," 17 *Tax Adviser* (No. 9) 585 (1986); Miller, "Legal Issues: New Rules for Funded Welfare Plans," 2 *Comp. & Benefits Man.* (No. 1) 185 (1985); Lurie, "Why Not a Salary-Reduction VEBA? Its Time Has Come," 1 *Comp. & Benefits Man.* (No. 2) 149 (1985); Sacks, "How Excess Assets of Terminating VEBAs May Best Be Utilized by the Employer," 62 *J. Tax.* (No. 4) 194 (1985); Eggertsen & Hainer, "1984 Tax Act: Changes Affecting Many Group Insurance Contracts and VEBAs," 64 *Mich. Bar J.* (No. 9) 932 (1985); Porcano, "Reconsidering Voluntary Employees' Beneficiary Associations Under the DRA," 16 *Tax Adv.* (No. 3) 130 (1985); Greenblatt, "VEBA Changes and Planning Under DEFRA," 37 *U.S.C. Inst. on Fed. Tax.* 2 (1985); Fuchs, "New VEBA Rules—Changes Under the 1984 Tax Act," 12 *Comp. Planning J.* (No. 9) 259 (1984); Tauber, "Voluntary Employees' Beneficiary Associations—Their Uses and Abuses," 10 *N.Y.U. Conf. on Employee Benefits Tax.* 11 (1984); Cole, Jr., "Voluntary Employee Beneficiary Associations and IRC Section 501(c)(9) Trusts," 42 *N.Y.U. Inst. on Fed. Tax.* 45 (1984); Boyers, "Using VEBAs to Complement Qualified Plan Benefits After TEFRA," 42 *N.Y.U. Inst. on Fed. Tax.* 43 (1984); Greenblatt, "Tax Planning for Fringe Benefits Provided by VEBAs Requires Changes Due to New Tax Law," 33 *Tax. Accts.* (No. 2) 82 (1984); Greenblatt, "Planning for VEBAs Under The Tax Reform Act of 1984," 62 *Taxes* (No. 9) 605 (1984); Smith, "An Examination of VEBAs and Deductions: Current or Deferred Compensation?," 17 *U.C. Davis L. Rev.* (No. 3) 925 (1984); Cirino, "Benefits: The Quiet Debut of 501(c)(9) Trusts," 11 *Institutional Investor* (No. 5) 57 (1977); Haneberg, "The 501(c)(9) Trust Revisited," 114 *Tr. & Est.* 622 (1975); Note, "Self-Insured Employee Welfare Plans and the 501(c)(9) Trust: The Specter of State Regulation," 43 *U. Cincinnati L. Rev.* 325 (1974); *501(c)(9) Trust Primer*, published by Northwestern National Life Insurance Co.; Stuchiver, "Using a 501(c)(9) Trust to Fund Employee Benefits," 112 *Tr. & Est.* 242 (1973).

A VEBA cannot be tax-exempt unless it meets certain nondiscrimination requirements.[50] However, this rule is inapplicable to a VEBA that is part of a plan maintained pursuant to one or more collective bargaining agreements between one or more employee organizations and one or more employers.[51]

A VEBA constitutes a *welfare benefit fund*[52] and therefore a *disqualified benefit*[53] provided by a VEBA will give rise to tax liability.[54]

VEBAs are subject to the unrelated income rules,[55] including the special rules by which only exempt function revenue is excluded from taxation.[56] Employer contributions to VEBAs are contributions to capital, rather than forms of gross income.[57] Net passive income of VEBAs constitutes unrelated business income, unless it is properly set aside for charitable purposes or to provide for the payment of life, sick, accident, or other benefits.[58]

§ 16.4 SUPPLEMENTAL UNEMPLOYMENT BENEFIT TRUSTS

The federal tax law provides tax exemption for certain trusts forming part of a plan providing for the payment of supplemental unemployment compensation benefits, which satisfy five basic requirements (as noted, SUBs[59]).[60] Among other criteria, the SUB must be part of a plan the eligibility conditions and benefits of which do not discriminate in favor of supervisory or highly compensated employees and that requires that benefits be determined according to objective standards. Also, the SUB must be a part of a plan that provides that the corpus and income of the SUB cannot (before the satisfaction of all liabilities to employees covered by the plan) be used for, or diverted to, any purpose other than the provision of supplemental unemployment compensation benefits; termination of a SUB, with distribution of its remaining assets to employees covered by the plan (after the satisfaction of all liabilities) will not result in loss of its tax-exempt status (even though technically the assets will not be used solely for the purpose of providing benefits).[61]

SUBs are intended to provide benefits to laid-off (or perhaps ill) employ-

---

[50] IRC § 505(a)(1), (b).

[51] IRC § 505(a)(2).

[52] IRC § 419(e)(3)(A).

[53] IRC § 4976(b).

[54] IRC § 4976(a).

[55] See Part Five.

[56] See § 28.3.

[57] Priv. Ltr. Rul. 8512058.

[58] IRC § 512(a)(3)(B). See § 28.3. IRC § 512(a)(3)(E)(i) limits the amount that can be treated as exempt function income because it is set aside to an amount that does not exceed the account limits imposed by IRC § 419A(c). However, these limits are inapplicable to collectively bargained plans (IRC § 419A(f)(5)(A)). Thus, there are no set-aside limits where the VEBA is a plan that is collectively bargained (e.g., Priv. Ltr. Rul. 9216033).

[59] See text accompanied by *supra* note 17.

[60] IRC § 501(c)(17); Reg. § 1.501(c)(17)-1(a).

[61] Rev. Rul. 81-68, 1981-1 C.B. 349.

ees, frequently in conjunction with other payments such as state unemployment benefits.

The term *supplemental unemployment compensation benefits* means separation-from-employment benefits and sick and accident benefits that are subordinate to the separation benefits.[62] These benefits encompass short-week benefits paid to employees not wholly separated from employment[63] and relocation payments to employees who would otherwise be separated from employment.[64] However, payments from a SUB to union members to compensate them for anticipated lost wages because of the adoption of a new industrial process were ruled to not qualify as this type of benefit since there was no showing that all union members receiving the benefits were involuntarily separated from employment or actually incurred a reduction in the number of hours worked because of the new process.[65]

An otherwise qualified SUB can invest in low-risk, income-producing investments that serve social purposes, do not accrue for the benefit of related parties, and are not contrary to the employees' interests without jeopardizing its tax exemption.[66] However, distribution to employees of funds representing contributions in excess of maximum funding will adversely affect a SUB's tax-exempt status.[67] The trustee of a tax-exempt plan may, upon authorization from an employee, deduct and pay the employee's union dues from his or her benefit payments.[68]

A SUB constitutes a *welfare benefit fund*[69] and therefore a *disqualified benefit*[70] provided by a SUB will give rise to tax liability.[71]

§ 16.5   BLACK LUNG BENEFITS TRUSTS

Another type of tax-exempt organization is the black lung benefits trust (BLBT).[72] The purpose of these rules is to provide income tax exemption for a qualifying trust used by a coal mine operator to self-insure for liabilities under federal and state black lung benefits laws. Under the federal black lung benefits statute, a coal mine operator in a state not deemed to provide adequate worker's compensation coverage for pneumoconiosis must secure the payment of benefits for which the operator may be found liable under the statute, either by means of commercial insurance or through self-insuring. Since no state laws are presently deemed ade-

---

[62] IRC § 501(c)(17)(D); Reg. § 1.501(c)(17)-1(b)(1).
[63] Rev. Rul. 70-189, 1970-1 C.B. 134. Also Rev. Rul. 80-124, 1980-1 C.B. 212; Rev. Rul. 56-249, 1956-2 C.B. 488.
[64] Rev. Rul. 70-188, 1970-1 C.B. 133.
[65] Rev. Rul. 77-43, 1977-1 C.B. 151.
[66] Rev. Rul. 70-536, 1970-2 C.B. 120.
[67] Rev. Rul. 71-156, 1971-2 C.B. 153.
[68] Rev. Rul. 73-307, 1973-2 C.B. 185.
[69] IRC § 419(e)(3)(A).
[70] IRC § 4976(b).
[71] IRC § 4976(a). Also, an organization described in IRC § 501(c)(17) cannot be tax-exempt if it engaged in a prohibited transaction as defined in IRC § 503(b) (IRC § 503(a)(1)(A), 503(a)(1)(B)).
[72] IRC § 501(c)(21).

quate for this purpose, all operators subject to this liability must obtain insurance or self-insure. Because this insurance is unavailable or is of high cost, Congress established this form of self-insurance program, with similar tax consequences (from the point of view of the operator) as would result if the operator had purchased noncancellable accident and health insurance.[73]

A qualified BLBT must be irrevocable, must be established by a written instrument, must be created or organized in the United States, and may be contributed to by any person (other than an insurance company). The trust instrument may be amended or restated for appropriate purposes, such as to enable subsidiaries of the corporation that initially created the BLBT to self-insure their obligations under the black lung benefits law.[74]

The tax-exempt BLBT has as its exclusive purpose the (1) satisfaction, in whole or in part, of the liability of a contributor to the trust for, or with respect to, claims for compensation for disability or death due to pneumoconiosis under Black Lung Acts;[75] (2) payment of premiums for insurance exclusively covering this type of liability; and (3) payment of administrative and other incidental expenses of the trust (including legal, accounting, actuarial and trustee expenses) in connection with the operation of the trust and the processing of claims under Black Lung Acts against a contributor to the trust.[76]

No part of the assets of a tax-exempt BLBT may be used for, or diverted to, any purpose other than the foregoing three purposes, or investment.[77] However, investment can occur only to the extent that the trustee determines that the invested assets are not currently needed for the trust's tax-exempt purposes. Moreover, the investment may only be in (1) public debt securities of the United States, (2) obligations of a state or local government that are not in default as to principal or interest, or (3) time or demand deposits in a bank[78] or an insured credit union located in the United States.[79] A division of a BLBT and the transfer of its assets to one or more new BLBTs is not a prohibited diversion of assets.[80]

The assets of a qualified BLBT may also be paid into the Black Lung Disability Trust Fund[81] or into the general fund of the United States Treasury (other than in satisfaction of any tax or other civil or criminal liability of the person who established or contributed to the trust).

The income of a qualified BLBT is not taxable to the operator making contributions to it. Similarly, the trust's income is not taxable to the trust, except that

---

[73] S. Rep. No. 95-336, 95th Cong., 2d Sess. 11–12 (1978).

[74] E.g., Priv. Ltr. Rul. 9428030.

[75] These laws are Part C, Title IV, of the Federal Coal Mine Health and Safety Act of 1969 and any state law providing compensation for disability or death due to pneumoconiosis.

[76] IRC § 501(c)(21)(A).

[77] IRC § 501(c)(21)(B).

[78] As defined in IRC § 581.

[79] As defined in the Federal Credit Union Act, 12 U.S.C. § 1752(b).

[80] E.g., Priv. Ltr. Rul. 9428029.

[81] See § 3 of the Black Lung Benefits Revenue Act of 1977, Pub. L. No. 227, 95th Cong.; 2d Sess. (1978).

the trust is subject to tax on any unrelated business taxable income.[82] The trust must, however, file annual information returns with the IRS.[83]

The contributions by a coal mine operator to a tax-exempt BLBT are deductible by the operator for federal income tax purposes.[84] This provision imposes alternative limitations on the deductibility of these contributions for a tax year, based on actual benefit claims approved or filed during the taxable year, as well as on the amount of anticipated liabilities for claims filed or expected to be filed in the future by past or present employees of the operator determined by using reasonable actuarial methods and assumptions, and any excess contributions may be taxable.[85] A contribution of property will be treated as a sale or exchange of the property for tax purposes, unless it is transferred without consideration and is not subject to a mortgage or similar lien.

A trust that is tax-exempt under these rules is subject to prohibitions on self-dealing[86] and the making of certain expenditures[87] (and is the only type of tax-exempt organization, other than a private foundation,[88] to be governed by these statutory restrictions). These prohibitions are similar to those imposed upon private foundations and are sanctioned by excise taxes upon the trust, its trustees, and/or the disqualified person(s) involved. The Senate Finance Committee observed that the investment limitations imposed on these trusts "are intended to preclude speculative or other investments of corpus or income which might jeopardize the carrying out of the trust's exempt purposes and permit the [C]ommittee [which authored these provisions] to simplify the self-dealing restrictions and avoid the necessity of certain other restrictions to prevent potential abuses."[89]

§ 16.6   OTHER BENEFIT FUNDS

Another type of tax-exempt organization is a trust established by the sponsors of a multiemployer pension plan as a vehicle to accumulate funds in order to provide withdrawal liability payments to the plan.[90]

Another type of tax-exempt organization is a trust described in section 4049 of the Employee Retirement Income Security Act of 1974 (as in effect on the date of the enactment of the Single-Employer Pension Plan Amendments Act of 1986).[91]

---

[82] See Part Five.
[83] See § 24.3. Although the exemption application and annual information returns of an IRC § 501(c)(21) trust are subject to the public disclosure requirements (IRC § 6104(a)(1), 6104(b); see § 24.4(b)), disclosure is not required of confidential business information of a coal mine operator who establishes and contributes to such a trust (Pub. L. No. 488, 95th Cong., 2d Sess. (1978) § (e); H. Rep. No. 1656, 95th Cong., 2d Sess. 6 (1978)).
[84] IRC § 192.
[85] IRC § 4953.
[86] IRC § 4951. Cf. IRC § 4941.
[87] IRC § 4952. Cf. IRC § 4945.
[88] See Chapter 11.
[89] S. Rep. No. 336, *supra* note 73 at 14.
[90] IRC § 501(c)(22).
[91] IRC § 501(c)(24). Section 4049 was repealed on Dec. 22, 1987 (Pub. L. No. 100-203, § 9312(a)).

The federal tax law references a trust or trusts, created before June 25, 1959, forming part of a plan providing for the payment of benefits under a pension plan funded only by employees' contributions, where three basic requirements are satisfied.[92]

Tax exemption is provided for teachers' retirement fund associations of a purely local character, if there is no private inurement (other than through payment of retirement benefits) and the income consists wholly of amounts received from public taxation, amounts received from assessments on the teaching salaries of members, and income from investments.[93]

No income tax regulations have been issued under this provision, nor have there been any IRS rulings or court opinions concerning this provision, leading the IRS to conclude that the section "has very limited application."[94] The phrase *of a purely local character* has the same meaning in this context as it does with respect to benevolent or mutual organizations.[95]

Congress in 1976 created a category of tax-exempt organization that was part of a qualified group legal services plan or plans.[96] This was part of an overall scheme according favorable tax treatment for prepaid group legal services provided by employers to their employees. However, the authorization for this type of tax exemption expired as of June 30, 1992.

§ 16.7 RETIREMENT PLANS

The federal tax law provides that "[a]n organization described in . . . [IRC] section 401(a) shall be exempt from taxation under this subtitle . . ." This provision of the Internal Revenue Code defines the qualified trust fund that is part of a stock bonus, pension, or profit-sharing plan[97] of an employer for the exclusive benefit of its employees or their beneficiaries. While the fund is the tax-exempt organization, the principal focus of the law in this area is on the terms and conditions of the retirement plan.

The law of retirement plans was substantially modified by the Employee Retirement Income Security Act of 1974.[98] Government supervision of retirement plans is largely the responsibility of the IRS and the Department of Labor. This body of law imposes requirements as respects employee participation, coverage, vesting of interests, funding, portability of benefits, fiduciary responsibility, prohibited transactions, preparation of plan summaries, and annual reporting and disclosure to the Department of Labor. The Pension Benefit Guaranty Corporation administers a program of plan termination insurance.

A Joint Pension Task Force is authorized to undertake studies in connection with continuing pension reform.

---

[92] IRC § 501(c)(18); Reg. § 1.501(c)(18)-1. An organization described in IRC § 501(c)(18) cannot be tax-exempt if it engaged in a prohibited transaction as defined in IRC § 503(b) (IRC § 503(a)(1)(C)).

[93] IRS § 501(c)(ii).

[94] IRS Exempt Organizations Handbook (IRM 7751) § (12) 21.

[95] Reg. § 1.501(c)(12)-1(b).

[96] IRC § 501(c)(20).

[97] Reg. § 1.401-1(b)(1).

[98] Pub. L. No. 406, 93d Cong., 2d Sess. (1974).

CHAPTER SEVENTEEN

Political Organizations*

Since the inception of the federal tax laws and until 1974, there were no rules as to whether political campaign committees and similar organizations were appropriate subjects of taxation. This absence of tax exposure resulted from the belief that virtually all of the receipts of political organizations were in the form of gifts and that, consequently, these organizations would not have taxable income.[1]

For many years, the IRS either failed or refused to assert tax liability against political campaign committees.[2] Early in 1974, however, the IRS ruled that an unincorporated campaign committee was not exempt from federal income taxation and must file tax returns, showing, as elements of gross income, items such as interest, dividends, and net gains from the sale of securities and related deductions (although contributions to the organization remained nontaxable).[3] This ruling

---

* The author wishes to acknowledge the assistance of D. Benson Tesdahl, Esq., in the preparation of this chapter.

[1] S. Rep. No. 1357, 93d Cong., 2d Sess. 25 (1974). The philosophy underlying the enactment of the tax rules concerning political organizations is much the same as that for social clubs (see Chapter 14) and homeowners' associations (see § 18.13). That is, in the case of social clubs and homeowners' associations, the law is designed to preclude income from sources other than members (i.e., nonmember and investment income) from subsidizing the members in their personal capacity.

[2] See Ann. 73-84, 1973-2 C.B. 461, which noted that it had been the historical practice of the IRS not to require the filing of tax returns by political parties and organizations and that this policy had been communicated to the field offices of the IRS more than 25 years previous, but was never made public.

[3] Rev. Rul. 74-21, 1974-1 C.B. 14. Also Rev. Rul. 74-23, 1974-1 C.B. 17, *mod. and clar. by* Rev. Rul. 74-475, 1974-2 C.B. 22.

was superseded by the enactment in 1974 of a specific tax law provision on the point[4] and related rules (including a per donee gift tax exclusion).[5]

Nonetheless, even after its 1974 ruling, the IRS continued to uphold the per donee gift tax exclusion for separate fund-raising campaign committees,[6] despite opposition in the courts.[7] Later in 1974, as noted, Congress exempted contributions to political parties or committees from the gift tax.[8]

The granting of tax exemption to political organizations by Congress in 1974 resulted from a congressional belief that "political activity (including the financing of political activity) as such is not a trade or business that is appropriately subject to tax."[9]

§ 17.1 *POLITICAL ORGANIZATIONS* DEFINED

(a) Political Organizations in General

This category of tax exemption is available for the *political organization*.[10] A political organization is a party, committee, association, fund, or other organization (whether or not incorporated) organized and operated primarily for the purpose

---

[4] IRC § 527.

[5] IRC §§ 84, 2501(a)(5). IRC § 84 and Reg. § 1.84-1 provide that if any person transfers appreciated property to a political organization, the transferor is treated as having sold the property to the political organization on the date of the transfer and as having realized an amount equal to the property's fair market value on that date.

[6] Rev. Rul. 72-355, 1972-2 C.B. 532; Rev. Rul. 74-199, 1974-1 C.B. 285.

[7] E.g., Tax Analysts and Advocates v. Schultz, 376 F. Supp. 889 (D.D.C. 1974), *vacated*, 75-1 U.S.T.C. ¶ 13,052 (D.C. Cir. 1975).

[8] IRC § 2501(a)(5); Reg. § 25.2501-1(a)(5). The IRS contended that gifts to political organizations made before May 8, 1974 (the effective date of the statutory revision), were subject to the gift tax. Litigation ensued, with the U.S. Tax Court holding that the gift tax did not apply to amounts contributed for political purposes during the period there at issue (1967–1971) (Carson v. Comm'r, 71 T.C. 252 (1978), aff'd, 641 F.2d 864 (10th Cir. 1981)). A similar decision had been reached by the U.S. Court of Appeals for the Fifth Circuit, for years 1959–1961 (Stern v. United States, 426 F.2d 1327 (5th Cir. 1971)). The *Carson* decision rejected the government's contention that the enactment of this gift tax exclusion represented a change in the law. The IRS subsequently acquiesced in the *Carson* decision (Rev. Rul. 82-216, 1982-2 C.B. 220). However, this acquiescence was as to the result of, and not necessarily in the rationale of, the decision. That is, in the acquiescence ruling, the IRS stated that it "continues to maintain that gratuitous transfers to persons . . . [other than political organizations] are subject to the gift tax absent any specific statute to the contrary, even though the transfers may be motivated by a desire to advance the donor's own social, political or charitable goals" (*id.* at 220). For example, the IRS stated that the gift tax exclusion in the charitable gift context (IRC § 2522(a)) is not available for transfers to organizations that have been disqualified from classification under IRC § 501(c)(3) for engaging in legislative or political campaign activities (*id.* at 220).

[9] S. Rep. No. 93-1357, *supra* note 1 at 26.

[10] Political organizations generally cannot qualify under any of the other categories of tax-exempt organizations, such as IRC § 501(c)(3) (e.g., Lonsdale v. Comm'r, 41 T.C.M. 1106 (1981); Cavell v. Comm'r, 40 T.C.M. 395 (1980), aff'd, 661 F.2d 71 (5th Cir. 1981)).

of directly or indirectly accepting contributions[11] or making expenditures[12] for an exempt function.[13]

Although the *political action committee* (PAC) is perhaps the most recognized form of the political organization, the term includes a much broader range of entities. For example, it has been held that a bank account used by a candidate for depositing political contributions and disbursing bona fide political campaign expenses qualifies as a tax-exempt political organization.[14] Additionally, a candidate's newsletter fund can constitute a political organization.[15]

As noted, a political organization is exempt from taxation when it accepts contributions or makes expenditures for an exempt function. An *exempt function* is the activity of influencing or attempting to influence the selection, nomination, election, or appointment of any individual to any federal, state, or local public office[16] or office in a political organization, or the election of presidential or vice-presidential electors, whether or not these individuals or electors are selected, nominated, elected, or appointed.[17] The term includes the making of expendi-

---

[11] The term *contribution* includes a gift, subscription, loan, advance, or deposit of money, or anything of value, and includes a contract, promise, or agreement to make a contribution, whether or not legally enforceable (IRC § 527(e)(3), which incorporated the definition in IRC § 271(b)(2)).

[12] The term *expenditures* includes a payment, distribution, loan, advance, deposit, or gift of money, or anything of value, and includes a contract, promise, or agreement to make an expenditure, whether or not legally enforceable (IRC § 527(e)(4), which incorporated the definition in IRC § 271)(b)(3)).

[13] IRC § 527(e)(1). Accordingly, a political organization may include a committee or other group that accepts contributions or makes expenditures for the purpose of promoting the nomination of an individual for an elective public office in a primary election, or in a meeting or caucus of a political party (Reg. § 1.527-2(a)).

[14] Rev. Rul. 79-11, 1979-1 C.B. 207. Also Rev. Rul. 79-12, 1979-1 C.B. 208; Rev. Rul. 79-13, 1979-1 C.B. 208. A nonprofit and nonpartisan committee organized to provide a corporation's employees, shareholders, and their families an opportunity to join together to financially support candidates for public office was ruled to be a political organization (Tech. Adv. Mem. 7742008).

[15] See *infra* § 1(b).

[16] The facts and circumstances of each case determine whether a particular federal, state, or local office is a *public office*. In making the determination, the IRS uses principles consistent with those found in Reg. § 52.4946-1(g)(2) (Reg. § 1.527-2(d)). This regulation, which is part of the private foundation rules, contains a definition of *public office* for purposes of determining who is a government official under IRC § 4946(c). The regulation states:

> In defining the term "public office" . . . such term must be distinguished from mere public employment. Although holding a public office is one form of public employment, not every position in the employ of a State or other governmental subdivision . . . constitutes a "public office." Although a determination whether a public employee holds a public office depends on the facts and circumstances of the case, the essential element is whether a significant part of the activities of a public employee is the independent performance of policymaking functions. In applying this subparagraph, several factors may be considered as indications that a position in the executive, legislative, or judicial branch of the government of a State, possession of the United States, or political subdivision or other area of any of the foregoing, or of the District of Columbia, constitutes a "public office." Among such factors to be considered in addition to that set forth above, are that the office is created by the Congress, a State constitution, or the State legislature, or by a municipality or other governmental body pursuant to authority conferred by the Congress, State constitution, or State legislature, and the powers conferred on the office and the duties to be discharged by such office are defined either directly or indirectly by the Congress, State constitution, or State legislature, or through legislative authority.

[17] IRC § 527(e)(2).

tures relating to an eligible office that, if incurred by the individual, would be a deductible business expense.[18]

The term *exempt function* has been construed by the IRS to encompass a wide range of activities. For example, the IRS ruled that exempt function expenditures include:

1. Expenses for parties or other celebrations given on election night by a candidate's campaign committee for the candidate's campaign workers;[19]

2. Cash awards to campaign workers after the election, if the amount is reasonable;[20]

3. Amounts expended to enable an elected legislator to attend a political party's national convention as a delegate;[21]

4. Amounts expended for voter research, public opinion polls, and voter canvasses on behalf of an elected legislator who becomes a candidate for another political office;[22]

5. Payments made for a direct mail campaign (for grass-roots lobbying purposes) in support of a nonbinding referendum promoting fiscal responsibility where a potential candidate's name, picture, and political philosophy were included in the mailing;[23]

6. Payments of salary to a candidate who took a leave of absence from his employment to campaign on a full-time basis, when the amounts are reasonable;[24]

7. Disbursements for the distribution of voter guides and incumbents' voting records;[25]

8. Expenditures for grassroots lobbying,[26] where the lobbying is of a "dual character," in that the targeting of materials and the timing of their distribution is in relation to one or more elections, so that there is a "link" between issues and candidates.[27]

The income tax regulations also contain several examples of exempt func-

---

[18] *Id.*, last sentence.

[19] Rev. Rul. 87-119, 1987-2 C.B. 151. However, an exempt function does not include the payment of an elected official's trade or business expenses (e.g., the cost of food for individuals working through lunch on legislative matters) and the payment of these expenses is gross income to the elected official (*id.*).

[20] *Id.* The amount of the cash award, however, is includible in the campaign worker's gross income.

[21] Rev. Rul. 79-12, *supra* note 14. The delegate's expenses were paid from surplus funds from an earlier campaign maintained in a separate bank account; these expenses are not includible in the delegate's gross income.

[22] Rev. Rul. 79-13, *supra* note 14. The voter research expenses were paid from surplus funds from an earlier campaign maintained in a separate bank account.

[23] Tech. Adv. Mem. 9130008.

[24] Priv. Ltr. Rul. 9516006.

[25] Priv. Ltr. Rul. 9652026.

[26] See § 20.2.

[27] E.g., Priv. Ltr. Rul. 9652026.

tion expenditures[28] and state that the individual for whom these expenditures are made does not have to be an announced candidate, "nor is it critical that he [or she] ever become a candidate for an office."[29] Even activities engaged in "between elections" can be exempt function activities, as long as they are directly related to the process of selection, nomination or election of an individual in the next applicable political campaign.[30] Also, *indirect expenses*[31] and *terminating activities*[32] fall within the definition of *exempt function*.

The IRS will look at all the facts and circumstances in determining whether an expenditure constitutes an exempt function.[33] For example, a proper exempt function expenditure includes expenses for "voice and speech lessons to improve [a candidate's] skills," but does not include expenses of a political incumbent for "periodicals of general circulation in order to keep himself informed on national and local issues."[34]

(b) Principal Campaign Committees and Newsletter Funds

There are two aspects of the tax law for political organizations that are of particular benefit to those seeking election or reelection to public office, especially office in the U.S. Congress. The first provision provides a more favorable rate of tax on the political organization taxable income of congressional candidate campaign committees, while the second provision includes within the definition of a *political organization* any newsletter funds established by candidates or incumbents at any level of elective public office. This latter provision alters tax rules that were perceived as unfairly distorting elected officials' taxable income.[35]

---

[28] Reg. § 1.527-2(c)(5).

[29] Reg. § 1.527-2(c)(1).

[30] *Id.* For example, funds held by a political organization and expended at the direction of a public officeholder after the individual had assumed office were found to be exempt function expenditures because the funds were expended for activities that were directly related to the process of influencing or attempting to influence the reelection of the individual (Tech. Adv. Mem. 8650001). The expenditures in question included a trip to a conference, where the political committee paid for the travel expenses of an entourage of political leaders, press staff, civic leaders, administrative staff, extra body guards, and certain spouses; the travel expenses of the family members of a politically influential official; donations to various charities and politically active groups; donations to certain families calculated to ingratiate the officeholder politically with certain ethnic constituencies; and the expenditure of funds to entertain certain political figures in an effort to facilitate fund-raising on behalf of the officeholder's upcoming reelection campaign (*id.*).

[31] Indirect expenses include items such as overhead, record keeping, and expenses incurred in soliciting contributions to the political organization (Reg. § 1.527-2(c)(2)).

[32] Terminating expenses are expenses incurred in furtherance of the process of terminating a political organization's existence. They can include payment of campaign debts after the conclusion of a campaign (Reg. § 527-2(c)(3)).

[33] Reg. § 1.527-2(c)(1); Tech. Adv. Mem. 8147009 (the determining factor in categorizing an activity as an exempt function is the character and nature of the activity itself and not the identity of the organization that is conducting the activity).

[34] Reg. §§ 1.527-2(c)(5)(iii), 1.527-2(c)(5)(v).

[35] Under tax laws prior to 1974, if an elected official received contributions to a fund established to pay for his or her newsletter, the IRS treated the contributions as income in the year received. Amounts spent in printing, addressing, and mailing the newsletter were deductible as ordinary and necessary business expenses, if the elected official itemized his or her deductions. The Senate Committee on Finance noted

As stated above, political organizations generally are subject to the highest rate, rather than the graduated rates, of corporate tax on their political organization taxable income. However, in 1981, Congress changed the law so that the political organization taxable income of a congressional candidate's *principal campaign committee*[36] is taxed at the graduated corporate income tax rates. A principal campaign committee is that designated by a congressional candidate pursuant to the federal election law.[37] A designation is not required where there is only one political committee with respect to a candidate.[38]

In addition, a *newsletter fund* is treated as if the fund constituted a political organization.[39] A newsletter fund is a fund established and maintained by an individual who holds, has been elected to, or is a candidate[40] for nomination or election to any federal, state, or local elective public office for use by the individual exclusively for the preparation and circulation of the individual's newsletter.[41] The exempt function of a newsletter fund is limited to the preparation and circulation of the newsletter, which includes secretarial services, printing, addressing, and mailing.[42] Thus, unlike other types of political organizations, newsletter fund assets may not be used for campaign activities.[43] Furthermore, newsletter fund assets used for purposes other than the preparation and circula-

---

that this tax treatment could unfairly distort an elected official's tax items. For example, since the official's gross income would be higher than normal due to the inclusion of the contributions to his or her newsletter fund, this would increase the amount of charitable deductions he or she could take, while raising the nondeductible floor for medical expense deductions. To avoid these and other distortions, the Committee decided not to make taxable the newsletter contributions received and not to allow any deductions for newsletter expenses paid by the official (S. Rep. No. 1357, *supra* note 1, at 33).

[36] IRC § 527(h); Reg. § 1.527-9. If a campaign committee is not a principal committee, it is taxed at the highest corporate rate.

[37] 2 U.S.C. § 432(e); IRC § 527(h)(2)(B). Designation is made by appending a copy of the Statement of Candidacy (Federal Election Form 2 or equivalent statement filed with the Federal Election Commission under 11 CFR § 101.1(a)) to the Form 1120-POL filed by the principal campaign committee (Reg. § 1.527-9(b)). This designation can only be revoked with the consent of the IRS (Reg. § 1.527-9(c)). In general, see Hopkins, *Charity, Advocacy, and the Law* (New York: John Wiley & Sons, Inc., 1992), Chapter 18.

[38] IRC § 527(h)(2)(B), last sentence.

[39] IRC § 527(g). However, the exempt function of a newsletter fund is narrower (see text accompanying *infra* notes 40 and 41) and the $100.00 specific deduction allowed to other political organizations is not applicable to a newsletter fund (Reg. § 1.527-7(b)).

[40] For purposes of newsletter funds, the term *candidate* means an individual who "publicly announces" that he or she is a candidate for nomination or election to an office and who meets the qualifications prescribed by law to hold such office (IRC § 527(g)(3)). This differs from the definition of *candidate for public office*, contained in Reg. § 1.501(c)(3)-1(c)(3)(iii), which does not require public announcement of a candidacy. (For a discussion of this term, see § 21.1(f).)

[41] IRC § 527(g)(1).

[42] Reg. § 1.527-7(c). Congressional incumbents also can mail their newsletters without charge under the congressional franking privilege, although these mailings are not supposed to be used to solicit political support (39 U.S.C. § 3210). Both the House and the Senate prohibit their members from making franked mass mailings that were printed or prepared with private or political funds, since the franking privilege is reserved for "official documents." See The Committee on Standards of Office Conduct, Ethics Manual for Members, Officers, and Employees of the U.S. House of Representatives, 100th Cong., 1st Sess., Chap. 6 (1987); Rule XL, Standing Rules of the Senate, S. Doc. No. 101-25, 101st Cong., 2d Sess. 59 (1990).

[43] Reg. § 1.527-7(d). Thus, a newsletter fund cannot transfer assets to another political organization, unless that organization also is a newsletter fund.

tion of the newsletter must be included in the gross income of the individual who established and maintained the fund.[44]

§ 17.2   ORGANIZATIONAL AND OPERATIONAL TESTS

A political organization satisfies the requisite organizational test if its articles of organization provide that the primary purpose of the organization is to carry on one or more exempt functions. If the organization has no formal articles of organization, consideration will be given to statements of the organization's members at the time it was formed that they intend to carry on an exempt function.[45]

To satisfy an operational test, a political organization does not have to engage exclusively in exempt function activities.[46] For example, a political organization may sponsor nonpartisan educational workshops, carry on social activities unrelated to an exempt function, support the enactment or defeat of a ballot proposition, or pay an incumbent's office expenses, as long as these are not the organization's primary activities.[47] In contrast, an organization that engages wholly in legislative activities cannot qualify as a political organization.[48]

§ 17.3   TAXATION OF ORGANIZATIONS

(a) Taxation of Political Organizations

Although political organizations are generally tax-exempt, they are subject to the highest rate[49] of corporate tax on their *political organization taxable income.*[50] A political organization's taxable income is its gross income,[51] less *exempt function income* and allowable deductions directly connected with the production of gross income (other than exempt function income).[52]

---

[44] Reg. § 1.527-7(a). Additionally, any future contributions to the fund also are treated as income to that individual (*id.*).

[45] Reg. § 1.527-2(a)(2).

[46] Reg. § 1.527-2(a)(3).

[47] *Id.* As noted, the payment of an incumbent's office expenses is not an exempt function and will be treated as gross income to the incumbent (*supra* note 19).

[48] E.g., Priv. Ltr. Rul. 9244003.

[49] Cf. *supra* §1(b).

[50] IRC § 527(b).

[51] *Gross income* can include amounts expended for other than an exempt function, if the expenditure results in direct or indirect financial benefit to the political organization. For example, a political organization must include in its gross income amounts expended for improvements to its facilities or for equipment that is not necessary for or used in carrying out an exempt function (Reg. § 1.527-5(a)(1)). Amounts expended for illegal activities also must be included in the political organization's taxable income (Reg. § 1.527-5(a)(2)).

[52] IRC § 527(c). A specific deduction of $100.00 is also allowed, but no net operating loss deduction and none of the special deductions for corporations may be taken (IRC § 527(c)(2)). The IRS ruled that state income taxes paid by a political organization on its nonexempt function income are deductible in computing its taxable income (Rev. Rul. 85-115, 1985-2 C.B. 172). A political organization's tax return is filed on Form 1120-POL (IRC § 6012(a)(6); Reg. 1.6012-6).

A political organization's exempt function income is any amount received as:

1. Contributions[53] of money or other property;[54]

2. Membership dues, fees, or assessments[55] from a member of the organization;

3. Proceeds from a political fund-raising or entertainment event;[56]

4. Proceeds from the sale of political campaign materials,[57] which are not received in the ordinary course of any trade or business;[58] or

5. Proceeds from the conduct of any bingo game,[59] to the extent the amount is segregated for use only for the exempt function of the political organization.[60]

---

[53] Generally, money or other property solicited personally, by mail, or through advertising will qualify as a *contribution*. Additionally, to the extent a political organization receives federal, state, or local funds under the $1.00 "checkoff" provisions of IRC §§ 9001–9003 or other provisions for campaign financing, those amounts are also treated as a contribution (Reg. § 1.527-3(b)).

[54] Some businesses establish "charity-PAC" matching programs, which allow employees of the business to designate a charitable organization to be the recipient of a contribution from the corporate employer; the contribution made by the corporation is an amount equal to the sum of the contributions that the employee made to the corporations political action committee during the previous year. The Federal Election Commission is of the view that this type of matching is not a means of exchanging corporate funds for voluntary contributions (which is illegal (11 C.F.R. 114.5(b))) but instead is a permissible solicitation expense (2 U.S.C. 441b(b)(2) (Federal Election Commission Advisory Opinion 1989-7)). However, it is the position of the IRS, as expressed by its Chief Counsel's Office, that a business corporation's contribution to a charitable organization, designated by an employee of the corporation, is not deductible as a charitable gift by the corporation where the contribution is made under a charity-PAC matching program (Gen. Couns. Mem. 39877). The reason for this lack of deduction is the fact that the corporation received a quid pro quo, for the payment to the charity, in the form of the contribution to the political action committee. In general, see Hopkins, *The Tax Law of Charitable Giving*, Chapter 4 § 1.

[55] For example, filing fees paid by an individual directly or indirectly to a political party in order that the individual may run as a candidate in a primary or general election as a candidate of that party are treated as exempt function income (Reg. § 1.527-3(c)).

[56] Events intended to rally and encourage support for an individual for public office would be proper political fund-raising events. Examples of these events are dinners, breakfasts, receptions, picnics, dances, and athletic exhibitions (Reg. § 1.527-3(d)(1)).

[57] Proceeds from the sale of political memorabilia, bumper stickers, campaign buttons, hats, shirts, political posters, stationery, jewelry, or cookbooks are related to political activity as long as these items can be identified as relating to distributing political literature or organizing voters to vote for a candidate for public office (Reg. § 1.527-3(e)).

[58] The IRS looks at all the facts and circumstances in determining whether an activity is in the ordinary course of a trade or business. Usually, proceeds from "casual, sporadic fund raising or entertainment events" are not considered in the ordinary course of a trade or business (Reg. § 1.527-3(d)(2)). However, the IRS ruled that the proceeds received by a political organization from the sales of art reproductions did not qualify as exempt function income, because the sales activity was considered to be a trade or business (Rev. Rul. 80-103, 1980-1 C.B. 120).

[59] This term uses the definition in IRC § 513(f)(2). See § 27.2(h).

[60] IRC § 527(c)(3). As noted above, exempt function income must be segregated. Reg. § 1.527-2(b) defines a *segregated fund* as any fund that is established and maintained by a political organization or an individual separate from the assets of the organization or the personal assets of the individual. The purpose of the fund must be to receive and segregate exempt function income (and earnings on this income) for use only for an exempt function or for an activity necessary to fulfill an exempt function. If an organization that has a segregated fund for purposes of segregating amounts referred to in IRC § 527(c) expends more than an insubstantial amount from the segregated fund for activities that are not for an exempt function during the taxable year, the fund will not be treated as a segregated fund for that tax year (*id.*).

For political organizations that limit their activities solely to exempt functions, the effect of the foregoing tax rules is to subject only their investment income to taxation. For example, assume that a political organization receives $100,000 in political contributions, which it keeps segregated for appropriate exempt function use. In addition, assume the organization earns $10,000 in interest income (for example, from depositing the political contributions in an interest-bearing account). Under these circumstances, the political organization taxable income would include only the $10,000 in interest income.

By contrast, where a political organization expends money that results in a direct or indirect benefit to the organization itself[61] or expends money for an illegal activity,[62] the entire amount of the expenditure will be included in the political organization's gross income. Further, where a political organization makes a dual use of facilities or personnel (that is, use for both an exempt function and for the production of political organization taxable income), the expenses, depreciation, and similar items attributable to the facility or personnel must be allocated between the two uses on a "reasonable and consistent basis."[63]

In addition to the above activities, which result in gross income to the political organization, certain activities by political organizations can result in gross income to a candidate or other individual affiliated with the political organization.[64] For example, where a political organization expends any amount for the personal use of any individual, such as for paying a candidate's income tax liability, the amount expended is included in the individual's gross income.[65] Also, excess funds controlled by a political organization or other person after a campaign or election are treated as expended for the personal use of the person having control over the ultimate use of the funds, unless the funds are held in reasonable anticipation of use by the political organization for future exempt functions or the funds are transferred within a reasonable period of time to certain political, tax-exempt, or governmental organizations described in the regulations.[66]

---

[61] An illustration would be the expenditure of exempt function income to purchase building improvements or equipment not necessary to carry on an exempt function.

[62] Although expenses for illegal activity are includable in the organization's gross income, expenses incurred in the defense of civil or criminal suits against the organization are not taxable to the organization (Reg. § 1.527-5(a)(2)). In addition, voluntary reimbursement to the participants in the illegal activity for similar expenses incurred by them are not taxable to the organization if it can demonstrate that such payments were not a part of the inducement to engage in the illegal activity or part of the agreed upon compensation for such activity (*id.*).

[63] Reg. § 1.527-4(c)(3).

[64] Activities that will not be treated as income to a candidate or other person affiliated with a political organization include contributions to another political organization or newsletter fund; contributions to organizations described in IRC § 509(a)(1) or §509(a)(2) (see § 11.3(a), (b)); and deposits in the general fund of the U.S. Treasury or the general fund of any state or local governments (IRC § 527(d); Reg. § 1.527-5(b)).

[65] Reg. § 1.527-5(a)(1).

[66] Reg. § 1.527-5(c)(1). The organizations to which funds can be transferred are described in Reg. § 1.527-5(b). For example, a political organization can contribute amounts "to or for the use of" a public or publicly supported charitable organization (i.e., those entities described in IRC § 509(a)(1) or § 509(a)(2) (see § 11.3(a), (b)) (Reg. § 1.527-5(b)(2)). The IRS ruled that campaign committees could

(b) Taxation of Exempt Organizations other than Political Organizations

Although a political organization is exempt from taxation on amounts expended for an exempt function, if another type of tax-exempt organization[67] expends any amount during a tax year, either directly[68] or through another organization,[69] for what would be a political organization exempt function, it must include in its gross income for the year an amount equal to the lesser of (1) its net investment income[70] for the year or (2) the aggregate amount expended during the year for the exempt function.[71] Generally, this amount is taxed at the highest corporate tax rate.[72]

The foregoing rules are not intended to change the prohibition on political activities applicable to charitable and social welfare organizations.[73] Indeed, public charities engaging in any amount of political campaign intervention stand to lose their tax-exempt status, in addition to facing the political organization tax. However, the concept of political organization exempt function is broader than

---

transfer funds to a private foundation and remain within this exception, where the foundation was obligated by its corporate documents to make grants only to these types of charitable entities; the foundation was characterized as a "trust" under state law, with the funds transferred "for the use of" the charitable organizations (Priv. Ltr. Rul. 9425032). Contributions to these organizations are not deductible (Reg. § 1.527-5(b)(2), last sentence). Where excess funds are held by an individual who dies before the funds have been properly transferred, the funds are generally considered income of the decedent and will be included in the decedent's gross estate, unless the estate transfers the funds within a reasonable period to an eligible organization in accordance with Reg. § 1.527-5(b) (Reg. § 1.527-5(c)(2)).

[67] That is, an organization described in IRC § 501(c) that is exempt from tax under IRC § 501(a).

[68] See Tech. Adv. Mem. 8502003 (contributions made by an exempt labor organization from its general checking fund directly to state and local candidates were taxable expenditures).

[69] Although an expenditure can be made for an exempt function "through another organization" (e.g., by making a contribution to another organization, which then uses the contribution for an exempt function), an IRC § 501(c) organization will not be absolutely liable for tax under IRC § 527(f)(1) for amounts transferred to an organization, as long as "reasonable steps" are taken to ensure that the transferee does not use these amounts for an exempt function (Reg. § 1.527-6(b)(1)(ii)).

[70] *Net investment income* is defined as the excess of gross income from interest, dividends, rents, and royalties, plus the excess of gains from the sale or exchange of assets over losses from the sale or exchange of assets, over allowable deductions directly connected with the production of investment income (IRC § 527(f)(2)). To avoid double taxation, however, items taken into account for purposes of the unrelated business income tax imposed by IRC § 511 are not taken into account when calculating net investment income (*id.*, last sentence).

[71] IRC § 527(f)(1). The IRS adopted protest and conference procedures for contesting the tax imposed by IRC § 527(f) (Rev. Proc. 90-27, 1990-1 C.B. 514).

[72] IRC § 527(b). However, special rules apply in cases where the organization has a net capital gain (IRC § 527(b)(2)). The IRS may revoke a ruling letter that recognized an organization's tax exemption, without retroactive effect, pursuant to IRC § 7805(b), but in this type of case the organization would be subject to taxation on any political activity during the IRC § 7805(b) relief period (Gen. Couns. Mem. 39811).

[73] S. Rep. No. 1357, *supra* note 1, at 29; Reg. 1.527-6(g). For example, the IRS ruled that a tax-exempt social welfare (IRC § 501(c)(4)) organization may, without adversely affecting its exempt status, participate in political campaign activities as long as it is primarily engaged in the promotion of social welfare but that the amounts expended for the activities may be treated as political organization taxable income (Rev. Rul. 81-95, 1981-1 C.B. 332) (see § 21.4).

The U.S. Tax Court held that a tax-exempt labor organization (see Chapter 31 § 1) was liable for the IRC § 527(f) tax as the result of the transfer of monies to its political action committee (Alaska Pub. Serv. Employees Local 71 v. Comm'r, 67 T.C.M. 1664 (1991)).

the political campaign intervention limitation.[74] For example, an exempt function includes an attempt to influence the appointment of an individual to a federal public office, such as a presidential nomination of a Supreme Court justice.[75] Since the effort to secure Senate confirmation of a Supreme Court nominee does not involve a political campaign, a charitable organization is not precluded from participating in that process.[76]

The purpose of taxing exempt organizations on their exempt function activity is to treat them on an equal basis for tax purposes with political organizations, and, at the same time, to ensure that they are taxed only to the extent they actually operate in a fashion similar to political organizations.[77] Tracing of funds is not required, and the tax will apply even though the tax-exempt organization uses its investment income exclusively for nonpolitical purposes and makes its political expenditures entirely out of other funds.[78]

However, not all politically related expenditures by exempt organizations are considered exempt function expenditures subject to taxation. For example, expenditures for nonpartisan activity are not considered exempt function expenditures. *Nonpartisan activities* include voter registration and "get-out-the-vote" campaigns, as long as they are not specifically identified with any candidate or political party.[79] Additionally, where an exempt organization appears before a legislative body in response to a "written request . . . for the purpose of influencing the appointment or confirmation of an individual to a public office," expenditures related to the appearance are not treated as exempt function expenditures.[80]

§ 17.4 AVOIDING THE POLITICAL ORGANIZATIONS TAX

Although tax-exempt organizations are subject to tax on their exempt function expenditures, these entities can avoid this political activities tax in a number of ways.

First, it may be possible for a tax-exempt organization to establish a related political organization (usually a political action committee, or PAC). From a tax law perspective, the law on this point is sparse. It is clear that tax-exempt organizations, such as social welfare organizations, trade and business associations, labor unions, and chambers of commerce can establish related PACs.[81] Presumably

---

[74] In general, § 21.1.

[75] *Id.*

[76] *Id.*

[77] S. Rep. No. 93-1357, *supra* note 1, at 29.

[78] *Id.*

[79] Reg. § 1.527-6(b)(5).

[80] Reg. § 1.527-6(b)(4).

[81] E.g., Priv. Ltr. Rul. 9652026 The Senate Finance Committee stated that "generally, a section 501(c) organization that is permitted to engage in political activities would establish a separate organization that would operate primarily as a political organization, and directly receive and disburse all funds related to nomination, etc. activities. In this way, the campaign-type activities would be taken entirely out of the section 501(c) organization, to the benefit both of the organization and the administration of the tax laws" (S. Rep. No. 1357, *supra* note 1, at 30).

this is also true with respect to other types of exempt organizations, such as social clubs and veterans' organizations.

Also, a tax-exempt organization will not be taxed where it merely receives contributions from its members for political action and promptly and directly[82] transfers the funds to the political organization that solicited them.[83] Furthermore, the IRS ruled that, where a tax-exempt organization deposits political contributions into an interest-bearing checking account for administrative efficiency before their transfer to a PAC, it has still satisfied the regulation's requirements to promptly and directly transfer the funds to the PAC.[84]

A separate segregated fund that is maintained by an eligible tax-exempt organization is treated as a separate entity from that organization for purposes of the rules pertaining to political organizations.[85] Thus, a tax-exempt organization that engaged in a political organization exempt function as a relatively small part of its operations may have much or all of its net investment income taxed, while the tax-exempt organization that maintains a separate segregated fund can segregate contributions for use in an exempt function, with the result that only the net investment income of the fund is subject to tax.[86]

A tax-exempt organization can make *soft-dollar* expenditures (i.e., expenditures for indirect expenses allowed by the federal election law) in support of a separate segregated fund. These expenditures generally are not considered an exempt function outlay and, thus, will not subject a tax-exempt organization to the political activities tax. It is important to note, however, that this type of expenditure is an exempt function outlay when made by a political organization.[87] There is some confusion on this point because of the dual use of the term *exempt function*

---

[82] A transfer is considered promptly and directly made if the organization's procedures satisfy requirements of applicable federal or state campaign laws, the organization maintains adequate records to demonstrate that amounts transferred are in fact political contributions or dues (rather than investment income), and the political contributions or dues transferred were not used to earn investment income for the organization (Reg. § 1.527-6(e)(3)).

[83] Reg. § 1.527-6(e).

[84] Tech. Adv. Mems. 9105001, 9105002. Also Gen. Couns. Mem. 39837, which is the background document for these two technical advice memoranda. The IRS stated that the primary objective of the test stated in Reg. § 1.527-6(e)(3) is to prevent tax-exempt organizations from needlessly retaining the PAC funds in order to invest those funds. In this case, even though a small amount of interest was earned and retained by the organization when it briefly held the PAC funds in its interest-bearing checking account, the PAC funds were placed in the checking account primarily for administrative efficiency, rather than for investment purposes (*id.*; *also* Tech. Adv. Mem. 9042004, reaching the same result with respect to a business league; Tech. Adv. Mem. 8628001, reaching the same result with respect to a labor union).

[85] IRC § 527(f)(3); Reg. § 1.527-6(f). A *separate segregated fund* is defined as a fund within the meaning of 18 U.S.C. § 610 or any similar state statute, or within the meaning of any state statute that permits the segregation of dues moneys for political organization exempt functions (IRC § 527(f)(3)). However, 18 U.S.C. § 610 was repealed by the Federal Election Campaign Act Amendments of 1976, Pub. L. No. 94-382. § 112, 90 Stat. 490, and was recodified at 2 U.S.C. § 441b. The term *separate segregated fund* is not further defined in the recodified section (see generally *infra* § 5). Although the focus of IRC § 527(f)(3) is on separate segregated funds that are maintained by an IRC § 501(c) organization, the IRS stated that there is nothing in the legislative history to indicate that was to be the only type of segregated fund to which amounts could be transferred (Tech. Adv. Mem. 8147008).

[86] Ann. 88-114, 1988-37 I.R.B. 26; S. Rep. No. 1357, *supra* note 1, at 30.

[87] Reg. § 1.527-6(b)(1).

expenditure, and the IRS has indicated that, if it should conclude in the future that some or all of the indirect expenses allowed by the federal election law constitute exempt function expenditures for purposes of the political activities tax, that interpretation of the law will apply only on a prospective basis.[88]

As discussed,[89] charitable organizations are not permitted to engage in political campaign activities; that is, they cannot intervene in a campaign on behalf of or in opposition to a candidate for public office.[90] However, a charitable organization may establish and use a political organization (such as a PAC) if the purpose of the PAC is to engage in political activities[91] that are not political campaign activities.[92] In other words, a noncampaign PAC affiliated with a charitable organization may be used to promote the organization's viewpoint on particular issues. However, in the view of the IRS, a corporate sponsor of a PAC may not deduct the organizational and administrative costs of the PAC.[93] In the instance under review, the expenses sought to be deducted were legal fees and interest expenses. The IRS concluded that the expenditures for the PAC were for intervention in political campaigns on behalf of candidates for public office and/or in connection with attempts to influence the general public, and thus were nondeductible.[94]

It is possible for the managers of a charitable organization and/or others, acting as individuals, to establish and use an *independent* political action committee, even if the PAC has the function of supporting a candidate's political campaign. While the IRS has yet to address this topic, the Federal Election Commission published an advisory opinion[95] sanctioning the concept of what the federal campaign law implicitly recognizes as a "non-connected political committee."[96] According to the FEC, a nonconnected political committee has the following characteristics:

1. It is established by the members of the governing board of the charitable organization acting in their individual capacities;

---

[88] Tech. Adv. Mem. 8516001. A soft-dollar expenditure by a tax-exempt membership organization, which is not an exempt function expenditure, may cause a portion of the members' dues to be nondeductible as a business expense, as a political campaign expense (IRC § 162(e)(2)). (Tech. Adv. Mem. 8202019). The same may be the case in connection with certain types of lobbying expenditures (Tech. Adv. Mem. 7946009). The business expenses deduction is disallowed where either of these disqualifying activities is substantial in relation to total activities (Reg. § 1.162-20(c)(3)).

[89] See Chapter 21.

[90] IRC § 501(c)(3).

[91] That is, IRC § 527 exempt functions.

[92] Ann. 88-114, 1988-37 I.R.B. 26.

[93] Priv. Ltr. Rul. 8202019. The IRS also held that the portion of the salaries of the corporation's officers and employees allocable to work on the PAC (including time spent after regular working hours) is nondeductible expenses. Further, the IRS also ruled as nondeductible the corporation's overhead expenses relating to the withholding of contributions to the PAC from employee's salaries and agents' commissions.

[94] IRC § 162(e)(2).

[95] FEC Advisory Opinion 1984-12.

[96] Cf. 2 U.S.C. §§ 431(7), 411b.

2. The committee operates and is governed independently of the charitable organization;

3. The committee is not financially supported by the charitable organization;

4. The committee appropriately reimburses the charitable organization for expenses incurred on behalf of the committee;

5. The committee pays a fair rent to the charitable organization for the use of any office space and/or facilities;

6. The committee pays a "commercially reasonable" consideration for the services of individuals who are employees or agents of the charitable organization;

7. The charitable organization does not engage in conduct that favors or appears to favor the solicitation activity of the committee; and

8. Neither the charitable organization nor the committee asserts a proprietary interest in or control over use of the name of the political committee.[97]

§ 17.5 RELATED FEDERAL ELECTION LAWS

The tax rules pertaining to political organizations are somewhat integrated with the federal law governing contributions made in connection with campaigns for election to federal office, as reflected in the Federal Election Campaign Act of 1971, as amended.[98] This Act broadly defines the terms *contribution* and *expenditure*,[99] and makes it unlawful for a corporation to make a contribution or expenditure in a federal election.[100] The term *corporation* includes tax-exempt corporations.

Despite the general prohibition in the Act against corporate contributions in connection with campaigns for federal office, the Act permits the establishment, administration, and solicitation of contributions to a separate segregated fund to be utilized for political purposes by a corporation or mem-

---

[97] *Id.* In general, Tesdahl, "Taxation and Representation—How to Use Political Organizations," 4 *J. Tax. Exempt Orgs.* 29 (Spring 1992); Forman, "PAC Contributions and Effective Corporate Tax Rates," 45 *Tax Notes* (No. 11) 1363 (1990); Schoenblum, "From De Facto to Statutory Exemption: An Analysis of the Evolution of Legislative Policy Regarding the Federal Taxation of Campaign Finance," 65 *Va. L. Rev.* 513 (1979); Golden, "Federal Taxation and the Political Process," 24 *Kan. L. Rev.* 221 (1976); Streng, "The Federal Tax Treatment of Political Contributions and Political Organizations," 29 *Tax Law.* 139 (1975); Kaplan, "Taxation and Political Campaigns: Interface Resolved," 53 *Taxes* 340 (1975); Boehm, "Taxes and Politics," 22 *Tax L. Rev.* 369 (1967).

[98] 2 U.S.C. Chapter 14 (for purposes of this chapter, "Act"). For a more complete discussion of the Act, see Hopkins, *supra*, note 37, Chapter 18.

[99] 2 U.S.C. § 441b(b)(2).

[100] 2 U.S.C. § 441b(a).

bership organization.[101] The term *separate segregated fund* is not defined in the statute or regulations, but the Federal Election Commission published campaign guidance in which the term is defined as "a political committee established by a corporation, labor organization, or incorporated membership organization which accepts voluntary contributions that are used to make contributions to or expenditures on behalf of Federal candidates and other political committees."[102] Separate segregated funds have come to be referred to as political action committees, or PACs[103] (a term that would encompass a tax-exempt political organization).

---

[101] 2 U.S.C. § 441b(b)(2)(C). An expenditure, such as the cost of establishing, administering, and soliciting contributions to a separate segregated fund, is sometimes referred to as a "soft-dollar expenditure" or "soft money." See *Corporate Political Activities 1990—PACs, Ethics, and Lobbying Laws*, 395 (Practicing Law Institute 1990).

[102] *Federal Election Commission Campaign Guide for Corporations and Labor Organizations*, 61 (Sept. 1986).

[103] *Id.*, at 2; see also *Corporate Political Activities—PACs, Ethics, and Lobbying Laws, supra* note 101, at 17; *The Washington Lobby, Cong. Quar.* 5th ed. (1987) 47. Technically, the term *PAC* refers to all noncandidate, nonparty political committees, including those that do not have corporate or labor sponsors (*nonconnected PACs*). See generally *Federal Election Commission Campaign Guide, supra* note 102; *Federal Election Commission Campaign Guide for Nonconnected Committees* (June 1985).

CHAPTER EIGHTEEN

Other Tax-Exempt Organizations

There are several categories of organizations that are exempt from federal income tax, other than those that have been discussed in previous chapters. These categories are summarized in this chapter, in order of the accompanying Internal Revenue Code section numbers.

§ 18.1 UNITED STATES INSTRUMENTALITIES

The federal tax law references "[c]orporations organized under Act of Congress, if such corporations are instrumentalities of the United States and if it is specifically provided in this title [Internal Revenue Title] (or under such Act as amended and supplemented before . . . [July 18, 1984]) that such corporations are exempt from Federal income taxes."[1] This third criterion was added to the Internal Revenue Code in 1984 to stipulate that tax exemptions for United States instrumentalities must be specified in the Code or in a revenue act. Under prior law

---

[1] IRC § 501(c)(1).

(and for pre-1984 instrumentalities), it was sufficient to have tax exemption provided in any act of Congress.

Organizations exempt from federal tax under this section include the Federal Deposit Insurance Corporation, the Reconstruction Finance Corporation, Federal Land Banks, Federal National Mortgage Association, Federal Reserve Banks, Federal Savings and Loan Insurance Corporation, and the Pennsylvania Avenue Development Corporation.[2]

Federal credit unions organized and operated under the Federal Credit Union Act are instrumentalities of the United States[3] and therefore are entitled to tax exemption under this provision. These credit unions are included in a group exemption ruling[4] issued to the National Credit Union Administration.[5] Certain other credit unions that fail to qualify under this provision may secure tax exemption under IRC § 501(c)(14) (see below).[6]

When Congress enacted the Employee Retirement Income Security Act of 1974 (ERISA), it established the Pension Benefit Guaranty Corporation (PBGC) primarily to administer a pension plan termination program. ERISA exempted the PBGC from state and local taxation but was silent on the matter of federal taxation. By enactment of the Tax Reform Act of 1976, Congress also exempted the PBGC from federal taxation.

Congress amended the ERISA[7] to specifically exempt the PBGC from taxation by the United States. (However, the PBGC remains subject to the taxes imposed under the Federal Insurance Contributions Act and the Federal Unemployment Tax Act.) This action by Congress qualified the PBGC for tax-exempt status as an instrumentality of the United States. The applicability of the PBGC provision was retroactive to September 2, 1974 (the date of enactment of ERISA).

§ 18.2 TITLE-HOLDING CORPORATIONS

The title-holding corporation is an entity that serves only one or more tax-exempt organizations. Its purpose, as the name indicates, is to function as a subsidiary organization, holding title to property that would otherwise be held by the parent organization or organizations and remitting any net income from the property to the parent or parents. Originally designed to circumvent state law restrictions on the holding of property by nonprofit organizations, the title-holding company today is used to house the title to property in the subsidiary for the purpose of reducing the exposure of liability from use of the property by the parent entity, otherwise facilitate administration, and increase borrowing power.[8]

---

[2] Tax exemption as a U.S. cooperative extends to the Central Liquidity Facility established under the Federal Credit Union Act, and the Resolution Trust Corporation and the Resolution Funding Corporation established under the Federal Home Loan Bank Act (IRC § 501(l)). By enactment of the Tax Reform Act of 1984 § 177, Congress repealed the federal income tax exemption for the Federal Home Loan Mortgage Corporation, effective January 1, 1985.

[3] Rev. Rul. 55-133, 1955-1 C.B. 138.

[4] See § 23.6.

[5] Rev. Rul. 89-94, 1989-2 C.B. 233.

[6] Rev. Rul. 69-283, 1969-1 C.B. 156.

[7] ERISA § 4002(g)(1).

[8] IRC § 501(c)(2); IRS Exempt Organizations Handbook (Internal Revenue Manual 7751) § 230.

Title-holding corporations are most useful where—for management and/or law reasons—it is deemed appropriate that the title to a property be held in the name of another organization. There is no limitation on the type of property the title to which may be held by a title-holding corporation; it may be real property, such as an office building, or an item of personal property, such as capital equipment. As the IRS once observed, the title-holding corporation "is by its nature responsive to the needs and purposes of its exempt parent which established it mainly to facilitate the administration of properties."[9] Wherever the administration of one or more organizations may be so served, the title-holding corporation is available as a useful tax planning mechanism.

Should one or more of the organizations to which a tax-exempt title-holding corporation makes income distributions cease to qualify for tax exemption, the holding company would, in turn, have its tax exemption revoked.[10] Likewise, the sale of all of the stock of a tax-exempt title-holding company to a private person would cause the organization to no longer qualify for tax-exempt status.[11]

(a) Single Parent Organizations

The federal tax law references "[c]orporations organized for the exclusive purpose of holding title to property, collecting income therefrom, and turning over the entire amount thereof, less expenses, to an organization which itself is" tax exempt. For this purpose, the term *expenses* includes a reasonable allowance for depreciation.[12]

In general, this type of organization cannot accumulate income.[13] That is, as a general rule, it must turn over the entire amount of its income, less expenses, to a tax-exempt parent.[14] If the organization is not specifically organized to do this, it cannot qualify as a tax-exempt title-holding corporation.[15] Moreover, if the entity does not operate in this fashion, it cannot constitute this type of exempt organization.[16] (Nonetheless, a tax-exempt title-holding corporation may receive unrelated business taxable income in an amount up to 10 percent of its gross income for a tax year, where the unrelated income is incidentally derived from the holding of real property.[17])

Despite the general prohibition on income accumulation, however, a tax-exempt title-holding corporation may retain part of its income each year to apply to indebtedness on property to which it holds title.[18] The transaction is treated as if the income had been turned over to the parent and the parent had used the income to

---

[9] Rev. Rul. 77-429, 1977-2 C.B. 189.

[10] Rev. Rul. 68-371, 1968-2 C.B. 204. Of course, a title-holding organization in this position could retain tax-exempt status by appropriately amending its articles of incorporation and other corporate documents.

[11] Priv. Ltr. Rul. 9414002.

[12] Rev. Rul. 66-102, 1966-1 C.B. 133.

[13] E.g., Kanawha-Roane Lands v. United States, 136 F. Supp. 631 (S.D. W.Va. 1955).

[14] Reg. § 1.501(c)(2)-1(b).

[15] E.g., Banner Bldg. Co., Inc. v. Comm'r, 46 B.T.A. 857 (1942).

[16] E.g., Eddie Cigelman Corp. v. Comm'r, 14 T.C.M. 1259 (1955); The Davenport Found. v. Comm'r, 6 T.C.M. 1335 (1947).

[17] See § 28.3, text accompanied by note 40.

[18] Rev. Rul. 77-429, *supra* note 9.

make a capital contribution to the title-holding corporation, which, in turn, applied the contribution to the indebtedness. In rationalizing this flexibility, the IRS observed that the title-holding corporation should not "be restricted in serving the needs of the parent in connection with the administration of properties."[19]

The IRS ruled that an organization formed as a subsidiary of a tax-exempt title-holding corporation, organized for the exclusive purpose of holding title to investment property that would otherwise be held by the parent, itself qualified as a tax-exempt title-holding corporation, since it collected the income from the property and turned it over to its parent (which was, of course, a tax-exempt organization).[20] In other words, an exempt title-holding organization can be the beneficiary of another exempt title-holding organization.

These organizations can be put to creative uses. In one instance, a title-holding corporation was utilized to hold and administer a scholarship and loan fund for a fraternity.[21] In another case, a stock corporation organized and operated to hold title to a chapter house of a college fraternity was held to qualify as a title-holding organization, even though the stock was owned by members of the fraternity.[22] (However, where a tax-exempt organization has no control over the title-holding organization, the latter cannot qualify for tax-exempt status.[23])

While the renting of real estate is usually treated as a business, the IRS determined that income from the rental of realty is a permissible source of income for tax-exempt title-holding corporations.[24] That is, this rental activity is not an unrelated business. However, the rental of personal property (unless leased with realty) is treated as the conduct of business.[25] Thus, title-holding organizations engaging in business activity—other than rental of real property—may be denied or lose their tax exemption.[26]

Consequently, the characterization of the nature of the property being rented can be determinative of an organization's status as a title-holding corporation. In one instance, a corporation that otherwise qualified for tax exemption as a title-holding entity held a leasehold interest in an office building, with all of its income derived from the subleasing of space in the building to the general public. Even though a leasehold of real property is generally classified as personal property, income derived from subleasing an office building was treated as income derived from the rental of real property.[27] The IRS reasoned that this type of income is similarly treated as rental income from real property for purposes of qualifica-

---

[19] *Id*. at 189–190.
[20] Rev. Rul. 76-335, 1976-2 C.B. 141.
[21] N.P.E.F. Corp. v. Comm'r, 5 T.C.M. 313 (1946).
[22] Rev. Rul. 68-222, 1968-1 C.B. 243. This stock was the type that did not provide any rights to receive profits (either as dividends or liquidating distributions).
[23] Rev. Rul. 71-544, 1971-2 C.B. 227; Citizens Water Works, Inc. v. Comm'r, 33 B.T.A. 201 (1935). Cf. Return Reality Corp. v. Ranieri, 359 N.Y.S. 2d 611 (N.Y. Cty. 1974).
[24] Rev. Rul. 69-381, 1969-2 C.B. 113. Also Reg. § 1.512(b)-1(c)(2); Rev. Rul. 66-295, 1966-2 C.B. 207.
[25] Rev. Rul. 69-278, 1969-1 C.B. 148.
[26] See § 28.3. Stanford Univ. Bookstore v. Comm'r, 29 B.T.A. 1280 (1934); Sand Springs Ry. Co. v. Comm'r, 21 B.T.A. 1291 (1931).
[27] IRC § 512(b)(3). See § 27.1(h).

tion for tax exemption as a title-holding corporation,[28] thereby concluding that the corporation was tax-exempt.[29]

A title-holding corporation that derives income from the rental of real property to the general public is not precluded from tax exemption. In one instance, a corporation held title to a building containing offices that were rented on annual leases to the general public. It collected the rents, paid the expenses incident to operation and maintenance of the building, and turned over the balance of the income to its tax-exempt parent. The rents were not forms of unrelated business income, because there were no substantial services to the tenants.[30] The "statutory language that requires them [tax-exempt title-holding corporations] to turn over the income from the property to an exempt organization contemplates that income will be received from parties other than the exempt organization for which they hold title."[31]

A tax-exempt title-holding corporation is subject to the unrelated business income tax if one of its parent organizations is subject to the tax. In one instance, a title-holding entity, with two parents, one subject to the tax, the other not, found itself in this position.[32]

Where a tax-exempt title-holding corporation holds title to property for the benefit of its parent tax-exempt organization, the property is encumbered with a debt, and the property is not utilized for the tax-exempt purposes of the parent organization, the title-holding corporation will be subject to the tax on unrelated debt-financed income.[33]

As noted, a title-holding corporation must, to be tax-exempt, not engage in any business other than that of holding title to property and collecting and remitting any resulting income.[34] For example, in one instance, an organization that held title to a building housing its tax-exempt parent, maintained the property, and operated social facilities located in the building, was held to not qualify for tax exemption, because the social activities were "outside the scope of" those allowed to an exempt title-holding entity.[35] Likewise, a title-holding corporation

---

[28] This reasoning proceeded as follows: An IRC § 501(c)(2) corporation generally cannot have unrelated business taxable income (Reg. § 1.501(c)(2)-1(a)). (However, this aspect of the law has been amended (see *supra* note 17).) For unrelated income purposes, the term *real property* includes property described in IRC § 1250(c) (Reg. § 1.512(b)-1(c)(3)(i)). That provision encompasses certain real property that is or has been property of a character subject to the depreciation allowance rules of IRC § 167. Qualifying depreciable real property includes intangible real property, which in turn includes a leasehold of land of IRC § 1250 property. Accordingly, such a leasehold is IRC § 1250 property and thus is real property for purposes of IRC § 501(c)(2).

[29] Rev. Rul. 81-108, 1981-1 C.B. 327.

[30] See § 27.1(h).

[31] Rev. Rul. 69-381, *supra* note 24, at 113.

[32] Rev. Rul. 68-490, 1968-2 C.B. 241.

[33] Priv. Ltr. Rul. 8145011. See § 29.1. An instance of the use of entities to hold title to property acquired with borrowed funds, prior to adoption of the unrelated debt-financed income rules, appears in Rev. Rul. 66-295, *supra* note 24; the rationale was that this type of activity was not a trade or business engaged in for profit, under the approach adopted in court opinions such as Bright Star Found., Inc. v. Campbell, 191 F. Supp. 845 (N.D. Tex. 1960).

[34] Reg. § 1.501(c)(2)-1(a).

[35] Rev. Rul. 66-150, 1966-1 C.B. 147, 148.

had its tax-exempt status revoked because it operated a bar and buffet in the building it maintained.[36]

A title-holding corporation may file a consolidated return with a parent entity for a tax year. When this occurs and the title-holding entity pays net income to the parent, or would pay net income but for the fact that the expenses of collecting the income exceed its income, the title-holding corporation is deemed, for purposes of the unrelated business income tax, as being organized and operated for the same purposes as the parent, as well as its title-holding purposes.[37]

Generally, contributions to a title-holding corporation are not deductible as charitable gifts. However, where a title-holding entity engages in a charitable activity, contributions to it for the express purpose of funding that activity are deductible as charitable gifts for federal income tax purposes.[38]

Indeed, if a title-holding corporation has a charitable organization as its parent and the corporation engages in one or more activities that the parent itself could undertake without loss of tax exemption, the title-holding entity may be eligible to itself be recognized as a charitable organization or can convert its basis for tax exemption from that as a title-holding organization to that of a charitable entity.[39]

It was the position of the IRS that a title-holding company is ineligible for tax exemption under these rules if it has multiple unrelated parents, inasmuch as that is evidence of a pooling of assets for an active corporate venture, not a mere holding of title.[40] However, this matter was subsequently resolved by legislation, as discussed next.[41]

(b) Multiparent Organizations

In 1986, Congress added to the categories of tax-exempt organizations the multiparent title-holding organization.[42] This is an otherwise eligible corporation or trust that is organized for the exclusive purposes of acquiring and holding title to real property, collecting income from the property, and remitting the entire amount of income from the property (less expenses) to one or more qualified tax-exempt organizations that are shareholders of the title-holding corporation or beneficiaries of the title-holding trust.[43] For this purpose, the term *real property*

---

[36] Knights of Columbus Bldg. Ass'n of Stamford, Conn., Inc. v. United States, 88-1 U.S.T.C. ¶ 9336 (D. Conn. 1988). Occasionally, the IRS or a court will not allow an organization to qualify under this category of exempt organization because of a violation of the private inurement doctrine (see Chapter 19) (e.g., Rev. Rul. 58-566, 1958-2 C.B. 261; The Davenport Found. v. Comm'r, *supra* note 16).

[37] IRC § 511(c).

[38] Priv. Ltr. Rul. 8705041.

[39] E.g., Priv. Ltr. Rul. 9242002. For example, a supporting organization (see § 11.3(c)) often can be utilized in this regard instead of a title-holding entity.

[40] Gen. Couns. Mems. 39341, 37351.

[41] In general, Blanchard, "Section 501(c)(2): Time for the Service To Clean House," 10 *Exempt Org. Tax Rev.* (No. 1) 101 (1994).

[42] IRC § 501(c)(25).

[43] IRC § 501(c)(25)(A)(iii). In 1988, the IRS modified and supplemented an earlier pronouncement (Notice 87-18, 1987-1 C.B. 455) concerning certain provisions that must be included in the articles of incorporation or trust document of an organization seeking recognition of federal tax exemption as an organization described in IRC § 501(c)(25) (Notice 88-121, 1988-2 C.B. 457). If state law prevents a corporation from including the required provisions in its articles of incorporation, the provisions must be

does not include any interest as a tenant in common (or similar interest) and does not include any indirect interest; this requirement means that the title-holding entity must hold real property directly, rather than, for example, as a partner in a partnership.[44] The term *real property* also includes any personal property that is leased under, or in connection with, a lease of real property, although this rule applies only if the rent attributable to the leasing of the personal property for a year does not exceed 15 percent of the total rent for the year attributable to both the real and personal property under the lease.[45]

Tax exemption under this category is available only if the corporation or trust has no more than 35 shareholders or beneficiaries, and has only one class of stock or beneficial interest.[46] Also, to be tax-exempt as this type of title-holding organization, the corporation or trust must permit its shareholders or beneficiaries to (1) dismiss the corporation's or trust's investment advisor, following reasonable notice, upon a vote of the shareholders or beneficiaries holding a majority of interest in the corporation or trust; and (2) terminate their interest in the corporation or trust by either (or both), as determined by the corporation or the trust, selling or exchanging their stock in the corporation or interest in the trust (subject to any federal or state securities law) to any qualified organization so long as the sale or exchange does not increase the number of shareholders or beneficiaries in the corporation or trust above 35, or having their stock or interest redeemed by the corporation or trust after the shareholder or beneficiary has provided 90 days' notice to the corporation or trust.[47]

Organizations that are eligible to acquire or hold interests in this type of title-holding organization are qualified pension, profit-sharing, or stock bonus plans,[48] governmental plans,[49] governments and their agencies and instrumentalities, and charitable organizations.[50]

For these purposes, a corporation that is a *qualified subsidiary* (wholly owned) of a multiparent title-holding organization is not treated as a separate organization.[51] In this instance, all assets, liabilities, and items of income, deduction, and credit of the qualified subsidiary are treated as assets, liabilities, and like items of the title-holding organization.[52] These rules allow a title-holding company to hold properties in separate corporations so as to limit liability with respect to each property.

---

included in the bylaws of the corporation. A nonstock corporation may qualify under IRC § 501(c)(25) if its articles of incorporation or bylaws provide members with the same rights as required for other qualifying entities. The 1988 pronouncement also stated that a multiparent title-holding organization may, under certain circumstances, acquire options to purchase real estate, hold reasonable cash reserves, and receive debt-financed income (see § 29.1) without loss of tax-exempt status.

[44] IRC § 501(c)(25)(A).
[45] IRC § 501(c)(25)(F).
[46] IRC § 501(c)(25)(A)(i), (ii).
[47] IRC § 501(c)(25)(D).
[48] That is, plans that meet the requirements of IRC § 401(a). See Chapter 16.
[49] That is, those plans described in IRC § 414(d).
[50] That is, organizations described in IRC § 501(c)(3). Originally, other tax-exempt multiparent title-holding organizations were qualified beneficiaries but Congress eliminated their participation in this regard in 1988 (§ 1016(a)(3)(B) of the Technical and Miscellaneous Revenue Act of 1988).
[51] IRC § 501(c)(25)(E)(i)(I).
[52] IRC § 501(c)(25)(E)(i)(II).

This category of tax-exempt organization was created in response to the position of the IRS that a title-holding company otherwise eligible for tax exemption under preexisting law[53] cannot be tax-exempt if two or more of its parent organizations are unrelated.[54] This body of law does not modify the preexisting law concerning the tax-exempt status of single- or related-parent title-holding corporations.[55]

§ 18.3 LOCAL EMPLOYEES' ASSOCIATIONS

The federal tax law provides exemption for "local associations of employees, the membership of which is limited to the employees of a designated person or persons in a particular municipality, and the net earnings of which are devoted exclusively to charitable, educational or recreational purposes."[56] The word *local* has the same meaning as is applicable with respect to certain benevolent and mutual organizations.[57]

A local association of employees can assume a variety of forms, such as the association that operated a gasoline station on property owned by its members' employer[58] and the organization that engaged only in social and recreational activities that met the approval of the members' employer.[59] A local employees' association whose membership was limited to the employees of a particular employer and that operated a bus for the convenience of its members was denied tax exemption,[60] as was an organization the purpose of which was to pay lump-sum retirement benefits to its members or death benefits to their survivors.[61] Employees can include retirees who were members of the association at the time of retirement.[62]

The IRS considered the tax status of an organization whose membership was limited to the employees of an employer in a particular municipality. The organization arranged with businesses to extend discounts to its members on their purchases of specified goods and services, and sold tickets to recreational and entertainment activities to them at a discount. Basing its position on legislative history,[63] the IRS dismissed the organization as a "cooperative buying service for members" and denied it tax exemption as an employees' association.[64]

The IRS took the position that a voluntary employees' beneficiary associa-

---

[53] See *supra* § 2(a).
[54] Gen. Couns. Mems. 39341, 37551.
[55] H. Rep. 99-841, 99th Cong., 2d Sess. II-824 (1986).
[56] IRC § 501(c)(4).
[57] Reg. § 1.501(c)(4)-1(b); Reg. § 1.501(c)(12)-1. These benevolent and mutual organizations are the subject of *infra* § 5.
[58] Rev. Rul. 66-180, 1966-1 C.B. 144.
[59] Rev. Rul. 70-202, 1970-1 C.B. 130. Also T.J. Moss Tie Co. v. Comm'r, 18 T.C. 188 (1952), *aff'd*, 201 F.2d 512 (8th Cir. 1953); Weil Clothing Co. v. Comm'r, 13 T.C. 873 (1949).
[60] Rev. Rul. 55-311, 1955-1 C.B. 72.
[61] Rev. Rul. 66-59, 1966-1 C.B. 142.
[62] Rev. Rul. 74-281, 1974-1 C.B. 133.
[63] Hearings Before House Ways and Means Committee on Revenue Revision of 1924, 68th Cong., 1st Sess. 5-12 (1924); 65 *Cong. Rec.* 2905–2906 (1924).
[64] Rev. Rul. 79-128, 1979-1 C.B. 197.

tion[65] that could not meet the 85 percent source-of-income test (deleted in 1969)[66] could not qualify for tax exemption as an employees' association.[67] Thus, the IRS does not follow a case holding that a cooperative electric company is tax-exempt as an employees' association even though it met all of the requirements for exemption under the rules for certain benevolent and mutual organizations[68] except for the 85 percent source-of-income test.[69]

Unlike the law pertaining to voluntary employee beneficiary associations, there are no membership restrictions for employees' associations. Thus, a health club available only to salaried employees qualified as an employees' association.[70] However, if the membership criteria are too exclusive, the organization may not qualify as a local employees' association because it may "not really [be] an association of employees at all."[71]

§ 18.4   FRATERNAL ORGANIZATIONS

(a) Fraternal Beneficiary Societies

The federal tax law provides tax exemption for fraternal beneficiary societies, orders, or associations operating under the lodge system or for the exclusive benefit of the members of a fraternity itself operating under the lodge system and providing for the payment of life, sick, accident, or other benefits to the members of the society, order, or association or their dependents.[72]

The classic definition of a fraternal beneficiary society was formulated by a federal court of appeals:

> We must accordingly assume that the words "fraternal-beneficial" were used in their ordinary sense—to designate an association or society that is engaged in some work that is of a fraternal and beneficial character. According to this view, a fraternal-beneficial society ... would be one whose members have adopted the same, or a very similar, calling, avocation, or profession, or who are working in unison to accomplish some worthy object, and who for that reason have banded themselves together as an association or society to aid and assist one another, and to promote the common cause. The term "fraternal" can properly be applied to such an association, for the reason that the pursuit of a common object, calling or profession usually has a tendency to create a brotherly feeling among those who are thus engaged. It is a well-known fact that there are at the present time many voluntary or incorporated societies which are made up exclusively of persons who are engaged in the same avocation. As a general rule such associations have been formed for the

---

[65] See § 16.3.

[66] See *id.*, text accompanied by note 49.

[67] Rev. Rul. 57-494, 1957-2 C.B. 315, subsequently declared obsolete in Rev. Rul. 82-148, 1982-2 C.B. 401.

[68] See *infra* § 5.

[69] United States v. Pickwick Elec. Membership Corp., 158 F.2d 272 (6th Cir. 1946).

[70] Gen. Couns. Mem. 39357.

[71] *Id.*

[72] IRC § 501(c)(8); Reg. § 1.501(c)(8)-1; Banner Bldg. Co., Inc. v. Comm'r, 46 B.T.A. 857 (1942); Royal Highlanders v. Comm'r, 1 T.C. 184 (1942).

purpose of promoting the social, moral, and intellectual welfare of the members of such associations, and their families, as well as for advancing their interests in other ways and in other respects . . . Many of these associations make a practice of assisting their sick and disabled members, and of extending substantial aid to the families of deceased members. Their work is at the same time of a beneficial and fraternal character, because they aim to improve the condition of a class of persons who are engaged in a common pursuit, and to unite them by a stronger bond of sympathy and interest. . . .[73]

On the basis of this definition, an organization of employees of a railroad company was denied tax exemption as a fraternal beneficiary society.[74] The organization was established to administer a relief fund for the payment of benefits to its members in case of sickness, accident, or death. The court involved characterized the organization's deficiencies in this regard as follows:

[The organization] is entirely without any social features. Its membership is made up of individuals whose vocations are as numerous and diverse as the classifications of employment of a great railway system; the section hand, the freight hustler, the brakeman, the conductor in charge of a fast trans-continental train, the locomotive engineer, the train dispatcher, the clerk in the office, all are entitled to membership in the Association for the mere asking, expressed in written application, provided no disability exists; and yet none of these look to the . . . [organization] for any betterment in social and laboring conditions. There is no fraternal object which moves them to seek membership in the . . . [organization] but rather the motive is mercenary. The . . . [organization] has neither lodges, rituals, ceremony, or regalia; and it owes no allegiance to any other authority or jurisdiction. It is not a "fraternal beneficiary association" operating under the lodge system . . . and, therefore, is not entitled to exemption. . . .[75]

Thus, an organization will not be classified as fraternal in nature for these purposes where the only common bond between the majority of its members is the fact of membership in the organization.[76] Moreover, mere recitation of common ties and objectives in an organization's governing instrument is insufficient; there must be specific activities in implementation of the appropriate purposes.[77]

As noted, a fraternal beneficiary organization, to qualify for tax exemption, must operate under the lodge system or for the exclusive benefit of members that so operate. The regulations state that "operating under the lodge system" means "carrying on its activities under a form of organization that comprises local branches, chartered by a parent organization and largely self-governing, called lodges, chapters, or the like."[78] Therefore, an organization without a parent organization or subordinate branches does not operate under the lodge system and

---

[73] National Union v. Marlow, 74 F. 775, 778 (8th Cir. 1896). Also Employees Benefit Ass'n of Am. Steel Foundries v. Comm'r, 14 B.T.A. 1166 (1929).

[74] Philadelphia & Reading Relief Ass'n v. Comm'r, 4 B.T.A. 713 (1926).

[75] Id. at 726.

[76] Polish Army Veterans Post 147 v. Comm'r, 24 T.C. 891 (1955), aff'd, 236 F.2d 509 (3d Cir. 1956).

[77] Fraternal Order of Civitans of Am. v. Comm'r, 19 T.C. 240 (1952).

[78] Reg. § 1.501(c)(8)-1. Also Western Funeral Benefit Ass'n v. Hellmich, 2 F.2d 367 (E.D. Mo. 1924).

cannot find tax exemption as a fraternal beneficiary society.[79] (Moreover, such a mutual, self-interest type of organization that may otherwise qualify as a tax-exempt fraternal beneficiary society cannot, for tax years beginning after June 2, 1975, qualify as a tax-exempt social welfare organization.[80]) Further, the parent and local organizations must be active, with mere provision for them in governing instruments insufficient.[81] Notwithstanding this requirement, however, an organization that did not operate under the lodge system was granted tax exemption as a fraternal beneficiary society because it operated exclusively for the benefit of the members of a fraternal beneficiary society that itself operated under the lodge system, by providing life, sick, and accident benefits to the members of the society or their dependents.[82]

Also, as noted, a tax-exempt fraternal beneficiary society must have an established system for the payment to its members or their dependents of life, sick, accident, or other benefits. While not every member of the society need be covered by the program of benefits,[83] a substantial number of members must be extended this type of coverage.[84] According to one federal court of appeals, the term *benefits* in this context is not confined to insurance for members against personal risks such as disability or death but may also extend to insuring them against property loss.[85] This decision overruled a lower court's determination that permissible benefits include only those insuring members against mishap to the person.[86] The IRS concluded that the term *other benefits* embraces the provision of legal expenses to defend members accused of criminal, civil, or administrative misconduct arising in the course of their employment (by a fraternal beneficiary society composed of law enforcement officers)[87] and the operation by a fraternal beneficiary society of an orphanage for surviving children of deceased members.[88] The IRS ruled that whole life insurance constitutes a life benefit that fraternal domestic societies can provide to members, even though the policies contain investment features such as cash surrender value and policy loans.[89]

Consequently, a tax-exempt fraternal beneficiary organization must both operate under the lodge system and provide for the payment of benefits to members or their dependents—although one of these features does not have to predominate over the other.[90] However, both features must be present in substantial form and neither may be a sham.[91]

As noted, the tax-exempt fraternal beneficiary society must be operated for

---

[79] Rev. Rul. 55-495, 1955-2 C.B. 259.
[80] Rev. Rul. 75-199, 1975-1 C.B. 160, *mod.* Rev. Rul. 55-495, *supra* note 79. Also Police Benevolent Ass'n of Richmond, Va. v. United States, 87-1 U.S.T.C. ¶ 9238 (E.D. Va. 1987); Rev. Rul. 81-58, 1981-1 C.B. 331.
[81] I.T. 1516, 1-2 C.B. 180 (1922).
[82] Rev. Rul. 73-192, 1973-1 C.B. 224.
[83] Rev. Rul. 64-194, 1964-2 C.B. 149.
[84] Polish Army Veterans Post 147 v. Comm'r, *supra* note 76.
[85] Grange Ins. Ass'n of Calif. v. Comm'r, 317 F.2d 222 (9th Cir. 1963).
[86] Grange Ins. Ass'n of Calif. v. Comm'r, 37 T.C. 582 (1961).
[87] Rev. Rul. 84-48, 1984-1 C.B. 133.
[88] Rev. Rul. 84-49, 1984-1 C.B. 134; also Gen. Couns. Mem. 39212.
[89] Rev. Rul. 86-75, 1986-1 C.B. 245; Gen. Couns. Mem. 39510.
[90] Rev. Rul. 73-165, 1973-1 C.B. 224.
[91] Commercial Travelers Life & Accident Ass'n v. Rodway, 235 F. 370 (N.D. Ohio 1913).

the exclusive benefit of its members. However, where benefits to others are incidental to the accomplishment of the society's tax-exempt purpose, the organization's tax exemption will not be jeopardized. Thus, for example, a society that conducted an insurance operation for its members in all 50 states was determined to not lose its tax exemption because it participated in a state-sponsored reinsurance pool that protected participating insurers from excessive losses on major medical health and accident insurance, since any benefit derived by other insurers from participation in the pooling arrangement was "incidental to" the society's tax-exempt purpose.[92] Similarly, the reinsurance of its policies is a fraternal beneficiary society's tax-exempt function.[93]

One federal district court held that fraternal organizations that are otherwise tax-exempt that practice racial discrimination as to membership may not be tax-exempt.[94] This holding was based on the fact that, unlike organizations that are tax-exempt as social clubs or voluntary employees' beneficiary associations,[95] the passive investment income of fraternal beneficiary organizations is not taxed; this the court found to be a governmental benefit warranting invocation of the Fifth Amendment. The case was initiated as a class action by a black individual allegedly denied, on the basis of race, membership in a local lodge of a fraternal beneficiary society.

Individuals' gifts to a domestic fraternal beneficiary organization are deductible where the gift is to be used exclusively for religious, charitable, scientific, literary, or educational purposes, or for the prevention of cruelty to children and animals.[96]

(b) Domestic Fraternal Societies

The federal tax law provides tax exemption for domestic fraternal societies, orders, or associations, operating under the lodge system, the net earnings of which are devoted exclusively to religious, charitable, scientific, literary, educational, and fraternal purposes, and that do not provide for the payment of life, sick, accident, or other benefits to its members.[97] An organization not providing these benefits but otherwise qualifying as a fraternal beneficiary society[98] qualifies as a

---

[92] Rev. Rul. 78-87, 1978-1 C.B. 160.

[93] Priv. Ltr. Rul. 7937002. Congress, by enactment of § 1012(c)(2) of the Tax Reform Act of 1986, directed the Department of the Treasury to audit and study fraternal beneficiary organizations that received gross insurance premiums in excess of $25 million in taxable years ending in 1984, and to report the results of the study and recommendations to Congress by January 1, 1988.

This report of this study was issued on January 15, 1993 ("Report to the Congress on Fraternal Beneficiary Societies"). The study found that the insurance functions of these organizations are income-producing activities that are similar in "nature and scope" to those provided by for-profit commercial insurance companies. Although the study concluded that the insurance policies of these societies "appear to serve the same markets as those served by commercial insurers" and that the large societies charge prices "that are not significantly less than those charged by comparable large mutual life insurers," it did not advocate repeal of the tax exemption for these organizations. Rather, it concluded that the "benefits of society from [their] charitable services . . . may justify continuation of tax exemption" for the insurance activities of fraternal beneficiary societies. Cf., in general, Chapter 25.

[94] McGlotten v. Connally, 338 F. Supp. 448, 459 (D.D.C. 1972).

[95] See IRC § 512(a)(3); § 28.3.

[96] IRC § 170(c)(4).

[97] IRC § 501(c)(10); Reg. § 1.501(c)(10)-1.

[98] See *supra* § 4(a).

domestic fraternal society. Thus, a domestic fraternal beneficiary society of farmers, which met the requirements of the fraternal beneficiary society rules except that it did not provide for the payment of the requisite benefits, although it did make its members eligible for favorable insurance rates, was denied classification as a tax-exempt fraternal beneficiary society and ruled to be a tax-exempt domestic fraternal society.[99] However, a social welfare organization[100] (for example, a national college fraternity) does not qualify for tax exemption under these rules.[101]

A domestic fraternal society meeting these basic requirements was organized to provide a fraternal framework for social contact among its members who are interested in the use of and the philosophy behind a method used in attempting to divine the future. The net income of the organization was used to provide instruction on the use of the method, supply information on the method to the public, and maintain a reference library—all charitable and educational uses. The IRS ruled that the organization qualified for tax exemption.[102]

The IRS ruled that an organization formed by a local lodge of a fraternal beneficiary society, both tax-exempt as domestic fraternal societies, to carry on the activities of the society in a particular geographical area, is itself tax-exempt as a domestic fraternal society.[103] Because the organization was chartered and supervised by the local lodge and was subject to the laws and edicts of the parent society, it was deemed to function "as part of the lodge system" of the fraternal society and hence qualify for the tax exemption.

The IRS also ruled that an organization that did not conduct any fraternal activities and did not operate under the lodge system, but operated exclusively for the benefit of the members of certain related domestic fraternal societies operating under the lodge system, could not qualify as a tax-exempt domestic fraternal society.[104] The rationale for the denial was that the tax rules for domestic fraternal societies lack the language in the tax rules for fraternal beneficiary societies providing exemption for an organization operating for the benefit of the members of a tax-exempt fraternity (a provision enacted to cover the separately organized insurance branches of a fraternal beneficiary society).

§ 18.5   BENEVOLENT OR MUTUAL ORGANIZATIONS

The federal tax law references tax-exempt benevolent life insurance associations of a purely local character, mutual ditch or irrigation companies, mutual or cooperative telephone companies, or like organizations.[105] In general, 85 percent or more of the income must consist of amounts collected from members for the sole

---

[99] Rev. Rul. 76-457, 1976-2 C.B. 155.
[100] See Chapter 12.
[101] Reg. § 1.501(c)(10)-1. This distinction was upheld by the U.S. Tax Court in Zeta Beta Tau Fraternity, Inc. v. Comm'r, 87 T.C. 421 (1986).
[102] Rev. Rul. 77-258, 1977-2 C.B. 195.
[103] Rev. Rul. 73-370, 1973-2 C.B. 184. In Hip Sing Ass'n, Inc. v. Comm'r, 43 T.C.M. 1092 (1982), an organization was found to be operating under the lodge system, even though the parent organization was created after the branches.
[104] Rev. Rul. 81-117, 1981-1 C.B. 346.
[105] IRC § 501(c)(12)(A).

purpose of meeting losses and expenses. As discussed below, there are some exceptions to this rule in the case of mutual or cooperative telephone companies.[106]

Thus, one type of organization described in these rules is the benevolent life insurance association of a purely local character. These associations basically operate to provide life insurance coverage to their members, albeit at cost because of the requirement that income be collected solely for the purpose of meeting losses and expenses.[107] Organizations *like* benevolent life insurance associations include burial and funeral benefit associations that provide benefits in cash,[108] but not in the form of services and supplies (although the latter type of organization may qualify for tax exemption as a mutual insurance company[109]), and an organization furnishing light and water to its members on a cooperative basis.[110] IRS rulings and court decisions provide examples of organizations considered not like benevolent life insurance associations.[111]

The phrase *of a purely local character* means "confined to a particular community, place, or district, irrespective, however, of political subdivisions,"[112] that is, a single identifiable locality.[113] This requirement does not mean that members of an otherwise qualifying benevolent life insurance association must continually reside in the local area to retain membership; it only means that persons applying for membership in the association must reside in the local geographic area at the time of application.[114] An organization is not local in character where its activities are limited only by the borders of a state,[115] although state lines are not controlling as to what constitutes a single locality. One organization lost its tax exemption as a benevolent life insurance association by advertising in four states.[116] Another organization was denied tax exemption because it operated in 14 counties, as did another conducting its affairs in 32 counties, including three separate metropolitan trade centers.[117]

The other type of organization exempt from federal income tax by virtue of these rules encompasses mutual ditch or irrigation companies, mutual or cooperative telephone companies, and similar organizations.[118] These organizations are

---

[106] *Id.* This rule was applied without taking into account any income attributable to the cancellation of any loan originally made or guaranteed to the United States (or any agency or instrumentality of the United States) if the cancellation occurred after 1986 and before 1990 (§ 6203 of the Technical and Miscellaneous Revenue Act of 1988).

[107] IRS Exempt Organizations Handbook (IRM 7751) § (12)21.

[108] Thompson v. White River Burial Ass'n, 178 F.2d 954 (8th Cir. 1950), *aff'g* 81 F. Supp. 18 (E.D. Ark. 1948).

[109] See *infra* § 8.

[110] Rev. Rul. 67-265, 1967-2 C.B. 205.

[111] Rev. Rul. 65-201, 1965-2 C.B. 170; Consumers Credit Rural Elec. Coop. Corp. v. Comm'r, 319 F.2d 475 (6th Cir. 1963); Shelby County Mut. Relief Ass'n v. Schwaner, 21 F.2d 252 (S.D. Ill. 1927); New Jersey Automobile Club v. United States, 181 F. Supp. 259 (Ct. Cl. 1960), *cert. den.*, 366 U.S. 964 (1961); Swedish Mission Friends' Aid Ass'n v. Comm'r, 12 B.T.A. 1152 (1928).

[112] Reg. § 1.501(c)(12)-1(b).

[113] Hardware Underwriters & National Hardware Serv. Corp. v. United States, 65 Ct. Cl. 267 (1928).

[114] Rev. Rul. 83-43, 1983-1 C.B. 108.

[115] Reg. § 1.501(c)(12)-1(b).

[116] Huff-Cook Mutual Burial Ass'n, Inc. v. United States, 327 F. Supp. 1209 (W.D. Va. 1971).

[117] Rev. Rul. 64-193, 1964-2 C.B. 151.

[118] Rev. Rul. 72-36, 1972-1 C.B. 151, *mod. by* Rev. Rul. 81-109, 1981-1 C.B. 347; Rev. Rul. 65-174, 1965-2 C.B. 169.

commonly mutual or cooperative electric companies and water companies.[119] Tax exemption was accorded an organization established to protect certain river banks against erosion,[120] an organization that provided and maintained a two-way radio system for its members,[121] and an electric generation and transmission cooperative that sold and serviced electric appliances.[122] The membership of cooperative companies need not be restricted to ultimate consumers,[123] nonmembers may be charged a higher rate for service than members,[124] and a government agency may be a member of a cooperative.[125] IRS rulings provide examples of organizations considered not like mutual and cooperative organizations.[126] In 1983, the IRS, ruling that a cooperative organization furnishing cable television service to its members qualified for tax exemption as a like organization under these rules, observed that this category of tax exemption "is applicable only to those mutual or cooperative organizations that are engaged in activities similar in nature to the benevolent life insurance or public utility type of service or business customarily conducted by the specified organizations."[127]

The IRS utilized a rather unusual rationale to allow a mutual ditch company tax exemption, notwithstanding the fact that it did not satisfy all of the requirements enunciated by the IRS in 1972.[128] The organization, created in 1874 to maintain and operate an irrigation system for the use and benefit of its members, was unable to meet standards concerning forfeiture of a member's rights and interest upon withdrawal or termination and distribution of gains from the sale of an appreciated asset upon dissolution, in that former shareholders were not entitled to any funds. However, the IRS said that it was nonetheless "necessary to give some consideration to the historical context within which mutual ditch and irrigation companies were created and have operated," because prior to the enactment of these rules in 1916 organizations such as the one at issue "were well established entities in a number of western states."[129] The IRS noted that, under applicable state law, these organizations (1) "issued stock representing both water rights and equitable interest in the organization's assets," which "was considered personal property and freely available," and (2) "had the power to assess the outstanding stock for the costs of operation and maintenance and to enforce any assessment lien through foreclosure and forced sale, thereby transferring a delinquent shareholder's interest to the purchaser."[130] Therefore, the IRS concluded that "[i]n view of the fact that such organizations were operating in this manner when Congress originally enacted legislation providing for their exemption from federal income

---

[119] Rev. Rul. 67-265, *supra* note 110. Also Rev. Rul. 73-453, 1973-2 C.B. 185.
[120] Rev. Rul. 68-564, 1968-2 C.B. 221.
[121] Rev. Rul. 57-420, 1957-2 C.B. 308.
[122] Priv. Ltr. Rul. 8109002.
[123] Rev. Rul. 65-174, *supra* note 118.
[124] Rev. Rul. 70-130, 1970-1 C.B. 133.
[125] Rev. Rul. 68-75, 1968-1 C.B. 271.
[126] Rev. Rul. 65-201, *supra* note 111; Rev. Rul. 55-311, *supra* note 60.
[127] Rev. Rul. 83-170, 1983-2 C.B. 97, 98 *mod'g* Rev. Rul. 55-716, 1955-2 C.B. 263.
[128] Rev. Rul. 72-36, *supra* note 118.
[129] Rev. Rul. 81-109, 1981-1 C.B. 347, 348.
[130] *Id.* at 348–349.

tax, and the fact that there have been no major changes in the applicable federal tax provisions in the intervening years, it is clear that Congress intended and still intends that mutual ditch and irrigation companies operated in the manner and under the circumstances described above would qualify for exemption from federal income tax under section 501(c)(12) of the Code."[131] The requirements promulgated in 1972 were consequently modified accordingly.

In another case, a mutual company formed for the purpose of supplying electric power to its members was recognized by the IRS as qualifying as a tax-exempt entity. Subsequently, part of the organization's distribution system located within a county was purchased by the county's public utility district. The organization's members located in that utility district were refunded their membership fee in full payment for their interest in the company, since they became served by the new utility. The company refused to meet the demand of the IRS that it distribute the gains realized from the sale on a patronage basis and thus had its tax-exempt status revoked. Upon review, a federal court of appeals held that the company need not credit or distribute its surplus or net gains on a patronage basis to maintain its classification as a tax-exempt mutual company.[132]

As noted,[133] the general rule is that all organizations, to be exempt from tax under these rules, must obtain at least 85 percent of their income from amounts collected from members for the sole purpose of meeting losses and expenses.[134] This requirement is applied on the basis of annual accounting periods.[135] Income from all sources is taken into account, including capital gains from the sale of assets[136] and investments;[137] amounts received as gifts or contributions are not regarded as income.[138] In one instance, the IRS ruled that, where an electric cooperative leased power facilities to a nonmember power company that in turn sold power to the cooperative, the entire rental income was income from a nonmember for purposes of the 85 percent requirement rather than an offset against the cost of acquiring power.[139] In another case, an organization in good faith failed to elect the installment method of treating gain from the sale of real property, with the result that the receipt of the entire gain caused less than 85 percent of its income to be derived from its members; over the government's objection, a court allowed the organization to amend its annual information return to make the election and thus preserve its tax exemption.[140] By contrast, the IRS determined that the income derived by a tax-exempt electric cooperative from the annual sale

---

[131] *Id*. at 349.

[132] Peninsula Light Co., Inc. v. United States, 552 F.2d 878 (9th Cir. 1977). The IRS, in Rev. Rul. 78-238, 1978-1 C.B. 161, announced that it would not follow this decision.

[133] See the text accompanied by *supra* note 106.

[134] IRC § 501(c)(12)(A).

[135] Rev. Rul. 65-99, 1965-1 C.B. 242.

[136] Cate Ditch Co. v. United States, 194 F. Supp. 688 (S.D. Cal. 1961); Mountain Water Co. of La Crescenta v. Comm'r, 35 T.C. 418 (1960).

[137] Reg. § 1.501(c)(12)-1(a).

[138] Gen. Couns. Mem. 35921.

[139] Rev. Rul. 65-174, *supra* note 118. It has been held that income from a cooperative's sale of non-firm power to a member entity constitute's member income (Buckeye Power, Inc. v. United States, 97-2 U.S.T.C. ¶ 50,580 (U.S. Ct. Fed. Cl. 1997)).

[140] Sunny Slope Water Co. v. United States, 78-2 U.S.T.C. ¶ 9685 (C.D. Cal. 1978).

of its excess fuel to a commercial pipeline company that was not a member of the cooperative was not to be taken into account in determining compliance with the 85 percent-of-income requirement, in that the excess fuel was sold at cost and thus no gross income was derived from the sales.[141] A federal district court held that the 85 percent requirement was satisfied where income from tenants of members of a mutual water and electric company was considered member income; the IRS took the position that the tenants did not have any participation in the management of the company and thus could not be regarded as *members*.[142] Court decisions provide examples of organizations that failed to meet the 85 percent-of-income requirement.[143]

Some exceptions to this 85-percent-of-income requirement are applicable in the case of mutual or cooperative telephone companies. One of these exceptions is that the requirement does not apply to income received or accrued from a nonmember telephone company for the performance of communication services that

---

[141] Rev. Rul. 80-86, 1980-1 C.B. 118.

[142] Modern Elec. Water Co. v. United States, 88-2 U.S.T.C. ¶ 9523 (E.D. Wash. 1988). The IRS elected to not have this case appealed (AOD 1990-07).

[143] Allgemeiner Arbeiter Verein v. Comm'r, 237 F.2d 604 (3d Cir. 1956), *aff'g* 25 T.C. 371 (1956); Family Aid Ass'n of the United States House of Prayer for All People v. United States, 36 F. Supp. 1017 (Ct. Cl. 1941). In Dial-Cab Taxi Owners Guild Ass'n, Inc. v. Comm'r, 42 T.C.M. 590 (1981), *aff'd in unpub. op.* (2d Cir. May 4, 1982), the organization was held to not qualify under IRC § 501(c)(12) because it was unable to carry its burden of proving that 85 percent of its income in the tax years involved was collected solely to cover losses and expenses. The court said the organization was "acquiring a substantial net worth far in excess of its reasonably anticipated needs" and that it failed to show that the retained earnings will be used to meet losses and expenses (*id.* at 592). The court also indicated that the organization—which provided a radio dispatching service to its member taxicab owners and operated a two-way radio station to dispatch its members—may not otherwise qualify as a "like organization" because its reliance on the *Peninsula Light Co., Inc.*, decision, *supra* note 132, was "tenuous" (*id.* at 592, note 3).

One court held that certain bond proceeds and items of interest income were not "income" for this purpose but were "capital investment funds" and thus that the 85 percent-of-income rule was not transgressed (Lockwood Water Users Ass'n v. United States (unreported) (D. Mont. 1990)), but the holding was reversed on appeal, with the appellate court finding that the monies were items of gross income for purposes of IRC § 501(c)(12)(A) (Lockwood Water Users Ass'n v. United States, 935 F.2d 274 (9th Cir. 1991)). The IRS ruled that a government grant to a tax-exempt electric power cooperative is excluded from the numerator and denominator of the 85 percent member-income fraction because it is excluded from income as a nonshareholder contribution to the capital of the cooperative (under IRC § 118(a)) (Priv. Ltr. Rul. 9401035).

The IRS held that income received by a cooperative telephone company from charges to third parties (such as interexchange carriers, local exchange carriers, or other exchange carriers) for billing or collecting intrastate, interstate, or international revenues is income from the provision of a service to nonmembers (Tech. Adv. Mems. 9110041, 9111001). Thus, this income is not member source income for purposes of the requirement that 85 percent of the cooperatives income is derived from members (see *supra* note 134). The IRS also ruled that the income is not excludable from the computation of the percentage of nonmember income under the rule that includes income from nonmember sources where the provision of the services involves members of the cooperative (IRC § 501(c)(12)(B)(i)). Thus, the cooperative involved did not qualify for tax exemption for the year unless the 15 percent limit was not exceeded, in which case this income would be unrelated business income (see Part Five). Subsequently, however, the IRS announced that these positions will apply for all tax years beginning after December 31, 1990 (Notice 92-33, 1992-2 C.B. 363). Income received by a telephone cooperative allocable to billing and collection services performed in respect of long-distance calls was held to qualify as income from communication services, enabling the organization to be tax-exempt (Golden Belt Telephone Ass'n, Inc. v. Comm'r., 108 T.C. 23 (1997)).

involve members of the mutual or cooperative telephone company.[144] These services pertain to the completion of long-distance calls to, from, or between members of the company.[145] This exception was legislated in response to (and to overrule) a ruling by the IRS in 1974, holding that a cooperative telephone company, providing only local telephone service to its members but obtaining connecting long-distance service by agreement with a nonmember company, could not adjust its gross income by offsetting income from long-distance tolls collected by both companies against expenses for services rendered by the nonmember company to the cooperative's members but had to include as part of its gross income all of the member and nonmember income from the long-distance service, to determine whether member income met the 85-percent-of-income requirement.[146] The statutory revision reflects the view that the performance of the "call-completion services" is a related activity and that the "payments" from another telephone company for the services should not disqualify otherwise eligible mutual or cooperative telephone cooperatives from tax-exempt status.[147]

Another exception is that the requirement does not apply to income received or accrued from qualified pole rentals.[148] A *qualified pole rental* is any rental of a pole (or other structure used to support wires) if the pole (or other structure) is used by the telephone or electric company to support one or more wires needed to provide telephone or electric services to its members and is used pursuant to the rental to support one or more additional wires for use in connection with the transmission by wire of electricity or of telephone or other communications.[149] For this purpose, the word *rental* includes any sale of the right to use the pole (or other structure).[150]

There are two other exceptions. One is for income received or accrued from the sale of display listings in a directory furnished to the members of the mutual or cooperative telephone company.[151] The other is for income received or accrued from the prepayment of certain loans.[152]

The IRS is of the opinion that an organization that meets all of the requirements for tax exemption under these rules except for the 85 percent-of-income test cannot qualify for exemption as a social welfare organization.[153] Also, an organization carrying on two functions, one qualifying under the social club rules[154] and the other under these rules, cannot qualify for exemption under either statute.[155]

---

[144] IRC § 501(c)(12)(B)(i).

[145] H. Rep. 95-742, 95th Cong., 1st Sess. (1977); S. Rep. 95-762, 95th Cong., 2d Sess. (1978).

[146] Rev. Rul. 74-362, 1974-2 C.B. 170.

[147] Consequently, Rev. Rul. 74-362, *supra* note 146, was declared obsolete by the IRS with respect to tax years beginning after December 31, 1974 (Rev. Rul. 81-291, 1981-2 C.B. 131).

[148] IRC §§ 501(c)(12)(B)(ii), 501(c)(12)(C)(i).

[149] IRC § 501(c)(12)(D).

[150] IRC § 501(c)(12), last sentence.

[151] IRC § 501(c)(12)(B)(iii).

[152] IRC §§ 501(c)(12)(B)(iv), 501(c)(12)(C)(ii).

[153] Cf. United States v. Pickwick Elec. Membership Corp., *supra* note 69.

[154] See Chapter 14.

[155] Allgemeiner Arbeiter Verein v. Comm'r, *supra* note 143. The IRS proposed examination guidelines to be followed by IRS agents when they are conducting examinations of tax-exempt rural electric cooperatives (Ann. 96-24, 1996-16 I.R.B. 30).

§ 18.6   CEMETERY COMPANIES

The federal tax law exemption rules reference cemetery companies owned and operated exclusively for the benefit of their members and that are not operated for profit.[156] This tax exemption also extends to a corporation chartered solely for the purpose of the disposal of bodies by burial or cremation that may not engage in any business not necessarily incident to that purpose. Thus, there are three types of cemetery companies that may gain tax exemption under these rules.

According to the IRS, a tax-exempt cemetery company is generally "one which owns a cemetery, sells lots therein for burial purposes, and maintains these and the unsold lots in a state of repair and upkeep appropriate to a final resting place."[157] With respect to the membership category of cemetery companies, its members are those who are "its lot owners who hold such lots for bona fide burial purposes and not for purpose of resale."[158] According to one court, a tax-exempt cemetery company need not be public nor serve exclusively public interests but may be a family cemetery organization.[159] Under certain circumstances, a cemetery company may be tax-exempt even though it has private preferred stockholders.[160] The tax exemption applies only to organizations providing for the burial or cremation of the remains of human bodies—not pets.[161]

An organization receiving and administering funds for the perpetual care of a nonprofit cemetery itself qualifies as a tax-exempt cemetery company.[162] A nonprofit organization that provides for the perpetual care of a burial area in a community may also become so classified, even though it is not associated with a nonprofit cemetery.[163]

One of the requirements for tax exemption as a cemetery company is that the company may not be permitted by its charter to engage in any business not necessarily incident to its tax-exempt (burial) purposes.[164] The IRS construed this requirement to extend to actual activities, thereby ruling, for example, that operation by a cemetery company of a mortuary will deprive the company of the tax exemption.[165] Under this rule, the IRS also held that operation of a crematorium would likewise adversely affect the exemption,[166] although this determination was subsequently withdrawn in view of the 1970 modification of the statute.[167]

---

[156] IRC § 501(c)(13).

[157] IRS Exempt Organizations Handbook (IRM 7751) § (13) 22.1. E.g., Resthaven Memorial Park & Cemetery Ass'n v. United States, 155 F. Supp. 539 (W.D. Ky. 1957); Forest Lawn Memorial Park Ass'n, Inc. v. Comm'r, 5 T.C.M. 738 (1946).

[158] Reg. § 1.501(c)(13)-1(a)(1). Also West Laurel Hill Cemetery Co. v. Rothensies, 139 F.2d 50 (3d Cir. 1943).

[159] The John D. Rockefeller Family Cemetery Corp. v. Comm'r, 63 T.C. 355 (1974); Du Pont de Nemours Cemetery Co. v. Comm'r, 33 T.C.M. 1438 (1974). Cf. Rev. Rul. 65-6, 1965-1 C.B. 229; Provident Nat'l Bank v. United States, 325 F. Supp. 1187 (E.D. Pa. 1971).

[160] Reg. § 1.501(c)(13)-1(b).

[161] Rev. Rul. 73-454, 1973-2 C.B. 185.

[162] Rev. Rul. 58-190, 1958-1 C.B. 15.

[163] Rev. Rul. 78-143, 1978-1 C.B. 161.

[164] Reg. § 1.501(c)(13)-1(b).

[165] Rev. Rul. 64-109, 1964-1 (Part 1) C.B. 190.

[166] Rev. Rul. 69-637, 1969-2 C.B. 127.

[167] Rev. Rul. 71-300, 1971-2 C.B. 238.

However, a cemetery company may sell monuments, markers, vaults, and flowers solely for use in the cemetery, where the sales proceeds are used for maintenance of the cemetery.[168]

The regulations provide that no part of the net earnings of a tax-exempt cemetery company may inure to the benefit of any private shareholder or individual.[169] The private inurement doctrine frequently is at play where a newly organized cemetery company is involved, in relation to payments to and other relationships with the organizers. The reasoning of the IRS is that (1) where a cemetery company acquires land at an indeterminable price, to be paid for on the basis of a percentage of the proceeds from the sale of individual lots from the tract, the vendor of the land has a continuing interest in the land; (2) any appreciation in value, whether it be due to the state of the market generally or the cemetery's own efforts to undertake capital improvements, etc., will result in a benefit to the vendor of the land; and (3) continuing participation in the earnings of the cemetery company will also ordinarily result in receipt by the vendor of a total price substantially in excess of the reasonable value of the land at the time of its sale to the cemetery company.[170]

Perhaps the most important issue in relation to these rules is one that emerged as many American cemeteries became transformed from noncommercial operations (such as by religious institutions and municipal governments) to commercial businesses. As part of that process, profit-oriented enterprises sought favorable tax consequences from bootstrap sales of assets to ostensibly tax-exempt cemetery companies. When this issue was first litigated, the courts were highly tolerant of these transactions,[171] thereby generating substantial criticism.[172] Subsequently, the courts began to scrutinize more carefully the substance of these transactions, concluding that the cemetery company was causing private inurement of net earnings by the creation of equity interests. That is, in considering transactions by which a cemetery acquires land under the terms of an open-ended or percentage arrangement contract in which the transferor receives a percentage of the sale price of each lot, the courts came to conclude that the substance of the transaction was to create an equity interest in the transferor because all the traditional elements of a true debt are missing: (1) There is no unqualified obligation on the part of the cemetery company to pay because the installments depend upon the sale of lots; (2) there is no maturity date because the obligation is to continue until all lots are sold; (3) there is no sum certain since the price of the lots is subject to change; (4) there is no stated interest rate; (5) there is no minimum annual payment; (6) there is no

---

[168] Rev. Rul. 72-17, 1972-1 C.B. 151.
[169] Reg. § 1.501(c)(13)-1(b). E.g., Branson v. Comm'r, 50 T.C.M. 1056 (1985). In general, see Chapter 19.
[170] Rev. Rul. 61-137, 1961-2 C.B. 118; Butler County Memorial Park, Inc. v. Comm'r, 45 T.C.M. 181 (1982).
[171] Forest Lawn Memorial Park Ass'n, Inc. v. Comm'r, 45 B.T.A. 1091 (1941); Kensico Cemetery v. Comm'r, 35 B.T.A. 498 (1937), aff'd, 96 F. 2d 594 (2d Cir. 1938). Also Rose Hill Memorial Park, Inc. v. Comm'r, 23 T.C.M. 1434 (1964); Washington Park Cemetery Ass'n, Inc. v. Comm'r, 22 T.C.M. 1345 (1963).
[172] Note, "Special Treatment of Cemeteries," 40 S.C. L. Rev. 716 (1967); Lanning, "Tax Erosion and the Bootstrap Sale of a Business," 108 U. Pa. L. Rev. 623 (1960).

right to share with general creditors; (7) there is no paid-in capitalization of the company; and (8) the transferors have control of the cemetery company.[173] Thus, the IRS ruled that a nonprofit cemetery company that acquired land from a for-profit cemetery company, under an agreement providing payment to the former owners on the basis of a percentage of the sales price of each cemetery lot sold, was not a tax-exempt cemetery company, because the transferors aquired an equity interest in the cemetery company, which constituted prohibited private inurement.[174]

Another issue concerns the ability of a commercial cemetery to sequester funds in a perpetual care trust fund that would qualify as a tax-exempt cemetery company. The matter seemed to have been resolved when the Court of Claims, enunciating the adjunct theory,[175] held in 1975 that this type of tax exemption was present by reason of the fact that the fund, which rendered services normally provided by the cemetery company, had the same tax status as the cemetery company itself.[176] This rationale had been espoused earlier by the IRS.[177] However, Congress in 1976 enacted a provision providing a deduction for amounts distributed by perpetual care trust funds to taxable cemetery companies for the care and maintenance of gravesites.[178] To qualify under this provision, the fund must be a trust established pursuant to local law by a taxable cemetery for the care and maintenance of the cemetery.[179]

Contributions to tax-exempt cemetery companies are deductible for federal income tax purposes.[180] The contributions must be voluntary and made to or for the use of a nonprofit cemetery, the funds of which are irrevocably dedicated to the care of the cemetery as a whole. Contributions made to a cemetery company for the perpetual care of a particular lot or crypt are not deductible.[181] While bequests or gifts to tax-exempt cemetery companies are generally not deductible for federal estate or gift tax purposes,[182] one court allowed the estate tax deduction for a bequest to a public nonprofit cemetery because of its osten-

---

[173] Restland Memorial Park of Dallas v. United States, 509 F.2d 187 (5th Cir. 1975); Evergreen Cemetery Ass'n v. United States, 375 F. Supp. 166 (W.D. Ky. 1974); Rose Hills Memorial Park Ass'n v. United States, 463 F.2d 425 (Ct. Cl. 1972), cert. den., 414 U.S. 822 (1973); Arlington Memorial Park Ass'n v. United States, 327 F. Supp. 344 (W.D. Ark. 1971); Knollwood Memorial Gardens v. Comm'r, 46 T.C. 764 (1966).

[174] Rev. Rul. 77-70, 1977-1 C.B. 150.

[175] See § 6.8.

[176] Trustees of Graceland Cemetery Improvement Fund v. United States, 515 F.2d 763 (Ct. Cl. 1975). Also Laurel Hill Cemetery Ass'n v. United States, 427 F. Supp. 679 (E.D. Mo. 1977), aff'd, 566 F.2d 630 (8th Cir. 1977); Endowment Care Trust Fund of Inglewood Park Cemetery Ass'n Bd. of Trustees v. United States, 76-2 U.S.T.C. ¶ 9516 (Ct. Cl. 1976); Au v. United States, 76-1 U.S.T.C. ¶ 9370 (Ct. Cl. 1976); Albuquerque Nat'l Bank v. United States, 75-1 U.S.T.C. ¶ 9294 (D.N.M. 1975).

[177] Rev. Rul. 64-217, 1964-2 C.B. 153; Rev. Rul. 58-190, supra note 162. Cf. Washington Trust Bank v. United States, 444 F.2d 1235 (9th Cir. 1971), cert. den., 404 U.S. 1059 (1972); Evergreen Cemetery Ass'n of Seattle v. United States, 444 F.2d 1232 (9th Cir. 1971), cert. den., 404 U.S. 1050 (1971); Mercantile Bank & Trust Co. v. United States, 441 F.2d 364 (8th Cir. 1971); Arlington Memorial Park Ass'n v. United States, supra note 173.

[178] Pub. L. No. 528, 94th Cong., 2d Sess. (1976). Also H. Rep. No. 1344, 94th Cong., 2d Sess. (1976).

[179] IRC § 642(j); Reg. § 1.642(j).

[180] IRC § 170(c)(5).

[181] Rev. Rul. 58-190, supra note 166.

[182] Rev. Rul. 67-170, 1967-1 C.B. 272.

sible characteristics as a charitable entity.[183] However, this decision was reversed on appeal.[184]

§ 18.7 CREDIT UNIONS AND MUTUAL RESERVE FUNDS

The federal tax law exemption rules reference credit unions without capital stock
organized and operated for mutual purposes and without profit.[185] As noted, federal credit unions organized and operated in accordance with the Federal Credit
Union Act are tax-exempt as instrumentalities of the United States.[186] Credit
unions exempt from federal tax under these rules generally are those chartered
under state law,[187] although in one instance the IRS recognized tax exemption under this provision for the benefit of an organization formed by a group at a
United States military base in a foreign country.[188] However, in addition to being
chartered under a state credit union law, a credit union, to qualify under these
rules, must operate without profit and for the mutual benefit of its members.[189]

The first credit union in the United States was chartered in New Hampshire
in 1909 and was recognized by the Treasury Department as a tax-exempt organization in 1935. The government attempted to revoke its tax-exempt status in 1966,
contending that the organization was operating as a commercial savings and loan
association, because of the nature of its services and the alleged absence of the requisite "common bond" among its members. The issues were litigated, with the
courts finding that the organization did not lose its tax-exempt credit union status
because it offers services such as checking accounts and real estate loans, and that
the members of the credit union in fact have a common bond (it primarily serves
the French-speaking residents of Manchester, New Hampshire) even though this
commonality was not reduced to a written requirement.[190] A federal court of appeals used the occasion of its decision in this case to define *credit union* as follows:

> A credit union is a democratically controlled, cooperative, nonprofit society
> organized for the purpose of encouraging thrift and self-reliance among its
> members by creating a source of credit at a fair and reasonable rate of interest
> in order to improve the economic and social conditions of its members. A

---

[183] Mellon Bank v. United States, 590 F. Supp. 160 (W.D. Pa. 1984).

[184] Mellon Bank v. United States, 762 F.2d 283 (3d Cir. 1985). One court held that a cemetery association
may not qualify as a charitable organization for estate tax deduction purposes because of its function
of selling burial plots and maintenance of grounds (Smith v. United States, 84-2 U.S.T.C. ¶ 13,595
(W.D. Mo. 1984)). Also Linwood Cemetery Ass'n v. Comm'r, 87 T.C. 1314 (1986). In general, Frederick
& Porcano, "Taxation of Cemetery Organizations," 57 *Taxes* 186 (1979); Lapin, "Golden Hills and
Meadows of the Tax-Exempt Cemetery," 44 *Taxes* 744 (1966).

[185] IRC § 501(c)(14); Reg. § 1.501(c)(14)-1. Also United States v. Cambridge Loan & Bldg. Co., 278 U.S.
55 (1928).

[186] Rev. Rul. 55-133, *supra* note 3.

[187] Rev. Rul. 69-282, 1969-1 C.B. 155.

[188] Rev. Rul. 69-283, *supra* note 6.

[189] Rev. Rul. 72-37, 1972-1 C.B. 152.

[190] La Caisse Populaire Ste. Marie v. United States, 425 F. Supp. 512 (D.N.H. 1976), *aff'd*, 563 F.2d 505
(1st Cir. 1977).

credit union is fundamentally distinguishable from other financial institutions in that the customers may exercise effective control.[191]

This category of tax exemption also extends to certain mutual organizations organized before September 1, 1957.[192] Prior to 1951, all savings and loan associations were exempt from taxation, as were the nonprofit corporations that insured these savings institutions. In that year, the tax exemption for savings and loan associations was repealed because Congress determined that the purpose of the exemption, which was to afford savings institutions that had no capital stock the benefit of a tax exemption so that a surplus could be accumulated to provide the depositors with greater security, was no longer applicable because the savings and loan industry had developed to the point where the ratio of capital account to total deposits was comparable to commercial banks, which, of course, do not have tax exemption.

However, the tax exemption for the insurers of these associations was continued for those that were organized prior to September 1, 1951.[193] In 1960, Congress extended the expiration date to September 1, 1957, to accommodate the Ohio Deposit Guaranty Fund, since that entity had been organized at a time when the savings and loan associations were essentially not taxed, due to generous bad debt reserve provisions.[194]

In 1962, a nonprofit corporation was established by the legislature of the State of Maryland for the purpose of insuring the accounts of depositors in savings and loan associations doing business in the state, which were not insured by the Federal Savings and Loan Insurance Corporation. Legislation was introduced and considered to advance the termination date to January 1, 1963,[195] but was never enacted, in part because Congress did not want to recreate a discrimination in favor of these financial institutions.[196] (This nonaction on the part of Congress was challenged, with the U.S. Supreme Court holding that Congress did not function in an arbitrary and unconstitutional manner in declining to extend the exemption beyond 1957.[197]) Similar legislation, to extend the cutoff period to January 1, 1969, for the benefit of the Maryland entity and a comparable North Carolina insurer, was introduced and considered in 1976 and 1978 but not enacted.[198] Thereafter, the Maryland organization attempted to secure a judicial determination that it was entitled to a deduction from its income for an addition to its loss reserves

---

[191] *Id.*, 563 F.2d at 509.

[192] IRC § 501(c)(14)(B).

[193] At that time, Congress understood that the exemption would be limited to four private insurers (two in Massachusetts, one in Connecticut, and one in New Hampshire). S. Rep. No. 781, 82d Cong., 1st Sess. 22–29 (1951).

[194] S. Rep. No. 1881, 87th Cong., 2d Sess. 40 (1962).

[195] H.R. 3297, 88th Cong., 1st Sess. (1963). Also H. Rep. No. 3297, 88th Cong., 1st Sess. (1963).

[196] Savings and loan associations, like other financial institutions, were entitled to establish tax-free reserves from their earnings for losses on loans; there was opposition to exemption of these insurers from tax on the earnings of their members' capital deposits because it would, in effect, provide a method whereby the associations could accumulate reserves free of tax. Also, there was concern about the financial stability of the FSLIC.

[197] Maryland Sav.-Share Ins. Corp. v. United States, 400 U.S. 4 (1970).

[198] H.R. 10612 (Senate version), 94th Cong., 1st Sess. (1976); H.R. 6989, 95th Cong., 1st Sess. (1978).

but this was rejected on the ground that the deduction would be the equivalent of exemption of the income from tax—a result Congress has repeatedly rejected.[199]

It is the position of the IRS that the only way that organizations providing insurance of shares or deposits can qualify for tax exemption is to satisfy these rules.[200] This position is predicated upon the rule of statutory construction that a specific statutory provision must prevail over more general provisions.[201] Thus, for example, the type of organization that cannot satisfy the requirements for exemption of these mutual organizations (for example, because it was organized after 1957) cannot be tax-exempt as a business league.[202] It has been held that this category of tax exemption is inapplicable to credit unions.[203]

§ 18.8   CERTAIN INSURANCE COMPANIES OR ASSOCIATIONS

(a) Existing Law

The federal tax law exemption rules reference insurance companies or associations, other than life insurance companies or associations (including interinsurers and reciprocal underwriters), if their net written premiums (or, if greater, their direct written premiums) for the year do not exceed $350,000.[204] Thus, this category of tax exemption applies not only to otherwise qualified mutual property and casualty organizations (the case previously) but also to otherwise qualified stock property and casualty organizations. For these purposes, a company or association is treated as receiving during the tax year qualifying premiums that are received during the year by all other companies or associations that are members of the same controlled group as the insurance company or association the tax exemption of which is being determined.[205]

(b) Pre-1987 Law

For tax years beginning before January 1, 1987, IRC § 501(c)(15) described *mutual insurance companies or associations* other than life or marine (including interinsurers and reciprocal underwriters), if their gross amount received during the tax year from certain items and premiums (including deposits and assessments) did not exceed $350,000. This amount received included[206] (1) interest, dividends, rents, and royalties; (2) amounts received as the result of entering into leases, mortgages, or other instruments or agreements from which the organization derived interest, rents, or royalties; (3) amounts received from altering or terminat-

---

[199] Maryland Sav.-Share Ins. Corp. v. United States, 644 F.2d 16 (Ct. Cl. 1981).

[200] Rev. Rul. 83-166, 1983-2 C.B. 96 (applicable to years beginning after November 7, 1983).

[201] E.g., HCSC-Laundry v. United States, 450 U.S. 1 (1981).

[202] See Chapter 13.

[203] Credit Union Ins. Corp. v. United States, 95-1 U.S.T.C. ¶ 50,286 (D. Md. 1995), *aff'd*, 96-2 U.S.T.C. ¶ 50,323 (4th Cir. 1996).

[204] IRC § 501(c)(15)(A).

[205] IRC § 501(c)(15)(B). The term *controlled group* is defined in IRC § 831(b)(2)(B)(ii) (IRC § 501(c)(15)(C)).

[206] See IRC § 822(b)(1)(A)-(C), (2).

ing these instruments or agreements; (4) gross income from a business (other than the insurance business) carried on by the company or by a partnership of which it was a partner; and (5) premiums,[207] including deposits and assessments.[208]

An insurance company that was tax-exempt under these rules was required to be a mutual organization; all of its policyholders had to be members having common equitable ownership.[209] Also, the members had to control the company; it would lose tax exemption if a substantial number of policyholders were denied the right to vote for management[210] or if nonpolicyholders enjoyed voting rights equal to policyholders.[211] Further, the tax-exempt mutual company had to provide its members with insurance at substantially actual cost, with any excess premiums eventually returned to the policyholders (as dividends or premium reductions).[212] The issuance of policies on a nonassessable basis (that is, at fixed premiums) was not a necessary prerequisite to mutuality.[213]

The requirement that insurance be provided at substantially actual cost could have operated to deny this tax exemption where the company had a guaranty fund evidenced by dividend-bearing stock entitling the holders to share in the profits of the organization or to share beyond the face amount of the certificates in the assets of the organization upon dissolution. Nonetheless, the holders of the certificate could have had voting rights without endangering the company's tax exemption as long as control in fact remained with its policyholder members.[214] Further, this requirement meant that tax-exempt mutual companies could not accumulate unreasonable reserves.[215]

§ 18.9   CROP OPERATIONS FINANCE CORPORATIONS

The federal tax law provides tax exemption for corporations organized by a tax-exempt farmers' cooperative or association[216] or members of these organizations, for the purpose of financing the ordinary crop operations of the members or other producers, and operated in conjunction with this type of an association.[217]

---

[207] See Reg. § 1.821-4(a).

[208] Reg. § 1.501(c)(15)-1(a). Cf. Young Men's Christian Ass'n Retirement Fund, Inc. v. Comm'r, 18 B.T.A. 139 (1929).

[209] Rev. Rul. 74-196, 1974-1 C.B. 140.

[210] Keystone Automobile Club Casualty Co. v. Comm'r, 122 F.2d 886 (3d Cir. 1941), cert. den., 315 U.S. 814 (1942).

[211] Rev. Rul. 55-240, 1955-1 C.B. 406; Rev. Rul. 58–616, 1958-2 C.B. 928.

[212] Penn Mutual Life Insurance Co. v. Lederer, 252 U.S. 523 (1920); Safeguard Mutual Fire Insurance Co. v. Comm'r, 4 T.C. 75 (1944). Also Estate of Moyer v. Comm'r, 32 T.C. 515 (1959).

[213] Ohio Farmers Indemnity Co. v. Comm'r, 108 F.2d 665 (6th Cir. 1940).

[214] Property Owners Mutual Insurance Co. v. Comm'r, 28 T.C. 1007 (1957); Holyoke Mutual Fire Insurance Co. v. Comm'r, 28 T.C. 112 (1957).

[215] Mutual Fire Ins. Co. of Germantown v. United States, 142 F.2d 344 (3d Cir. 1944); Keystone Mutual Casualty Co. v. Driscoll, 137 F.2d 907 (3d Cir. 1943); MacLaughlin v. Philadelphia Contributionship for Ins. of Houses from Loss by Fire, 73 F.2d 582 (3d Cir. 1934), cert. den., 294 U.S. 718 (1935); The Mutual Fire, Marine and Inland Insurance Co. v. Comm'r, 8 T.C. 1212 (1947); Baltimore Equitable Soc. v. United States, 3 F. Supp. 427 (Ct. Cl. 1933), cert. den., 290 U.S. 662 (1933).

[216] See infra § 11.

[217] IRC § 501(c)(16); Reg. § 1.501(c)(16)-1.

The finance corporation may retain its tax exemption even though it issues capital stock, where certain statutory conditions are met, or it accumulates and maintains a reasonable reserve. A tax-exempt crop financing corporation may own all the stock of a business corporation without jeopardizing its tax-exempt status.[218]

One court denied tax exemption under these rules to a crop financing corporation, which was organized by fruit growers who were members of tax-exempt cooperatives, because the growers did not perform their activities as members of the cooperatives.[219]

§ 18.10 VETERANS' ORGANIZATIONS

(a) General Rules

The federal tax law provides tax exemption for a post or organization of past or present members of the armed forces of the United States, or an auxiliary unit or society of these entities, or a trust or foundation operated for these entities, where (1) it is organized in the United States or any of its possessions; (2) at least 75 percent of its members are past or present members of the U.S. armed forces and substantially all of the other members are individuals who are cadets or spouses, widows, or widowers of these past or present members or of cadets; and (3) there is no private inurement.[220] These rules were revised in 1982 to enable certain veterans' organizations to qualify for tax exemption without having a principal amount of members who are war veterans.[221] Some veterans groups may nonetheless continue to have tax exemption as social welfare organizations.[222]

Although the accompanying tax regulations have not been altered to reflect revision of the statute, presumably, a veterans' organization, to qualify for tax exemption under these rules, must operate exclusively to (1) promote the social welfare of the community; (2) assist disabled and needy veterans and members of the U.S. armed forces and their dependents, and the widows and widowers and orphans of deceased veterans; (3) provide entertainment, care, and assistance to hospitalized veterans or members of the U.S. armed forces; (4) carry on programs to perpetuate the memory of deceased veterans and members of the armed forces and comfort their survivors; (5) conduct programs for religious, charitable, scientific, literary, or educational purposes; (6) sponsor or participate in activities of a patriotic nature; (7) provide insurance benefits for their members or dependents thereof, or both; and/or (8) provide social and recreational activities for their members.[223]

---

[218] Rev. Rul. 78-434, 1978-2 C.B. 179.

[219] Growers Credit Corp. v. Comm'r, 33 T.C. 981 (1970).

[220] IRC § 501(c)(19).

[221] Under pre-1982 law, the membership of a tax-exempt veterans' organization had to be composed of at least 97.5 percent of war veterans or the other qualifying individuals (Reg. § 1.501(c)(19)-1(b)(2)). The term *war veteran* was defined at Reg. § 1.501(c)(19)-1(b)(1) and *war period* was defined in Rev. Rul. 78-239, 1978-1 C.B. 162.

[222] See Chapter 12.

[223] Reg. § 1.501(c)(19)-1(c). The IRS held that a veterans' organization engaged in unrelated activities in renting its hotel to nonmembers, selling bottled liquor, and providing banquet services to civic groups (Priv. Ltr. Rul. 8539091).

Exempted from the unrelated business income tax is income derived from members of these organizations attributable to payments for life, accident, or health insurance with respect to its members or their dependents, where the net profits are set aside for charitable purposes.[224] The enactment of this general income tax exemption thus provides a category of organizations entitled to use the unrelated business income tax exemption.

A contribution to a post or organization of war veterans, or an auxiliary unit or society of, or trust or foundation for, any of these posts or organizations is deductible as a charitable gift, if the donee is organized in the United States or any of its possessions and none of its net earnings inures to the benefit of any private shareholder or individual.[225]

Prior to enactment of the specific exemption for war veterans' organizations in 1972, veterans' organizations found their tax exemption as social welfare organizations,[226] social clubs,[227] or charitable and educational organizations.[228] It is not clear from the legislative history underlying the specific exemption whether the exemption is to be the exclusive basis for tax exemption for veterans' groups or whether they may continue to be eligible for exemption under one or more of the other categories. One judicial opinion treated this specific exemption as if it is the exclusive ground for tax exemption for veterans' organizations,[229] although the better view appears to be that this exemption was originally written for war veterans' organizations and that other veterans' organizations may, if they are otherwise qualified to do so, base their tax exemption upon the social welfare organization, social club, or charitable and educational organization categories.

When this tax exemption category was first proposed in the House of Representatives,[230] the descriptive language was the same as that in the provision making veterans' groups eligible charitable donees.[231] In both the House Committee on Ways and Means report[232] and in statements on the House floor,[233] there were repeated references to creation of a separate category of exemption for *veterans' organizations*. The House-passed measure was amended by the Senate, which added the 75 percent membership requirement.[234] This membership requirement

---

[224] IRC § 512(a)(4); Reg. § 1.512(a)-4. See § 28.3, text accompanied by note 26.

[225] IRC § 170(c)(3). Also Rev. Rul. 84-140, 1984-2 C.B. 56, *mod. and sup.*, Rev. Rul. 59-151, 1959-1 C.B. 53. One federal court of appeals concluded that a contribution to a qualifying veterans' organization by an individual of long-term capital gain appreciated property was subject to the 30 percent-of-contribution base limitation (see § 2.5), because the donee satisfied the publicly supported organization test of (i.e., is "described in") IRC § 509(a)(2) (see § 11.3(b)(iv)) and thus was described in IRC § 170(b)(1)(A)(viii) (Weingarden v. Comm'r, 825 F.2d 1027 (6th Cir. 1987)). The appellate court thus rejected the conclusion of the U.S. Tax Court that the gift was limited by the 20-percent-of-contribution base limitation on the ground that Congress intended that only organizations described in IRC § 501(c)(3) are charitable donees eligible for the more liberal limitation (Weingarden v. Comm'r, 86 T.C. 669 (1986)).

[226] See Chapter 12.

[227] See Chapter 14.

[228] See Chapters 6, 7.

[229] Taxation With Representation of Wash. v. Regan, 676 F.2d 715 (D.C. Cir. 1982).

[230] H.R. 11185, 92d Cong., 2d Sess. (1972).

[231] H. Rep. No. 851, 92d Cong., 2d Sess. (1972).

[232] 118 *Cong. Rec.* 6033 (1972).

[233] 118 *Cong. Rec.* 29076 (1972).

[234] 118 *Cong. Rec.* 29076 (1972).

was added by the Senate Committee on Finance, which regarded the amendment as an expansion of the specific exemption. (The Senate Finance Committee report characterized the House bill as providing the exemption for *war veterans' organizations*.[235]) The Finance Committee report also stated that "[t]he committee intends this provision to cover any veterans organization whose membership is composed almost exclusively of military associated individuals."[236]

Nonetheless, there is nothing in the legislative history of this specific tax exemption for certain types of veterans' organizations that expressly precludes a veterans' organization that cannot or may not qualify under it from tax exemption pursuant to some other classification of tax-exempt organization where the criteria for that classification are satisfied.

There is no federal tax law restriction on the extent of lobbying by veterans' organizations. This feature has been characterized by the U.S. Supreme Court as a "subsidy" enacted by Congress as part of the nation's long standing policy of compensating veterans for their past contributions by providing them with numerous advantages.[237] Presumably, tax exemption for their organizations is likewise a subsidy, for those who have "been obliged to drop their own affairs and take up the burdens of the nation"[238] and have subjected "themselves to the mental and physical hazards as well as the economic and family detriments which are peculiar to military service and which do not exist in normal life."[239] "This policy [of subsidization]," wrote the Court, "has 'always been deemed to be legitimate.' "[240]

(b) Pre-1880 Veterans' Organizations

In 1982, Congress established another category of tax-exempt veterans' organizations, which is available for any association organized before 1880, more than 75 percent of the members of which are present or past members of the U.S. Armed Forces and a principal purpose of which is to provide insurance and other benefits to veterans or their dependents.[241]

§ 18.11 FARMERS' COOPERATIVES

An eligible farmers' cooperative organization is exempt from federal income taxation.[242] These farmers' cooperatives are farmers', fruit growers', or like associations organized and operated on a cooperative basis for the purpose of (1) marketing the products of members or other producers and returning to them the proceeds of sales, less the necessary marketing expenses, on the basis of either the quantity or the value of the products furnished by them; or (2) purchasing sup-

---

[235] S. Rep. No. 1082, 92d Cong., 2d Sess. 1, 3 (1972).
[236] *Id*. at 5.
[237] Regan v. Taxation With Representation of Wash., 461 U.S. 540, 550 (1983).
[238] Boone v. Lightner, 319 U.S. 561, 575 (1943).
[239] Johnson v. Robison, 415 U.S. 361, 380 (1974).
[240] Personnel Admin. v. Feeney, 442 U.S. 256, 279, note 25 (1979).
[241] IRC § 501(c)(23).
[242] IRC § 521.

plies and equipment for the use of members or other persons and turning over the supplies and equipment to them at actual cost plus necessary expenses.[243] A farmers' cooperative may pay dividends on its capital stock in certain circumstances,[244] may permit proxy voting by its shareholders,[245] and may maintain a reasonable reserve.[246] The earnings of cooperatives generally are taxed to them or their patrons; these rules give tax-exempt farmers' cooperatives certain advantages in computing the tax that are not available to other cooperatives.[247]

Farmers' cooperatives came into being because of the economic fact that "[a] farmer sells his products in a producers' market and makes his purchases in a retail market."[248] Thus, a farmers' marketing cooperative markets farmers' products at a price nearer retail price and makes their purchases at wholesale rather than retail. A farmers' purchasing cooperative sells supplies and equipment to its patrons at a price that leaves a balance after expenses. The cooperative's net earnings or savings are distributed to the patrons on the basis of the amount of business transacted by them, in the form of *patronage dividends*. Patronage dividends are the profits of a cooperative that are rebated to its patrons pursuant to a preexisting obligation of the cooperative to do so; the rebate must be made in some equitable fashion on the basis of the quantity or value of business done with the cooperative.

Farmers' cooperatives are associations of individuals such as farmers, fruit growers, livestock growers, and dairymen. Illustrations of these organizations include associations operated to facilitate the artificial breeding of members' livestock,[249] acquire and apportion the beneficial use of land for the grazing of members' livestock,[250] furnish its members a place to market their farm products,[251] process and market poultry for members and other producers,[252] market farm-raised fish,[253] operate a grain elevator and feed yard and process soybeans,[254] purchase raw materials for processing into completed products before their transfer to patrons,[255] and produce and market range grasses.[256] The term *like association* is limited to associations that market agricultural products or purchase supplies and equipment for those engaged in producing agricultural products.[257] Thus, the admission to membership of a substantial number of nonproducers in an otherwise

---

[243] Reg. § 1.521-1. In general, Liberty Whse. Co. v. Burley Tobacco Growers' Coop. Mktg. Ass'n, 276 U.S. 71, 92–96 (1928).

[244] IRC § 521(b)(2); Reg. § 1.521-1(a)(2). Also Rev. Rul. 75-388, 1975-2 C.B 227; Rev. Rul. 73-148, 1973-1 C.B. 294. Also Agway, Inc. v. United States, 524 F.2d 1194 (Ct. Cl. 1975).

[245] Rev. Rul. 75-97, 1975-1 C.B. 167.

[246] IRC § 521(b)(3); Reg. § 1.521-1(a)(3). Also Rev. Rul. 76-233, 1976-1 C.B. 173.

[247] According to the U.S. Tax Court, in determining the amount to be paid as patronage dividends, a cooperative may allocate all of its gain from the sale of equipment to its patrons in the year of the sale in proportion to their patronage during that year (Lamesa Coop. Gin v. Comm'r, 78 T.C. 894 (1982)).

[248] IRS Exempt Organizations Handbook (IRM 7751) § (44) 12 (1).

[249] Rev. Rul. 68-76, 1968-1 C.B. 285.

[250] Rev. Rul. 67-429, 1967-2 C.B. 218.

[251] Rev. Rul. 67-430, 1967-2 C.B. 220.

[252] Rev. Rul. 58-483, 1958-2 C.B. 277.

[253] Rev. Rul. 64-246, 1964-2 C.B. 154.

[254] Rev. Rul. 74-567, 1974-2 C.B. 174.

[255] Rev. Rul. 54-12, 1954-1 C.B. 93.

[256] Rev. Rul. 75-5, 1975-1 C.B. 166.

[257] Sunset Scavenger Co., Inc. v. Comm'r, 84 F.2d 453 (9th Cir. 1936).

tax-exempt producers' cooperative would destroy the association's tax exemption.[258] This, in turn, raises questions as to what constitutes a *farm*[259] and a *farmer*.[260]

The specific rules in this area of the federal tax law do not define these terms. However, these terms are referenced elsewhere in the federal tax law.[261] On the basis of these other definitions, the IRS concluded that these terms do not apply to forestry, so that a federated cooperative marketing newsprint and its member cooperatives supplying pulpwood cut from timber grown by the patron members did not qualify as tax-exempt farmers' cooperatives.[262]

Examples of organizations denied this tax exemption as not being like a farmers' cooperative include an association that maintained its patrons' orchards and harvested their crops,[263] that marketed lumber for the independent lumber producing companies that controlled it,[264] that marketed building materials on a cooperative basis,[265] and an association of advertising agencies[266] and of garbage collectors.[267] An organization may be recognized as a cooperative association under state law and still be denied this tax exemption.[268]

Other requirements must be met to achieve this tax exemption, including the requirements that the association be organized and operated on a cooperative basis,[269] that there be bona fide members,[270] and that (where appropriate) there be producers.[271] One federal court of appeals held that a person who merely stores items in the cooperative's facilities but does not market any products or purchase any supplies from the cooperative is not a producer.[272]

To be tax-exempt as a farmers' cooperative, an organization must establish that it has no taxable income for its own account other than that reflected in an authorized reserve or surplus.[273] An organization engaged in both marketing farm products and purchasing supplies and equipment is tax-exempt if as to each of its functions it meets the tax law requirements.[274] An organization cannot be tax-exempt under these rules if it nets losses between the marketing function and the purchasing function.[275]

---

[258] Cooperative Cent. Exch. v. Comm'r, 27 B.T.A. 17 (1932).

[259] Rev. Rul. 64-246, *supra* note 253.

[260] Rev. Rul. 55-611, 1955-2 C.B. 270.

[261] IRC §§ 61 (also Reg. § 1.61-4(d)), 175 (Reg. § 1.175-3), 180, 182 (Reg. § 1.182-2), 464(e)(1).

[262] Rev. Rul. 84-81, 1984-1 C.B. 135.

[263] Rev. Rul. 66-108, 1966-2 C.B. 154.

[264] Rev. Rul. 73-570, 1973-2 C.B. 195.

[265] Rev. Rul. 73-308, 1973-2 C.B. 193.

[266] National Outdoor Advertising Bur., Inc. v. Helvering, 89 F.2d 878 (2d Cir. 1937).

[267] Sunset Scavenger Co., Inc. v. Comm'r, *supra* note 257.

[268] Lyeth v. Hoey, 305 U.S. 188 (1938).

[269] Reg. § 1.521-1(a)(1); Rev. Rul. 71-100, 1971-1 C.B. 159; Rev. Rul. 68-496, 1968-2 C.B. 251; Rev. Rul. 55-558, 1955-2 C.B. 270; Eugene Fruit Growers Ass'n v. Comm'r, 37 B.T.A. 993 (1938).

[270] Reg. § 1.521-1(a)(3); Producers Livestock Mktg. Ass'n of Salt Lake City v. Comm'r, 45 B.T.A. 325 (1941).

[271] Rev. Rul. 72-589, 1972-2 C.B. 282; Rev. Rul. 67-422, 1967-2 C.B. 217; Rev. Rul. 58-483, *supra* note 252; Farmers Coop. Creamery Ass'n of Cresco, Iowa v. United States, 81-1 U.S.T.C. ¶ 9457 (N.D. Iowa 1981); Dr. P. Phillips Coop. v. Comm'r, 17 T.C. 1002 (1951).

[272] West Cent. Coop. v. United States, 758 F.2d 1269 (8th Cir. 1985), *aff'g per curiam* (N.D. Iowa 1983).

[273] Reg. § 1.521-1(c).

[274] *Id.*

[275] Union Equity Coop. Exch. v. Comm'r, 481 F.2d 812 (10th Cir. 1973), *cert. den.*, 414 U.S. 1028 (1973).

With respect to a farmers' cooperative that issues stock, for the cooperative to be tax-exempt, substantially all of the capital stock must be owned by producers who market their products or purchase their supplies and equipment through the cooperative.[276] Also, the farmers' cooperative must be able to demonstrate that the ownership of its capital stock has been restricted to participating shareholders "as far as possible."[277] While the phrase *substantially all* is not defined in the statute or regulations, it is the view of the IRS that, for this rule to be satisfied, at least 85 percent of the capital stock must be held by producers,[278] with a court holding that a 91 percent holding satisfies the requirement[279] and that neither a 78 percent nor a 72 percent holding meets the requirement.[280]

Subsequently, one court agreed with the IRS' 85-percent test "in concept," emphasizing that the "favorable tax treatment offered cooperatives is intended to benefit the member producers, not the cooperative as a business entity."[281] A federal court of appeals twice concluded that the test is reasonable.[282] In so concluding, this appellate court wrote that, since this tax exemption is available "only to those cooperatives in which participation in the direction and decision making process of the cooperative is strictly limited to patrons," "[o]f primary importance, therefore, is a shareholder's right to vote."[283] Consequently, the court of appeals enunciated this rule:

> [F]or purposes of applying the 85% test, the relevant consideration is whether the right to vote has actually accrued or been terminated by the time of the annual shareholders' meeting following the close of the tax year. In other words, if a producer who sufficiently patronizes a cooperative during the tax year to become entitled to a share of capital stock is actually entitled to vote that share at the annual shareholders' meeting following the close of that tax year, that producer should be counted as both a shareholder and as a patron for the tax year in which the right to the share accrued. Conversely, if a shareholder, by failing to patronize a cooperative, ceases to be entitled to own a share and thereby actually loses the right to vote at the annual shareholders' meeting following the close of the tax year, that shareholder should not be counted as a shareholder or patron for the tax year in which the right to the share was lost.[284]

Specifically, the law provides that an "[e]xemption shall not be denied any such association because it has capital stock . . . if substantially all such stock . . . is owned by producers who market their products or purchase their supplies and

---

[276] IRC § 521(b)(2).

[277] Reg. § 1.521-1(a)(2).

[278] Rev. Rul. 73-248, 1973-1 C.B. 295.

[279] Farmers Co-Op. Creamery v. Comm'r, 21 B.T.A. 265 (1930). Also Farmers' Co-Op. Milk Co. v. Comm'r, 9 B.T.A. 696 (1927).

[280] Co-Operative Grain & Supply Co. v. Comm'r, 32 T.C.M. 795 (1973), *on remand*, 407 F.2d 1158 (8th Cir. 1969), *rev'g in part and rem'g*, 26 T.C.M. 593 (1967); Petaluma Co-Op. Creamery v. Comm'r, 52 T.C. 457 (1969).

[281] Farmers Coop. Co. v. Comm'r, 85 T.C. 601, 613, 614 (1985).

[282] Farmers Coop. Co. v. Comm'r, 87-2 U.S.T.C. ¶ 9404 (8th Cir. 1987); West Cent. Coop. v. United States, *supra* note 272.

[283] Farmers Coop. Co. v. Comm'r, *supra* note 282, at 89, 116.

[284] *Id.*

equipment through the association." It is, as noted, the position of the IRS that at least 85 percent of capital stock must be held by producers to satisfy the *substantially all* test.[285] This requirement has been upheld by the courts, with the courts agreeing that, as noted, a person that merely stores items in the cooperative's storage facilities but marketed no products nor purchased any supplies from the cooperative is not a producer.[286]

The IRS issued guidelines[287] to determine whether a patron is a producer patron of a farmers' cooperative for purposes of applying these stock ownership requirements.[288] These guidelines, which were subsequently abandoned, stated that the qualifying stockholders will be persons who, during the cooperative's tax year, market through the cooperative more than 50 percent of their products or who purchase from the cooperative more than 50 percent of their products or who purchase from the cooperative more than 50 percent of their supplies and equipment of the type handled by the cooperative.[289] A person who did not meet this 50 percent requirement could nonetheless be considered a producer for purposes of the ownership requirements if certain facts and circumstances, as stated in a 1977 IRS ruling, are present.[290] However, a court voided the 50 percent patronage requirement,[291] causing the IRS to revoke the 50 percent patronage test[292] and the 1977 ruling.[293] Thus, stock owned by persons who transact any amount of current and active patronage with a tax-exempt cooperative during the cooperative's tax year will be considered stock that is counted toward the stock ownership requirement. Moreover, a person who does not transact any patronage during the cooperative's tax year may still be considered a producer for these purposes if, upon consideration of all the facts and circumstances, it is determined that the person was unable to transact any patronage during the year because (1) the person encountered a crop failure and had nothing to market; (2) sickness, disability, death, or other hardship prevented the person from transacting any patronage; or (3) the cooperative deals in items (such as farm machinery) that are not normally purchased on an annual basis.[294]

Still other requirements concern the nature of permissible activities. As respects marketing cooperatives, questions have been raised as to what constitutes *marketing*.[295] The IRS has a long-standing policy of allowing farmers' cooperatives, in connection with their marketing function, to manufacture or otherwise change the basic form of their members' products, as illustrated by the tax-exempt farmers' cooperative operating a cannery and facilities for drying fruit and a cooperative operating a textile mill, both of which marketed the processed or unprocessed products of their member growers and distributed the proceeds to

---

[285] Rev. Rul. 73-248, *supra* note 278.

[286] West Cent. Coop. v. United States, *supra* note 272.

[287] Rev. Proc. 73-39, 1973-2 C.B. 502.

[288] IRC § 521(b)(2). Also *supra* note 244.

[289] Rev. Proc. 73-39, *supra* note 287.

[290] Rev. Rul. 77-440, 1977-2 C.B. 199.

[291] Farmers Coop. Co. v. Comm'r, 89 T.C. 682 (1987).

[292] Rev. Proc. 90-29, 1990-1 C.B. 533.

[293] Rev. Rul. 90-42, 1990-1 C.B. 117.

[294] See Rev. Proc. 90-29, *supra* note 292; Rev. Rul. 90-42, *supra* note 293.

[295] Treasure Valley Potato Bargaining Ass'n v. Ore-Ida Foods, Inc., 497 F.2d 203 (9th Cir. 1974); Rev. Rul. 67-430, *supra* note 251; Rev. Rul. 66-108, *supra* note 263; Mim. 3886, X-2 C.B. 164 (1931).

them on the basis of the quantity of product furnished, less a charge to cover the cost of processing.[296] Subsequently, this policy was further illustrated by a ruling from the IRS allowing qualification as a tax-exempt farmers' cooperative of a cooperative association that, in connection with its marketing function, processed its members' agricultural products into alcohol.[297]

Concerning the purchasing cooperative, the issue may be what is encompassed by the term *supplies and equipment*.[298] Business done for or with the United States or any of its agencies is disregarded in determining the right to this tax exemption.[299] Because hedging is an activity that is incidental to the marketing function of a tax-exempt farmers' cooperative, it may establish a commodity trading division to serve as a commodity broker to facilitate hedging transactions for its marketing patrons without adversely affecting its tax exemption.[300]

Tax exemption for a farmers' cooperative may not be denied because it has capital stock, if the dividend rate of the stock is fixed at a rate not to exceed the legal rate of interest in the state of incorporation or 8 percent per annum, whichever is greater, on the value of the consideration for which the stock was issued, and if substantially all of the stock (other than nonvoting preferred stock, the owners of which are not entitled or permitted to participate, directly or indirectly, in the profits of the organization, upon dissolution or otherwise, beyond the fixed dividends) is owned by producers who market their products or purchase their supplies and equipment through the organization.[301] It is the position of the IRS that this *substantially all* test can be satisfied only where at least 85 percent of the capital stock (other than the nonvoting preferred stock) is held by producers.[302] This test has been upheld by a federal court of appeals.[303]

A tax-exempt farmers' cooperative may establish and control a subsidiary corporation as long as the activities of the subsidiary are activities that the cooperative itself might engage in as an integral part of its operations without adversely affecting its tax-exempt status.[304] For this reason, the IRS ruled that a cooperative may establish and control a Domestic International Sales Corporation.[305]

One rule that has generated considerable attention is the limitation on the purchasing of supplies and equipment for nonmembers and nonproducers to 15 percent of the value of all of the tax-exempt cooperative's purchase of supplies and equipment.[306] By contrast, a marketing cooperative will generally not qualify for this

---

[296] Rev. Rul. 77-384, 1977-2 C.B. 198.

[297] Rev. Rul. 81-96, 1981-1 C.B. 359.

[298] Rev. Rul. 68-76, *supra* note 249; Rev. Rul. 67-429, *supra* note 250; Rev. Rul. 54-12, *supra* note 255; S.M. 2288, III-2 C.B. 223 (1924); Farmers Union Coop. Ass'n, Fairbury, Neb. v. Comm'r, 44 B.T.A. 34 (1941).

[299] IRC § 521(b)(5); Rev. Rul. 65-5, 1965-1 C.B. 244.

[300] Rev. Rul. 76-298, 1976-2 C.B. 179.

[301] IRC § 521(b)(2).

[302] Rev. Rul. 73-248, 1973-2 C.B. 295.

[303] West Cent. Coop. v. United States, *supra* note 272. Also Cooperative Grain & Supply Co. v. Comm'r, 407 F.2d 1158 (8th Cir. 1969).

[304] Rev. Rul. 69-575, 1969-2 C.B. 134.

[305] Rev. Rul. 73-247, 1973-1 C.B. 294.

[306] IRC § 521(b)(4). Also Rev. Rul. 69-417, 1969-2 C.B. 132; Rev. Rul. 67-346, 1967-2 C.B. 216; Rev. Rul. 67-223, 1967-2 C.B. 214. As for the effect of the use of subsidiaries in relation to this limitation, see Rev. Rul. 73-148, *supra* note 244; Rev. Rul. 69-575, *supra* note 304.

tax exemption if it markets the goods of nonproducers.[307] However, there are exceptions to the limitation on marketing nonproducer goods, which may be categorized into sideline,[308] ingredient,[309] and emergency[310] purchases from nonproducers.

Still another requisite for entitlement to this tax exemption is that any excess of gross receipts over expenses and payments to patrons (termed *earnings*) must be returned to the patrons in proportion to the amount of business done for them. The income and expenses for each function (primarily marketing and purchasing) must be accounted for separately.[311] In computing earnings, the tax-exempt cooperative must experience only necessary expenses associated with marketing and purchasing (frequently undertaken in different departments or branches), rather than for items such as the purchase of life insurance for members.[312] Nonpatronage income may be allocated to the appropriate department of the cooperative.[313]

Also, a tax-exempt farmers' cooperative must treat its nonmember patrons the same as member-patrons as respects patronage dividends. There are several cases where an association has been denied tax exemption under these rules because of this type of discrimination,[314] as well as a number of instances where inequality among patrons was deemed to be not present.[315]

A discussion of the circumstances under which a federated farmers' cooperative (an association the membership of which includes tax-exempt farmers' cooperative associations) may qualify for this tax exemption is the subject of a 1969 IRS ruling.[316] Two 1972 revenue procedures set forth methods acceptable for a federated cooperative and its members to establish tax exemption (involving the look through principle[317]) and setting forth the general requirements in this regard.[318]

The federal tax law provisions for cooperatives generally[319] operate to treat these organizations more like a conduit than a separate taxable business enterprise. The primary reason for this treatment is to avoid penalizing (by taxing) a group of persons for collectivizing their marketing or purchasing efforts in order to take advantage of economies of scale. The conduit treatment is derived from the ability of a cooperative to deduct from its taxable income patronage divi-

---

[307] IRC § 521(b)(1). Also Rev. Rul. 67-152, 1967-1 C.B. 147.

[308] Rev. Proc. 67-37, 1967-2 C.B. 668; Land O'Lakes, Inc. v. United States, 362 F. Supp. 1253 (S.D. Minn. 1973), *rev. and rem.* 514 F.2d 134 (8th Cir. 1975), *cert. den.*, 423 U.S. 926 (1975); Eugene Fruit Growers Ass'n v. Comm'r, *supra* note 269.

[309] Rev. Rul. 75-4, 1975-1 C.B. 165; Rev. Rul. 67-152, *supra* note 307, Dr. P. Phillips Coop. v. Comm'r, *supra* note 271.

[310] Rev. Rul. 69-222, 1969-1 C.B. 161; Producer's Produce Co. v. Crooks, 2 F. Supp. 969 (W.D. Mo. 1932).

[311] Rev. Rul. 67-253, 1967-2 C.B. 214; Rev. Rul. 75-110, 1975-1 C.B. 167.

[312] Rev. Rul. 55-558, *supra* note 269. Also Rev. Rul. 73-93, 1973-1 C.B. 292.

[313] Rev. Rul. 67-128, 1967-1 C.B. 147; Juanita Farmers Coop. Ass'n v. Comm'r, 43 T.C. 836 (1965). Cf. Rev. Rul. 75-228, 1975-1 C.B. 278; Rev. Rul. 74-327, 1974-2 C.B. 66.

[314] E.g., Farmers Coop. Creamery Ass'n of Cresco, Iowa v. United States, *supra* note 271; Fertile Coop. Dairy Ass'n v. Huston, 119 F.2d 274 (8th Cir. 1951); Farmers Coop. Co. of Wahoo, Neb. v. United States, 23 F. Supp. 123 (Ct. Cl. 1938); Rev. Rul. 73-59, 1973-1 C.B. 292.

[315] E.g., Rev. Rul. 69-52, 1969-1 C.B. 161; Rev. Rul. 66-152, 1966-1 C.B. 155. Also Rev. Rul. 76-388, 1976-2 C.B. 180.

[316] Rev. Rul. 69-651, 1969-2 C.B. 135.

[317] Rev. Ruls. 72-50, 51, 52, 1972-1 C.B. 163, 164, 165.

[318] Rev. Procs. 72-16, 17, 1972-1 C.B. 738, 739.

[319] IRC § 1381 *et seq.*

dends paid. (A farmers' cooperative generally may deduct patronage dividends to the full extent of its net income and may also deduct, to a limited extent, dividends on common stock.)

An unresolved issue pertains to the fact that a cooperative may make purchases or market goods in several product lines and/or several geographic areas, or both make purchases and market goods. Many cooperatives of this type will calculate net income on an aggregate basis, netting gains from profitable products or geographic areas with losses from unprofitable ones, and thus pay patronage dividends based upon the net income so computed. It is the position of the IRS that a cooperative may not net gains and losses from different operations in any manner it chooses and that netting is not permitted unless it is equitable under the circumstances.[320]

§ 18.12   SHIPOWNERS' PROTECTION AND INDEMNITY ASSOCIATIONS

The federal tax law provides that "[t]here shall not be included in gross income the receipts of shipowners' mutual protection and indemnity associations not organized for profit, and no part of the net earnings of which inures to the benefit of any private shareholder; but such corporations shall be subject as other persons to the tax on their taxable income from interest, dividends, and rents."[321]

The return of excess dues by a fishing vessel owners' association to its members was ruled by the IRS to not be inurement of earnings to the members; therefore, the dues paid to the association were not includible in its gross income.[322]

---

[320] The caselaw is more supportive of the cooperatives', rather than the government's, position. E.g., Ford-Iroquois FS v. Comm'r., 74 T.C. 1213 (1980); Lamesa Cooperative Gin v. Comm'r, *supra* note 247; Associated Milk Producers v. Comm'r, 68 T.C. 729 (1977). In general, Butwill, "IRS Expands Availability of Patronage Dividend Deductions and Tax-Exempt Status for Cooperatives but Restricts Benefit of Package Design Expenditures," 12 *J. Agric. Tax. & Law* (No. 4) 342 (1991); Fleck, "Cooperatives—Accounting and Tax Developments: Distribution of Nonpatronage Retained Earnings," 11 *J. Agric. Tax. & Law* (No. 2) 181 (1989); Fleck, "Cooperatives—Accounting and Tax Developments: Losses and Netting," 9 *J. Agric. Tax. & Law* (No. 4) 374 (1988); Frederick, "Qualifying Farmers' Cooperatives for Section 521 Tax Status," 10 *J. Agric. Tax. & Law* (No. 1) 16 (1988); Locke, "Cooperatives—Accounting and Tax Developments: 'Substantially All' Test of Section 521 Cooperatives Clarified," 10 *J. Agric. Tax. & Law* (No. 2) 181 (1988); Sedo, "Cooperative Mergers and Consolidations: A Consideration of the Legal and Tax Issues," 63 *N.D.L. Rev.* (No. 3) 377 (1987); Katz, "Buying Through Cooperatives Has Tax Benefits for the Cooperative and Its Owners," 16 *Tax Accts.* 115 (1976); Comment, "Agricultural Cooperative Associations and the Equal Treatment Requirement of Section 521," 27 *Ala. L. Rev.* 611 (1976); Note, "Section 521—Exemption of Farmers Cooperatives from Tax," 25 *Drake L. Rev.* 705 (1976); Schrader & Goldberg, *Farmers' Cooperatives and Federal Income Taxes* (1975); Pearson, "Farm Cooperatives and the Federal Income Tax," 44 *N.D.L. Rev.* 490 (1968); Logan, "Federal Income Taxation of Farmers' and Other Cooperatives," 44 *Tex. L. Rev.* 250, 1269 (1965–1966); Wile, "Taxation of Farmers' Cooperatives and Their Patrons," 18 *S.C. Tax Inst.* 449 (1966); Blair, "Farmers' Cooperatives and Their Patrons Face New Problems in Reporting Income," 28 *J. Tax.* 180 (1968); Asbill, "Cooperatives: Tax Treatment of Patronage Refunds," 42 *Va. L. Rev.* 1087 (1956); Paul, "The Justifiability of the Policy of Exempting Farmers' Marketing and Purchasing Cooperatives for Federal Income Taxation," 29 *Minn. L. Rev.* 343 (1945).
[321] IRC § 526.
[322] Rev. Rul. 70-566, 1970-1 C.B. 128.

The amount paid by a member of a tax-exempt association to its reserve fund to provide certain insurance protection was deemed deductible.[323]

§ 18.13 HOMEOWNERS' ASSOCIATIONS

Homeowners' associations, for decades, were treated as social welfare organizations. It is common for these associations to be formed as part of the development of a real estate subdivision, a condominium project, or a cooperative housing project. These associations enable their members (usually individual homeowners) to act together in managing, maintaining, and improving areas where they live. The associations' purposes include the administration and enforcement of covenants for preserving the physical appearance of the development, the ownership and management of common areas (for example, sidewalks and parks), and the exterior maintenance of property owned by the members.

Originally, as noted, the IRS regarded homeowners' associations as tax-exempt social welfare organizations.[324] However, the IRS, concerned that the requisite *community* was not being served, issued a countervailing ruling in 1974.[325] Most homeowners' associations found it difficult to meet the requirements of the 1974 determination.[326] The IRS also ruled that condominium management associations did not qualify for tax exemption.[327]

Congress responded to this situation with a special elective tax exemption provision for condominium management and residential real estate associations.[328] This provision is in the mode of the present tax treatment of exempt social clubs[329] and political organizations,[330] in that only *exempt function income* escapes unrelated business income taxation.

To qualify as a tax-exempt homeowners' association, an organization must be a condominium[331] management association or a residential real estate management association.[332] Generally, membership in a condominium management association or a residential real estate management association is con-

---

[323] Rev. Rul. 55-189, 1955-1 C.B. 265.

[324] Rev. Rul. 72-102, 1972-1 C.B. 149.

[325] Rev. Rul. 74-199, 1974-1 C.B. 131.

[326] Frank, "IRS Takes Harsh Position on Exempting Condominium and Homeowners' Associations," 44 *J. Tax.* 306 (1976).

[327] Rev. Rul. 74-17, 1974-1 C.B. 130.

[328] IRC § 528; Reg. § 1.528-8. In Priv. Let. Rul. 8429049, the IRS refused to excuse a homeowners' association from the requirement of filing a timely refund claim, under the mitigation rules of IRC §§ 1311–1314, in the face of the argument that the claim is dependent upon a future event, namely, the grant of permission to revoke the IRC § 528 election on the ground of inadequate accounting advice. In Priv. Let. Rul. 8433077, the IRS refused to grant a homeowners' association an extension of time within which to make the IRC § 528 election, where three management companies failed to file tax returns for the association. The IRS ruled that a homeowners' association may revoke an IRC § 528 election because of incorrect tax advice provided by a professional tax advisor (Rev. Rul. 83-74, 1983-1 C.B. 112). There is an automatic 12-month extension to make the election (Rev. Proc. 92-85, 1992-2 C.B. 490 § 4.01).

[329] IRC § 512(a)(3). See § 28.3.

[330] IRC § 527(b). See § 17.3(a).

[331] The term *condominium* is defined for these purposes in Reg. § 1.528-1(b).

[332] Reg. § 1.528-1(a). The term *residential real estate management association* is defined in Reg. § 1.528-1(c).

fined to the developers and the owners of the units, residences, or lots.[333] Membership in either type of association is normally required as a condition of this ownership.[334]

A homeowners' association must meet certain requirements: (1) It must be organized and operated primarily to provide for the acquisition, construction, management, maintenance, and care of association property;[335] (2) an income test, whereby at least 60 percent of the association's gross income for a tax year consists of exempt function income;[336] (3) an expenditure test, whereby at least 90 percent of the annual expenditures of the association must be to acquire, construct, manage, maintain, and care for or improve its property;[337] (4) no part of the association's net earnings may inure to the benefit of any private shareholder or individual;[338] and (5) substantially all of the dwelling units in the condominium project or lots and buildings in a subdivision, development, or similar area must be used by individuals for residences.[339] The acts of acquiring, constructing, or providing management, maintenance, and care of association property, and of rebating excess membership dues, fees, or assessments, do not constitute private inurement. Association property means not only property held by it but also property commonly held by its members, property within the association privately held by the members, and property owned by a governmental unit and used for the benefit of residents of the unit.[340]

In this context, *exempt function income* means any amount received as membership dues, fees, or assessments from persons who are members of the association, namely, owners of condominium housing units (in the case of a condominium management association) or owners of real property (in the case of a residential real estate management association).[341] Taxable income includes investment income and payments by nonmembers for the use of the association's facilities, subject to a specific $100 deduction and deductions directly connected with the production of gross income (other than exempt function income).[342] The taxable income of a qualified homeowners' association is taxable at the rate of 30 percent, rather than the regular corporate rates (ranging from 15 to 34 percent, the latter for taxable income over $75,000).[343]

---

[333] Reg. § 1.528-1(a).

[334] *Id*. Effective as to years beginning after December 31, 1996, associations of holders of timeshare interests (IRC § 528(c)(4)) are treated as homeowners' associations.

[335] Reg. § 1.528-2.

[336] Reg. § 1.528-5.

[337] Reg. § 1.528-6.

[338] Reg. § 1.528-7.

[339] Reg. § 1.528-4.

[340] Reg. § 1.528-3.

[341] Reg. § 1.528-9. Annual assessments paid to a homeowners' association by its members are not deductible as real property taxes (Rev. Rul. 76-495, 1976-2 C.B. 43). An amount received by a homeowners' association in settlement of litigation on behalf of individual lot owners was deemed to constitute membership fees for this purpose (Rev. Rul. 88-56, 1988-1 C.B. 126). In contrast, interest earned by a homeowners' association on funds received in settlement of a pending lawsuit and held for certain repairs was ruled to be taxable (Priv. Ltr. Rul. 9042036).

[342] Reg. § 1.528-10. Qualified homeowners' associations that elect to be taxed under IRC § 528 file tax return Form 1120-H (IRC § 6012(a)(7); Ann. 77-42, 1977-13 I.R.B. 23).

[343] IRC § 528(b). However, timeshare associations (see *supra* note 334) are taxed at a 32 percent rate.

The House version of the Tax Reform Act of 1969 would have applied the foregoing rules to cooperative housing corporations,[344] but the 1969 Act in its final form followed the Senate bill in not allowing the exemption for these corporations.[345] Instead, the Act clarified existing law to ensure that a cooperative housing corporation is entitled to a deduction for depreciation[346] with respect to property it leases to a tenant-stockholder even though the tenant-stockholder may be entitled to depreciate his or her stock in the corporation to the extent the stock is related to a proprietary lease or right of tenancy that is used by the tenant-stockholder in a trade or business or for the production of income.[347]

§ 18.14 HIGH-RISK INDIVIDUALS HEALTH CARE COVERAGE ORGANIZATIONS

Tax-exempt status is available for a membership organization established by a state exclusively to provide coverage for medical care[348] on a nonprofit basis to high-risk individuals through insurance issued by the organization or a health maintenance organization under an arrangement with the organization.[349]

The individuals, who must be residents of the state, must be—by reason of the existence or history of a medical condition—unable to acquire medical care coverage for the medical condition through insurance or from a health maintenance organization, or able to acquire the coverage only at a rate that is substantially in excess of the rate for the coverage through the membership organization.[350] The composition of the membership in the organization must be specified by the state.[351] For example, a state could mandate that all organizations that are subject to insurance regulation by the state must be members of the organization.[352] The private inurement doctrine[353] is applicable to this type of organization.[354]

---

[344] IRC § 216(b).

[345] Thus, "[c]ooperative housing corporations and organizations based on a similar form of ownership are not eligible to be taxed as homeowners' associations" (Reg. § 1.528-1(a)).

[346] IRC § 167(a).

[347] Park Place, Inc. v. Comm'r, 57 T.C. 767(1972). In general, Cowan, "Working with New Rules for Condominiums, Cooperatives and Homeowners Associations," 46 *J. Tax.* 204 (1977); IRS Publication 588 (rev. ed. 1980), which includes discussion of the treatment of individual condominium owners' tax situations and homeowners' associations' tax alternatives; Reinstein, "Federal Tax Implications of Condominium Associations," 50 *Fla. Bar J.* 219 (1976); Redemske, "Income Tax Considerations for the Condominium Corporation," 7 *Tax Adv.* 608 (1976); Garrett, "The Taxability of Condominium Owners' Associations," 12 *San Diego L. Rev.* 778 (1975).

[348] This term is defined in IRC § 213(d).

[349] IRC § 501(c)(26)(A).

[350] IRC § 501(c)(26)(B).

[351] IRC § 501(c)(26)(C).

[352] H. Rep. 736, 104th Cong., 2d Sess. 36 (1996).

[353] See Chapter 19.

[354] IRC § 501(c)(26)(D).

§ 18.15   WORKERS' COMPENSATION REINSURANCE ORGANIZATIONS

(a) State-sponsored Organizations

Tax-exempt status is available for a membership organization established before June 1, 1996, by a state exclusively to reimburse its members for losses arising under workers' compensation acts.[355]

The state must require that the membership of the organization consist of all persons who issue insurance covering workers' compensation losses in the state, and all persons and governmental entities who self-insure against these losses.[356] The organization must "operate as a nonprofit organization" by returning surplus income to its members or workers' compensation policyholders on a periodic basis and reducing initial premiums in anticipation of investment income.[357]

(b) Certain Insurance Companies

Tax exemption is also available to any organization (including a mutual insurance company) if it is created by state law and is organized and operated under state law exclusively to (1) provide workers' compensation insurance which is required by state law or with respect to which state law provides significant disincentives if the insurance is not purchased by an employer, and (2) provide related coverage which is incidental to worker's compensation insurance.[358]

The organization must provide workers' compensation insurance to any employer in the state (for employees in the state or temporarily assigned out-of-state) which seeks the insurance and meets other reasonable requirements relating thereto.[359] The state must make a financial commitment with respect to the organization, either by extending the full faith and credit of the state to the initial debt of the organization or by providing the initial operating capital of the organization.[360] In the case of periods after August 5, 1997, the assets of the organization must revert to the state upon dissolution, unless state law does not permit the dissolution of the organization.[361] The majority of the board of directors or oversight body of the organization must be appointed by the chief executive officer or other executive branch official of the state, by the state legislature, or by both.[362]

§ 18.16   STATE TUITION PROGRAMS

Tax-exempt status is accorded to *qualified state tuition programs.*[363] These are programs established and maintained by a state (or an agency or instrumentality of a

---

[355] IRC § 501(c)(27)(A)(i).

[356] IRC § 501(c)(27)(A)(ii).

[357] IRC § 501(c)(27)(A)(iii). This exemption is available with respect to tax years ending after August 21, 1996, and to tax years beginning before January 1, 1998 (as IRC § 501(c)(27)), and is available with respect to tax years beginning after December 31, 1997 (as IRC § 501(c)(27)(A)).

[358] IRC § 501(c)(27)(B)(i).

[359] IRC § 501(c)(27)(B)(ii).

[360] IRC § 501(c)(27)(B)(iii)(I).

[361] IRC § 501(c)(27)(B)(iii)(II).

[362] IRC § 501(c)(27)(B)(iv). This exemption is available with respect to tax years beginning after December 31, 1997.

[363] IRC § 529(a).

state) under which persons may (1) purchase tuition credits or certificates on behalf of a designated beneficiary that entitle the beneficiary to the waiver or payment of qualified higher education expenses of the beneficiary or (2) make contributions to an account that is established for the sole purpose of meeting qualified higher education expenses of the designated beneficiary of the account.[364] The phrase *qualified higher education expenses* means tuition, fees, books, and equipment required for the enrollment or attendance at a college, university, or certain vocational schools.[365]

This type of program must provide that purchases or contributions may be made only in cash.[366] Contributors and beneficiaries are not allowed to direct any investments made on their behalf by the program.[367] The program is required to maintain a separate accounting for each designated beneficiary.[368] A specified individual must be designated as the beneficiary at the commencement of participation in a qualified state tuition program (that is, when contributions are first made to purchase an interest in the program), unless interests in the program are purchased by a state or local government or a tax-exempt charitable organization as part of a scholarship program operated by the government or charity under which beneficiaries to be named in the future will receive the interests as scholarships.[369] A transfer of credits (or other amounts) from one account benefiting one designated beneficiary to another account benefiting a different beneficiary is considered a distribution (as is a change in the designated beneficiary of an interest in a qualified state tuition program) unless the beneficiaries are members of the same family.[370]

Earnings on an account may be refunded to a contributor or beneficiary, but the state or instrumentality must impose a more than de minimis monetary penalty unless the refund is used for qualified higher education expenses of the beneficiary, made on account of the death or disability of the beneficiary, or made on account of a scholarship received by the designated beneficiary to the extent the amount refunded does not exceed the amount of the scholarship used for higher education expenses.[371] These programs may not allow any interest in the program or any portion of it to be used as security for a loan.[372]

A program cannot be treated as a qualified state tuition program unless it provides adequate safeguards to prevent contributions on behalf of a designated beneficiary in excess of those necessary to provide for the qualified higher education expenses of the beneficiary.[373]

In general, no amount is includable in the gross income of a designated beneficiary under a qualified state tuition program or a contributor to the program on behalf of a designated beneficiary with respect to any distribution or earnings

---

[364] IRC § 529(b)(1).

[365] IRC § 529(e)(3).

[366] IRC § 529(b)(2).

[367] IRC § 529(b)(5).

[368] IRC § 529(b)(4).

[369] IRC § 529(e)(1). An interest in a qualified state tuition program is not regarded as a debt for purposes of the unrelated debt-financed income rules (see § 29.1) (IRC § 529(e)(4)).

[370] The phrase *member of the family* is defined in IRC § 2032A(e)(2).

[371] IRC § 529(b)(3).

[372] IRC § 529(b)(6).

[373] IRC § 529(b)(7).

under the program.[374] A contribution to a qualified state tuition program on behalf of a designated beneficiary is not a taxable gift.[375] A distribution under a qualified state tuition program is includable in the gross income of the distributee in the manner as prescribed under the annuity taxation rules[376] to the extent not excluded from gross income under other federal tax law.[377] Thus, if matching-grant amounts are distributed to or on behalf of a beneficiary as part of a qualified state tuition program, the matching-grant amounts still may be excluded from the gross income of the beneficiary as a scholarship.[378]

Amounts contributed to a qualified state tuition program (and earnings on those amounts) are included in the contributor's estate for federal estate tax purposes in the event that the contributor dies before the amounts are distributed under the program.[379]

§ 18.17 STATES, POLITICAL SUBDIVISIONS, INSTRUMENTALITIES, ETC.

Still another type of tax-exempt entity, in a loose sense of the term, is a state. This tax exemption does not derive from any specific provision in the federal tax law, but is the result of the doctrine of *intergovernmental immunity*—the doctrine implicit in the U.S. Constitution that the federal government will not tax the states. The general principle is that the "United States may not tax instrumentalities which a state may employ in the discharge of her essential governmental duties."[380]

This tax exemption extends not only to the states but to integral parts thereof: political subdivisions, instrumentalities, agencies, and the like. This tax exemption is also available to the District of Columbia and to any territory. The IRS issues private letter rulings concerning organizations that do or do not qualify as governmental instrumentalities by reason of the intergovernmental immunity doctrine.[381]

The constitutional law basis for tax exemption or immunity is not unlimited; however, its scope has not been specifically delineated. The position of the U.S. Supreme Court was first that all "governmental" functions of a state were encompassed by the immunity and that only its "proprietary" activities could be taxed by the federal government.[382] Subsequently, the Court ruled that Congress could tax any "source of revenue by whomsoever earned and not uniquely capable of being earned only by a State," even though the tax "incidence falls also on a State."[383] Apparently, the *uniquely capable* test remains the standard.[384]

---

[374] IRC § 529(c)(1).
[375] IRC § 529(c)(2).
[376] IRC § 72.
[377] IRC § 529(c)(3).
[378] H. Rep. 737, 104th Cong., 2d Sess. 122 (1996).
[379] IRC § 529(c)(4).
[380] Helvering v. Therrell, 303 U.S. 218, 223 (1938). In general, Tucker & Rombro, "State Immunity from Federal Taxation: The Need for Re-examination," 43 *Geo. Wash. L. Rev.* 501 (1975).
[381] E.g., Priv. Ltr. Rul. 8842071.
[382] South Carolina v. United States, 199 U.S. 437 (1905).
[383] New York v. United States, 326 U.S. 572, 582 (1946).
[384] Massachusetts v. United States, 435 U.S. 44 (1978); Willmette Park Dist. v. Campbell, 388 U.S. 411 (1949). Cf. Davis v. Michigan Dept. of Treasury, 89-2 U.S.T.C. ¶ 9456 (Mich. Ct. App. 1989); State of S.C. v. Baker, 485 U.S. 505 (1988). Also Flint v. Stone Tracy Co., 220 U.S. 107, 172 (1911).

Notwithstanding the existence of a constitutional law immunity, Congress in 1913 enacted a broader statutory immunity. In its relevant portions,[385] this statutory immunity is available only for entities that exercise an "essential governmental function," and where the income thereby generated accrues to a state or political subdivision thereof. The IRS has long maintained that, by enacting the statutory immunity, "Congress did not desire in any way to restrict a State's participation in enterprises which might be useful in carrying out those projects desirable from the standpoint of the State Government . . ."[386] Thus, the IRS ruled that the income of an investment fund established by a state is excludable from gross income; even though more than one governmental entity participated in the fund, the requisite accrual was found.[387] Likewise, the IRS held that the income of an organization formed, operated, and funded by one or more political subdivisions (or by a state and one or more political subdivisions) to pool their risks in lieu of purchasing insurance to cover their public liability, workers' compensation, or employees' health obligations was excluded from gross income, as long as private interests did not, except for incidental benefits to employees of the participating state and political subdivisions, participate in or benefit from the organization.[388]

The question thus becomes: What type of entity can avail itself of the broader immunity? Commentators wrote that only a state or political subdivision of a state, and not a private corporation, may invoke this immunity, because only the former can perform an essential governmental function.[389] The courts appear to have reached the same conclusion, albeit for a different reason, namely, on the theory that the interposition of a corporation operates to prevent the requisite *accrual* from taking place.[390] These analyses, however, leave unanswered the question as to whether a corporation, such as a nonprofit corporation, can qualify for tax purposes as a political subdivision. The answer to this question has several ramifications, not the least of which is the ability of this type of entity to incur debt the interest on which is excludable from the recipient's gross income.[391]

In its narrowest sense, the term *political subdivision* connotes a jurisdictional or geographical component of a state, such as counties, cities, and sewer districts. Perhaps a more realistic definition of the term was provided by a federal court of appeals: The term *political subdivision* is broad and comprehensive and denotes any division of the state made by the proper authorities thereof, acting within their constitutional powers, for the purpose of carrying out a portion of these functions of the state that by long usage and the inherent necessities of government have always been regarded as public.[392]

---

[385] IRC § 115(a)(1).

[386] Gen. Couns. Mem. 14407.

[387] Rev. Rul. 77-261, 1977-2 C.B. 45, as *clar.* (on another point) by Rev. Rul. 78-316, 1978-2 C.B. 304.

[388] Rev. Rul. 90-74, 1990-2 C.B. 34.

[389] Tucker & Rombro, *supra* note 380 at 546–547.

[390] E.g., Troy State Univ. v. Comm'r, 62 T.C. 493, 497 (1974).

[391] IRC § 103. The U.S. Supreme Court ruled that the federal income tax exemption for mutual bond interest is not mandated by the Tenth Amendment to the U.S. Constitution or by the doctrine of intergovernmental immunity (State of S.C. v. Baker, *supra* n. 379).

[392] Comm'r v. Estate of Alexander J. Shamburg, 3 T.C. 131 (1944), *aff'd*, 144 F.2d 998 (particularly 1005) (2d Cir. 1944), *cert. den.*, 323 U.S. 792 (1944). Cf. Rev. Rul. 76-550, 1976-2 C.B. 331; Rev. Rul. 76-549, 1976-2 C.B. 330. Also Crilly v. Southeastern Pa. Transp. Auth., 529 F.2d 1355 (3d Cir. 1976); Popkin v. New York State Health & Mental Hygiene Facilities Improvement Corp., 409 F. Supp. 430 (S.D.N.Y. 1976).

These considerations take on greater coloration when applied in the context of organizations that are state-owned but have charitable counterparts, such as state schools, colleges, universities, hospitals, and libraries.[393] Certainly these entities are generally exempt from tax; the tax exemption derives in part, of course, from the constitutional immunity accorded the revenue of integral units of states. Can the exemption be likewise traced to this statutory immunity? Presumably, there is the requisite accrual; the provision of education has been regarded as the exercise of an essential governmental function.[394] By contrast, courts have held that, under certain circumstances, operation of a hospital is not an essential governmental function.[395] There is no case that specifically holds that, for example, a state college or university is a political subdivision, although this conclusion may be reached by a process of negative implication.[396] However, the IRS has asserted that a state university cannot qualify as a political subdivision because it fails to possess a substantial right to exercise the power to tax, the power of eminent domain, or the police power.[397]

The IRS issues private letter rulings on an ongoing basis as to organizations that do or do not qualify as political subdivisions.[398]

A third way for an organization to qualify for this type of tax-exempt status is to be an integral part of a state. The IRS issues private letter rulings on this subject on an ongoing basis.[399]

The rules as to whether an entity is a political subdivision, instrumentality, agency, or integral part of a state continue to become more inconsistent and confusing. One court of appeals evaluated the tax status of an organization established to receive advance payments of college tuition, invest the money, and ultimately make disbursements under a program that allows its beneficiaries to attend any of

---

[393] See Chapters 6, 7.

[394] Page v. Regents of Univ. Sys. of Ga., 93 F.2d 887 (5th Cir. 1937), *rev. on other grounds sub nom.* Allen v. Regents of the Univ. Sys. of Ga., 304 U.S. 339 (1938).

[395] Liggett & Myers Tobacco Co. v. United States, 13 F. Supp. 143 (Ct. Cl. 1936), *aff'd*, 299 U.S. 383 (1937), *reh. den.*, 300 U.S. 686 (1937); Cook v. United States, 26 F. Supp. 253 (D. Mass. 1939).

[396] Troy State Univ. v. Comm'r, *supra* note 390; Iowa State Univ. of Science & Technology v. United States, 500 F.2d 508 (Ct. Cl. 1974).

[397] Rev. Rul. 77-165, 1977-1 C.B. 21. In Tech. Adv. Mem. 8119061, the IRS held that a state university was not a political subdivision of the state (for purposes of eligibility for the interest exclusion for the university's obligations) because the university possessed no more than an insubstantial part of any sovereign power. The university did not have the power to tax nor the power of eminent domain, and the IRS concluded that the possession of certain powers to promulgate and enforce regulations in the areas of health and safety on the university's campus did not constitute the police power (citing Manigault v. Springs, 119 U.S. 473 (1905); Barbier v. Connelly, 113 U.S. 27 (1885)). The IRS noted that the campus police operated at the university under a scope of authority defined by state law rather than by the university, and that the campus police had the power to make arrests only for violations of the state's criminal law and not for violations of the university's rules and regulations that are not criminal in nature. The university also failed with its argument that the interest on its obligations should be tax-excludable because the obligations were issued "on behalf of" the state (principally inasmuch as the university was a state instrumentality and a land grant institution), with the IRS determining that the requisite degree of control by the state is absent, in that fewer than one third of the university's board of trustees are government officials or appointees of the governor of the state (see § 6.9). In general, Henze, "State Universities As Political Subdivisions," 9 *J. Coll. & U.L.* 341 (1982–1983).

[398] E.g., Priv. Ltr. Rul. 8737090. In general, Aprill, "Excluding the Income of State and Local Governments: The Need for Congressional Action," 26 *Ga. L. Rev.* 421 (Winter 1992).

[399] E.g., Priv. Ltr. Rul. 9507037 (updated by Priv. Ltr. Rul. 9522039).

the state's public colleges and universities without further tuition cost. The appellate court, having found that the entity was an instrumentality of the state, concluded that it was also an integral part of the state, so that its investment income is not taxable.[400] The court ruled that a state or political subdivision of a state is not a corporation for purposes of the federal corporate income tax.[401] It wrote that the "broad constitutional immunity from federal taxation once thought to be enjoyed by states and their instrumentalities has been severely eroded by the passage of time."[402] As to the law concerning the exclusion from taxation of income accruing to the state, the court characterized the rules as "very old and somewhat cryptic."[403]

§ 18.18 NATIVE AMERICAN TRIBES

Native American tribes generally are not taxable entities for federal income tax purposes.[404] These tribes generally have governing instruments, a council, operational rules, a formal membership arrangement, and various governmental powers, such as the rights to levy taxes, enact ordinances, and maintain a police force. The assets of an Indian tribe are owned by the tribe as a community (not by the individual members) and the right to participate in the enjoyment of tribal property depends on continuing membership in the tribe.[405]

Any income earned by an unincorporated tribe (including that from gambling and other commercial business activities), regardless of the location of the business activities that produced the income (that is, whether on or off the tribe's reservation), is not subject to federal income tax.[406] Tribal income not otherwise exempt from federal income tax is includible in the gross income of the Indian tribal member when distributed to, or constructively received by, the member.[407]

A native American tribal corporations organized under the Indian Reorganization Act of 1934[408] share the same tax status as the native American tribe and is not taxable on income from activities carried on within the boundaries of the reservation.[409] Thus, any income earned by this type of corporation, regardless of

---

[400] Michigan v. United States, 40 F.3d 817 (6th Cir. 1994). The district court ruled that this entity was not tax-exempt under the doctrine of intergovernmental immunity because it was not an integral part of the state and that its income could not be excluded from taxation pursuant to IRC § 115 because there was no accrual of income to the state (Michigan v. United States, 92-2 U.S.T.C. ¶ 50,424 (W.D. Mich. 1992)).

[401] IRC § 11. The court relied on Gen. Couns. Mem. 14407 (issued in 1935) as authority for this proposition.

[402] Michigan v. United States, *supra* note 400, at 822.

[403] *Id.* at 829. Subsequently, as discussed *supra* § 16, a statutory basis for tax-exempt status for tuition programs of this nature was enacted.

[404] Rev. Rul. 67-284, 1967-2 C.B. 55, *mod. on another issue*, Rev. Rul. 74-13, 1974-1 C.B. 14. Cf. Lummi Indian Tribe v. Whatcom County, Wash., 5 F.3d 1355 (9th Cir. 1993) (real property of a tribe was held not exempt from state property tax).

[405] Gritts v. Fisher, 224 U.S. 640 (1912).

[406] Rev. Rul. 94-16, 1994-1 C.B. 19.

[407] *Id.* E.g., Beck v. Comm'r, 67 T.C.M. 2469 (1994) (income received by a member of the Eastern Band of Cherokee Indians from the rental of apartment buildings located on a Cherokee reservation was held to not be exempt from federal income taxation).

[408] 25 U.S.C. § 477.

[409] Rev. Rul. 81-295, 1981-2 C.B. 15, which relied on Mescalero Apache Tribe v. Jones, 411 U.S. 145 (1973).

the location of the business activities that produced the income, is not subject to federal income tax.[410] Tribal corporations organized under the Oklahoma Welfare Act[411] have the same tax status.[412]

A corporation organized by a native American tribe under state law is not the same as a native American tribal corporation organized under the Indian Reorganization Act and does not share the same tax status as the native American tribe for federal income tax purposes. This type of corporation is subject to federal income tax on any income earned, regardless of the location of the income-producing activities.[413]

§ 18.19 OTHER TAX-EXEMPT ORGANIZATIONS

There are several other types of organizations or entities that may be regarded as tax-exempt organizations in the broadest sense of the term.

Some organizations are tax-exempt as a matter of practice, not because of any specific grant of tax exemption but because of the ability to utilize sufficient deductions to effectively eliminate taxation. As noted, this is the principle on which the general tax exemption for cooperatives is premised.[414] Likewise, a pooled income fund[415] is generally a nontaxpaying entity because it is entitled to a deduction for distributions to beneficiaries and for long-term capital gain set aside.[416] (By contrast, a charitable remainder annuity trust or unitrust[417] is an organization expressly exempt from tax except in years in which it has unrelated business taxable income.[418]) As discussed earlier, this approach will also provide "tax exemption" for perpetual care trust funds operated in conjunction with taxable cemeteries.[419]

Other entities achieve federal income tax exemption because the law regards them as organizations that, while they may have to file tax returns, do not

---

[410] Rev. Rul. 94-16, *supra* note 406.

[411] 25 U.S.C. § 503.

[412] Rev. Rul. 94-65, 1994-2 C.B. 14. Earlier law was clear that the fact that a native American tribe was incorporated did not alter its federal tax status (Maryland Cas. Co. v. Citizens Nat'l Bank of W. Hollywood, 361 F.2d 517 (5th Cir. 1966), *cert den.*, Maryland Cas. Co. v. Seminole Tribe of Fla. Inc. 385 U.S. 918 (1966); Parker Drilling Co. v. Metlakatla Indian Community, 451 F. Supp. 1127 (D. Alaska 1978); Rev. Rul. 81-295, 1981-2 C.B. 15).

[413] *Id.* However, the portion of Rev. Ru. 94-16, *supra* note 401, that applies to a corporation organized by an Indian tribe under state law is not applicable to income earned before October 1, 1994, from activities conducted within the boundaries of the reservation, including gain or loss properly allocable to the activities from the sale or exchange of assets (*id.*). IRC § 7871 provides that a qualified native American tribal government is treated as a state for certain federal income tax purposes, including the private foundation rules, unrelated business income rules, and the charitable contribution deductions. Although native American tribal governments do not have an inherent exemption from federal excise taxes, the IRS issued a ruling, founded on IRC § 7871, granting limited exemptions from some of these taxes (Rev. Rul. 94-81, 1994-2 C.B. 412).

[414] See § 3.4.

[415] IRC § 642(c)(5).

[416] Reg. § 1.642(c)-5(a)(2).

[417] IRC § 664.

[418] Reg. § 1.664-1(c).

[419] Also IRC § 852(a) (concerning regulated investment companies).

have taxable income but instead pass that liability on to others. It is this principle that operates to exempt partnerships[420] and small business ("S") corporations[421] from federal taxation.

§ 18.20 PROPOSED EXEMPT ORGANIZATIONS

Proposals continue to abound for statutory authorization of new types of tax-exempt organizations. These proposals include the following:

1. Tax exemption for public utilities that furnish electrical power (S. 2213 (1975)).

2. Same tax exemptions and other tax treatment to recognized native American tribes as are available for governmental units (H.R. 8989 (1975); H. Rep. No. 94-1693 (1976)).

3. Tax exemption for a trust established by a taxpayer for the purpose of providing care for certain mentally incompetent relatives (H.R. 584 (1979); H.R. 10582 (1978); H.R. 3932 (1977); H.R. 9736 (1975)).

4. Tax credit for contributions to "neighborhood corporations" (S. 2192 (1975)).

5. Tax exemption for certain nonprofit corporations all of the members of which are tax-exempt credit unions (H.R. 1153 (1977); H.R. 13532 (1976)).

6. Tax exemption for certain nonprofit organizations operated for mutual purposes to provide reserve funds for and insurance of shares or deposits in certain credit unions and domestic building and loan associations (H.R. 6989 (1978); H.R. 14039 (1976)).

7. Tax exemption for certain state and local government retirement systems (S. 1587 (1977); H.R. 9109 (1977)).

8. Tax exemption for associations operated exclusively to provide worker's compensation for state and local employees (H.R. 1074 (1979); H.R. 8470 (1977)).

9. Tax exemption for a product liability self-insurance reserve trust (H.R. 394, 1677, 1678, 1947, 2341, 2693, 2926, 2935, 3252, 4729, 6489 (1979–1980); H.R. 12471 (1978); H.R. 7711 (1977)).

10. Tax exemption for certain organizations furnishing computer and fiscal management services to social service organizations (H.R. 7207 (1978)).

---

[420] IRC § 701.
[421] IRC § 1372.

11. Tax exemption for an Energy Company of America (H.R. 3885, 4649, and 5622 (1979)).

12. Tax exemption for organizations of professionals (H.R. 990, 4724 (1979)).

13. Tax exemption for professional liability insurance organizations (H.R. 4427 (1979)).

14. Special tax treatment of certain physicians' and surgeons' mutual protection and indemnity associations ((Senate version of Tax Reform Act of 1984, H.R. 4170, 98th Cong., 2d Sess. (1984) § 866)).

15. Tax exemption for local police and fire associations that provide pension and other benefits that would otherwise be provided by a state or local government, to its members ((Senate version of Tax Reform Act of 1984, H.R. 4170, 98th Cong., 2d Sess. (1984)).

16. Tax exemption for certain nonprofit corporations and associations organized to provide reserve funds for domestic savings and loan associations (H.R. 6199 (1984)).

17. Separate category of tax exemption for college and university fraternities and sororities (H.R. 2189 (1985)).

18. Tax exemption for trust or corporation to facilitate collective investment in real estate by tax-exempt organizations, pension plans, and state and local governments (H.R. 3301 (1986)).

19. Tax exemption for organizations that assist in introducing into public use technology developed by operating research organizations (S. 2195 (1986)).

20. Tax exemption for self-insured workers' compensation associations (H.R. 1489 (1987); H.R. 1709 (1987)).

21. Tax exemption for certain Blue Cross and Blue Shield organizations (H.R. 2191 (1989)).

22. To deny tax-exempt status to certain politically active organizations that are linked to candidates for federal office and to require that contributions to separate political organizations that are linked to these candidates be treated as direct contributions (S. 2148 (1990)).

23. Tax exemption for industrial recapitalization funds for manufacturing industries (S. 2765 (1990)).

24. Imposition of a requirement that tax-exempt hospitals provide a certain amount of charity care and care to Medicare and Medicaid patients in order to maintain tax-exempt status (H.R. 5686 (1990), H.R. 790 (1991)).

25. Denial of tax-exempt status to educational institutions which have been found to have a policy of racial discrimination against any group in enrollment, hiring, or in other areas, until these institutions clearly and convincingly demonstrate their abandonment of the policy through the

enrollment, hiring, or the taking of other vigorous, affirmative, and continued corrective action with respect to such group (H.R. 181 (1991)).

26. Denial of tax-exempt status to rural electric cooperatives that have gross receipts in excess of $25 million (H.R. 1355 (1991)).

27. Linkage of a hospital's tax-exempt status with the level of charity care that the hospital provides (H.R. 1374 (1991)).

28. Denial of tax-exempt status, and charitable donee status, to organizations which directly or indirectly perform or finance procedures which take the life of a pre-born child other than procedures required to prevent the death of either the pregnant woman or pre-born child, so long as every reasonable effort is made to preserve the life of each (H.R. 1458 (1991)).

29. Tax exemption for common investment funds for private and community foundations (H.R. 2608 (1989), H.R. 1733, S. 588 (1991)). This proposal was the subject of § 4664 of the Revenue Act of 1992 (H.R. 11 (1992)), which passed Congress but was vetoed by the President.

30. Tax exemption for regional health alliances, as part of the Clinton Administration's health care reform legislation (H.R. 3600 (1993)).

31. Tax exemption for health risk pools (H.R. 3507 (1993); S. 539 (1995)).

32. Tax exemption (reinstitution of it) for the Teacher's Insurance and Annuity Association-College Retirement Equities Fund (S. 1142 (1997)).

General Exempt Organization Laws

Private Inurement, Private Benefit, and Excess Benefit Transactions

The doctrine of *private inurement* is the fundamental defining principle distinguishing *nonprofit organizations* from for-profit entities.[1] As a statutory criterion for tax exemption, it is applicable to nine types of tax-exempt organizations: charitable organizations,[2] social welfare organizations,[3] associations and other business leagues,[4] social clubs,[5] voluntary employees' beneficiary associations,[6]

---

[1] See § 1.1.
[2] See Part Two.
[3] See Chapter 12.
[4] See Chapter 13.
[5] See Chapter 14.
[6] See § 16.3.

teachers' retirement fund associations,[7] cemetery companies,[8] certain veterans' organizations,[9] and state-sponsored organizations providing health care to high-risk individuals.[10] That is, aside from being organized and operated primarily for an exempt purpose and otherwise meeting the appropriate statutory requirements, an exempt organization subject to the doctrine must comport with the federal tax law proscribing *private inurement*.

The oddly phrased and somewhat antiquated language of the private inurement doctrine requires that the tax-exempt organization be organized and operated so that "no part of . . . [its] net earnings . . . inures to the benefit of any private shareholder or individual."[11] In fact, it is rare for a tax-exempt organization to have any shareholders,[12] and the private inurement doctrine can be triggered by the involvement of persons other than individuals. The meaning of the statutory language today is that none of the income or assets of a tax-exempt organization subject to the doctrine may be permitted to unduly benefit a person who has some close relationship to the organization. The law pertaining to the private inurement doctrine, while applicable to many categories of exempt organizations, is the most developed in connection with charitable organizations.

To date, the body of law reflected in the *private benefit doctrine* has been applied only to charitable organizations. The rules pertaining to *excess benefit transactions* are applicable to public charities and social welfare organizations.

§ 19.1 ESSENCE OF PRIVATE INUREMENT

The concept of *private inurement*, while lacking precise definition,[13] is broad and wide-ranging. The word *inure* means to gravitate toward, flow to or through, or transfer to something. The term *private* is used in this setting to mean personal benefits and other forms of "nonexempt" uses and purposes. Consequently, the private inurement doctrine forbids the flow or transfer of income or assets of a tax-exempt organization (that is subject to the doctrine) through or away from the organization, *and* the use of such income or assets by one or more persons associated with, or for the benefit of one or more persons with some significant relationship to, the organization, for nonexempt purposes.

One pronouncement on the point from the IRS states that private "[i]nure-

---

[7] See § 16.6, text accompanied by note 93.

[8] See § 18.6.

[9] See § 18.10(a).

[10] See § 18.14.

[11] This phraseology has been characterized as a "nondistribution constraint" (Hansmann, "The Role of Nonprofit Enterprise," 89 *Yale L.J.* 835, 838 (1980)).

[12] The law in a few states permits a nonprofit corporation to issue stock; however, this type of stock does not carry with it rights to dividends. Thus, this body of law is not in automatic conflict with the private inurement doctrine.

[13] The U.S. Tax Court stated: "The boundaries of the term 'inures' have thus far defied precise definition" (Variety Club Tent No. 6 Charities, Inc. v. Comm'r, 74 T.C.M. 1485 (1997)). The advent and applicability of the rules concerning *excess benefit transactions* (see *infra* § 11) will undoubtedly bring some precision to the private inurement doctrine. Also, the specificity of the rules pertaining to self-dealing with private foundations (see § 11.4(a)) has brought additional examples of private inurement transactions.

ment is likely to arise where the financial benefit represents a transfer of the organization's financial resources to an individual solely by virtue of the individual's relationship with the organization, and without regard to accomplishing exempt purposes."[14] Another of these observations, more bluntly expressed, stated that the "inurement prohibition serves to prevent anyone in a position to do so from siphoning off any of a charity's [or other exempt organization subject to the doctrine] income or assets for personal use."[15]

The purpose of the private inurement rule is to ensure that the tax-exempt organization involved is serving exempt interests and not private interests. It thus becomes necessary for an organization subject to the doctrine to establish that it is not organized and operated for the benefit of private persons such as the creators of the organization, trustees, directors, officers, members of their families, persons controlled by these individuals, or any other persons having a personal and private interest in the activities of the organization.[16]

In ascertaining the presence of any proscribed private inurement, the law looks to the ultimate purpose of the organization involved: If its basic purpose is to benefit individuals in their private capacity (without thereby serving exempt purposes[17]), then it cannot be tax-exempt, even though exempt activities may also be performed. Conversely, incidental benefits to private individuals will not defeat the exemption, if the organization otherwise qualifies for tax-exempt status.[18]

The private inurement doctrine does not prohibit transactions between a tax-exempt organization subject to the doctrine and those who are *insiders* with respect to it.[19] Rather, the doctrine requires that these transactions be tested against a standard of *reasonableness*.[20] The *reasonableness* standard focuses essentially on comparisons, that is, on how similar organizations, acting prudently, transact their affairs in comparable circumstances. Usually, the terms of one or more of these transactions are tested against ordinary commercial practices; an overarching test is whether these transactions were negotiated on an arm's-length basis. Of course, a tax-exempt organization may incur ordinary and necessary expenditures in its operations without forfeiting its exempt status.[21]

---

[14] Gen. Couns. Mem. 38459.

[15] Gen. Couns. Mem. 39862.

[16] Reg. §§ 1.501(a)-1(c), 1.501(c)(3)-1(c)(1)(ii), 1.501(c)(3)-1(c)(2); Ginsburg v. Comm'r, 46 T.C. 47 (1966); Rev. Rul. 76-206, 1976-1 C.B. 154.

[17] In one instance, a court, in concluding that an organization that purchased and sold products manufactured by blind individuals constituted a tax-exempt organization, was not deterred in reaching this finding because of the fact that the organization distributed a portion of its "net profits" to qualified workers at a state agency; the court appeared to hold that these profit distributions were in furtherance of exempt purposes and were insubstantial (Industrial Aid for the Blind v. Comm'r, 73 T.C. 96 (1979)).

[18] Reg. § 1.501(c)(3)-1(d)(1)(ii).

[19] See *infra* § 3.

[20] This is also the standard underlying excess benefit transactions (see *infra* § 11) and private benefit transactions (see *infra* § 10); it usually is not the standard with respect to self-dealing transactions in the private foundation context (see § 11.4(a)).

[21] E.g., Birmingham Business Coll., Inc. v. Comm'r, 276 F.2d 476 (5th Cir. 1960); Enterprise Ry. Equip. Co. v. United States, 161 F. Supp. 590 (Ct. Cl. 1958); Mabee Petroleum Corp. v. United States, 203 F.2d 872 (5th Cir. 1953); Broadway Theatre League of Lynchburg, Va., Inc. v. United States, 293 F. Supp. 346 (W.D. Va. 1968).

Currently, the law generally holds that the relative insignificance of the private benefit conveyed does not serve as a defense to a charge of impermissible inurement, although that precept is undergoing reevaluation.[22]

§ 19.2 CONCEPT OF *NET EARNINGS*

In general, the term *net earnings* refers to gross earnings less expenses—a meaning that applies the term in a technical, accounting sense.[23] For example, a state supreme court addressed this definition at length in the early decades of the federal tax law. In one opinion, this court wrote that, since the term is not defined in the statute, it "must be given its usual and ordinary meaning of what is left of earnings after deducting necessary and legitimate items of expense incident to the corporate business."[24] This approach was followed in the early years by other state courts and by federal courts.[25]

However, in the context of tax-exempt organizations law, this technical definition of the term was never quite adequate as its sole meaning. Some courts applied the term in this restricted manner, where the facts particularly lent themselves to this approach,[26] but most court opinions on the point reflect the broader, and certainly contemporary, view that there can be inurement of *net earnings* in the absence of transfers of net income.[27] An early proponent of this view was another state supreme court, which observed that the *net earnings* phraseology "should not be given a strictly literal construction, as in the accountant's sense" and that the "substance should control the form," so that tax exemption should not be available where private inurement is taking place, "irrespective of the means by which that result is accomplished."[28] Likewise, a federal court foresaw today's application of the term when it held that *private inurement* "may include more than the term net profits as shown by the books of the organization or than the difference between the gross receipts and disbursements in dollars," and that "[p]rofits may inure to the benefit of shareholders in ways other than dividends."[29] This view represents the current application of the term

---

[22] See *infra* § 11(c), text accompanied by note 269.

[23] The statute, as originally written, employed the term *net income*. In 1918, the word *earnings* was substituted for *income*. There is nothing in the legislative history to suggest that this change had any substantive significance, and the commonality of the meanings of the two terms indicates that none was intended.

[24] Bank of Commerce & Trust Co. v. Senter, 260 S.W. 144, 151 (Tenn. 1924). Likewise, Southern Coal Co. v. McCanless, 192 S.W.2d 1003, 1005 (Tenn. 1946); National Life & Accident Ins. Co. v. Dempster, 79 S.W.2d 564, 567 (Tenn. 1935).

[25] E.g., Inscho v. Mid-Continent Dev. Co., 146 P. 1014, 1023 (Kan. 1915); United States v. Riely, 169 F.2d 542, 543 (4th Cir. 1948); Winkelman v. General Motors Corp., 44 F. Supp. 960, 1000 (S.D.N.Y. 1942).

[26] E.g., Birmingham Business Coll., Inc. v. Comm'r, *supra* note 20 at 480–481; Gemological Inst. of Am. v. Comm'r, 17 T.C. 1604, 1609 (1952), *aff'd*, 212 F.2d 205 (9th Cir. 1954); Putnam v. Comm'r, 6 T.C. 702, 706 (1946).

[27] E.g., Gemological Inst. of Am. v. Riddell, 149 F. Supp. 128, 130 (S.D. Cal. 1957); Edward Orton, Jr., Ceramic Found. v. Comm'r, 9 T.C. 533 (1947), *aff'd*, 173 F.2d 483 (6th Cir. 1949).

[28] Virginia Mason Hosp. Ass'n v. Larson, 114 P.2d 978, 983 (Wash. 1941).

[29] Northwestern Mun. Ass'n v. United States, 99 F.2d 460, 463 (8th Cir. 1938).

net earnings—as part of a standard assessing the use of a tax-exempt organization's income and assets[30]—although occasionally the term is still given a somewhat literal interpretation.[31]

Therefore, the contemporary concept of private inurement goes far beyond any mechanical computation and dissemination of *net earnings*, and embraces a wide range of transactions and other activities.

§ 19.3   THE REQUISITE *INSIDER*

It is clear that the concept of private inurement contemplates a type of transaction between a tax-exempt organization subject to the doctrine and one or more persons who have some special, close relationship to the organization. The federal tax law has borrowed the term *insider* from the federal securities laws (which prohibit, among other uses of the term, *insider trading*) and applies it to describe persons of this nature. Generally, an *insider* is a person who has a unique relationship with the organization involved, by which that person can cause the application of the organization's funds or assets for the private purposes of the person by reason of the person's exercise of control of or influence over the organization.[32] An *insider* includes an organization's founders, trustees, directors, officers, key employees, members of the family of these individuals, and certain entities controlled by them.[33] All of these persons have been swept into the insider category, from the starting point of the statutory language referencing "private shareholder or individual."

The caselaw is rich with opinions concerning the involvement of insiders in private inurement transactions.

Five individuals leased property to a school, which constructed improvements on the property; of this group, one was the school's president, two were

---

[30] E.g., Harding Hospital, Inc. v. United States, 505 F.2d 1068, 1072 (6th Cir. 1974).

[31] One federal court found that the term *net earnings* signifies funds used for expenses over and above expenses that are "ordinary and necessary" in the operation of a charitable organization (Hall v. Comm'r, 729 F.2d 632, 634 (9th Cir. 1984); Carter v. United States, 973 F.2d 1479, 1487 (9th Cir. 1992)).

A most unliteral interpretation of these rules occurred when a court held that "paying over a portion of *gross* earnings to those vested with the control of a charitable organization constitutes private inurement as well," adding that "[a]ll in all, taking a slice off the top should be no less prohibited than a slice out of net" (People of God Community v. Comm'r, 75 T.C. 127, 133 (1980) (emphasis in original)).

[32] American Campaign Academy v. Comm'r, 92 T.C. 1053, 1066 (1989). It was subsequently stated that the "case law appears to have drawn a line between those who have significant control over the organization's activities and those who are unrelated third parties" (Variety Club Tent No. 6 Charities, Inc. v. Comm'r, *supra* note 11, at 1492).

[33] In the setting of excess benefit transactions (see *infra* § 11) and self-dealing involving private foundations (see § 11.4(a)), the term *disqualified person* is used rather than *insider*.

The IRS expressed the view that all persons performing services for a tax-exempt organization are *insiders* with respect to that organization (Gen. Couns. Mem. 39670); this obviously is an overly broad reading of the concept. It was the position of the IRS that all physicians on the medical staff of an exempt hospital are insiders in relation to the hospital (Gen. Couns. Mem. 39498); however, this stance was ameliorated in the aftermath of enactment of the intermediate sanctions law (see *infra* § 11(c), text accompanied by note 268).

vice-presidents, and one was its secretary-treasurer. These four individuals were also directors of the school and constituted its executive committee. Private inurement was found in the form of "excessive rent payments [by which] part of the net earnings of . . . [the school] inured to the benefit of the members of the . . . group . . . and that part of the net earnings of . . . [the school] also inured to their benefit because of the construction at its expense of buildings and improvements on real estate owned by them."[34]

A foundation failed to achieve tax-exempt status because part of its net earnings was determined to have inured to its founder. The foundation made loans for the personal benefit of this individual and his family members and friends, made research expenditures to advance his personal hobby, and purchased stock in a corporation owned by a friend of his. A court concluded that the foundation was "organized in such a fashion that . . . [its founder] held control of its activities and expenditures; it was operated to carry out projects in which . . . [he] was interested and some of its funds were expended for . . . [his] benefit . . . or [for the benefit of] members of his family."[35]

Tax exemption was denied to a college that had five family members as all of its trustees and three of them as its shareholders, because of private inurement in the form of "constant commingling of the funds of the shareholders and the [c]ollege."[36] A court found that the college was "operated as a business producing, or ultimately producing, substantial revenues for its operators . . . [;] the net earnings, or substantial portions, were to be, and were in fact, distributed to these shareholders for their own personal benefit."[37]

A foundation, bearing the name of a radio personality, was established to provide musical instruction, proper living quarters, and medical assistance to young people interested in the entertainment field and who were featured in the shows of this entertainer. The foundation was found to be engaging in private inurement, inasmuch as in "these circumstances . . . [the entertainer] received a great benefit by establishing an organization whereby the recipients of the organization's charitable services were in his employ and benefiting him" and that "it was to . . . [his] advantage as a director of a radio program and as an employer to provide these services."[38]

An ostensible scientific research foundation was established by a physician; he and his father were two of its three trustees. A court found private inurement in the form of benefits to the physician in his medical practice. The foundation's laboratory, located next door to the physician's office, was, according to the government, used "on numerous occasions in his practice"; the foundation's principal activities were the treatment of patients (chiefly those of the physician). The court accepted the government's contention that the physician's "practice and the income therefrom were materially enhanced by the establishment of the laboratory."[39]

A church disbursed substantial sums to its founder and members of his

---

[34] Texas Trade School v. Comm'r, 30 T.C. 642, 647 (1958), *aff'd*, 272 F.2d 168 (5th Cir. 1959).

[35] Best Lock Corp. v. Comm'r, 31 T.C. 1217, 1236 (1959).

[36] Birmingham Business Coll., Inc. v. Comm'r, *supra* note 21, at 479.

[37] *Id.* at 480.

[38] Horace Heidt Found. v. United States, 170 F. Supp. 634, 638 (Ct. Cl. 1959).

[39] Cranley v. Comm'r, 20 T.C.M. 20, 25 (1961).

family, as fees, commissions, royalties, compensation for services, rent, reimbursement for expenses, and loans; the church maintained a personal residence for these individuals. Finding impermissible private inurement, a court observed that '[w]hat emerges from these facts is the inference that the . . . [founder's] family was entitled to make ready personal use of the corporate earnings. . . . [N]othing we have found in the record dispels the substantial doubts the court entertains concerning the receipt of benefit by . . . [this family] from . . . [the church's] net earnings."[40] With respect to certain of the disbursements, the court stated that the "logical inference can be drawn that these payments were disguised and unjustified distributions of . . . [the church's] earnings."[41]

A hospital's tax exemption was barred by a court, in part because of the advantages obtained by the physicians who organized the institution. Most of the patients admitted into the hospital were attended to by the founding physicians; the court's concern was an arrangement for management services by which these physicians were paid and a lease of office space. The court concluded that the hospital was the "primary source of the doctor's professional income" and that "this virtual monopoly by the . . . [physicians] of the patients permitted benefits to inure to . . . [them] within the intendment of the statute."[42]

The IRS revoked, on private inurement grounds, the tax-exempt status of a hospital organized and operated by a physician. The institution was held by a court to have distributed its earnings to the physician in the form of direct payments (compensation and loans), improvements to the property of a corporation he owned, administrative services relating to his private practice, and the free use of its facilities.[43] The same fate befell an organization established to study chiropractic methods, where the founding chiropractor sold his home, automobile, and medical equipment to the entity, and caused it to pay his personal expenses and a salary while he continued his private practice.[44] Likewise, the exemption of an organization was revoked because of several transactions, including the receipt of property from the founder's mother and payment to her of an annuity, payment of a son's college education, payment of the founder's personal expenses, and purchasing and leasing real estate owned by the founder.[45]

Private inurement precluded an ostensible religious organization from achieving tax-exempt status; its governing board consisted of its founder, his spouse, and their daughter. It conducted some ministry through its founder (who was also its principal donor) and made some grants to needy individuals selected by the founder. A court concluded that the founder's activities were "more personal than church oriented."[46] In similar circumstances, a court rejected an organization's claim of tax exemption because the organization provided its founder

---

[40] Founding Church of Scientology v. United States, 412 F.2d 1197, 1202 (Ct. Cl. 1969), *cert. den.*, 397 U.S. 1009 (1970).

[41] *Id.* at 1201.

[42] Harding Hosp., Inc. v. United States, *supra* note 30, at 1078.

[43] Kenner v. Comm'r, 33 T.C.M. 1239 (1974).

[44] The Labrenz Found., Inc. v. Comm'r, 33 T.C.M. 1374 (1974).

[45] Rueckwald Found., Inc. v. Comm'r, 33 T.C.M. 1383 (1974).

[46] Western Catholic Church v. Comm'r, 73 T.C. 196, 211 (1979), *aff'd*, 631 F.2d 736 (7th Cir. 1980), *cert. den.*, 450 U.S. 981 (1981).

and his family with "housing, food, transportation, clothing and other proper needs as may from time to time arise."[47]

A court's finding that a church was ineligible for tax-exempt status was based in part on its conclusion that a portion of the net earnings of the church inured to the benefit of its founder and his family. Indicia of this private inurement included unreasonable increases in salaries and payments of directors' fees, management fees, and other payments in support of the family. The court also labeled as private inurement the founder's practice of marketing books and other items in the name of the church, and being paid royalties for the sales, as well as to personally be paid royalties attributable to the literary efforts of employees of the church. Still other forms of private inurement were analyzed by the court, including "repayment of alleged debts in unspecified amounts and unfettered control over millions of dollars in funds" belonging to entities affiliated with the church.[48]

A community organization, with homeowners as members, was held to be engaging in private inurement transactions by providing "comfort and convenience" to the residents who, by reason of being the "intended beneficiaries" of the facilities and services of the organization, were found to have a "personal interest" in the activities of the organization.[49]

An ostensibly independent entity, such as a vendor of services, can be an insider with respect to a tax-exempt organization. This occurred, for example, when a fund-raising firm was found to be an insider in relation to a charitable organization for which it provided fund-raising services because of the extent to which the firm controlled and manipulated the charity. By reason of the arrangement between the parties, the charity was funded and otherwise kept in existence by the firm; this relationship, involving "extensive control" by the firm, was found to be "in many ways analogous to that of a founder and major contributor to a new organization."[50]

The IRS likewise has adopted the view that the private inurement prohibition relates only to circumstances where unwarranted benefits are provided to insiders. Thus, the IRS ruled that there was no private inurement where a tax-exempt hospital compensated a hospital-based radiologist on the basis of a fixed percentage of the revenue of the radiology department. This conclusion was arrived at, in part, because the radiologist "did not control" the hospital.[51] By contrast, a trust that was required to pay out its net income for tax-exempt purposes for a period of years or the lives of specified individuals was ruled by the IRS to not qualify for tax-exempt status. At the end of the income payment period, the trust terminated and the principal reverted to the founder of the trust or his es-

---

[47] Parshall Christian Order v. Comm'r, 45 T.C.M. 488, 492 (1983).
[48] Church of Scientology of Calif. v. Comm'r, 83 T.C. 381, 492 (1984), *aff'd*, 823 F.2d 1310 (9th Cir. 1987).
[49] Columbia Park & Recreation Ass'n, Inc. v. Comm'r, 88 T.C. 1, 24, 26 (1987), *aff'd*, 838 F.2d 465 (4th Cir. 1988).
[50] United Cancer Council, Inc. v. Comm'r, 109 T.C. No. 17 (1997). Indeed, the court wrote that, for these purposes, an insider is a person who has "significant control of the [exempt] organization's activities"; this definition is striking close to that of a disqualified person in the context of the excess benefit transaction rules (see *infra* § 19.11(c)). The court subsequently found an individual to be an insider where he "had a significant formal voice in . . . [a charitable organization's] activities generally and had substantial formal and practical control over most of . . . [the organization's] income" (Variety Club Tent No. 6 Charities, Inc. v. Comm'r, *supra* note 11).
[51] Rev. Rul. 69-383, 1969-2 C.B. 113, 114.

tate. The disqualifying feature in this regard was this reversionary interest, which resulted in inurement of investment gains over the life of the trust to the benefit of the creator of the trust.[52] The IRS observed that the "inurement issue . . . focuses on benefits conferred on an organization's insiders through the use or distribution of the organization's financial resources."[53]

Consequently, a tax-exempt organization subject to the private inurement doctrine should be concerned with the doctrine only where there is a transaction or transaction involving one or more *insiders* with respect to the organization. The most explicit court opinion on the point expressed the matter thus: The "concept of private benefit [inurement] . . . [is] limited to the situation in which an organization's *insiders* . . . [are] benefited."[54]

§ 19.4 TYPES OF PRIVATE INUREMENT

The concept of private inurement has many manifestations. While the most common example is excessive compensation, there are several other forms of private inurement, including sales of property, and transactions involving lending and rental arrangements. Although the concepts of private inurement and private foundation self-dealing are by no means precisely the same, the following summary of self-dealing transactions offers a useful sketch of the scope of transactions that may, in appropriate circumstances, amount to instances of private inurement: (1) sale or exchange, or leasing, of property between an organization and a private individual; (2) lending of money or other extension of credit between an organization and a private individual; (3) furnishing of goods, services, or facilities between an organization and a private individual; (4) payment of compensation (or payment or reimbursement of expenses) by an organization to a private individual; and (5) transfer to, or use by or for the benefit of, a private individual of the income or assets of an organization.[55]

An instance of a situation that distinguishes between private inurement and

---

[52] Rev. Rul. 66-259, 1996-2 C.B. 214.

[53] Gen. Couns. Mem. 38459.

[54] Sound Health Ass'n v. Comm'r, 71 T.C. 158, 185 (1978) (emphasis in original). Occasionally, the overwhelming domination of a tax-exempt organization and wrongdoing by an insider can lead a court into finding private inurement when in fact it is not present, usually because the court fails to apply a standard of reasonableness (e.g., Airlie Found., Inc. v. United States, 826 F. Supp. 537 (D.D.C. 1993), *aff'd*, 95-1 U.S.T.C. ¶ 50,279 (D.C. Cir. 1995)).

[55] IRC § 4941(d)(1)(A)–(E). See § 11.4(a). The IRS applied the self-dealing rationale on one occasion in an instance of a transaction involving a public charity and its directors (Rev. Rul. 76-441, 1976-2 C.B. 147), and the U.S. Tax Court essentially did the same (without expressly using the term) in a case concerning a church and its ministers (Church by Mail, Inc. v. Comm'r, 48 T.C.M. 471 (1984), *aff'd*, 765 F.2d 1387 (9th Cir. 1985)).

Private inurement does not occur when an insider steals money from a charitable organization. In a case where insiders stole proceeds from a charity's bingo games, private inurement was not found; the court wrote: "[W]e do not believe that the Congress intended that a charity must lose its exempt status merely because a president or a treasurer or an executive director of a charity has skimmed or embezzled or otherwise stolen from the charity, at least where the charity has a real-world existence apart from the thieving official" (Variety Club Tent No. 6 Charities, Inc. v. Comm'r, supra note 11).

self-dealing was provided in a case involving a museum that was structured as a private foundation. The museum made a low-interest loan to an incoming director, who was a disqualified person with respect to the museum. The IRS determined that, for every year the loan principal remained outstanding, an act of self-dealing occurs, inasmuch as an extension of credit by a private foundation to a disqualified person is an act of self-dealing.[56] However, the museum became qualified as a public charity (thus rendering the self-dealing rules inapplicable); the IRS valued the loan as part of the director's compensation package and found the package reasonable, thus causing the arrangement to not entail private inurement.

(a) Compensation for Services

The payment of reasonable compensation by a tax-exempt organization for services rendered does not constitute private inurement. (A tax-exempt organization subject to the private inurement doctrine may pay compensation to an employee in the form of a salary, hourly wage, bonus, commission, and/or the like, or make payments to a vendor, consultant, or other independent contractor.) Conversely, excessive compensation can result in private inurement.[57] Of course, whether the compensation paid is reasonable is a question of fact, to be decided in the context of each case.[58] One court observed that the "law places no duty on individuals operating charitable organizations to donate their services; they are entitled to reasonable compensation for their efforts."[59]

The process for determining reasonable compensation is much like that of appraising an item of property: It is an evaluation of factors that have a bearing on its value. That is, it is an exercise of comparing a mix of variables pertaining to the compensation of others; this alchemy is supposed to yield the determination as to whether a particular item of compensation is *reasonable* or *excessive*.

While the law is relatively clear as to the criteria to be used in ascertaining the reasonableness of compensation,[60] application of these principles is not always easy. Some preliminary concepts are relatively obvious. One is, as noted, that charitable and other exempt organizations can compensate individuals for services rendered. Another is that all forms of compensation paid to an individual by a tax-exempt organization are aggregated for this purpose; it is not merely a matter of the salary or the wage—bonuses, commissions, royalties, fringe bene-

---

[56] Priv. Ltr. Rul. 9530032.

[57] E.g., Harding Hosp., Inc. v. United States, *supra* note 30; Birmingham Business Coll., Inc. v. Comm'r, *supra* note 21; Mabee Petroleum Corp. v. United States, *supra* note 21; Texas Trade School v. Comm'r, *supra* note 34; Northern Ill. Coll. of Optometry v. Comm'r, 2 T.C.M. 664 (1943).

[58] E.g., Jones Bros. Bakery, Inc. v. United States, 411 F.2d 1282 (Ct. Cl. 1969), Home Oil Mill v. Willingham, 68 F. Supp. 525 (N.D. Ala. 1945), *aff'd*, 181 F.2d 9 (5th Cir. 1950), *cert. den.*, 340 U.S. 852 (1950).

[59] World Family Corp. v. Comm'r, 81 T.C. 958, 969 (1983).

[60] Nearly all of the law to date addressing the reasonableness of compensation is found in cases concerning payments by for-profit corporations. This is because a payment of compensation, to be deductible as a business expense (IRC § 162(a)), must be an *ordinary and necessary* outlay; the concepts of *reasonableness* and *ordinary and necessary* are essentially the same. If the IRS or a court finds that a portion of a payment constitutes excessive compensation, that amount is regarded as a dividend and thus is not deductible by the payor corporation. E.g., Rapco, Inc. v. Comm'r, 85 F.3d 950 (2d Cir. 1990); Leonard Pipeline Contractors, Ltd. v. Comm'r, 72 T.C.M. 83 (1996).

fits, retirement benefits, and the like are also taken into account. A third concept is that the amount of time an individual devotes to the task is a factor: An amount of compensation may be reasonable when paid to a full-time employee, yet be unreasonable when the employee is only providing services on a part-time basis.

There is a scheme of statutory law that is likely to clarify the process of determining reasonable compensation, both the procedure and the substantive elements to be evaluated. This body of law—termed *intermediate sanctions*[61]—is an alternative to the sanction of revocation of the tax exemption of the organization that participated in the private inurement transaction. The enactment of these rules is forcing clarification of the means by which reasonableness of compensation is determined.

The intermediate sanctions rules include a rebuttable presumption of reasonableness with respect to a compensation arrangement with a disqualified person if the arrangement was approved by an independent board of directors (or an independent committee authorized by the board) that (1) was composed entirely of individuals unrelated to and not subject to the control of the disqualified person(s) involved in the arrangement, (2) obtained and relied upon appropriate data as to comparability, and (3) adequately documented the basis for its determination (such as a record that includes an evaluation of the individual whose compensation was being established and the basis for determining that the compensation was reasonable in light of that evaluation and data).

As to the second criterion, the *appropriate data* are items such as (1) the compensation levels paid by similarly situated organizations, both tax-exempt and taxable, for functionally comparable positions; (2) the location of the organization, including the availability of similar specialties in the geographic area; (3) independent compensation surveys by nationally recognized independent firms; and (4) actual written offers from similar organizations competing for the services of the disqualified person.

The payment of personal expenses and benefits to disqualified persons, and nonfair-market value transactions benefiting these persons, are treated under these rules as compensation only if it is clear that the organization intended and made the payments as compensation for services. In determining whether the payments of transactions are, in fact, compensation, the relevant factors include whether the appropriate decision-making body approved the transfer as compensation in accordance with established procedures, and whether the organization and the recipient reported the transfer as compensation on the relevant federal tax forms.[62]

These criteria and processes for assessing the reasonableness of compensation are equally applicable in the private inurement setting.

A large salary or wage (in absolute dollar amount, not as a percentage of gross receipts) can be considered the receipt by the employee of the organization's net earnings, particularly where the employee is concurrently receiving other forms of compensation from the organization (for example, fees, commissions, royalties) and more than one member of the same family are compensated

---

[61] See *infra* § 11.

[62] These forms include the organization's annual information return (Form 990), the information return provided by the organization to the recipient (Form W-2 or Form 1099), and the recipient's individual income tax return (Form 1040).

employees.[63] Thus, where the control of an organization was in two ministers who contributed all of its receipts, all of which were paid to them as housing allowances, the tax exemption of the organization was revoked; the court said that the compensation was not "reasonable" although it may not be "excessive."[64] Yet large salaries and noncash benefits received by an organization's employees can be reasonable, considering the nature of their services and skills, such as payments to physicians by a nonprofit group that is an incorporated department of anesthesiology of a hospital.[65] Another basis for construing the presence of private inurement is where the compensation paid is reasonable but the year-to-year increases in it are not justifiable. For example, a court considered a case where three executives of a nonprofit organization had salaries in 1970 of $25,000, $16,153, and $5,790, and in 1978 of $100,000, $72,377, and $42,896, respectively. This was held to be an "abrupt increase" in the salaries and a "substantial amount" of compensation, leading to the conclusion that the salaries "are at least suggestive of a commercial rather than nonprofit operation."[66]

Other forms of compensation are subject to the private inurement doctrine. For example, although one court had held that an excessive parsonage allowance may constitute private inurement,[67] the same court ruled subsequently that another parsonage allowance was "not excessive as a matter of law."[68] Also, a split-dollar life insurance plan benefiting, in part, an organization's directors is considered a form of compensation.[69]

In one instance, a compensation arrangement based upon a percentage of gross receipts was held by a court to constitute private inurement, where there was no upper limit as to total compensation.[70] However, the court subsequently restricted the reach of this decision by holding that private inurement does not occur when a tax-exempt organization pays its president a commission determined by a percentage of contributions procured by him. The court held that the standard is whether the compensation is reasonable, not the manner in which it is ascertained. Fund-raising commissions, that "are directly contingent on success

---

[63] E.g., Founding Church of Scientology v. United States, *supra* note 40; Bubbling Well Church of Universal Love, Inc. v. Comm'r, 74 T.C. 531 (1980), *aff'd*, 670 F.2d 104 (9th Cir. 1981); Unitary Mission Church of Long Island v. Comm'r, 74 T.C. 507 (1980), *aff'd*, 647 F.2d 163 (2d Cir. 1981).

[64] Church of the Transfiguring Spirit, Inc. v. Comm'r, 76 T.C. 1, 6 (1981). Cf. Universal Church of Scientific Truth, Inc. v. United States, 74-1 U.S.T.C. ¶ 9360 (N.D. Ala. 1973) (where the organization retained tax exemption in part because its revenues came from charges for published materials and the expenses were not entirely for the compensation of its ministers).

[65] B.H.W. Anesthesia Found., Inc. v. Comm'r, 72 T.C. 681 (1979). Also University of Mass. Med. School Group Practice v. Comm'r, 74 T.C. 1299 (1980).

[66] The Incorporated Trustees of the Gospel Worker Soc. v. United States, 510 F. Supp. 374, 379 (D.D.C. 1981), *aff'd*, 672 F.2d 894 (D.C. Cir. 1981), *cert. den.*, 456 U.S. 944 (1982).

The IRS revoked the tax-exempt status of a health care institution on the ground of several instances of private inurement and private benefit, including several forms of compensation (Tech. Adv. Mem. 9451001; the institution is challenging this revocation (LAC Facilities, Inc. v. United States (No. 94-604T, U.S. Ct. Fed. Cl.)). In general, Griffith, "Compensation and Fraud Issues Trigger First Health Care Audit Revocation of the 1990s," 6 *J. Tax. Exempt Orgs.* (No. 6) 259 (May/June 1995).

[67] Hall v. Comm'r, 729 F.2d 632, 634 (9th Cir. 1984).

[68] Carter v. United States, 973 F.2d 1479, 1487 (9th Cir. 1992).

[69] Priv. Ltr. Rul. 9539016.

[70] People of God Community v. Comm'r, 75 T.C. 127, 132 (1980).

in procuring funds," were held to be an "incentive well suited to the budget of a fledgling organization."[71] In reaching this conclusion, the court reviewed states' charitable solicitation acts governing payments to professional solicitors, which the court characterized as "sanction[ing] such commissions and in many cases endors[ing] percentage commissions higher than" the percentage commission paid by the organization involved in the case.[72] Another court subsequently introduced even more confusion on these points when it held that "there is nothing insidious or evil about a commission-based compensation system" and thus that an arrangement, by which those who successfully procure contributions to a charitable organization are paid up to 6 percent of the gift amounts, is "reasonable," despite the absence of any limit as to an absolute amount of compensation (and despite the fact that the law requires the compensation to be reasonable, not the percentage by which it is determined).[73]

The IRS will closely scrutinize compensation programs of tax-exempt organizations that are predicated on an incentive feature by which compensation is a function of revenues received by the organization, is guaranteed, or is otherwise outside the boundaries of conventional compensation arrangements. These programs seem to occur most frequently in the health care context. For example, the IRS concluded that the establishment of incentive compensation plans for the employees of a hospital, with payments determined as a percentage of the excess of revenues over the budgeted level, will not constitute private inurement, where the plans are not devices to distribute profits to principals and are the result of arm's-length bargaining, and do not result in unreasonable compensation.[74] Using similar reasoning, the IRS approved of guaranteed minimum annual salary contracts under which physicians' compensation was subsidized in order to induce them to commence employment at a hospital.[75] Likewise, the IRS has explored other forms

---

[71] World Family Corp. v. Comm'r, *supra* note 59, at 970.

[72] *Id.* at 969. In general, see Hopkins, *The Law of Fund-Raising, Second Edition* (New York: John Wiley & Sons, Inc., 1996), Chapter 4 § 8.

[73] National Found., Inc. v. United States, 87-2 U.S.T.C. ¶ 9602 (Ct. Cl. 1987). In general, Steinberg, "Profits and Incentive Compensation in Nonprofit Firms," 1 *Nonprofit Mgmt. & Leadership* (No. 2) 137 (1990).

[74] Gen. Couns. Mem. 39674. In general, Lorain Avenue Clinic v. Comm'r, 31 T.C. 141 (1958).

[75] Gen. Couns. Mem. 39498. In general, Woodhill & Jones, "Hospital Recruitment Policies Can Endanger a Hospital's Exemption," 4 *J. Tax. Exempt Orgs.* 31 (Nov./Dec. 1992); Hyatt, "Physician Recruitment and Retention for Charitable Hospitals: In the Midst of a Sea Change?," 6 *Exempt Org. Tax Rev.* (No. 6) 1314 (1992). In the context of entering into a closing agreement with the tax-exempt Hermann Hospital, in Houston, Texas (reproduced in *Daily Tax Report* (BNA) (No. 200), Oct. 19, 1994, at L-1), the IRS promulgated physician recruitment guidelines by which certain permissible incentives are allowed, the others being forms of private inurement or private benefit.
   Subsequent to the issuance of these guidelines, the IRS promulgated guidance concerning the tax consequences of physician recruitment incentives (Rev. Rul. 97-21, 1997-18 I.R.B. 8). In general, Washlick, "Physician Recruitment Incentives and Tax Exemption—More Than the Code Is Involved," 7 *J. Tax. Exempt Orgs.* 212 (Nov./Dec. 1996); Mancino, "How to Retain Both Physicians and Exemption," 7 *J. Tax. Exempt Orgs.* 57 (Sept./Oct. 1995); Kaufman & Curry, "IRS Proposed Guidelines Allow for Reasonable Physician Recruitment Incentives," 83 *J. Tax.* (No. 3) 162 (Sept. 1995); Mancino, "Diverse Physician Recruitment Incentives Involve Common Tax Exemption Issues," 6 *J. Tax. Exempt Orgs.* 243 (May/June 1995); Peregrine, "The Proposed 'Physician Recruitment' Revenue Ruling: A Base Hit Instead of a Home Run," 11 *Exempt Org. Tax Rev.* 1025 (May 1995); Hyatt, "The New Physician Recruitment Revenue Ruling: The Right Approach," 11 *Exempt Org. Tax Rev.* 725 (Apr. 1995).

of productivity incentive programs[76] and contingent compensation plans.[77] Outside the health care setting, for example, the IRS concluded that a package of compensation arrangements for the benefit of sports coaches for schools, colleges, and universities, including deferred compensation plans, payment of life insurance premiums, bonuses, and moving expenses, did not amount to impermissible private inurement.[78] In one instance, the IRS approved of a "sharable income policy" by which a scientific research organization provided one-third of the revenue derived from patents, copyrights, processes, or formulae to the inventors and 15 percent of the revenue received from the licensing or other transfer of the organization's technology to valuable employees.[79]

Hospital audit guidelines issued by the IRS in 1992 contain a substantive review of the law, summarized above, concerning the form of private inurement known as "unreasonable compensation."[80] These guidelines specifically address private inurement transactions between hospitals and their physicians and senior executives (who, in the view of the IRS, are nearly always insiders), but they also apply to any category of tax-exempt organization where the private inurement rules are applicable. These guidelines reflect the fact that contemporary concerns at the IRS in this regard embrace incentive compensation plans, recruiting and retention incentives, purchases of physicians' practices, open-ended employment contracts, and compensation based on a percentage of the institutions' profits. IRS agents have been urged to review compensation contracts to determine whether they were negotiated at arm's length; where that is not the case (such as where a physician is also a member of the hospital's board of trustees or is a department head), the contracts are said to require "closer scrutiny."[81]

On occasion, private inurement entails excessive compensation coupled with some other impermissible element in the transaction. Thus, for example, not only was compensation paid by a charitable organization to a fund-raising firm (an insider with respect to it) determined to be excessive, private inurement was found in the manner in which the firm manipulated the use of the charity's mailing list for its own ends.[82]

In some instances, an individual will receive compensation (including fringe benefits) and/or other payments from more than one organization, whether or not tax-exempt. A determination as to the reasonableness of this compensation or other payments is made in the aggregate. Thus, for example, in the college and university examination guidelines developed by the IRS,[83] auditing agents are advised that, "[i]f an employee is compensated by several entities,

---

[76] E.g., Gen. Couns. Mem. 36918.

[77] E.g., Gen. Couns. Mem. 32453.

[78] Gen. Couns. Mem. 39670. Cf. Copperweld Steel Co.'s Warren Employees' Trust v. Comm'r, 61 T.C.M. 1642 (1991) (organization denied tax-exempt status by reason of IRC § 501(c)(3) because its primary purpose is the provision of compensatory fringe benefits).

[79] Priv. Ltr. Rul. 9316052.

[80] IRS Audit Guidelines for Hospitals ("hospital audit guidelines"), Manual Transmittal 7(10)69-38 for Exempt Organizations Examinations Guidelines Handbook (Mar. 27, 1992) §§ 333.2, 333.3. In general, Flynn, "Audit Guidelines Send Agents to All Corners of Hospital Operations," 4 J. Tax. Exempt Orgs. 9 (Nov./Dec. 1992).

[81] Hospital audit guidelines, *supra* note 80 § 333.2(2).

[82] United Cancer Council, Inc. v. Comm'r, *supra* note 50.

[83] See § 24.8(d).

even if the entities have independent boards or representatives, examine the total compensation paid to such person by all entities over which the institution has significant control or influence."[84]

Aside from the reasonableness of compensation, it is fundamental that a tax-exempt organization subject to the private inurement doctrine may not, without transgressing the doctrine, pay compensation where services are not actually rendered. For example, an organization was denied tax-exempt status because it advanced funds to telephone solicitors, to be offset against earned commissions, where some of the solicitors resigned before earning commissions equal to or exceeding their advances.[85]

(b) Equity Distributions

With the emphasis of the federal tax law, in the private inurement area, on *net earnings* and the reference to private shareholders, it is clear that the most literal and obvious form of private inurement would be the division of an organization's net earnings among those akin to shareholders, such as members of the board of directors. It is rare that such a blatant form of private inurement occurs. However, in one instance, this type of private inurement was identified.[86]

In that case, the assets of a tax-exempt hospital relating to a pharmacy were sold to an organization, which then sold pharmaceuticals to the hospital at higher prices. The court held that that practice amounted to the "siphoning off" of the hospital's income for the benefit of its stockholders.[87] Thereafter, apparently according to a preconceived plan, the corporation was dissolved and the sales proceeds distributed to its shareholders. While the court's reasoning is far from clear, the court observed that "[i]t is doubtful, too, whether an organization's operation can be 'exclusively' for charitable purposes . . . when its income is being accumulated to increase directly the value of the interests of the stockholders which they expect, eventually, to receive beneficially."[88] This separation of the pharmacy from the hospital resulted in the retroactive revocation of the tax-exempt status of the hospital. Moreover, the shareholders were held to have received capital gain on the transaction, because of the proprietary rights in the hospital evidenced by the stock.

In most states, nonprofit corporations, especially charitable and educational organizations, may not be organized as stock corporations. Even in the instances where tax-exempt organizations may have formal stockholders, the organizations may not pay dividends. Where the individual stockholders derive income from the

---

[84] Hospital audit guidelines, *supra* note 80 § 342.(15)(2).

[85] Senior Citizens of Mo., Inc. v. Comm'r, 56 T.C.M. 479 (1988). In general, Broeck, "Preventing Private Inurement by Measuring the Reasonableness of Compensation for Executives," 6 *J. Tax. Exempt Orgs.* (No. 1) 21 (July/Aug. 1994).

[86] Maynard Hosp., Inc. v. Comm'r, 52 T.C. 1006 (1969).

[87] *Id.* at 1027, 1032.

[88] *Id* at 1031. In another case, memberships in a tax-exempt charitable hospital were found to not entitle the members to a beneficial interest in the capital or earnings of the hospital because the law of the state prohibited the corporation from paying any part of its income to members and required transfer of the assets upon dissolution for charitable purposes (Estate of Grace M. Scharf v. Comm'r, 316 F.2d 625 (7th Cir. 1963), *aff'g* 38 T.C. 15 (1962)).

By contrast, a tax-exempt social club (see Chapter 14) may make liquidating distributions to its members following a sale of assets (e.g., Mill Lane Club, Inc. v. Comm'r, 23 T.C. 433 (1954)).

organization's operations through the medium of dividend payments, the organization cannot qualify as a charitable or many other types of tax-exempt organization.

(c) Retained Interests

A charitable organization may not be organized so that an individual or individuals retains a reversionary interest, by which the principal would flow to a private individual upon dissolution or liquidation; instead, in this event, net assets must pass for charitable or public, governmental purposes.[89] However, the acceptance of an income-producing asset subject to a reserved life estate will not result in private inurement, because only the charitable remainder interest is acquired; likewise, annuity payments in return for a gift of an income-producing asset are not a form of undue inurement, because the payment of the annuity merely constitutes the satisfaction of the charge upon the transferred asset.[90]

(d) Rental Arrangements

A tax-exempt organization subject to the doctrine of private inurement generally may lease property and make rental payments for the use of the property.[91] However, the rental payments must be reasonable, and the arrangement must be beneficial and desirable to the exempt organization. That is, inflated rental prices may amount to a private benefit inuring to the lessor.[92]

The above-noted hospital audit guidelines point out that one form of private inurement is "payment of excessive rent"[93] and state that "[a]reas of concern" include "below market leases."[94] The guidelines observe that auditing agents should be alert to the existence of "rent subsidies," noting that "[o]ffice space in the [tax-exempt] hospital/medical office building for use in the physician's private practice generally must be provided at a reasonable rental rate gauged by market data and by actual rental charges to other tenants in the same facility."[95] The guidelines state that it is permissible for a physician to use an exempt organization's facility for both hospital duties and private practice, as long as the "time/use of [the] office . . . [is] apportioned between hospital activities and private practice activities and a reasonable rent . . . [is] charged for the private practice activities."[96]

The factors to be considered include the duration of the lease and the amount and frequency of the rent payments, with all elements of the rental arrangement assessed in relation to comparable situations in the community.

---

[89] Rev. Rul. 66-259, 1966-2 C.B. 214.

[90] Rev. Rul. 69-176, 1969-1 C.B. 150. Also IRC §§ 642(c)(5), 664 (charitable contributions of remainder interests by means of pooled income funds and charitable remainder trusts).

[91] However, a rental arrangement between a disqualified person and a private foundation may constitute an act of self-dealing (see § 11.4(a)).

[92] E.g., Founding Church of Scientology v. United States, *supra* note 40, at 1202; Texas Trade School v. Comm'r, *supra* note 34.

[93] Hospital audit guidelines, *supra* note 80, § 333.2(1).

[94] *Id.* § 333.3(1)

[95] *Id.* § 333.3(7)(b).

[96] *Id.*

(e) Loans

A loan arrangement involving the assets of a tax-exempt organization subject to the private inurement doctrine are likely to be skeptically reviewed.[97] Like rental arrangements, the terms of this type of loan should be reasonable, that is, financially advantageous to the organization, and should be commensurate with the organization's purposes.[98] The factors to be considered when assessing reasonableness are the duration of the indebtedness, the rate of interest to be paid, the security underlying the loan, and the repayment amount—all in relation to similar circumstances in the community. If a loan is not timely repaid, questions of private inurement will almost assuredly be raised.[99] As has been noted, "the very existence of a private source of loan credit from an organization's earnings may itself amount to inurement of benefit."[100] Thus, for example, a school's tax exemption was revoked in part because two of its officers were provided by the school with interest-free, unsecured loans that subjected the school to uncompensated risks for no business purpose.[101]

A court found private inurement resulting from a loan where a nonprofit corporation, formed to take over the operations of a school conducted up to that time by a for-profit corporation, required parents of its students to make interest-free loans to the for-profit corporation. Private inurement was detected in the fact that the property to be improved by the loan proceeds would revert to the for-profit corporation after a 15-year term and that the interest-free feature of the loans was an unwarranted benefit to private individuals.[102]

This court earlier found private inurement in a case involving a tax-exempt hospital and its founder, who was a physician who operated a clinic located in the hospital building.[103] The hospital and the clinic shared supplies and services, and most of the hospital's patients were also patients of the founding physician and his partner. The hospital made a substantial number of unsecured loans to a nursing home owned by the physician and a trust for his children at below-market interest rates. The court held that there was private benefit to the physician because this use of the hospital's funds reduced his personal financial risk in and lowered the interest costs for the nursing home. The court also found inurement in the fact that the hospital was the principal source of financing for the nursing home, since an equivalent risk incurred for a similar duration could be expected to produce higher earnings elsewhere. In general, the court observed, "[w]here a doctor or group of doctors dominate the affairs of a corporate hospital otherwise exempt from tax, the courts have closely scrutinized the underlying relationship

---

[97] A loan arrangement between a disqualified person and a private foundation may constitute an act of self-dealing (see § 11.4(a)).

[98] Griswold v. Comm'r, 39 T.C. 620 (1962).

[99] Best Lock Corp. v. Comm'r, *supra* note 35; Rev. Rul. 67-5, 1967-1 C.B. 123.

[100] Founding Church of Scientology v. United States, *supra* note 63, 412 F.2d, at 1202. Also Unitary Mission Church of Long Island v. Comm'r, *supra* note 63; Western Catholic Church v. Comm'r, *supra* note 46; Church in Boston v. Comm'r, 71 T.C. 102, 106–107 (1978).

[101] John Marshall Law School v. United States, 81-2 U.S.T.C. ¶ 9514 (Ct. Cl. 1981).

[102] Hancock Academy of Savannah, Inc. v. Comm'r, 69 T.C. 488 (1977).

[103] Lowry Hosp. Ass'n v. Comm'r, 66 T.C. 850 (1976).

to insure that the arrangements permit a conclusion that the corporate hospital is organized and operated *exclusively* for charitable purposes without any private inurement."[104]

The above-noted hospital audit guidelines state that another form of private inurement is "inadequately secured loans,"[105] and that a loan used as a recruiting subsidy is appropriate (assuming the requisite need for the physician in the first instance) as long as the recruitment contract "'re(quire[s] full repayment (at prevailing interest rates)."[106] These guidelines provide the following factors, which the IRS is considering in determining whether a loan made to an insider is reasonable: (1) Generally, the loan agreement should specify a reasonable rate of interest (the prime rate of interest plus one or 2 percent) and provide for adequate security, (2) the loan decision should be reviewed by the board of directors of the tax-exempt organization and should include consideration of the history of payment of prior loans by the insider, and (3) even if determined reasonable, any variance in the terms of the loan from what the borrower could obtain from a typical lending institution must be treated, and appropriately reported, as compensation.[107]

(f) Provision of Goods, Refreshments

A tax-exempt organization subject to the private inurement doctrine cannot have as its primary purpose the provision of goods or refreshments (in the nature of social or recreational activities) to private individuals. Of course, the organization may incidentally bear the expense of meals and refreshments (for example, working luncheons, annual banquets), and the like, but, in general, "[r]efreshments, goods and services furnished to the members of an exempt corporation from the net profits of the business enterprise are benefits inuring to the individual members."[108] Thus, a discussion group that held closed meetings at which personally oriented speeches were given, followed by the serving of food and other refreshments, was ruled not to be tax-exempt, since the public benefits were remote at best and the "functions of the organization are to a significant extent fraternal and designed to stimulate fellowship among the membership."[109] Likewise, a school's tax exemption was revoked in part because the school paid for a variety of household items and furnishings used in the home of one of its officers.[110]

This aspect of private inurement frequently surfaces in the context of tax-exempt social clubs. These clubs must be organized and operated for pleasure, recreation, and other nonprofitable purposes, and the private inurement prohibition applies.[111] They must have an established membership of individuals, personal contacts and fellowship, and a commingling of members must play a

---

[104] *Id.* at 859.
[105] Hospital audit guidelines, *supra* note 80, § 333.2(1).
[106] *Id.* § 333.3(4).
[107] *Id.* § 333.3(10).
[108] Spokane Motorcycle Club v. United States, 222 F. Supp. 151, 1202 (E.D. Wash. 1963).
[109] Rev. Rul. 73-439, 1973-2 C.B. 176.
[110] John Marshall Law School v. United States, *supra* note 101.
[111] IRC § 501(c)(7). See Chapter 14.

material part in the life of the organization.[112] For example, this commingling requirement was satisfied in the case of a membership organization that provided bowling tournaments and recreational bowling competition for its members.[113] However, in this case, the IRS ruled that the awarding of cash prizes paid from entry fees did not constitute inurement of the organization's net income but was in furtherance of the members' pleasure and recreation.

(g) Services Rendered

An organization, the primary purpose of which is to render services to individuals in their private capacity, generally cannot qualify as a charitable entity. There are exceptions to this principle, such as where the individuals benefited constitute a bona fide charitable class, the individual beneficiaries are considered merely instruments or means to a charitable objective, or the private benefit is merely incidental.

This type of private inurement takes many forms and involves judgments governing in individual cases that are difficult to quantify. For example, the advancement of the arts has been seen to be a charitable activity.[114] However, a cooperative art gallery that exhibited and sold only its members' works was ruled to be serving the private purposes of its members ("a vehicle for advancing their careers and promoting the sale of their work") and hence not tax-exempt, even though the exhibition and sale of paintings may otherwise be an exempt purpose.[115]

Similarly, although the rendering of housing assistance for low-income families may qualify as an exempt purpose,[116] an organization that provided this form of assistance but gave preference for housing to employees of a farm proprietorship operated by the individual who controlled the organization was ruled to be not a charitable organization.[117] Also, a school's tax exemption was revoked in part because the school awarded scholarships to the children of two of its officers, yet made no scholarship awards to anyone else.[118]

The provision of services to individuals, as precluded by the private inurement proscription, takes many forms. For example, an organization created to provide bus transportation for school children to a tax-exempt private school was ruled to not be tax-exempt itself.[119] The IRS said that the organization served a private rather than a public interest, in that it enabled the participating parents to fulfill their individual responsibility of transporting children to school. The IRS concluded: "When a group of individuals associate to provide a cooperative ser-

---

[112] Rev. Rul. 58-589, 1958-2 C.B. 266.
[113] Rev. Rul. 74-148, 1974-1 C.B. 138.
[114] See § 6.7.
[115] Rev. Rul. 71-395, 1971-2 C.B. 228.
[116] See § 6.1.
[117] Rev. Rul. 72-147, 1972-1 C.B. 147.
[118] John Marshall Law School v. United States, *supra* note 101.
[119] Rev. Rul. 69-175, 1969-1 C.B. 149. Also Chattanooga Automobile Club v. Comm'r, 182 F.2d 551 (6th Cir. 1950).

vice for themselves; they are serving a private interest."[120] A testamentary trust established to make payments to charitable organizations and to use a fixed sum from its annual income for the perpetual care of the testator's burial lot was ruled to be serving a private interest.[121] Further, an organization that operated a subscription "scholarship" plan, whereby "scholarships" were paid to preselected, specifically named individuals designated by subscribers, was ruled to not be tax-exempt, since it was operated for the benefit of designated individuals.[122] Likewise, the furnishing of farm laborers for individual farmers, as part of the operation of a labor camp to house transient workers, was held not to be an agricultural purpose under federal tax law but rather the provision of services to individual farmers that they would otherwise have to provide for themselves.[123] Also, a nonprofit corporation was deemed to be serving private purposes where it was formed to dredge a navigable waterway, little used by the general public, fronting the properties of its members.[124] Further, an organization that provided travel services, legal services, an insurance plan, an antitheft registration program, and discount programs to its members was held to be serving the interests of the members, thereby precluding the organization from qualifying as a tax-exempt educational organization.[125] Morever, an organization was denied tax-exempt status because a substantial portion of its funds was to be used to pay for the medical and rehabilitative care of an individual who was related to each of the trustees of the organization.[126]

On occasion, the rule that unwarranted services to members can cause denial or loss of an organization's tax-exempt status leads to bizarre consequences. This general limitation is, from time to time, stretched—to bring about adverse consequences for the organization involved—far beyond what Congress surely intended in legislating the proscription on private inurement.

A classic illustration of this expansionist reading of the private inurement clause is the holding by a court that a genealogical society, the membership of which was composed of those interested in the migrations of persons with a common name (by birth or marriage) to and within the United States, failed to qualify as a charitable organization on the ground that its genealogical activities served the private interests of its members.[127] The society's activities included research of the

---

[120] Rev. Rul. 69-175, *supra* note 119, at 149.

[121] Rev. Rul. 69-256, 1969-1 C.B. 150.

[122] Rev. Rul. 67-367, 1967-2 C.B. 188.

[123] Rev. Rul. 72-391, 1972-2 C.B. 249. See § 15.2.

[124] Ginsburg v. Comm'r, *supra* note 14. Cf. Rev. Rul. 70-186, 1970-1 C.B. 128.

[125] U.S. CB Radio Ass'n, No. 1, Inc. v. Comm'r, 42 T.C.M. 1441 (1981).

[126] Wendy L. Parker Rehabilitation Found., Inc. v. Comm'r, 52 T.C.M. 51 (1986). This type of organization is, since 1987, precluded from tax-exempt status under either IRC §§ 501(c)(3) or (4) by reason of IRC § 501(m) (see § 22.1.).

[127] The Callaway Family Ass'n, Inc. v. Comm'r, 71 T.C. 340 (1978). This opinion presumably reinforces the published IRS ruling that genealogical societies in general qualify as IRC § 501(c)(7) organizations (see Chapter 14) (Rev. Rul. 67-8, 1967-1 C.B. 142). However, in an opinion handed down less than one month prior to the *Callaway Family Association* case, the U.S. Tax Court expressly recognized that a membership organization can qualify under IRC § 501(c)(3) where it provides information and services to both members and nonmembers (National Ass'n for the Legal Support of Alternative Schools v. Comm'r, 71 T.C. 118 (1978)).

"family's" development (primarily by collecting and abstracting historical data), preparation and dissemination of publications containing the research, promotion of scholarly writing, and instruction (by means of lectures and workshops) in the methodology of compiling and preserving historical, biographical, and genealogical research. The organization's underlying operational premise was that the growth and development of the continental United States can be understood by tracing the migratory patterns of a typical group of colonists and their descendants.

While the IRS and the court conceded that some of the society's activities were charitable and educational, they determined that the compilation and publication of the genealogical history of this "family" group was an activity that served the private interests of the organization's members. The court "note[d] specifically . . . [the organization's] emphasis on compiling members' family lives and the . . . [group's] family history" and held that "[a]ny educational benefit to the public created by . . . [the organization's] activities is incidental to this private purpose."[128] This rationale ignored the discipline of "kinship studies," in which social history focuses extensively on families and family-related institutions and strained to place a negative, private orientation on the term "family" when in fact the use of a family is merely a research technique whereby the tracings of genealogy are undertaken pursuant to an objective standard. This case presented a major threat to genealogical societies—particularly "family associations"—because of the opinion's characterizing of genealogical study as private inurement.[129]

Following this court holding, the IRS publicly ruled that a genealogical society may qualify as a tax-exempt educational organization by conducting lectures, sponsoring public displays and museum tours, providing written materials to instruct members of the general public on genealogical research, and compiling a geographical area's pioneer history. However, the organization's membership was open to all interested persons in the area, rather than members of any one "family," and the society did not conduct genealogical research for its members, although its members researched genealogies independently using the society's research materials.[130] By contrast, the IRS also ruled that an organization cannot qualify as a charitable or educational entity where its membership was limited to descendants of a particular family, it compiled family genealogical research data for use by its members for reasons other than to conform to the religious precepts of the family's denomination, it presented the data to designated libraries, it published volumes of family history, and it promoted occasional social activities among family members.[131]

---

[128] *Id.* at 344. Also Manning Ass'n v. Comm'r, 93 T.C. 596 (1989); Benjamin Price Genealogical Ass'n v. Internal Revenue Service, 79-1 U.S.T.C. ¶ 9361 (D.D.C. 1979).

[129] The U.S. Tax Court distinguished the general family association from the type of family association that engages in genealogical activities for religious purposes, usually one that is operated to collect and furnish information needed by the Mormon Church to advance its religious precepts (The Callaway Family Ass'n Inc. v. Comm'r, *supra* note 127, at 345). The IRS has ruled that the latter type of family association is a charitable entity because it advances religion (see § 6.4) (Rev. Rul. 71-580, 1971-2 C.B. 235.) Yet the definition of the term *charitable* also includes the advancement of education (see § 6.5) and the private inurement restrictions apply equally to all categories of *charitable* and other classes of tax-exempt organizations.

[130] Rev. Rul. 80-301, 1980-2 C.B. 180.

[131] Rev. Rul. 80-302, 1980-2 C.B. 182. In general, Johnstone, "Section 501(c)(3) Status for Nonreligious Family Associations Barred by Recent Cases," 53 J. Tax. 168 (1980).

Charitable organizations frequently provide services to individuals in their private capacity when they dispense financial planning advice in the context of designing planned gifts. This type of personal service made available by a tax-exempt organization has never been regarded as jeopardizing the organization's tax exemption. However, the IRS refused to accord tax exemption to an organization that engaged in financial counseling by providing tax planning services (including charitable giving considerations) to wealthy individuals referred to it by subscribing religious organizations. The court involved upheld the government's position, finding that tax planning is not an exempt activity and that the primary effect of the advice is to reduce individuals' liability for taxes—a private benefit.[132] The court rejected the contention that the organization was merely doing what the subscribing members can do themselves without endangering their tax exemption: fund-raising.[133]

The private inurement proscription may apply not only to separate individuals in their private capacity but also to corporations, industries, professions, and the like. Thus, an organization primarily engaged in the testing of drugs for commercial pharmaceutical companies was ruled not to be engaged in scientific research or testing for public safety but to be serving the private interests of the manufacturers.[134] Similarly, an organization composed of members of a particular industry to develop new and improved uses for existing products of the industry was ruled to be operated primarily to serve the private interests of its creators and thus not tax-exempt.[135] Further, an association of professional nurses that operated a nurses' registry was ruled to be affording greater employment opportunities for its members and thus to be substantially operated for private ends.[136]

(h) Assumption of Liability

As a general proposition, a tax-exempt organization can incur debt to purchase an asset at fair market value and subsequently retire the debt with its receipts, and not thereby violate the private inurement proscription.[137] However, if the purchase price for the asset is in excess of the property's fair market value, private inurement may result.[138]

In one instance, a nonprofit corporation was formed to take over the operations of a school conducted up to that time by a for-profit corporation. The organization assumed a liability for goodwill that the court involved determined was an excessive amount. The court held that this assumption of liability was a violation of the prohibition on private inurement because it benefited the private inter-

---

[132] Christian Stewardship Assistance, Inc. v. Comm'r, 70 T.C. 1037 (1978).

[133] Cf. discussion in § 26.5(i).

[134] Rev. Rul. 68-373, 1968-2 C.B. 206. Also Rev. Rul. 65-1, 1965-1 C.B. 266.

[135] Rev. Rul. 69-632, 1969-2 C.B. 120.

[136] Rev. Rul. 61-170, 1961-2 C.B. 112.

[137] E.g., Shiffman v. Comm'r, 32 T.C. 1073 (1959); Estate of Howes v. Comm'r, 30 T.C. 909 (1958), *aff'd sub nom.* Commissioner v. Johnson, 267 F.2d 382 (1st Cir. 1959); Ohio Furnace Co., Inc. v. Comm'r, 25 T.C. 179 (1955), *app. dis.* (6th Cir. 1956). Nonetheless, the acquisition of property by means of debt-financing may generate unrelated business income (see § 29.1).

[138] Kolkey v. Comm'r, 27 T.C. 37 (1956), *aff'd*, 254 F.2d 51 (7th Cir. 1958).

ests of the owners of the for-profit corporation.[139] (In a footnote, the court strongly suggested that any payment by a nonprofit corporation for goodwill constitutes a private inurement, since goodwill is generally a measure of the profit advantage in an established business and the profit motive is, by definition, not supposed to be a factor in the operation of a nonprofit organization.[140])

(i) Employee Benefits

The IRS looks skeptically on allegedly charitable organizations established to benefit employees, particularly where the entity is controlled and funded by the employer. Thus, a trust created by an employer to pay pensions to retired employees was ruled to not be a charitable organization.[141] This same result would obtain where the recipients are present employees,[142] in part because they do not constitute a charitable class.[143] Perhaps the best example of this rule is that of the foundation that lost its tax exemption because it devoted its funds to the payment of expenses of young performers employed by the foundation's founder, who was in show business.[144] However, organizations such as these (and also those that are supported by employees) may nonetheless qualify for tax exemption under other aspects of federal tax law.[145]

In one case, a school's tax exemption was revoked because, for one or more of its officers, it provided interest-free, unsecured loans, paid for household items and furnishings used in the private residence, made scholarship awards to their children, paid personal travel expenses, paid for their personal automobile expenses, paid the premiums on life and health insurance policies (where the premiums were not paid for anyone else), and purchased season tickets to sports events.[146] Yet, in another instance, a court concluded that the payment by a church of medical expenses for its minister and family did not constitute private inurement.[147] Likewise, a court found that the payment for medical insurance is an "ordinary and necessary" expense of a tax-exempt employer.[148]

Nonetheless, the IRS has come around to the view that charitable organizations (and thus other categories of tax-exempt organizations) may establish profit-sharing and similar compensation plans without causing prohibited private inurement,[149] having earlier taken the position that the establishment of qualified profit-sharing plans resulted in private inurement per se.[150] This alteration of position is based on the reasoning that the principles of qualification of

---

[139] Hancock Academy of Savannah, Inc. v. Comm'r, *supra* note 102.

[140] *Id.* at 494, note 6.

[141] Rev. Rul. 56-138, 1956-1 C.B. 202.

[142] Watson v. United States, 355 F.2d 269 (3d Cir. 1965); Rev. Rul. 68-422, 1968-2 C.B. 207.

[143] See § 5.5(a).

[144] Horace Heidt Found. v. United States, *supra* note 38.

[145] See IRC § 501(c)(9), (17). See §§ 16.3, 16.4.

[146] John Marshall Law School v. United States, *supra* note 101. Also Chase v. Comm'r, 19 T.C.M. 234 (1960).

[147] Brian Ruud Int'l v. United States, 733 F. Supp. 396 (D.D.C. 1989).

[148] Carter v. United States, *supra* note 68, at 1487.

[149] Gen. Couns. Mem. 39674.

[150] E.g., Gen. Couns. Mem. 35869.

pension and profit-sharing plans[151] and Title I of the Employee Retirement Income Security Act of 1974 are sufficient to ensure that operation of these plans would not jeopardize the tax-exempt status of the nonprofit organizations involved. Thereafter, legislation enacted in 1986 amended the employee plan rules to make it clear that tax-exempt organizations can maintain qualified profit-sharing plans[152] and extended certain deferred compensation rules to make them applicable to tax-exempt organizations.[153]

Tax-exempt organizations may maintain the qualified cash or deferral arrangements known as 401(k) plans.[154] A charitable organization may maintain a tax-sheltered annuity program[155] for its employees. In general, tax-exempt organizations may pay reasonable pensions to retired employees without adversely affecting their tax-exempt status.[156]

(j) Tax Avoidance Schemes

The IRS classifies tax avoidance schemes involving nonprofit organizations as representing a category of private benefit. Here, the IRS is concerned about the business or professional person who transfers his or her business assets to a controlled nonprofit entity solely for the purpose of avoiding taxes and then continues to operate the business or profession as an employee of the transferee organization. The IRS characterizes these schemes as follows:

> Transactions of this type are lacking in substance in the sense that the transferor is still, in effect, engaging in his business or profession in his individual capacity. Since the organization is operated by the transferor essentially as an attempt to reduce his personal Federal income tax liability while still enjoying the benefits of his earnings, the organization's primary function is to serve the private interest of its creator rather than a public interest.[157]

In one instance, a physician transferred his medical practice and other assets to a controlled organization, which then hired him to conduct "research," that is, examine and treat patients; tax exemption for the organization was denied.[158] In another case, an organization characterized as a church was formed by a professional nurse (who was the organization's minister, director, and principal officer). It held assets and liabilities formerly owned and assumed by the

---

[151] IRC § 401.

[152] IRC § 401 (a)(27).

[153] IRC § 457.

[154] IRC § 401(k)(4)(B)(i), effective for plan years beginning after December 31, 1996. Maintenance of these plans by exempt organizations was prohibited in 1986, although this prohibition did not apply to arrangements adopted before July 2, 1986 (Tax Reform Act of 1986 § 1116(f)(2)(B)). However, rural telephone cooperatives (see § 18.8) and certain other rural entities (as defined in IRC § 401(k)(7)) have been, as of November 10, 1988, eligible to maintain 401(k) plans.

[155] IRC § 403(b).

[156] Rev. Rul. 73-126, 1973-1 C.B. 220.

[157] IRS Exempt Organizations Handbook (IRM 7751) § 343.4.

[158] Rev. Rul. 69-266, 1969-1 C.B. 151. Also Nittler v. Comm'r, 39 T.C.M. 422 (1979); Walker v. Comm'r, 37 T.C.M. 1851 (1978); Boyer v. Comm'r, 69 T.C. 521 (1977).

nurse and provided the nurse with a living allowance and use of the assets (including a house and automobile). The organization was ruled to not be tax-exempt because the corporation "serves as a vehicle for handling the nurse's personal financial transactions."[159] A court in one case found that "tax avoidance" is a "substantial nonexempt purpose" of an organization, as evidenced by its promotional literature and seminars, and for that reason revoked the organization's tax-exempt status.[160]

Another court, unwilling to recognize an organization as a church because most of the organization's support was derived from its founder and the organization paid the living expenses of the founder, wrote that "[p]rohibited inurement is strongly suggested where an individual or small group is the principal contributor to an organization and the principal recipient of the distributions of the organization, and that individual or small group has exclusive control over the management of the organization's funds."[161]

(k) Joint Ventures with Commercial Entities

Tax-exempt organizations frequently become involved in partnerships or joint ventures with individuals and/or nonexempt entities.[162] Real estate ventures, with the tax-exempt organization as the general partner in a limited partnership, are a common manifestation of this practice. The IRS has a concern that some of these ventures may be a means for conferring unwarranted benefit on the private participants.

Nonetheless, one court decision sanctioned the involvement of a charitable organization as a general partner in a limited partnership. The case concerned an arts organization that, to generate funds to pay its share of the capital required to produce a play with a tax-exempt theater, sold a portion of its rights in the play to outside investors by means of a limited partnership. The arts organization was the general partner, with two individuals and a for-profit corporation as limited partners. Only the limited partners were required to contribute capital and they collectively received a share of any profits or losses resulting from production of the play. In disagreeing with the IRS position that the organization, solely by involvement in the limited partnership, was being operated for private interests, the court noted that the sale of the interest in the play was for a reasonable price, the transaction was at arm's-length, the organization was not obligated for the return of any capital contribution made by the limited partners, the limited partners had no control over the organization's operations, and none of the limited partners nor any officer or director of the for-profit corporation was an officer or director of the arts organization.[163]

---

[159] Rev. Rul. 81-94, 1981-1 C.B. 330. Also Rev. Rul. 78-232, 1978-1 C.B. 69. These two rulings concern the *personal church* (see § 8.2).

[160] Freedom Church of Revelation v. United States, 588 F. Supp. 693 (D.D.C. 1984).

[161] The Church of Eternal Life & Liberty, Inc. v. Comm'r, 86 T.C. 916 (1986). Also McFall v. Comm'r, 58 T.C.M. 175 (1989) (funds transferred to a "church" used to furnish a sports car for donor/pastor); Good Friendship Temple v. Comm'r, 55 T.C.M. 1310 (1988); Church of Modern Enlightenment v. Comm'r, 55 T.C.M. 1304 (1988); Petersen v. Comm'r, 53 T.C.M. 235 (1987).

[162] See Chapter 32.

[163] Plumstead Theatre Society, Inc. v. Comm'r, 74 T.C. 1324 (1980). Cf. Broadway Theatre League of Lynchburg, Va., Inc. v. United States, *supra* note 20.

In one instance, the IRS approved of a joint undertaking between a blood plasma fractionation facility and a commercial laboratory, by which the parties would acquire a building site and construct a blood fractionation facility on it. This arrangement enabled the facility to become self-sufficient in its production of blood fractions, to reduce the costs of fractionating blood, and thus to be able more effectively to carry out its charitable blood program. Each party had an equal ownership of, and shared equally in the production capacity of, the facility. The IRS concluded that the organization's participation in the joint undertaking was substantially related to its tax-exempt purposes.[164]

(l) Asset Sales to Insiders

Another application of the private inurement doctrine involves sales of assets of tax-exempt organizations to their insiders. It is becoming common for a charitable (and perhaps other tax-exempt) organization to decide to sell assets relating to a particular program activity, because the organization no longer wishes to engage in that activity. Sometimes, for a variety of reasons, these assets are sold to one or more individuals who are directors, officers, and/or other types of insiders with respect to the organization. An IRS private letter ruling issued in 1991 illustrates how the doctrine may apply in this setting.[165] This private letter ruling offers a case in point: A tax-exempt organization that operated a hospital, and had research and educational functions, determined to sell the hospital to gain income for the other exempt programs. Because of the highly specialized nature of the hospital facility, there was a limited market for its sale. Thus, the hospital was sold to a for-profit entity controlled by its board of directors.

Basically, the organization went about this process in the proper manner. It secured a valuation from a qualified independent appraiser. The property was sold at that value, which was $8.3 million (principally in cash and notes). No loan abatements or other special concessions were offered to the directors as purchasers of the hospital facility. The exempt organization took steps to ensure that it would use arm's-length standards in future dealings with the hospital. A ruling from the IRS was obtained to the effect that the transaction would not adversely affect the tax exemption of the organization.[166]

Soon after the sale, the purchasing organization began receiving inquiries as to resale of the facility. The new organization added beds to the hospital and obtained a certificate of need for additional beds. Less than two years after the initial sale of the hospital facility, it was resold. The resale price was $29.6 million. Each member of the board of the selling organization received in excess of $2.3 million as his or her share of the sales proceeds. The attorney general of the state involved filed a lawsuit, alleging that the initial sale price was not fair and reasonable. The court agreed, also concluding that the directors of the tax-exempt organization acted with a lack of due diligence. At trial, the facilities

---

[164] Priv. Ltr. Rul. 7921018.
[165] Priv. Ltr. Rul. 9130002.
[166] Priv. Ltr. Rul. 8234084.

were appraised using five appraisal methodologies; the conclusion was that the value of the assets at the time of the initial sale was approximately $18 to $21 million. A subsequent analysis by the IRS set the value of the facility at $24 million.

The factual question before the IRS was whether the tax-exempt organization received fair market value when it sold its hospital facility. A detailed analysis of the appraisals led the IRS to the conclusion that fair market value had not been received. The appraisals done for the court and the IRS were based on various appraisal methodologies; the appraisal relied upon by the tax-exempt organization used one. The IRS conceded that "no single valuation method is necessarily the best indicator of value in a given case." However, added the IRS, "it would be logical to assume that an appraisal that has considered and applied a variety of approaches in reaching its 'bottom line' is more likely to result in an accurate valuation than an appraisal that focused on a single valuation method." Having resolved that factual issue, the IRS concluded as a matter of law that the tax-exempt organization, in selling the hospital facility for substantially less than fair market value, contravened the private inurement doctrine. Accordingly, the organization's tax-exempt status was revoked, effective as of the date of sale of the facility.

In so doing, the IRS observed: "There is no absolute prohibition against an exempt section 501(c)(3) organization dealing with its founders, members, or officers in conducting its economic affairs." There is no doubt, however, that transactions of this nature will be subject to special scrutiny, with the IRS concerned about a (in the language of the ruling) "disproportionate share of the benefits of the exchange" flowing to the insiders. Thus, in this case, there was nothing inherently improper about the organization's decision to cease being a hospital and to sell the appropriate assets to an organization controlled by its directors.

Second, the organization followed the correct approach in acquiring an independent appraisal. In most circumstances, this would have been enough.[167] However, when the directors resold the hospital facility after approximately only a two-year period and experienced a $21.3 million dollar profit and a lawsuit by the state's attorney general (with the court having found a breach of fiduciary responsibility), the IRS determined that private inurement occurred.

This private letter ruling offers two points of IRS thinking that previously were not known. One is that a breach of fiduciary responsibility by the directors or trustees of a tax-exempt charitable organization under state law principles can be the basis for a finding of private inurement. The other is that the IRS prefers an appraisal that has "considered and applied a variety of approaches" in reaching a valuation rather than an appraisal that "focused on a single valuation method."

---

[167] For example, in the charitable giving setting, where an appraisal of contributed property is mandated, only a single appraisal is required (see Hopkins, *The Tax Law of Charitable Giving* (New York: John Wiley & Sons, Inc., 1993), Chapter 21 § 2.

§ 19.5 PRIVATE INUREMENT AND SOCIAL WELFARE ORGANIZATIONS

The private inurement doctrine was expressly added to the criteria for tax-exempt status for social welfare organizations[168] in 1996. Nonetheless, the IRS and the courts applied a generic version of the doctrine beforehand. For example, a social welfare organization was found to have not engaged in private benefit practices when it conferred most of its benefits on the employees of one corporation, with which the organization's founder had been affiliated, and the board of directors of which was composed solely of employees of the same corporation.[169]

A related body of law requires that a tax-exempt social welfare organization not be operated primarily for the economic benefit or convenience of its members.[170]

§ 19.6 PRIVATE INUREMENT AND BUSINESS LEAGUES

The private inurement doctrine is applicable with respect to business leagues.[171] This rule is related to the proscription on services to members. For example, private inurement was deemed present with respect to an organization that used its funds to provide financial assistance and welfare benefits to its members,[172] that paid its members for expenses incurred in malpractice litigation,[173] and that distributed royalties to its members.[174]

A related inurement concept concerns the impact on the level of members' dues as the result of the organization's receipt of nonmember income (that is, income other than membership dues). Basically, the question resolves itself on the issue of whether the activity is an unrelated trade or business,[175] although prior to the advent of those rules (in 1950) it had been held that a dues reduction occasioned by business earnings constituted private inurement.[176] Also, a business league may receive income from nonmember sources without losing its tax exemption where the income-producing activity is related to the tax-exempt purpose, such as a sports organization operating public championship tournaments,[177] a veterinarians' association operating a public rabies clinic,[178] an insurance agents association receiving commissions from handling insurance

---

[168] These organizations are the subject of Chapter 12.
[169] Eden Hall Farm v. United States, 389 F. Supp. 858 (W.D. Pa. 1975).
[170] See § 12.1(b).
[171] These organizations are the subject of Chapter 13.
[172] Rev. Rul. 67-251, 1967-2 C.B. 196.
[173] National Chiropractor Ass'n v. Birmingham, 96 F. Supp. 874 (N.D. Iowa 1951).
[174] Wholesale Grocers Exch. v. Comm'r, 3 T.C.M. 699 (1944).
[175] See Part Five.
[176] National Automobile Dealers Ass'n v. Comm'r, 2 T.C.M. 291 (1943). The IRS ruled that a tax-exempt association may have a tiered dues structure, with members paying varied amounts and those making payments to a related business league paying less dues, without causing private benefit (Priv. Ltr. Rul. 9448036).
[177] Rev. Rul. 58-502, 1958-2 C.B. 271.
[178] Rev. Rul. 66-222, 1966-2 C.B. 223.

programs,[179] and a professional association conducting a training program for nonmembers.[180] Thus, for example, an otherwise qualified tax-exempt business league can derive its support primarily from the sale of television broadcasting rights to the tournaments it conducts without imperiling its tax exemption, because the "sponsorship of tournaments and the sale of broadcasting rights with respect thereto by the organization directly promotes the interests of those engaged in the sport by encouraging participation in the sport and by enhancing awareness of the general public of the sport as a profession."[181]

Another private inurement issue of pertinence to tax-exempt trade associations concerns the tax consequences of cash rebates to exhibitors who participate in their trade shows. As a general principle, a qualified business league may make cash distributions to its members without loss of tax exemption where the distributions represent no more than a reduction in dues or contributions previously paid to the league to support its activities.[182] The IRS extrapolated from this principle in ruling that a trade association may, without adversely affecting its tax-exempt status, make cash rebates to member and nonmember exhibitors who participate in the association's annual trade show, where the rebates (1) represent a portion of an advance floor deposit paid by each exhibitor to insure the show against financial loss, (2) are made to all exhibitors on the same basis, and (3) may not exceed the amount of the deposit.[183] Because the "effect of refunding a portion of the floor deposits is to reduce the exhibitors' cost of participating in the trade show," the IRS concluded that the return of funds did not constitute inurement of net earnings.[184] If, however, a tax-exempt business league sponsoring an industry trade show, involving both member and nonmember exhibitors who are charged identical rates, makes space rental rebates only to its member-exhibitors, the rebates are considered proscribed inurement of income.[185]

§ 19.7   PRIVATE INUREMENT AND SOCIAL CLUBS

The private inurement doctrine is applicable with respect to social clubs.[186] For the most part, the application of this doctrine to tax-exempt social clubs focuses on the question as to whether nonmember use is generating revenue, the use of which (such as for maintenance and improvement of club facilities) is redounds unduly to the personal advantage of the members (as represented by reduced dues, improved facilities, and the like).[187] Even in this context, how-

---

[179] Rev. Rul. 56-152, 1956-1 C.B. 56.
[180] Rev. Rul. 67-296, 1967-2 C.B. 22.
[181] Rev. Rul. 80-294, 1980-2 C.B. 187, 188.
[182] E.g., King County Ins. Ass'n v. Comm'r, 37 B.T.A. 288 (1938).
[183] Rev. Rul. 77-206, 1977-1 C.B. 149. Also Rev. Rul. 81-60, 1981-1 C.B. 335.
[184] Rev. Rul. 77-206, *supra* note 183, at 149.
[185] Michigan Mobile Home & Recreational Vehicle Inst. v. Comm'r, 66 T.C. 770 (1976).
[186] These organizations are the subject of Chapter 14.
[187] See Chapter 14 § 2. Also Aviation Club of Utah v. Comm'r, 162 F.2d 984 (10th Cir. 1947); Knights of Columbus Council 3660 v. United States, 83-2 U.S.T.C. ¶ 16,410 (S.D. Ind. 1983), *aff'd*, 783 F.2d 69 (7th Cir. 1986).

ever, use of club facilities by the general public may not constitute proscribed inurement where the club contributes any net profits from a function (for example, a steeplechase[188]) to charity.[189] Infrequent public use is permissible as long as it is incidental and basically in furtherance of the club's purposes[190]—although considerable effort has gone into the matter of defining what is *incidental*.

The private inurement doctrine in this context can also become applicable where an otherwise tax-exempt social club has more than one class of members. It is the position of the IRS that, where membership classes in a club that enjoy the same rights and privileges in the club facilities are treated differently as respects dues and initiation fees, there is prohibited private inurement because the membership class that pays the lower dues and fees is being subsidized by the members of the other class(es).[191] Similarly, private inurement can arise where a club increases its services without a corresponding increase in dues or other fees paid for club support.[192]

Another dimension to the private inurement doctrine in this context invokes undue dealings between a tax-exempt social club and its members. For example, a social club was denied tax exemption because it regularly sold liquor to its members, for consumption off the club premises.[193] Likewise, a club that leased building lots to its members in addition to providing them recreation facilities was deemed not entitled to tax exemption.[194] In a somewhat comparable set of circumstances, the IRS ruled nonexempt a club operating a cocktail lounge and cafe as an integral part of a motel and restaurant business; about one-fourth of the club's "membership" was composed of persons temporarily staying at the motel.[195] However, private inurement is not involved where a tax-exempt social club pays a fixed fee to each club member who brings a new member into the club, as long as the payments are "reasonable compensation for performance of a necessary administrative service."[196]

A tax-exempt social club may provide social and recreational facilities to its members who are limited to homeowners of a housing development and nonetheless qualify for tax exemption. However, the exemption will be precluded where any of the following services are provided by the club: (1) owning and maintaining residential streets, (2) administering and enforcing covenants for the preservation of the architecture and appearance of the housing development, or (3) providing police and fire protection and a trash collection service to residential areas.[197]

---

[188] Rev. Rul. 68-119, 1968-1 C.B. 268.
[189] Rev. Rul. 69-636, 1969-2 C.B. 126.
[190] Rev. Rul. 60-323, 1960-2 C.B. 173.
[191] Rev. Rul. 70-48, 1970-1 C.B. 133.
[192] Rev. Rul. 58-589, 1958-2 C.B. 266.
[193] Rev. Rul. 68-535, 1968-2 C.B. 219. Also Santa Barbara Club v. Comm'r, 68 T.C. 200 (1977).
[194] Rev. Rul. 68-168, 1968-1 C.B. 269; Lake Petersburg Ass'n v. Comm'r, 33 T.C.M. 259 (1974).
[195] Rev. Rul. 66-225, 1966-2 C.B. 227.
[196] Rev. Rul. 80-130, 1980-1 C.B. 117.
[197] Rev. Rul. 75-494, 1975-2 C.B. 214.

§ 19.8 PER SE PRIVATE INUREMENT

As discussed, most instances of private inurement arise where a payment—such as compensation for services, rent, or interest—to one or more insiders is not reasonable or is excessive. However, there are forms of private inurement that have that status because they amount to *per se* private inurement. This means that the structure of the transaction is inherently deficient; private inurement is found in the very nature of the transaction. Thus, it is irrelevant, under this rule, that the benefit conferred on the insiders in some way also furthers the organization's exempt purposes and/or that the amount paid is reasonable. To date, this rationale has not been applied with respect to forms of compensation.

The doctrine of per se private inurement was publicly articulated when the IRS made known the view of its Chief Counsel's office on the impact on the tax-exempt status of a hospital involved in a joint venture with members of its medical staff, where the venture was sold, by the hospital, the gross or net revenue stream derived from operation of an existing hospital department or service for a defined period.[198] The IRS's view: The hospital jeopardized its tax exemption, on the ground of private inurement, solely by entering into the transaction.[199]

In arriving at this conclusion, the IRS Chief Counsel's office revisited the position taken in three private letter rulings issued in the 1980s. Essentially, the facts in these cases involved the purchase, by a joint venture or partnership, of the revenue stream of a hospital program.

For example, in the facts underlying one of these rulings, a limited partnership purchased the net revenue stream of a hospital's outpatient surgical program and gastroenterology laboratory.[200] The partnership consisted of a subsidiary of the hospital as the general partner and the limited partners were members of the hospital's medical staff. Likewise, in the facts of another of these rulings, a limited partnership (involving a hospital and members of its medical staff) acquired the gross revenue stream derived from operation of the hospital's outpatient surgery facility.[201] This was done to provide an investment incentive to the physicians to use the hospital's facilities. A for-profit venture had established a competing ambulatory surgery center less than five miles from the nonprofit hospital and was offering physicians on the hospital's medical staff ownership interests in the surgicenter to attract their business.

In these situations, the hospital continued to own and operate the facilities and to establish the amounts charged patients for their use. In these cases, the hospital paid the partnership the net revenue from operation of the facilities. At the time of the ruling request, the surgical facility in the first of these cases was only 54 percent utilized. The arrangement was undertaken to allow the hospital's

---

[198] Gen. Couns. Mem. 39862.

[199] Priv. Ltr. Ruls. 8942099, 8820093, and one unpublished 1984 ruling.

[200] Priv. Ltr. Rul. 8820093 (subsequently withdrawn (Priv. Ltr. Rul. 9231047)).

[201] Priv. Ltr. Rul. 8942099 (subsequently withdrawn (Priv. Ltr. Rul. 9233037)). Thus, the IRS is now of the view that these and other private letter rulings on the point were issued in error and they have been withdrawn (e.g., Priv. Ltr. Rul. 9231047, withdrawing Priv. Ltr. Rul. 8820093, *supra* notes 199, 200, and Priv. Ltr. Rul. 9233037, withdrawing Priv. Ltr. Rul. 8942099, *supra* note 199 and this footnote).

medical staff physicians to participate, on an investment basis, in the technical or facility charge component of the outpatient surgery program and gastroenterology laboratory. As part of the ruling request, the IRS was told that this arrangement would offer a financial incentive to the physicians to increase usage of the hospital's facilities. In each instance, the purchase price for the revenue stream was established at fair market value as the result of arm's-length negotiations, and was discounted to present value.

The IRS recognized that "there often are multiple reasons why hospitals are willing to engage in joint ventures and other sophisticated financial arrangements with physicians."[202] Two of these reasons are the "need to raise capital and to give physicians a stake in the success of a new enterprise or service." The hospital, in addition "to the hope for or expectation of additional admissions and referrals," may act "out of fear that a physician will send patients elsewhere or, worse, establish a new competing provider." However, the IRS added: "Whenever a charitable organization engages in unusual financial transactions with private parties, the arrangements must be evaluated in light of applicable tax law and other legal standards."

Its analysis of net revenue stream arrangements led the IRS to conclude that "there appears to be little accomplished that directly furthers the hospitals' charitable purposes of promoting health." The reason the hospitals entered into these arrangements is noted above: to retain and reward the physicians. However, wrote the IRS, "[g]iving (or selling) medical staff physicians a proprietary interest in the net profits of a hospital under these circumstances creates a result that is indistinguishable from paying dividends on stock." Thus, the private inurement prohibition was considered violated because "[p]rofit distributions are made to persons having a personal and private interest in the activities of the organization and are made out of the net earnings of the organization."

The IRS added that, in these cases, the "hospital's profit interests in those [charitable] assets have been carved out largely for the benefit of the physician-investors." The IRS' lawyers opined that "[t]his is enough to constitute inurement and is per se inconsistent with exempt status."[203]

Per se private inurement thus cannot be successfully defended with the argument that the amounts being paid (in the above cases, to the physicians) are reasonable. (It was the hospitals' position that the physicians were being paid to admit or refer patients or for giving up the right to establish or invest in a competing provider, and that these payments were reasonable.)

---

[202] Gen. Couns. Mem. 39862.

[203] In general, Mancino, "New GCM Suggests Rules for Ventures Between Nonprofit Hospitals and Doctors," 76 J. Tax. 164 (Mar. 1992); Bromberg, "IRS Announces New Position on Hospital-Physician Joint Ventures," 5 Exempt Org. Tax Rev. (No. 1) 31 (1992). In an unusual move, the IRS established a temporary "amnesty program" in connection with these net-revenue-stream joint ventures, by which a hospital could, prior to September 1, 1992, rescind the arrangement and enter into a closing agreement with the IRS concerning the tax consequences of the transaction (Ann. 92-70, 1992-19 I.R.B. 89).

§ 19.9 INCIDENTAL PRIVATE INUREMENT

It is the position of the IRS that there is no de minimis exception to the private in-urement doctrine; that is, there is no defense to an allegation of private inurement that it was merely *incidental*.[204]

Nonetheless, even though private inurement may be present in a situation, an argument can be made that tax exemption should not be denied for that reason if the private inurement is *incidental*. As an illustration, the IRS, having reversed an initial decision, ruled that an organization of accredited educational institutions was exempt as a charitable entity because the development of standards for ac-creditation of colleges is a charitable activity in that it constitutes the advancement of education.[205] The relevance of this ruling is that, although "very few" schools that had been approved for membership in the organization were proprietary in-stitutions, the IRS ruled that any benefit that may accrue to them because of ac-creditation was incidental to the purpose of improving the quality of education.

Similarly, where a business donated lands and money to a charitable entity to establish a public park, its exemption was not jeopardized by the donor reten-tion of the right to use a scenic view in the park as a brand symbol.[206] Also, in a situation involving a business corporation that provided a substantial portion of the support of a charitable organization operating a replica of a nineteenth cen-tury village, where the corporation benefited by having the village named after it, by having its name associated with the village in conjunction with its own adver-tising program, and by having its name mentioned in each publication of the or-ganization, the IRS ruled that "such benefits are merely incidental to the benefits flowing to the general public . . ."[207] Likewise, the IRS determined that a chil-dren's day-care center, operated in conjunction with an industrial company that enrolled children on the basis of financial need and the children's needs for the care and development program of the center, was tax-exempt because any benefit derived by the company or the parents of enrolled children was incidental to the public benefits resulting from the center's operation.[208] In another example, the IRS concluded that an otherwise tax-exempt educational organization may pro-duce public interest programs for viewing via public educational channels of commercial cable television companies because any benefit to the companies is "merely incidental."[209] Also, the IRS concluded that the sale of items on consign-ment by a thrift shop does not result in the loss of tax-exempt status, in that any benefit to the consignors is "clearly incidental" to the organization's charitable

---

[204] E.g., Gen. Couns. Mem. 35855. In Gen. Couns. Mem. 39862, the IRS's lawyers stated: "There is no de minimis exception to the inurement prohibition." (However, as indicated in the text, as a matter of law and practice, there is some minimal threshold embodied in the private inurement rule, per-haps analogous to the "incidental and tenuous" standard applied in the self-dealing context (see § 11.4(a).)

[205] Rev. Rul. 74-146, 1974-1 C.B. 129. Also Rev. Rul. 74-575, 1974-2 C.B. 161. Cf. Rev. Rul. 81-29, 1981-1 C.B. 329. See § 6.5.

[206] Rev. Rul. 66-358, 1966-2 C.B. 218.

[207] Rev. Rul. 77-367, 1977-2 C.B. 193.

[208] Rev. Rul. 70-533, 1970-2 C.B. 112.

[209] Rev. Rul. 76-4, 1976-1 C.B. 145.

purposes.[210] Likewise, a consortium of universities and libraries was advised by the IRS that it may, without jeopardizing its tax exemption, make its information dissemination services available to private businesses, since "[a]lthough there is some benefit to the private institutions such benefit is incidental to this activity and, in fact, may be said to be a logical by-product of it."[211]

By contrast, some courts—particularly the U.S. Tax Court—take the position that any element of private inurement can cause an organization to lose or to be deprived of tax exemption. For example, in one opinion, the court stated that "even if the benefit inuring to the members is small, it is still impermissible."[212] This interpretation of the law is reflected in other opinions as well[213] and, as noted, represents the formal position of the IRS.

The state—or future—of the law on this point is probably reflected in the view of one federal court of appeals, which observed that "[w]e have grave doubts that the de minimis doctrine, which is so generally applicable, would not apply in this situation [that is, in the private inurement setting]."[214]

§ 19.10 PRIVATE BENEFIT DOCTRINE

An organization cannot qualify as a charitable organization[215] where it transgresses the *private benefit doctrine*. The concept of private benefit, a derivative of the operational test,[216] is separate from the private inurement doctrine, yet is broader than, and in many respects subsumes, that doctrine.[217]

---

[210] Rev. Rul. 80-106, 1980-1 C.B. 113.

[211] Priv. Ltr. Rul. 7951134.

[212] McGahen v. Comm'r, 76 T.C. 468, 482 (1981), *aff'd*, 720 F.2d 664 (3d Cir. 1983).

[213] E.g., Gookin v. United States, 707 F. Supp. 1156, 1158 (N.D. Cal. 1988) ("any inurement, however small the benefit to the individual, is impermissible"); Unitary Mission Church of Long Island v. Comm'r, *supra* note 63, Beth-El Ministries, Inc. v. United States, 79-2 U.S.T.C. ¶ 9412 (D.D.C. 1979).

[214] Carter v. United States, *supra* note 68, at 1486, note 5, citing Texas State Teachers Ass'n v. Garland Independent School Dist., 489 U.S. 782 (1989) (civil rights plaintiff held to not be a prevailing party for purposes of an award of attorneys' fees where the success was technical or de minimis); Withrow v. Concannon, 942 F.2d 1385 (9th Cir. 1991) (only if a state's noncompliance with statutorily prescribed time periods for administrative action is de minimis does a court have the discretion not to issue an injunction); United States v. Johns, 891 F.2d 243 (9th Cir. 1989) (if the role of illegally obtained leads in discovery of evidence is de minimis, suppression of the evidence held to be inappropriate); Lindow v. United States, 738 F.2d 1057 (9th Cir. 1984) (de minimis rule applies in relation to total sum involved in litigation, precluding overtime compensation recovery for tasks otherwise compensable under the Fair Labor Standards Act where the time spent on tasks is de minimis).

In general, Hutton & Rowland, "The Inurement Rule and Ownership of Copyrights," 9 *Exempt Org. Tax Rev.* (No. 4) 813 (1994); Sevcik, "Inurement of Net Earnings to Shareholders or Individuals: A Challenge and a Danger to Exempt Organizations," 65 *Taxes* (No. 8) 519 (1987); Etzioni & Doty, "Profit in Not-For-Profit Institutions," 9 *Philanthropy Monthly* (No. 2) 22 (1976); Bromberg, "The Effect of Tax Policy on the Delivery and Cost of Health Care," 53 *Taxes* 452, 469–475 (1975); Note, "Section 501(c)(3) and Incidental Social and Recreational Activities," 22 *St. Louis U. L.J.* 225 (1967); Note, "'Inurement of Earnings to Private Benefit' Clause of Section 501(c)(3): A Standard Without Meaning?," 48 *Minn. L. Rev.* 1149 (1964).

[215] That is, an organization described in IRC § 501(c)(3).

[216] See § 4.5.

[217] E.g., Church of Ethereal Joy v. Comm'r, 83 T.C. 20, 21 (1984); Canada v. Comm'r, 82 T.C. 973, 981 (1984); Goldsboro Art League, Inc. v. Comm'r, 75 T.C. 337, 345, note 10 (1980); Aid to Artisans, Inc. v. Comm'r, 71 T.C. 202, 215 (1978).

The private benefit rule was articulated most fully by the U.S. Tax Court in a 1989 opinion.[218] The case concerned an otherwise tax-exempt school that trained individuals for careers as political campaign professionals; at issue was the benefit that accrued to entities of the Republican Party and its candidates, since nearly all of the school's graduates became employed by or consultants to these entities or candidates. The court concluded that the school was not primarily engaging in activities that accomplish educational purposes, because it benefited private interests to more than an insubstantial extent. That is, the school was found to substantially benefit the private interests of Republican Party entities and candidates.

The court noted that the prohibition against private benefit is not limited to circumstances where the benefits accrue to an organization's insiders. That is, the court held that this prohibition is not limited to persons having a personal and private interest in the activities of the organization, and embraces benefits to what the court labeled "disinterested persons."[219] Having thus defined the bounds (or lack thereof) of the private benefit doctrine, the court ruled that it was violated in this case. The court wrote that the school "conducted its educational activities with the partisan objective of benefiting Republican candidates and entities."[220] Elsewhere in the opinion, the court wrote that the school operated to "advance Republican interests."[221]

The heart of this opinion is the analysis of the concept of *primary* private benefit and *secondary* private benefit. In this setting, the beneficiaries of primary private benefit were the students and the beneficiaries of secondary private benefit were the employers of the graduates. It was the secondary private benefit that caused the school to fail to acquire tax exemption.

The court accepted the IRS's argument that "where the training of individuals is focused on furthering a particular targeted private interest, the conferred secondary benefit ceases to be incidental to the providing organization's exempt purposes."[222] The beneficiaries, at the secondary level, were found to be a "select group."[223] The "particular targeted private interest" and the "select group" were, in the court's view, the Republican entities and candidates served by the school's graduates.

The school unsuccessfully used as precedent several IRS revenue rulings holding tax-exempt, as educational organizations, entities that provide training to individuals in a particular industry or profession.[224] The court accepted the IRS characterization of these rulings, which was that the "secondary benefit provided in each ruling was broadly spread among members of an industry . . ., as opposed to being earmarked for a particular organization or person."[225] The court

[218] American Campaign Academy v. Comm'r, 92 T.C. 1053 (1989).
[219] *Id*. at 1069.
[220] *Id*. at 1070.
[221] *Id*. at 1072.
[222] *Id*. at 1074.
[223] *Id*. at 1076.
[224] Rev. Rul. 75-196, 1975-1 C.B. 155; Rev. Rul. 72-101, 1972-1 C.B. 144; Rev. Rul. 68-504, 1968-2 C.B. 211; Rev. Rul. 67-72, 1967-1 C.B. 125.
[225] American Campaign Academy v. Comm'r, *supra* note 218, at 1074.

said that the secondary benefit in each of these rulings was because of the spread, "therefore incidental to the providing organization's exempt purpose."[226]

Although charitable and certain other types of tax-exempt organizations may provide benefits to private individuals, benefits of this nature must—to avoid jeopardizing tax-exempt status—be incidental both quantitatively and qualitatively in relation to the furthering of tax-exempt purposes. To be quantitatively incidental, the private benefit must be insubstantial, measured in the context of the overall tax-exempt benefit conferred by the activity.[227] To be qualitatively incidental, private benefit must be a necessary concomitant of the exempt activity, in that the exempt objectives cannot be achieved without necessarily benefiting certain private individuals.[228] As an illustration, a nonprofit organization was formed to generate community interest in retaining classical music programs on a commercial radio station, by seeking sponsors for the programs, urging listeners to patronize the sponsors, and soliciting listener subscriptions to promote the programs; the IRS ruled that the organization could not qualify for tax exemption because these activities increased the station's revenues and thus benefited it in more than an incidental manner.[229] By contrast, a charitable organization that allocated Medicaid patients to physicians in private practice was held to provide qualitatively and quantitatively incidental private benefits to the physicians, including some on the organization's board of directors, since it would be "impossible" for the organization to accomplish its exempt purposes without providing some measure of benefit to the physicians.[230]

Thus, the principal distinctions between the private inurement doctrine and the private benefit doctrine are that the law is clear that there can be incidental private benefit and that the private benefit doctrine can operate without the involvement of insiders.

§ 19.11 INTERMEDIATE SANCTIONS

The concept of *intermediate sanctions* involving public charities and social welfare organizations—an emphasis on the taxation of those persons who engaged in impermissible private transactions with these entities, rather than revocation of the entities' tax exemption—was added to the federal tax law in 1996. With this approach, tax sanctions—structured as penalty excise taxes—may be imposed on the disqualified persons (defined below) who improperly benefited from the transaction and on the organization managers (defined below) who participated in the transaction knowing that it was improper.

---

[226] *Id.*

[227] E.g., Ginsburg v. Comm'r, *supra* note 16; Rev. Rul. 75-286, 1975-2 C.B. 210; Rev. Rul. 70-186, 1970-1 C.B. 128; Rev. Rul. 68-14, 1968-1 C.B. 243.

[228] E.g., Rev. Rul. 70-186, *supra* note 227.

[229] Rev. Rul. 76-206, *supra* note 16.

[230] Priv. Ltr. Rul. 9615030.

This body of law[231] represents the most dramatic and important package of rules concerning exempt charitable organizations since Congress enacted the basic statutory scheme in this field in 1969.[232] In addition to reshaping and expanding the private inurement and private benefit doctrines, intermediate sanctions are likely to impact the composition and functioning of many boards of directors of tax-exempt organizations.

(a) Exempt Organizations Involved

As noted, these sanctions apply with respect to tax-exempt public charities[233] and tax-exempt social welfare organizations.[234] These entities are termed, for this purpose, *applicable tax-exempt organizations*.[235] Organizations of this nature include any organization described in either of these two categories of exempt organizations at any time during the five-year period ending on the date of the transaction.[236]

There are no exemptions from these rules. That is, all tax-exempt public charities and all tax-exempt social welfare organizations are applicable tax-exempt organizations.[237]

(b) Excess Benefit Transactions

This tax scheme has as its heart the *excess benefit transaction*. In the instance of one of these transactions, tax sanctions are imposed on the disqualified person or persons who improperly benefited from the transaction and perhaps on any organization managers who participated in the transaction knowing that it was improper.

An excess benefit transaction is any transaction in which an economic bene-

---

[231] IRC § 4958, enacted by § 1311(a) of the Taxpayer Bill of Rights 2, Pub. L. No. 168, 104th Cong., 2d Sess. (1996), 110 Stat. 1452 (for purposes of this § 11, "Act"). The report of the House Committee on Ways and Means, dated March 28, 1996 (H. Rep. 104-506, 104th Cong., 2d Sess. (1996)) (for purpose of this § 11, "House Report"), constitutes the totality of the legislative history of the intermediate sanctions rules. The IRS provided a brief summary of the intermediate sanctions rules in Notice 96-46, 1996-2 C.B. 212.

[232] A substantial portion of the Tax Reform Act of 1969 consists of enactment of law defining *public charities* and *private foundations* and imposing stringent rules of operations concerning these foundations. Much of the motivation for creation of the foundation rules—fear of considerable abuses—is mirrored in the reason for adoption of the intermediate sanctions rules.

[233] A *public charity* is an organization that is tax-exempt for federal income tax purposes (IRC § 501(a)) because it is a charitable, educational, scientific, or like organization (that is, is described in IRC § 501(c)(3)); this type of charitable organization is not (by reason of IRC § 509(a)) a private foundation. The law of public charities is the subject of § 11.3.

[234] A *social welfare organization* is an organization that is tax-exempt for federal income tax purposes (IRC § 501(a)) because it is described in IRC § 501(c)(4). The law of social welfare organizations is the subject of Chapter 12.

[235] IRC § 4958(e)(1).

[236] IRC § 4958(e)(2).

[237] Private foundations (see *supra* note 232) are not included in this tax regime because a somewhat similar system—that involving self-dealing rules (IRC § 4941)—is applicable to them. The self-dealing rules are the subject of § 11.4(a).

fit is provided by an applicable tax-exempt organization directly or indirectly to or for the use of any disqualified person, if the value of the economic benefit provided by the exempt organization exceeds the value of the consideration (including the performance of services) received for providing the benefit.[238] This type of benefit is known as an *excess benefit*.[239]

An economic benefit may not be treated as consideration for the performance of services unless the organization clearly intended and made the payments as compensation for services.[240] Items of this nature include the payment of personal expenses, transfers to or for the benefit of disqualified persons, and non-fair-market-value transactions benefiting these persons.[241] In determining whether payments or transactions of this nature are in fact forms of compensation, the relevant factors include whether (1) the appropriate decision-making body approved the transfer as compensation in accordance with established procedures and (2) the organization and the recipient reported the transfer (other than in the case of nontaxable fringe benefits) as compensation on relevant returns or other forms.[242]

With the exception of nontaxable fringe benefits[243] and certain other types of nontaxable transfers (such as employer-provided health benefits and contributions to qualified pension plans), an organization is not permitted to demonstrate at the time of an IRS audit that it intended to treat economic benefits provided to a disqualified person as compensation for services merely by claiming that the benefits may be viewed as part of the disqualified person's total compensation package. Rather, the organization is required to provide substantiation that is contemporaneous with the transfer of the economic benefits at issue.[244]

The phraseology *directly or indirectly* means the provision of an economic benefit directly by the organization or indirectly by means of a controlled entity. Thus, an applicable tax-exempt organization cannot avoid involvement in an excess benefit transaction by causing a controlled entity to engage in the transaction.[245]

Also, to the extent to be provided in tax regulations, the term *excess benefit transaction* includes any transaction in which the amount of any economic benefit provided to or for the use of a disqualified person is determined in whole or in part by the revenues of one or more activities of the organization, but only if the transaction results in impermissible private inurement.[246] In this context, the excess benefit is the amount of impermissible private inurement.[247]

Thus, excess benefit transactions include (1) transactions in which a disqual-

---

[238] IRC § 4958(c)(1)(A).

[239] IRC § 4958(c)(1)(B).

[240] IRC § 4958(c)(1)(A).

[241] House Report at 57.

[242] These returns or forms include the organization's annual information return filed with the IRS (usually Form 990), the information return provided by the organization to the recipient (Form W-2 or Form 1099), and the individual's income tax return (Form 1040) (House Report at 57).

[243] IRC § 132.

[244] House Report at 57, note 8.

[245] *Id.* at 56, note 3.

[246] IRC § 4958(c)(2).

[247] *Id.*

ified person engages in a non-fair-market-value transaction with an applicable tax-exempt organization or receives unreasonable compensation, and (2) financial arrangements (to the extent to be provided in tax regulations) under which a disqualified person receives payment based on the organization's income in a transaction that violates the private inurement rules. This latter category of arrangement is known as a *revenue-sharing arrangement*. The Department of the Treasury has been instructed to promptly issue guidance providing examples of revenue-sharing arrangements that violate the private inurement prohibition. This guidance will be applicable prospectively.[248]

Under preexisting law, certain revenue-sharing arrangements have been determined by the IRS to not constitute private inurement;[249] it is to continue to be the case that not all revenue-sharing arrangements are improper private inurement. However, the Department of the Treasury and the IRS are not bound by any particular prior rulings in this area.[250]

Existing tax law standards[251] apply in determining reasonableness of compensation and fair market value.[252] In this regard, an individual need not necessarily accept reduced compensation merely because he or she renders services to a tax-exempt, as opposed to a taxable, organization.[253]

There is a rebuttable presumption of reasonableness, with respect to a compensation arrangement with a disqualified person.[254] This presumption arises where the arrangement was approved by a board of directors or trustees (or a committee of the board) that was composed entirely of individuals unrelated to and not subject to the control of the disqualified person(s) involved in the arrangement, obtained and relied upon appropriate data as to comparability, and adequately documented the basis for its determination.[255]

As to the first of these criteria, which essentially requires an independent board (as opposed to a captive board), a reciprocal approval arrangement does not satisfy the independence requirement. This arrangement occurs where an individual approves compensation of a disqualified person and the disqualified person, in turn, approves the individual's compensation.[256]

As to the second of these criteria, appropriate data includes compensation levels paid by similarly situated organizations, both tax-exempt and taxable, for functionally comparable positions; the location of the organization, including the availability of similar specialties in the geographic area; independent compensation surveys by nationally recognized independent firms;

---

[248] House Report at 56.

[249] For example, Gen. Couns. Mems. 39674, 38905, and 38283. House Report at 56, note 4.

[250] House Report at 56, note 4.

[251] This includes those standards established under the law concerning ordinary and necessary business expenses (IRC § 162). House Report at 56. See the text accompanied by *infra* note 257.

[252] This concept is essentially the same as that in the private foundation context (Reg. § 53.4941(d)-3(c)(1)).

[253] House Report at 56, note 5.

[254] This rebuttable presumption is not a matter of statute (that is, it is not in the Act); it is provided in the House Report.

[255] House Report at 56–57.

[256] House Report at 57, note 6.

and written offers from similar institutions competing for the services of the disqualified person.[257]

As to the third of these criteria, adequate documentation includes an evaluation of the individual whose compensation was being established, and the basis for determining that the individual's compensation was reasonable in light of that evaluation and data).[258] The fact that a state or local legislative or agency body may have authorized or approved a particular compensation package paid to a disqualified person is not determinative of the reasonableness of the compensation paid.[259]

If these three criteria are satisfied, penalty excise taxes can be imposed only if the IRS develops sufficient contrary evidence to rebut the probative value of the evidence put forth by the parties to the transaction. For example, the IRS could establish that the compensation data relied upon by the parties was not for functionally comparable positions or that the disqualified person in fact did not substantially perform the responsibilities of the position.[260] A similar rebuttable presumption arises with respect to the reasonableness of the valuation of property sold or otherwise transferred (or purchased) by an organization to (or from) a disqualified person if the sale or transfer (or purchase) is approved by an independent board that uses appropriate comparability data and adequately documents its determination. The Department of the Treasury and the IRS have been instructed to issue guidance in connection with the reasonableness standard incorporating this presumption.[261]

(c) Disqualified Persons

For these purposes, the term *disqualified person* means (1) any person who was, at any time during the five-year period ending on the date of the transaction involved, in a position to exercise substantial influence over the affairs of the organization (whether by virtue of being an organization manager or otherwise),[262] (2) a member of the family of an individual described in the preceding category,[263] and (3) an entity in which individuals described in the preceding two categories own more than a 35 percent interest.[264]

As to the first of these categories, a person can be in a position to exercise substantial influence over a tax-exempt organization despite the fact that the person is not an employee of (and does not receive any compensation directly from) a tax-exempt organization but is formally an employee of (and is directly com-

---

[257] *Id.* at 57. As noted (see *supra* notes 251–253), the rules applicable to taxable entities are generally followed in this context (e.g., Elliotts, Inc. v. Comm'r, 716 F.2d 1241 (9th Cir. 1983); Rapco, Inc. v. Comm'r, *supra*; Leonard Pipeline Contractors, Ltd. v. Comm'r, *supra* note 60.

[258] *Id.*

[259] *Id.*, note 7. Likewise, this type of authorization or approval is not determinative of whether a revenue-sharing arrangement violates the private inurement proscription (see text accompanied by *supra* note 248). *Id.*

[260] *Id.* at 57.

[261] *Id.*

[262] IRC § 4958(f)(1)(A).

[263] IRC § 4958(f)(1)(B).

[264] IRC § 4958(f)(1)(C).

pensated by) a subsidiary—including a taxable subsidiary—controlled by the parent tax-exempt organization.[265]

An individual having the title of "trustee," "director," or "officer" does not automatically have the status as a disqualified person.[266] Although it has been the view of the IRS that all physicians who are on the medical staff of a hospital or similar organization are insiders for purposes of the private inurement proscription,[267] a physician is a disqualified person under the intermediate sanctions rules only where he or she is in a position to exercise substantial influence over the affairs of the organization.[268]

The Department of the Treasury is granted the authority to promulgate rules exempting broad categories of individuals from the category of disqualified persons (such as full-time bona fide employees who receive economic benefits of less than a threshold amount or individuals who have taken a vow of poverty).[269]

An *organization manager* is a trustee, director, or officer of the applicable tax-exempt organization, as well as an individual having powers or responsibilities similar to those of trustees, directors, or officers of the organization.[270] Principles similar to those under the law pertaining to private foundations are to be followed in determining who is an organization manager.[271]

The term *member of the family* is defined as being the following: (1) spouses, ancestors, children, grandchildren, great grandchildren, and the spouses of children, grandchildren, and great grandchildren—namely, those individuals so classified under the private foundation rules,[272] and (2) the brothers and sisters (whether by the whole- or half-blood) of the individual and their spouses.[273] Thus, this term is defined more broadly in the public charity setting than is the case with private foundations.[274]

The entities that are disqualified persons because one or more disqualified persons own more than a 35 percent interest in them are termed *35 percent controlled entities*.[275] They are (1) corporations in which one or more disqualified persons own more than 35 percent of the total combined voting power, (2) partnerships in which one or more disqualified persons own more than 35 percent of the profits interest, and (3) trusts or estates in which one or more disqualified persons own more than 35 percent of the beneficial interest. The term *voting power* includes voting power represented by holdings of voting stock, actual or constructive, but does not include voting rights held only as a director or trustee.[276] In general, constructive ownership rules apply for purposes of determining 35 percent controlled entities.[277]

---

[265] House Report at 58, note 10.

[266] *Id*. at 58.

[267] Gen. Couns. Mem. 39862.

[268] House Report at 58, note 12.

[269] *Id*. at 58.

[270] IRC § 4958(f)(2).

[271] House Report at 59, note 13. See § 11.2(b).

[272] IRC § 4946(d). See § 11.2(d).

[273] IRC § 4958(f)(4).

[274] See § 11.2(d).

[275] IRC § 4958(f)(3)(A).

[276] House Report at 58, note 11. This rule is identical to that in the private foundation context (Reg. § 53.4946-1(a)(5)).

[277] IRC § 4958(f)(3)(B). In general, see § 11.2(e)-(g).

(d) Tax Structure

A disqualified person who benefited from an excess benefit transaction is subject to and must pay an initial excise tax equal to 25 percent of the amount of the excess benefit.[278] Again, the excess benefit is the amount by which a transaction differs from fair market value, the amount of compensation exceeding reasonable compensation, or (pursuant to tax regulations) the amount of impermissible private inurement resulting from a transaction based on the organization's gross or net income.[279] (In addition, as noted below, the matter must be rectified—corrected—by a return of the excess benefit to the applicable tax-exempt organization.)

An organization manager who participated in an excess benefit transaction, knowing that it was such a transaction, is subject to and must pay an initial excise tax of 10 percent of the excess benefit (subject to a maximum amount of tax as to a transaction of $10,000[280]), where an initial tax is imposed on a disqualified person.[281] As to the latter, the tax is not imposed where the participation in the transaction was not willful and was due to reasonable cause.[282]

An additional excise tax may be imposed on a disqualified person where the initial tax was imposed and if there was no correction of the excess benefit transaction within a specified period. This period is the *taxable period*, which means—with respect to an excess benefit transaction—the period beginning with the date on which the transaction occurred and ending on the earliest of (1) the date of mailing of a notice of deficiency[283] with respect to the initial tax or (2) the date on which the initial tax is assessed.[284] In this situation, the disqualified person is subject to and must pay a tax equal to 200 percent of the excess benefit involved.[285]

For this purpose, the term *correction* means undoing the excess benefit to the extent possible and taking any additional measures necessary to place the organization in a financial position not worse than that in which it would be if the disqualified person were dealing under the highest fiduciary standards.[286] If more than one organization manager or other disqualified person is liable for an excise tax, then all such persons are jointly and severally liable for the tax.[287]

(e) Returns for Payment of Excise Taxes

Under the law in existence prior to the enactment of intermediate sanctions, charitable organizations and other persons liable for certain excise taxes must file re-

---

[278] IRC § 4958(a)(1).
[279] House Report at 58–59. See text accompanied by *supra* notes 246–250.
[280] IRC § 4958(d)(2).
[281] IRC § 4958(a)(2).
[282] *Id.*
[283] IRC § 6212.
[284] IRC § 4958(f)(5).
[285] IRC § 4958(b).
[286] IRC § 4958(f)(6). See § 11.4(f).
[287] IRC § 4958(d)(1).

turns by which the taxes due are calculated and reported. These taxes are those imposed on public charities for excessive lobbying[288] and for political campaign activities,[289] and on private foundations and/or other persons for a wide range of impermissible activities.[290] The returns are on Form 4720.

Disqualified persons and organization managers liable for payment of excise taxes as the result of excess benefit transactions are required to file Form 4720 as the return by which these taxes are paid.[291] In general, returns on Form 4720 for a disqualified person or organization manager liable for an excess benefit transaction tax must be filed on or before the 15th day of the fifth month following the close of that person's tax year.[292]

(f) Reimbursements and Insurance

Any reimbursements by an applicable tax-exempt organization of excise tax liability are treated as an excess benefit unless they are included in the disqualified person's compensation during the year in which the reimbursement is made.[293] (This rule is consistent with that noted above, which is that payments of personal expenses and other benefits to or for the benefit of disqualified persons are treated as compensation only if it is clear that the organization intended and made the payments as compensation for services.) The total compensation package, including the amount of any reimbursement, is subject to the requirement of reasonableness. Similarly, the payment by an applicable tax-exempt organization of premiums for an insurance policy providing liability insurance to a disqualified person for excess benefit taxes is an excess benefit transaction unless the premiums are treated as part of the compensation paid to the disqualified person and the total compensation (including premiums) is reasonable.[294]

Because individuals may be both members of and disqualified persons with respect to a nonexclusive applicable tax-exempt organization (for example, a museum or neighborhood civic organization) and receive certain benefits (for example, free admission or discounted gift shop purchases) in their capacity as members (rather than in their capacity as disqualified persons), the Treasury Department is to provide guidance clarifying that these membership benefits may be excluded from consideration under the private inurement proscription and intermediate sanctions rules.[295]

---

[288] IRC § 4911 or 4912. See § 20.6.

[289] IRC § 4955. See § 21.2.

[290] IRC § 4940–4948. See Chapter 11.

[291] Reg. § 53.6011-1(b) (as amended by T.D. 8705).

[292] Reg. § 53.6071-1(f)(1). A Form 4720 for a disqualified person or organization manager liable for the tax on an excess benefit transaction occurring in the person's tax year ending September 13, 1995 (see *infra* § 11(h)), and on or before July 30, 1996, was due on or before December 15, 1996 (Reg. § 53.6071-1(f)(2)).

[293] House Report at 58.

[294] *Id.*

[295] *Id.* at note 9.

(g) Scope of the Sanctions

These intermediate sanctions may be imposed by the IRS in lieu of or in addition to revocation of an organization's tax-exempt status.[296] In general, these intermediate sanctions are to be the sole sanction imposed in those cases in which the excess benefit does not rise to such a level as to call into question whether, on the whole, the organization functions as a charitable or social welfare organization.

In practice, the revocation of tax-exempt status, with or without the imposition of these excise taxes, is to occur only when the organization no longer operates as a charitable or social welfare organization, as the case may be.[297] Existing law principles apply in determining whether an organization no longer operates as an exempt organization. For example, in the case of a charitable organization, the loss of tax-exempt status would occur in a year, or as of a year, the entity was involved in a transaction constituting a substantial amount of private inurement.

As under preexisting law, a three-year statute of limitations applies, except in the case of fraud.[298] The IRS has the authority to abate an excise tax penalty if it is established that the violation was due to reasonable cause and not due to willful neglect, and the transaction at issue was corrected within the specified taxable period.[299]

(h) Effective Dates

These intermediate sanctions generally are effective with respect to excess benefit transactions occurring on or after September 14, 1995.[300] The sanctions do not apply to any benefits arising out of a transaction pursuant to a written contract that was binding on that date and continued in force through the time of the transaction, and the terms of which have not materially changed.[301]

However, parties to transactions entered into after September 13, 1995, and before January 1, 1997, were entitled to rely on the above-discussed rebuttable presumption of reasonableness if, within a reasonable period (such as 90 days) after entering into the compensation package, the parties satisfied the criteria that give rise to the presumption. After December 31, 1996, the rebuttable

---

[296] *Id*. at 59.

[297] *Id*. at 59, note 15.

[298] IRC § 6501.

[299] IRC § 4962. The term *taxable period* is the subject of the text accompanied by *supra* note 284.

There was a mistake in the statute, which forestalled the ability of the IRS to abate excess benefit transaction taxes until the matter was corrected. The error stemmed from the fact that the term *first tier tax* was defined twice in the Internal Revenue Code—and inconsistently. IRC § 4962(b) defined *qualified first tier tax* as "any first tier tax imposed by subchapter A or C of this chapter . . ." (IRC Chapter 42). The difficulty was that the intermediate sanctions tax (IRC § 4958) is lodged in subchapter D of IRC Chapter 42. By contrast, IRC § 4963(a) defines *first tier tax* as including any tax imposed by IRC § 4958(a). This error was corrected by technical corrections legislation enacted in 1997 (Taxpayer Relief Act of 1997 § 1603).

[300] Act § 1311(d)(1).

[301] *Id*. § 1311(d)(2).

presumption arises only if the criteria are satisfied prior to payment of the compensation (or, to the extent provided by tax regulations, within a reasonable period thereafter).[302]

§ 19.12   INTERRELATIONSHIP OF DOCTRINES

The coming months and years will bring interpretations and amplifications of the concept of the excess benefit transaction. At least in the short term, this process will draw heavily on existing law as shaped by the private inurement doctrine. From a larger perspective, however, the applications of intermediate sanctions are certain to also meaningfully inform the substance and boundaries of the doctrine of private inurement. Decision-makers in either setting will not be able to ignore the impact of the policymaking on the other doctrine. For the most part, the intermediate sanctions rules will supplant actual application of the private inurement doctrine to public charities and social welfare organizations (that is, revocation of the tax-exempt status of the organization).[303]

The law concerning self-dealing in the private foundation context[304] also will be heavily interrelated with the law pertaining to excess benefit transctions. The structure of the intermediate sanctions penalties is obviously patterned after the foundation rules. Of greater substance, however, is that a significant amount of the private foundation self-dealing law is directly usable in discerning the contours of the excess benefit transaction. (Likewise, developments in interpreting intermediate sanctions will have an impact on the shaping of the self-dealing law.) This is certainly the case with respect to the various transactions that are embraced by the foundation self-dealing rules. Yet this amounts to more than that: the self-dealing rules can be looked to in defining *disqualified persons*, determining the existence of *indirect* excess benefit transac-

---

[302] House Report at 60. In general, Hopkins & Tesdahl, *Intermediate Sanctions: Curbing Nonprofit Abuse* (John Wiley & Sons, Inc., 1997); Polito, "Private Inurement and the Intermediate Sanctions Regime," 18 *Exempt Orgs. Tax Rev.* (No. 3) 219 (Dec. 1997); Henzke and Davis, "Assessing the Reasonableness of Compensation Under the Intermediate Sanctions," 9 *J. Tax. Exempt Orgs.* (No. 3) 118 (Nov./Dec. 1997); Faber, "The Effect of Intermediate Sanctions on the Ultimate Sanction for Tax-Exempt Organizations," 16 *Exempt Org. Tax Rev.* (No. 4) 587 (April 1997); Kalick, "Influence Determines When a Physician is a Disqualified Person," 8 *J. Tax. Exempt Orgs.* (No. 4) 152 (Jan./Feb. 1997); McGovern, "Intermediate Sanctions—The New Law's Effect on Colleges," 15 *Exempt Org. Tax Rev.* (No. 3) 365 (1996); Davis, Jr., and Thomas, "Exempt Organizations Should Support Intermediate Sanctions Legislation," 8 *J. Tax. Exempt Orgs.* 51 (Sept./Oct. 1996); Crozier, "Intermediate Sanctions Will Affect Exempt Organizations' Hiring and Compensation Practices," 8 *J. Tax. Exempt Orgs.* (No. 2) 61 (Sept./Oct. 1996); Schoenfeld & Repass, "'Intermediate Sanctions'—Issues, Pitfalls, and Protective Measures," 72 *Tax Notes* 1033 (Aug. 19, 1996); Peregrine, Nilles, & Palmer, "Complying with the New Intermediate Sanctions Law," 14 *Exempt Org. Tax Rev.* (No. 2) 245 (1996); Fremont-Smith, "Current Proposals for Public Charity Intermediate Sanctions," 10 *Exempt Org. Tax Rev.* (No. 1) 115 (1994); Boisture & Cerny, "Treasury Proposes Intermediate Sanctions on Public Charities and Section 501(c)(4) Organizations," 63 *Tax Notes* (No. 3) 353 (1994); Suhrke, "What's Wrong With Intermediate Sanctions?," XXVI *Philanthropy Monthly* (No. 9) 5 (Nov. 1993).

[303] See *supra* § 11(g).

[304] See § 11.4(a).

tions, transactions *for the use of* or *for the benefit of* disqualified persons, the process of *correction*, and whether an individual *knew* that an excess benefit was being provided.

Thus, one of the unappreciated aspects of the advent of the intermediate sanctions rules is the extent to which the doctrines of private inurement, self-dealing, and excess benefit transactions are going to interrelate and fertilize the evolution of the law in the three fields.

CHAPTER TWENTY

Legislative Activities by Exempt Organizations

Tax policy and attempts to influence legislation have, at best, an uneasy relationship: There are many who criticize use of the tax system to subsidize lobbying and legislators often do not want to encourage the practice. This antipathy is reflected in the law of tax-exempt organizations, which, among other restraints, places limitations on the extent to which charitable organizations[1] can engage in lobbying and discourages lobbying by membership associations by curbing the deductibility of dues paid to them, yet encourages lobbying by veterans' organizations.

    The federal law contains six discrete bodies of law that can pertain to attempts to influence legislation by tax-exempt organizations: two sets of rules ap-

---

[1] That is, organizations described in IRC § 501(c)(3) and exempt from federal income taxation by reason of IRC § 501(a).

plicable to public charities,[2] rules applicable to private foundations,[3] rules pertaining to membership associations,[4] law regulating attempts to influence legislation in the U.S. Congress,[5] law concerning lobbying by recipients of federal grants and similar payments,[6] and rules established by the Office of Management and Budget concerning the use of federal funds for lobbying by nonprofit organizations.[7] These various sets of rules contain law by which *legislation* and *attempts to influence* it are defined, and costs associated with lobbying are ascertained. While there is considerable overlap as to the content of the rules, in several instances there are varied definitions of the concepts.

Public charities may engage in legislative activities to the extent that lobbying is not a *substantial* part of their overall functions. The rules applicable to public charities are termed the *substantial part test* and the *expenditure test*. The essence of these tests is the basis by which substantiality in this context is measured. A charitable organization is subject to the substantial part test, unless the expenditure test is elected.

§ 20.1 MEANING OF *LEGISLATION*

A threshold concept in this setting is the meaning of the term *legislation*. In the law of tax-exempt organizations, there are three sources of law on the point.

(a) Substantial Part Test

The term *legislation*, as defined for purposes of the substantial part test, includes action by Congress, a state legislature, a local council or similar governing body, and the general public in a referendum, initiative, constitutional amendment, or similar procedure.[8]

Legislation generally does not include action by an executive branch of a government, such as the promulgation of rules and regulations, nor does it include action by independent regulatory agencies. Appropriations bills are items of legislation for federal tax purposes. Also, the term *legislation* includes proposals for the making of laws in countries other than the United States.[9]

It is the view of the IRS that an attempt to influence the confirmation, by the U.S. Senate, of a federal judicial nominee constitutes, for these purposes, an attempt to influence legislation.[10] This position is based upon the definition of the

---

[2] See *infra* §§ 2–4.

[3] See § 11.4(e).

[4] See *infra* § 6.

[5] 2 U.S.C. § 1601 et seq. (the "Lobbying Disclosure Act of 1995").

[6] 31 U.S.C. § 1352 (the "Byrd Amendment"). This law is the subject of Hopkins, *Charity, Advocacy, and the Law* (John Wiley & Sons, Inc., 1992), Chapter 10.

[7] Circular A-122, "Cost Principles for Nonprofit Organizations," 45 Fed. Reg. 46,022 (July 8, 1980), particularly Revised Transmittal Memorandum No. 2 (May 19, 1987). This law is the subject of Hopkins, *supra* note 6, Chapter 9.

[8] Reg. § 1.501(c)(3)-1(c)(3)(ii). Cf. Smith v. Comm'r, 3 T.C. 696 (1944).

[9] Rev. Rul. 73-440, 1973-2 C.B. 177.

[10] Notice 88-76, 1988-2 C.B. 392.

term *legislation* found in the expenditure test, where the term is defined to include resolutions and similar items.[11]

(b) Expenditure Test

The statute in connection with the expenditure test states that the term *legislation* includes "action with respect to Acts, bills, resolutions, or similar items by the Congress, any State legislature, any local council, or similar governing body, or by the public in a referendum, initiative, constitutional amendment, or similar procedure."[12]

The position of the IRS that an attempt to influence the confirmation, by the U.S. Senate, of a federal judicial nominee constitutes an attempt to influence legislation is reflected in the expenditure test, in examples in the regulations.[13]

(c) Associations' Dues Deductibility Test

The term *legislation*, as defined for purposes of the rules concerning the deductibility of associations' members' dues, means the same as is the case with respect to the expenditure test.[14] Thus, the term includes any action with respect to acts, bills, resolutions, or other similar items by a legislative body.[15] Also, legislation includes a "proposed treaty required to be submitted by the President to the Senate for its advice and consent from the time the President's representative begins to negotiate its position with the prospective parties to the proposed treaty."[16]

However, because of the breadth of these rules,[17] legislative bodies are "Congress, state legislatures, and other similar governing bodies, excluding local councils (and similar governing bodies), and executive, judicial, or administrative bodies."[18] *Administrative bodies* include "school boards, housing authorities, sewer and water districts, zoning boards, and other similar Federal, State, or local special purpose bodies, whether elective or appointive."[19]

§ 20.2   LOBBYING BY CHARITABLE ORGANIZATIONS

As noted, one of the criteria for qualification as a tax-exempt charitable organization is that "no substantial part of the activities" of the organization may constitute "carrying on propaganda, or otherwise attempting, to influence leg-

---

[11] IRC § 4911(e)(2).

[12] IRC § 4911(e)(2). Also Reg. § 56.4911-2(d)(1).

[13] Reg. § 56.4911-2(b)(4)(ii)(B), Example (6). Also Reg. § 53.4945-2(d)(2)(iii), Examples (5)–(7).

[14] IRC § 162(e)(4)(B).

[15] Reg. § 1.162-29(b)(4).

[16] *Id.*

[17] As discussed *infra* § 8(a), these rules encompass certain lobbying efforts with respect to the federal executive branch but do not apply with respect to direct lobbying with respect to local legislation.

[18] Reg. § 1.162-29(b)(6).

[19] *Id.*

islation."[20] It is irrelevant, for purposes of classification of an organization as a charitable entity under federal tax law, that the legislation advocated would advance the charitable purposes for which the organization was created to promote.[21] This position should be contrasted with the state of the law prior to enactment of the Revenue Act of 1934.[22]

(a) Legislative History

The provision limiting lobbying by charitable organizations was added to the federal tax law in 1934, without benefit of congressional hearings, as the result of a floor amendment adopted by the Senate. During debate on the legislation that became the Revenue Act of 1934, Senator David A. Reed of Pennsylvania, on April 2, 1934, spoke to an amendment to restrict "partisan politics" and lobbying by charitable organizations. On that occasion, he stated that the purpose of the amendment was to prohibit tax exemption for "any organization that is receiving contributions, the proceeds of which are to be used for propaganda purposes or to try to influence legislation."[23] He said that the intent of the Committee on Finance, where the amendment originated, was to deny deductibility of a contribution as a charitable gift "if it is a selfish one made to advance the personal interests of the giver of the money."[24] Observing that he did "not reproach the draftsmen" as "I think we gave them an impossible task," Senator Reed said that "this amendment goes much further than the committee intended to go."[25] He noted: "Mr. President, as that amendment is worded it would apply to the Society for the Prevention of Cruelty to Children, to the Society for the Prevention of Cruelty to Animals, or any of the worthy institutions that we do not in the slightest mean to affect."[26]

The Senate abandoned its consideration of the amendment that day and deferred it to later in the debate; on April 4, 1934, it was again taken up. At that time, Senator Byron P. Harrison of Mississippi observed that the intent of the Finance Committee was to stop deductible contributions for legislative ends.[27] Senator Reed stated that he did "not think that the committee is proud of the language in which this amendment is couched" and that the "legislative drafting counsel who drew it expressed no pride whatsoever in their product."[28] The amendment was adopted; thereafter, Senator Reed said that "we will have from now until the conference to study the project and prepare better phraseology."[29] The language was indeed changed in conference, with deletion of the reference to

---

[20] IRC § 501(c)(3). This subject is treated in greater detail in Hopkins, *supra* note 6, Chapter 5.
[21] Rev. Rul. 67-293, 1967-2 C.B. 185. Also Cammarano v. United States, 358 U.S. 498 (1959).
[22] There is nothing in the English common law of charity that prohibits a charitable organization from engaging in legislative activities. One federal court opinion, issued in 1930, held that charitable organizations may not engage in "[p]olitical agitation" (Slee v. Comm'r, 42 F.2d 184, 185 (2d Cir. 1930)).
[23] 78 *Cong. Rec.* 5861 (1934).
[24] *Id.*
[25] *Id.*
[26] *Id.*
[27] 78 *Cong. Rec.* 5959 (1934).
[28] *Id.*
[29] *Id.*

"partisan politics," and the language enacted in that regard remains in the federal tax law today.

(b) Substantial Part Test

Although legislative activities take many forms, the law distinguishes between *direct* lobbying and *grassroots* lobbying. Direct lobbying includes the presentation of testimony at public hearings held by legislative committees, correspondence and conferences with legislators and their staffs, and publication of documents advocating specific legislative action. Grassroots lobbying consists of appeals to the general public or segments of the general public, to contact legislators or take other specific action as regards legislative matters.[30]

An organization is regarded as attempting to influence legislation if it (1) contacts, or urges the public to contact, members of a legislative body for the purpose of proposing, supporting, or opposing legislation; or (2) advocates the adoption or rejection of legislation.[31] If a substantial part of an organization's activities is attempting to influence legislation, the organization is denominated an *action organization* and hence cannot qualify as a charitable entity.[32]

For an organization to be denied or lose tax-exempt status because of lobbying activity, the legislative activities must be undertaken as an act of the organization itself. Thus, for example, the IRS recognized that the legislative activities of a student newspaper were not attributable to the sponsoring university.[33] Similarly, during the course of the anti-Vietnam war efforts on many college and university campuses, which included legislative activities, the principle was established that the activities by students and faculty were not official acts of the particular institutions.[34]

(c) Expenditure Test

Under the expenditure test, the definition of *legislation* includes the term *action*. The term action is "limited to the introduction, amendment, enactment, defeat, or repeal of Acts, bills, resolutions, or similar items."[35]

(i) Influencing Legislation. These rules define the term *influencing legislation* in two ways. One is any attempt to influence any legislation through

---

[30] Roberts Dairy Co. v. Comm'r, 195 F.2d 948 (8th Cir. 1952), *cert. den.*, 344 U.S. 865 (1952); American Hardware & Equip. Co. v. Comm'r, 202 F.2d 126 (4th Cir. 1953), *cert. den.*, 346 U.S. 814 (1953). In certain circumstances, grassroots lobbying is also political campaign activity (e.g., Priv. Ltr. Rul. 9652026); see § 17.1(a), text accompanied by note 27.

[31] Reg. § 1.501(c)(3)-1(c)(3)(ii).

[32] See § 4.5(b). Also Reg. § 1.501(h)-1(a)(4).

[33] Rev. Rul. 72-513, 1972-2 C.B. 246.

[34] American Council on Education Guidelines, CCH Stand. Fed. Tax Rep. ¶ 3033.197. In general, Hopkins & Myers, "Governmental Response to Campus Unrest," 22 *Case W. Res. L. Rev.* 408 (1971); Broughton, "New Politics on the Campus, Reconstitution, The Princeton Plan," VI *The College Counsel* 119 (1971); Field, "Tax Exempt Status of Universities: Impact of Political Activities by Students," 24 *Tax Law.* 157 (1970); Goldberg, "Guarding Against Loss of Tax Exempt Status Due to Campus Politics," 33 *J. Tax* 232 (1970); Note, "Taxation—University Political Activities and Federal Tax Exemption: American Council on Education Guidelines," 84 *Harv. L. Rev.* 463 (1970).

[35] IRC § 4911(e)(3); Reg. § 56.4911-2(d)(2).

communication with any member or employee of a legislative body[36] or with any other governmental official or employee who may participate in the formulation of the legislation (a *direct lobbying communication*).[37] The other is any attempt to influence any legislation through an attempt to affect the opinions of the general public or any segment of the public (a *grassroots lobbying communication*).[38]

A communication with a legislator or government official is a direct lobbying communication only where the communication refers to *specific legislation* and reflects a view on the legislation.[39] Where a communication refers to and reflects a view on a measure that is the subject of a referendum, ballot initiative, or similar procedure, and is made to the members of the general public in the jurisdiction where the vote will occur, the communication is a direct lobbying communication (unless certain exceptions apply).[40]

A communication is regarded as a grass-roots communication only where the communication refers to specific legislation, reflects a view on the legislation, and encourages the recipient of the communication to take action with respect to the legislation.[41] The regulations define the phrase "encouraging the recipient to take action."[42] The IRS considers this definition to be "very lenient," because it "will permit many clear advocacy communications to be treated as NONlobbying."[43]

The term *specific legislation* is defined as (1) legislation that has already been introduced in a legislative body and (2) a specific legislative proposal that the organization supports or opposes.[44] In the case of a referendum, ballot initiative, constitutional amendment, or other measure that is placed on the ballot by petitions, an item becomes specific legislation when the petition is first circulated among the voters for signature.[45]

The regulations contain a rebuttable presumption that a *paid mass media advertisement*[46] is grass roots lobbying if it (1) is made within two weeks before a vote by a legislative body, or committee of a legislative body, on highly publicized legislation, (2) reflects a view on the general subject of the legislation, and (3) either refers to the legislation or encourages the public to communicate with

---

[36] This term is defined in Reg. § 56.4911-2(d)(3).

[37] IRC § 4911(d)(1)(B); Reg. § 56.4911-2(b)(1)(i).

[38] IRC § 4911(d)(1)(A); Reg. § 56.4911-2(b)(2)(i).

[39] Reg. § 56.4911-2(b)(1)(ii).

[40] Reg. § 56.4911-2(b)(1)(iii). This type of communication may be treated as nonpartisan analysis, study, or research (see text accompanying *infra* note 100).

[41] Reg. § 56.4911-2(b)(2)(ii).

[42] Reg. § 56.4911-2(b)(2)(iii), 56.4911-2(b)(2)(iv).

[43] 55 *Fed. Reg.* 35580 (Aug. 31, 1990) (emphasis in original). The IRS commentary on this definition adds: "This is part of the Service's attempt to maintain a careful balance between the statutory limits on electing public charities' lobbying expenditures and the desire of those organizations to involve themselves in the public policy making process to the greatest extent consistent with those statutory limits" (*id.*).

[44] Reg. § 56.4911-2(d)(1)(ii).

[45] *Id.*

[46] Certain large-scale in-house publications and broadcasts are considered *paid mass media advertisements*.

legislators on the general subject of the legislation. The presumption is rebutted either by showing that the charitable organization regularly makes similar mass media communications without regard to the timing of legislation or that the timing of the communication was unrelated to the upcoming vote.[47]

There are rules concerning the situation where expenses incurred for non-lobbying communications can subsequently be characterized as grass roots lobbying expenditures where the materials or other communications are later used in a lobbying effort. For this result to occur, the materials must be "advocacy communications or research materials," where the primary purpose of the organization in undertaking or preparing the communications or materials was for use in lobbying; in the case of subsequent distribution of the materials by another organization, there must be "clear and convincing" evidence of collusion between the two organizations to establish that the primary purpose for preparing the communication was for use in lobbying. In any event, this subsequent use rule applies only to expenditures paid less than six months before the first use of the nonlobbying material in the lobbying campaign.[48]

A communication between an organization and any bona fide member of the organization made to directly encourage the member to engage in direct lobbying is itself considered direct lobbying.[49] A communication between an organization and any bona fide member of the organization made to directly encourage the member to urge persons other than members to engage in direct or grass-roots lobbying is considered grassroots lobbying.[50]

A transfer is a grassroots expenditure to the extent it is earmarked[51] for grassroots lobbying purposes.[52] A transfer that is earmarked for direct lobbying purposes, or for direct lobbying and grassroots lobbying purposes, is regarded as a grassroots expenditure in full, unless the transferor can demonstrate that all or part of the amounts transferred were expended for direct lobbying purposes, in which case that part of the amounts transferred is a direct lobbying expenditure by the transferor.[53] There are rules for treating as a lobbying (direct or grass roots) expenditure transfers for less than fair market value from a public charity that has elected the expenditure test, to any noncharity that makes lobbying expenditures.[54]

(ii) Allocation Rules.   There are two allocation rules for communications that have a lobbying and a bona fide nonlobbying purpose.

One rule requires that the allocation be *reasonable*. This rule applies to an electing public charity's communications primarily with its bona fide members.

---

[47] Reg. § 56.4911-2(b)(5).
[48] Reg. § 56.4911-2(b)(2)(v).
[49] IRC § 4911(d)(3)(A).
[50] IRC § 4911(d)(3)(B).
[51] Reg. § 56.4911-4(f)(4).
[52] Reg. § 56.4911-3(c)(1).
[53] Reg. § 56.4911-3(c)(2).
[54] Reg. § 56.4911-3(c)(3).

More than one half of the recipients of the communication must be members of the electing public charity for this rule to apply.[55]

The other allocation rule is for nonmembership communications. Where a nonmembership lobbying communication also has a bona fide nonlobbying purpose, the regulations provide that an organization must include as lobbying expenditures all costs attributable to those parts of the communication that are on the same specific subject as the lobbying message. The rules define the phrase *same specific subject*.[56]

If a communication (other than to an organization's members) is both a direct lobbying communication and a grassroots lobbying communication, the communication is treated as a grassroots lobbying expenditure, unless the electing public charity demonstrates that the communication was made primarily for direct lobbying purposes, in which case a reasonable allocation is permitted.[57]

§ 20.3 MEASURING ALLOWABLE LOBBYING BY CHARITABLE ORGANIZATIONS

The rules concerning legislative activities by charitable organizations, other than private foundations, contain three essential elements: the meaning of the term *legislation*, the meaning of the term *influencing legislation*, and the concept of a *substantial* part of a charitable organization's activities.

(a) Substantial Part Test

A determination as to whether a specific activity or category of activities of a charitable organization is substantial must basically be a factual one, and until enactment of the expenditure test, discussed below, the law offered no formula for computing substantial or insubstantial legislative undertakings. Thus, the Senate Finance Committee, in its report accompanying the Tax Reform Act of 1969, said that the "standards as to the permissible level of [legislative] activities under the present law are so vague as to encourage subjective application of the sanction."[58] In its report accompanying the Tax Reform Act of 1976, the Senate Finance Committee portrayed the dilemma this way: "Many believe that the standards as to the permissible level of [legislative] activities under present law are too vague and thereby tend to encourage subjective and selective enforcement."[59]

One approach to attempting to measure substantiality in this context is to determine what percentage of an organization's spending is devoted on an annual basis to efforts to influence legislation. Yet the limitation on influencing legislation involves more than simply a curb on expenditures or diversions of funds; it includes restrictions on certain levels of activity as well. A portion of an organization's efforts and activities devoted to legislative activities may well be re-

---

[55] Reg. § 56.4911-3(a)(2)(ii).
[56] Reg. § 56.4911-3(a)(2)(i).
[57] Reg. § 56.4911-3(a)(3).
[58] S. Rep. No. 552, 91st Cong., 1st Sess. 47 (1969).
[59] S. Rep. No. 938 (Part 2), 94th Cong., 2d Sess. 80 (1976).

garded as more important than the organization's expenditures for the purpose.[60] It was once suggested that five percent of an organization's time and effort that involves legislative activities is not "substantial."[61]

However, in the context of activities, a percentage standard may be of less utility. An exempt organization enjoying considerable prestige and influence might be considered as having a substantial impact on the legislative process solely on the basis of a single official position statement, an activity considered negligible when measured according to a percentage standard of time expended.[62] A standard such as this, however, would tend to place undue emphasis on whether or not a particular legislative effort was successful.[63]

In 1972, a federal court of appeals provided a new dimension to the concept of attempting to influence legislation, when it upheld the revocation of tax exemption of a ministry organization.[64] The court, after holding that the income tax regulations properly interpreted the intent of Congress (before enactment of the expenditure test), found the following substantial legislative activities: articles constituting appeals to the public to react to certain issues, support or opposition to specific terms of legislation and enactments, and efforts to cause members of the public to contact members of Congress on various matters. Of particular consequence was the court's explicit rejection of a percentage test in determining substantiality, which was dismissed as obscuring the "complexity of balancing the organization's activities in relation to its objectives and circumstances."[65] Said the court: "The political [i.e., legislative] activities of an organization must be balanced in the context of the objectives and circumstances of the organization to determine whether a substantial part of its activities was to influence or attempt to influence legislation."[66]

A subsequent court decision offered authority for the proposition that *substantiality* is not always measured by the factor of funds or time expended. The court wrote, albeit reviewing the term in a different context,[67] that "[w]hether an activity is substantial is a facts-and-circumstances inquiry not always dependent upon time or expenditure percentages."[68]

(b) Expenditure Test

The expenditure test utilizes a mechanical test for measuring permissible and impermissible ranges of lobbying expenditures[69] by eligible charitable organiza-

---

[60] League of Women Voters v. United States, 180 F. Supp. 379 (Ct. Cl. 1960), *cert. den.*, 364 U.S. 822 (1960).

[61] Seasongood v. Comm'r, 227 F.2d 907, 912 (6th Cir. 1955).

[62] Kuper v. Comm'r, 332 F.2d 562 (3d Cir. 1964), *cert. den.*, 379 U.S. 920 (1964).

[63] Haswell v. United States, 500 F.2d 1133, 1142 (Ct. Cl. 1974), *cert. den.*, 419 U.S. 1107 (1974); Dulles v. Johnson, 273 F.2d 362, 367 (2d Cir. 1959), *cert. den.*, 364 U.S. 834 (1960).

[64] Christian Echoes Nat'l Ministry, Inc. v. United States, 470 F.2d 849 (10th Cir. 1972), *cert. den.*, 414 U.S. 864 (1973).

[65] *Id.* 470 F.2d at 855.

[66] *Id.*

[67] See § 7.2, particularly text accompanied by notes 34–51.

[68] The Nationalist Movement v. Comm'r, 102 T.C. 558, 589 (1994), *aff'd*, 37 F.3d 216 (5th Cir. 1994).

[69] IRC § 4911(c)(1); Reg. § 1.501(h)-3(c)(1).

tions, and does so in terms of the expenditure of funds and sliding scales of percentages. (The basic concept that legislative activities cannot be a substantial portion of the undertakings of a charitable organization was not altered by enactment of the expenditure test.)

These standards are formulated in terms of declining percentages of total *exempt purpose expenditures*.[70] In general, an expenditure is an exempt purpose expenditure for a tax year if it is paid or incurred by an electing public charity to accomplish the organization's exempt purposes.[71] These expenditures include (1) those expended for one or more charitable purposes, including most grants made for charitable ends; (2) amounts paid as employee compensation (current or deferred) in furtherance of a charitable purpose; (3) the portion of administrative expenses allocable to a charitable purpose; (4) all lobbying expenditures; (5) amounts expended for nonpartisan analysis, study, or research; (6) amounts expended for examinations of broad social, economic, and similar problems; (7) amounts expended in response to requests for technical advice; (8) amounts expended pursuant to the *self-defense exception*; (9) amounts expended for communications to members that are not lobbying expenditures; (10) a reasonable allowance for straight-line depreciation or amortization of charitable assets;[72] and (11) certain fund-raising expenditures.[73]

The term *exempt purpose expenditure* does not include (1) amounts expended that are not for purposes described in the preceding items (1) through (9), or (11); (2) the amount of transfers to members of an affiliated group, made to artificially inflate the amount of exempt purpose expenditures, or to certain noncharitable organizations; (3) amounts paid to or incurred for a *separate fundraising unit* of the organization or an affiliated organization; (4) amounts paid to or incurred for any person that is not an employee or any organization that is not an affiliated organization, if paid primarily for fund-raising, but only if the person or organization engages in fund-raising, fund-raising counseling, or the provision of similar advice or services; (5) amounts paid or incurred that are properly chargeable to a capital account with respect to an unrelated trade or business; (6) amounts paid or incurred for a tax that is not imposed in connection with the organization's efforts to accomplish charitable purposes (such as the unrelated business income tax); and (7) amounts paid or incurred for the production of income, where the income-producing activity is not substantially related to exempt purposes (such as the costs of maintaining an endowment).[74]

For this purpose, the term *fundraising* embraces three practices: (1) the solicitation of dues or contributions from members of the organization, from persons whose dues are in arrears, or from the general public; (2) the solicitation of gifts from businesses or gifts or grants from other organizations, including charitable ones; or (3) the solicitation of grants from governmental units or any agency or instrumentality of the units.[75]

---

[70] IRC § 4911(e)(1); Reg. § 56.4911-4(a).
[71] IRC § 4911(e)(1)(A).
[72] IRC § 4911(e)(4).
[73] IRC § 4911(e)(1)(B); Reg. § 56.4911-4(b). Cf. Reg. § 56.4911-3(a)(1).
[74] IRC § 4911(e)(1)(C); Reg. § 56.4911-4(c).
[75] Reg. § 56.4911-4(f)(1).

A *separate fundraising unit* of an organization "must consist of either two or more individuals a majority of whose time is spent on fundraising for the organization, or any separate accounting unit of the organization that is devoted to fundraising." In addition, "amounts paid to or incurred for a separate fundraising unit include all amounts incurred for the creation, production, copying, and distribution of the fundraising portion of a separate fundraising unit's communication."[76]

The basic permitted annual level of expenditures for legislative efforts (the *lobbying nontaxable amount*[77]) is determined by using a sliding scale percentage of the organization's exempt purpose expenditures, as follows: 20 percent of the first $500,000 of an organization's expenditures for an exempt purpose, plus 15 percent of the next $500,000, 10 percent of the next $500,000, and 5 percent of any remaining expenditures. These calculations generally are made on the basis of a four-year average.[78] However, the total amount spent for legislative activities in any one year by an eligible charitable organization may not exceed $1 million.[79] A separate limitation—amounting to 25 percent of the foregoing amounts—is imposed upon attempts to influence the general public on legislative matters[80] (the *grassroots nontaxable amount*).[81]

A charitable organization that has elected the expenditure test and that exceeds either or both of these limitations becomes subject to an excise tax in the amount of 25 percent of the excess lobbying expenditures,[82] which tax falls on the greater of the two excesses.[83] If an electing organization's lobbying expenditures normally (that is, on an average over a four-year period[84]) exceed 150 percent of either limitation (the *lobbying ceiling amount*[85] and the *grassroots ceiling amount*[86]), it will lose its tax-exempt status as a charitable entity.[87] A charitable organization in this circumstance is not able to convert to a tax-exempt social welfare organization.[88]

§ 20.4   EXCEPTIONS TO FEDERAL TAX DEFINITION OF LOBBYING BY CHARITABLE ORGANIZATIONS

(a) Substantial Part Test

A charitable organization found to have engaged in legislative activities to a prohibited extent is deemed an *action organization* and thus is not entitled to continu-

[76] Reg. § 56.4911-4(f)(2).
[77] Reg. §§ 1.501(h)-3(c)(2), 56.4911-1(c)(1).
[78] IRC § 501(h)(1). This averaging is used as the consequence of the word *normally*; the general measuring period is termed the *base years* (Reg. § 1.501(h)-3(c)(7)).
[79] IRC § 4911(c)(2); Reg. § 56.4911-1(c)(1).
[80] IRC § 4911(c)(3); Reg. § 56.4911-1(c)(2); Reg. § 1.501(h)-3(c)(4).
[81] IRC § 4911(c)(4). Reg. §§ 1.501(h)-3(c)(5), 56.4911-1(c)(2).
[82] IRC § 4911(a); Reg. § 56.4911-1(a); Reg. § 1.501(h)-1(a)(3).
[83] IRC § 4911(b); Reg. § 56.4911-1(b).
[84] Reg. § 1.501(h)-3(c)(7).
[85] Reg. § 1.501(h)-3(c)(3).
[86] Reg. § 1.501(h)-3(c)(6).
[87] IRC § 501(h)(1), 501(h)(2); Reg. § 1.501(h)-3(b).
[88] IRC § 504; Reg. §§ 1.504-1, 1.504-2. See Chapter 12. Cf. Reg. § 1.501(c)(3)-1(c)(3)(v).

ing tax exemption. Likewise, legislative activities may preclude tax exemption. One form of action organization is one as to which a "substantial part of its activities is attempting to influence legislation by propaganda or otherwise."[89] Another type of action organization is one to which its "main or primary objective or objectives (as distinguished from its incidental or secondary objectives) may be attained only by legislation or a defeat of proposed legislation," and "it advocates, or campaigns for, the attainment of such main or primary objective or objectives as distinguished from engaging in nonpartisan analysis, study or research and making the results thereof available to the public."[90]

The IRS stated in 1970 that a charitable organization that does not initiate any action with respect to pending legislation but merely responds to a request from a legislative committee to testify is not, solely because of this activity, an action organization.[91] The IRS observed that (1) proscribed attempts to influence legislation "imply an affirmative act and require something more than a mere passive response to a Committee invitation," and (2) "it is unlikely that Congress, in framing the language of this position [IRC § 501(c)(3)], intended to deny itself access to the best technical expertise available on any matter with which it concerns itself."[92]

An organization may engage in nonpartisan analysis, study, and research and publish its results (that is, perform educational activities[93]), where some of the plans and policies formulated can only be carried out through legislative enactments, without being an action organization, as long as it does not advocate the adoption of legislation or legislative action to implement its findings.[94] That is, an organization may evaluate a subject of proposed legislation or a pending item of legislation and present to the public an objective analysis of it, as long as it does not participate in the presentation of suggested bills to the legislature and does not engage in any campaign to secure enactment of the legislation.[95] However, if the organization's primary objective can be attained only by legislative action, it is an action organization.[96] In general, promoting activism instead of promoting educational activities can deny an organization classification as a charitable entity.[97]

As for the specific connotation of the term *propaganda*, it appears quite clear that the term is not as expansive as merely spreading particular beliefs, opinions, or doctrines. Rather, the word "connotes public address with selfish or ulterior purpose and characterized by the coloring or distortion of facts."[98] To avoid

---

[89] Reg. § 1.501(c)(3)-1(c)(3)(ii).

[90] Reg. § 1.501(c)(3)-1(c)(3)(iv). In general, McClintock-Trunkey Co. v. Comm'r, 19 T.C. 297 (1952), *rev'd on other issue*, 217 F.2d 329 (9th Cir. 1955).

[91] Rev. Rul. 70-449, 1970-2 C.B. 111.

[92] Curtis, "The House Committee on Ways and Means: Congress Seen Through a Key Committee," 1966 *Wis. L. Rev.* 121, 132 (1966).

[93] See Chapter 7.

[94] Reg. § 1.501(c)(3)-1(c)(3)(iv); Rev. Rul. 70-79 1970-1 C.B. 127; Weyl v. Comm'r, 48 F.2d 811 (2d Cir. 1931).

[95] Rev. Rul. 64-195, 1964-2 C.B. 138; I. T. 2654, XI-2 C.B. 39 (1932).

[96] Rev. Rul. 62-71, 1962-1 C.B. 85; Haswell v. United States, *supra* note 63, at 1143–1145.

[97] Rev. Rul. 60-193, 1960-1 C.B. 195, as modified by Rev. Rul. 66-258, 1966-2 C.B. 213.

[98] Seasongood v. Comm'r, *supra* note 61, at 910–912. Also Cochran v. Comm'r, 78 F.2d 176, 179 (4th Cir. 1935).

stigmatization as propaganda, therefore, a presentation must be fairly well balanced as to stating alternative viewpoints and solutions, and be motivated more by a purpose to educate than by a "selfish" purpose.[99]

(b) Expenditure Test

Five categories of activities are excluded from the term *influencing legislation* for purposes of the expenditure test: (1) making available the results of nonpartisan analysis, study, or research;[100] (2) providing technical advice or assistance to a governmental body or legislative committee in response to a written request by the body or committee;[101] (3) appearances before or communications to any legislative body with respect to a possible decision of that body that might affect the existence of the organization, its powers and duties, its tax-exempt status, or the deduction of contributions to it (the *self-defense exception*);[102] (4) communications between the organization and its bona fide members[103] with respect to legislation or proposed legislation of direct interest to it and them, unless the communications directly encourage the members to influence legislation or directly encourage the members to urge nonmembers to influence legislation;[104] and (5) routine communications with government officials or employees.[105]

In amplification of the fourth exception, expenditures for a communication that refers to, and reflects a view on, specific legislation are not lobbying expenditures if the communication satisfies the following requirements: (1) The communication is directed only to members of the organization; (2) the specific legislation the communication refers to, and reflects a view on, is of direct interest to the organization and its members; (3) the communication does not directly encourage the member to engage in direct lobbying;[106] and (4) the communication does not directly encourage the member to engage in grassroots lobbying.[107] An expenditure that meets all of these requirements, other than the third one, is treated as an expenditure for direct lobbying.[108] An expenditure that satisfies all of these requirements, other than the fourth one, is treated as an expenditure for grassroots lobbying.[109] The regulations provide rules for treatment, as expenditures for direct or grassroots lobbying, expenditures for any written communication that is designed primarily for members of an organization, and that refers to, and reflects a view on, specific legislation of direct interest to the organization and its members.[110]

The regulations create another exception, excusing examinations and dis-

---

[99] Rev. Rul. 68-263, 1968-1 C.B. 256. In general, see § 7.2.
[100] IRC § 4911(d)(2)(A); Reg. § 56.4911-2(c)(1). See text accompanied by notes 93–97.
[101] IRC § 4911(d)(2)(B); Reg. § 56.4911-2(c)(3).
[102] IRC § 4911(d)(2)(C); Reg. § 56.4911-2(c)(4).
[103] Reg. §§ 56.4911-5(f)(1)–(4).
[104] IRC § 4911(d)(2)(D).
[105] IRC § 4911(d)(2)(E).
[106] Reg. § 56.4911-5(f)(6).
[107] Reg. § 56.4911-5(b).
[108] Reg. § 56.4911-5(c).
[109] Reg. § 56.4911-5(d).
[110] Reg. § 56.4911-5(e).

cussions of broad social, economic, and similar problems from the ambit of direct lobbying communications and grassroots lobbying communications, even if the problems are of the type with which government would be expected to deal ultimately.[111]

§ 20.5 OTHER ASPECTS OF THE EXPENDITURE TEST

Previous sections of this chapter contain summaries of various aspects of the expenditure test. However, there are some additional aspects of this test.

(a) The Election

An eligible charitable organization[112] that desires to avail itself of the expenditure test must elect to come within these standards and can do so on a year-to-year basis.[113] Charitable organizations that may not or that choose not to make the election are governed by the substantial part test.[114] Churches, conventions or associations of churches, integrated auxiliaries of churches, certain supporting organizations of noncharitable entities,[115] and private foundations may not elect to come under these rules[116]—the latter having been made subject to stringent regulation in this regard by legislation enacted in 1969.[117]

If a charitable organization is denied tax exemption by reason of the expenditure test and thereafter is again recognized as an exempt charitable organization, it may again elect the expenditure test.[118]

(b) Record Keeping

An electing public charity must keep a record of its lobbying expenditures for a tax year. These records must include (1) expenditures for grassroots lobbying, (2) amounts paid for direct lobbying, (3) the portion of amounts paid or incurred as compensation for an employee's services for direct lobbying, (4) amounts paid for out-of-pocket expenditures incurred on behalf of the organization and for direct lobbying, (5) the allocable portion of administration, overhead, and other general expenditures attributable to direct lobbying, (6) expenditures for publications or for communications with members to the extent the expenditures are treated as expenditures for direct lobbying, and (7) expenditures for direct lobbying of a controlled organization[119] to the extent in-

---

[111] Reg. § 56.4911-2(c)(2).
[112] Reg. §§ 1.501(h)-2(b), 1.501(h)-2(e).
[113] IRC §§ 501(h)(3), 501(h)(4), 1.501(h)(6). This election, and any revocation or reelection of it, is made by filing Form 5768 with the IRS. Reg. §§ 1.501(h)-2(a), 1.501(h)-2(c), 1.501(h)-2(d).
[114] Reg. § 1.501(h)-1(a)(4).
[115] See § 11.3(c).
[116] IRC § 501(h)(5).
[117] IRC § 4945(d)(1), (e). See Chapter 11.
[118] Reg. § 1.501(h)-3(d)(4).
[119] Reg. § 56.4911-10(c).

cluded by a controlling organization[120] in its lobbying expenditures.[121] Identical record keeping requirements apply with respect to grassroots expenditures.[122]

(c) Affiliated Organizations

The expenditure test contains methods of aggregating the expenditures of related organizations, so as to forestall the creation of numerous organizations for the purpose of avoiding the limitations of the foregoing tests. Where two or more charitable organizations are members of an affiliated group[123] and at least one of the members has elected coverage under the expenditure test, the calculations of lobbying and exempt purpose expenditures must be made by taking into account the expenditures of the group.[124] If these expenditures exceed the permitted limits, each of the electing member organizations must pay a proportionate share of the penalty excise tax, with the nonelecting members treated under the substantial part test.[125]

Generally, under these rules, two organizations are deemed *affiliated* where (1) one organization is bound by decisions of the other on legislative issues pursuant to its governing instrument,[126] or (2) the governing board of one organization includes enough representatives of the other (an *interlocking governing board*[127]) to cause or prevent action on legislative issues[128] by the first organization.[129] Where a number of organizations are affiliated, even in chain fashion, all of them are treated as one group of affiliated organizations.[130] However, if a group of autonomous organizations controls an organization but no one organization in the controlling group alone can control that organization, the organizations are not considered an affiliated group by reason of the interlocking directorates rule.[131]

(d) Reporting

In order to make information about the legislative activities of electing charitable organizations obtainable by the public, the required contents of annual information returns were expanded.[132] Thus, an electing organization must disclose in its

---

[120] *Id.*
[121] Reg. § 56.4911-6(a).
[122] Reg. § 56.4911-6(b).
[123] Reg. § 56.4911-7(e).
[124] IRC § 4911(f)(1); Reg. §§ 56.4911-8, 56.4911-10.
[125] IRC § 4911(f)(1)(B).
[126] Reg. § 56.4911-7(c).
[127] Reg. § 56.4911-7(b).
[128] Reg. § 56.4911-7(a)(3).
[129] IRC § 4911(f)(2); Reg. § 56.4911-7(a)(1).
[130] Reg. § 56.4911-7(d).
[131] IRC § 4911(f)(3).
[132] See § 24.3(a).

information return the amount of its lobbying expenditures (total and grass-roots), together with the amount that it could have spent for legislative purposes without becoming subject to the 25 percent excise tax. An electing organization that is a member of an affiliated group must provide this information with re-spect to both itself and the entire group.[133]

(e) When Should the Election Be Made?

Consequently, a charitable organization (that is not a private foundation) may at-tempt to influence the legislative process as long as the organization stays within the bounds of insubstantiality. Thus, a charitable organization desiring to engage in legislative activities must, in assessing insubstantiality, decide whether to uti-lize the substantial part test or elect the expenditure test and must determine whether one or more exceptions provided by either test are available. In an opti-mum situation, a charitable organization can expend 20 percent or more of its to-tal expenditures on attempts to influence legislation.[134]

There are many variables to consider when deciding whether to elect the ex-penditure test. For example, a charitable organization that seeks to engage en-tirely in grassroots lobbying is undoubtedly best advised to not make the election, because the limitation on that type of lobbying is probably more strin-gent under the expenditure test than under the substantial part test.[135] Other fac-tors to consider are these: (1) the relative certainty as to allowable lobbying afforded by the expenditure test, (2) the possibility that the IRS may enforce the substantial part test using one or more standards other than the volume of leg-islative activity, (3) the fact that the time expended by volunteers for lobbying is taken into account for purposes of the substantial part test and is disregarded for purposes of the expenditure test, (4) the fact that lobbying is assessed annually pursuant to the substantial part test and over a four-year average under the ex-penditure test, (5) the potential impact of the affiliation rules in the expenditure test,[136] (6) the additional reporting responsibilities imposed by the expenditure test,[137] (7) the potential of applicability of the taxes that may be imposed in in-stances of substantial lobbying,[138] (8) the fact that a public charity that has elected the expenditure test may satisfy its requirement to report lobbying activities to Congress using the definition of lobbying under the test,[139] and (9) the fact that a public charity that has elected the expenditure test may satisfy its requirement to

---

[133] IRC § 6033(b)(8).

[134] Presumably, a 20 percent lobbying expenditure, allowed by the expenditure test, is greater than what would be allowed under the substantial part test. Whether lobbying can exceed 20 percent in any one year (disregarding the expenditure test's averaging rule), without adversely affecting a chari-table organization's tax-exempt status, will essentially depend upon the availability and use of one or more of the exceptions from the limitation (see the text accompanying *supra* notes 100–111).

[135] See text accompanied by *supra* notes 80–81,

[136] See text accompanied by *supra* notes 123–131,

[137] See text accompanied by *supra* notes 132–133,

[138] See *infra* § 6.

[139] Lobbying Disclosure Act of 1995, *supra* note 5 ("Act") § 1610(a)(2).

report lobbying expenses to Congress by filing a copy of the schedule[140] to the entity's annual information return.[141]

Finally, a nonelecting charitable organization desiring to engage in a substantial amount of lobbying can convert to a social welfare organization[142] to pursue those activities.[143]

§ 20.6 LOBBYING EXPENDITURES BY CHARITABLE ORGANIZATIONS AND TAX SANCTIONS

If an otherwise charitable organization that has not elected to come under the expenditure test or that is ineligible to make the election, fails to meet the tax law definition of *charity* because of attempts to influence legislation, a tax in the amount of 5 percent of the *lobbying expenditures* is to be imposed, for each year involved, on the organization.[144] A lobbying expenditure is any amount paid or incurred by a charitable organization in carrying on propaganda or otherwise attempting to influence legislation.[145]

A separate tax is applicable to each of the organization's managers (basically, its officers and directors) who agreed to the making of the lobbying expenditures (knowing that they were likely to result in revocation of its exemption), unless the agreement was not willful and was due to reasonable cause.[146] This tax is also an amount equal to 5 percent of the lobbying expenditures and can be imposed only where the tax on the organization is imposed.

---

[140] See § 24.3(a).

[141] Act § 1610(c)(1). In making its good faith estimate of lobbying expenditures as required by the Act, this type of public charity may use the amounts reported under the expenditure test reporting requirements (*id.* § 1610(a)(1)). An organization that has elected to use tax law information for Act reporting purposes must inform the Secretary of the Senate and the Clerk of the House of that fact; all estimates for a year must be made under the elected procedures (*id.* § 1610(c)(1)).

[142] In general, see Chapter 12.

[143] Cf. text accompanying *supra* note 88. In general, Kusma & Jackson, "Lobbying By Exempt Organizations: A Realistic Alternative to the 'Substantial Part' Test," 69 *Taxes* (No. 7) 422 (July 1991); Bouchillon, "Guiding Lobbying Charities into a Safe Harbor: Final Section 501(h) and 4911 Regulations Set Limits for Tax-Exempt Organizations," 61 *Miss. L. J.* 157 (Spring 1991); Troyer, Slocombe & Mallon, "Final Lobbying Regulations Provide Workable Guidance," 74 *J. Tax.* (No. 2) 124 (1991); McGovern, Accettura & Walsh Skelly, "The Final Lobbying Regulations: A Challenge for Both the IRS and Charities," 48 *Tax Notes* (No. 10) 1305 (1990); Asher & Fountain, "Lobbying by Public Charities—Living With (or Without) the New IRS Regulations," 3 *Exempt. Org. Tax Rev.* (No. 11) 1261 (1991); Asher & Fountain, "Lobbying by Public Charities—Living With (or Without) the New IRS Regulations," 3 *Exempt Org. Tax Rev.* (No. 9) 1011 (1991); Murdich, "The Final Lobbying Regulations—Finally," 2 *J. Tax. Exempt Orgs.* 23 (Fall 1990); Hallenberg & Murdich, "A Second Look at the Second Set of Lobbying Regulations," 1 *J. Tax. Exempt Orgs.* 29 (Winter 1990).

[144] IRC § 4912(a).

[145] IRC § 4912(d)(1).

[146] IRC § 4912(b). According to the conference report accompanying this legislation, the burden of proof as to whether a manager knowingly participated in the lobbying expenditure is on the IRS and the fact that the excise tax is imposed on an organization does not itself establish that any manager of the organization is subject to the excise tax (H. Rep. 495, 100th Cong., 1st Sess. 1024 (1987)).

§ 20.7   LOBBYING BY SOCIAL WELFARE ORGANIZATIONS

There are no federal tax law limitations on attempts to influence legislation by tax-exempt social welfare organizations. In other words, a social welfare organization can be what a charitable organization cannot be—an action organization.[147]

Thus, a tax-exempt social welfare organization may draft proposed legislation, present petitions for the purpose of having legislation introduced, and circulate speeches, reprints, and other material concerning legislation.[148] This type of organization may appear before a federal or state legislative body, or a local council, administrative board or commission, and may encourage members of the community to contact legislative representatives in support of its programs.[149]

The IRS ruled that a tax-exempt social welfare organization can operate to inform the public on controversial subjects, "even though the organization advocates a particular viewpoint."[150] The IRS noted that "seeking of legislation germane to the organization's program is recognized by the regulations . . . as permissible means of attaining social welfare purposes."[151] Offering a rationale for allowing a tax-exempt social welfare organization to engage in legislative activities, the IRS stated: "The education of the public on [controversial subjects] is deemed beneficial to the community because society benefits from an informed citizenry."[152] Likewise, the IRS extended tax-exempt status as a charitable entity to an organization formed to educate the public on the subject of abortions, promote the rights of the unborn, and support legislative and constitutional changes to restrict women's access to abortions, recognizing that the organization "advocates objectives that are controversial."[153]

Similarly, an organization that engaged in attempts to influence legislation intended to benefit animals, animal owners, persons interested in the welfare of animals, and the community at large was considered a tax-exempt social welfare organization, although it was denied tax-exempt status as a charitable entity (as an organization operated for the prevention of cruelty to animals) because it was deemed to be an action organization.[154]

§ 20.8   LOBBYING BY ASSOCIATIONS

There is no restriction, from the standpoint of the tax exemption for membership associations and other business leagues, on the amount of legislative activity these organizations may conduct. Indeed, the IRS recognized attempts to influence legislation as a valid function for a tax-exempt business league.[155]

---

[147] See § 12.3.
[148] Rev. Rul. 68-656, 1968-2 C.B. 216.
[149] Rev. Rul. 67-6, 1967-1 C.B. 135.
[150] Rev. Rul. 68-656, *supra* note 148, at 216.
[151] *Id.* at 216–217.
[152] *Id.* at 216.
[153] Rev. Rul. 76-81, 1976-1 C.B. 156.
[154] Rev. Rul. 67-293, 1967-2 C.B. 185.
[155] Rev. Rul. 61-177, 1961-2 C.B. 117.

However, the federal tax law rules stringently restricting the deductibility of business expenses for legislative activities[156] have meaningful consequences in this context, in that they can operate as an indirect limitation on lobbying activities by business leagues. The inability to fully deduct membership dues may have an impact on the extent of an association's membership.

(a) General Business Expense Deduction Disallowance Rules

Under these rules, generally there is no business expense deduction for any amount paid or incurred in connection with influencing legislation (whether by direct or grass roots lobbying); any attempt to influence the general public, or segments of it, with respect to legislative matters or referendums; or any direct communication with a covered executive branch official in an attempt to influence the official actions or positions of the official.[157] However, this deduction disallowance rule basically does not apply to local legislation[158] or with respect to Indian tribal governments.[159]

In this setting, *influencing legislation* means (1) any attempt to influence legislation through a lobbying communication and (2) all activities, such as research, preparation, planning, and coordination, including deciding whether to make a lobbying communication, engaged in for a purpose of making or supporting a lobbying communication, even if not yet made.[160] A *lobbying communication* is any communication (other than one compelled by subpoena or otherwise compelled by federal or state law) with any member or employee of a legislative body or any other government official or employee who may participate in the formulation of the legislation[161] that (1) refers to specific legislation and reflects a view on that legislation or (2) clarifies, amplifies, modifies, or provides support for views reflected in a prior lobbying communication.[162] The term *specific legislation* includes a specific legislative proposal that has not been introduced in a legislative body.[163]

Covered executive branch official describes the President, the Vice President, any officer or employee of the White House Office of the Executive Office of the President, the two most senior-level officers of each of the other agencies within the Executive Office of the President, any individual serving in a position in level I of the Executive Schedule (for example, a member of the Cabinet),[164] any other individual designated by the President as having Cabinet-level status, and an immediate deputy of an individual in the preceding two categories.[165]

---

[156] IRC § 162(e).
[157] IRC § 162(e)(1)(A), (C), (D). These rules apply with respect to expenses paid or incurred beginning in 1994. Thus, the tax regulations reflecting prior law (Reg. § 1.162-20(c)(1)–1.162-20(c)(3)) are, with two exceptions (see *infra* notes 158 and 159), no longer operational.
[158] IRC § 162(e)(2). The regulations developed under prior law (Reg. § 1.162-20) generally are pertinent to the costs of lobbying in connection with local legislation.
[159] IRC § 162(e)(7).
[160] Reg. § 1.162-29(b)(1).
[161] The term *legislation* is the subject of *supra* § 1(c).
[162] IRC § 162(e)(4)(A); Reg. § 1.162-29(b)(3).
[163] Reg. § 1.162-29(b)(5).
[164] 5 U.S.C. § 5312.
[165] IRC § 162(e)(6).

The purposes for engaging in an activity are determined on the basis of all the facts and circumstances, including whether the activity and the lobbying communication are proximate in time; the activity and the lobbying communication relate to similar subject matter; the activity is performed at the request of, under the direction of, or on behalf of a person making the lobbying communication; the results of the activity are also used for a nonlobbying purpose; and, at the time the person engages in the activity, there is specific legislation to which the activity relates.[166] In instances of activities involving lobbying and nonlobbying purposes, costs must be allocated.[167] Certain activities, such as determining the status of legislation or summarizing legislation, do not constitute lobbying.[168]

Any amount paid or incurred for research for, or preparation, planning, or coordination of, any lobbying activity subject to the general disallowance rule is treated as paid or incurred in connection with the lobbying activity.[169] The apparent intent of this rule is to convert what might otherwise be a function constituting nonpartisan analysis, study, or research[170] into a lobbying undertaking where the research is subsequently used in an attempt to influence legislation. It is not clear how this rule is to be applied where the research is performed by one organization and the lobbying using that research is done by another, particularly where the two organizations are related.[171]

There is a *de minimis* exception for certain in-house expenditures where the organization's total amount of these expenditures for a tax year does not exceed $2,000 (computed without taking into account general overhead costs otherwise allocable to most forms of lobbying).[172] The term *in-house expenditures* means expenditures for lobbying (such as labor and materials costs) other than payments to a professional lobbyist to conduct lobbying for the organization and dues or other similar payments that are allocable to lobbying (such as association dues).[173]

An organization, although able to use any reasonable method of allocation of labor costs and general and administrative costs to lobbying activities, is authorized to use a *ratio method*, a *gross-up method*, or tax rules concerning allocation of service costs.[174] An organization may disregard time spent by an individual on lobbying activities if less than 5 percent of his or her time was so spent, although this de minimis test is not applicable with respect to *direct contact lobbying*, which is a meeting, telephone conversation, letter, or other similar means of communication with a federal or state legislator or a covered executive branch official and which otherwise qualifies as a lobbying activity.[175]

Other than a general exclusion for charitable organizations, there are no

---

[166] Reg. § 1.162-29(c)(1).
[167] Reg. § 1.162-29(c)(2). See text accompanied by *infra* note 174.
[168] Reg. § 1.162-29(c)(3).
[169] IRC § 162(e)(5)(C).
[170] See *supra* § 4(a), text accompanied by notes 93–97; § 4(b), text accompanied by note 100.
[171] See, by contrast, *supra* § 2(c)(i), text accompanied by note 48.
[172] IRC § 162(e)(5)(B)(i).
[173] IRC § 162(e)(5)(B)(ii).
[174] Reg. § 1.162-28(a)–(f). The third of these methods is the subject of IRC § 263A.
[175] Reg. § 1.162-28(g).

specific statutory exceptions to these rules. However, as noted, any communication compelled by subpoena, or otherwise compelled by federal or state law, does not constitute an attempt to influence, legislation or an official's actions.[176]

A provision prevents a cascading of the lobbying expense disallowance rule to ensure that, when multiple parties are involved, the rule results in the denial of a deduction at only one level. Thus, in the case of an individual engaged in the trade or business of providing lobbying services or an individual who is an employee and receives employer reimbursements for lobbying expenses, the disallowance rule does not apply to expenditures of the individual in conducting the activities directly on behalf of a client or employer. Instead, the lobbying payments made by the client or employer to the lobbyist or employee are nondeductible under the general disallowance rule.[177]

This anticascading rule applies where there is a direct, one-on-one relationship between the taxpayer and the entity conducting the lobbying activity, such as a client or employment relationship. It does not apply to dues or other payments to membership organizations that act to further the interests of all of their members rather than the interests of any one particular member. These organizations are themselves subject to the general disallowance rule, based on the amount of their lobbying expenditures.[178]

There is an antiavoidance rule designed to prevent donors from using charitable organizations[179] as conduits to conduct lobbying activities, the costs of which would be nondeductible if conducted directly by the donor. That is, no deduction is allowed as a charitable contribution deduction (nor as a business expense deduction) for amounts contributed to a charitable organization if (1) the charitable organization's lobbying activities regard matters of direct financial interest to the donor's trade or business, and (2) a principal purpose of the contribution is to avoid the general disallowance rule that would apply if the contributor directly had conducted the lobbying activities.[180] The application of this anti-avoidance rule to a contributor would not adversely affect the tax-exempt status of the charitable organization as long as the activity qualified as nonpartisan analysis, study, or research[181] or was not substantial under either the substantial part test or the expenditure test[182] of the rules limiting the legislative activities of charitable organizations.[183]

The determination regarding a *principal* purpose of the contribution is to be

---

[176] See *supra* note 162. Also H. Rep. 213, 103d Cong., 1st Sess. 607 (1993).

[177] IRC § 162(e)(5)(A).

[178] H. Rep. 213, *supra* note 176, at 610.

[179] See Part Two.

[180] IRC § 170(f)(9).

[181] See *supra* § 4(a), text accompanied by notes 93–97; § 4(6), text accompanied by note 100.

[182] See *supra* §§ 1-6. There are exemptions for these four categories of organizations based on refinements of the 90-percent-of-dues test; organizations can avail themselves of this exemption by satisfying record-keeping and annual return filing requirements or by obtaining a private letter ruling from the IRS on the point. For example, social welfare organizations, and agricultural and horticultural organizations, are treated as satisfying the exemption requirements if either (1) more than 90 percent of all annual dues are received from persons who each pay less than $50 or (2) more than 90 percent of all annual dues are received from certain tax-exempt entities. (This $50 amount is indexed for inflation; for tax years beginning in 1998, the amount is $55 (Rev. Proc. 97-57, 1997-52 I.R.B. 20). The IRS occasionally issues rulings as to the availability of the exemption (e.g., Priv. Ltr. Rul. 9429016).

[183] H. Rep. 213, *supra* note 176, at 610, note 70.

based on the facts and circumstances surrounding the contribution, including the existence of any formal or informal instructions relating to the charitable organization's use of the contribution for lobbying efforts (including nonpartisan analysis), the "temporal nexus" between the making of the contribution and the conduct of the lobbying activities, and any historical pattern of contributions by the donor to the charity.[184]

(b) Association Flow-Through and Proxy Tax Rules

A flow-through rule applicable with respect to membership associations disallows a business expense deduction for the portion of the membership dues (or voluntary payments or special assessments) paid to a tax-exempt organization that engages in lobbying activities.[185] Trade, business, and professional associations, and similar organizations, generally are required to provide annual information disclosure to their members, estimating the portion of their dues that is allocable to lobbying and thus nondeductible.

The organization must disclose in its annual information return both the total amount of its lobbying expenditures and the total amount of dues (or similar payments) allocable to these expenditures.[186] For this purpose, an organization's lobbying expenditures for a taxable year are allocated to the dues received during the taxable year.[187] Any excess amount of lobbying expenditures is carried forward and allocated to dues received in the following taxable year.[188]

The organization also is generally required to provide notice to each person paying dues (or similar payments), at the time of assessment or payment of the dues, of the portion of dues that the organization reasonably estimates will be allocable to the organization's lobbying expenditures during the year and that is, therefore, not deductible by the member.[189] This estimate must be reasonably calculated to provide organization members with adequate notice of the nondeductible amount. The notice must be provided in conspicuous and easily recognizable format.[190] These requirements of annual disclosure and notice to members are applicable to all tax-exempt organizations other than those that are charitable entities.[191]

If an organization's actual lobbying expenditures for a tax year exceed the estimated allocable amount of the expenditures (either because of higher-

---

[184] *Id*. at 610.

[185] IRC § 162(e)(3).

[186] IRC § 6033(e)(1)(A)(i). An organization that is subject to these rules may satisfy its requirement to report lobbying activities to Congress using the definition of lobbying under these rules and may satisfy its requirement to report lobbying expenses to Congress by using the amounts that are nondeductible under these rules (Lobbying Disclosure Act of 1995, *supra* note 5 § 1610(b)).

[187] IRC § 6033(e)(1)(C)(i).

[188] IRC § 6033(e)(1)(c)(ii).

[189] IRC § 6033(e)(1)(A)(ii).

[190] H. Rep. 213, *supra* note 176, at 608, note 65. As to the standard of "conspicuous and easily recognizable," the IRC § 6113 rules are used (see § 22.2).

[191] IRC § 6033(e)(1)(B). The term *charitable* in this context means all organizations that are tax-exempt by reason of IRC § 501(c)(3).

than-anticipated lobbying expenses or lower-than-projected dues receipts), the organization must pay a *proxy tax* on the excess amount[192] or seek permission from the IRS to adjust the following year's notice of estimated expenditures.[193] The proxy tax rate is equal to the highest corporate tax rate in effect for the taxable year;[194] the highest corporate tax rate is 35 percent.[195] If an organization does not provide its members with reasonable notice of anticipated lobbying expenditures allocable to dues, the organization is subject to the proxy tax on its aggregate lobbying expenditures for the year.

If an organization elects to pay the proxy tax rather than provide the requisite information disclosure to its members, no portion of any dues or other payments made by members of the organization is rendered nondeductible because of the organization's lobbying activities. That is, if the organization pays the tax, the dues payments are fully deductible by the members as business expenses (assuming they otherwise qualify).

However, this disclosure and notice element is not required in the case of an organization that (1) incurs only *de minimis* amounts of in-house lobbying expenditures, (2) elects to pay the proxy tax on its lobbying expenditures incurred during the taxable year,[196] or (3) establishes, pursuant to an IRS regulation or procedure, that substantially all of its dues monies are paid by members who are not entitled to deduct the dues in computing their taxable income. The concept of *de minimis* in-house expenditures in this setting is the same as that in the disallowance rules (including the $2,000 maximum).[197] Amounts paid to outside lobbyists, or as dues to another organization that lobbies, do not qualify for this exception.

Regarding this third component, if an organization establishes, to the satisfaction of the IRS, that substantially all of the dues monies it receives are paid by members who are not entitled to deduct their dues in any event (and obtains a waiver from the IRS), the organization is not subject to the disclosure and notice requirements (or the proxy tax).[198] In this context, the term *substantially all* means at least 90 percent.[199] Examples of organizations of this nature are (1) an organization that receives at least 90 percent of its dues monies from members that are tax-exempt charitable organizations; and (2) an organization that receives at least 90 percent of its dues monies from members who are individuals not entitled to deduct the dues payments because the payments are not ordinary and necessary business expenses. Indeed, by IRS pronouncement,[200] there is a complete exemption from the reporting and notice requirements (and proxy tax) for all tax-exempt organizations, other than social welfare organizations that are not veterans'

---

[192] IRC § 6033(e)(2)(A)(ii).
[193] IRC § 6033(e)(2)(B).
[194] IRC § 6033(e)(2)(A).
[195] IRC § 11.
[196] IRC § 6033(e)(2)(A)(i).
[197] IRC § 6033(e)(1)(B)(ii). See the text accompanied by *supra* note 172.
[198] IRC § 6033(e)(3).
[199] H. Rep. 213, *supra* note 176, at 609.
[200] Rev. Proc. 95-35, 1995-2 C.B. 391.

organizations;[201] agricultural organizations;[202] horticultural organizations;[203] and trade, business, and professional associations, other business leagues, chambers of commerce, and boards of trade.[204]

If the amount of lobbying expenditures exceeds the amount of dues or other similar payments for the taxable year, the proxy tax is imposed on an amount equal to the dues and similar payments; any excess lobbying expenditures are carried forward to the next taxable year.[205]

§ 20.9 CONSTITUTIONAL LAW CONSIDERATIONS

It has been asserted that the proscription on substantial legislative activities applicable to public charities is violative of constitutional law principles.[206] While the issues were repeatedly presented to the courts, it was not until 1982 that a litigant was successful in securing a decision finding that this provision is constitutionally deficient. Nonetheless, even that remarkable occurrence ultimately failed—almost with unintended consequences for other categories of tax-exempt organizations.

Representative of these decisions was one handed down in 1979.[207] The issues involved were the following: does this tax law limitation on legislative activities (1) impose an unconstitutional condition upon the exercise of First Amendment rights (i.e., the right to engage in legislative activity), (2) restrict the exercise of First Amendment rights as being a discriminatory denial of tax exemption for engaging in speech, (3) deny organizations so restricted the equal protection of the laws in violation of the Fifth Amendment, and/or (4) lack a compelling governmental interest that would justify the restrictions on First Amendment rights?

The approach of the courts on the First Amendment question has been to recognize that the lobbying of legislators constitutes an exercise of the First Amendment right of petition[208] and thus that the Amendment protects legislative activities. Oft-cited in this context is the Supreme Court declaration that the general advocacy of ideas is constitutionally protected as part of this nation's "pro-

---

[201] See Chapter 12.

[202] See § 15.2.

[203] See § 15.3.

[204] See Chapter 13.

[205] H.R. Rep. No. 213, *supra*, note 176, at 608–609. In general, Dillon, "Lobbying Provisions of H.R. 2264 for Tax-Exempt Membership Organizations," 8 Exempt Org. Tax Rev. (No. 5) 895 (1993); Cummings, Jr., "Tax Policy, Social Policy, and Politics: Amending Section 162(e)," 9 *Exempt Org. Tax Rev.* (No. 1) 137 (1994).

[206] E.g., Troyer, "Charities, Law-Making, and the Constitution: The Validity of the Restrictions on Influencing Legislation," 31 *N.Y.U. Inst. on Fed. Tax.* 1415 (1973); Note, "Regulating the Political Activities of Foundations," 83 *Harv. L. Rev.* 1843 (1970).

[207] Taxation With Representation of Wash. v. Blumenthal, 79-1 U.S.T.C. ¶ 9185 (D.D.C. 1979), *aff'd*, 81-1 U.S.T.C. ¶ 9329 (D.C. Cir. 1981), *rev. en banc sub nom.*, Taxation With Representation of Wash. v. Regan, 676 F.2d 715 (D.C. Cir. 1982).

[208] E.g., Eastern R.R. Presidents Conference v. Noerr Motor Freight, Inc., 365 U.S. 127 (1961); Liberty Lobby, Inc. v. Pearson, 390 F.2d 489 (D.C. Cir. 1968).

found national commitment to the principle that debate on public issues should be uninhibited, robust, and wide-open."[209] However, the courts inevitably go on to observe that the tax law limitation does not violate First Amendment rights because it does not on its face prohibit organizations from engaging in substantial efforts to influence legislation.[210]

This position is based on a 1959 Supreme Court pronouncement upholding the constitutionality of a regulation that excluded from deduction as business expenses amounts expended for the promotion or defeat of legislation.[211] There, the Court stated that the taxpayers "are not being denied a tax deduction because they engage in constitutionally protected activities, but are simply being required to pay for these activities entirely out of their own pocketbook, as everyone else engaging in similar activities is required to do under the provisions of the Internal Revenue Code."[212] Thus, when it comes to substantial legislative activities, charitable organizations are required to fund these efforts from their own (after-tax) resources, and this result is not regarded as a denial of a deduction for engaging in constitutionally protected activities.

As regards the second aspect of the First Amendment question, this argument is premised in part upon the fact that several categories of tax-exempt organizations are free to lobby without jeopardizing their tax-exempt status.[213] Thus, the proposition is that the lobbying condition on charitable groups is a discriminatory denial of a tax exemption for engaging in protected speech. The courts hold that this principle relates to legislative efforts "aimed at the suppression of dangerous ideas"[214] and not to denials or revocation of tax exemptions for charitable organizations.

Similar short shrift has been given to the equal protection challenge, which is based upon the fact that similarly situated (that is, tax-exempt) organizations are accorded different treatment with respect to lobbying activities. The courts usually concede that this involves a classification that accords differing treatment to classes but that it is permissible since the classification does not affect a "fundamental" right nor involve a "suspect" class.[215] The applicable standard of scrutiny—which this statutory limitation has been repeatedly ruled to satisfy—is whether the challenged classification is reasonably related to a legitimate governmental purpose.[216]

This standard is also deemed met where the courts evaluate the constitu-

---

[209] New York Times Co. v. Sullivan, 376 U.S. 254, 270 (1964).

[210] Taxation With Representation v. United States, 585 F.2d 1219 (4th Cir. 1978), *cert. den.*, 441 U.S. 905 (1979).

[211] Cammarano v. United States, *supra* note 21.

[212] *Id.* at 513.

[213] E.g., the organizations described in IRC §§ 501(c)(4), 501(c)(5), 501(c)(6), 501(c)(8), 501(c)(9), 501(c)(19). See Chapters 12, 15, 13, § 18.4(a), § 16.3, and § 18.10(a), respectively.

[214] Speiser v. Randall, 357 U.S. 513, 519 (1958), where the U.S. Supreme Court struck down a state statute that required veterans to take a loyalty oath as a condition to the receipt of a veterans' property tax exemption.

[215] E.g., San Antonio Independent School District v. Rodriguez, 411 U.S. 1 (1973); Dunn v. Blumstein, 405 U.S. 330 (1972); Shapiro v. Thompson, 394 U.S. 618 (1969).

[216] E.g., United States Dep't of Agric. v. Moreno, 413 U.S. 528 (1973); Frontiero v. Richardson, 411 U.S. 677 (1973).

tionality of the proscription on legislative activity as respects legislative activities in relation to the requirement that it be rationally related to a legitimate government purpose.[217] Several of these purposes are usually found served: "assurance of governmental neutrality with respect to the lobbying activities of charitable organizations; prevention of abuse of charitable lobbying by private interests; and preservation of a balance between the lobbying activities of charitable organizations and those of non-charitable organizations and individuals."[218]

Thus, until 1982, all courts that considered the matter had made it clear that there is no constitutional imperfection in the federal tax antilobbying clause.[219] In that year, however, a federal court of appeals changed the complexion of the constitutional law concerning the antilobbying rule applicable to charitable organizations. The appellate court agreed that this restriction on legislative activities is not violative of free speech (First Amendment) rights but—after concluding that an organization that acquires tax exemption and charitable donee status is thereby receiving a government subsidy—held that this subsidy cannot constitutionally be accorded on a discriminatory basis and that to do so is violative of equal protection (Fifth Amendment) rights.[220] Therefore, the court held, the fact that charitable organizations are required to limit their lobbying to an insubstantial extent, while certain other organizations—such as veterans' organizations—can lobby without these limits, is an unconstitutionally discriminatory allocation of this "government subsidy."[221]

The appellate court held that "[b]y subsidizing the lobbying activities of veterans' organizations while failing to subsidize the lobbying of . . . charitable groups, Congress has violated the equal protection guarantees of the Constitution."[222] While the court decided that the challenge to the lobbying restriction is "weak" if based solely on free speech claims and is "weak" if based solely on equal protection claims,[223] it concluded that "the whole of . . . [the] argument well exceeds the sum of its parts" and that a "First Amendment concern must inform the equal protection analysis in this case."[224]

As a prelude to its findings, the court concluded that a "high level of scrutiny is required" because the lobbying restriction on charitable organizations "constitutes a limitation on protected First Amendment activity" and because the equal protection argument involves "what is clearly a fundamental right."[225] Under law, this "scrutiny" requires a determination as to whether "a substantial

---

[217] E.g., United States v. O'Brien, 391 U.S. 367 (1968); Schenk v. United States, 249 U.S. 47 (1919).

[218] Taxation With Representation of Wash. v. Blumenthal, *supra* note 207.

[219] Haswell v. United States, *supra* note 63, at 500 F.2d 1147–1150; Tax Analysts & Advocates v. Shultz, 74-2 U.S.T.C. ¶ 9601 (D.D.C. 1974), *aff'd*, 512 F.2d 992 (D.C. Cir. 1975) (suit to declare legislative activities provision of IRC § 501(c)(3) dismissed).

[220] Taxation With Representation of Wash. v. Regan, *supra* note 207.

[221] Charitable organizations are those that are tax-exempt by reason of IRC § 501(c)(3) and that are charitable donees by reason of IRC § 170(c)(2); veterans' organizations are tax-exempt by reason of IRC § 501(c)(3), (4), or (19), and are charitable donees by reason of IRC § 170(c)(3).

[222] Taxation With Representation of Wash. v. Regan, *supra* note 207, at 717.

[223] *Id.* As to the equal protection aspect, the court conceded that "Congress has vast leeway under the Constitution to classify the recipients of its benefits and to favor some groups over others" (*id.* at 740).

[224] *Id.* at 715.

[225] *Id.* at 730.

governmental interest supports the classification."[226] The court based its conclusion on the premise that nonprofit organizations that embody both features of tax exemption and eligibility to attract tax-deductible contributions are essentially alike. Inasmuch as the court was unpersuaded that there is a valid governmental interest to be served by treating charitable groups and veterans' groups differently on the matter of lobbying, the court ruled that the distinctions between the two classes of entities are "post hoc rationales" that are "constitutionally illegitimate."[227] Hence, the court found an unconstitutional denial of equal protection rights.

The remedy desired by the organization that initiated this case was the invalidation of the lobbying restrictions on charitable organizations. This the court was disinclined to do. First, it wrote that unfettered lobbying by charitable organizations would increase the likelihood of "selfish" contributions made solely to advance the donors' personal legislative interests.[228] Second, the court concluded that Congress believes that the public interest requires limitations on lobbying by charitable organizations and that "[e]ven when they attempt to remedy constitutional violations, courts must resist ordering relief that clearly exceeds the legitimate expectations of Congress."[229] The reverse approach—to place the same restrictions on veterans' groups as are presently imposed upon charitable groups—was far more appealing to the court and received serious consideration, but the court hesitated to strike down what it termed the "preferential treatment now accorded the lobbying of veterans' organizations," since veterans' groups were not parties to the litigation.[230] Instead, the case was ordered remanded to the district court "with the instruction that it cure the constitutionally invalid operation of Section 501(c) after inviting veterans' organizations to participate in framing the relief."[231] However, before the remand could occur, the decision was appealed to the U.S. Supreme Court.

The Supreme Court reacted swiftly, in 1983 unanimously reversing the court of appeals.[232] In so holding, the Court reiterated its position that the lobbying restriction on charitable organizations does not infringe First Amendment rights or regulate any First Amendment activity, that Congress did not violate the equal protection doctrine in the Fifth Amendment, and that Congress acted rationally in subsidizing (by means of tax exemption and charitable deductions) lobbying by veterans' organizations while not subsidizing lobbying by charitable organizations generally.

---

[226] *Id*. at 731.

[227] *Id*. at 739.

[228] *Id*. at 742.

[229] *Id*.

[230] *Id*. at 743.

[231] *Id*. at 744. In general, Brower, "Whose Voice Shall Be Heard? Lobbying Limitations on Section 501(c)(3) Charitable Organizations Held Unconstitutional in Regan v. Taxation With Representation," 28 *St. Louis U. L.J.* (No. 4) 1017 (1984); Cerasani, "Lobbying of Charitable Organizations: *Regan v. Taxation With Representation*," 37 *Tax Law*. (No. 2) 399 (1984); Crockett, "Lobbying Restrictions on Section 501(c)(3) Organizations Held Unconstitutional: First Amendment Implications of Taxation With Representation of Washington v. Regan," 1983 *B.Y.U. L. Rev.* 442 (1983); Hopkins, "Nonprofit Lobbying: Are the Rules Changing?," 23 *Foundation News* (No. 3) 46 (May/June 1982).

[232] Regan v. Taxation With Representation of Wash., 461 U.S. 540 (1983).

As to the free speech issue, the Court held that the federal tax law "does not deny . . . [a charitable organization] the right to receive deductible contributions to support its non-lobbying activity, nor does it deny . . . [a charitable organization] any independent benefit on account of its intention to lobby" but that "Congress has merely refused to pay for the lobbying out of public moneys."[233]

Noting that "[l]egislatures have especially broad latitude in creating classifications and distinctions in tax statutes,"[234] the Court concluded that the distinctions in the lobbying context made by Congress between charitable and veterans' organizations do not employ any "suspect classification," are not violative of equal protection principles, and are "within Congress' broad power in this area."[235] Moreover, the Court accepted the views that "Congress was concerned that exempt [charitable] organizations might use tax-deductible contributions to lobby to promote the private interests of their members"[236] and that "[o]ur country has a long standing policy of compensating veterans for their past contributions by providing them with numerous advantages."[237] Consequently, it appears that the proscription on substantial legislative activities by charitable organizations, contained in the federal tax rules, is beyond further constitutional law challenge in the courts.[238]

---

[233] *Id.* at 545, thus restating its position in Cammarano v. United States, *supra* note 21.

[234] *Id.* at 547.

[235] *Id.* at 548–550.

[236] *Id.* at 550.

[237] *Id.* at 551.

[238] A concurring opinion authored by Justice Blackmun took the position that the lobbying restriction in IRC § 501(c)(3) is—viewed in isolation—unconstitutional but that the defect is cured by the presence of IRC § 501(c)(4) (see § 12.3). This position rests upon the premises that an IRC § 501(c)(3) organization may utilize an IRC § 501(c)(4) affiliate for lobbying purposes and that contemporary administrative policy is to allow this in-tandem relationship to function relatively unfettered (see § 30.2(b)). And, this concurring opinion states, "[a]ny significant restriction on this channel of communication, however, would negate the saving effect of [IRC] § 501(c)(4)" (*id.* at 553).

[239] In general, Fuller & Abbott, "Political Activity and Lobbying Rules for Section 501(c) Organizations," 15 *Exempt Org. Tax. Rev.* (No. 3) 383 (1996); Cobb & King, "Working Through the Maze of Lobbying Requirements for Nonprofit Organizations," 7 *J. Tax. Exempt Orgs.* 243 (May/June 1996); Knight, Knight & Marshall, "Lobbying, Campaigning, and Section 501(c)(3)—What Is Allowed?," 2 *J. Tax. Exempt Orgs.* 17 (Fall 1990); Haight, "Lobbying for the Public Good: Limitations on Legislative Activities by Section 501(c)(3) Organizations," 23 *Gonzaga L. Rev.* (No. 1) 77 (1987); Robinson, "Charitable Lobbying Restraints and Tax-Exempt Organizations: Old Problems, New Directions?," 1984 *Utah L. Rev.* 337 (1984); Clark, "Church Lobbying: The Legitimacy of the Controls," 16 *Houston L. Rev.* 480 (1979); Webster & Krebs, *Associations and Lobbying Regulation* (1979); Nix, "Limitations on the Lobbying of Section 501(c)(3) Organizations—A Choice for Public Charities," 81 *W. Va. L. Rev.* 407 (1978–1979); Montgomery, "Lobbying by Public Charities Under the Tax Reform Act of 1976," 50 *Taxes* 449 (1978); Washburn, "New Tax Act Defines 'Substantial' Lobbying—But Charities Must Elect to be Covered," 55 *Taxes* 291 (1977); Bostick, "Lobbying By Non-Profit Groups," 1 *District Lawyer* (No. 3) 21 (1977); Whaley, "Political Activities of Section 501(c)(3) Organizations," *Proceedings of Univ. S. Cal. Law Center 29th Tax Institute* 195 (1977); Weithorn, "Practitioners' Planning Guide to the New Lobbying Rules for Public Charities," 46 *J. Tax.* 294 (1977); Hyslop & Ebell, "Public Interest Lobbying and the Tax Reform Act of 1976," 7 *Envtl. Law* 283 (1977); Note, "Lobbying by Section 501(c)(3) Organizations Under the Tax Reform Act of 1976: A Proposal for Change," 30 *Tax Law.* 214 (1976); Moore, Washburn & Goldman, "Restrictions on Lobbying Activities by Charitable Organizations: Proposed Legislative Remedies," 3 *Notre Dame J. Legis.* 17 (1976); Fogel, "To the I.R.S., 'Tis Better to Give than to Lobby," 61 *A.B.A. J.* 960 (1975); Caplin & Timbie, "Legislative Activities of Public Charities," 39 *Law and Contemp.*

The enactment of the expenditure test, liberalizing the ability of public charities to engage in legislative activities, did not stem the flow of comment on this subject. This segment of the law of tax-exempt organizations has always been a fertile field for commentators[239] and is likely to remain so.

Probs. 183 (1975); Note, "Political Speech of Charitable Organizations under the Internal Revenue Code," 41 *U. Chi. L. Rev.* 352 (1974); Geske, "Direct Lobbying Activities of Public Charities," 26 *Tax Law.* 305 (1973); Green, "Activism and the Tax Status of Exempt Organizations," 44 *P. B.A.Q.* 500 (1973); Wachtel, "David Meets Goliath in the Legislative Arena: A Losing Battle for an Equal Charitable Voice?," 9 *San Diego L. Rev.* 933 (1972); Garrett, "Federal Tax Limitations on Political Activities of Public Interest and Educational Organizations," 59 *Geo. L. J.* 561 (1971); Goldberg, "Guarding Against Loss of Tax Exempt Status Due to Campus Politics," 33 *J. Tax.* 232 (1970); Hauptman, "Tax-Exempt Private Educational Institutions: A Survey of the Prohibition Against Influencing Legislation and Intervening in Political Matters," 37 *Brooklyn L. Rev.* 107 (1970); Lehrfeld, "The Taxation of Ideology," 19 *Cath. U. L. Rev.* 50 (1969); Note, "Sierra Club, Political Activity, and Tax-Exempt Charitable Status," 55 *Geo L. J.* 1128 (1967); Note, "Income Taxes-Deductions: In General—IRS Proposes to Revoke Sierra Club's Eligibility to Receive Deductible Contributions Because of the Club's Political Activities," 80 *Harv. L. Rev.* 1793 (1967); Borod, "Lobbying for the Public Interest—Federal Tax Policy and Administration," 42 *N.Y.U.L. Rev.* 1087 (1967); Grant, "Sierra Club: The Procedural Aspects of the Revocation of its Tax Exemption," 15 *U.C.L.A. L. Rev.* 200 (1967); Boehm, "Taxes and Politics," 22 *Tax L. Rev.* 369 (1967); Clark, "The Limitation on Political Activities: A Discordant Note in the Law of Charities," 46 *Va. L. Rev.* 439 (1960); Note, "The Effect of Legislative Activity on the Tax Status of Religious, Charitable and Scientific Organizations," 10 *Ohio State L. J.* 414 (1957); Note, "Tax Treatment of Lobbying Expenses and Contributions," 67 *Harv. L. Rev.* 1408 (1954).

Political Campaign Activities by Tax-Exempt Organizations

With one exception—the political organization[1]—the federal tax laws concerning tax-exempt organizations do not encourage their involvement in political campaign activities. The limitations with respect to charitable organizations[2] are particularly stringent. Moreover, the law of tax-exempt organizations in this regard interrelates to, and sometimes is inconsistent with, the federal law regulating the financing and conduct of political campaigns.[3]

§ 21.1 POLITICAL CAMPAIGN ACTIVITIES OF PUBLIC CHARITIES

One of the criteria for qualification as a tax-exempt charitable organization is that it must "not participate in, or intervene in (including the publishing or distributing of statements), any political campaign on behalf of (or in opposition to) any candidate for public office."[4] If a charitable organization engages in a political campaign activity, it becomes classified as an *action organization*[5] and thus may be disqualified for tax-exempt status.

---

[1] See Chapter 17.

[2] That is, organizations described in IRC § 501(c)(3) and exempt from federal income taxation by reason of IRC § 501(a).

[3] This law is the subject of Hopkins, *Charity, Advocacy, and the Law* (New York: John Wiley & Sons, Inc. 1992), Chapter 18.

[4] IRC § 501(c)(3). This subject is treated in greater detail in Hopkins, *supra* note 3, Chapter 14.

[5] Reg. § 1.501(c)(3)-1(c)(3)(iii).

(a) Legislative History

This provision forbidding political campaign activity by charitable organizations was added to the federal tax law in 1954, without benefit of congressional hearings, in the form of a floor amendment adopted in the Senate.[6] During consideration of the legislation that became the Revenue Act of 1954, Senator Lyndon B. Johnson of Texas, on July 2, 1954, offered the amendment out of concern that funds provided by a charitable foundation were being used to help finance the campaign of an opponent in a primary election. Senator Johnson said only that the purpose of the amendment is to "deny[] tax-exempt status to not only those people who influence legislation but also to those who intervene in any political campaign on behalf of any candidate for any public office."[7] The phrase "(in opposition to)" was added to the provision in 1987.

(b) Scope of the Proscription

The prohibition on involvement by a tax-exempt charitable organization in a political campaign is generally considered by the IRS to be absolute, although neither the legislative history of the provision nor the regulations provide any clarification.[8] The IRS stated that "this is an absolute prohibition," adding that "[t]here is no requirement that political campaigning be substantial."[9] Thus, the Chief Counsel of the IRS opined that "an organization described in section 501(c)(3) is precluded from engaging in *any* political campaign activities."[10] However, analogy may be made to a comparable statute that was also absolute on its face: section 610 of the Federal Corrupt Practices Act. That act made "[i]t . . . unlawful for . . . any corporation whatever . . . to make a contribution or expenditure in connection with" various federal elections. Nonetheless, the courts read a substantiality test into the absolute proscription of this law.[11] Further, it has been stated that "a slight and comparatively unimportant deviation from the narrow furrow of tax approved activity is not fatal."[12] It was also observed that "courts recognize that a nonexempt purpose, even 'somewhat beyond a de minimis level,' may be permitted without loss of exemption."[13] Thus, the Commissioner of Internal Revenue stated, in congressional testimony describing the political campaign limitation: "If political intervention is involved, the prohibition is absolute; however, some consideration may be given to whether, qualitatively or quantitatively, the organization is in the cir-

---

[6] 100 *Cong. Rec.* 9604 (1954).

[7] *Id.* There is no analysis of this provision in the conference report (H. Rep. 2543, 83d Cong., 2d Sess. 46 (1954).

[8] Reg. §§ 1.501(c)(3)-1(b)(3)(ii), 1.501(c)(3)-1(c)(iii).

[9] IRS Exempt Organizations Handbook (IRM 7751) § 370(2).

[10] Gen. Couns. Mem. 39694 (emphasis supplied).

[11] United States v. Construction Local 264, 101 F. Supp. 873 (W.D. Mo. 1951); United States v. Painters Local 481, 172 F.2d 854 (2d Cir. 1949). The subsequent repeal of the Federal Corrupt Practices Act does not alter the analysis on this point.

[12] St. Louis Union Trust Co. v. United States, 374 F.2d 427, 431–432 (8th Cir. 1967).

[13] Living Faith, Inc. v. Comm'r, 950 F.2d 365, 370 (7th Cir. 1991).

cumstance where the activity is so trivial it is without legal significance and, therefore, de minimus."[14]

There is an anomaly in this aspect of the federal tax law. This prohibition on political campaign activities is considered, at least by the IRS, to be absolute, yet there is very little law and guidance as to the scope of the prohibition.[15] As discussed next, this scope is believed to be very broad—even though there is considerable difference between political campaign activities and political activities.

(c) Political Campaign Activities

The political campaign activities prohibition applicable to charitable organizations embodies four elements, all of which must be present for the limitation to become operative. These elements are that a charitable organization may not *participate* or *intervene* in a political campaign, the political activity that must be involved is a political *campaign*, the campaign must be with respect to an individual who is a *candidate*, and the individual must be a candidate for a *public office*.[16]

(d) Participation or Intervention

The requirement that a charitable organization not engage in political campaign activities is relatively clear as to meaning. Because of this relative clarity, the matter has infrequently been the subject of discussion in court opinions or in IRS rulings. The most obvious way for a charitable organization to participate or intervene in a political campaign is to make a contribution to the political campaign of a candidate. However, this is clearly forbidden as a condition of tax exemption.

The IRS ruled that a charitable organization may not evaluate the qualifications of potential candidates in a school board election and then support particular slates in the campaign.[17] Also, a court held that an organization established with the dominant aim of bringing about world government as rapidly as possible did not qualify as a charitable organization.[18] On the other hand, the IRS ruled that a university does not intervene in a political campaign by conducting a political science course that required the students' participation in political campaigns of their choice[19] nor by the provision of faculty advisors and facilities for a campus newspaper that published the students' editorial opinions on polit-

---

[14] Statement of Lawrence B. Gibbs before the House Subcommittee on Oversight, March 12, 1987, in "Lobbying and Political Activities of Tax-Exempt Organizations," Hearings before the Subcommittee on Oversight, Committee on Ways and Means, House of Representatives, Serial 100-5, 100th Cong., 1st Sess. 96-97 (1987).

[15] Reg. § 1.501(c)(3)-1(c)(3)(iii).

[16] "It should be noted that exemption is lost . . . by participation in any political campaign on behalf of *any* candidate for public office" (United States v. Dykema, 666 F.2d 1096, 1101 (7th Cir. 1981), *cert. den.*, 456 U.S. 983 (1982) (emphasis in original)).

[17] Rev. Rul. 67-71, 1967-1 C.B. 125.

[18] Estate of Blaine v. Comm'r, 22 T.C. 1195 (1954).

[19] Rev. Rul. 72-512, 1972-2 C.B. 246.

ical matters.[20] Also, a tax-exempt broadcasting station that provided equal air time to all electoral candidates in compliance with the Federal Communications Act was ruled to not be in violation of the proscription against partisan political activities.[21]

Despite the requirement of a political campaign and a candidate for public office, the IRS denominated as an action organization (and thus denied tax exemption to) an organization formed for the purpose of implementing an orderly change of administration of the office of governor of a state in the most efficient and economical fashion possible by assisting the governor-elect during the period between his election and inauguration.[22] The IRS ruled that the organization's "predominant purpose is to effectuate changes in the government's policies and personnel which will make them correspond with the partisan political interests of both the Governor-elect and the political party he represents."[23] Without any statement of its reasoning, the IRS ruled that a presidential inaugural committee that sponsored inaugural activities, some of which were open to the public and some by invitation only, where donations to it were commingled with the proceeds from various fund-raising affairs and activities, was not an organization organized and operated exclusively for charitable purposes.[24]

An expansion of this prohibition on political activities was furthered by a federal court of appeals, in denying tax-exempt status to a religious ministry organization for engaging in legislative activities and intervening in political campaigns.[25] The organization, by means of publications and broadcasts, attacked candidates and incumbents (presidents and members of Congress) considered too liberal and endorsed conservative officeholders. The court summarized the offense: "These attempts to elect or defeat certain political leaders reflected . . . [the organization's] objective to change the composition of the federal government."[26] The IRS Chief Counsel's office "reluctantly" concluded in 1989 that an organization "probably" did not intervene in a political campaign on behalf of or in opposition to a candidate for public office, even though the organization ran a political advertising program that (1) was, in the words of the IRS, "mostly broadcast during a two week period around the Reagan/Mondale foreign and defense policy debate on October 21, 1984," (2) contained statements that "could be viewed as demonstrating a preference for one of the debating candidates" [Mondale], (3) "could be viewed" as having content such that "individuals listening to the ads would generally understand them to support or oppose a candidate in an election campaign," (4) involved statements that were released so close to the November

---

[20] Rev. Rul. 72-513, 1972-2 C.B. 246.
[21] Rev. Rul. 74-574, 1974-2 C.B. 160.
[22] Rev. Rul. 74-117, 1974-1 C.B. 128.
[23] *Id.*
[24] Rev. Rul. 77-283, 1977-2 C.B. 72.
[25] Christian Echoes Nat'l Ministry, Inc. v. United States, 470 F.2d 849 (10th Cir. 1972), *cert. den.*, 414 U.S. 864 (1973).
[26] *Id.* at 856. Also Monsky v. Comm'r, 36 T.C.M. 1046 (1977); Giordano v. Comm'r, 36 T.C.M. 430 (1977).

vote as to be "troublesome," and (5) was clearly in violation of the IRS' voter education rules.[27]

Inasmuch as organizations function only through individuals, who have the freedom to engage in political activities, the law distinguishes between activities that are undertaken in conjunction with "official" responsibilities and those that are "personal"; only the former activities are relevant in assessing an organization's qualification for tax exemption in the face of political campaign efforts.[28] However, political activities of individuals (such as officers or members) will be imputed to the organization if it has, directly or indirectly, authorized or ratified the acts.[29]

It is the view of the IRS that an attempt to influence the confirmation, by the U.S. Senate, of a federal judicial nominee does not constitute participation or intervention in a political campaign, inasmuch as the individual involved is not a contestant for elective public office.[30]

The proscription on political campaign activity by public charities is particularly controversial as applied to religious organizations. Thus, one observer wrote: "Religion and politics have been intertwined since the birth of our nation. In a democracy created to reflect the social fabric of its citizens, religious groups have always advocated moral positions to further or impede political causes and political campaigns."[31] Another commentator wrote: "Under some circumstances, nearly every religious group will be motivated by sincere belief to engage in substantial political activity. Moreover, political activity of some sort implicitly is required by many religions; indeed, a religion which did not have moral standards which it believed should be followed by the society would be an anomaly."[32] A similar viewpoint is reflected in this passage: Churches and other religious organizations "consider their efforts to influence the making of public policy to be an integral part of their religious enterprise. For some religious persons, political activity may even be a form of worship."[33] Still another said: "The involvement of religious organizations in the political process . . . has long been a reality in American society."[34] The situation has been aptly summed up as follows: "[T]he IRS interpretations [of the political campaign prohibition] make compliance extremely difficult and are highly intrusive on 'free exercise' and other constitutional rights. In particular, churches must act at their peril as they attempt to walk the obscure line be-

---

[27] Tech. Adv. Mem. 8936002.

[28] Gen. Couns. Mem. 34631.

[29] Gen. Couns. Mem. 33912.

[30] Notice 88-76, 1988-2 C.B. 392.

[31] Note, "Religion and Political Campaigns: A Proposal to Revise Section 501(c)(3) of the Internal Revenue Code," 49 *Fordham L. Rev.* 536 (1981) (footnotes omitted).

[32] Note, "Religion in Politics and the Income Tax Exemption," 42 *Fordham L. Rev.* 397 (1973) (footnotes omitted).

[33] West, "The Free Exercise Clause and the Internal Revenue Code's Restrictions on the Political Activity of Tax-Exempt Organizations," 21 *Wake Forest L. Rev.* 395, 396 (1986).

[34] Note, "Conflicts Between the First Amendment Religion Clauses and the Internal Revenue Code: Politically Active Religious Organizations and Racially Discriminatory Private Schools," 61 *Wash. U. L. Q.* 503, 508–509 (1983) (footnote omitted).

tween loss of exemption and faithfulness to the obligation to speak out on the moral dimension of important social issues."[35]

(e) Voter Education Activities

A charitable organization may instruct the public on matters useful to the individual and beneficial to the community.[36] In carrying out this form of an educational purpose, an organization may cautiously enter the political milieu. Thus, organizations have been permitted to assemble and donate to libraries the campaign speeches, interviews, and other materials of an individual who was a candidate for a "historically important elective office,"[37] conduct public forums at which debates and lectures on social, political, and international questions are considered,[38] and conduct public forums involving congressional candidates, where there is a fair and impartial treatment of the candidates.[39] By contrast, the organization will imperil its tax exemption if it solicits the signing or endorsing of a fair campaign practices code by political candidates.[40]

However, in performing activities such as these, the organization must present a sufficiently full and fair exposition of pertinent facts to permit the public to form its own opinion or conclusion independent of that presented by the organiza-

---

[35] Caron & Dessingue, "I.R.C. § 501(c)(3): Practical and Constitutional Implications of 'Political' Activity Restrictions," II *J. Law & Politics* (No. 1) 169, 178 (1985). In general, Colvin, "An Election-Year Guide to Exempt Organization Political Activities," 7 *J. Tax. Exempt Orgs.* (No. 2) 74 (Sept./Oct. 1995); Hopkins, *supra* note 3, particularly Chapter 21; Rosenthal, "Prelates and Politics: Current Views on the Prohibition Against Campaign Activity," 52 *Tax Notes* 1122 (1991); Chisholm, "Politics and Charity: A Proposal for Peaceful Coexistence," 58 *Geo. Wash. L. Rev.* (No. 2) 308 (1990); Tesdahl, "Intervention in Political Campaigns by Religious Organizations After the Pickle Hearings—A Proposal for the 1990s," 4 *Exempt Org. Tax Rev.* (No. 9) 1165 (1991).

It is the position of the IRS that a distinction is to be made between political campaign involvement by religious institutions and the free expression on political matters by leaders of religious organizations speaking for themselves as individuals; the latter certainly is permitted. Thus, the IRS stated that "[m]inisters and others who commonly speak or write on behalf of religious organizations should clearly indicate, at the time they do so, that public comments made by them in connection with political campaigns are strictly personal and are not intended to represent their organization" ("Tax Guide for Churches and Other Religious Organizations" (Pub. 1828) (Ann. 94-112, 1994-42 I.R.B. 20, modifying Ann. 94-111, 1994-37 I.R.B. 36)). The IRS added: "Partisan comments by the employees or other representatives of an organization regarding political candidates must be avoided in official organization publications and at official church functions" (id.). A lawsuit challenging the constitutionality of the political campaign proscription as it applies to churches, and asserting selective prosecution, was filed on April 17, 1995 (Branch Ministries, Inc. v. Richardson, No. 95-0724 (D.D.C. Apr. 17, 1995)). As to the latter claim, the court held that the organization made a "colorable showing" that the entity's "political and/or religious beliefs may have played an impermissible role in the revocation of their tax-exempt status" and thus that it was entitled to additional discovery on the issue of intent (Branch Ministries, Inc. v. Richardson, 970 F. Supp. 11, 17 (D.D.C. 1997)).

[36] Reg. § 1.501(c)(3)-1(d)(3). See §§ 7.4, 7.5.

[37] Rev. Rul. 70-321, 1970-1 C.B. 129.

[38] Rev. Rul. 66-256, 1966-2 C.B. 210.

[39] Rev. Rul. 86-95, 1986-1 C.B. 332. In one instance, the IRS approved of a forum where less than all of the candidates were invited because the decision "accentuate[d] the educational nature of the forums and still ensure[d] a meaningful field of candidates for worthwhile forums, while allocating for the organization's limited space and time" (Tech. Adv. Mem. 9635003).

[40] Rev. Rul. 76-456, 1976-2 C.B. 151, *supra.* Rev. Rul. 66-258, 1966-2 C.B. 213. Also Rev. Rul. 60-193, 1960-1 C.B. 195.

tion, although the organization may also advocate a particular position or viewpoint.[41] Thus, while a charitable organization may seek to educate the public on patriotic, political, and civic matters and even alert the citizenry to the dangers of an extreme political doctrine, it may not do so by the use of disparaging terms, insinuations, innuendoes, and suggested implications drawn from incomplete facts.[42]

There is, therefore, a tension between the concepts of political campaign activities and voter education activities. This is illustrated by a case involving the practice of a bar association (otherwise qualified as a charitable organization) of rating candidates for public office in a state's judiciary. The candidates were rated as "approved," "not approved," or "approved as highly qualified"; more than one candidate for the same office may receive the same rating. The ratings were disseminated to the public in press releases and by means of the publications of the association. A court held that this rating process did not constitute prohibited participation or intervention in political campaigns on behalf of or in opposition to candidates; the court found that the "ratings do not support or oppose the candidacy of any particular individual or recommend that the public vote for or against a specific candidate."[43] The court added that "we do not believe that the mere practice of rating candidates for elective office without more is, per se, a prohibited political activity."[44] However, on appeal, this opinion was reversed, with the appellate court concluding that the rating activity did constitute participation or intervention in the political campaigns for the judgeships.[45] The court of appeals characterized the ratings as "[p]ublished expressions of . . . opinion, made with an eye toward imminent elections."[46]

One traditional distinction between political campaign activity and voter education activity has been that the latter is *nonpartisan*. This bar association case focused on this aspect of the law as well, with the appellate court finding that the prohibition on political campaign activity for charitable organizations embraces nonpartisan activity; it wrote that "the statute and pertinent regulations thereunder are not limited in their application to the partisan campaigns of candidates representing recognized political parties."[47] Writing of the rating process, the court of appeals noted that a "candidate who receives a 'not qualified' rating will derive little comfort from the fact that the rating may have been made in a nonpartisan manner."[48] By contrast, the lower court took the position that the rating activity was not campaign activity because the association engaged in the "totally passive, not active" function of merely reporting its ratings (which were not, according to that court, based on partisan or political preferences) and did "not actively seek to influence the outcome of elections."[49]

The IRS published a ruling allowing organizations that operate broadcast sta-

---

[41] Reg. § 1.501(c)(3)-1(d)(3). Also Haswell v. United States, 500 F.2d 1133, 1143–1145 (Ct. Cl. 1974), *cert. den.*, 419 U.S. 1107 (1974).

[42] Rev. Rul. 68-263, 1968-1 C.B. 256.

[43] Association of the Bar of the City of N.Y. v. Comm'r, 89 T.C. 599, 609–610 (1987).

[44] *Id.* at 610.

[45] Association of the Bar of the City of N.Y. v. Comm'r, 858 F.2d 876 (2d Cir. 1988), *cert. den.*; 490 U.S. 1030 (1989).

[46] *Id.* 858 F.2d at 880.

[47] *Id.*

[48] *Id.*

[49] Association of the Bar of the City of N.Y. v. Comm'r, *supra* note 43, at 611.

tions to provide equal air time to political candidates.[50] However, the import of this ruling as a matter of tax policy is uncertain, in that these organizations were required by federal communications law to provide free air time to political candidates.[51]

An IRS ruling contains two examples of voter education activities that a charitable organization may carry on without loss of tax exemption. These examples indicate that a charitable organization can (1) prepare and disseminate a compilation of the voting records of all members of Congress on a wide variety of major subjects, as long as there is no editorial comment and no approval or disapproval of the voting records is implied, and (2) publish the responses to its questionnaire on a wide variety of subjects from all candidates for an office, as long as no preference for a candidate is expressed. This ruling also contains two illustrations of prohibited activities: an organization may not (1) publish candidates' answers to questions that indicate a bias on the issues, or (2) publish a voter guide reflecting the voting records of members of Congress on selected issues of interest to the organization.

Notwithstanding these latter two illustrations, the IRS subsequently ruled that a charitable organization may publish a newsletter containing the voting records of congressional incumbents on selected issues without prohibited involvement in political campaigns.[52] The IRS indicated that the format and content of the publication need not be neutral, in that each incumbent's votes and the organization's views on selected legislative issues can be reported, and the publication may indicate whether the incumbent supported or opposed the organization's view. Nonetheless, the IRS considered the following factors as demonstrating the absence of political campaign activity: (1) The voting records of all incumbents will be presented, (2) candidates for reelection will not be identified, (3) no comment will be made on an individual's overall qualifications for public office, (4) no statements expressly or impliedly endorsing or rejecting any incumbent as a candidate for public office will be offered, (5) no comparison of incumbents with other candidates will be made, (6) the organization will point out the inherent limitations of judging the qualifications of an incumbent on the basis of certain selected votes, by stating the need to consider such unrecorded matters as performance on subcommittees and constituent service, (7) the organization will not widely distribute its compilation of incumbents' voting records, (8) the publication will be distributed to the organization's normal readership (who number only a few thousand nationwide), and (9) no attempt will be made to target the publication toward particular areas in which elections are occurring nor to time the date of publication to coincide with an election campaign.

The position of the IRS on this issue in general is that "in the absence of any expressions of endorsement for or opposition to candidates for public office, an organization may publish a newsletter containing voting records and its opinions on issues of interest to it provided that the voting records are not widely distributed to the general public during an election campaign or aimed, in view of all the facts and circumstances, towards affecting any particular elections."[53]

The IRS concluded that the use by a charitable organization of panels of citi-

---

[50] Rev. Rul. 74-574, *supra* note 21.
[51] See Rev. Rul. 78-160, 1978-1 C.B. 153, *rev.* by Rev. Rul. 78-248, 1978-1 C.B. 154.
[52] Rev. Rul. 80-282, 1980-2 C.B. 178.
[53] Gen. Couns. Mem. 38444.

zens to review and rate political candidates is a form of intervention or participation in their campaigns.[54] These groups of individuals questioned expert witnesses and candidates, analyzed the information and views presented, and prepared reports for public dissemination. Most of these reports included a rating of the candidates by members of the panels, including an analysis of their stands on several major issues in a box score style. The organization viewed these processes as forms of issue education and means to stimulate public dialogue, but the IRS determined that the candidates' ratings provided "political editorial opinions to the general public and went beyond the neutral forums" that are permissible.

A charitable organization was found to have engaged in prohibited political campaign activity because of language in and the timing of mailing of fund-raising letters.[55] This organization had a variety of programs, all focused on a certain side of the political spectrum; its direct-mail fund-raising letters were mailed mostly to individuals of this political persuasion. These letters, sent contemporaneously with election periods, implied—in the view of the IRS—that a contribution to the organization will help candidates for public office who share this political view. The IRS wrote that the letters were biased against candidates of opposing political aims or in favor of the candidates supporting its view of political issues; one letter was found to not entail voter education but rather "voter direction."

(f) Treatment of Activist Organizations

Aside from the types of activity traditionally considered by the federal tax laws to be action efforts—legislative and political campaign activities—there is a broad range of clearly action or political undertakings that may be described as the type of speech or activities sheltered by the First Amendment. These undertakings may be manifested in a variety of ways, such as writings, demonstrations, boycotts, strikes, picketing, and litigation, all protected by the rights of free speech and association and the right to petition (assuming the absence of any illegal activities). These activities frequently give the IRS pause in evaluating the status of an organization as a charitable entity but, unless the activities may be fairly characterized as being impermissible lobbying or electioneering, there is no basis in the law concerning action organizations (as that term is used in its technical sense) for denying an organization engaging in these activities tax-exempt status or for revoking this type of organization's tax-exempt status.

The position of the IRS on this point apparently is that this type of activity can be a permissible method by which to further tax-exempt purposes.[56] These activities will jeopardize tax exemption, however, where they are illegal or otherwise contrary to public policy.[57] Nonetheless, where an activity is legal, the IRS generally will not deem it contrary to public policy.[58]

The tolerance of the courts in this area in general was classically illustrated by a federal district court finding that the anticonvention boycott orchestrated by the National Organization for Women (NOW), in states the legislatures of which

---

[54] Tech. Adv. Mem. 9635003.
[55] Tech. Adv. Mem. 9609007.
[56] Gen. Couns. Mem. 37858.
[57] See §§ 5.3, 5.5(f).
[58] Gen. Couns. Mem. 37858.

had not ratified the proposed Equal Rights Amendment, was not in violation of antitrust laws, even though the boycott or concerted refusal to deal has been held to be an unlawful combination in restraint of trade.[59] Because the objective of NOW's convention boycott campaign was the ratification of the proposed amendment, by means of demonstrating support and generating widespread publicity for the proposed amendment, the court found that the boycott activities "were not intended as punitive . . . and were not motivated by any type of anti-competitive purpose."[60] NOW was successful in asserting that the antitrust laws do not apply to boycotts that take place in a political rather than a commercial context.[61] The essence of the NOW case is summed up in one sentence from an article quoted by the court: "There are areas of our economic and political life in which the precepts of antitrust must yield to other social values."[62]

Coincidentally, at the same time the NOW litigation was unfolding, the IRS had before it the tax status of an organization that conducted a consumer boycott. Prior to the decision in the NOW case, the IRS concluded that the organization, which conducted a national campaign against the purchase of products from companies that manufacture infant formula and market it in developing countries by means of allegedly unethical business practices, could not qualify as a charitable entity because it is an action organization. Consequently, the organization took the matter into court,[63] but just before the case reached the briefing stage, the IRS suddenly reversed its position and issued a favorable ruling, thereby mooting the case.

Presumably, therefore, the case stands as a basis for the proposition that an organization may conduct a boycott in furtherance of charitable ends.[64] The operative legal principle appears to be that, while the conduct of a boycott may not itself be an exempt function, a boycott can further an exempt purpose and thereby lead to charitable status. As the IRS recognized, the "performance of a particular activity that is not inherently charitable may nonetheless further a charitable purpose [and the] . . . overall result in any given case is dependent on why and how that activity is actually being conducted."[65]

Moreover, the IRS recognized that an otherwise tax-exempt charitable organization can further its exempt purposes by instituting litigation, even where the organization employs private lawyers to represent it in bringing and maintaining the litigation.[66] The IRS insists, however, that an organization's litigation activities be a "reasonable means" of accomplishing its tax-exempt purposes, and that

---

[59] State of Mo. v. National Org. for Women, Inc., 467 F. Supp. 289 (W.D. Mo. 1978).

[60] Id. at 296.

[61] Also Eastern R.R. Presidents Conf. v. Noerr Motor Freight, Inc., 365 U.S. 127 (1961); Register of Wills for Baltimore City v. Cook, 216 A.2d 542 (Md. 1966).

[62] Handler, "Annual Review of Antitrust Developments," 71 Yale L.J. 75, 88 (1961).

[63] The Infant Formula Action Coalition v. United States (D.D.C. No. 79-0129).

[64] Some organizations, already possessing IRC § 501(c)(3) classification, engage in consumer boycotts (relating to, for example, the purchase of tuna, products that exploit animals, and products produced in whaling nations) but The Infant Formula Action Coalition case, supra note 63, involved an organization that conducted a boycott as its primary activity and that had its tax status reviewed by the IRS at the outset of its existence.

[65] Rev. Rul. 69-572, 1969-2 C.B. 119.

[66] In general, Bachmann, Nonprofit Litigation (New York: John Wiley & Sons, Inc., 1991), Chapter 4.

the program of litigation not be illegal, contrary to a clearly defined and established public policy, or violative of express statutory provisions.[67]

This means-to-an-end principle thus characterizes activities like demonstrations, boycotts, and litigation as "neutral" activities—from a federal tax standpoint—and allows the tax status of the organization conducting them to depend on its ability to show how tax-exempt purposes are thereby furthered. (In some instances, the IRS has publicly recognized the tax-exempt status of organizations engaging in this type of activity, such as litigation conducted by public interest law firms.[68])

This principle has also been recognized in the courts. One court discussed the point that the purpose towards which an organization's activities are directed, and not the nature of the activities themselves, is ultimately dispositive of the organization's right to be classified as a charitable organization.[69] In a similar case, this court found that an activity (sale of handicrafts) was neither an exempt purpose nor a nonexempt purpose but an activity carried on by . . . [the organization] in furtherance of its exempt purposes.[70]

The U.S. Supreme Court applied this principle in an analogous context. Perhaps the most applicable of the Court's opinions is the holding that litigation activities as conducted in the public interest context of that case are modes of expression and association protected by constitutional law and may not be barred by state authority to regulate the legal profession.[71] The Court distinguished this type of litigation from that normally instituted to resolve private differences, stating that the former is a "means for achieving lawful objectives."[72] In that case, litigation activities were perceived as neutral activities, engaged in as a means for accomplishment of the organization's ends. Likewise, boycotts, demonstrations, and the like can serve as vehicles for carrying forward charitable purposes. As the Court repeatedly observed, the First Amendment protects advocacy, certainly of lawful ends, against governmental intrusion.[73]

A court specifically held that litigation is an "appropriate vehicle for an organization to accomplish" its tax-exempt purpose, in a case involving the tax-exempt

---

[67] Rev. Rul. 80-278, 1980-2 C.B. 175. The IRS, in Rev. Rul. 80-279, 1980-2 C.B. 176, took a like stance with respect to an organization that conducted mediation of international environmental disputes.

[68] See § 6.10(d).

[69] Pulpit Resource v. Comm'r, 70 T.C. 594 (1978).

[70] Aid to Artisans, Inc. v. Comm'r, 71 T.C. 202, 214 (1978).

[71] N.A.A.C.P. v. Button, 371 U.S. 415 (1963).

[72] *Id.* at 429.

[73] E.g., Thomas v. Collins, 323 U.S. 516 (1945); Herndon v. Lowry, 301 U.S. 242 (1937). Also Pratt v. Robert S. Odell & Co., 122 P.2d 684, 692 (Cal. Dist. Ct. App. 1942), where it was held that a corporation may expend funds in the prosecution of litigation to which it is not a party where the expenditure is a means for furthering its objects; and Register of Wills for Baltimore City v. Cook, *supra* note 61, at 546, where it was held that advocacy of passage of the Equal Rights Amendment is one method of accomplishing the charitable objectives of a tax-exempt trust. In this context, it should be noted that, in Village of Schaumburg v. Citizens for a Better Environment, 444 U.S. 620 (1980), the Supreme Court held that acts of fund-raising are among the most protected forms of free speech. Also, as to the latter point, Riley v. National Fed. of the Blind of N.C., 487 U.S. 781 (1988); Secretary of State of Md. v. Joseph H. Munson Co., Inc., 467 U.S. 947 (1984). In general, Hopkins, *The Law of Fund-Raising, Second Edition* (New York: John Wiley & Sons, Inc., 1996), Chapter 5 § 3.

status of an organization that provided legal assistance to employees whose rights were violated under compulsory unionism arrangements.[74]

In one case, the IRS had taken the position that engaging in proxy contest activities was not a charitable activity. There was no dispute over the fact that proxy contests are not inherently charitable or educational endeavors. However, upon review, the court placed the organization's activities in context, that is, in light of its overall purposes.[75] The court recognized that the purpose of the organization "is to make corporate management, and thus corporations, responsible."[76] The court continued:

> It is only reasonable that corporations begin to realize that they have duties beyond simply making money for their stockholders. A corporation does not exist in a vacuum, but is part of the community for better or for worse. In the past, it has been for worse. Large corporations have contributed to many of the social problems affecting the community both directly, in hiring practices, effects on the environment, non-compliance with regulations, indifference to the consumer safety, etc. and indirectly through use of their economic power in socially irresponsible ways. As a member of the community, it is incumbent upon corporations to use their substantial economic power for the community good, rather than solely for self-enrichment, at the community's expense. The need for a swift re-orientation of the corporate perspective to its community responsibilities is imperative. The general public is in no financial, organizational or power position to undertake the task with any effectiveness.[77]

With that as background, the court discussed the proxy voting process and its impact on corporate management. After commenting that proposals to promote socially responsible programs and policies may not be voted in by stockholders, the court concluded:

> But the questions will have been raised, the shareholders will have been educated to the wider horizon, and the seed may have been planted for future change that will require the corporation to assume some of its duties as a member of the community. The beneficiary of this activity and educational process to promote socially responsible corporations will be the public. . . .
>
> As the Court views them, proxy contests appear to be the more direct and effective instrument of achieving the . . . [organization's] purposes, and when conducted in the public interest, as the . . . [organization] has done, they are charitable activities, in that they are the instruments (both legal and not against public policy) by which the charitable purposes are accomplished for the public good.[78]

---

[74] National Right to Work Legal Defense & Educ. Found., Inc. v. United States, 487 F. Supp. 801 (E.D.N.C. 1979). Cf. Retired Teachers Legal Defense Fund, Inc. v. Comm'r, 78 T.C. 280 (1982).
[75] Center on Corporate Responsibility, Inc. v. Shultz, 368 F. Supp. 863 (D.D.C. 1973).
[76] Id. at 874, note 21.
[77] Id. at 874–875, note 21.
[78] Id. at 875, note 21.

Thus, certain activities—activist in nature—can avoid classification as political campaign activities, thereby enabling the organizations involved to qualify for tax-exempt status as public charities.[79]

(g) Requirement of a Candidate

The Internal Revenue Code does not define the term *candidate*. The income tax regulations address the term in the context of defining the phrase *candidate for public office*, as "an individual who offers himself, or is proposed by others, as a contestant for an elective public office, whether such office be national, State, or local."[80]

An analysis of the political campaign intervention rules by the staff of the Joint Committee on Taxation, U.S. Congress, stated that "[c]lear standards do not exist for determining precisely at what point an individual becomes a candidate for purposes of the rule."[81] This analysis continued: "On the one hand, once an individual declares his candidacy for a particular office, his status as a candidate is clear."[82] The analysis added: "On the other hand, the fact that an individual is a prominent political figure does not automatically make him a candidate, even if there is speculation regarding his possible future candidacy for particular offices."[83]

(h) Requirement of a Campaign

A federal court of appeals observed that a "campaign for a public office in a public election merely and simply means running for office, or candidacy for office, as the word is used in common parlance and as it is understood by the man in the street."[84]

The term *campaign* is not otherwise defined in the federal tax law.

---

[79] E.g., Priv. Ltr. Rul. 8936002. In general, Fuller & Abbott, "Political Activity and Lobbying Rules for Section 501(c) Organizations," 15 *Exempt Org. Tax Rev.* (No. 3) 383 (1996); Bird, "The Exempt Organization Rules on Political Activities," 7 *J. Tax Exempt Orgs.* 195 (Mar./Apr. 1996); Colvin, "An Election-Year Guide to Exempt Organization Political Activities," 7 *J. Tax Exempt Orgs.* 74 (Sept./Oct. 1995); Washlick, "Political Activities of Tax-Exempt Organizations," 3 *J. Tax. Exempt Orgs.* 4 (Spring 1991); Knight, Knight & Marshall, "Lobbying, Campaigning, and Section 501(c)(3)—What is Allowed?," 2 *J. Tax. Exempt Orgs.* 17 (Fall 1990); Rosenblum, "Religion and Political Campaigns: A Proposal to Revise Section 501(c)(3) of the Internal Revenue Code," 49 *Fordham L. Rev.* 536 (1981); Crumplar, "Tax Consequences of Political Activity by Religious Organizations," V *Christian Law.* (No. 2) 29 (1975); Bailey, "Religion in Politics and the Income Tax Exemption," 42 *Fordham L. Rev.* 397 (1974); Garrett, "Federal Tax Limitations on Political Activities of Public Interest and Educational Organizations," 59 *Geo. L. J.* 561 (1971); Note, "Political Activity and Tax-Exempt Organizations Before and After The Tax Reform Act of 1969," 38 *Geo. Wash. U. L. Rev.* 1114 (1970); Amer. Ent. Inst., *Political Activities of Colleges and Universities* (1970); Lehrfeld, "How Much 'Politicking' Can a Charitable Organization Engage In?," 20 *J. Tax.* 236 (1968); Boehm, "Political Expenditures by Tax-Exempt Organizations," 14 *Prac. Law.* 13 (1968); Note, "Income Tax Disadvantages of Political Activities," 57 *Col. L. Rev.* (1957).

[80] Reg. § 1.501(c)(3)-1(c)(3)(iii).

[81] Joint Committee on Taxation, "Lobbying and Political Activities of Tax-Exempt Organizations" 14 (JCS-5-87, Mar. 11, 1987).

[82] *Id.*

[83] *Id.*

[84] Norris v. United States, 86 F.2d 379, 382 (8th Cir. 1936), *rev'd on other grounds*, 300 U.S. 564 (1937).

(i) Requirement of a Public Office

Neither the Internal Revenue Code nor the income tax regulations define the term *public office* for purposes of the political campaign activity prohibition applicable to charitable organizations.

However, the private foundation rules defining disqualified persons make reference to the phrase an *elective public office*.[85] While the statute does not define the term public office in this setting, the tax regulations state:

> In defining the term "public office" . . ., such term must be distinguished from mere public employment. Although holding a public office is one form of public employment, not every position in the employ of a State or other governmental subdivision . . . constitutes a "public office." Although a determination whether a public employee holds a public office depends on the facts and circumstances of the case, the essential element is whether a significant part of the activities of a public employee is the independent performance of policymaking functions. In applying this subparagraph, several factors may be considered as indications that a position in the executive, legislative, or judicial branch of the government of a State, possession of the United States, or political subdivision or other area of any of the foregoing, or of the District of Columbia, constitutes a "public office." Among such factors to be considered in addition to that set forth above, are that the office is created by the Congress, a State constitution, or the State legislature, or by a municipality or other governmental body pursuant to authority conferred by the Congress, State constitution, or State legislature, and the powers conferred on the office and the duties to be discharged by such office are defined either directly or indirectly by the Congress, State constitution, or State legislature, or through legislative authority.[86]

The only other instance, in the law of tax-exempt organizations, where the tax regulations make reference to the term *public office* is in the context of the rules concerning political organizations, where the term public office is used in the definition of a political organization exempt function.[87] The accompanying regulations use the same definition of the term public office as is used in the setting of the private foundations' rules defining disqualified persons.[88]

The IRS Chief Counsel's office took the position that precinct committeemen in an unidentified state were holders of a public office.[89] This position is based on the content of the state's law, which accorded them the following characteristics: (1) The position was created by statute, (2) holders of the position swear an oath to uphold the state and U.S. constitutions in the performance of their duties, (3) they assist in the selection of election officers (characterized as an "essential function in the State's regulation of elections"), (4) they participate in the party's county central committee and state committee (characterized as "essential to the electoral process"), (5) there is a fixed term of office, and (6) the positions are "not occasional or contractual." The IRS observed that, if the above-quoted regulation was

---

[85] IRC §§ 4946(c)(1), (5). See § 11.2(i).
[86] Reg. § 53.4946-1(g)(2)(i).
[87] IRC § 527(e)(2). See § 17.2.
[88] Reg. § 1.527-2(d).
[89] Gen. Couns. Mem. 39811.

applied to these facts, the precinct committeemen "would not be considered as holding public office because their duties entail no independent policymaking functions." Nonetheless, the IRS pronouncement continued: "However, the additional factors to be considered as indicative of a public office and which are listed in the latter part of that regulation would support the Service's position." Thus, the IRS chief counsel's office advised that the tax exemption of the organization involved should be revoked because it encourages its members to seek election to precinct committees and to support these candidacies.

A state court of appeals held that an individual who is a candidate for delegate to a county political convention is a candidate for state law purposes but is not a candidate for a public office.[90] The court pointed out that the state's election law does not define the word *candidate*. Thus, the court concluded, applying a "general rule of statutory construction . . . that words and phrases should be construed according to their common meaning," "[l]ogically, most people would believe that if an individual's name is listed on an election ballot, that individual is a candidate for something."[91] In the court's opinion, the "common meaning" of the word *candidate* includes state precinct delegates,[92] although, as noted, they are not seekers of a "public office."

Another federal appellate court has held that the phrase *candidate for office* is "used in common parlance and as it is understood by the man in the street."[93] Relying on this observation, the above IRS pronouncement stated that, "[t]o the average person, the appearance of precinct candidates on the general election ballot indicates that the position is a public office."[94]

§ 21.2   POLITICAL EXPENDITURES BY CHARITABLE ORGANIZATIONS AND TAX SANCTIONS

The federal tax law authorizes the levy of taxes in situations where a charitable organization makes a political expenditure.[95] Generally, a *political expenditure* is any amount paid or incurred by a charitable organization in any participation in, or intervention in (including the publication or distribution of statements), any political campaign on behalf of or in opposition to any candidate for public office.[96]

In an effort to discourage the use of ostensibly educational organizations operating in tandem with political campaigns, the concept of a political expenditure was expanded, so as to apply with respect to "an organization which is formed primarily for purposes of promoting the candidacy (or prospective candidacy) of an individual for public office (or which is effectively controlled by a candidate or prospective candidate and which is availed of primarily for such

---

[90] Templin v. Oakland City Clerk, 387 N.W.2d 156 (Mich. Ct. App. 1986).
[91] *Id*. at 159.
[92] *Id*.
[93] Association of the Bar of the City of N.Y. v. Comm'r, *supra* note 45, 858 F.2d at 880.
[94] Gen. Couns. Mem. (*supra* note 89).
[95] IRC § 4955.
[96] Reg. § 53.4955-1(c)(1).

purposes)."[97] In these circumstances, the term *political expenditure* includes any of the following amounts paid or incurred by the organization: (1) amounts paid to or incurred by the individual for speeches or other services; (2) the travel expenses of the individual; (3) the expenses of conducting polls, surveys, or other studies, or the preparation of papers or other materials, for use by the individual; (4) the expenses of advertising, publicity, and fund-raising for the individual; and (5) any other expense "which has the primary effect of promoting public recognition, or otherwise primarily accruing to the benefit, of" the individual.[98]

A political expenditure triggers an *initial tax*, payable by the organization, of 10 percent of the amount of the expenditure. An initial tax of $2^1/_2$ percent of the expenditure is also imposed on each of the organization's managers (such as directors and officers), where he or she knew it was a political expenditure, unless the agreement to make the expenditure was not willful and was due to reasonable cause.[99] The IRS has the discretionary authority to abate these initial taxes where the organization can establish that the violation was due to reasonable cause and not to willful neglect, and timely corrects the violation.[100]

An *additional tax* is imposed on a charitable organization, at a rate of 100 percent of the political expenditure. This tax is levied where the initial tax was imposed and the expenditure was not timely corrected. An additional tax is imposed on the organization's manager, at a rate of 50 percent of the expenditure. This tax is levied where the additional tax was imposed on the organization and where the manager refused to agree to part or all of the correction.

---

[97] Reg. § 53.4955-1(c)(2)(i), (ii). The conference report accompanying these rules stated that, for this purpose, an "organization is to be considered as effectively controlled by a candidate or prospective candidate only if the individual has a continuing, substantial involvement in the day-to-day operations or management of the organization" (H. Rep. 495, 100th Cong., 1st Sess. 1021 (1987).) The report added that an organization "is not to be considered as effectively controlled by a candidate or a prospective candidate merely because it is affiliated with such candidate, or merely because the candidate knows the directors, officers, or employees of the organization" (*id.*). The report additionally stated that, "[l]ikewise, the effectively controlled test is not met merely because the organization carries on its research, study, or other educational activities with respect to subject matter or issues in which the individual is interested or with which the individual is associated" (*id.*).

This conference report also stated that the "determination of whether the primary purposes of an organization described in . . . [these rules] are promoting the candidacy or prospective candidacy of an individual for public office is to be made on the basis of all relevant facts and circumstances" (*id.*). The report added that the "factors to be considered include whether the surveys, studies, materials, etc. prepared by the organization are made available only to one individual (the candidate) or are made available to the general public; and whether the organization pays for speeches and travel expenses for only one individual, or for speeches or travel expenses of several persons" (*id.*). The report concluded: "The fact that a candidate or prospective candidate utilizes studies, papers, materials, etc. prepared by the organization (for example, in speeches by the individual) is not to be considered as a factor indicating that the organization has a purpose of promoting the candidacy or prospective candidacy of such individual where such studies, papers, materials, etc. are not made available only to that individual" (*id.* at 1021–1022).

[98] The conference report accompanying this legislation made it clear that these rules do not alter the preexisting rules as to the qualification of voter registration and voter education activities as exempt functions of charitable organizations (H. Rep. 495, *supra* note 97, at 1021). Also Reg. § 53.4955-1(c)(2)(iii).

[99] Reg. § 53.4955-1(b).

[100] IRC § 4962; Reg. § 53.4955-1(d).

As to management and as to any one political expenditure, the maximum initial tax is $5,000 and the maximum additional tax is $10,000.[101]

In this context, the concept of *correction* means "recovering part or all of the expenditure to the extent recovery is possible, establishment of safeguards to prevent future political expenditures, and where full recovery is not possible, such additional corrective action" as may be prescribed by federal tax regulations.[102]

Although a charitable organization can be required to pay these taxes and forfeit tax-exempt status for the tax years involved, the IRS frequently imposes the political expenditures tax without revoking the organization's tax exemption.[103]

If a tax is imposed with respect to a political expenditure under these rules, the expenditure will not be treated as a taxable expenditure under the private foundation rules.[104]

An organization that loses its federal tax status as a charitable organization because of substantial lobbying may be precluded from becoming tax-exempt as a social welfare organization.[105] This rule includes loss of tax-exempt status due to political campaign activities.

Under certain circumstances, the IRS is empowered to commence an action in federal district court to enjoin a charitable organization from the further making of political expenditures and for other relief to ensure that the assets of the organization are preserved for tax-exempt purposes.[106] The circumstances are the following: (1) The IRS has notified the organization of its intention to seek this injunction if the making of the political expenditures does not immediately cease; and (2) the Commissioner of Internal Revenue has personally determined that the organization has "flagrantly" participated or intervened in a political campaign on behalf of or in opposition to any candidate for public office and that injunctive relief is appropriate to prevent future political expenditures. If the federal district court finds, on the basis of "clear and convincing" evidence, the same facts as the Commissioner found, the court is authorized to enjoin the expenditures and grant other appropriate relief.

If the IRS finds that a charitable organization has flagrantly violated the prohibition against the making of political expenditures, the IRS is required to determine and assess any income and/or excise tax(es) due immediately, by terminating the organization's tax year.[107]

---

[101] A tax paid under this section is reported on Form 4720 (Reg. §§ 53.6011-1(b), 53.6071-1(e)).

[102] Reg. § 53.4955-1(e). The conference report note that the "adoption of the excise tax sanction does not modify the present-law rule that an organization is not tax-exempt under [IRC] section 501(c)(3), or eligible to receive tax-deductible charitable contributions, if the organization engages in any political campaign activity" (H. Rep. 495, *supra* note 97, at 1020). Also Reg. § 53.4955-1(a).

[103] E.g., Tech. Adv. Mem. 9635003. See, however, Branch Ministries Inc. v. Richardson, *supra* note 35.

[104] See § 11.4(e).

[105] IRC § 504. See § 20.3(b), text accompanied by note 88. Cf. § 20.9, text accompanied by note 238.

[106] IRC § 7409; Reg. § 301.7409-1.

[107] IRC § 6852; Reg. § 301.6852-1. In general, Chisholm, "Sinking the Think Tanks Upstream: The Use and Misuse of Tax Exemption Law to Address the Use and Misuse of Tax-Exempt Organizations by Politicians," 51 *U. Pitt. L. Rev.* (No. 3) 577 (1990); Sabbath, "Tax Exempt Political Education Organizations: Is the Exemption Being Abused?," 41 *Tax Law.* (No. 4) 847 (1988); Christopher, "Political Activities Become More Risky for Tax-Exempts Due to RA '87," 68 *J. Tax.* (No. 3) 136 (1988).

§ 21.3 TAXATION OF POLITICAL ACTIVITIES

A tax-exempt organization[108] that makes an expenditure for a *political* activity is subject to a tax.[109] This tax is determined by computing an amount equal to the lesser of the organization's net investment income[110] for the year involved or the amount expended for the political activity. This amount constitutes *political organization taxable income*[111] and is taxed[112] at the highest corporate rates.[113]

The concept of political activity for purposes of this tax is the same as that used for defining the exempt functions of political organizations.[114] Thus, political activity includes the function of influencing or attempting to influence the selection, nomination, election, or appointment of any individual to any federal, state, or local public office.[115] Consequently, this concept of political activity is broader than the concept of political campaign activity made applicable, as a prohibition, to charitable organizations.[116]

The prohibition applicable to charitable organizations concerns interventions or participations in political campaigns on behalf of or in opposition to candidates for public office. This prohibition is not necessarily a bar on political activity. For example, a charitable organization can attempt to influence the nomination of an individual to a public office; this would be *political activity* (and thus could attract this special tax) but not *political campaign activity*. Indeed, it is the position of the IRS that the function of influencing or attempting to influence the appointment of any individual to a public office, where confirmation by the legislative branch is involved, constitutes influencing or attempting to influence legislation, rather than political activity.[117]

The IRS has recognized the distinction between the concept of *political campaign activity* and the broader concept of *political activity*, in the context of noting that a charitable organization can establish a separate segregated fund for the purpose of conducting political activities that are not political campaign activities. On this occasion, the IRS Chief Counsel's office wrote that an "organization described in section 501(c)(3) is precluded from engaging in any political campaign activities."[118]

Political activity that is not political campaign activity can constitute a charitable, educational, religious, or like activity, undertaken in furtherance of the tax-exempt functions of a charitable organization. Thus, the income tax regulations

---

[108] That is, an organization described in IRC § 501(c) and exempt from federal income taxation by reason of IRC § 501(a).

[109] IRC § 527(f)(1).

[110] This term is defined in IRC § 527(f)(2).

[111] IRC § 527(c)(1), (2).

[112] IRC § 527(b).

[113] IRC § 11(b).

[114] IRC § 527(e)(2). In general, see Chapter 17.

[115] *Id.*

[116] This chapter, *passim.* (The term *charitable* organization means an organization described in IRC § 501(c)(3).)

[117] Notice 88-76, 1988-2 C.B. 392.

[118] Gen. Couns. Mem. 39694.

state that, where the prohibited activities are not engaged in as a "primary objective," the organization is not an action organization but can be regarded as "engaging in nonpartisan analysis, study, or research and making the results thereof available to the public."[119]

§ 21.4   POLITICAL ACTIVITIES OF SOCIAL WELFARE ORGANIZATIONS

Tax-exempt social welfare organizations generally are forbidden from participating or intervening in any political campaign on behalf of or in opposition to any candidate for public office.[120] The IRS has traditionally been strict in applying this restriction, as illustrated by the denial of classification as a tax-exempt social welfare organization to a group that rated candidates for public office on a nonpartisan basis and disseminated its ratings to the general public, on the theory that its rating process was intervention or participation on behalf of those candidates favorably rated and in opposition to those less favorably rated.[121]

Nor will objectivity necessarily ward off an unfavorable determination, as evidenced by the nonprofit group that selected slates of candidates for school board elections and engaged in campaigns on their behalf, and that was accordingly denied tax exemption as a charitable organization (and thus presumably as a social welfare organization) because of these political activities, "even though its process of selection may have been completely objective and unbiased and was intended primarily to educate and inform the public about the candidates."[122]

The foregoing does not mean, however, that a tax-exempt social welfare organization is completely foreclosed from participation in governmental and political affairs. An organization the activities of which were primarily directed, on a nonprofit and nonpartisan basis, toward encouraging individuals in business to become more active in politics and government and toward promoting business, social, or civic action was held to qualify for tax exemption as a social welfare organization.[123] Likewise, a group that engaged in nonpartisan analysis, study, and research, made the results available to the public, and publicized the need for a code of fair campaign practices, was ruled to be a tax-exempt educational organization.[124] Also, an organization that recruited college students for an internship program providing employment with local municipal agencies qualified as a tax-exempt educational and charitable organization.[125] Thus, a tax-exempt social welfare organization could similarly undertake these activities.

The IRS, therefore, in determining an organization's tax-exempt status in light of the requirements for a social welfare entity, carefully adheres to the dis-

---

[119] Reg. § 1.501(c)(3)-1(c)(3)(iv).
[120] Reg. § 1.501(c)(4)-1(a)(2)(ii). See Chapter 12.
[121] Rev. Rul. 67-368, 1967-2 C.B. 194.
[122] Rev. Rul. 67-71, 1967-1 C.B. 125.
[123] Rev. Rul. 60-193, 1960-1 C.B. 145.
[124] Rev. Rul. 66-258, 1966-2 C.B. 213.
[125] Rev. Rul. 70-584, 1970-2 C.B. 114.

tinction between those groups that actively participate or intervene in a political campaign for or against candidates for public office and those that more passively seek to stimulate public interest in improved government, better campaign practices, and the like.

However, this prohibition on political campaign activities by tax-exempt social welfare organizations is not absolute, in that the requirement is that these organizations must be *primarily* engaged in activities that promote social welfare. Thus, a tax-exempt organization primarily engaged in social welfare functions may carry on activities (such as financial assistance and in-kind services) involving participation and intervention in political campaigns on behalf of or in opposition to candidates for nomination or election to public office.[126]

§ 21.5 POLITICAL ACTIVITIES OF ASSOCIATIONS

Rules similar to those concerning expenditures for lobbying by associations and other business leagues are applicable with respect to certain political campaign expenditures by these organizations.[127]

There is no business expense deduction for any amount paid or incurred in connection with participation in, or intervention in, any political campaign on behalf of or in opposition to any candidate for public office or for any attempt to influence the general public, or segments of it, with respect to elections.[128]

Political activity by a business league can give rise to the tax on political campaign activities.[129] Many associations and other business leagues elect to maintain affiliated political organizations for the purpose of conducting political activities. In this fashion, the associations can avoid the tax on political activities, as well as not violate the federal campaign regulation laws.

---

[126] Rev. Rul. 81-95, 1981-1 C.B. 332. However, these political campaign activities will cause the organization to be subject to the tax imposed by IRC § 527(f) on the expenditures for political activities that are within the meaning of IRC § 527(e)(2) (see § 21.3).

[127] See § 20.

[128] IRC § 162(e)(1)(B), (C).

[129] See *supra* § 3.

CHAPTER TWENTY-TWO

Insurance and Fund-Raising Activities

§ 22.1   Insurance Activities   § 22.2   Fund-Raising Disclosure

The federal tax law contains bodies of law applicable to tax-exempt organizations that engage in certain insurance activities and certain fund-raising activities. The former is a set of rules that can affect qualification for tax-exempt status, while the latter is a disclosure requirement. Also, the law concerning the taxation of unrelated business income can apply with respect to both insurance and fund-raising activities.[1]

§ 22.1   INSURANCE ACTIVITIES

An otherwise tax-exempt charitable organization or social welfare organization will lose or be denied tax exemption if a substantial part of its activities consists of the provision of *commercial-type insurance*.[2] Otherwise, the activity of providing commercial-type insurance is treated as the conduct of an unrelated trade or business[3] and the income from it is taxed under the rules pertaining to taxable insurance companies.[4]

The term *commercial-type insurance* generally is any insurance of a type provided by commercial insurance companies.[5] For example, an organization was held to not qualify as a tax-exempt social welfare organization because its sole activity was the provision of certain benefits to students in a school who were injured in the course of school-related activities, in that the coverage was similar to contingent or excess insurance coverage.[6] However, this term does not include insurance provided at substantially below cost to a class of charitable recipients, incidental health insurance provided by an HMO of a kind

---

[1] See Part Five.
[2] IRC § 501(m).
[3] IRC § 501(m).
[4] IRC Subchapter L. The application of these rules may require organizations affected by them to change their accounting methods; the process for doing so is the subject of Rev. Proc. 87-51, 1987-2 C.B. 650.
[5] H. Rep. 99-841, 99th Cong., 2d Sess. II-345 (1986).
[6] Gen. Couns. Mem. 39703.

customarily provided by these organizations,[7] property or casualty insurance provided (directly or through a qualified employer)[8] by a church or convention or association of churches for the church or convention or association of churches, and the provision of retirement or welfare benefits (or both) by a church or a convention or association of churches (directly or through a qualified organization[9]) for the employees of the church or convention or association of churches or the beneficiaries of these employees.[10] This rule is also inapplicable to income from an insurance activity conducted by a political subdivision of a government.[11]

The IRS endeavored to define the term *commercial-type insurance*, since the phrase is undefined in the statute. Following a review of tax cases defining the term insurance, the Chief Counsel's office at the IRS concluded that the definition of commercial-type insurance "should include some form of risk-sharing and risk-distribution."[12] The IRS's lawyers also said that, despite the statutory exception for HMO insurance, "it is our opinion that in certain circumstances a health maintenance organization may be found to provide" commercial-type insurance.

Of course, for these rules to apply, the underlying activity must be the provision of *insurance* in the first instance. (The essence of the concept of insurance is that the risk of liability is shifted to at least one third party (the insurer), and that the risk is shared and distributed across a group of persons.[13]) For these purposes, the issuance of annuity contracts is considered the provision of insurance.[14] However, these rules do not apply to a charitable gift annuity, which is defined for this purpose as an annuity where a portion of the amount paid in connection with the issuance of the annuity is allowable as a charitable deduction for federal income or estate tax purposes, and the annuity is described in the special rule for annuities in the unrelated debt-financed income provisions[15] (determined as if any amount paid in cash in connection with the issuance were property).[16]

A court ruled that a nonprofit organization established to create and administer a group self-insurance pool for the benefit of tax-exempt social service paratransit providers, to provide the necessary financing for comprehensive automobile liability, risk management, and related services for pool members, did not qualify for exemption as a charitable organization because it provided

---

[7] E.g., Priv. Ltr. Rul. 9246004.

[8] That is, an organization described in IRC § 414(e)(3)(B)(ii).

[9] That is, an organization described in IRC § 414(e)(3)(A) or § 414(e)(3)(B)(ii).

[10] IRC § 501(m)(3). The management, by supporting organizations (see § 11.3(c)), for a church of regulated investment companies to provide benefits for church employees was ruled by the IRS to not cause loss of tax-exempt status of the organizations by reason of IRC § 501(m) (Priv. Ltr. Rul. 9645007).

[11] Priv. Ltr. Rul. 8836038.

[12] Gen. Couns. Mem. 39828.

[13] E.g., Sears, Roebuck & Co. v. Comm'r, 96 T.C. 61 (1991); The Harper Group v. Comm'r, 96 T.C. 45 (1991); Americo & Subsidiaries v. Comm'r, 96 T.C. 18 (1991); Humana, Inc. v. Comm'r, 88 T.C. 197 (1987), *aff'd in part, rev'd in part*, 881 F.2d 276 (6th Cir. 1989); Beech Aircraft Corp. v. United States, 797 F.2d 920 (10th Cir. 1986); Clougherty Packing Co. v. Comm'r, 84 T.C. 948 (1985), *aff'd*, 811 F.2d 1297 (9th Cir. 1987); Stearns-Roger Corp. v. United States, 774 F.2d 414 (10th Cir. 1985); Carnation Co. v. Comm'r, 71 T.C. 400 (1978), *aff'd*, 640 F.2d 1010 (9th Cir. 1981), *cert. den.*, 454 U.S. 965 (1981); Helvering v. LeGierse, 312 U.S. 531 (1941).

[14] IRC § 501(m)(4).

[15] IRC § 514(c)(5) (see § 29.3).

[16] IRC §§ 501(m)(3)(E), (5).

commercial-type insurance.[17] The court observed that the purpose of the insurance pool "is to shift the risk of potential tort liability from each of the individual insured paratransit organizations" to the entity, which "diversifies the risk of liability for each individual member."[18] It added that the type of insurance offered "is basic automobile liability insurance, a type of insurance provided by a number of commercial insurance carriers."[19] The court, writing that the phrase commercial-type insurance encompasses "every type of insurance that can be purchased in the commercial market," rejected the contention that the rules as to commercial-type insurance apply only where the insurance is offered to the general public. As to substantiality, the court, having found claims expenses to be as high as 75 percent, held that these insurance activities "are unquestionably a substantial part of its operations."[20]

This court subsequently held that three types of hospital membership funds cannot qualify as tax-exempt because they provided forms of commercial-type insurance. One fund enabled hospitals to self-insure on a group basis against hospital professional liability; this fund and another provided centralized cooperative insurance services to its member hospitals through the employment of actuaries, risk managers, underwriters, accountants, and other insurance consultants. The third fund was created as a vehicle for member hospital employers to self-insure on a group basis against workers' compensation claims. Finding the commercial-type insurance rules applicable, the court observed that the funds "provide actuarial, accounting, underwriting, claims payment, and similar services" that are "essential to the administration of the insurance programs."[21] The court said that there "is no dispute that hospital professional liability and workers' compensation insurance are normally offered by commercial insurers."[22]

Another case concerned an organization that administered a group self-insurance risk pool for a membership of nearly 500 charitable organizations that operate to fund or provide health or human services. It was formed to provide its membership with affordable insurance, which had endured periods of large premium increases, coverage reductions, and cancellations. The organization also develops educational materials and makes educational presentations, provides loss control and risk management services without charge, and serves as a resource for insurance-related questions. As to the insurance coverage, the organization provided commercial general liability, automobile liability, employer's non-owned and hired automobile liability, and miscellaneous professional liability. Observing that the organization "exists solely for the purpose of selling insurance to nonprofit exempt organizations at the lowest possible cost on a continued, stable basis," the court wrote that "[s]elling insurance undeniably is an inherently commercial activity ordinarily carried on by a commercial for-

---

[17] Paratransit Ins. Corp. v. Comm'r, 102 T.C. 745 (1994).
[18] *Id*. at 754.
[19] *Id*.
[20] *Id*.
[21] Florida Hosp. Trust Fund v. Comm'r, 103 T.C. 140 (1994).
[22] *Id*. at 158. This opinion was affirmed on appeal (71 F.3d 808 (11th Cir. 1996)).

profit company."[23] The court said that, despite the fact that the insurance is provided on a low-cost basis and that loss control and risk management services are provided without charge, the "nature and operation" of the organization are commercial in nature.[24] It was noted that the organization engages in the actual underwriting of insurance policies, contracts with other firms to secure reinsurance for high claims, and ceases membership benefits when a member fails to timely pay the required premium payments.

However, the foregoing body of caselaw[25] has been somewhat supplanted by statutory law providing tax-exempt status for charitable risk pools.[26]

As noted,[27] these rules are inapplicable to the provision of insurance by a nonprofit organization at substantially below cost to a class of charitable recipients.[28] The courts are placing great emphasis on a ruling by the IRS, issued in a different context, that the phrase *substantially below cost* entails a subsidy of at least 85 percent.[29] Thus, in one case, while the court declined to "draw a bright line" defining that phrase, it rejected the proposition that a subsidy of about 35 percent qualified.[30] In another instance, this exception was ruled not applicable where member contributions for one year were in excess of 80 percent.[31]

§ 22.2 FUND-RAISING DISCLOSURE

Federal tax law includes a provision concerning fund-raising by most tax-exempt organizations.[32] However, these rules are not applicable with respect to charitable organizations.[33]

---

[23] Nonprofits' Ins. Alliance of Calif. v. United States, 94-2 USTC § 50,593 (Ct. Fed. Cl. 1994).

[24] *Id.*

[25] See the text accompanied by *supra* notes 17–24,

[26] See § 10.6.

[27] See *supra* note 10.

[28] IRC § 501(m)(3)(A).

[29] Rev. Rul. 71-529, 1971-2 C.B. 234.

[30] Nonprofits' Ins. Alliance of Calif. v. United States, *supra* note 23.

[31] Paratransit Ins. Corp. v. Comm'r, *supra* note 17. In general, Shill, "Revocation of Blue Cross & Blue Shield's Tax-Exempt Status an Unhealthy Change? An Analysis of the Effect of the Tax Reform Act of 1986 on the Taxation of Blue Cross & Blue Shield and Health Insurance Activities," 6 *B. U. J. Tax Law* 147 (1988).

[32] IRC § 6113.

[33] That is, this element of the legislation does not apply to organizations described in IRC § 501(c)(3). Nonetheless, the report of the House Committee on Ways and Means accompanying the legislation (H. Rep. 391, 100th Cong., 1st Sess. (1987)) observed that the Committee "is concerned that some charitable organizations may not make sufficient disclosure, in soliciting donations, membership dues, payments for admissions or merchandise, or other support, of the extent (if any) to which the payors may be entitled to charitable deductions for such payments" (at 1607). The report discussed these matters in some detail, concluding with an exhortation to the organizations representing the charitable community to "further educate their members as to the applicable tax rules and provide guidance as to how charities can provide appropriate information to their supporters in this regard" (at 1608).

However, less than five years later, fund-raising regulation law was enacted for charitable organizations. These rules include a gift substantiation requirement (IRC § 170(f)(8)) and rules pertaining to

This body of law is designed to prevent noncharitable (principally, social welfare) organizations from engaging in public fund-raising activities under circumstances where donors are likely to assume that the contributions are tax deductible as charitable gifts, when in fact they are not.

Thus, under these rules, each *fundraising solicitation* by (or on behalf of) a noncharitable tax-exempt organization is required to "contain an express statement (in a conspicuous and easily recognizable format)" that gifts to it are not deductible as charitable contributions for federal income tax purposes.[34] A fund-raising solicitation that is in conformity with rules promulgated by the IRS (concerning the format of the disclosure statement in instances of use of print media, telephone, television, and radio), which include guidance in the form of "safe harbor" provisions, is deemed to satisfy the statutory requirements.[35]

Generally, this rule applies to any organization to which contributions are not deductible as charitable gifts and that (1) is tax-exempt,[36] (2) is a political organization,[37] (3) was either type of organization at any time during the five-year period ending on the date of the fund-raising solicitation, or (4) is a successor to this type of an organization at any time during the five-year period.[38] However, this rule is inapplicable to any organization that has annual gross receipts that are normally no more than $100,000. Also, where all of the parties being solicited are tax-exempt organizations, a solicitation need not include the disclosure statement (inasmuch as these grantors do not utilize a charitable contribution deduction).[39]

Further exempt from this disclosure rule is the billing of those who advertise in an organization's publications, billings by social clubs for food and beverages, billing of attendees at a conference, billing for insurance premiums of an insurance program operated or sponsored by an organization, billing of members of a community association for mandatory payments for police and fire (and similar) protection, or billing for payments to a voluntary employees' beneficiary association, as well as similar payments to a trust for pension and/or health benefits.[40]

The IRS is accorded the authority to treat any group of two or more organi-

---

quid pro quo contributions (IRC §§ 6115, 6714). These bodies of law are the subject of Hopkins, *The Tax Law of Charitable Giving* (New York: John Wiley & Sons, Inc., 1993), 1996 Cum. Supp., Chs. 21 § 1(b), 22 § 1(b).

[34] IRC § 6113(a).

[35] Notice 88-120, 1988-2 C.B. 454. In one instance, a political organization (see Chapter 17) that conducted fund-raising by means of telemarketing and direct mail was found to be in violation of these rules; a notice of nondeductibility of contributions was not included in its telephone solicitations or pledge statements, and the print used in some of its written notices was too small (Priv. Ltr. Rul. 9315001).

[36] That is, is described in IRC § 501(c) (other than, as noted, *supra* note 33, IRC § 501(c)(3)).

[37] That is, an organization described in IRC § 527. See Chapter 17.

[38] IRC § 6113(b). For this purpose, a fraternal organization (one described in IRC § 170(c)(4); see § 18.4) is treated as a charitable organization only with respect to solicitations for contributions which are to be used exclusively for purposes referred to in IRC § 170(c)(4).

[39] Notice 88-120, *supra* note 35.

[40] *Id.*

zations as one organization for these purposes where "necessary or appropriate" to prevent the avoidance of these rules through the use of multiple organizations. The term *fundraising solicitation* means any solicitation of gifts made in written or printed form, or by television, radio, or telephone. An exclusion is provided for letters or calls not part of a "coordinated fundraising campaign soliciting more than 10 persons during the calendar year."[41]

Failure to satisfy this disclosure requirement can result in imposition of penalties.[42] The penalty is $1,000 per day (maximum of $10,000 per year), albeit with a reasonable cause exception. However, in the case of an "intentional disregard" of these rules, the penalty for the day on which the offense occurred is the greater of $1,000 or 50 percent of the aggregate cost of the solicitation that took place on that day and the $10,000 limitation would be inapplicable. For these purposes, the days involved are those on which the solicitation was telecast, broadcast, mailed, otherwise distributed, or telephoned.

---

[41] IRC § 6113(c).
[42] IRC § 6710.

Exemption Recognition Process

Every element of gross income received by a person, including a corporation or trust, is subject to the federal income tax.[1] The presumption is that all income is taxed; income that is not taxable is exempt by virtue of a specific tax law provision to that effect. Examples of this are the provisions for tax-exempt organizations.

An organization is not exempt from the federal income tax merely because it is organized and operated as a *nonprofit* entity.[2] Tax exemption is achieved only where the organization satisfies the requirements of a particular provision in the Internal Revenue Code.[3] Thus, in general, an organization that meets the appropriate statutory criteria qualifies—for that reason alone—as a tax-exempt organization. That is, whether an organization is entitled to tax exemption, on an initial or ongoing basis, is a matter of law. It is Congress that, by statute, defines the categories of organizations that are eligible for tax exemption[4] and it is Congress that determines whether a type of tax exemption should be continued.[5]

---

[1] IRC § 61(a).

[2] See discussion at § 1.1.

[3] IRC §§ 501(c), 521, or 526–529.

[4] E.g., HCSC-Laundry v. United States, 450 U.S. 1 (1981) (Congress had the authority to exclude nonprofit laundry organizations from the scope of the tax exemption accorded to cooperative hospital service organizations (see § 10.4)).

[5] E.g., Maryland Sav.-Share Ins. Corp. v. United States, 400 U.S. 4 (1970) (Congress did not exceed its power to tax nor violate the Fifth Amendment to the Constitution in denying tax-exempt status to

§ 23.1 CONCEPT OF RECOGNITION OF TAX EXEMPTION

The tax law contains the concept of *recognition* of tax-exempt status. This is a function of the IRS, which it exercises, where appropriate, by making a written determination that an entity constitutes a tax-exempt organization. (The role of the IRS in recognizing the tax-exempt status of organizations is part of its overall practice of evaluating the tax status of organizations.[6]) However, eligibility for tax-exempt status is different than recognition of that status. Thus, Congress, as noted, and not the IRS, is responsible for *granting* tax-exempt status.

As a general rule, an organization desiring tax-exempt status pursuant to the federal tax law is not required to secure recognition of tax exemption from the IRS.[7] Nonetheless, organizations of this nature may seek recognition of tax-exempt status, and are often well-advised to do so (following standards used in ascertaining whether to seek any type of ruling from the IRS[8]). By contrast, in order for an organization to be granted tax exemption as a charitable entity or as an employee benefit organization, it must file an application for recognition of the exemption with the IRS and receive a favorable determination. Consequently, when an organization makes application to the IRS for a determination as to tax-exempt status, it is requesting the IRS to recognize its tax exemption, not to grant tax exemption.

Subject only to the authority of the IRS to revoke a ruling for good cause (usually a change in the facts or law), an organization whose tax-exempt status has been recognized by the IRS can rely on that determination as long as there are no substantial changes in its character, purposes, or methods of operation.[9] (Upon the occurrence of any one of these changes, the organization is required to notify the IRS and obtain a reevaluation of its tax-exempt status.[10])

§ 23.2 RECOGNITION APPLICATION PROCEDURE

The IRS promulgated rules by which a determination letter or ruling may be issued to an organization in response to the filing of an application for recognition of tax-exempt status.[11] Nearly all determinations by the IRS recognizing the tax-

---

nonprofit insurers of deposits in savings banks and similar entities where the insurers were organized after September 1, 1957 (see § 18.5)). Likewise, for example, IRC § 501(c)(18) (see § 16.6) is applicable only to trusts created before June 25, 1959; IRC § 501(c)(20) (see § 16.6) is available to provide tax exemption for trusts under a qualified group legal services plan for tax years beginning before July 1, 1992; and IRC § 501(c)(27)(A) (see § 18.15) is applicable only to entities established before June 1, 1996.

[6] Reg. §§ 601.201(a)(1), 601.201(d)(1).

[7] E.g., Savings Feature of Relief Dep't of B&O R.R. Co. v. Comm'r, 32 B.T.A. 295 (1935); Rev. Rul. 80-108, 1980-1 C.B. 119 (reflecting the fact that an organization qualifying for tax exemption as a social welfare organization (see Chapter 12) is not required to seek recognition of tax exemption).

[8] In this context, the advantages to be gained by obtaining recognition of tax-exempt status include acknowledgment by the IRS that the entity qualifies for tax exemption, exemption from certain state taxes, and eligibility for nonprofit mailing privileges. As to the latter, see Hopkins, *The Law of Fund-Raising, Second Edition* (New York: John Wiley & Sons, Inc., 1996), Chapter 6 § 20.

[9] Reg. § 1.501(a)-1(a)(2).

[10] See § 4.5(a).

[11] Rev. Proc. 90-27, 1990-1 C.B. 514. These rules apply with regard to organizations seeking recognition of tax exemption under IRC §§ 501 and 521, and with respect to revocation and modification of ex-

exempt status of organizations are in the form of *determination letters*. This is a document issued by the IRS in response to an application for recognition of exemption.[12] Where a determination as to an organization's tax exemption is made by the National Office of the IRS, the document is a *ruling*.[13]

In most instances, an organization seeking recognition of tax exemption by the IRS must file a particular form of application. An organization seeking recognition of exemption as a charitable organization is required to file Form 1023.[14] Nearly all other applicant organizations[15] file Form 1024,[16] although homeowners' associations file Form 1120-H and farmers', fruit growers', and like associations file Form 1028.[17] For a few categories of tax-exempt organization, there is no application form by which to seek recognition of tax exemption; instead, the request is made by letter.[18]

Historically, these applications were filed with the appropriate IRS key district director's office, determined in relation to the district in which the principal place of business of the organization was located.[19] However, as part of a reorganization of the IRS, which was completed in 1997, all applications for recognition of tax exemption are filed with the IRS Service Center in Cincinnati, Ohio.[20]

These rules as to application for recognition of tax-exempt status are separate from those concerning requests for determination letters or rulings in the tax-exempt organizations context generally.[21] They are also separate from the

---

emption determination letters and rulings. Rev. Proc. 72-5, 1972-1 C.B. 709, states the information that must be included on applications for recognition of tax exemption filed by certain religious and apostolic organizations (see § 8.7). Rev. Proc. 80-30, 1980-1 C.B. 685, applies in instances involving the tax exemption of funds underlying pension, annuity, profit-sharing, and stock bonus plans.

Occasionally, the IRS will announce a process for the expediting of applications for recognition of tax exemption for charitable organizations, in aid of entities that are quickly formed to solicit contributions and provide programs in response to an emergency. For example, this type of a process was implemented in the aftermath of Hurricane Opal in 1995 (Notice 95-66, 1995-2 C.B. 343), Hurricane Marilyn in 1995 (Notice 95-56, 1995-2 C.B. 343), the floods in Virginia in 1995 (Notice 95-47, 1995-2 C.B. 331), the bombing of a federal building in Oklahoma City, Oklahoma, on April 19, 1995 (Notice 95-33, 1995-1 C.B. 309), the floods in California in late 1994 and early 1995 (Notice 95-7, 1995-1 C.B. 292; Notice 95-16, 1995-2 C.B. 300), the floods in the southeastern United States in 1994 (Notice 94-87, 1994-2 C.B. 555), the earthquake in Los Angeles earlier that year (Notice 94-15, 1994-1 C.B. 337), Hurricane Andrew in 1992 (Notice 92-45, 1992-2 C.B. 375; Ann. 92-128,1992-38 I.R.B. 42), and Hurricane Iniki in that same year (Ann. 92-140, 1992-41 I.R.B. 75; Notice 92-45, *supra*).

[12] Reg. § 601.201(a)(3).

[13] Reg. § 601.201(a)(2).

[14] The present Form 1023 is dated April 1996.

[15] Generally, those listed in IRC § 501(c), other than in IRC § 501(c)(3).

[16] The present Form 1024 is dated April 1996.

[17] The present Form 1028 is dated March 1994.

[18] E.g., that is the procedure in the case of multiemployer pension plan trusts (Ann. 80-163, 1980-52 I.R.B. 50).

[19] Reg. § 601.201(n)(1)(i).

[20] See Ann. 96-92, 1996-38 I.R.B. 151; Ann. 96-133, 1996-53 I.R.B. 60; Ann. 97-20, 1997-11 I.R.B. 22.

[21] The IRS generally will issue determination letters, rulings, and information letters on any aspect of the law of tax-exempt organizations, transactions that may have an impact on an organization's tax-exempt or public charity status, or that may involve unrelated trade or business matters. The administrative rules in this regard are issued at the beginning of each year (currently Rev. Proc. 98-4, 1998-1 I.R.B. 113), as are the related rules concerning the seeking of technical advice from the IRS (currently Rev. Proc. 98-5, 1998-1 I.R.B. 155).

procedures followed by the IRS for the issuance of determination letters and the like generally.[22]

(a) General Procedures

A determination letter or ruling recognizing tax-exempt status will be issued by the IRS to an organization, where its application for recognition of exemption and supporting documents establish that it meets the requirements of the category of exemption that it claimed as provided in the Internal Revenue Code and other related law.[23] Any oral representations of additional facts or modification of facts as represented or alleged in the application must be reduced to writing over the signature of an authorized individual.[24]

Tax-exempt status for an organization will be recognized by the IRS in advance of operations where the entity's proposed activities are described in sufficient detail to permit a conclusion that the organization will clearly meet the pertinent statutory requirements. A mere restatement of purposes or a statement that proposed activities will be in furtherance of the organization's purposes does not satisfy this requirement. An applicant organization must fully describe the activities in which it expects to engage, including the standards, criteria, procedures, or other means adopted or planned for carrying out the activities, the anticipated sources of receipts, and the nature of contemplated expenditures.[25]

An organization seeking a determination letter or ruling as to recognition of its tax-exempt status has the burden of proving that it satisfies all of the requirements of the particular tax exemption category.[26]

The IRS, generally supported by the courts, usually will refuse to recognize an organization's tax-exempt status unless the entity tenders sufficient information regarding its operations and finances. For example, an organization submitted an application for recognition of tax exemption, stating its "long-range plan" to form a school; it was unable to substantively respond to any of the requests from the IRS for additional information. The IRS refused to recognize the organization as a tax-exempt entity; a court agreed, holding that the organization "failed to supply such information as would enable a conclusion that when operational, if ever, . . . [the organization] will conduct all of its activities in a manner which will accomplish its exempt purposes."[27] The court chided the entity for having only "vague generalizations" of its ostensibly planned activities and strongly suggested that the organization had "no plan to operate a school in the foreseeable future."[28] Likewise, a court concluded that an organization failed to

---

[22] These procedures are also issued at the outset of each year (currently Rev. Proc. 98-1, 1998-1 I.R.B. 11), along with the general rules for seeking technical advice (currently Rev. Proc. 98-2, 1998-1 I.R.B. 64).

[23] Reg. § 601.201(n)(1)(ii).

[24] Rev. Proc. 90-27, *supra* note 11 § 5.01.

[25] Reg. § 601.201(n)(1)(ii); Rev. Proc. 90-27, *supra* note 11 § 5.02. See § 24.8.

[26] E.g., Harding Hosp., Inc. v. United States, 505 F.2d 1068 (6th Cir. 1974); Church of Spiritual Technology v. United States, 92-1 U.S.T.C. ¶ 50,305 (Fed. Cl. 1992).

[27] Pius XII Academy, Inc. v. Comm'r, 43 T.C.M. 634, 636 (1982).

[28] *Id.*

meet its burden of proof as to its eligibility for tax exemption because it did not provide a "meaningful explanation" of its activities to the IRS.[29] In another such instance, a court concluded that an organization's failure to respond "completely or candidly" to many of the inquiries of the IRS precluded it from receiving a determination as to its tax-exempt status.[30]

However, an organization is considered to have made the required "threshold showing" where it describes its activities in "sufficient detail" to permit a conclusion that the entity will meet the pertinent requirements,[31] particularly where it answered all of the questions propounded by the IRS.[32] In another instance, a court observed that, although the law "requires that the organization establish reasonable standards and criteria for its operation as an exempt organization," the standard does not necessitate "some sort of metaphysical proof of future events."[33]

When the representatives of a would-be tax-exempt organization fail to submit its books and records to the IRS, an inference arises that the facts involved would denigrate the organization's cause.[34] (At the same time, it has been held that the refusal by an organization to turn records over to the IRS, in response to a summons, does not give the IRS the authority to summarily revoke the organization's tax-exempt status.[35])

Where an organization cannot demonstrate, to the satisfaction of the IRS, that its proposed activities will qualify it for tax exemption, a record of actual operations may be required before a determination letter or ruling is issued.[36] In cases where an organization is unable to fully describe its purposes and activities, a refusal by the IRS to issue a determination letter or ruling is considered an initial adverse determination from which administrative appeal or protest rights will be afforded.[37]

If an application for recognition of tax exemption does not contain the requisite information, the application usually will be returned to the applicant organization (rather than to anyone on a power of attorney) without being considered

---

[29] Public Indust., Inc. v. Comm'r, 61 T.C.M. 1626, 1629 (1991).

[30] National Ass'n of Am. Churches v. Comm'r, 82 T.C. 18, 32 (1984). Also United Libertarian Fellowship, Inc. v. Comm'r, 65 T.C.M. 2178 (1993); Church of Nature in Man v. Comm'r, 49 T.C.M. 1393 (1985); LaVerdad v. Comm'r, 82 T.C. 215 (1984); The Basic Unit Ministry of Alma Karl Schurig v. United States, 511 F. Supp. 166 (D.D.C. 1981).

[31] Rev. Proc. 90-27, *supra* note 11 § 5.02.

[32] E.g., The Church of the Visible Intelligence That Governs the Universe v. United States, 83-2 U.S.T.C. ¶ 9726 (Ct. Cl. 1983).

[33] American Science Found. v. Comm'r, 52 T.C.M. 1049, 1051 (1986).

[34] E.g., New Concordia Bible Church v. Comm'r, 49 T.C.M. 176 (1984) (*app. dis.*, 9th Cir. (1985)). Also Chief Steward of the Ecumenical Temples & the Worldwide Peace Movement & His Successors v. Comm'r, 49 T.C.M. 640 (1985); Basic Bible Church of Am., Auxiliary Chapter 11004 v. Comm'r, 46 T.C.M. 223 (1983); McElhannon v. Comm'r, 44 T.C.M. 1392 (1982); Bubbling Well Church of Universal Love, Inc. v. Comm'r, 74 T.C. 531 (1980), *aff'd*, 670 F.2d 104 (9th Cir. 1981); Founding Church of Scientology v. United States, 412 F.2d 1197 (Ct. Cl. 1969), *cert. den.*, 397 U.S. 1009 (1970); Parker v. Comm'r, 365 F.2d 792 (8th Cir. 1966), *cert. den.*, 385 U.S. 1026 (1967).

[35] Church of World Peace, Inc. v. Internal Revenue Serv., 715 F.2d 492 (10th Cir. 1983).

[36] Reg. § 601.201(n)(1)(ii).

[37] Rev. Proc. 90-27, *supra* note 11 § 5.02.

on its merits, with a letter of explanation.[38] In the case of a would-be charitable organization, where an application is returned, the IRS will inform the organization of the time within which the completed application must be resubmitted in order for the application to be considered a timely notice to the IRS.[39]

A determination letter or ruling recognizing tax exemption ordinarily will not be issued if an issue involving the organization's tax-exempt status is pending in litigation or is under consideration within the IRS.[40]

An application for recognition of tax exemption may be withdrawn, upon the written request of an authorized representative of the organization, at any time prior to the issuance of an initial adverse determination letter or ruling. Where an application is withdrawn, it and all supporting documents are retained by the IRS.[41]

An organization may reapply for recognition of tax exemption if it was previously denied the recognition, where the facts involved are materially changed so that the organization is in compliance with the requirements. For example, an organization that was refused recognition of exemption because of excessive lobbying activities, by reason of the expenditure test,[42] may subsequently reapply for recognition of exemption as a charitable organization for any tax year following the first tax year as to which the recognition was denied.[43] The reapplication form must include information demonstrating that the organization was in compliance with the expenditure test during the full tax year immediately preceding the date of reapplication,[44] and that the organization will not knowingly operate in a manner that would disqualify it from exemption by reason of attempts to influence legislation.[45]

The IRS has an expedited determination process, whereby an experienced employee reviews applications for determination letters recognizing tax-exempt status and decides which applications can be processed quickly without further review by an exempt organization specialist or contact with the applicant organization.[46] A properly prepared application for recognition of tax-exempt status can thus be processed by the IRS in a shorter period than might otherwise be the case.

The proper preparation of an application for recognition of tax exemption involves far more than merely responding to the questions on a government form. It is a process not unlike the preparation of a prospectus for a business in conformity with securities law requirements. Every statement made in the application should be carefully considered. Some of the questions may force the applicant organization to focus on matters that good management practices should cause it to consider, even in the absence of the application requirements.

---

[38] *Id.* at § 5.03.
[39] Reg. § 601.201(n)(1)(iii). See *infra* § 3.
[40] Reg. § 601.201(n)(1)(iv); Rev. Proc. 90-27, *supra* note 11 § 5.04.
[41] *Id.* at § 7.01.
[42] See § 20.2(c).
[43] Reg. § 1.501(h)-3(d)(1).
[44] Reg. § 1.501(h)-3(d)(2).
[45] Reg. § 1.501(h)-3(d)(3).
[46] This process is discussed in "Tax Administration: IRS Can Improve Its Process for Recognizing Exempt Organizations," 4 General Accounting Office (GAO/GCD-90-55 (June 1990)).

The prime objective must be accuracy; it is essential that all material facts be correctly and fully disclosed. Of course, the determination as to which facts are material and the marshaling of these facts requires judgment. Also, the manner in which the answers are phrased can be extremely significant; in this regard, the exercise can be more one of art than science. The preparer or reviewer of the application should be able to anticipate the concerns the contents of the application may cause the IRS and to see that the application is properly prepared, while simultaneously minimizing the likelihood of conflict with the IRS. Organizations that are entitled to tax-exempt status have been denied recognition of exemption by the IRS, or at least have caused the process of gaining the recognition more protracted, because of unartful phraseologies in the application that motivated the IRS to muster a case that the organization does not qualify for exemption. Therefore, the application for recognition of tax exemption should be regarded as an important legal document and prepared accordingly. The fact that the application is available for public inspection only underscores the need for the thoughtful preparation of it.[47]

(b) The *Substantially Completed* Application

The application for recognition of tax exemption as submitted by a tax-exempt organization will not be processed by the IRS until the application is at least *substantially completed*.[48] Likewise, for purposes of the declaratory judgment rules,[49] it is the position of the IRS that the 270-day period[50] does not begin until the date a substantially completed application is filed with the IRS.[51]

A substantially completed application for recognition of tax exemption is one that:

- Is signed by an authorized individual;

- Includes an employer identification number or a completed application for the number (Form SS-4);

- Includes information regarding any previously filed federal income and/or exempt organization information returns;

- Includes a statement of receipts and expenditures and a balance sheet for the current year and the three preceding years (or the years the organization was in existence, where that period is less than four years), although if the organization has not yet commenced operations, or has not completed one full accounting period, a proposed budget for two full ac-

---

[47] See § 15.3. It is the view of the IRS that the estimated average time required to keep records underlying the Form 1023 (not including the schedules) is 55 hours and 29 minutes, to learn about the law in this regard or the form is 4 hours and 37 minutes, and to prepare the form and send it to the IRS is 8 hours and 7 minutes (instructions accompanying Form 1023).

[48] Rev. Proc. 90-27, *supra* note 11 § 5.06.

[49] See § 24.6(b).

[50] IRC § 7428(b)(2).

[51] Rev. Proc. 90-27, *supra* note 11 § 5.05.

counting periods and a current statement of assets and liabilities is acceptable;

- Includes a narrative statement of proposed activities[52] and a narrative description of anticipated receipts and contemplated expenditures[53];

- Includes a copy of the document by which the organization was established that is signed by a principal officer or is accompanied by a written declaration signed by an authorized individual certifying that the document is a complete and accurate copy of the original or otherwise meets the requirement that it be a *conformed* copy[54];

- If the organizing document is a set of articles of incorporation, includes evidence that it was filed with and approved by an appropriate state official (such as a copy of the certificate of incorporation) or includes a copy of the articles of incorporation accompanied by a written declaration signed by an authorized individual that the copy is a complete and accurate copy of the original document that was filed with and approved by the state, and stating the date of filing with the state;

- If the organization has adopted bylaws,[55] includes a current copy of that document, verified as being current by an authorized individual; and

- Is accompanied by the correct user fee.[56]

Of particular significance to charitable organizations, the application for recognition of tax exemption requests information concerning the composition of the entity's governing body, any relationship with other organizations, the nature of its program activities, its fund-raising program, and a variety of other matters.

Where an application for recognition of tax exemption involves an issue where significant contrary authorities (such as court opinions) exist, the applicant organization is encouraged by the IRS to disclose and discuss them. Failure to do so can result in requests for additional information and may delay action on the application.[57]

If an application for recognition of tax exemption is revised at the request of the IRS, the 270-day period that applies in the declaratory judgment context[58] will not be considered by the IRS as starting until the date the application is refiled with the IRS with the requested information. If the upgraded application is mailed and a postmark is not evident, the period starts on the date the IRS received the substantially completed application.

Even though an application for recognition of tax exemption is substantially

---

[52] Also Reg. §§ 1.501(a)-1(b)(1), 1.501(c)(3)-1(b)(1)(v).
[53] Also Reg. § 1.501(a)-1(a)(3).
[54] Rev. Proc. 68-14, 1968-1 C.B. 768.
[55] Reg. § 1.501(a)-1(a)(3).
[56] Rev. Proc. 90-27, *supra* note 11 § 5.05. As to user fees, see *infra* § 2(d).
[57] Rev. Proc. 90-27, *supra* note 11 § 5.08.
[58] See § 24.6(b).

complete, the IRS has reserved the authority to obtain additional information before a determination letter or ruling is issued.[59]

The standards for a substantially completed application also apply with respect to the notice requirements for charitable organizations.[60]

(c) Issuance of Determination Letters and Rulings

Generally, an organization acquiring recognition of tax-exempt status does so by means of issuance of a determination letter by the IRS.[61] That is, the National Office of the IRS relatively infrequently issues a ruling recognizing the tax-exempt status of an organization.[62]

An IRS representative must refer to the National Office of the IRS an application for recognition of tax exemption that (1) presents questions the answers to which are not specifically covered by the Internal Revenue Code, Department of the Treasury regulations, an IRS revenue ruling, or court decision published in the *Internal Revenue Bulletin*, or (2) has been specifically reserved by an IRS revenue procedure and/or *Internal Revenue Manual* instructions for handling by the National Office for purposes of establishing uniformity or centralized control of designated categories of cases. In this instance, the National Office is to consider the application, issue a ruling directly to the organization, and send a copy of the ruling to the appropriate IRS office.[63]

If, during the course of consideration of an application for recognition of tax exemption, the applicant organization believes that its case involves an issue on which there is no published precedent, the organization may ask the IRS to request technical advice[64] from the IRS National Office.[65] If the IRS proposes to recognize the tax exemption of an organization to which the National Office had previously issued a contrary ruling or technical advice memorandum (a highly unlikely event), the IRS representative must seek technical advice from the National Office before issuing a determination letter.[66]

Some determination letters issued by the IRS are reviewed by the Exempt Organizations Division in the IRS National Office for the purpose of assuring uniform application of the statutes, regulations, rulings, and court opinions published in the *Internal Revenue Bulletin*.[67] Where the IRS National Office takes exception to a determination letter, the IRS representative involved must be advised. If the organization disagrees with the exception taken, the file is returned to the National Office. The referral is treated as a request for technical advice.[68]

---

[59] Rev. Proc. 90-27, *supra* note 11 § 5.07. Also Reg. §§ 1.501(a)-1(b)(2), 601.201(h)(1)(ii), 601.201(h)(1)(iii). Cf. text accompanied by *supra* notes 27–35.

[60] Rev. Proc. 90-27, *supra* note 11 § 5.07. See § 24.3.

[61] Reg. § 601.201(n)(2)(i); Rev. Proc. 90-27, *supra* note 11 § 6.01.

[62] See text accompanied by *infra* note 69.

[63] Reg. § 601.201(n)(2)(ii); Rev. Proc. 90-27, *supra* note 11 § 6.02.

[64] Reg. § 601.201(n)(2)(iv); Rev. Proc. 97-5, *supra* note 21.

[65] Rev. Proc. 90-27, *supra* note 11 § 6.03.

[66] *Id.* at § 6.04.

[67] *Id.* at § 8.01.

[68] *Id.* at § 8.02.

Occasionally, the IRS issues exemption letters (rulings) out of its National Office. These documents are available for public inspection, along with the underlying application for recognition of exemption.[69]

A determination letter or ruling recognizing tax exemption usually is effective as of the date of formation of the organization where its purposes and activities during the period prior to the date of the determination letter or ruling were consistent with the requirements for tax exemption.[70] If the organization is required to alter its activities or to make substantive amendments to its enabling instrument, the determination letter or ruling recognizing its tax-exempt status is effective as of the date specified in the determination letter or ruling. If a nonsubstantive amendment is made, tax exemption is ordinarily recognized as of the date the entity was formed.[71]

In general, an organization can rely on a determination letter or ruling from the IRS recognizing its tax exemption. However, this is not the case if there is a material change, inconsistent with exemption, in the character, purpose, or method of operation of the organization.[72]

(d) User Fees

Congress enacted a program of user fees, payable to the IRS for requests for rulings, information letters, determination letters, and similar requests. These fees must be accompanied by the filing of an IRS form (Form 8718). This program became effective as of February 1, 1988,[73] was extended until October 1, 2000, and is certain to be extended thereafter.

Under the current schedule, the fee for the processing of an application for recognition of tax exemption is $465, where the applicant has gross receipts that annually exceed $10,000. For smaller organizations, the fee is $150. A group exemption[74] letter fee is $500. A user fee of $100 is charged for a request for a ruling to modify the terms or stipulations stated in an initial ruling, issued by the National Office of the IRS, recognizing the tax-exempt status of an organization.[75]

---

[69] Notice 92-28, 1992-1 C.B. 515.

[70] Reg. § 601.201(n)(3)(i); Rev. Proc. 90-27, *supra* note 11 § 13.01. There are special requirements in this regard for charitable organizations (see §§ 24.3, 24.4).

[71] Rev. Proc. 90-27, *supra* note 11 § 13.01. *Nonsubstantive* amendments include correction of a clerical error in the enabling instrument or the addition of a dissolution clause (see § 4.3(b)), where the activities of the organization prior to the determination letter or ruling are consistent with the requirements for tax exemption (*id.*).

[72] Reg. § 601.201(n)(3)(ii); Rev. Proc. 90-27, *supra* note 11 § 13.02.

[73] The program was first described in Rev. Proc. 88-8, 1988-1 C.B. 628.

[74] See *infra* § 6.

[75] Rev. Proc. 98-8, 1998-1 I.R.B. 225. Other ruling requests in the tax-exempt organizations area generally generate a user fee of $1,775. However, where the requesting organization has annual gross receipts that are less than $150,000, the fee is $500.

Advance approval of scholarship grant-making procedures of a private foundation (see § 11.4(e), text accompanied by notes 301–307) that has an agreement for the administration of the scholarship program with the National Merit Scholarship Corporation or similar organization administering a scholarship program shown to meet the IRS requirements entails a user fee of $100 (*id.*).

(e) The Application Form

The application forms are available from the IRS, as part of a packet that includes general instructions as to the preparation of them.[76]

The pertinent parts of the application form for charitable organizations (Form 1023) are the following:

- Part I, which requests basic information about the applicant organization, such as its name, address, employer identification number, form of entity, and date of formation;

- Part II, which requests a description of activities, composition of and other information about the governing body, assets, and other operational information about the applicant organization;

- Part III, which requests information concerning the period of time the determination letter or ruling will cover[77] and the public charity/private foundation status of the applicant organization[78]; and

- Part IV, which requests certain financial data, including revenue, expenses, assets, and liabilities, which new applicant organizations may instead submit by means of a budget.

The application also contains the following:

- The form that is used to extend the statute of limitations for the assessment of the private foundation investment income tax[79] during the pendency of the advance ruling period (Form 872-C);[80]

- Schedule A, to be prepared by applicant organizations that are churches;[81]

- Schedule B, to be prepared by applicant organizations that are schools, colleges, and universities;[82]

- Schedule C, to be prepared by applicant organizations that are hospitals and medical research organizations;[83]

- Schedule D, to be prepared by applicant organizations that are supporting organizations;[84]

---

[76] Also "How to Apply for Recognition of Exemption for an Organization," IRS Pub. No. 557.
[77] See *infra* § 3, 4.
[78] See Chapter 11.
[79] See § 11.4(f).
[80] See *infra* § 4(b).
[81] See § 8.3.
[82] See § 7.3.
[83] See § 6.2(a), (c).
[84] See § 11.3(c).

- Schedule E, to be prepared by applicant organizations that are private operating foundations;[85]

- Schedule F, to be prepared by applicant organizations that are homes for the aged or disabled;[86]

- Schedule G, to be prepared by applicant organizations that are child care organizations;[87]

- Schedule H, to be prepared by applicant organizations that provide scholarships and comparable benefits;[88]

- Schedule I, to be prepared by applicant organizations that are successors to for-profit organizations;[89] and

- A schedule of activity codes.[90]

Once the IRS has recognized the tax exemption of an organization, the entity cannot voluntarily relinquish it.[91] That is, there is no provision in the law for voluntary termination of tax-exempt status. The only ways an organization can shed its tax exemption is to violate the applicable organizational test[92] or the applicable operational test,[93] or to dissolve.[94]

Applications for recognition of tax exemption submitted by most tax-exempt organizations must be made available for public inspection.[95]

§ 23.3   SPECIAL REQUIREMENTS FOR CHARITABLE ORGANIZATIONS

There are special requirements in this regard for charitable organizations[96] that desire to be tax-exempt under federal law.

(a) General Rules

An organization that desires to be tax-exempt as a charitable organization generally must obtain a determination letter or a ruling from the IRS to that effect.[97] An

---

[85] See § 11.1(b).

[86] See § 6.2(d).

[87] See § 7.7.

[88] See § 6.5.

[89] See § 33.4.

[90] An applicant organization is requested to select up to three of these codes, that best correlate to the applicant organization's actual and/or planned activities, and insert them in Form 1023, Part I, question 6.

[91] Priv. Ltr. Rul. 9141050.

[92] See § 4.3.

[93] See § 4.5.

[94] See § 4.3(b).

[95] See § 24.4(b). In general, Hopkins, "A Practical Guide on How to Apply for Section 501(c)(3) Status," 4 J. Tax. Exempt Orgs. (No. 4) 8 (Jan./Feb. 1993); Gessay, "Tracking a Pending Application for Federal Income Tax Exemption," 2 J. Tax. Exempt Orgs. 4 (Winter 1991); Gardner, "The Determination Process—Current Changes and Some in the Wind," 2 J. Tax. Exempt Orgs. 7 (Fall 1990).

[96] That is, entities described in IRC § 501(c)(3) and tax-exempt by reason of IRC § 501(a).

[97] IRC § 508(a).

organization that desires recognition as a tax-exempt charitable organization as of the date of its formation generally must notify the IRS that it is applying for recognition of exemption on that basis, in conformity with a threshold notice rule. Thus, where the IRS recognizes the tax exemption of an organization that made a timely filing of the notice, the exemption is effective as of the date the organization was created. (The requisite notice is given by the timely filing with the IRS of a properly completed and executed application for recognition of tax exemption.[98]) Otherwise, the recognition of tax exemption as a charitable organization by the IRS generally is effective only on a prospective basis.[99]

This *threshold notice rule* is of two parts. The general rule is that the notice to the IRS must be given within 15 months from the end of the month in which the organization was organized.[100] However, the IRS provided an automatic 12-month extension of time for this filing,[101] thereby converting it to a 27-month period. If this extension is used, the application must be marked to claim it.

An organization is considered *organized* on the date it became a charitable entity.[102] In determining the date on which a corporation is organized for purposes of this exemption recognition process, the IRS looks to the date the entity came into existence under the law of the state in which it was incorporated, which usually is the date its articles of incorporation were filed in the appropriate state office.[103] This date is not the date the organizational meeting was held, by-laws adopted, or actual operations began.

In general, if any return, claim, statement, or other document is required by law to be filed before a specified date, and the document is delivered by mail after that date to the agency, officer, or office with which the document is required to be filed, it is deemed to have been filed on or before that date if the postmark stamped on the envelope or other cover in which the document was mailed was dated on or before the date prescribed for filing.[104] In application of this standard, the date of notice for purposes of the threshold notice rule is the date of the postmark stamped on the cover in which the application for recognition of tax exemption was mailed; in the absence of a postmark, the date of notice is the date the application was stamped as received by the IRS.[105]

If an organization made a nonsubstantive amendment to a governing instrument,[106] that action is not taken into account for purposes of the threshold notice rule.[107] For example, an organization may have submitted an application for recognition of tax exemption within the 15-month period and subsequently made

---

[98] See *supra* § 2(b).

[99] IRC §§ 508(a)(2), 508(d)(2)(B); Reg. § 1.508-2. E.g., Priv. Ltr. Rul. 8518067. However, as discussed *infra*, there are two exceptions to this rule: the automatic 12-month extension procedure (see the text accompanied by *infra* notes 100–101) and the grant of an extension of this filing time by the IRS (see the text accompanied by *infra* notes 108–110).

[100] Reg. § 1.508-1(a)(2)(i). E.g., Peek v. Comm'r, 73 T.C. 912 (1980); Rev. Rul. 90-100, 1990-2 C.B. 156.

[101] Rev. Proc. 92-85, 1992-2 C.B. 490 § 4.01.

[102] Reg. § 1.508-1(a)(2)(iii). See Form 1023, Part I, question 5.

[103] Rev. Rul. 75-290, 1975-2 C.B. 215.

[104] IRC § 7502(a)(1).

[105] Rev. Rul. 77-114, 1977-1 C.B. 152.

[106] Rev. Proc. 90-27, *supra* note 11 § 13.01.

[107] Rev. Proc. 84-47, 1984-1 C.B. 545.

a nonsubstantive amendment to its governing instrument; its tax exemption is still effective as of the date of its formation. Likewise, an organization may have submitted an application for recognition of tax exemption after expiration of the 27-month period and thereafter made a nonsubstantive amendment to its governing instrument; its tax exemption is effective as of the date the application was mailed to or received by the IRS, as the case may be. If an organization made a nonsubstantive amendment to its governing instrument after expiration of the threshold notice rule period, then applied for recognition of exemption within 27 months after the date of the amendment, the organization will be recognized as tax-exempt as of the date the application was mailed to or received by the IRS, not the date the amendment was made. Where a substantive amendment is made to the governing instrument, recognition of exemption is effective as of the date of the change.

The IRS has general discretionary authority, upon a showing of good cause, to grant a reasonable extension of a time fixed by the tax regulations for making an election or application for relief in respect of the federal income tax law.[108] This discretionary authority may be exercised where the time for making the election or application is not expressly prescribed by statute, the request for the extension is filed with the IRS within a period the IRS considers reasonable under the circumstances, and it is shown to the satisfaction of the IRS that granting the extension will not jeopardize the interests of the federal government. The IRS acknowledged that it can exercise this discretionary authority to extend the time for satisfaction of the threshold notice period requirement (which, as noted, is not fixed by statute).[109] The IRS outlined the information and representations that must be furnished and some factors that will be taken into consideration in determining whether an extension of this nature will be granted.[110]

An organization's eligibility to receive deductible charitable contributions also is governed by the threshold notice rule. Thus, where a charitable organization timely files the application for recognition of tax exemption, and the determination letter or ruling ultimately is favorable, the ability to receive deductible charitable gifts is effective as of the date the organization was formed.

An organization that qualifies for tax exemption as a charitable organization but files for recognition of exemption after the threshold notice period can be tax-exempt as a social welfare organization[111] for the period commencing on the date of its inception to the date tax exemption as a charitable organization becomes effective.[112] However, contributions to social welfare organizations are generally

---

[108] Reg. § 1.9100-1.

[109] Rev. Proc. 84-47, *supra* note 107 § 4; Rev. Rul. 80-259, 1980-2 C.B. 192.

[110] Rev. Proc. 92-85, *supra* note 101, *mod. by* Rev. Proc. 93-28, 1993-2 C.B. 344. A request for this extension is built into the application for recognition of tax exemption (Form 1023, Part III, questions 13 (c), 13(d)).

[111] See Chapter 12.

[112] Rev. Rul. 80-108, *supra* note 7. This is because, as noted (see the text accompanied by *supra* notes 7–8), social welfare organizations are not required to apply for recognition of tax-exempt status. The IRS requests an organization in this circumstance to file Form 1024, page 1, with its application for recognition of exemption (Form 1023, Part III, instructions accompanying line 6).

not deductible as charitable gifts,[113] so this approach is of little utility to charitable organizations that rely significantly on contributions.[114]

(b) Exceptions

The threshold notice requirement is not applicable to

- Churches, interchurch organizations of local units of a church, conventions or associations of churches, and integrated auxiliaries of churches;[115]

- Organizations whose gross receipts in each tax year are normally not more than $5,000 (as long as they are not private foundations[116]);[117] and

- Subordinate organizations covered by a group exemption letter where the central organization has submitted to the IRS the requisite notice covering the subordinates.[118]

The IRS is authorized to exempt from the notice requirement operating educational institutions[119] and any other class of organizations as to which compliance with the requirement is not necessary to the efficient administration of the tax law rules pertaining to private foundations.[120] The IRS has not exercised this authority.

The exception in these rules for organizations with gross receipts that are normally no more than $5,000 can operate to relieve a small organization from the requirement of filing an application for recognition of tax exemption during the initial years of its operation but expire as the organization receives greater amounts of financial support. Once an organization fails to meet this exception, it is required to file the notice (application for recognition of exemption) within 90 days after the close of the year in which its gross receipts exceeded the amounts permitted under the exemption.[121] Thus, this notice period is used in this circumstance instead of the general threshold notice rule. An organization in this situation can, therefore, be tax-exempt as a charitable entity from its inception—no matter how many years have passed—as long as it files the application on a timely basis.

The term *normally* embodies an averaging mechanism. That is, the gross re-

---

[113] E.g., Smith v. Comm, 51 T.C.M. 1114 (1986).

[114] For example, nearly all private foundations are funded at the time of their inception; the charitable contribution deduction is, of course, desired for these initial gifts. However, if a private foundation is formed and minimally funded during the grantor's lifetime, with the vast bulk of the funding to come later, this preliminary use of the social welfare organization status may be appropriate.

[115] IRC § 508(c)(1), (2); Reg. § 1.508-1(a)(3)(i)(A). Also Gen. Couns. Mems. 36078, 37458. See §§ 8.3–8.5.

[116] See Chapter 11.

[117] IRC § 508(c)(1).

[118] See *infra* § 6.

[119] IRC § 508(c)(3)(A). These are entities described in IRC § 170(b)(1)(A)(ii). See § 7.3.

[120] IRC § 508(c)(2)(B).

[121] Reg. § 1.508-1(a)(3)(ii).

ceipts of an organization are normally not more than $5,000 if, during its first tax year, it received gross receipts of no more than $7,500; during its first two tax years, it received gross receipts of no more than $12,000; and, in the case of an organization that has been in existence for three tax years, the gross receipts received by it during its immediately preceding two tax years plus the current year are not more than $15,000.[122] The IRS provided three examples of the applicability of this 90-day rule, one involving an organization that did not receive any financial support until its third year[123] and two illustrating the consequences of failing to timely satisfy the rule.[124]

§ 23.4 NONPRIVATE FOUNDATION STATUS

(a) Notification to IRS

In general, every charitable organization is presumed to be a private foundation unless it is able to rebut the presumption.[125] The rebuttal process entails the filing of the requisite notice with the IRS;[126] this is done as part of the application for recognition of tax exemption.[127] Thus, generally, a charitable organization endeavoring to be a public charity[128] must successfully rebut this presumption. The time for the giving of this notice is, by IRS rule, the same as for the notice requirement with respect to tax exemption—the threshold notice rule or the 90-day rule.

The requirement of notification to the IRS as to nonprivate foundation status does not apply to churches, conventions or associations of churches, and integrated auxiliaries of churches.[129]

The law is vague as to the time when a notice of nonprivate foundation status must be filed to be effective. As noted, a charitable organization that is not a private foundation is able to rebut the presumption that it is a foundation by showing that it is a public charity. An organization that failed to timely file a notice may nonetheless establish its public charity status by submitting a request for a determination as to that status to the IRS.[130]

In one instance, a charitable organization (not exempt from the notice requirement) did not apply for recognition of tax exemption until after expiration of the threshold notice rule. Tax exemption of this organization was ultimately approved; it was a private foundation. However, inasmuch as the organization could be treated as a charitable organization only as of the date the application was filed, it could not be classified as a private foundation until that date.[131] The same result obtains with respect to an organization's public charity status.[132]

---

[122] *Id.*

[123] Rev. Rul. 85-173, 1985-2 C.B. 164.

[124] Rev. Rul. 81-177, 1981-2 C.B. 132; Rev. Rul. 80-259, *supra* note 109.

[125] IRC § 508(b). See § 11.1.

[126] IRC § 508(a).

[127] Form 1023, Part III, questions 7–14.

[128] See § 11.2.

[129] IRC § 508(c)(1)(A).

[130] Rev. Rul. 73-504, 1973-2 C.B. 190.

[131] Rev. Rul. 77-207, 1977-1 C.B. 152.

[132] Rev. Rul. 80-113, 1980-1 C.B. 58; Rev. Rul. 77-208, 1977-1 C.B. 153.

When an applicant organization withdraws its application for recognition of exemption in the face of issuance of an adverse determination, it also cancels its notification to the IRS that it is seeking public charity status, so that the threshold notice rule period continues to run.[133]

The IRS promulgated rules with respect to the issuance of determination letters and rulings as to public charity/private foundation status, as well as to reconsiderations, modifications, and revocations of these determinations.[134]

(b) Advance and Definitive Rulings

A tax-exempt charitable organization (not exempt from the notice requirements) that is not a private foundation will (if the notice has been given) have its public charity status evidenced in either an advance ruling or a definitive ruling. Whether the ruling is an advance or definitive one is dependent on the basis on which the organization is classified as a public charity. This ruling usually is in the same document by which the organization's tax exemption was recognized by the IRS.

A *definitive ruling* is a permanent (or final) determination as to public charity status, which remains in effect absent a material change in the facts or change in the law. An *advance ruling* is a preliminary (or probationary) determination as to an organization's status as a publicly supported charity[135] that is in effect for a sufficient period—the *advance ruling period*—to enable the organization to attempt to qualify for a definitive ruling as to public charity status. An organization with an advance ruling that meets the applicable public support requirements during the advance ruling period becomes entitled to receive a definitive ruling on the point.[136]

A charitable organization will receive a definitive ruling at the outset if it is one of the institutions,[137] has been publicly supported during the requisite period,[138] or constitutes a supporting organization.[139] Otherwise, the charitable organization must start the process with an advance ruling.

A newly created organization seeking recognition as a tax-exempt charitable entity and also seeking nonprivate foundation status as a publicly supported organization is entitled to receive (if it so elects) a definitive ruling as to public

---

[133] Rev. Rul. 90-100, *supra* note 100.

[134] Rev. Proc. 90-27, *supra* note 11.

[135] There are three categories of publicly supported charitable organizations: the donative charity, the service provider charity, and the foundation supportive of state colleges and universities (see § 11.3(b)).

[136] As part of the process of filing the application for recognition of exemption, a charitable organization will submit a budget projecting its financial support. If the projection indicates that the applicable public support test will be met, the IRS will rule that it is reasonable to conclude that the organization will qualify as a publicly supported charity, and will issue an advance ruling. Within 90 days following expiration of the advance ruling period, the organization is expected to submit to the IRS a summary of its financial support during the period (preferably on Form 8734). If that data shows that the organization has been publicly supported, the IRS will issue a definitive ruling to the organization.

[137] See § 11.3(a).

[138] See § 11.3(b).

[139] See § 11.3(c).

charity status if it has completed a tax year consisting of at least eight full months (as of the time of filing the application) and if the applicable public support test is met.

This type of organization that does not satisfy a public support test over the eight-month period must request an advance ruling covering its first five tax years. (Unlike the eight-month rule, the first tax year of this five-year period can consist of any number of days.)

A charitable organization that has been in existence for at least eight full months has two options in this regard. One, as noted, is to request a definitive ruling at the outset, in which instance the organization's qualification as a publicly supported charity is initially based on the support the organization has received as of the application date. The other is to request an advance ruling; the organization's public support computation, for purposes of obtaining a definitive ruling, is based on the financial support it receives during its first five tax years. As to this choice, the IRS offers this advice: "An organization should consider this [second] option if it has not received significant public support during its first tax year or during its first and second tax years, but it reasonably expects to receive such support by the end of its fifth tax year."[140] (In both instances, the organization must, to avoid subsequent classification as a private foundation, constitute a public charity on an ongoing basis.)

A charitable "foundation" that is related to a state college or university[141] is not subject to the foregoing eight-month requirement.[142] Thus, a newly created organization, prior to the close of its first tax year consisting of at least eight months, may be issued a definitive ruling that it qualifies as this type of publicly supported charity, assuming the requisite support requirements are met.

Where an incorporated charitable organization is claiming qualification as a publicly supported entity, it is the successor to an unincorporated charitable organization, and incorporation is the only significant change in the facts, the period of time that the predecessor organization was in operation may be taken into consideration in determining qualification of the successor organization under the time requirements[143] of the rules concerning publicly supported charity classification.[144] In other words, the IRS permits the public support data for the unincorporated entity to be tacked to the public support data for the incorporated entity for purposes of ascertaining whether the corporation qualifies as a publicly supported charity.

After a decade or so after the creation by statute of the concepts of public charities and private foundations, Congress began receiving complaints from donors and grantors about the stringency of the rules concerning newly created publicly supported charities, in that the advance ruling period that was in the law

---

[140] Instructions accompanying Form 1023, Part III, line 10. The description of eligibility for definitive and advance rulings accompanied by *supra* notes 135–139 is based on the rules as stated in these instructions. However, the rules in this regard contained in the tax regulations are quite different.

[141] See § 11.3(b)(v).

[142] Rev. Rul. 77-407, 1977-2 C.B. 77.

[143] Reg. §§ 1.170A-9(e)(4)(vi), 1.509(a)-3(c)(1)(iv).

[144] Rev. Rul. 73-422, 1973-2 C.B. 70. Cf. Rev. Rul. 77-116, 1977-1 C.B. 155.

at that time[145] was thought to be too short, thereby not according these new entities adequate time to qualify as publicly supported entities. Congress was reluctant to legislate on this subject, however, because the underlying rules as to advance and definitive rulings are not statutory ones. That is, Congress did not want to codify the entire procedure solely for the purpose of lengthening the advance ruling period.

This matter of expanding the opportunities for reliance by donors and grantors on the nonprivate foundation status of new charitable organizations was rectified in 1984. The conference committee finalizing the Tax Reform Act of that year directed the Department of the Treasury to extend this advance ruling period to five years.[146] The IRS, in 1986, adopted the single five-year advance ruling period discussed above. The tax regulations on this topic have yet to be amended to reflect this change in policy.

§ 23.5   SPECIAL REQUIREMENTS FOR EMPLOYEE BENEFIT ORGANIZATIONS

An organization that desires status as an *employee benefit organization*[147] as of the date of its establishment must timely notify the IRS that it is applying for recognition of tax exemption on that basis.[148] The 15-month rule[149] is applicable in this context, including its exceptions.[150]

These rules as to notification are generally the same as those in place for charitable organizations.[151] That is, the 15-month rule also applies in this context and the organization's tax exemption will be recognized retroactively to the date the organization was organized, where the notice is timely filed.[152]

§ 23.6   GROUP EXEMPTION

An organization (such as a chapter, local, post, or unit) that is affiliated with and is subject to the general supervision or control of a central organization (usually, a state, regional, or national organization) may be recognized as a tax-exempt organization solely by reason of its relationship with the parent organization. Tax-exempt status acquired in this manner is referred to as tax exemption on a *group basis*. The advantage of the group exemption is that each of the organizations cov-

---

[145] See *supra* note 140.

[146] H. Rep. 861, 98th Cong., 2d Sess. 109 (1984).

[147] That is, one described in IRC § 501(c)(9) (a voluntary employees' beneficiary association—see § 16.3), IRC § 501(c)(17) (a supplemental unemployment compensation benefit trust—see § 16.4), or IRC § 501(c)(20) (a group legal service organization—see IRC § 16.6).

[148] IRC § 505(c)(1).

[149] See *supra* § 2.

[150] *Id.* (particularly text accompanied by *supra* notes 100–101, 108–110).

[151] See *supra* §§ 2, 3.

[152] Reg. § 1.505(c)-1T. The notice that is required by IRC § 505(c)(1) is given by submitting a properly completed and executed Application for Recognition of Exemption (Form 1024) to the IRS.

ered by a group exemption letter—termed *subordinate* organizations[153]—is relieved from filing its own application for recognition of tax exemption.

The procedures by which a group exemption may be recognized by the IRS[154] contemplate a functioning of the parent organization as an agent of the IRS, requiring that the parent organization responsibly and independently evaluate the tax-exempt status of its subordinate organizations from the standpoint of the organizational and operational tests applicable to them.[155] A parent organization is required to annually file with the IRS a list of its qualifying tax-exempt subordinate organizations; this listing amounts to an attestation by the central organization that the subordinate organizations qualify as tax-exempt organizations so that the IRS need not carry out an independent evaluation as to the tax-exempt status of the organizations. Therefore, it is essential that the central organization, in performing this agency function, exercise responsibility in evaluating the tax status of its subordinates.

Assuming that the general requirements for recognition of tax-exempt status[156] are satisfied, a group exemption letter will be issued to a central organization where the above requirements as to subordinate organizations are met, the exemption to be recognized is under the general exemption rules,[157] and each of the subordinate organizations has an organizing document (although they do not have to be incorporated). Private foundations may not be included in a group exemption letter, nor may an organization that is organized and operated in a foreign country.

Thus, a central organization applying for a group exemption letter must first obtain recognition of its own tax-exempt status and establish that all of the subordinate organizations to be included in the group exemption letter are affiliated with it, subject to its general supervision or control, exempt under the same paragraph of the general exemption rules (although not necessarily the section under which the central organization is tax-exempt), not private foundations or foreign organizations, on the same accounting period as the central organization if they are not to be included in group returns, and formed within the 15-month period prior to the date of submission of the group exemption application (assuming this is the case and these entities are claiming charitable status and are subject to the requirements for application for recognition of tax exemption).[158] For example, with respect to this third requirement, a central organization may be tax-exempt as a charitable entity with all of the subordinates thereof exempt as social welfare organizations. Concerning the sixth requirement, the procedures state that if one or more of the subordinates have not been organized within the 15-month period, the group exemption letter will be issued only if all of the subordinates agree to be recognized as tax-exempt from the date of the ap-

---

[153] This is an unfortunate choice of terminology, in that many organizations and those who manage them do not care to be regarded as *subordinates*; a preferable term would have been *affiliates*.

[154] Rev. Proc. 80-27, 1980-1 C.B. 677. Also Reg. § 601.201(n)(7).

[155] See §§ 4.3, 4.5.

[156] Rev. Proc. 90-27, *supra* note 11.

[157] IRC § 501(c). Thus, the group exemption procedures are unavailable to organizations described in IRC §§ 521 (see § 18.11), 526 (see § 18.12), 527 (see Chapter 17), 528 (see § 18.13), 529 (see § 18.16).

[158] See *supra* § 2.

plication rather than the date of their creation. Subordinate charitable organizations are exempt from the notice requirements generally applicable to charitable organizations.[159]

Each subordinate organization must authorize, in writing, the central organization to include it in the application for the group exemption letter.

A central organization may be involved in more than one group exemption arrangement, such as a charitable parent organization having both charitable and social welfare/civic organization subordinates. Also, a central organization may be a subordinate organization with respect to another central organization, such as a state organization that has subordinate units and is itself affiliated with a national organization.

An instrumentality or agency of a political subdivision that exercises control or supervision over a number of organizations similar in purposes and operations, each of which may qualify for tax exemption under the same category of exempt organizations, may obtain a group exemption letter covering the organizations in the same manner as a central organization. With this approach the group exemption for organizations such as federal credit unions, state chartered credit unions, and federal land bank associations may be established.[160]

A central organization must submit to the IRS, in addition to certain information about itself, the following information on behalf of its group exemption subordinates: (1) a letter signed by a principal officer of the central organization setting forth or including as attachments (a) information verifying the existence of the foregoing six relationships and requirements, (b) a detailed description of the principal purposes and activities of the subordinates, including financial information, (c) a sample copy of a uniform or representative governing instrument adopted by the subordinates, (d) an affirmation that, to the best of the officer's knowledge, the subordinates are operating in accordance with the stated purposes, (e) a statement that each subordinate to be included within the group exemption letter has furnished the requisite written authorization, (f) a list of subordinates to be included in the group exemption letter to which the IRS has issued an outstanding ruling or determination letter relating to tax exemption, and (g), if relevant, an affirmation that no subordinate organization is a private foundation; and (2) a list of the names, addresses, and employer identification numbers of subordinates to be included in the group exemption letter (or, in lieu thereof, a satisfactory directory of subordinates). Certain additional information is required if a subordinate is claiming tax-exempt status as a school. In the only court decision involving the group exemption rules, the U.S. Tax Court upheld the requirement that detailed information concerning the activities and finances of subordinates be submitted to the IRS, in holding that an organization is not eligible for classification as a central organization because the requisite information was not provided.[161]

Once a group exemption letter is issued, certain information must be submitted annually by the central organization (at least 90 days before the close of its

---

[159] Reg. § 1.508-1(a)(3)(i)(c); Rev. Rul. 90-100, *supra* note 100.
[160] See § 18.7.
[161] National Ass'n of Am. Churches v. Comm'r, *supra* note 30.

annual accounting period) to the IRS so as to maintain the letter. This information consists of (1) information regarding any changes in the purposes, character, or method of operation of the subordinates; (2) lists of (a) subordinates that have changed their names or addresses during the year, (b) subordinates no longer to be included in the group exemption letter (for whatever reason), and (c) subordinates to be added to the group exemption letter (for whatever reason); and (3) the information summarized in the foregoing paragraph (items (1)(a) through (g)) with respect to subordinates to be added to the group exemption letter.[162]

A subordinate organization may, in lieu of filing a separate annual information return (Form 990), file in combination with the central organization. (This is an optional practice; combined filing is not required under the group exemption rules.) However, for this option to be available, each of the subordinates must be tax-exempt under the same federal tax law provision and the consolidated return must relate solely to unrelated income tax matters.[163]

There are two ways in which a group exemption letter may be terminated. When a termination occurs, the tax-exempt status of the subordinate organizations is no longer recognized by the IRS, thereby requiring (where continuing recognition of tax-exempt status is required or desired) each subordinate to file an application for recognition of tax exemption, the central organization to file for a new group exemption letter, or the subordinates (or a portion of them) to become tax-exempt by reason of their status with respect to another qualifying central organization. Termination of a group exemption letter will be occasioned where (1) the central organization dissolves or otherwise ceases to exist, (2) one or more of the subordinates fail to fulfill the qualification requirements, or (3) the central organization fails to qualify for tax exemption, to submit the information required to obtain the letter, to file the annual information return, or to otherwise comply with the reporting requirements.[164]

If the IRS revokes the tax-exempt status of a central organization, the group exemption letter involved is also revoked, thereby simultaneously revoking the tax-exempt status of all of the subordinates. To regain recognition of tax exemption in this instance, or in the case of its withdrawal from the group exemption, a subordinate organization must file an application for recognition of exemption or become a member of another tax-exempt group. As of the date an organization is no longer in a group, the 27-month notice period begins to run, so that an organization desiring to maintain tax exemption on an ongoing basis must file the application within that period or timely join another group.[165]

Where a subordinate organization has an outstanding ruling of tax exemp-

---

[162] Historically, these annual filings were made with the appropriate IRS service center. However, group exemption reports submitted on or after July 1, 1996, are filed with the IRS Service Center in Ogden, Utah (Rev. Proc. 96-40, 1996-2 C.B. 301).

[163] Tech. Adv. Mem. 8514001. See text accompanied by *infra* notes 168–170.

[164] IRC §§ 6001, 6033. Loss of tax exemption by some members of the group does not adversely affect the group exemption ruling as it pertains to the other members in the group (Tech. Adv. Mem. 9711004).

[165] Rev. Rul. 90–100, *supra* note 100.

tion and becomes included in a group exemption letter, the prior exemption letter is superseded.[166] The central organization, in this circumstance, is obligated to notify the affected subordinate organization(s) of this supersession.

Where the subordinates are charitable organizations, their publicly supported charity status must be considered, inasmuch as, as noted, they may not be private foundations and qualify under the group exemption rules. On the basis of standardized paragraphs promulgated by the IRS National Office, the IRS will assume—and so rule—that the subordinates have the same nonprivate foundation status as the parent charitable organization. Moreover, the IRS will, in the case of classification of subordinates as publicly supported entities, do so on the basis of definitive rulings.[167]

The group exemption arrangement is distinguishable from the consolidated return rules pertaining to the filing requirements of an affiliated group of organizations.[168] Generally, the consolidated return rules are applicable only with respect to taxable entities.[169] However, tax-exempt organizations can use the consolidated return option as respects unrelated business income tax returns.[170]

A central organization must, as a general rule, file an annual information return.[171] Also as a general rule, this reporting obligation is imposed upon a subordinate organization. However, one or more of the subordinates may file with the central organization as part of a group annual information return.[172] Organizations with gross receipts not normally in excess of $25,000 each year are not required to file an annual information return.[173] Thus, a central organization may exclude from its group return those subordinates the annual gross receipts of which are normally not in excess of $25,000 per year.[174]

The group exemption generally is very favorable for clusters of nonprofit organizations that are affiliated. This approach to tax exemption obviates the need for each member entity in the group to file a separate application for recognition of tax exemption, and this can result in savings of time, effort, and expenses—for the organizations and for the IRS. It is, then, a streamlined approach to the establishment of tax-exempt status for related organizations.

However, there are some disadvantages to a tax-exempt status based on the group exemption. One concerns the fact that the members of the group do not individually possess determination letters as to their tax exemption. This can pose difficulties for donors and grantors,[175] as well as problems for the organization in

---

[166] Internal Revenue Manual, Part 7600 § 7667, 23 (3).

[167] See *supra* § 4(b).

[168] IRC § 1501.

[169] IRC § 1504(b)(1); cf. IRC § 1504(e).

[170] Tech. Adv. Mem. 8514001. See § 24.3(a)(v).

[171] See § 24.3.

[172] Reg. § 1.6033-2(d).

[173] See § 24.3(b)(ii).

[174] Priv. Ltr. Rul. 8337094.

[175] A donor of a major gift may want the security of a determination letter so as to have the requisite basis for relying on the organization's representation that it is a charitable entity. A private foundation grantor may desire similar assurance to be certain that the grant constitutes a qualifying distribution (see § 11.4(b)), is not an expenditure responsibility grant (see § 11.4(e)), or is not otherwise a taxable expenditure (*id.*).

securing state tax exemptions. Second, there is no separate assessment of these organizations' publicly supported status.[176] Third, if a member of the group is found liable for damages, the existence of the group exemption may be used in an effort to assert "ascending" liability on the part of the central organization.

§ 23.7 INTEGRAL PART DOCTRINE

The *integral part doctrine* is a basis in law for the acquisition of tax-exempt status, by means of recognition of that status by the IRS or otherwise. There are two variants of this doctrine. One concerns an organization that obtained tax exemption because of its relationship with one or more tax-exempt entities. This type of organization is, in law, a separate entity, with tax exemption a function of the affiliation. The other application of the doctrine pertains to tax-exempt organizations that have component entities that, while appearing to be separate organizations, are not, in law, separate but are instead *integral parts* of the larger organization. These component entities are in the nature of divisions of a tax-exempt organization.

(a) Affiliated Organizations

As noted, in general, the entitlement of a nonprofit organization to tax-exempt status is derived solely from the entity's own characteristics.[177] There is, however, an exception to this general rule, which is one of two aspects of the integral part doctrine. This facet of the doctrine, applied largely with respect to tax exemption as a charitable organization, enables an organization which functions as an integral part of the exempt activities of a related entity or entities to derive tax exemption by reason of the relationship with its affiliate or affiliates. Tax exemption of this nature is also known as a *derivative* or *vicarious* exemption.

The genesis of this element of the doctrine is language in the federal tax regulations on the subject of feeder organizations.[178] There it is stated that, as an exception to these rules, a "subsidiary" of a tax-exempt organization can be exempt "on the ground that its activities are an integral part of the activities of the parent organization."[179] As an illustration, the regulations describe a "subsidiary organization that is operated for the sole purpose of furnishing electric power used by its parent, a tax-exempt organization, in carrying out its educational activities."[180] These regulations also state that an entity seeking tax exemption as an integral part of another entity cannot primarily be engaged in an activity that would generate more than insubstantial unrelated business income for the other entity.[181]

---

[176] This point relates to the ones in *supra* note 175. For example, private foundations rarely make grants to other private foundations and a private foundation grantor usually wants meaningful assurance that the grantee is a public or publicly supported charity.

[177] See *supra* § 1.

[178] See § 28.6.

[179] Reg. § 502-1(b). Also Gen. Couns. Mem. 39830.

[180] Reg. § 1.502-1(b).

[181] *Id.*

Because of recent developments, the criteria for achieving tax exemption by reason of an affiliation with a charitable entity are in flux. The traditional view is that this aspect of the integral part doctrine applies where the activities of the organization whose tax status is being evaluated are carried on under the supervision or control of an exempt organization and could be carried on by the exempt parent organization without materially constituting an unrelated trade or business.[182] Interpretations along this line from the IRS include tax exemption for a trust existing solely as a repository of funds set aside by a nonprofit hospital for the payment of malpractice claims against the hospital and as the payor of those claims,[183] a corporation that published and sold law journals as an adjunct to a tax-exempt law school,[184] and a bookstore used almost exclusively by the faculty and students of a university with which it was associated.[185] This traditional explication of the doctrine is also found in court opinions. For example, one court ruled that a corporation operating a bookstore and restaurant that sold college texts, was wholly owned by a tax-exempt college, used college facilities without charge, served mostly faculty and students, and devoted its earnings to educational purposes was tax-exempt because it "obviously bears a close and intimate relationship to the functioning of the [c]ollege itself."[186]

The reason that the criteria associated with this doctrine seems to be in transition is that, despite this tax regulation, and wealth of caselaw and IRS rulings, a court decided that the law is not clear as to "whether there are any other necessary qualifications" surrounding the doctrine.[187] Indeed, the court also concluded that there is one additional criterion—and, "[d]istilling . . . [this body of law] into a general rule," wrote that "a subsidiary that is not entitled to exempt status on its own may only receive such status as an integral part of its . . . [charitable] parent if (i) it is not carrying on a trade or business that would be an unrelated trade or business (that is, unrelated to exempt activities) if regularly carried on by the parent, and (ii) its relationship to its parent somehow enhances the subsidiary's own exempt character to the point that, when the boost provided by the parent is added to the contribution made by the subsidiary itself, the subsidiary would be entitled to . . . [tax-exempt, charitable] status"[188] Applying this new *boost principle*, the court held that a health maintenance organization could not qualify for tax exemption on the ground that it is an integral part of a hospital system, because the plan did not receive

---

[182] E.g., Geisinger Health Plan v. Comm'r, 100 T.C. 394, 402 (1993), *aff'd*, 30 F.3d 494 (3d Cir. 1994).

[183] Rev. Rul. 78-41, 1978-1 C.B. 148. See, however, § 22.1.

[184] Rev. Rul. 63-235, 1963-2 C.B. 210.

[185] Rev. Rul. 58-194, 1958-1 C.B. 240.

[186] Squire v. Students Book Corp., 191 F.2d 1018, 1020 (9th Cir. 1951). Also University of Md. Physicians, P.A., v. Comm'r, 41 T.C.M. 732 (1981); University of Mass. Med. School Group Practice v. Comm'r, 74 T.C. 1299 (1980); B.H.W. Anesthesia Found. Inc. v. Comm'r, 72 T.C. 681 (1979); B.S.R Group, Inc. v. Comm'r, 70 T.C. 352 (1978); Brundage v. Comm'r, 54 T.C. 1468 (1970).

[187] Geisinger Health Plan v. Comm'r, 30 F.3d 494 (3d Cir. 1994).

[188] *Id.* at 501.

any boost from its association with the system.[189] Noting that an entity's "mere financing of the exempt purposes of a related organization does not constitute furtherance of that organization's purpose so as to justify exemption," the court observed that "it is apparent that . . . [the plan] merely seeks to 'piggyback' off of the other entities in the [s]ystem, taking on their charitable characteristics in an effort to gain exemption without demonstrating that it is rendered 'more charitable' by virtue of its association with them.[190] Reviewing the prior caselaw, this court wrote that the electric company referenced in the tax regulations received a boost from its association with the educational institution, as did the bookstore and law journal organizations. This new articulation of the integral part doctrine prevents "an organization that is not entitled to an exemption on its own" from becoming "tax-exempt *merely* because it happens to be controlled by an organization that is itself exempt."[191]

---

[189] The court concluded that the association of the health maintenance organization with the other entities in the hospital system "does nothing to increase the portion of the community for which . . . [the plan] promotes health—it serves no more people as a part of the [s]ystem than it would serve otherwise. It may contribute to the [s]ystem by providing more patients than the [s]ystem might otherwise have served, thus arguably allowing the [s]ystem to promote health among a broader segment of the community than could be served without it, but its provision of patients to the [s]ystem does not enhance its own promotion of health; the patients it provides—its subscribers—are the same patients it serves without its association with the [s]ystem. To the extent it promotes health among non- . . . [plan]-subscriber patients of the [s]ystem, it does so only because . . . [plan] subscribers' payments to the [s]ystem help finance the provision of health care to others" (*id*. at 502).

This appellate court earlier held that this health maintenance organization could not qualify as a charitable entity on its own merits (Geisinger Health Plan v. Comm'r, 985 F.2d 1210 (3d Cir. 1993) (see § 6.2(e)).

[190] *Id*. at 503.

[191] *Id*. at 502 (emphasis by the court). When this court of appeals remanded the case to the U.S. Tax Court for decision as to application of the integral part doctrine, it said the doctrine "provides a means by which organizations may qualify for exemption vicariously through related organizations, as long as they are engaged in activities which would be exempt if the related organizations engaged in them, and as long as those activities are furthering the exempt purposes of the related organizations" (Geisinger Health Plan v. Comm'r, *supra* note 190, at 1220). No mention was there made of any boost principle. (Likewise, Texas Learning Technology Group v. Comm'r, 958 F.2d 122, 126 (5th Cir. 1992).) In its subsequent opinion, the appellate court dismissed its previous summary of the doctrine as simply "dicta" and pronounced that it was "not bound by" it (Geisinger Health Plan v. Comm'r, *supra* note 188, at 499).

As to the prior law, one IRS ruling (Rev. Rul. 78-41, *supra* note 183) did not comport with the boost theory, so the court elected to "not rely on . . . [it] in our analysis" (Geisinger Health Plan v. Comm'r, *supra* note 188, at 502, note 8).

When the U.S. Tax Court considered this issue, it sought to determine whether the organization's overall functions were substantially related to the exempt function of its tax-exempt affiliates in the system; it stated that, if the organization's activities are conducted on a scale larger than is reasonably necessary to accomplish the purposes of the affiliates (see § 26.4(b)), the requisite substantial relationship would not be present (Geisinger Health Plan v. Comm'r, *supra* 182, at 394, 406 (1993)). The court concluded that, because the health maintenance organization made sales to and provided services for individuals who are not patients of the exempt entities within the health care system, the organization's operations were not substantially related to the other components of the system and thus it could not be considered an integral part of the system (*id*. at 406–407). On appeal, this unrelated business argument was not reviewed, because the appellate court held that, inasmuch as the boost principle of the doctrine was not satisfied, there was no need to assess the other prong of this integral part test. In general, Levine, "*Geisinger Health Plan* Likely to Adversely Affect HMOs and Other Health Organizations," 79 *J. Tax.* (No. 2) 90 (Aug. 1993).

There are other instances where this variant of the integral part doctrine has been applied that escaped the analysis of the boost principle court. One is the determination by the IRS that a vending machine management organization was an integral part of a tax-exempt university.[192] Another is an IRS ruling that an organization formed and controlled by a tax-exempt conference of churches, that borrowed funds from individuals and made mortgage loans at less than the commercial rate of interest to affiliated churches to finance the construction of church buildings, qualified as an integral part of the parent organization.[193] A court subsequently held, without reference to the boost principle, that two organizations did not qualify for tax exemption on the basis of the integral part doctrine; indeed, the entities were dismissed as "appendages rather than integral parts" and "superfluous corporate shells that make no cognizable contribution" to the exempt organizations's purposes.[194]

(b) Divisions

An organization may be viewed as a composite of integrated components—being "composed of constituent parts making a whole."[195] In comparable instances, the law regards an item of property as an integral part of a larger property or process, such as bottles and cartons being an integral part of manufactured beer for purpose of state use tax exemptions[196] and executed contracts being an integral part of a baseball team for purposes of defining the team's "raw materials."[197] The fragmentation rule utilized in the unrelated business setting is predicated on this view of an organization.[198]

A tax-exempt organization may have component entities that are not separate organizations (although they may appear to be) and thus are "exempt" from tax because of the tax exemption of the host organization. For example, a tax-exempt university may have scholarship funds, a tax-exempt hospital may have research funds, and a tax-exempt charitable organization may have one or more endowment funds; these funds may have separate names and be recipients of contributions made in those names. These component entities may be little more than one of several accounts carried on a tax-exempt organization's financial records. By analogy to the terminology in the for-profit setting, these component entities are akin to divisions (as is the case with the schools of a university or the departments of a hospital).[199] The principal distinction from a tax standpoint is that the entity that is an integral part of a tax-exempt organization as a division is

---

[192] Rev. Rul. 81-19, 1981-1 C.B. 353.

[193] Rev. Rul. 75-282, 1975-2 C.B. 201. In general, Rasman, "Third Circuit's 'Boost' Test Denies Section 501(c)(3) Status to HMO," 6 *J. Tax. Exempt Orgs.* (No. 4) 147 (Jan./Feb. 1995).

[194] University Medical Resident Serv., P.C. v. Comm'r, 71 T.C.M. 3130, 3131-3135 (1996).

[195] Application of Larson, 340 F.2d 965, 967 (U.S. Ct. Cust. Pat. Appl. 1965).

[196] Zoller Brewing Co. v. State Tax Comm'r, 5 N.W.2d 643 (Iowa 1942).

[197] Hollywood Baseball Ass'n v. Comm'r, 423 F.2d 494 (9th Cir. 1970), *cert. den.*, 400 U.S. 848 (1970).

[198] See § 26.2(d).

[199] By contrast, the organizations that are tax-exempt by reason of the other application of the integral part doctrine (see text accompanied by *supra* notes 177–194) or the group exemption procedures (see *supra* § 6) are comparable to a for-profit organization's subsidiaries. A somewhat similar body of federal tax law is that concerning the supporting organization (see § 11.3(c)).

itself tax-exempt solely by virtue of the exemption of the home organization, while the tax exemption of a subsidiary must be obtained (if it can) by reason of the other definition of the integral part doctrine or on the merits of its own characteristics.[200]

It has been held that a principal element leading to a finding that one organization functions as an integral part of another organization is the fact that the function of the integrated organization is "essential" to the operation of the larger organization, and is an "ordinary and proper" function of the larger organization.[201] While this may be the case in general, in the tax-exempt organizations context it is largely an irrelevant criterion, inasmuch as the decision as to whether to establish the would-be integrated organization will nearly always be that of the larger organization.

Thus, the use of the integral part doctrine can be an efficient manner in which to acquire tax exemption for an organization, being a considerably speedier approach than the conventional exemption application process and even more rapid than the group exemption approach.[202]

§ 23.8 ADMINISTRATIVE PROCEDURES WHERE DETERMINATION IS ADVERSE

The filing of an application for recognition of tax exemption with the IRS can, of course, lead to the issuance of an initial adverse determination. In this instance, or in the case of the issuance of a letter proposing revocation or modification of tax-exempt status,[203] the IRS will advise the organization of its right to appeal the determination by requesting appeals office consideration.[204] To initiate an appeal, the organization must submit to the IRS, within 30 days from the date of the letter, a statement of the facts, law, and arguments in support of its position. At this time, the organization must also state whether it wishes an appeals office conference.

Upon receipt of an organization's request for appeals office consideration, the person with responsibility for the case will forward the request and case file to the chief of the appropriate appeals office.[205] However, any determination letter that is issued on the basis of IRS National Office technical advice may not be

---

[200] The *division* aspect of the doctrine assumes that the attributes of this type of component entity do not cause it to be considered a separate organization; for example, one nonprofit corporation cannot be a division of another nonprofit corporation (although it can be an integral part of one).

[201] E.g., Schwarz v. United States, 284 F. Supp. 792, 797 (U.S. Customs Ct. 1968); also Matczak v. Secretary of Health, Educ. & Welfare, 299 F. Supp. 409 (E.D.N.Y. 1969).

[202] One of the current issues involving the integral part doctrine is whether the many unincorporated congregations established by the Universal Life Church are tax-exempt by reason of the Church's tax-exempt status (see § 8.3). To date, the U.S. Tax Court (the only court to consider the issue) has held that the congregations cannot partake of the Church's tax exemption (Stephenson v. Comm'r, 79 T.C. 995 (1982), *aff'd*, 748 F.2d 331 (6th Cir. 1984); Murphy v. Comm'r, 45 T.C.M. 621 (1983); Riemers v. Comm'r, 42 T.C.M. 838 (1981)).

[203] Reg. § 601.201(n)(6).

[204] Rev. Proc. 90-27, *supra* note 11 § 10.01.

[205] *Id.* at § 10.03.

appealed to an appeals office as regards issues that were the subject of the technical advice.[206]

The appeals office, after considering the organization's appeal and any additional information developed in conference, will advise the organization of its decision and issue the appropriate determination letter to the organization.[207]

An organization is expected to make full presentation of the facts, circumstances, and arguments at the initial level of consideration by the appeals office, since submission of additional facts, circumstances, and arguments may result in suspension of appeal procedures and referral of the case back to the key district for additional consideration. Any oral representation of additional facts or modification of facts originally represented or alleged must be reduced to writing.[208]

If an appeals office believes that a tax exemption or private foundation status issue is not covered by published precedent, the appeals office must request technical advice from the IRS National Office. Unless the appeals office believes that the conclusions reached by the National Office should be reconsidered and promptly requests the reconsideration, the case will be disposed of by the appeals office on the basis of the decision in the technical advice memorandum.[209]

If at any time during the course of appeals office consideration, the organization believes that its case involves an issue as to which there is no published precedent, the organization may ask the appeals office to request technical advice from the National Office.[210]

If the proposed disposition by the appeals office is contrary to a prior National Office technical advice memorandum or ruling concerning tax exemption, the proposed disposition will be submitted through the Office of the Regional Director of Appeals to the Assistant Commissioner (Employee Plans and Exempt Organizations) or, in the case of farmers' cooperatives,[211] the Assistant Chief Counsel (Technical).[212] Unless the appeals office believes that the conclusions reached by the National Office should be reconsidered and promptly requests that consideration, the decision of the National Office must be followed by the appeals office.[213] In any event, it is clear that the appropriate Assistant Commissioner (and perhaps, ultimately, the Commissioner of Internal Revenue) will make the final decision.

A ruling or determination letter recognizing tax exemption may be revoked or modified by (1) a notice to the organization involved, (2) enactment of legislation, (3) ratification of a tax treaty, (4) a decision of the U.S. Supreme Court, (5) is-

---

[206] *Id.* at § 10.02.
[207] *Id.* at § 11.01.
[208] *Id.* at § 11.02.
[209] *Id.* at § 11.03.
[210] *Id.* at § 11.04. Reg. §§ 601.201(n)(2)(iv), (9).
[211] See § 18.11.
[212] Reg. § 601.201(n)(5)(iii).
[213] Rev. Proc. 90-27, *supra* note 11 § 11.05.

suance of temporary or final regulations, or (6) the issuance of a revenue ruling, a revenue procedure, or other statement published in the Internal Revenue Bulletin. The revocation or modification may be retroactive[214] if the organization omitted or misstated a material fact, operated in a manner materially different from that originally represented, or, in certain instances,[215] engaged in a prohibited transaction with the purpose of diverting corpus or income of the organization from its tax-exempt purpose and the transaction involved a substantial part of the corpus or income of the organization. Where there is a material change, inconsistent with tax exemption, in the character, purpose, or method of operation of an organization, revocation or modification will ordinarily take effect as of the date of the material change.[216]

Once the IRS has acted to revoke recognition of the tax exemption of an organization, it will expect the entity to begin paying income taxes.[217] Should the organization not do so, however, the IRS may be expected to commence proceedings to assess and collect the tax due. This activity is begun by the mailing to the organization of a statutory notice of deficiency. This the IRS is authorized to do following a determination that there is a tax deficiency.[218] However, because there cannot be general income tax liability for a tax-exempt organization, it is essential to the government's efforts to collect the tax that the statutory notice of deficiency be preceded by a valid letter of revocation. To have this letter, the IRS is required to act in conformity with certain procedures[219] and at least generally apprise the organization of the basis for the revocation. However, the revocation itself must be in conformity with all requirements of law, so that if, for example, the grounds upon which the revocation is based were erroneous, the revocation is not proper.[220] Likewise, if the letter of revocation was prompted by political or similar considerations that demonstrate lack of objectivity by the IRS, the revocation becomes null and void.[221] Thus, a letter of revocation can be shown to be void *ab initio* because of the considerations governing its issuance. Also, subsequent actions by the IRS

---

[214] See § 24.1.

[215] Namely, where IRC § 503 applies; that provision denies tax exemption to supplemental unemployment benefit trusts (see § 16.4) and to certain funded pension trusts (see § 16.6) where the organization engaged in one or more *prohibited transactions* (as defined in IRC § 503(b)).

[216] Rev. Proc. 90-27, *supra* note 11 § 14.01.

[217] See, e.g., § 24.2(a) (concerning the tax consequences of retroactive revocation of tax-exempt status of public charities). Usually, when an organization's exemption is revoked, it becomes a taxable nonprofit organization, liable for the regular federal income tax imposed on corporations. However, when the tax exemption of a social club (see Chapter 14) was revoked, the issue arose as to whether the club should be treated as a personal holding company. One of the tests for a personal holding company is that, at any time during the last half of the tax year, more than 50 percent in value of its stock is owned by or for no more than five individuals (IRC § 542(a)). The IRS treated the club's members as shareholders for this purpose, found that the stock ownership test was met, and held that the club, as a nonexempt entity, was a personal holding company (Tech. Adv. Mem. 9728004). The result was that the club became liable, not only for the regular corporate income tax, but also for a tax of 39.6 percent of the club's undistributed personal holding company income.

[218] IRC § 6212.

[219] Internal Revenue Manual § 7(10)(12).

[220] A. Duda & Sons Coop. Ass'n v. United States, 504 F.2d 970, 975 (5th Cir. 1974).

[221] Center on Corporate Responsibility, Inc. v. Schultz, 368 F. Supp. 863, 871–873 (D.D.C. 1973).

indicating a continuing recognition of tax-exempt status can operate to make a prior revocation of recognition nugatory. In either event, the letter of revocation is not valid, so that the tax exemption has not been properly revoked, meaning that any notice of deficiency based upon the letter of revocation is of no force and effect.[222]

Still other procedures have been promulgated for appeals from the attempted imposition of certain taxes on most tax-exempt organizations and on certain individuals under the private foundation rules. These taxes are the excise taxes imposed by the federal tax law pertaining to private foundations,[223] the unrelated income tax,[224] the private foundation termination tax,[225] the political activities tax,[226] and the tax[227] on charitable and split-interest trusts.[228]

---

[222] Cf. Church of Scientology of Calif. v. Comm'r, 83 T.C. 381 (1984), *aff'd*, 823 F.2d 1310 (9th Cir. 1987).
[223] See § 11.4.
[224] See § 28.1
[225] See § 11.4(f).
[226] See § 17.3.
[227] IRC § 641.
[228] IRC § 4947.

CHAPTER TWENTY-FOUR

Operational Considerations

The federal tax law imposes a battery of operational requirements on tax-exempt organizations, irrespective of whether they have received recognition of tax-exempt status from the IRS.[1] For most exempt organizations, the principal responsibility is the filing of an annual information return with the IRS. Other reporting obligations are imposed on tax-exempt organizations, such as in instances of material changes and mandated disclosures. Most ominous is the possibility of an IRS audit and the potential revocation of tax exemption.

---

[1] Reg. § 1.501(a)-1(a)(2). Also Rev. Proc. 90-27, 1990-1 C.B. 514 § 13.02; Rev. Rul. 68-217, 1968-2 C.B. 260. The IRS may revoke a ruling letter that recognized an organization's tax exemption, without retroactive effect, pursuant to IRC § 7805(b), but in this case the organization would be subject to taxation on any unrelated business taxable income (see Part Five) during the IRC § 7805(b) relief period (Rev. Rul. 78-289, 1978-2 C.B. 180). It is the view of the IRS that the principle of this 1978 ruling is applicable with respect to the political activities tax (see § 17.3) (Gen. Couns. Mem. 39811).

§ 24.1 CHANGES IN OPERATIONS OR FORM

Once an organization achieves tax-exempt status, that qualification can be maintained as long as the entity does not materially change its character, purposes, or methods of operation. A change in an organization's form is likely to have tax consequences. An organization's tax-exempt status may be affected by a change in the law.

(a) Changes in Operations

An organization's tax-exempt status remains in effect as long as there are no substantial—*material*—changes in the organization's character, purposes, or methods of operation.[2] An organization and its advisors have the burden of determining whether or not a change of this nature is material or immaterial.

A material change should be communicated to the IRS as soon as possible after the change is made or becomes effective. Other changes should be reflected in due course in the organization's annual information return.[3]

A substantial change in an organization's character, purposes, or methods of operation may result in modification or revocation of the organization's tax-exempt status.[4] As noted, a change in the law may afford the IRS a basis for modifying or revoking an organization's tax-exempt status.

Occasionally, the IRS attempts to cause a retroactive revocation of tax exemption. The government's procedural regulations state that a revocation of tax exemption may be retroactive in three instances: where (1) the organization omitted or misstated a material fact in the process of acquiring recognition of exemption, (2) the organization operated in a manner materially different from that originally represented, or (3) the organization engaged in a prohibited transaction.[5] A *prohibited transaction* is one in which the organization entered into the process of pursuing tax exemption for the purpose of diverting substantial corpus or income from its exempt purpose.[6]

One of the infrequent cases on the point was decided in 1979. A nonprofit organization was recognized as a tax-exempt educational entity in 1959; its function was to operate a school. In 1970, when the rules prohibiting schools from maintaining racially discriminatory policies were introduced,[7] the IRS advised the school of its concerns that the school may be engaging in discriminatory practices. In 1976, the IRS commenced a revocation procedure, which culminated in loss by the organization of its tax exemption by court order. The IRS attempted to revoke the school's exempt status retroactively to 1959, the date the IRS initially recognized the entity's tax-exempt status. However, the court upheld revocation

---

[2] Reg. §§ 1.501(a)-1(a)(2), 601.201(n)(3)(ii).

[3] See *infra* § 3. E.g., Form 990, Part VI, question 77.

[4] Rev. Proc. 90-27, *supra* note 1 § 14.

[5] Reg. § 601.201(n)(6)(i). E.g., West Cent. Coop. v. United States, 758 F.2d 1269 (8th Cir. 1985); Stevens Bros. Found. Inc. v. Comm'r, 324 F.2d 633, 641 (8th Cir. 1963), *cert. den.*, 376 U.S. 969 (1964).

[6] Reg. § 601.201(n)(6)(vii); Rev. Proc. 90-27, *supra* note 1 § 14.01.

[7] See § 5.4(a).

retroactively to 1970, inasmuch as the IRS had expressly provided the organization with notice of the law change in that year, rather than to 1959.[8]

Thereafter, the same court upheld a retroactive revocation of tax exemption, effective as of the date the IRS determined that the exempt functions had ceased. The case involved an organization that was granted tax exemption in 1936 as a religious organization engaging in missionary activities, with the exemption upheld in 1953. In 1976, the IRS proposed to revoke the exemption on the grounds that the missionary activities had ceased and were replaced by commercial publishing operations, with the revocation retroactive to 1963, the year in which the tax-exempt functions were determined to have stopped. This court agreed with the IRS and held that the organization failed to meet its burden of showing that the IRS's action of retroactive revocation of exemption was erroneous. The IRS had also determined that the organization's records showed drastic increases in salaries and accumulated surplus by 1970 and ordered the filing of tax returns by the organization as of that year; this determination was also upheld by the court.[9]

Subsequently, another court adopted a like stance with respect to a religious publishing company. The organization was formed in 1931 and was recognized as tax-exempt in 1939; in 1980, the IRS proposed to revoke the exemption, on the grounds that the organization had become operated in a commercial manner, retroactive to 1969. The court agreed with the IRS as to revocation of tax exemption, but held that the IRS abused its discretion in making the revocation effective as of 1969; instead, the court concluded that the retroactivity should extend back only to 1975.[10] However, the court was reversed on appeal, with the appellate court concluding that the organization was engaged in tax-exempt functions, thereby voiding this retroactive revocation of tax-exempt status.[11]

A comparable line of law holds that the IRS has the power to retroactively revoke a determination as to tax-exempt status if it becomes contrary to law.[12] However, the cases involve situations where the change in the law was made by Congress.[13] Also, retroactivity of tax exemption may occur where the law was clear at the time the ruling was issued and the issuance was an error.[14]

An aspect of this subject that is by no means clear is the authority of the IRS

---

[8] Prince Edward School Found. v. United States, 80-1 U.S.T.C. ¶ 9295 (D.D.C. 1979), *aff'd in unpub. op.* (D.C. Cir. 1980), *cert. den.*, 450 U.S. 944 (1981). Also Virginia Educ. Fund v. Comm'r, 85 T.C. 743 (1985), *aff'd*, 799 F.2d 903 (4th Cir. 1986); Estate of Clopton v. Comm'r, 93 T.C. 275 (1989).

[9] Incorporated Trustees of Gospel Worker Soc'y v. United States, 510 F. Supp. 374 (D.D.C. 1981), *aff'd*, 672 F.2d 894 (D.C. Cir. 1981), *cert. den.*, 456 U.S. 944 (1982). Also Freedom Church of Revelation v. United States, 588 F. Supp. 693 (D.D.C. 1984).

[10] Presbyterian & Reformed Publishing Co. v. Comm'r, 79 T.C. 1070 (1982).

[11] 743 F.2d 148 (3d Cir. 1984). In another case, the IRS recognized the tax-exempt status of an organization in 1969, revoked the determination letter in 1990, and caused the revocation to be retroactive to 1984 (United Cancer Council, Inc. v. Comm'r, 100 T.C. 162 (1993)).

[12] This authority is predicated upon the authority of the IRS to apply withdrawal of an acquiescence retroactively (e.g., Dixon v. United States, 381 U.S. 68 (1965)).

[13] E.g., Bornstein v. United States, 345 F.2d 558 (Ct. Cl. 1965) (where a ruling was issued one month after a statute was enacted, the matter was reconsidered months later, and the ruling was retroactively revoked).

[14] E.g., Automobile Club of Mich. v. Comm'r, 353 U.S. 180 (1957), *aff'g* 230 F.2d 585 (6th Cir. 1956), *aff'g* 20 T.C. 1033 (1955).

to retroactively revoke the tax exemption of an organization solely for the reason that the IRS has prevailed in a case of first impression. While this type of victory for the government may be a basis for revocation, it does not appear to be a "change" in the law that would trigger retroactive revocation of exemption. Even a decision by the U.S. Supreme Court should not lead to automatic revocation of exemption of all similarly situated organizations, retroactive to the date they were established. In part, the rationale for a more reasoned approach is that an organization receiving a favorable ruling is permitted, in most circumstances, to rely upon the position stated in the ruling in planning and/or consummating a transaction.[15]

Retroactive revocation of tax exemption can produce harsh results, particularly where the period embraced by the revocation covers several years. Moreover, comparable adverse tax consequences may result under state law. Also, for nearly all charitable organizations, retroactive revocation of tax exemption would operate to likewise retroactively revoke the organization's eligibility to receive deductible contributions, which could lead to disallowance of the tax deductions taken by the organization's donors.

The facts and circumstances of a given case determine whether, in retroactively revoking an organization's tax exemption, the IRS has abused its discretion[16] and thus has caused the government to be estopped from causing a revocation to be retroactive.[17]

(b) Changes in Form

A change in organizational form generally is regarded by the IRS as the creation of a new legal entity requiring the filing of an application for recognition of exemption for the successor entity, even though the organization's purposes, methods of operation, sources of support, and accounting method remain the same as they were in its predecessor form.[18] In this determination, the IRS stated that in each of the following changes in the structure of organizations, a new application for recognition of tax exemption is warranted: (1) conversion of a trust to a corporation; (2) conversion of an unincorporated association to a corporation; (3) reincorporation of an organization, incorporated under state law, by an act of Congress; and (4) reincorporation of an organization, incorporated under the laws of one state, under the laws of another state. This determination has been explicitly endorsed by a court.[19]

Absent a change in the law or in the rulings policy of the IRS, the tax-exempt status of the predecessor entity will, in effect, be transmitted to the successor entity. This assumes, however, that the predecessor entity itself was a tax-exempt organization and, in the case of a charitable entity, held a ruling from the IRS to that effect. Where the predecessor lacks the ruling, the organization is

---

[15] Rev. Proc. 62-28, 1962-2 C.B. 496.

[16] IRC § 7805.

[17] E.g., Lesavoy Found. v. Comm'r, 238 F.2d 589 (3d Cir. 1957), rev'g 25 T.C. 924 (1956).

[18] Rev. Rul. 67-390, 1967-2 C.B. 179.

[19] American New Covenant Church v. Comm'r, 74 T.C. 293 (1980). Also Smith v. Comm'r, 51 T.C.M. 1114 (1986).

treated as a charitable entity only as of the date of formation of the successor entity (assuming a ruling to that effect is timely secured).[20]

When the IRS issues a ruling or determination letter recognizing the tax-exempt status of a corporation, generally the effective date is the date of incorporation or the date when the entity became organized and operated for exempt purposes.[21] However, when prior to incorporation an organization was formed and operated in an exempt manner and its incorporation merely had the effect of changing the form of organization from that of an unincorporated organization to a corporation, the ruling or determination letter embraces the period during which the organization operated in an unincorporated status.[22]

However, it should not be assumed that the tax status of a predecessor entity will automatically be transmitted to a successor entity. For example, as noted, the policies and views of the IRS may change, and the IRS may deny recognition of tax exemption to an organization even though it granted recognition of tax exemption to a predecessor organization and the material facts did not differ.[23]

The law also imposes comparable requirements in other areas. Thus, an organization that remains in existence after terminating its private foundation status[24] must file a new application for recognition of exemption if it wishes to be treated as a charitable organization, since the IRS regards it as a newly created entity.[25] Similarly, a tax-exempt corporation formed to take over the operations of an exempt unincorporated association is regarded as a new organization for purposes of filing the Social Security (FICA) tax waiver certificate.[26]

The continuity of existence of a charitable organization is of extreme importance, notwithstanding a change in form. This is particularly the case where the organization has its nonprivate foundation status predicated on classification as a publicly supported organization, which classification contemplates a history of required financial support.[27] Where certain requirements are met, the IRS allows the financial history of the predecessor entity to be used in establishing a public support record for the successor entity.[28]

If a tax-exempt organization converts to a taxable entity,[29] the termination of exempt status is ordinarily operative prospectively; retroactive loss of exemption would occur only if there had been a material misrepresentation of fact or material difference in actual operation.[30]

---

[20] Rev. Rul. 77-469, 1977-2 C.B. 196; Rev. Rul. 77-208, 1977-1 C.B. 153.

[21] Rev. Rul. 54-134, 1954-1 C.B. 88.

[22] *Id.*

[23] E.g., MIB, Inc. v. Comm'r, 734 F.2d 71 (1st Cir. 1984); National Right to Work Legal Defense Educ. Found., Inc. v. United States, 487 F. Supp. 801 (E.D.N.C. 1979).

[24] See Chapter 11.

[25] Rev. Rul. 74-490, 1974-2 C.B. 171.

[26] Rev. Rul. 77-159, 1977-1 C.B. 302. Also Rev. Rul. 71-276, 1971-1 C.B. 289.

[27] See § 11.3(b).

[28] Rev. Rul. 73-422, 1973-2 C.B. 70.

[29] See § 33.3.

[30] E.g., Priv. Ltr. Rul. 8446047.

§ 24.2 TAX CONSEQUENCES OF RETROACTIVE REVOCATION OF TAX-EXEMPT STATUS OF PUBLIC CHARITIES

There are numerous federal tax consequences that can flow from the revocation of the tax-exempt status of an organization that is not a private foundation,[31] where the revocation is retroactive.[32] In general, revocation of the tax exemption of an organization is made retroactive if the organization omitted or misstated a material fact in seeking recognition of exemption or operated in a manner materially different from that originally represented.[33] (The IRS, however, has the authority to grant relief in this regard.[34])[35]

Generally, a public charity that has its tax-exempt status retroactively revoked will be treated as a corporation for tax purposes.[36] Some organizations, however, are established as charitable trusts.[37] In addition, the corporate form may be disregarded and the tax liabilities passed through to another entity where the revoked corporation is in substance a sham that should be disregarded as the "alter ego" of a controlling individual or group[38] or where the corporation is functioning as an agent with respect to contributed funds.[39]

(a) Tax Treatments: Corporations

Where a charitable organization loses its tax-exempt status because it is operating on a "commercial" basis, it becomes taxed under the rules normally applicable to taxable corporations.

When a revoked charitable organization is engaged in tax-exempt activities, nonprofit, nonexempt (for example, political) activities, and/or for-profit activities, the tax outcome is dependent upon whether the income is business income, investment income, or contribution income.

As to income from a related or unrelated business, a revoked organization would have gross income to the extent of receipts from trade or business activity,

---

[31] An organization is not a private foundation where it is an organization that is tax-exempt by reason of IRC § 501(c)(3), where it is also classified under IRC § 509(a)(1), 509(a)(2), 509(a)(3), or 509(a)(4) as being other than a private foundation. See Chapter 11.

[32] Many of these considerations are also applicable with respect to private foundations. However, in those circumstances, rules pertaining to the termination of private foundation status may be applicable. See § 11.4(f).

[33] Rev. Proc. 84-86, 1984-1 C.B. 541 § 14.01.

[34] IRC § 7805(b).

[35] In these circumstances (retroactive revocation), charitable contribution deductions generally are protected until public announcement of the revocation of charitable donee status; however, the IRS may disallow a contribution deduction where the donor knew of actual or imminent revocation or was responsible for or aware of the activities that gave rise to the revocation (Rev. Proc. 82-39, 1982-2 C.B. 759, note 5 § 3.01). In the context of declaratory judgment litigation (see *infra* § 6(b)), contributions not in excess of $1,000 are deductible after notice of revocation and during the pendency of the litigation (see text accompanied by *infra* notes 322–324).

[36] IRC § 7701.

[37] IRC § 4947.

[38] Generally, however, the corporate form is respected. See § 4.1.

[39] E.g., Commissioner v. Bollinger, 485 U.S. 340 (1988); National Carbide Corp. v. Comm'r, 336 U.S. 422 (1949).

offset by deductions for related expenses.[40] Investment income, net of related expenses, would be taxable, including passive income that generally is excluded from taxation when received by a tax-exempt organization.[41]

The law on this point is more complicated where the receipts are voluntary contributions intended, by the donor or donors, to further the organization's stated tax-exempt purposes.

Generally, donated funds and the value of donated property are not considered items of income to the recipient organization.[42] For this purpose, a *gift* is a payment where the donor does not receive something of equivalent value in return. Thus, the U.S. Supreme Court wrote that a "payment of money [or transfer of property] generally cannot constitute a charitable contribution if the contributor expects a substantial benefit in return."[43] Essentially, the same rule was subsequently articulated by the Court, when it ruled that an exchange having an "inherently reciprocal nature" is not a gift and thus cannot be a charitable gift, where the recipient is a charity.[44] An earlier Supreme Court opinion stated that a gift proceeds from a "detached and disinterested generosity" and is "out of affection, respect, admiration, charity or like impulses."[45]

Therefore, while a true gift to an organization is not income,[46] the IRS may contend that the payments are in fact gross income, such as where contributions are considered income to individuals associated with an organization rather than gifts to the organization[47] or where the "contributions" are considered payments in exchange for a quid pro quo.[48] Another contention may be that the "contributions" are items of unrelated business income.[49]

It is the position of the IRS that contributions given in good faith are generally excludable by a revoked tax-exempt organization, as long as the organization also acted in good faith in soliciting the contributions.[50] It is also the view of the IRS that the intent of the donor is not determinative of the gift issue in instances of "misrepresentation or fraud" where "it is clear that from the outset an organization intentionally misrepresented in its solicitations that it was validly tax-exempt and would use all the donations for exempt purposes."[51] By contrast, it has been held that excludable gift treatment is not appropriate where the recipient organization, "misrepresenting itself to be a tax-exempt charity, seeks and obtains donations which it plans to, and does, use in carrying on business activities for

---

[40] See § 28.2.

[41] See § 27.1.

[42] IRC § 102.

[43] United States v. American Bar Endowment, 477 U.S. 105, 116–117 (1986).

[44] Hernandez v. Comm'r, 490 U.S. 680, 692 (1989).

[45] Commissioner v. Duberstein, 363 U.S. 278, 285–286 (1960).

[46] E.g., Bail Fund of the Civil Rights Congress of N.Y. v. Comm'r, 26 T.C. 482 (1956).

[47] E.g., Webber v. Comm'r, 21 T.C. 742 (1954), aff'd, 219 F.2d 834 (10th Cir. 1955).

[48] E.g., Foundation for Divine Mediation, Inc. v. Comm'r, 24 T.C.M. 411 (1965); Publishers New Press, Inc. v. Comm'r, 42 T.C. 396 (1964); Teleservice Co. of Wyoming Valley v. Comm'r, 27 T.C. 722 (1957), aff'd, 254 F.2d 105 (3d Cir. 1958).

[49] E.g., Veterans of Foreign Wars, Dep't of Mich. v. Comm'r, 89 T.C. 7 (1987), app. dis. (6th Cir. 1988).

[50] Gen. Couns. Mem. 39813.

[51] Id.

profit and thereby enriches itself."[52] Thus, where the "mispresentation exception" is applicable, contributions to the revoked exempt organization are not excludable gifts but are items of gross income. This exception will apply where the fraudulent acts and intentions are attributable to the organization,[53] as opposed to actions by individuals in their separate capacities.[54]

The determination as to this type of corporate-level responsibility is a matter of fact. Nonetheless, it is the view of the IRS's lawyers that "misrepresentation by an organization should be presumed to exist when the facts show that an organization soliciting contributions was engaged in a pattern of activities inconsistent with the basis for its exemption."[55] It is also their view that contributions are taxable pursuant to the misrepresentation exception when the organization's exemption is revoked for engaging in nonprofit, nonexempt (for example, political) activities, inasmuch as this type of activity does not "benefit" the organization.[56] However, under these views, the misrepresentation rationale does not extend to situations where contributions initially obtained through "sincere representations" are diverted to noncharitable uses.[57]

Some "contributions" will not be regarded as gifts but as contributions to the capital of the corporation involved.[58] Contributions to capital, whether by a shareholder or a nonshareholder, are not includable in the recipient's gross income.[59] It is unlikely, however, that contributions to a revoked exempt organization would qualify as contributions to capital. Should a contribution potentially so qualify, the contribution would usually be by a "nonshareholder"; even then, the contribution probably would not be a contribution to capital, if only because the contribution would not have become a permanent part of the recipient's working capital structure.[60]

If contributions are included in the gross income of a revoked organization, the organization's tax would depend upon its ability to offset expenditures against that income. Where the expenditures (including an allocable portion of fund-raising costs) were for exempt purposes, a deduction will be allowed to the extent of income from the related activity.[61] Charitable expenditures that are at-

---

[52] Synanon Church v. Comm'r, 57 T.C.M. 602, 628 (1989). Also Altman v. Comm'r, 475 F.2d 876 (2d Cir. 1973); Peters v. Comm'r, 51 T.C. 226 (1968); Zips v. Comm'r, 38 T.C. 620 (1962), *app. dis.* (5th Cir. 1963).
[53] E.g., Asphalt Indust., Inc. v. Comm'r, 384 F.2d 229 (3d Cir. 1967).
[54] E.g., Sherin v. Comm'r, 13 T.C. 221 (1949).
[55] Gen. Couns. Mem. 39813 (see text accompanied by *supra* note 50).
[56] *Id.*
[57] *Id.* An alternative approach that would bypass the IRC § 102 issue rests on the basic principle that funds or assets received by persons acting under the control and for the benefit of others are not includable in the gross income of the initial recipients under the "conduit" doctrine. See § 3.4.
[58] E.g., Veterans Found. v. Comm'r, 38 T.C. 66 (1962), *aff'd,* 317 F.2d 456 (10th Cir. 1963).
[59] IRC § 118.
[60] The characteristics of nonshareholder contributions to capital are analyzed in United States v. Chicago, Burlington & Quincy R.R., 412 U.S. 401 (1973) . Another consequence of this classification is that a gift accords the donee the donor's basis in the property (carryover basis) (IRC § 1015), while a contribution to capital results in zero basis to the recipient (IRC § 362(c)). Also, generally, the basis of an asset acquired or held in periods during which the organization was exempt from income tax would be the original cost or other basis of the asset, reduced by depreciation (IRC § 1016(a)(3)(B); Reg. § 1.1016-4; Polish Am. Club, Inc. v. Comm'r, 33 T.C.M. 925, 931–932 (1974)).
[61] Gen. Couns. Mem. 39813.

tributable to income from other sources (such as business or investment income) would be subject to other income tax restrictions.[62] If the expenditures represent reasonable compensation for services, the expenditures would be deductible; however, amounts in excess of reasonable compensation for services, or otherwise found not to have been intended as compensation for services, would not be deductible.[63] Amounts for expenditures by public charities that are specifically disallowed by federal tax law (such as political campaign expenses[64] or substantial lobbying expenses[65]) would not be deductible. Most expenditures for illegal activities could not be offset against contribution income.

In addition to income tax consequences, there may be excise tax consequences when the tax-exempt status of a public charity is retroactively revoked. For example, where the tax-exempt status is revoked due to excessive lobbying, an excise tax is applicable to the organization,[66] as is the case when the revocation occurs because the organization participated in political campaign activities.[67]

(b) Tax Treatments: Individuals

If a purported organization is no more than a sham or "alter ego" for an individual, upon the retroactive revocation of the tax exemption of the "organization," there would not be any tax at the organizational level.[68] Should this occur, all income (including charitable contributions) and expenditures would be attributed to the individual.[69] This result would also occur should the "organization" be considered merely a conduit in relation to an individual.[70]

Where an organization is a separate entity, and a principal of the organization obtains dominion and control over its funds (other than as a borrower or agent), the individual is taxable on the payment (unless it is a return of capital). Likewise, payments made by the organization to others, where made for the benefit of an individual, would constitute constructive payments includible in the individual's income. For these rules to apply, however, the payment must confer benefit (usually financial in nature) to the individual rather than to the corporation[71]; these rules do not apply simply because an individual has control over an organization's income and expenditures in his or her capacity as a director, officer, or employee. Thus, "a principal of a revoked exempt organization would not realize income merely by virtue of having authorized, or acquiesced in, a diver-

---

[62] IRC § 162 (business expense deduction) and/or § 170 (charitable contribution deduction).

[63] E.g., Kenner v. Comm'r, 33 T.C.M. 1239 (1974); Synanon Church v. Comm'r, *supra* note 52, at 633–635.

[64] See Chapter 21.

[65] See Chapter 20.

[66] IRC § 4912. See § 20.6.

[67] IRC § 4955. See § 21.2. In general, Summers, "Retroactive Loss of Exemption—The Effect on Organizations," 2 *J. Tax. Exempt Orgs.* 18 (Summer 1990).

[68] As discussed, however, this type of characterization of an organization is unlikely (see text accompanied by *supra* note 38).

[69] E.g., Universal Church of Jesus Christ, Inc. v. Comm'r, 55 T.C.M. 144 (1988); Sly v. Comm'r, 56 T.C.M. 209 (1988).

[70] See text accompanied by *supra* note 57.

[71] E.g., Knott v. Comm'r, 67 T.C. 681 (1977); Rev. Rul. 79-9, 1979-1 C.B. 125.

sion of funds to nonexempt purposes, in the absence of a financial or economic benefit."[72]

Usually, this type of a payment (direct or constructive) to an individual is regarded as ordinary income in the nature of compensation for services provided. However, it is possible for the payment to be taxed as capital gain (where made in return for property furnished to the organization) or as a dividend.[73] Nonetheless, there is authority for the conclusion that, when controlling persons divert corporate funds to their personal use, the persons are taxable in full on the amount involved without regard to the technicalities of dividend treatment.[74]

Principals of a revoked exempt organization may be liable for the organization's taxes and/or penalties, to the extent that they obtained assets of the organization and are liable as transferees.[75] Also, courts have occasionally disregarded the corporation to collect a corporate liability from a controlling individual, under an "alter ego" theory, even though the corporate entity was considered viable for purposes of imposing a corporate-level tax.[76]

Aside from income tax consequences, an individual who is a manager of a public charity that has its tax-exempt status retroactively revoked can be liable for an excise tax where the organization lost its exemption because of substantial lobbying[77] or political campaign activities.[78]

§ 24.3 ANNUAL REPORTING REQUIREMENTS

Nearly every organization that is exempt from federal income taxation must file an annual information return.[79] This return generally is as follows:

---

[72] Gen. Couns. Mem. 39813.

[73] As to dividend treatment, see, e.g., Sly v. Comm'r, *supra* note 69; Kenner v. Comm'r, *supra* note 63; Grant v. Comm'r, 18 T.C.M. 601 (1959). Also Stevens Bros. Found. v. Comm'r, 39 T.C. 93 (1962), *rev'd* 324 F.2d 633 (8th Cir. 1963), *cert. den.*, 376 U.S. 919 (1964).

[74] Truesdell v. Comm'r, 89 T.C. 1280 (1987). Cf. Benes v. Comm'r, 42 T.C. 358 (1964), *aff'd*, 355 F.2d 929 (6th Cir. 1966), *cert. den.*, 384 U.S. 961 (1966); Weir v. Comm'r, 283 F.2d 675 (6th Cir. 1960); Davis v. United States, 226 F.2d 331 (6th Cir. 1955). Also DiZenzo v. Comm'r, 348 F.2d 122 (2d Cir. 1965); Leaf v. Comm'r, 33 T.C. 1093 (1960), *aff'd*, 295 F.2d 503 (6th Cir. 1961); Simon v. Comm'r, 248 F.2d 869 (8th Cir. 1957).

[75] IRC § 6901. E.g., Wade v. Comm'r, 16 T.C.M. 308 (1957).

[76] E.g., Wolfe v. United States, 798 F.2d 1241, *amended,* 806 F.2d 1410 (9th Cir. 1986), *cert. den.*, 482 U.S. 927 (1987); Harris v. United States, 764 F.2d 1126 (5th Cir. 1985).

[77] IRC § 4912. See § 20.6.

[78] IRC § 4955. See § 21.2. An IRS analysis of this aspect of the law stated that the Internal Revenue Code "does not provide clear-cut answers to many of these questions," in that the "statutory scheme is oriented toward normal, profit-making corporations." The memorandum concluded: "If the treatment of revoked [exempt] organizations continues to pose a problem, a legislative solution may be appropriate." Gen. Couns. Mem. 39813.

[79] IRC § 6033(a)(1); Reg. § 1.6033-2(a)(1). This filing requirement applies to organizations that are tax-exempt by reason of IRC § 501(a). Thus, it is not applicable to those entities that are exempt pursuant to IRC §§ 521 (see § 18.11), 526 (§ 18.9), 527 (Chapter 17), 528 (§ 18.3), or 529 (§ 18.16).

1. Most tax-exempt organizations—Form 990[80]

2. Small tax-exempt organizations[81]—Form 990-EZ

3. Private foundations[82]—Form 990-PF.

4. Black lung benefit trusts[83]—Form 990-BL

Political organizations[84] file tax returns on Form 1120-POL and homeowners" associations[85] file tax returns on Form 1120-H.

The annual information return must state the organization's items of gross income, disbursements, and other information, and it must keep appropriate records, render under oath statements, make other returns, and comply with other requirements, as the tax regulations, return instructions, and the return itself prescribes.[86] Generally, an organization must file an annual information return irrespective of whether it is chartered by, or affiliated or associated with, any central, parent, or other organization.[87]

(a) Contents of Annual Information Return

The annual information return filed with the IRS by most tax-exempt organizations—Form 990—is not merely akin to a tax return that principally requires the submission of financial information. There is also a substantial amount of other factual information that is required to be provided. This annual return is often the document that is principally used to evaluate an exempt organization.[88]

(i) Form 990.   The annual information return filed by most exempt organizations must include the following items: a summary of the types of gross revenue received for the year involved;[89] its expenses for the year;[90] its net assets as of the close of the year;[91] a statement of program service accomplishments;[92] a list of trustees, directors, officers, and key employees;[93] an analysis of income-producing activities;[94] and information concerning taxable subsidiaries.[95] Expenses

---

[80] The Form 990 is also generally filed by nonexempt charitable trusts (IRC § 4947(a)(1)). The filing requirements for charitable trusts (IRC § 4947) are the subject of Rev. Proc. 73-29, 1973-2 C.B. 474.

[81] See *infra* § 3(a)(iii).

[82] See Chapter 11.

[83] See § 16.5.

[84] See Chapter 17.

[85] See § 18.3.

[86] IRC § 6033(a)(1); Reg. § 1.6033-2. The contents of the return for charitable organizations (entities described in IRC § 501(c)(3) and tax-exempt by reason of IRC § 501(a)) are stated in IRC § 6033(b); Reg. § 1.6033-2(a)(2).

[87] Reg. § 1.6033-2(a)(1).

[88] In general, see Dylewsky, "Form 990 Offers Opportunity for Exempts to Position Themselves Favorably," 6 *J. Tax. Exempt Orgs.* 120 (Nov./Dec. 1994).

[89] Form 990, Part I, lines 1–12.

[90] *Id.*, Part I, lines 13–17.

[91] *Id.*, Part I, lines 18–21; Part IV.

[92] *Id.*, Part III.

[93] *Id.*, Part V.

[94] *Id.*, Part VII.

[95] *Id.*, Part IX.

must be reported on a functional basis.[96] Information is required with respect to cost allocations where there are joint costs for educational and fund-raising purposes.[97] An organization must report aggregate compensation of directors and the like from the reporting organization and related organizations, where more than $10,000 was provided by a related organization.[98]

An exempt organization is required to inventory its sources of revenue (such as program service revenues identified by discrete activities, membership dues, investment income, special fund-raising events, and sales of inventory).[99] These items of revenue must be characterized as either unrelated business income or related (exempt function) income.[100] Each type of related income must be accompanied by an explanation as to how the income-producing activities relate to the accomplishment of exempt purposes.[101] A *business code* must be assigned to each item of unrelated business income.[102] Some revenue received by tax-exempt organizations is excluded from unrelated business income taxation.[103] If an exempt organization has income of this nature, it must report the amount and identify an *exclusion code* corresponding with the section of the Internal Revenue Code that provides the exclusion.[104]

In determining whether an activity of a tax-exempt organization is a *business*, the IRS and the courts look to the presence or absence of a *profit motive* prompting the conduct of the activity.[105] An activity that is not conducted with this motive is not regarded as a *business*. (This means that any net loss from an activity of this nature cannot be offset against net gain from a business undertaking.[106]) To induce exempt organizations to disclose any activities that do not qualify as businesses for this purpose, the IRS utilizes a special business code.[107]

A tax-exempt organization is required to report certain other facts, including a statement as to any new activities, any changes made in governing documents, a liquidation or substantial contraction, relationship with another organization, political expenditures, receipt of nondeductible gifts, compliance with the requirement to disclose its application for recognition of exemption and recent annual information returns, deductibility of membership dues (in the case of social welfare, labor, agricultural, and horticultural organizations, and business leagues), revenue items unique to social clubs, payment of taxes for excessive lobbying or political campaign activities (in the case of public charities),

---

[96] *Id.*, Part II.
[97] *Id.*, Part II, last question.
[98] *Id.*, Part V, last question.
[99] *Id.*, Part VII.
[100] *Id.*, Part VII, columns (B), (E).
[101] *Id.*, Part VIII.
[102] *Id.*, Part VII, column (A).
[103] See Chapter 27.
[104] Form 990, Part VII, columns (C), (D).
[105] See § 26.2(a).
[106] As reflected on Form 990-T, net income and net losses from unrelated businesses conducted in a year can be netted in determining any unrelated business taxable income. See § 28.1.
[107] Form 990 instructions, exclusion code 41.

ownership of an interest in a taxable corporation or partnership, and information about any excess benefit transaction (in the case of public charities and social welfare organizations).[108]

The accounting system used by a tax-exempt organization to maintain its books and records may be different from that reflected on the annual information return, particularly because of recent changes in generally accepted accounting principles.[109] A portion of the annual information return is used to reconcile these two approaches.[110]

(ii) Form 990, Schedule A. In addition to filing the annual information return, a charitable organization[111] must file an accompanying schedule requiring other information.[112]

This schedule is the means by which charitable organizations report on the compensation of the five highest paid employees,[113] the compensation of the five highest paid independent contractors for professional services,[114] certain activities[115] eligibility for nonprivate foundation status,[116] compliance by private schools with the antidiscrimination rules,[117] and on information regarding transfers, transactions, and relationships with other organizations.[118]

Charitable organizations that elected the expenditure test with respect to their lobbying activities[119] must report their lobbying expenses, including those over the four-year averaging period.[120] Organizations that have not made this election, and thus remain subject to the substantial part test,[121] are subject to other reporting requirements.[122]

(iii) Form 990-EZ. To alleviate the annual reporting burden for smaller tax-exempt organizations, the IRS promulgated a less extensive annual information return. This is the two-page Form 990-EZ.

This return may be used by tax-exempt organizations that have gross receipts that are less than $100,000 and total assets that are less than $250,000 in value at the end of the reporting year.[123]

An organization can use this annual information return in any year in

---

[108] Form 990, Part VI, questions 76–77 (see *supra* § 1), 79 (§ 4.3(b)), 80 (Chapters 30–33), 81 (Chapter 17), 82, 83 (*infra* § 4), 84 (§ 22.2), 85 (§ 20.8), 86 (Chapter 14), 87 (§ 18.5), 88 (Chapters 31, 32), and 89 (§§ 20.6, 21.2, 19.11(d)).
[109] Financial Accounting Standards Board Statements Nos. 116, 117.
[110] Form 990, Parts IV-A, IV-B.
[111] That is, an organization that is tax-exempt under IRC § 501(a) by reason of IRC § 501(c)(3).
[112] Form 990, Schedule A.
[113] Schedule A, Part I.
[114] Schedule A, Part II.
[115] Schedule A, Part III.
[116] Schedule A, Part IV. See Chapter 11.
[117] Schedule A, Part V. See § 5.4(a).
[118] Schedule A, Part VII.
[119] See § 20.5(a).
[120] Form 990, Schedule A, Part VI-A.
[121] See § 20.2(b).
[122] Form 990, Schedule A, Part VI-B.
[123] This is not a statutory rule; it is a threshold established by the IRS.

which it meets the two criteria, even though it was, and/or is, required to file a Form 990 in other years. The Form 990-EZ cannot be filed by private foundations (see below). A charitable organization filing a Form 990-EZ must also file a Schedule A (Form 990) (see above).

(iv) *Form 990-PF.* Private foundations[124] must file an annual information return.[125] This return is on Form 990-PF.

Private foundations must report their revenue and expenses,[126] assets and liabilities,[127] fund balances,[128] and information about trustees, directors, officers, foundation managers, other highly paid employees, and contractors.[129] Private foundations must report as to qualifying distributions,[130] calculation of the minimum investment return,[131] computation of the distributable amount,[132] undistributed income,[133] and grants programs and other activities.[134]

A private foundation must calculate the tax on its investment income[135] (unless it is an exempt operating foundation) and its qualification for the reduced tax on net investment income (assuming it is reporting that lower tax).[136] A private foundation must provide certain information regarding foundation managers,[137] loan and scholarship programs,[138] grants and contributions paid during the year or approved for future payment,[139] transfers, transactions, and relationships with other organizations,[140] and compliance with the public inspection requirements.[141]

A private foundation must report as to certain activities. These requirements are largely the same as for all reporting tax-exempt organizations.[142] However, the annual information return for private foundations also requests information about self-dealing transactions,[143] failure to distribute income as required,[144] excess business holdings,[145] investments that jeopardize charitable pur-

---

[124] See Chapter 11.
[125] IRC §§ 6033(a), 6033(b), 6033(c).
[126] Form 990-PF, Part I.
[127] Form 990-PF, Part II.
[128] Form 990-PF, Part III.
[129] Form 990-PF, Part VIII.
[130] Form 990-PF, Part XIII.
[131] Form 990-PF, Part IX.
[132] Form 990-PF, Part X.
[133] Form 990-PF, Part XIV.
[134] Form 990-PF, Part XVII.
[135] Form 990-PF, Part IV, VI.
[136] Form 990-PF, Part V.
[137] Form 990-PF, Part XVI.
[138] *Id.*
[139] *Id.*
[140] Form 990-PF, Part XVIII.
[141] Form 990-PF, Part XIX.
[142] See text accompanying *supra* notes 107–115.
[143] Form 990-PF, Part VII, question 10.
[144] Form 990-PF, Part VII, question 11.
[145] Form 990-PF, Part VII, question 12.

poses,[146] taxable expenditures,[147] political expenditures,[148] and substantial contributions.[149]

Additional reporting requirements are applicable to private operating foundations.[150]

Additionally, the Form 990-PF must include the following items: (1) an itemized statement of the private foundation's assets; (2) an itemized list of all grants and contributions made or approved, showing the amount of each grant or contribution, the name and address of each recipient, any relationship between any recipient and the foundation's managers or substantial contributors, and a concise statement of the purpose of each grant or contribution; (3) the address of the principal office of the foundation and (if different) of the place where its books and records are maintained; and (4) the names and addresses of the foundation's managers that are substantial contributors with respect to the foundation or that own 10 percent or more of the stock of any corporation of which the foundation owns 10 percent or more of the stock, or corresponding interests in partnerships or other entities, in which the foundation has a 10 percent or greater interest.[151]

(v) Form 990-T. Revenue and expenses associated with unrelated business activity by a tax-exempt organization are reported to the IRS on Form 990-T.[152]

An exempt organization with unrelated business taxable income[153] must file, in addition to the Form 990 or Form 990-EZ (or, in the case of a private foundation, the Form 990-PF), a Form 990-T. It is on this form that the source (or sources) of unrelated income is reported and any tax computed.[154]

Tax-exempt organizations must report their unrelated trade or business income.[155] These reporting obligations are less where the unrelated trade or business gross income is no more than $10,000.

All forms of unrelated trade or business gross income must be reported, along with associated deductions.[156] Separate schedules pertain to rental income,[157] unrelated debt-financed income,[158] investment income of those organizations that must treat that type of income as unrelated business income,[159] income

---

[146] Form 990-PF, Part VII, question 13.
[147] Form 990-PF, Part VII, question 14.
[148] Form 990-PF, Part VII, question 14.
[149] Form 990-PF, Part VII, question 15.
[150] Form 990-PF, Part XV.
[151] IRC § 6033(c); Reg. § 1.6033-3(a).
[152] IRC § 6012(a)(2), (4); Reg. §§ 1.6012-2(e), 1.6012-3(a)(5), 1.6033-2(i).
[153] See Chapters 26, 27.
[154] Reg. § 1.6012-2(e).
[155] See § 28.2.
[156] Form 990-T, Parts I, II.
[157] Form 990-T, Schedule C. See § 27.1(h).
[158] Form 990-T, Schedule E. See §§ 29.1–29.4.
[159] Form 990-T, Schedule F. See § 28.3. These organizations are social clubs (see Chapter 14), voluntary employees beneficiary associations (see § 16.3), supplemental unemployment benefit trusts (see § 16.4), and group legal services organizations (see § 16.6).

(other than dividends) from controlled organizations,[160] exploited exempt activity income (other than advertising income),[161] and advertising income.[162]

Under certain guidelines,[163] tax-exempt labor organizations may file copies of U.S. Department of Labor forms in lieu of Form 990, Part II, and tax-exempt employee benefit plans may file for that purpose copies of forms otherwise filed with the IRS pursuant to the requirements of the Employee Retirement Income Security Act.

(vi) Due Dates. The annual information return (Form 990, Form 990-EZ, or Form 990-PF) and any unrelated business income tax return (Form 990-T) are due on or before the fifteenth day of the fifth month following the close of the tax year.[164] Thus, the return for a calendar year organization should be filed by May 15 of each year. One or more extensions may be obtained.

Historically, tax-exempt organizations have filed their annual information and tax returns with the appropriate IRS service center. However, as of January 1, 1997, all of these returns are filed with the IRS service center in Ogden, Utah.[165] This development is part of an overall centralization of IRS functions; it is also intended to consolidate expertise in the processing and review of exempt organization returns.

At the time a private foundation files its annual return, a copy of the return must be sent to the attorney general of one or more states, including the state in which the foundation was created and in which the foundation's principal office is located.[166]

The filing date for an annual information return (Form 990, Form 990-EZ, or Form 990-PF) may fall due while the organization's application for recognition of tax-exempt status is pending with the IRS. In that instance, the organization should nonetheless file the information return (rather than a tax return) and indicate on it that the application is pending.[167]

(vii) Penalties. Failure to timely file the appropriate information return, or failure to include any information required to be shown on the return (or failure to show the correct information) absent reasonable cause, can, for pre-1996 years, give rise to a $10 penalty, payable by the organization, for each day the failure continues, with a maximum penalty for any one return not to exceed the

---

[160] Form 990-T, Schedule G. See §§ 27.1(n), 33.1.

[161] Form 990-T, Schedule H. See § 26.4(e).

[162] Form 990-T, Schedule I. See § 26.5(f).

[163] Rev. Proc. 79-6, 1979-1 C.B. 485.

[164] IRC § 6072(e); Reg. § 1.6033-2(e). This due date is also applicable with respect to Form 4720 (the tax return by which certain excise taxes imposed on private foundations, public charities, and others are paid).

[165] Ann. 96-63, 1996-29 I.R.B. 18.

[166] Reg. § 1.6033-3(c).

[167] Reg. § 1.6033-2(c).

lesser of $5,000 or five percent of the gross receipts of the organization for one year.[168] An additional penalty may be imposed at the same rate and maximum of $5,000 on the individual(s) responsible for the failure to file, absent reasonable cause, where the return remains unfiled following demand for the return by the IRS.[169] An addition to tax for failure to timely file a federal tax return, including a Form 990-T, may also be imposed.[170]

For tax years ending on or after July 30, 1996, the penalties as described in the foregoing paragraph are increased. In general, the new penalties are a doubling of the previous ones;[171] thus, the $10 per day penalty is, as of the effective date, generally $20 per day,[172] and the $5,000 limitation is, as of the effective date, $10,000.[173] However, there is, as of the effective date, a much larger penalty on organizations having gross receipts in excess of $1 million for a year; in this circumstance, the per-day penalty is $100 and the maximum penalty is $50,000.[174]

In one instance, an organization required to file a Form 990 submitted an incomplete return by omitting material information from the form, and failed to supply the missing information after being requested to do so by the IRS and did not establish a reasonable cause for its failure to file a complete return. Under these circumstances, the filing of the incomplete return is a failure to file the return for purposes of the penalty.[175] The IRS observed that the legislative history underlying the pertinent law "shows that Congressional concern was to ensure that information requested on exempt organization returns was provided timely and completely so that the Service would be provided with the information needed to enforce the tax laws."[176] The IRS added:

> Form 990 and accompanying instructions issued by the Service request information that is necessary in order for the Service to perform the duties and responsibilities placed upon it by Congress for proper administration of the revenue laws. These duties and responsibilities include making exempt organization returns available for public inspection as well as conducting audits of

---

[168] IRC § 6652(c)(1)(A), (c)(3). A private foundation is deemed to have reasonable cause for failure to comply with the requirements of IRC § 6033, as well as §§ 6011, 6056, 6104 and 6151, for filing of returns and payment of taxes until 90 days after it is issued a letter containing a determination of private foundation status from the IRS, thereby immunizing it from application of penalty provisions IRC §§ 6651 and 6652 with respect to a tax year for which, prior to the due date for filing Form 990-PF, the organization has filed notice (on Form 1023) claiming not to be a private foundation (Rev. Proc. 79-8, 1979-1 C.B. 487).

[169] IRC § 6652(c)(1)(B); Reg. § 301.6652-2. Two or more organizations exempt from taxation under IRC § 501, one or more of which is described in IRC § 501(c)(2) (see § 18.2(a) and the other(s) of which derive income from IRC § 501(c)(2) organization(s), are eligible to file a consolidated return Form 990 (and/or Form 990-T) in lieu of separate returns (IRC § 1504(e)).

[170] IRC § 6651(a)(1).

[171] The increases in these penalties were occasioned by enactment of the Taxpayer Bill of Rights 2 (Pub. L. No. 168, 104th Cong., 2d Sess. (1996)).

[172] IRC § 6652(c)(1)(A). (The reasonable cause rule was not adjusted by the law change in 1996.)

[173] *Id.* (The alternative 5 percent threshold was not altered.)

[174] IRC § 6652(c)(1)(A), last sentence.

[175] Rev. Rul. 77-162, 1977-1 C.B. 400.

[176] *Id.*, citing S. Rep. 552, 91st Cong., 1st Sess. 52 (1969).

exempt organizations to determine their compliance with statutory provisions. When a return is submitted that has not been satisfactorily completed, the Service's ability to perform its duties is seriously hindered, and the public's right to obtain meaningful information is impaired. Thus, when material information is omitted, a return is not completed in the manner prescribed by the form and instructions and the organization has not met the filing requirements of section 6033(a)(1) of the Code.[177]

A related point is that, in the case of failure to file a return, the tax may be assessed, or a proceeding in court for the collection of the tax may be begun without assessment, at any time.[178] In the above-discussed situation, the organization was considered[179] to have failed to file any return at all and, therefore, the period of limitations on assessment and collection of the tax[180] was ruled to have not started.[181]

(viii) Assessments. The IRS generally must assess any tax within three years of the due date of the return or the date on which the return involved is actually filed, whichever is later.[182] However, a six-year statute of limitations applies if an excise tax return "omits an amount of such tax properly includible thereon which exceeds 25 percent of the amount of such tax reported thereon"; this extended period does not apply, in the case of the private foundation and certain other taxes, where there is adequate disclosure in the return to the IRS.[183] In one case, a private foundation timely filed its annual information return, reflecting certain salary payments to an officer; believing the payments to be reasonable, the foundation did not file a return showing any excise taxes due. The U.S. Tax Court held that, under these facts, only the annual information return was due, that adequate disclosure was made on that return, and that the six-year statute of limitations was inapplicable (thereby precluding the IRS from assessing the tax because the deficiency notice was mailed more than three years after the organization's returns were filed).[184]

It is the practice of the IRS to omit from its listing of organizations to which deductible gifts may be made[185] those organizations that fail to establish their nonfiling status with the IRS. This practice was upheld by the Chief Counsel of the IRS.[186] The continuing validity of this procedure was temporarily cast

---

[177] Rev. Rul. 77-162, *supra* note 175 at 401.

[178] IRC § 6501(c)(3).

[179] IRC § 6652(c)(1)(A).

[180] IRC § 6501(c)(3).

[181] In general, reliance on the advice of a competent tax advisor can constitute reasonable cause for a failure to file a return, for purposes of the IRC § 6651(a)(1) addition to tax, and the IRC § 6652(c)(1)(A) or § 6652(c)(1)(B) penalty (e.g., Waco Lodge No. 166, Benevolent & Protective Order of Elks v. Comm'r, 42 T.C.M. 1202 (1981), *aff'd in part and rev'd in part*, 696 F.2d 372 (5th Cir. 1983); Coldwater Seafood Corp. v. Comm'r, 69 T.C. 966 (1978); West Coast Ice Co. v. Comm'r, 49 T.C. 345 (1968)).

[182] IRC § 6501(a).

[183] IRC § 6501(e)(3).

[184] Cline v. Comm'r, 55 T.C.M. 540 (1988).

[185] Publication No. 78, "Cumulative List of Organizations Described in Section 170(c) of the Internal Revenue Code."

[186] Gen. Couns. Mem. 39389.

in doubt because of a court opinion,[187] although the lawyers at the IRS ultimately concluded that the opinion did not raise any concerns with respect to the practice.[188]

(ix) Miscellaneous.   The filing of an annual information return is also the opportunity for the changing of annual accounting periods by most tax-exempt organizations. An exempt organization desiring to change its annual accounting period may effect the change by timely filing its annual information return with the IRS for the short period for which the return is required, indicating in the return that a change of accounting period is being made. If an organization is not required to file an annual information return or a tax return reflecting unrelated income, it is not necessary to otherwise notify the IRS that a change of accounting period is being made. However, if an organization has previously changed its annual accounting period at any time within the 10 calendar years ending with the calendar year that includes the beginning of the short period resulting from the change of an annual accounting period, and if the organization had a filing requirement at any time during the 10-year period, it must file an application for a change in accounting period (Form 3115) with the IRS.[189]

Special rules apply with respect to the filing of annual information returns by organizations under a group exemption.[190]

(b)   Exceptions to Reporting Requirements

This requirement of filing an annual information return does not apply to several categories of tax-exempt organizations.

Some of these exceptions are mandatory,[191] while others are at the discretion of the IRS.[192]

(i) Churches and Certain Other Religious Organizations.   Churches (including an interchurch organization of local units of a church), their integrated auxiliaries, and conventions or associations of churches do not have to file annual information returns.[193]

---

[187] Estate of Clopton v. Comm'r, *supra* note 8.

[188] Gen. Couns. Mem. 39809.

[189] Rev. Proc. 85-58, 1985-2 C.B. 740, *sup.* Rev. Proc. 76-9, 1985-1 C.B. 547, as *mod. by* Rev. Proc. 79-2, 1979-1 C.B. 482. This simplified procedure is inapplicable to farmers' cooperatives (see § 18.11), shipowners' protective associations (see § 18.12), political organizations (see Chapter 17), or homeowners' associations (see § 18.13). These entities change their annual accounting period by filing the form with the IRS National Office.

The IRS provided relief from the filing of an application for change in accounting method for tax-exempt organizations changing their method so as to comply with the Statement of Financial Accounting Standards No. 116 issued by the Financial Accounting Standards Board (Notice 96-30, 1996-1 C.B. 378).

[190] Reg. § 1.6033-2(d). The group exemption rules are the subject of § 23.6.

[191] IRC § 6033(a)(2)(A).

[192] IRC § 6033(a)(2)(B).

[193] IRC § 6033(a)(2)(A)(i); Reg. § 1.6033-2(g)(1)(i). Religious orders (see § 8.6) do not file Form 990; instead, because they are treated as partnerships for tax purposes, they file the partnership return (Form 1065).

The definitions given the terms *church, integrated auxiliary of a church*, and *convention or association of churches* are discussed elsewhere.[194]

Also, the reporting requirements do not apply to the exclusively religious activities of any *religious order*.[195]

(ii) Small Organizations. The requirement of filing an annual information return is inapplicable to certain organizations (other than private foundations) the gross receipts[196] of which in each year are normally not more than $5,000.[197]

Other organizations may be relieved from filing annual information returns where a filing of these returns by them is not necessary to the efficient administration of the internal revenue laws, as determined by the IRS.[198] This category of organizations[199] embraces:

1. Religious organizations;[200]

2. Educational organizations;[201]

3. Charitable organizations or organizations for the prevention of cruelty to children or animals,[202] if the organizations are supported by funds contributed by the federal or a state government or are primarily supported by contributions from the general public;

4. Organizations operated, supervised, or controlled by or in connection with a religious organization;

5. Certain fraternal beneficiary organizations;[203] and

6. A corporation organized under an act of Congress if it is wholly owned by the United States or any agency or instrumentality of the United States or a wholly owned subsidiary of the United States.[204]

---

[194] See §§ 8.3–8.5.

[195] IRC § 6033(a)(2)(A)(iii); Reg. § 1.6033-2(g)(1)(iii). See § 8.6.

[196] The term *gross receipts* means total receipts without any reduction for costs or expenses, including costs of goods sold (Form 990, part 1, line 8). For this purpose, insurance premiums collected by the local lodge of a tax-exempt fraternal beneficiary society from its members, maintained separately without use or benefit, and remitted to its parent organization that issued the insurance contracts, were ruled by the IRS to not be gross receipts of the local lodge (Rev. Rul. 73-364, 1973-2 C.B. 393).

[197] IRC § 6033(a)(2)(A)(ii). The rules for calculating this $5,000 limitation appear in Reg. § 1.6033-2(g)(3). This threshold amount is, in actuality, $25,000 (see *infra* note 204).

[198] IRC § 6033(a)(2)(B); Reg. § 1.6033-2(g)(6).

[199] IRC § 6033(a)(2)(C).

[200] See Chapter 8.

[201] IRC § 170(b)(1)(A)(ii). See Chapter 7, § 11.3(a).

[202] IRC § 501(c)(3). See § 10.1.

[203] IRC § 501(c)(8). See § 18.4(a).

[204] IRC § 501(c)(1). Also Reg. § 1.6033-2(g)(1)(vi). See § 18.1. The IRS ruled that the National Credit Union Administration and the tax-exempt federal credit unions under its supervision are organizations described in IRC § 501(c)(1) and thus are not required to file annual information returns (Rev. Rul. 89-94, 1989-2 C.B. 233).

In the exercise of this discretionary authority, the IRS announced that organizations, other than private foundations, with gross receipts not normally in excess of $25,000, will not have to file a Form 990 for tax years ending on or after December 31, 1982.[205]

(iii) Other Exempted Organizations.   As noted, other organizations may be relieved from filing annual information returns where a filing of these returns by them is not necessary to the efficient administration of the internal revenue laws, as determined by the IRS.[206] This discretion in the IRS also has been exercised to except from the filing requirement:

1. An educational organization (below college level) that is qualified as a school, has a program of a general academic nature, and is affiliated with a church or operated by a religious order;[207]

2. Mission societies sponsored by or affiliated with one or more churches or church denominations, more than one-half of the activities of which are conducted in, or directed at persons in, foreign countries;[208]

3. State institutions, the income of which is excluded from gross income on the ground that the income is accruing to the state;[209]

4. A foreign organization (other than a private foundation) which normally does not receive more than $25,000 in gross receipts annually from sources within the United States[210] and which does not have any significant activity (including lobbying or political activity) in the United States;[211]

5. A governmental unit;[212] and

6. An affiliate of a governmental unit.[213]

For purposes of the fifth of these items, an entity is a *governmental unit* if it is (1) a state or local governmental unit as defined in the rules providing an exclusion from gross income for interest earned on bonds issued by these units,[214] (2) it

---

[205] Ann. 82-88, 1982-25 I.R.B. 23. For purposes of the $25,000 rule, a tax-exempt organization is exempt from filing an annual information return where (1) during its first year, it received (including pledges) gross receipts of $37,500 or less; (2) during a period of more than one year of its existence and less than three years, it received, as an average of gross receipts experienced in the first two tax years, gross receipts of $30,000 or less; and (3) during its existence of more than three years, it received, as an average of gross receipts, $25,000 or less (*id.*).

[206] IRC § 6033(a)(2)(B).

[207] Reg. § 1.6033-2(g)(1)(vii). See § 7.3. Also Rev. Rul. 78-316, 1978-2 C.B. 304. For this purpose, the rules as to *affiliation* are the same as those discussed in § 8.5.

[208] IRC § 115; Reg. § 1.6033-2(g)(1)(iv).

[209] Reg. § 1.6033-2(g)(1)(v).

[210] IRC §§ 861–865; Reg. § 53.4948-1(b).

[211] Rev. Proc. 94-17, 1994-1 C.B. 579.

[212] Rev. Proc. 95-48, 1995-2 C.B. 418, *supp'g* Rev. Proc. 83-23, 1983-1 C.B. 687.

[213] *Id.*

[214] Reg. § 1.103-1(b). See § 6.9.

is entitled to receive deductible charitable contributions as a unit of government,[215] or (3) it is an Indian tribal government or a political subdivision of this type of government.[216]

For purposes of the sixth of these items, an entity is an *affiliate of a governmental unit* if it is a tax-exempt organization[217] and meets one of two sets of requirements. One is that it has a ruling or determination letter from the IRS that (1) its income, derived from activities constituting the basis for its exemption, is excluded from gross income under the rules for political subdivisions and the like,[218] (2) it is entitled to receive deductible charitable contributions[219] on the basis that contributions to it are for the use of governmental units, or (3) it is a wholly owned instrumentality of a state or political subdivision of a state for employment tax purposes.[220] The other is available for an entity that does not have a ruling or determination letter from the IRS but (1) it is either operated, supervised, or controlled by governmental units, or by organizations that are affiliates of governmental units, or the members of the organization's governing body are elected by the public at large, pursuant to local statute or ordinance, (2) it possesses two or more of certain affiliation factors,[221] and (3) its filing of an annual information return is not otherwise necessary to the efficient administration of the internal revenue laws.[222] An organization can (but is not required to) request a ruling or determination letter from the IRS that it is an affiliate of a governmental unit.[223]

§ 24.4 DOCUMENT AVAILABILITY REQUIREMENTS

As this chapter and the previous one indicate, the following general categories of documents containing information about tax-exempt organizations must be filed with the IRS: the application for recognition of tax exemption and supporting documents (such as governing instruments, exhibits, and legal memoranda), any statements as to changes in material facts, and annual information returns. Another document on file at the IRS is, of course, a copy of the ruling as to tax-exempt (and, where applicable, private foundation) status. These several documents are likely to collectively comprise a wealth of information about the organization.

---

[215] IRC § 170(c)(1). See § 18.18.

[216] IRC §§ 7701(a)(40), 7871. This tripartite definition of *governmental unit* is in Rev. Proc. 95-48, *supra* note 212, § 4.01.

[217] That is, is described in IRC § 501(c).

[218] IRC § 115. See § 18.17.

[219] IRC § 170(c)(1).

[220] IRC §§ 3121(b)(7), 3306(c)(7). This definition is provided by Rev. Proc. 95-48, *supra* note 212, § 4.02(a).

[221] Rev. Proc. 95-48, *supra* note 212 § 4.03.

[222] *Id.* § 4.02(b). Relevant facts and circumstances as to whether an annual return is necessary include those provided at *id.* § 4.04.

[223] *Id.* § 5.

§ 24.4   DOCUMENT AVAILABILITY REQUIREMENTS

(a) Availability Through IRS

The application for recognition of tax exemption and any supporting documents filed by most tax-exempt organizations[224] must be made accessible to the public by the IRS where a favorable determination letter is issued to the organization.[225] Where there is no prescribed application form, the documents filed with the IRS that led to the issuance of an exemption ruling become publicly available under these rules. These rules are triggered by a finding that an organization is tax-exempt for any one year, even though the organization may subsequently lose its tax exemption.

Information contained in the application or supporting documents may relate to a trade secret, patent, process, style of work, or apparatus. An organization, the application for recognition of exemption of which is open to public inspection, may request in writing that the information be withheld. The information will be withheld from public inspection if the IRS determines that disclosure of it would adversely affect the organization.[226]

Once an organization's exemption application, and related and supporting documents, become open to public inspection, the determination letter (ruling) issued by the IRS also becomes publicly available. Also open to inspection under these rules are any technical advice memoranda issued with respect to any favorable ruling. A favorable ruling recognizing an organization's tax-exempt status may be issued by the National Office; these rulings and the underlying applications for recognition of tax exemption are available for inspection in the IRS Freedom of Information Reading Room in Washington, D.C.[227]

However, certain determinations issued by the IRS in the tax-exempt organizations context are not open to public inspection. These include (1) unfavorable rulings issued in response to applications for recognition of tax exemption, (2) rulings revoking or modifying a favorable ruling, (3) technical advice memoranda relating to a disapproved application for recognition of tax exemption, and (4) any letter filed with or issued by the IRS relating to an organization's status as a nonprivate foundation or as a private operating foundation.[228]

An application and related materials may be inspected at the appropriate IRS service center. Inspection may also occur at the National Office of the IRS; a request for inspection should be directed to the Assistant to the Commissioner (Public Affairs), 1111 Constitution Avenue, N.W., Washington, D.C. 20224.[229]

The excise tax return filed by private foundations (Form 4720) is disclosable to the public.[230] However, this return as filed by a person other than a foundation

---

[224] Those described in IRC § 501(c) or § 501(d).
[225] IRC § 6104(a)(1)(A). This disclosure requirement is confined to papers submitted in support of the application by the organization (Reg. § 301.6104(a)-1(e)). It does not apply to papers submitted by any other person, such as a member of Congress (Lehrfeld v. Richardson, 1998 WL 15282 (D.C. Cir. 1998)).
[226] Reg. § 301.6104(a)-5.
[227] Notice 92-28, 1992-1 C.B. 515.
[228] Reg. § 301.6104(a)-1(i).
[229] Reg. § 301.6104(a)-6.
[230] Reg. § 1.6033-2(a)(2)(ii)(j).

is not disclosable. Therefore, if disclosure of the return filed by a person other than a private foundation is not desired, the person should file separately rather than jointly with the foundation, inasmuch as the joint filing is disclosable.[231]

(b) Access at Exempt Organization

The annual information returns and applications for recognition of tax exemption of tax-exempt organizations other than private foundations must be made available for public inspection.[232] This requirement does not cause disclosure of the names or addresses of donors. As to annual information returns, a tax-exempt organization is required to make a copy of each return available for inspection during regular business hours by any individual at its principal office for three years.[233] If an exempt organization regularly maintains one or more regional or district offices having at least three employees, this inspection requirement applies with respect to each office.[234] The penalty for failure to so provide access to copies of the annual return is $10 per day for pre-1996 years, absent reasonable cause, with a maximum penalty per return of $5,000.[235] Similar rules apply with respect to public inspection of copies of applications for recognition of exemption, along with supporting documents and IRS communications. However, certain information can be withheld from public inspection, such as trade secrets and patents.[236] The penalty for failure to so provide access to copies of the application, payable by the person failing to meet the requirements, is $10 per day for pre-1996 years, absent reasonable cause, without any limitation.[237] Any person who willfully fails to comply with these inspection requirements is subject to a $1,000 penalty with respect to each return or application.[238]

For tax years ending on or after July 30, 1996, the penalties described in the foregoing paragraph are increased. Any person failing to allow inspection of annual returns must pay $20 per day for each day the failure continues, up to $10,000.[239] Any person failing to allow inspection of an organization's application

---

[231] T.D. 7785, 1981-2 C.B. 233.

[232] IRC § 6104(e). There are separate publicity requirements applicable to private foundations (IRC § 6104 (d)).

[233] IRS rules (Notice 88-120, 1988-2 C.B. 454) reinforce the point that exact copies of these documents are required. This means that, for IRC § 501(c)(3) (charitable and the like) organizations, the compensation of major employees must be disclosed as part of public access to the returns.

[234] Organizations that are covered by a group exemption and do not file their own annual information returns (see § 23.6), and that receive a request for inspection, must acquire a copy of the group return from the central organization and make the material available to the requestor within a reasonable amount of time (Notice 88-120, *supra*, note 233.) Also, the requestor has the option of requesting, from the central organization, inspection of the group return at the principal office of the parent organization (*id.*)

[235] IRC § 6652(c)(1)(C).

[236] IRC § 6104(a)(1)(D).

[237] IRC § 6652(c)(1)(D).

[238] IRC § 6685. These rules are applicable to annual information returns for years beginning after December 31, 1986, and on and after January 22, 1988, in the case of applications for recognition of tax exemption submitted to the IRS after July 15, 1987, or on or before July 15, 1987, if the organization has a copy of the application on July 15, 1987.

[239] IRC § 6652(c)(1)(C).

for recognition of tax exemption must pay $20 per day for each day the failure continues.[240]

The disclosure requirement is in the process of expansion.[241] If an individual makes the request at the principal, regional, or district office of a tax-exempt organization, copies of one or more of the three most recent annual information returns and the application for recognition of exemption will have to be provided to the individual.[242] This request will have to be made in person or in writing. The copies of the documents will have to be provided without charge, other than a reasonable fee for any reproduction and mailing costs. Where the request is made in person, the copy of the return will have to be made available immediately. If the request is made in writing, a copy of the return will have to be provided within 30 days.[243]

This requirement as to the provision of copies of exemption applications and annual information returns will be inapplicable where the organization has made the documents *widely available* or the IRS determines that the request is part of a *harassment campaign* and that compliance with the request is not in the public interest.[244] The effective date of these rules is for requests made on or after the 60th day following issuance of tax regulations.[245] Until that time, the existing law governs the manner in which a tax-exempt organization must allow inspection by the public of its annual information returns and exemption application.[246]

The penalty in this context will be substantially increased. The present-day $1,000 penalty for willful failure to comply with the public inspection rules[247] will, as to requests made on or after the 60th day following issuance of the final version of the anti-harassment regulations,[248] become $5,000.[249] However, the legislative history of this law stated that the House Committee on Ways and Means

---

[240] IRC § 6652(c)(1)(D). The increase in this penalty and the one reflected in *supra* note 239, was intended to be made as part of the Taxpayer Bill of Rights 2, *supra* note 171; however, the revisions were inadvertently omitted. Congress corrected this omission by adding the penalty revisions by enactment of the Small Business Job Protection Act of 1996 (Pub. L. No. 188, 104th Cong., 2d Sess. (1996)).

[241] The following requirements will, once the new law becomes effective (see the text accompanied by *infra* note 246), be the subject of IRC § 6104(e)(1)(A)(i).

[242] IRC § 6104(e)(1)(A)(ii) (not yet effective; see the text accompanied by *infra* note 246). The IRS provided a brief summary of these rules in Notice 96-48, 1996-2 C.B. 214.

[243] IRC § 6104(e)(1)(A), final two sentences (not yet effective; see the text accompanied by *infra* note 246).

[244] IRC § 6104(e)(3) (not yet effective; see the text accompanied by *infra* note 246).

[245] Taxpayer Bill of Rights 2, *supra* note 171 § 1313(c).

[246] Regulations explaining these two exceptions were issued in proposed form on September 25, 1997 (REG-246250-96). Under this proposal, an organization can make the documents widely available by posting them on a World Wide Web page on the Internet or by having the documents posted on another organization's Web page as part of a database of similar materials, where certain criteria are satisfied (Prop. Reg. § 301.6104(e)-2). Generally, a harassment campaign would exist when an organization received a group of requests, and the relevant facts and circumstances show that the purpose of these requests was to disrupt the operations of the exempt organization rather than to collect information (Prop. Reg. § 301.6104(e)-3). In general, Boisture & Mayer, "Treasury Releases Proposed Disclosure Regulations," 9 *J. Tax Exempt Orgs.* (No. 4) 148 (Jan./Feb. 1998).

[247] See text accompanied by note 239.

[248] See text accompanied by note 245.

[249] Prospective IRC § 6685.

"expects" that tax-exempt organizations will "comply voluntarily" with the public inspection provisions prior to the issuance of the regulations.[250]

With the annual information return a public document, it is important that it be accurately and completely prepared. This is easier to state than to do, for the preparers of today's annual information return are expected to make determinations as to which there is little guidance, in law and in accounting, as to how to do them. These judgments include functional accounting of expenses,[251] allocations as between types of legislative activities,[252] separation of related and unrelated activities,[253] and the availability of a host of exceptions to unrelated income taxation.[254] Nonetheless, the annual information return is now an excellent means by which to present an organization's programs and other activities in the best possible light to the public, the media, and the IRS (perhaps thereby avoiding an audit). The return also is an effective tool for the management of a tax-exempt organization to use to assess the programmatic and financial progress of the organization.

§ 24.5 DISCLOSURE REGARDING CERTAIN INFORMATION OR SERVICES

A tax-exempt organization[255] must pay a penalty if it fails to disclose that information or services it is offering is available without charge from the federal government.

Specifically, if (1) a tax-exempt organization offers to sell (or solicits money for) specific information or a routine service for any individual that could be readily obtained by the individual without charge (or for a nominal charge) from an agency of the federal government, (2) the tax-exempt organization, when making the offer or solicitation, fails to make an "express statement (in a conspicuous and easily recognizable format)" that the information or service can be so obtained, and (3) the failure is due to "intentional disregard" of these requirements, the organization must pay a penalty.[256]

This requirement applies only if the information to be provided involves the specific individual solicited. Thus, for example, the requirement applies with respect to obtaining the social security earnings record or the social security identification number of an individual solicited, while the requirement is inapplicable with respect to the furnishing of copies of newsletters issued by federal agencies

---

[250] H. Rep. 506, 104th Cong., 2d Sess. 61 (1996).

[251] See *supra* § 3(a)(i).

[252] See § 20.2.

[253] See Chapter 26.

[254] See Chapter 27.

[255] That is, an entity described in IRC §§ 501(c) or (d) and exempt from federal income tax under IRC § 501(a) (see Part Two), or a political organization as defined in IRC § 527(e) (see Chapter 17).

[256] IRC § 6711(a). These rules apply to offers and solicitations made after January 31, 1988. IRS guidelines (Notice 88-120, *supra* note 233) state that if materials and/or services are available from the federal government for less than $2.50 (including postage and handling costs), the materials are considered by the IRS as being available from the federal government at a nominal charge.

or providing copies of or descriptive material on pending legislation. Also, this requirement is inapplicable to the provision of professional services (such as tax return preparation, grant application preparation, or medical services), as opposed to routine information retrieval services, to an individual even if they may be available from the federal government without charge or at a nominal charge.[257]

The penalty, which is applicable for each day on which the failure occurred, is the greater of $1,000 or 50 percent of the aggregate cost of the offers and solicitations that occurred on any day on which the failure occurred and with respect to which there was this type of failure.[258]

§ 24.6   REVOCATION OF EXEMPTION: ADMINISTRATIVE AND LITIGATION PROCEDURES

The IRS is authorized to revoke an organization's tax exemption, notwithstanding an earlier recognition of its exemption by IRS ruling or court order, where the organization violates one or more of the requirements for the applicable tax-exempt status. If the recognition of tax exemption was by court order, the IRS is not collaterally estopped from subsequently revoking the exemption where the ground for disqualification is different from that asserted in the prior court proceeding.[259]

If an organization's tax-exempt (or, where applicable, nonprivate foundation) status is revoked (or adversely modified) by the IRS, its administrative remedies are much the same as if the original application for that status had been denied.[260]

The principle of procedural due process, embodied in the Fifth Amendment to the U.S. Constitution, does not require the IRS to initiate a judicial hearing on the qualification of an organization for tax-exempt status before revoking the organization's favorable determination letter. This point was addressed by the Supreme Court in 1974.[261] It was reaffirmed nearly 20 years later, when another court found that the Supreme Court's analysis is still the law, that the revocation did not infringe on the organization's exercise of First Amendment rights,[262] and that, even if the organization had a property interest in the IRS's prior recognition

---

[257] Notice 88-120, *supra* note 233.

[258] IRC § 6711(b).

[259] Universal Life Church, Inc. v. United States, 86-1 U.S.T.C. ¶ 9271 (Cl. Ct. 1986).

[260] Rev. Proc. 90-27, *supra* note 1 § 14.02; § 23.8. The protest and conference rights before a final revocation notice is issued are not applicable to matters where delay would be prejudicial to the interests of the IRS (such as in cases involving fraud, jeopardy, or the imminence of the expiration of the statute of limitations, or where immediate action is necessary to protect the interests of the federal government) (Rev. Proc. 90-27, *supra* note 1 § 14.03). In general, Sanders, "What to Do About the Loss of Exemption: Effect Upon the Organization and Its Members," 24 *N.Y.U. Inst. Fed. Tax.* 167 (1966).

[261] Bob Jones Univ. v. Simon, 416 U.S. 725 (1974), *aff'g* 472 F.2d 903 (4th Cir. 1973), *reh. den.*, 476 F.2d 259 (4th Cir. 1973).

[262] This argument was based on the fact that the organization involved, a charitable (IRC § 501(c)(3)) entity, has a First Amendment (free speech) right to solicit charitable contributions. See Hopkins, *The Law of Fund-Raising, Second Edition* (New York; John Wiley & Sons, Inc., 1996), Chapter 5 § 3.

of its tax-exempt status, the revocation was not a deprivation of property without procedural due process.[263]

(a) General Rules

Facing revocation of tax-exempt status and having exhausted its administrative remedies, an organization's initial impulse may be to seek injunctive relief in the courts, to restrain the IRS from taking such action. However, the Anti-Injunction Act[264] provides that, aside from minor exceptions, "no suit for the purpose of restraining the assessment or collection of any tax shall be maintained in any court by any person. . . ."[265] Despite the explicitly inflexible language of the statute, the U.S. Supreme Court carved out a narrow exception, in that a preenforcement injunction against tax assessment or collection may be granted only if it is clear that under no circumstances could the government ultimately prevail and if equity jurisdiction otherwise exists (that is, a showing of irreparable injury, no adequate remedy at law, and advancement of the public interest).[266] Generally, loss of tax-exempt status will not bring an organization within the ambit of this exception, under Supreme Court rulings[267] and other cases.[268] An exception may be available in this context but success will require rather unusual factual circumstances.[269]

An organization facing loss of tax-exempt status or similar adverse treatment from the IRS may petition the U.S. Tax Court for relief following the issuance of notice of tax deficiency (if one can be found)[270] or may pay the tax and sue for a refund in federal district court or the U.S. Court of Federal Claims following expira-

---

[263] United Cancer Council, Inc. v. Comm'r, *supra* note 11.

[264] IRC § 7421(a).

[265] Also the Tax Exception to the Declaratory Judgment Act, 28 U.S.C. § 2201. E.g., American Soc'y of Ass'n Executives v. Bentsen, 848 F. Supp. 245 (D.D.C. 1994) (holding that both statutes deprived the court of jurisdiction over challenge of the constitutionality of the law denying the business expense deduction for dues paid to exempt associations that engaged in lobbying (see § 20.8)); Alpine Fellowship Church of Love & Enlightenment v. United States, 87-1 U.S.T.C. ¶ 9203 (N.D. Cal. 1987).

[266] Enochs v. Williams Packing & Navigation Co., 370 U.S. 1 (1962). E.g., Investment Annuity v. Blumenthal, 437 F. Supp. 1095 (D.D.C. 1977), 442 F. Supp. 681 (D.D.C. 1977), *rev'd*, 609 F.2d 1 (D.C. Cir. 1979); State of Minn., Spannaus v. United States, 525 F.2d 231 (8th Cir. 1975). Also Notes at 30 *Wash. & Lee L. Rev.* 573 (1973), 73 *Col. L. Rev.* 1502 (Part 2)(1973), 1 *Tulsa L.J.* 88 (1964).

[267] Bob Jones Univ. v. Simon, *supra*; note 261; "Americans United" Inc. v. Walters, 416 U.S. 752 (1974), *rev'g* 477 F.2d 1169 (D.C. Cir. 1973). Also Note, 46 *Temp. L. Q.* 596 (1974); United States v. American Friends Serv. Comm., 419 U.S. 7 (1974); Cattle Feeders Tax Comm. v. Shultz, 504 F.2d 462 (10th Cir. 1974); Vietnam Veterans Against the War, Inc. v. Voskuil, 389 F. Supp. 412 (E.D. Mo. 1974).

[268] E.g., Crenshaw County Private School Found. v. Connally, 474 F.2d 1185 (5th Cir. 1973); National Council on the Facts of Overpopulation v. Caplin. 224 F. Supp. 313 (D.D.C. 1963); Israelite House of David v. Holden, 14 F.2d 701 (W.D. Mich. 1926).

[269] Center on Corporate Responsibility, Inc. v. Shultz, 368 F. Supp. 863 (D.D.C. 1973). In The Founding Church of Scientology of Washington, D.C., Inc. v. Director, Federal Bureau of Investigation et al., 84-1 U.S.T.C. ¶ 9468 (D.D.C. 1984), the organization was permitted to seek an injunction against the IRS for allegedly engaging in illegal law enforcement and information-gathering activities in violation of the organization's constitutional rights, inasmuch as the lawsuit was not related to tax assessment or collection.

[270] IRC §§ 6212, 6213. E.g., Golden Rule Church Ass'n, v. Comm'r, 41 T.C. 719 (1964). The role and responsibilities of the Chief Counsel of the IRS in tax-exempt organization cases docketed in the U.S. Tax Court is the subject of Rev. Proc. 78-9, 1978-1 C.B. 563.

tion of the statutory six-month waiting period.[271] However, the organization may well become defunct before any relief can be obtained in this fashion, particularly where the ability to attract charitable contributions is a factor, since denial of tax-exempt status also means (where applicable) loss of advance assurance by the IRS of deductibility of contributions. The U.S. Supreme Court recognized the seriousness of this dilemma but concluded that "although the congressional restriction to postenforcement review may place an organization claiming tax-exempt status in a precarious financial position, the problems presented do not rise to the level of constitutional infirmities, in light of the powerful governmental interests in protecting the administration of the tax system from premature judicial interference . . . and of the opportunities for review that are available."[272]

(b) Declaratory Judgment Rules

The federal tax law provides for declaratory judgments as to the tax status of charitable organizations.[273] This law authorizes federal court jurisdiction in cases of actual controversy involving determinations (or failures to make a determination) by the IRS with respect to the tax status of charitable organizations. This jurisdiction is vested in the U.S. District Court for the District of Columbia, the U.S. Court of Federal Claims, and the U.S. Tax Court.[274]

This declaratory judgment procedure is designed to facilitate relatively prompt judicial review of four categories of tax-exempt organizations issues.[275] However, this procedure is not intended to supplant the preexisting avenues available for exempt organizations for judicial review. Jury trials are not available in these types of cases.[276]

These rules create a remedy in a case of actual controversy involving a determination by the IRS with respect to the initial qualification or classification or continuing qualification or classification of an entity as a charitable organization for tax exemption purposes[277] and/or charitable contribution deduction pur-

---

[271] IRC § 7422; 28 U.S.C. §§ 1346(a)(1), 1491. In the absence of the timely filing of a claim for refund (a jurisdictional prerequisite to this type of court action), this type of suit may not be maintained. Also The American Ass'n of Commodity Traders v. Department of the Treasury, 79-1 U.S.T.C. ¶ 9183 (D.N.H. 1978), aff'd, 598 F.2d 1233 (1st Cir. 1979).

[272] Bob Jones University v. Simon, supra note 261, 416 U.S., at 747–748.

[273] IRC § 7428. E.g., The Church of the New Testament v. United States, 783 F.2d 771 (9th Cir. 1986).

[274] The U.S. Tax Court is the only one of these courts where a declaratory judgment case can be pursued without the services of a lawyer; these pro se cases will be dismissed for that reason in the other two courts (Point of Wisdom No. 1 v. United States, 77 A.F.T.R. 2d 986 (D.D.C. 1996)).

[275] Congress in 1974 enacted a similar declaratory judgment procedure for ascertaining the tax qualifications of employee retirement plans, as part of the Employee Retirement Income Security Act (IRC § 7476). E.g., Federal Land Bank Ass'n of Asheville, N.C. v. Comm'r, 67 T.C. 29 (1976), rev. and rem., 573 F.2d 179 (4th Cir. 1978), 74 T.C. 1106 (1980) (on remand).

[276] The Synanon Church v. United States, 83-1 U.S.T.C. ¶ 9230 (D.D.C. 1983).

[277] That is, an organization described in IRC § 501(c)(3) and exempt from federal income taxation by reason of IRC § 501(a). Reasoning that the question as to whether a trust is a charitable trust within the meaning of IRC § 4947(a)(1) (see § 11.4(f)) is "inextricably related" to the issue of whether it is qualified under IRC § 501(c)(3), the Tax Court held that it has declaratory judgment jurisdiction to decide the IRC § 4947(a)(1) issue (Allen Eiry Trust v. Comm'r, 77 T.C. 1263, 1267 (1981)). However, in the case, the court declined to take jurisdiction over the question as to whether the trust is qualified to

poses,[278] a private foundation,[279] or a private operating foundation.[280] The remedy is also available in the case of a failure by the IRS to make a determination as respects one or more of these issues.[281] The remedy is pursued in one of the three above-noted courts, which is authorized to "make a declaration" with respect to the issues.

A *determination* within the meaning of these rules[282] is a final decision by the IRS affecting the tax qualification of a charitable organization.[283] The term does not encompass an IRS ruling passing on an organization's proposed transactions; in that this type of ruling does not constitute a denial or revocation of an organization's tax-exempt status nor does it jeopardize the deductibility of contributions to it; thus, absent a final determination, a declaratory judgment is premature.[284] The same principle applies to an IRS ruling concerning an organization's public charity entity classification.[285] In the case of a church, a final report of an IRS agent (the *30-day letter*) constitutes the requisite final determination.[286]

A topic of some controversy is whether an organization can litigate, under the declaratory judgment rules, its public charity classification where the IRS accords public charity status to it but in a category different from that requested by the organization. In the first case on the point, the U.S. Tax Court held that it is a justiciable issue[287] for an organization to assert that it is not a private foundation because it is a church rather than a publicly supported organization.[288] The court said that, in such an instance, the organization has received the requisite adverse ruling, if only because the organization had requested a definitive ruling yet received only an advance ruling;[289] the IRS unsuccessfully asserted that the declaratory judgment jurisdiction becomes available only where the ruling is "fully adverse."[290]

---

have its income exempt from tax under IRC § 115 (see § 18.17) (*id.*, at 1270). The court also declined jurisdiction in an instance where the organization was dissolved prior to the filing of the petition for declaratory relief, on the ground that there was not an actual controversy (National Republican Found. v. Comm'r, 55 T.C.M. 1395 (1988)). Likewise, where an audit by the IRS is undertaken and the organization's tax-exempt status is not altered, there is no actual controversy (Founding Church of Scientology of Washington, D.C., Inc. v. United States, 92-1 U.S.T.C. ¶ 50,302 (Cl. Ct. 1992)).

[278] IRC § 170(c)(2).

[279] IRC § 509(a).

[280] IRC § 4942(j)(3).

[281] IRC § 7428(a)(2). Thus, the rulings and determination letters in cases subject to the declaratory judgment procedure of IRC § 7428 are those issued pursuant to the procedures stated in Rev. Proc. 90-27, *supra* note 1. The withdrawal of an application for recognition of tax exemption is not a failure to make a determination under IRC § 7428(a)(2) (*id.* § 7.02).

[282] IRC § 7428(a)(1).

[283] Rev. Proc. 90-27, *supra* note 1, § 12.04.

[284] New Community Senior Citizen Hous. Corp. v. Comm'r, 72 T.C. 372 (1979). In one case, the U.S. Tax Court held that the requirement that there be a final adverse determination means that the court lacks jurisdiction to review a determination issued by the IRS only after the organization agreed to not conduct a certain activity in consideration of receipt of the otherwise favorable determination, because the ruling is not "adverse" in relation to the proposed activity (AHW Corp. v. Comm'r, 79 T.C. 390 (1982)).

[285] Urantia Found. v. Comm'r, 77 T.C. 507 (1981), *aff'd*, 684 F.2d 521 (7th Cir. 1982).

[286] IRC § 7611(g).

[287] Under IRC § 7428(a)(1)(B).

[288] See § 11.3.

[289] See § 23.4(b).

[290] Friends of the Soc'y of Servants of God v. Comm'r, 75 T.C. 209 (1980). Also Foundation of Human Understanding v. Comm'r, 88 T.C. 1341 (1987).

However, the U.S. Court of Appeals for the Fifth Circuit endeavored to narrow the reach of this Tax Court decision.[291] While the appellate court agreed that "the receipt of a favorable ruling on a non-private [foundation] status that is a different and less advantageous status that [sic] the one which is the subject of the ruling request will not defeat" declaratory judgment jurisdication,[292] the court said it would "not . . . [interpret] the statute to allow court review of an adverse holding by the Service which has no present effect on a taxpayer's classification" as a private foundation or nonfoundation.[293] The principal issue before the court of appeals concerned an organization that was ruled to be a donative publicly supported organization; however, the IRS had also ruled, contrary to the position of the organization, that contributions from another organization were subject to the 2 percent limitation on allowable "public" contributions.[294] The court rejected the contention that the Tax Court had jurisdiction to entertain the action, concerning proper application of the two percent limitation, since the organization was accorded initial classification as a publicly supported charity and since the IRS had not failed to make the requisite determination. Thus, the court concluded that the necessary *actual controversy* was not present and that the organization can litigate the applicability of the 2 percent rule when and if that rule causes the IRS to attempt to adversely classify the organization under the public charity classification rules.[295] Likewise, the U.S. Court of Appeals for the Sixth Circuit held that the courts lack declaratory judgment jurisdiction where an organization is seeking reclassification under the public charity rules.[296]

A pleading may be filed under these rules "only by the organization the qualification or classification of which is at issue."[297] Prior to utilizing the declaratory judgment procedure, an organization must have exhausted all administrative remedies available to it within the IRS.[298] It was held that the refusal by an

---

[291] CREATE, Inc. v. Comm'r, 634 F.2d 803 (5th Cir. 1981).

[292] *Id.* at 813.

[293] *Id.* at 812.

[294] See Chapter 11.

[295] Inherent in the opinion is the court's concern about overburdening the judicial system with too many IRC § 7428 declaratory judgment cases, for it speaks of a contrary holding giving rise to "a significant volume of § 7428 litigation, some of which would be needless" (CREATE, Inc. v. Comm'r, *supra* note 291, at 812).

[296] Ohio County & Ind. Agric. Soc's v. Comm'r, 610 F.2d 448 (6th Cir. 1979), *cert. den.*, 446 U.S. 965 (1980).

[297] IRC § 7428(b)(1). Thus, for example, as regards an unincorporated organization that applied for tax exemption and subsequently, during the administrative process, incorporated, when the IRS denied tax exemption for the unincorporated entity, the corporation (being a separate legal entity) was held to lack standing to seek a declaratory judgment on the qualification as an exempt organization of the unincorporated organization (American New Covenant Church v. Comm'r, *supra* note 19). By contrast, a surviving tax-exempt corporation in a merger was held to be able to litigate, under these rules, the issue of tax exemption of the merged entity; the appellate court looked to state law to determine that the suit could be said to be maintained by "the organization" (Baptist Hosp. Inc. v. United States, 851 F.2d 1397 (Fed. Cir. 1988), *rev'g* 87-1 U.S.T.C. ¶ 9290 (Ct. Cl. 1987)).

[298] In The Sense of Self Soc. v. United States, 79-2 U.S.T.C. ¶ 9673 (D.D.C. 1979), the court ruled that the organization failed to exhaust its administrative remedies because it did not respond to the IRS' "repeated" requests for information. Cf. Change-All Souls Hous. Corp. v. United States, 671 F.2d 463 (Ct. Cl. 1982).

organization to turn records over to the IRS, during the pendency of a contest of the IRS summons, cannot be considered a failure to exhaust administrative remedies that could result in a loss of declaratory judgment rights.[299] For the first 270 days after a request for a determination is made, an organization is deemed to not have exhausted its administrative remedies, assuming no determination is actually made during that period.[300] After this 270-day period has elapsed, the organization may initiate an action for a declaratory judgment. However, if the IRS makes an adverse determination during the jurisdictional period, an action could be initiated immediately thereafter. Nonetheless, all actions under these rules must be initiated within 90 days after the date on which the final determination by the IRS is made.[301] In the case of a church, the receipt of a final report of an IRS agent is deemed to constitute the exhaustion of administrative remedies.[302]

A *determination* can, in this context, include a proposed revocation of an organization's tax-exempt status or public charity classification. In one case, an organization received a letter in which the IRS proposed to revoke its public charity status; in response, it filed a written protest and thereafter filed a petition for a declaratory judgment (under the 270-day rule). After the court petition was filed, the IRS issued a final determination letter revoking the classification of the organization. At issue was whether the U.S. Tax Court had jurisdiction as the result of the filing of the petition. The IRS contended the court did not, inasmuch as the petition was filed before the final adverse letter was issued. The court disagreed, finding that the proposed revocation was sufficient to create the requisite actual controversy and that the written protest constituted the requisite request for a determination.[303]

In the case, the Tax Court concluded that the administrative appeals process had been completed and that the 270-day period had run its course. By contrast, where the administrative process is ongoing and where the IRS has merely threatened to issue a notice of proposed revocation, the courts will decline to assume declaratory judgment jurisdiction.[304] Emphasizing the requirement of an "actual controversy," the Tax Court observed that " [w]e find no grounds for believing that Congress intended this [declaratory judgment] section to grant us plenary authority to supervise examinations of exempt organizations."[305] This determination was upheld by the U.S. Court of Appeals for the Ninth Circuit, rejecting the claim of jurisdiction in that the "IRS is still only in the investigative stage and has not issued any ruling affecting . . . [the organization's] tax exempt status, directly or indirectly."[306]

---

[299] Church of World Peace, Inc. v. Internal Revenue Service, 715 F.2d 492 (10th Cir. 1983).

[300] IRC § 7428(b)(2). Withdrawal of an application for recognition of tax exemption (Form 1023) is not an exhaustion of administrative remedies (Rev. Proc. 90-27, *supra* note 1 § 7.02). The filing of an application for tax exemption is not a required administrative step for organizations claiming status as a church (see § 23.3(b)), according to the U.S. Tax Court in Universal Life Church, Inc. (Full Circle) v. Comm'r, 83 T.C. 292 (1984).

[301] IRC § 7428(b)(3). E.g., Metropolitan Community Serv., Inc. v. Comm'r, 53 T.C.M. 810 (1987).

[302] IRC § 7611(g).

[303] J. David Gladstone Found. v. Comm'r, 77 T.C. 221 (1981).

[304] High Adventure Ministries, Inc. v. Comm'r, 80 T.C. 292 (1983).

[305] *Id*. at 302.

[306] 726 F.2d 555, 557 (9th Cir. 1984).

In one instance, a court concluded that it had declaratory judgment jurisdiction over a case, where the IRS notified a tax-exempt organization that the IRS was considering revocation of its tax-exempt status, even though the complaint in the case was filed before the IRS issued its final adverse determination letter to the organization.[307] Prior to the filing of the court petition, the IRS issued a technical advice memorandum stating that the organization's tax exemption should be revoked. The government argued that, at the time the petition was filed, there was no actual controversy because the IRS had not yet revoked or officially "proposed revocation" of the organization's tax-exempt status. However, the court held that the organization's "continuing classification was unquestionably at issue between the parties throughout the entire administrative proceeding."[308] Reviewing the facts, the court wrote that, "[a]fter the issuance of the technical advice memorandum, final revocation was inevitable" and thus "[t]here can be no other conclusion but that an actual controversy existed on the date . . . [the organization] filed its petition herein."[309]

In this case, there was no "failure to make a determination" and there was no "request for a termination." The government did not issue a "proposed revocation" and the organization never filed a "written protest." However, the court examined the administrative status of the case and compared it to the administrative status of an organization that receives a proposed revocation, and concluded that the correspondence from the IRS was "in substance, procedurally the same" as a proposed revocation and that the organization's written response was "in substance, procedurally the same" as a written protest.[310] The court concluded that, by the time the matter was substantively considered by the IRS, a full and complete administrative record had been developed.

In the course of issuance of a favorable determination letter recognizing an organization's tax-exempt status, the IRS not infrequently conditions its ruling on the organization's agreement to not engage in a particular activity. The U.S. Tax Court held that this type of favorable final ruling does not constitute the requisite adverse determination.[311] Indeed, the court starkly wrote that "[o]rganizations which have an exempt status have been left with only one means of obtaining judicial review: to engage in the proposed activities despite . . . [the IRS's] adverse ruling, thereby to risk revocation, and to test . . . [the IRS's] position in court in the event of actual revocation."[312] If an organization concludes that it cannot risk loss of tax exemption, the court suggested that a new entity be formed to undertake the activities at issue and, if necessary, litigate the matter.[313]

According to the IRS, this 270-day period does not begin until the date a *substantially completed* application for recognition of tax exemption is sent to the appropriate key district director.[314]

---

[307] Anclote Psychiatric Center, Inc. v. Comm'r, 98 T.C. 374 (1992).

[308] *Id.* at 377.

[309] *Id.*

[310] *Id.* at 378.

[311] AHW Corp. v. Comm'r, 79 T.C. 390 (1982).

[312] *Id.* at 394–395.

[313] *Id.* at 398, note 5.

[314] Rev. Proc. 90-27, *supra* note 1 at § 5.05.

As respects the exhaustion of administrative remedies requirements, the IRS determined that the following steps and remedies must be exhausted prior to proper initiation of a declaratory judgment action:

1. The filing of a substantially completed application for recognition of tax exemption,[315] or the filing of a request for a determination of private foundation status;

2. The timely submission of all additional information requested to perfect an application for recognition of exemption or request for determination of private foundation status;

3. In appropriate cases, requesting appropriate relief under the rules[316] regarding applications for extensions of the time for making an election or application for relief from tax;[317] and

4. Exhaustion of all administrative appeals available within the IRS,[318] as well as appeal of a proposed adverse ruling in National Office original jurisdiction exemption application cases.[319]

According to the IRS, an organization cannot be deemed to have exhausted its administrative remedies prior to the earlier of (1) the completion of the foregoing four steps and the sending of a notice of final determination by certified or registered mail, or (2) the expiration of the 270-day period in a case where the IRS has not issued a notice of final determination and the organization has taken, in a timely manner, all reasonable steps to secure a ruling or determination.[320]

Further, the IRS states that the foregoing steps "will not be considered completed until the Service has had a reasonable time to act upon the appeal or protest, as the case may be."[321] (As noted, nonetheless, once the statutory 270 days have elapsed, the action can be initiated, without regard to the pace of the IRS in relation to these steps.)

To protect the financial status of an allegedly charitable organization during the litigation period, the law provides for circumstances under which contributions made to the organization during that period are deductible[322] even though the court ultimately decides against the organization.[323] Basically, this relief can only be accorded where the IRS is proposing to revoke, rather than initially deny,

---

[315] See § 23.2(b)

[316] Reg. § 1.9100.

[317] Rev. Proc. 79-63, 1979-2 C.B. 578.

[318] Rev. Proc. 90-27, *supra* note 1 §§ 10, 11.

[319] *Id*. at § 12.01.

[320] *Id*. at § 12.02.

[321] *Id*. at § 12.03. The U.S. District Court for the District of Columbia, in New York County Health Servs. Review Org., Inc. v. Comm'r, 80-1 U.S.T.C. ¶ 9398 (D.D.C. 1980), held that the court lacks subject matter jurisdiction until the IRS makes an adverse determination or the 270-day period (commenced by the filing of a substantially completed application for recognition of exemption) has elapsed.

[322] IRC § 170(c)(2).

[323] IRC § 7428(c)(1).

an organization's charitable status. However, the total deductions to any one organization from a single donor to be so protected during this period may not exceed $1,000.[324] (Where an organization ultimately prevails in a declaratory judgment case, this $1,000 limitation on deductibility becomes inapplicable, so that all gifts are fully deductible within the general limitations of the charitable deduction rules.[325]) Further, this benefit is not available to any individual who was responsible, in whole or in part, for the actions (or failures to act) on the part of the organization that were the basis for the revocation of tax-exempt status.[326]

When the IRS revokes an organization's tax exemption, that action is usually the result of an audit of the organization's activities for one or more tax years. When a revocation of exemption occurs, the IRS inevitably makes a public announcement that the organization is no longer tax-exempt and that contributions to it are no longer deductible. Thus, for example, once such a revocation occurs, and the organization takes no affirmative steps to restore its tax exemption, a gift to the organization would not be tax-deductible, even when made in a year subsequent to one of the audit years. A court in a declaratory judgment case only has jurisdiction in relation to the audit years, inasmuch as the requisite determination has been made. As to the subsequent years, there is no jurisdiction because there is no determination with respect to those years. The remedy available to an organization in these circumstances is to file an application for recognition of exemption for the subsequent period. The manner in which the IRS responds to the filing will determine whether or not the organization needs to proceed in court for those years—in any event, that response will be the determination needed to invest a court with declaratory judgment jurisdiction.[327]

The U.S. Tax Court is the only one of the three jurisdictions to adopt procedural rules for actions filed under these rules.[328] The single most significant feature of these rules is the decision of the court to generally confine its role to review of the denial by the IRS of a request for a determination of exemption based solely on the facts contained in the administrative record, that is, not to conduct a trial *de novo* at which new evidence may be adduced.[329] (This approach

---

[324] IRC § 7428(c)(2)(A).

[325] See § 2.5.

[326] IRC § 7428(c)(3). The IRS publishes the names of organizations that are challenging, under IRC § 7428, the revocation of their status as organizations entitled to receive deductible charitable contributions, so as to inform potential donors to these organizations of the protection, to the extent provided under IRC § 7428(c), for their contributions made during the litigation period (Ann. 85-169, 1985-48 I.R.B. 40). In general, Kittrell, "Administrative Prerequisites for Declaratory Judgments about Tax Issues," 66 *A.B.A.J.* 1570 (1980); Roady, "Declaratory Judgments for 501(c)(3) Status Determinations: End of a 'Harsh Regime'," 30 *Tax Law.* 765 (1977).

[327] *The Synanon Church v. United States, supra* note 266.

[328] Rules of Practice and Procedure, U.S. Tax Court, Title XXI.

[329] *Id.,* Rule 217(a). E.g., The Nationalist Movement v. Comm'r, 64 T.C.M. 1479 (1992); Dr. Erol Bastug, Inc. v. Comm'r, 57 T.C.M. 562 (1989); Colorado State Chiropractic Soc'y, Inc. v. Comm'r, 56 T.C.M. 1018 (1989); Liberty Ministries Int'l v. Comm'r, 48 T.C.M. 105 (1984); Unitary Mission Church v. Comm'r, 74 T.C. 507 (1980). The U.S. Tax Court is concerned about "fishing expeditions" in these situations (e.g., Wisconsin Psychiatric Servs. v. Comm'r, 76 T.C. 839, 846 (1981)). The U.S. Tax Court has allowed supplementation of the administrative record in one denial case (First Libertarian Church v. Comm'r, 74 T.C. 396 (1980)). However, the U.S. District Court for the District of Columbia appears more willing to review facts beyond the administrative record (Freedom Church of Revelation v. United States, 588 F.

does not apply where the tax exemption has been revoked.) Thus, in one case, the court refused to permit information orally furnished to IRS representatives during a conference at the administrative level to be introduced in evidence during the pendency of the case before the court.[330] Likewise, it was held that the administrative record can consist only of material submitted by either the applicant organization or the IRS, so that materials submitted by third parties are inadmissible.[331] Similarly, the court is to base its decision upon only theories advanced in the IRS notice or at trial, and not upon arguments advanced anew by the IRS during the litigation.[332]

The U.S. Tax Court suggested that, if an organization that has been denied tax exemption and did not prevail before it has material information previously excluded from the administrative record, the organization may file a new application for recognition of exemption and that the principles of *res judicata* would not preclude the court from reviewing a denial of the subsequent application.[333]

The general Tax Court scheme for the processing of these declaratory judgment cases is being adopted, on a case-by-case basis, by both the U.S. District Court for the District of Columbia and the U.S. Court of Federal Claims. This approach includes basic reliance upon the administrative record, with court review *de novo* only in unusual cases.[334]

An organization's fate before a court may well depend on the quality of the contents of the administrative record. It is highly significant that the applicant organization generally controls what comprises the administrative record. Even when the record includes responses to IRS inquiries, it is the organization that de-

---

Supp. 693 (D.D.C. 1984); Incorporated Trustees of the Gospel Worker Soc'y v. United States, *supra* note 9; cf. Airlie Found., Inc. v. United States, 92-2 U.S.T.C. ¶ 50,462 (D.D.C. 1992)). Because the Tax Court will render a declaratory judgment in a nonrevocation case upon the petition, the answer, and the administrative record, it has held that a motion for summary judgment in that court is "superfluous" and "pointless" (Pulpit Resource v. Comm'r, 70 T.C. 594, 602 (1978)).

[330] Houston Lawyer Referral Serv., Inc. v. Comm'r 69 T.C. 570 (1978). Also Church in Boston v. Comm'r, 71 T.C. 102 (1979).

[331] Church of Spiritual Technology v. United States, 90-1 U.S.T.C. ¶ 50,097 (Ct. Cl. 1989). In one case, a court ruled that transcripts from the criminal trials and the grand jury materials from the criminal case, involving the founder and executive director of an organization, were part of the administrative record in a subsequent case where the organization's ongoing tax-exempt status was at issue (Airlie Found., Inc. v. United States, *supra* note 329).

[332] Peoples Translation Service/Newsfront Int. v. Comm'r, 72 T.C. 42 (1979); Goodspeed Scholarship Fund v. Comm'r, 70 T.C. 515, 520–525 (1978); Schuster's Express, Inc. v. Comm'r, 66 T.C. 588, 593 (1976), *aff'd*, 562 F.2d 39 (2d Cir. 1977).

[333] Houston Lawyer Referral Serv., Inc. v. Comm'r, *supra* note 330, at 577–578.

[334] E.g. Southwest Va. Professional Standards Review Org., Inc. v. United States, 78-2 U.S.T.C. ¶ 9747 (D.D.C. 1978); Animal Protection Inst., Inc. v. United States, 78-2 U.S.T.C. ¶ 9709 (Ct. Cl. 1978).

In Synanon Church v. United States, 579 F. Supp. 967 (D.D.C. 1984), *aff'd*, 87-1 U.S.T.C. ¶ 9347 (D.C. Cir. 1987), the court dismissed the case on the ground of fraud upon the court, based upon the court's finding that the organization destroyed material records.

The U.S. Tax Court will not consolidate a declaratory judgment case with a regular deficiency case, even where the issues are the same and a trial may be available in both instances, according to the opinion in Centre for Int'l Understanding v. Comm'r, 84 T.C. 279 (1985).

The Tax Court ruled that an IRC § 7428 declaratory judgment petition may be dismissed for failure of the organization to prosecute the case, in Basic Bible Church of Am. v. Comm'r, 86 T.C. 110 (1986).

cides the phraseology of the answers and what, if anything, to attach as exhibits. It is, therefore, highly important that the administrative record be carefully crafted, particularly in instances where there is a reasonable likelihood that an initial determination case will be unsuccessful at the IRS level and thus ripen into a declaratory judgment case.

As an illustration, a court had before it the issue as to whether an organization that operated a mountain lodge as a retreat facility could qualify as a religious organization. The opinion in the case clearly reflected the court's view that this type of an organization can so qualify under appropriate circumstances, yet the particular organization involved lost the case primarily because the administrative record did not show that the recreational facilities were used for tax-exempt purposes or otherwise used only in an insubstantial manner.[335] By contrast, where the administrative record is able to show that an organization is advancing exempt purposes by means of a religious retreat, the courts will not deprive the organization of tax exemption, even where the retreats are held in an environment somewhat more attractive than the wilderness.[336]

The impact of this declaratory judgment procedure on the administrative practice before the IRS cannot be underestimated. In the past, the IRS could be confident that, with rare exception, its determination as to a charitable organization's status was the final one. That is, because of the large amount of legal fees, expenses, and time required to litigate, the IRS knew that judicial review of one of its decisions in this area would be highly unlikely.

With the advent of the declaratory judgment rules, all this has dramatically changed. No longer can the IRS make its decisions with the luxury of assuming their finality. Now, the IRS, in approaching this decision-making process, must do so with awareness of the greatly increased possibility of a challenge in court. This means that the IRS, obviously reluctant to have a total rebuff in the casebooks as precedent, may well be forced to issue favorable rulings in instances where the contrary would otherwise be the case. Also, these procedures can force the IRS to act more quickly than it may otherwise be disposed to do.

In a 1979 episode, the IRS refused to rule on an exemption request, saying that the issue raised was under study. Once the 270-day administrative remedies period expired, the organization launched a lawsuit. Within 60 days after the complaint was filed, the Department of Justice made it known that the IRS was willing to issue a favorable ruling (thereby mooting the case). Thus, within $2^1/_2$ months after instituting a declaratory judgment request, the organization came into possession of a favorable ruling, under circumstances where, if this form of relief were not available, the IRS probably would not have acted for some time or would have issued an unfavorable determination.[337]

---

[335] The Schoger Foundation v. Comm'r, 76 T.C. 380 (1981). The organization attempted the argument that the administrative record did not show that the recreational facilities were used in more than an insubstantial manner but this failed because, under the U.S. Tax Court Rules of Practice and Procedure (Rule 217 (c)(2)(i)), the organization has the burden of showing that the determination of the IRS is incorrect. Cf. Alive Fellowship of Harmonious Living v. Comm'r, 47 T.C.M. 1134 (1984).

[336] Junaluska Assembly Hous., Inc. v. Comm'r, 86 T.C. 1114 (1986).

[337] Infant Formula Action Coalition v. United States (C.A. No. 79-0129, D.D.C.); also Fair Campaign Practices Comm., Inc. v. United States (C.A. No. 77-0830, D.D.C.).

These procedures are not solely of consequence to the new organization that is struggling to obtain its tax exemption and/or its private foundation/public charity status. They are also of immense significance to the established charitable (including educational, religious, and scientific) organization or institution, the tax status of which is, or appears to be, immune from revocation or other disturbance. This declaratory judgment provision is having a considerable impact on development of the law applicable to charitable organizations.

The courts are holding a variety of organizations to be tax-exempt entities, in rejection of IRS positions. As illustrations, the courts have concluded, notwithstanding the opposition of the IRS, that health maintenance organizations,[338] professional standards review organization foundations,[339] consumer credit counseling agencies,[340] and private schools providing custodial services for young pupils[341] can qualify for tax exemption. Not surprisingly, courts are also upholding the IRS position, such as in the case of genealogical societies,[342] communal groups,[343] and certain scholarship funds.[344] Interpretations of the private foundation definition rules have gone for and against the government.[345]

Consequently, the growing use of these procedures creates a significant impact on the law encompassing the reach of the tax exemption for charitable organizations. This can be of considerable importance in the continuing preservation of organizations' tax-exempt and/or private foundation classifications.

Moreover, the breadth of the issues being raised by these cases is fostering the rapid development of law in areas related to tax exemption other than as respects the exemption categories themselves. Chief among these areas being explored and expounded upon is the doctrine of private inurement.[346] Many of these cases under review and being decided are turning on the question of whether private interests are being unduly served. Thus, two courts have found that genealogical societies improperly (for tax exemption purposes) provide personal services to members when the societies help their members research their ancestry.[347] One set of cases has resulted in opinions that there is unwarranted private inurement with respect to a religious organization because of its communal structure, where meals, lodging, and other life necessities are provided to the ministers.[348] Other decisions contain analyses as to why particular facts may con-

---

[338] Sound Health Assn v. Comm'r, 71 T.C. 158 (1978).

[339] Virginia Professional Standards Review Found. v. Blumenthal, 466 F. Supp. 1164 (D.D.C. 1979).

[340] Consumer Credit Counseling Serv. of Ala., Inc. v. United States, 78-2 U.S.T.C. ¶ 9660 (D.D.C. 1978).

[341] San Francisco Infant School, Inc. v. Comm'r, 69 T.C. 957 (1978); Michigan Early Childhood Center, Inc. v. Comm'r, 37 T.C.M. 808 (1978). Also § 7.7.

[342] The Callaway Family Ass'n, Inc. v. Comm'r, 71 T.C. 340 (1978); Benjamin Price Genealogical Ass'n v. Internal Revenue Service, 79-1 U.S.T.C. ¶ 9361 (D.D.C. 1979). Also Manning Ass'n v. Comm'r, 93 T.C. 596 (1989) (holding that an association of descendants of a settler from England in the United States in the 1600s did not qualify for tax exemption as an educational organization, in part because of the compilation of genealogical information).

[343] Beth-El Ministries, Inc. v. United States, 79-2 U.S.T.C. ¶ 9412 (D.D.C. 1979).

[344] Miss Georgia Scholarship Fund, Inc. v. Comm'r, 72 T.C. 267 (1979).

[345] E.g., William F., Mabel E., & Margaret K. Quarrie Charitable Fund v. Comm'r, 70 T.C. 182 (1978), aff'd, 603 F.2d 1274 (7th Cir. 1979).

[346] See Chapter 19.

[347] See supra note 342.

[348] See supra note 343.

cern educational efforts,[349] or may involve private inurement, or why the inurement that is present is either insubstantial or unavoidable and incidental.[350]

These cases are also triggering examinations of the requirement that charitable organizations be organized and operated exclusively for tax-exempt purposes. The parameters of this requirement are being tested by cases that involve questions such as whether, or the extent to which, a charitable organization can operate at a profit or can provide services to members.[351]

The courts in these declaratory judgment cases are also paying close attention to the technical essentials of the organizational test.[352] In one case, a court ruled that an organization could not qualify for tax exemption because of a defect in its articles of organization, in that the articles did not expressly preclude the possibility of a violation of the test by operation of state law.[353]

Both current and future developments will have an enormous impact on the revision and expansion of the federal tax law applicable to charitable organizations. All indications are that representatives of charitable organizations are acquiring a better understanding of the declaratory judgment procedures—not only the basics, but the planning aspects, such as shaping the administrative record, timely (albeit prudent) introduction at the administrative level of the possibility of a declaratory judgment action, and selection of the proper forum. These procedures are rewriting federal tax law affecting charitable organizations on many fronts, and the organizations and their advisors should monitor these cases to glean applicable legal principles—and not be reluctant to initiate a declaratory judgment action where the organization's interests warrant doing so.

(c) Other Approaches

Other jurisdictional options are open to the organization confronted with revocation (or denial) of tax-exempt status. Where charitable contributions are involved, a "friendly donor" may bring an action contesting the legality of the IRS disal-

---

[349] Big Mama Rag, Inc. v. United States, 631 F.2d 1030 (D.C. Cir. 1980), *rev'g and rem'g*, 494 F. Supp. 473 (D.D.C. 1979); Afro-American Purchasing Center, Inc. v. Comm'r, 37 T.C.M. 184 (1978).

[350] Christian Stewardship Assistance, Inc. v. Comm'r, 70 T.C. 1037 (1978), *aff'd*, 647 F.2d 170 (9th Cir. 1981); Est of Hawaii v. Comm'r, 71 T.C. 1067 (1979); Federation Pharmacy Servs. Inc. v. Comm'r, 72 T.C. 687 (1979), *aff'd*, 625 F.2d 804 (8th Cir. 1980).

[351] Pulpit Resource v. Comm'r, *supra* note 329, *supra*; National Ass'n for the Legal Support of Alternative Schools v. Comm'r, 71 T.C. 118 (1978); Aid to Artisans, Inc. v. Comm'r, 71 T.C. 202 (1978); Christian Manner Int'l, Inc. v. Comm'r, 71 T.C. 661 (1979); Peoples Translation Service/Newsfront Int'l v. Comm'r, *supra* note 332;, Industrial Aid for the Blind v. Comm'r, 73 T.C. 96 (1979); The Schoger Found. v. Comm'r, *supra* note 335.

[352] See § 4.3.

[353] General Conference of the Free Church of Am. v. Comm'r, 71 T.C. 920 (1979). In general, Lehrfeld, "Section 501(c)(3) Appeals—Declaratory Judgments for Establishing Exemption," 43 *N.Y.U. Inst. on Fed. Tax.* 18 (1985); Winslow & Ash, "Forum Shopping Has Distinct Advantages in Seeking Declaratory Judgments on Exemption," 51 *J. Tax.* 112 (1979); McGovern, "The New Declaratory Judgment Provision for 501(c)(3) Organizations: How It Works," 47 *J. Tax.* 222 (1977); Black, "Exempt Organizations—Declaratory Judgments," 1976 *Tax No. 14* 2 (1976); Colvin, "Contesting Loss of Exemption Under I.R.C. Section 501(c)(3) After *Bob Jones University* and *'Americans United' Inc.,*" 34 *Fed. Bar J.* 182 (1975); Lewis, "Revocation of Tax Exemptions—Current Problems," 1974 *Tax Mgmt. (BOSA) Memo. No. 20* 3 (1974); Schroer, "Applicability of Prohibition of Suits to Restrain Assessment and Collection of Taxes to Revocation of Tax Exemptions Under Section 501(c)(3) of the Internal Revenue Code," 73 *Col. L. Rev.* 1502 (1973).

lowance of the charitable deduction, which generally will involve the same is-sue(s) as those relating to the exemption.[354] However, a donor suit requires a plaintiff who is also willing to be subjected to a tax audit and the organization may lose control over the management of the litigation. An organization may also sue for refund of FUTA taxes,[355] excise taxes[356], or wagering taxes.[357] While these avenues of review can take much more time than a declaratory judgment action, they do offer the distinct advantage of enabling the organization to initiate the lit-igation in a federal court geographically proximate to it.

Conventional declaratory judgment suits[358] are of no avail in this setting, as the Declaratory Judgment Act expressly excludes controversies over federal taxes from its purview.[359]

One of the considerations in determining the nature of litigation in the tax-exempt organizations context is the likelihood of the award of reasonable litiga-tion costs. This type of award can be made in the case of a civil proceeding brought by or against the United States in connection with the determination, col-lection, or refund of any federal tax.[360] This award is accorded to the prevailing party that establishes that the position of the government in the proceeding "was not substantially justified" and has substantially prevailed with respect to the amount in controversy or the "most significant issue or set of issues presented."[361] However, an award is not available with respect to any declaratory judgment proceeding, other than a proceeding that involves the revocation of a determina-tion that the organization is a charitable entity.[362]

Once an organization has secured a final determination from the courts that it is tax-exempt, and if the material facts and law have not changed since court consideration, the IRS will, upon request, issue a ruling or determination letter recognizing the tax exemption. However, if the organization did not previously file an application for recognition of exempt status, the IRS will not issue a ruling or determination letter until the application is submitted.[363]

Absent relief administratively or in the courts, an organization facing loss of tax-exempt status may have no choice but to accept the revocation, discontinue the disqualifying activity (if its activities are sufficiently separable), and reestab-

---

[354] E.g., Teich v. Comm'r, 48 T.C. 963 (1967), *aff'd*, 407 F.2d 815 (7th Cir. 1969); Krohn v. United States, 246 F. Supp. 341 (D. Col. 1965); Kuper v. Comm'r, 332 F.2d 562 (3d Cir. 1964), *cert. den.*, 379 U.S. 902 (1964); Bolton v. Comm'r, 1 T.C. 717 (1943).

[355] IRC § 3306(c)(8).

[356] IRC § 4253(h).

[357] IRC § 4421. Also Rochester Liederkranz, Inc. v. United States, 456 F.2d 152 (2d Cir. 1972); Hessman v. Campbell, 134 F. Supp. 415 (S.D. Ind. 1955).

[358] 28 U.S.C. §§ 2201–2202.

[359] E.g., Ecclesiastical Order of the ISM of AM, Inc. v. Internal Revenue Service, 725 F.2d 398 (6th Cir. 1984); Mitchell v. Riddell, 401 F.2d 842 (9th Cir. 1968), *cert. den.*, 394 U.S. 456 (1969); In re Wingreen Co., 412 F.2d 1048 (5th Cir. 1969); Jolles Found., Inc. v. Moysey, 250 F.2d 1966 (2d Cir. 1957); The Church of the New Testament, Its Members & Friends v. United States, 85-1 U.S.T.C. ¶ 9227 (E.D. Col. 1984); In-ternational Tel. & Tel. Corp. v. Alexander, 396 F. Supp. 1150 (D. Del. 1975); Kyron Found. v. Dunlop, 110 F. Supp. 428 (D.D.C. 1952).

[360] IRC § 7430(a).

[361] IRC § 7430(c)(2).

[362] IRC § 7430(b)(3).

[363] Rev. Proc. 80-28, 1980-1 C.B. 680.

lish its exemption,[364] or spin the disqualifying activity off into a taxable subsidiary[365] or auxiliary exempt organization[366] and reestablish its exemption. Or, the organization may attempt an alternative to formal tax-exempt status, such as by operating as a nonexempt cooperative.[367]

§ 24.7   THIRD-PARTY LITIGATION

As noted at the outset, an organization's tax-exempt status may be maintained absent a material change in the pertinent facts or a change in the law.[368] The organization generally will have control over the former circumstances but relatively little opportunity to affect the latter. One way, however, to have an impact on the development of the law of tax-exempt organizations is to bring a third-party lawsuit.

(a) Third-Party Lawsuits in General

A third-party suit in this context is an action brought by one or more persons as a challenge to an IRS policy in administering the tax-exempt organizations or other tax law. The person bringing suit is rarely a taxpayer, and this type of a suit is not framed as a conventional U.S. Tax Court or refund suit. Those sued are the Secretary of the Treasury and/or the Commissioner of Internal Revenue. Depending on the outcome of the suit, the resulting change in law can have considerable implications for one or more categories of tax-exempt organizations.

The present-day third-party policy suit challenging a principle of the law of tax-exempt organizations is an amalgam of a series of "public interest" suits in the tax field[369] and a variety of tax suits raising constitutional questions. As respects the latter, in the principal case, the courts involved concluded that racially discriminatory private schools were not entitled to federal tax exemption.[370] Comparable cases, with fainter relationships to constitutional principles, led to decisions that racially discriminatory fraternal organizations were not entitled to

---

[364] Compare Danz v. Comm'r, 18 T.C. 454 (1952), aff'd, 231 F.2d 673 (9th Cir. 1955), cert. den., 352 U.S. 828 (1956), reh. den., 353 U.S. 951 (1957), with John Danz Charitable Trust v. Comm'r, 32 T.C. 469 (1959), aff'd, 284 F.2d 726 (9th Cir. 1960).

[365] American Inst. for Economic Research, Inc. v. United States, 302 F.2d 934 (Ct. Cl. 1962), cert. den., 372 U.S. 976 (1963); Rev. Rul. 54-243, 1954-1 C.B. 92.

[366] Center on Corporate Responsibility, Inc. v. Shultz, supra note 269.

[367] See § 3.4. In general, Friedland, "Constitutional Issues in Revoking Religious Tax Exemptions: Church of Scientology of California v. Comm'r," 39 U. Fla. L. Rev. 565 (1985); Yaffa, "The Revocation of Tax Exemptions and Tax Deductions for Donations to 501(c)(3) Organizations on Statutory and Constitutional Grounds," 30 U.C.L.A. L. Rev. 156 (1982).

[368] See text accompanied by supra notes 2–4.

[369] E.g., Tax Analysts & Advocates v. Shultz, 376 F. Supp. 889 (D.D.C. 1974); Tax Analysts & Advocates v. Internal Revenue Service., 362 F. Supp. 1298 (D.D.C. 1973); Common Cause v. Shultz, 73-2 U.S.T.C. ¶ 9592 (D.D.C. 1973).

[370] Green v. Kennedy, 309 F. Supp. 1127 (D.D.C. 1970); app. dis. sub nom. Cannon v. Green, 398 U.S. 956 (1970), cont. sub nom. Green v. Connally, 330 F. Supp. 1150 (D.D.C. 1971), aff'd on intervenors' appeal sub nom. Coit v. Green, 404 U.S. 997 (1971). See § 5.4(a).

tax exemption,[371] although racially discriminatory social clubs[372] were not barred from tax-exempt status,[373] that charitable organizations will not lose their tax law categorization because they discriminate in their membership policies on the basis of sex,[374] and that unions that expend membership dues for partisan political campaigns do not for that reason forfeit their tax-exempt status.[375]

These cases have given rise, however, to cases that strictly involve "policy" questions—questions previously answered only by the Department of the Treasury in its regulations, the IRS in its rulings, or the courts in passing on the tax status of particular organizations who were parties to the suit. The most prominent case in this category caused the U.S. Court of Appeals for the District of Columbia Circuit to consider IRS policy as to the criteria for a tax-exempt hospital and pronounce a revision of that policy valid.[376] A comparable case initiated in 1974 unsuccessfully sought to enjoin Treasury and IRS officials from granting charitable status to otherwise charitable organizations that substantially provide commercial travel services and from refusing to enforce the unrelated business income tax provisions.[377] Similarly, a for-profit consulting company failed in its attempt to cause the revocation of the tax-exempt status of a nonprofit research organization for the latter's refusal to include the company's product in its research and testing program.[378] Likewise, individuals who claimed they were forced out of the restaurant business because of the competitive activities of tax-exempt social clubs were unsuccessful in their effort to have the clubs' tax exemptions revoked.[379]

The continuing viability of these types of cases is somewhat questionable, since the U.S. Supreme court is seeking to extinguish this type of third-party litigation.[380] It has chosen to accomplish this end by issuing opinions articulating its concept of the law of standing.[381] In one instance, the court, in a case initiated by indigents and organizations of indigents seeking judicial review of IRS criteria for exempting nonprofit hospitals from income tax, held that the plaintiffs lacked standing to bring the suit within the framework of Article III of the U.S. Constitution, which requires the existence of an authentic "case or controversy." Nonetheless, the court stated that "[we] do not reach. . . . the question of whether a third party *ever* may challenge the IRS treatment of another. . . ."[382]

---

[371] See § 18.4(a).

[372] See Chapter 14.

[373] McGlotten v. Connally, 338 F. Supp. 448 (1972).

[374] McCoy v. Shultz, 73-1 U.S.T.C. ¶ 9233 (D.D.C. 1973).

[375] IRC § 501(c)(5). Marker v. Connally, 485 F.2d 1003 (D.C. Cir. 1973), aff'g 837 F. Supp. 1301 (D.D.C. 1972).

[376] Eastern Kentucky Welfare Rights Org. v. Simon, 560 F.2d 1278 D.C. Cir. 1974), rev'g 370 F. Supp. 325 (D.D.C. 1973). Also Penn v. San Juan Hosp. Inc., 528 F.2d 1181 (10th Cir. 1975).

[377] American Soc'y of Travel Agents v. Simon, 75-1 U.S.T.C. ¶ 9484 (D.D.C. 1975), aff'd, 556 F.2d 145 (D.C. Cir. 1977), *cert. den.*, 435 U.S. 947 (1978). Also Pharmaceutical & Diagnostic Serv's, Inc. v. The Univ. of Utah, 1989 U.S. Dist. LEXIS 11857 (D. Utah 1989); Council of British Soc. in S. Calif. v. United States, 78-2 U.S.T.C. ¶ 9744 (C.D. Cal. 1978).

[378] Research Consulting Assocs., Inc. v. Electric Power Research Inst., 626 F. Supp. 1330 (D. Mass. 1986).

[379] Drake v. North Dakota, 1995 U.S. Dist. LEXIS 8967 (D.N.D. 1995).

[380] Simon v. Eastern Ky. Welfare Rights Org., 426 U.S. 26 (1976).

[381] See text accompanied by *infra* notes 398–437.

[382] Simon v. Eastern Ky. Welfare Rights Org., *supra* note 380 at 37 (emphasis added).

Still, the standing test as formulated in this decision was designed to curb the type of litigation represented by that case. The Court summarized the standing requirement as follows: ". . . when a plaintiff's standing is brought into issue the relevant inquiry is whether, assuming justiciability of the claim, the plaintiff has shown an injury to himself that is likely to be redressed by a favorable decision."[383] The court's interpretation of that requirement in this context means that "an organization's abstract concern with a subject that could be affected by an adjudication does not substitute for the concrete injury required by Article III."[384] Thus, the plaintiffs in the case lost because they could not demonstrate the needed "concrete injury" (stated in a previous decision as the requisite "personal stake in the outcome of the controversy"[385]) and because, even if the hospitals had caused injury, the plaintiffs proceeded not against those institutions but against federal officials. (The second, "non-constitutional" standing requirement that the interest of a plaintiff be "arguably within the zone of interests to be protected or regulated" by the statutory framework within which his or her claim arises[386] went unconsidered in the opinion.[387])

The author of a concurring opinion in this case observed that "I cannot now imagine a case, at least outside the First Amendment area, where a person whose own tax liability was not affected ever could have standing to litigate the federal tax liability of someone else."[388] However, this gratuitous comment is unduly broad. For example, an organization ruled by the IRS to be a supported organization pursuant to the public charity/private foundation rules[389] would have standing to bring suit against the Secretary of the Treasury and Commissioner of Internal Revenue contesting the legality of the determination on the ground that the alleged supporting organization was not in compliance with the statute's essentials (thereby depriving the alleged supported organization of funds) and thus is liable for the taxes imposed on private foundations.

One justice criticized his brethren for not deciding the case against the plaintiffs on the ground that the case involved largely hypothetical situations and hence not a ripe controversy. He also complained that the majority unnecessarily and erroneously treated the "injury-in-fact" standing requirement in a manner in direct conflict with prior decisions of the court, in part by laying down a standard of pleading of facts not "in keeping with modern notions of civil procedure."[390]

---

[383] *Id.* at 38.

[384] *Id.* at 40, citing Sierra Club v. Morton, 405 U.S. 727 (1972).

[385] Warth v. Seldin, 422 U.S. 490, 498 (1975).

[386] Association of Data Processing Serv. Org. v. Camp, 397 U.S. 150, 153 (1969). In Wright v. Regan, 81-2 U.S.T.C. ¶ 9504 (D.C. Cir. 1981), the U.S. Court of Appeals for the District of Columbia Circuit held that the parents of black public school children had standing to bring a class action suit claiming that IRC § 501(a) promoted discrimination by permitting recognition of tax exemption of racially discriminatory private schools. Also Tax Analysts v. Blumenthal, 566 F.2d 130 (D.C. Cir. 1977), *cert. den.*, 434 U.S. 1086 (1977).

[387] Commentary on the *Eastern Kentucky* case appears in Note, 30 *Tax Law.* 490 (1977); Note, 1977 *Wis. L. Rev.* 247 (1977); Note, 29 *Tax Law.* 361 (1976); Note, 7 *U. Toledo L. Rev.* 278 (1975); Note, 73 *Col. L. Rev.* 1502 (1973).

[388] Simon v. Eastern Ky. Welfare Rights Org., *supra* note 380, at 46.

[389] See Chapter 11.

[390] Simon v. Eastern Ky. Welfare Rights Org., *supra* note 380, at 62.

On this latter point, this justice stated that, in Administrative Procedure Act cases, "standing is not to be denied merely because the ultimate harm alleged is a threatened future one rather than an accomplished fact."[391] (The "ultimate harm" alleged in the case was that tax-exempt hospitals, as encouraged by the IRS, would cease providing medical services to indigents.) The justice did some hypothesizing of his own,[392] wondering if, as the result of the opinion, "minority school children [will] now have to plead and show that in the absence of illegal governmental 'encouragement' of private segregated schools, such schools would not 'elect to forego' their favorable tax treatment, and that this will 'result in the availability' to complainants of an integrated educational system"[393] or if "black Americans [will] be required to plead and show that in the absence of illegal government encouragement, private institutions would not 'elect to forego' favorable tax treatment, and that this will 'result in the availability' to complain[an]ts of services previously denied."[394]

This justice found the "most disturbing aspect" of the opinion to be the court's "insistence on resting its decision regarding standing squarely on the irreducible Art. III minimum of injury in fact, thereby effectively placing its holding beyond congressional power to rectify."[395] He added: "Thus, any time Congress chooses to legislate in favor of certain interests by setting up a scheme of incentives for third parties, judicial review of administrative action that allegedly frustrates the congressionally intended objective will be denied, because any complainant will be required to make an almost impossible showing."[396] What this augurs for the future is unclear. He stated the ultimate objective well: "In our modern-day society, dominated by complex legislative programs and large-scale governmental involvement in the everyday lives of all of us, judicial review of administrative action is essential both for protection of individuals illegally harmed by that action. . . . and to ensure that the attainment of congressionally mandated goals is not frustrated by illegal action."[397]

(b) Standing

The impact of the U.S. Supreme Court's pronouncement on this subject has been somewhat moderated as the result of enactment by Congress of the declaratory judgment procedures for contesting loss or denial of tax-exempt and similar status for charitable organizations. Although third-party suits are not involved as such, these procedures are greatly enhancing the likelihood and frequency of court review of IRS determinations in the tax-exempt organizations field.

Although generally outside the scope of this work, it may be helpful to

---

[391] *Id.* at 61.

[392] *Id.* at 63.

[393] Citing Green v. Kennedy, *supra* note 370.

[394] Citing McGlotten v. Connally, *supra* note 373; Pitts v. Wisconsin Dep't of Revenue, 333 F. Supp. 662 (E.D. Wis. 1971).

[395] Simon v. Eastern Ky. Welfare Rights Org., *supra* note 380, at 64.

[396] *Id.*

[397] *Id.* at 65. In general, Sheldon & Bostock, "Supreme Court Severely Limits Third Party's Right to Contest Exempt Status," 45 J. Tax. 140 (1976).

briefly summarize the jurisdictional and related issues raised by these third-party cases. Despite the government's attempts to invoke the doctrine of sovereign immunity, the courts have generally held that the doctrine does not bar actions against government officials who allegedly are acting in excess of their statutory authority or discretion or in an unconstitutional manner.[398] The general prohibition on injunctive relief[399] was held to not be a bar to these suits because they bear no relation to assessment or collection of taxes.[400] The Declaratory Judgment Act likewise was found to not be a bar to jurisdiction, on the ground that its scope is coterminous with the injunctive relief rule.[401]

Aside from these and other alleged bars to jurisdiction, the courts have held that various statutes provide jurisdiction. Thus, jurisdiction in these cases has been fully asserted on the basis of the Administrative Procedure Act[402] and the Declaratory Judgment Act, the pendent jurisdiction rules,[403] and the more conventional jurisdictional basis.[404] Still another hurdle these suits, in many instances, have cleared is *standing*, which is a prerequisite of any court action. Basically, a plaintiff must be able to demonstrate a direct injury and the requisite personal stake in the controversy.[405] The focus of these principles is far from clear,[406] as the above-discussed U.S. Supreme Court decision indicates.

The future of third-party suits in the tax-exempt organizations field is uncertain, in view of the above-discussed Supreme Court opinion and the decision of Congress to confine the tax-exempt organizations declaratory judgment procedure to use "by the organization the qualification or classification of which is at issue."[407] In the first case to be considered by a court of appeals following the Supreme Court's ruling, the appellate court had deferred its consideration of the case pending the Supreme Court's determination and, once the Supreme Court acted, affirmed the lower court's dismissal of the case but on the ground of lack of standing.[408] The court concluded that the plaintiff organization failed to demonstrate any actual injury resulting from the administration of the tax laws, with respect to third parties, governing tax-exempt organizations.

Certainly this line of litigation produced much uncertainty about the appro-

---

[398] E.g., Dugan v. Rank, 372 U.S. 609 (1963); State Highway Comm'n of Mo. v. Volpe, 479 F.2d 1099 (8th Cir. 1973). So held in Eastern Ky. Welfare Rights Org. v. Simon, *supra* note 376; McGlotten v. Connally, *supra* note 373.

[399] IRC § 7421(a).

[400] Eastern Ky. Welfare Rights Org. v. Simon, *supra* note 376; McGlotten v. Connally, *supra* note 373.

[401] E.g., Jules Hairstylists of Md. v. United States, 268 F. Supp. 511 (D. Md. 1967), *aff'd*, 389 F.2d 389 (4th Cir. 1968), *cert. den.*, 391 U.S. 934 (1968). So held in, e.g., Eastern Ky. Welfare Rights Org. v. Simon, *supra* note 376; "Americans United" Inc. v. Walters, *supra* note 267, at 447 F.2d 1176.

[402] 5 U.S.C. §§ 702, 703. Also Eastern Ky. Welfare Rights Org. v. Simon, *supra* note 376.

[403] 28 U.S.C. §§ 2282, 2284. E.g., Zemel v. Rusk, 381 U.S. 1 (1965).

[404] 28 U.S.C. §§ 1331, 1340, 1361.

[405] Frothingham v. Mellon, 262 U.S. 447 (1923); Flast v. Cohen, 392 U.S. 83 (1968); Association of Data Processing Serv. Org. v. Camp, *supra* note 325; Tax Analysts Advocates v. Simon, 390 F. Supp. 927 (D.D.C. 1975).

[406] United States v. Richardson, 418 U.S. 166 (1974); Schlesinger v. Reservists Comm. to Stop the War, 418 U.S. 208 (1974); United States v. Students Challenging Regulatory Agency Procedures, 412 U.S. 669 (1973).

[407] IRC § 7428(b)(1).

[408] American Soc'y of Travel Agents, Inc. v. Simon, *supra* note 377.

priate tax treatment of particular activities and programs of tax-exempt organizations.[409] Moreover, these cases generated considerable controversy as to the proper roles of the courts, the IRS, and the Department of the Treasury in formulating the law of tax-exempt organizations.[410]

Nonetheless, third-party litigation over tax exemption issues continues. As illustrations, the debate over the tax status of private schools with racially discriminatory policies was resumed, in part, because the original litigation was reopened,[411] and the challenge on equal protection grounds to the disparate treatment of charitable and veterans' groups that lobby was, for a while, successful.[412]

One of the most striking examples of third-party litigation in the tax-exempt organizations setting arose in mid-1982, when a federal district court ruled that a variety of organizations and individuals had standing to challenge the constitutionality of the government's alleged refusal to enforce the restrictions in the general rules for charitable organizations on legislative and political campaign involvements[413] against a church.[414] The plaintiffs in the case sued the Secretary of the Treasury and the Commissioner of Internal Revenue on the ground that they failed in their responsibility to revoke the tax-exempt status of the church because of its alleged legislative and electioneering activities. These activities were seen by the plaintiffs, which included a charitable organization, as being in direct conflict with the limitations on lobbying and electioneering in the tax law under which the church and its affiliates continue to be tax-exempt. By contrast, the plaintiffs assered that the IRS has refused to grant to organizations with opposing views (such as the plaintiff tax-exempt organization) tax exemption as charitable entities where they engage in comparable legislative and electioneering activities. The plaintiffs contended that this was discriminatory tax policy that was unconstitutional, illegal, and unfair.

Before considering the claims of these plaintiffs on their merits, the court had to dispose of a variety of motions, including the government's motion to dismiss for lack of standing. The court considered three bases for standing: establishment clause standing, voter standing, and equal protection standing. The essential elements for standing, said the court, are a "distinct and palpable injury" to the plaintiff, a "fairly traceable causal connection between the claimed injury and the challenged conduct," and a showing that the "exercise of the Court's remedial powers would redress the claimed injuries."[415]

As to establishment clause standing, most of the plaintiffs were found to have failed the injury-in-fact test. Said the court: "Plaintiffs' devotion to . . . [its]

---

[409] E.g., Jackson v. Statler Found., 496 F.2d 623 (2d Cir. 1974).

[410] Tannenbaum, "Public Interest Tax Litigation Challenging Substantive I.R.S. Decisions," 27 *Nat'l Tax J.* 373 (1974); Worthy, "Judicial Determinations of Exempt Status: Has the Time Come for a Change of Systems?," 40 *J. Tax.* 324 (1974).

[411] Wright v. Regan, 656 F.2d 820 (D.C. Cir. 1981).

[412] Taxation With Representation of Wash. v. Regan, 676 F.2d 715 (D.C. Cir. 1982).

[413] See Chapters 20, 21.

[414] Abortion Rights Mobilization, Inc. v. Regan, 544 F. Supp. 471 (S.D.N.Y. 1982). Also 552 F. Supp. 364 (S.D.N.Y. 1982).

[415] *Id.* at 476–477.

position does not identify an interest that the allegedly illegal activities have damaged; it only explains why plaintiffs have chosen to complain about a particular government impropriety—renewal of the church defendants' [IRC] § 501(c)(3) status. . . ."[416] However, the plaintiffs who are members of the clergy were found to have shown "compelling and personalized injuries flowing from the tacit government endorsement of the . . . [church's] position on . . . [issues] that are sufficient to confer standing on them to complain of the alleged establishment clause violations."[417] In language that suggested the government was going to lose the case on the merits in this court, the court ruled that the "causation" and "redressability" tests were also satisfied. As to the former, the court said: "The granting of a uniquely favored tax status to one religious entity is an unequivocal statement of preference that gilds the image of that religion and tarnishes all others."[418] As to the latter, the court observed: "A decree ordering the termination of this illegal practice and restoring all sects to equal footing will redress this injury."[419]

Concerning voter standing, the underlying issue was whether some arbitrary government action diluted the strength of voters in one group at the expense of those in another group. Finding this type of standing in the plaintiffs, the court concluded: "Plaintiffs claim that allegedly unconstitutional government conduct and illegal private conduct has distorted the electoral and legislative process by creating a system in which members of the public have greater incentive to donate funds to the . . . [church] than to politically active . . . groups and in which each dollar contributed to the church is worth more than one given to non-exempt [that is, noncharitable donee] organizations."[420] Once again, in language highly suggestive of victory to the plaintiffs (at least at the district court level), the court stated: "An injunction against that discriminatory policy will restore the proper balance between adversaries in the abortion debate."[421]

As to the equal protection basis for standing, the court rejected the contention that the plaintiffs can prevail on any Fifth Amendment grounds. The court also found that the litigation was outside the reach of the Anti-Injunction Act[422] and that conventional declaratory relief[423] was not available to the plaintiffs.[424]

---

[416] *Id.* at 478.

[417] *Id.* at 479.

[418] *Id.* at 480.

[419] *Id.*

[420] *Id.* at 482.

[421] *Id.* Cf. Keane v. Baker, 1987 W.L. 8052 (W.D.N.Y. 1987), where, in holding that a defeated candidate for public office lacks standing to sue the IRS in an attempt to cause revocation of the tax-exempt status of an organization allegedly involved in political campaign activities on behalf of his opponent, a court rejected broad applicability of the concept of voter standing.

[422] IRC § 7421. E.g., In re Heritage Village Church & Missionary Fellowship, Inc., 851 F.2d 104 (4th Cir. 1988).

[423] IRC § 2201.

[424] A similar suit, challenging the tax-exempt status of the World Zionist Organization American Section, Inc., Jewish Agency American Section, Inc., United Israel Appeal, Inc., United Jewish Appeal, Inc., Jewish National Fund, Inc., and Americans for a Safe Israel, Inc., was filed in 1983. However, the case was dismissed in early 1985, shortly after the Supreme Court decisions finding any correlation between tax exemption for allegedly racially discriminatory public schools and denigration of black individuals to be "speculative" (see *infra* notes 425–428) with the court observing that it would be

However, in 1984, the U.S. Supreme Court issued an opinion that made successful third-party lawsuits more difficult to structure.[425] The Court held that parents of black public school children lacked standing to bring an action to force the IRS to adopt more stringent rules to deny tax-exempt status and deductible contributions to racially discriminatory private schools.[426] While the proponents of this litigation did not claim their children were denied access to private schools, they claimed direct injury in the form of denigration suffered by reason of the grant of tax-exempt status to educational institutions that discriminate against members of their race.

The Court analyzed the case or controversy requirement of Article III of the U.S. Constitution, from which is derived the concept of standing. To successfully achieve standing, wrote the Court, a plaintiff must allege personal injury "fairly traceable" to a defendant's allegedly unlawful conduct and likely to be redressed by the requested relief.[427] In the case, the Court ruled that this denigration injury does not constitute judicially cognizable injury, nor does any adverse impact on the plaintiffs' "equal educational opportunities" that may be occasioned as the result of the tax exemption and charitable deduction. As to the latter claim, the Court ruled that the injury alleged is not fairly traceable to any conduct of the IRS.

It thus appeared that lawsuits brought solely to challenge governmental policies, absent the requisite direct injury, would fail on the standing issue. The Court counseled "against recognizing standing in a case brought, not to enforce specific legal obligations whose violation works in direct harm, but to seek a restructuring of the apparatus established by its legal duties."[428]

However, notwithstanding this Supreme Court decision, the court in the church case maintained its position on the standing issue.[429] Unlike the Supreme Court, the district court found the requisite direct link between the injury that was the subject of the complaint and governmental action. Finding a "quasi-offi-

---

"more fanciful still to assume here that the government of Israel is so responsive to changes in U.S. tax laws that the withdrawal of benefits from U.S. contributors will work any alteration whatsoever in the character of its occupation of territory it now holds by force in the Middle East" (Khalaf et al. v. Regan et al., 85-1 U.S.T.C. ¶ 9269 (D.D.C. 1985)). Likewise, a tax-exempt organization formed to advance civil and religious liberties, other religious organizations and then-officials, and individual members of the clergy of various denominations were found to lack standing as taxpayers, citizens, and voters, and as victims of stigmatization, to sue the President, the Secretary of the Treasury, and the United States Ambassador to the Vatican to enjoin the funding of a diplomatic mission to the Vatican and to enjoin the ambassador from engaging in ambassadorial activity (Americans United for Separation of Church & State v. Reagan, 786 F.2d 194 (3d Cir. 1986)).

Litigation against other employees of the Department of the Treasury and IRS is likely to be unsuccessful, in that the employees of these agencies are insulated from lawsuits where reasonable grounds existed for the belief that the challenged actions were appropriate and they acted in good faith (E.g., The Ecclesiastical Order of the ISM of AM, Inc. v. Chasin, 653 F. Supp. 1200 (E.D. Mich. 1986), *aff'd*, 845 F.2d 113 (6th Cir. 1988)).

[425] Allen v. Wright, 468 U.S. 737 (1984).

[426] See § 5.4(a).

[427] Allen v. Wright, *supra* note 425, at 751.

[428] *Id.* at 761. In general, Simon, "Supreme Court Limits Ability of Third Parties to Sue Agencies Such as the IRS," *J. Tax.* (No. 7) 400 (1984).

[429] Abortion Rights Mobilization, Inc. et al. v. Regan, 603 F. Supp. 970 (S.D.N.Y. 1985).

cial imprimatur accorded the anti-abortion activities of the [c]hurch through tax exemptions and the restrictions placed on the establishment clause plaintiffs' political activities by [IRC] § 501(c)(3)," the court held that "[r]edress will come directly from the government's consistent enforcement of the tax laws, not from any change in the political activities of the [c]hurch."[430] Added the court: "The injury alleged . . . [in the case] is unequal footing in the political arena, a condition completely traceable [to] and within the control of the IRS."[431] The court in the case wrote that, "the [Supreme] Court did not close the door on private suits challenging government grants of tax exemption."[432]

Subsequently, however, a federal court of appeals decided that the district court in this case lacked jurisdiction over the matter because the plaintiffs failed to satisfy the standing requirements.[433] The appellate court explored the principles of clergy standing, taxpayer standing, and voter standing as they applied in the context of this case, as well as jurisdiction predicated upon the doctrine of "competitive advocate standing." The court wrote that the clergy plaintiffs "have not been injured in a sufficiently personal way to distinguish themselves from other citizens who are generally aggrieved by a claimed constitutional violation." Taxpayer standing was rejected because of violation of the "basic rule . . . that taxpayers do not have standing to challenge how the federal government spends tax revenue." Voter standing was not found since the "plaintiffs' asserted basis for standing has nothing to do with voting." Competitive advocate standing was held absent "since by their [plaintiffs'] own admission they choose not to match the [c]hurch's alleged electioneering with their own," so that the plaintiffs are not competitors. Addressing the point that, if no one among this diverse group of plaintiffs has standing in this case, then no one could have standing to raise these issues, the appellate court summarily observed that the "lack of a plaintiff to litigate an issue may suggest that the matter is more appropriately dealt with by Congress and the political process." By reason of this holding that none of the plaintiffs in this case had standing, the appellate court concluded that the district court lacked subject matter jurisdiction. Subsequently, the U.S. Supreme Court declined to review this case, thereby ending a decade of litigation over the issue.[434]

---

[430] *Id.* at 973.

[431] *Id.* at 974, 971.

[432] In general, Atkinson, Jr., "Third Parties' Tax-Exempt Status *Can* Be Challenged According to New Decisions," 63 *J. Tax.* (No. 3) 166 (1985).

[433] In re: United States Catholic Conference & Natl Conference of Catholic Bishops, 885 F.2d 1020 (2d Cir. 1989).

[434] Abortion Rights Mobilization, Inc. v. United States Catholic Conference, *cert. den.*, 495 U.S. 918 (1990). In general, Dunec, "Voter Standing: A New Means for Third Parties to Challenge the Tax-Exempt Status of Nonprofit Organizations?," 16 *Hastings Const. L. Quar.* (No. 3) 453 (1989); Shimazaki, "Abortion Politics: The Roman Catholic Church's Tax-Exempt Status in Jeopardy Under Section 501(c)(3) of the Internal Revenue Code," 1988 *B. Y. U. L. Rev.* (No. 4) 799 (1988); Lowenheim, "Challenging the Determination of Another Taxpayer's Status: The Effect of *Eastern Kentucky Welfare Rights Organization,*" 9 *N. C. Cent. L. J.* 227 (1978); Goldberg, "Standing for Public and Quasi-Public Interest Tax Litigants," 1978 *Wash. U. L. Q.* 571 (1978); Harper, "Non-Taxpayer Standing to Challenge Revenue Ruling—Insufficient Allegation of Nexus between Affirmative Action and Injury," 30 *Tax Law.* 490 (1977); Matava, "The Supreme Court's Seeming Disposal of Quasi-Public Interest Tax Litigation," 13 *Wake Forest L. Rev.* 602 (1977); Wang, "Constitutional Law—Standing of Indigents in Need of Hospital Care to Challenge the Charitable Tax Status

Consequently, it appears that nearly all forms of third-party litigation will not satisfy the requirements of standing as interpreted by the Supreme Court.[435] In any event, a somewhat functional equivalent of the third-party suit is available. The congressional committee reports constituting part of the legislative history of the Tax Reform Act of 1976 stated that Congress's silence on third-party litigation "constitutes neither an implied endorsement nor an implied criticism of such 'third-party' suits."[436] Nonetheless, Congress indicated its intent that the courts should be reasonably "generous" in accepting amicus curiae briefs and permitting appearances by third parties in these suits.[437]

§ 24.8 THE IRS AUDIT

(a) General Rules

The IRS is empowered to audit the activities and records of tax-exempt organizations. This examination activity is designed to assure that exempt organizations are in compliance with all pertinent requirements of the federal tax law.[438] Consequently, the likelihood of an IRS audit continues to be a concern to organizations as a factor affecting continuation of their tax exemption (and, where applicable, their private foundation status), susceptibility to the tax on unrelated income, and proper administration of their payroll.

The audit is usually initiated "in the field," that is, by a local IRS office. The individuals involved are supposed to be specialists in tax-exempt organization matters and are under the direction of a supervisor in the particular office. The Exempt

---

of Hospitals," 1977 *Wis. L. Rev.* 247 (1977); Sheldon & Bostick, "Supreme Court Severely Limits Third Party's Right to Contest Exempt Status," 45 *J. Tax.* 140 (1976).

[435] A candidate for the U.S. presidency was found to lack standing to sue the Secretary of the Treasury to revoke the tax-exempt status of a debate-sponsoring organization on the ground that she was excluded from the debates (Fulani v. Brady, 729 F. Supp. 158 (D.D.C. 1990), *aff'd*, 935 F.2d 1324 (D.C. Cir. 1991)). Also Fulani v. Bentsen, 809 F. Supp. 1112 (S.D.N.Y. 1994), *aff'd*, 35 F.3d 49 (2d Cir. 1994); Fulani v. League of Women Voters Educational Fund, 882 F.2d 621 (2d Cir. 1989), Fulani v. Brady, 809 F. Supp. 1112 (S.D.N.Y. 1993); Fulani v. Brady, 149 F.R.D. 501 (S.D.N.Y. 1993). In general, Note, "Fighting Exclusion from Televised Presidential Debates: Minor Party Candidates' Standing to Challenge Sponsoring Organizations' Tax-Exempt Status," 90 *Mich. L. Rev.* 838 (Feb. 1992).

[436] E.g., S. Rep. 938, 94th Cong., 2d Sess. 212, note 6 (1976).

[437] *Id.*

[438] In general, McGovern, "IRS Audits of Exempt Organizations: News and Tips for the General Practitioner," 17 *Exempt Org. Tax Rev.* (No. 1) 125 (1997); Faber, "How to Handle an IRS Audit of a Tax-Exempt Organization," 16 *Exempt Org. Tax Rev.* (No. 5) 753 (1997); Arnold, Jr., "How the IRS Approves, Processes and Audits Tax-Exempt Organizations," 20 *Prac. Acct.* (No. 10) 62 (1987); Gershon, "Tax-Exempt Entities: Achieving and Maintaining Special Status Under the Watchful Eye of the Internal Revenue Service," 16 *Cumberland L. Rev.* (No. 2) 301 (1985–86); Lurie, "Charities Begin at the IRS: The Forms and Substance of Their Regulation," 9 *Tax Adv.* 536 (1978); Arnold, Jr., "The IRS' Exempt Organization Program: How It's Working," 9 *Prac. Acct.* (No. 4) 46 (1976); Bacon, "Working with the I.R.S. in the New Exempt Organizations Program in Audit," 1 *Tax Adv.* 69 (1970); Lehrfeld, "IRS' New Large Private Foundation Audit Program: How to Prepare for It," 33 *J. Tax.* 16 (1970). For pre-1970 audit practices, see Stratton, "A Guide to Dealing With The IRS," 31 *Ass'n Mgt.* 45 (Aug. 1979); Wolfe, "Federal Policing of Exempt Organizations," *N.Y.U. 28th Ann. Inst. on Fed. Tax.* 1387 (1969); Lehrfeld, "Administration by the IRS of Nonprofit Organization Matters," 21 *Tax Law.* 591 (1968); Panel Discussion, "What to Do When the Revenue Agent Appears to Make an Audit," *N.Y.U. Sixth Ann. Inst. on Char. Fdns.* 251 (1963).

Organization Division of the Office of Employee Plans and Exempt Organizations at the IRS National Office has the responsibility for establishing the procedures and policy for the conduct for exempt organization audit programs.

While there is some coordination within the IRS as to the timing and focus of audits, a tax-exempt organization can generally expect one at any time, particularly if a significant period has elapsed since any prior audit.

The records that must be produced upon audit are likely to include all organizational documents (such as articles of organization, bylaws, resolutions, and minutes of meetings), documents relating to tax status (such as the application for recognition of exemption and IRS rulings as to exempt and private foundation status), financial statements (including underlying entry books and records), and newsletters and/or other publications. The items that must be produced will depend upon the type of audit being conducted; the audit may or may not encompass payroll records, pension plan matters, returns of associated individuals or subsidiary organizations, and the like. A related element is the attitude and competence of the revenue agent(s), and the degree to which the organization is prepared to cooperate in the audit. In some circumstances, the organization may find it appropriate to produce information only upon the presentation of a subpoena.[439]

The techniques for coping with IRS personnel on the occasion of an audit are easily summarized but their deployment and success are likely to depend heavily on the personalities involved. Certainly, the key staff personnel and legal counsel of the audited organization should be in the process from the beginning, and it is advisable to select one person who will serve as liaison with the IRS during the audit. The duration of and the procedures to be followed during the audit should be ascertained at the outset and records should be carefully maintained as to information and documents examined or copies by the revenue agents. All interviews should be monitored by the liaison person, with appropriate records made; at least some of the questioning should occur only in the presence of legal counsel.

Where issues arise, one or both sides may decide to pursue the technical advice procedure[440] or the matter may be taken up with the IRS by means of the conference(s) procedure.[441]

(b) Church Audits

Special statutory rules govern federal tax inquiries and examinations of churches.[442] These rules pertain to inquiries and examinations of a church's tax-

---

[439] A discussion of enforcement proceedings in connection with IRS administrative summonses appears in United States v. Church of Scientology of Calif., 520 F.2d 818 (9th Cir. 1975). In general, the U.S. Supreme Court broadly construes the IRS summons power (e.g., United States v. LaSalle Natl Bank, 437 U.S. 298 (1978), rev'g and rem'g 554 F.2d 302 (7th Cir. 1977)).

[440] See § 23.2(a).

[441] Details of the IRS Audit Procedures for Exempt Organizations appear in the Internal Revenue Manual. IR Manual MT 4(11) 00-6.

[442] IRC § 7611. These rules supersede restrictions on the audits of churches for unrelated income tax purposes (IRC § 7605(c)) (e.g., United States v. Church of World Peace, 85-2 U.S.T.C. ¶ 9749 (10th Cir. 1985)). However, these rules are inapplicable where the inquiry is directed at one or more church leaders personally, rather than the church (St. German of Alaska E. Orthodox Catholic Church et al. v. United States, 653 F. Supp. 1342 (S.D.N.Y. 1987), aff'd, 840 F.2d 1087 (2d Cir. 1988)). Cf. Assembly of Yahveh Beth Israel et al. v. United States, 87-1 U.S.T.C. ¶ 9353 (D. Col. 1984).

exempt status, as to whether a church may be engaged in activities that give rise to unrelated business taxable income, and otherwise whether a church is engaged in taxable activities.[443]

For these purposes, a *church* includes any organization claiming to be a church or a convention or association of churches[444] but the term does not include church-supported schools or other organizations that are incorporated separately from the church.[445]

An inquiry of a church's tax liabilities—a *church tax inquiry*—may be commenced by the IRS only where the appropriate IRS regional commissioner (or higher official) reasonably believes, on the basis of facts and circumstances recorded in writing, that the organization may not qualify for tax exemption as a church, may be carrying on an unrelated trade or business,[446] or otherwise be engaged in taxable activities.[447]

Prior to commencement of an investigation, the IRS must provide written notice to the church of the beginning of the inquiry, containing a general explanation of the federal statutory tax law provisions authorizing the investigation or that may otherwise be involved in the inquiry, a general explanation of the church's administrative and constitutional rights in connection with the audit (including the right to a conference with the IRS before any examination of church records), and an explanation of the concerns that gave rise to the investigation and the general subject matter of the inquiry.[448]

The explanation of the concerns and general subject matter of the inquiry must be "sufficiently specific to allow the church to understand the particular area of church activities or behavior which is at issue in the inquiry."[449] For example, as to an inquiry regarding unrelated business income, the notice should indicate the general activities of the church that may result in unrelated income, and, as to an inquiry regarding tax-exempt status, the notice should indicate the general aspects of the church's operations or activities that have given rise to questions regarding its tax-exempt status. The IRS "is not to be precluded from expanding its inquiry beyond the concerns expressed in the notice as a result of facts and circumstances which subsequently come to its attention (including, where appropriate, an expansion of an unrelated income inquiry to include questions of tax-exempt status, or vice-versa)."[450]

The notice requirement does not require the IRS to share particular items of evidence with a church or to identify its sources of information regarding church activities, where provision of the information would be damaging to the inquiry

---

[443] One court characterized these rules as follows: "The IRS has broad authority with respect to tax inquiries. Congress, however, has scaled back these powers with respect to church tax inquiries." IRC § 7611 "provides certain procedural protections to [e]nsure that the IRS does not embark on an impermissibly intrusive inquiry into church affairs." United States v. Church of Scientology of Boston, Inc., 739 F. Supp. 46, 47 (D. Mass. 1990), *aff'd*, 933 F.2d 1074 (1st Cir. 1991).

[444] IRC § 7611(h)(1). See §§ 8.3, 8.4.

[445] H. Rep. No. 861, 98th Cong., 2d Sess. 1102 (1984).

[446] See Part Five.

[447] IRC §§ 7611(a)(1)(A), (2).

[448] IRC §§ 7611(a)(1)(B), (3).

[449] H. Rep. No. 861, *supra* note 445, at 1102.

[450] *Id.*

or to the sources of IRS information. For example, in an inquiry regarding unrelated business income, the IRS might indicate that its inquiry was prompted by a local newspaper advertisement regarding a church-owned business, yet would not be required to reveal the existence or identity of any informers within the church (including present or past employees).[451]

The general explanation of applicable administrative and constitutional provisions "should make reference to the various stages of the church audit procedures . . . (including the right to a preexamination conference) and the principle of separation of church and state under the First Amendment," although the explanation "is not required to explain the possible legal or constitutional ramifications of any particular church audit."[452]

A *church tax inquiry* is any inquiry to a church (other than an examination) that serves as a basis for determining whether the organization qualifies for tax exemption as a church, is engaged in unrelated activities, or is otherwise engaged in taxable activities. A church tax inquiry commences when the IRS requests information or materials from a church of a type contained in church records, other than routine requests for information or inquiries regarding matters that do not primarily concern the tax status or liability of the church.[453]

The facts and circumstances that form the basis for a reasonable belief under these rules must be derived from information lawfully obtained by the IRS and the information obtained from informants used by the IRS for this purpose must not be known to be unreliable.[454]

The IRS may examine church records or religious activities—a *church tax examination*—only if, at least 15 days prior to the examination, the IRS provides written notice to the church and to the appropriate IRS regional counsel of the proposed examination.[455] This notice is in addition to the notice of commencement of a tax inquiry previously provided to the church. A church tax examination is any examination, for purposes of making a determination as described in the *church tax inquiry* definition, of church records at the request of the IRS or of the religious activities of any church.[456]

The notice of examination must include a copy of the church tax inquiry notice previously provided to the church, a description of the church records and activities that the IRS seeks to examine, and a copy of all documents that were collected or prepared by the IRS for use in the examination, and that are required to be disclosed under the Freedom of Information Act[457] and supplemented by the federal tax law concerning disclosure and confidentiality of tax return information.[458] The documents that must be supplied under this requirement are "limited to documents specifically concerning the church whose records are to be examined and will not include documents relating to other inquiries or examina-

[451] *Id.*
[452] *Id.*
[453] IRC § 7611(h)(2).
[454] H. Rep. No. 861, *supra* note 445, at 1101.
[455] IRC §§ 7611(b)(1), (2)(A).
[456] IRC § 7611(h)(3).
[457] U.S.C. § 552.
[458] IRC § 6103.

tions or to IRS practices and procedures in general."[459] Disclosure to the church is "subject to the restrictions of present law regarding the disclosure of the existence or identity of informers."[460] The description of materials to be examined in the notice of examination and the documents disclosed by the IRS to the church do not restrict the ability of the IRS to examine the church records or religious activities that are properly within the scope of the examination.

The appropriate IRS regional commissioner is required, as part of the notice of examination, to offer the church an opportunity to meet with an IRS official to discuss, and attempt to resolve, the concerns that gave rise to the examination and the general subject matter of the inquiry. The organization may request this meeting at any time prior to the examination. If the church requests a meeting, the IRS is required to schedule the meeting within a reasonable time and may proceed to examine church records only following that meeting.[461] The holding of one meeting with the church "is sufficient to satisfy the requirement" and churches cannot utilize this requirement "in order to unreasonably delay an examination."[462]

The purpose of a meeting between the church and the IRS is to discuss the relevant issues that may arise as part of the inquiry, in an effort to resolve the issues of tax exemption or liability without the necessity of an examination of church records. The church and the IRS are expected to "make a reasonable effort to resolve outstanding issues at the meeting" and the IRS is expected to "remind the church at the meeting, in general terms, of the stages of the church audit procedures and the church's rights under such procedures," although the IRS is not required to "reveal information at the meeting of a type properly excludable from a written notice (including information regarding the identity of third-party witnesses or evidence provided by such witnesses)."[463]

The notice of examination may be sent to a church not less than 15 days after the notice of commencement of a church tax inquiry was provided.[464] Thus, at least 30 days must pass between the first notice and the actual examination of church records. If the IRS does not send a notice of examination within 90 days after sending the notice of inquiry, the inquiry must be terminated.[465] This 90-day period is suspended during any period for which the two-year period for duration of a church audit (discussed below) would be suspended;[466] however, the 90-day period "is not to be suspended because of the church's failure to comply with requests for information made prior to the notice of examination."[467] If an inquiry or examination is terminated under this rule, any further inquiry or examination regarding the same or similar issues within a five-year period must have the approval of the IRS Assistant Commissioner for Employee Plans and Exempt Organizations.[468]

---

[459] H. Rep. No. 861, *supra* note 445, at 1103–1104.
[460] *Id.* at 1104.
[461] IRC §§ 7611(b)(2), (3)(A)(iii).
[462] H. Rep. No. 861, *supra* note 445, at 1104.
[463] *Id.*
[464] IRC § 7611(b)(3)(B).
[465] IRC § 7611(c)(1)(B).
[466] IRC § 7611(c)(2).
[467] H. Rep. No. 861, *supra* note 445, at 1104.
[468] IRC § 7611(f).

At the same time as the notice of an examination is provided to a church, the IRS is required to provide a copy of the same notice to the appropriate IRS regional counsel. The regional counsel is then allowed 15 days from issuance of the notice in which to file an advisory objection to the examination.[469] (This is concurrent with the 15-day period during which the IRS is prohibited from examining church records pending a request for a conference.) This regional commissioner is expected to "take any objection by the regional counsel into account when determining whether to proceed with the examination."[470]

The IRS may examine church records only to the extent necessary to determine the liability for, and the amount of, any federal tax.[471] This may include examinations to determine the initial or continuing qualification of the organization as a tax-exempt entity,[472] to determine whether the organization qualifies to receive tax-deductible contributions, or to determine the amount of tax, if any, to be imposed upon the organization.[473]

All regularly kept church corporate and financial records, including (but not limited to) corporate minute books, contributor lists, and membership lists, constitute church records.[474] The term *church records* includes "private correspondence between a church and its members that is in the possession of the church" but does "not include records previously filed with a public official or . . . newspapers or newsletters distributed generally to the church members."[475] Records held by third parties (such as cancelled checks or other records in the possession of a bank) are not church records, so that the IRS is permitted access to these records without regard to the church audit procedures. As under general law, either the IRS or a third-party record keeper generally is required to inform a church of any IRS requests for materials.[476]

The IRS may not determine that a church is not entitled to an exemption or assess tax for unrelated business income against a church solely on the basis of third-party records, without complying with the church audit procedures. (This rule does not apply to assessments of tax other than for unrelated business income, such as for social security or other employment taxes.) The IRS may not use information obtained from third-party bank records to avoid the purposes of the church audit procedures.[477]

The IRS may examine the religious activities of an organization claiming to

---

[469] IRC § 7611(b)(3)(C).
[470] H. Rep. No. 861, *supra* note 445, at 1105.
[471] IRC § 7611(b)(1)(A).
[472] That is, exempt from federal income tax pursuant to IRC § 501(a) by reason of description in IRC § 501(c)(3).
[473] The scope of the records of a church that the IRS may examine is discussed in United States v. C.E. Hobbs Found. for Religious Training & Educ., Inc., 93-2 U.S.T.C. ¶ 50,588 (9th Cir. 1993); United States v. Church of Scientology W. United States, 973 F.2d 715 (9th Cir. 1992), petition to U.S. Supreme Court (No 92-2002) dismissed on Oct. 6, 1993.
[474] IRC § 7611(h)(4).
[475] H. Rep. No. 861, *supra* note 445, at 1106.
[476] *Id.*
[477] *Id.*

be a church (or a convention or association of churches) only to the extent necessary to determine if the organization actually is a church for any period.[478]

The IRS is required to complete any church tax inquiry or examination, and make a final determination with respect to the examination or inquiry, not later than two years after the date on which the notice of examination is supplied to the church.[479] The running of this two-year period is suspended for any period during which (1) a judicial proceeding brought by the church against the IRS with respect to the church tax inquiry or examination is pending or being appealed, (2) a judicial proceeding brought by the IRS against the church or any official of the church to compel compliance with any reasonable IRS request for examination of church records or religious activities is pending or being appealed, or (3) the IRS is unable to take actions with respect to the church tax inquiry or examination by reason of an order issued in a suit involving access to third-party records.[480] The two-year period is also suspended for any period in excess of 20 days, but not in excess of six months, in which the church fails to comply with any reasonable IRS request for church records or other information. This two-year period can be extended by mutual agreement of the church and the IRS.[481]

For examinations regarding revocation of tax-exempt status, where no return is filed, the IRS is limited initially to an examination of church records that are relevant to a determination of tax status or liability for the three most recent taxable years preceding the date on which the notice of examination (the second notice) is sent to the church.[482] If the church is proven to not be tax-exempt for any of these years, the IRS may examine relevant records and assess tax (or proceed without assessment), as part of the same audit, for a total of six years preceding the notice of examination date.[483]

For examinations relating to unrelated business income, where no return is filed, the IRS may assess or collect tax for the six most recent years preceding the date on which the notice of examination is sent, with no additional limit on the period of church records that may be examined.[484] For examinations involving issues other than revocation of tax-exempt status or unrelated business income (such as examinations relating to Social Security or other employment taxes), there is no limitation period where a return has not been filed.

The special limitation periods for church tax liabilities are not to be construed to increase an otherwise applicable limitation period.[485] Thus, as under general law, a three-year limitation period applies where a church filed a tax return before an examination was held and did not substantially understate income. There is no limitation period in a case of fraud, willful tax evasion, or knowing failure to file a return that should have been filed. The applicable limitation period may be extended by mutual agreement of the church and the IRS.

---

[478] IRC § 7611(b)(1)(B).
[479] IRC § 7611(c)(1)(A).
[480] IRC § 7609.
[481] IRC § 7611(c)(2).
[482] IRC § 7611(d)(2)(A)(i).
[483] IRC § 7611(d)(2)(A)(ii).
[484] IRC § 7611(d)(2)(B).
[485] IRC § 7611(d)(2)(C).

The appropriate IRS regional counsel must approve, in advance and in writing, (1) any determination as to whether an organization has tax-exempt status as a church, (2) the determination of whether the organization is a church that is eligible to attract tax-deductible contributions, or (3) the issuance of a notice of tax deficiency to a church following a church tax examination (or in cases where the deficiency procedures are inapplicable, the assessment of any underpayment of tax by the church following a church tax examination). The regional counsel must state in writing that the IRS has substantially complied with the church audit procedures.[486]

The appropriate IRS assistant commissioner must approve, in writing, any second investigation or examination of a church, unless the first investigation or examination resulted in (1) revocation of tax exemption or an assessment of tax or (2) a request by the IRS for any significant changes in church operational practices (including the adequacy or sufficiency of records maintained to reflect income). This rule applies only to second audits involving the same or similar issues as the prior audit. This requirement of assistant commissioner approval is inapplicable where the second audit does not involve the same or similar issues as the preceding inquiry or examination and the requirement applies only to second audits beginning within five years of the date on which the notice of examination was sent to the church during the prior audit (or, if no notice of examination was sent, the date of the notice of commencement of inquiry). This five-year period is suspended for periods during which the two-year period for completion of an audit is suspended (unless the prior audit was actually concluded within two years of the notice of examination). The approval of any second audit under these rules must be made by the IRS Assistant Commissioner for Employee Plans and Exempt Organizations.[487] In determining whether a second audit involves issues similar to those of a prior audit, the "substantive factual issues involved in the two audits, rather than legal classifications, will govern" and, specifically, "unrelated business income from different sources will be considered different issues" for these purposes.[488]

The church audit procedures are inapplicable to any inquiry or examination of any person other than a church, any termination assessment[489] or jeopardy assessment,[490] any case involving a knowing failure to file a return or a willful attempt to defeat or evade tax, or a criminal investigation.[491]

Inquiries or examinations "which relate primarily to the tax status or liability of persons other than the church (including the tax status or liability of a contributor or contributors to the church), rather than the tax status or liability of the church itself, will not be subject to the church audit procedures"; these inquiries or examinations may include those regarding the "inurement of church funds to a particular individual or to another organization, which may result in the denial of all or part of such individual's or organization's deduction for charitable con-

---

[486] IRC § 7611(d)(1).
[487] IRC § 7611(f).
[488] H. Rep. No. 861, *supra* note 445, at 1110.
[489] IRC § 6851.
[490] IRC § 6861.
[491] IRC § 7611(i).

tributions to the church," the "assignment of income or services or excessive contributions to a church," or a "vow of poverty by an individual or individuals followed by a transfer of property or an assignment of income or services to the church."[492] The IRS "may require of a church regarding these matters without being considered to have commenced a church tax inquiry and may proceed to examine church records relating to these issues (including enforcement of a summons for access to such records) without following the requirements applicable to church tax examinations, subject to the general rules regarding examinations of taxpayer books and records."[493]

Inquiries or examinations "conducted outside the church audit procedures will be limited to the determination of facts and circumstances specifically relating to the tax liabilities of the individuals or other organizations in question" and the IRS may not "make use of inquiries or examinations regarding individuals' or other organizations' tax liabilities to avoid the intended purpose of the church audit procedures."[494] However, the "failure of a church to respond to repeated inquiries regarding individuals' or other organizations' tax liabilities will be considered a reasonable basis for commencement of a church tax inquiry."[495]

"[R]outine IRS inquiries to a church will not be considered to commence a church tax inquiry and therefore will not trigger application of the church audit procedures."[496] Nonetheless, "[r]epeated failure by a church or its agents to reply to such routine inquiries will be considered a reasonable basis for commencement of a church tax inquiry under the applicable church audit procedures."[497] Also, the IRS may "request a church to provide information necessary to locate third-party records (for example, bank records), including information regarding the church's chartered name, state and year of incorporation, and location of checking and savings accounts, without following the church audit procedures; failure to provide this type of information is to be a factor, but not a conclusive factor, in determining if there is reasonable cause for commencing a church tax inquiry."[498]

As stated, the church audit procedures do not apply to any case involving a knowing failure to file a return or a willful attempt to defeat or evade tax. "[N]othing in the church audit procedures will inhibit IRS inquiries, examinations, or criminal investigations of tax protestor or other tax avoidance schemes posing as religious organizations, including (but not limited to) tax avoidance schemes posing as mail-order ministries or storefront churches,

---

[492] H. Rep. No. 861, *supra* note 445, at 1111.

[493] *Id.* at 1111–1112.

[494] *Id.* at 1112.

[495] *Id.*

[496] *Id.* "Routine questions for the [this] include (but are not limited to) questions regarding (1) the filing or failure to file any tax return or information return by the church, (2) compliance with income tax or FICA tax withholding responsibilities by the church, (3) any supplemental information needed to complete the mechanical processing of any incomplete or incorrect return filed by the church, (4) information necessary to process applications for exempt status, letter ruling requests, or employment tax exemption requests by the church, and information identifying a church that is used by the IRS to update its Cumulative List of Tax Exempt Organizations and other computer files, and (5) confirmation that a specific business is or is not owned or operated by a church" (*id.*).

[497] *Id.*

[498] *Id.*

whether such schemes are limited to one particular taxpayer or encompass a group of taxpayers."[499]

The exclusive remedy for any IRS violation of the church audit procedures is as follows: failure of the IRS to substantially comply with (1) the requirement that two notices be sent to the church, (2) the requirement that the appropriate regional commissioner approve the commencement of a church tax inquiry, or (3) that an offer of an IRS conference with the church be made (and a conference held if requested), will result in a stay of proceedings in a summons proceeding to gain access to church records (but not in dismissal of the proceeding) until a court determines that these requirements have been satisfied.[500] The two-year limitation on the duration of a church audit is not suspended during these stays of summons proceedings; however, the IRS may correct the violations without regard to the otherwise applicable time limits prescribed under the church examination procedures.[501] In determining whether a stay is necessary, "a court will consider the good faith of the IRS and the effect of any violation of the proper examination procedures."[502]

Otherwise, there is no judicial remedy for IRS violation of the church examination procedures. The failure of the IRS to comply with these rules may not be raised as a defense or as an affirmative ground for relief in a judicial proceeding, including a summons proceeding to gain access to church records, a declaratory judgment proceeding involving a determination of tax-exempt status,[503] or a proceeding to collect unpaid tax. Additionally, failure to substantially comply with the requirement that two notices be sent, that the assistant commissioner approve an inquiry, and that a conference be offered (and the conference held if requested) may not be raised as a defense or as an affirmative ground for relief in a summons proceeding or any other judicial proceeding other than as specifically previously stated.[504] A church or its representatives cannot "litigate the issue of the reasonableness of the assistant commissioner's belief in approving the commencement of a church tax inquiry . . . in a summons proceeding or any other judicial proceeding," although this does not derogate from "a church's right to raise any substantive or procedural argument which would be available to taxpayers generally in the appropriate proceeding."[505]

---

[499] *Id.* at 1113.

[500] IRC § 7611(e)(1).

[501] *Id.*

[502] H. Rep. No. 861, *supra* note 395, at 1114.

[503] That is, a proceeding under IRC § 7428. See *supra* § 6(b).

[504] IRC § 7611(e)(2).

[505] H. Rep. No. 861, *supra* note 395, at 1114. The final regulations to accompany the church audit rules were promulgated on February 20, 1986 (T.D. 8013). An illustration of the applicability of these rules so as to preclude an audit of a church appears in United States v. Church of Scientology of Boston, Inc., *supra* note 443, interpreting, in this context, United States v. Powell, 679 U.S. 48 (1964). Also United States v. Church of World Peace, 775 F.2d 265 (10th Cir. 1985); United States v. Church of Scientology Flag Serv. Org. Inc., 90-1 U.S.T.C. ¶ 50,019 (M.D. Fla. 1989); United States v. Church of Scientology Western United States, 92-2 U.S.T.C. ¶ 50,441 (9th Cir. 1992).

In general, Walker & Holub, "Audit of Church-Related Schools and Churches," 24 *Cath. Law.* 184 (1979); Worthing, "The Internal Revenue Service as a Monitor of Church Institutions: The Excessive Entanglement Problem," 45 *Fordham L. Rev.* 929 (1977); Shaw, "Tax Audits of Churches," 22 *Cath. Law.* 247 (1976).

(c) Hospital Audits

The IRS, in recent years, has been making the audit of tax-exempt hospitals and other health care entities a matter of special priority. In reflection of this, the IRS developed audit guidelines specific to these types of tax-exempt organizations (although many of the guidelines are equally applicable to other types of exempt entities).[506]

The guidelines encompass nearly all aspects of qualification for tax-exempt status by hospitals, with emphasis on private inurement and private benefit situations;[507] they also focus on joint venture arrangements[508] and unrelated business income circumstances.[509]

The tax exemption of nonprofit hospitals today rests on the *community benefit standard*.[510] In determining whether a hospital meets this standard, IRS agents are expected to consider the following factors: (1) whether the hospital has a governing board composed of "prominent civic leaders" rather than hospital administrators, physicians, and the like (the agents are requested to review the minutes of the board meetings to determine how active the members are), (2) if the organization is part of a multi-entity hospital system, whether the minutes reflect "corporate separateness" (and whether the minutes show that the board members understand the purposes and activities of the various entities), (3) whether admission to the medical staff is open to all qualified physicians in the area, consistent with the size and nature of the facilities, (4) whether the hospital operates a full-time emergency room open to everyone, regardless of ability to pay, and (5) whether the hospital provides nonemergency care to everyone in the community who is able to pay either privately or through third parties (such as Medicare and Medicaid).[511]

The guidelines contain criteria for assessing whether an "open staff policy" exists at a hospital, for determining whether use of an emergency room is restricted, and for examining whether nonemergency services are available to everyone in the community who has the ability to pay. Examining agents are admonished to determine whether a hospital engages in the practice known as patient dumping.[512]

The guidelines contain a discussion of private inurement and private benefit, and differentiate between the two doctrines. The IRS recognized two key distinctions between these two concepts. First, the Service reiterated its position that even a "minimal amount" of private inurement will result in loss of tax-exempt status, while private benefit is tested against an "insubstantiality" threshold. Second, private inurement applies only with respect to "insiders," while private benefit can accrue to anyone. An *insider* is defined in these guidelines as individuals

---

[506] IRS Audit Guidelines for Hospitals ("hospital audit guidelines"), Manual Transmittal 7(10)69-38 for Exempt Organizations Examinations Guidelines Handbook (Mar. 27, 1992).
[507] See Chapter 19.
[508] See § 32.3.
[509] See Part Five.
[510] See § 7.6.
[511] Hospital audit guidelines, *supra* note 506, § 333.1(1).
[512] *Id*. §§ 333.1(2), (3).

"whose relationship with an organization offers them an opportunity to make use of the organization's income or assets for personal gain." (The IRS considers a physician an insider in relation to a hospital in which he or she practices and/or is a member of the hospital's governing body.)[513]

The following guidelines for determining private inurement or private benefit are applicable with respect to any tax-exempt organization where either set of rules applies:

1. Identify the members of the board of directors or trustees and key staff members. Examine any business relationships or dealings with the hospital. Note transactions where supplies or services are provided at prices exceeding competitive market prices or on preferred terms. Be alert for any loan agreement at less than prevailing interest rates. Scrutinize any business arrangements under which hospitals finance the construction of medical buildings owned by staff doctors on favorable financial terms.

2. Review contracts and leases. Scrutinize any contracts under which the hospital requires doctors to conduct private practices on hospital premises.

3. Review the minutes of the board of directors' executive committee and finance committee for indications of transactions with physicians, administrators, and board members.

4. Review the articles of incorporation, bylaws, minutes, filings with regulatory authorities, correspondence, brochures, newspaper articles, and the like, to determine the existence of related parties.

5. Determine whether the hospital is engaged in commercial or industrial research or testing benefiting private individuals or firms rather than scientific or medical research benefiting the general public.

6. Review third-party reports (such as CPA audit reports, management letters, and annual reports) to determine whether the hospital's activities further an exempt purpose or serve private interests.

7. To determine whether medical staff or board members have an economic interest in, or significant dealings with, the hospital, review any conflict-of-interest statements.[514]

These guidelines focus on the matter of unreasonable compensation and require examining agents to inquire as to recruiting incentives, incentive compensation arrangements, below-market loans, below-market leases, and hospital purchases of a physician's practice. An extensive list of "common compensation arrangements" between physicians and hospitals is provided.[515]

The guidelines also focus on joint ventures, pointing out that a variety of

---

[513] *Id.* § 333.2(1)–333.2(3). See, however, § 19.11(c), text accompanied by notes 267–268.
[514] *Id.* § 333.2(4)–333.2(10).
[515] *Id.* § 333.3.

forms may be involved, such as a cooperative agreement or the creation of a separate legal entity. Examples of the items or services involved in these joint ventures are said to include clinical diagnostic laboratory services, medical equipment leasing, durable medical equipment, and other outpatient medical or diagnostic services.[516]

Agents are advised to carefully examine joint ventures between taxable and tax-exempt parties in search of private inurement or private benefit. The facts must be reviewed to determine whether the partnership involved (if any) serves a charitable purpose, whether and how participation by the exempt entity furthers an exempt purpose, and whether the arrangement permits the exempt entity to act exclusively in furtherance of its exempt purposes. A variety of private inurement issues in this context are explored, as are possible violations of the federal anti-kickback law.[517]

Sixteen types of "financial analyses" by examining agents are requested.[518] These include

1. Review income and expenditures of affiliated entities, to determine whether nonexempt purposes, inurement, serving of private interests, or unrelated business income may be present.

2. Look for lobbying or political activities or expenditures; determine whether the hospital has elected the expenditure test as to lobbying expenditures.

3. Reconcile the hospital's books with the figures on its information return (Form 990).

4. Review Medicare cost reports for indications of insider transactions or unrelated activities.

5. Review the correspondence files on large gifts and grants; look for unusual transactions that may prohibit the "donor" from receiving a charitable deduction.

6. Check the value shown on the books for donated property against any appraisals in the file; if any property was sold, note the difference between the book value and the selling price.

7. Review the travel ledger accounts of the administrative department and the board of directors; be alert for personal items such as spouse's travel and ensure that there has been "proper accounting."

8. Where private individuals or outside entities operate the hospital cafeteria, gift shop, pharmacy, parking lot, etc., determine whether the agreements with these individuals or firms provide for reasonable payments to the hospital.

---

[516] *Id.* § 333.4.
[517] *Id.*
[518] *Id.* § 333.5.

The guidelines contain rules for analyzing a hospital's balance sheet.[519] These are

1. Review the general ledger control account for receivables from officers, trustees, and members of the medical staff, and analyze for private benefit and additional compensation; review loan or other agreements underlying these transactions.

2. Check notes receivable for interest-free loans to insiders (for example, a mortgage loan to an administrator given as an inducement to accept or continue employment at the hospital); these arrangements must be scrutinized for inurement, proper reporting, etc.

3. Review property records to determine whether any assets are being used for personal purposes that should be taxable income to the user (for example, vehicles, residential property held for future expansion, etc.).

4. Review trust funds to see whether the trusts should be filing separate returns.

5. Review investment portfolios and check for controlled entities.

6. Review the ledger accounts and check for notes and mortgages payable that could lead to unrelated debt-financed income[520] issues.

7. Analyze any self-insurance trust or fund set up by the hospital to provide liability insurance.[521]

The guidelines also contain rules for determining whether physicians are employees of the hospital (rather than independent contractors).[522] According to these guidelines, if the following factors are present, the physician is "most likely" an employee (even if the contract describes the position as an independent contractor): (1) the physician does not have a private practice, (2) the hospital pays wages to the physician, (3) the hospital provides supplies and professional support staff, (4) the hospital bills for the physician's services, (5) there is a percentage division of the physician's fees with the hospital (or vice versa), (6) there is hospital regulation of, or right to control, the physician, (7) the physician is on-duty at the hospital during specified hours, and/or (8) the physician's uniform bears the hospital name or insignia.

Concerning the unrelated income aspects of audits, IRS agents are advised to be particularly inquisitive as respects these "[s]pecific examples common in [the] health care field"[523]: laboratory testing, pharmacy sales, cafeterias, coffee

---

[519] *Id.* § 333.6

[520] See §§ 29.1–29.4.

[521] See, however, § 10.6.

[522] Hospital audit guidelines, *supra* note 506 § 333.7.

[523] *Id.* § 333.8(1). In general, Bedard & Gribens, "CEP Audits Often Are Revenue Raisers for IRS and Bad News for Health Organizations," 8 *J. Tax. Exempt Orgs.* 3 (July/Aug. 1996); Theisen & Pelfrey, "Preparing an Exempt Health Care Organization for an IRS Audit," 6 *J. Tax. Exempt Orgs.* 208 (Mar./Apr. 1995); Bedard & Gribens, "Coordinated Examinations Highlight Current Scrutiny of Health Care Organizations," 6 *J. Tax. Exempt Orgs.* 28 (July/Aug. 1994); Broccolo & Peregrine, "New Hospital Audit Guidelines: The IRS Gets Down to Business," 5 *Exempt Org. Tax Rev.* 653 (1992).

shops, gift shops, parking facilities, medical research, laundry services, leasing of medical buildings, supply departments, and services to other hospitals.

(d) College and University Audits

The IRS, in September 1994, issued examination guidelines for its agents to use during the audits of colleges and universities.[524] These guidelines provide factors to be considered in determining how a college or university is structured. Emphasis was placed on accounting methods, financial information, compensation arrangements, fringe benefit issues, joint ventures,[525] scholarships and fellowships, and unrelated business income issues.[526] Attention was also placed on the fund-raising efforts of, and contributions to, these entities. Like the guidelines for hospital audits,[527] the college and university examination guidelines contain material that is equally applicable to other types of tax-exempt organizations.

These guidelines[528] apply with respect to three categories of exempt colleges and universities: (1) private institutions that are tax-exempt[529] and are not private foundations,[530] (2) public institutions the income (other than unrelated business income) of which is excluded from federal taxation,[531] and (3) public institutions that have received recognition of tax exemption from the IRS.[532]

Agents are instructed to obtain and review the following items in analyzing the institution's size, structure, and activities: the school bulletin and course catalogue, the school telephone directory, minutes of meetings of the governing board, as well as committees and other groups, student newspapers, alumni bulletins and magazines, any catalogue or descriptive list of the publications of the institution, a description of the institution's accounting system, the requisition and purchase order files, information that must be disclosed by coaches concerning athletically related income from sources outside the institution, possible conflicts of interest involving federally sponsored research, a description of the computer hardware and software, and formats of files and records maintained, and the institution's materials as to its racially nondiscriminatory policies.[533] Other documentation to be reviewed includes the appropriate audited financial statements, reports prepared for accreditation audits, information concerning state and local real property tax exemptions and information required by the U.S. Office of Management and Budget.[534] The guidelines contain detailed instruction

---

[524] Examination Guidelines for Colleges and Universities, (college and university audit guidelines), Internal Revenue Manual, Exempt Organizations Handbook 7(10)(69), reproduced in Ann. 94-112, 1994-37 I.R.B. 36.

[525] See § 32.3.

[526] See Part Five.

[527] See *supra* § 8(c).

[528] College and university audit guidelines, *supra* note 523, § 342.

[529] That is, are tax-exempt under IRC § 501(a) by reason of being described in IRC § 501(c)(3). See § 7.3.

[530] That is, are classified under IRC § 509(a)(1) by reason of description in IRC § 170(b)(1)(A)(ii). See § 11.3(a).

[531] This exclusion of income is by reason of IRC § 115. See §§ 6.9, 18.17.

[532] This refers to tax exemption pursuant to IRC § 501(c)(3).

[533] College and university audit guidelines, *supra* note 524, §§ 342.2, 342.31.

[534] *Id.* at §§ 342.32, 342.33.

on examination of financial statements,[535] employment taxes and fringe benefits,[536] cafeteria plans, retirement and pension plans, and other deferred compensation arrangements[537] contributions to the institution and other aspects of fund-raising,[538] research and contracts,[539] scholarships and fellowships,[540] legislative and political expenses,[541] bookstores,[542] other unrelated business income tax considerations,[543] and related entities.[544]

As to the matter of related entities, the examining agents are advised to interpret the term *related* broadly and to include any organization the primary activity of which is to support a college or university or its programs.[545] These related entities will include separately incorporated schools or departments, athletic booster clubs, foundations, endowment funds, scholarship funds, joint ventures (including those with unitrusts), and partnerships.[546] Auditors are encouraged to identify related entities.[547]

---

[535] *Id.* at § 342.4.

[536] *Id.* at §§ 342.5, 342.7.

[537] *Id.*, § 342.6. See Chapter 16.

[538] *Id.* at § 342.9.

[539] *Id.* at § 342.10.

[540] *Id.* at § 342.11.

[541] *Id.* at § 342.12. See Chapters 20, 21.

[542] *Id.* at § 342.13. See § 26.5(a)(i).

[543] *Id.* at § 342.14.

[544] *Id.* at § 342.15.

[545] *Id.* at § 342.15(1).

[546] *Id.* at § 342.15(4)-(9).

[547] *Id.* at § 342.45. In general, Cerny & Mallon, "Extensive New IRS Audit Guidelines Intensify Scrutiny of Colleges and Universities," 78 *J. Tax.* (No. 5) 298 (May 1993); Harding, Jr., & McClellan, "Commentary on the IRS Proposed Examination Guidelines for College and University Audits," 9 *Exempt Org. Tax Rev.* (No. 3) 589 (1994); Whaley, "IRS Proposes Strict College and University Examination Guidelines," 4 *J. Tax. Exempt Orgs.* (No. 6) 3 (May/June 1993).

The Commerciality Doctrine and Unrelated Business Income Taxation

CHAPTER TWENTY-FIVE

The Commerciality Doctrine

Occasionally, as part of the law of tax-exempt organizations, the courts will create new law or develop law that is engrafted onto statutory criteria. This phenomenon is most obvious and extensive in connection with the evolution and application of the *commerciality doctrine*. These principles are impacting the law concerning qualification for tax exemption, principally for charitable organizations, and in the process helping shape the law of unrelated business activities.

Despite its enormous effect to date, the commerciality doctrine is somewhat of an enigma. In writing the law of tax-exempt organizations over the decades, Congress did not create the doctrine. With one exception,[1] the word *commercial* does not appear in the federal statutory law concerning exempt organizations. Nor, with one mostly irrelevant exception (discussed below), is the term to be found in the applicable income tax regulations. It is, then, a doctrine created by the courts.

§ 25.1 ORIGIN OF DOCTRINE

The commerciality doctrine, as it relates to the activities of tax-exempt organizations, is an overlay body of law that the courts have engrafted onto the statutory and regulatory rules. The time is likely to come when Congress legislates some variant of the commerciality doctrine; when this occurs, Congress will essentially be codifying this law configured by the courts over the better part of this century.

(a) Nature of Doctrine

The commerciality doctrine is essentially this: A tax-exempt organization is engaged in a nonexempt activity when that activity is engaged in in a manner that is considered *commercial*. An act is a commercial one if it has a direct counterpart

---

[1] IRC § 501(m), denying tax exemption to certain organizations that provide *commercial-type* insurance. See § 22.1.

in, or is conducted in the same manner as is the case in the realm of for-profit organizations. (Having stated the essence of the doctrine, it must also be said that the doctrine is unevenly applied.)

The doctrine appears to be born of the basic fact that United States society is composed of three sectors: the business (for-profit) sector, the governmental sector, and the nonprofit sector. Generally, the governmental sector is not viewed as an operator of businesses (there are, of course, many exceptions to this), so that sector is not a factor in this analysis (other than as the source of regulation).

The United States is essentially a capitalist society, so the business sector is, in several ways, the preferred sector. While entities in the business sector are seen as being operated for private ends (for example, profits to shareholders), with the overall result a capitalist (albeit rather regulated) economy for the society, the nonprofit sector is seen as being operated for public ends (the general good of society).[2] Many today still perceive of nonprofit organizations as entities that do not and should not earn a profit, are operated largely by volunteers, and are not "run like a business."[3]

Out of these precepts (some of which are false) is emanating the view that organizations in the nonprofit sector should not "compete" with organizations in the business sector. Thus, over recent years, the nonprofit community has heard much about competition between for-profit organizations (usually, "small" business) and nonprofit organizations—with the word "competition" almost always preceded by the word "unfair."[4]

This doctrine thus involves a *counterpart* test. When a court sees an activity being conducted by a member of the business sector and the same activity being conducted by a member of the nonprofit sector, it often, motivated by some form of intuitive offense at the thought that a nonprofit organization is doing something that "ought to" be done or is being done by a for-profit organization, concludes that the nonprofit organization is conducting that activity in a commercial manner. This conclusion then leads to a finding that the commercial activity is a nonexempt function with adverse consequences in law for the nonprofit organization, either as respects unrelated income taxation or tax exemption.

Consequently, the federal tax law pertaining to nonprofit organizations is being shaped by a doctrine that rests in part upon untrue premises and that has crept into the law by actions of courts which, consciously or unconsciously, ignored the Internal Revenue Code and the underlying regulations, and developed law with these premises in mind.

For example, the ongoing debate over whether credit unions should continue to be tax-exempt is a classic illustration of the counterpart test. A report from the Congressional Research Service, a division of the Library of Congress, makes reference to the fact that "many believe that an economically neutral tax system requires that financial institutions engaged in similar activities should have the same tax treatment."[5] Citing differences between credit unions and other financial institutions, organizations like the National Credit Union Admin-

---

[2] See § 1.1(b).
[3] See § 4.9.
[4] See § 26.2(b).
[5] "Should Credit Unions Be Taxed?," CRS Analysis No. I B 89066 (Sept. 18, 1990).

istration argue for the ongoing exemption, while organizations like the American Bankers Association disagree.

Another example is the debate over the criteria for tax exemption for hospitals. This issue concerns the question as to whether the basis for tax exemption for hospitals should continue to be the community benefit standard[6] or whether it should be revised to reflect a charity care standard.[7]

(b) Internal Revenue Code

Usually, when endeavoring to understand a point of federal tax law, one first turns to the Internal Revenue Code. However, in searching for the law embodied by the commerciality doctrine as it applies to tax-exempt organizations, a perusal of the pages of the Code is basically futile. That is, the commerciality doctrine, as a general standard of law, is not in the Code.

However, a significant element of the doctrine was added to the Internal Revenue Code in 1986. This occurred as the result of the decision by Congress to deny tax-exempt status to organizations such as Blue Cross and Blue Shield organizations that are providers of health care insurance. The thought was that this type of insurance is being provided by the business sector, that these types of nonprofit organizations "look like" and compete with for-profit organizations, and that tax exemption for insurance providers is no longer appropriate.[8] This legislation is a classic illustration of the points made above, concerning the business sector preference and the counterpart test.

Thus, Congress wrote a rule that provides that an organization cannot be tax-exempt as a charitable organization[9] or a social welfare organization[10] if a substantial part of its activities consists of the provision of *commercial-type* insurance.[11] Although this term is not defined in the Internal Revenue Code, the legislative history stated that "commercial-type insurance generally is any insurance of a type provided by commercial insurance companies."[12] This is an appli-

---

[6] See § 6.2(a).

[7] See Hyatt & Hopkins, *The Law of Tax-Exempt Healthcare Organizations* (New York: John Wiley & Sons, Inc., 1995), Chapter 6. Still another illustration of the point is the question of the ongoing tax exemption for fraternal beneficiary societies. A study conducted by the Department of the Treasury, which led to a report in early 1993 (see § 18.4 (a), note 93), concluded that the insurance products offered by these organizations are essentially the same as those provided by commercial insurers; it observed that the large fraternal beneficiary societies "conduct their insurance operations in a manner similar to commercial insurers." However, the report dismissed this commerciality, stating that these societies "do not use their exemption to compete unfairly with commercial insurers in terms of price or to operate inefficiently." Nonetheless, this conclusion is wholly inconsistent with contemporary court opinions and IRS policy. As will be discussed, in those quarters, commercial practices are automatically considered unrelated activities, leading to denial or revocation of exemption or to unrelated income taxation. This report concluded that there must be more than commerciality—there must also be unfair competition.

[8] See § 22.1.

[9] That is, an organization described in IRC § 501(c)(3) (see Part Two).

[10] That is, an organization described in IRC § 501(c)(4) (see Chapter 12).

[11] IRC § 501(m).

[12] H. Rep. 841, 99th Cong., 2d Sess. II-345 (1986).

cation of the counterpart test: if the activity is found in the business sector, it is an inappropriate activity for conduct in the nonprofit organization sector.

Organizations that seek to be tax-exempt must meet an *operational test*—a test that facilitates an evaluation of activities in relation to the achievement of tax-exempt functions.[13] The operational test is most refined in the body of law concerning charitable organizations.[14] The regulations also amplify the Internal Revenue Code usage of words such as *charitable* and *educational*.[15]

A provision of the Internal Revenue Code taxes the net income derived from tax-exempt organizations from *unrelated business activities*.[16] These activities are those that are not substantially related to the exercise or performance by the exempt organization of its exempt purpose or function.[17] The need of the organization for the revenue derived from a business or the use it makes of the profits derived from it cannot be used as a basis for demonstrating relatedness.[18]

Absent an applicable statutory exception, an activity is taxable as an unrelated one where the activity is a trade or business, the business is regularly carried on, and the conduct of the business is not substantially related (other than through the production of funds) to the organization's performance of its exempt function.[19]

Pursuant to the statutory law, "an activity does not lose identity as trade or business merely because it is carried on within a larger aggregate of similar activities or within a larger complex of other endeavors that may, or may not, be related to the exempt purposes of the organization."[20] This is the *fragmentation rule*.

(c) Tax Regulations

The tax regulations exist to explain and, in some instances, amplify the law as stated in the statutory law. Yet, when it comes to the commerciality doctrine as it is being conceived and interpreted by the courts today, it is nowhere to be found in the regulations.

The income tax regulations are silent on the matter of commercial operations as the concept relates to a determination as to whether an activity is substantially related to the accomplishment of exempt purposes.[21] With one minor and irrelevant exception (concerning commercial advertising), the same is true with respect to the definition of the term *trade or business*.[22]

The term *commercial* is used in the regulations as part of the elements for determining whether or not a business is regularly carried on. Thus, the regulations state that specific business activities of an exempt organization are ordinarily

---

[13] See § 4.5.
[14] Reg. § 1.501(c)(3)-1(c).
[15] Reg. § 1.501(c)(3)-1(d)(2), (3).
[16] IRC § 511(a).
[17] IRC § 513(a); Reg. § 1.513-1(a).
[18] *Id.*
[19] Reg. § 1.513-1(a).
[20] IRC § 513(c).
[21] Reg. § 1.513-1(d).
[22] Reg. § 1.513-1(b).

deemed to be regularly carried on if they "manifest a frequency and continuity, and are pursued in a manner, generally similar to comparable commercial activities of nonexempt organizations."[23]

To determine whether an activity is substantially related to an organization's exempt purposes, it is necessary to examine the "relationship between the business activities which generate the particular income in question—the activities, that is, of producing or distributing the goods or performing the services involved—and the accomplishment of the organization's exempt purposes."[24]

A business is related to exempt purposes where the conduct of the business activity has a *causal relationship* to the achievement of exempt purposes and it is substantially related where the causal relationship is a substantial one.[25] For a business to be substantially related to exempt purposes, the production or distribution of the goods or the performance of the sevices from which the gross income is derived must "contribute importantly to the accomplishment of those purposes."[26] Whether activities productive of gross income contribute importantly to the accomplishment of one or more exempt purposes "depends in each case upon the facts and circumstances involved."[27]

As noted, this regulatory definition of relatedness does not make any reference to the commerciality doctrine. Rather, this definition of relatedness is a causal relationship test. Thus, under the regulations, a business may be regularly carried on (that is, be commercially conducted) and not be taxed, where there is a substantial causal relationship between the activity and the accomplishment of exempt purposes. In other words, the IRS regulations contemplate a nontaxable, related business that is commercially carried on.

(d) Beginnings of the Doctrine

The commerciality doctrine is not the consequence of some grand pronouncement by the Supreme Court or, for that matter, any court. The doctrine just evolved, growing from loose language in court opinions, which in turn seems to have reflected judges' personal views as to what the law ought to be (rather than what it is). The commerciality doctrine appears to be the product of what is known in the law as *dictum*: a gratuitous remark by a judge that need not have been uttered to resolve the case. The term stems from the Latin "simplex dictum," meaning an "assertion without proof," and later "obiter dictum," which means a statement "lacking the force of an adjudication." However, the commerciality doctrine has, over the years, very much taken on the force of an adjudication.

The doctrine was initiated far before Congress enacted the unrelated income rules in 1950. It was first mentioned, at the federal level, in 1924, by the U.S. Supreme Court.[28] The case concerned a religious order that was operated for reli-

---

[23] Reg. § 1.513-1(c)(1), (2)(ii).

[24] Reg. § 1.513-1(d)(1).

[25] Reg. § 1.513-1(d)(2).

[26] *Id.*

[27] *Id.*

[28] Trinidad v. Sagrada Orden de Predicadores de la Provincia del Santisimo Rosario de Filipinas, 263 U.S. 578 (1924).

gious purposes, but that engaged in other activities, which the government alleged destroyed the basis for its exemption; the order had extensive investments in real estate and stockholdings that returned a profit, as well as some incidental sales of wine, chocolate, and other articles. The Supreme Court found that the order was tax-exempt as a religious entity, justifying its investment and business efforts by writing that "[s]uch [religious] activities cannot be carried on without money."[29]

In this case, the Court did not articulate any commerciality doctrine. The Court characterized the government's argument as being that the order "is operated also for business and *commercial* purposes."[30] The Court rejected this characterization, writing that there is no "competition" and that while "the transactions yield some profit [it] is in the circumstances a negligible factor."[31] Thus, in this case, the Supreme Court did not enunciate the commerciality doctrine; however, by using the word in describing the government's position, the commerciality doctrine was born.

The rules that flowed out of this Supreme Court opinion are known today as the *operational test*, which is stated in the tax regulations.[32] The opinion laid down the rule that a charitable organization can engage in business activities for profit, without loss of exemption, if its net income is destined for charitable uses. This rule, known as the *destination-of-income test*, was ended by Congress in 1950, when it enacted the law of *feeder organizations*.[33] An analysis of the cases applying the destination-of-income test and of its transition out of existence was provided in a 1957 appellate court opinion.[34]

However, repeal of the destination-of-income test did not extinguish what has been termed the *activities standard*.[35] This standard is used where a nonprofit organization engages in activities that, while commercial, further exempt purposes.[36] Today, the activities standard survives as the operational test.

The 1924 Supreme Court opinion established another point: where an organization's activities are a "negligible factor" (as was the sale by the order of wine and chocolate), they are considered "incidental" in relation to exempt purposes and thus have no adverse effect on the exemption.[37] This aspect of the law is today reflected in the rule that a charitable organization must be operated exclusively for exempt purposes, with today's understanding that the word *exclusively* actually means *primarily*. The word exclusively is in the Internal Revenue Code and in the tax regulations the word is primarily.[38]

The Supreme Court formally articulated the commerciality doctrine in 1945,

---

[29] *Id*. at 581.

[30] *Id*. (emphasis added).

[31] *Id*. at 582.

[32] Reg. § 1.501(c)(3)-1(c)(1). See § 4.5.

[33] IRC § 502. See § 28.6.

[34] Lichter Found. v. Welch, 247 F.2d 431 (6th Cir. 1957).

[35] Fides Publishers Ass'n v. United States, 263 F. Supp. 924 (N.D. Ind. 1967).

[36] *Id*. at 933–934.

[37] Trinidad v. Sagrada Orden de Predicadores de la Provincia del Santisimo Rosario de Filipinas, *supra* note 28, at 582.

[38] Reg. § 1.501(c)(3)-1(c)(1). See § 4.6.

when reviewing a case concerning the tax exemption of a chapter of the Better Business Bureau, which was seeking exempt status as an educational organization.[39] On this occasion, the Court said that the "exclusivity" requirement "plainly means that the presence of a single non-educational purpose, if substantial in nature, will destroy the exemption regardless of the number or importance of truly educational purposes."[40] The Court found a noneducational purpose in the promotion of a profitable business community. The Court, in the closest that it has come to expressly articulating the commerciality doctrine, said that the organization had a "commercial hue" and that its "activities are largely animated by this commercial purpose."[41]

(e) Focus on Publishing

The commerciality doctrine flourished during a period in the early 1960s, in the context of the courts' scrutiny of nonprofit publishing organizations, which is understandable given the fact that publishing occurs in both the business and nonprofit sectors, and thus facilitates easy application of the counterpart doctrine.

An early case to invoke the commerciality doctrine, replete with the counterpart test, was decided in 1961.[42] The organization published and sold religious literature in furtherance of the purpose of upgrading the quality of teaching materials for Bible instruction in Sunday schools. It generated what the court termed "very substantial" profits.[43] The court rejected the argument that profits alone preclude tax exemption. The court wrote: "If the defendant [IRS] seeks by this distinction ["slight" versus "very substantial" profits] to suggest that where an organization's profits are very large a conclusion that the organization is noncharitable must follow, we reject such a suggestion."[44] But then the court added these fateful words: "If, however, defendant means only to suggest that it is at least some evidence indicative of a *commercial* character we are inclined to agree."[45]

This court found the organization to be directly involved in the conduct of a trade or business for profit, with religious objectives "incidental."[46] Application of the counterpart test was articulated in a footnote, with the court observing "that there are many commercial concerns which sell Bibles, scrolls, and other religious and semi-religious literature which have not been granted exemption as to that part of their businesses."[47] Consequently, the court found that the organization's activities were of a "nonexempt character."[48] The court declined to apply the unrelated income tax rules to these facts. Thus, this 1961 opinion is devoid of

---

[39] Better Business Bureau of Wash., D.C. v. United States, 326 U.S. 279 (1945).
[40] *Id.* at 283.
[41] *Id.* at 283–284.
[42] Scripture Press Found. v. United States, 285 F.2d 800 (Ct. Cl. 1961).
[43] *Id.* at 803.
[44] *Id.*
[45] *Id.* (emphasis added).
[46] *Id.* at 805.
[47] *Id.* at 806, note 11.
[48] *Id.* at 807.

any discussion of related and unrelated activities. The court obviously thought that the organization's primary activities were unrelated ones, since the exemption was revoked, but the word *commercial* was used rather than the word *unrelated*. The opinion offers no definition of the word commercial and contains no indication as to why the court used it.

In one of these cases, decided in 1956, a court held that an organization that sold religious publications and charged admission fees to conclaves was tax-exempt because the "activities bear an intimate relationship to the proper functioning of" the organization.[49] The court made no mention of a commerciality doctrine. Earlier, in 1954, this court held that an organization organized to prepare and publish a widely accepted system for indexing library collections (the Dewey Decimal Classification System) was tax-exempt.[50] Again, there was no mention of any commerciality doctrine. The commerciality doctrine appears, on the basis of this 1961 opinion, to take into account at least three elements: the scope of an organization's net profits, the extent of accumulated surplus revenue (capital), and amounts expended for what the court deems to be tax-exempt functions.

As it turned out, another court had another nonprofit publishing organization before it the next year. This organization disseminated publications (principally newsletters and books) containing investment advice to subscribers and other purchasers. Rejecting the argument that the organization was engaged in educational activities, the court held that the organization was not entitled to tax exemption because "its purpose is primarily a business one."[51] Once again, there was no discussion by the court as to whether the business was related or unrelated.

This court did not need to use the word *commercial*; the proper terminology would have been *unrelated business*. Instead, in this 1962 opinion, the court wrote passages such as the organization is "in competition with other commercial organizations providing similar services,"[52] the organization's "investment service in all its ramifications may be educational, but its purpose is primarily a business one,"[53] and the "totality of these activities is indicative of a business, and . . . [the organization's] purpose is thus a commercial purpose and nonexempt."[54] With that, the commerciality doctrine, and its counterpart test and the concern about competition between the sectors, was irrevocably launched. The doctrine was becoming a part of the law of tax-exempt organizations, although Congress had nothing to do with it.

In 1963, a court rejected the government's contention that the publication and sale of religious magazines, books, pamphlets, Bibles, records, tape recordings, and pictures amounted to commercial activity.[55] In 1964, this court was faced with another case involving the operation of alleged commercial enter-

---

[49] Saint Germain Found. v. Comm'r, 26 T.C. 648, 658 (1956).

[50] Forest Press, Inc. v. Comm'r, 22 T.C. 265 (1954).

[51] American Inst. for Economic Research v. United States, 302 F.2d 934, 938 (Ct. Cl. 1962).

[52] *Id.* at 938.

[53] *Id.*

[54] *Id.* at 937.

[55] A.A. Allen Revivals, Inc. v. Comm'r, 22 T.C. 1435 (1963).

prises, this time concerning a religious organization that conducted training projects. The court rejected the commerciality doctrine, with the observation that "we regard consistent nonprofitability as evidence of the absence of commercial purposes."[56]

Still another case involving a religious publishing organization was considered by a federal district court in 1967. This court refined the commerciality doctrine by distinguishing between organizations that have commercial activities as a part of their overall activities and those that have commercial activities as their sole activity.[57] Organizations that retained their tax exemption in the prior cases were grouped in the first category;[58] the other organizations were placed in the second category. The court thus relied on the other cases[59] in concluding that the publishing company was not exempt. The nonexempt purpose[60] was portrayed as the "publication and sale of religious literature at a profit."[61] The court said its conclusion could not be otherwise—"If it were, every publishing house would be entitled to an exemption on the ground that it furthers the education of the public."[62]

In 1968, another federal district court came to the identical result. A publisher of religious materials was denied tax exemption because it was "clearly engaged primarily in a business activity, and it conducted its operations, although on a small scale, in the same way as any commercial publisher of religious books for profit would have done."[63] The fact that the organization's ultimate purpose was a religious one did not, for that court, confer exemption.

The next year, this opinion was reversed on appeal. The case was won before the appellate court on the ground that the organization did not have "operational profits."[64] The court concluded that the "deficit operation reflects not poor business planning nor ill fortune but rather the fact that profits were not the goal of the operation."[65] Although the nonprofit organization involved in the case prevailed, this opinion went a long way toward establishment of the point that the existence of profit is evidence of commerciality.

Thus, the 1960s witnessed court cases that invoked and solidified the commerciality doctrine. After this flurry of activity involving publishing organizations, not much happened with the doctrine for over a decade. Then, in 1978, came the first of the contemporary commerciality doctrine cases.

In 1978, a court had occasion to review the previous cases discussing the commerciality doctrine. Once again, it had before it an organization the sole ac-

---

[56] The Golden Rule Church Ass'n v. Comm'r, 41 T.C. 719, 731 (1964).

[57] Fides Publishers Ass'n v. United States, 263 F. Supp. 924 (N.D. Ind. 1967).

[58] This includes cases like Saint Germain Found. v. Comm'r, *supra* note 49; The Golden Rule Church Ass'n v. Comm'r, *supra* note 56; A.A. Allen Revivals, Inc. v. Comm'r, *supra* note 55.

[59] Scripture Press Found. v. United States, *supra* note 42; American Inst. for Economic Research v. United States, *supra* note 51.

[60] Following the rationale in Better Business Bureau of Wash., *D.C. v.* United States, *supra* note 39.

[61] Fides Publishers Ass'n v. United States, *supra* note 57, at 935.

[62] *Id.*

[63] Elisian Guild, Inc. v. United States, 292 F. Supp. 219, 221 (D. Mass. 1968).

[64] Elisian Guild, Inc. v. United States, 412 F.2d 121, 125 (1st Cir. 1969).

[65] *Id.* at 125.

tivity of which was religious publishing. Essentially, the purpose of the organization under review was to disseminate sermons to ministers to improve their religious teachings. The court allowed the organization to be tax-exempt on the ground that the sale of religious literature was an "integral part of and incidental to" the entity's religious purpose.[66]

That same year, the court was called upon to determine whether an organization that purchased, imported, and sold artists' crafts could be tax-exempt. The IRS contended that the organization was a "commercial import firm."[67] The organization argued that its purpose was to help disadvantaged artisans in poverty stricken countries to subsist and preserve their craft and to furnish services to tax-exempt museums by providing museum stores with representative handicrafts from disadvantaged countries. Once again, the court came down on the side of tax exemption, concluding that the organization engaged in the purchase, import, and sale activities, not as an end unto themselves, but as a means of accomplishing exempt purposes. This organization thus escaped characterization as a commercial organization.

In early 1979, this court went the other way. The court concluded that the primary purpose of the organization involved was the publication and sale of books written by its founder. In concluding that the principal purpose served by this organization was commercial in nature, the court focused on the fact of annual profits and its distribution and marketing practices. Although the conclusion reached was that the organization was principally commercial, the case had considerable overtones of private inurement.[68]

Later that same year, the court analyzed the facts involving an organization operated to purchase and sell products manufactured by blind individuals. The court found that the principal purpose of the organization was to provide employment for the blind, thereby alleviating the hardship these disabled individuals experience in securing and holding regular employment. The fact that the organization generated a profit was disregarded.[69]

Early in 1980, the same court considered the case of an organization that benefited the poor of the Navajo Nation by assisting in the organization and operation of businesses that employ or are owned by residents of the Navajo Reservation. Its most substantial source of revenue was the leasing of oil well drilling equipment. The court denied the organization tax exemption on the ground that it was operated primarily for commercial purposes. The court articulated the commerciality doctrine as follows: "Profits may be realized or other nonexempt purposes may be necessarily advanced incidental to the conduct of the commercial activity, but the existence of such nonexempt purposes does not require denial of exempt status so long as the organization's dominant purpose for conducting the activity is an exempt purpose, and so long as the nonexempt activity is merely incidental to the exempt purpose."[70] The organization's activities were found to be in violation of the operational test.

---

[66] Pulpit Resource v. Comm'r, 70 T.C. 594, 611 (1978).
[67] Aid to Artisans, Inc. v. Comm'r, 71 T.C. 202, 208 (1978).
[68] Christian Manner Int'l v. Comm'r, 71 T.C. 661 (1979).
[69] Industrial Aid for the Blind v. Comm'r, 73 T.C. 96 (1979).
[70] Greater United Navajo Dev. Enters., Inc. v. Comm'r, 74 T.C. 69, 79 (1980).

The next year, a federal district court concluded that an organization that published religious literature should lose its tax exemption because it evolved into a commercial entity. Originally formed as a missionary organization, it, the court ruled, became an organization with a "commercial hue" and a "highly efficient business venture."[71] In reaching this conclusion, the court noted that the organization adhered to publishing and sales practices followed by comparable commercial publishers, had shown increasing profits in recent years, experienced a growth in accumulated surplus, and had been paying substantially increased salaries to its top employees.

Late in 1982, this court issued an opinion concerning still another religious publishing house, again concluding that its exemption should be revoked. The court decided that the organization had become too profitable and thus commercial.[72] Once again, the court found a "commercial hue," derived from profits, wide profit margins, development of a professional staff, and competition with commercial publishers.[73] However, the opinion was reversed on appeal, with the appellate court "troubled by the inflexibility of the Tax Court's approach."[74] The court of appeals proffered no clarity; while it was bothered by the facts, it could not bring itself to revoke the exemption of the organization. Thus, the court of appeals said that "success in terms of audience reached and influence exerted, in and of itself, should not jeopardize the tax-exempt status of organizations which remain true to their stated goals."[75] Yet the court also wrote that if an exempt "organization's management decisions replicate those of commercial enterprises, it is a fair inference that at least one purpose is commercial."[76]

In 1983, a court concluded that an ostensibly religious organization could not qualify for tax exemption because its principal purpose is "tax avoidance" counseling.[77] The court was clearly displeased at that element of the facts and, in a sense, the case is more one of private benefit rather than commerciality. However, the court noted that the information provided by the organization "is no different from that furnished by a commercial tax service."[78]

About three years went by before a court considered another commerciality case. Before a court was an organization that was formed to assist in the process of technology transfer, which is the transfer of technology from universities and research institutions to industry.[79] The court concluded that its major activity was the provision of patenting and licensing services, and that the activity was primarily commercial in nature.[80]

In 1986, a court held that a religious retreat center was not an organization

---

[71] Incorporated Trustees of Gospel Worker Soc'y v. United States, 510 F. Supp. 374, 381 (D.D.C. 1981), aff'd, 672 F.2d 894 (D.C. Cir. 1981), cert. den., 456 U.S. 944 (1981).

[72] Presbyterian & Reformed Publishing Co. v. Comm'r, 79 T.C. 1070 (1982).

[73] Id. at 1083.

[74] Presbyterian & Reformed Publishing Co. v. Comm'r, 743 F.2d 148, 152 (3d Cir. 1984).

[75] Id. at 158.

[76] Id. at 155.

[77] The Ecclesiastical Order of the Ism of Am, Inc. v. Comm'r, 80 T.C. 833, 843 (1983).

[78] Id. at 839.

[79] See § 9.5.

[80] Washington Research Found. v. Comm'r, 50 T.C.M. 1457 (1985). (This opinion was "overturned" by Congress when it enacted § 1605 of the Tax Reform Act of 1986 (see H. Rep. 841, 99th Cong., 2d Sess. II-827 (1986)).)

that is commercial in nature, because it did not compete with commercial entities.[81] The entity was held to be an integral part of a conference of the United Methodist Church. The organization was portrayed as a general contractor for the construction of housing on its own property to promote increased religious activity. The fact that the organization charged fair market prices was held to be required to avoid charges of private inurement.

(f) Contemporary Application of the Doctrine

The latter half of the 1980s brought little attention to the commerciality doctrine. The focus instead, particularly with respect to religious organizations, was on unrelated business activities, rather than loss of exemption. In none of these opinions did the court involved endeavor to discuss the origins and scope of the commerciality doctrine.

The 1990s continue to bring cases involving the commerciality doctrine. In the first of these cases, the court concluded that the commerciality doctrine was the basis for denial of tax-exempt status, as a charitable and religious entity, to an organization associated with the Seventh-day Adventist Church that operated, in advancement of church doctrine, vegetarian restaurants and health food stores.[82] The court wrote that the organization's "activity was conducted as a business and was in direct competition with other restaurants and health food stores."[83] The court added: "Competition with commercial firms is strong evidence of a substantial nonexempt purpose."[84]

When this case was considered on appeal, the appellate court affirmed the lower court decision.[85] The appellate court opinion specifically stated the factors that the court relied upon to find commerciality and thus offered the best contemporary explication of the commerciality doctrine. These factors were that (1) the organization sold goods and services to the public (this factor alone was said to make the operations "presumptively commercial"), (2) the organization was in "direct competition" with for-profit restaurants and food stores, (3) the prices set by the organization were based on pricing formulas common in the retail food business (with the "profit-making price structure loom[ing] large" in the court's analysis and the court criticizing the organization for not having "below-cost pricing"), (4) the organization utilized promotional materials and "commercial catch phrases" to enhance sales, (5) the organization advertised its services and food ($15,500 expended for advertising over two years), (6) the organization's hours of operation were basically the same as for-profit enterprises, (7) the guidelines by which the organization operated required that its management have "business ability" and six months training, (8) the organization did not uti-

---

[81] Junaluska Assembly Hous., Inc. v. Comm'r, 86 T.C. 1114 (1986).

[82] Living Faith, Inc. v. Comm'r, 60 T.C.M. 710 (1990).

[83] *Id.* at 713.

[84] *Id.*

[85] Living Faith, Inc. v. Comm'r, 950 F. 2d 365 (7th Cir. 1991). In another case, a court concluded that an organization's principal activity was the "operation of a number of canteen-style lunch trucks," which is a commercial activity, and upheld revocation of the organization's tax exemption (New Faith, Inc. v. Comm'r, 64 T.C.M. 1050 (1992)).

lize volunteers but paid salaries (totalling $63,000 in one year and more than $25,000 in another year), and (9) the organization did not receive charitable contributions.

The IRS is beginning to apply the commerciality doctrine in the context of ascertaining whether a tax-exempt charitable organization should lose its tax-exempt status because its fund-raising costs are too "high."[86] Further, it has been held that an organization selling religious tapes was a nonexempt commercial organization,[87] and that an organization operating prisoner rehabilitation programs is not eligible for tax exemption because of commercial activities.[88]

The commerciality doctrine is being applied in some of the cases involving the provision of *commercial-type insurance*.[89] For example, in one of these cases, the court wrote that the "various factors to consider in determining whether an organization promotes a forbidden nonexempt purpose" under the rules concerning charitable organizations include the "manner in which an organization conducts its activities; the commercial hue or nature of those activities; the competitive nature of the activities; the existence of accumulated profits; and the provision of free or below cost services."[90] The organization, the tax status of which was at issue in the case, was characterized by the court as existing "solely for the purpose of selling insurance to nonprofit exempt organizations at the lowest possible cost on a continued, stable basis"; the court continued with the observation that "[s]elling insurance undeniably is an inherently commercial activity ordinarily carried on by a commercial for-profit company."[91] The court added that, although the organization "may not possess every attribute characteristic of a mutual insurance company, it possesses a majority of the qualifying characteristics, which only further enhances the determination that . . . [it] is presumptively commercial in nature."[92] In another of these cases, a court concluded that a group of self-insurance pools had a "commercial hue."[93]

The commerciality doctrine, as a court-founded rule of law, has come to be widely accepted in the courts. This phenomenon has occurred, and is occurring, as other judicial and administrative doctrines are coming to the fore. These other doctrines include competition between nonprofit and for-profit organizations,[94] the private benefit standard,[95] and the commensurate test.[96]

---

[86] E.g., United Cancer Council, Inc. v. Comm'r, 109 T.C. No. 17 (1997); this opinion is discussed at § 19.4(a). In general, Hopkins, *The Law of Fund-Raising, Second Edition* (New York: John Wiley & Sons, Inc. 1996), Chapters 6 § 15, 8 § 12.

[87] United Missionary Aviation, Inc. v. Comm'r, 60 T.C.M. 1152 (1990), *rev'd and rem'd*, 985 F.2d 564 (8th Cir. 1989), *cert. den.*, 506 U.S. 816 (1992).

[88] Public Indust., Inc. v. Comm'r, 61 T.C.M. 1626 (1991).

[89] See § 22.1.

[90] Nonprofits' Ins. Alliance of Calif. v. United States, 94-2 U.S.T.C. ¶ 50,593 (Fed. Cl. 1994).

[91] *Id.*

[92] *Id.*

[93] Paratransit Ins. Corp. v. Comm'r, 102 T.C. 745, 754 (1994). Subsequently, Congress enacted a limited tax exemption for certain charitable risk pools (see § 10.6).

[94] See *supra* note 4.

[95] See § 19.10.

[96] See § 4.7.

§ 25.2 CONTEMPORARY PERSPECTIVE ON DOCTRINE

One of the requirements for qualification as a tax-exempt charitable organization is that the entity be operated exclusively for one or more tax-exempt purposes.[97] This is, in essence, a *primary purpose* rule.[98]

Pursuant to the exclusively doctrine, the IRS or a court may conclude that an organization is not operated exclusively for a tax-exempt purpose because its operation is similar to a commercial enterprise operated on a for-profit basis.[99] In many of the court opinions focusing on this point, the courts have expressed concern about the "commercial hue" of the organization.[100]

There is more to the commerciality doctrine than the generation of profits. It partakes, as well, of other doctrines discussed throughout, such as, as noted, the matter of competition with for-profit organizations, the private inurement and private benefit rules, and the commensurate test. However, the IRS may use the existence of a profit to characterize the activity as being commercial in nature, thus placing at issue the question as to whether the organization's activities are devoted exclusively to tax-exempt purposes.

The competition issue is the most troublesome, particularly when the lines of demarcation between nonprofit and for-profit organizations are blurring. Nonprofit organizations are becoming increasingly reliant on revenue in the form of fees for services. For-profit organizations are more concerned than ever about their public image and the extent to which they can provide assistance to their communities. For-profit organizations are entering domains of producing and providing services that were once the sole province of nonprofit organizations. Laws are changed to promote greater parity between the sectors, such as the Office of Management and Budget regulations, which require tax-exempt organizations pursuing government contracts to calculate tax revenues foregone. Management of nonprofit organizations is becoming more sophisticated.

Two categories of charitable organizations continue to evolve: Those that are supported largely by gifts (*donative* organizations)[101] and those that are supported principally by exempt function revenue (*service provider* organizations).[102] As this trend continues, it will force new pressures on the concept of tax exemption. New rationales for exemption may emerge. The battles that are building over the ground rules for tax exemptions for hospitals[103] and credit unions[104] must be appreciated from this perspective. A sort of "domino theory" may be in the works in this setting. One commentator is of the view that "if nonprofit hospitals lose their exemption, federal corporate tax exemption for most or all of the second [commercial] nonprofit sector may then be in doubt."[105]

---

[97] See § 4.6.

[98] See § 4.4.

[99] See Chapter 25.

[100] See § 26.2(b).

[101] See § 11.3(b)(i).

[102] See § 11.3(b)(iv).

[103] See text accompanying *supra* notes 6–7.

[104] See text accompanying *supra* note 5.

[105] Hansmann, "The Two Nonprofit Sectors: Fee for Service Versus Donative Organizations," in *The Future of the Nonprofit Sector* 95 (San Francisco: Jossey-Bass, Inc., 1989).

The undermining effect of the commerciality doctrine on the future of the nonprofit sector cannot be underestimated. Recall the underlying premise of the commerciality doctrine, which is that there are two sectors that can engage in commercial activities but the bias is that those activities should be conducted only by the for-profit sector—the United States being a capitalist society. The business sector is, in several ways, the preferred sector. This view is that of the Treasury Department, such as was expressed in 1987, where an assistant secretary testified before the House Subcommittee on Oversight that the "role of the quasi-governmental, not-for-profit sector should . . . be restricted to that of supplementing, and not supplanting, the activities of for-profit businesses."[106]

The emerging commerciality doctrine is the backdrop against which the unrelated business laws can be viewed. This is in part because, in the view of some, the concept of relatedness and unrelatedness is outmoded, and should be replaced by a commerciality test.[107] Even if the commerciality doctrine does not operate to cause denial or loss of tax-exempt status, the doctrine remains a significant force in determining what is an unrelated trade or business.[108]

---

[106] "Unrelated Business Income Tax," Statement of O. Donaldson Chapeton, Deputy Assistant Secretary (Tax Policy), Department of the Treasury, Hearings before the Subcommittee on Oversight, House Committee on Ways and Means, House of Representatives, 100th Cong., 1st Sess. 35 (1987).

[107] Bennett & Rudney, "A Commerciality Test to Resolve the Commercial Nonprofit Issue," 36 *Tax Notes* (No. 14) 1065 (1987).

[108] In general, Washlick, "The Commerciality Standard Changes the Rules of UBIT Planning," 4 *J. Tax. Exempt Orgs.* 15 (Nov./Dec. 1992); Hopkins, "Is the Rationale for Tax-Exempt Organizations Changing?," 4 *J. Tax. Exempt Orgs.* 13 (Spring 1992); Hopkins, "The Most Important Concept in the Law of Tax-Exempt Organizations Today: The Commerciality Doctrine," 5 *Exempt Org. Tax Rev.* (No.3) 459 (1992); Brown, "Religious Nonprofits and the Commercial Manner Test," 99 *Yale L. J.* (No. 7) 1631 (1990);

CHAPTER TWENTY-SIX

Unrelated Business Activities

One of the most significant aspects of the law of tax-exempt organizations is the body of law that defines, and taxes the net income from, exempt organizations' unrelated trade or business activities.

The term *unrelated trade or business* means any trade or business the conduct of which is not substantially related to the exercise or performance, by the tax-exempt organization carrying on the business activity, of its exempt purposes.[1] The fact that an exempt organization may need the income from a business for its program operations, or the way in which the organization uses the revenue derived from the business activity, does not cause the conduct of a business to be substan-

---

[1] IRC § 513(a).

tially related to an organization's exempt purpose.[2] There are special rules in this area for certain trusts.[3]

The portion of a tax-exempt organization's gross income that is subject to the tax on unrelated business income[4] is generally includable in the computation of unrelated business taxable income where three factors are present: (1) The income is from a *trade or business*; (2) the trade or business is *regularly carried on* by the organization; and (3) the conduct of the trade or business is not *substantially related* to the performance by the organization of its tax-exempt functions.[5] However, there are certain types of income and certain activities that are exempt from unrelated business income taxation.[6]

§ 26.1 BASIC RATIONALES

The taxation of unrelated income, a feature of the federal tax law since 1950, is based on the concept that the approach is a more effective and workable sanction for enforcement of the law of exempt organizations than denial or revocation of tax-exempt status.[7] It is fundamentally a simple concept: the unrelated business income tax applies only to active business income that arises from activities that are *unrelated* to the organization's tax-exempt purposes. That is, income generated by a tax-exempt organization from the conduct of one or more activities that are undertaken for reasons other than the furtherance of the organization's exempt purposes is taxed in the same manner as the income would have been if received by a taxable entity. (These activities are often termed *unrelated business activities* and the income they yield is often termed *unrelated business income*.)

Conventional thinking has it that, if a substantial portion of an exempt organization's income is from unrelated sources, the organization will not qualify for tax exemption in the first instance.[8] This is a logical outcome when viewed in light of the *primary purpose test*.[9] Thus, even though there generally are no specific percentage limitations in this area,[10] the IRS may deny or revoke the tax-exempt status of an organization where it regularly derives over one-half of its annual revenue from unrelated activities.[11] One court barred an organization from

---

[2] *Id.*
[3] IRC § 513(b).
[4] See § 28.1.
[5] Reg. § 1.513-1(a).
[6] See Chapter 27.
[7] An analysis of developments leading to enactment of the unrelated business income tax provisions appears in Myers, "Taxing the Colleges," 38 *Cornell L.Q.* 388 (1953).
[8] E.g., Indiana Retail Hardware Ass'n v. United States, 366 F.2d 998 (Ct. Cl. 1966); People's Educ. Camp Soc'y, Inc. v. Comm'r. 331 F. 2d 923 (2d Cir. 1964), *cert. den.*, 379 U.S. 839 (1964), Rev. Rul. 69-220, 1969-1 C. B. 154
[9] See § 4.4.
[10] However, see § 28.3, text accompanied by notes 36–40.
[11] E.g., Gen. Couns. Mem. 39108.

achieving tax-exempt status where the organization received about one third of its revenue from an unrelated business.[12]

However, this is not always the case. The IRS also applies the *commensurate test*[13] in this context. That is, an organization may derive a substantial portion of its revenue in the form of unrelated income, yet be tax-exempt because it also expends a significant amount of its time on exempt functions. In one instance, a charitable organization derived 98 percent of its income from an unrelated business but remained exempt because 41 percent of the organization's activities constituted exempt programs.[14]

An organization may qualify as a tax-exempt entity, although it operates a trade or business as a substantial part of its activities, where the operation of the business is in furtherance of the organization's tax-exempt purposes and where the organization is not organized or operated for the primary purpose of carrying on a trade or business. In determining the existence or nonexistence of a primary purpose, all of the circumstances must be considered, including the size and extent of the trade or business and of the activities that are in furtherance of one or more tax-exempt purposes.[15] For example, an organization that purchased and sold at retail products manufactured by blind persons was held by a court to qualify as a charitable organization because its activities resulted in employment for the blind, notwithstanding its receipt of net profits and its distribution of some of these profits to qualified workers.[16]

At the other end of the spectrum, incidental trade or business activity will not alone cause an organization to lose or be denied tax exemption, although the income derived from the activity may be taxable.[17] It is common to measure substantiality and insubstantiality in terms of percentages of time or expenditures.[18] However, it is clear that, as noted, "[w]hether an activity is substantial is a facts-and-circumstances inquiry not always dependent upon time or expenditure percentages."[19]

Prior to 1969, the unrelated business income tax applied only to certain tax-exempt organizations, including charitable,[20] educational,[21] some religious,[22] and

---

[12] Orange County Agric. Soc'y, Inc. v. Comm'r, 893 F.2d 647 (2d Cir 1990), *aff'g* 55 T. C.M. 1602 (1988). In general, Horvitz, "Financing Related Commercial Activities of Exempt Universities," 55 *Taxes* 457 (1977), Note, "Profitable Related Business Activities and Charitable Exemption Under Section 501(c)(3)," 44 *Geo. Wash. L. Rev.* 270 (1976).

[13] See § 4.7.

[14] Tech. Adv. Mem. 9711003.

[15] Reg. § 1.501(c)(3)-1(e)(1).

[16] Industrial Aid for the Blind v. Comm'r., 73 T. C. 96 (1979).

[17] E.g., Rev. Rul. 66-221, 1966-2 C.B. 220 (holding that a volunteer fire department is tax-exempt notwithstanding an incidental amount of unrelated business activities).

[18] Similar definitional issues pertain with respect to the limits on allowable lobbying by public charitable organizations (see § 20.3).

[19] The Nationalist Movement v. Comm'r, 102 T.C. 558, 589 (1994), *aff'd*, 37 F.3d 216 (5th Cir. 1994). Also Manning Ass'n v. Comm'r, 93 T.C. 596, 610–611 (1989); Church in Boston v. Comm'r, 71 T.C. 102, 108 (1978).

[20] See Chapter 6.

[21] See Chapter 7.

[22] See Chapter 8.

comparable organizations; labor, agricultural, and horticultural organizations;[23] and business leagues and similar organizations.[24] However, the tax on unrelated business income is now almost uniformly applicable, its coverage having been extended by Congress in that year.[25] The applicability of the unrelated business income tax was broadened for the following reason:

> In recent years, many of the exempt organizations not subject to the unrelated business income tax—such as churches, social clubs, fraternal beneficiary societies, etc.—began to engage in substantial commercial activity. For example, numerous business activities of churches were brought to the attention of the Congress. Some churches are engaged in operating publishing houses, hotels, factories, radio and TV stations, parking lots, newspapers, bakeries, restaurants, etc. Furthermore, it is difficult to justify taxing a university or hospital which runs a public restaurant or hotel or other business and not tax a country club or lodge engaged in similar activity.[26]

The unrelated business income tax is, as noted, now applicable to nearly all tax-exempt organizations. This tax also applies to any college or university that is an agency or instrumentality of any government or political subdivision of a government, or that is owned or operated by a government or any political subdivision of a government or by any agency or instrumentality of one or more governments or political subdivisions of them, and applies to any corporation wholly owned by one or more of these colleges or universities.[27] Excepted from the tax are federal government instrumentalities,[28] certain religious and apostolic organizations,[29] farmers' cooperatives,[30] and shipowners' protection and indemnity associations.[31]

The primary objective of the unrelated business income tax is to eliminate a source of unfair competition by placing the unrelated business activities of covered tax-exempt organizations on the same tax basis as the nonexempt business endeavors with which they compete.[32] The House Ways and Means Committee report on the Revenue Act of 1950 observed:

> The problem at which the tax on unrelated business income is directed here is primarily that of unfair competition. The tax-free status of [IRC § 501] organizations enables them to use their profits tax-free to expand operations, while

---

[23] See Chapter 15.
[24] See Chapter 13.
[25] IRC § 511(a)(2)(A).
[26] Joint Committee on Internal Revenue Taxation. *General Explanation of Tax Reform Act of 1969*, 91st Cong., 2d Sess. 66–67 (1970).
[27] IRC § 511(a)(2)(B).
[28] See § 18.1.
[29] See § 8.7.
[30] See § 18.11.
[31] See § 18.12.
[32] Reg. § 1.513-(b). In general, IRS Pub. No. 598, "Tax on Unrelated Business Income of Exempt Organizations"; Steinfeld, "Unrelated Business Income Tax An Increased Hazard for Qualified Trusts," 36 *J. Tax* 110 (1972); Webster, "Unrelated Business Income Tax," 48 *Taxes* 844 (1970); Newland, "Profit in Nonprofit Corporations," 22 *Tax L. Rev.* 687 (1967); Rogovin, "Charitable Enigma: Commercialism," 17 *S. C. Tax Inst.* 61 (1965).

their competitors can expand only with the profits remaining after taxes. Also, a number of examples have arisen where these organizations have, in effect, used their tax exemption to buy an ordinary business. That is, they have acquired the business with no investment on their own part and paid for it in installments out of subsequent earnings—a protection which usually could not be followed if the business were taxable.[33]

(The problem discussed by the Committee in the latter portion of the foregoing quotation was further addressed by enactment of the unrelated debt-financed income rules.)[34] The Senate Finance Committee reaffirmed this position in 1976 when it noted that one "major purpose" of the unrelated income tax "is to make certain that an exempt organization does not commercially exploit its exempt status for the purpose of unfairly competing with taxpaying organizations."[35]

These rationales for the unrelated business income rules have begun to be supplanted by the view that other objectives—including the raising of revenue—are equally important. Thus, as one federal appellate court observed, "although Congress enacted the . . . [unrelated income rules] to eliminate a perceived form of unfair competition, that aim existed as a corollary to the larger goals of producing revenue and achieving equity in the tax system."[36] Another appellate court has elected to be somewhat more reticent, observing that "while the equalization of competition between taxable and tax-exempt entities was a major goal of the unrelated business income tax, it was by no means the statute's sole objective."[37]

In recent years, considerable attention has been accorded the phenomenon of tax-exempt organizations that are considered to be operating in a commercial manner[38] or unfairly competing with for-profit organizations.[39] Many of the activities that are under review as being commercial or competitive are those that are related, rather than unrelated, businesses.

§ 26.2 DEFINITION OF *TRADE OR BUSINESS*

As noted, gross income of a tax-exempt organization may be includable in the computation of unrelated business income where it is income from a *trade or business*.

---

[33] H. Rep. 2319, 81st Cong., 2d Sess. 36–37 (1950). Also S. Rep. No. 2375, 81st Cong., 2d Sess. 28–29 (1950).

[34] See §§ 29.1–29.4.

[35] S. Rep. No. 94-938, 94th Cong., 2d Sess. 601 (1976). The United States General Accounting Office, by letter to the IRS dated July 8, 1985, stated its conclusion that the resources of the IRS are not being fully deployed in the pursuit of unrelated business taxable income, in that the "IRS does not have sufficient information on UBI tax noncompliance to fully understand the nature and magnitude of UBI noncompliance and develop profiles of high noncompliant tax-exempt organizations engaging in UBI activity," with the recommendation that the "IRS may want to focus more on UBI organizations with a high potential for being noncompliant in addition to assuring that exempt organizations are operating in accordance with their exempt purposes."

[36] Louisiana Credit Union League v. United States, 693 F.2d 525, 540 (5th Cir. 1982).

[37] American Medical Ass'n. v. United States, 887 F.2d 760, 772 (7th Cir. 1989).

[38] See Chapter 25.

[39] See *infra* § 2(b).

(a) General Principles

The definition of the term *trade or business* is of two parts. The term includes "any activity which is carried on for the production of income from the sale of goods or the performance of services."[40] However, the definition also embraces an activity that otherwise possesses the characteristics of a *trade or business* as that term is defined by the federal income tax law in the business expense deduction setting.[41] This definition, then, is informed by the considerable body of law that has accreted in the federal tax law generally.

The first component of this definition is very broad and encompasses nearly every activity that a tax-exempt organization may undertake. As discussed below, nonetheless, the term does have its boundaries.[42]

The most important standard as to whether an activity is a trade or business for purposes of the business expense deduction is the presence of a *profit motive*. This profit objective standard has been carried over into the tax-exempt organizations setting. Thus, as the Supreme Court stated, the principal test in this regard is that the "taxpayer's primary purpose for engaging in the activity must be for income or profit."[43] In the exempt organizations context, the Court wrote that the inquiry should be whether the activity "was entered into with the dominant hope and intent of realizing a profit."[44] An appellate court stated that the "existence of a genuine profit motive is the most important criterion for . . . a trade or business."[45]

Various federal courts of appeal have applied the profit motivation element to ascertain whether an activity of a tax-exempt organization is a trade or business for purposes of the unrelated business rules. For example, the U.S. Court of Appeals for the Fourth Circuit—the most vociferous on the point—employs an *objective profit motivation test* to ascertain whether an activity is a business. This appellate court wrote that "there is no better objective measure of an organization's motive for conducting an activity than the ends it achieves."[46] Subsequently, this court held that a tax-exempt organization's activity was a business because it "received considerable financial benefits" from performance of the activity, which was found to be "persuasive evidence" of a business endeavor.[47] On this latter occasion, the court explicitly defined as a business the situation where a "non-profit entity performs comprehensive and essential business services in return for a fixed fee."[48] Thereafter, this appellate court wrote simply that, for an activity of a tax-exempt organization to be a trade or business, it must be conducted with a "profit objective."[49]

---

[40] IRC § 513(c).

[41] Reg. § 1.513-1(b). The business expense deduction is the subject of IRC § 162.

[42] See infra § 2(e).

[43] Comm'r v. Groetzinger, 480 U.S. 23, 35 (1987).

[44] United States v. American Bar Endowment, 477 U.S. 105, 110, note 1 (1986). The Court cited for this proposition the opinion in Brannen v. Comm'r, 722 F.2d 695, 704 (11th Cir. 1984).

[45] Professional Ins. Agents v. Comm'r, 726 F.2d 1097, 1102 (6th Cir. 1984).

[46] Carolinas Farm & Power Equip. Dealers Ass'n, Inc. v. United States, 699 F.2d 167, 170 (4th Cir. 1983).

[47] Steamship Trade Ass'n of Baltimore, Inc. v. Comm'r, 757 F.2d 1494, 1497 (4th Cir. 1985).

[48] *Id.*

[49] West Va. State Medical Ass'n v. Comm'r, 882 F.2d 123, 125 (4th Cir. 1989), *cert. den.*, 493 U.S. 1044 (1990).

Other courts of appeal have adopted this *profit motive* test. In varying forms of intensity, it has been cited favorably and applied by the Fifth Circuit,[50] Sixth Circuit,[51] and Eighth Circuit.[52]

It had been thought, until recent years, that the *profit motive* element was not pertinent to the definition of the term *trade or business* in the unrelated business income setting. This was because the statutory criteria for imposition of the unrelated business tax does not include a profit motivation factor. However, the law has changed dramatically and recently on this point, stimulated by caselaw redefining the term *trade or business* in another federal tax setting.

One of the principal characteristics of the concept of a trade or business had been that the activity "involves holding one's self out to others as engaged in the selling of goods or services."[53] However, the U.S. Tax Court rejected that test in 1983, terming it "overly restrictive," and adopted a "facts and circumstances" standard.[54] The case involved the tax status of a full-time gambler who was found to be in the business of gambling, notwithstanding the fact that he did not hold himself out as providing services to others. This approach has spread to the exempt organizations setting, so that the sale of goods or the performance of services can be a business activity, even when undertaken only by the tax-exempt organization for itself. As noted,[55] the Tax Court's position on this point was adopted by the U.S. Supreme Court and thereafter taken up by various courts of appeal.[56]

The IRS adheres to the application of the profit motive test. In one example, an exempt health care provider sold a building to another provider organization; it was used to operate a skilled nursing and personal care home. The selling entity provided food service to the patients for about seven months, at a net loss; the IRS characterized the food service operation as an "accommodation" to the purchasing entity.[57] Finding the activity to not be conducted in a manner characteristic of a commercial enterprise—that is, with a profit motive—the IRS looked

---

[50] Louisiana Credit Union League v. United States, 693 F.2d 525 (5th Cir. 1982).

[51] Professional Ins. Agents v. Comm'r, *supra* note 45.

[52] American Academy of Family Physicians v. United States, 91 F.3d 1155 (8th Cir. 1996).

[53] Gentile v. Comm'r, 65 T. C. 1, 5 (1975), quoting from the concurring opinion in Deputy v. DuPont, 308 U.S. 488, 499 (1940).

[54] Ditunno v. Comm'r, 80 T.C. 362, 366–367 (1983).

[55] See text accompanied by *supra* notes 43–44.

[56] In Comm'r v. Groetzinger, *supra* note 43, the Supreme Court held that a full-time gambler who made wagers solely for his own account was engaged in a trade or business for purposes of the business expense deduction (IRC § 162(a)) because the "primary purpose for engaging in the activity . . . [was] for income or profit" (at 35). The Court stated that this profit motive test was not a "test for all situations" (at 36), that its interpretation of the phrase *trade or business* was "confined to the specific sections of the [Internal Revenue] Code at issue here" (at 27, note 8) (namely, the business expense deduction), and that "[w]e do not purport to construe the phrase [*trade or business*] where it appears in other places" (*id.*). Yet the lower courts, ignoring the Court's admonitions, quickly exported that definition of the phrase from the business expense setting into the law of tax-exempt organizations. This process was stimulated by the Tax Court (e.g., West Va. State Medical Ass'n v. Comm'r, 91 T.C. 651 (1988), *aff'd* as noted *supra* note 49; National Water Well Ass'n, Inc. v. Comm'r, 92 T.C. 75 (1989). In general, Hopkins & Kaplan, "Could *Ditunno* and *Hoopengarner* Result in Expanding the Scope of Unrelated Business?," 60 *J. Tax.* (No. 1) 40 (1984).

[57] Tech. Adv. Mem. 9719002.

to the following factors: there was no evidence, such as a business plan, that a food service business was being started; the organization did not take any steps to expand the food service to other unrelated organizations; the organization did not actively solicit additional clientele for a meal (or food catering) business; the organization did not take any steps to increase the per-meal charge, which was substantially below cost; and there was not any contract between the organizations.

Where an activity carried on for profit constitutes an unrelated trade or business, no part of the trade or business may be excluded from classification as a business merely because it does not result in profit.[58]

There may be a third element to consider in this regard, also stemming from the view that, to be a *trade or business*, an income-producing activity of a tax-exempt organization must have the general characteristics of a trade or business. Some courts of appeals have recognized that an exempt organization must carry out extensive business activities over a substantial period of time to be considered engaged in a trade or business.[59] However, this aspect of the analysis is close to a separate test altogether, which is whether the business activities are regularly carried on.[60]

(b) Competition and Commerciality

The presence or absence of unfair competition is not among the formal criteria applied in assessing whether an activity is an unrelated business. This is the case even though concern about competition between tax-exempt and for-profit organizations is the underpinning of the unrelated business rules.[61] Thus, an activity of a tax-exempt organization may be wholly uncompetitive with an activity of a taxpaying organization and nonetheless be an unrelated business. For example, in an opinion finding that the operation of a bingo game by an exempt organization was an unrelated business, the court wrote that the "tax on unrelated business income is not limited to income earned by a trade or business that operates in competition with taxpaying entities."[62]

Yet, on occasion, the IRS takes the position that, where an activity of a tax-exempt organization constitutes a business and is not substantially related to the performance of exempt functions, there is sufficient likelihood—something akin to a presumption—that unfair competition is present. Where there is competition, a court may well conclude that the activity is being conducted in a commercial manner and thus is an unrelated business.[63]

---

[58] *Id.*

[59] In the business expense deduction context, Zell v. Comm'r, 763 F.2d 1139 (10th Cir. 1985); McDowell v. Ribicoff, 292 F.2d 174 (3d Cir. 1961), *cert. den.*, 368 U.S. 919 (1961). In the tax-exempt organizations setting, American Academy of Family Physicians v. United States, *supra* note 52; Professional Ins. Agents v. Comm'r, *supra* note 45.

[60] See *infra* § 3.

[61] See *supra* § 1.

[62] Clarence LaBelle Post No. 217 v. United States, 580 F.2d 270, 272 (8th Cir. 1978).

[63] E.g., Iowa State Univ. of Science & Technology v. United States, 500 F.2d 508 (Ct. Cl. 1974) (holding that the operation of a television station by an exempt university was done in a commercial manner (the station was an affiliate of a national television broadcasting company)).

(c) Charging of Fees

Many tax-exempt organizations charge fees for the services they provide; where the business generating this revenue is a related one, the receipts are characterized as *exempt function revenue*.[64] Universities, colleges, hospitals, museums, planetariums, orchestras, and like institutions generate exempt function revenue, without adverse impact as to their exempt status.[65] Organizations such as medical clinics, homes for the aged, and blood banks impose charges for their services and are not subject to unrelated income taxation (or deprived of tax exemption) as a result.[66] Indeed, the revenue ruling discussing the tax status of homes for the aged as charitable organizations observed that the "operating funds [of these homes] are derived principally from fees charged for residence in the home."[67] Similarly, the IRS ruled that a nonprofit theater may charge admission for its performances and nonetheless qualify as a charitable organization.[68] Other fee-based exempt charitable entities include hospices,[69] organizations providing specially designed housing for the elderly,[70] and organizations providing housing for the disabled.[71] Moreover, for some types of publicly supported charities, exempt function revenue is regarded as support enhancing public charity status.[72] Several categories of exempt organizations, such as business associations, unions, social clubs, fraternal groups, and veterans' organizations are dues-based entities.

Yet the receipt of fee-for-service revenue occasionally is regarded in some quarters as evidence of the conduct of an unrelated business. For example, the contention is made from time to time that an organization, to be charitable in nature, must provide its services and/or sell its goods without charge. In fact, the test is, for charitable and other exempt organizations, how the fees received are expended; the rendering of services without charge is not a prerequisite to tax-exempt status.

In one instance, the IRS opposed tax exemption for nonprofit consumer credit counseling agencies. The agencies asserted that their services, provided to individuals and families, as well as facilitating speakers and disseminating publications, are educational in nature as being forms of instruction of the public on subjects (such as budgeting) useful to the individual and beneficial to the community.[73] They also contended that their activities are charitable because they advance education and promote social welfare.[74] The IRS sought to deny these agencies tax-exempt status on the ground that they charge a fee for certain services, even though the fee is nominal and waived in instances of economic hard-

---

[64] See, e.g., § 11.3(b)(iv).

[65] IRC § 170(b)(1)(A)(ii), (iii); Reg. § 1.170A-9(e)(1)(ii); Reg. § 1.501(c)(3)-1(d)(3)(ii), Ex. (4).

[66] E.g., Rev. Rul. 72-124, 1972-1 C.B. 145; Rev. Rul. 70-590, 1970-2 C.B. 116; Rev. Rul. 66-323, 1966-2 C.B. 216, *mod. by* Rev. Rul. 78-145, 1978-1 C.B. 169.

[67] Rev. Rul. 72-124, *supra* note 66, at 145.

[68] Rev. Rul. 73-45, 1973-1 C.B. 220.

[69] Rev. Rul. 79-17, 1979-1 C.B. 193.

[70] Rev. Rul. 79-18, 1979-1 C.B. 194.

[71] Rev. Rul. 79-19, 1979-1 C.B. 195.

[72] IRC § 509(a)(2). See § 11.3(b)(iv).

[73] Reg. § 1.501(c)(3)-1(d)(3) (i) (b). See § 7.4.

[74] Reg. § 1.501(c)(3)-1(d)(2). See § 6.6.

ship. This effort was rebuffed in court.[75] Thereafter, the IRS's office of chief counsel advised that "[i]f the activity [of consumer credit counseling] may be deemed to benefit the community as a whole, the fact that fees are charged for the organization's services will not detract from the exempt nature of the activity" and that the "presence of a fee is relevant only if it inhibits accomplishment of the desired result."[76] (Earlier, the chief counsel's office wrote that the fact that a charitable organization charges a fee for a good or service "will be relevant in very few cases," that the "only inquiry" should be whether the charges "significantly detract from the organization's charitable purposes," and that the cost issue is pertinent only where the activities involved are commercial in nature.[77]) At about the same time, the IRS ruled that an organization that is operated to provide legal services to indigents may charge, for each hour of legal assistance provided, a "nominal hourly fee determined by reference to the client's own hourly income."[78]

There have been instances where the IRS determined that an organization is charitable in nature, and thus tax-exempt, because it provides services that are free to the recipients. However, this is an independent basis for finding a charitable activity, usually invoked where the services, assistance, or benefits provided are not inherently charitable in nature. This distinction may be seen in the treatment by the IRS of cooperative service organizations established by colleges and universities. In one instance, a computer services sharing organization was ruled to be a charitable organization because the IRS concluded that the services provided to the participating institutions of higher education were charitable as advancing education; no requirement was imposed that the services be provided without charge.[79] In another instance, a similar organization was found to be charitable even though the services it rendered to the participating educational institutions were regarded as non-exempt functions (being "administrative"); the distinguishing feature was that the organization received less than 15 percent of its financial support from the colleges and universities that received the services.[80] Thus, the recipient entities were receiving the services for, at most, a nominal charge. Had this latter organization been providing only an insubstantial extent of administrative services and a substantial amount of exempt services, its tax exemption would have been predicated on the basis that it was engaging in inherently exempt activities; the 15-percent rule was employed only as an alternative rationale for exemption as a charitable entity.[81]

Thus, the law does not require, as a condition of tax exemption or avoidance of unrelated income, that the organization provide services without charge.[82]

---

[75] Consumer Credit Counseling Service of Ala., Inc. v. United States, 78-2 U.S.T.C. ¶ 9660 (D.D.C. 1978).

[76] Gen. Couns. Mem. 38459.

[77] Gen. Couns. Mem. 37257.

[78] Rev. Rul. 78-428, 1978-2 C.B. 177.

[79] Rev. Rul. 74-614, 1974-2 C.B. 164, *amp. by* Rev. Rul. 81-29, 1981-1 C.B. 329.

[80] Rev. Rul. 71-529, 1971-2 C.B. 234.

[81] In general, see § 10.5.

[82] The "position that the test of a charitable institution is the extent of free services rendered, is difficult of application and unsound in theory" (Southern Methodist Hosp. & Sanatorium of Tucson v. Wilson, 77 P.2d 458, 462 (Ariz. 1943)).

Likewise, the fact that a tax-exempt organization charges a fee for the provision of goods or services, while a certain indicator that the underlying activity is a *business*, should not lead to an automatic conclusion that the business is an unrelated one.

(d) Fragmentation Rule

The IRS long contended that income from an activity can be taxed as unrelated business income even where the activity is an integral part of a larger activity that is in furtherance of a tax-exempt purpose. To ferret out unrelated activity, the IRS said that it had the authority to regard a tax-exempt organization as a bundle of discrete activities and could evaluate each of the activities in isolation to determine if one or more of them constitutes a trade or business. This approach, which is reflected in the tax regulations[83] and subsequently codified in 1969, is known as the *fragmentation* rule.

The statutory law embracing the *fragmentation* rule states that "an activity does not lose identity as trade or business merely because it is carried on within a larger aggregate of similar activities or within a larger complex of other endeavors which may, or may not, be related to the exempt purposes of the organization."[84] Thus, as noted, the IRS is empowered to fragment the operations of a tax-exempt organization, operated as an integrated whole, into its component parts in search of one or more unrelated businesses. This provision was initially directed at, but is by no means confined to, activities of soliciting, selling, and publishing commercial advertising, even where the advertising is published in a publication of a tax-exempt organization that contains editorial matter related to the exempt purposes of the organization.[85] That is, the advertising functions constitute an unrelated business even though the overall publishing function is a related business; the advertising is an integral part of the larger publication activity. The IRS appears to be unrestrained as to the level of detail it may pursue in application of the fragmentation rule. A telling illustration of this was a case involving a tax-exempt blood bank that sold blood plasma to commercial laboratories. The blood bank maintained inventories of blood and blood products that were furnished to hospitals for patient use. Because medical techniques have been perfected by which red blood cells are transfused into a patient in lieu of whole blood, the blood bank was left with a large supply of plasma after these cells were removed. Since the hospitals serviced by the blood bank required little of this by-product plasma, most of it was sold to commercial laboratories. The blood bank also obtained plasma (1) from donors by means of plasmapheresis, a procedure where blood is drawn, the red cells are separated and replaced in the donors, and the plasma collected; (2) in the form of salvage plasma, which is unused whole blood maintained in the inventory of the bank that is nearing the end of its shelf life; and (3) by purchase from other blood banks. The IRS ruled that "where the

---

[83] Reg. § 1.513-1 (b).
[84] IRC § 513(c).
[85] The caption of IRC § 513(c) (see text accompanied by *supra* note 19) is "Advertising, etc." The rules by which advertising revenue is cast as unrelated business income are the subject of *infra* § 5(f).

blood bank is merely disposing of products which result from the performance of its exempt functions, it will not be considered to be engaging in unrelated trade or business."[86] Consequently, the sale of by-product plasma was determined to not be an unrelated business; the same treatment was accorded the sale of salvage plasma. However, the sale of plasmapheresed plasma and purchased plasma was ruled to be an unrelated business, since this plasma was not a product resulting from the performance of the bank's tax-exempt functions.

In another instance, the IRS considered the activities of a tax-exempt organization, the primary purpose of which was to retain and stimulate trade in the downtown area of a city where adequate parking facilities were lacking. This organization—formed by professional, business, and other civic leaders—operated fringe parking facilities and a shuttle bus service to and from the downtown area. No merchant or group of merchants was favored by the manner in which the parking lot and bus were operated or in the selection of discharge and pickup points; they were not able to offer patrons free or discount parking or bus fares. The organization operated a park-and-shop plan by which patrons of particular downtown member merchants were able to park free at certain parking lots. Merchants participating in this plan purchased parking stamps, which were distributed to their customers and subsequently surrendered to the parking lot management instead of money. The IRS ruled that the operation of the fringe parking lot and shuttle bus service contributed importantly to the accomplishment of the organization's exempt purposes because it provided "easy and convenient access to the downtown area and, thus, stimulates and improves business conditions in the downtown area generally."[87] However, the IRS fragmented the park-and-shop plan activity, finding that it "constitutes the provision of a particular service to individual members of the organization" and therefore did not further the organization's exempt purposes and consequently was an unrelated business.[88]

There are other examples of application of the fragmentation rule. In one, the IRS determined that use of the golf course of a university by its students and employees was not unrelated business, while use of the course by alumni of the university, members of its President's Club, other major donors, and guests of these individuals was unrelated business.[89] In another, the IRS used the fragmentation rule to differentiate between related and unrelated educational and religious tours conducted by a tax-exempt organization.[90]

(e) Non-Business Activities

Not every activity of a tax-exempt organization that generates a financial return is a trade or business for purposes of the unrelated business rules. As the U.S. Supreme Court observed, the "narrow category of trade or business" is a "con-

---

[86] Rev. Rul. 78-145, 1978-1 C.B. 169, 170.
[87] Rev. Rul. 79-31, 1979-1 C.B. 206, 207.
[88] *Id.*
[89] Tech. Adv. Mem. 9645004.
[90] Tech. Adv. Mem. 9702004.

cept which falls far short of reaching every income or profit making activity."[91] More specifically, an appellate court wrote that "there are instances where some activities by some exempt organizations to earn income in a noncommercial manner will not amount to the conduct of a trade or business."[92]

Probably the most obvious of these non-business activities is the management by a tax-exempt organization of its own investment properties. Under the general rules (pertaining to the business expense deduction) defining *business* activity, it is clear that the management of an investment portfolio composed wholly of the manager's own securities does not constitute the carrying on of a trade or business. The Supreme Court held that the mere keeping of records and collection of income from securities, through managerial attention to the investments, is not the operation of a business.[93] On that occasion, the Court sustained the government's position that "mere personal investment activities never constitute carrying on a trade or business."[94] Subsequently, the Court stated that "investing is not a trade or business."[95] Likewise, a court of appeals observed that the "mere management of investments . . . is insufficient to constitute the carrying on of a trade or business."[96]

This concept is clearly applicable in the tax-exempt organizations context. For example, the IRS ruled that the receipt of income by an exempt employees' trust from installment notes purchased from the employer-settlor is not income derived from the operation of a business.[97] The IRS noted that the trust "merely keeps the records and receives the periodic payments of principal and interest collected for it by the employer."[98] For a time, there was controversy over whether the practice engaged in by some tax-exempt organizations of lending securities to brokerage houses for compensation was an unrelated business.[99] However, the IRS came around to the view that securities lending is a form of "ordinary or routine investment activities" and thus is not a business.[100] This matter was subsequently further resolved by statute.[101]

There are other rationales as to why a particular activity does not rise to

---

[91] Whipple v. Comm'r, 373 U.S. 193, 197, 201 (1963).

[92] Steamship Trade Assn of Baltimore, Inc. v. Comm'r, *supra* note 47, at 1497. Also Blake Constr. Co., Inc. v. United States, 572 F.2d 820 (Ct. Cl. 1978); Monfore v. United States, 77-2 U.S.T.C. ¶ 9528 (Ct. Cl. 1977); Adirondack League Club v. Comm'r, 458 F.2d 506 (2d Cir. 1972); Oklahoma Cattlemen's Ass'n, Inc. v. United States, 310 F. Supp. 320 (W.D. Okla. 1969); McDowell v. Ribicoff, *supra* note 59.

[93] Higgins v. Comm'r, 312 U.S. 212, 218 (1941).

[94] *Id.* at 215.

[95] Whipple v. Comm'r, *supra* note 91 at 202.

[96] Continental Trading, Inc. v. Comm'r, 265 F.2d 40, 43 (9th Cir. 1959), *cert. den.*, 361 U.S. 827 (1959). Also VanWart v. Comm'r, 295 U.S. 112 (1935); Deputy v. duPont, 308 U.S. 488 (1940) (concurring opinion); Moller v. United States, 721 F.2d 810 (Fed. Cir. 1983); Comm'r v. Burnett, 118 F.2d 659 (5th Cir. 1941); Rev. Rul. 56-511, 1956-2 C.B. 170.

[97] Rev. Rul. 69-574. 1969-2 C.B. 130.

[98] *Id.* at 131. Also The Marion Found. v. Comm'r, 19 T.C.M. 99 (1960) (holding that certain investment activities were not businesses).

[99] E.g., Stern & Sullivan, "Exempt Organizations Which Lend Securities Risk Imposition of Unrelated Business Income Tax," 45 *J. Tax.* 240 (1976).

[100] Rev. Rul. 78-88, 1978-1 C.B. 163.

[101] See § 27.1(d).

the level of a trade or business. One is that the exempt organization did not engage in the activity with the requisite profit motive.[102] The most significant case on this point involved an association, representing family physicians and promoting quality health care, that was held not taxable on certain payments it received through its sponsorship of group insurance plans that were available to its members and their employees.[103] A for-profit company administered the insurance plans; the company reported twice a year to a committee of the association and was required to obtain the committee's approval before making any changes to the policies. These payments were based on a specified annual fixed percentage of insurance reserves and were generated by the insurance company's investment of the reserves. The payments were held to not be compensation for services rendered and not "profit in a commercial sense."[104] Interest was payable without regard to the profitability of the group insurance plans. The court wrote that the annual payments "were neither brokerage fees nor other compensation for commercial services, but were the way the parties decided to acknowledge the . . . [association's] eventual claim to the excess reserves while . . . [the insurance company] was still holding and using the reserves."[105] The court also found that this activity did not constitute a business because the association's involvement in the insurance plans was not extensive and did not possess the general characteristics of a trade or business.[106]

Another case involved a tax-exempt dental society that sponsored a payment plan to finance dental care. The society received refunds for income taxes and interest on amounts paid as excessive reserve funds from a bank and as collections on defaulted notes. Thwarting an IRS attempt to tax the net revenue from the program as unrelated income, a court held that this activity of the society did not amount to a business because the organization lacked any control over the possible financial results of the bank's efforts.[107] A comparable position was taken by a court in concluding that a tax-exempt organization did not engage in an unrelated business by making health insurance available to its members, in that the organization did not control the financial result of the insurance activities.[108]

Funds received by a tax-exempt organization as an agent for another orga-

---

[102] See *supra* § 2(a).
[103] American Academy of Family Physicians v. United States, *supra* note 52.
[104] *Id*. at 1158.
[105] *Id*. at 1159.
[106] *Id*. The court additionally observed that, even if the insurance company made the payments to the association for the latter's sponsorship, the payments would not be taxable, in that "it does not matter whether the payments were brokerage fees, gratuities to promote goodwill, or interest"—they were not taxable because the association was not engaging in business activity for a profit (American Academy of Family Physicians v. United States, *supra* note 52, at 1159–1160).

Nonetheless, the IRS remains of the view that these types of oversight and like activities with respect to insurance programs constitute unrelated business (e.g., Tech. Adv. Mem. 9612003, concerning a charitable organization fostering competition in a sport that provided certain administrative services in connection with an insurance program covering its members for practices and other sport activities). See § 10.2.
[107] San Antonio Dist. Dental Soc'y v. United States, 340 F. Supp. 11 (W.D. Tex. 1972).
[108] Carolinas Farm & Power Equip. Dealers Ass'n, Inc. v. United States, 541 F. Supp. 86 (E.D.N. Car. 1982), *aff'd, supra* note 46.

nization are not taxable income to the exempt organization and thus are not unrelated business income.[109]

Another illustration of a transaction involving a tax-exempt organization that is not a business undertaking is the occasional sale of an item of property.[110] This aspect of the law is closely analogous to the *regularly carried on* test.[111]

(f) Efficiencies of Operation

On occasion, a court will focus on the fact that a tax-exempt organization is operating in a fashion that is considered "efficient," "effectively managed," "run like a business," and the like.[112] This can lead to a finding that the organization, or an activity of it, is—for that reason alone—a business undertaking. Conclusions of this nature are reflected in opinions of the U.S. District Court for the District of Columbia[113] and the U.S. Tax Court.[114]

§ 26.3   DEFINITION OF *REGULARLY CARRIED ON*

As noted, gross income of a tax-exempt organization may be includable in the computation of unrelated business income where the trade or business that produced the income is *regularly carried on* by the organization.

(a) General Principles

In determining whether a trade or business from which a particular amount of gross income is derived by a tax-exempt organization is *regularly carried on*,[115] regard must be had to the frequency and continuity with which the activities productive of the income are conducted and the manner in which they are pursued. This requirement is applied in light of the purpose of the unrelated business income rules, which is to place tax-exempt organization business activities on the same tax basis as the nonexempt business endeavors with which they compete.[116] Thus, for example, specific business activities of a tax-exempt organization will ordinarily be deemed to be *regularly carried on* if they manifest a frequency and continuity, and are pursued in a manner generally similar to comparable commercial activities of nonexempt organizations.[117]

---

[109] Priv. Ltr. Rul. 7823048.

[110] E.g., Priv. Ltr. Rul. 9316032 (in which the IRS held that a sale of property was not under circumstances where the property was held primarily for sale to customers in the ordinary course of business, following the standard articulated in Malat v. Riddell, 383 U.S. 569 (1966)). See § 27.1(j).

[111] See *infra* § 3.

[112] See § 4.9.

[113] E.g., The Incorporated Trustees of the Gospel Worker Soc'y v. United States, 510 F. Supp. 374 (D.D.C. 1981), *aff'd*, 672 F.2d 894 (D.C. Cir. 1981), *cert. den.*, 456 U.S. 944 (1981).

[114] E.g., Presbyterian and Reformed Publishing Co. v. Comm'r, 79 T.C. 1070 (1983).

[115] IRC § 512.

[116] See *supra* § 1. This is one of only two aspects of the unrelated business rules where the commerciality doctrine (see Chapter 25) is expressly taken into account in the statute or tax regulations. The other aspect is the subject of § 22.1.

[117] Reg. § 1.513-1(c)(1).

An illustration of this body of law is the case of a tax-exempt organization that published a yearbook for its membership. The publication contained advertising; the organization contracted on an annual basis with a commercial firm for solicitation of advertising sales, printing, and collection of advertising charges. Although the editorial materials were prepared by the staff of the organization, the organization, by means of its contract with the commercial firm, was ruled by the IRS to be "engaging in an extensive campaign of advertising solicitation" and thus to be "conducting competitive and promotional efforts typical of commercial endeavors."[118] Therefore, the income derived by this organization from the sale of advertising in its yearbook was deemed to be unrelated business income.

By contrast, a one-time sale of property (as opposed to an ongoing income-producing program) is not an activity that is regularly carried on and thus does not give rise to unrelated business income. For example, a tax-exempt organization that was formed to deliver diagnostic and medical health care and that developed a series of computer programs concerning management and administrative matters, such as patient admissions and billings, payroll, purchases, inventory, and medical records, sold some or all of the programs to another exempt organization comprising three teaching hospitals affiliated with a university; the income derived from the sale was held to be from a "one-time only operation" and thus not taxable as unrelated business income.[119] Likewise, the transfer of investment assets from a public charity to its supporting organization[120] is exempt from unrelated business taxation under this rule,[121] as is the infrequent sale of parcels of real estate.[122]

(b) Determining Regularity

Where income-producing activities are of a kind normally conducted by nonexempt commercial organizations on a year-round basis, the conduct of the activities by a tax-exempt organization over a period of only a few weeks does not constitute the regular carrying on of a business.[123] For example, the operation of a sandwich stand by a hospital auxiliary organization for two weeks at a state fair is not the regular conduct of a business.[124] However, the conduct of year-round business activities for one day each week, such as the operation of a commercial parking lot once a week, constitutes the regular carrying on of a business.[125]

If income-producing activities are of a kind normally undertaken by nonexempt commercial organizations only on a seasonal basis, the conduct of the activities by a tax-exempt organization during a significant portion of the season

---

[118] Rev. Rul. 73-424, 1973-2 C.B. 190, 191.

[119] Priv. Ltr. Rul. 7905129.

[120] See § 11.3(c).

[121] E.g., Priv. Ltr. Rul. 9425030.

[122] The gain from transactions of this nature may be protected from taxation by the exclusion for capital gain (see § 27.1(j)). In general, Roha, "Exempt Organizations and Real Estate Sales—How Many Bricks Build a UBIT Liability?," 4 J. Tax. Exempt Orgs. 5 (Spring 1992).

[123] Reg. § 1.513-1(c)(2)(i).

[124] Id.

[125] S. Rep. No. 2375, 81st Cong., 2d Sess. 106–107 (1950).

ordinarily constitutes the regular conduct of a business.[126] For example, the operation of a track for horse racing for several weeks in a year is the regular conduct of a business where it is usual to carry on the business only during a particular season.[127] Likewise, where a distribution of greeting cards celebrating a holiday was deemed to be an unrelated business, the IRS measured regularity in terms of that holiday's season.[128]

In determining whether intermittently conducted activities are regularly carried on, the manner of conduct of the activities must, as noted, be compared with the manner in which commercial activities are normally pursued by nonexempt organizations.[129] In general, tax-exempt organization business activities that are engaged in only discontinuously or periodically will not be considered regularly carried on if they are conducted without the competitive and promotional efforts typical of commercial endeavors.[130] As an illustration, the publication of advertising in programs for sports events or music or drama performances will not ordinarily be deemed to be the regular carrying on of a business.[131] Conversely, where the nonqualifying sales are not merely casual but are systematically and consistently promoted and carried on by the organization, they meet the requirement of regularity.[132]

In determining whether a business is regularly carried on, the functions of a service provider with which a tax-exempt organization has contracted may be attributed to the exempt organization for these purposes. This is likely to be the case where the contract denominates the service provider as an agent of the exempt organization, in that the activities of an agent are attributed to the principal for law analysis purposes. In such a circumstance, the time expended by the service provider is attributed to the exempt organization for purposes of determining regularity.[133]

It has been held that noncompetition under a covenant not to compete, characterized as a "one-time agreement not to engage in certain activities," is not a taxable business inasmuch as the "activity" is not "continuous and regular."[134]

(c) Fund-Raising and Similar Activities

Fund-raising activities, by charitable and other tax-exempt organizations, can constitute unrelated business activities.[135] Inasmuch as these activities rarely are

---

[126] *Id.*

[127] *Id.* Also Rev. Rul. 68-505, 1968-2 C.B. 248.

[128] Priv. Ltr. Rul. 8203134.

[129] Reg. § 1.513-1(c)(1), (2)(ii).

[130] Reg. § 1.513-1(c)(2)(ii). Also Adam v. Comm'r, 60 T.C. 996 (1973).

[131] *Id.*

[132] *Id.*

[133] National Collegiate Athletic Ass'n v. Commr, 92 T.C. 456 (1989), *aff'd, infra* note 142.

[134] Ohio Farm Bureau Fed. Inc. v. Comm'r, 106 T.C. 222, 234 (1996). This opinion caused the IRS to issue Gen. Couns. Mem. 39891, revoking Gen. Couns. Mem. 39865 (which held that refraining from competition in this context was a business activity).

[135] See *infra* § 5(g); Hopkins, *The Law of Fund-Raising, Second Edition* (New York: John Wiley & Sons, 1996), Chapter 6 § 6.

inherently exempt functions, the rules as to *regularity* are often the only basis on which the income from these activities is not taxed as unrelated business income.

Certain intermittent income-producing activities occur so infrequently that neither their recurrence nor the manner of their conduct will cause them to be regarded as trades or businesses that are regularly carried on.[136] For example, fund-raising activities lasting only a short time are not ordinarily treated as being regularly carried on if they recur only occasionally or sporadically.[137] Furthermore, activities will not be regarded as regularly carried on merely because they are conducted on an annual basis.[138] It is for this reason that many special event fund-raising activities, such as dances, auctions, tournaments, car washes, and bake sales, do not give rise to unrelated business income.[139] In one instance, a court concluded that a vaudeville show conducted one weekend per year was an intermittent fund-raising activity and thus not regularly carried on.[140]

(d) Preparatory Time

An issue of some controversy is whether the time expended by a tax-exempt organization in preparing for a business undertaking should be taken into account in assessing whether the activity is regularly carried on. The IRS asserts that this preparatory time should be considered, even where the event itself occupies only one or two days each year.[141] However, this preparatory time argument has been rejected on the occasions it was considered by a court.[142] In the principal case, a federal court of appeals held that the preparatory time argument is inconsistent with the tax regulations, which do not mention the concept. The court referenced the example concerning operation of the sandwich stand at a state fair,[143] denigrating the thought that preparatory time should be taken into account as follows: "The regulations do not mention time spent in planning the activity, building the stand, or purchasing the alfalfa sprouts for the sandwiches."[144]

Nonetheless, the IRS is in disagreement with these holdings, writes private letter rulings and technical advice memoranda that are openly contrary to these cases, and continues to litigate the issue.[145] One of these instances concerned a tax-exempt organization which sponsored a concert series open to the public occupying two weekends each year, one in the spring and one in the fall. The preparation and ticket solicitation for each of the concerts usually occupies up to six months. Taking into account the preparatory time involved, the IRS

---

[136] Reg. § 1.513-1(c)(2)(iii).
[137] *Id.*
[138] *Id.*
[139] E.g., Orange County Builders Ass'n, Inc. v. United States, 65-2 U.S.T.C. ¶ 9679 (S.D. Cal. 1965).
[140] Suffolk County Patrolmen's Benevolent Ass'n, Inc. v. Comm'r, 77 T.C. 1314 (1981).
[141] E.g., Tech. Adv. Mem. 9147007; Priv. Ltr. Rul. 9137002.
[142] National Collegiate Athletic Ass'n v. Comm'r, 914 F.2d 1417 (10th Cir. 1990); Suffolk County Patrolmen's Benevolent Assn, Inc. v. Comm'r, *supra* note 140.
[143] See text accompanied by *supra* note 124.
[144] National Collegiate Athletic Assn v. Comm'r, *supra* note 140, at 1423.
[145] AOD No. 1991-015.

concluded that the concerts were unrelated business activities that were regularly carried on.[146]

§ 26.4   DEFINITION OF *SUBSTANTIALLY RELATED*

As noted, gross income of a tax-exempt organization may be includible in the computation of unrelated business income where it is income from a trade or business that is regularly carried on and that is not *substantially related* to the exempt purposes of the organization.[147] (The fact that the organization needs or uses the funds for an exempt purpose does not make the underlying activity a related business.) Thus, it is necessary to examine the relationship between the business activity that generates the income in question—the activity, that is, of producing or distributing the goods or performing the services involved—and the accomplishment of the organization's exempt purposes.[148]

(a) General Principles

A trade or business is *related* to tax-exempt purposes of an organization only where the conduct of the business activity has a causal relationship to the achievement of an exempt purpose (again, other than through the production of income); it is *substantially related* only if the causal relationship is a substantial one.[149] Thus, for the conduct of a business from which a particular amount of gross income is derived to be substantially related to tax-exempt purposes, the production or distribution of the goods or the performance of the services from which the gross income is derived must contribute importantly to the accomplishment of these purposes.[150] Where the production or distribution of the goods or the performance of services does not contribute importantly to the accomplishment of the exempt purposes of an organization, the income from the sale of the goods or the performance of the services does not derive from the conduct of related business.[151] A court wrote that resolution of the substantial relationship test requires "an examination of the relationship between the business activities which generate the particular income in question . . . and the accomplishment of the organization's exempt purposes."[152]

Certainly, gross income derived from charges for the performance of a tax-exempt function does not constitute gross income from the conduct of an unrelated business.[153] Thus, income is not taxed when it is generated by functions

---

[146] Tech. Adv. Mem. 9712001. The IRS acquiesced in the *Suffolk County Patrolmen's Ass'n* case (*supra* note 140) (AOD 1249 (1984). However, that acquiescence had no bearing in this instance, the IRS said, inasmuch as the preparatory time in that case was "much shorter."

[147] IRC § 513(a) ; Reg. § 1.513-1(a).

[148] Reg. § 1.513-1(d)(1).

[149] Reg. § 1.513-1(d)(2).

[150] *Id.*

[151] *Id.*

[152] Louisiana Credit Union League v. United States, 693 F.2d 525, 534 (5th Cir. 1982).

[153] Reg. § 1.513-1(d)(4)(i).

such as performances by students enrolled in a school for training children in the performing arts, the conduct of refresher courses to improve the trade skills of members of a union, and the presentation of a trade show for exhibiting industry products by a trade association to stimulate demand for the products.[154] Also, dues paid by bona fide members of a tax-exempt organization are forms of related income.[155]

Whether activities productive of gross income contribute importantly to the accomplishment of an organization's exempt purpose depends in each case upon the facts and circumstances involved.[156] One court observed that each of these instances requires a case-by-case identification of the exempt purpose involved and an analysis of how the activity contributed to the advancement of that purpose.[157] By reason of court opinions and IRS rulings, there have been many determinations over the years as to whether particular activities are related businesses[158] or unrelated businesses.[159]

(b) Size and Extent Test

In determining whether an activity contributes importantly to the accomplishment of a tax-exempt purpose, the *size and extent* of the activity must be considered in relation to the nature and extent of the exempt function that it purportedly serves.[160] Thus, where income is realized by a tax-exempt organization from an activity that is generally related to the performance of its exempt functions, but the activity is conducted on a scale that is larger than reasonably necessary for performance of the functions, the gross income attributable to the portion of the activity that is in excess of the needs associated with exempt functions constitutes gross income from the conduct of an unrelated business.[161] This type of income is not derived from the production or distribution of goods or the performance of services that contribute importantly to the accomplishment of any exempt purpose of the organization.[162]

For example, one of the activities of a trade association, which had a membership of businesses in a particular state, was to supply companies (members and nonmembers) with job injury histories on prospective employees. Despite the association's contention that this service contributed to the accomplishment of its exempt purposes, the IRS ruled that the operation was an unrelated business, in that the activity went "well beyond" any mere development and promo-

---

[154] *Id.*

[155] E.g., Rev. Rul. 67-109, 1967-1 C.B. 136. However, certain forms of associate members dues are taxable as unrelated business income (see *infra* § 5(d)(iii), § 27.2(l)).

[156] Reg. § 1.513-1(d)(2).

[157] Hi-Plains Hosp. v. United States, 670 F.2d 528 (5th Cir. 1982). Also Huron Clinic Foundation v. United States, 212 F. Supp. 847 (D.S.D. 1962).

[158] See *infra* § 4(f).

[159] See *infra* § 4(g).

[160] Reg. § 1.513-1(d)(3). One court discussed the point that, in a search for unrelated activity, there should be an examination of the scale on which the activity is conducted (Hi-Plains Hosp. v. United States, *supra* note 157).

[161] Reg. § 1.513-1(d)(3).

[162] *Id.* In essence, the size and extent test is an application of the fragmentation rule (see *supra* § 2(d)).

tion of efficient business practices.[163] The IRS adopted a similar posture in ruling that a retail grocery store operation, formed to sell food in a poverty area at below-market prices and to provide job training for unemployed residents in the area, could not qualify for tax exemption because the operation was conducted "on a much larger scale than reasonably necessary" for the training program.[164] Similarly, the IRS ruled that the provision of private duty nurses to unrelated tax-exempt organizations, by an exempt health care organization that provided temporary nurses and private duty nurses to patients of related organizations as related businesses, was an activity performed on a scale "much larger" than necessary for the achievement of exempt functions.[165]

By contrast, a tax-exempt organization formed to provide a therapeutic program for emotionally disturbed adolescents was the subject of a ruling from the IRS that a retail grocery store operation, almost fully staffed by adolescents to secure their emotional rehabilitation, was not an unrelated business because it was operated on a scale no larger than reasonably necessary for its training and rehabilitation program.[166] A like finding was made in relation to the manufacture and marketing of toys, which was the means by which an exempt organization accomplished its charitable purpose of training unemployed and underemployed individuals.[167]

(c) Same State Rule

Ordinarily, gross income from the sale of products that result from the performance of tax-exempt functions does not constitute gross income from the conduct of an unrelated business if the product is sold in substantially the *same state* it is in upon completion of the exempt functions.[168] Thus, in the case of a charitable organization engaged in a program of rehabilitation of disabled individuals, income from the sale of items made by them as part of their rehabilitation training is not gross income from the conduct of an unrelated business. The income in this instance is from the sale of products, the production of which contributes importantly to the accomplishment of the organization's exempt purposes, namely, rehabilitation of the disabled.[169] Conversely, if a product resulting from an exempt function is utilized or exploited in further business endeavors beyond that reasonably appropriate or necessary for disposition in the state it is in upon completion of exempt functions, the gross income derived from these endeavors would be from the conduct of unrelated business.[170]

---

[163] Rev. Rul. 73-386, 1973-2 C.B. 191, 192.
[164] Rev. Rul. 73-127, 1973-1 C.B. 221, 222. Under similar facts, a nonprofit organization that operated restaurants and health food stores in accordance with the tenets of a church was denied tax-exempt status as a charitable entity on the ground that it was operated for substantially commercial purposes (Living Faith, Inc. v. Comm'r, 60 T.C.M. 710 (1990), *aff'd*, 950 F.2d 365 (7th Cir. 1991).
[165] Priv. Ltr. Rul. 9535023.
[166] Rev. Rul. 76-94, 1976-1 C.B. 171.
[167] Rev. Rul. 73-128, 1973-1 C.B. 222.
[168] Reg. § 1.513-1(d)(4)(ii).
[169] *Id.*
[170] *Id.*

As an illustration, in the case of an experimental dairy herd maintained for scientific purposes by an exempt organization, income from the sale of milk and cream produced in the ordinary course of operation of the project is not gross income from the conduct of unrelated business. However, if the organization utilized the milk and cream in the further manufacture of food items, such as ice cream and pastries, the gross income from the sale of these products would be from the conduct of unrelated business—unless the manufacturing activities themselves contributed importantly to the accomplishment of an exempt purpose of the organization.[171] Similarly, a charitable organization that operated a salmon hatchery as an exempt function was able to sell a portion of its harvested salmon stock in an unprocessed condition to fish processors in an untaxed business. By contrast, when it converted the fish into salmon nuggets (fish that was seasoned, formed into nugget shape, and breaded), the sale of the fish in that state was an unrelated business.[172]

(d) Dual Use Rule

An asset or facility of a tax-exempt organization that is necessary to the conduct of exempt functions may also be utilized for commercial purposes. In these *dual use* instances, the mere fact of the use of the asset or facility in an exempt function does not, by itself, make the income from the commercial endeavor gross income from a related business. The test is whether the activities productive of the income in question contribute importantly to the accomplishment of exempt purposes.[173] For example, a tax-exempt museum may have an auditorium that is designed and equipped for showing educational films in connection with its program of public education in the arts and sciences. The theater is a principal feature of the museum and is in continuous operation during the hours the museum is open to the public. If the museum were to operate the theater as a motion picture theater for public entertainment during the evening hours when the museum is otherwise closed, gross income from that operation would be gross income from the conduct of an unrelated business.[174] Similarly, a mailing service operated by a tax-exempt organization was ruled to be an unrelated trade or business even though the mailing equipment was also used for exempt purposes.[175]

Another illustration is the athletic facilities of a college or university, which, while used primarily for educational purposes, may also be made available for members of the faculty, other employees of the institution, and members of the general public. Income derived from the use of the facilities by those who are not students or employees of the institution is likely to be unrelated business income.[176] For example, the IRS ruled that the operation by an exempt school of a

---

[171] *Id.*
[172] Priv. Ltr. Rul. 9320042.
[173] Reg. § 1.513-1(d)(4)(iii).
[174] *Id.*
[175] Rev. Rul. 68-550, 1968-2 C.B. 249.
[176] E.g., Tech. Adv. Mem. 9645004 (concerning dual use of a university's golf course).

ski facility for the general public was the conduct of an unrelated business, while use of the facility by the students of the school for recreational purposes and in its physical education program were related activities.[177] Likewise, a college that made available its facilities and personnel to an individual not associated with the institution for the conduct of a summer tennis camp was ruled to be engaged in the conduct of an unrelated business.[178]

The provision of athletic or other activities by an educational institution to outsiders may be a tax-exempt function, inasmuch as the instruction of individuals on the subject of a sport can be an educational activity.[179] As illustrations, the IRS held that the following were exempt educational activities: the conduct of a summer hockey camp for youths by a college,[180] the conduct of four summer sports camps by a university,[181] and the operation of a summer sports camp by a university-affiliated athletic association.[182] Similarly, the IRS determined that a college may operate a professional repertory theater on its campus that is open to the general public[183] and that a college may make its facilities available to outside organizations for the conduct of conferences[184]—both activities being in furtherance of exempt purposes.

This area of the law intertwines with the exclusion from unrelated income taxation for rent received by tax-exempt organizations.[185] For example, a college may lease its facilities to a professional sports team for the conduct of a summer camp and receive nontaxable lease income, as long as the college does not provide food or cleaning services to the team.[186] By contrast, where the institution provides services, such as cleaning, food, laundry, security, and grounds maintenance, the exclusion for rent is defeated.[187]

This dichotomy is reflected in the treatment the IRS accorded a school that used its tennis facilities, which were utilized during the academic year in the institution's educational program, in the summer as a public tennis club operated by employees of the school's athletic department. Because the school not only furnished its facilities, but operated the tennis club through its own employees who rendered substantial services for the participants in the club, the IRS held that the operation of the club was an unrelated business and that the income derived from the club's operation was not sheltered by the exclusion for rental income.[188] However, the IRS also observed that, if the school had furnished its tennis facilities to an unrelated individual without the provision of services (leaving it to the lessee to hire the club's administrators) and for a fixed fee not dependent on the income or profits derived from the leased property, the rental income

---

[177] Rev. Rul. 78-98, 1978-1 C.B. 167.
[178] Rev. Rul. 76-402, 1976-2 C.B. 177.
[179] E.g., Rev. Rul. 77-365, 1977-2 C.B. 192. In general, see § 7.4.
[180] Priv. Ltr. Rul. 8024001.
[181] Priv. Ltr. Rul. 7908009.
[182] Priv. Ltr. Rul. 7826003.
[183] Priv. Ltr. Rul. 7840072.
[184] Priv. Ltr. Rul. 8020010.
[185] See § 27.1(h).
[186] Priv. Ltr. Rul. 8024001.
[187] Priv. Ltr. Rul. 7840072.
[188] Rev. Rul. 80-297, 1980-2 C.B. 196.

exclusion would have been available.[189] In a comparable ruling, the IRS determined that, when a university that leased its stadium to a professional sports team for several months of the year and provided the utilities, grounds maintenance, and dressing room, linen, and stadium security services, it was engaged in an unrelated business and was not entitled to the rental income exclusion.[190]

(e) Exploitation Rule

Activities carried on by a tax-exempt organization in the performance of exempt functions may generate good will or other intangibles that are capable of being exploited in commercial endeavors. Where an exempt organization exploits this type of intangible in commercial activities, the mere fact that the resultant income depended in part upon an exempt function of the organization does not make it gross income from a related business. In these cases, unless the activities contribute importantly to the accomplishment of an exempt purpose, the income that they produce is gross income from the conduct of an unrelated business.[191]

Thus, the rules with respect to taxation of advertising revenue received by tax-exempt organizations treat advertising as an exploitation of exempt publication activity.[192] As another illustration of this *exploitation rule*, where access to athletic facilities of an educational institution by students is covered by a general student fee, outside use may trigger the exploitation rule; if separate charges for use of the facilities are imposed on students, faculty, and outsiders, any unrelated income is a product of the dual-use rule.[193]

(f) Related Business Activities

There are many determinations by the courts and the IRS that activities by tax-exempt organizations are related businesses. For example, a furniture shop operated by an exempt halfway house and staffed by its residents was found to be a related business.[194] An organization that promoted professional automobile racing was held to not receive unrelated business income from the conduct of a product certification program, because the program was part of the organization's regulatory activities designed to prevent trade abuses in the automobile racing business.[195] The certification of the accuracy and authenticity of export documents by a tax-exempt chamber of commerce, for the purpose of providing an independent verification of the origin of exported goods, was ruled to be a related business because the activity "stimulates international commerce by facili-

---

[189] *Id.*

[190] Rev. Rul. 80-298, 1980-2 C.B. 197. The dual use rule is, in some ways, an application of the fragmentation rule (see *supra* § 2(d)).

[191] Reg. § 1.513-1(d)(4)(iv).

[192] See *infra* § 5(f).

[193] E.g., Priv. Ltr. Rul. 7823062.

[194] Rev. Rul. 75-472, 1975-2 C.B. 208.

[195] Priv. Ltr. Rul. 7922001.

tating the export of goods and, thus, promotes and stimulates business conditions in the community generally."[196]

A national conservation education organization was ruled to be engaging in related activities, by the sale of stationery items, serving items, desk accessories, nature gift items, emblem items, toys, and wearing apparel, because each of the product lines served to stimulate the public about wildlife preservation.[197] The operation of a restaurant and cocktail lounge by tax-exempt organizations, such as social clubs and veterans' organizations, for their members is an activity that is in furtherance of their exempt purposes.[198]

Other court opinions and IRS rulings providing illustrations of related business activities include these: the sponsorship of championship tournaments by a tax-exempt association organized to promote a sport;[199] the charging of activity fees to libraries of for-profit organizations for computer-stored library cataloging services;[200] the operation of a beauty shop and barber shop by a tax-exempt senior citizens' center:[201] the sale of members' horses by a tax-exempt horsebreeders' association,[202] the sale of greeting cards and art reproductions by a tax-exempt museum,[203] the conduct of weekly dances by a tax-exempt volunteer fire company;[204] the tax collection activities by a tax-exempt social welfare organization on behalf of its member municipalities;[205] sponsorship of a bank payment plan for the membership of a tax-exempt professional society;[206] gambling receipts from members of tax-exempt social and fraternal organizations;[207] loan organization and servicing activities;[208] a project to facilitate court proceedings by telephone;[209] the operation of a lawyer referral service by a tax-exempt bar association;[210] the performance of management services for a tax-exempt charitable organization;[211] the provision of group insurance and workers' compensation self-insurance for member counties by a tax-exempt social welfare organization;[212] the provision of worker's compensation insurance coverage to county government employees by a tax-exempt social welfare organization;[213] the provision of veterinary services

---

[196] Rev. Rul. 81-127, 1981-1 C.B. 357, 358.

[197] Priv. Ltr. Rul. 8107006.

[198] Priv. Ltr. Rul. 8120006.

[199] Rev. Rul. 58-502, 1958-2 C.B. 271, as clarified by Rev. Rul. 80-294, 1980-2 C.B. 187. Cf. Mobile Arts & Sports Ass'n v. United States, 148 F. Supp. 315 (S.D. Ala. 1957).

[200] Priv. Ltr. Rul. 7816061.

[201] Rev. Rul. 81-61, 1981-1 C.B. 355.

[202] Priv. Ltr. Rul. 8112013.

[203] Rev. Rul. 73–104, 1973-1 C.B. 263.

[204] Rev. Rul. 74–361, 1974-2 C.B. 159. Also Rev. Rul. 68–225, 1968-1 C.B. 283; Rev. Rul. 67–296, 1967-2 C.B. 212; Rev. Rul. 67–219, 1967-2 C.B. 1967-2 C.B. 210; Rev. Rul. 64–182, 1964-1 (Part 1) C.B. 186. Maryland State Fair & Agric. Soc'y, Inc. v. Chamberlin, 55-1 U.S.T.C. ¶ 9399 (D. Md. 1955).

[205] Kentucky Mun. League v. Comm'r, 81 T.C. 156 (1983).

[206] San Antonio Dist. Dental Soc'y v. United States, *supra* note 107.

[207] Gen. Couns. Mem. 39061.

[208] Priv. Ltr. Rul. 8349051.

[209] Priv. Ltr. Rul. 8351160.

[210] Priv. Ltr. Rul. 8417003.

[211] Priv. Ltr. Rul. 8422168.

[212] Priv. Ltr. Rul. 8442092.

[213] Tech. Adv. Mem. 8443009.

by a tax-exempt humane society;[214] a low-cost animal neutering service;[215] the operation of a health club for individuals reflective of the community;[216] the conduct of research and counseling activities for the purpose of promoting business in foreign countries;[217] the sales of products in connection with the conduct of educational programs;[218] the sale of computer software by a tax-exempt orgnization formed to make new scientific technology widely available for the benefit of the public;[219] the sale of life memberships in a rural lodge used only for religious and educational purposes;[220] the operation of an arena (including concessions and leases);[221] the management of a project to restore historic property;[222] the operation of golf courses to promote rehabilitation of disadvantaged youth;[223] the construction and operation of a recreational complex and ancillary activities;[224] the performance of art conservation services for private collectors;[225] the conduct of an employment program providing training and work experience to the handicapped;[226] the sale of posters and other promotional items carrying the tax-exempt organization's program message;[227] the publication and sale by a tax-exempt shipowners' and operators' organization of common tariffs:[228] the operation of a medical malpractice peer review program by a tax-exempt medical society;[229] the operation of a mobile cancer screening program;[230] the activities of a tax-exempt trade association as a "certified frequency coordinator" (as designated by the Federal Communications Commission) for its industry;[231] the leasing of a theater by a tax-exempt performing arts organization for musical productions;[232] the sale of insurance by a tax-exempt charitable organization on the lives of donors;[233] the licensing of a tax-exempt educational institution's curriculum to other colleges and universities;[234] the teaching of computer programming courses for employees of a corporation;[235] the conduct of teleconferencing activities;[236] the operation of a second-hand store;[237] the operation of physical, oc-

[214] Tech. Adv. Mem. 8450006.
[215] Tech. Adv. Mem. 8501002.
[216] Tech. Adv. Mem. 8505002.
[217] Priv. Ltr. Rul. 8505047.
[218] Priv. Ltr. Rul. 8512084.
[219] Priv. Ltr. Rul. 8518090.
[220] Priv. Ltr. Rul. 8523072.
[221] Priv. Ltr. Rul. 8623081.
[222] Priv. Ltr. Rul. 8628049.
[223] Priv. Ltr. Rul. 8626080.
[224] Priv. Ltr. Rul. 8624127.
[225] Priv. Ltr. Rul. 8606074.
[226] Priv. Ltr. Rul. 8332072.
[227] Priv. Ltr. Rul. 8633034.
[228] Priv. Ltr. Rul. 8709072.
[229] Priv. Ltr. Rul. 8730060.
[230] Priv. Ltr. Rul. 8749085.
[231] Priv. Ltr. Rul. 8802079.
[232] Gen. Couns. Mem. 39715.
[233] Priv. Ltr. Rul. 8820061.
[234] Priv. Ltr. Rul. 8824018.
[235] Priv. Ltr. Rul. 9137002.
[236] Priv. Ltr. Rul. 8643091.
[237] Priv. Ltr. Rul. 8643049.

cupational, and speech therapy, injury prevention, pediatric services, and adult day-care programs;[238] the cleaning up of spills of oil and oil products;[239] the conduct of services relating to the use of a tax-exempt organization's mailing list;[240] the operation of a birthing center by a church;[241] the sponsorship of gospel concerts by a broadcast ministry;[242] the operation of nursing homes by a health care organization;[243] the receipt of income from Medicare, Medicaid, or private insurance programs for the operation of intermediate care facilities;[244] the operation by a charitable organization of a parking garage for the benefit of its member charities;[245] the performance of pre-acquisition student loan services by a public charity;[246] the provision by a health care entity of temporary nurses to a related exempt organization;[247] the sale of books by a religious organization that were written by its founder;[248] the provision of services by a community development organization to a community development bank;[249] the conduct by an agricultural organization of activities promoting cooperative programs among farmers in a state;[250] the development and operation by a business league of a tracking system for alimony and support payments;[251] and the conduct by a public charity of market development and investment programs intended to promote investment in foreign countries.[252]

Private letter rulings from the IRS provide additional illustrations of related business activity.[253]

(g) Unrelated Business Activities

There are many determinations by the courts and the IRS that activities by tax-exempt organizations are unrelated businesses. For example, the presentation of commercial programs and the sale of air time were ruled to be activities not substantially related to the exempt purposes of a tax-exempt broadcasting station.[254] A charitable organization operating to promote the physical fitness of young individuals was held to have unrelated activity in the form of a health club, since the dues and fees charged were sufficiently high so as to restrict the club's use to a limited number of the members of the community.[255] The operation of a miniature

---

[238] Priv. Ltr. Rul. 9241055.
[239] Priv. Ltr. Rul. 9242035.
[240] Priv. Ltr. Rul. 9249001.
[241] Priv. Ltr. Rul. 9252037.
[242] Priv. Ltr. Rul. 9325062.
[243] Priv. Ltr. Rul. 9237090.
[244] Priv. Ltr. Rul. 9335061.
[245] Priv. Ltr. Rul. 9401031.
[246] Priv. Ltr. Rul. 9403022.
[247] Priv. Ltr. Rul. 9535023.
[248] Priv. Ltr. Rul. 9535050.
[249] Priv. Ltr. Rul. 9539015.
[250] Ohio Farm Bur. Fedn. Inc. v. Comm'r, *supra* note 134.
[251] Priv. Ltr. Rul. 9633044.
[252] Priv. Ltr. Rul. 9651046.
[253] E.g., Priv. Ltr. Rul. 8640007.
[254] Rev. Rul. 78-385, 1978-2 C.B. 174.
[255] Rev. Rul. 79-360, 1979-2 C.B. 236.

golf course in a commercial manner, by a charitable organization operating to provide for the welfare of young individuals, was determined to constitute an unrelated business.[256] The operation of dining facilities for the general public by a tax-exempt social club or exempt veterans' organization is an unrelated business.[257]

Other court opinions and IRS rulings providing illustrations of unrelated business activities include these: the provision of pet boarding and grooming services, for pets owned by the general public, by a tax-exempt organization operated to prevent cruelty to animals;[258] carrying on of commercially sponsored research, where the publication of the research is withheld or delayed significantly by the tax-exempt organization beyond the time reasonably necessary to establish ownership rights;[259] weekly operation of a bingo game by a tax-exempt social welfare organization;[260] sale of membership lists to commercial companies by tax-exempt educational organizations;[261] publication of academic works;[262] receipt of commissions from sales of cattle by a tax-exempt agricultural organization for its members;[263] sale of certain blood and blood components by a tax-exempt blood bank to commercial laboratories;[264] management of health and welfare plans by a tax-exempt business league for a fee;[265] furnishing of laborers by a tax-exempt religious organization (usually its members) to forest owners to plant seedlings on cleared forest land;[266] the sale of heavy-duty appliances to senior citizens by a tax-exempt senior citizens' center;[267] the performance of administrative services performed by a tax-exempt business league in connection with vacation pay and guaranteed annual income accounts established by a collective bargaining agreement;[268] the provision of veterinary services for a fee by a tax-exempt animal cruelty prevention society;[269] the operation of a commuting program by a tax-exempt labor union for its members;[270] the distribution of business direc-

---

[256] Rev. Rul. 79-361, 1979-2 C.B. 237.

[257] Rev. Rul. 68-46, 1968-1 C.B. 260.

[258] Rev. Rul. 73-587, 1973-2 C.B. 192.

[259] Rev. Rul. 76-296, 1976-2 C.B. 141.

[260] Clarence LaBelle Post No. 217 v. United States, *supra* note 62, Smith-Dodd Businessman's Ass'n, Inc. v. Comm'r, 65 T.C. 620 (1975). Also Rev. Rul. 59-330, 1959-2 C.B. 153.

[261] Rev. Rul. 72-431, 1972-2 C.B. 281.

[262] Priv. Ltr. Rul. 7839042. Also Oklahoma Dental Ass'n v. United States, 75-2 U.S.T.C. ¶ 9682 (W.D. Okla. 1975); Western Catholic Church v. Comm'r, 73 T.C. 196 (1979), *aff'd*, 631 F.2d 736 (7th Cir. 1980), *cert. den.*, 450 U.S. 981 (1981).

[263] Rev. Rul. 69-51, 1969-1 C.B. 159.

[264] Rev. Rul. 66-323, 1966-2 C.B. 216, as *mod. by* Rev. Rul. 78-145, *supra* note 86.

[265] Rev. Rul. 66-151, 1966-1 C.B. 152. Also Cooper Tire & Rubber Co., Employees' Retirement Fund v. United States, 306 F.2d 20 (6th Cir. 1962); Rev. Rul. 69-633, 1969-2 C.B. 121, Rev. Rul. 69-69, 1969-1 C.B. 159, Rev. Rul. 68-505, 1968-2 C.B. 248; Rev. Rul. 68-267, 1968-1 C.B. 284; Duluth Clinic Foundation v. United States, 67-1 U.S.T.C. ¶ 9226 (D. Minn. 1967); Rev. Rul. 66-47, 1966-1 C.B. 149; Rev. Rul. 62-191, 1962-2 C.B. 146; Rev. Rul. 60-228, 1960-1 C.B. 200; Rev. Rul. 60-86, 1960-1 C.B. 198; Rev. Rul. 58-482, 1958-2 C.B. 273; Rev. Rul. 57-466, 1957-2 C.B. 311; Rev. Rul. 57-313, 1957-2 C.B. 316; Rev. Rul. 55-449, 1955-2 C.B. 599.

[266] Rev. Rul. 76-341, 1976-2 C.B. 307. Also Shiloh Youth Revival Centers v. Comm'r, 88 T.C. 565 (1987).

[267] Rev. Rul. 81-62, 1981-1 C.B. 355.

[268] Steamship Trade Ass'n of Baltimore, Inc. v. Comm'r, 81 T.C. 303 (1983).

[269] Priv. Ltr. Rul. 8303001.

[270] Tech. Adv. Mem. 8226019.

tories to new residents in a community;[271] the sale of work uniforms by a tax-exempt union;[272] the operation of a central payroll and records system;[273] the sale of printing services to other persons (including tax-exempt organizations);[274] the provision of commercial hospitalization review services by a tax-exempt professional standards review organization;[275] the sales of liquor by a tax-exempt veterans' organization;[276] the sale of a computer-based information retrieval and message service provided by a for-profit business;[277] the sale of information about real estate used to prepare market evaluations and house appraisals;[278] the provision of arbitration and mediation, and other alternative dispute resolution services for the benefit of consumers;[279] the conduct of utilization review services and drug-free workplace programs for private businesses by a professional standards review organization;[280] and the sale of herbs and herb products by an exempt scientific research organization to private practitioners and the general public.[281]

Private letter rulings from the IRS provide additional illustrations of unrelated business activity.[282]

Occasionally, a situation will arise where monies are paid to an agent of a tax-exempt organization, who in turn pays the monies over to the organization, with the monies taxable as unrelated business income. This situation occurs, for example, in connection with a tax-exempt religious order, which requires its members to provide services for a component of the supervising church and to turn over their remuneration to the order under a vow of poverty. Under these circumstances, the payments for services are income to the order and not to the member.[283] However, where the individual is not acting as agent for the order and is performing services (as an employee) of the type ordinarily required by members of the religious order, the income is to the individual, and the unrelated income tax is avoided, because the monies are received by the orders as charitable contributions.

§ 26.5   CONTEMPORARY APPLICATIONS OF THE UNRELATED BUSINESS RULES

Myriad activities undertaken by various types of tax-exempt organizations provide contemporary applications of the unrelated business income rules. Traditionally, colleges and universities raised the most issues as to related and unrelated

---

[271] Priv. Ltr. Rul. 8433010.
[272] Tech. Adv. Mem. 8437014.
[273] Tech. Adv. Mem. 8446004.
[274] Priv. Ltr. Rul. 8452074.
[275] Priv. Ltr. Rul. 8511082.
[276] Priv. Ltr. Rul. 8530043.
[277] Priv. Ltr. Rul. 8814004.
[278] Priv. Ltr. Rul. 9043001.
[279] Priv. Ltr. Rul. 9145002.
[280] Priv. Ltr. Rul. 9436002.
[281] Tech. Adv. Mem. 9550001.
[282] E.g., Priv. Ltr. Rul. 9128003.
[283] Rev. Rul. 76-323, 1976-2 C.B. 18, *clar. by* Rev. Rul. 77-290, 1977-2 C.B. 26. Also Rev. Rul. 77-436, 1977-2 C.B. 25; Rev. Rul. 68-123, 1968-1 C.B. 35.

business endeavors, although in recent years health care institutions have achieved the dubious distinction of being first in this regard. Other tax-exempt organizations that are currently generating significant unrelated business issues are museums, associations, and labor, agricultural, and horticultural organizations. Heading the list of activities that invoke contemporary issues in this field are operation of taxable subsidiaries, advertising services, and fund-raising activities.

(a) Educational Institutions

The principal business of colleges, universities, and schools[284] is the education of students; income generated by this related activity in the form of tuition, fees, assessments, dormitory rent, and food service revenue is not taxable. Another major exempt function at these institutions is research; this activity is not normally taxed, either because it is inherently an exempt function or is sheltered from tax by statute.[285]

The legislative history of the unrelated business income rules states that a wheat farm operated by a tax-exempt agricultural college as part of its educational program is a related business and income from a university press is tax-exempt "in the ordinary case" since it is derived from an activity that is substantially related to the purposes of the university.[286]

By contrast, an activity such as the manufacture and sale of automobile tires by a tax-exempt college ordinarily is an unrelated business; this type of activity does not become substantially related simply because some students performed minor clerical or bookkeeping functions as part of their educational program.[287] By contrast, the IRS determined that the sale of handicraft articles by a tax-exempt vocational school, made by its students as part of their regular courses of instruction, is a related trade or business.[288] Likewise, the IRS held that a tax-exempt university may publish as a related business, scholarly works written by its faculty and students.[289]

(i) Bookstore Operations. For colleges, universities, and some schools, operation of their bookstores yields opportunities for unrelated business income issues.[290] While the operation of these stores generally is a tax-exempt function,[291] there are some sales that can attract the tax on unrelated business income. There are three categories of business activities in this context: related business, business activities that are protected from taxation by a statutory exception, and unrelated business.

---

[284] Essentially, these are institutions referenced in IRC § 170(b)(1)(A)(ii) (see § 11.3(a)).

[285] See §§ 9.2, 27.1(l).

[286] S. Rep. No. 2375, *supra* note 125, at 107.

[287] *Id.* A college or university may operate a health and physical fitness center, with many of its programs qualifying as related business activities (Priv. Ltr. Rul. 9732032).

[288] Rev. Rul. 68-581. 1968-2 C.B. 250

[289] IRS Priv. Ltr. Rul. 9036025.

[290] Some institutions lease the bookstore operation to unrelated parties, with the resulting rent nontaxable (see § 27.1(h)).

[291] Squire v. Students Book Corp., 191 F.2d 1018 (9th Cir. 1951); Rev. Rul. 58-194, 1958-1 C.B. 240.

Related business activities include the sale of items such as course books, supplies, tapes, compact discs, athletic wear necessary for participation in the institution's athletic, and physical education programs, computer hardware and software,[292] and items that induce school spirit, including t-shirts, tote bags, pennants, and mugs.

Another category of sales that are not taxable are those that are within the ambit of the *convenience doctrine*, in that the business activity is for the benefit of the students.[293] Items protected from taxation by this doctrine include sundry articles, film, cards, health and beauty aids, and novelty items.

For the most part, all other sales are unrelated business transactions. It is the view of the IRS that items that have a useful life of more than one year cannot be the subject of the convenience doctrine.[294] Taxable sales can thus be those of articles such as wearing apparel, appliances, stuffed animals, wall posters, wristwatches, and plants.[295] Sales of items to the general public, as opposed to students and faculty, can be unrelated business activity.

(ii) Athletic Events.   It is an understatement to say that the preparation for and participation in athletic events is a major function of today's educational institution. The revenue that a college, university, or school derives as charges for admission to athletic events is income from a related business inasmuch as the activities are substantially related to the institution's educational program.[296]

Revenue generated by the telecasting and radio broadcasting of these events also is not taxable, in that this activity is related to the institutions' educational mission.[297] As the IRS observed, "an audience for a game may contribute importantly to the education of the student-athlete in the development of his/her physical and inner strength." Further, "[a]ttending the game enhances student interest in education generally and in the institution because such interest is whetted by exposure to the school's athletic activities." Finally, the "games (and the opportunity to observe them) foster those feelings of identification, loyalty, and participation typical of a well-rounded educational experience."[298]

---

[292] The IRS, in its college and university examination guidelines (see § 24.8(d)), stated that "[a]lthough the sale of one computer to a student or faculty member may be substantially related to exempt purposes, the sale of multiple computers, in a single year, to a single student or the sale of a computer to someone who is not a student, officer or employee of the institution may result in unrelated business income" (*id.* § 342.(13)(5)).

[293] See § 27.2(b).

[294] Gen. Couns. Mem. 35811.

[295] E.g., Priv. Ltr. Rul. 8025222.

[296] H. Rep. No. 2319, 81st Cong., 2d Sess. 37, 109 (1950); S. Rep. No. 2375, *supra* note 125, at 107. "[A] university would not be taxable on income derived from a basketball tournament sponsored by it, even where the teams were composed of students from other schools" (H. Rep. No. 2319, *supra*, at 37; S. Rep. No. 2375, *supra* note 125, at 29).

[297] Tech. Adv. Mem. 7851004. However, the original position of the IRS on this point was that the income from telecasting and radio broadcasting of athletic events, including bowl games, was unrelated business income. This view was altered in the face of enactment of legislation to the contrary.

[298] Priv. Ltr. Rul. 7930043.

The IRS ruled that a tax-exempt organization that sponsored a post-season all-star college football game for the benefit of a state university did not jeopardize its tax-exempt status because of, nor realize unrelated income from the sale of, television broadcast rights of the games since broadcasting of the games "contributes importantly" to the accomplishment of its tax-exempt purposes;[299] that payments received by a state university for the sale of radio and television broadcasting rights to its basketball and football games were not unrelated business income because the carrying on the sporting events was substantially related to the university's tax-exempt purposes;[300] that income received by a tax-exempt organization that promoted professional automobile racing from the sale of television broadcast rights to the races it sanctions did not constitute unrelated income because the television coverage effectively popularized automobile racing;[301] that income derived from the sale by a tax-exempt organization that sponsored and sanctioned amateur athletics of television rights to broadcast its athletic events was not unrelated income because the television medium was used to disseminate its goals and purposes to the public;[302] that a tax-exempt organization promoting interest in a particular sport that sold television rights to championship golf tournaments that it sponsored did not incur unrelated income because the grant of the rights was directly related to its tax-exempt purposes;[303] that the income received by a tax-exempt amateur sports organization for the licensing of television broadcasting rights was not unrelated income because the broadcasting of the sports events was substantially related to the organization's tax-exempt purpose of promoting international goodwill;[304] and that payments to be received from the sale of radio and television broadcasting rights to an athletic event were not items of unrelated income because the promotion of the event (the organization's tax-exempt purpose) was furthered by the broadcasting of it.[305]

Thereafter, the IRS issued a public ruling, holding that the sale of exclusive television and radio broadcasting rights to athletic events to an independent producer by a tax-exempt national governing body for amateur athletics was not unrelated business because the "broadcasting of the organization's sponsored, supervised, and regulated athletic events promotes the various amateur sports, fosters widespread public interest in the benefits of its nationwide amateur athletic program, and encourages public participation" and, therefore, the sale of the broadcasting rights and the broadcasting of the events was a tax-exempt function.[306] The IRS issued a similar ruling with respect to the sale of broadcasting rights to a national radio and television network by an organization created by a

---

[299] Priv. Ltr. Rul. 7948113 (which also held that the proceeds from admissions to the game, sales of the program of the game, and sales of advertising in the program were not taxable as unrelated income).
[300] Priv. Ltr. Rul. 7930043.
[301] Priv. Ltr. Rul. 7922001.
[302] Priv. Ltr. Rul. 7851003.
[303] Priv. Ltr. Rul. 7845029.
[304] Priv. Ltr. Rul. 8303078.
[305] Priv. Ltr. Rul. 7919053.
[306] Rev. Rul. 80-295, 1980-2 C.B. 194.

regional collegiate athletic conference composed of tax-exempt universities to hold an annual athletic event.[307]

The IRS asserted that the payment by a business, of a sponsorship fee to a college, university, or bowl association in connection with the telecasting or radio broadcasting of an athletic event, was unrelated business income because the package of "valuable services" received by the business was not substantially related to exempt purposes and amounted to advertising services.[308] However, this matter was generally resolved by the enactment of legislation concerning the *qualified sponsorship payment*.[309]

(iii) Travel Tours. The IRS is concerned that a college, university, or school, or alumni or alumnae association, will offer a travel tour as an educational experience, yet in fact it is a social, recreational, or other form of vacation opportunity and thus an unrelated business.

In a 1977 unpublished technical advice memorandum, the IRS ruled that a travel tour program conducted by an alumni association of a university was an unrelated trade or business. The program was available to all members of the association and their families; in the year at issue, the association made four mailings announcing nine tours to between 27,500 and 34,900 individuals. The memorandum stated that "[al]though the tours include sightseeing, there is no formal educational program conducted in connection with them; nor is there any program for contacting and meeting with alumni in the countries visited." The IRS determined that (1) the activities of the alumni association in working with commercial travel agencies in the planning and preparation of the tours, mailing out the tour announcements, and receiving reservations constituted a trade or business; the travel tours were inherently recreational, not educational,[310] and thus did not contribute importantly to a tax-exempt (educational) purpose; the unrelated business was regularly carried on; and this commercial endeavor exploited an intangible asset, namely, the association's membership.[311]

An alumni association travel tour program that is structured as an authentic educational activity is not an unrelated trade or business.[312] The policy of the IRS

---

[307] Rev. Rul. 80-296, 1980-2 C.B. 195. These two public rulings, along with Rev. Rul. 80-294, 1980-2 C.B. 187, capture the essence of the foregoing (notes 300–305) and like private letter rulings. In general, Jensen, "Taxation, the Student Athlete, and the Professionalization of College Athletics," 1987 *Utah L. Rev.* (No. 1) 35 (1987); Thompson & Young, "Taxing the Sale of Broadcast Rights to College Athletics— An Unrelated Trade or Business?," 8 *J. Coll. & U.L.* 331 (1981–2); Kaplan, "Intercollegiate Athletics and the Unrelated Business Income Tax," 80 *Col. L. Rev.* 1430 (1980); Note. "University TV Receipts Not Unrelated Business Income," 50 *J. Tax.* 184 (1979).

[308] Tech. Adv. Mem. 9147007.

[309] See § 27.2(n). The taxation of advertising revenue is the subject of *infra* § 5f.

[310] Rev. Rul. 67-327, 1967-2 C.B. 187. Also Rev. Rul. 84-55, 1984-1 C.B. 29, holding that the travel expenses incurred by an alumnus in participation in a university's continuing education program in foreign countries are not deductible because they are personal outlays. Cf. IRC § 170(k).

[311] This technical advice memorandum is the basis of Rev. Rul. 78-43, 1978-1 C.B. 164. The IRS revoked the tax-exempt status of a charitable organization in 1995, because of the extent of its conduct of golf and tennis tours, ostensibly undertaken in furtherance of exempt purposes (Tech. Adv. Mem. 9540002).

[312] Rev. Rul. 70-534, 1970-2 C.B. 113.

with respect to travel tours generally is that some are related and some unrelated, depending on how they are structured, what they consist of, and what they accomplish. Tours that feature "bona fide educational methodologies"—such as organized study, reports, lectures, library access, and reading lists—are likely to be considered educational in nature. Pursuant to a primary purpose test, tours that devote a significant amount of time to endeavors such as sightseeing are not usually exempt functions. Tours that are "not significantly different from commercially sponsored" tours are probably unrelated businesses, as are extension (or add-on) tours.[313]

(iv) Rental of Facilities. A tax-exempt educational institution may provide athletic facilities, dormitories, and other components of the campus to persons other than its students, such as for seminars or the training of professional athletes. The income derived from the provision of the facilities in these circumstances is likely to be regarded by the IRS as unrelated business income where the institution is providing collateral services such as meals or maintenance; a mere leasing of facilities would likely generate passive rental income excluded from taxation.[314] However, the provision of dormitory space may be an activity that is substantially related to a tax-exempt purpose, as the IRS ruled in an instance of rental of dormitory rooms primarily to individuals under age 25 by a tax-exempt organization the purpose of which was to provide for the welfare of young people.[315]

(b) Hospitals and Other Health Care Providers

Hospitals and other health care providers[316] have as their principal business the promotion of health; income generated by this related activity in the form of revenue from patients (whether by means of Medicare, Medicaid, insurance, or private pay) is not taxable.[317]

(i) Various Related Businesses. Tax-exempt hospitals operate many businesses that are necessary to their tax-exempt function. Thus, a hospital may operate a gift shop, which is patronized by patients, visitors making purchases for patients, and its employees, without incurring the unrelated business income tax.[318] The IRS observed: "By providing a facility for the purchase of merchandise and services to improve the physical comfort and mental well-being of its patients, the hospital is carrying on an activity that encourages their recovery and therefore contributes importantly to its exempt purposes."[319] The same rationale is extended

---

[313] Tech. Adv. Mem. 9702004.
[314] See § 27.1(h).
[315] Rev. Rul. 76-33, 1976-1 C.B. 169. In general, Keeling, "Property Taxation of Colleges and Universities: The Dilemma Posed by the Use of Facilities for Purposes Unrelated to Education," 16 *J. Coll. & Univ. L.* 623 (1990). Behrsin; "College and University Leasing Activities Evoke IRS Scrutiny," 57 *Taxes* 431 (1979).
[316] Essentially, these are institutions referenced in IRC § 170(b)(1)(A)(iii) (see § 11.3(a)).
[317] S. Rep. No. 2375, *supra* note 125, at 107.
[318] Rev. Rul. 69-267, 1969-1 C.B. 160.
[319] *Id.*

to the hospital operation of a cafeteria and coffee shop primarily for its employees and medical staff,[320] the hospital operation of a parking lot for its patients and visitors,[321] and the hospital operation of a guest accommodation facility.[322]

In one instance, a tax-exempt hospital had as its primary activity the operation of a clinic that provided various rehabilitation services to handicapped persons, including those with hearing deficiencies. The hospital tested and evaluated the hearing of its patients with the deficiencies and recommended types of hearing aids as may be necessary in each case. The hospital also sold hearing aids and fitted them to ensure maximum assistance to the patients in the correction or alleviation of their hearing deficiencies. The IRS ruled that the sale of hearing aids as an integral part of the hospital's program was not an unrelated business because it "contributes importantly to the organization's purpose of promoting the health of such persons."[323] Likewise, the IRS determined that a hospital was not conducting an unrelated business when it allowed its physicians and facilities to be used in reading and diagnosing electrocardiogram tests for a hospital that lacked the physicians and facilities to provide the service.[324] Similarly, a health care provider was held to not be engaging in an unrelated trade or business when it provided supplemental staffing services to hospitals and nursing homes.[325]

The *convenience doctrine*—applicable with respect to businesses that are conducted for the benefit of patients—is of considerable import in the health care setting.[326] The IRS defined the term *patient* of a health care provider.[327]

A hospital may be able to develop real estate by constructing condominium residences to be used as short-term living quarters by its patients, as a related business.[328]

(ii) Sales of Pharmaceuticals. The sale of pharmaceutical supplies by a tax-exempt hospital to private patients of physicians who have offices in a medical building owned by the hospital is considered by the IRS to constitute the conduct of an unrelated business.[329] The IRS also outlined the circumstances in which a tax-exempt hospital derives unrelated business income from the sale of pharmaceutical supplies to the general public.[330] By contrast, the sale of pharmaceutical supplies by a hospital pharmacy to its patients is not the conduct of an unrelated trade or business.

A federal court of appeals considered this issue and concluded that sales of pharmaceuticals by a hospital to members of the general public give rise to unre-

---

[320] Rev. Rul. 69-268, 1969-1 C.B. 160.
[321] Rev. Rul. 69-269, 1969-1 C.B. 160. Also Ellis Hosp. v. Fredette, 279 N.Y.S. 925 (N.Y. 1967); Rev. Rul. 81-29, 1981-1 C.B. 329.
[322] Priv. Ltr. Rul. 9404029.
[323] Rev. Rul. 78-435, 1978-2 C.B. 181.
[324] Priv. Ltr. Rul. 8004011.
[325] Tech. Adv. Mem. 9405004.
[326] Rev. § 27.2(b).
[327] Rev. Rul. 68-376, 1968-2 C.B. 246.
[328] Priv. Ltr. Rul. 8427105.
[329] Rev. Rul. 68-375, 1968-2 C.B. 245. Cf. Rev. Rul. 69-463, 1969-2 C.B. 131.
[330] Rev. Rul. 68-374, 1968-2 C.B. 242.

lated business taxable income.[331] The concept of the "general public" encompassed the private patients of the hospital-based physicians, on the rationale that sales by the pharmacy to the patients were related to the purchaser's visit to his or her private physician at offices rented from the hospital and were not related to the use of services provided by the hospital. Another consideration was that tax-exempt hospital-operated pharmacies unfairly compete with commercial pharmacies.

By contrast, another appellate court concluded that sales of pharmaceuticals by a hospital to nonhospital private patients of physicians located in the hospital did not produce unrelated business income because the sales were important in attracting and holding physicians in a community that lacked any medical services for eight years prior to the establishment of the hospital.[332] This appellate court ruled that the trial court was in error in defining the organization's function solely as that of providing a hospital, and held that another purpose was to attract physicians to the community and provide facilities to retain them. Thus, this appellate court concluded that the "availability of the hospital's pharmacy for use by the doctor's private patients is causally related to inducing doctors to practice" at the hospital.[333] The court distinguished this case from the holding of the other court of appeals, stating that the facts in the previous case "give no indication that the hospital had any difficulty in attracting doctors to its staff."[334]

(iii) Testing Services. It is the view of the IRS that the performance of diagnostic laboratory testing, otherwise available in the community, by a tax-exempt hospital, upon specimens from private office patients of the hospital's staff physicians, generally constitutes an unrelated business.[335] The IRS concluded that there was no substantial causal relationship between the achievement of a hospital's tax-exempt purposes and the provision of the testing to nonpatients, and that there are commercial laboratories that can perform the testing services on a timely basis. Nonetheless, the IRS noted that there may exist "unique circumstances" that cause the testing to be related activities, such as emergency laboratory diagnosis of blood samples from nonpatient drug overdose or poisoning victims in order to identify specific toxic agents, where referral of these specimens to other locations would be detrimental to the health of hospital nonpatients, or in situations where other laboratories are not available within a reasonable distance from the area served by the hospital or are clearly unable or inadequate to conduct tests needed by hospital nonpatients.[336]

A court held that income received by a tax-exempt teaching and research hospital for the performance of pathological diagnostic tests on samples submitted by physicians associated with the hospital was not unrelated business taxable

---

[331] Carle Found. v. United States, 611 F.2d 1192 (7th Cir. 1979), *cert. den.*, 449 U.S. 824 (1980).

[332] Hi-Plains Hosp. v. United States, 670 F.2d 528 (5th Cir. 1982), *rev'g and rem'g* 81-1 U.S.T.C. ¶ 9214 (N.D. Tex. 1981).

[333] *Id.* at 531.

[334] *Id.* at 533.

[335] Rev. Rul. 85-110, 1985-2 CB. 166.

[336] *Id.* at 168. Laboratory testing services provided by a university's dental school were ruled to be related activities because a unique type of diagnostic dental service and testing was provided, and there were no commercial laboratories that provided a comparable service (Priv. Ltr. Rul. 9739043).

income.[337] The court found that the performance and interpretation of these outside pathology tests by the hospital's pathology department were substantially related to the performance by the hospital of its tax-exempt functions because the tests contributed importantly to the teaching functions of the hospital. Further, the court concluded that the testing was a related activity because it increased the doctors' confidence in the quality of the work performed by the pathology department and it was convenient in the event of surgery, in that the pathologist who interpreted the test could interpret the biopsy.[338]

(iv) Fitness Centers and Health Clubs.   Another area of controversy is whether fitness centers and health clubs, operated as a program of a hospital, are unrelated businesses. In this setting, the IRS looks to the breadth of the group of individuals being served. If the fees for use of a health club are sufficiently high to restrict use of the club's facilities to a limited segment of a community, the club operation will be a non-exempt one or an unrelated business activity.[339] By contrast, where the health club provides a community-wide benefit for the community the organization serves, operation of the club is an exempt function or a related business.[340] This latter position is predicated on the rule in the general law of charity that the promotion of the happiness and enjoyment of the members of the community is considered to be a charitable purpose.[341] Thus, in one instance, the IRS blended these two definitions of *charity* in finding that a health club was tax-exempt because its "operations promote health in a manner which is collateral to the providing of recreational facilities which advances the well-being and happiness of the community in general."[342] Similarly, a fitness center was held to be tax-exempt inasmuch as it furthered the accomplishment of certain of the other programs of the health organization that operated it (including an occupational and physical therapy program), its facilities and programs were specially designed for the needs of the handicapped and the treatment plans of patients in other programs, its fee structure was designed to make it available to the general public, and it offered a range of programs and activities that focused on wellness.[343]

(v) Physical Rehabilitation Programs.   Organizations that maintain physical rehabilitation programs often provide housing and other services which are available commercially. Yet, the IRS ruled that an organization which provided specially designed housing to physically handicapped individuals at the lowest feasible cost and maintained in residence those tenants who subsequently

---

[337] St. Luke's Hosp. of Kansas City v. United States, 494 F. Supp. 85 (W.D. Mo. 1980). The IRS agreed to follow this aspect of the decision (Rev. Rul. 85-109, 1985-2 C.B. 165).

[338] Also Anateus Lineal 1948, Inc. v. United States, 366 F. Supp. 118 (W.D. Ark. 1973). In general, Mancino, "The Unrelated Business Income Taxation of Nonprofit Hospitals," 4 *Exempt Org. Tax Rev.* (No. 1) 35 1991; Kannry, "How Hospitals Can Minimize Their Potential Exposure to the Unrelated Business Income Tax," 43 *J. Tax.* 166 (1975).

[339] Rev. Rul. 79-360, 1979-2 C.B. 236.

[340] Tech. Adv. Mem. 8505002.

[341] *Restatement (Second) of Trusts* § 374 (1959); IV Scott, *The Law of Trusts* § 374.10 (3d ed. 1967).

[342] Tech. Adv. Mem. 8505002. A similar facility operated by a university was ruled to entail related business activities (Priv. Ltr. Rul. 9732032).

[343] Priv. Ltr. Rul. 9329041.

became unable to pay the monthly fees was a tax-exempt charitable entity.[344] The IRS similarly ruled that the rental to individuals under age 25 and low-income individuals of all ages of dormitory rooms and similar residential accommodations was a related business.[345] The IRS likewise ruled that a halfway house, organized to provide room, board, therapy, and counseling for individuals discharged from alcoholic treatment centers was a tax-exempt charitable organization; its operation of a furniture shop to provide full-time employment centers for its residents was considered a related business.[346] Also, the IRS ruled that an organization which provided a residence facility and therapeutic group living program for individuals recently released from a mental institution was an exempt charitable organization.[347] An organization with the purpose of providing rehabilitative and pre-vocational counseling to the handicapped and developmentally disabled received a ruling that its residential and day care facilities were related activities.[348] Another entity, a charitable organization which maintained nursing homes and ancillary health facilities, was ruled to be engaged in the following related businesses: programs offering physical therapy, occupational therapy, speech therapy, injury prevention, pediatric services, and adult care, as well as the provision of day care for its employees.[349]

Lifestyle rehabilitation programs can also present this dichotomy. For example, the IRS ruled that the operation of a miniature golf course in a commercial manner by a tax-exempt organization, the purpose of which was to provide for the welfare of young people, constituted an unrelated trade of business.[350] However, the IRS also ruled that a tax-exempt organization, formed to improve the life of abused and otherwise disadvantaged children by means of the sport and business of golf, did not conduct an unrelated activity in operation of a golf course because the opportunity to socialize and master skills through the playing of the game were "essential to the building of self-esteem and the ultimate rehabilitation of the young people" in the organization's programs.[351]

(vi) Other Health Care Activities. In other instances, the IRS ruled that the rental of pagers to staff physicians by a hospital is not unrelated business;[352] the sale by a hospital of silver recovered from x-ray film is not an unrelated activity;[353] and the leasing of space and the furnishing of services to practitioners is not an unrelated activity by the lessors.[354] Still other related business in the health care setting are operation of mobile cancer screening units;[355] sales and rentals of

---

[344] Rev. Rul. 79-19, 1979-1 C.B. 195.
[345] Rev. Rul. 76-33, *supra* note 315.
[346] Rev. Rul. 75-472, 1975-2 C.B. 208.
[347] Rev. Rul. 72-16, 1972-1 C.B. 143.
[348] Priv. Ltr. Rul. 9335061.
[349] Priv. Ltr. Rul. 9241055.
[350] Rev. Rul. 79-361, *supra* note 256.
[351] Priv. Ltr. Rul. 8626080.
[352] Tech. Adv. Mem. 8452011.
[353] Tech. Adv. Mem. 8452012.
[354] Priv. Ltr. Rul. 8452099.
[355] Priv. Ltr. Rul. 8749085.

durable medical equipment to patients of a health care organization;[356] and the provision by an exempt hospital of services such as ultrasound and general radiology, outpatient dialysis, acute dialysis, critical life support, home health, occupational health, electrocardiogram computer, wellness and prevention, employee physicals, and storage of medical and administrative records.[357]

The provision of services by and among organizations within a hospital system,[358] such as the leasing of property and the sale of services, generally will not give rise to unrelated business taxable income.[359]

(c) Museums

Tax-exempt museums operate related businesses when they maintain collections and make them accessible to the general public; admissions fees and the like are not taxable. Some museum business operations are nontaxable by reason of the lines of law referenced above, pertaining to parking lots, snack bars, and the like. The IRS ruled that the operation of a dining room, cafeteria, and snack bar by an exempt museum for use by its staff, employees, and members of the public were related activities.[360]

The most difficult issues in the unrelated trade or business context presented by museum operations relate to sales to the general public. Where, for example, a museum sells to the public greeting cards that display printed reproductions of selected works from the museum's collection and from other art collections, the sales activity is substantially related to the museum's tax-exempt purpose.[361] The rationale for this conclusion is twofold: (1) The sale of the cards "contributes importantly to the achievement of the museum's exempt educational purposes by stimulating and enhancing public awareness, interest, and appreciation of art"; and (2) a "broader segment of the public may be encouraged to visit the museum itself to share in its educational functions and programs as a result of seeing the cards."[362]

The IRS applies the fragmentation rule, to segment the retailing activities of tax-exempt museums.[363] In so doing, the IRS evidences a readiness to isolate a particular type of sale and presume it is an unrelated activity because of one or more characteristics of the items being sold.[364] For example, museums traditionally have sold greeting cards, slides, instructional literature, and metal, wood, and ceramic copies of art works. In recent years, some museums have begun selling novelty items, clothing, and the like. To the extent that the items being sold

---

[356] Priv. Ltr. Rul. 8736046.

[357] E.g., Priv. Ltr. Rul. 8736046.

[358] In general, see Hyatt & Hopkins, *The Law of Tax-Exempt Healthcare Organizations* (New York: John Wiley & Sons, Inc., 1995), Chapter 20.

[359] E.g., Priv. Ltr. Rul. 8822065.

[360] Rev. Rul. 74-399, 1974-2 C.B. 172. Cf. Rev. Rul. 69-268, 1969-1 C.B. 160.

[361] Rev. Rul. 73-104, *supra* note 203.

[362] *Id.*

[363] Rev. Rul. 73-105, 1973-1 C.B. 264.

[364] E.g., "Exempt Organizations Annual Technical Review Institute for 1979," Training 3177-01 and 02 (3-79).

are "expensive," "lavish," or otherwise "luxury" items, there is a greater likelihood that the IRS will presume the sales activity to be an unrelated business.

Where an item sold by a museum is priced at a "low cost,"[365] and bears the museum's logo, the IRS generally finds the sales activity to be related, because it enhances public awareness of and encourages greater visitation to the museum. Again, however, as the price of items bearing a museum's logo increases, so too will the likelihood that the IRS will find the sales activity to be substantially unrelated to the museum's tax-exempt purposes. Nonetheless, the sale of, for example, clothing bearing a reference to a museum is arguably *per se* substantially related to the museum's tax-exempt purposes—since it publicizes the museum and attracts visitors—irrespective of the price paid for the clothing.

One of the most difficult issues in this context lies in the distinction drawn by the IRS between museum *reproductions* and *adaptations*. For the most part, the IRS considers the sales of reproductions to be sales that are related to the museum's tax-exempt purposes, although the IRS may resist that conclusion where the items, while copies of items originally created by master period craftsmen, are not contemporaneously made in a manner commensurate with the period. The IRS is much more likely to question the relatedness of sales of adaptations, which are items that may incorporate or reflect original art but differ significantly in form from the original work. Nonetheless, an adaptation may have intrinsic artistic merit or historical significance in its adaptive form (so that a sale of it by a museum is a related activity) or it may bear a museum's logo or otherwise reference the museum (so that it enhances public awareness of the museum and encourages the public to visit the museum, thereby making the sale of it a related activity).[366]

In application of the fragmentation rule, the IRS will attempt to determine the motivation behind the museum's sale of an item. For example, the IRS's general counsel has advised the IRS that it should apply a test to determine whether or not the primary purpose of the article sold is "utilitarian."[367] According to this test, "[i]f the primary purpose of the article is utilitarian and the utilitarian aspects are the predominant reasons for the production and sale of the article, it should not be considered related." Conversely, "if the utilitarian or ornamental aspects are merely incidental to the article's relation to an exempt purpose, then the article should be considered related." In most instances, the IRS finds that a museum regularly sells both related and unrelated items. The IRS counsel readily admitted that application of the "utilitarian" standard is easiest when "reproductions or adaptations of items contained in the [m]useum's collection" are considered (sales of them are clearly related) or when "items of a souvenir, trivial, or convenience nature" are considered (sales of these are clearly unrelated). "The difficult task," conceded the IRS counsel, "lies in identifying those items that

---

[365] Reg. § 1.513-1(b). See text accompanying *infra* note 532. Also § 27.2(j).
[366] In general, Murphy, "New Pronouncements from the IRS." 62 *Museum News* (No. 1) 55 (Oct. 1983); Yanowitz & Purcell, "IRS's Recent Approaches to Retail Sales by Exempt Organizations: Analyzing Standards, "58 *J. Tax.* 250 (Oct. 1983); Liles & Roth, "The Unrelated Business Income Problems of Art Museums," 10 *Conn. L. Rev.* 638 (1978).
[367] Gen. Couns. Mem. 38949.

raise classification problems, such as those that are arguably reproductions with utilitarian, ornamental, or decorative aspects and those that present an interpretation of some theme related to an exempt purpose."

The museum evaluated by the IRS counsel and the IRS agreed that the items sold in the museum can be classified as follows: (1) replicas or reproductions of items or artifacts in the collections or exhibitions; (2) reproductions, adaptations, or examples of items that are not on exhibit, but that are representative of, and designed to encourage interest in, historical periods or artistic, scientific, or technological developments that are featured in the museum collections, or that are related to areas of museum involvements; (3) arts and crafts works by artists, or by native and/or foreign groups, whose works are in the collections or have been included in museum exhibitions; (4) arts and crafts items representing similar forms that can be found in the various museum collections designed to illustrate the techniques and historical development of these forms; (5) arts and crafts kits, tools, and instruments designed to encourage a personal experience of various arts and crafts forms; (6) books and records relating to art, science, history, and other areas of museum involvement; (7) educational toys and games for children, based on museum exhibits or relating to areas of museum involvement; (8) scientific and aviation models, tools and specimens, and other educational items that encourage interest and personal participation in the sciences; (9) posters, postcards, note cards, and calendars, with photographs, drawings, or depictions relating to areas of museum involvement; (10) souvenirs of the museum; and (11) convenience items. The IRS counsel did not attempt to classify the sale of each of these categories of sale items as related or unrelated business but, instead, noted that "[t]hese judgments are not, of course, easy to make."

Thus the IRS, in application of the fragmentation rule, also applies a primary purpose test. If the article sold by a tax-exempt museum is predominantly utilitarian, sales of it produce unrelated income, as is the case with items sold primarily to generate income. If an article is primarily related to the museum's exempt function and any utilitarian aspects are incidental, sales income is related income. One specific guideline is provided: "If the primary purpose of an article that interprets some facet of the [m]useum's collection is to encourage personal learning experiences about the [m]useum's collection even though not an accurate depiction of an item in the collection, the article should be considered related."

The current emphasis of the IRS in this regard is on the primary purpose for the production and sale of each item in the museum. As noted, the sale of reproductions of items found in the collection is not unrelated business, as is the case with the sales of adaptations of artistic utilitarian items in the collection, particularly where the items are sold with descriptive literature showing their artistic, cultural, or historic connections with the museum's collections or exhibits. However, museum sales of original art or craft is unrelated business, since these activities are inconsistent with the purpose of exhibiting art for the public benefit.[368]

The IRS in 1986 again addressed the subject of the tax treatment of retail sales of items by a tax-exempt museum.[369] In that instance, the IRS inventoried

---

[368] Priv. Ltr. Rul. 8326008. Cf. (on this last point) Goldsboro Art League v. Comm'r, 75 T.C. 337 (1980).
[369] Tech. Adv. Mem. 8605002.

the various items sold by the museum, fragmenting them into categories such as furniture, china, fabrics, wallpaper, lamps, note cards, cooking accessories, handicrafts, and gift items. The IRS observed that, to be exempt from the tax on unrelated income, items sold in museum gift shops must be substantially related to the accomplishment of the museum's tax-exempt purpose. This relationship, said the IRS, "must extend specifically to the particular subject matter of the museum in which the items are sold as contrasted to being educational generally." The IRS added: "The characterization of a sales activity as an unrelated trade or business does not hinge on whether the activities may have a commercial hue or are in competition with for-profit entities such as furniture stores, or roadside gift stands offering souvenir items with a regional flavor."

In this case, the IRS said that the museum's retail sales inventory is to be evaluated in the context of its tax-exempt purpose (to preserve and protect the cultural and historical heritage unique to a particular city in the seventeenth through nineteenth centuries). The IRS proceeded through the various categories of items, finding the sale of nearly all of them related. Thus, all of the furniture sales were held to be related activities because of the educational value, despite the fact that the "items are sturdy enough for practical use in the home." The china sales were found related because of the design of the items and accompanying descriptive literature. The sales of fabric and wallpaper were found related because of the original designs and derivations from documented research. Lamp sales were related despite the "utilitarian adaptation of the modern electric lamps from various artifacts" because the original design was not distorted. Most of the sales of the other items were held related because of authenticated design motifs, decorations portraying historical scenes, and/or accompanying literature. This rationale embraced chandeliers, artwork, kitchen accessories, cookbooks, lawn furniture, toys, and games. The only sales that were found unrelated were those of a cast iron trivet (merely bearing the museum's logo), soaps, colognes, and bath oils.

This museum did more than sell at retail from its store; it also engaged in catalog sales. Applying the fragmentation rule, the IRS found that the catalog itself was a tax-exempt function, in that it is of educational value because it carried articles and illustrations generally supportive of the museum's tax-exempt purpose. Rejected was the view that the income from catalog sales should be divided into related and unrelated income on an allocable basis in relation to the listing of related and unrelated items. However, under these facts, less than one and one-half pages out of 80 were devoted to unrelated items.

In technical advice made public late in 1995, the IRS once again had occasion to review the tax treatment of sales of items by a tax-exempt museum.[370] As before, the IRS stated that the museum's primary purpose for selling a particular item is determinative of whether the sale is a related or unrelated activity. Thus, where the primary purpose behind the production and sale of an item is to further the organization's exempt purpose, the sale is a related one. In a departure from previous pronouncements, however, the IRS added that this is the case even though the item has a utilitarian function or value.[371] By contrast, where the pri-

---

[370] Tech. Adv. Mem. 9550003.
[371] See text accompanied by *supra* note 367.

mary purpose underlying production and sale of an item is to generate income, the activity is an unrelated business. In this document, the IRS stated that there are a number of differing factors to be considered in ascertaining this primary purpose, including (1) the degree of connection between the item and the museum's collection, (2) the extent to which the item relates to the form and design of the original item, and (3) the overall impression conveyed by the article. If the "dominant impression" individuals gain from viewing or using the article relates to the subject matter of the original article, picture, or likeness, substantial relatedness would be established. However, if the noncharitable use or function predominated, the sale is an unrelated business activity.

In this case, the IRS addressed the fact that much of the museum's sales are off-site. The IRS wrote that the museum "has many outlets and utilizes many vehicles to advertise and sell its wares," namely, retail stores, gift shops, an outlet located in another city, mail order catalogues, advertisements in various publications, a corporate/conference program, and more. However, the IRS held that the sole fact that sales are off-site does not make them unrelated; this is true even when the sales are in a commercial manner and in competition with for-profit companies. The reason: the off-site sales enhance a broader segment of the public's understanding of the collection and may encourage more individuals to visit the museum.

In another of these instances, an exempt museum, which sponsored programs for children, maintained a shop; the IRS found that the sale of certain tots' and childrens' items constituted unrelated businesses. Nonetheless, items that were reproductions or adaptations of articles displayed in the collections and exhibits were held saleable in related business. The IRS reiterated its general view that, where the primary purpose behind the production and sale of an item is utilitarian, ornamental souvenir in nature, or only generally educational, the matter entails unrelated business activity.[372]

The IRS ruled that a tax-exempt museum may operate an art conservation laboratory and perform conservation work for other institutions and collectors for a fee, without incurring unrelated business income.[373] Likewise, the IRS ruled that a museum store may sell items in furtherance of the tax-exempt museum's exempt purpose, other than those that have utilitarian purposes.[374]

(d) Associations

A tax-exempt association (or business league[375]) is subject to the unrelated income rules. The basic related business function of an exempt association is the provision of services to its members in exchange for dues; thus, this type of dues income is related revenue.

(i) *Service to Members.*   The IRS ruled that a variety of services performed by tax-exempt associations for their members are unrelated businesses.[376] Illustra-

---

[372] Tech. Adv. Mem. 9720002.
[373] Priv. Ltr. Rul. 8432004.
[374] Tech. Adv. Mem. 8605002.
[375] See Chapter 13.
[376] See § 13.4.

tions of this approach include the sale of equipment by a tax-exempt association to its members,[377] the management of health and welfare plans for a fee by a tax-exempt business league,[378] the provision of insurance for the members of a tax-exempt association,[379] the operation of an executive referral service,[380] the publication of ordinary commercial advertising for products and services used by the legal profession in a tax-exempt bar association's journal,[381] the conduct of a language translation service by an exempt trade association that promoted international trade relations,[382] the publication and sale, by an association of credit unions to its members, of a consumer-oriented magazine designed as a promotional device for distribution to the members' depositors,[383] the provision of mediation and arbitration services by an exempt business league,[384] the advertising and administrative services provided by an exempt business league with respect to a for-profit discount purchasing service,[385] and the operation by an association of members in the trucking industry of an alcohol and drug testing program for members and nonmembers.[386] Nonetheless, the IRS is not always successful in this context, as illustrated by the finding of a court that the sales of preprinted lease forms and landlord's manuals by a tax-exempt association of apartment owners and managers is a related activity.[387] By contrast, the IRS concluded that the sale of television time to governmental and nonprofit organizations at a discount by a tax-exempt association of television stations was a related business.[388]

Sometimes, there can be a direct conflict between the IRS and the courts in this setting. For example, the sale of standard legal forms by a local bar association to its member lawyers, which purchased the forms from the state bar association, was ruled by the IRS to be an unrelated business because the activity did not contribute importantly to the accomplishment of the association's exempt functions.[389] However, a court held that the sale of standard real estate legal forms to lawyers and law students by an exempt bar association was an exempt function because it promoted the common business interests of the legal profession and improved the relationship among the bench, bar, and public.[390]

In one instance, the IRS examined seven activities of a tax-exempt trade association and found all of them to be productive of unrelated income. These activities were the sale of vehicle signs to members, the sale to members of embossed tags for inventory control purposes, the sale to members of supplies

---

[377] Rev. Rul. 66-338, 1966-2 C.B. 226.
[378] Rev. Rul. 66-151, *supra* note 265.
[379] Rev. Rul. 74-81, 1974-1 C.B. 135.
[380] Tech. Adv. Mem. 8524006.
[381] Rev. Rul. 82-139, 1982-2 C.B. 108. In this ruling, the IRS also held that the publication of legal notices by a bar association was not an unrelated trade or business.
[382] Rev. Rul. 81-75, 1981-1 C.B. 356.
[383] Rev. Rul. 78-52, 1978-1 C.B. 166.
[384] Priv. Ltr. Rul. 9408002.
[385] Tech. Adv. Mem. 9440001.
[386] Tech. Adv. Mem. 9550001.
[387] Texas Apartment Ass'n v. United States, 869 F.2d 884 (5th Cir. 1989).
[388] Priv. Ltr. Rul. 9023081.
[389] Rev. Rul. 78-51, 1978-1 C.B. 165.
[390] San Antonio Bar Ass'n v. United States, 80-2 U.S.T.C. ¶ 9594 (W.D. Tex. 1980).

and forms, the sale to members of kits to enable them to retain sales tax information, the sale of price guides, the administration of a group insurance program,
and the sale of commercial advertising in the association's publications. Moreover, since the majority of the income of the organization was derived from these
activities and the majority of the time of the organization's employees was devoted to them, the IRS revoked the association's tax exemption.[391]

(ii) Insurance Programs.   It is common for an association to be involved in
the provision of various forms of insurance for its members. The state of the law
on this point is that nearly any form of insurance program of an association—endorsement or otherwise—is an unrelated activity.

An association can become involved in a variety of insurance programs in
several ways. An association may have little relationship to an insurance offering except to make its name and membership records available to the insurer. It
may endorse a particular insurance policy or have a role in the processing of
claims. By contrast, the association may be directly involved in the management
of an insurance program or may operate a self-insurance fund. The insurance
coverage (on a group basis or otherwise) may range over life, health, disability,
legal liability, worker's compensation, product liability, and similar subjects. The
insureds may be the association's employees, members, and/or employees of
members.

At the outset of the evolution of the development of law on this issue, where
an insurance company provided insurance coverage for a tax-exempt association's
members (and/or its employees) and the association was the mere sponsor, it appeared that this minimal involvement in the insurance process was not an unrelated trade or business. In one instance, an association provided an insurance
company with information about its membership, mailed a letter about the insurance coverage, and allowed the insurer to use the association's name and insignia
on brochures. For this, the association received a percentage of the premiums paid
by its members to the insurance company. The matter was litigated, with the court
concluding that the association was merely passively involved and thus that the
activity did not become a trade or business.[392] Another court concluded that this
type of remuneration, sometimes termed an "administrative allowance," paid to a
tax-exempt association for its efforts in administering an accident and health insurance program for its members, did not constitute unrelated income, because
the association's activities in this regard did not rise to the level of a business,[393]
but this holding was reversed on appeal.[394] Similar logic was applied in a decision
regarding fees received by a tax-exempt business league in return for its sponsorship of a bank payment plan made available to its members.[395]

Today, however, it is clear that, where an association actively and regularly
manages an insurance program for its members, for a fee, and a substantial por-

---

[391] Priv. Ltr. Rul. 7902006.
[392] Oklahoma Cattlemen's Ass'n v. United States, *supra* note 92.
[393] Carolinas Farm & Power Equip. Dealers Ass'n., Inc. v. United States, *supra* note 108.
[394] *Supra*, note 46.
[395] San Antonio Dist. Dental Soc'y v. United States, *supra* note 107.

tion of its income and expenses is traceable to the activity, the management undertaking will be regarded by the IRS as an unrelated business.[396] The IRS initially permitted tax-exempt associations to escape taxation of insurance income by structuring the payments as royalties,[397] but subsequently reversed its position and ruled that the payments are taxable income for services rendered.[398] If the provision of insurance is an association's sole or principal activity, the IRS will deny recognition of, or deprive it of, tax exemption, as illustrated by the denial of tax exemption to an organization that provided group worker's compensation insurance to its members[399] and to an organization that provided insurance and similar plans for its members.[400]

The approach of the courts in this area is essentially the same as that of the IRS. The Court of Claims, for example, found that a significant portion of an association's income was from the performance of services to members, including billing and collecting insurance premiums and distributing claim forms (with the association's income set as a percentage of premiums collected) and therefore held that the association did not qualify for tax exemption.[401] The U.S. Tax Court adopted a like rationale, combining insurance activities with the sale of educational materials, jewelry, emblems, and supplies to conclude that an association failed to qualify for tax exemption because of substantial unrelated business activity.[402] This decision was followed by a holding that the promotional and administrative fees received by a tax-exempt professional association of independent insurance agents for the promotion of group insurance programs for its members constituted unrelated business income.[403]

One of the first courts to rule directly on the point upheld the IRS position. The court determined that a commission paid a tax-exempt organization upon the writing of new and renewal insurance policies by an insurance company, the coverage plans of which the organization endorsed, was unrelated business income.[404] Subsequently, the U.S. Tax Court echoed that decision, holding that the promotional and administrative fees received by a tax-exempt business league from insurance companies for the sponsorship of insurance programs for the ben-

---

[396] Rev. Rul. 66-151, *supra* note 265. Also Rev. Rul. 60-228, *supra* note 265.

[397] See § 27.1(g). This position of the IRS was stated in Priv. Ltr. Rul. 8828011.

[398] Priv. Ltr. Rul. 9029047. In reaching this conclusion, the IRS took into consideration not only the insurance-related activities of the association but also the activities of its agent, which the IRS attributed to the association under authority of National Water Well Ass'n, Inc. v. Comm'r, *supra* note 56. Further, the IRS held that the membership list exception (see § 27.2(k)) governed the tax consequences of the transaction, in that the payments for services were inseparable from payments for use of the association's membership list; the IRS held that the exception was inapplicable.

[399] Rev. Rul. 76-81, 1976-1 C.B. 156.

[400] Rev. Rul. 67-176, 1967-1 C.B. 140.

[401] Indiana Retail Hardware Ass'n v. United States, 366 F.3d 998 (Ct. Cl. 1966).

[402] Associated Master Barbers & Beauticians of America, Inc. v. Comm'r, 69 T.C. 53 (1977).

[403] Professional Ins. Agents of Mich. v. Comm'r, 78 T.C. 246 (1982), *aff'd*, 726 F.2d 1097 (6th Cir. 1984). Also Professional Ins. Agents of Wash. v. Comm'r, 53 T.C.M. 9 (1987); Long Island Gasoline Retailers Ass'n, Inc. v. Comm'r, 43 T.C.M. 815 (1982).

[404] Louisiana Credit Union League v. United States, 501 F. Supp. 934 (E.D.La. 1980), *aff'd*; 693 F.2d 525 (5th Cir. 1982).

efit of its membership were taxable as unrelated income.[405] In so holding, the Tax Court expressly rejected the reasoning of the two decisions finding that this type of income is merely passively derived and thus not taxable.[406] The court held that, since the activity was engaged in with the intent to earn a profit, the activity must be considered a trade or business.[407] Also, the court was of the view that the enactment in 1969 of a statutory definition of the term *trade or business* overruled the passive income concept utilized in the other cases.[408] An appellate court agreed, holding that the organization was engaged in a taxable business activity because it "engaged in extensive activity over a substantial period of time with intent to earn a profit."[409]

Thus, the remaining major substantive issue in this area is no longer whether a tax-exempt association can have its tax status adversely affected by, or must treat as an unrelated trade or business, the active conduct of an insurance program, but whether there is a way for an association to be only passively involved in an insurance activity. The IRS does not believe the court decision finding this passive involvement[410] to be correct; rather, the IRS holds that initiation of an insurance program by an association, negotiation with the broker, and general support of and promotion of the program are services to the association's members, in the private capacity, and thus an unrelated business.[411] Consequently, in the view of the IRS, once the insurance activity rises to the level of a business,[412] it is an unrelated activity, and all association insurance activities constitute more than mere passive involvements.[413]

One solution may be to have the insurance program conducted by a separate entity, such as a trust or corporation, albeit controlled by the parent tax-exempt association. This approach requires care that the separate entity is in fact a true legal entity, with its own governing instruments, governing board, and separate tax return filing obligation.[414] If it is a mere trusteed bank account or the like of the association, the IRS will regard the program as an integral part of the association itself.[415] If it is an authentic separate legal entity, any tax liability would be confined to that imposed on the net income of the entity, which presumably

---

[405] Professional Ins. Agents of Mich. v. Comm'r, *supra* note 403.

[406] See *supra* notes 392, 393.

[407] See *supra* § 2(a).

[408] *Id.*

[409] Professional Ins. Agents of Mich. v. Comm'r, 726 F.2d 1097, 1102 (6th Cir. 1984). Also Professional Ins. Agents of Wash. v. Comm'r, *supra*, note 403; Texas Farm Bur. v. United States, 822 F. Supp. 371 (W.D. Tex. 1993); Independent Ins. Agents of Huntsville, Inc. v. Comm'r, 63 T.C.M. 2468 (1992), *aff'd*, 998 F.2d 898 (11th Cir. 1993), *rev'd*. 95-1 U.S.T.C. ¶ 50,297 (5th Cir. 1995); Illinois Ass'n of Professional Ins. Agents, Inc. v. Comm'r, 49 T.C.M. 925 (1985).

[410] See *supra* note 392.

[411] E.g., Priv. Ltr. Rul. 7840014.

[412] See *supra* § 2.

[413] In the first appellate court decision following the pronouncement of the Supreme Court in the *American Bar Endowment* case (*infra* note 600), a court concluded that the performance of promotional and administrative services by an association in connection with the sale of insurance to its members is an unrelated activity (Illinois Ass'n of Professional Ins. Agents, Inc. v. Comm'r, 86-2 U.S.T.C. ¶ 9702 (7th Cir. 1986), *aff'g* 49 T.C.M. 925 (1985)). Also National Water Well Ass'n, Inc. v. Comm'r, *supra* note 56.

[414] See § 24.3.

[415] Priv. Ltr. Rul. 7847001.

would have no basis for securing tax exemption.[416] However, if the entity transfers funds to the parent association, the funds may be taxable to the association as unrelated business income.[417] Likewise, the funds may be taxable to the association if the separate entity is regarded as an agent of the association.[418]

One court case recognized that the acquisition and provision of insurance can be an exempt function of a tax-exempt business league.[419] In this instance, the organization's purposes included counseling governmental agencies with regard to insurance programs, accepting and servicing insurance written by the agencies, and otherwise acting as an insurance broker for the governmental agencies. Finding this function to be "an important public service" (because the activity resulted in the best comprehensive insurance program for each agency and eliminated political corruption in the procurement of insurance), the court held that the net brokerage commissions received by the business league were not taxable as being from an unrelated trade or business. In so holding, the court placed some reliance on an IRS ruling that the provision for equitable distribution of high-risk insurance policies among member insurance companies is a tax-exempt undertaking.[420]

If a tax-exempt association provides insurance for its own employees, it can do so without adverse tax consequences by contracting with an insurance provider or by establishing a voluntary employees beneficiary association, which is itself tax-exempt.[421] This type of organization is one that provides "for the payment of life, sick, accident, or other benefits to the members of such association or their dependents or designated beneficiaries. . . ."[422]

Separate consideration must be given the insurance programs of tax-exempt fraternal beneficiary societies,[423] as their exempt purpose is to provide for the payment of qualifying benefits to their members and their dependents.[424] The IRS recognized that these benefits are in the nature of insurance, in holding that a society may not, as an exercise of an exempt function, provide additional insurance for terminated members.[425]

(iii) Associate Member Dues. Another issue for tax-exempt associations is the tax treatment of dues derived from associate members (or affiliate or patron members). In some instances, the IRS will tax these dues as forms of unrelated business income, on the ground that the member is paying for a specific service or

---

[416] North Carolina Oil Jobbers Ass'n, Inc. v. United States, 78-2 U.S.T.C. ¶ 9658 (E.D.N.C. 1978); New York State Ass'n of Real Estate Bds. Group Ins. Fund v. Comm'r, 54 T.C. 1325 (1970).

[417] See §§ 27.1(n).

[418] See *supra* § 3(b), text accompanied by note 133.

[419] Independent Ins. Agents of N. Nev., Inc. v. United States, 79-2 U.S.T.C. ¶ 9601 (D. Nev. 1979). This position of the IRS extends to insurance programs maintained by tax-exempt social welfare membership organizations (see Chapter 12) (e.g., Priv. Ltr. Rul. 9441001).

[420] Rev. Rul. 71-155, 1971-1 C.B. 152.

[421] See § 16.3.

[422] In general, Greif & Goldstein, "Rulings Holding Insurance Plans of Exempt Orgs. Taxable May Threaten Exemptions," 50 *J. Tax.* 294 (1979); Claytor, "When Will Business Activities Cause Trade Associations to Forfeit Their Exempt Status?," 49 *J. Tax.* 104 (1978).

[423] See § 18.4(a).

[424] *Id.*

[425] Priv. Ltr. Rul. 7937002.

to gain access to the regular membership for purposes of selling products or services.[426] Thus, in one instance, the IRS recommended taxation of associate member dues, where the associates allegedly joined only to obtain coverage under the association's automobile, health, dental, and farm owners' insurance programs.[427] In another instance, the IRS recommended taxation as advertising income the dues paid by associate members for listings in a variety of publications, allegedly to make them accessible to the regular members; the IRS recast the dues as *access fees*.[428] Taxation of dues is more likely where the associate members do not receive exempt function benefits, serve as directors or officers, vote on association matters, or otherwise lack any meaningful right or opportunity to participate in the affairs of the organization. The first court opinion on the point held that dues collected by a tax-exempt labor organization[429] from persons who were not regular active members of the organization, who became members so as to be able to participate in a health insurance plan sponsored by the organization, constituted unrelated business income.[430] The court concluded that this special class of members was created to generate revenue and not to contribute importantly to an exempt purpose. The fact that the organization generated substantial net revenues through the sale of these memberships was considered evidence that revenue-raising was the principal intent underlying the establishment of the membership category.[431]

The IRS stated that, in the case of tax-exempt labor, agricultural, and horticultural organizations,[432] dues payments from associate members will not be regarded as unrelated business income unless, for the relevant period, the membership category was formed or availed of for the principal purpose of producing unrelated income.[433] However, this aspect of the law was subsequently altered by statute, in that certain dues payments to exempt agricultural or horticultural organizations are exempt from unrelated business income taxation.[434] Nonetheless, this IRS position continues to be its view with respect to labor organizations (and to agricultural and horticultural entities that do not qualify for the exception); indeed, the IRS indicated that it will follow this approach with respect to associations generally.[435]

---

[426] This issue is identical to that raised in the context of tax-exempt labor unions (see text accompanied by *infra* notes 443–444).

[427] Tech. Adv. Mem. 9416002.

[428] Tech. Adv. Mem. 9345004.

[429] See § 15.1.

[430] National League of Postmasters v. Comm'r, 69 T.C.M. 2569 (1995), *aff'd*, 86 F.3d 59 (4th Cir. 1996).

[431] The Tax Court has this issue under consideration in National Alliance of Postal and Federal Employees v. Comm'r (No. 12911-94).

[432] See Chapter 15.

[433] Rev. Proc. 95-21, 1995-1 C.B. 686.

[434] See § 27.2(l).

[435] Rev. Proc. 97-12, 1997-4 I.R.B. 7., *mod.* Rev. Proc. 95-21, *supra* note 433. Associate member dues received by a professional association were found to not be taxable because the associate member category was not formed or availed of for the principal purpose of producing unrelated business income; votings rights were held to not be the sole criterion in this evaluation (Tech. Adv. Mem. 9742001). However, associate member dues received by a union were held taxable as unrelated income because the membership category was availed of for the principal purpose of producing this type of income (Tech. Adv. Mem. 9751001). In general, Tenenbaum, "Tax Treatment of Associate Member Dues: An Update and Review of the Rules," 16 *Exempt Org. Tax Rev.* (No. 4) 583 (April 1997).

(iv) Other Association Business Activity. It is the position of the IRS that a tax-exempt business league can engage in charitable activities, without incurring an unrelated income tax, even though the activities are technically unrelated to the business league's purposes.[436]

The position of the IRS is that the operation of an employment service by a tax-exempt association is an unrelated activity.[437] This approach embraces registry programs[438] but not job training programs.[439]

Tax-exempt associations are experiencing a conflict in the federal tax law as respects the classification of an activity as being a related service for members or an unrelated business. In the absence of statutory or administrative regulatory authority on the point, the courts are formulating standards. For example, the U.S. Court of Appeals for the Fourth Circuit applies the following three factors in resolving the issue as to whether an activity is substantially related to an association's exempt purposes: (1) whether the fees charged are directly proportionate to the benefits received; (2) whether participation is limited to members and thus is of no benefit to those in the industry who are nonmembers; and (3) whether the service provided is one commonly furnished by for-profit entities.[440] In subsequent application of these criteria, the court found that an association's administration of vacation pay and guaranteed annual income accounts for its members under a collective bargaining agreement was unrelated to its exempt negotiation and arbitration activities, because each member benefited in proportion to its participation in the activity, only the association's members were eligible to participate in the service, and the functions could be performed by for-profit entities.[441]

(e) Labor and Agricultural Organizations

One of the principal issues in the unrelated income context for labor unions[442] is the taxation of revenue (dues) derived from associate members (sometimes termed limited benefit members) who joined the organization solely to be able to participate in the organization's health insurance plans. The evolving view is that this dues revenue is taxable.[443] When this issue was initially litigated, the government lost, basically on the ground that the courts lacked the authority to define bona fide membership of tax-exempt labor unions.[444] However, the prevailing

---

[436] Tech. Adv. Mem. 8418003.

[437] Rev. Rul. 61-170, 1961-2 C.B. 112.

[438] Priv. Ltr. Rul. 8503103.

[439] Rev. Rul. 67-296, 1967-2 C.B. 22.

[440] Carolinas Farm & Power Equip. Dealers Ass'n, Inc. v. United States, *supra* note 108, at 171.

[441] Steamship Trade Ass'n of Baltimore, Inc. v. Comm'r, *supra* note 47, where the appellate court endorsed Rev. Rul. 66-151, *supra* note 265. Cf. Rev. Rul. 82-138, 1982-2 C.B. 106; Rev. Rul. 65-164, 1965-1 C.B. 238.

[442] See § 15.1.

[443] American Postal Workers Union, AFL-CIO v. United States, 925 F.2d 480 (D.C. Cir. 1991); National Ass'n of Postal Supervisors v. United States, 90-2 U.S.T.C. ¶ 50,445 (Ct. Cl. 1990), *aff'd*, 944 F. 2d 859 (Fed. Cir. 1991).

[444] American Postal Workers Union, AFL-CIO, v. United States, 90-1 U.S.T.C. ¶ 50,013 (D.D.C. 1989), *rev'd*, *supra* note 443. In general, Note, "Insurance Benefits for Limited 'Members' Results in UBIT," 5 *Ins. Tax Rev.* (No. 7) 597 (Sept.–Oct. 1991).

view is that the same rules that apply with respect to associations[445] apply in the case of labor organizations.

In other applications of the unrelated income rules to labor organizations, the IRS found to be taxable income derived by a tax-exempt labor organization from the operation of semiweekly bingo games[446] and from the performance of accounting and tax services for some of its members.[447]

Tax-exempt agricultural organizations are likewise subject to the tax on unrelated business income. As an illustration, the IRS ruled that the following is taxable: income received by a tax-exempt agricultural organization from the sale of supplies and equipment to members,[448] commissions from the sale of members' cattle,[449] income from the sale of supplies to seedsmen,[450] and income from the operation of club facilities for its members and their guests.[451]

Federal tax law provides an exclusion from the unrelated income taxation rules for income received by a tax-exempt organization used to establish, maintain, or operate a retirement home, hospital, or similar facility for the exclusive use and benefit of the aged and infirm members of the organization, where the income is derived from agricultural pursuits and conducted on grounds contiguous to the facility and where the income does not provide more than 75 percent of the cost of maintaining and operating the facility.[452]

(f) Advertising Activities

Generally, the net income derived by a tax-exempt organization from the sale of advertising is taxable as unrelated business income.[453] However, despite the extensive body of regulatory and case law in this area concerning when and how advertising revenue may be taxed, there is little law on the question as to what constitutes *advertising*. In one instance, a court considered the publication of "business listings," consisting of "slogans, logos, trademarks, and other information which is similar, if not identical in content, composition and message to the listings found in other professional journals, newspapers, and the 'yellow pages' of telephone directories," and found them to qualify as advertising.[454]

Under the rules defining what is a *trade or business*,[455] income from the sale of advertising in publications of tax-exempt organizations (even where the publications are related to the exempt purpose of the organization) generally constitutes unrelated business income, taxable to the extent it exceeds the expenses

---

[445] See *supra* § 5(d).
[446] Rev. Rul. 59-330, 1959-2 C.B. 153. Cf. § 27.2(h).
[447] Rev. Rul. 62-191, 1962-2 C.B. 146.
[448] Rev. Rul. 57-466, 1957-2 C.B. 311.
[449] Rev. Rul. 69-51, 1969-1 C.B. 159.
[450] Priv. Ltr. Rul. 8429010.
[451] Rev. Rul. 60-86, 1960-1 C.B. 198.
[452] Pre-1976 IRC § 512(b)(4). Although this provision was removed from the Internal Revenue Code as one of the "deadwood" provisions of the Tax Reform Act of 1976, it remains preserved in the law.
[453] IRC § 513(c).
[454] Fraternal Order of Police, Illinois State Troopers Lodge No. 41 v. Comm'r, 87 T.C. 747, 754 (1986), *aff'd*, 833 F.2d 717 (7th Cir. 1987).
[455] IRC § 513(c). See *supra* § 2.

directly related to the advertising. However, if the editorial aspect of the publication is carried on at a loss, the editorial loss may be offset against the advertising income from the publication. Thus, there will be no taxable unrelated trade or business income because of advertising where the publication as a whole is published at a loss. This rule embodies a preexisting regulation[456] that was promulgated in an effort to carve out (and tax) income from advertising and other activities in competition with taxpaying business, even though the advertising may appear in a periodical related to the educational or other tax-exempt purpose of the organization.

These rules are not intended to encompass the publication of a magazine with little or no advertising, which is distributed free or at a nominal charge not intended to cover costs. This type of publication would likely be published basically as a source of public information and not for the production of income. For a publication to be considered an activity carried on for the production of income, it must be contemplated that the revenues from advertising in the publication or the revenues from sales of the publication, or both, will result in net income (although not necessarily in a particular year). Nonetheless, for the tax on unrelated business income to apply, the advertising activity must also constitute a trade or business that is regularly carried on. Further, the tax is inapplicable where the advertising activity is a tax-exempt function.[457]

As an example, an association of law enforcement officials published a monthly journal containing conventional advertising featuring the products or services of a commercial enterprise. The IRS ruled that the regular sale of space in the journal for the advertising was carried on for the production of income and constituted the conduct of trade or business, which was not substantially related to the organization's tax-exempt functions.[458] The "controlling factor in this case," said the IRS, was that the "activities giving rise to the income in question constitute the sale and performance of a valuable service on the part of the publisher, and the purchase of that service on the part of the other party to the transaction."[459]

In a similar situation, the IRS ruled that income derived by a tax-exempt membership organization from the sale of advertising in its annual yearbook was unrelated business income.[460] Preparation of the editorial materials in the yearbook was largely done by the organization's staff, which also distributed it. However, an independent commercial firm was used, under a full year contract, to conduct an intensive advertising solicitation campaign in the organization's name and the firm was paid a percentage of the gross advertising receipts for selling the advertising, collecting from advertisers, and printing the yearbook. The

---

[456] Reg. § 1.513-1(b). This regulation became effective on December 13, 1967. IRC § 513(c) became effective on December 31, 1969. As respects tax years beginning between these dates, the regulation is of no effect, as an impermissible administrative enlargement of the scope of the statutory unrelated business income law (Massachusetts Medical Soc'y v. United States, 514 F.2d 153 (1st Cir. 1975); American College of Physicians v. United States, 530 F.2d 930 (Ct. Cl. 1976)).

[457] E.g., Priv. Ltr. Rul. 7948113 (holding that proceeds from the sale of advertising in the program published in promotion of a postseason all-star college football game are not unrelated income).

[458] Rev. Rul. 74-38, 1974-1 C.B. 144, *clar. by* Rev. Rul. 76-93, 1976-1 C.B. 170.

[459] Rev. Rul. 74-38, *id.*, at 145.

[460] Rev. Rul. 73-424, *supra* note 118.

IRS stated that "[b]y engaging in an extensive campaign of advertising solicitation, the organization is conducting competitive and promotional efforts typical of commercial endeavors."[461]

Initially, it appeared that the courts were willing to accede to this approach by the IRS. In the principal case, a tax-exempt medical organization was found to be engaging in an unrelated business by selling advertising in its scholarly journal. The court rejected the contention that the purpose of the advertising was to educate physicians, holding instead that its primary purpose was to raise revenue. In reaching this conclusion, the court reviewed the content, format, and positioning of the advertisements, and concluded they were principally commercial in nature. The court, however, set forth some standards as to when journal advertising might be a tax-exempt function, such as advertising that comprehensively surveys a particular field or otherwise makes a systematic presentation on an appropriate subject.[462]

These findings of the court were reversed on appeal, with the appellate court holding that the content of the advertisements was substantially related to the organization's educational purpose.[463] The court noted that the advertisements only appeared in bunches, at the beginning and end of the publications; were screened with respect to subject matter, with the contents controlled; and were indexed by advertiser. Also, only advertisements directly relevant to the practice of internal medicine were published. This decision, then, clearly established the principle that advertising is like any other trade or business, in that it is not automatically an unrelated activity, in that it can be an information dissemination (educational) function.

This dispute as to the tax treatment of advertising revenue in the unrelated income context, specifically whether the IRS is correct in asserting that all net income from advertising in tax-exempt publications is always taxable, was resolved by the U.S. Supreme Court, in 1986, when it held, after reviewing the history of the regulations promulgated in 1967[464] and of the statutory revisions authored in 1969,[465] that it is possible to have related advertising.[466] The Court said that the standard is whether the conduct of the tax-exempt organization in selling and publishing the advertising is demonstrative of a related function, rather than a determination as to whether the advertising is inherently educational.

The Supreme Court observed that in ascertaining relatedness, it is not sufficient to merely cluster the advertising in the front and back of the tax-exempt

---

[461] *Id*. at 191.
[462] The American College of Physicians v. United States, 83-2 U.S.T.C. ¶ 9652 (Ct. Cl. 1983).
[463] The American College of Physicians v. United States, 743 F.2d 1570 (Fed. Cir. 1984).
[464] See *supra* note 456.
[465] IRC § 513(c).
[466] United States v. American College of Physicians, 475 U.S. 834 (1986). Subsequently, a court found the advertising of a tax-exempt trade association to be taxable because it was not substantially related to the organization's exempt purposes and there is "[n]o systematic effort" made "to advertise products that relate to the editorial content of the magazine, and no effort . . . made . . . to limit the advertisements to new products" (Florida Trucking Ass'n, Inc. v. Comm'r, 87 T.C. 1039 (1986)). Displays and listings in a yearbook published by a tax-exempt labor organization (see § 15.1) were found to be the result of unrelated business (State Police Ass'n of Massachusetts v. Comm'r, 97-2 U.S.T.C. ¶ 50,627 (1st Cir. 1997)).

publication. Other facts that tended to mitigate against relatedness were that all advertising was paid, the advertising was for established products or services, advertising was repeated from one month to another, or the advertising concerned matters having "no conceivable relationship" to the exempt purpose of the sponsoring tax-exempt organization.[467] The test, said the Court, quoting from the trial court's opinion, is whether the organization uses the advertising "to provide its readers a comprehensive or systematic presentation of any aspect of the goods or services publicized."[468] As the Court wrote, a tax-exempt organization can "control its publication of advertisements in such a way as to reflect an intention to contribute importantly to its . . . [exempt] functions."[469] This can be done, said the Court, "[b]y coordinating the content of the advertisements with the editorial content of the issue, or by publishing only advertisements reflecting new developments . . ."[470]

The foregoing may be contrasted with the situation involving a charitable organization that raised funds for a tax-exempt symphony orchestra. As part of this effort, the organization published an annual concert book that was distributed at the orchestra's annual charity ball. The IRS ruled that the solicitation and sale of advertising by volunteers of the organization was not an unrelated taxable activity because the activity was not regularly carried on and because it was conducted as an integral part of the process of fund-raising for charity.[471] Thus, part of a successful contention that the unrelated income tax should not apply in the advertising context would seem to be a showing that the advertising activity ties in with other organization activity. Yet the same type of organization that engaged in the sale of advertising over a four-month period by its paid employees, for publication in concert programs distributed free at symphony performances over an eight-month period, was found by the IRS to be carrying on an unrelated business.[472] In that ruling, the IRS observed:

> It is a matter of common knowledge that many non-exempt organizations make a regular practice of publishing and distributing a seasonal series of special interest publications covering only a portion of each year with a format that includes substantial amounts of advertising matter. It would not be unusual for such an organization to concentrate its efforts to sell the advertising space thus made available during similar periods of intensive activity that would frequently last for no more than three or four months of each year. Since it is likewise further apparent that the activities giving rise to the adver-

---

[467] United States v. American College of Physicians, *supra* note 466, at 849.

[468] *Id.*

[469] *Id.*

[470] *Id.*, at 849–850. Subsequently, a court found that a tax exempt organization's advertising did not contribute importantly to the carrying out of any of its tax-exempt purposes, although it was willing to explore the argument to the contrary and found that the subject matter of some of the advertising was related to the organization's exempt purpose (Minnesota Holstein-Friesian Breeders Ass'n v. Comm'r, 64 T.C.M. 1319 (1992)). The court concluded that the primary purposes underlying the advertising were commercial: stimulating demand for the advertised products and raising revenue for the tax-exempt organization.

[471] Rev. Rul. 75-201, 1975-1 C.B. 164.

[472] Rev. Rul. 75-200, 1975-1 C.B. 163.

tising income here in question do not otherwise substantially differ from the comparable commercial activities of nonexempt organizations, those activities of the subject organization are regularly carried on within the meaning of section 512 of the Code.[473]

Similarly, a business league that sold a membership directory, but only to its members, was held to not be engaged in an unrelated trade or business.[474] The directory was considered to contribute importantly to the achievement of the organization's tax-exempt purposes by facilitating communication among its members and encouraging the exchange of ideas and expertise, resulting in greater awareness of collective and individual activities of the membership. The principal aspect governing the outcome of this matter, however, was the fact that the sale of the directory, done in a noncommercial manner, did not confer any private benefit on the organization's members.

Income attributable to a publication of a tax-exempt organization basically is regarded as either *circulation income* or (if any) *gross advertising income*.[475] Circulation income is the income attributable to the production, distribution, or circulation of a publication (other than gross advertising income), including amounts realized from the sale of the readership content of the publication. Gross advertising income is the amount derived from the unrelated advertising activities of an exempt organization publication.

Likewise, the costs attributable to a tax-exempt organization publication are characterized as *readership costs* and *direct advertising costs*.[476] A reasonable allocation may be made as between cost items attributable both to an exempt organization publication and to its other activities (such as salaries, occupancy costs, and depreciation).[477] Readership costs are, therefore, the cost items directly connected with the production and distribution of the readership content of the publication, other than the items properly allocable to direct advertising costs. Direct advertising costs include items that are directly connected with the sale and publication of advertising (such as agency commissions and other selling costs, artwork, and copy preparation), the portion of mechanical and distribution costs attributable to advertising lineage, and any other element of readership costs properly allocable to the advertising activity.

As noted, a tax-exempt organization (assuming it is subject to the unrelated business income rules in the first instance) is not taxable on its advertising income where its direct advertising costs equal such (gross) income. Even if gross advertising income exceeds direct advertising costs, costs attributable to the readership content of the publication qualify as costs deductible in computing (unre-

---

[473] *Id.* at 164.

[474] Rev. Rul. 79-370, 1979-2 C.B. 238.

[475] Reg. § 1.512(a)-1(f)(3).

[476] Reg. § 1.512(a)-1(f)(6).

[477] Once a reasonable method of allocation is adopted, it must be used consistently (Reg. § 1.512(a)-1(f)(6)(i)). One court held that the application of a ratio used in previous years for this purpose is not a "method"; it is the output of a method which cannot be automatically applied each year (National Ass'n of Life Underwriters, Inc. v. Comm'r, 94-2 U.S.T.C. ¶ 50,412 (D.C. Cir. 1994), *rev'g* 64 T.C.M. 379 (1992)).

lated) income from the advertising activity, to the extent that the costs exceed the income attributable to the readership content.[478] There are limitations on this rule, however, including the conditions that its application may not be used to realize a loss from the advertising activity nor to give rise to a cost deductible in computing taxable income attributable to any other unrelated activity. If the circulation income of the publication exceeds its readership costs, any unrelated business taxable income attributable to the publication is the excess of gross advertising income over direct advertising costs.

Another set of rules requires an allocation of membership dues to circulation income where the right to receive the publication is associated with membership status in the tax-exempt organization for which dues, fees, or other charges are received.[479] There are three ways of determining the portion of membership dues that constitute a part of circulation income (*allocable membership receipts*):

1. If 20 percent or more of the total circulation of the publication consists of sales to nonmembers, the subscription price charged to the nonmembers is the amount allocated from each member's dues to circulation income. It was held that the term *total circulation* means paid circulation, that is, it does not include distribution of a publication without charge to a tax-exempt organization's nonmembers.[480] It has also been held that this term means the actual number of copies of the publication distributed for compensation without regard to how the copies were purchased; in the case, members of a tax-exempt association paid for subscriptions, by means of dues, and they designated nonmember recipients of the publication, who were considered part of the total circulation base.[481]

2. If rule (1) is inapplicable and if the membership dues from 20 percent or more of the members of the organization are less than the dues received from the remaining members because the former category of members does not receive the publication, the amount of the dues reduction is the amount used in allocating membership dues to circulation income.

3. Otherwise, the portion of membership receipts allocated to the publication is an amount equal to the total amount of the receipts multiplied by a fraction, the numerator of which is the total costs of the publication and

---

[478] Reg. § 1.512(a)-1(f)(2)(ii), (d)(2).

[479] Reg. § 1.512(a)-1(f)(4). The IRS initially took the position that the requirement that membership receipts must be allocated on a pro rata basis to circulation income of a tax-exempt organization's periodical (Reg. § 1.512(a)-1(f)(4)(iii)) requires that the "cost of other exempt activities of the organization" must be offset by the income produced by the activities (the "net cost" rule) (IRS Gen. Couns. Mem. 38104), but subsequently concluded that the gross cost of the other tax-exempt activities must be used in computing the denominator of the formula (Gen. Couns. Mems. 38205, 38168).

[480] American Hosp. Ass'n v. United States, 654 F. Supp. 1152 (N.D. Ill. 1987).

[481] North Carolina Citizens for Business & Indus. v. United States, 89-2 U.S.T.C. ¶ 9507 (Cl. Ct. 1989).

the denominator of which is these costs plus the costs of the other tax-exempt activities of the organization.[482]

These rules become even more intricate where a tax-exempt organization publishes more than one publication for the production of income. (A publication is published for the production of income if the organization generally receives gross advertising income from the publication equal to at least 25 percent of its readership costs and the publication activity is engaged in for profit.) In this case, the organization may treat the gross income from all (but not just some) of the publications and the deductible items directly connected with the publications on a consolidated basis in determining the amount of unrelated business taxable income derived from the sale of advertising. (Thus, an organization cannot consolidate the losses of a publication not published for the production of income with the profit of other publications that are so published.) This treatment must be followed consistently and, once adopted, is binding, unless the organization obtains the requisite permission from the IRS to change the method.[483]

It is the position of the IRS, as supported by the U.S. Tax Court, that the specific rules concerning the computation of net unrelated income derived from advertising are inapplicable in a case where the "issue of whether the . . . [organization's] publication of the readership content of the magazines is an exempt activity has not been decided, stipulated to, or presented for decision" and where the IRS "has not sought to apply such regulations, maintaining that they cannot be applied due to the . . . [organization's] failure to produce credible evidence of its advertising and publishing expenses."[484]

---

[482]The reference to the "costs of the other exempt activities" means the total costs or expenses incurred by an organization in connection with its other tax-exempt activities, not offset by any income earned by the organization from the activities (Rev. Rul. 81-101, 1981-1 C.B. 352).

An organization, such as a business league (Chapter 13), may have within it an integral fund that is a charitable organization, and the costs of the fund can be included in the formula used to calculate the business league's net unrelated business taxable income derived from advertising, thereby reducing the tax liability of the business league (American Bar Ass'n v. United States, 84-1 U.S.T.C. ¶ 9179 (N.D. Ill. 1984)).

These regulations, particularly the third pro rata allocation method rule, were challenged in court on substantive and procedural grounds; while the challenge was initially successful, it essentially failed on appeal (American Medical Ass'n v. United States, 887 F.2d 760 (7th Cir. 1989), aff'g and rev'g 608 F. Supp. 1085 (N.D. Ill. 1987), 668 F. Supp. 1101 (N. D. Ill. 1987), 668 F. Supp. 358 (N.D. Ill. 1988), 691 F. Supp. 1170 (N.D. Ill. 1988)). The basic assertion, which was ultimately rejected, was that a tax-exempt organization can deduct, as direct advertising costs, the readership content costs of periodicals distributed for the purpose of generating advertising revenue.

[483] IRC § 446(e); Reg. § 1.446-1(e).

[484] CORE Special Purpose Fund v. Comm'r, 49 T.C.M. 626, 630 (1985). Notwithstanding the differences in the manner in which tax-exempt social clubs are treated for purposes of unrelated taxation (see § 28.3), the rules concerning the taxation of advertising revenue are applicable to them (Chicago Metropolitan Ski Council v. Comm'r, 104 T.C. 341 (1995)). In general, Reap, "Getting the Most from Periodical Advertising Income," 4 *Exempt Org. Tax Rev.* (No. 8) 1065 (1991); Geske, "Unrelated Business Taxable Income and Advertising Revenue of Exempt Organization Periodicals," 4 *Exempt Org. Tax Rev.* (No. 3) 311 (1991); Schnee & Brock, "Opportunities Exist to Reduce Unrelated Business Income from Advertising Revenue," 74 *J. Tax.* (No. 4) 240 (1991); Littman, "Advertising and the Unrelated Business Income Tax after *United States v. American College of Physicians*," 49 *Ohio St. L. Jour.* (No. 2) 625 (1988); Gallagher, " 'Substantially Related': The Magic Words for Nonprofit Organizations: *United*

(h) Share-Crop Leasing

An unrelated business tax issue that is of concern to the IRS and that is being addressed in the courts is the proper tax treatment to be accorded share-crop revenue received by tax-exempt organizations.

This subject is informed by two bodies of law: (1) the existence or nonexistence of a general partnership or joint venture for tax purposes[485] and (2) the interpretation of the *passive rent rules*.[486]

A share-crop lease arrangement may involve land that is owned by a tax-exempt organization and leased by the organization to a farmer. Under the terms of the lease, the tenant is exclusively responsible for managing and operating the farm property. The tenant is also required to prepare a farm operating plan, including a schedule of crops to be grown on the land and seeding or planting rates, chemicals and fertilizers to be used, conservation practices and tillage plans, livestock breeding and market schedules, nutrition and feeding schedules, and harvesting and storage plans. After the operating plan is complete, the tenant is usually required to submit the plan to the tax-exempt organization for review.[487]

Operation of all aspects of the farm is the sole responsibility of the tenant. The tenant is responsible for general farming operations, including cultivation of the land, planting, fertilizing, harvesting and marketing crops, and all aspects of livestock husbandry. The tax-exempt organization is generally responsible for all of the costs associated with the land and fixed improvements, including the costs of wells and pumps, irrigation equipment, and initially required limestone and rock phosphates. The tenant or the landlord may provide equipment and tools required to farm the land. The allocation of the proceeds of the sale of any crops and/or livestock raised on the property between the tax-exempt organization and the tenant is negotiated between them and is generally comparable to per-

---

States v. American College of Physicians," 21 *U.S.F.L. Rev.* (No. 4) 795 (1987): Huffaker & Gut, "Supreme Court Holds Advertising Revenue Was Not Substantially Related Income," 65 *J. Tax.* (No. 1) 2 (July 1986); Gross, "New Developments Regarding Advertising Income of Tax-Exempt Organizations," 24 *Am. Bus. L. J.* (No. 1) 116 (1986); Shillingburg, *"American College of Physicians v. United States*: An Ending—A Beginning—Or?," 64 *Taxes* (No. 9) 539 (1986); Simpson, "Taxation of Income from Advertising in Exempt Organizations' Publications," 10 *Estates, Gifts, & Trusts J.* (No. 6) 184 (1985); Weinberg & Nixon, "What Are the Implications of the Federal Circuit's Holding in *American College*?," 62 *J. Tax.* (No. 4) 242 (1985); Gregory, Jr., "Fed. Circuit Holds ABE Insurance Program Does Not Constitute Unrelated Business Income," 63 *J. Tax.* (No. 4) 244 (1985); Kannry, "Taxing Advertising," IX *The Philanthropy Monthly* (No. V) 26 (1976); Kannry, "How to Mitigate the Impact of New Regs. on Exempt Organization's Advertising Income," 45 *J. Tax.* 304 (1976); Sugarman & Vogt, "The New Advertising Regulations and Their Application to Exempt Organizations," 54 *Taxes* 196 (1976); Spevack, "Taxation of Advertising Income of Exempt Organizations' Publications," 21 *Cath. Law.* 268 (1975); Endicott, "Proposed Changes in the Taxation of Advertising Income of Exempt Organization Publications," 2 *Tax Adv.* 710 (1971); Lehrfeld, "The Unfairness Doctrine: Commercial Advertising Profits as Unrelated Business Income," 23 *Tax Law.* 349 (1970); Weithorn & Liles, "Unrelated Business Income Tax: Changes Affecting Journal Advertising Revenues," 45 *Taxes* 791 (1967).

[485] See Chapter 32.

[486] See § 27.1(h).

[487] The final college and university examination guidelines omitted a discussion of crop leasing, due to the litigation throughout 1993 (see text accompanied by *infra* notes 497–511. However, the proposed guidelines (Ann. 93-2, 1993-2 I.R.B. 39) contained this analysis (in § 342.12(2)): the text is based on that summary.

centage crop rents negotiated between other landlords and farm operators in the community.[488]

Under the terms of the typical share-crop lease, although the tenant farmer is required to submit a detailed farm operating plan to the tax-exempt organization for review, which provides an opportunity for control to some extent by the tax-exempt organization over the farming operations, the IRS is of the view that "it does not follow that under the terms of such a farm lease that the exempt organization manages and directs the operation of the property to a significant extent."[489] The IRS also stated that, even if the requirement of a farm operating plan provides control over how a tenant conducts the farming activity, "it does not rise to a level of control that would require treating crop shares as other than rental from real property."[490] The IRS observed that "[i]t is significant that under such a farm lease there is no sharing of expense and the exempt organization does not provide financing for its tenants."[491]

The determination of whether an amount received pursuant to a share-crop lease constitutes excludable rent is a two-step process. First, there must be a determination as to whether a particular share-crop arrangement constitutes a lease or some other arrangement. It is necessary to compare the particular share-crop arrangement with standard share-crop arrangements in a particular locality to determine whether the agreement constitutes a lease under local law and whether an amount received according to the agreement constitutes rent. However, most share-crop arrangements are in the nature of leases that produce rental income. There are cases where the IRS will find that a particular sharecrop agreement creates a joint venture rather than a lease; in these circumstances, it will be asserted that the income under the agreement does not constitute rent,[492] so that the income is taxable.[493] Second, if it is found that a share-crop agreement constitutes a lease producing rental income, the determination must be made as to whether the exclusion for rental income applies. In cases where the IRS asserts that the underlying agreement is not a lease, it generally will be asserted as a back-up argument that the exclusion for rent does not apply because the rent is in any event based on the profit from the farm.[494]

When a tax-exempt organization shares the crop produced by a tenant farmer, the rent is in fact based on a percentage of receipts or sales and is not barred from treatment as rent from real property for these purposes. However, when the sharing is combined with a substantial sharing of farm costs with the tenant, the rent is in effect based on the profit from the farm and the income is not protected by the exclusion.[495]

One federal district court was the first to issue an opinion grappling with the question as to whether income received by a tax-exempt organization, as rent

---

[488] *Id.*

[489] *Id.*

[490] *Id.*

[491] *Id.*

[492] *Id.* § 342.12(3)(a).

[493] See § 27.1(h).

[494] Ann. 93-2, *supra* note 487 § 342.12(3)(b).

[495] *Id.* § 342.12(4).

from a share-crop lease, was a form of passive income (and thus not subject to unrelated income taxation) or revenue from participation in a joint venture that is not in furtherance of an exempt purpose (and thus subject to the tax). The court concluded that the income was "true rent" that is based on a fixed percentage of receipts from the farm production within the scope of the statutory exclusion[496] and thus was not taxable.[497]

The tax-exempt organization in this case owned a farm that was managed by a bank; the organization entered into a share-crop agreement with two individuals. Their rent was 50 percent of farm production after the crop was divided at the grain elevator. They made the farming decisions; they and the bank were billed separately for the shared expenses and never assumed one another's debts. The parties to the lease did not share in each other's profits or losses. The court reviewed the applicable state law and concluded that there was no evidence that this relationship was a joint venture or a partnership.

The government's alternative argument was that the rent from the share-crop agreement was based on a percentage of income or profits and thus was not exempt from tax under a special exception.[498] This assertion led the court to review the legislative history of this provision and to conclude that, in enacting it, Congress sought to tax property rentals that are measured by reference to the net income from the property. The court again reviewed the terms of the lease and state law which recognized that rent may be paid as a portion of crops. It said that if the farm were leased on a cash-rent basis, the rent would be excludable from tax.[499] It wrote that "[i]t seems anomalous that identical activities undertaken on a share-crop lease should be taxable."[500] The court noted the "long history" of share-crop leases in the particular state; the absence of "a clear directive from Congress to the contrary" led it to hold that division of the crops under this share-crop lease was a receipt of rent and not a division of profits.[501]

In a subsequent case, another court held that rents received under share-crop leases by a charitable trust were excluded from unrelated business income taxation.[502] The trust, by means of a bank that managed the property, operated farmland, paid necessary expenses, made necessary improvements, and rented the farmland; the land was rented under share-crop leases. Thus, the trust supplied the farm and buildings on it, materials necessary for repairs and improvements on the farm, and skilled labor for making permanent improvements. The trust was responsible for 50 percent of the cost of seed, fertilizer, limestone, herbicides, and insecticides. These leases obligated the tenant to be responsible for all machinery, equipment, power, and labor necessary to farm the land. The parties were to confer for the purpose of planning land use and sharing certain costs. Li-

---

[496] IRC § 512(b)(3)(A)(i), (B)(ii).
[497] Harlan E. Moore Charitable Trust v. United States, 812 F. Supp. 130, 135 (C.D. Ill. 1993), aff'd, 9 F.3d 623 (7th Cir. 1993). The IRS Office of Chief Counsel recommended acquiesence in this case (AOD 1994-001).
[498] IRC § 512(b)(3)(B)(ii).
[499] IRC § 512(b)(3)(A)(i).
[500] Harlan E. Moore Charitable Trust v. United States, *supra* note 497, 812 F. Supp. at 135.
[501] *Id.*
[502] Trust U/W Emily Oblinger v. Comm'r, 100 T.C. 114 (1993).

ability for all accidents relative to farming was conferred on the tenant. The amount of rent payable to the trust under these leases was fixed at 50 percent of the harvested corn, oats, soybean, and wheat.

Generally, to be excluded from unrelated income taxation, rent must be passive income. Thus, rent is taxable as unrelated income if the "determination of the amount of such rent depends in whole or in part on the income or profits derived by any person from the property leased."[503] Nonetheless, rent may be excluded from unrelated income taxation when the amount of rent is based on a "fixed percentage or percentages of receipts or sales."[504] These two provisions were termed by the court the "passive rent test."[505] The court wrote that, "[i]n order to exclude rents from . . . [unrelated business income taxation], rents must in substance qualify as rent, as opposed to actually representing a return of profits by the tenant or a share of profits retained by the landlord as either a partner or joint venturer . . . and not violate the . . . passive income test."[506]

The IRS contended that these arrangements were either general partnerships or joint ventures and that the payments under the leases represented a return of profits that were taxable. This contention was rested largely on the provisions in the leases concerning land use planning and cost sharing.

The court disagreed with the IRS's characterization of the facts. It found that the trust "did not itself or through its managing agent participate in the day-to-day operations of the farm to a degree which would support the existence of a joint venture or partnership with the tenant."[507] The court specifically singled out the provision concerning liability for farming accidents as evidence that the arrangement was not a joint venture or a partnership. Also, the court noted that the trust was not required to contribute to losses, there were no provisions to carry over losses from one year to reduce payments to the trust in later years, and the leases were typical of share-crop leases used in the region. The court then found that the rent involved did not violate the passive rent test. The tax regulations state that an amount is excluded from "rents from real property" if, considering the lease and the surrounding circumstances, the arrangement does not conform with normal business practice and is in reality used as a means of basing the rent on income or profits.[508] The court wrote that this test "is intended to prevent avoidance of unrelated business income tax where a profit-sharing arrangement will, in effect, make the lessor an active participant in the operation of the property."[509]

As noted, an exception is provided for amounts based on a fixed percentage or percentages of receipts or sales. In asserting that the arrangements violated the passive rent test, the IRS emphasized the trust's splitting of the expenses, its involvement in the farming operations, and its receipt of a percentage of production as rent, rather than a percentage of receipts. The court disagreed, finding the leases to amount to the "equivalent of the tenant's reducing the crops to cash and

---

[503] IRC § 512(b)(3)(B)(ii).
[504] *Id.*
[505] Trust U/W Emily Oblinger v. Comm'r, *supra* note 502, at 121.
[506] *Id.* at 117.
[507] *Id.* at 120.
[508] Reg. § 1.512(b)-1(c)(2)(iii)(b).
[509] Trust U/W Emily Oblinger v. Comm'r, *supra* note 502, at 122.

then giving . . . [the trust] its share of the total receipts collected."[510] In conclusion, wrote the court, the "passive rent test was not violated since . . . [the trust's] rent was not determined, in whole or in part, on the net profits or income derived from the property."[511]

(i) Retirement Plan Reversions

A tax-exempt organization may maintain a qualified pension or other retirement plan to provide retirement benefits to its employees.[512] Generally, the assets of the plan must be used exclusively for the employees and their beneficiaries,[513] and the contributions of an employer to a qualified plan are deductible in the year in which the contributions are paid.[514] This type of plan may be terminated; in that instance, all benefits accrued to the date of termination must become completely vested and nonforfeitable, and plan benefits must be distributed to the participants in the plan or annuities providing for the payment of comparable benefits must be purchased and distributed to the participants. Where the plan is terminated and assets remain after the satisfaction of all liabilities to plan participants and other beneficiaries, and if the excess of assets is attributable to actuarial error, the employer is permitted to recover the excess assets.[515] Generally, this excess must be included in the gross income of the employer.

Where the employer organization is a tax-exempt organization that is subject to the rule that all income other than exempt function income is taxable as related business income,[516] such as a social club,[517] generally the amount of the reversion is includable in the organization's unrelated business income because it is not exempt function income.[518] This body of law does not contain the general requirement that there must be a *trade or business* before the income can be taxable.[519]

However, this type of income of a tax-exempt organization with these characteristics may be excluded from taxation by reason of the *tax benefit rule* Under the exclusionary portion of this rule, gross income does not include income attributable to the recovery during a tax year of any amount deducted in any prior tax year to the extent that amount did not reduce the amount of income tax involved.[520] By contrast, under the inclusionary aspect of this rule, where the amount previously deducted from gross income generates a tax benefit and is then recaptured in a subsequent year, the recaptured amount is includable in

---

[510] *Id.* at 123.
[511] *Id.* In so holding, the court favorably cited the opinion in Harlan E. Moore Charitable Trust v. Comm'r, *supra* note 497. Also Independent Order of Odd Fellows Grand Lodge of Iowa v. United States, 93-2 U.S.T.C. ¶ 50,448 (S.D. Iowa 1993); White's Iowa Manual Labor Inst. v. Comm'r, 66 T.C.M. 389 (1993).
[512] See § 16.1.
[513] IRC § 401(a)(2).
[514] IRC § 401(a)(1)(A).
[515] Reg. § 1.401-2(b)(1).
[516] See § 28.3.
[517] See Chapter 14.
[518] Gen. Couns. Mem. 39717.
[519] See § 14.3.
[520] IRC § 111(a).

gross income in the year of the recapture.[521] Consequently, to the extent that this type of tax-exempt organization deducted contributions to a defined benefit plan in determining its taxable nonexempt function income, the inclusionary aspect of the tax benefit rule would be applicable.[522]

Where the employer organization is a tax-exempt organization that is not subject to this rule concerning taxation of nonexempt function income, the tax consequences of a reversion of plan assets are different. Because (1) the operation of the plan is not a business[523] but rather an administrative function that is part of the overall operations of the exempt organization and (2) the funds that revert upon termination of the plan are a one-time source of income rather than income from an activity that is regularly carried on,[524] the reverted funds are generally not taxable as unrelated business income.[525]

The tax benefit rule can apply in this setting as well. In general, an organization that is not subject to this special rule of unrelated income taxation is usually exempt from taxation and thus would not derive any tax benefit from contributions to a qualified pension plan. This is another application of the exclusionary aspect of the tax benefit rule. However, this type of organization could receive a tax benefit from a contribution to a qualified plan if it deducted the amount of the contribution from any unrelated business taxable income.[526] In that case, by operation of the inclusionary aspects of the tax benefit rule, the recovery of the previously deducted amounts would be unrelated business taxable income to the tax-exempt organization.[527]

(g) Fund-Raising Activities

Fund-raising practices for charitable organizations and the unrelated business rules have a precarious relationship.[528]

For many years, the IRS exercised restraint in this area by refraining from applying the unrelated income rules to charitable gift solicitation efforts. However, the IRS now utilizes the unrelated business income rules to characterize the receipts from certain fund-raising activities as taxable income. This utilization of these rules is one of the chief means by which the IRS is embarking upon regulation of fund-raising for charity.[529]

---

[521] IRC § 61; Rev. Rul. 68-104, 1968-1 C.B. 361; Gen. Couns. Mem. 39744.

[522] Gen. Couns. Mem. 39717.

[523] See § 14.3.

[524] See *supra* § 3.

[525] Gen. Couns. Mem. 39806.

[526] See § 28.2.

[527] Gen. Couns. Mem. 39806.

[528] The federal tax law does not generally define the term *fund-raising*. However, the tax regulations promulgated in connection with the *expenditure test* provide that the term fund-raising embraces three practices: (1) the solicitation of dues or contributions from members of the organization, from persons whose dues are in arrears, or from the general public: (2) the solicitation of gifts from businesses or gifts or grants from other organizations, including charitable entities, or (3) the solicitation of grants from a governmental unit or any agency of instrumentality of the unit (Reg. § 56.4911-4(f)(1)). See § 20.2(c).

[529] In general, Hopkins, *The Law of Fund-Raising, Second Edition* (New York: John Wiley & Sons, Inc. 1996), Chapter 6 § 6.

At the outset, it must be conceded that some charitable fund-raising practices possess all of the technical characteristics of an unrelated trade or business. Reviewing the criteria for unrelated income taxation,[530] some fund-raising activities are (1) trades or businesses, (2) regularly carried on, and (3) not efforts that are substantially related to the performance of tax-exempt functions. Further, applying some of the tests often used by the IRS and the courts, there is no question but that some fund-raising endeavors (4) have a commercial counterpart and they are being conducted in competition with that counterpart, and (5) are being undertaken with the objective of realizing a profit.[531]

The rationale that fund-raising activities are not businesses was expressed by the Senate Committee on Finance in 1969, when it stated that "where an activity does not possess the characteristics of a trade or business within the meaning of IRC [§] 162, such as when an organization sends out low-cost articles incidental to the solicitation of charitable contributions, the unrelated business income tax does not apply, since the organization is not in competition with taxable organizations."[532] However, an examination of this rationale reveals two elements that substantially undermine its widespread application: (1) The funds received by the organization are in the form of gifts, not payments for the articles or services provided, and (2) the activity is not in competition with commercial endeavors. These two elements are frequently absent in a fund-raising endeavor.

Thus, a tax-exempt organization may well engage in fund-raising efforts that have their commercial counterparts. Some of these activities are sheltered by law from consideration as taxable businesses, such as a business (1) in which substantially all of the work is performed for the organization by volunteers,[533] (2) carried on primarily for the convenience of the organization's members, students, patients, officers, or employees,[534] or (3) that consists of the sale of merchandise substantially all of which has been received by the organization as gifts.[535] Also, the receipts from certain types of bingo games are exempted from unrelated business income taxation.[536]

The beginning of serious regard of fund-raising activities as businesses can be traced to the Tax Reform Act of 1969, whereby Congress authorized the taxation of revenue from the acquisition and publication of advertising in the magazines of tax-exempt organizations.[537] To accomplish this result, Congress codified two rules previously contained in the income tax regulations: it enacted laws that state that (1) the term *trade or business* includes any activity carried on for the production of income from the sale of goods or the performance of services, and (2)

---

[530] See *supra* §§ 2–4.
[531] See § 4.9, Chapter 25. The fact that the "profits" of an activity are destined for use in furtherance of tax-exempt functions cannot be taken into consideration in assessing whether an activity is an unrelated one (IRC §§ 502, 513(a)).
[532] S. Rep. No. 522, 91st Cong., 1st Sess. 71 (1969), quoted as part of the IRS Exempt Organizations Handbook (IRM 7751) at (36) 21 (2); Reg. § 1.513-1(b).
[533] See § 27.2(a).
[534] See § 27.2(b).
[535] See § 27.2(c). E.g., Rev. Rul. 71–581, 1971–2 C.B. 236.
[536] See § 27.2(h).
[537] See *supra* § 5(f).

an activity of producing or distributing goods or performing services from which gross income is derived does not lose identity as a trade or business merely because it is carried on within a larger aggregate of similar activities or within a larger complex of other endeavors that may or may not be related to the exempt purposes of the organization.[538]

The IRS observed that the definition of the term "is not limited to integrated aggregates of assets, activities, and good will which comprise businesses" for purposes of other tax rules.[539] In addition to the breadth of this definition, the IRS is, as noted, authorized by statute to examine the activities of a tax-exempt organization one-by-one (rather than as a single bundle of activities) and fragment its operations in search of unrelated business endeavors. As the result of both of these rules, the fund-raising practices of charitable organizations are exposed and thus more vulnerable to the charge that they are unrelated businesses.

More directly, the IRS held that the regular sales of membership mailing lists by a tax-exempt educational organization to colleges and business firms for the production of income is an unrelated trade or business.[540] By contrast, the IRS ruled that the exchange of mailing lists by an exempt organization with similar exempt organizations does not give rise to unrelated business income (namely, barter income of an amount equal to the value of the lists received).[541] In this ruling, the IRS ruled that the activity was not a business because it was not carried on for profit but rather to obtain the names of potential donors. Likewise, this exchange function was held to be substantially related to the organization's exempt function as being a "generally accepted method used by publicly supported organizations to assist them in maintaining and enhancing their active donor files."[542] Nonetheless, where a tax-exempt organization exchanges mailing lists so as to produce income, it is the position of the IRS that the transaction is economically the same as a rental and thus is an unrelated trade or business.[543]

The rationale that fund-raising activities are not taxable businesses because they are not regularly carried on also finds support in the early IRS literature. The basic position of the IRS is that "exempt organization business activities which are engaged in only discontinuously or periodically will not be considered regularly carried on if they are conducted without the competitive and promotional efforts typical of commercial endeavors."[544] For example, the operation of a sandwich stand by a hospital auxiliary for two weeks at a state fair is not the regular conduct of a trade or business,[545] while the operation of a parking lot for commercial purposes one day each week on a year-round basis is the regular conduct of a

---

[538] IRC § 513(c); also Reg. § 1.513-1(b). See *supra* § 2(a).
[539] Exempt Organizations Handbook, *supra* note 532, at (36) 21 (1).
[540] Rev. Rul. 72-431, *supra* note 26.
[541] Priv. Ltr. Rul. 8127019.
[542] *Id.*
[543] Priv. Ltr. Rul. 8216009.
[544] Exempt Organizations Handbook, *supra* note 532, at (36)30(2)(d).
[545] *Id.* at (36)30(2)(a).

trade or business.[546] Thus, the IRS observed that "[a]n annually recurrent dance or similar fund-raising event for charity would not be regular since it occurs so infrequently."[547]

In one case, a court concluded that the annual fund-raising activity of a tax-exempt charitable organization, consisting of the presentation and sponsoring of a professional vaudeville show (one weekend per year), was not regularly carried on.[548] The court concluded: "The fact that an organization seeks to [e]nsure the success of its fundraising venture by beginning to plan and prepare for it earlier should not adversely affect the tax treatment of the income derived from the venture."[549]

However, just as many fund-raising practices are *trades or businesses*, so are many *regularly carried on*. Inasmuch as the other rationales for avoiding unrelated income taxation (principally, the contention that the activity is *substantially related* or that the income is *passive*) are unlikely to apply in the fund-raising context, it is today quite possible for a fund-raising activity to be deemed a trade or business that is regularly carried on and an undertaking that is not substantially related to the exercise of a charitable organization's tax-exempt purposes.

There are several instances of the assumption by the IRS of this position. One is a 1979 private letter ruling concerning a tax-exempt religious organization that conducted, as its principal fund-raising activity, bingo games and related concessions.[550] Players were charged a fixed amount for the use of bingo cards, the games were held three nights each week, and the receipts from the expenses of the games were substantial. The IRS concluded that the "bingo games constitute a trade or business with the general public, the conduct of which is not substantially related to the exercise or the performance by the organization of the purpose for which it was organized other than the use it makes of the profits derived from the games."[551]

A court of appeals held that a solicitation of charitable contributions by means of the mailing of greeting cards to potential contributors does not constitute the conduct of an unrelated trade or business.[552] The case concerned a school that, unsuccessful in its attempt to raise funds from private foundations and other organizations, turned to a program of mailing packages of greeting cards to prospective donors, with information about the school and a request for contribu-

---

[546] *Id.* at (36)30(2)(b).

[547] *Id.* at (36)30(2)(f). However, a charitable organization may be found to be engaged in an unrelated trade or business for conducting this type of a fund-raising event where it is done for the benefit of another charity (Rev. Rul. 75-201, 1975-1 C.B. 164).

[548] Suffolk County Patrolmen's Benevolent Ass'n, Inc. v. Comm'r, *supra* note 140. The court took the opportunity of this case to observe: The IRS "apparently believes that all fundraisers of exempt organizations are conducted by amateurs in an amateurish manner. We do not believe that this is, nor should be, the case. It is entirely reasonable for an exempt organization to hire professionals in an effort to insure the success of a fundraiser. . . ." (at 1323).

[549] *Id.* at 1324.

[550] Priv. Ltr. Rul. 7946001. Also P.L.L. Scholarship Fund v. Comm'r, 82 T.C. 196 (1984); Piety, Inc. v. Comm'r, 82 T.C. 193 (1984).

[551] The organization was unable to utilize the exemption from unrelated income taxation accorded to bingo games because, under the law of the state in which it was organized (Texas), the games constituted, at that time, an illegal lottery. See § 27.2(h).

[552] The Hope School v. United States, 612 F.2d 298 (7th Cir. 1980).

tions. An outside firm printed, packaged, and mailed the greeting cards and the accompanying solicitation letter. The court rejected the government's contention that the solicitation was a trade or business, finding that the greeting cards were not being sold but were distributed incidental to the solicitation of charitable contributions. As noted, the income tax regulations provide that "an activity does not possess the characteristics of a trade or business . . . when an organization sends out low cost articles incidental to the solicitation of charitable contributions."[553] The government argued that this rule was inapplicable in this case because the funds involved were not "gifts," but the court said that to read the law in that narrow manner would "completely emasculate the exception."[554] The court held that the case turned on the fact that the unrelated income rules were designed to prevent nonprofit organizations from unfairly competing with for-profit companies, and that the school's fund-raising program did not give it "an unfair competitive advantage over taxpaying greeting card businesses."[555]

Another court subsequently examined application of the unrelated income rules as they relate to certain fund-raising efforts of a national veterans organization.[556] The case focused on two fund-raising practices of the organization. The first was its practice of offering items (termed *premiums*) to potential donors as part of its semiannual direct mail solicitation. The premiums, offered in exchange for contributions of $2, $3, or $5, were maps, charts, calendars, and books. The rationale for this use of premiums was that it gained the attention of the recipients so that more initial responses were obtained or, in instances involving prior donors, the level of contributions was upgraded. The second practice was the rental of names on the organization's mailing list to both tax-exempt and commercial organizations. The court found that certain of the organization's solicitation activities using premiums constituted a trade or business because they were conducted in a competitive and commercial manner. In making the differentiation, the court ruled that "if the contribution required for any one premium was set at an amount greatly in excess of the retail value of the premium concerned, a competitive situation would not be present."[557] Because the $2 premium items were valued at $0.85 to $1 and the $3 items were valued at $1.50, the court concluded that there was not a trade or business. However, because the $5 premium items were valued at $2.95 to $5.45, the court found the requisite trade or business, noting that the sending of a $5 contribution "may well have formed a contract binding . . . [the organization] to furnish the premium item."[558] Also finding that the solicitation was regularly carried on (because of "sufficient similarity to a commercial endeavor"[559]) and was not an activity related to the organization's tax-exempt purposes notwithstanding the utility of the premiums as attention-

---

[553] See text accompanied by *supra* note 365.
[554] The Hope School v. United States, *supra* note 552, at 302.
[555] *Id.* at 304. An appeal of this decision was not authorized, with the government believing a preferential appeal vehicle on the issue was Veterans of Foreign Wars of the United States, Department of Michigan v. Comm'r, which turned out to be accurate (see text accompanied by *infra* note 568).
[556] Disabled American Veterans v. United States, 80-2 U.S.T.C. ¶ 9568 (Ct. Cl. 1980).
[557] *Id.*, at 84,855.
[558] *Id.*
[559] *Id.*, at 84,856.

getting devices), the court declared the presence of an unrelated trade or business. The court also determined that the rental of the organization's donor list was a trade or business that was regularly carried on and that was not substantially related to the accomplishment of its tax-exempt purposes.[560]

It is clear, from these two court cases, that there is much less of a likelihood that the use of premium items as part of a fund-raising activity will be considered an unrelated trade or business if the items are mailed with the solicitation. That is, where the recipients are informed that the premiums can be retained without any obligation to make a contribution, the activity is not conducted in a competitive manner and hence presumably is not a trade or business. However, as one court observed, "when premiums are advertised and offered only in exchange for prior contributions in stated amounts, the activity takes on much more of a commercial nature."[561]

Subsequently, this court adopted the trial judge's report, with some modifications but none concerning the substantive unrelated business income issues. Thus, the position of the entire court in the case was that the amounts received by the veterans' organization from a semiannual gift solicitation program utilizing premium items constituted unrelated business income and that the amounts received by the organization from the rental of its mailing list constituted unrelated business income. Consequently, the law appears to be that "when premiums are advertised and offered only in exchange for prior contributions in stated amounts,"[562] the activity becomes a commercial one, but if the organization "had mailed the premiums with its solicitations and had informed the recipients that the premiums could be retained without any obligation arising to make a contribution," the activity is not a business because it is not a competitive practice.[563]

Armed with this victory, the IRS began to apply the rule concerning premium items to situations where tax-exempt organizations distribute greeting cards to raise funds. Some charitable groups engraft onto their greeting card distribution program some elements that go beyond the mere sending of cards in the hope that a contribution will ensue. Some of these factors include a "suggested" minimum contribution that is equivalent to the retail value of the cards and invoicing of the recipient of the cards for the amount requested. In one instance, an organization entered into a contract with an independent card distributor that distributed cards to the organization's members. A minimum contribution was requested per box of cards and follow-up notices were sent for nonresponsive recipients, requesting either payment for the cards or their return. The distributor was paid a fixed amount for each box of cards mailed. In another instance, an organization solicited orders for cards at the time it mailed its newsletter. In some years, a commercial supplier processed the orders; in other years, the organization fulfilled the requests. In all instances, a "minimum price" was suggested.

---

[560] This determination thus upheld the IRS policy on the point proclaimed in Rev. Rul. 72-431, *supra* note 261.

[561] Disabled American Veterans v. United States, *supra* note 556, at 84,855.

[562] Disabled American Veterans v. United States, 650 F.2d 1179, 1187 (Ct. Cl. 1981).

[563] *Id.* at 1186. Also Hope School v. United States, *supra* note 552.

Persons who returned money that was less than the suggested price were invoiced for the difference.

In the first instance, the IRS held that the program involved sale of the cards.[564] The IRS noted that commercial practices were being employed—namely, payment for or return of the cards and the sending of follow-up notices. Because of these practices, the IRS concluded that the payments were not gifts because they were not voluntary and because the amount paid exceeded the fair market value of the cards. The receipts were thus characterized as a sale of the cards at their fair market value in a competitive manner. In the second instance, the IRS stressed the same factors. Again, the program was said to be "indistinguishable from normal commercial operations."[565] Therefore, it appears clear that the IRS will treat a greeting card distribution program as an unrelated business where there is a "suggested" price equivalent to the retail value of the cards and where the recipients are invoiced for the payment. However, where the cards are distributed without any obligation to the recipient and where there is no subsequent invoicing, the better view is that the activity is not an unrelated business and that any support provided in response to the appeal is a deductible charitable contribution.[566]

This matter developed further when the IRS embarked on litigation characterizing card distribution programs of tax-exempt veterans' organizations as unrelated businesses, in the face of the contention that the programs constitute forms of fund-raising. Although the government lost the first case in this series,[567] the U.S. Tax Court subsequently ruled that the revenue derived by a veterans' organization from the distribution of Christmas cards to its members constituted unrelated business taxable income.[568] While recipients of the boxes of cards were not under any legal obligation to pay for them, the literature was written to convey the impression that the cards cannot be considered by the recipients as being unsolicited. This card program involved the organization for about one week of time per month from September through February of each year. The program produced substantial profits, being the second largest revenue source for the organization (behind dues). The veterans' organization contended that the boxes of cards were gifts to its members (in the nature of premiums) and that the monies sent to it from the members also were gifts. It rejected the thought that it was selling the cards and thus that a business was involved. Other contentions were that the activity was not regularly carried on (and therefore not taxable) and that the card dissemination program was related activity in that it promoted comradeship

---

[564] Priv. Ltr. Rul. 8203134.

[565] Priv. Ltr. Rul. 8232011.

[566] For an unrelated trade or business to give rise to taxable income, the business activity must be regularly carried on (see *supra* § 3). In both instances, the cards distributed were Christmas cards and thus the IRS determined that the period of time within which to measure regularity is the "Christmas season," not the full year. In both instances also, the organization attempted to cast the greeting card program as a related activity (see *supra* § 4). One group placed its logo on the cards. The other organization mailed literature about its program along with the cards. The IRS was not persuaded that either exercise made the card distribution program a related activity.

[567] Veterans of Foreign Wars of the United States, Dep't of Mo., Inc. v. United States, 85-2 U.S.T.C. ¶ 9605 (W.D. Mo. 1984).

[568] Veterans of Foreign Wars, Department of Mich. v. Comm'r, 89 T.C. 7 (1987).

among its members. In finding the activity to be a business, the court concluded that the organization had a profit motive and that the card program constituted the "sale of goods," noting that 85–90 percent of those who paid for the cards paid precisely the amount requested. It further found that the exception in the tax regulations for low-cost articles[569] was inapplicable, in part because of its rejection of the thought that there was any solicitation of contributions. The card program was held to be regularly carried on because of the extent of its activities on a seasonal basis[570] and because it was not related to the advancement of the organization's purposes. Without citing either of these two cases, another court ruled that the revenue derived by a veterans' organization from the dissemination of greeting cards was not income from an unrelated business but rather contributions resulting from a fund-raising program.[571]

In one instance, a court ruled that the conduct by a charitable organization of weekly and monthly lotteries was activity regularly carried on and thus was a taxable business because the "gambling activities" were not substantially related to the organization's charitable purposes.[572]

A fundamental precept of the federal tax law concerning charitable organizations is that they may not, without imperiling their tax-exempt status, be operated in a manner that causes persons to derive a private benefit from their operations.[573] Yet, the provision of services that amount to personal financial and tax planning—an essential element of the appreciated property and planned gift techniques[574]—may not be considered a tax-exempt activity but rather the provision of private benefit. While it would seem nearly inconceivable to contend that, when a charitable organization works with a donor to effect a sizable gift that will generate significant tax savings for the donor by reason of a charitable contribution deduction and other benefits, the organization is jeopardizing its tax-exempt status because it is providing a private benefit, this conclusion is the import of a 1978 court opinion.

The case concerned the tax status of an organization that engaged in financial counseling by providing tax planning services (including charitable giving considerations) to wealthy individuals referred to it by subscribing religious organizations. The counseling given by the organization consisted of advice on how a contributor may increase current or planned gifts to the religious organizations, including the development of a financial plan that, among other objectives, resulted in a reduction of federal income and estate taxes. The position of the IRS was that this organization could not qualify for federal income tax exemption be-

---

[569] See text accompanied by *supra* notes 367, 555.

[570] See *supra* § 3(b).

[571] The American Legion Department of N.Y. v. United States, 93-2 U.S.T.C. ¶ 50,417 (N.D.N.Y. 1993).

[572] United States v. Auxiliary to the Knights of St. Peter Claver, Charities of the Ladies Court No. 97, 92-1 U.S.T.C. ¶ 50,176, at 83,666 (S.D. Ind. 1992). The exception for businesses carried on by volunteers (see § 27.2(a)) was not available because the organization paid commissions and salaries to lottery ticket sales agents.

[573] See Chapter 19.

[574] Planned giving includes the use of charitable remainder trusts, pooled income funds, and charitable gift annuities. In general, Hopkins, *The Tax Law of Charitable Giving* (New York: John Wiley & Sons, Inc., 1993), particularly Chapters 11–16.

cause it served the private interests of individuals by enabling them to reduce their tax burden. The organization's position was that it was merely engaging in activities that tax-exempt organizations may themselves undertake without loss of their tax exemption.[575] The court agreed with the government, finding that the organization's "sole financial planning activity, albeit an exempt purpose further-ing . . . [exempt] fundraising efforts, has a nonexempt purpose of offering advice to individuals on tax matters that reduces an individual's personal and estate tax liabilities."[576] As the court dryly stated: "We do not find within the scope of the word charity that the financial planning for wealthy individuals described in this case is a charitable purpose."[577]

In this opinion, the Tax Court singled out the planned giving techniques for portrayal as methods that give rise to unwarranted private benefit. Thus, the court observed:

> For example, when . . . [the organization] advises a contributor to establish a charitable unitrust gift, the contributor ultimately forfeits the remainder. Nev-ertheless, this loss is voluntarily exchanged for considerable lifetime advan-tages. Unitrusts generate substantial income and estate and gift tax benefits, such as retained income for life, reduced capital gains tax, if any, on the ex-change of appreciated investments, favorable tax rates for part or all of the in-come payments on certain investments, and lower probate costs. Consequently, there are real and substantial benefits inuring to the contribu-tors by the . . . [organization's] activities.[578]

The court concluded this discourse by stating: "We think the tax benefits inuring to the contributors are . . . substantial enough to deny exemption."[579]

The Tax Court returned to this theme in 1983, holding that an admittedly re-ligious organization is not tax-exempt because it engaged in a substantial nonex-empt purpose, which was the counseling of individuals on the purported tax benefits accruing to those who become ministers of the organization.[580] The court found the organization to be akin to a "commercial tax service, albeit within a narrower field (i.e., tax benefits to ministers and churches) and a narrower class of customers (i.e., . . . [the organization's] ministers)," and thus that it served pri-vate purposes.[581] The many detailed discussions, by the organization in its litera-ture, of ways to maximize tax benefits led the court to observe that "although . . .

---

[575] This rationale has ample support in the law. See § 6.8.

[576] Christian Stewardship Assistance, Inc. v. Comm'r, 70 T.C. 1037, 1041 (1978).

[577] *Id.* at 1043.

[578] *Id.* at 1044.

[579] *Id.* This is a preposterous conclusion for the Tax Court to have reached. Congress has provided the benefits to donors of making contributions by means of charitable remainder trusts (IRC § 664); it is absurd to conclude that, because donors decide to avail themselves of these benefits, the donee chari-table organization should lose its tax exemption because it brings these gift techniques to the attention of prospective donors. Indeed, the Tax Court subsequently somewhat trimmed the reach of this con-clusion (see text accompanying *infra* note 584).

[580] The Ecclesiastical Order of The Ism of Am, Inc. v. Comm'r, 80 T.C. 833 (1983), *aff'd*, 740 F.2d 967 (6th Cir. 1984), *cert. den.*, 471 U.S. 1015 (1985).

[581] *Id.*, 80 T.C. at 839. Also Universal Life Church v. United States, 87-2 U.S.T.C. ¶ 9617 (Cl. Ct. 1987).

[the organization] may well advocate belief in the God of Am [the diety worshipped by the members of the organization], it also advocates belief in the God of Tax Avoidance."[582] In words that have considerable implications for fund-raising for charitable purposes generally, the court wrote that "a substantial nonexempt purpose does not become an exempt purpose simply because it promotes the organization in some way."[583] The court somewhat recognized the larger meaning of its opinion and attempted to narrow its scope by noting that "[w]e are not holding today that any group which discusses the tax consequences of donations to and/or expenditures of its organization is in danger of losing or not acquiring tax-exempt status."[584]

The U.S. Tax Court revisited this theme early in 1984, holding that an organization, the membership of which was religious missions, was not entitled to tax-exempt status as a religious organization because it engaged in the substantial nonexempt purpose of providing financial and tax advice.[585] Once again, the court was heavily influenced by the recent rush of cases before it concerning, in the words of the court, "efforts of taxpayers to hide behind the cover of purported tax-exempt religious organizations for significant tax avoidance purposes."[586] As the court saw the facts of the case, each member "mission" was the result of individuals attempting to create churches involving only their families so as to convert after-tax personal and family expenses into deductible charitable contributions; the central organization provided sample incorporation papers, tax seminars, and other forms of tax advice and assistance to those creating the missions. Consequently, the court was persuaded that the "pattern of tax avoidance activities which appears to be present at the membership level, combined with . . . [the organization's] admitted role as a tax advisor to its members" justified the conclusion that the organization was ineligible for tax exemption.

Subsequently, the U.S. Tax Court issued an opinion that once again raised questions about the imposition of the unrelated income tax in the fund-raising context.[587] At issue was the tax status of a membership organization for citizens' band radio operators, which used insurance, travel, and discount plans to attract new members. The organization contended that it was only doing what many tax-exempt organizations do to raise contributions, analogizing these activities to fund-raising events such as rallies and dinners. The court rejected this argument, defining a *fund raising event* as a "single occurrence that may occur on limited occasions during a given year and its purpose is to further the exempt activities of the organization."[588] These events were contrasted with activities that "are continuous or continual activities which are certainly more pervasive a part of the organization than a sporadic event and [that are] . . . an end in themselves."[589]

---

[582] *Id.* at 840.
[583] *Id.* at 841.
[584] *Id.* at 842. This decision was affirmed on appeal (740 F.2d 967, 6th Cir. 1984), *cert. den.*, 471 U.S. 1015 (1985)).
[585] National Association of American Churches v. Comm'r, 82 T.C. 18 (1984).
[586] *Id.* at 29–30.
[587] U.S. CB Radio Association, No. 1, Inc. v. Comm'r, 42 T.C.M. 1441 (1981).
[588] *Id.* at 1444.
[589] *Id.*

The Tax Court subsequently concluded that a novel fund-raising scheme was an unrelated business.[590] A nonprofit school consulted with a tax-shelter investments firm in search of fund-raising methods, with the result being a program in which individuals would purchase various real properties from the school, which the school would simultaneously purchase from third parties; both the sellers and the buyers were clients of the investments firm. There were about 22 of these transactions during the years at issue, from which the school received income reflecting the difference between the sales prices and the purchase prices. Finding the "simultaneous purchase and sale of real estate . . . not substantially related to the exercise or performance of [the school's] . . . exempt function," the court held that the net income from the transactions was unrelated, taxable income.[591]

The U.S. Claims Court was the first court to squarely face and analyze the difference, for tax purposes, between a fund-raising activity and a business activity.[592] The specific issue before this court in the case was whether income, received by a charitable organization as the result of assignments to it of dividends paid in connection with insurance coverages purchased by members of a related professional association at group rates, is to be taxed as unrelated income; the court ruled that the program constituted fund-raising, not a commercial venture. While, as will be discussed,[593] this particular holding was subsequently overturned, the opportunity was presented to develop a contrast between fund-raising efforts and business undertakings.

At the outset, the court wrote that, where the tax-exempt organization involved in an unrelated income tax case is a charitable one, the "court must distinguish between those activities that constitute a trade or business and those that are merely fundraising."[594] Admittedly, said the court, this distinction is not always readily apparent, as "[c]haritable activities are sometimes so similar to commercial transactions that it becomes very difficult to determine whether the organization is raising money 'from the sale of goods or the performance of services' [the statutory definition of a *business* activity[595]] or whether the goods or services are provided merely as an incident to a fund-raising activity."[596] Nonetheless, the court held that the test is whether the activity in question is "operated in a competitive, commercial manner," which is a "question of fact and turns upon the circumstances of each case."[597] "At bottom," the court wrote, the "inquiry is whether the actions of the participants conform with normal assumptions about how people behave in a commercial context" and "[i]f they do not, it may be because the participants are engaged in a charitable fundraising activity."[598]

---

[590] Parklane Residential School, Inc. v. Comm'r, 45 T.C.M. 988 (1983).

[591] *Id.* at 992.

[592] American Bar Endowment v. United States, 84-1 U.S.T.C. ¶ 9204 (Cl. Ct. 1984).

[593] See text accompanied by *infra* note 600.

[594] American Bar Endowment v. United States, *supra* note 592, at 83,350.

[595] See *supra* § 2(a).

[596] American Bar Endowment v. United States, *supra* note 592, at 83,350. Indeed, the court observed that, "[o]ver the years, charities have adopted fundraising schemes that are increasingly complex and sophisticated, relying on many business techniques" (*id.*).

[597] *Id.* at 83,351. Also Disabled American Veterans v. United States, *supra* note 556.

[598] American Bar Endowment v. United States, *supra* note 592, at 83,351.

In the specific case and in application of these rules, the court stressed five elements: (1) The activity under examination was a pioneering idea at its inception, (2) the activity was originally devised as a fund-raising effort and has been so presented since then, (3) the "staggering amount of money" and "astounding profitability" that is generated by the activity, (4) the degree of the organization's candor toward its members and the public concerning the operation and revenue of the program, and (5) the fact that the activity is operated with the consent and approval of the association's membership. Concerning the third element, as has been discussed previously,[599] substantial profits and consistently high profit margins are usually cited as reasons for determining that the activity involved is a business. However, in this case, the amounts of money involved were so great that they could not be rationalized in conventional business analysis terms; the only explanation that was suitable to the court was that the monies were the result of successful charitable fund-raising.

Despite the findings of the lower courts, the U.S. Supreme Court held that the provision of group insurance policies, underwritten by major insurance companies, by a tax-exempt charitable organization to the members of a related tax-exempt professional association constituted the carrying on of an unrelated trade or business.[600] The Court noted that the organization negotiated premium rates with insurers, selected the insurers that provided the coverage, solicited the association's membership, collected the premiums, transmitted the premiums to the insurer, maintained files on each policyholder, answered members' questions concerning insurance policies, and screened claims for benefits. In finding the activity to be an unrelated business, the Court observed that the charitable organization "prices its insurance to remain competitive with the rest of the market," that the Court "can easily view this case as a standard example of monopoly pricing," and that the case "presents an example of precisely the sort of unfair competition that Congress intended to prevent."[601] The Court concluded that the "only valid argument in the charitable organization's favor, therefore, is that the insurance program is billed as a fund-raising effort."[602] But the Court summarily rejected this contention: "That fact, standing alone, cannot be determinative, or any exempt organization could engage in a tax-free business by 'giving away' its product in return for a 'contribution' equal to the market value of the product."[603]

Currently popular fund-raising techniques that raise questions as to application of the unrelated income rules are forms of *commercial co-venturing* and *cause-related marketing*. The former involves situations where a charitable organization consents to be a recipient of funds under circumstances where a commercial business agrees to make payments to it, with that agreement advertised, where the amount of the payment is predicated on the extent of products sold or

---

[599] See § 4.9.
[600] United States v. American Bar Endowment, 447 U.S. 105 (1986).
[601] *Id.* at 112–114.
[602] *Id.* at 115.
[603] *Id.* Revisions in this program led the IRS to conclude that it is no longer an unrelated business (Priv. Ltr. Rul. 8725056). In general, Dolan, "Charitable Donations or Unrelated Business Income?: *United States v. American Bar Endowment*," 21 *U.S.F. L. Rev.* (No. 4) 817 (1987); Note, 15 *Balt. L. Rev.* 604 (1986).

services provided by the business to the public during a particular time period.[604] The latter involves the public marketing of products or services by or on behalf of a tax-exempt organization, or some similar other use of an exempt organization's resources. A manifestation of the latter can be seen in the participation by tax-exempt organizations in affinity card programs, in which an exempt membership organization is paid a portion of the revenues derived from the marketing of credit cards to its members, where the initial position of the IRS was that, while the participation (licensing of mailing lists) is an exploitation of the organization's exempt function,[605] the resultant revenues are not taxable because they constitute passive royalty income.[606] However, the IRS subsequently determined that an affinity card program is an unrelated business, that the payments are not exempt royalty income, and that the resulting revenue is taxable as income from a third party's use of the organization's membership mailing lists.[607]

Nonetheless, the U.S. Tax Court, following its stance with respect to the exclusion for royalty income in general,[608] ruled that affinity card revenue is excludable from unrelated income taxation when it is structured, as reflected in the pertinent agreement with one or more for-profit participants, as royalty income.[609] The court rejected the government's arguments that the exempt organization involved participated in a joint venture with regard to the affinity card program or that it was engaged in the business of selling financial services to its members. Finding that the organization made available its name, marks, and mailing list for use by the for-profit participant, and that those items were intangible property, the court ruled that the "financial consideration received by . . . [the organization] under the agreement was in consideration of such use" and thus that the resulting revenue was excludable royalty income.[610]

However, on appeal, the appellate court crafted a different definition of the term *royalty*,[611] and reversed the Tax Court as to the affinity card revenue, remanding the case for reconsideration.[612] The court of appeals disapproved of the way in which the Tax Court resolved certain factual issues, namely, in favor of the exempt organization. The Tax Court's grant of summary judgment was reversed and the case returned to the lower court so that it could once again make findings of fact, by means of a trial.

Consequently, nearly all fund-raising efforts by tax-exempt charitable orga-

---

[604] In general, Hopkins, *supra* note 529, Chapter 4 § 7; Chapter 8 § 4.

[605] See *supra* § 4(e).

[606] Priv. Ltr. Rul. 8747066.

[607] Gen. Couns. Mem. 39727. Priv. Ltr. Rul. 8747066 (see *supra* note 606) was revoked by Priv. Ltr. Rul. 8823109. As to the mailing list approach, the IRS determined that the statutory exception (see § 27.2(k)) was not available because the lists were provided to noncharitable organizations. In general, Cerny & Lauber, "Logos, UBIT, and a Strict IRS Approach to Affinity Card Programs," 2 *J. Tax. Exempt Orgs.* 9 (Winter 1991).

[608] See § 27.1(a), text accompanied by notes 17–21.

[609] Sierra Club, Inc. v. Comm'r, 103 T.C. 307 (1994). Also Mississippi State University Alumni, Inc. v. Comm'r, 74 T.C.M. 458 (1997); Oregon State University Alumni Assn, Inc. v. Comm'r, 71 T.C.M. 1935 (1996); Alumni Ass'n of the Univ. of Oregon, Inc. v. Commr, 71 T.C.M. 2093 (1996).

[610] Sierra Club, Inc. v. Comm'r, *supra* note 609 at 344.

[611] See § 27.1(g), text accompanied by notes 42–44.

[612] Sierra Club, Inc. v. Comm'r, 86 F.3d 1526 (9th Cir. 1996).

nizations will escape taxation as unrelated businesses. Those that are taxed are held frequently, are operated in a commercial manner, and utilize paid assistance. Nonetheless, this still leaves the fact that fund-raising is not "program" and is a "nonexempt function." Two other principles of tax law apply in this setting. One is that the existence of a single nonexempt purpose, if substantial in nature, will destroy a tax exemption regardless of the number or importance of truly exempt purposes.[613] The other is that a tax-exempt organization must serve public purposes and will lose its exemption if it serves private purposes.[614]

(j) Provision of Services

In general, net income from the provision of services by a tax-exempt organization to another organization, including another exempt organization, is unrelated business income. This is because it is not automatically an exempt function for one exempt organization to provide services to another, even where both organizations have the same category of tax-exempt status. For example, the IRS ruled that the provision of administrative services by a tax-exempt association to a tax-exempt voluntary employees' beneficiary association, where the latter entity provided a health and welfare benefit plan for the former entity's members' employees, was an unrelated business.[615]

There are two exceptions to this general rule. One is that, under certain circumstances, it can be a related business for a tax-exempt organization to provide services of this nature to another exempt entity. As an illustration, a business association with an aggressive litigation strategy placed the litigation function in a separate exempt organization because of a substantial risk of counterclaims and other retaliatory actions against the association and its members; the IRS concluded that the provision by the association of management and administrative services to the other exempt organization was in furtherance of the association's exempt purposes.[616] Likewise, the IRS ruled that a national charitable organization engaged in related business activities when it provided certain coordination services for its chapters in connection with a new program it was implementing.[617] Additionally, a tax-exempt organization that was an arm of an association of public school boards which administered the association's cash/risk management funds was found to be engaged in the charitable activity of lessening the burdens of government.[618]

The other exception is where the exempt organizations are related entities, usually as parent or subsidiary. In the health care context, for example, the IRS has long had a ruling policy that the provision of services by and to related entities is not an unrelated business. This policy was articulated in a private letter rul-

---

[613] See § 4.6.
[614] See Chapter 19. The Internal Revenue Manual § 331(2), as amended in 1982, directs internal revenue agents to, as part of their examination of public charities, "[c]onsider the [charities'] method of raising funds and whether such income is subject to unrelated business income tax."
[615] Tech. Adv. Mem. 9550001.
[616] Tech. Adv. Mem 9608003.
[617] Priv. Ltr. Rul. 9641011.
[618] Tech. Adv. Mem. 9711002.

ing concerning the tax consequences of creation of a health care delivery system by means of a joint operating agreement. The arrangement entails what the IRS terms the provision of *corporate services* by and among tax-exempt organizations (in the case of this type of system, several hospitals and a parent supporting organization). The IRS stated that, if the participating exempt organizations are in a parent and subsidiary relationship, corporate services provided between them necessary to their accomplishment of their exempt purposes are treated as other than an unrelated business and the financial arrangements between them are viewed as "merely a matter of accounting."[619] Indeed, in this ruling, the IRS extended the matter-of-accounting rationale to relationships that are analogous to parent-subsidiary arrangements, which was the case under the facts involved under this particular joint operating agreement.

---

[619] Priv. Ltr. Rul. 9651047. In constructing this rationale, the IRS utilized the accounting concept heretofore reserved for the unrelated debt-financed income rules (see § 29.3).

In general, Hansmann, Kaplan & Jett, "Handling the UBIT Problems of Churches and Religious Organizations," 6 *J. Tax. Exempt Orgs.* (No. 2) 74 (Sep./Oct. 1994); Tesdahl, "Three Easy Ways to Avoid UBIT," 8 *Exempt Org. Tax Rev.* (No. 5) 937 (Nov. 1993); "Unfair Competition and the Unrelated Business Income Tax," 75 *Va. L. Rev.* (No. 3) 605 (1989); Gallagher III, "The Taxation of Investments by Pension Funds and Other Tax-Exempt Entities," 67 *Taxes* (No. 12) 981 (1989); Jones, Shortway, & Borhorst, "When Pension Trusts Participate: The Impact of the Unrelated Business Income Rules," 5 *Real Estate Finance* (No. 2) 91 (1988); Bennett, "Unfair Competition and the UBIT," 41 *Tax Notes* (No. 7A) 759 (1988); Rosen, "When Will Business Income of an Organization Be Sheltered by Its Tax-exempt Status?," 40 *Tax. for Accts.* (No. 4) 222 (1988); Wittenbach & Gallagher, "The Tax Implications to Exempt Organizations of Six Income-producing Activities," 16 *Tax Adv.* (No. 3) 170 (1985); Fant III, "Doing Well While Doing Good, and the Pitfalls of the Unrelated Business Income Tax," 63 *Taxes* (No. 12) 862 (1985); Walter, "Unrelated Business Income—Division, Characterization and Allocation," 19 *Univ. of Miami Philip E. Heckerling Inst. on Est. Plan.* 7 (1985); Kennedy, "Considerations in the Determination of Tax on Unrelated Business Income," 15 *Tax Adv.* (No. 6) 342 (1984).

In recent years, there have been efforts to revise the statutory law concerning the taxation of unrelated business income. In general, Comment, "Making Tax-Exempts Pay: The Unrelated Business Income Tax and the Need for Reform," 4 *Admin. L. J. Am. U.* 527 (Winter 1991); Owens, "Current Developments in the Unrelated Business Area—IRS Perspective," 4 *Exempt Org. Tax Rev.* (No. 7) 923 (1991); Sanders & Cobb, "Impact of Proposals To Revise the Unrelated Business Income Rules," 2 *Exempt Org. Tax Rev.* (No. 6) 694 (1990); Haley, "The Taxation of the Unrelated Business Activities of Exempt Organizations: Where Do We Stand? Where Do We Seem To Be Headed?," 7 *Akron Tax J.* (No. 2) 61 (1990); Spitzer, "Reform of the UBIT: An Open Letter to Congress," 43 *Tax Notes* (No. 2) 195 (1989); Aprill, "Lessons from the UBIT Debate," 45 *Tax Notes* (No. 9) 1105 (1989); Turner & Lambert, "Why the Furor Over UBIT." 165 *J. Act.* (No. 5) 78 (1988); Troyer, "Changing UBIT: Congress in the Workshop," 41 *Tax Notes* (No. 11) 1221 (1988); Kalick, "Reorganizing for the UBIT," 41 *Tax Notes* (No. 7A) 771 (1988); Hasson, Jr., "An Early Warning: UBIT Changes Ahead," 127 *Tsr. & Ests.* (No. 7) 43 (1988).

Exceptions to Unrelated Income Taxation

Notwithstanding the fact that an activity may constitute an unrelated trade or business that is regularly carried on, the activity may escape federal income taxation under one or more specific statutory exceptions.

§ 27.1 MODIFICATIONS

In determining unrelated business taxable income, both gross income derived from an unrelated trade or business and business deductions are computed with certain *modifications*.[1]

---

[1] IRC § 512(b).

EXCEPTIONS TO UNRELATED INCOME TAXATION

(a) Concept of Passive Income

The unrelated business rules were enacted to ameliorate the effects of competition between tax-exempt organizations and for-profit (taxable) organizations by taxing the net income of exempt organizations from unrelated business activities.[2] The principle underlying this statutory scheme is that the business endeavors must be *active* ones for competitive activity to result. Correspondingly, income derived by a tax-exempt organization in a *passive* manner generally is income that is not acquired as the result of competitive activity and, consequently, most forms of passive income are not taxed as unrelated business income.[3]

Therefore, passive income, such as dividends, interest, payments with respect to securities loans, annuities, royalties, certain rents (generally of real estate), income from certain option-writing activities, income from interest rate and currency swaps, income from equity and commodity swaps, income from notional principal contracts, and the like, and gain from the disposition of property, is generally excluded from unrelated business taxable income, along with directly connected deductions.[4]

The legislative history of these provisions indicates that Congress believed that passive income should not be taxed under these rules "where it is used for exempt purposes because investments producing incomes of these types have long been recognized as proper for educational and charitable organizations."[5]

It is because of these rules that a tax-exempt organization can own all of the stock of a for-profit corporation without endangering its tax exemption;[6] the for-profit corporation can pay dividends to the tax-exempt organization without jeopardizing the tax exemption of the nonprofit entity; the income received by the for-profit corporation will not be taxable as unrelated income to the tax-exempt organization; dividends paid by the for-profit organization to the tax-exempt organization generally will not be taxable to the tax-exempt entity; and a tax-exempt organization can capitalize a for-profit corporation without endangering the tax exemption of the tax-exempt organization.[7]

There may be forms of passive income incurred by tax-exempt organizations that may not be strictly within the technical meaning of one of the specific

---

[2] See § 26.1.

[3] Two significant exceptions to this rule concern income from debt-financed property (see *infra* notes 56, 81, and 87, §§ 29.1–29.4) and income from controlled subsidiaries (§§ 27.1(b), 31.3).

[4] IRC §§ 512(b)(1), 512(b)(2), 512(b)(3), 512(b)(5). Also Reg. § 1.512(b)-1(a)-(d); State National Bank of El Paso v. United States, 509 F.2d 832 (5th Cir. 1975); Rev. Rul. 69-430, 1969-2 C.B. 129; Rev. Rul. 69-178, 1969-1 C.B. 158; Rev. Rul. 69-69, 1969-1 C.B. 159; Rev. Rul. 67-218, 1967-2 C.B. 213; Rev. Rul. 60-206, 1960-1 C.B. 201; Louis W. Hill Family Found. v. United States, 347 F. Supp. 1225 (D. Minn. 1972).

A 1983 U.S. Tax Court decision expanded the possibility that what once may have been considered a passive activity is now to be treated as an active business enterprise, by holding that nearly any activity engaged in for the production of income (the expenses of which are deductible under IRC § 212) can be converted into a business activity by the intensification of participation by the taxpayer in the activity (Hoopengarner v. Comm'r, 80 T.C. 538 (1983)). In general, Hopkins & Kaplan, "Could *Ditunno* and *Hoopengarner* result in expanding the scope of unrelated business?," 60 *J. Tax.* (No. 1) 40 (1984).

[5] H. Rep. No. 2319, 81st Cong., 2d Sess. 38 (1950). Also S. Rep. No. 2375, 81st Cong., 2d Sess. 30–31 (1950).

[6] See, however, special rules for private foundations in this regard (See § 11.4(c)).

[7] E.g., Priv. Ltr. Rul. 8244114. See Chapter 31.

terms referenced in the passive income rules, yet which are nonetheless outside the framework of unrelated income taxation.

Occasionally, the IRS takes the position that the only items of income that can be regarded as passive income are those that are specifically referenced in the statutory modification rules. This has led to conflict, with the matter usually resolved in favor of tax-exempt organizations by Congress, such as in the instances of the writing of options[8] and the lending of securities.[9]

The legislative history of the unrelated business income tax provisions is clear on the point that Congress, in enacting these rules, did not intend and has not authorized taxation of the receipt of passive income by tax-exempt organizations, and that a technical satisfaction of the definitional requirements of the terms used in the passive income rules is not required. Thus, the Senate Finance Committee observed in 1950 that the unrelated income tax was to apply to "so much of . . . [organizations'] income as rises from *active business enterprises* which are unrelated to the tax exempt purposes of the organizations."[10] The Committee added: "The problem at which the tax on unrelated business income is directed is primarily that of unfair competition."[11] Speaking of the exclusion for passive sources of income, the Committee stated:

> Dividends, interest, royalties, most rents, capital gains and losses and *similar items* are excluded from the base of the tax on unrelated income because your committee believes that they are "passive" in character and are not likely to result in serious competition for taxable businesses having similar income. Moreover, investment-producing incomes of these types have long been recognized as a proper source of revenue for educational and charitable organizations and trusts.[12]

Therefore, it seems unmistakable that passive income, regardless of type, is generally excluded from taxation.[13]

The most recent illustration of the IRS acceptance of this viewpoint is the development of regulations[14] concerning the exclusion of income derived from certain notional principal contracts[15] and other forms of a tax-exempt organization's ordinary and routine investments.[16]

The foregoing analysis notwithstanding, a line of law may be developing

---

[8] See text accompanied by *supra* note 4 and *infra* notes 109–110.

[9] See *infra* § 1(d).

[10] S. Rep. No. 2375, *supra* 5, at 27 (emphasis supplied).

[11] *Id.* at 28.

[12] *Id.* at 30–31 (emphasis supplied).

[13] Also H. Rep. No. 2319, *supra* note 5, at 36–38.

[14] Reg. § 1.512(b)-1(a)(2). The exclusion for income from notional principal contracts took effect for amounts received after August 30, 1991. However, an organization can apply this exclusion of income from notional principal contracts prior to that date, as long as the amounts are treated consistently for all open tax years. Unless otherwise provided, the exclusion of income that the IRS determines to be substantially similar income from ordinary and routine investments is effective for amounts received after the date of the IRS's determination (Reg. § 1.512(b)-1(a)(3)).

[15] Reg. § 1.512(b)-1(a).

[16] See text accompanied by *infra* notes 93–100.

that rejects the premise that, for an item of income to be excluded from unrelated business income taxation (absent a specific statutory exclusion), it must be passive in nature. That is, there is a view that an item of income—once classified as a royalty or other similar item—is excludable from unrelated income taxation irrespective of whether it is passively derived.

At the present, only the U.S. Tax Court has expressed this view, which has arisen in the course of consideration of whether payments for the use of mailing lists and payments from the operation of an affinity card program constitute *royalties*. This court held that, if the arrangement is *properly* structured, mailing lists payments are royalties and thus that they are excludable even if they are not forms of passive income.[17] The court also so held in the case of affinity card program payments.[18] The essence of this view is that, although Congress *believed* these types of income to be passive,[19] that does not necessarily mean that they always must be passive.[20] Stated in the reverse, this view holds that a statutorily classified item of excludable income remains excludable irrespective of whether the income is passive or is derived from the active conduct of a trade or business. However, the validity of this view was substantially eroded by a subsequent appellate court opinion.[21]

(b) Dividends

Dividends paid to a tax-exempt organization generally are not taxable.[22] Basically, a *dividend* is a share allotted to each of one or more persons who are entitled to share in the net profits generated by a business undertaking, usually a corporation; it is a payment out of the payor's net profits.

There are some exceptions to this exclusion, principally `dividends that are unrelated debt-financed income[23] and those that are from controlled foreign offshore insurance captives.[24] However, generally, dividends from controlled corporations are not taxable.[25]

(c) Interest

Interest paid to a tax-exempt organization generally is not taxable.[26] Basically, *interest* is compensation that one person pays to another for the use of money.

---

[17] Sierra Club, Inc. v. Comm'r, 65 T.C.M. 2582 (1993); Disabled American Veterans v. Comm'r, 94 T.C. 60 (1990), *rev'd on other grounds*, 942 F.2d 309 (6th Cir. 1991).

[18] Sierra Club, Inc. v. Comm'r, 103 T.C. 307 (1994). See *infra* § 1(g).

[19] See text accompanied by *supra* note.

[20] This view is based on additional language in the committee reports indicating that the exception for dividends, interest, annuities, royalties, and the like "applies not only to investment income [a concept broader than passive income], but also to such items as business interest on overdue open accounts receivable" (S. Rep. No. 2375, *supra* note 5, at 108; H. Rep. No. 2319, *supra* note 5, at 110).

[21] See text accompanied by *infra* notes 42–44.

[22] IRC § 512(b)(1).

[23] See § 29.1–29.4.

[24] See *infra* § 1(p).

[25] See *infra* § 1(n), § 31.3.

[26] IRC § 512(b)(1).

There are some exceptions to this exclusion, principally interest that is unrelated debt-financed income[27] and that is paid by a controlled corporation.[28]

The IRS from time to time issues private letter rulings as to what constitutes excludable interest in this context.[29]

(d) Payments with Respect to Securities Loans

Qualified payments with respect to securities loans are generally excluded from unrelated business income taxation.[30] However, these amounts are not excluded if they constitute unrelated debt-financed income.[31]

This exclusion is available for the lending of securities to a broker and the return of identical securities.[32] For this nontaxation treatment to apply, the security loans must be fully collateralized and must be terminable on five business days' notice by the lending organization. Further, an agreement between the parties must provide for reasonable procedures to implement the obligation of the borrower to furnish collateral to the lender with a fair market value on each business day the loan is outstanding in an amount at least equal to the fair market value of the security at the close of business on the preceding day.

(e) Certain Consideration

Amounts received or accrued as consideration for entering into agreements to make loans are excluded from unrelated business income taxation.[33] This exclusion is not available where the income is unrelated debt-financed income.[34]

(f) Annuities

Income received by a tax-exempt organization as an annuity generally is not taxable.[35] Basically, an *annuity* is an amount of money, fixed by contract between the annuitor and the annuitant, that is paid annually, either in one sum or in installments (such as semiannually or quarterly).

This exclusion is not available where the income is unrelated debt-financed income[36] or is from a controlled corporation.[37]

---

[27] See §§ 29.1–29.4.
[28] See *infra* § 1(n), § 31.3.
[29] E.g., Priv. Ltr. Rul. 9108021.
[30] IRC § 512(b)(1).
[31] See §§ 29.1–29.4.
[32] IRC § 512(a)(5).
[33] IRC § 512(b)(1).
[34] See §§ 29.1–29.4.
[35] IRC § 512(b)(1).
[36] See §§ 29.1–29.4.
[37] See *infra* § 1(n), § 31.3.

(g) Royalties

Generally, a royalty paid to a tax-exempt organization is excludible from unrelated income taxation.[38]

Basically, a royalty is a payment for the use of a valuable right, such as a trademark, trade name, service mark, or copyright, regardless of whether the property represented by the right is used; royalties also include the right to a share of production reserved to the owner of property for permitting another to work mines and quarries or to drill for oil or gas.[39] Royalties have also been characterized as payments that constitute passive income, such as the compensation paid by a licensee to the licensor for the use of the licensor's patented invention.[40]

It is the stance of the U.S. Tax Court that a royalty is a payment for the use of valuable intangible property rights.[41] However, one court of appeals is of the view that the Tax Court's definition of the term is too broad, in that a royalty "cannot include compensation for services rendered by the owner of the property."[42] This position, then, is a compromise between the approach of the Tax Court and that of the IRS on the point. Thus, the appellate court wrote that, to the extent the IRS "claims that a tax-exempt organization can do nothing to acquire such fees," the agency is "incorrect."[43] Yet, the court continued, "to the extent that . . . [the exempt organization involved] appears to argue that a 'royalty' is any payment for the use of a property right—such as a copyright—regardless of any additional services that are performed in addition to the owner simply permitting another to use the right at issue, we disagree."[44]

Despite the exclusion for royalty income, it is the position of the IRS that monies will be taxed, even if they are characterized as royalties, when the tax-exempt organization is actively involved in the enterprise that generates the revenue, such as through the provision of services.[45] Frequently, the IRS will view the relationship between the parties as that of partners or joint venturers. This interpretation of the tax law is at odds with the position being taken by the Tax Court.[46] Nonetheless, during the pendency of this litigation, the IRS is adhering to this view in its letter ruling policies.[47] A common instance of this treatment is the insistence by the IRS that the funds an exempt organization receives for an endorsement are taxable, while the organization asserts that the monies are royalties for the use of its name and logo.[48] A growing practice is to make partial use of

---

[38] IRC § 512(b)(2).

[39] E.g., Fraternal Order of Police Ill. State Troopers Lodge No. 41 v. Comm'r, 833 F.2d 717, 723 (7th Cir. 1987).

[40] Disabled Am. Veterans v. United States, 650 F.2d 1178, 1189 (Ct. Cl. 1981).

[41] Sierra Club, Inc. v. Comm'r, *supra* note 18 at 337; Sierra Club, Inc. v. Comm'r, *supra*, note 17 at 2586-2588; Disabled Am. Veterans v. Comm'r, *supra* note 17, 94 T.C. at 70.

[42] Sierra Club, Inc. v. Comm'r, 86 F.3d 1526, 1532 (9th Cir. 1996).

[43] *Id.* at 1535.

[44] *Id.*

[45] E.g., National Water Well Ass'n, Inc. v. Comm'r, 92 T.C. 75 (1989).

[46] See text accompanied by *supra* notes 17–20.

[47] E.g., Tech. Adv. Mem. 9509002.

[48] E.g., Priv. Ltr. Rul. 9450028.

the royalty exclusion by the use of two contracts: one for the taxable services and one for the royalty arrangement.[49]

Mineral royalties, whether measured by production or by gross or taxable income from the mineral property, are excludable in computing unrelated business taxable income. However, where a tax-exempt organization owns a working interest in a mineral property, and is not relieved of its share of the development costs by the terms of any agreement with an operator, income received is not excludable.[50] The holder of a mineral interest is not liable for the expenses of development (or operations) for these purposes where the holder's interest is a net profit interest not subject to expenses that exceed gross profits. Thus, a tax-exempt university was ruled to have excludable royalty interests, where the interests it held in various oil and gas producing properties were based on the gross profits from the properties reduced by all expenses of development and operations.[51]

The IRS ruled that patent development and management service fees deducted from royalties collected from licensees by a tax-exempt charitable organization for distribution to the beneficial owners of the patents were not within this exception for royalties; the IRS said that "although the amounts paid to the [tax-exempt] organization are derived from royalties, they do not retain the character of royalties in the organization's hands" for these purposes.[52] Similarly, the IRS decided that income derived by a tax-exempt organization from the sale of advertising in publications produced by an independent firm was properly characterized as royalty income.[53] By contrast, the IRS determined that amounts received from licensees by a tax-exempt organization, which was the legal and beneficial owner of patents assigned to it by inventors for specified percentages of future royalties, constituted excludable royalty income.[54] A federal court of appeals held that income consisting of 100 percent of the net profits in certain oil properties, received by a tax-exempt organization from two corporations controlled by it, constituted income from overriding royalties and thus was excluded from taxation.[55]

A matter of some concern to the IRS has been the proper tax treatment of payments to a tax-exempt organization, the principal purpose of which is the development of a U.S. team for international amateur sports competition, in return for the right to commercially use the organization's name and logo. The organization entered into licensing agreements that, in consideration of the annual payment of a stated sum, authorized use of the organization's name and logo in connection with the sale of products. The initial position of the IRS was that payments must be mea-

---

[49] There is some support for this approach in Texas Farm Bureau, Inc. v. United States, 53 F.3d 120 (5th Cir. 1995), in which the contracts involved did not expressly cast the revenues at issue as royalties.

[50] Reg. § 1.512(b)-1(b).

[51] Priv. Ltr. Rul. 7741004.

[52] Rev. Rul. 73-193, 1973-1 C.B. 262, 263. Also Rev. Rul. 69-179, 1969-1 C.B. 158.

[53] Priv. Ltr. Rul. 7926003.

[54] Rev. Rul. 76-297, 1976-2 C.B. 178. Also J. E. and L. E. Mabee Found., Inc. v. United States, 533 F.2d 521 (10th Cir. 1976), aff'g 389 F. Supp. 673 (N.D. Okla. 1975).

[55] United States v. The Robert A. Welch Found., 334 F.2d 774 (5th Cir. 1964), aff'g 228 F. Supp. 881 (S.D. Tex. 1963). The IRS does not follow this decision, as stated in Rev. Rul. 69-162. 1969-1 C.B. 158. In general, Holloman, "Are Overriding Royalties Unrelated Business Income?," 24 Oil & Gas Tax Q. 1 (1975).

sured according to the use made of a valuable right to be characterized as a royalty and thus be excludable from unrelated income taxation. However, the IRS became sufficiently persuaded, on the basis of caselaw precedent,[56] that fixed-sum payments for the right to use an asset qualify as excludable royalties, although it continues to adhere to the position that absent the statutory exclusion, the income would be taxable as being from an unrelated trade or business.[57]

Subsequently, the IRS ruled that certain payments a labor organization received from various business enterprises for the use of its trademark and similar properties were royalties.[58] This conclusion was reached even though the organization retained the right to approve the quality or style of the licensed products and services, and the payments were sometimes set as flat annual payments.[59]

The U.S. Tax Court held that a tax-exempt organization that received income from the rental of mailing lists was not taxable on that income because it was properly characterized as royalties, notwithstanding the extent of activities the organization engaged in to preserve and enhance the list.[60] The court seemed to state that it was irrelevant in this setting as to whether or not the royalty income was passive. It appears, nonetheless, that the active endeavors of the organization that the court acknowledged were activities to preserve and enhance the asset (maintain the list) rather than the provision of services to others in connection with rental activities. However, on appeal, it was held that the organization was collaterally estopped from bringing the case in the first instance, in that the same issue was litigated previously.[61]

The IRS from time to time issues private letter rulings as to what constitutes excludable royalties in this context.[62]

Unrelated debt-financed income is not subject to this exclusion,[63] nor is royalty income from a controlled corporation.[64]

---

[56] Comm'r v. Affiliated Enters., Inc., 123 F.2d 665 (10th Cir. 1941), *cert. den.*, 315 U.S. 812 (1942). Also Comm'r v. Wodehouse, 337 U.S. 369 (1949); Rohmer v. Comm'r, 153 F.2d 61 (2d Cir. 1946), *cert. den.*, 328 U.S. 862 (1946); Sabatini v. Comm'r, 98 F.2d 753 (2d Cir. 1938).

[57] Priv. Ltr. Rul. 8006005.

[58] Rev. Rul. 81-178, 1981–2 C.B. 135. By contrast, other payments were held to not be royalties because the personal services of the organization's members were required.

[59] The IRS cited the following authority for its conclusion: Uhlaender v. Henrickson, 316 F. Supp. 1277 (D. Minn. 1970); Cepeda v. Swift & Co., 415 F.2d 1205 (8th Cir. 1969); Comm'r v. Wodehouse, *supra* note 56; Rohmer v. Comm'r, *supra* note 56; Sabatini v. Comm'r, *supra* note 56; Comm'r v. Affiliated Enters., Inc., *supra* note 56.

[60] Disabled Am. Veterans v. Comm'r, 94 T.C. 60 (1990). In general, Sperzman & Washlick, "Mailing Lists Revisited: The Disabled American Veterans in Tax Court," 47 *Tax Notes* (No. 11) 1377 (1990).

[61] Disabled Am. Veterans v. Comm'r, 942 F.2d 309 (6th Cir. 1991). The previous litigation is reflected in Disabled Am. Veterans v. United States, 650 F.2d 1178 (Ct. Cl. 1981), *aff'd and rem'd*, 704 F.2d 1570 (Fed. Cir. 1983). In general, Elfenbein & Crigler, "*Sierra Club* Provides Trailmarks for Royalties," 8 *J. Tax. Exempt Orgs.* 99 (Nov./Dec. 1996); Cerny & Lauber, "Ninth Circuit Rules On Sierra Club Mailing List and Affinity Card Income," 14 *Exempt Org. Tax Rev.* (No. 2) 255 (Aug. 1996); Desilets, Jr., "Payments Received for Use of an Exempt Organization's Name and Logo: Royalties or UBTI?" 13 *Exempt Org. Tax Rev.* (No. 6) 967 (June 1996); Elfenbein & Crigler, "*Sierra* Case Stirs Up More Royalty Issues," 7 *J. Tax. Exempt Orgs.* 147 (Jan./Feb. 1996); Kirschten & Brown, "The IRS Narrows the UBIT Royalty Exclusion," 1 *J. Tax. Exempt Orgs.* 20 (Spring 1989).

[62] E.g., Priv. Ltr. Rul. 8708031.

[63] IRC §§ 29.1–29.4.

[64] See *infra* § 1(n), § 31.3.

(h) Rent

Another exclusion is available with respect to certain rents.[65] The principal exclusion is for rents from real property.[66]

(i) General Rules. Rent is a form of income that is paid for the occupation or other use of property. In general, this exclusion is available for rental income where the tax-exempt organization is not actively involved in the enterprise that generates the revenue, such as through the provision of services.

The exclusion from unrelated business taxable income for rents is sometimes misunderstood, since not all income labeled *rent* qualifies for the exclusion. Where a tax-exempt organization carries on activities that constitute an activity carried on for trade or business, even though the activities involve the leasing of real estate, the exclusion will not be available.[67] For example, a tax-exempt organization may own a building and lease space in it, and the income from this activity will constitute excludable rent even where the organization performs normal maintenance services, such as the furnishing of heat, air conditioning, and light, the cleaning of public entrances, exits, stairways, and lobbies, and the collection of trash. Where, however, the organization undertakes functions beyond these maintenance services, such as services rendered primarily for the convenience of the occupants (for example, the supplying of cleaning services), the payments will not be considered as being from a passive source but instead from an unrelated trade or business (assuming that the activity is regularly carried on and is not substantially related to the organization's tax-exempt purposes).[68]

The contractual relationship between the parties, from which the ostensible rental income is derived, must be that as reflected in a *lease*, rather than a *license*, for the exclusion for rental income to be available. A lease "confers upon a tenant exclusive possession of the subject premises as against all the world, including the owner."[69] The difference is the conferring of a privilege to occupy the owner's property for a particular use, rather than general possession of the premises. Thus, a tax-exempt organization that conferred to an advertising agency the permission to maintain signs and other advertisements on the wall space in the organization's premises was held to receive income from a license arrangement, rather than a rental one, so that the exclusion for rental income was not available.[70]

As a general rule, the exclusion for rent will not be available where the relationship between the parties is a partnership[71] or a joint venture.[72]

Consequently, where the requisite profit motive is absent, even if the arrangement is a partnership or joint venture in the broad sense of ownership of

---

[65] IRC § 512(b)(3).

[66] IRC § 512(b)(3)(a)(i).

[67] In general the rental of real estate can constitute the carrying on of a trade or business (e.g., Hazard v. Comm'r, 7 T.C. 372 (1946)).

[68] Reg. § 1.512(b)-1(c)(5). Rev. Rul. 69-69, *supra* note 4; Rev. Rul. 58-482, 1958-2 C.B. 273. The distinction between these permitted and impermissible services is discussed in Rev. Rul. 69-178, *supra* note 4.

[69] Union Travel Associates, Inc. v. International Associates, Inc., 401 A.2d 105 (D.C. Ct. App. 1979).

[70] Priv. Ltr. Rul. 9740032.

[71] See §§ 32.1, 32.2.

[72] See § 32.3.

property and sharing of net rents, there presumably is no partnership or joint venture for federal tax purposes because of the lack of an intent of a return of profits and because the relationship does not involve a working interest or operational control of the "business." Thus, where the income is truly rent and where the relationship is a passive one (of investor only), the exclusion for rental income is available.[73]

The exclusion from unrelated business taxable income for rents of personal property leased with real property is limited to instances where the rent attributable to the personalty is "incidental" (no more than 10 percent).[74] Moreover, the exclusion is not available where the rent attributable to personalty is tied into the user's income or profits or if more than 50 percent of the total rent is attributable to the personalty leased. Thus, where the rent attributable to personalty is between 10 percent and 50 percent of the total, only the exclusion with respect to personalty is lost.[75]

However, unrelated debt-financed income is not subject to this exclusion,[76] nor is royalty income from a controlled corporation.[77]

(ii) Passive Rent Test. Notwithstanding these general rules, the exclusion for rent does not apply if the determination of the amount of the rent depends in whole or in part on the income or profits derived by any person from the property leased (other than an amount based on a fixed percentage or percentages of receipts or sales).[78] This is the *passive rent test.*

An amount is excluded from consideration as rents from real property if, considering the lease and all of the surrounding circumstances, the arrangement does not conform with normal business practice and is in reality used as a means of basing the rent on income or profits.[79] This rule is intended to prevent avoidance of the unrelated business income tax where a profit-sharing arrangement would, in effect, make the lessor an active participant in the operation of the property.

As noted, an exception is provided for amounts based on a fixed percentage or percentages of sales. These amounts are customary in rental contracts and are generally considered to be different from the profit or loss of the lessee. Generally, rents received from real property would not be disqualified solely by reason of

---

[73] United States v. Myra Found., 382 F.2d 107 (8th Cir. 1967), where it was held that a foundation that was a lessor of farmland and received a portion of the crops produced by the tenant as rent was not subject to the unrelated business tax on the rent. Also Rev. Rul. 67-218, *supra* note 4. Cf. Reg. § 1.512(c)-1.

[74] IRC § 512(b)(3).

[75] Reg. § 1.512(b)-1(c)(2). Also Rev. Rul. 67-218, *supra* note 4; Rev. Rul. 60-206, *supra* note 4. In general, Greif, "Tax Implications of an Exempt Organization Constructing and Operating a Building," 6 *Tax Adv.* 354 (1975); Reed, "Exemptions from Unrelated Business Tax—Rental Income," 21 *Cath. Law.* 282 (1975); Johnson, "Rental and Investment Income of Many Exempt Organizations May Be Taxable," 41 *J. Tax.* 170 (1974).

[76] IRC § 512(b)(4). See §§ 29.1–29.4.

[77] See *infra* § 1(n), § 31.3.

[78] IRC § 512(b)(3)(B)(ii).

[79] Reg. §§ 1.512(b)-1(c)(2)(iii)(b), 1.856-4(b)(3), 1.856-4(b)(6) (other than (b)(6)(ii)). The latter set of regulations is part of the rules pertaining to real estate investment trusts.

the fact that the rent is based on a fixed percentage of total receipts or sales of the lessee. However, the fact that a lease is based on a percentage of total receipts would not necessarily qualify the amount received or accrued as rent from real property. For example, an amount would not qualify as rent from real property if the lease provided for an amount measured by varying percentages of receipts and the arrangement did not conform with normal business practices but was used as a means of basing the rent on income or profits.[80]

This passive rent test can be applied, for example, in determining whether income from share-crop leasing is excludable rent or taxable rental income.[81] In one of these instances, the IRS argued that, even if there was a landlord-tenant relationship, the rents were nonetheless taxable as unrelated business income because they were not in conformance with the passive rent test.[82] The government contended that, because of the splitting of the expenditures by the tax-exempt organization/landlord, its involvement in the farming operation, and its receipt of a percentage of production as rents, rather than a percentage of receipts, the exempt organization violated the passive rent test. The court disagreed. The tax-exempt organization's rental fee was based solely on a fixed percentage of the crops. The organization shared the costs of some of the expenses related to farming; the tenant, however, bore the entire cost of damages, claims, interest, and other liabilities. The share-crop lease explicitly exonerated the tax-exempt organization from any liability, claim, and/or damages. Thus, the court held that the crop shares to the tax-exempt organization were rental income based on a percentage of the receipts of the harvest. This, wrote the court, is the "equivalent of the tenant's reducing the crops to cash and then giving . . . [the tax-exempt organization] its share of the total receipts collected."[83] "It is not," the court continued, "a percentage of profits or net income."[84]

However, income passively received from the rental of real property, such as that from a valid landlord-tenant relationship where the landlord receives nothing more than net rental payments, is not taxable.[85]

The IRS from time to time issues private letter rulings as to what constitutes excludable rent in this context.[86]

On occasion, rental income is derived from the operation of a related business, so that the revenue is nontaxable. In one instance, a public charity with a training program shared office space with a business league that owned the building, in part because the tenants of the league provided volunteer teaching faculty to the charitable organization; the charity accorded the business league the right to allow the tenants use of its research equipment in exchange for main-

---

[80] Reg. § 1.856 4(b)(3).
[81] The law concerning share-crop leases in the unrelated business income tax context is the subject of § 26.5(h).
[82] Trust U/W Emily Oblinger v. Comm'r, 100 T.C. 114 (1993).
[83] Id. at 123.
[84] Id. Also Harlan E. Moore Charitable Trust v. United States, 812 F. Supp. 130 (C.D. Ill. 1993), aff'd, 9 F.3d 623 (7th Cir. 1993).
[85] The State National Bank of El Paso v. United States, 75-2 U.S.T.C. ¶ 9868 (W.D. Tex. 1975). Cf. Rev. Rul. 54-420, 1954-2 C.B. 128, rendered obsolete by Rev. Rul. 77-278, 1977-2 C.B. 485.
[86] E.g., Priv. Ltr. Rul. 9246032.

tenance of the equipment; the IRS held that the value of the maintenance services was phantom rent that was not taxable.[87]

(i) Other Investment Income

The IRS ruled that the interest earned by a tax-exempt organization pursuant to the *interest rate swap agreements* is not taxable as unrelated business income.[88]

A typical transaction of this type proceeds as follows: The tax-exempt organization purchases a debt security; the instrument evidencing the indebtedness provides that the organization will receive interest payments from the issuer that are keyed to the six-month Eurodollar rate; the organization contracts with an unrelated third party to provide it with payments equal to a fixed rate of return on all or a specified part of the principal amount of the debt security; the fixed rate of return is set so as to provide the organization with a return that is a specified spread of basis points over the seven-year U.S. Treasury bill rate; the organization provides the third party with payments equal to a floating rate of return on all or part of the principal amount of the debt security; the floating rate of return is calculated in the same manner as the floating rate interest payments described in the second stage of the transaction; the funds used to acquire the debt security and the funds used to make the swap payments are not borrowed;[89] and all payments made and received by the organization are in U.S. dollars.

The anticipated result of the interest rate swap is to provide the tax-exempt organization with interest payments that are preferable, from its investment standpoint, to those provided for in the floating rate note.

The IRS concluded that these swap transactions are "ordinary or routine investment activities undertaken in connection with the management of . . . [the organization's] securities portfolio." The IRS analogized to the securities lending practice,[90] finding the swap transaction "similar," in that the "securities will be acquired and the swap agreements will be entered into as part of an investment strategy designed to stabilize the return on the floating rate debt securities."

In addition to the foregoing forms of investment income, income from notional principal contracts,[91] and other substantially similar income from ordinary and routine investments to the extent determined by the IRS, are excluded in computing unrelated business taxable income.[92] This exclusion embraces interest rate and currency swaps, as well as equity and commodity swaps.

These exclusions do not apply to income derived from (and deductions in connection with) debt-financed property,[93] gains or losses from the sale, exchange, or other disposition of any property,[94] gains or losses from the lapse or

---

[87] Priv. Ltr. Rul. 9615045.
[88] Priv. Ltr. Rul. 9042038.
[89] This is done to prevent debt-financed income taxation. See §§ 29.1–29.4.
[90] See *supra* § 1(d).
[91] Reg. § 1.863-7; the term may also be defined in regulations issued under IRC § 446.
[92] Reg. § 1.512(b)-1(a)(2).
[93] See §§ 29.1–29.4.
[94] See *infra* § 1(j).

termination of options to buy or sell securities,[95] interest and annuities derived from (and deductions in connection with) controlled organizations,[96] and income earned by brokers or dealers (including organizations that make a market in derivative financial products[97]).[98]

(j) Capital Gains

Excluded from taxation generally are all gains from the sale, exchange, or other disposition of capital gain property.[99]

(i) Certain Gains and Losses.   This exclusion for capital gains does not extend to dispositions of inventory or property held primarily for sale to customers in the ordinary course of a business.[100] The IRS applies eight factors in determining whether property is being sold in the ordinary course of business: the purpose for which the property was acquired, the cost of it, the activities of the owner in the improvement and disposition of the property, the extent of improvements made to the property, the proximity of the sale to the purchase, the purpose for which the property was held, prevailing market conditions, and the frequency, continuity, and size of the sales.[101] For example, the IRS ruled that the gain from the sale by tax-exempt organizations of leased fee interests in condominium apartments to lessees is not taxed because of the exclusion for capital gain.[102]

Nonetheless, effective for property acquired on or after January 1, 1994, there is an exception from this second limitation[103] that excludes gains and losses from the sale, exchange, or other disposition of certain real property and mortgages acquired from financial institutions that are in conservatorship or receivership.[104] Only real property and mortgages owned by a financial institution (or held by the financial institution as security for a loan) at the time when the institution entered conservatorship or receivership are eligible for the exception.

This exclusion is limited to properties designated as *foreclosure property* within nine months of acquisition and disposed of within $2\frac{1}{2}$ years of acquisition.[105] The $2\frac{1}{2}$-year disposition period may be extended by the IRS if the extension is necessary for the orderly liquidation of the property. No more than one half by value of properties acquired in a single transaction may be designated as

---

[95] *Id.*
[96] See *infra* § 1(n), § 31.3.
[97] Reg. § 1.954-2T(a)(4)(iii)(B).
[98] In general, Note, "Tax-Exempt Entities, Notional Principal Contracts, and the Unrelated Business Income Tax," 105 *Har v. L. Rev.* 1265 (April 1992); Ben-Ami, "UBIT and Portfolio Investments for Exempt Organizations," 2 *J. Tax. Exempt Orgs.* 12 (Spring 1990).
[99] IRC § 512(b)(5).
[100] IRC § 512(b)(5)(A), (B) 512(b)(5); Reg. § 1.512(b)-1(d). In general Kaltreider v. Comm'r, 255 F.2d 833 (3d Cir. 1958), *aff'g* 28 T.C. 121 (1957); Buono v. Comm'r, 74 T.C. 187 (1980).
[101] E.g., Priv. Ltr. Rul. 9619069.
[102] E.g., Priv. Ltr. Rul. 9629030.
[103] IRC § 512(b)(5)(B).
[104] IRC § 512(b)(16).
[105] IRC §§ 512(b)(16)(B), 514(c)(9)(H)(v). As to the latter reference, see § 29.3.

disposal property. This exception is not available for properties that are improved or developed to the extent that the aggregate expenditures on development do not exceed 20 percent of the net selling price of the property.[106] This rule concerning an exclusion of gains from certain dispositions of property also excludes all gains, in connection with the organization's investment activities, from the lapse or termination of options to buy or sell securities or real property, as well as all gains from the forfeiture of good-faith deposits (that are consistent with established business practice) for the purchase, sale, or lease of real property in connection with the organization's investment activities.[107] Under prior law, the income from the writing of options (premiums) was generally treated as ordinary income—and thus was subject to the unrelated business income tax.[108] (Premiums received for options that are exercised are treated as part of the gain or loss on the sale of the property involved, that is, usually as capital gain or loss.) In the opinion of the Senate Committee on Finance, a law change was necessary because "[t]axing such income is inconsistent with the generally tax-free treatment accorded to exempt organizations' income from investment activities."[109]

The IRS from time to time issues private letter rulings as to what constitutes excludable capital gains in this context.[110]

However, unrelated debt-financed income is not subject to this exclusion.[111]

(k) Loan Commitment Fees

The law has been unclear as to whether loan commitment fees constitute unrelated business taxable income. (A loan commitment fee is a nonrefundable charge made by a lender to reserve a sum of money with fixed terms for a specified period of time. Such a charge compensates the lender for the risk inherent in committing to make the loan (such as for the lender's exposure to interest rate changes and for potential lost opportunities).) However, effective for these fees received on or after January 1, 1994, an exclusion from such tax treatment applies; the reference is to "amounts received or accrued as consideration for entering into agreements to make loans."[112]

(l) Research Income

Income derived from research[113] for government is excluded, as is income derived from research for anyone in the case of a tax-exempt college, university, or hospital, and "of fundamental research" units.[114] According to the legislative history, *re-*

---

[106] IRC § 512(b)(16)(A).

[107] IRC § 512(b)(5). This rule does not apply to the cutting of timber, which is considered (IRC § 631) a sale or exchange of the timber (*id.*).

[108] Rev. Rul. 66-47, 1966-1 C.B. 137. In general, Oifer & Coleman, "Option Writing by Exempt Organizations: An Analysis of the Tax Problems," 44 *J. Tax.* 42 (1976).

[109] S. Rep. No. 1172, 94th Cong., 2d Sess. 3 (1976), accompanying Pub. L. No. 94-396.

[110] E.g., Priv. Ltr. Rul. 9247038.

[111] IRC § 512(b)(4). See §§ 29.1–29.4.

[112] IRC § 512(b)(1).

[113] A discussion of scientific research is in § 9.2.

[114] IRC § 512(b)(7), (8), (9). See Reg. § 1.512(b)-1(f). Also Rev. Rul. 54–73, 1954-1 C.B. 160; IIT Research Inst. v. United States, 9 Cl. Ct. 13 (1985).

search includes "not only fundamental research but also applied research such as testing and experimental construction and production."[115] As respects the separate exemption for college, university, or hospital research, it is clear that "funds received for research by other institutions [do not] necessarily represent unrelated business income," such as a grant by a corporation to a foundation to finance scientific research if the results of the research were to be made freely available to the public.[116] Without defining the term *research*, the IRS was content to find applicability of this rule because the studies are not "merely quality control programs or ordinary testing for certification purposes, as a final procedural step before marketing."[117]

In employing the term *research* in this context, the IRS generally looks to the body of law defining the term in relation to what is considered tax-exempt scientific research.[118] Thus, the issue is usually whether the activity is being carried on as an incident to commercial or industrial operations; if it is, it will almost assuredly be regarded by the IRS as an unrelated trade or business.[119] In one instance, the IRS found applicability of the exclusion because the studies undertaken by a tax-exempt medical college in the testing of pharmaceutical products under contracts with the manufacturers were held to be more than "mere quality control programs or ordinary testing for certification purposes, as a final procedural step before marketing."[120] In another instance, the exclusion was held applicable to contract work done by a tax-exempt educational institution for the federal government in the field of rocketry.[121]

The college and university audit guidelines issued by the IRS[122] include a section on research activities by these institutions. The auditing agent is directed to determine whether "purported research is actually the conduct of an activity incident to a commercial enterprise (e.g., testing, sampling or certifying of items to a known standard)";[123] determine whether the research is conducted by the institution or by a separate entity;[124] review the institution's safeguards for managing and reporting conflicts of interest and any requirements imposed by any federal agency sponsoring research;[125] review the institution's policy regarding ownership of intellectual property;[126] review research arrangements with government sponsors and joint venture or royalty-sharing

---

[115] H. Rep. No. 2319, *supra* note 5, at 37.

[116] S. Rep. No. 2375, *supra* note 5, at 30.

[117] Priv. Ltr. Rul. 7936006.

[118] Rev. Rul. 76-296, 1976-2 C.B. 141. Cf. IRC § 41 (tax credit for certain research). In general, Kertz, "University Research and Development Activities: The Federal Income Tax Consequences of Research Contracts, Research Subsidiaries and Joint Ventures," 13 *J. Coll. & Univ. L.* 109 (1986); Kertz, "Tax Exempt Organizations and Commercially Sponsored Scientific Research," 9 *J. Coll. & Univ. L.* 69 (1982–1983).

[119] Rev. Rul. 68-373, 1968-2 C.B. 206.

[120] Priv. Ltr. Rul. 7936006.

[121] Priv. Ltr. Rul. 7924009.

[122] See § 24.8(d).

[123] *Id.* § 342.(10)(3).

[124] *Id.* § 342.(10)(2).

[125] *Id.* § 342.(10)(4).

[126] *Id.* § 342.(10)(5).

arrangements with industry sponsors;[127] determine who holds the patent or right to license technology derived from the research;[128] determine whether the institution is investing in licensee firms, either directly or through venture capital funds;[129] obtain a list of all publications that discuss the institution's research activities;[130] if the institution conducts government-funded research, review copies of audit reports from the funding agency;[131] and review sample closed research projects.[132]

(m) Certain Deductions

Also excluded are all deductions directly connected with income in the form of dividends, interest, payments with respect to securities loans, amounts received or accrued as consideration for entering into agreements to make loans, annuities, royalties, and rents.[133] Similarly excluded are capital losses.[134]

There are limitations on the availability of the charitable contribution deduction, as allowed in the unrelated income tax context.[135] This deduction may not exceed 10 percent of unrelated business taxable income, otherwise computed.

In computing unrelated business taxable income, there is a specific deduction of $1,000.[136] The specific deduction is allowed, in the case of a diocese, province of a religious order, or a convention or association of churches, with respect to each parish, individual church, district, or other local unit.[137] This deduction is intended to eliminate imposition of the unrelated income tax in cases where the exaction of it would involve excessive costs of collection in relation to any payments received by the government.[138]

(n) Revenue from Controlled Organizations

Payments of interest, annuities, royalties, and/or rents (but not dividends) by a controlled organization to a tax-exempt, controlling organization can be taxable as unrelated income, notwithstanding the fact that these forms of income are generally nontaxable as passive income.[139] The purpose of this provision is to prevent a tax-exempt organization from housing an unrelated activity in a separate but controlled organization and receiving nontaxable income by reason of the passive income rules (for example, by renting unrelated income property to a sub-

---

[127] *Id.* § 342.(10)(6)(a).

[128] *Id.* § 342.(10)(6)(b).

[129] *Id.* § 342.(10)(7).

[130] *Id.* § 342.(10)(8).

[131] *Id.* § 342.(10)(9).

[132] IRC § 512(b)(1)–(3).

[133] IRC § 512(b)(5).

[134] College and university audit guidelines § 342(10)(10).

[135] IRC § 512(b)(10); Reg. § 1.512(b)-1(g).

[136] IRC § 512(b)(12); Reg. § 1.512(b)-1(h)(1).

[137] Reg. § 1.512(b)-1(h)(2). Also Rev. Rul. 68-536, 1968-2 C.B. 244.

[138] H. Rep. No. 2319, *supra* note 5, at 37; S. Rep. No. 2375, *supra* note 5, at 30.

[139] IRC § 512(b)(13); Reg. § 1.512(b)-1(1). Also *J.E. & L.E. Mabee Found. Inc.* v. *United States, supra* note 54; The Robert A. Welch Found. v. United States, *supra* note 58.

sidiary).[140] If the subsidiary is a tax-exempt organization, these rules apply in the proportion that the subsidiary's income is unrelated business income; likewise, where the subsidiary is a nonexempt organization, income from an activity related to the parent's tax-exempt function can be treated as related income in proportion to the subsidiary's total receipts.

The rules in this regard changed dramatically in 1997.[140a]

(i) Pre-1998 Law. Pursuant to the law before its revision in 1997, a tax-exempt organization *controlled* another organization where it had at least an 80 percent interest.[141] This control element can be manifested by stock or by an interlocking of directors, trustees, or other representatives of the two organizations.[142]

When stock was the control mechanism, it had to constitute at least 80 percent of the total combined voting power of all classes of stock entitled to vote and at least 80 percent of the total number of shares of all other classes of stock of the corporation.[143] Thus, this type of control was not present when the classes of stock issued by the subsidiary were split between tax-exempt organizations that are related. For example, a tax-exempt trade association with a related supporting foundation was not considered to control a for-profit subsidiary when the association held all of the subsidiary's voting stock and the foundation held all of its nonvoting stock (such as preferred shares). Likewise, there was no control element applied where a second-tier subsidiary paid income to a tax-exempt organization.[144]

(ii) Post-1997 Law. The law in this regard changed in 1997, with the control test revised to entail a considerably reduced percentage threshold. Now, control in the case of a stock corporation means ownership by vote or value of more than 50 percent of the stock; in the case of a partnership or other unincorporated entity, control means ownership of more than 50 percent of the profits, capital, or beneficial interests.[145]

Constructive (indirect) ownership rules have been engrafted onto this area.[146] Thus, a parent exempt organization is deemed to control a subsidiary organization that holds more than 50 percent of the voting power or value directly or indirectly.[147]

---

[140] S. Rep. No. 91-552, 91st Cong., 1st Sess. 73 (1969); In general, Crosby Valve & Gage Co. v. Comm'r, 380 F.2d 146 (1st Cir. 1967); Bird, "Exempt Organizations and Taxable Subsidiaries," 4 *Prac. Tax Law.* (No. 2) 53 (1990); Heinlen, "Commercial Activities of Exempt Organizations—Joint Ventures and Taxable Subsidiaries," *N. Ky. L. Rev.* (No. 2) 285 (1989); Nagel, "The Use of For-Profit Subsidiaries by Non-Profit Corporations," 17 *Col. Law.* (No. 7) 1293 (1998).

[140a] The Taxpayer Relief Act of 1997 altered the rules in this context, effective for tax years beginning after August 5, 1997. The prior law is referred to as *pre-1998 law.*

[141] IRC § 368(c).

[142] Reg. § 1.512(b)-1(1)(4).

[143] Reg. § 1.512(b)-1(1)(4)(i)(a).

[144] See § 31.3.

[145] IRC § 512(b)(13)(D)(i).

[146] IRC §§ 512(b)(13)(D)(ii), 318.

[147] This law change was directed particularly at the prior law concerning first-tier and second-tier subsidiaries (see § 31.3).

(o) Commercial-Type Insurance Activities

In the case of tax-exempt charitable and social welfare organizations, commercial-type insurance activities are treated as unrelated trades or businesses.[148] These exempt organizations are subject to tax on the income from these insurance activities (including investment income that might otherwise be excluded from taxation) under the rules by which for-profit insurance companies are taxed.[149]

(p) Foreign Source Income

A look-through rule characterizes certain foreign source income, namely, income from insurance activities conducted by offshore captives of tax-exempt organizations, as unrelated business income.[150] Generally, U.S. shareholders of controlled foreign corporations must include in income their shares of the foreign entities' income, including certain insurance income.[151] However, the IRS treated these income inclusions as dividends, so that the income to tax-exempt organizations was excludible from tax.[152] For tax years beginning after December 31, 1995, this look-through rule overrides the former treatment of this income as dividends.[153]

    This rule is not applicable to amounts that are attributable to the insurance of risks of the tax-exempt organization itself, certain of its exempt affiliates,[154] or an officer or director of, or an individual who (directly or indirectly) performs services for, the exempt organization (or certain exempt affiliates), provided that the insurance primarily covers risks associated with the individual's performance of services in connection with the tax-exempt organization (or exempt affiliates).[155]

(q) Miscellaneous Provisions

The unrelated business income tax does not apply to a tax-exempt religious order or educational institution maintained by the order, with respect to a trade or business, even though the business is unrelated, if the business provides services under license issued by a federal regulatory agency, if less than 10 percent of its net income is used for unrelated activities, and if the business was carried on before May 27, 1969.[156]

---

[148] If these commercial-type insurance activities constitute a substantial part of the organization's activities, the organization cannot be tax-exempt (see § 22.1).

[149] IRC § 501(m)(2).

[150] IRC § 512(b)(17)(A).

[151] IRC §§ 951(a)(1)(A), 953.

[152] E.g., Priv. Ltr. Rul. 8819034. See text accompanied by *supra* note 4.

[153] This look-through rule was enacted as part of the Small Business Job Protection Act of 1996 (Pub. L. No. 188, 104th Cong., 2d Sess. (1996)).

[154] The determination as to whether an entity is an affiliate of an organization is made under rules similar to those applied in the tax-exempt entity leasing context (see § 29.5(c)). Also, two or more organizations generally are regarded as affiliates if the organizations are colleges, universities, hospitals, or other medical entities and they participate in an insurance arrangement that provides for any profits from the arrangement to be returned to the policyholders in their capacity as such (see § 29.5(c)).

[155] IRC § 512(b)(17)(B). In general, Stretch, Cooper, & Snowling, "UBIT Rules Are Expanded to Include Income From Foreign Captives: Congressional Revenue Raisers Pick Another Pocket," 16 *Exempt Org. Tax Rev.* (No. 16) 29 (Jan. 1997).

[156] IRC §512(b)(15).

However, the "deadwood" amendments of the Tax Reform Act of 1976 deleted a provision that excluded from the definition of *unrelated business taxable income* certain income received by tax-exempt trusts created by the wills of individuals who died between August 16, 1954, and January 1, 1957, if that income is received by the trusts as limited partners.[157] Also deleted was a provision that provided a similar exclusion for income used by tax-exempt labor, agricultural, or horticultural organizations to establish, maintain, or operate a retirement home, hospital, or similar facility, if the income was derived from agricultural pursuits on grounds contiguous to the facility and if the income did not provide more than 75 percent of the cost of operating or maintaining the facility.[158] Nonetheless, the Tax Reform Act of 1976 contains a savings provision continuing both of these exclusions.[159]

§ 27.2 EXCEPTIONS

In addition to those provided in the rules concerning the modifications, there are various other exceptions from unrelated business income taxation.

(a) Businesses Conducted by Volunteers

Exempt from the scope of taxable unrelated trade or business is a business in which substantially all of the work in carrying on the business is performed for the tax-exempt organization without compensation.[160] An example involving this exception is a tax-exempt orphanage operating a second-hand clothing store and selling to the general public, where substantially all of the work in running the store is performed by volunteers.[161] Another illustration is the production and sale of phonograph records by a medical society, where the services of the performers were provided without compensation.[162] Still another illustration concerned a trade association that sold advertising in a commercial, unrelated manner, but avoided unrelated income taxation of the activity because the work involved was provided solely by volunteers.[163] As to the scope of this exception, Congress apparently intended to provide an exclusion from the definition of unrelated trade or business only for those unrelated business activities in which the performance of services is a material income-producing factor in carrying on the business and substantially all of the services are performed without compensation.[164] In reliance upon the legislative history underlying this rule, the IRS ruled

---

[157] Pre-1969 IRC § 512(b)(13).
[158] Pre-1969 IRC § 512(b)(14).
[159] Tax Reform Act of 1976 § 1951(b)(8).
[160] IRC § 513(a)(1). Also Rev. Rul. 56-152, 1956-1 C.B. 56.
[161] S. Rep. No. 2375, *supra* note 5, at 108.
[162] Greene County Med. Soc'y Found. v. United States, 345 F. Supp. 900 (W.D. Mo. 1972).
[163] Priv. Ltr. Rul. 9302023.
[164] H. Rep. No. 2319, *supra* note 5, at 37; S. Rep. No. 2375, *supra* note 5, at 107–108.

that the rental of heavy machinery under long-term lease agreements requiring the lessees to provide insurance, pay the applicable taxes, and make and pay for most repairs, with the functions of securing leases and processing rental payments performed without compensation, was not an unrelated trade or business excluded under this exception since "there is no significant amount of labor regularly required or involved in the kind of business carried on by the organization" and thus the performance of services in connection with the leasing activity is not a material income-producing factor in the business.[165]

The U.S. Tax Court ruled that the exemption was defeated in part because free drinks provided to the collectors and cashiers in connection with the conduct of a bingo game by a tax-exempt organization were considered "liquid compensation."[166] However, this position was rejected on appeal.[167] The court subsequently held that this exception was not available, in the case of an exempt organization that regularly carried on gambling activities, because the dealers and other individuals received tips from patrons of the games.[168] In another case, this court found that a tax-exempt religious order that operated a farm was not taxable on the income derived from the farming operations because the farm was maintained by the uncompensated labor of the members of the order.[169]

(b) Convenience Businesses

Also excluded is a business, in the case of a tax-exempt charitable organization or a state college or university, that is carried on by the organization primarily for the convenience of its members, students, patients, officers, or employees.[170] An example involving this exception is a laundry operated by a tax-exempt college for the purpose of laundering dormitory linens and the clothing of students.[171] (However, a laundry operated by a college apart from its campus primarily for the purpose of making a profit from laundering the clothing of the general public would be an unrelated business and outside the scope of this limitation.) One court expanded this concept by holding that physicians on the staff of a teaching hospital are "members" of the hospital, in that the term "refers to any group of persons who are closely associated with the entity involved and who are necessary to the achievement of the organization's purposes."[172] However, the IRS disagrees with this opinion, taking the position that the "hospital's staff physicians

---

[165] Rev. Rul. 78-144, 1978-1 C.B. 168.

[166] Waco Lodge No. 166, Benevolent & Protective Order of Elks v. Comm'r, 42 T.C.M. 1202 (1981).

[167] 696 F.2d 372 (5th Cir. 1983).

[168] Executive Network Club, Inc. v. Comm'r, 69 T.C.M. 1680 (1995).

[169] St. Joseph Farms of Ind. Bros. of the Congregation of Holy Cross, Southwest Province, Inc. v. Comm'r, 85 T.C. 9 (1985), *app. dis.* (7th Cir. 1986). Cf. Shiloh Youth Revival Centers v. Comm'r, 88 T.C. 565 (1987).

[170] IRC § 513(a)(2). Also Rev. Rul. 81-19, 1981-1 C.B. 354; Rev. Rul. 69-268, 1969-1 C.B. 160; Rev. Rul. 55-676, 1955-2 C.B. 266; college and university audit guidelines, *supra* note 122, § 342 (13). Cf. Carle Found. v. United States, 611 F.2d 1192 (7th Cir. 1979), *cert. den.,* 449 U.S. 824 (1980).

[171] Reg. § 513-2(6); S. Rep. No. 2375, *supra* note 5, at 108.

[172] St. Luke's Hosp. of Kansas City v. United States, 494 F. Supp. 85, 92 (W.D. Mo. 1980).

are neither 'members' nor 'employees' of the hospital in their capacities as private practitioners of medicine."[173]

The exemption for revenue derived from an activity carried on primarily for the convenience of an organization's members has been unsuccessfully invoked in a situation involving advertising in the organization's monthly journal. The lower court rejected the argument, deciding that the primary purpose of the advertising was to raise revenue.[174] On appeal, the higher court wrote that it could not conclude that the finding was clearly erroneous.[175]

Read literally, this exception pertains only to the classes of individuals who have the requisite relationship directly with the exempt organization; for example, it applies with respect to services carried on by a hospital for the convenience of *its* patients. However, the IRS ruled that the doctrine was available when an exempt organization's activities were for the convenience of patients of another, albeit related, exempt entity.[176] At the same time, the IRS refused to extend the doctrine to embrace spouses and children of a university's students.[177]

(c) Thrift Stores and the Like

Further, unrelated trade or business does not include a business that is the selling of merchandise, substantially all of which has been received by the organization as gifts or contributions.[178] This exception is available for thrift shops that sell donated clothes and books to the general public.[179]

(d) Businesses of Employees' Associations

Likewise excluded is a business, in the case of a tax-exempt local association of employees[180] organized before May 27, 1969, that is the selling by the organization of items of work-related clothing and equipment and items normally sold through vending machines, through food-dispensing facilities, or by snack bars, for the convenience of its members at their usual places of employment.[181] The IRS ruled that this type of association may change its form, from unincorporated entity to a corporation, without losing its grandfathered status.[182]

---

[173] Rev. Rul. 85-109, 1985-2 C.B. 165, 166.

[174] The American College of Physicians v. United States, 83-2 U.S.T.C. ¶ 9652 (Cl. Ct. (1983)).

[175] The American College of Physicians v. United States, 743 F.2d 1570 (Fed. Cir. 1984), *rev'd*, 475 U.S. 834 (1986).

[176] Priv. Ltr. Rul. 9535023.

[177] Tech. Adv. Mem. 9645004.

[178] IRC § 513(a)(3). Also Disabled Veterans Serv. Found. v. Comm'r, 2 T.C.M. 202 (1970). In general, "Panel Discussion on Unrelated Business Income Tax," 21 *Cath. Law.* 287 (1975); Cooper, "Trends in the Taxation of Unrelated Business Activity," 29 *N.Y.U. Inst. Fed. Tax.* 1999 (1971).

[179] Rev. Rul. 71-581, 1971-2 C.B. 236.

[180] IRC § 501(c)(4). See § 18.3.

[181] IRC § 513(a)(2).

[182] Priv. Ltr. Rul. 9442013. In so ruling, the IRS relied on Rev. Rul. 54-134, 1954-1 C.B. 88 (holding that an IRS ruling recognizing the tax-exempt status of a corporation, where there was a mere change in form from unincorporated status, embraces the period of unincorporation as well).

(e) Entertainment Activities

Another exception is applicable with respect to the conduct of entertainment at fairs and expositions. The rule, with respect to entertainment at fairs and expositions,[183] applies to charitable, social welfare, labor, agricultural, and horticultural organizations[184] that regularly conduct, as a substantial tax-exempt purpose, an agricultural and educational fair or exposition.[185] This exemption from the unrelated income tax overrode an earlier IRS pronouncement.[186]

The term unrelated trade or business does not include qualified *public entertainment activities* of an eligible organization.[187] This term is defined to mean "any entertainment or recreational activity of a kind traditionally conducted at fairs or expositions promoting agricultural and educational purposes, including, but not limited to, any activity one of the purposes of which is to attract the public to fairs or expositions or to promote the breeding of animals or the development of products or equipment."[188]

No unrelated income taxation is to occur with respect to the operation of a *qualified public entertainment activity* that meets one of the following conditions: the public entertainment activity is conducted (1) in conjunction with an international, national, state, regional, or local fair or exposition, (2) in accordance with state law that permits that activity to be conducted solely by an eligible type of tax-exempt organization or by a governmental entity, or (3) in accordance with state law that permits that activity to be conducted under license for not more than 20 days in any year and that permits the organization to pay a lower percentage of the revenue from this activity than the state requires from other organizations.[189]

To qualify under this rule, the organization must regularly conduct, as a substantial tax-exempt purpose, a fair or exposition that is both agricultural and educational. The Senate Finance Committee report that accompanied these rules stated that a book fair held by a tax-exempt university does not come within this provision since this type of a fair is not agricultural in nature.[190]

A charitable, social welfare, labor, agricultural, or horticultural organization is not to be considered as not entitled to tax exemption solely because of its qualified public entertainment activities.

(f) Trade Show Activities

Another exception is applicable with respect to the conduct of trade shows by certain tax-exempt organizations. The rule with respect to trade show activi-

---

[183] IRC § 513(d)(1), (2).
[184] IRC § 501(c)(3), 501(c)(4), or 501(c)(5). See Chapters 5–10, 12, 15, respectively.
[185] IRC § 513(d)(2)(C).
[186] Rev. Rul. 68-505, 1968-2 C.B. 248.
[187] IRC § 513(d)(1).
[188] IRC § 513(d)(2)(A).
[189] IRC § 513(d)(2)(B).
[190] S. Rep. 938, 94th Cong., 2d Sess. 602 (1976).

ties[191] is available for tax-exempt labor, agricultural, and horticultural organizations, business leagues,[192] and charitable and social welfare organizations[193] that regularly conduct, as a substantial tax-exempt purpose, shows that stimulate interest in and demand for the products of a particular industry or segment of industry or that educate persons in attendance regarding new developments or products or services related to the tax-exempt activities of the organization. This provision overrules contrary and previous IRS determinations.[194]

Under these rules, the term unrelated trade or business does not include qualified *convention and trade show activities* of an eligible organization.[195] This term is defined to mean "any activity of a kind traditionally conducted at conventions, annual meetings, or trade shows, including but not limited to, any activity one of the purposes of which is to attract persons in an industry generally (without regard to membership in the sponsoring organization) as well as members of the public to the show for the purpose of displaying industry products or services, or to educate persons engaged in the industry in the development of new products and services or new rules and regulations affecting the industry."[196]

A *qualified convention and trade show activity* is a convention and trade show activity (as defined) that is (1) carried out by a qualifying organization (as defined); (2) conducted in conjunction with an international, national, state, regional, or local convention, annual meeting, or show; (3) sponsored by a qualifying organization that has as one of its purposes in sponsoring the activity the promotion and stimulation of interest in and demand for the products and services of the industry involved in general or the education of persons in attendance regarding new developments or products and services related to the tax-exempt activities of the organization; and (4) designed to achieve this purpose through the character of the exhibits and the extent of the industry products displayed.[197]

The income that is excluded from taxation by these rules is derived from the rental of display space to exhibitors. This is the case even though the exhibitors who rent the space are permitted to sell or solicit orders, as long as the show is a qualified trade show or a qualified convention and trade show.[198] This exclusion is also available with respect to a "supplier's exhibit" that is conducted by a qualifying organization in conjunction with a qualified convention

---

[191] IRC § 513(d)(1), (3).

[192] IRC § 501(c)(5), (6). See Chapters 15, 13, respectively.

[193] IRC § 501(c)(3), (4). See Chapters 5–10, 12, respectively.

[194] Rev. Ruls. 75-516 through 75-520, 1975-2 C.B. 220–226. Also Rev. Rul. 67-219, 1967-1 C.B. 210; Rev. Rul. 58-224, 1958-1 C.B. 242. An analysis of these rulings appears in Kannry, "Trade Shows Must Bar All Selling to Avoid Unrelated Business Income Tax," 44 *J. Tax.* 300 (1976). Subsequently, these rulings were revoked or obsoleted by the IRS (Rev. Rul. 85-123, 1985-2 C.B. 168).

[195] IRC § 513(d)(1).

[196] IRC § 513(d)(3)(A); Reg. § 1.513-3(c)(4).

[197] IRC § 513(d)(3)(B). E.g., Orange County Agric. Soc'y Inc. v. Comm'r, 893 F.2d 647 (2d Cir. 1990), *aff'g* 55 T.C.M. 1602 (1988); Ohio County & Independent Agricultural Soc'y Delaware County Fair v. Comm'r, 43 T.C.M. 1126 (1982).

[198] Reg § 1.513-3(d)(1).

or trade show.[199] However, this exclusion is not available to a stand-alone suppliers' exhibit that is not a qualified convention show.[200] Nonetheless, income from a suppliers' show is not taxable where the displays are educational in nature and are displays at which soliciting and selling are prohibited.[201]

There is, moreover, an aspect of this issue that has received inadequate consideration and may resolve the tax issue for many organizations not expressly covered by these rules. This relates to the fact that an unrelated business must be *regularly carried on* before the revenue from the business can be taxed as unrelated income.[202] Thus, the net income derived by a tax-exempt organization (irrespective of the statutory basis for its tax exemption) from the conduct of a trade show would not be taxable as unrelated income if the trade show is not regularly carried on. A case decided by the U.S. Tax Court gives great support to the premise that the conduct of a trade show is not an activity that is regularly carried on.[203] This decision held that an organization that annually sponsors a vaudeville show did not generate any unrelated income from the activity because the show was not regularly carried on—rather, it was an "intermittent activity."[204] Consequently, to the extent that an annual trade show of a tax-exempt organization can be regarded as an intermittent activity, it would not give rise to unrelated income, irrespective of the tax-exempt status of the organization and without regard to invocation of these special rules. It must be noted, however, that in measuring regularity, the IRS looks not only to the time expended in conducting the activity itself but also to the time expended in preparing for the activity and any time expended after, yet related to, the activity.[205]

A tax-exempt organization may sponsor and perform educational and supporting services for a trade show (such as use of its name, promotion of attendance, planning of exhibits and demonstrations, and provision of lectures for the exhibits and demonstrations) without having the compensation for its efforts taxed as unrelated income, as long as the trade show is not a sales facility.[206] The IRS has ruled that this type of activity both stimulates interest in and demand for services of the profession involved in the ruling (the organization being a tax-exempt business league) and educates the members on matters of professional interest.

---

[199] Reg. § 1.513-3(c), Ex. (2). A *supplier's exhibit* is one in which the exhibitor displays goods or services that are supplied to, rather than by, the members of the qualifying organization in the conduct of the members' own trade or business (Reg. § 1.513-3(d)(2)).

[200] Reg § 1.513-3(e), Ex. (4). However, the legislative history of these statutory rules suggests that the exclusion is applicable with respect to wholly suppliers' shows (S. Rep. No. 94-938, 94th Cong., 2d Sess., 601–603 (1976).

[201] Rev. Rul. 75-516, *supra* note 194. In general, Fones, "Taxation of Trade Shows and Public Entertainment Activities," 64 *A.B.A.J.* 913 (1978).

[202] See § 26.3.

[203] Suffolk County Patrolmen's Benevolent Ass'n, Inc. v. Comm'r, 77 T.C. 1314 (1982).

[204] *Id.* at 1321, 1322.

[205] See § 26.3(d).

[206] Rev. Rul. 78-240, 1978-1 C.B. 170.

(g) Hospital Services

Another exception is applicable with respect to the performance of certain services for small hospitals. It generally is the position of the IRS that income that a tax-exempt hospital derives from providing services to other tax-exempt hospitals constitutes unrelated business income to the hospital providing the services, on the theory that the providing of services to other hospitals is not an activity that is substantially related to the tax-exempt purpose of the hospital providing the services.[207] Congress acted to reverse this rule in the case of small hospitals.

This special rule[208] applies where a hospital[209] provides services only to other tax-exempt hospitals, as long as each of the recipient hospitals has facilities to serve not more than 100 inpatients and the services would be consistent with the recipient hospitals' tax-exempt purposes if performed by them on their own behalf. The services provided must be confined to certain ones.[210]

This law change was implemented to enable a number of small hospitals to receive services from a single institution instead of providing them directly or creating a separate organization to provide the services. However, language in the legislative history is somewhat broader than the specifics of the statutory rule, inasmuch as the Senate Finance Committee explanation stated that "a hospital is not engaged in an unrelated trade or business simply because it provides services to other hospitals if those services could have been provided on a tax-free basis, by a cooperative organization consisting of several tax-exempt hospitals."[211]

Another requirement for this exception for services provided to small hospitals is that the service must be provided at a fee not in excess of actual cost, including straight-line depreciation and a reasonable rate of return on the capital goods used to provide the service.[212] The Medicare program formulations are a "safe harbor" for use in complying with the limitations on fees. Thus, a rate of return on capital goods will be considered reasonable as long as it does not exceed, on an annual basis, a percentage that is based on the average of the rates of interest on special issues of public debt obligations issued to the Federal Hospital Insurance Trust Fund for each of the months included in the tax year of the hospital during which the capital goods are used in providing the service. Determinations as to the cost of services and the applicable rate of return are to be made as prescribed in the Medicare rules,[213] which permit a health care facility to be reimbursed under the Medicare program for the reasonable cost of its services, including, in the case of certain proprietary facilities, a reasonable return on equity capital. For years beginning on or before

---

[207] Rev. Rul. 69-633, 1969-2 C.B. 121. See § 26(j).

[208] IRC § 513(e).

[209] IRC § 170(b)(1)(A)(iii). See §§ 6.2(a), 11.3(a).

[210] IRC § 501(e)(1)(A). See § 10.4.

[211] S. Rep. No. 94-938 (Part 2), 94th Cong., 2d Sess. 76 (1976).

[212] IRC § 513(e)(3).

[213] 42 USC 1395x(v)(1)(A), (B).

May 14, 1986, the rate of return is 1.5 times the average of the rates of interest on the previously referenced public debt obligations that were in effect on or before April 20, 1983.[214]

(h) Bingo and Other Games of Chance

Bingo game income realized by most tax-exempt organizations is not subject to the unrelated business income tax.[215] This exclusion applies where the bingo game[216] is not conducted on a commercial basis and where the games do not violate state or local laws.[217] It is the view of the IRS that this exception applies only to gambling activities in which all wagers are placed, all winners are determined, and all prizes are distributed in the presence of the players of the game, so that the conduct of a "pull-tab operation" is not embraced by the exception.[218] This view was subsequently reflected in a court opinion holding that proceeds attributable to an organization's "instant bingo" activities were not protected by the exception because individuals could play and win in isolation.[219] By virtue of the way the organizations are taxed, the bingo game rule is not applicable to social clubs, voluntary employees' beneficiary associations, political organizations, and homeowners' associations.[220]

The term *unrelated trade or business* does not include any trade or business which consists of the conduct of games of chance, conducted after June 30, 1981, which, under state law (in effect as of October 5, 1983), can be conducted only by nonprofit organizations.[221] However, this exception is applicable only with respect to North Dakota law.[222]

---

[214] Reg. § 1.513-6(a)(3).

[215] IRC § 513(f).

[216] IRC § 513(f)(2)(A).

[217] H. Rep. No. 95-1608, 95th Cong., 2d Sess. (1978). E.g., Waco Lodge No. 166. Benevolent & Protective Order of Elks v. Comm'r, *supra* note 217 (where this exception was held unavailable because the bingo game was illegal under state law (Texas) as being a "lottery").

[218] Tech. Adv. Mem. 8602001.

[219] Julius M. Israel Lodge of B'nai B'rith No. 2113 v. Comm'r, 70 T.CM. 673 (1995), *aff'd*, 98 F.3d 190 (5th Cir. 1996). Also Variety Club Tent No. 6 Charities, Inc. v. Comm'r, T.C. Mem. 1997-575.

[220] See, Chapter 14, § 16.3, Chapter 17, and § 18.13. Cf. Clarence LaBelle Post No. 217 v. United States, 580 F.2d 270 (8th Cir. 1978); Smith-Dodd Businessman's Association, Inc. v. Comm'r, 65 T.C. 620 (1975).

[221] Tax Reform Act of 1984 § 311.

[222] Tax Reform Act of 1986 § 1834. This clarification in 1986 would have caused retroactive taxation of this type of revenue derived by tax-exempt organizations in states other than North Dakota. However, the Technical Corrections and Miscellaneous Revenue Act of 1988 (§ 6201) made the 1986 clarification effective for games of chance conducted after October 22, 1986 (the date of enactment of the 1986 technical correction), so that revenue derived by tax-exempt organizations from games of chance conducted prior to the 1986 effective date in any state is governed by rules enacted in 1984. The IRS issued an explanation of the law on this point (Ann. 89-138, 1989-45 I.R.B. 41).

(i) Pole Rental Activities

In the case of a mutual or cooperative telephone or electric company,[223] the term *unrelated trade or business* does not include engaging in qualified pole rentals.[224]

(j) Low-Cost Articles

Another exception is available only to tax-exempt organizations eligible to receive tax-deductible charitable contributions,[225] for activities relating to certain distributions of *low cost* articles incidental to the solicitation of charitable contributions.[226] While this statutory provision is generally reflective of a similar rule stated in the income tax regulations,[227] there is one important refinement, which is that the term *low-cost article* is defined as any article (or aggregate of articles distributed to a single distributee in a year) that has a cost not in excess of $5 to the organization that distributes the item or on behalf of which the item is distributed (with that amount adjusted for inflation[228]).[229] These rules also require that the distribution of the items be unsolicited and be accompanied by a statement that the distributee may retain the low cost article irrespective of whether a charitable contribution is made.[230]

(k) Mailing Lists

Another exception available to the same category of tax-exempt organizations eligible for the low-cost articles exception[231] is applicable to the exchanging or renting of membership or donor mailing lists with or to other of these tax-exempt organizations.[232]

Absent this exception, however, the rental or exchange of a mailing list by a tax-exempt organization, when regularly carried on, is considered by the IRS

---

[223] See § 18.5.

[224] IRC § 513(g). For the definition of *qualified pole rentals*, see § 18.5.

[225] That is, an organization described in IRC § 501, where it qualifies as a charitable donee under IRC § 170(c)(2) or § 170(c)(3) (namely, as a charitable or veterans' organization).

[226] IRC § 513(h)(1)(A).

[227] Reg. § 1.513-1(b).

[228] IRC § 513(h)(2)(C). The IRS calculated that the low-cost-article cost threshold is $5.71 for years beginning in 1991 and $6.01 for years beginning in 1992 (Rev. Proc. 92-58, 1992-2 C.B. 410), is $6.20 for years beginning in 1993 (Rev. Proc. 92-102, 1992-2 C.B. 579), is $6.40 for years beginning in 1994 (Rev. Proc. 93-49, 1993-2 C.B. 581), is $6.60 for years beginning in 1995 (Rev. Proc. 94-72, 1994-2 C.B. 811), is $6.70 for years beginning in 1996 (Rev. Proc. 95-53, 1995-2 C.B. 445), is $6.90 for years beginning in 1997 (Rev. Proc. 96-59, 1996-2 C.B. 390) and is $7.10 for years beginning in 1998 (Rev. Proc. 97-57, 1997-52 I.R.B. 20).

[229] IRC § 513(h)(2).

[230] IRC § 513(h)(3).

[231] See *supra* § 2(j).

[232] IRC § 513(h)(1)(B). The purpose of this provision is to "overrule" the decision of the U.S. Claims Court in Disabled American Veterans v. United States, *supra* note 56. Also Disabled American Veterans v. Comm'r, 68 T.C. 95 (1994).

to be a taxable unrelated business. This is not a problem from an economic standpoint when the activity involves a list rental,[233] in that taxes can be paid from the resulting net income. When the activity is a list exchange, there is no income flowing from the transaction to pay the tax; it is nonetheless the view of the IRS that these exchanges are unrelated businesses.[234] In calculating the amount of "income" of this nature, the IRS advised that the method to use should be in accordance with the rules concerning facilities used for related and unrelated purposes; thus, expenses and deductions are to be allocated between the two uses on a reasonable basis.[235] According to the IRS, the "actual calculating of the costs and expenses associated with or allocable to the rental or exchange activities and the income they generate is a factual determination."[236]

If properly structured, however, a mailing list rental or exchange program involving a noncharitable tax-exempt organization apparently can avoid unrelated business income taxation by reason of treatment of the income as an excludable royalty.[237]

(l) Certain Associate Member Dues

If a tax-exempt agricultural or horticultural organization[238] requires annual dues not exceeding $100 to be paid in order to be a member of the organization, no portion of the dues may be considered unrelated business income because of any benefits or privileges to which these members are entitled.[239] This rule is applicable to tax years beginning after December 31, 1986;[240] for years beginning after 1995, this $100 threshold is indexed for inflation.[241]

The term *dues* is defined as "any payment required to be made in order to be recognized by the organization as a member of the organization."[242] If a person makes a single payment that entitles the person to be recognized as a member of the organization for more than 12 months, the payment can be prorated for pur-

---

[233] Rev. Rul. 72-431, 1972-2 C.B. 281.

[234] Tech. Adv. Mem. 9502009.

[235] See § 28.2.

[236] In the technical advice memorandum (*supra* note 234), the IRS ruled that these exchanges are not a disposition of property causing the realization of gain or loss for tax purposes (IRC § 1001), in that capital assets (IRC § 1222) are not involved; this holding precluded application of the exception from income taxation for capital gains (see *supra* § 1(j)). It also held that the nontaxation rules concerning like-kind exchanges (IRC § 1031) are inapplicable, because the title to the lists does not pass and the rights to the properties acquired by the parties are not perpetual (Koch v. Comm'r, 37 T.C.M. 1167 (1978); Rev. Rul. 55-749, 1955-2 C.B. 295). An earlier technical advice memorandum, concluding that exchanges of mailing lists between tax-exempt organizations did not give rise to unrelated business income (8128004), was thereafter prospectively revoked by the IRS (Tech. Adv. Mem. 9635001).

[237] So held in Sierra Club, Inc. v. Comm'r, 86 F.3d 1526 (9th Cir. 1996). Also American Academy of Ophthalmology, Inc. v. Comm'r (Tax Ct. No. 21657-94) (where the IRS abandoned its mailing list revenue taxation stance in the aftermath of the *Sierra Club* holding). See the discussion in *supra* § 1(g).

[238] See §§ 15.2, 15.3.

[239] IRC § 512(d)(1).

[240] Small Business Job Protection Act of 1996 Pub. L. No. 104-188, 104th Cong., 2d Sess. (1996) § 1115(b)(1).

[241] IRC § 512(d)(2). For years beginning in 1998, this threshold is $109 (Rev. Proc. 97-57, *supra* note 228).

[242] IRC § 512(d)(3).

poses of applying the $100 cap.[243] Transitional relief was provided for these tax-exempt organizations that had a reasonable basis for not treating membership dues received prior to January 1, 1987, as unrelated business income.[244]

(m) S Corporations

A tax-exempt organization may be a shareholder in an *S corporation*, which is a corporation that is treated for federal income tax purposes as a partnership.[245] The authorization to own this type of a security is a revision of prior law.[246]

This type of interest is considered as an interest in an unrelated business.[247] Items of income, loss, or deduction of an S corporation flow through to exempt organization shareholders as unrelated business income.[248] Gain or loss on the disposition of stock in an S corporation results in unrelated business income.[249]

(n) Qualified Sponsorship Payments

Qualified sponsorship payments received by tax-exempt organizations and state colleges and universities are exempt from the unrelated business income tax. That is, the activity of soliciting and receiving these payments is not an unrelated business.[250]

A *qualified sponsorship payment* is a payment made by a person engaged in a trade or business, with respect to which there is no arrangement or expectation that the person will receive any substantial return benefit other than the use or acknowledgment of the name or logo (or product lines) of the person's trade or business in connection with the organization's activities.[251] It is irrelevant whether the sponsored activity is related or unrelated to the organization's exempt purpose.[252]

This use or acknowledgment does not include advertising of the person's products or services, including messages containing qualitative or comparative language, price information or other indications of savings or value, an endorsement, or an inducement to purchase, sell, or use the products or services.[253] For example, if in return for receiving a sponsorship payment, an exempt organization promises to use the sponsor's name or logo in acknowledging the sponsor's support for an educational or fund-raising event con-

---

[243] H. Rep. No. 104-737, 104th Cong., 2d Sess. 14 (1996).

[244] Pub. L. No. 104-188, *supra* note 240 § 1115(b)(2), (3).

[245] IRC §§ 1361–1363.

[246] IRC § 1361(c)(7). This law was altered by enactment of the Small Business Job Protection Act of 1996 (Pub. L. No. 104-188).

[247] IRC § 512(e)(1)(A).

[248] IRC § 512(e)(1)(B)(i).

[249] IRC § 512(e)(1)(B)(ii).

[250] IRC § 513(i)(1).

[251] IRC § 513(i)(2)(A).

[252] H. Rep. No. 105-220, 105th Cong., 1st Sess. 69 (1997).

[253] IRC § 513(i)(2)(A).

ducted by the organization, the payment is not taxable. However, if an organization provides advertising of a sponsor's products, the payment made to the organization by the sponsor in order to receive the advertising is subject to unrelated business income tax (assuming that the other requirements for taxation are satisfied).[254]

A qualified sponsorship payment does not include any payment where the amount of the payment is contingent on the level of attendance at one or more events, broadcast ratings, or other factors indicating the degree of public exposure to one or more events.[255] However, the fact that a sponsorship payment is contingent on an event actually taking place or being broadcast, in and of itself, does not cause the payment to fail to qualify. Also, mere distribution or display of a sponsor's products by the sponsor or the exempt organization to the general public at a sponsored event, whether for free or for remuneration, is considered a *use or acknowledgment* of the sponsor's product lines—and not advertising.[256]

This law does not apply to a payment which entitles the payor to the use or acknowledgment of the name or logo (or product line) of the payor's trade or business in a tax-exempt organization's periodical. A *periodical* is regularly scheduled and printed material published by or on behalf of the payee organization that is not related to and primarily distributed in connection with a specific event conducted by the payee organization.[257] Thus, the exclusion does not apply to payments that lead to acknowledgments in a monthly journal but applies if a sponsor received an acknowledgment in a program or brochure distributed at a sponsored event.[258] The term *qualified sponsorship payment* also does not include a payment made in connection with a qualified convention or trade show activity.[259]

To the extent that a portion of a payment would (if made as a separate payment) be a qualified sponsorship payment, that portion of the payment is treated as a separate payment.[260] Therefore, if a sponsorship payment made to a tax-exempt organization entitles the sponsor to product advertising and use or acknowledgment of the sponsor's name or logo by the organization, the unrelated business income tax does not apply to the amount of the payment that exceeds the fair market value of the product advertising provided to the sponsor.[261]

The provision of facilities, services, or other privileges by an exempt organization to a sponsor or the sponsor's designees (such as complimentary tickets, pro-am playing spots in golf tournaments, or receptions for major donors) in connection with a sponsorship payment does not affect the determination of whether the payment is a qualified one. Instead, the provision of the goods or

---

[254] H. Rep. No. 105-220, *supra* note 252, at 68.
[255] IRC § 513(i)(2)(B)(i).
[256] H. Rep. No. 105-220, *supra* note 252, at 69.
[257] IRC § 513(i)(2)(B)(ii)(I).
[258] H. Rep. No. 105-220, *supra* note 252, at 69.
[259] IRC § 513(i)(2)(B)(ii)(II). This type of activity is the subject of *supra* § 2(f).
[260] IRC § 513(i)(3).
[261] H. Rep. No. 105-220, *supra* note 252, at 69.

services is evaluated as a separate transaction in determining whether the organization has unrelated business income from the event. In general, if the services or facilities do not constitute a substantial return benefit (or if the provision of the services or facilities is a related business activity), the payments attributable to them are not to be subject to the unrelated business income tax.[262]

Likewise, a sponsor's receipt of a license to use an intangible asset (such as a trademark, logo, or designation) of the tax-exempt organization is treated as separate from the qualified sponsorship transaction in determining whether the organization has unrelated business taxable income.[263]

This statutory exemption from taxation for qualified sponsorship payments is in addition to other exceptions from the unrelated business tax. These exceptions include the one for activities substantially all the work for which is performed by volunteers[264] and for activities not regularly carried on.[265]

---

[262] *Id.*

[263] *Id.*

[264] See *infra* § 2(a).

[265] See § 26.3. This rule became effective with respect to qualified sponsorship payments solicited or received after December 31, 1997. Although there is no inference as to whether a sponsorship payment received prior to 1998 was taxable, the IRS has dedicated that it will follow the statutory rules in disposing of the previous cases.

A history of the law leading to this legislation is at Hopkins, *The Law of Fund-Raising, Second Edition* (New York: John Wiley & Sons, Inc. 1996), Chapter 6 § 17(b); Henderson, "The Tax Treatment of Corporate Sponsorship Payments and the Aftermath of the Cotton Bowl Ruling," 13 *Exempt Org. Tax Rev.* (No. 5) 789 (May 1996).

CHAPTER TWENTY-EIGHT

Unrelated Income Taxation and Feeder Organizations

Even though a nonprofit organization achieves exemption from the federal income tax,[1] it nonetheless remains potentially taxable on any unrelated business income.[2]

§ 28.1 TAX STRUCTURE

The unrelated income rates payable by most tax-exempt organizations are the corporate rates.[3] Some organizations, such as trusts, are subject to the individual income rates.[4]

The tax law features the following three-bracket structure for corporations:

Taxable Income	Rate (percent)
$50,000 or less	15
$50,000–$75,000	25
Over $75,000	34

An additional 5 percent surtax is imposed on taxable income between $100,000 and $335,000, causing a marginal tax rate of 39 percent on taxable income in that range.[5] This tax structure is inapplicable to the taxation of insurance companies,[6] which is the tax paradigm that is used to tax organizations that cannot qualify as charitable organizations or social welfare organizations because a sub-

---

[1] IRC § 501(a).
[2] IRC § 501(b).
[3] IRC § 11. See IRC § 12(1).
[4] IRC § 1(d).
[5] IRC § 11(b).
[6] IRC § 11(c)(2). See IRC § 801 *et seq.* (IRC Subchapter L).

stantial part of their activities consists of the provision of commercial-type insurance.[7]

Tax-exempt organizations must make quarterly estimated payments of the tax on unrelated business income, under the same rules that require quarterly estimated payments of corporate income taxes.[8] Revenue and expenses associated with unrelated business activity are reported to the IRS on a tax return (Form 990-T).[9]

§ 28.2   DEDUCTION RULES

Generally, the term *unrelated business taxable income* means the gross income derived by an organization from an unrelated trade or business, regularly carried on by the organization, less business deductions that are directly connected with the carrying on of the trade or business.[10] For purposes of computing unrelated business taxable income, both gross income and business deductions are computed with certain modifications.[11]

Generally, to be *directly connected with* the conduct of an unrelated business, an item of deduction must have a proximate and primary relationship to the carrying on of that business. In the case of an organization that derives gross income from the regular conduct of two or more unrelated business activities, unrelated business taxable income is the aggregate of gross income from all unrelated business activities, less the aggregate of the deductions allowed with respect to all unrelated business activities.[12] Expenses, depreciation, and similar items attributable solely to the conduct of unrelated business are proximately and primarily related to that business and therefore qualify for deduction to the extent that they meet the requirements of relevant provisions of the federal income tax law.[13] However, the emerging law is that a loss incurred in the conduct of an unrelated activity may be offset against the net gain occasioned by the conduct of another unrelated activity only where each activity is a business in the sense that each activity must be conducted with a profit objective.[14]

---

[7] IRC § 501(m)(2)(B). See § 22.1.

[8] IRC §§ 6655(a)–(d). A tax-exempt organization is generally subject to an addition to tax for any underpayment of estimated tax on its unrelated business income (IRC § 6655(a), (g)(3)). The law was revised by enactment of the Omnibus Budget Reconciliation Act of 1993 (§ 13225), for years beginning after December 31, 1993, to provide that a tax-exempt organization does not have an underpayment of estimated tax if it makes four timely estimated tax payments that total at least 100 percent of the tax liability shown on its return for the current taxable year (IRC § 6655(d)(1)(B)). A tax-exempt organization may determine its estimated unrelated income tax payments (filed by means of Form 990-W) under one of three annualized income installment methods: a standard option, option 1, and option 2; Form 8842 (introduced by Ann. 94-36, 1994-9 I.R.B. 53) must be annually filed to elect option 2.

[9] IRC § 6012(a)(2), 6012(a)(4). See § 24.3(a)(v).

[10] IRC § 512(a)(1).

[11] See § 27.1. A tax-exempt organization is not entitled to an expense deduction for funds transferred from one internal account to another (Women of the Motion Picture Industry v. Comm'r, T.C. Mem. 1997-518).

[12] Reg. § 1.512(a)-1(a).

[13] E.g., IRC §§ 162, 167. Reg. § 1.512(a)-1(b).

[14] E.g., West Va. State Med. Ass'n v. Comm'r, 91 T.C. 651 (1988), *aff'd*, 882 F.2d 123 (4th Cir. 1989), *cert. den.*, 493 U.S. 1044 (1990). See § 26.2(a).

Where facilities and/or personnel are used both to carry on tax-exempt activities and to conduct unrelated trade or business, the expenses, depreciation, and similar items attributable to the facilities and/or personnel, such as overhead or items of salary, must be allocated between the two uses on a reasonable basis.[15] Despite the statutory rule that an expense must be directly connected with an unrelated business, the regulations merely state that the portion of the expense allocated to the unrelated business activity is, where the allocation is on a reasonable basis, proximately and primarily related to the business activity.[16] Once an item is proximately and primarily related to a business undertaking, it is allowable as a deduction in computing unrelated business income in the manner and to the extent permitted by federal income tax law generally.[17]

Both the U.S. Tax Court and the U.S. Court of Appeals for the Second Circuit found the regulations to be in conformity with the statutory requirements, in a case concerning the proper allocation of fixed expenses of the operation of a fieldhouse by a university where the facility was used for both tax-exempt and unrelated purposes.[18] Therefore, the critical question in this context is whether a particular method of allocation is *reasonable*. The university contended that fixed expenses should be allocated on the basis of relative times of actual use, so that the portion of the deductible expenses is determined by means of a ratio, the numerator of the fraction of which is the total number of hours the facility is used for unrelated purposes and the denominator of which is the total number of hours the fieldhouse is used for both related and unrelated activities. By contrast, the IRS argued that the allocation should be on the basis of total time available for use, so that the denominator of the fraction is the total number of hours in the tax year. The two courts found for the university.

The essential argument of the IRS was that the allocation is not reasonable because the outcome is a deductible expense that is not directly connected with the unrelated activity. However, the appellate court reasoned that it was merely following the government's own regulations. A dissent took the position that the regulation must be read in conjunction with the statute, so that the "directly connected with" language is a requirement that is in addition to those expressly contained in the regulations.[19]

Gross income may be derived from an unrelated trade or business that exploits a tax-exempt function. Generally, in these situations, expenses, depreciation, and similar items attributable to the conduct of the tax-exempt function are not deductible in computing unrelated business taxable income. Since the items are incident to a function of the type that is the chief purpose of the organization to conduct, they do not possess a proximate and primary relationship to the unre-

---

[15] Reg. § 1.512(a)-1(c). In Disabled American Veterans v. United States, 704 F.2d 1570 (Fed. Cir. 1983), *aff'g and rem'g* 82-2 U.S.T.C. ¶ 9440 (Cl. Ct. 1982), the U.S. Court of Appeals for the Federal Circuit approved an allocation of expenses proposed by the Claims Court whereby the veterans' organization is to allocate its fund-raising expenses between the taxable and tax-exempt portions of its solicitation program.

[16] Reg. § 1.512(a)-1(c).

[17] *Id.*

[18] Rensselaer Polytechnic Inst. v. Comm'r, 732 F.2d 1058 (2d Cir 1984), *aff'g* 79 T.C. 967 (1982).

[19] *Id.*, 732 F.2d 1058 at 1063–1066.

lated trade or business. Therefore, they do not qualify as being directly connected with that business.[20]

A tax-exempt organization will be denied business expense deductions in computing its unrelated business taxable income if it cannot adequately substantiate that the expenses were incurred or that they were directly connected with the unrelated activity. In one instance, an organization derived unrelated business income from the sale of advertising space in two magazines, and incurred expenses in connection with solicitation of the advertising and publication of the magazines. A court basically upheld the position of the IRS, which disallowed all of the claimed deductions (other than those for certain printing expenses) because the organization failed to establish the existence or relevance of the expenses.[21] The court found that the organization did not maintain adequate books and records, failed to accurately allocate expenses among accounts, and had insufficient accounting practices. During pretrial discovery, the organization failed to provide the requisite documentation. This led to a court order to produce the material, the response to which was labeled by the court as "evasive and incomplete."[22] Consequently, the court imposed sanctions, which essentially prevented the organization from introducing at trial any documentary evidence embraced by the government's request in discovery. The court rejected the organization's effort to prove its expenses at trial by testimony and to use its accountant's audit as evidence of the facts stated in the report. Thus, most of the claimed expenses were not allowed. Those that the court allowed over the government's objection were ascertained by the court on the basis of an approximation by the court.[23]

§ 28.3 SPECIAL RULES

Federal tax law provides a definition of *unrelated business taxable income* specifically applicable to foreign organizations that are subject to the tax on unrelated income.[24] Basically, foreign organizations are taxed on their unrelated business taxable income that is *effectively connected* with the conduct of a trade or business within the United States and on unrelated income derived from sources within the United States even though not so effectively connected.

In the case of certain veterans' organizations,[25] the term *unrelated business taxable income* does not include any amount attributable to payments for life, sick, accident, or health insurance with respect to members of the organizations or

---

[20] Reg. § 1.512(a)-1(d).

[21] CORE Special Purpose Fund v. Comm'r, 49 T.C.M. 626 (1985).

[22] *Id.*, at 629.

[23] In general, Lyons & Hall, "Allocating and Substantiating Income and Expenses for Tax-Exempt Organizations," 8 *J. Tax Exempt Orgs.* 107 (Nov./Dec. 1996): Bloom, "Offsetting Expenses Against UBI Can Be an Allocation Headache for Tax-Exempts," 8 *J. Tax. Exempt Orgs.* 33 (July/Aug. 1996); Blazek. "Accentuate the Negative: Maximizing Deductions on Form 990-T," 4 *J. of Tax. Exempt Orgs.* (No. 6) 24 (May/June 1993).

[24] IRC § 512(a)(2).

[25] See § 18.

their dependents that is set aside for the purpose of providing for the payment of insurance benefits or for a charitable purpose.[26]

Special rules are applicable to social clubs,[27] voluntary employees' beneficiary associations,[28] supplemental unemployment benefit trusts,[29] and group legal services organizations.[30] These rules[31] apply the unrelated business income tax to all of these organizations' net income other than so-called *exempt function income*.[32] For example, a tax-exempt voluntary employees' beneficiary association was required to pay the unrelated business income tax on revenue allocable to temporary excess office space, notwithstanding the court's belief that the space was acquired, in the exercise of sound business judgment, in anticipation of growth of the organization.[33]

Exempt function income is of two types: gross income from amounts (such as dues or fees) paid by members of the organization as consideration for the provision of goods, facilities, or services in furtherance of tax-exempt purposes, and income that is set aside for a charitable[34] purpose or (other than in the case of a social club) to provide for the payment of life, sick, accident, or other benefits, subject to certain limitations.[35]

It had been the position of the IRS that a title-holding company[36] must lose its tax-exempt status if it generates any amount of certain types of unrelated business taxable income.[37] However, the federal tax law was amended in 1993 to permit a tax-exempt title-holding company to receive unrelated business taxable income (that would otherwise disqualify the company for tax exemption) in an amount up to 10 percent of its gross income for the tax year, provided that the unrelated business taxable income is incidentally derived from the holding of real property.[38] For example, income generated from fees for parking or from the operation of vending machines located on real property owned by a title-holding company generally qualifies for the 10 percent *de minimis* rule, but income derived from an activity that is not incidental to the holding of real property (such as manufacturing) does not qualify.[39] Permissible unrelated business income is nonetheless subject to taxation.

Also, a tax-exempt title holding company will not lose its tax exemption if unrelated business taxable income that is incidentally derived from the hold-

---

[26] IRC § 512(a)(4).
[27] IRC § 501(c)(7) (see Chapter 14).
[28] IRC § 501(c)(9) (see § 16.3).
[29] IRC § 501(c)(17) (see § 16.4).
[30] IRC § 501(c)(20) (see § 16.6).
[31] IRC § 512(a)(3), as amended by Tax Reform Act of 1984 § 511(b).
[32] IRC § 512(a)(3)(B). Interest on obligations of a state (see IRC § 103(a)) received by a tax-exempt social club is not included in gross income for purposes of IRC § 512(a)(3) (Rev. Rul. 76-337, 1976-2 C.B. 177).
[33] Uniformed Serv. Benefit Ass'n v. United States, 727 F. Supp. 533 (W. D. Mo. 1990).
[34] IRC § 170(c)(4).
[35] IRC § 512(a)(3)(E).
[36] See § 18.2.
[37] IRS Notice 88-121, 1988-2 C.B. 457. Also Reg. § 1501(c)(2)-1(a).
[38] IRC § 501(c)(2), last sentence; IRC § 501(c)(25)(G)(i).
[39] H. Rep. No. 103-111, 103d Cong., 1st Sess. 618 (1993).

ing of real property exceeds the 10 percent limitation, where the organization establishes to the satisfaction of the IRS that the receipt of unrelated business taxable income in excess of the 10 percent limitation was "inadvertent and reasonable steps are being taken to correct the circumstances giving rise to such income."[40]

A tax-exempt organization and a single-parent title-holding corporation[41] may file a consolidated annual information return for a tax year. When this is done, and where the title-holding corporation pays any amount of its net income over the year to the exempt organization (or would have paid the amount but for the fact that the expenses of collecting the income exceeded its income), the corporation is treated as if it was organized and operated for the same purpose(s) as the other exempt organization (in addition to its title-holding purpose).[42] The effect of this rule is to exclude from any unrelated income taxation the income received by the exempt parent organization from the title-holding corporation.

§ 28.4 PARTNERSHIP RULES

If a trade or business regularly carried on by a partnership, of which a tax-exempt organization is a member, is an unrelated trade or business with respect to the organization, in computing its unrelated business taxable income the organization must include its share (whether or not distributed and subject to certain modifications[43]) of the gross income of the partnership from the unrelated trade or business and its share of the partnership deductions directly connected with the gross income.[44] This rule (known as a *look-through rule*) applies irrespective of whether the tax-exempt organization is a general or limited partner.[45] The courts are rejecting the thought that income derived by a tax-exempt organization from a limited partnership interest is, for that reason alone, not taxable because a limited partnership interest is a passive investment by which the organization lacks any ability to actively engage in the management, operation, or control of the partnership.[46]

However, with respect to partnership interests acquired after December 17, 1987, through partnership years ending on December 31, 1993, or thereafter in 1994, a tax-exempt organization's share (whether or not distributed) of the gross income of a publicly traded partnership must be treated as gross income derived from an unrelated trade or business, and its share of the partnership

---

[40] IRC § 501(c)(2), last sentence; IRC § 501(c)(25)(G)(ii).
[41] See §18.2(a).
[42] IRC § 511(c).
[43] See § 27.1.
[44] IRC § 512(c)(1), Reg. § 1.512(c)-1. E.g., IRS Priv. Ltr. Rul. 7934008.
[45] Rev. Rul. 79-222, 1979-2 C.B. 236; Service Bolt & Nut Co. Profit Sharing Trust et al. v. Comm'r, 78 T.C. 812 (1982).
[46] Service Bolt & Nut Co. Profit Sharing Trust v. Comm'r, 724 F.2d 519 (6th Cir. 1983), *aff'g* 78 T.C. 812 (1982).

deductions is allowed in computing unrelated business income.[47] (A publicly traded partnership is a partnership where interests in the partnership are traded on an established securities market or are readily tradable on a secondary market (or the substantial equivalent of a secondary market).[48]) The amounts includible or deductible under this rule are based on the income and deductions of the partnership for the tax year of the partnership ending within or with the tax year of the tax-exempt organization.[49] Thus, effective for partnership years beginning on or after January 1, 1994, investment income received by tax-exempt organizations from publicly traded partnerships is treated the same as investments in other partnerships for purposes of the unrelated business income rules; that is, the look-through rule applies in this setting as well.[50]

§ 28.5   SMALL BUSINESS CORPORATION RULES

Tax-exempt charitable organizations are allowed to be shareholders in small business corporations (also known as *S corporations*[51]).[52] Items of income or loss of a small business corporation flow through to these organizations as unrelated business income, irrespective of the source or nature of the income.[53] Thus, for example, unlike the partnership rules,[54] passive income of a small business corporation flows to an exempt charitable organization as unrelated business income.

If a charitable organization has acquired by purchase stock in a small business corporation (whether the stock was acquired when the corporation was a regular corporation—also known as a *C corporation*[55]—or an S corporation) and receives a dividend distribution with respect to the stock, except as to be provided in regulations, the shareholder must reduce its basis in the stock by the

---

[47] Former IRC § 512(c)(2). This rule was initiated as an outgrowth of Congress's decision in 1987 to treat publicly traded partnerships as corporations (IRC § 7704) but was repealed in 1993, when Congress decided to enact tax laws to enhance investment in real estate.

[48] IRC § 469(k)(2).

[49] IRC § 512(c)(3).

[50] In general, Kennedy, "Guidelines for Avoiding the Unrelated Business Income Tax on Exempt Organizations," 12 *Tax Law.* (No. 1) 56 (1983); Van Wert, "Retail Sales by Exempt Organizations: When Will They Be Subject to the UBT?", 56 *J. Tax.* 104 (Feb. 1982); Myers & Myers, Jr., "How Art-Oriented Exempt Organizations Can Skirt the Unrelated Business Income Tax," 49 *J. Tax.* 150 (Sept. 1978); Warren, "Taxable Income of Qualified Trusts," 61 *A.B.A.J.* 981 (1975); Webster, "Unrelated Business Income," 23 *Tax Law.* 471 (1970); Note, "Unrelated Business Income of Tax Exempt Organizations," 19 *De Paul L. Rev.* 525 (1970); Note, "The Macaroni Monopoly: The Developing Concept of Unrelated Business Income of Exempt Organizations," 81 *Harv. L. Rev.* 1280 (1968); Comment, "Preventing the Operation of Untaxed Business by Tax-Exempt Organizations," 32 *U. Chi. L. Rev.* 581 (1965).

[51] That term is derived from the fact that the tax treatment of these corporations is the subject of IRC Subtitle A, Chapter 1, subchapter S (§§ 1361–1363).

[52] See § 27.2(m).

[53] *Id.*

[54] See *supra* § 4.

[55] That term is derived from the fact that the tax treatment of these corporations is the subject of IRC Subtitle A, Chapter 1, subchapter C (§§ 301–385).

amount of the dividend.[56] Tax regulations may provide that the basis reduction would apply only to the extent the dividend is deemed to be allocable to subchapter C earnings and profits that accrued on or before the date of acquisition of the stock.[57]

§ 28.6 FEEDER ORGANIZATIONS

Federal tax law provides that an "organization operated for the primary purpose of carrying on a trade or business for profit shall not be exempt from taxation under [IRC] section 501 on the ground that all of its profits are payable to one or more organizations exempt from taxation under section 501."[58] This type of nonexempt entity is a *feeder organization*, inasmuch as it is a business operation that "feeds" monies to one or more tax-exempt organizations. In determining the primary purpose of an organization, all pertinent circumstances are considered, including the size and extent of the trade or business and the size and extent of the activities of the tax-exempt organization.[59] If an organization carries on a trade or business but not as a primary function, the organization may be tax-exempt, although the income from the trade or business may be taxed as unrelated business taxable income.[60]

The feeder organization rules were added to the federal tax law in 1950, as a legislative overturning of the court-derived *destination-of-income test*. Pursuant to this test, as articulated by the U.S. Supreme Court in 1924,[61] the destination of an organization's income was considered to be of greater consequence than the source and use of the income (the emphasis now as the result of enactment of the feeder organization rules) for purposes of determining exemption from taxation. That is, under this test, where a for-profit organization contributed all of its net income for charitable purposes, the organization itself was considered a charity.

---

[56] IRC § 512(e)(2).

[57] H. Rep. 104-737, 104th Cong., 2d. Sess. 61 (1996).

[58] IRC § 502(a).

[59] Reg. § 1.502-1(a).

[60] Reg. § 1.502-1(c). See Chapters 26–27.

[61] Trinidad v. Sagrada Orden de Predicadores de la Provincia del Santisimo Rosario de Filipinas, 263 U.S. 578 (1924). Cases involving application of the destination-of-income test, for the benefit of the organizations involved, are Roche's Beach, Inc. v. Comm'r 96 F.2d 776 (2d Cir. 1938); Bohemian Gymnastic Ass'n Sokol of City of New York v. Higgins, 147 F.2d 774 (2d Cir. 1945); Debs Memorial Radio Fund, Inc. v. Comm'r 148 F.2d 948 (2d Cir. 1945); Comm'r v. Orton, 173 F.2d 483 (6th Cir. 1949); Consumer-Farmer Milk Coop. v. Comm'r 186 F.2d 68, 70 (2d Cir. 1950), *cert. den.*, 341 U.S. 931 (1951); Willingham v. Home Oil Mill, 181 F.2d 9 (5th Cir. 1950); Scofield v. Rio Farms, Inc., 205 F.2d 68 (5th Cir. 1953); Lichter Found. v. Welch, 247 F.2d 431 (6th Cir. 1957). Cases where the government prevailed, the test notwithstanding, are Universal Oil Prods. Co. v. Campbell, 181 F.2d 451 (7th Cir. 1950), *cert den.*, 340 U.S. 850 (1950); United States v. Community Servs. 189 F.2d 421 (1951), *cert. den.*, 342 U.S. 932 (1952); Ralph H. Eaton Found. v. Comm'r, 219 F.2d 527 (9th Cir. 1955); John Danz Charitable Trust v. Comm'r, 231 F.2d 673 (9th Cir. 1955), *cert. den.*, 352 U.S. 828 (1956); Riker v. Comm'r, 244 F.2d 220 (9th Cir. 1957).

A summary of the law prior to enactment of the destination-of-income test and the transition into the feeder organization rules is provided in Lichter Found. v. Welch, *supra* at 434–437.

However, the principal problem with this standard was that tax-exempt business operations were able to competitively undercut for-profit organizations that were not related to or otherwise supporting tax-exempt organizations.

The House Committee on Ways and Means report accompanying the Revenue Act of 1950 stated that the feeder organization provision was intended to

> prevent the exemption of a trade or business organization under . . . [the predecessor to IRC § 501(c)(3)] on the grounds that an organization actually described in . . . [that section] receives the earnings from the operations of the trade or business organization. In any case it appears clear to your committee that such an organization is not itself carrying out an exempt purpose. Moreover, it obviously is in direct competition with other taxable business.[62]

The impact of the feeder organization rules may be vividly seen in the case of the SICO Foundation, which was a nonstock corporation that owned controlling interests in several corporations engaged in the business of selling and distributing petroleum products.[63] Its net income was distributed to teachers' colleges for scholarship purposes. The SICO Foundation was before the Court of Claims for tax years prior to 1951, seeking tax-exempt status, in 1952. Following the destination of income test, the court found the organization to be educational in nature and hence tax-exempt.[64] But, when its tax status for years 1951, 1952, and 1953 was litigated in the Court of Claims, the court held that enactment of the feeder organization rules in 1950[65] caused the organization to lose its tax-exempt status. Concluded the court: "That it gave all its profits to an educational institution availeth it nothing [except perhaps a charitable contribution deduction] in the mundane field of taxation, however much the children in our schools have profited from its beneficence."[66]

One vestige of the destination of income test remains, however. Under the rules defining the meaning of the term *gross income*,[67] the value of services is not includible in gross income when the services are rendered directly and gratuitously to a charitable organization.[68] Thus, a parimutuel race track corporation was able to distribute charity day race proceeds to a charitable organization, which agreed to absorb any losses arising from the event and to assume all responsibility for the promotion, and not include any of the proceeds in its gross income for federal income tax purposes.[69] Where, by contrast, the race track corporation was the promoter of the charity day racing event,

---

[62] H. Rep. No. 2319, 81st Cong., 2d Sess. 41 (1950). Also S. Rep. No. 2375, 81st Cong., 2d Sess. 35 (1950).
[63] SICO Found. v. United States, 295 F.2d 924 (Ct. Cl. 1961), *reh den*, 297 F.2d 557 (Ct. Cl. 1962).
[64] The SICO Co. v. United States, 102 F. Supp. 197 (Ct. Cl. 1952).
[65] 26 U.S.C. § 101.
[66] *Supra* note 7, at 925.
[67] IRC § 61(a).
[68] Reg. § 1.61-2(c).
[69] Rev. Rul. 77-121, 1977-1 C.B. 17.

rather than the agent of the charity, the proceeds from the event were taxable to the corporation.[70]

The distinctions at play in the feeder organization context are frequently difficult to initially discern. For example, the IRS accorded tax-exempt status to a nonprofit corporation controlled by a church, where the organization's function was to print and sell educational and religious material to the church's parochial system at a profit, with the profits returned to the system.[71] But, an organization formed by a church to operate a commercial printing business (which generated a substantial profit) and to print religious materials for the church at cost (about 10 percent of its activities), where all net income was paid over to the church, was ruled a feeder organization and thus not tax-exempt.[72] The distinguishing feature was the fact that an overwhelming percentage of the organization's activities in the latter instance were the provision of commercial services to other than the related tax-exempt organization.

The government's position is that where a subsidiary organization of a tax-exempt parent would itself be tax-exempt, because its activities are an integral part of the activities of the parent, the tax-exempt status of the subsidiary will not be lost because the subsidiary derived a profit from its dealings with the parent.[73] For example, the income tax regulations contain an illustration of a subsidiary organization operated for the sole purpose of furnishing electric power used by the parent organization (a tax-exempt educational institution) in carrying on its tax-exempt activities, the subsidiary is itself a charitable entity. However, where a subsidiary of a tax-exempt parent is operated for the primary purpose of carrying on a trade or business that would be an unrelated trade or business if regularly carried on by the parent, the subsidiary would not be tax-exempt.[74] The regulations contain the example of a subsidiary of a tax-exempt parent that is not exempt because it is operated primarily for the purpose of furnishing electric power to consumers other than the parent.

The income tax regulations accompanying the feeder organizations law contain an observation that has no basis in statutory law and that has nothing to do with that rule. This is the comment that "if the subsidiary organization is owned by several [that is, more than one] unrelated exempt organizations, and is operated for the purpose of furnishing electric power to each of them, it is not exempt since such business would be an unrelated trade or business if regularly carried on by any one of the tax-exempt organizations."[75] On this point, the regulations have it backwards, for the feeder organization rules do not even apply until there is an organization "operated for the primary purpose of carrying on a

---

[70] Rev. Rul. 72-542, 1972-2 C.B. 37. In this instance, however, the corporation receives a business expense deduction under IRC § 162 or a charitable contribution deduction under IRC § 170 for the proceeds turned over to charity (Rev. Rul. 77-124, 1977-1 C.B. 39; Rev. Rul. 72-542 *supra*).

[71] Rev. Rul. 68-26 1968-1 C.B. 272 Also Pulpit Resource v. Comm'r 70 T C 594 (1978).

[72] Rev. Rul. 73-164, 1973-1 C.B. 223.

[73] Reg. § 1.502-1(b). A technical parent-subsidiary relationship need not be present (Rev. Rul. 68-26, *supra* note 71).

[74] *Id.*

[75] *Id.*

trade or business for profit." Thus, the Senate Finance Committee report accompanying the Senate version of the measure that became the Revenue Act of 1950 stated that the provision "applies to organizations operated for the primary purpose of carrying on a trade or business for profit, as for example, a feeder corporation whose business is the manufacture of automobiles for the ultimate profit of an educational institution."[76] These rules do not purport to define this type of organization and nothing in its history indicates that it was intended to denominate as a feeder an organization controlled by and serving only tax-exempt organizations. As discussed,[77] this statement is one of the rationales of the IRS for denying tax-exempt status to consortia and other organizations performing joint activities for tax-exempt organizations,[78] even though this rationale was explicitly rejected in the first cases where it was considered.[79] In one of these cases, the court first questioned the relationship of this regulation to the statute. "Charitably put (no pun intended), the Court has difficulty in finding any basis in the statute . . . [concerning feeder organizations] for . . . [this] portion of the regulations."[80] Second, the court dismissed the applicability of these rules in the context of "shared services" organizations consortia. "What does this [the feeder organization rule] have to do with two or more such [tax-exempt] organizations setting up a not-for-profit corporation, wholly controlled by them, and not serving the public, in order to effect economies in their own charitable operations? The Court in . . . [a prior case] gave no effect to the regulation, nor does this Court."[81]

As the government progressed to ultimate success in defeating tax exemption for cooperative hospital laundry organizations,[82] it abandoned its argument against consortia based on this interpretation of the feeder rules. The argument was rejected by the federal district court involved,[83] jettisoned by the government on appeal,[84] and thus not considered by the U.S. Supreme Court.[85] However, the U.S. Tax Court accepted this argument.[86]

With the emphasis on determination of unrelated business taxable income, rather than deprivation of tax-exempt status, the IRS has retreated somewhat as concerns vigorous assertion of the feeder organization rules.[87] Also, the

---

[76] S. Rep. No. 2375, *supra* note 62 at 116.

[77] See § 6.8.

[78] Rev. Rul. 69–528, 1969-2 C.B. 127.

[79] Hospital Bur. of Standards & Supplies v. United States, 158 F. Supp. 560, 563 (Ct. Cl. 1958); United Hosp. Serv., Inc. v. United States, 384 F. Supp. 776 (S.D. Ind. 1974).

[80] United Hosp. Serv., Inc. v. United States, *supra* note 79, at 782.

[81] *Id.*

[82] See §§ 6.8. 10.4.

[83] HCSC Laundry v. United States, 473 F. Supp. 250 (E.D. Pa. 1979).

[84] HCSC Laundry v. United States, 624 F.2d 428, 432, note 6. (3d Cir. 1980).

[85] HCSC Laundry v. United States, 450 U.S. 1 (1981).

[86] Associated Hosp. Servs., Inc. v. Comm'r, 74 T.C. 213 (1980), *aff'd unrep. dec.* (5th Cir. 1981). In a case involving a cooperative organization outside the health care setting, the IRS advanced, then withdrew, the feeder organization argument (The Council for Bibliographic and Information Technologies v. Comm'r, 63 T.C.M. 3186, 3187–3188 (1992)).

[87] E.g., Rev. Rul. 66–296, 1966-2 C.B. 215; Rev. Rul. 66–295, 1966-2 C.B. 207.

courts have infrequently construed the feeder rules against the affected organizations.[88]

For purposes of these rules,[89] the term *trade or business* does not include (1) the derivation of most types of rents,[90] (2) any trade or business in which substantially all the work in carrying on the trade or business is performed for the organization without compensation,[91] or (3) any trade or business that consists of the selling of merchandise, substantially all of which has been received by the organization as gifts or contributions.[92] For example, a thrift shop may avoid feeder organization status because the work is performed by volunteers[93] or because the merchandise was received as gifts.[94]

[88] Cases where IRC § 502 was not applied include Industrial Aid for the Blind v. Comm'r, 73 T.C. 96 (1979); E. Orton, Jr. Ceramic Found. v. Comm'r, 56 T.C. 147 (1971); Duluth Clinic Found. v. United States, 67-1, U.S.T.C. ¶ 9926 (D. Minn. 1967); Bright Star Found. v. Campbell, 191 F. Supp. 845 (N.D. Tex 1960). The feeder organization rule was applied in, e.g., Veterans Found. v. United States, 281 F.2d 912 (10th Cir. 1960); Disabled Veterans Serv. Found., Inc. v. Comm'r, 29 T.C.M. 202 (1970).

[89] IRC § 502(b).

[90] See § 27.1(h).

[91] See § 27.2(a).

[92] See § 27.2(c).

[93] Rev. Rul. 80-106, 1980-1 C.B. 113.

[94] Rev. Rul. 71-581, 1971-2 C.B. 236.

CHAPTER TWENTY-NINE

Unrelated Debt-Financed Income and Tax-Exempt Entity Leasing Rules

The unrelated debt-financed income rules cause certain forms of income received by tax-exempt organizations, which income would otherwise be exempt from taxation, to be subject to the unrelated business income tax. The tax-exempt entity leasing rules require certain persons who engage in certain leasing transactions involving exempt organizations to compute their depreciation deduction over a longer recovery period than might otherwise be the case.

§ 29.1 OVERVIEW OF DEBT-FINANCED INCOME RULES

Prior to the enactment of the Tax Reform Act of 1969, most charitable organizations and certain other tax-exempt organizations were subject to the unrelated business income tax on rental income from real property to the extent the property was acquired with borrowed funds. However, there was an important exception that excluded rental income from a lease of five years or less and, further, the tax was not applicable to all tax-exempt organizations. Moreover, there was a question as to whether the tax applied to income from the leasing, by a tax-exempt organization, of assets constituting a going business.

In the years immediately preceding enactment of the 1969 Act, some tax-exempt organizations were using their tax privileges to purchase businesses and investments on credit, frequently at what was more than the market price, while contributing little or nothing themselves to the transaction other than their tax exemption. A typical factual situation in this regard is as follows:

> A sells an incorporated business to B, a charitable foundation, which makes a small (or no) down payment and agrees to pay the balance of the purchase price only out of profits to be derived from the property. B liquidates the corporation and then leases the business assets to C, a new corporation formed to operate the business. A (collectively, the stockholders of the original business) manages the business for C and frequently holds a substantial minority interest in C. C pays 80 percent of its business profits as "rent" to B, who then passes on 90 percent of those receipts to A until the original purchase price is paid in full. B has no obligation to pay A out of any funds other than the "rent" paid by C.[1]

The tax results of this type of transaction provided capital gain to the seller, a rent deduction for the operator, and no tax on the tax-exempt organization.

In this manner, a business was able to realize increased after-tax income and a tax-exempt organization was able to acquire the ownership of a business valued at $1.3 million without the investment of its own funds.[2] Immediately prior to the Tax Reform Act of 1969, the U.S. Tax Court upheld the acquisition of 24 businesses by the University Hill Foundation in this manner in the period 1945 to 1954.[3]

The response of Congress to the problems in this area was enactment of the unrelated debt-financed income rules by means of a revamped IRC § 514. In 1969, Congress acted to impose a tax on the investment income of tax-exempt institutions that is traceable in one way or another to borrowed funds. This was done by the addition to the Internal Revenue Code of rules that impose a tax on *unrelated debt-financed income.*[4]

In computing a tax-exempt organization's unrelated business taxable income, there must be included with respect to each debt-financed property that is unrelated to the organization's exempt function—as an item of gross income derived from an unrelated trade or business—an amount of income from the property, subject to tax in the proportion in which the property is financed by the debt.[5] Basically, deductions are allowed with respect to each debt-financed property in the same proportion.[6] The allowable deductions are those that are directly connected with the debt-financed property or its income, although any depreciation may only be computed on the straight-line method.[7] For example, if a commercial business property is acquired by a tax-exempt organization subject to an 80 percent mortgage, 80 percent of the income and 80 percent of the deductions are taken into account for these tax purposes. As the mortgage is paid, the percentage taken into account usually diminishes. Capital gains on the sale of unrelated debt-financed property are also taxed in the same proportions.[8]

---

[1] H. Rep. 91-413 (Part 1), 91st Cong., 1st Sess. 45 (1969).

[2] Comm'r v. Brown, 380 U.S. 563 (1965).

[3] University Hill Found. v. Comm'r, 51 T.C. 548 (1969), *rev'd.* 446 F.2d 701 (10th Cir. 1971), *cert. den.*, 405 U.S. 965 (1972). Also Anderson Dairy, Inc. v. Comm'r, 39 T.C. 1027 (1963); Shiffman v. Comm'r, 32 T.C. 1073 (1959); Ohio Furnace Co., Inc. v. Comm'r, 25 T.C. 179 (1955).

[4] An example of an interpretation of pre-1969 IRC § 514 appears in Rev. Rul. 70-132, 1970-1 C.B. 138.

[5] IRC §§ 514(a)(1), 512(b)(4).

[6] IRC § 514(a)(2).

[7] IRC § 514(a)(3).

[8] Reg. § 1.514(a)-1.

§ 29.2 DEBT-FINANCED PROPERTY

The term *debt-financed property* means, with certain exceptions, all property (for example, rental real estate, tangible personalty, and corporate stock) that is held to produce income (for example, rents, royalties, interest, and dividends) and with respect to which there is an acquisition indebtedness[9] at any time during the tax year (or during the preceding 12 months, if the property is disposed of during the year).[10]

Excepted from the term debt-financed property is (1) property where substantially all (at least 85 percent) of its use is substantially related (aside from the need of the organization for income or funds) to the exercise or performance by the organization of its tax-exempt purpose or, if less than substantially all of its use is related, to the extent that its use is related to the organization's exempt purpose,[11] (2) property to the extent that its income is already subject to tax as income from the conduct of an unrelated trade or business,[12] (3) property to the extent that the income is derived from research activities and therefore excluded from unrelated business taxable income,[13] and (4) property to the extent that its use is in a trade or business exempted from tax because substantially all the work is performed without compensation, the business is carried on primarily for the convenience of members, students, patients, officers, or employees, or the business is the selling of merchandise, substantially all of which was received as gifts or contributions.[14] For purposes of item (1), substantially all of the use of property is considered substantially related to the exercise or performance of an organization's tax-exempt purpose if the property is real property subject to a lease to a medical clinic, where the lease is entered into primarily for purposes that are substantially related to the lessor's exempt purposes.[15] For purposes of items (1), (3), and (4), the use of any property by a tax-exempt organization that is related to an organization is treated as use by the related organization.[16]

An illustration of a situation where property that is debt-financed did not yield unrelated debt-financed income, because the use of the property was substantially related to a tax-exempt use, was provided by the case of an exempt organization, created to encourage business development in a particular area, that constructed a building to lease, at below-market rates, to an industrial tenant for the purpose of attracting new industry to the area. Once the lease was executed, the organization completed the building (which was initially financed by the

---

[9] See *infra* § 3.
[10] IRC § 514(b)(1).
[11] IRC § 514(b)(1)(A). Unrelated debt-financed income is triggered to the extent that the financing occurred in connection with the acquisition of property used for an exempt purpose but the loan proceeds were instead invested (Southwest Tex. Elec. Coop., Inc. v. Comm'r, 95-2 U.S.T.C. ¶ 50,565 (5th Cir. 1995), *aff'g* 68 T.C.M. 285 (1994)).
[12] IRC § 514(b)(1)(B). This rule does not apply in the case of income excluded under IRC § 512(b)(5) (principally, capital gain). See § 27.1(j).
[13] IRC § 514(b)(1)(C). See § 27.1(l).
[14] IRC § 514(b)(1)(D). See § 27.2(c).
[15] IRC § 514(b), last sentence.
[16] IRC § 514(b)(2).

business community) to suit the needs of the tenant; the completion of the building was financed by subjecting the property to a mortgage. Because the leasing of the building under these circumstances was an activity designed to attract industry to the community, the IRS concluded that the activity contributed importantly to the organization's tax-exempt purpose and hence did not constitute debt-financed property subject to these tax rules.[17] Another example of this rule was provided in the case of a tax-exempt medical foundation that rented mortgaged property to a medical clinic that had a close working relationship with the foundation; the leased property was held to be related to the foundation's tax-exempt purpose of providing medical training, so that the rental income was determined to be nontaxable.[18]

Also, for purposes of the foregoing item (1), the principles established under the general unrelated income rules[19] are applicable in determining whether there is a substantial relationship between the property and the tax-exempt purposes of the organization.[20] These principles were adversely applied to a tax-exempt organization that was operated for educational purposes essentially in the same manner as a museum in that it promoted the appreciation of history and architecture by acquiring, restoring, and preserving buildings of historical and/or architectural significance and opened the restored buildings to the general public for a nominal admission fee. The organization acquired certain historically or architecturally significant buildings by assumption of outstanding mortgages and leased them at a fair rental value, subject to a covenant to ensure that the historical architecture of the buildings was maintained by the lessees, for uses that neither bear any relationship to the buildings' historical or architectural significance nor accommodate viewing by the general public. Because this leasing did not contribute importantly to the accomplishment of the organization's educational purpose and had no causal relationship to the achievement of that purpose, the IRS found that substantially all the use of the buildings was not substantially related to the organization's exempt purposes and thus that the leased buildings constituted debt-financed property.[21]

Property owned by a tax-exempt organization and used by a related tax-exempt organization or by an exempt organization related to the related exempt organization is not treated as debt-financed property to the extent the property is used by either organization in furtherance of its tax-exempt purpose.[22] Two tax-exempt organizations are related to each other if more than 50 percent of the members of one organization are members of the other organization.[23] In one instance, the IRS held that a charitable organization may acquire a building, use a portion of it, and lease the other portion to a related charitable organization

[17] Rev. Rul. 81-138, 1981-1 C.B. 358, *amplifying* Rev. Rul. 70-81, 1970-1 C.B. 131. Cf. Rev. Rul. 58-547, 1958-2 C.B. 275.
[18] Gundersen Med. Found., Ltd. v. United States, 536 F. Supp. 556 (W.D. Wis. 1982). Also Rev. Rul. 69-464, 1969-1 C.B. 132.
[19] IRC § 513. See Chapter 26.
[20] Reg. § 1.514(b)-1(b)(1). See § 26.4.
[21] Rev. Rul. 77-47, 1977-1 C.B. 157.
[22] Reg. § 1.514(b)-1(c)(2)(i).
[23] Reg. § 1.514(b)-1(c)(2)(ii)(c).

and a related business league for their offices and activities and that the building will not be treated as debt-financed property.[24] The organization acquiring the building had as its membership all of the active members of the business league who had contributed to it, and the membership of the other charitable organization consisted of those active members of the business league who were elected to and served on the governing body of the business league; the members of one of the charitable organizations would not necessarily be members of the other.

The *neighborhood land rule* provides an exemption from the debt-financed property rules for interim income from neighborhood real property acquired for a tax-exempt purpose. The tax on unrelated debt-financed income does not apply to income from real property, located in the neighborhood of other property owned by the tax-exempt organization, which it plans to devote to exempt uses within 10 years of the time of acquisition.[25] This rule applies after the first five years of the 10-year period only if the exempt organization satisfies the IRS that future use of the acquired land in furtherance of its exempt purposes before the expiration of the period is reasonably certain;[26] this process is to be initiated by filing a ruling request at least 90 days before the end of the fifth year.[27] A more liberal 15-year rule is established for churches and it is not required that the property be in the neighborhood of the church.[28]

If debt-financed property is sold or otherwise disposed of, a percentage of the total gain or loss derived from the disposition is included in the computation of unrelated business taxable income.[29] The IRS recognizes, however, that the unrelated debt-financed income rules do not render taxable a transaction that would not be taxable by virtue of a nonrecognition provision of the federal tax law if it were carried out by an entity that is not tax-exempt.[30] The occasion was a transfer, subject to an existing mortgage, of an apartment complex, which had appreciated in value, by a tax-exempt hospital to its wholly owned taxable subsidiary in exchange for additional stock in the subsidiary. Because of the operation of federal tax rules that provide for the nonrecognition of gain or loss in certain circumstances,[31] including those involving this hospital, the transaction did not result in a taxable gain for the hospital.

---

[24] Priv. Let. Rul. 7833055. The IRS cautioned that the charitable organization should charge the business league a fair market value rent, for if it did not it would be conferring a financial benefit upon a non–IRC § 501(c)(3) organization, which might adversely affect its tax-exempt status.

[25] IRC § 514(b)(3)(A)-(C). Where a tax-exempt organization did not own the original site property in the neighborhood, since the property was owned by a supporting organization (see § 11.3(c)) with respect to the organization, the IRS concluded that the neighborhood land rule nonetheless applied because of the supported organization's "interrelated nature" with the property by means of the supporting organization (Priv. Ltr. Rul. 9603019).

[26] IRC § 514(b)(3)(A).

[27] Reg. § 1.514(b)-1(d)(1)(iii). Where an exempt organization failed to seek this ruling, because the IRS was satisfied with the plans the organization submitted for the future use of the property, it granted administrative relief (Reg. § 301.9100-1(a)) by extending the filing period (Priv. Ltr. Rul. 9603019).

[28] IRC § 514(b)(3)(E). In general, Reg. § 1.514(b)-1.

[29] Reg. § 1.514(a)-1(a)(1)(v).

[30] Rev. Rul. 77-71, 1977-1 C.B. 156.

[31] IRC §§ 351, 357.

§ 29.3 ACQUISITION INDEBTEDNESS

Income-producing property is considered to be unrelated debt-financed property (making income from it, less deductions, taxable) only where there is an *acquisition indebtedness* attributable to it. Acquisition indebtedness, with respect to debt-financed property, means the unpaid amount of the indebtedness incurred by the tax-exempt organization in acquiring or improving the property, the indebtedness incurred before any acquisition or improvement of the property if the indebtedness would not have been incurred but for the acquisition or improvement, and the indebtedness incurred after the acquisition or improvement of the property if the indebtedness would not have been incurred but for the acquisition or improvement and the incurring of the indebtedness was reasonably foreseeable at the time of the acquisition or improvement.[32]

If property is acquired by a tax-exempt organization subject to a mortgage or other similar lien, the indebtedness thereby secured is considered an acquisition indebtedness incurred by the organization when the property is acquired, even though the organization did not assume or agree to pay the indebtedness.[33] However, some relief is provided with respect to mortgaged property acquired as a result of a bequest or devise. That is, the indebtedness secured by this type of mortgage is not treated as acquisition indebtedness during the 10-year period following the date of acquisition. A similar rule applies to mortgaged property received by gift, where the mortgage was placed on the property more than five years before the gift and the property was held by the donor more than five years before the gift.[34]

A tax-exempt charitable organization acquired an undivided interest in income-producing rental property subject to a mortgage; the property was leased for purposes unrelated to the organization's tax-exempt purposes. To liquidate its share of the mortgage, the organization prepaid its proportionate share of the mortgage indebtedness, thereby receiving releases of liability from the mortgagee and the co-owners. The lien securing payment of the mortgage nonetheless extended to the entire rental property and the mortgagee was not to release the lien until the entire principal of the mortgage was paid by the co-owners. The IRS ruled that the organization, by satisfying the full amount of its indebtedness under the mortgage, did not have any acquisition indebtedness.[35]

By contrast, a charitable organization purchased mineral production payments with borrowed funds to obtain income for its grant-making program, receiving from each payment the difference between the aggregate amount payable to the lender of the borrowed funds and the total amount of the production payment, with the difference generally amounting to 1/16 of 1 percent of each payment purchased. The IRS held that the indebtedness incurred to purchase the

---

[32] IRC § 514(c)(1). An interest in a qualified state tuition program (see § 18.16) is not regarded as a debt for purposes of these rules (IRC § 529(e)(4)). Trading in commodity futures contracts by a tax-exempt organization does not give rise to acquisition indebtedness (Gen. Couns. Mem. 39620).

[33] IRC § 514(c)(2)(A).

[34] IRC § 514(c)(2)(B).

[35] Rev. Rul. 76-95, 1976-1 C.B. 172.

production payment was an acquisition indebtedness and that, accordingly, the payments were debt-financed property.[36]

The regulations accompanying the statutory unrelated debt-financed income rules provide, in effect, a special rule for debts for the payment of taxes, stating that "in the case where State law provides that a tax lien attaches to property prior to the time when such lien becomes due and payable, such lien shall not be treated as similar to a mortgage until after it has become due and payable and the organization has had an opportunity to pay such lien in accordance with State law."[37] However, prior to enactment of the Tax Reform Act of 1976, the IRS took the position that a lien arising from a special assessment imposed by a state or local government on land for the purpose of making improvements on the land, with the improvements financed by the sale of bonds secured by the lien, constituted acquisition indebtedness, even though (like the property tax lien) the installment payments were due in future periods. In 1976, Congress took action to reverse this position so that, as respects tax years that began after December 31, 1969, where state law provides that a lien for taxes or for assessments made by the state or a political subdivision of the state attaches to property prior to the time when the taxes or assessments become due and payable, the indebtedness does not become acquisition indebtedness (that is, the lien is not regarded as similar to a mortgage[38]) until and to the extent that the taxes or assessments become due and payable and the organization has had an opportunity to pay the taxes or assessments in accordance with state law.[39] The Senate Finance Committee noted that "it is not intended that this provision apply to special assessments for improvements which are not of a type normally made by a State or local governmental unit or instrumentality in circumstances in which the use of the special assessment is essentially a device for financing improvements of the sort that normally would be financed privately rather than through a government."[40]

Other exemptions from the scope of acquisition indebtedness are as follows:

1. The term does not include indebtedness that was necessarily incurred in the performance or exercise of an organization's tax-exempt purpose or function, such as the indebtedness incurred by a tax-exempt credit union[41] in accepting deposits from its members.[42] It has been held, however, that the purchase of securities on margin and with borrowed funds is not inherent in (meaning essential to) the performance or exercise of a credit union's exempt purposes or function, so that a portion of the resulting income is taxable as debt-financed income.[43]

2. The term does not include an obligation to pay an annuity that (a) is the sole consideration issued in exchange for property if, at the time of the

---

[36] Rev. Rul. 76-354, 1976-2 C.B. 179.
[37] Reg. § 514(c)-1(b)(2).
[38] IRC § 514(c)(2)(A).
[39] IRC § 514(c)(2)(C).
[40] S. Rep. No. 94-938 (Part 2), 94th Cong., 2d Sess. 86 (1976).
[41] See § 18.7.
[42] IRC § 514(c)(4).
[43] Alabama Central Credit Union v. United States, 646 F. Supp. 1199 (N.D. Ala. 1986).

exchange, the value of the annuity is less than 90 percent of the value of the property received in the exchange; (b) is payable over the life of one individual who is living at the time the annuity is issued, or over the lives of two individuals living at that time; and (c) is payable under a contract that does not guarantee a minimum amount of payments or specify a maximum amount of payments and does not provide for any adjustment of the amount of the annuity payments by reference to the income received from the transferred property or any other property.[44]

3. The term does not include an obligation to finance the purchase, rehabilitation, or construction of housing for low and moderate income persons to the extent that it is insured by the Federal Housing Administration.[45]

4. The term does not include a tax-exempt organization's obligation to return collateral security pursuant to a securities lending arrangement, thereby making it clear that, in ordinary circumstances, payments on securities loans are not debt-financed income.[46]

The IRS ruled that a tax-exempt employees' trust (which was, in general, subject to tax on unrelated business taxable income[47]), which was a partner in a partnership that was organized to make investments in securities, could experience unrelated debt-financed income.[48] The partnership borrowed money to invest in securities and became primarily liable for repayment of the debt and for payment of interest on the debt, with the partners secondarily liable on a pro rata basis. The IRS held that the indebtedness was an acquisition indebtedness because it was incurred to acquire property for investment purposes, the incurring of the debt was not inherent in the performance of the trust's tax-exempt function (namely, to receive employer and employee contributions and to use them and increments on them to provide retirement benefits to the plan participants[49]), and the investment property was not substantially related to the exercise of the trust's tax-exempt purposes. Thus, whether the trust's investment activity can result in unrelated business taxable income under these rules is determined by whether its share of any partnership income was derived from or on account of debt-financed property.[50] Subsequently, a court held that the income from securities purchased on margin by a qualified profit sharing plan was unrelated debt-financed income, in that this type of indebtedness was not inherent in the exercise of the trust's exempt function.[51] Similarly, another court concluded that, when a tax-exempt or-

---

[44] IRC § 514(c)(5).
[45] IRC § 514(c)(6). In general, Reg. § 1.514(c)-1.
[46] IRC § 514(c)(8). See § 27.1(d).
[47] Rev. Rul. 71-311, 1971-2 C.B. 184.
[48] Rev. Rul. 74-197, 1974-1 C.B. 143.
[49] Reg. § 1.401-1(a)(2)(i).
[50] Reg. § 1.702-1(a).
[51] Elliot Knitwear Profit Sharing Plan v. Comm'r, 71 T.C. 765 (1979), aff'd, 614 F.2d 347 (3d Cir. 1980). Also Ocean Cove Corp. Retirement Plan & Trust v. United States, 657 F. Supp. 776 (S.D. Fla. 1987); Alabama Central Credit Union v. United States, *supra* note 43.

ganization withdrew the accumulated cash values in life insurance policies and reinvested the proceeds in income-paying investments, it created an acquisition indebtedness and thus unrelated debt-financed income, even though the organization did not have an obligation to repay the funds.[52] Likewise, a court held that the interest earned on certificates of deposit obtained by a tax-exempt organization was taxable as debt-financed income because the certificates were acquired using the proceeds of a loan that was collateralized with other certificates of deposit previously purchased by the organization.[53]

By contrast, the IRS examined similar practices engaged in by a trust forming part of a leveraged employee stock ownership plan (ESOP).[54] (An ESOP is a technique of corporate finance designed to build beneficial equity ownership of shares in an employer corporation into its employees substantially in proportion to their relative income without requiring any cash outlay on their part, any reduction in pay or other employee benefits, or the surrender of any rights on the part of the employees.[55]) This type of trust generally acquires stock of the employer with the proceeds of a loan made to it by a financial institution. Consequently, the IRS concluded that a leveraged ESOP's capital growth and stock ownership objectives were part of its tax-exempt function[56] and "borrowing to purchase employer securities is an integral part of accomplishing these objectives."[57] Thus, the borrowing was not acquisition indebtedness and the securities thereby purchased were not debt-financed property. But the IRS cautioned that these circumstances are "distinguishable from a situation in which a pension or profit sharing plan that satisfies the requirements of [IRC] section 401(a) borrows money to purchase securities of the employer; in the latter situation the exempt trusts borrowing to purchase employer securities could result in unrelated business income within the meaning of [IRC] section 512."[58]

For these purposes, the term *acquisition indebtedness* generally does not include indebtedness incurred by a qualified organization in acquiring or improving any real property.[59] A *qualified organization* is an operating educational institution,[60] any affiliated support organization,[61] and a tax-exempt multiparent title-holding organization,[62] as well as any trust that constitutes a pension trust.[63] Nonetheless, in computing the unrelated income of a shareholder or beneficiary

---

[52] Mose & Garrison Siskin Memorial Found., Inc. v. United States, 603 F. Supp. 91 (E.D. Tenn. 1985), aff'd, 790 F.2d 480 (6th Cir. 1986).

[53] Kern County Elec. Pension Fund v. Comm'r, 96 T.C. 845 (1991), *aff'd in unpub opinion* (9th Cir. 1993).

[54] IRC § 4975(e)(7).

[55] S. Rep. No. 94-938, 94th Cong., 2d Sess. (1976).

[56] IRC § 401(a).

[57] Rev. Rul. 79-122, 1979-1 C.B. 204, 206.

[58] *Id*. Cf. Rev. Rul. 79-349, 1979-2 C.B. 233.

[59] IRC § 514(c)(9)(A).

[60] That is, one described in IRC § 170(b)(1)(A)(ii). See § 11.3(a).

[61] That is, one described in IRC § 509(a)(3). See § 11.3(c).

[62] That is, one described in IRC § 501(c)(25). See § 18.2(b).

[63] That is, one described in IRC § 401. The definition of *qualified organization* is the subject of IRC § 514(c)(9)(C).

of a disqualified holder (namely, a multiparent title-holding organization[64]) of an interest in a multiparent title-holding entity attributable to the interest, the holder's pro rata share of the items of income that are treated as gross income derived from an unrelated business (without regard to the exception for debt-financed property) is taken into account as gross income of the disqualified holder derived from an unrelated business; the holder's pro rata share of deductions are likewise taken into account.[65]

Thus, under this exception, income from investments in real property is not treated as income from debt-financed property and therefore as unrelated business income. Mortgages are not considered real property for purposes of this exception.[66]

This exception for real property in the debt-financed income rules is available for investments only if the following six restrictions are satisfied:

1. Where the purchase price for an acquisition or improvement of real property is a fixed amount determined as of the date of the acquisition or completion of the improvement (the *fixed price restriction*);[67]

2. Where the amount of the indebtedness, any amount payable with respect to the indebtedness, or the time for making any payment of that amount, is not dependent (in whole or in part) on revenues, income, or profits derived from the property (the *participating loan restriction*);[68]

3. Where the property is not, at any time after the acquisition, leased by the qualified organization to the seller or to a person related[69] to the seller (the *leaseback restriction*);[70]

4. In the case of a pension trust, where the seller or lessee of the property is not a disqualified person[71] (the *disqualified person restriction*);[72]

5. Where the seller or a person related to the seller (or a person related to the plan with respect to which a pension trust was formed) is not providing financing in connection with the acquisition of the property (the *seller-financing restriction*);[73]

6. If the investment in the property is held through a partnership, where certain additional requirements are satisfied by the partnership, namely,

---

[64] IRC § 514(c)(9)(F)(iii). However an entity that is this type of shareholder or beneficiary is not a disqualified holder if it otherwise constitutes a qualified organization by reason of being an educational institution, a supporting organization of an educational institution, or a pension trust (*id.*).

[65] IRC § 514(c)(9)(F)(i), (ii). The purpose of this rule is to prevent the benefits of this exception from flowing through the title-holding company to its shareholders or beneficiaries (unless those organizations themselves are qualified organizations (see *supra* note 63).

[66] IRC § 514(c)(9)(B), last sentence.

[67] IRC § 514(c)(9)(B)(i).

[68] IRC § 514(c)(9)(B)(ii).

[69] As described in IRC § 267(b) or IRC § 707(b).

[70] IRC § 514(c)(9)(B)(iii).

[71] As described in IRC § 4975(e)(2)(C), (E), (H).

[72] IRC § 514(c)(9)(B)(iv).

[73] IRC § 514(C)(9)(B)(v).

(a) the partnership satisfies the rules in the foregoing five circumstances, and (b)(i) all of the partners are qualified organizations,[74] (ii) each allocation to a partner of the partnership is a qualified allocation,[75] or (iii) the partnership meets the rules of a special exception (the *partnership restrictions*).[76]

However, for acquisitions (and leases entered into) on or after January 1, 1994, (1) the leaseback restriction and the disqualified person restriction are relaxed to permit a limited leaseback of debt-financed real property to the seller (or a person related to the seller) or to a disqualified person;[77] and (2) the fixed price restriction and the participating loan restriction are relaxed for certain sales of real property foreclosed on by financial institutions.[78]

An example of the flexibility of the potential application of the unrelated debt-financed income rules was the suggestion made by some within the IRS that this type of income is realized by tax-exempt organizations in the lending of securities transaction.[79] This conclusion was arrived at by way of the contention that the tax-exempt institution is not actually lending the securities but is "borrow-

---

[74] For this purpose, an organization cannot be treated as a qualified organization if any income of the organization is unrelated business income (IRC § 514(c)(9)(B), penultimate sentence).

[75] A *qualified allocation* is one described in IRC § 168(h)(6) (see *infra* § 5(g), text accompanied by note 130).

[76] IRC § 514(c)(9)(B)(vi). This special exception is the subject of IRC § 514(c)(9)(E). Rules similar to those of this situation also apply in the case of any pass-thru entity other than a partnership and in the case of tiered partnerships and other entities (IRC § 514(c)(9)(D)).

[77] This exception applies only where (1) no more than 25 percent of the leasable floor space in a building (or complex of buildings) is leased back to the seller (or related party) or to the disqualified person and (2) the lease is on commercially reasonable terms, independent of the sale and other transactions (IRC § 514(c)(9)(G)). A leaseback to a disqualified person remains subject to the prohibited transaction rules (IRC § 4975).

The fixed price restriction and the participating loan restriction are not subject to this refinement. Thus, for example, income from real property acquired with seller financing, where the timing or amount of payment is based on revenue, income, or profits from the property, generally continues to be treated as income from debt-financed property, unless another exception applies.

[78] For this purpose, the term *financial institutions* includes financial institutions in conservatorship or receivership, certain affiliates of financial institutions, and government corporations that succeed to the rights and interests of a receiver or conservator (IRC § 514(c)(9)(H)(iv)).

This exception is limited to instances where (1) a qualified organization obtained real property from a financial institution that acquired the property by foreclosure (or after an actual or imminent default), or the property was held by the selling financial institution when it entered into conservatorship or receivership; (2) any gain recognized by the financial institution with respect to the property is ordinary income; (3) the stated principal amount of the seller financing does not exceed the financial institution's outstanding indebtedness (including accrued but unpaid interest) with respect to the property at the time of foreclosure or default; and (4) the present value of the maximum amount payable pursuant to any participation feature cannot exceed 30 percent of the total purchase price of the property (including contingent payments) (IRC § 514(c)(9)(H)(i)–(iii), (v)).

In general, Ferguson & Brown, "More Investment Options Are Available for Tax-Exempt Organizations," 4 *J. Tax. Exempt Orgs.* (No. 4) 22 (Jan./Feb. 1993); McDowell, "Taxing Leveraged Investments of Charitable Organizations: What Is the Rationale?," 39 *Case W. Res. L. Rev.* (No. 3) 705 (1988–1989).

[79] See § 27.1(d).

ing" the collateral, thereby making—so the argument goes—the entire interest (and perhaps the dividend or interest equivalent) taxable.

However, this matter was clarified by the enactment of a special rule[80] and earlier by an IRS ruling that the income from the investment of the collateral posted by the broker is not unrelated debt-financed income, since the organization did not incur the indebtedness "for the purpose of making additional investments."[81]

The intent of these rules is to treat an otherwise tax-exempt organization in the same manner as an ordinary business enterprise to the extent that the exempt organization purchases property through the use of borrowed funds.[82] The IRS recalled this intent in passing on the tax status of indebtedness owed to a tax-exempt labor union by its wholly owned subsidiary title-holding company resulting from a loan to pay debts incurred to acquire two income-producing office buildings. The IRS ruled that this *interorganizational indebtedness* was not an acquisition indebtedness because the "very nature of the title-holding company as well as the parent-subsidiary relationship show this indebtedness to be merely a matter of accounting between the organizations rather than an indebtedness as contemplated by" these rules.[83]

The income of a tax-exempt organization that is attributable to a short sale of publicly traded stock through a broker is not unrelated debt-financed income and thus is not taxable as unrelated business income.[84] This is because, although a short sale creates an obligation, it does not create an indebtedness for tax purposes[85] and thus there is no acquisition indebtedness. This position of the IRS is not intended to cause any inference with respect to a borrowing of property other than publicly traded stock sold short through a broker.

§ 29.4 COMPUTATION OF UNRELATED DEBT-FINANCED INCOME

The computation of unrelated debt-financed income (the amount subject to tax) is made by applying to the total gross income (and deductions attributable) to debt-financed property the following fraction: the average acquisition indebtedness for the tax year over the average adjusted basis of the property during the tax year.

For purposes of the numerator of this fraction, acquisition indebtedness is to be averaged over the tax year.[86] This averaging mechanism precludes a tax-exempt organization from avoiding a tax by using other available funds to pay off the indebtedness immediately before any fixed determination date. If debt-

---

[80] IRC § 514(c)(8) (see text accompanied by *supra* note 45).

[81] Rev. Rul. 78–88, 1978-1 C.B. 163, 164.

[82] H. Rep. No. 91-413, 91st Cong., 1st Sess. 46 (1969).

[83] Rev. Rul. 77-72, 1977-1 C.B. 157, 158. The Department of Treasury is authorized to prescribe regulations to prevent the circumvention of these rules through the use of *segregated asset accounts* (IRC § 514(g)).

[84] Rev. Rul. 95-8, 1995-1 C.B. 107.

[85] Deputy v. du Pont, 308 U.S. 488 (1940).

[86] IRC § 514(c)(7).

financed property is disposed of during the year, *average acquisition indebtedness* means the highest acquisition indebtedness during the preceding 12 months. Absent this rule, a tax-exempt organization could avoid tax by using other resources to discharge indebtedness before the end of one tax year and dispose of property after the beginning of the next tax year.

For purposes of the denominator of this fraction, adjusted basis is the average adjusted basis for the portion of the year during which the property is held by the tax-exempt organization. The use of average adjusted basis is only for purposes of determining the fraction. Where property is disposed of, gain or loss will, as usual, be computed with reference to adjusted basis at the time of disposition.

The essence of the foregoing rules[87] may be illustrated by the following example:

A tax-exempt organization acquires property for the production of income on July 1, 1998, for $100,000, of which $80,000 is financed (that is, there is an $80,000 acquisition indebtedness). As of December 31, 1998, the organization has satisfied $10,000 of the debt, by one payment (on September 1, 1998) and has claimed $2,500 in straight-line depreciation. For 1998, 75.9 percent of the income (less appropriate deductions) from the property is taxable.

To determine this percentage, the average acquisition indebtedness for 1998 must be computed. This amount is $75,000, ascertained as follows:

(1) Debt	(2) Months Outstanding	(3) (1) × (2)
$80,000	3	$240,000
70,000	3	210,000
	6	$450,000

(3) divided by (2) equals $75,000, which is the weighted average for the six-month period involved.

To determine the average adjusted basis, it is necessary to compute the basis at the beginning (here, $100,000) and at the end of the tax year ($97,500, that is, original basis less depreciation). The average adjusted basis ($100,000 divided by $97,500 divided by 2) is $98,750.

The applicable percentage thus becomes 75.9 percent ($75,000/$98,750).

If property is distributed by a corporation in liquidation to a tax-exempt organization, the exempt organization uses the basis of the distributing corporation, with adjustment for any gain recognized on the distribution either to the exempt organization or to the taxable corporation. An example of the former would be where a tax-exempt organization had an acquisition indebtedness applicable to its stock in the distributing corporation and an illustration of the latter would be an instance of recapture of depreciation.[88] This rule prevents a tax-exempt organization from acquiring the property in a taxable subsidiary to secure

---

[87] IRC § 514(a)–(c).
[88] IRC §§ 1245, 1250.

accelerated depreciation during the first several years of the life of the property, enabling the subsidiary to pay off a large part of the indebtedness during those years, after which the exempt organization would obtain a stepped-up basis on liquidation of the subsidiary.[89] If property is used partly for tax-exempt and partly for nonexempt purposes, the income and deductions attributable to the exempt uses are excluded from the computation of unrelated debt-financed income and allocations are made, where appropriate, for acquisition indebtedness, adjusted basis, and deductions assignable to the property.[90]

§ 29.5 TAX-EXEMPT ENTITY LEASING RULES

The federal income tax law contains a body of law concerning certain situations where tax-exempt organizations lease real and/or personal property in practices known as *tax-exempt entity leasing*. These rules have two purposes. One is to impose restrictions on the federal tax benefits of leasing property (including relationships evidenced by service contracts) to tax-exempt organizations. The other is to place restrictions on the federal tax benefits available to investors in partnerships composed of taxable and tax-exempt entities.

These rules were designed to remedy three perceived abuses. One concern was that lessors indirectly made investment tax incentives available to tax-exempt organizations through reduced rents. Another concern was that tax-exempt organizations were being encouraged to enter into sale-leaseback transactions with taxpayers that resulted in substantial revenue losses to the federal government. The third perceived abuse was that partnerships that included tax-exempt and taxable entities could allocate all tax losses to taxable entities, while tax-exempt entities shared in profits and cash distributions.

(a) Introduction

During the early 1980s, Congress became concerned that, in some cases, the tax-exempt status of nonprofit organizations was being abused by techniques designed to shift to taxpaying persons the tax benefits of ownership of property (chiefly, the depreciation deduction[91]) that in actuality was owned by the tax-

---

[89] IRC § 514(d); Reg. § 1.514(d)-1.
[90] IRC § 514(e); Reg. §1.514(e)-1. Also Florida Farm Bur. Fed'n. v. Comm'r, 65 T.C. 1118 (1975). In general, Krasity & Indenbaum, "Tax-Exempt Organizations and Section 514: The Taxation of Income Generated by Bond Reserve Funds and Similar Accounts," 19 *J. Real Estate Tax.* (No. 2) 137 (1992); Indenbaum & Krasity, "Tax-Exempt Entities and Limited Partnerships; Section 514(c)(9)(E)'s Inadequate Response to the Problem of Unrelated Debt-Financed Income," 18 *J. Real Estate Tax.* (No. 1) 37 (1990); Weitz, "Unresolved Issues Remain for Qualified Organizations in Real Estate Partnerships," 73 *J. Tax.* 332 (1990); Williamson, Duren & Grigorian, "How Exempt Organizations Can Avoid Unrelated Debt-Financed Income on Realty," 6 *J. Tax. Inv.* (No. 4) 236 (1989); Larson, "Tax Exempt Organizations and Unrelated Debt Financed Income: Does the Problem Persist?," 61 *N. D. L. Rev.* (No. 1) 31 (1985); Beller, "Exempt Organizations: Taxation of Debt-Financed Income," 24 *Tax Law.* 489 (1971).
[91] IRC § 168.

exempt organizations. Generally, of course, the depreciation deduction and other tax benefits of property ownership (such as the former investment tax credit[92]) are not available for property owned by tax-exempt organizations inasmuch as they are not usually taxable, and thus usually do not have a need for deductions and credits. A specific provision disallowed the investment tax credit for property leased to or otherwise used by a tax-exempt organization.[93] However, until the federal tax law was revised in 1984, a comparable provision was not in the depreciation deduction rules.

A number of transactions involving sales and leasebacks by tax-exempt organizations or governmental units achieved considerable publicity in the months preceding the 1984 tax law revisions.[94] One result of this attention was a congressional report on the subject.[95]

Consequently, even though a tax-exempt organization is not generally permitted to have the benefits of the depreciation deduction that normally accompany the ownership of property, Congress believed that some tax-exempt organizations were indirectly enjoying these tax benefits by leasing property, with the value of the tax deductions available to the lessor reflected in the lease payments. The result was enactment of the tax-exempt entity leasing rules.[96]

In general, the depreciation deduction is determined by utilizing, as phrased in the statute, the applicable depreciation method, the applicable recovery period, and the applicable convention.[97] The applicable recovery periods run from 3 years to 31.5 years, with the 31.5-year period for nonresidential real property.[98]

The law embodies the concept of *alternative depreciation systems*.[99] The alternative depreciation systems utilize the straight line method (without regard to salvage value), the applicable convention, and recovery periods that run from the appropriate class life[100] to 40 years, with the 40-year period for nonresidential real property.[101] The alternative depreciation system is to be used, *inter alia*, with respect to tax-exempt use property.[102]

---

[92] Pre-1986 IRC § 38.

[93] Pre-1986 IRC § 48(a)(4).

[94] For example, Doyle & Hartle, "Tax Avoidance 101," *Wash. Post*, June 2, 1983; "Selling a Bridge," *N. Y. Times*, April 10, 1983; "Financing of Art Center Is Somewhat Convoluted," *Wash. Post*, April 3, 1983; Curran, "Intriguing Twists in Real Estate," *Fortune*, March 21, 1983; Webb, Jr., "Associations Can Use the Tax Benefits of Leasing—At Least for Now," 34 *Ass'n Mgmt.* 141 (Aug. 1982). In general, Henze II & Simpkins, "Should Tax-Exempt Lessees Profit from Tax Benefits?," 8 *Review of Tax. of Indiv.* (No. 3) 240 (Summer 1984); McIlwain, "The Sale and Leasing Back of Real Estate by Tax-Exempt Organizations," 14 *Coll. Law Digest* (No. 6) 154 (1984).

[95] "Tax and Budget Issues Related to Leasing by Non-taxable Entities," Report of Subcommittee on Oversight, House Committee on Ways and Means, U.S. House of Representatives, May 25, 1983.

[96] IRC § 168(h).

[97] IRC § 168(a).

[98] IRC § 168(c).

[99] IRC § 168(g).

[100] IRC § 168(g)(3).

[101] IRC § 168(g)(2).

[102] IRC § 168(g)(1)(B).

(b) Summary of Rules

The essence of the tax-exempt entity leasing rules is to force investors to compute their depreciation deduction over a longer recovery period where the property is *tax-exempt use property.*

(c) Definition of *Tax-Exempt Entity*

For purposes of these rules, the term *tax-exempt entity* includes any organization that is tax-exempt under the federal income tax law (other than a farmer's cooperative[103]).[104]

(d) Definition of *Related Entity*

For purposes of these rules, one entity is *related* to another entity if the two entities have "significant common purposes and substantial common membership" or "directly or indirectly substantial common direction or control."[105]

An entity is related to another entity if either entity owns (directly or through one or more entities) a 50 percent or greater interest in the capital or profits of the other entity.[106]

An entity is related to another entity with respect to a transaction if the transaction is part of an attempt by the entities to avoid the application of these rules.[107]

(e) Recovery Periods

The tax-exempt entity rules apply with respect to both tangible personal property and real property. Where these rules apply, the depreciation deduction must be determined by using the straight-line method (without regard to salvage

---

[103] See § 18.11.

[104] IRC § 168(h)(2)(A)(ii). Governmental bodies and their instrumentalities are also considered tax-exempt entities (IRC § 168(h)(2)(A)(i), (D)), as are certain foreign organizations (IRC §§ 168(h)(2)(A)(iii), 168(h)(2)(B), 168(h)(2)(C)). Special rules deem certain previously tax-exempt organizations to be tax-exempt entities where they were tax-exempt during the five-year period ending on the date the property involved was first leased to the organization (IRC § 168(h)(2)(E)(i)), with a special election for IRC § 501(c)(12) organizations (IRC § 168(h)(2)(E)(ii)). This rule applies to successor corporations (IRC § 168(h) (2) (E) (iii)). Property is *first used* by an organization when the property is first placed in service under a lease to the organization (IRC § 168(h)(2)(E) (iv) (I)). Also, property is first used by an organization, in the case of property leased to (or held by) a partnership (or other pass-through entity) in which the organization is a member, on the later of when the property is first used by the partnership (or other pass-through entity) or when the organization is first a member of the partnership (or other pass-through entity) (IRC § 168(h) (2) (E) (iv) (II)).

[105] IRC § 168(h)(4)(B).

[106] IRC § 168(h)(4)(C).

[107] IRC § 168(h)(4)(D).

value).[108] However, the recovery period must always be at least 125 percent of the lease term.[109]

Real property must be depreciated over a 40-year recovery period if it is subject to these rules.[110] Again, the recovery period must always be at least 125 percent of the lease term.[111]

(f) Definition of *Tax-Exempt Use Property*

Tax-exempt use property means that portion of any tangible property (other than nonresidential real property) that is leased[112] to a tax-exempt entity.[113]

In the case of nonresidential real property, the term *tax-exempt use property* means any portion of the property that is leased to a tax-exempt organization by means of a disqualified lease.[114] However, these rules apply to property only if the portion of the property leased to a tax-exempt entity by means of a disqualified lease is more than 35 percent of the property.[115]

A *disqualified lease* is any lease of a property to a tax-exempt organization, where one or more of the following four features or events are or were present:

1. Part or all of the property was financed (directly or indirectly) by a tax-exempt obligation[116] and the exempt organization (or a related entity) participated in the financing.

2. Under the lease, there is a fixed or determinable price purchase or sale option that involves the entity (or a related entity) or there is the equivalent of a sale option.

3. The lease has a lease term in excess of 20 years.[117]

---

[108] IRC § 168(g)(2)(C)(iii). The recovery period for qualified technological equipment (see *infra* note 113) is generally five years (IRC § 168(h)(3)).

[109] IRC § 168(g)(3)(A). Options to renew are taken into account in determining a lease term and two or more successive leases that are part of the same transaction (or a series of related transactions) with respect to the same or substantially similar property are treated as one lease (IRC § 168(i)(3)(A)).

[110] IRC § 168(g)(2). Earlier, this property would otherwise be depreciable over a 15-year recovery period under pre-1984 rules. However, the Tax Reform Act of 1984 (§ 111) generally converted the recovery period to 18 years, with the recovery period extended to 19 years in 1985 (Pub. L. No. 99-121, § 103) (pre-1986 IRC § 168(j)(2)(F)).

[111] IRC § 168(g)(3)(A). For purposes of the definition of a *lease term* (see *supra* note 109) in the case of real property, an option to renew at fair market value, determined at the time of renewal, is not taken into account (IRC § 168(i)(3)(B)).

[112] The term *lease* includes any grant of a right to use property (IRC § 168(h)(7)) and may include *service contracts* (IRC § 7701(e)).

[113] IRC § 168(h)(1)(A). Property is not considered tax-exempt use property merely by reason of a *short-term lease* (IRC § 168(h)(1)(C)), nor if it is a certain type of *qualified technological equipment* (IRC § 168(h)(3)).

[114] IRC § 168(h)(1)(B)(i).

[115] IRC § 168(h)(1)(B)(iii). For purposes of these rules, improvements to a property (other than land) are not treated as a separate property (IRC § 168(h)(1)(B)(iv)).

[116] That is, an obligation the interest on which is exempt from tax under IRC § 103.

[117] See *supra* notes 109, 111.

4. The lease occurs after a sale (or other transfer) of the property by, or lease of the property from, the tax-exempt entity (or a related entity) and the property has been used by the entity (or a related entity) before the sale (or other transfer) or lease.[118]

The fourth of these items embraces the sale-leaseback feature that triggered the invocation of these rules. It requires that the property be *used* by the tax-exempt organization (or a related entity) prior to the sale or other transfer and any subsequent leasing arrangement. Also, this type of leasing arrangement does not become a disqualified lease where the property is leased within three months after the date the property is first used by the tax-exempt organization (or a related entity).[119]

In the case of any property that is leased to a partnership, the determination as to whether any portion of the property is tax-exempt use property is made by treating each tax-exempt organization partner's share[120] of the property as if it is being leased to the partner.[121] This rule also applies in the case of any pass-through entity other than a partnership and in the case of tiered partnerships and other entities.[122]

The term *tax-exempt use property* does not include any portion of a property if the portion is predominantly used by the tax-exempt entity (directly or through a partnership of which the entity is a partner) in an unrelated business.[123] As respects nonresidential real property, the rule that tax-exempt use property means that portion of the property leased to a tax-exempt entity in a disqualified lease[124] applies only if the portion of the property leased to a tax-exempt entity in a disqualified lease is more than 35 percent of the property.[125] Any portion of a property used in unrelated business is not to be treated as leased to a tax-exempt entity in a disqualified lease.[126]

This is best illustrated by an example. Assume that a tax-exempt entity leases 100 percent of a building for a term of 21 years (a disqualified lease). Eighty percent of the building is used in the tax-exempt organization's unrelated trade or business and 20 percent is used in its tax-exempt function. No portion of the building constitutes tax-exempt use property because the portion used in a disqualified lease (20 percent) is less than 35 percent of the property.[127]

(g) Partnership Arrangements

It is becoming more common for a tax-exempt organization to utilize property owned by a partnership in which the organization is a partner.[128] However, the

---

[118] IRC § 168(h)(1)(B)(ii).
[119] IRC § 168(h)(1)(B)(v).
[120] IRC § 168(h)(6)(C).
[121] IRC § 168(h)(5)(A).
[122] IRC § 168(h)(5)(B).
[123] IRC § 168(h)(1)(D).
[124] IRC § 168(h)(1)(B)(i).
[125] IRC § 168(h)(1)(B)(iii).
[126] IRC § 168(h)(1)(D), last sentence.
[127] H. Rep. 99-426, 99th Cong., 1st Sess. 878 (1986); S. Rep. 99-313, 99th Cong., 2d Sess. 895 (1986).
[128] See Chapter 32.

tax-exempt entity leasing rules may cause the property in a partnership to be treated as tax-exempt use property.

The rules provide that if any property, which would not otherwise be tax-exempt use property, is owned by a "partnership which has both a tax-exempt entity and a person who is not a tax-exempt entity as partners," and any allocation to the tax-exempt entity of partnership items is not a qualified allocation, an amount equal to the tax-exempt organization's proportionate share of the property is treated as tax-exempt use property.[129]

A *qualified allocation* is any allocation to a tax-exempt organization that (1) is consistent with allocation to the organization of the same distributive share of each item of income, gain, loss, deduction, credit, and basis, and the share remains the same during the entire period the organization is a partner in the partnership, and (2) has substantial economic effect.[130]

A tax-exempt organization's *proportionate share* of property owned by a partnership is determined on the basis of the organization's share of partnership items of income or gain, whichever results in the largest proportionate share.[131] If a tax-exempt organization's share of partnership items of income or gain varies during the period the organization is a partner in a partnership, the proportionate share is the highest share the organization may receive.[132]

These rules also apply in the case of any *pass-thru* entity other than a partnership and in the case of tiered partnerships and other entities.[133]

Proposed and temporary regulations to accompany the tax-exempt entity leasing rules were issued in 1985.[134] These regulations, issued in question-and-answer format, pertain to a variety of matters, including the computation of recovery deductions,[135] the application of the rules with respect to buildings that are partially tax-exempt use property,[136] application of the *predominantly used* test,[137] the rules concerning qualified technological equipment,[138] the rules used to determine the length of a lease,[139] and the rules applicable to property owned by a partnership in which one or more partners is a tax-exempt entity.[140]

Following the creation of these rules, there were efforts to avoid them by causing a taxable entity controlled by a tax-exempt organization to be a partner in a partnership (where the allocation of partnership items was not a qualified one[141] in lieu of the tax-exempt organization. Congress acted to thwart this technique by

---

[129] IRC § 168(h)(6)(A).

[130] IRC § 168(h)(6)(B). The concept of *substantial economic effect* is the subject of IRC § 704(b)(2).

[131] IRC § 168(h)(6)(C)(i).

[132] IRC § 168(h)(6)(C)(ii).

[133] IRC § (168)(h)(6)(E).

[134] Reg. § 1.168(j)-1T (T.D. 8033).

[135] *Id.*, Q-1, A-1.

[136] *Id.*, Q-4, A-4.

[137] *Id.*, Q-9, A-9.

[138] *Id.*, Q-12, A-12.

[139] *Id.*, Q-17, A-17.

[140] *Id.*, Q-21, A-21. In general, Yanowitz & Purcell, "An Analysis of the Just-issued Temporary Regulations on Tax-Exempt Entity Leasing," 63 *J. Tax.* (No. 2) 112 (1985).

[141] See *supra* note 130.

causing the taxable subsidiary to be considered a tax-exempt organization for purposes of the tax-exempt entity leasing rules.

This result was occasioned by introduction of the term tax-exempt controlled entity.[142] A *tax-exempt controlled entity* means any corporation (not otherwise a tax-exempt entity) if 50 percent or more (in value) of the stock in the corporation is held by one or more tax-exempt entities.[143] In the case of a corporation the stock of which is publicly traded on an established securities market, stock held by a tax-exempt entity is not taken into account for this purpose unless the entity holds at least five percent (in value) of the stock in the corporation.[144] Also, related entities[145] are treated as one entity[146] and a tax-exempt entity is treated as holding stock that it holds constructively.[147]

A tax-exempt controlled entity can irrevocably elect to not be treated as a tax-exempt entity for these purposes.[148] The consequence of this election is that any gain recognized by a tax-exempt entity on any disposition of an interest in a tax-exempt controlled entity (and any dividend or interest received or accrued by a tax-exempt entity from the tax-exempt controlled entity) is treated as unrelated business taxable income.[149]

---

[142] IRC § 168(h)(6)(F)(i).

[143] IRC § 168(h)(6)(F)(iii)(I).

[144] IRC § 168(h)(6)(F)(iii)(II).

[145] See *supra* notes 105–107.

[146] IRC § 168(h)(6)(F)(iii)(II).

[147] IRC § 168(h)(6)(F)(iii)(III). The constructive ownership rules are those of IRC § 318, determined without regard to the 50-percent limitation in IRC § 318(a)(2)(C).

[148] IRC § 168(h)(6)(F)(ii)(I).

[149] IRC § 168(h)(6)(F)(ii)(II). For this purpose, only dividends that are properly allocable to income of the tax-exempt controlled entity that was not taxed are taken into account (IRC § 168(h)(6)(F)(ii)). (The unrelated business income rules are the subject of Part Five; see, particularly, IRC § 512(b)(13), discussed in §§ 27.1(n), 31.3.)

Inter-Organizational Structures and Operational Forms

Combinations of Tax-Exempt Organizations

One of the most striking and significant practices of tax-exempt organizations today is the structuring of activities, which in an earlier era were or would have been in a single tax-exempt entity, so that they are undertaken by two or more related organizations, either tax-exempt or taxable.

This chapter contains an analysis of combinations of tax-exempt organizations, while the following two chapters discuss the utilization by tax-exempt organizations of other types of entities.

§ 30.1 OVERVIEW OF BIFURCATION

The reasons for the advent of combinations of tax-exempt organizations are varying and manifold. In the early years, the law guided most of the structuring, such as the placement of lobbying activities by a charitable organization[1] into a separate organization[2] or the placement of property with a potential for incurring liability into a title-holding corporation.[3] Likewise, as discussed in the next chapter, the law frequently dictated the placement by a tax-exempt organization of a substantially unrelated business into a for-profit subsidiary.

---

[1] That is, an organization described in IRC § 501(c)(3) and exempt from federal income taxation under IRC § 501(a).

[2] See § 20.7.

[3] See § 18.2.

Cutbacks in government funding and reductions in traditional forms of revenue (such as dues) have caused many tax-exempt organizations to become more innovative and entrepreneurial in the search for operating monies, spawning both tax-exempt and for-profit subsidiaries. More sophisticated management of and advisors to tax-exempt organizations have also led to extensive utilization of one or more separate organizations.

Underlying the concept of interorganizational forms is the precept that a tax-exempt organization may be perceived as a bundle of activities.[4] In this setting, then, the management, legal, and/or other considerations should be regarded as determining whether the activities of a tax-exempt organization are properly housed in one legal entity or whether one or more of the activities of the organization are to be spun off and placed in one or more other legal entities. For example, a charitable organization may consist of a bundle of publication, seminar, research, scholarship, administrative, and lobbying activities; to retain its tax-exempt status, it may, as noted, have to place the legislative activities in a separate organization. As another example, a business association[5] may consist of a bundle of membership service, industry promotion, certification, lobbying, administrative, and research activities; to attract deductible charitable gifts and foundation grants to support its research activities, it generally will have to place the research activities in a separate organization.[6]

The early manifestation of this phenomenon as reflected in federal tax law was simple *bifurcation*: the assignment of activities to two related organizations. Frequently, both of the organizations were tax-exempt, such as, as noted, the use of a tax-exempt title-holding corporation by another tax-exempt organization or the use of a tax-exempt fund-raising organization by a government college or university.[7] In some instances, as noted in the next chapter, one of the two related organizations is taxable, such as a for-profit business with a related foundation or a tax-exempt organization with a for-profit subsidiary.

The concept of bifurcation in the tax-exempt organizations context was given a meaningful boost and degree of acceptance by Congress when the supporting organization rules[8] were enacted in 1969. On that occasion, Congress gave recognition to the widespread application of the bifurcation principle in the exempt organizations setting. These rules gave another official sanction to the idea of housing related activities in two (or more) tax-exempt organizations.[9]

As managers of and planners for tax-exempt organizations became more sophisticated, they utilized the bifurcation concept more readily. Thus, it became more common, for example, for the leadership of a trade or business association to establish a related foundation, political action committee, and/or for-profit subsidiary. Soon, however, the pattern of using two organizations, where before

---

[4] This is the principle underlying the *fragmentation rule* (see § 26.2(d)).
[5] See Chapter 13.
[6] See *infra* § 2.
[7] See §§ 17.2, 11.3(b)(v).
[8] See § 11.3(c).
[9] As noted in Chapter 31, Congress earlier recognized the use by a tax-exempt organization of a related for-profit subsidiary but, until recently, that technique was not frequently utilized.

there might be or was only one, began to be augmented by the use of many organizations. Thus, for example, today the leadership of that association would be likely to more readily implement the utilization of all three related entities, so that the association's activities become allocated among four organizations.

Today, the health care community is leading the way in organizational restructuring. Yesterday's hospital often is today's multiorganizational system, replete with several health care entities, a fund-raising foundation, a management company, and an array of other tax-exempt and taxable organizations. These systems may well entail twenty, thirty, or more organizations, coordinated by a tax-exempt managing entity.[10] Frequently, in a structure that is also being utilized outside the health care setting, there is a *holding company*, or management company, that coordinates the system.

While it is by no means necessary for a tax-exempt organization to spread its activities over tens of tax-exempt and taxable organizations, the basic concepts of restructuring and the potential for use of various operational forms offer great opportunities and flexibility for today's tax-exempt organization in the performance of its exempt functions and in the financing of its operations in the most legally efficacious and efficient manner. As an illustration of these points, a tax-exempt fraternal beneficiary society[11] that conducted a variety of charitable activities deemed it appropriate to reorganize and establish five additional exempt organizations, including four public charities: a school,[12] a home for the aged,[13] a title-holding company,[14] a publicly supported charity,[15] and a supporting organization[16] for the three other charitable entities.[17]

§ 30.2   CHARITABLE ORGANIZATIONS AS SUBSIDIARIES

One of the more common developments in recent years in the law of tax-exempt organizations is the establishment by a tax-exempt organization, which is not itself a charitable organization, of an auxiliary charitable organization for program operation and/or fund-raising purposes. The auxiliary charitable organization functions in tandem with the sponsoring (or parent) organization to achieve com-

---

[10] Health care provider reorganizations and combinations are discussed in Hyatt & Hopkins, *The Law of Tax-Exempt Healthcare Organizations* (New York: John Wiley & Sons, Inc., 1995), Chapter 20. In general, Hill, "Separation Is the Key to Using Complex Structures in Exempt Organizations," 6 *J. Tax. Exempt Orgs.* (No. 5) 195 (Mar./Apr. 1995).

[11] See § 18.4(a).

[12] See § 11.3(a).

[13] See § 11.3(b)(iv).

[14] See § 18.2(a).

[15] See § 11.3(b)(i).

[16] See § 11.3(c).

[17] Priv. Ltr. Rul. 9527043. A court case that the IRS lost could have had enormous adverse implications for these forms of restructuring had the IRS prevailed, in that the government asserted six forms of private benefit in the arrangement, including the payment of rent, use of common employees, overlapping boards of directors, and similarity of organizations' names (Bob Jones Univ. Museum & Gallery, Inc. v. Comm'r, 71 T.C.M. 3120 (1996)). In the case, a taxable nonprofit university spun off a tax-exempt educational museum to be operated on the university's campus.

mon objectives.[18] Frequently termed a *related foundation*, the related charitable organization is rarely a private foundation, due to its ability to qualify as a publicly supported organization or a supporting organization.[19]

(a) Charitable Subsidiaries of Associations

Typical of this pattern is the charitable organization related to a trade, business, or professional association that qualifies as a tax-exempt business league.[20] The association-related foundation can engage in many activities, principally publishing, seminars, research, scholarships, fellowships, awards, and a variety of services. These activities—which can qualify as charitable, educational, and/or scientific programs—are either activities previously undertaken by the association or activities initiated by the foundation, or a combination of both. The foundation's activities can be funded by gifts and grants, leaving the association's revenues (such as membership dues) to support the remaining association activities.

When properly organized and operated, the auxiliary charitable organization is eligible to receive deductible charitable contributions and grants from private foundations and others. The foundation can administer its own programs, can make grants to other entities (including its parent organization) in furtherance of charitable purposes, or can utilize a combination of both approaches. Of course, where the auxiliary charitable organization is not properly organized or operated, it will lose or not obtain recognition of tax-exempt status.[21]

Many business leagues engage in charitable activities. While doing so will not adversely affect their tax-exempt status as long as the charitable activities are in furtherance of their exempt purposes, deductible charitable gifts cannot and private foundation grants most likely will not be made available to a business league.[22] However, by transferring the charitable activities to a separate foundation, the programs become eligible for a variety of tax-enhanced fund-raising undertakings. For example, a medical society may wish to have a scholarship fund for medical students, which, by being placed in a separate organization, can qualify as a charitable organization for both tax exemption and tax-deductible charitable giving purposes. In addition to the tax advantages, this technique has the virtue of concentrating the fund-raising function in a separate organization, where its governing board realizes (or should realize) that fund-raising is a principal reason for the existence of the subsidiary.

As noted, the auxiliary charitable organization may properly make grants to its parent association, as long as it can be clearly demonstrated that the grants are for one or more qualifying charitable purposes. This type of grant must be targeted for specific charitable programs and not used by the association to defray the cost of general operations.

---

[18] Historically, the IRS has been tolerant of the use by a tax-exempt organization of a related subsidiary organization (e.g., Rev. Rul. 58-143, 1958-1 C.B. 239 (revoked on another issue)).

[19] See § 11.3(b), (c).

[20] See Chapter 13. In general, Tenenbaum, "Subsidiaries and Related Foundations: Maximizing the Returns and Minimizing the Risks to Your Association," 14 *Exempt Org. Tax. Rev.* (No. 1) 105 (July 1996).

[21] E.g., Priv. Ltr. Rul. 9017003.

[22] See Chapter 13.

In most instances, the auxiliary charitable organization is a true subsidiary of the related association, meaning that it is controlled by the association.[23] Of course, control of this nature is not mandatory, in that the foundation can be a freestanding organization, but most associations, taking into account the investment in the related foundation, are unwilling to forgo the opportunity to at least loosely control the foundation.

Also, as noted, the association-related foundation will almost certainly not be a private foundation. These foundations are frequently publicly supported, in that they receive the requisite amount of gifts, grants, and/or exempt function revenue. For example, an association-related foundation may have a program of conferences and publications, and generate sufficient qualifying support in the form of admissions fees and publications sales.[24] If an association-related foundation relies on gifts and grants for nonprivate foundation status, the related association and/or its members can be contributors, although this form of support will generally be confined as to its qualification as public support.[25] If these two approaches are unavailable, the association-related foundation can usually qualify as a supporting organization in relation to the association, where the association itself satisfies the first of these support tests.[26]

Despite the need to adhere to certain legal requirements as to organization and operation of an association-related foundation,[27] the advantages to a business league associated with an auxiliary charitable organization usually outweigh the few complexities. The ability of the association-related foundation to attract grants and deductible charitable contributions, and perhaps forms of exempt function revenue, means that, for the furtherance of the objectives concurrently served by the two organizations, there is access to financial support that otherwise would not be forthcoming. The use of a charitable organization by a business league makes support of eligible programs by private foundations much more likely, since (assuming the charitable organization is not a private foundation) the administrative rigors of the expenditure responsibility rules[28] are thereby avoided.

The growing complexity of the law of tax-exempt organizations is offering the managers of these organizations more opportunities to properly structure the organizations' functions. Developing law is producing greater flexibility in these regards, making use of the auxiliary charitable organization for trade and professional associations an extremely useful management and fund-raising technique.

(b) Charitable Subsidiaries of Other Noncharitable Exempt Organizations

Despite the growing frequency of the practice, business leagues are by no means the only type of noncharitable tax-exempt organization that can make effective

---

[23] See Chapter 31.
[24] See § 11.3(b)(iv).
[25] See § 11.3(b)(i).
[26] See § 11.3(c).
[27] See Chapter 33.
[28] See § 11.4(e).

use of an auxiliary charitable organization. Indeed, any tax-exempt organization that operates or otherwise funds charitable programs is in this category.

Auxiliary charitable organizations are usually most useful to membership organizations, because they provide the means by which the members can assist in the funding of programs of direct consequence to themselves and simultaneously deduct the payments as charitable gifts. This is one of the principal reasons that an auxiliary charitable organization can be so useful in relation to the objectives of a business league.

However, business leagues are not the only form of tax-exempt membership organizations. Membership organizations also include social welfare organizations,[29] labor organizations,[30] social clubs,[31] and veterans' organizations.[32] For example, an organization may be classified as a social welfare organization solely because of the extent of its legislative activities; its charitable functions may be housed in a related foundation. Similarly, a college or university fraternity or sorority can make effective use of an auxiliary charitable organization as a source of funding of charitable and educational programs of, or sponsored by, the fraternity or sorority,[33] and/or by means of the set-aside deduction for the funding of charitable programs.[34]

Nonetheless, there is no requirement that a tax-exempt organization must be a membership organization to utilize an auxiliary charitable organization. Indeed, any type of tax-exempt organization (or, for that matter, a taxable organization) can potentially make effective use of a related foundation. The same federal tax considerations that are discussed in the context of foundations related to business leagues[35] apply with respect to any auxiliary charitable organization, including the rules pertaining to nonprivate foundation status (although the special rule for supporting organizations of noncharitable entities also applies only with respect to social welfare organizations and labor organizations).[36]

(c) Charitable Subsidiaries of U.S. Charitable Organizations

The general reason for the establishment, by a noncharitable organization (whether tax-exempt or taxable), of a charitable organization is to attract deductible charitable contributions and perhaps private foundation and other grants. Thus, it may appear that the establishment of a charitable organization by a charitable organization solely for fund-raising purposes would be of little utility inasmuch as the qualifying gifts and grants could be made directly to the parent entity.

However, in some instances, the establishment of a separate fund-raising entity by a charitable organization is warranted. Usually the objective in these circumstances is to concentrate the fund-raising function in a single organization, essentially by creating a governing board and other support systems and re-

---

[29] See Chapter 12.
[30] See § 15.1.
[31] See Chapter 14.
[32] See § 18.10.
[33] E.g., Priv. Ltr. Rul. 8739055.
[34] See §§ 11.4(b), 28.3.
[35] See *supra* § 2(a).
[36] See Chapter 12 and § 15.1.

sources that are present principally or solely to enhance fund-raising. This enhancement can also occur by creating a governing body of which substantial contributors (and/or those that can lead to them) can be members and by giving the fund-raising entity a name that is more conducive to fund-raising than that of the parent. Further, the subsidiary may have a characteristic that the parent entity lacks, such as the ability to maintain a pooled income fund.[37]

Many of the federal tax considerations reflected above likewise pertain to the auxiliary charitable organization of a charitable parent. Thus, for example, the auxiliary charitable organization can avoid private foundation classification by using one of the three approaches generally available.[38] In some situations, the charitable parent will be one of the tax-recognized institutions, such as a church, university, college, or hospital. Indeed, the auxiliary charitable organization serving a governmental college or university is expressly referenced in the federal tax law.[39] Likewise, the supporting organization rules generally contemplate a charitable parent and a charitable subsidiary.[40]

For the most part, however, the use of an auxiliary charitable organization by a charitable organization is done to enhance the nontax aspects of fund-raising, by concentrating the fund-raising function with a group that has fund-raising as its principal, if not sole, responsibility.[41] Other uses include a function that the charitable organization parent could itself perform without jeopardizing its tax-exempt status, such as the maintenance by a hospital of a separate charitable fund from which to pay malpractice claims[42] or the maintenance by a college of an endowment fund in a separate charitable organization.[43]

Another application of the charitable subsidiary approach in this context can be seen in the reorganization phenomenon, where management considerations dictate the use of several charitable organizations.[44] While this relationship can result in instances of derivative tax exemptions, the exemption as a charitable organization may not be available on this basis where the entity is providing services to both tax-exempt and nonexempt organizations, without suitable limitations on the scope of the latter.[45]

(d) Charitable Subsidiaries of Foreign Charitable Organizations

A U.S. organization that otherwise qualifies as a charitable entity and that carries on part or all of its charitable activities in foreign countries is not precluded because of these activities from qualifying as a charitable organization.[46] For example, the charitable activity of "relief of the poor and distressed or of the underprivileged" is nonetheless charitable where the beneficiaries of the assis-

---

[37] See § 18.19.
[38] See Chapter 11.
[39] See § 11.3(b)(v).
[40] See § 11.3(c).
[41] E.g., Priv. Ltr. Rul. 9019004.
[42] Rev. Rul. 78-41, 1978-1 C.B. 148.
[43] E.g., Priv. Ltr. Rul. 9242002.
[44] See *supra* § 1.
[45] E.g., Gen. Couns. Mem. 39684. In general, see § 23.7(a).
[46] Rev. Rul. 71-460, 1971-2 C.B. 231.

tance are outside the United States. Thus, the IRS ruled tax-exempt as a charitable group an organization formed to help poor rural inhabitants of developing countries[47] and an organization created for the purpose of assisting underprivileged people in Latin America to improve their living conditions through educational and self-help programs.[48]

The foregoing distinctions are well illustrated by the tax treatment accorded the *friends organization*. This is an organization formed to solicit and receive contributions in the United States and to expend the funds on behalf of a charitable organization in another country. Its support may be provided in a variety of ways, including program or project grants, provision of equipment or materials, or scholarship or fellowship grants.

Charitable contributions made directly to an organization not created or organized in the United States, a state or territory, the District of Columbia, or a possession of the United States are not deductible.[49] Also, contributions to a United States charity that transmits the funds to a foreign charity are deductible only in certain limited circumstances.

An IRS ruling provided five illustrations of supporting domestic charities and the tax treatment to be given contributions to them.[50] Example (1) involved a mere conduit entity formed by a foreign organization. Example (2) involved a mere conduit entity formed by individuals in the United States. Example (3) involved a tax-exempt U.S. charitable organization that agrees to solicit and funnel contributions to a foreign organization. Example (4) involved a U.S. charitable organization that frequently makes grants to charities in a foreign country in furtherance of its exempt purposes, following review and approval of the uses to which the funds are to be put. Example (5) involved a U.S. charitable organization that formed a subsidiary organization in a foreign country to facilitate its tax-exempt operations there, with certain of its funds transmitted directly to the subsidiary.

This ruling stated a rationale of earmarking and of nominal as opposed to real donees, and thus concluded that contributions to the U.S. entities in examples (1), (2), and (3) in that ruling were not deductible. Contributions to the U.S. organization described in example (4) were deductible because there is no earmarking of contributions and "use of such contributions will be subject to control by the domestic organization."[51] Contributions to the U.S. organization described in example (5) were deductible because the "foreign organization is merely an administrative arm of the domestic organization,"[52] with the domestic organization considered the "real recipient"[53] of the contributions.

These rules were amplified, with the IRS describing the necessary attributes of the friends organization (in essence, the entity in example (4) of the earlier ruling).[54]

---

[47] Rev. Rul. 68-117, 1968-1 C.B. 251.

[48] Rev. Rul. 68-165, 1968-1 C.B. 253. Also Rev. Rul. 80-286, 1980-2 C.B. 179.

[49] IRC § 170(c)(2)(A); Rev. Rul. 63-252, 1963-2 C.B. 101. Also Tobjy v. Comm'r, 51 T.C.M. 449 (1986); Erselcuk v. Comm'r, 30 T.C. 962 (1958); Welti v. Comm'r, 1 T.C. 905 (1943).

[50] Rev. Rul. 63-252, *supra* note 49.

[51] *Id.*, at 104.

[52] *Id.*, at 105.

[53] *Id.*

[54] Rev. Rul. 66-79, 1966-1 C.B. 48.

Again, the IRS emphasized the earmarking problem,[55] stating that the "test in each case is whether the organization has full control of the donated funds, and discretion as to their use, so as to insure that they will be used to carry out its functions and purposes."[56] The point of this example (4) was subsequently illustrated.[57]

However, these rules concerning prohibited *earmarking* and *conduits* contemplate two separate organizations: the domestic (United States) entity and the foreign entity. Where, therefore, the domestic and foreign activities are housed in one entity (such as a corporation), and that entity qualifies as a domestic charitable organization, the rules do not apply and the contributions to the organization are deductible as charitable gifts. Thus, in one case, a court held that a corporation (a recognized charitable entity) organized under the law of a state and operating a private school in France was fully qualified as a recipient of deductible contributions from U.S. sources.[58] The organization did not have any employees, activities, or assets in the United States and all expenditures were in France. These facts led the IRS to contend that the U.S. corporation was a mere "shell" and functioned solely to funnel contributions to a foreign organization (namely, the school). But the court refused to go much beyond the fact that the corporation was a valid legal entity[59] and that the charitable giving rules do not require a substantial operational nexus in the United States in order to qualify as an eligible recipient of deductible gifts.[60]

Assuming, however, that the friends organization has been properly created

---

[55] Citing Rev. Rul. 62-113, 1962-2 C.B. 10.

[56] Rev. Rul. 66-79, *supra* note 54, at 51.

[57] Rev. Rul. 75-65, 1975-1 C.B. 79. A lawsuit challenging the deductibility of contributions made by U.S. donors to U.S.-based Jewish organizations, claiming that these organizations were mere conduits of the contributions to Israel, was initiated in 1983. However, the case was dismissed in early 1985, shortly after the Supreme Court decisions finding any correlation between tax exemption for allegedly racially discriminatory public schools and denigration of black individuals to be "speculative" (see § 5.4(a)), with the court observing that it would be "more fanciful still to assume here that the government of Israel is so responsive to changes in U.S. tax laws that the withdrawal of benefits from U.S. contributors will work any alteration whatsoever in the character of its occupation of territory it now holds by force in the Middle East" (Khalaf et al. v. Regan et al., 85-1 U.S.T.C. ¶ 9269, at 87,592 (D.D.C. 1985)).

[58] Bilingual Montessori School of Paris, Inc. v. Comm'r, 75 T.C. 480 (1980).

[59] IRC § 170(c)(2)(A).

[60] This holding created a substantial exception to the IRS's conduit rationale and exalts much form over substance (e.g., Maryland Savings-Share Insurance Corp. v. United States, 644 F.2d 16, 31 (Ct. Cl. 1981), where the court wrote of mere "different mechanics for achieving the same result"). The charitable giving rules do not differentiate between corporations but rather between organizations, and in any event a corporation for tax purposes can be different from a corporation for state law purposes. Thus, irrespective of the status of the U.S. corporation, it would not have been difficult for the court to find the school to be a "corporation" for federal tax law purposes. The fact that the domestic entity was recognized as an IRC § 501(c)(3) organization eligible for gifts deductible for estate and gift tax purposes would not have precluded this finding. Also, the court explored the legislative history and found that the rationale expressed in it—that the charitable deduction for gifts to foreign charities is not available because there are no economic and social benefits for the U.S. government—supports its conclusions. However, there can be no such U.S. benefits resulting from the conduct of a school in France, whether operated by a U.S. entity or not. Also, the legislative history states that if the gift recipient "is a domestic organization the fact that some portion of its funds is used in other countries for charitable and other purposes . . . will not affect the deductibility of the gift" (H. Rep. No. 1860, 75th Cong., 3d Sess. (1938)) but this statement does not necessarily mean that the same result occurs where all of the funds, and assets, are so used in other countries.

and operated so as to qualify as a charitable entity for purposes of charitable giving and tax exemption, a determination must also be sought as to whether it is a private foundation.[61] This type of entity can qualify as a publicly supported organization if it can demonstrate sufficient support from the general public.[62] However, since grants from substantial contributors often cannot be fully utilized in computing the public support fraction, a form of publicly supported charity status may not be available. This leaves the supporting organization rules.

These rules require the supporting organization to stand in one of three required relationships to the supported organization (the foreign organization). Because the charitable giving rules stress the independence of the qualified friends organization from the foreign charity, the weakest of the supporting relationships should be relied upon in establishing its nonprivate foundation status. This is the relationship defined in the regulations accompanying the supporting organization rules as *operated in connection with*. In connection with this relationship, the *responsiveness test* can be met by causing one or more of the officers of the foreign organization to be a director or officer of the U.S. organization.[63] The *integral part test* can be met by demonstrating that the U.S. entity makes payments of substantially all of its income to the foreign entity.[64] In essence, the difficulty is to show independence between the U.S. and foreign entities to qualify for deductible contributions but to establish a sufficient relationship between them to satisfy the requirements of the supporting organization rules.

As to the charitable contribution deduction, however, the IRS ruled that contributions to a U.S. charity that solicits contributions for a specific project of a foreign charity are deductible only under certain circumstances. Contributions made directly to a foreign organization are not deductible.[65] Organizations formed in the United States for the purpose of raising funds and merely transmitting them as a conduit to a foreign charity are not eligible to attract deductible charitable contributions.[66] Conversely, where a domestic organization makes grants to a foreign charity out of its general fund following review and approval of the specific grant or where the foreign organization is merely an administrative arm of the domestic organization, contributions to the domestic charity would be deductible.[67] The test is whether the domestic organization is the real recipient of the contributions, as it must be for the charitable contribution deduction to be allowed. The domestic organization must have full control over the donated funds and discretion as to their use.[68]

---

[61] See Chapter 11.

[62] IRC §§ 509(a)(1) (§ 170(b)(1)(A)(vi)), and 509(a)(2).

[63] Reg. § 1.509(a)-4(i)(2)(ii)(b). See § 11.3(c). The IRS, not overly enamored of the operated in connection with relationship, tends to strictly construe the responsiveness test and the integral part test (e.g., Tech. Adv. Mem. 9730002).

[64] Reg. § 1.509(a)-4(i)(3)(iii)(a). See § 11.3(c).

[65] IRC § 170(c)(2)(A).

[66] Rev. Rul. 63-252, *supra* note 49.

[67] *Id.*

[68] Rev. Rul. 75-434, 1975-2 C.B. 205; Rev. Rul. 66-79, *supra* note 54. Also see Rev. Rul. 75-65, *supra* note 57. A related issue is the availability of the estate tax deduction for charitable transfers to foreign governments or political subdivisions thereof, as discussed in Rev. Rul. 74-523, 1974-2 C.B. 304, and the cases cited therein. In general, Sanders, "Support and Conduct of Charitable Operations Abroad," *1st Annual Notre Dame Inst. on Charitable Giving, Foundations, & Trusts* 33 (1976).

As a general rule, a contribution by a corporation to a charitable organization is deductible only if the gift is to be used within the United States or its possessions exclusively for permissible charitable purposes.[69] However, where the recipient charitable organization is itself a corporation, this restriction is inapplicable.[70]

Because of the United States–Canada tax treaty, the general rule that contributions to a foreign charity are not deductible does not apply in the case of certain contributions to Canadian charities.[71] In order for the contribution to be deductible, the Canadian organization must be one that, if it were a U.S. organization, would be eligible for deductible charitable contributions. In addition, the deduction may not exceed the charitable deduction allowable under Canadian law, computed as though the corporation's taxable income from Canadian sources was its aggregate income.

§ 30.3   TAX-EXEMPT SUBSIDIARIES OF CHARITABLE ORGANIZATIONS

The previous section of this chapter summarized circumstances where, in an intandem relationship between two tax-exempt organizations, the parent exempt organization is a noncharitable organization and the subsidiary is a charitable organization. However, this arrangement can be reversed.

Thus, another application of these precepts occurs where a charitable organization has a noncharitable, albeit tax-exempt, subsidiary. This will occur where a charitable organization, which is engaging in or planning to engage in an activity that may or would jeopardize its tax-exempt status, spins off to or initiates that potentially disqualifying activity in a separate organization that qualifies under another category of tax exemption. For example, a charitable organization may be concerned about the extent of its legislative activities[72] and thus elect to operate them out of a tax-exempt social welfare organization.[73] Other functions that a charitable organization cannot properly pursue itself can be housed in a noncharitable tax-exempt organization, such as a title-holding corporation or a business league.[74] For example, as to the use of a business league (although not as a subsidiary) by a charitable organization, the IRS ruled that a charitable entity could advance its charitable purpose of lessening the burdens of government[75] by

---

[69] IRC § 170(c)(2), last sentence. This limitation does not apply with respect to contributions by individuals nor to contributions from a small business corporation (an *S corporation*) (IRS Priv. Ltr. Rul. 9703028).

[70] This results from the fact that IRC § 170(c)(2) opens with the phrase that a "corporation, trust, or community chest, fund, or foundation" may qualify as a charitable donee, while the restriction in the last sentence of IRC § 170(c)(2) applies to a gift to a "trust, chest, fund, or foundation." E.g., Rev. Rul. 69-80, 1969-1 C.B. 65.

[71] Rev. Proc. 59-31, 1959-2 C.B. 949.

[72] See Chapter 20.

[73] See Chapter 12.

[74] See § 18.2, Chapter 13, respectively.

[75] See § 6.3.

purchasing an office building and leasing it to a business league for job creation and world trade purposes, where the business league would sublease the property to appropriate businesses.[76] This technique generally cannot work, however, in the context of political activities,[77] in that a charitable organization usually cannot properly establish a related political action committee.[78]

The use by a charitable organization of entities such as charitable remainder trusts and pooled income funds[79] can also be viewed as illustrative of this technique.

Thus, the use by a charitable organization of noncharitable tax-exempt subsidiaries is still another application of the concept of bifurcation in the tax-exempt organizations setting. When coupled with other combinations of tax-exempt organizations, as well as with the use of taxable subsidiaries by tax-exempt organizations,[80] it is clear that there are many occasions and opportunities warranting the splitting of functions of tax-exempt organizations and the housing of them in separate entities.

§ 30.4 OTHER COMBINATIONS OF TAX-EXEMPT ORGANIZATIONS

There are combinations of tax-exempt organizations where none of the entities involved are charitable ones. The most common of these arrangements entails the use of political action committees, title-holding corporations, and employee benefit funds.

As discussed, several types of tax-exempt organizations utilize political action committees.[81] The usual users of these entities are business leagues[82] and labor organizations;[83] occasionally, social welfare organizations[84] and other exempt organizations will have occasion to create and operate a related political organization.

Any type of tax-exempt organization can have a related title-holding corporation. The usual model is a parent exempt organization and a title-holding entity.[85] However, unrelated exempt organizations can share a title-holding corporation.[86]

Various employee benefit funds are themselves tax-exempt organizations[87] and can be related to other tax-exempt organizations. This includes pension and retirement funds in general, and voluntary employees' beneficiary associations.[88]

---

[76] Priv. Ltr. Rul. 9246032.

[77] See Chapter 21.

[78] See Chapter 17.

[79] See § 18.19.

[80] See Chapter 31.

[81] See § 17.1(a).

[82] See Chapter 13.

[83] See § 15.1.

[84] See Chapter 12.

[85] See § 18.2(a).

[86] See § 18.2(b).

[87] See Chapter 16.

[88] *Id.* at § 3. There can be combinations of entities where some are tax-exempt and some are taxable. This includes the use of for-profit subsidiaries (see Chapter 31) and partnerships (see Chapter 32). Related to a for-profit organization can be a political action committee, a private foundation, and/or one or more employee benefit funds.

§ 30.5 TREATMENT OF CONTRIBUTIONS AND OTHER PAYMENTS

As a consequence of these in-tandem arrangements, it is not uncommon for a payment by a third party to be made to one organization, with some or all of the payment directed to another organization. The tax treatment accorded some or all of the payment (such as deductibility as a charitable contribution) can depend on whether the payment is deemed made to the initial payee or whether it or a portion of it is deemed made to another, sometimes related, organization that is the transferee of the initial payee. In many of these instances, the initial payee organization is regarded as the agent of the organization that is the ultimate recipient of the payment, so that the payor is considered, for tax purposes, to have made the payment directly to the ultimate transferee, notwithstanding the flow of the payment through one or more intermediate organizations (conduit entities).[89]

For example, a contribution to a tax-exempt organization is deductible as a charitable gift only where the recipient is a qualified donee.[90] Nonetheless, contributions to a tax-exempt social club[91] were held to be so deductible, where the club functioned as an authorized agent for one or more charitable organizations, enabling the members of the club to, when purchasing tickets for a social event, direct that the amount of their total payment in excess of the price of the tickets be transferred to charitable organizations and deduct, as charitable gifts, that portion of the payment to the club that was paid over to the charitable organizations.[92] In this type of instance, the initial payee organization is considered the mere conduit of some or all of the payments and thus the federal tax consequences of the payment are determined as if the payment (or a portion of it) was made directly to the ultimate recipient.

Likewise, charitable gift deductibility treatment was accorded additional amounts paid by customers of a utility company, when paying their bills to the company, where the additional amounts were earmarked for a charitable organization that assisted individuals with emergency energy-related needs.[93] Again, the utility company was considered the agent of the charitable organization; the company did not exercise any control over the funds and segregated them from its own funds. In a similar instance, contributions paid to a title-holding company[94] for purposes of maintaining and operating a historic property were once ruled by the IRS to be deductible as charitable gifts, where the gifts were segregated from the company's funds and otherwise clearly devoted to charitable ends.[95] However, in this instance, the ruling was subsequently withdrawn,[96] although the effect of the withdrawal was not made retroactive.[97]

---

[89] Cf. *supra* § 2(d).
[90] IRC § 170(c). See § 2.5.
[91] See Chapter 14.
[92] Rev. Rul. 55-192, 1955-1 C.B. 294.
[93] Rev. Rul. 85-184, 1985-2 C.B. 84.
[94] See § 18.2(a).
[95] Priv. Ltr. Rul. 8705041.
[96] Priv. Ltr. Rul. 8826012.
[97] Priv. Ltr. Rul. 8836040. The IRS did not provide any explanation for the withdrawal of this ruling, although it may be surmised that the IRS was concerned that this form of deductible charitable giving could become prevalent, with difficulties inherent in enforcing the rules.

Similarly, a contribution to a charitable entity is not deductible as a charitable gift where the ultimate recipient is not a qualified donee. For example, a contribution to a university for the general use of a fraternity or sorority on its campus is not deductible, in that the recipient of the funds is a social club. By contrast, a contribution of this nature would be deductible if the use of the funds is confined to charitable or educational purposes.[98] Thus, where a university owns the property and leases it to fraternities and sororities as part of its overall program of provision of student housing, contributions to the university for fraternity or sorority housing are deductible.[99]

Another variant of these principles is the rule that amounts paid to a tax-exempt organization for transfer to a political action committee do not, when promptly and directly transferred, constitute political campaign expenditures by the exempt organization.[100] A transfer is considered *promptly* and *directly* made if (1) the procedures followed by the organization satisfy the requirements of applicable federal and state campaign laws; (2) the organization maintains adequate records to demonstrate that the amounts transferred do in fact consist of political contributions or dues, rather than investment income; and (3) the political contributions or dues transferred were not used to earn investment income for the payor organization.[101]

Consequently, a payment to an organization (whether or not tax-exempt) can be treated, for federal tax purposes, as a payment to another organization (whether or not tax-exempt) where the initial payee is the agent of the ultimate transferee, the funds are clearly earmarked by the payor for the ultimate payee, and the funds are not subject to the control of (for example, invested for the benefit of) the initial payee.

§ 30.6 MERGERS

Notwithstanding the variety of these in-tandem arrangements, occasionally two of these organizations are merged. Likewise, on occasion, two unrelated tax-exempt organizations merge. With one exception, there is not any statutory law on the point.[102]

When a merger of this nature occurs, both of the organizations involved often have the same tax-exempt status. Usually, the two organizations in this type of a merger are public charitable organizations.[103] The rationale for these mergers varies. In one instance, the merger served to change the state of incorporation.[104] In another, the merger was intended to reduce the administrative burdens of op-

---

[98] Rev. Rul. 60-367, 1960-2 C.B. 73.

[99] E.g., Priv. Ltr. Rul. 9733015.

[100] See § 17.4. E.g., Priv. Ltr. Rul. 7903079.

[101] Reg. § 1.527-6(e).

[102] This exception pertains to the special termination tax rules that apply with respect to the mergers of private foundations (see § 11.4(f)).

[103] That is, public institutions, publicly supported charitable organizations, or supporting organizations (see Chapter 11).

[104] Priv. Ltr. Rul. 9309037.

erating two or more organizations.[105] In still another, the merger was undertaken to eliminate what had become a superfluous organization.[106] In one instance, a supporting organization for a boys' school and a supporting organization for a girls' school merged to form one supporting organization, following a merger of the two schools.[107]

Occasionally, both of the merging organizations will be tax-exempt organizations, but under differing categories. For example, a lobbying organization[108] related to a public charitable organization may merge into the public charity, or a foundation related to a trade or professional organization[109] may merge into the association.

These mergers usually do not adversely affect the tax-exempt status or the public charity status of the surviving organization, or cause any unrelated business income.[110]

An infrequent occurrence will be a merger of a for-profit organization into a tax-exempt organization. This can be done without endangering the tax-exempt status of the surviving organization, and generally without causing unrelated business income for the tax-exempt organization.[111] In one instance, a taxable corporation was merged into a tax-exempt social welfare organization.[112] The activities of the corporation were consistent with the exempt organization's purposes.[113] The tax-exempt organization issued "special notes" to the shareholders of the for-profit corporation in exchange for their stock. Again, the rationale for the merger was that the combination would reduce duplicative operations and expenses.[114]

---

[105] E.g., Priv. Ltr. Rul. 9314059.

[106] Priv. Ltr. Rul. 9303030 (a supporting organization (see § 11.3(c)) merged into a supported organization).

[107] Priv. Ltr. Rul. 9317054.

[108] That is, an organization described in IRC § 501(c)(4) (see Chapter 12).

[109] That is, an organization described in IRC § 501(c)(6) (see Chapter 13).

[110] E.g., Priv. Ltr. Ruls. 9738055, 9738056 (hospitals (see § 6.2(a)) merging into unrelated supporting organizations (see § 11.3(c)); Priv. Ltr. Rul. 9522022 (merger of two supplemental unemployment benefit trusts (see § 16.4)); Priv. Ltr. Rul. 9530008 (merger of a supporting organization into a private foundation (see § 11.3(c))); Priv. Ltr. Rul. 9530036 (merger of two trade associations (see Chapter 13)); Priv. Ltr. Rul. 9533015 (merger of a social club into a public charity (see Chapter 14)); Priv. Ltr. Rul. 9548019, as modified by Priv. Ltr. Rul. 9551009 (merger of two supporting organizations, followed by transfer to the survivor entity of the assets of a private foundation and 14 charitable trusts).

[111] See, however, § 31.2(d) (discussion of liquidations of for-profit subsidiaries into tax-exempt parents).

[112] That is, an organization described in IRC § 501(c)(4)(see Chapter 12).

[113] Priv. Ltr. Rul. 9346015.

[114] In general, Harris, "Structuring Affiliations Between Exempt and Nonexempt Organizations," 6 *J. Tax. Exempt Orgs.* (No. 4) 155 (Jan./Feb. 1995).

CHAPTER THIRTY-ONE

Tax-Exempt Organizations and For-Profit Subsidiaries

It is common, if not frequently essential, for a tax-exempt organization to utilize one or more for-profit, taxable subsidiaries.

The reasons for this phenomenon are manifold, including situations where the activity to be housed in the subsidiary is an unrelated one and the activity is too extensive to be conducted within the tax-exempt organization, the management of an exempt organization does not want to report the receipt of any unrelated income and so shifts it to a separate subsidiary, insulation of the assets of the parent exempt organization from potential liability, expansion of the sources of capital, use of it in a partnership, and/or the management of an exempt organization simply is enamored with the idea of use of a for-profit subsidiary.[1]

In most instances, the first of these three reasons is the prevalent if not the sole one. An unrelated business may be operated as an activity within a tax-exempt organization, as long as the primary purpose of the organization is the carrying out of one or more exempt functions or the commensurate test is satisfied.[2] With one exception, there is no fixed percentage of unrelated activity that may be engaged in by a tax-exempt organization.[3]

Therefore, if a tax-exempt organization engages in one or more unrelated activities where the activities are substantial in relation to exempt activities, the

---

[1] See Sanders, *Partnerships & Joint Ventures Involving Tax-Exempt Organizations* (New York: John Wiley & Sons, Inc., 1994) (hereinafter *Partnerships & Joint Ventures*), at 119.

[2] Reg. § 1.501(c)(3)-1(e)(1). Also Reg. § 1.501(c)(3)-1(c)(1).

[3] The one exception is a 10 percent limit on the unrelated business activities of title-holding companies (see § 28.3). Also, an active business enterprise may not be carried on by a private foundation (see § 11.4(c)).

use of a for-profit subsidiary is unavoidable, assuming exemption is to be retained.[4] Indeed, tax exemption cannot be maintained if there is a substantial non-exempt activity or set of activities.[5]

§ 31.1 STRUCTURAL CONSIDERATIONS

There are several matters of structure to be taken into account when contemplating the use of a for-profit subsidiary by a tax-exempt organization. These include choice of form and the control mechanism.

(a) Establishing a For-Profit Subsidiary

Essentially, the factors to be considered in determining whether a particular activity should be housed in a tax-exempt organization or a for-profit organization are the same as those that should be weighed when one is contemplating the commencement of a business that potentially may be conducted in either a tax-exempt or for-profit form. These factors are the value of or need for tax exemption, the motives of those involved in the enterprise (for example, a profit motive), the desirability of creating an asset (such as stock that is appreciating in value and/or the means for transfer of ownership) for equity owners of the enterprise (usually shareholders), and the compensatory arrangements contemplated for the employees.

The law is clear that a tax-exempt organization can have one or more tax-exempt (or at least non-profit) subsidiaries and/or one or more for-profit subsidiaries.[6] Indeed, the IRS acknowledged that the "number of subsidiaries or related entities an exempt organization can create for the purpose of conducting business activities is not set."[7] With respect to for-profit subsidiaries, the tax-exempt parent organization can own some or all of the equity (usually stock) of the for-profit subsidiary (unless the parent is a private foundation, in which case special rules apply[8]).[9] For example, a public charity created a for-profit management corporation, to provide services to it and two other exempt organizations, and provided it operating funds in exchange for 100 percent of the subsidiary's stock.[10]

---

[4] In Orange County Agric. Soc'y. Inc. v. Comm'r, 893 F.2d 529 (2d Cir. 1990), the court discussed the fact that the operation of a substantial unrelated business by a tax-exempt organization is likely to result in loss of the organization's tax exemption.

[5] Better Business Bur. of Washington, D.C. v. United States, 326 U.S. 279 (1945).

[6] E.g., Priv. Ltr. Rul. 9016072 (where a tax-exempt organization owned a for-profit subsidiary and that subsidiary in turn owned a network of for-profit subsidiaries).

[7] Priv. Ltr. Rul. 8706012.

[8] See § 11.4(c).

[9] The extent of stock ownership may determine whether income from a subsidiary to a tax-exempt parent is taxable (see infra § 3). A transfer without consideration from a taxable corporation to a charitable organization, which is its sole stockholder, is a dividend rather than a charitable contribution (Rev. Rul. 68-296, 1968-1 C.B. 105).

[10] Priv. Ltr. Rul. 9308047.

The IRS issues private determinations concerning the use of for-profit subsidiaries by tax-exempt organizations.[11]

There are several matters of structure to be taken into account when the use of a for-profit subsidiary by a tax-exempt organization is contemplated. These include choice of form and the control mechanism.

(b) Choice of Form

Just as in forming a tax-exempt organization, consideration must be given to choice of organizational form when establishing a for-profit subsidiary. Most will be corporations, inasmuch as a corporation is the most commonplace of business forms, provides a shield against liability for management and the exempt parent, and enables the tax-exempt parent to own the subsidiary by holding all or at least a majority of its stock.[12]

Some taxable businesses are organized as sole proprietorships; however, this approach is of no avail in the tax-exempt organization context since the business activity conducted as a sole proprietorship is an undertaking conducted directly by the exempt organization and thus does not lead to the desired goal of having the unrelated activity in a separate entity.

Some taxable businesses are structured as partnerships;[13] however, the participation by a tax-exempt organization in a partnership can involve unique legal complications.[14]

Some states allow businesses to be conducted by means of "business trusts," so this approach may be available to a tax-exempt organization. However, before this approach (or any other approach involving a vehicle other than a corporation) is used, it is imperative that those involved are certain that the corporate form is not the most beneficial. One important consideration must be that of stock ownership, as stock in and of itself is an asset that can appreciate in value and can be sold in whole or in part.

In some instances, an activity can be placed in a taxable nonprofit organization.[15] This approach is a product of the distinction between a nonprofit organization and a tax-exempt organization.[16] The former is a state law concept; the latter essentially is a federal tax concept. Assuming state law permits (in that an activity may be *unrelated* to the parent's tax-exempt functions, yet still be a *nonprofit* one), a business activity may be placed in a nonprofit, albeit taxable, corpo-

---

[11] E.g., Priv. Ltr. Rul. 8706012.

[12] In tax years beginning after December 31, 1997, charitable organizations may be shareholders in small business corporations (*S corporations*) (IRC § 1361(b)(1)(B), (c)(7)(B)). The applicability of the unrelated business income rules in this context is the subject of § 27.2(m).

[13] See Chapter 32.

[14] A new business form is the limited liability company, which may have some utility in structuring an exempt organization's for-profit subsidiary (e.g., Priv. Ltr. Rul. 9637050).

[15] Another approach—when appropriate—is use of a tax-exempt subsidiary. This technique is discussed throughout (e.g., § 11.3(c) (supporting organizations), § 18.2 (title-holding companies), § 20.7 (lobbying arms of charitable organizations), and § 30.2(d) (fund-raising vehicles for foreign charitable organizations)).

[16] See §§ 1.1(a), 1.2.

ration.[17] There may be some advantage (such as public relations) to this approach.

(c) Control

Presumably, a tax-exempt organization will, when forming a taxable subsidiary, intend to maintain control over the subsidiary. Certainly, after capitalizing the enterprise,[18] nurturing its growth and success, and desiring to enjoy some profits from the business, the prudent tax-exempt organization parent usually would not want to place the activity in a vehicle over which it cannot exercise control.

Where the taxable subsidiary is structured as a business corporation, the tax-exempt organization parent can own the entity and ultimately control it simply by owning the stock (received in exchange for the capital contributed).[19] The exempt organization parent as the stockholder can thereafter select the board of directors of the corporation and, if desired, its officers.

If the taxable subsidiary is structured as a nonprofit corporation, three choices are available. The tax-exempt organization parent can control the subsidiary by means of interlocking directorates. Alteratively, the subsidiary can be a membership corporation, with the parent entity the sole member. In the third—and least utilized—approach, the entity can be structured as a nonprofit organization that can issue stock, in which case the exempt organization parent would control the subsidiary by holding its stock. If the latter course is chosen and if the nonprofit subsidiary is to be headquartered in a (foreign) state where stock-based nonprofit organizations are not authorized, the subsidiary can be incorporated in a state that allows nonprofit organizations to issue stock and thereafter be qualified to do business in the home (domestic) state.

(d) Attribution Considerations

For federal income tax purposes, a parent corporation and its subsidiary are respected as separate entities as long as the purposes for which the subsidiary is formed are reflected in authentic business activities.[20] That is, where an organization is established with the bona fide intention that it will have some real and substantial business function, its existence will generally not be disregarded for tax purposes.[21] By contrast, where the parent organization so controls the affairs of the subsidiary that it is merely an extension of the parent, the subsidiary may not be regarded as a separate entity.[22] In an extreme situation (such as where the

---

[17] Of course, in this situation, the subsidiary, then, is not a for-profit one.

[18] See *infra* § 2(a).

[19] E.g., text accompanied by *supra* note 4. There are special rules in this regard for private foundations (see § 11.4(c)).

[20] E.g., Moline Properties, Inc. v. Comm'r, 319 U.S. 436 (1943); National Carbide Corp. v. Comm'r, 336 U.S. 422 (1949); Britt v. United States, 431 F.2d 227 (5th Cir. 1970). Also Sly v. Comm'r, 56 T.C.M. 209 (1988), Universal Church of Jesus Christ, Inc. v. Comm'r, 55 T.C.M. 143 (1988) (where a debt collection business was said to be "operating under the thinnest of veils in an attempt to give itself the appearance of a religious enterprise" (at 153)).

[21] Britt v. United States, *supra* note 10.

[22] E.g., Krivo Industrial Supply Co. v. National Distillers & Chemical Corp., 483 F.2d 1098 (5th Cir. 1973); Orange County Agric. Soc'y, Inc. v. Comm'r, 55 T.C.M. 1602 (1988); *aff'd, supra* note 4.

parent is directly involved in the day-to-day management of the subsidiary), the establishment and operation of an ostensibly separate subsidiary may be regarded as a sham perpetrated by the parent and thus ignored for tax purposes; with this outcome, the tax consequences are the same as if the two "entities" were one.[23]

The position of the IRS on this subject can be traced through three pronouncements from its Office of Chief Counsel. In 1968, the IRS was advised by its lawyers that an attempt to attribute the activities of a subsidiary to its parent "should be made only where the evidence clearly shows that the subsidiary is merely a guise enabling the parent to carry out its . . . [disqualifying] activity or where it can be proven that the subsidiary is an arm, agent, or integral part of the parent."[24] In 1974, the IRS Chief Counsel advised that "[t]o disregard the corporate entity requires a finding that the corporation or transaction involved was a sham or fraud without any valid business purpose, or the finding of a true agency or trust relationship between the entities."[25] In 1984, the IRS's lawyers reviewed a situation where a separate for-profit corporation provided management and operations services to several hospitals. Although the IRS was inclined otherwise, its lawyers advised that where a subsidiary is organized for a bona fide business purpose and the tax-exempt parent is not involved in the day-to-day management of the subsidiary, the activities of the subsidiary cannot be attributed to the parent for purposes of determining the parent's tax-exempt status.[26] In the third instance, this was the outcome irrespective of the fact that the parent tax-exempt organization owned all of the stock of the subsidiary corporation.

Thus, the contemporary posture of the IRS in this regard can be distilled to two tests, which are that, for the legitimacy of a for-profit subsidiary to be respected, it must engage in an independent, bona fide function and not be a mere instrumentality of the exempt parent. As to the former, the IRS's lawyers wrote that

> the first aspect [in determining the authenticity of a for-profit subsidiary] is the requirement that the subsidiary be organized for some bona fide purpose of its own and not be a mere sham or instrumentality of the [exempt] parent. We do not believe that this requirement that the subsidiary have a bona fide business purpose should be considered to require that the subsidiary have an inherently commercial or for-profit activity. The term "business" . . . is not synonymous with "trade or business" in the sense of requiring a profit motive.[27]

As to the latter, the IRS's lawyers observed that

---

[23] Gen. Couns. Mem. 39598. In a similar set of circumstances, courts are finding nonprofit organizations to be the alter ego of the debtor, with the result that the assets of the organization are made available to IRS levies (see the cases collected in § 4.1, note 25).

   In the reverse situation, where a for-profit entity controls an exempt organization (such as by day-to-day management of it), the tax exemption of the controlled entity may be jeopardized (see, e.g., United Cancer Council, Inc. v. Comm'r, 109 T.C. No. 17 (1997); §§ 19.4, 33.3). Nonetheless, management of a tax-exempt organization by a for-profit company generally does not raise these concerns (e.g., Priv. Ltr. Rul. 9715031).

[24] Gen. Couns. Mem. 33912.

[25] Gen. Couns. Mem. 35719.

[26] Gen. Couns. Mem. 39326. Also IRS Gen. Couns. Mem. 39866.

[27] Gen. Couns. Mem. 39598.

the second aspect of the test is the requirement that the parent not be so involved in, or in control of, the day-to-day operations of the subsidiary that the relationship between parent and subsidiary assumes the characteristics of the relationship of principal and agent, i.e., that the parent not be so in control of the affairs of the subsidiary that it is merely an instrumentality of the parent.[28]

At one point, the IRS demonstrated some proclivity to treat two organizations in this situation as one where the entities' directors and officers are the same. For example, the IRS privately ruled that the activities of a for-profit subsidiary are to be attributed to its tax-exempt parent, for purposes of determining the ongoing tax exemption of the parent, where the officers and directors of the two organizations are identical.[29]

The rationale underlying this ruling rests on the premise that, when the tax-exempt parent is involved in the day-to-day management of the subsidiary, the activities of the subsidiary are imputed to the parent. In this ruling, the IRS stated that an exempt parent is "necessarily" involved in the day-to-day management of the subsidiary simply because the officers and directors of the parent serve as the officers and directors of the subsidiary. Thus, because of this structural overlap, the IRS attributed the activities of the subsidiary to the parent. Once this attribution occurs, the impact of this attribution must be ascertained to determine whether the parent will remain tax-exempt.

In the case, the attribution to the tax-exempt parent of the activities of the for-profit subsidiary was not fatal to the parent because the involvement was deemed to be insubstantial. (The parent was a scientific research organization; the subsidiary developed and manufactured products that were derived from patentable technology generated out of the parent's research activities. The parent's average annual income was $50,000,000; the subsidiary's was $10,000–$70,000.) The for-profit subsidiary was capitalized by the parent (for between $10,000 and $100,000). The parent maintained a controlling interest in the subsidiary. There was an overlapping of employees as between the parent and subsidiary. Likewise, there was a sharing of facilities and equipment. These relationships were evidenced by employment contracts and lease agreements. Separate books and records of the two entities were maintained.

However, the principles of law do not lead to the conclusion of the IRS in this ruling, which is that overlapping directors and officers of two organizations automatically results in an attribution of the subsidiary's activities to the parent. The case law is instructive in that this can be the consequence where the facts show that the arrangement is a sham; however, this cannot be a mechanical and inexorable outcome. Indeed, in subsequent rulings, the IRS's rulings division has been guided by this advice from its lawyers:

> Control through ownership of stock, or power to appoint the board of directors, of the subsidiary will not cause the attribution of the subsidiary's activities to the parent. We do not believe that . . . [a prior general counsel memorandum] should be read to suggest, by negative inference, that when the board of directors of a wholly owned subsidiary is made up entirely of

---

[28] *Id.*
[29] Priv. Ltr. Rul. 8606056.

board members, officers, or employees of the parent there must be attribution of the activities of the subsidiary to the parent.[30]

Contemporary rulings from the IRS evidence an abandonment of this earlier approach.[31]

Thus, the IRS is highly unlikely to attribute the activities of a for-profit subsidiary of a tax-exempt organization to the parent entity, by reason of the foregoing elements of law. The use of for-profit subsidiaries in the contemporary exempt organizations setting has become too customary for this form of attribution to occur, absent the most egregious of facts.[32]

§ 31.2 FINANCIAL CONSIDERATIONS

(a) Capitalization

Assets of a tax-exempt organization that are currently being used in an unrelated business activity may, with little (if any) legal constraint,[33] be spun off into an affiliated for-profit organization. However, the extent to which a for-profit corporation can be capitalized using tax-exempt assets (particularly charitable ones) is a matter involving far more strenuous confines.

A tax-exempt organization can, of course, invest a portion of its assets and engage in a certain amount of unrelated activities. At the same time, the governing board of a tax-exempt organization must act in conformity with basic fiduciary responsibilities, and the organization cannot (without jeopardizing its exemption) contravene the prohibitions on private inurement and private benefit.[34]

IRS private letter rulings suggest that perhaps only a very small percentage of an organization's resources ought to be transferred to controlled subsidiaries.[35] However, these percentages approved by the IRS are usually unduly low and, in any event, probably pertain only to cash. (Many IRS rulings in this area do not state the amount of capital involved.[36]) In some cases, a specific asset may—indeed, perhaps must—be best utilized in an unrelated activity, even though its value represents a meaningful portion of the organization's total re-

---

[30] Gen. Couns. Mem. 39598.

[31] E.g., Priv. Ltr. Rul. 9245031 ("[t]he activities of [the] subsidiary cannot be attributed to [the] [p]arent . . .").

[32] This does not mean that revenue from a for-profit subsidiary to an exempt parent is not taxable; in fact, just the opposite is often the case (see *infra* § 3).

[33] It goes without saying that this mechanism should not be used to assist in fraud or other wrongdoing. A manager of a tax-exempt organization may decide that a for-profit subsidiary is a useful device for creating additional compensation or to accumulate funds to be used for other private ends, such as travel and property ownership. The conviction of the former president of the United Way of America was based on these and other inappropriate uses of a taxable subsidiary, Partnership Umbrella. In general, Glaser, *An Insider's Account of the United Way Scandal: What Went Wrong and Why* (New York: John Wiley & Sons, Inc., 1994), particularly Chapter 6.

[34] See Chapter 19.

[35] E.g., Priv. Ltr. Rul. 8505044.

[36] E.g., Priv. Ltr. Rul. 9305026.

sources.[37] Also, the exempt parent may want to make subsequent advances or loans to the subsidiary.

The best guiding standard in these regards is that of the prudent investor. In capitalizing a subsidiary, a tax-exempt organization should only part with an amount of resources that is reasonable under the circumstances and that can be rationalized in relation to amounts devoted to programs and invested in other fashions. Relevant to all of this is the projected return on the investment, in terms of both income and capital appreciation. If a contribution to a subsidiary's capital seems unwise, the parent-to-be should consider a loan (albeit one bearing a fair rate of interest and accompanied by adequate security).

In all instances, it is preferable that the operation of the subsidiary furthers (if only by providing funds for) the exempt purpose of the parent.[38] Certainly, circumstances where exempt purposes are thwarted by reason of operation of a for-profit subsidiary are to be avoided.

(b) Compensation

The structure of a tax-exempt parent and a taxable subsidiary may generate questions and issues as to compensation of employees.

The compensation of the employees of the taxable subsidiary is subject to an overarching requirement that the amounts paid may not exceed a reasonable salary or wage.[39] The compensation of the employees of the parent tax-exempt organization is subject to a like limitation, by reason of the private inurement, private benefit, and/or excess benefit transaction doctrines.[40] An individual may be an employee of both the parent and subsidiary organizations; in that circumstance, a reasonable allocation of compensation as between the entities is required.[41] Also, if an officer, director, trustee, or key employee received aggregate compensation of more than $100,000 from a tax-exempt organization and one or more of its related organizations, of which more than $10,000 was provided by a related organization, that fact must be reported to the IRS, with an explanation.[42] The employees of a for-profit subsidiary of a parent tax-exempt organization may be included in the medical and dental plan of the parent, without endangering the tax-exempt status of the parent, as long as the costs of the plan are allocated among the two employers on a per-capita basis.[43]

The employees of the tax-exempt parent could participate in deferred com-

---

[37] In one instance, the amount of capital transferred was characterized by the IRS as "substantial," although the exempt parent was not a charitable entity; it was a tax-exempt social welfare organization (see Chapter 12); (Priv. Ltr. Rul. 9245031).

[38] E.g., Priv. Ltr. Rul. 8709051.

[39] IRC § 162.

[40] See Chapter 19.

[41] One of the burgeoning issues in this regard is potential misuse of for-profit subsidiaries, such as by unduly shifting expenses to them, excess and/or additional compensation paid by them, and lack of disclosure of the relationship; sometimes, there are also conflict-of-interest issues.

[42] Form 990, Part V. In general, see § 24.3.

[43] Priv. Ltr. Rul. 9242039.

pensation plans[44] or perhaps tax-sheltered annuity programs.[45] Deferred salary plans may also be used by the subsidiary, as may qualified pension plans. Both the parent and the subsidiary may utilize 401 (k) plans.[46]

Use of a taxable subsidiary may facilitate the offering of stock options to employees, to enable them to share in the growth of the corporation. The subsidiary similarly may offer an employee stock ownership plan, which is a plan that invests in the stock of the sponsoring company.[47] The subsidiary may issue unqualified options to buy stock or qualified incentive stock options.[48]

(c) Sharing of Resources

Generally, a tax-exempt organization and a for-profit subsidiary may share resources without adverse consequences to the exempt entity. That is, the two organizations may share office facilities, equipment, supplies, and the like. However, particularly where the exempt entity is a charitable one, all relevant costs must be allocated on the basis of actual use and each organization must pay fair market value for the resources used.[49]

It is generally preferable for the tax-exempt organization to reimburse the for-profit entity for the exempt organization's use of resources, to avoid even a perception that the funds of a tax-exempt organization are being used to subsidize a for-profit organization. Nonetheless, this approach often is impractical where the exempt organization is the parent entity.

(d) Liquidations

The federal tax law causes recognition of gain or loss by a for-profit corporation in an instance of a liquidating distribution of its assets (as if the corporation had sold the assets to the distributee at fair market value) and in the event of liquidating sales. There is an exception for liquidating transfers within an affiliated group (which is regarded as a single economic unit), so that the basis in the property is carried over from the distributor to the distributee in lieu of recognition of gain or loss.

This nonrecognition exception is modified for eligible liquidations in which an 80 percent corporate shareholder receives property with a carryover basis, to provide for nonrecognition of gain or loss with respect to any property actually distributed to that shareholder. Nonetheless, this nonrecognition rule under the exception for 80 percent corporate shareholders is generally not available where the shareholder is a tax-exempt organization. That is, any gain or loss generally must be recognized by the subsidiary on the distribution of its assets in liquidation as if the assets were sold to the exempt parent at their fair market

---

[44] IRC § 457.
[45] IRC § 403(b).
[46] See § 16.1, text accompanied by note 14.
[47] IRC § 4975(e)(7).
[48] E.g., Priv. Ltr. Rul. 9242038.
[49] E.g., Priv. Ltr. Rul. 9308047. Where, however, the charitable organization is a private foundation, extreme caution is required in this regard, in that this type of resource sharing is likely to be self-dealing (see § 11.4(a)).

value.[50] (No gain or loss is recognized by the parent on its receipt of the subsidiary's assets pursuant to the liquidation.[51]) However, this nonrecognition treatment is available in the tax-exempt organizations context where the property distributed is used by the tax-exempt organization in an unrelated business immediately after the distribution. If the property subsequently ceases to be used in an unrelated business, the tax-exempt organization will be taxed on the gain at that time.[52]

In one instance, a tax-exempt home health and hospice agency had formed a wholly owned for-profit subsidiary to provide home companion services and operate an assisted living facility. Years later, the parent organization expanded its programs and facilities, and determined that the activities conducted by the subsidiary could be undertaken by the parent without adversely affecting the parent's exempt status. The parent organization proceeded to liquidate the subsidiary and transfer to it all of the assets in the subsidiary, which had appreciated in value. The IRS ruled that the gain attributable to the distribution of the subsidiary's assets to the parent organization upon liquidation would be excludable from taxation as unrelated business income by reason of the exclusion from taxation of capital gains.[53] This ruling was silent on the tax consequences of transfer of the appreciated assets by the subsidiary.[54] In another instance, one of the functions of a charitable entity was the publication and circulation of religious materials. This organization had a for-profit subsidiary that engaged in both exempt and commercial printing activities. Once it was decided to discontinue the commercial printing operations, the exempt parent decided to liquidate the subsidiary and distribute its assets to the parent organization. The IRS ruled that any gain or loss must be recognized by the subsidiary on the distribution of its assets in liquidation (as if they were sold to the exempt parent at fair market value) to the extent the assets are to be used in related business activities.[55]

---

[50] IRC § 337(b)(2)(A).

[51] IRC § 332(a). In one instance, the IRS erroneously ruled that the nonrecognition of gain by a tax-exempt organization receiving assets as the result of a liquidation was based on IRC § 512(b)(5) (see § 27.1(j)) (Priv. Ltr. Rul. 9438029).

[52] IRC § 337(b)(2)(B)(ii) Cf. Centre for Int'l Understanding v. Comm'r, 62 T.C.M. 629 (1991) (applying the liquidation rules of IRC § 337(c)(2)(A)). The IRS proposed regulations, under authority of IRC § 337 (d), concerning the liquidations of for-profit entities into tax-exempt organizations, where the relationship is not that of parent and subsidiary; although the rules in this regard would be essentially the same as those that apply to liquidations of subsidiaries, they would also apply where a for-profit corporation converts to a tax-exempt entity (see § 33.4(b)) (REG-209121-89). In general, Royalty & Colton, "Treasury Proposes Regulations on Exempt Organizations and the Repeal of *General Utilities*," 9 J. Tax. Exempt Orgs. (No. 2) 51 (Sep./Oct. 1997); Royalty, Tracy, Latkovic & Levenson, "Proposed Regulations Address Conversions and Other Transfers to Tax-Exempt Entities," 16 *Exempt Org. Tax Rev.* (No. 2) 207 (Feb. 1997); Silk, "Conversions of Tax-Exempt Nonprofit Organizations: Federal Tax Law and State Charitable Law Issues," 13 *Exempt Org. Tax Rev.* (No. 5) 745 (May 1996).

[53] See *supra* note 51.

[54] This ruling did not utilize the liquidation rules of IRC §§ 332 and 337. It is not clear from this ruling whether the assets in the subsidiary were to be used in related or unrelated activities by the exempt parent after the liquidation. If the assets were to be used in related activities, the gain should have been recognized and taxable to the subsidiary (IRC § 337(b)(2)(A)).

[55] Priv. Ltr. Rul. 9645017. This ruling expressly addressed the point that, to the extent the assets were to be used by the parent in unrelated activities, any gain would not be recognized during the pendency of that type of use (IRC § 337(b)(2)(B)(ii)).

§ 31.3 TREATMENT OF REVENUE FROM SUBSIDIARY

While not always the case, most tax-exempt organizations develop an unrelated activity in the anticipation that it will serve as a source of revenue. Thus, the development within, or shifting of the unrelated business to, a taxable subsidiary should be done in such a way as to not preclude or inhibit the flow of income from the subsidiary to the parent.

The staff and other resources of an affiliated business are usually those of the tax-exempt organization parent. Thus, the headquarters of the taxable subsidiary are likely to be the same as its parent. This means that the taxable subsidiary may have to reimburse the exempt organization parent for the subsidiary's occupancy costs, share of employees' time, and use of the parent's equipment and supplies. Therefore, one way for dollars to flow from the subsidiary to the parent is as this form of reimbursement, which would include an element of rent.

Another type of relationship between a tax-exempt organization parent and a taxable subsidiary is that of lender and borrower. That is, in addition to funding its subsidiary by means of a capital contribution (resulting in a holding of equity by the parent), the parent may find it appropriate to lend money to its subsidiary. Inasmuch as a no-interest loan to a for-profit subsidiary by a tax-exempt organization parent may endanger the tax-exempt status of the parent, and trigger problems under the below-market interest rules,[56] it would be appropriate for a loan to bear a fair market rate of interest. Therefore, another way for dollars to flow from the subsidiary to the parent is in the form of interest.

The business activities of a for-profit subsidiary may be to market and sell a product or service. When done in conformity with its tax-exempt status, the parent can license the use of its name, logo, acronym, and/or some other feature that would enhance the sale of the product or service provided by the subsidiary. For this license, the subsidiary would pay to the parent a royalty—another way of transferring dollars from a for-profit subsidiary to a tax-exempt parent.

A conventional way of transferring money from a corporation to its stockholders is for the corporation to distribute its earnings and profits to them. These distributions are dividends and represent still another way in which a taxable subsidiary can transfer dollars to its tax-exempt parent.

As related earlier, certain types of income are exempted from taxation as unrelated income—principally the various forms of passive income. Were it not for a special rule of federal tax law, a tax-exempt organization could have it both ways: avoid taxation of the exempt organization on unrelated income by housing the activity in a subsidiary and thereafter receive passive, nontaxable income from the subsidiary.

Congress, however, was mindful of this potential double benefit and thus legislated a rule that is an exception to the general rule that exempts passive income from taxation: otherwise passive nontaxable income that is derived from a controlled taxable subsidiary is generally taxed as unrelated income. Thus,

---

[56] IRC § 7872.

when a tax-exempt organization parent receives rents, interest, or most other forms of passive income from a controlled taxable subsidiary, those revenues will generally be taxable.[57]

There is, nonetheless, an exception to the exception. This rule is predicated upon the fact that the payment of rents, interest, or royalties gives rise to a tax deduction for the payment of them for the payor organization. So, for example, when a for-profit subsidiary pays interest to its tax-exempt organization parent in connection with a loan, the interest payments are deductible by the subsidiary.

However, there is no tax deduction for the payment of dividends. Consequently, when a for-profit subsidiary pays a dividend to its tax-exempt organization parent, the dividend payments are not deductible by the subsidiary. Therefore, Congress determined that it would not be appropriate to tax revenue to an exempt organization parent where it is not deductible by the taxable subsidiary.

Thus, this principle has developed (facilitating tax planning as to which entity, if any, is to be taxed): if the income paid to a tax-exempt organization parent is deductible by the subsidiary, it is unrelated income to the parent; by contrast, if the income paid is not deductible by the subsidiary, it is not taxable to the parent. The exception to the exception, then, is for dividend income, which is not taxable to an exempt organization parent even when derived from a controlled taxable subsidiary.

The IRS privately ruled that payments of passive income by a for-profit subsidiary of a tax-exempt organization, which would be taxable if paid to the exempt parent, are not taxable when paid to another tax-exempt organization, even where the payee is related to the parent organization.[58]

§ 31.4 SUBSIDIARIES IN PARTNERSHIPS

There is a dimension to the use of a taxable subsidiary by a tax-exempt organization parent that is alluded to in the discussion of exempt organizations in partnerships.[59] This is the attempt by a charitable organization to avoid endangering its tax-exempt status because of involvement in a partnership as a gen-

---

[57] IRC 512(b)(13). Prior to a law revision in 1997, the rules that applied with respect to the tax treatment of revenue from a for-profit subsidiary to a tax-exempt parent organization did not apply when the exempt parent entity received revenue from a *second-tier subsidiary*, which is a for-profit subsidiary of a subsidiary (a *first-tier subsidiary*) of a tax-exempt parent. Thus, an exempt museum was able to receive tax-free rent from a store operated in a second-tier subsidiary (Tech. Adv. Mem. 9338003) and an association was likewise the recipient of nontaxable rent from a golf course management company (Priv. Ltr. Rul. 9506046). However, by adding an indirect control rule in this context, this use of second-tier subsidiaries is no longer effective (see § 27.1(n)(ii)).

[58] Priv. Ltr. Rul. 8842025. Today, the ruling in this instance would likely be that the income is taxable, in accordance with the indirect control rules (see *supra* note 57).

[59] See § 29. 5(g), Chapter 32.

eral partner by causing a taxable subsidiary to be the general partner in its stead.[60]

This can be an effective stratagem as long as all of the requirements of the law as to the bona fides of the subsidiary are satisfied, including the requirement that the subsidiary be an authentic business entity. However, as discussed,[61] if the tax-exempt organization parent is too intimately involved in the day-to-day management of the subsidiary, the IRS may impute the activities of the subsidiary to the parent, thereby endangering the tax-exempt status of the parent by treating it as if it were directly involved as a general partner of the limited partnership.[62]

One commentator, discussing this subject in the health care context but with implications for all charitable parent organizations, observed that, for this approach to be successful, "it is preferable for the affiliate's [subsidiary's] participation to be funded through a source other than the hospital, because the IRS analyzes such transactions as if the hospital itself were participating directly in the venture to the extent of any funding traceable to it."[63] This commentator inventoried the factors establishing the independent status of the subsidiary in this setting; they are that the hospital should refrain from active involvement in the day-to-day business affairs of the for-profit subsidiary, the subsidiary should be formed for a true business purpose and not as a mere instrumentality of the hospital, the terms of all transactions between the hospital and the subsidiary are at arm's length, the costs of any shared assets, services, or facilities should be allocated according to actual use, and the subsidiary should maintain separate minutes and other formal documentation.[64]

An illustration of this use of a partnership was presented in an IRS private letter ruling.[65] A community hospital wanted to expand its provision of medical rehabilitation services; a for-profit corporation that managed the rehabilitation program at the hospital was a subsidiary of the nation's largest independent provider of comprehensive rehabilitation services. The hospital, through this subsidiary, sought a joint venture with its for-profit parent to utilize its expertise and methodologies, and to operate the rehabilitation facility as a venture so that the expansion would not jeopardize the institution's role as a community hospital. The joint venture was structured so that it was between the hospital and a system of which it was a component, and a wholly owned for-profit subsidiary of the for-

---

[60] E.g., Gen. Couns. Mems. 39866, 39598; Priv. Ltr. Rul. 9105029. One area of the federal tax law concerning tax-exempt organizations where the use of a for-profit subsidiary in a partnership, instead of an exempt organization, generally will not alter the tax outcome is the set of rules pertaining to tax-exempt entity leasing (see § 29.5(g)). On occasion, some or all of these results can be accomplished by the use of a tax-exempt subsidiary (e.g., Priv. Ltr. Rul. 8638131).

[61] See *supra* § 1(d).

[62] In one instance, the IRS, without explanation, expressly ignored a tax-exempt organization's use of a for-profit subsidiary as the general partner in a partnership, reviewing the facts as though the exempt organization was directly involved in the partnership (Tech. Adv. Mem. 8939002).

[63] *Partnerships & Joint Ventures* at 267–268, citing Gen. Couns. Mems. 39646, 39598, and Priv. Ltr. Ruls. 9303030, 8621059, 8604006.

[64] *Id.*

[65] Priv. Ltr. Rul. 9352030.

profit parent entity and its subsidiary. The IRS ruled favorably in the case, concluding that the hospital's participation in the venture was consistent with its purposes of promoting health.[66]

§ 31.5 EFFECT OF FOR-PROFIT SUBSIDIARIES ON PUBLIC CHARITY STATUS

Just as it is possible for the existence of a for-profit subsidiary to have an adverse impact on the exempt status of a tax-exempt organization (by an attribution of the activities for tax purposes),[67] so too is there potential that the presence of a for-profit subsidiary will have a pernicious effect on the public charity status of the exempt charitable parent organization.

(a) Publicly Supported Organizations

Any impact of a for-profit subsidiary organization on the status of a tax-exempt charitable organization that is its parent, where the parent is classified as a publicly supported organization, is derived from funding of the parent by the subsidiary. If the funding is in the form of a charitable contribution, it may be regarded for tax purposes as a dividend.[68]

Where a parent charitable organization has its non-private foundation status based on classification as a donative type of publicly supported charity,[69] a transfer of money or property to it by a subsidiary will, if treated as a dividend, not qualify as public support.[70] Moreover, where the item or items transferred to the publicly supported donative parent are considered gifts, they would not constitute public support to the extent the amount exceeded the two percent limitation threshold.[71]

If the parent organization is not a private foundation by reason of categorization as a service provider type of publicly supported charity,[72] any amount paid to it by a subsidiary would not be public support if the amount was regarded as a dividend.[73] Moreover, a payment of this nature accorded dividend treatment would be investment income, as to which there is a one-third limitation with respect to receipt of this type of revenue.[74] If the item or items transferred to the publicly supported service provider parent are considered gifts, they would not constitute public support where the subsidiary is a disqualified person[75] with respect to the parent organization.[76]

---

[66] In general, see § 6.2.
[67] See *supra* § 1(d).
[68] See *supra* § 1, note 9.
[69] See § 11.3(b)(i).
[70] Reg. § 1.170A-9(e)(2)
[71] Reg. § 1.170A-9(e)(6)(i).
[72] See § 11.3(b)(iv).
[73] IRC § 509(a)(2)(A); Reg. § 1.509(a)-3(a)(2).
[74] IRC § 509(a)(2)(B): Reg. § 1.509(a)-3(a)(3)(i).
[75] See § 11.2.
[76] IRC § 509(a)(2)(A); Reg. § 1.509(a)-3(b)(2).

(b) Supporting Organizations

Some tax-exempt charitable organizations are able to become classified as public charities by virtue of the rules concerning supporting organizations.[77]

Because the public charity status of a supporting organization is not derived from the nature of its funding, the considerations pertaining to publicly supported organizations discussed previously are inapplicable (although a transfer from a for-profit subsidiary to a supporting organization may nonetheless be considered a dividend).

The public charity classification of a charitable organization that is a supporting organization is rested on the rule that it be operated exclusively to support or benefit one or more eligible public charitable organizations.[78] There was a school of thought that held that a supporting organization cannot have a for-profit subsidiary because, to do so, would be a violation of the exclusively requirement. There was some merit to this position, since the term *exclusively* means, in this setting, *solely*,[79] as opposed to its definition in the context of charitable organizations generally, where the term means *primarily*.[80] Contentions to the contrary include the view that, where the reason for organizing and utilizing the subsidiary is to assist in the supporting or benefiting of one or more eligible public charities, there should not be a prohibition on the use of for-profit subsidiaries in this manner. This issue arose when the IRS ruled that, as long as a supporting organization does not actively participate in the day-to-day management of a for-profit subsidiary and both entities have a legitimate economic and business purpose and operations, the supporting organization can utilize a for-profit subsidiary without jeopardizing its tax-exempt status;[81] the ruling was silent on the matter of the impact of the use of the subsidiary on the organization's supporting organization status. However, the IRS subsequently held that a supporting organization can have a for-profit subsidiary and not disturb its classification as a supporting entity.[82]

---

[77] See § 11.3(c).
[78] IRC § 509(a)(3)(A). See § 11.3(c), text accompanied by notes 188, 191.
[79] Reg. § 1.509(a)-4(e)(1).
[80] See § 4.6.
[81] Priv. Ltr. Rul. 9305026.
[82] Priv. Ltr. Rul. 9637051. The IRS ruled as to the tax consequences of a liquidation of a for-profit subsidiary into a supporting organization (Priv. Ltr. Rul. 9645017) (in general, see *supra* § 2(d)).

CHAPTER THIRTY-TWO

Tax-Exempt Organizations, Partnerships, and Joint Ventures

§ 32.1 Partnerships Basics

§ 32.2 The Tax Exemption Issue
  (a) Evolution of the Law
  (b) Current State of the Law
     (i) General Rules
     (ii) Health Care Institutions

§ 32.3 Joint Ventures

§ 32.4 Whole Hospital Joint Ventures

§ 32.5 Information Reporting

§ 32.6 Alternatives to Partnerships

One of the most important phenomena involving tax-exempt organizations in the modern era is the use of related organizations. There is nothing particularly revolutionary about this technique, as reflected in the discussion about the use of subsidiaries by tax-exempt organizations.[1] What is different is the contemporary willingness of many tax-exempt organizations to simultaneously use many different forms of related entities, be they for-profit or nonprofit, trust or corporation, taxable or nontaxable. This includes participation by tax-exempt organizations in partnerships.

§ 32.1 PARTNERSHIPS BASICS

A partnership is a business form, recognized in law as an entity, as is a corporation or trust. It is usually evidenced by a document, which is a partnership agreement, executed between persons who are the partners; the persons may be individuals, corporations, and/or other partnerships. Each partner owns one or more interests, called units, in the partnership.

The term *partnership* is defined in the federal tax law to include "a syndicate, group, pool, joint venture, or other unincorporated organization, through or by means of which any business, financial operation, or venture is carried on, and which is not . . . a trust or estate or a corporation."[2] This term is applied in a broad fashion. For example, co-owners of income-producing real estate who operate the property (either through an agent of one or more of them) for their joint profit are

---

[1] See Chapters 30 and 31.
[2] IRC § 7701(a)(2).

operating a partnership.[3] A partnership usually entails a profit motive. Thus, one court defined a partnership as a "contract of two or more persons to place their money, efforts labor, and skill, or some or all of them, in lawful commerce or business, and to divide the profit and bear the loss in definite proportions."[4]

Partners are of two types: general and limited. The types are delineated principally by the extent of the partners' liability for the acts of the partnership. Generally, liability for the consequences of the partnership's operations rests with the general partner(s), while the exposure to liability for the functions of the partnership for the limited partners is confined to the amount of the limited partner's contribution to the partnership. A general partner is liable for satisfaction of the ongoing obligations of the partnership and can be called upon to make additional contributions of capital to it. Every partnership must have at least one general partner. Sometimes where there is more than one general partner, one of them is designated the managing general partner.

Many partnerships have only general partners, who contribute cash, property, and/or services. This type of partnership is the *general partnership*. The interests of the general partners may or may not be equal. In this type of partnership, which is essentially a joint venture, generally all of the partners are equally liable for satisfaction of the obligations of the partnership and can be called upon to make additional capital contributions to the partnership.

Some partnerships, however, need or want to attract capital from sources other than the general partners. This capital can come from investors, who are termed limited partners. Their interest in the partnership is, as noted, limited in the sense that their liability is limited. The liability of a limited partner is confined to the amount of the capital contribution—the investment. The limited partners are involved to obtain a return on their investment and perhaps to procure some tax advantages. A partnership with both general and limited partners is termed a *limited partnership*.

The partnership is the entity that acquires the property, develops it (if necessary), and sometimes continues to operate and maintain the property. Where a tax-exempt organization is the general partner, it is not the owner of the property (the partnership is) but nonetheless it can have many of the incidents of ownership, such as participation in the cash flow generated by the property, a preferential leasing arrangement, and/or the general perception by the outside world that the property is owned by the tax-exempt organization. The tax-exempt organization leases space in the property owned by the partnership. Often, the tax-exempt organization will have the option to purchase the property from the partnership after the passage of a stated period of time.

Partnerships do not pay taxes. They are merely conduits of net revenue to the partners, who bear the responsibility for paying tax on the net income. Partnerships are also conduits of the tax advantages of the ownership of property, and thus pass through preference items such as depreciation and interest deductions.

If an entity fails to qualify under the federal tax laws as a partnership, it will be treated as an *association*, which means taxed as a corporation. When that hap-

---

[3] Rev. Rul. 54-369, 1954-2 C.B. 364; Rev. Rul. 54-170, 1954-1 C.B. 213.
[4] Whiteford v. United States, 61-1 U.S.T.C. ¶ 9301, at 79,762 (D. Kan. 1960).

pens, as a general rule the entity will have to pay taxes and the ability to pass through tax advantages to the equity owners is lost.[5]

In many instances, it is clear that the parties in an arrangement intend to create and operate a partnership. However, in some cases, the law will treat an arrangement as a partnership (usually a general partnership) for tax purposes, even though the parties involved insist that their relationship is something else (such as landlord and tenant or payor and payee of royalties). (When a partnership form is imposed as a matter of law, sometimes the arrangement is termed a *joint venture*;[6] the terms are synonymous in this setting.) The issue arises often in the unrelated business income context, where a tax-exempt organization is asserting that certain income is passive in nature (most frequently, rent or royalty income) and the IRS is contending that the income was derived from active participation in a partnership (or joint venture).

The federal tax law is inconsistent in stating the criteria for ascertaining whether a partnership is to be found as a matter of law. The U.S. Supreme Court stated that "[w]hen the existence of an alleged partnership arrangement is challenged by outsiders, the question arises whether the partners really and truly intended to join together for the purpose of carrying on business and sharing in the profits or losses or both."[7] The Court added that the parties' "intention is a question of fact, to be determined from testimony disclosed by their 'agreement considered as a whole, and by their conduct in execution of its provisions.' "[8] In one instance, a court examined state law and concluded that the most important element in determining whether a landlord-tenant relationship or joint venture agreement exists is the intention of the parties. This court also held that the burden of proving the existence of a partnership is on the party who claims that that type of relationship exists (usually, the IRS).[9]

Yet, another court declared that "it is well settled that neither local law nor the expressed intent of the parties is conclusive as to the existence or nonexistence of a partnership or joint venture for federal tax purposes."[10] The court then described the test to follow:

> . . . "whether, considering all the facts—the agreement, the conduct of the parties in execution of its provisions, their statements, the testimony of disinterested persons, the relationship of the parties, their respective abilities and

---

[5] Moreover, the partnership must have effective ownership of the property for these deductions to be available, rather than have the ownership be by the exempt organization/general partner (e.g., Smith v. Comm'r, 50 T.C.M. 1444 (1985)).

[6] See *infra* § 3.

[7] Commissioner v. Tower, 327 U.S. 280, 286–287 (1946).

[8] *Id.* at 287 (citations omitted). These principles are equally applicable in determining the existence of a joint venture (see *infra* § 3) (e.g., Estate of Smith v. Comm'r, 313 F.2d 724, 729 (8th Cir. 1963), *aff'g in part, rev'g in part, and remanding* 33 T.C. 465 (1959); Luna v. Comm'r, 42 T.C. 1067 (1964); Beck Chemical Equip. Corp. v. Comm'r, 27 T.C. 840 (1957).

[9] Harlan E. Moore Charitable Trust v. United States, 812 F. Supp. 130, 132 (C.D. Ill. 1993), *aff'd*, 9 F.3d 623 (7th Cir. 1993).

[10] Trust U/W Emily Oblinger v. Comm'r, 100 T.C. 114 (1993). The court cited a number of court opinions as authority for this proposition, relying principally on Haley v. Comm'r, 203 F.2d 815 (5th Cir. 1953), *rev'g and rem'g* 16 T.C. 1509 (1951).

capital contributions, the actual control of income and the purposes for which it is used, and any other facts throwing light on their true intent—the parties in good faith and acting with a business purpose intended to join together in the present conduct of the enterprise."[11]

The court wrote that the "realities of the taxpayer's economic interest rather than the niceties of the conveyancer's art should determine the power to tax."[12] The court added: "Among the critical elements involved in this determination are the existence of controls over the venture and a risk of loss in the taxpayer."[13] Finally, the court said that it is not bound by the "nomenclature used by the parties," so that a document titled, for example, a lease, may in law be a partnership agreement.[14]

This dichotomy is well-illustrated in a case involving a charitable organization and its tenant-farmer; the issue was whether the relationship was landlord-tenant, partnership, or joint venture.[15] The specific question before the court was whether the rent, equaling 50 percent of the crops and produce grown on the farm, constituted rent that was excludable from taxation as unrelated business income.[16] The court looked to state law to ascertain the meaning to be given the term *rent*. It observed that the written contracts at issue contained provisions usually found in leases, the tenant furnished all of the machinery and labor in the production of crops, and the tenant generally made decisions with a farm manager as to the day-to-day operations of the farm. The court concluded that the contracts as a whole clearly reflected the intention of the parties to create a landlord-tenant relationship, rather than a partnership.

The IRS unsuccessfully contended that the charitable organization, by furnishing the seed and one-half of the cost of fertilizer, weed spray, and combining, had engaged in farming as a partner or joint venturer. The court observed that these types of arrangements were not uncommon in share-crop leases, and noted that the furnishing of these items ordinarily increased the crop yield and the net return of both the landlord and tenant substantially more than the amount invested by each for the items. The court also analyzed the effect on the landlord-tenant relationship of the hiring by the charitable organization of a farm manager for the supervision of the tenant-farmer. The farm manager advised the tenant on topics such as crops, seed, weed spray, and fertilizer; decisions were made by the mutual agreement of the tenant and manager. The court concluded that the fact of the farm manager did not adversely affect the landlord-tenant relationship, and generally found that the arrangement was not that of a partnership (or joint venture).

As a general rule, a partnership is a very useful and beneficial way for one or more individuals or organizations to acquire, own, and operate property. However, there can be problems with this approach in the tax-exempt organizations context.[17]

---

[11] Trust U/W Emily Oblinger v. Comm'r, *supra* note 10 at 118, citing Comm'r v. Culbertson, 337 U.S. 733, 742 (1949). Also Luna v. Comm'r, *supra* note 8, at 1077–1078.

[12] Trust U/W Emily Oblinger v. Comm'r, *supra* note 10 at 118.

[13] *Id*. at 118–119.

[14] *Id*. at 119.

[15] United States v. Myra Found., 382 F.2d 107 (8th Cir. 1967).

[16] See § 27.1(h)(i). This case was decided before enactment of the "passive rent rules".

[17] The foregoing is, by necessity, an overview of the law of partnerships. For a comprehensive analysis

§ 32.2   THE TAX EXEMPTION ISSUE

The IRS is not enamored with the thought of tax-exempt organizations (particularly charitable ones) in partnerships, other than as limited partners in a prudent investment vehicle.[18] To date, all of the controversy has focused on charitable organizations in partnerships, although some or all of the principles of law being developed may become applicable to other types of tax-exempt organizations, such as social welfare organizations and business leagues.[19]

It is the view of the IRS that substantial benefits can be provided to the for-profit participants in a partnership (usually the limited partners) with a tax-exempt organization where the exempt organization is a general partner. This concern has its origins in arrangements involving hospitals and physicians, such as a limited partnership formed to build and manage a medical office building, with a hospital as the general partner and investing physicians as limited partners.[20] Where these substantial benefits are present, the IRS will—upon discovering them—not be hesitant to assert private inurement and private benefit.[21] Yet the law is clear that a tax-exempt charitable organization may participate as a partner in a partnership.[22]

It is the position of the IRS that a charitable organization will lose its federal income tax exemption if it participates as the, or a, general partner in a limited partnership, unless the principal purpose of the limited partnership itself is to further charitable purposes.[23] Even where the partnership can so qualify, the exemption is revoked if the charitable organization/general partner is not adequately insulated from the day-to-day management responsibilities of the partnership and/or if the limited partners are to receive an undue economic return. The IRS recognizes that a charitable organization can be operated exclusively for exempt purposes, and simultaneously be a general partner and satisfy its fiduciary responsibilities with respect to the other partners.[24]

---

of these entities (from a tax-exempt organizations perspective), see Sanders, *Partnerships & Joint Ventures Involving Tax-Exempt Organizations* (New York: John Wiley & Sons, Inc., 1994) (*Partnerships & Joint Ventures*), particularly Chapters 1, 3, and 4.

[18] E.g., Gordanier, Jr., "Structuring Securities Partnerships for Tax-Exempt and Foreign Investors," 7 *J. Partnership Tax.* (No. 2) 24 (1990); Menna, "Leveraged Real Estate Investments by Tax-Exempt and Taxable Investors: Comparing the Forms of Investment," 17 *J. Real Estate Tax.* (No. 3) 231 (1990); Williamson & Blum, "Tax Planning for Real Estate Ownership and Investment by Tax-Exempt Entities," 16 *J. Real Estate Tax.* (No. 2) 139 (1989).

[19] See Chapters 12, 13.

[20] The history of the position of the IRS in these regards is detailed in *Partnerships & Joint Ventures*, at 260–268.

[21] The IRS is not averse to using its authority in this context. For example, the agency created the private inurement per se doctrine in the health care context as a basis for revocation of hospitals' tax-exempt status (see § 19.8). The IRS revoked the tax exemption of hospitals for engaging in private inurement transactions (e.g., Priv. Ltr. Rul. 9130002). In general, the IRS concludes from time to time that the tax-exempt status of other types of charitable organizations should be terminated because of private inurement (e.g., see Tech. Adv. Mem. 9335001 (concerning a private foundation)). In general, Chapter 19.

[22] On one occasion, the IRS ruled that the tax-exempt status of a charitable organization should not be revoked because of its participation as a general partner in seven limited partnerships (Priv. Ltr. Rul. 8938001).

[23] Gen. Couns. Mem. 39005. Cf. Yanowitz & Purcell, "Using the Investment Partnership as a Charitable Activity: A Means/End Analysis," 60 *J. Tax.* (No. 5) 214 (1984).

[24] Gen. Couns. Mem. 39546.

Confusion as to the ability of tax-exempt charitable organizations to participate as general partners in limited partnerships was added when the U.S. Tax
Court held, in 1993, that an organization did not qualify as a charitable entity
where it was a co-general partner in limited partnerships, where the other general
partner was a for-profit corporation and the limited partners were individuals, and
where the purpose of the partnerships was to operate low-income housing projects.
The court said that the organization's participation violated the operational test[25] in
that the operation of the partnerships would cause federal and state tax benefits to
flow to the nonexempt partners.[26] By reason of the organization's involvement in
the partnerships, the underlying properties would receive property tax reductions.
The partnership would be eligible, under federal tax law, for general business credits and low-income housing credits; pursuant to management agreements, the organization had the responsibility for ensuring that the partnership complied with
the business tax credit requirements. The organization received, as compensation,
percentages of state tax savings. The court concluded that the "keystone of . . . [this]
entire plan is of course to lend its [the organization's] exempt status to achieving
the objective of property tax reduction."[27] The organization also was deprived of
tax-exempt status by reason of the private inurement doctrine[28] because its "activities here serve the commercial purposes of the for-profit partners in the limited
partnerships of which . . . [the organization] is a general partner."[29]

Prior to a review of the law concerning charitable organizations in partnerships, it is appropriate to trace the evolution of the doctrine.

(a) Evolution of the Law

Originally, the IRS was of the view that involvement by a charitable organization
in a limited partnership as general partner was the basis for automatic revocation
of tax exemption, irrespective of the purpose of the partnership. This view, predicated upon the private inurement doctrine, is known as the *per se rule*.

The *per se rule* surfaced in 1978, when the IRS privately ruled that participation by a charitable organization in a partnership, where the organization was the
general partner and private investors were limited partners, was contrary to the
organization's tax-exempt status in that private economic benefit resulted to the
limited partners.[30] In this ruling, the IRS staked out this position:

> . . . [I]f you entered [into] the proposed partnership, you would be a direct par-
> ticipant in an arrangement for sharing the net profits of an income producing
> venture with private individuals and organizations of a non-charitable nature.
> By agreeing to serve as the general partner of the proposed . . . project, you

---

[25] See § 4.5.
[26] Housing Pioneers, Inc. v. Comm'r, 65 T.C.M. 2191 (1993).
[27] *Id*. at 2195.
[28] See Chapter 19.
[29] Housing Pioneers, Inc. v. Comm'r, *supra* note 26, at 2196. This opinion was affirmed but on the
ground that the organization failed to show that it was a qualified nonprofit organization for purposes of the low-income housing tax credit (IRC § 42(h)(5)(B)) (95-1 U.S.T.C. ¶ 50,126 (9th Cir. 1995)).
[30] Priv. Ltr. Rul. 7820058.

would take on an obligation to further the private financial interests of the other partners. This would create a conflict of interest that is legally incompatible with you being operated exclusively for charitable purposes.

Thus, the IRS posture on the matter was clear: A tax-exempt charitable organization would lose its tax exemption if it functioned as the general partner of a limited partnership on the ground that it was furthering the private interests of the limited partners. This was the IRS position, even though the purpose of the partnership was to advance a charitable objective (in the case, the development and operation of a low-income housing project).

The *per se rule* was advanced again in 1979, with the IRS issuing an adverse ruling to a charitable organization that was the general partner in a limited partnership (also again, having the purpose of maintaining a low-income housing project). As before, the IRS pronounced the organization a "direct participant in an arrangement for sharing the net profits of an income producing venture" with private individuals, so that the organization is "further[ing] the private financial interest of the [limited] partners."[31]

Several months later, the issue became the subject of litigation in the then-named U.S. Court of Claims.[32] Before that court was the case of the charitable organization that was the subject of the 1979 ruling and that held a one percent interest in a partnership as a general partner, a for-profit corporation that held a 4.5 percent interest as the other general partner, and an unspecified number of individuals that held the balance of the partnership interests as limited partners. At issue was the tax-exempt status of the tax-exempt organization. However, there is no opinion in the case because it was settled and the matter dismissed in 1980.

The *per se rule* was temporarily abandoned by the IRS and, as the result of the settlement, the charitable organization was allowed to serve as a general partner in the limited partnership without endangering its tax exemption. The organization ultimately prevailed because it was able to demonstrate a relatively limited involvement in both the finances, and overall control and management, of the project. The organization was successful in showing that the other general partner was, by reason of provisions in the partnership agreement, primarily responsible for managing the financial and business aspects of the project, thereby permitting it to work primarily in furtherance of its tax-exempt purposes without having to become unduly involved in the nonexempt aspects of the venture.

The terms of the settlement proved to be a harbinger of the IRS position to come. Nonetheless, the IRS continued to pursue application of the *per se rule* in other cases.

For example, an IRS private letter ruling issued in 1979, concerning the issue as to whether certain fees derived by tax-exempt lawyer referral services were items of unrelated income, reflected this IRS position.[33] The IRS ruled that, while flat counseling fees paid by clients and registration fees paid by lawyers were not taxable, the fees paid by lawyers to the organization based on a percent-

---

[31] Priv. Ltr. Rul. dated Feb. 6, 1979.
[32] Strawbridge Square, Inc. v. United States (Ct. Cl. No. 471-79T).
[33] Priv. Ltr. Rul. 7952002.

age of the fees received by the lawyers for providing legal services to clients referred to them constituted unrelated income. The reason: The subsequently established lawyer-client relationship was a commercial undertaking and the ongoing fee arrangement with the percentage feature placed the organization in the position of being in a joint venture in furtherance of those commercial objectives.

This perseverance on the part of the IRS also is mirrored in another case, this one concerning syndication of a play. In this instance, a tax-exempt theater group was struggling in its efforts to stage a play at the Kennedy Center in Washington, D.C. Needing financial assistance, it underwrote its production costs with funds provided by private investors. The IRS sought to revoke the organization's tax-exempt status for attempting to sustain the arts in this fashion but lost, both at trial and on appeal.[34] Again, the matter involved a partnership that was being used to further the tax-exempt ends of the general partner. The courts in the case placed some emphasis on the facts that the partnership had no interest in the tax-exempt organization or its other activities, the limited partners had no control over the way in which the exempt organization operated or managed its affairs, and none of the limited partners nor any officer or director of a corporate limited partner was an officer or director of the charitable organization.

The first manifestation of a relaxation of the stance of the IRS in these regards appeared in 1983 in the form of an IRS general counsel memorandum.[35] On that occasion, the IRS chief counsel's office opined that it is possible for a charitable organization to participate as a general partner in a limited partnership without jeopardizing its tax exemption. The IRS's lawyers advised that two aspects of the matter should be reviewed: (1) whether the participation may be in conflict with the goals and purposes of the charitable organization, and (2) whether the terms of the partnership agreement contain provisions that "insulate" the charitable organization from certain of the obligations imposed on a general partner. In the instance involved, the limited partnership (another low-income housing venture) was found to further the organization's charitable purposes and several specific provisions of the partnership agreement were deemed to provide the requisite insulation for the charitable organization/general partner. Thus, the organization was permitted to serve as the partnership's general partner and simultaneously retain its tax exemption.

This position of the IRS Chief Counsel opened the way for many favorable private letter rulings concerning charitable organizations in partnerships. Each of these partnerships, however, was held to be in furtherance of charitable objectives, such as the construction and operation of a medical office building on the grounds of a hospital, the purchase and operation of a CAT scanner at a hospital, and low-income housing projects. To date, the IRS has yet to issue a private letter ruling denying a charitable organization tax-exempt status because of its involvement as a general partner in a limited partnership.[36] Indeed, the IRS frequently concludes that a tax-exempt charitable organization can participate as a general

---

[34] Plumstead Theatre Soc'y, Inc. v. Comm'r, 74 T.C. 1324 (1980), aff'd, 675 F.2d 244 (9th Cir. 1982).

[35] Gen. Couns. Mem. 39005.

[36] This observation is made with the understanding that the facts in some of these rulings are altered at the request of the IRS and that some ruling requests in this area are withdrawn in anticipation of the issuance of an adverse ruling.

partner in a limited partnership without endangering its tax-exempt status.[37] Also, on occasion, a charitable organization can achieve exempt purposes by involvement in a partnership as a limited partner.[38]

(b) Current State of the Law

(i) General Rules.   The current position of the IRS as to whether a charitable organization will have its tax-exempt status revoked (or recognition denied) if it functions as a general partner in a limited partnership is the subject of a three-part test,[39] which is the successor to the *per se rule*.[40]

Under this three-part test, the IRS first looks to determine whether the charitable organization/general partner is serving a charitable purpose by means of the partnership. If the partnership is serving a charitable purpose, the IRS applies the remainder of the test. Should the partnership fail to adhere to the charitability standard, however, the charitable organization/general partner will be deprived of its tax-exempt status.

The balance of the test is designed to ascertain whether the charity's role as general partner inhibits its charitable purposes. Here, the IRS looks to means by which the organization may, under the particular facts and circumstances, be insulated from the day-to-day responsibilities as general partner and whether or not the limited partners are receiving an undue economic benefit from the partnership. It is the view of the IRS that there is an inherent tension between the ability of a charitable organization to function exclusively in furtherance of its exempt functions and the obligation of a general partner to operate the partnership for the benefit of the limited partners. This tension is the same perceived phenomenon that the IRS, when applying its *per se rule*, chose to characterize as a conflict of interest.

An instance of application of this test appeared in an IRS private letter ruling made public in 1985.[41] In that case, a charitable organization became a general partner in a real estate limited partnership that leased all of the space in the property to the organization and a related charitable organization. The IRS applied the first part of the test and found that the partnership was serving charitable ends because both of the tenants were charitable organizations. (The IRS general counsel memorandum underlying this private ruling[42] noted that, if the lessee organization that was not the general partner had not been a charitable entity, the general partner would have forfeited its tax exemption.) Upon application of the rest of the test, the IRS found that the general partner was adequately insulated from the day-to-day management responsibilities of the partnership and that the limited partners' economic return was reasonable.

---

[37] E.g., Priv. Ltr. Rul. 8338127.

[38] E.g., Priv. Ltr. Rul. 9608039.

[39] This was articulated in Gen. Couns. Mem. 39005 (see text accompanying *supra* note 35).

[40] In general, Hopkins, "Tax Consequences of a Charity's Participation as a General Partner in a Limited Partnership Venture: A Commentary on the McGovern Analysis," 30 *Tax Notes* (No. 4) 361 (1986), written in response to McGovern, "The Tax Consequences of a Charity's Participation as a General Partner in a Limited Partnership Venture," 29 *Tax Notes* 1261 (1985).

[41] Priv. Ltr. Rul. 8541108.

[42] Gen. Couns. Mem. 39444.

In this private letter ruling, the IRS offered this guidance in explication of the second and third elements of the test:

> If a private interest is served [by a limited partnership in which a charitable organization is the general partner], it must be incidental in both a qualitative and quantitative sense. In order to be incidental in a qualitative sense, it must be a necessary concomitant of the activity which benefits the public at large. In other words, the activity can be accomplished only by benefiting certain private individuals. To be incidental in a quantitative sense, the private benefit must not be substantial after considering the overall public benefit conferred by the activity.

Added the IRS: "[I]f the [charitable] organization is serving a private interest, other than incidentally, then its participation in a limited partnership [as general partner] will [adversely] affect its exempt status." However, as discussed next, considerable clarity has been subsequently provided in this area of the federal tax law as the IRS has formulated its policies concerning the involvement of hospitals and other health care institutions in partnerships where physicians practicing at the hospitals are limited partners in these partnerships.

As to means by which the requisite insulation may be created, a commentator suggested one or more of nine provisions in a partnership agreement involving a tax-exempt organization: a requirement of income distributions to the organization at least in proportion to its capital contribution, a ceiling on losses allocable to the organization equal to its share of total capital, a requirement that all transactions between the partnership and other parties be at fair market value, a limit on the exposure of the organization to liabilities of the venture and corresponding indemnification, exoneration of the organization from repayments of amounts invested by the other partners, a prohibition against loans by the organization to the partnership to finance operations (at least not without full security) or to the nonexempt partners to finance contributions, options (puts, calls, or rights of first refusal) granted to the organization upon disposition of the partnership property or interests, no such options in the nonexempt partners unless the exempt organization is to receive at least fair market value, and powers in the organization to appoint a majority of the governing body of the partnership.[43]

Until mid-1994, the IRS position with respect to charitable organizations in partnerships was represented solely by the three-part test. However, at that time, a private letter ruling appeared which added requirements to the basic test.[44] The IRS observed that the organization was "governed by an independent board of directors" composed of church and community leaders, and that it had no other relationship with any of the commercial companies involved in the project. The

---

[43] *Partnerships & Joint Ventures*, at 266–267. If the tax-exempt organization/general partner is shielded too much, however, the partnership may lose its tax status as a partnership (that is, as a nontaxable flow-through entity). Should that occur, the entity may become an "association" taxable as a corporation (IRC § 7701(a)(3)) (see text accompanied by *supra* note 2). The IRS's office of Chief Counsel raised this issue for the benefit of the agency's reviewers (Gen. Couns. Mem. 39546).

[44] Priv. Ltr. Rul. 9438030.

IRS added that no information indicated that the organization was controlled by or "otherwise unduly influenced" by the limited partners or any company involved in the development or management of the project.

(ii) Health Care Institutions. Recently, nearly all of the federal tax law in this setting has developed as the result of innovative financing techniques, including partnerships, by or for the benefit of hospitals and other health care organizations, institutions, and systems.

One of the most recent manifestations of this phenomenon is the IRS's position with respect to the sale of a hospital department's net revenue stream to a limited partnership (or joint venture) involving the hospital and physicians practicing in the department. The IRS holds that this use of hospital assets is private inurement per se (that is, the amount of the funds flowing to the physicians is not evaluated against a standard of reasonableness), causing the hospital to lose its tax exemption.[45] In formulating its position in this regard, the chief counsel's office of the IRS used the occasion (in late 1991) to restate and update the analysis the IRS uses in evaluating the participation of hospitals in a partnership arrangement.

The IRS's lawyers emphasized that the participation by a tax-exempt hospital as a general partner in a limited partnership is not inconsistent with tax exemption on a per-se basis.[46] In each partnership situation, the IRS determines the presence or absence of private inurement or more than incidental private benefit[47] by evaluating all of the facts and circumstances, applying a standard of review termed "careful scrutiny." This three-step analysis is as follows:

1. Does the partnership further a charitable purpose?

2. If so, does the partnership agreement reflect an arrangement that permits the tax-exempt organization to act primarily in furtherance of its exempt (charitable) purposes?

3. If so, does the arrangement cause the tax-exempt organization to convey an impermissible private benefit to the limited partners?[48]

The third criterion requires a finding, if the hospital is to continue to be tax-exempt, that the benefits received by the limited partners are incidental to the exempt purposes advanced by the partnership. Thus, according to this analytical approach, a hospital's participation in a partnership or joint venture is inconsistent with its tax exemption if it does not further a charitable purpose, or if there is either inadequate protection against financial loss by the hospital or inappropriate or excessive financial gain flowing to the limited partners (investors/physicians).

The IRS, in evaluating these situations, looks to see "what the hospital gets

---

[45] See § 19.8.

[46] Gen. Couns. Mem. 39862. The IRS bluntly stated that it "no longer contends that participation as a general partner in a partnership is *per se* inconsistent with [tax] exemption."

[47] E.g., Gen. Couns. Mem. 37789.

[48] In stating these factors, the IRS reaffirmed the ongoing validity of Gen. Couns. Mem. 39005 (see *supra* note 35), 39444 (see *supra* note 42), 39546 (see *supra* note 43).

in return for the benefit conferred on the physician-investors." The IRS is least likely to find a basis for revocation of tax exemption because of hospital partnerships where a "new health care provider or resource was made available to the community."[49] Of importance also is whether the partnership itself became a "property owner or service provider, subject to all the attendant risks, responsibilities, and potential rewards." By contrast, in the net revenue stream partnerships, the IRS saw insufficient community benefit; the partnership was viewed as "a shell type of arrangement where the hospital continues to own and operate the facilities in question and the joint venture invests only in a profits interest." The arrangement was perceived as only incidentally promoting health; the IRS believed that the "hospitals engaged in these ventures largely as a means to retain and reward members of their medical staffs; to attract their admissions and referrals; and to pre-empt the physicians from investing in or creating a competing provider."

Another feature the IRS deplores is the situation where the general partner (such as a hospital or a taxable subsidiary of the hospital) is liable for partnership losses and is required to maintain a loss reserve, while the limited partners are not burdened with much risk. The net revenue stream arrangement did not result in "improved patient convenience, greater accessibility of physicians, or any other direct benefit to the community."

The IRS has identified the following legitimate purposes (absent private inurement per se) for involvement of a hospital in a partnership (or joint venture): the raising of needed capital, the bringing of new services or a new provider to a community, the sharing of a risk inherent in a new activity, and/or the pooling of diverse areas of expertise. Prior pronouncements from the IRS reflect the following factors favored by the IRS: a limited contractual liability of the tax-exempt partner, a limited (reasonable) rate of return on the investment by the limited partners, a right in the tax-exempt organization of first refusal on the disposition of an asset of the partnership, the involvement of other general partners obligated to protect the interests of the limited partners, and the absence of any obligation to return the limited partners' capital from the resources of the tax-exempt general partner. The IRS's audit guidelines for the examination of hospitals[50] summarize the fact situations that may cause private inurement to arise: where participation in the venture imposes on the tax-exempt organization obligations that conflict with its exempt purposes; where there is a disproportionate allocation of profits and losses to the nonexempt (usually, limited) partners; where the tax-exempt partner makes loans to the partnership that are commercially unreasonable (that is, they have a low interest rate or inadequate security); where the tax-exempt partner provides property or services to the partnership at less than fair market value; and/or where a nonexempt partner receives more than reasonable compensation for the sale of property or services to the joint venture.[51]

The IRS will pursue a private inurement rationale where there is a "com-

---

[49] E.g., Gen. Couns. Mem. 39732.
[50] IRS Audit Guidelines for Hospitals, Manual Transmittal 7(10)69–38 for Exempt Organizations Examinations Guidelines Handbook (March 27, 1992). See § 24.8(c).
[51] Id. § 342.

plete lack of symmetry in upside opportunities and downside risks for the physician-investors." At the same time, the position struck by the IRS in the context of hospitals and physicians in partnerships should not "be read to imply that a typical joint venture that involves true shared ownership, risks, responsibilities, and rewards and that demonstrably furthers a charitable purpose should be met automatically with suspicion or disapproved merely because physician-investors have an ownership interest."

On occasion, a hospital or hospital system will create a taxable subsidiary and cause that entity to be a (or the) general partner in a limited partnership.[52]

These pronouncements by the IRS in the health care context have added considerable clarity to the dimensions of the federal tax law concerning the permissible and impermissible participation, in general, of charitable organizations in partnerships.

§ 32.3   JOINT VENTURES

A tax-exempt organization may enter into a joint venture with a for-profit organization, without adversely affecting its tax-exempt status, as long as doing so furthers exempt purposes and the joint venture agreement does not prevent it from acting exclusively to further those purposes. A joint venture does not present the private inurement problems that the IRS associates with participation by exempt organizations in limited partnerships (discussed above). By contrast, an involvement in a joint venture by a tax-exempt organization would lead to loss (or denial) of tax exemption if the primary purpose of the exempt organization is to participate in the venture and if the function of the venture is unrelated to the exempt purposes of the tax-exempt organization.

One court defined a *joint venture* as an association of two or more persons with intent to carry out a single business venture for joint profit, for which purpose they combine their efforts, property, money, skill, and knowledge, but they do so without creating a formal partnership, trust, or corporation.[53] Thus, two or more entities (including tax-exempt organizations) may operate a business enterprise as a joint venture.[54]

Generally, when a tax-exempt organization acquires an interest in a joint venture (such as by transfer of funds), the event is not a taxable one, because the action is a one-time activity and thus is not a business that is regularly carried on.[55] That is, the exempt organization is not likely to be characterized as being in the business of establishing or investing in partnerships.[56]

Where the purpose of the joint venture is investment, the joint venture will be looked through to determine the nature of the revenue being received by the exempt organization. It is rare that the investment income will be exempt func-

---

[52] In general, see § 31.4.
[53] Whiteford v. United States, *supra* note 4, at 79,762.
[54] Stevens Bros. Found., Inc. v. Comm'r, 324 F.2d 633 (8th Cir. 1963).
[55] See § 26.3.
[56] E.g., Priv. Ltr. Rul. 8818008.

tion revenue. Usually, the income is passive investment income and thus is not taxed.[57] But if the participation in the joint venture is the principal activity of the exempt organization and the purpose of the venture is not an exempt one for the organization, it will, as observed, lose (or be denied) its tax-exempt status by reason of participation in the venture.

A tax-exempt organization may become involved in a joint venture with a for-profit organization in advancement of an exempt purpose. Again, the look-through principle applies, with the revenue derived by the exempt organization from the venture characterized as related revenue. For example, a charitable organization participating as a general partner in a venture, with a for-profit entity, to own and operate an ambulatory surgical center was determined by the IRS to be engaging in a related activity.[58] Likewise, the IRS ruled that a joint venture between a charitable organization and a for-profit one, for the purpose of organizing and operating a free-standing alcoholism/substance abuse treatment center, would not jeopardize the tax-exempt status of the charitable organization.[59] Still another illustration is the IRS ruling that a tax-exempt hospital may, without endangering its exempt status, participate with a for-profit organization for the purpose of providing magnetic resonance imaging services in an underserved community.[60] Other IRS private letter rulings provide examples of joint ventures that did not adversely affect the tax-exempt status of the tax-exempt organization involved.[61]

A joint venture of this nature may be structured as a limited liability company.[62]

The IRS is concerned, nonetheless, about situations where the involvement of a tax-exempt organization in a joint venture gives rise, or may give rise, to private inurement.[63] For example, it is the view of the IRS that a tax-exempt hospital endangers its tax exemption because of its involvement in a joint venture with members of its medical staff, where the hospital sold to the joint venture the net revenue stream of a hospital department for a stated period of time.[64] In this situation and similar others, the application of the private inurement doctrine is triggered by the inherent structure of the joint venture and not by the reasonableness of the compensation.[65]

Also, in some instances, the IRS will characterize an arrangement between parties as a joint venture, for tax purposes.[66]

A tax-exempt organization may also enter into a joint venture with another tax-exempt organization, in furtherance of the tax-exempt purposes of both of them.[67]

---

[57] See § 27.1.
[58] Priv. Ltr. Rul. 8817039.
[59] Priv. Ltr. Rul. 8521055.
[60] Priv. Ltr. Rul. 8833038.
[61] E.g., Priv. Ltr. Rul. 8621059.
[62] E.g., Priv. Ltr. Rul. 9637050.
[63] See Chapter 19.
[64] Gen. Couns. Mem. 39862.
[65] See § 19.8.
[66] See text accompanied by *supra* notes 6–16.
[67] E.g., Priv. Ltr. Rul. 9249026. In general, Sanders and Cobb, "Recent IRS Rulings Provide New Standards for Joint Ventures Involving Charities," 18 *Exempt Org. Tax Rev.* (No. 2) 213 (Nov. 1997); Korman

§ 32.4   WHOLE HOSPITAL JOINT VENTURES

There are developments brewing in the health care field that could have significant implications for all public charities and perhaps other types of tax-exempt
organizations. This matter concerns the *whole hospital joint venture*.

As discussed, a tax-exempt health care organization, as well as any other
type of exempt organization, can participate in a joint venture with a for-profit
person and not adversely affect the organization's tax-exempt status, as long as
the purpose of involvement of the exempt organization in the joint venture is furtherance of exempt purposes.[68] In this type of joint venture, in the health care context, the exempt entity utilizes its assets (usually only some of them) in
furtherance of a charitable purpose.

The whole hospital joint venture—in some respects, a misnomer—is much
different from a conventional joint venture. With this approach, the hospital or
other exempt entity transfers its assets to the joint venture, with the for-profit organization assuming control over the assets and managing the day-to-day operations of the venture. For example, ownershp of one or more hospitals might be
transferred. The tax-exempt health care organization does not directly engage in
health care activities; it receives income and other distributions attributable to its
ownership interest in the venture. There usually is a board of directors of this joint
venture. Technically, the venture is a partnership[69] or a limited liability company.[70]

Essentially, a whole hospital joint venture is another form of hospital network;[71] it is a way of integrating a nonprofit hospital into the activities of a large,
for-profit entity. This can lead to access to managed care contracts, greater efficiency of operations, and additional funding of charitable programs. From the
standpoint of the for-profit entity, the venture provides a means to "acquire" a
hospital without having to engage in an outright purchase of the institution.

Thus, the fundamental distinction between joint ventures in general and
whole hospital joint ventures—one that may determine whether the exempt organization is able to obtain or maintain tax exemption—is that, in instances of the
former, the exempt entity continues to engage in health care functions while, in
the latter case, the entity is an owner of the venture which itself controls the assets
and operates the programs underlying the health care activity. This raises the
question, unresolved at this time, as to whether participation in a whole hospital
joint venture would cause the hospital or other health care organization to lose or
be denied tax-exempt status. Other issues are the possibility of private inurement
or private benefit to the for-profit entity in the venture[72] and the likelihood that
income from the venture is unrelated business income to the exempt hospital.[73]

Guidance is expected from the IRS as to the tax consequences of whole hos-

---

& Gaske, "Joint Ventures Between Tax-Exempt and Commercial Health Care Providers," 16 *Exempt
Org. Tax Rev.* (No. 5) 773 (May 1997).

[68] See *supra* § 3.

[69] See *supra* § 1.

[70] See *supra* § 3, text accompanied by note 62.

[71] See, e.g., § 6.2(f).

[72] See Chapter 19.

[73] See Part Five.

pital joint ventures. Complicating this process is the impact of any new rules on entities outside the health care field, such as on tax-exempt organizations that are managed by for-profit companies[74] and the entanglement with the excess benefit transactions rules in that these management organizations are often disqualified persons.[75]

§ 32.5 INFORMATION REPORTING

If a partnership in which a tax-exempt organization is a partner regularly carries on a trade or business that would constitute an unrelated trade or business if directly carried on by the exempt organization, the organization generally must include its share of the partnership's income and deductions from the business in determining its unrelated income tax liability. Special rules apply where the tax-exempt organization is a partner in a publicly traded partnership.[76]

A partnership generally must furnish to each partner a statement reflecting the information about the partnership required to be shown on the partner's tax return or information return.[77] The statement must set forth the partner's distributive share of the partnership income, gain, loss, deduction, or credit required to be shown on the partner's return, along with any additional information as provided by IRS forms or instructions that may be required to apply particular provisions of the federal tax law to the partner with respect to items related to the partnership.[78]

The instructions accompanying the statement for partners (Schedule K-1, Form 1065) require the partnership to identify whether the partner is a tax-exempt organization. Also, the partnership must attach a statement furnishing any other information needed by the partner to file its return that is not shown elsewhere on the schedule.

The federal tax statutory law was amended in 1988 to expressly provide that, in the case of any partnership regularly carrying on a trade or business, the partnership must furnish to the partners the information necessary to enable each tax-exempt partner to compute its distributive share of partnership income or

---

[74] Under current law, this utilization of management companies is quite common and appropriate (see, e.g., Priv. Ltr. Rul. 9715031).

[75] See § 19.11(c). The IRS denied tax-exempt status in a case involving an ancillary services joint venture, on the ground that the nonprofit organization was operating for a substantial nonexempt purpose and was conferring private benefits to more than an incidental extent, and that the arrangement was basically an investment in a for-profit entity (Redlands Surgical Services v. Comm'r (Tax Ct. 11025-97X). Cf. Priv. Ltr. Rul. 9709014.

In general, Boisture & Varley, "Emphasis on Control by Exempt General Partners May Indicate Restrictive Rules on Joint Ventures," 9 *J. Tax. Exempt Orgs.* (No. 3) 109 (Nov./Dec. 1997); Sullivan, "Whole-Hospital Joint Ventures," 19 *Exempt Org. Tax Rev.* (No. 1) 45 (Jan. 1998); Tsilas, "Whole Hospital Joint Ventures—Do Exempt Organizations Really Know What They're Getting Themselves Into?," 17 *Exempt Org. Tax Rev.* (No. 2) 273 (Aug. 1997); Greenwalt & Legget, "Whole-Hospital Joint Ventures With Taxable Entities Raise Tax Questions for Exempts," 6 *J. Tax. Exempt Orgs.* (No. 4) 163 (Jan./Feb. 1995).

[76] See § 28.4.

[77] IRC § 6031(b).

[78] Temp. Reg. § 1.6031(b)-1T.

loss from the business.[79] The conference report accompanying this law change states that it "will emphasize that the IRS should monitor and enforce the present-law reporting requirements and, where appropriate, should provide further guidance to partnerships through regulations or instructions as to how such information must be furnished" and that "information that must be furnished to tax-exempt partners under this provision is to be reflected by such organization on Form 990 or Form 990-T in the manner prescribed by Treasury regulations or by the IRS instructions for such Forms."[80]

Partnerships of tax-exempt organizations, including those comprised wholly of tax-exempt organizations, must annually file federal information returns (Form 1065).[81]

§ 32.6   ALTERNATIVES TO PARTNERSHIPS

Until or unless the IRS revises its rules in this area, charitable organizations must avoid participation in partnerships where the purpose of the partnership is not itself charitable (or else test the government's position in court).

One way for a charitable organization to avoid the dilemma is to establish a wholly owned organization, usually a for-profit corporation, that would serve as the general partner in the partnership. This approach has been upheld by the IRS in private letter rulings.[82] However, as discussed,[83] the tax-exempt entity leasing rules were revised to make this approach somewhat less attractive.

Another approach is to avoid partnerships altogether and utilize a leasing arrangement. This works best where a tax-exempt organization acquires unimproved land and subsequently desires to have it improved, such as for its offices. The organization can acquire land and enter into a long-term ground lease with a developer or development group. The developer would construct the building, perhaps giving it the organization's name and otherwise providing all external appearances of the structure being the organization's own building. This leaves the developer or development group in the position of fully utilizing all of the tax benefits. The tax-exempt organization leases space in the building, perhaps pursuant to a "sweetheart" lease, and may be accorded an option to purchase the building after the passage of years.[84]

In this way, the organization fixes its headquarters expenses and—for all practical purposes—owns the building from the outset, while at the same time

---

[79] IRC § 6031(d). This reporting requirement applies without regard to the modifications of IRC §§ 512(b)(8)–512(b)(15) (see § 27.1(l)-(n), (q)).

[80] H. Rep. 100-1104, 100th Cong., 2d Sess. 13. (1988). As to these reporting requirements, see § 24.3.

[81] IRC § 6031. This return is Form 1065. E.g., Priv. Ltr. Rul. 8925092.

[82] E.g., Priv. Ltr. Rul. 7820057. In general, Rev. Rul. 68-296, 1968-1 C.B. 105.

[83] See § 29.5(g).

[84] E.g., Priv. Ltr. Rul. 8715055.

avoiding jeopardizing its tax exemption and allocating all of the tax benefits to those who can utilize them.[85]

In some instances, a pooled income fund can be employed as an alternative to a limited partnership. However, where the facts cause the relationship between the pooled income fund and the charitable organization that is the remainder interest beneficiary of the pooled income fund to be manifested in a lease, the tax-exempt entity leasing rules make the fund, as an investment vehicle, somewhat unattractive.[86]

---

[85] Pooled income funds are the subject of IRC § 642(c)(5). In general, see Hopkins, *The Tax Law of Charitable Giving* (John Wiley & Sons, Inc., 1993), Chapter 12.

[86] The depreciation deduction (and perhaps other tax benefits) can flow through a pooled income fund to the income beneficiaries of the fund in determining their federal income tax liability (e.g., Priv. Lt. Rul. 8347010). This feature can provide useful tax incentives to donors to charity by means of a pooled income fund, when coupled with the income tax charitable deduction that is occasioned by reason of the transfer of cash or property to the pooled income fund. As a general rule, the depreciation deduction available to the income beneficiaries is not computed by applying the tax-exempt entity leasing rules. However, where the property that is the (or a) medium of investment of the pooled income fund is located on the premises of the charitable organization that maintains the fund or is otherwise available to those who are served by that charity, the tax-exempt entity leasing rules are likely to be applicable. This is because of the provision of these rules that includes within the definition of a *lease* the grant of the *right to use* property, thereby causing the grant of a right to use property to be a *disqualified lease* (Reg. § 1.168(j)-1T, Q-5, A-5). In general, Bean, "Tax Exempt Organizations' Investment in Leveraged Real Estate," 5 *Prac. Tax Law.* (No. 2) 67 (1991); Brenman, "A Lesson in Fractions: How to Attract Capital from Tax-Exempt Investors," 8 *J. Part. Tax.* (No. 1) 70 (1991); Weitz, "Unresolved Issues Remain for Qualified Organizations in Real Estate Partnerships," 73 *J. Tax.* (No. 5) 332 (1990); Kirchick & Cavell, "Tax-Exempt Organizations in Real Estate Transactions: A General Survey," 41 *U. S. C. Inst. on Fed. Tax.* 24 (1989); Gartrell, "Unrelated Business Taxable Income in Limited Partnerships After the Revenue Act of 1987," 16 *J. Real Estate Tax.* (No. 1) 29 (1988); Odell, "Special Partners—Exempt and Foreign Entities," 46 *N.Y. U. Inst. on Fed. Tax.* 29 (1988); Hardee, Jacobson, & Talisman, "Tax-Exempt Organizations: Use of Pass-Through Entities," 2 *Prac. Tax Law.* (No. 4) 23 (1988); Feder & Scharfstein, "Leveraged Investment in Real Property Through Partnerships by Tax Exempt Organizations after the Revenue Act of 1987—A Lesson in How the Legislative Process Should Not Work," 42 *Tax Law.* (No. 1) 55 (1988); Kertz & Hasson, Jr., "University Research and Development Activities: The Federal Income Tax Consequences of Research Contracts, Research Subsidiaries and Joint Ventures," 13 *J. Coll. & Univ. Law* (No. 2) 109 (1986); Lehrfeld, "Charities and Partnerships: A Many-Faceted Issue," 44 *NYU Ann. Inst. on Fed. Tax.* 39-1 (1986); Sanders, "Syndication with Tax-Exempt Organizations as Partners," 2 *J. Tax. Inv.* (No. 4) 341 (1985); Charyk, "The Partnership Corner: New Problems Involving Real Estate Partnerships With Tax-Exempt Partners," 12 *J. Real Estate Tax.* (No. 4) 380 (1985); Flaherty, "Exempt Organizations and Real Estate Syndications After the Tax Reform Act of 1984," 12 *J. Coll. & Univ. Law* (No. 1) 61 (1985); Schill, "The Participation of Charities in Limited Partnerships," 93 *Yale L. J.* 1355 (1984); Kaplan, "Real Estate Opportunities for Tax-Exempt Organizations: Potential and Pitfalls After *Plumstead Theatre*," 61 *Taxes* 291 (1983); Braitman, "Creative Uses of Real Estate for Financing Tax-Exempt Organizations," 13 *NYU Conf. on Char. Orgs.*, Chapter 8 (1983); Bromberg, "Federal Income Tax Consequences of Medical Office Buildings," *Official J. Healthcare Financial Mgmt. Ass'n* (No. 11) 11 (1982); Becker, "Partnerships with Historic Preservation Organizations in Real Estate Development," 1 *Preservation Law Rep.* 2052 (1982); Stoner & Pineo, "Tax-Exempt Organizations and Limited Partnerships," 54 *Taxes* 339 (1976).

CHAPTER THIRTY-THREE

Organizational and Operational Considerations

With respect to the interrelationships between tax-exempt and other organizations, there are a variety of organizational and operational considerations.

§ 33.1 ORGANIZATIONAL CONSIDERATIONS

The organizational considerations in these regards involve the form of the organizations, the composition of the governing boards, and the matter of control (if any) as between the various organizations.

(a) Form

To be a separate legal entity, an organization must fit within a legally recognized form. (In some instances, the law will treat an activity or bundle of activities as a separate organization, despite the intent and/or the preferences of those who administer the activity or activities.[1]) Therefore, the context of interorganizational structures dictates the presence of two or more separate legal entities, as contrasted with the structure where an activity (although accorded some form of formal recognition) is an integral component of an organization.[2]

    As noted, a tax-exempt organization must be structured in one of three

---

[1] For example, the IRS has the authority to classify an activity as a corporation for federal income tax purposes under IRC § 7701(a)(3).
[2] See § 23.7.

forms: a corporation, a trust, or an unincorporated association.[3] If a corporation, the organization almost always must be a nonprofit, nonstock corporation; some states provide for a stock-based nonprofit corporation. Occasionally, a for-profit organization will convert to a tax-exempt organization.[4]

A for-profit entity can be structured as a corporation, partnership, or other type of joint venture. While a business can be operated as a sole proprietorship, this approach is of no utility in this context because, by definition, it means that the for-profit activity will be housed in the tax-exempt organization.[5]

Therefore, assuming the presence of a tax-exempt organization (in one of the three forms), in this context it will be presumed to be either the parent or subsidiary of or under common control with, another legal entity, be it tax-exempt or taxable.

(b) Governing Boards

Both tax-exempt organizations and for-profit organizations must have one or more managers.[6] Depending upon the form of the legal entity, the requirements of state law, the nomenclature preferred by the individuals involved, and similar considerations, there will be one or more directors or trustees.

A trust may well have only one trustee. In some states, a corporation need only have one director. However, in most instances, both a tax-exempt organization and a for-profit organization will have a governing board of three or more individuals, and that body is termed the *board of directors* or *board of trustees*.

Of course, an individual may be a member of the governing board of more than one organization. Therefore, an individual may be a member of the boards of two or more related tax-exempt organizations and for-profit organizations. Indeed, the governing boards of organizations may be identical. (However, the law may regard two or more organizations as one under certain circumstances and identical boards would likely be one criterion used to reach that conclusion.[7])

As a generalization, the objective should be to minimize the extent to which the governing boards of two or more organizations (where at least one is a tax-exempt organization) are overlapping. It is clear that there can be interlocking of

---

[3] See § 4.1. There is one minor exception to this statement: The IRS is indicating, in the health care context, that it will recognize professional corporations of physicians as exempt charitable organizations; this has typically occurred in connection with states where the corporate practice of medicine doctrine requires physicians to use the professional corporation vehicle.

The IRS recognized that a tax-exempt business league (see Chapter 13) may have within it a fund that can be recognized as a charitable entity for federal income tax purposes (Rev. Rul. 54-243, 1954-1 C.B. 92). However, this type of fund may not be a legal entity for other law purposes, such as state law (e.g., eligibility to take title to property).

[4] E.g., Priv. Ltr. Rul. 8851039. See see *infra* § 4.

[5] Depending essentially upon the nature and size of the for-profit activity, it may or may not adversely affect the tax-exempt organization's tax-exempt status or cause unrelated business income.

[6] The term *manager* is used in this context because of the use of that term in federal tax law in referencing both directors and officers of organizations (IRC §§ 4946(a)(1)(B), 4946(b)(1), 4958(f)(1)) (see §§ 11.2(b), 19.11(c)).

[7] In Greater United Navajo Development Enterprises, Inc. v. Comm'r, 74 T.C. 69 (1980), *aff'd in unpub. op.* (9th Cir., Dec. 23, 1981), two corporations with the same directors, officers, and staff were regarded by both the IRS and the court as one organization. However, the IRS subsequently ruled that the directors and/or officers of a tax-exempt organization and a controlled for-profit company may be the same individuals (Priv. Ltr. Rul. 8244114). See § 31.1(d).

these directorates without jeopardizing an organization's tax-exempt status but the prudent practice is to have interlocking boards only to the extent necessary to achieve control (assuming that is desired). In some instances, interlocking directorates are required to achieve a particular result in the law, such as supporting organization classification.[8] Yet, in other circumstances, there may be reasons to keep the overlap to a minimum, such as with a charitable fund-raising organization associated with a charitable parent, where the intent is to broaden the fund-raising base of the charitable subsidiary.

The law, in some contexts, regards the existence of overlapping directorates as significant, such as in determining the tax treatment of income received by one organization from another[9] or the extent of the depreciation deduction allowed to partners in a partnership involving a controlled subsidiary of a tax-exempt organization.[10]

Particularly with respect to public charities, there is almost no federal tax law regulating the composition of the organizations' board of directors. Two exceptions prove this general rule: the body of law pertaining to the required and/or permissible configuration of the governing board of a supporting organization[11] and that relating to the board of an organization seeking to qualify as a donative publicly supported organization by means of the facts-and-circumstances test.[12] Nonetheless, despite the absence of any statutory authority[13] the IRS is more frequently utilizing the concept of the *independent board* or the *community-represented board* in the development of tax policy in the exempt organizations field.

This is most frequently the case in instances of private inurement and private benefit.[14] For example, the make-up of the board of directors is being invoked by the IRS in instances of examinations for private inurement and benefit activities and transactions by tax-exempt hospitals and other health care providers. As an illustration, as part of the development of its policy with respect to physician recruitment and retention arrangements, the IRS forced a hospital to concede that its board of trustees lacked awareness of and control over these transactions by the institution, agree to have the board's executive committee review and approve the major physician service agreements, adopt a conflict of interest policy applicable to the hospital's trustees and officers, and agree to a set of recruitment guidelines requiring board approval of every financial package provided to recruited physicians.[15] In another instance, the IRS found private inurement at a hospital, including unreasonable compensation; the IRS observed that the salary of the chief executive officer and president of the institution was "not determined by an independent compensation committee."[16] Further, a reorganization of a hospital sys-

---

[8] See § 11.3(c).

[9] See §§ 27.1(n), 31.3.

[10] See § 29.5(g).

[11] See § 11.3(c).

[12] See § 11.3(b)(ii).

[13] See § 19.11.

[14] In general, see Chapter 19.

[15] Closing agreement with Hermann Hospital, dated Sept. 16, 1994, in *Daily Tax Report* (BNA) (No. 200), Oct. 19, 1994, at L-1.

[16] Tech. Adv. Mem. 9451001, recommending revocation of the tax-exempt status of Modern Health Care Services, Inc.

tem was approved by the IRS,[17] with any private benefit found to be incidental; the IRS emphasized the fact that "there is broad community representation on the boards of directors of the . . . [exempt, charitable] members of the system."[18]

However, the IRS is increasingly invoking a requirement of an independent or community-based board in other settings. For example, the involvement of a public charity as a general partner in a limited partnership was sanctioned by the IRS, using pre-existing criteria[19] but inexplicably adding the observation that the organization was governed by an "independent board of directors made up of church and community leaders," in finding the absence of any unwarranted service of private interests.[20] In another instance, concerning a close operating relationship between a charitable organization and a for-profit fund-raising company where the IRS had raised questions as to private inurement and private benefit, the IRS became satisfied that the organization could retain tax exemption once its board of directors was enlarged to provide for control by individuals other than its founder (who was also the sole shareholder of the fund-raising company) and her family; the IRS noted that this alteration of board composition "should do much to provide assurance" that the charity will operate "independently" of the company.[21]

(c) Control

One organization may control another organization, or two or more organizations may be under common control. This is the case irrespective of whether the organizations are tax-exempt or taxable. Thus, a tax-exempt organization may control one or more other tax-exempt organizations and/or for-profit organizations, just as a for-profit organization may control one or more tax-exempt organizations.[22]

Essentially, there are three ways by which one organization controls another: interlocking directorates, a membership, or stock.

Inasmuch as few nonprofit organizations are stock-based, a tax-exempt organization is usually controlled by another tax-exempt organization by means of an interlocking directorate. This control mechanism can take many forms, such as by enabling the board of directors of the parent tax-exempt organization to name at least a majority of the board of directors of the subsidiary tax-exempt organization or by causing at least a majority of the board of directors of the subsidiary tax-exempt organization to consist of individuals holding named offices (for example, president, past-president, or treasurer) of the parent tax-exempt organization. Any combinations of these or other forms is permissible; it is the mere fact of the majority overlap of directors that vests control in the parent organization.

On occasion, one tax-exempt organization will control another exempt organization by means of a membership feature. With this approach, the controlled entity is structured as a membership organization; the controlling entity usually is the sole member of the membership entity. The control element in this instance is manifested in the power and authority accorded the member.

[17] See § Hyatt & Hopkins, *The Law of Tax-Exempt Healthcare Organizations* (New York: John Wiley & Sons, Inc., 1995), particularly Chapter 20.
[18] Priv. Ltr. Rul. 9426040.
[19] See § 32.2.
[20] Priv. Ltr. Rul. 9438030.
[21] Priv. Ltr. Rul. 9417003.
[22] See *supra* notes 8, 9.

Where a tax-exempt organization is formed pursuant to a nonprofit corporation act that allows the issuance of stock, the tax-exempt organization can be controlled by another tax-exempt organization by reason of ownership of at least a majority of the stock. In this situation, the control is achieved by the stock ownership, so that the composition of the board of directors of the tax-exempt subsidiary is, in a sense, irrelevant, although in many instances the parent tax-exempt organization will want more immediate control over the operations of the tax-exempt subsidiary than mere stock ownership can give and thus will also have a substantial representation on the board of directors of the subsidiary.[23]

The control mechanism represented by the interlocking directorate and/or a membership feature will be provided for in the governing instruments of the tax-exempt subsidiary.

A for-profit organization can control a tax-exempt organization by means of the same two devices: interlocking directorates and/or stock ownership.

Most for-profit organizations are corporations, so that the ownership of a for-profit organization by a tax-exempt organization will likely be the subject of stock ownership. Just as above, a tax-exempt organization may control a for-profit organization by means of an interlocking directorate (although ultimate control is always vested in the stockholders(s)).[24]

§ 33.2 OPERATIONAL CONSIDERATIONS

There are certain criteria that must be met to ensure that the appropriate relationship between a noncharitable organization and an auxiliary charitable organization is maintained. Some of these criteria are dependent on whether the charitable organization is to be operated as a subsidiary of the noncharitable organization or whether the two organizations are to operate as independent entities.

In most instances, where a tax-exempt organization controls and operates another organization (whether tax-exempt or taxable), the headquarters of both organizations will be at the same location. Thus, for example, the foundation that is related to a trade association will usually be located in the same offices as is the association. This fact gives rise to several operational considerations, mostly involving money.

(a) Expenses

Again, the organizations involved are separate legal entities, with their own governing boards, officers, bank accounts, and the like. Unless the organizations involved have the same federal tax status (and even then it is not a desirable practice), their monies should not be commingled (as contrasted with exchanged). This prohibition against commingling dictates the use of separate bank accounts.[25]

---

[23] This aspect of the structure may cause attribution problems. See § 31.1(d).

[24] Special rules apply in this regard to private foundations. See § 11.4(c).

[25] E.g., Regan v. Taxation With Representation of Wash., 461 U.S. 540, 544, note 6 (1983). Nonetheless, a group of tax-exempt organizations, including those with differing exempt statuses, may maintain a single general operating account into which funds are deposited and subsequently allocated, as long as the transfers are accomplished on a timely basis, the assets of each entity are separately maintained, and the resources of a charitable organization are not utilized to provide economic benefits for noncharitable purposes (e.g., Women of the Motion Picture Industry v. Comm'r, T.C. Mem. 1997-518).

These considerations, however, do not preclude the organizations from functioning in close operational conjunction. Therefore, whether it is a professional society in relation to its foundation or a charitable organization in relation to its lobbying arm, the two organizations may share office space, personnel, furniture, equipment, and the like.[26] Indeed, this is the case irrespective of the number of organizations involved. Moreover, it is the practice of the IRS to rule that the sharing of assets, personnel, facilities, and services, and the allocation of costs, among the organizations will not produce unrelated business income—even when there might be this type of income were the organizations unrelated.[27]

Where the parent is a tax-exempt organization other than a charitable organization[28] and the subsidiary is a charitable organization, the subsidiary may reimburse the parent for its allocable use of the resources of the parent, as long as the reimbursement amounts are reasonable. (When this is done, a desirable practice is to have a written agreement between the parties stating the terms of the relationship.[29]) This is not a form of commingling of funds but rather a reasonable expenditure of funds for administrative and program purposes. Alternatively, the parent may forgo reimbursement, with the amounts involved regarded as a grant of the funds by the parent to the subsidiary.[30]

It is preferable to avoid having a noncharitable organization reimburse a charitable organization for expenses incurred on its behalf to eliminate the potential contention that charitable funds are being expended for noncharitable purposes. However, where this practice cannot be avoided, the relationship should be memorialized in writing, and the terms and conditions of the relationship must be fair and reasonable.

There is not a prescribed accounting practice for allocating expenses in this context.[31] Therefore, a system should be used that is reasonable.[32] For example, the costs associated with occupancy can be reimbursed on the basis of floor space utilized by the parties, the costs associated with the utilization of personnel can be reimbursed on the basis of time records, and the costs associated with the use of equipment can be reimbursed on the basis of actual use.[33]

---

[26] Center on Corp. Responsibility, Inc. v. Schultz, 368 F. Supp. 863, 866, note 2 (D.D.C. 1973).

[27] E.g., Priv. Ltr. Rul. 9527043. See § 26.5(j).

[28] That is, an organization described in IRC § 501(c)(3) (see Part Two).

[29] E.g., Priv. Ltr. Rul. 9012045.

[30] If the parent organization is forgoing revenue that might be taxable (such as rent that would be unrelated business taxable income), the IRS may apply the rules concerning allocation of income and deductions among taxpayers (IRC § 482) to cause the parent to have taxable income. These allocation rules are applicable to tax-exempt organizations (Reg. § 1.482-1(a)(1)).

[31] See Gross, Jr., Larkin, Bruttomesso & McNally, *Financial and Accounting Guide for Not-For-Profit Organizations, Fifth Edition* (New York: John Wiley & Sons, Inc., 1995), at 242.

[32] It would not be inappropriate to analogize to the concept of the *mixed purpose expenditure* contained in the regulations that accompany the expenditure test lobbying rules (see Chapter 20), which require, in the case of this type of an expenditure, "a reasonable allocation, based on all the facts and circumstances" (Reg. § 56.4911-2(d)). Also, there are cost allocation rules available to membership associations and certain other organizations that can be alluded to in this setting (see § 20.8).

[33] These principles are not unlike the rules pertaining to the allocation of expenses between tax-exempt and unrelated activities (see § 28.2), although those rules may be somewhat more strict due to the requirement that the expenses allocable to an unrelated activity are only those that are incurred directly in connection with the unrelated activity.

Of course, an organization can avoid allocations and reimbursements to the extent that services and supplies can be acquired and paid for directly. But avoidance of interorganizational sharing may be undesirable or impractical, if not impossible, particularly in the early years of the relationship.

The foregoing considerations also apply to a relationship between a tax-exempt organization and a for-profit organization. Where the services and supplies are provided by the for-profit organization to the tax-exempt organization, there may be reimbursement; where the circumstances are reversed, there must be reimbursement, and it must be fair and reasonable.

When a tax-exempt organization performs administrative or management tasks for another organization, the general position of the IRS is that any net revenue resulting from the provision of the services is unrelated business taxable income. This is the case irrespective of whether the organization receiving the services is tax-exempt. In other words, it is not automatically an exempt function for one exempt organization to provide services to another, even where both organizations have the same category of tax-exempt status. Yet, under certain circumstances, it can be a related business for a tax-exempt organization to provide services to another exempt entity or it can be other than an unrelated business where services are provided by and among related entities.[34]

(b) Gifts and Grants

A charitable organization may be the recipient of one or more gifts or grants from its parent, whether or not the parent is tax-exempt.[35] Where the parent is a taxable organization, the payment may be regarded by the parties as a gift (although it may be characterized for tax purposes as a (nondeductible) dividend).

Where the charitable organization is endeavoring to be a publicly supported organization,[36] the parent will be considered a donor or grantor for purposes of measuring public support. This is presumably the case irrespective of whether the grant is made directly or by means of reimbursements forgone. Consequently, where the parent is a tax-exempt organization, the related charitable organization may have to be structured as a supporting organization[37] where the organization is to receive a large portion of its funding from the parent.[38] There are exceptions to this precept, such as grants from a tax-exempt hospital[39] or university[40] to a publicly supported organization.[41] Where the parent is a for-profit organization, the related charitable organization will probably be a private foundation.[42]

---

[34] See § 26.5(j).

[35] E.g., Priv. Ltr. Rul. 8640052.

[36] See § 11.3(b).

[37] See § 11.3(c).

[38] For example, a parent organization that is a large donor or grantor will likely be considered a *substantial contributor* and thus a *disqualified person* for purposes of qualification under IRC § 509(a)(2) (see § 11.2(a)).

[39] IRC § 170(b)(1)(A)(iii).

[40] IRC § 170(b)(1)(A)(ii).

[41] IRC § 509(a)(2)(A).

[42] See Chapter 11.

A charitable organization can make a grant to a noncharitable organization (although this is generally inadvisable where the grantor is a private foundation[43]), as long as the grant is properly restricted for charitable purposes. For example, a "foundation" related to a trade association can make a grant to the association as long as the grant is restricted for charitable purposes (such as a seminar or a research project). Generally, however, the preferable practice is for the charitable program to be maintained and funded directly by the charitable organization.

§ 33.3 CONVERSION FROM EXEMPT TO NONEXEMPT STATUS

As has been discussed throughout, organizations can be nonprofit, tax-exempt entities or for-profit entities. On occasion, an entity of one type is desirous of converting to an entity of the other type. While both can be accomplished, the federal and state law on the point is scant.[44]

The state law on the subject concerns form and procedure. Most states have separate nonprofit corporation acts and business (for-profit) corporation acts; mergers from one to the other are not always permissible. Thus, a change in form is often required, entailing liquidations and reformations. The federal tax law on the subject focuses primarily on the need for new determinations as to tax status and disclosure of certain facts as part of any new application for recognition of exempt status.[45]

A tax-exempt organization may decide to shed that status and convert to a for-profit entity. (There is no prohibition in law as to doing that.) For example, a public charity may determine that the rules for maintaining tax-exempt status as a charitable entity are too onerous or those involved in its operations may wish to partake of its profits; operation as a for-profit entity may thus be more attractive.

(a) State Law

Nearly every tax-exempt organization is a creature of the law of a state or the District of Columbia. (In a rare instance, an exempt organization is established by a specific state statute or, even less frequently, is created by federal law.) These organizations are shaped as one of three types of entity: nonprofit corporation, unincorporated association, or trust.[46]

---

[43] See § 11.4(b).

[44] The law on this subject is most pronounced when it involves the termination of a charitable organization's status as a private foundation (IRC § 507; see § 11.4(f)). This is a separate body of law that is uniquely applicable to private foundations; this chapter assumes that the charitable organizations discussed in it are not private foundations.

[45] The process for obtaining a determination or ruling as to recognition by the IRS of tax-exempt status is the subject of § 23.2.

[46] See *supra* § 1(a).

The unincorporated association is the least likely option for a nonprofit entity. The articles of organization of this type of organization is termed a constitution. It will undoubtedly have bylaws and otherwise function much in the nature of a corporation.

Some organizations are formed as trusts. The articles of organization of this type of entity will be a declaration of trust or a trust agreement. Trusts, particularly charitable ones, are uniquely treated under state law and this treatment may vary from state to state.

The third form that a tax-exempt entity can assume is that of the nonprofit corporation—the form that is most commonly used today. (The balance of this chapter is predicated on the assumption that the nonprofit and for-profit entities involved are corporations.) The corporate form is advantageous because the law as to its formation and operation is usually quite clear, and because it can provide a shield against personal liability for those individuals who are its directors and officers.[47]

As noted, nearly every state has a nonprofit corporation act and a for-profit corporation act. These are separate statutes; the extent of any interplay between them is a matter of state law, which can vary from state to state. For example, it may not be possible for a nonprofit corporation in a particular state to amend its articles of organization so as to become a for-profit corporation under the law of that state. This is because of the fundamental difference between the two types of corporations.[48]

Likewise, the issue of whether a nonprofit corporation can merge into a for-profit corporation, particularly where the survivor of the merger is the for-profit entity, can be problematic. In any event, the transformation of a tax-exempt charitable organization can easily attract the attention of a state's attorney general.

Suppose a tax-exempt charitable entity, organized as a nonprofit corporation, is desirous of becoming a for-profit organization, organized as a for-profit corporation. Theoretically, the easiest way to accomplish this is to amend the corporate documents and convert to the for-profit form. However, as noted, state law may not allow for this transformation, and it raises great problems under the federal tax law.[49]

Another approach would be to create a for-profit corporation and then merge the nonprofit corporation into it. Again, state law may preclude the merger of a nonprofit and a for-profit organization.

A third approach would be to create the for-profit corporation, liquidate the nonprofit corporation, and transfer the remaining assets and income of the nonprofit corporation to the for-profit corporation. However, as discussed next, this type of transfer must, for federal tax reasons, entail a sale or exchange of the assets for fair market value.

---

[47] The subject of personal liability in the nonprofit organization context is outside the scope of this book. See, however, Hopkins, *A Legal Guide to Starting and Managing A Nonprofit Organization, Second Edition* (New York: John Wiley & Sons, Inc., 1993), Chapter 19.

[48] However, an IRS private letter ruling reflects a factual situation in which a state's law apparently permits a nonexempt nonprofit corporation to convert to a stock-based for-profit corporation (Priv. Ltr. Rul. 9545014).

[49] See text accompanied by *infra* § 3(b).

(b) Federal Tax Law

There is no federal law procedure by which an exempt organization has its tax-exempt status withdrawn; while the IRS recognizes the exempt status of nonprofit organizations, it does not "de-recognize" them.[50] Thus, the only way for a tax-exempt organization to lose its tax exemption is to violate one or more aspects of the organizational test and/or the operational test. These tests find their origin in the language of the statute giving rise to the exemption, which speaks of an organization being both *organized* and *operated* for one or more exempt purposes.[51]

The organizational test focuses on the organizing instrument of the entity, to determine the presence of all required provisions in the document (such as a clause preserving the assets for charitable purposes upon dissolution) and to assure that prohibited language is not present.[52] If, for example, the articles of organization[53] of a tax-exempt charitable organization are amended to allow its net earnings to inure to one or more persons in their private capacity,[54] the organization is no longer qualified for tax exemption.[55] In general, an organization's articles of organization must limit its purposes to one or more exempt ones and may not empower the organization to engage in nonexempt activities other than insubstantially.[56]

The concern of the operational test is with an organization's programs. In the case of a charitable organization, the requirement is that the entity be operated at least primarily for exempt purposes.[57] For example, the rationale for tax exemption for a charitable organization might be that it is engaged in activities that primarily promote health.[58] Where, however, the operational test is violated so that the organization is no longer functioning primarily for exempt purposes (such as by engaging in one or more forms of private inurement), the organization is no longer qualified for tax exemption.[59]

---

[50] Moreover, once the IRS has recognized the tax-exempt status of an organization, the organization cannot voluntarily relinquish it (Priv. Ltr. Rul. 9141050). That is, there is no provision in the law for voluntary termination of tax-exempt status.

[51] IRC § 501(c)(3); Reg. § 1.501(c)(3)-1(a)(1). If an organization fails to meet either of these tests, it is not tax-exempt (*id.*). These tests thus are applicable with respect to tax-exempt charitable organizations. In a sense, most other categories of exempt organizations have organizational and operational tests as well, although none of them are as well-developed as those for charitable entities.

[52] Reg. § 1.501(c)(3)-1(b)(1). See § 4.3.

[53] An organization's *articles of organization* is the document (articles of incorporation, constitution, trust agreement, and the like) by which an organization is created (Reg. § 1.501(c)(3)-1(b)(2)).

[54] The private inurement doctrine is the subject of Chapter 19.

[55] Reg. § 1.501(c)(3)-1(b)(4).

[56] Reg. § 1.501(c)(3)-1(b)(1). Although the statute (IRC § 501(c)(3)) states that a charitable organization must be organized and operated *exclusively* for charitable purposes, the true state of the law is that the word *substantially* or *primarily* is substituted for the word *exclusively* (Better Business Bur. v. United States, 326 U.S. 279 (1945)) (see § 4.4). This construction of the terminology not only tolerates an *incidental* amount of nonexempt activity, it allows for a meshing of the unrelated business rules (see Part Five). (This is the case even though the U.S. Supreme Court articulated the principle five years before the unrelated business law was enacted.)

[57] Reg. § 1.501(c)(3)-1(c)(1). The term *exempt purposes* means those charitable purposes for which the organization was organized and is operated (Reg. § 1.501(c)(3)-1(a)(2)). See § 4.5.

[58] Rev. Rul. 69-545, 1969-2 C.B. 117.

[59] Reg. § 1.501(c)(3)-1(c)(2).

In addition, an organization is not organized or operated exclusively for one or more exempt purposes unless it serves a public, rather than a private, interest.[60] This rule, like the private inurement prohibition, requires the absence of transactions that benefit insiders with respect to the organization, such as directors, officers, substantial contributors, and persons controlled by insiders.[61] (Particularly where the membership is small, insiders can include members.)

In the case of transgression of either the organizational test or the operational test, the organization becomes a non-tax-exempt (that is, taxable) entity. However, it nonetheless remains a nonprofit organization under state law. Therefore, without additional action, the entity is a taxable, nonprofit organization. Further steps under state law are usually required to convert the entity to a for-profit corporation or to merge it into a new or existing for-profit corporation.[62]

Where the exempt organization is a charitable one, the most difficult problem to overcome is the proscription of the dissolution clause. The organization, to be initially recognized as a charitable entity, was required to have this clause in its articles of organization. This clause mandates that, upon dissolution or liquidation, the net assets and remaining income of the organization be preserved for charitable purposes.[63] A blatant violation of this rule would be transfer, upon dissolution, of assets to an organization's members or shareholders.[64] This aspect of the organizational test prevents a charitable organization from accumulating assets and income in the tax-exempt charitable mode and then simply converting to a taxable entity.[65]

There may be conflict between federal and state law on this point. That is, state law may allow certain liquidating distributions that are impermissible under federal tax precepts. For example, where the articles of organization of a church failed to contain the requisite dissolution clause, tax-exempt status was denied, particularly in light of the fact that the law in the state of organization permitted certain distributions of assets to members of nonprofit corporations.[66]

---

[60] Reg. § 1.501(c)(3)-1(d)(1)(ii).

[61] *Id.* The federal tax regulations do not specifically use the term *insider*; the term used is "private shareholder or individual" (Reg. § 1.501(a)-1(c)) or "private interests" (Reg. § 1.501(c)(3)-1(d)(1)(ii)).

[62] Where this type of conversion is allowable under state law, the IRS regards it as a non-taxable reorganization within the meaning of IRC § 368(a)(1)(E) (Priv. Ltr. Rul. 9545014).

[63] Reg. § 1.501(c)(3)-1(b)(4).

[64] *Id.*, last sentence.

[65] In a sense, this statement is overly broad. A statement of law or a provision in articles of organization does not, in a literal sense, "prevent" an individual from doing anything. This form of violation of the organizational test would, from a federal tax standpoint, merely cause loss of the organization's tax-exempt status—a result that is to occur in any event because of the organization's conversion to a taxable entity. Nonetheless, this development would still leave the organization as a nonprofit one, with potential problems under state law (see *supra* § 3(a)). Further, the attorney general of the particular state may intervene to preserve the assets for charitable purposes.

For certain other categories of tax-exempt organizations, the federal tax law is not so stringent. For example, a social club (see Chapter 14) may make liquidating distributions to its members (e.g., Mill Lane Club, Inc. v. Comm'r, 23 T.C. 433 (1954); Rev. Rul. 58-501, 1958-2 C.B. 262). Also, a fraternal beneficiary association (see § 18.4(a)) may convert to a for-profit entity (Priv. Ltr. Rul. 8938072).

[66] General Conference of Free Church of Am. v. Comm'r, 71 T.C. 920 (1979).

In another case, a charitable contribution deduction was denied where the donee organization could, under state law, distribute its assets upon dissolution to its founders (in this instance, the donors).[67] As one appellate court stated, "if there is substantial possibility that upon dissolution, accumulated assets will find their way into private hands, exemption is barred."[68] That statement is equally applicable in the revocation context.

Suppose, for example, that a tax-exempt charitable hospital decides to convert to a taxable for-profit hospital. It cannot merely create a for-profit corporation and transfer all of the income and assets of the charitable entity to it.[69] While the assets of the charitable organization may be transferred to the for-profit corporation, the recipient corporation must pay fair market value for them. This outcome leaves the charitable entity with no assets other than an amount of funds equal to the fair value of the assets (property) it once had.

To continue with this example, the charitable organization will no longer function as a hospital (although it may continue to operate in a manner that promotes health). Thus, there will almost certainly be a material change in circumstances, requiring the charitable entity to report the development to the IRS[70] and perhaps submit another application for recognition of tax exemption. The surviving charitable organization may, as illustrations, become a freestanding medical research organization, a foundation operating in tandem with the newly formed for-profit organization, or an entity operating a gift shop in conjunction with the for-profit hospital.[71] This new mode of operation may cause the charitable entity to become another type of public charity or become a private foundation.[72]

This matter becomes more complex where the successor for-profit entity is controlled by physicians who are insiders with respect to the tax-exempt hospital.

---

[67] Calvin K. of Oakknoll v. Comm'r, 69 T.C. 770 (1978).

[68] Monterey Pub. Parking Corp. v. United States, 27 A.F.T.R. 2d 71-378, 380 (6th Cir. 1971).

[69] See *supra* note 65.

[70] See § 24.1(a).

[71] It is the position of the IRS that a nonprofit organization, the primary activity of which is the operation of a gift shop and a gift cart within a proprietary hospital for the purpose of selling candy, flowers, newspapers, books, magazines, sundries, and other small gift items to patients, visitors, and employees of the hospital is a charitable entity because the organization's activity primarily improves the physical comfort and mental well-being of the hospital's patients, thereby encouraging their recovery and only incidentally benefits the proprietary hospital (Gen. Couns. Mem. 39762). The IRS termed these "recuperative sales of nonmedical items" (*id.*) and found the private benefit derived by the for-profit hospital to be incidental in both a qualitative and quantitative sense, in that the overall benefit to the general public substantially overrode any benefit to private individuals and that the private benefit was a necessary concomitant of the beneficial activity, following the criteria stated in Gen. Couns. Mem. 37789. (The doctrine of private benefit is the subject of § 19.10).

[72] E.g., Hoyt, "Creating Supporting Organizations of Community Foundations from Hospital Sales," 17 *Exempt Org. Tax Rev.* (No. 2) 265 (Aug. 1997). If the entity became a free-standing medical research organization, it presumably would gain tax-exempt status by reason of IRC § 501(c)(3) as a scientific organization (see Chapter 9) and become a publicly supported organization by reason of IRC §§ 170(b)(1)(A)(vi) and 509(a)(1) or IRC § 509(a)(2) (see § 11.3(b)). (An example where the successor public charity status in these circumstances, was that of IRC § 509(a)(2) is in Priv. Let. Rul. 8234085.) It could not, however, be a medical research organization as that term is used in IRC § 170(b)(1)(A)(iii) (see § 11.3(a)) because the required related hospital must be a tax-exempt one. If the entity became a foundation in relation to the for-profit institution, it may well become a private foundation as is the case with most company-related foundations.

In one case, a tax-exempt, charitable hospital transferred its pharmacy operations to an organization controlled by its trustees to function on a for-profit basis. The for-profit entity sold pharmaceuticals to the hospital at prices higher than those previously paid by it. Subsequently, the assets of the pharmacy were sold to another charitable organization. The exemption of the hospital was retroactively revoked, on the basis of private inurement, on the ground that the transaction was merely a device to funnel profits from the exempt hospital to its trustees.[73]

Although it is infrequent, a tax-exempt organization may decide to sell one or more of its assets; generally, it can do so as long as fair value is received on the sale. For the most part, the status of the purchaser is irrelevant.[74] For example, the IRS approved the sale of assets from a tax-exempt hospital to another tax-exempt organization,[75] to a partnership formed by the board of directors of a hospital,[76] and to unrelated purchasers.[77]

Nonetheless, where the purchaser of assets from a tax-exempt, charitable entity is an organization that was created by individuals related to it to the extent that they are treated as insiders,[78] such as physicians practicing at a hospital or members of the hospital's governing board, the transaction will be accorded strict scrutiny. This type of transaction has several ramifications, other than the matter of tax exemption; they include the impact on the qualification for any tax-exempt bond financing[79] and conflicts of interest.

As to the bounds of this scrutiny, it is frequently advised in these circumstances that the services of one or more competent appraisers be obtained. The purpose of this is to be able to demonstrate that the fair market value of the transferred assets was obtained on an independent basis.[80] However, in one instance, that act of prudence proved inadequate to preclude loss of the selling hospital's tax-exempt status.

In that case, a tax-exempt organization that operated a hospital, and had research and educational functions, determined to sell the hospital to gain income for the other exempt functions. Because of the highly specialized nature of the hospital facility, there was a limited market for its sale. Thus, the hospital was

---

[73] Maynard Hosp., Inc. v. Comm'r, 52 T.C. 1006 (1969).

[74] Again, the assumption of this chapter is that the selling organization is not a private foundation (see *supra* note 44). In instances where the selling organization is a private foundation and one or more of the purchasers are disqualified persons with respect to it, the sale would almost certainly be an act of self-dealing, with resulting adverse federal tax consequences (see § 11.4(a)).

[75] Priv. Ltr. Rul. 9010073.

[76] Priv. Ltr. Rul. 8234084.

[77] Priv. Ltr. Rul. 8519069.

[78] See text accompanied by *supra* note 61.

[79] IR-90-60. In Rev. Rul. 77-416, 1977-2 C.B. 34, the IRS ruled that interest on municipal bonds continued to be excludable from gross income under IRC § 103 following the sale by a city of an electric system to a private utility company, where the sale proceeds were placed in an escrow account as substituted security for the system revenues originally pledged as security for the bonds. The full reasoning underlying this ruling is contained in Gen. Couns. Mem. 37158 (with heavy emphasis on the facts that considerable time passed before the facility was sold and other evidence that the transaction was "legitimate," that is, "nonprearranged"), with a somewhat similar situation analyzed in Gen. Couns. Mem. 37783.

[80] This approach to sales to insiders will become even more critical now that intermediate sanctions have been enacted into law (see § 19.11).

sold to a for-profit entity controlled by its board of directors. Basically, the organization went about this process in the appropriate manner. It secured a valuation from a qualified independent appraiser; the property was sold at that value, which was $8.3 million (principally in cash and notes). No loan abatements or other special concessions were offered to the directors as purchasers of the hospital facility. The exempt organization took steps to ensure that it would use arm's-length standards in future dealings with the hospital. A ruling was obtained from the IRS to the effect that the transaction would not adversely affect the tax exemption of the organization.[81]

Soon after the sale, the purchasing organization began receiving inquiries as to resale of the facility. The new organization added beds to the hospital and obtained a certificate of need for additional beds. Less than two years after the initial sale of the hospital facility by the exempt organization, it was resold; the resale price was $29.6 million. Each member of the board of the for-profit selling organization received in excess of $2.3 million as his or her share of the sales proceeds. The attorney general of the state involved filed a lawsuit, alleging that the initial sales price was not fair and reasonable. The court agreed, also concluding that the directors of the exempt organization acted with a lack of due diligence. At trial, the facilities were appraised using five appraisal methodologies; the conclusion was that the value of the assets at the time of sale by the exempt organization was approximately $18 million to $21 million. A subsequent analysis by the IRS set the value of the facility at $24 million.

The factual issue before the IRS was whether the tax-exempt organization received fair market value when it sold its hospital facility. A detailed analysis of the appraisals led the IRS to the conclusion that fair market value had not been received. The appraisals done for the court and the IRS were based on various appraisal methodologies; the appraisal relied upon by the selling exempt organization used one of these methods. The IRS conceded that "no single valuation method is necessarily the best indicator of value in a given case."[82] But, added the IRS, "it would be logical to assume that an appraisal that has considered and applied a variety of approaches in reaching its 'bottom line' is more likely to result in an accurate valuation than an appraisal that focused on a single valuation method." Having resolved that factual issue, the IRS concluded as a matter of law that the tax-exempt organization, in selling the hospital facility for substantially less than its fair market value, contravened the private inurement doctrine. Accordingly, the organization's tax-exempt status was revoked, effective as of the date of the sale of the facility.[83] In so doing, the IRS observed: "There is no absolute prohibition against an exempt section 501(c)(3) organization dealing with its founders, members, or officers in conducting its economic affairs." There is no doubt, however, that transactions of this nature will be subject to special scrutiny,

---

[81] Priv. Ltr. Rul. 8234085 (in which the IRS stated that the "proposed sale as described will not benefit those in a controlling position with respect to you by virtue of the ability of such persons to unfairly manipulate the transaction"). In this ruling, the IRS observed that the transaction presented the converse of the situations in Rev. Rul. 76-441, 1976-2 C.B. 147 (see text accompanied by *infra* notes 88–89).
[82] Priv. Ltr. Rul. 9130002.
[83] *Id.*

with the IRS concerned about a (in the language of the ruling) "disproportionate share of the benefits of the exchange" flowing to the insiders. Thus, in this case, there was nothing inherently improper about the organization's decision to cease being a hospital and to sell the appropriate assets to an organization controlled by its directors.

The organization in this case followed the correct approach in acquiring an independent appraisal. In most circumstances, this should have been enough.[84] However, when the directors resold the hospital facility after approximately only a two-year period and experienced a $21.3 million profit and a lawsuit by the state's attorney general (with the court having found a breach of fiduciary responsibility), the IRS found private inurement.

This type of sale of assets, in whole or in part, does not give rise to taxable gain or loss under the unrelated trade or business tax rules. The one-time sale of an asset, principal or otherwise, used directly in furtherance of the selling organization's exempt function lacks the frequency, continuity, and commercial manner to be considered as an unrelated trade or business.[85]

As an alternative to sale of assets and/or total conversion, a tax-exempt organization may lease assets to a non-exempt organization, particularly where doing so advances the lessor's exempt purposes.[86] In one instance, a tax-exempt hospital leased its clinic facilities to a for-profit corporation controlled by physicians formally employed by the clinics without endangering its exempt status.[87]

§ 33.4 CONVERSION FROM NONEXEMPT STATUS TO EXEMPT STATUS

A for-profit organization may decide to convert to a tax-exempt organization. (Like the reverse, there is no prohibition in law as to doing so.)

(a) State Law

Nearly every for-profit organization is subject to the law of a state or the District of Columbia. These organizations are usually organized as corporations. (Again, the balance of this chapter is predicated on the assumption that the nonprofit and for-profit entities involved are corporations.)

Nearly every state has a nonprofit corporation act and a for-profit corpora-

---

[84] For example, in the charitable contribution deduction context, gifts of property in excess of $5,000 in value are generally required to be the subject of a *qualified appraisal* by a *qualified appraiser* (Reg. § 1.170A-13(c)). There is no requirement for more than one appraisal nor is there a requirement that an appraisal be based on a "variety of approaches." Indeed, these rules require a qualified appraisal to state "the" method of valuation (Reg. § 1.170A-13(c)(3)(ii)). Moreover, these rules allow a donor to obtain more than one appraisal and use the most desirous one in substantiating the charitable deduction (Reg. § 1.170A-13(c)(5)(iii)). In general, Hopkins, *The Tax Law of Charitable Giving* (New York: John Wiley & Sons, 1993), Chapter 21 § 2. In subsequent private letter rulings, moreover, the IRS approved the use of a single valuation method (e.g., Priv. Ltr. Ruls. 9538026, 9538031). In general, see Hyatt & Hopkins, *supra* note 17, 1998 Cum. Supp.

[85] Reg. § 1.513-1(c)(1). E.g., Priv. Ltr. Rul. 8234084. In general, Mancino, "Converting the Status of Exempt Hospitals and Health Care Organizations," 9 *J. Tax Exempt Orgs.* (No. 1) 16 (July/Aug. 1997).

[86] E.g., Gundersen Med. Found. Ltd. v. United States, 536 F. Supp. 556 (W.D. Wis. 1982).

[87] Priv. Ltr. Rul. 8204057.

tion act. These are separate statutes; the extent of any interplay between them is a matter of state law, which can vary from state to state. For example, it may not be possible for a for-profit corporation in a particular state to amend its articles of incorporation so as to become a nonprofit corporation under the law of that state. Likewise, it can be problematic as to whether a for-profit corporation can merge into a nonprofit corporation.[88]

Suppose a hospital, organized as a for-profit corporation, is desirous of becoming a tax-exempt organization, organized as a charitable entity. As is the case when the conversion is to be the reverse, theoretically, the easiest way to accomplish this is to amend the corporate documents and convert to the nonprofit form. However, as noted, state law may not allow for this transformation.

Another approach would be to create a nonprofit corporation and then merge the for-profit corporation into it. Again, state law may preclude the merger of a nonprofit and a for-profit organization.

A third approach would be to create the nonprofit corporation, transfer the assets and income of the for-profit corporation to the nonprofit corporation, and dissolve the for-profit corporation. Presumably, there would not be a state law prohibition as to this type of transaction.

(b) Federal Tax Law

Unlike the state of the law concerning the process by which a tax-exempt organization converts to a for-profit one, there are considerable guidelines at the federal tax level for converting a for-profit entity to an exempt one.

The essential principles in this area in the healthcare context are reflected in a revenue ruling published by the IRS in 1976.[89] The transaction in that ruling involved the purchase by a nonprofit hospital corporation of all of the assets of a for-profit hospital; the purchase was not at arm's length, in that the owners of the for-profit entity created the nonprofit organization and over one half of the board of directors of the nonprofit entity were stockholders of the for-profit institution. The nonprofit entity was held to qualify as an exempt charitable organization; the IRS ruled that there was no private inurement.

The chief tax issue in a transaction of this nature is the appropriate selling price. In this case, the owners obtained an independent appraisal of the tangible assets and then computed the value of the intangible assets (which was substantial) by the capitalization of excess earnings formula.[90] The purchase was made using the price arrived at by this method. The nonprofit organization satisfied the IRS that the intangible assets had a direct and substantial relationship to the performance of the exempt functions of the hospital. These assets, in the case of a hospital, were said to include accreditation for an internship or residency program, good labor relations, an active medical staff, and a favorable location.

Another example of these principles is contained in a subsequent revenue

---

[88] See text accompanied by *supra* § 4(a).
[89] Rev. Rul. 76-91, 1976-1 C.B. 149.
[90] This formula is the subject of Rev. Rul. 68-609, 1968-2 C.B. 327.

ruling also published by the IRS in 1976.[91] One aspect of the ruling concerned an otherwise qualifying nonprofit organization that purchased or leased the assets of a former for-profit school and employed the former owners, who were not related to the directors of the nonprofit entity, at salaries commensurate with their responsibilities. The IRS determined that the nonprofit school operated to serve a public interest where it purchased the for-profit school's personal property at fair market value in an arm's-length transaction and paid a fair rental value for use of the land and buildings. In the ruling, the IRS concluded that the organization was operating exclusively for educational and charitable purposes.

However, the ruling also discussed another situation concerning a nonprofit organization which, after receiving as a gift all of the stock of a for-profit school, dissolved the school and assumed all of its liabilities, which included notes owed to the former owners, all of whom comprised the board of directors of the recipient organization. Financial information showed that the liabilities of the school exceeded the fair market value of its assets; consequently, the IRS ruled that the nonprofit donee organization was substantially serving the directors' private interests in honoring the notes and thus that the organization failed to qualify for tax exemption. Said the IRS, "The directors were, in fact, dealing with themselves and will benefit financially from the transaction."[92]

In general, it is the view of the IRS that where an organization purchases assets from an independent party, a presumption exists that the purchase price (arrived at through negotiations) represents fair market value. However, where the purchaser is controlled by the seller (or there is a close relationship between the two) at the time of the sale, this presumption will not be made because the elements of an arm's length transaction are not present.[93]

Although there are no regulations or rulings on the subject, the IRS, in the application for recognition of tax-exempt status as a charitable organization,[94] established an inventory of the items of information it must have concerning the predecessor and successor organizations in order to issue a favorable ruling or determination letter to the nonprofit organization. (This body of information is in addition to the information requested of all nonprofit organization applicants.) The form presupposes that the applicant nonprofit organization is an entity separate from the predecessor for-profit organization,[95] thus reflecting the presumption that a for-profit organization cannot be transformed into a nonprofit organization.[96]

The specific items of information a successor nonprofit organization must provide the IRS as part of the exemption recognition process are (1) the name of the predecessor organization; (2) the nature of the activities of the predecessor or-

---

[91] Rev. Rul. 76-441, *supra* note 81.
[92] *Id.* at 148.
[93] Rev. Rul. 76-91, *supra* note 89.
[94] Form 1023, Schedule I.
[95] For this purpose, a *for-profit* organization includes any organization in which a person may have a proprietary or partnership interest, hold corporate stock, or otherwise exercise an ownership interest (Form 1023, Schedule I, last sentence). The organization need not have operated for the purpose of making a profit (*id.*).
[96] See *supra* §§ 3(a), 4(a).

ganization; (3) the names and addresses of the owners or principal stockholders of the predecessor organization; (4) their share or interest in the predecessor organization; (5) the business or family relationship between the owners or principal stockholders and principal employees of the predecessor organization and the officers, directors, and principal employees of the applicant nonprofit organization; (6) whether any property or equipment formerly used by the predecessor organization has been or will be rented to the successor organization (if so, copies of leases and like contracts must be attached); (7) whether the successor organization is or will be leasing or otherwise making available any space or equipment to the owners, principal stockholders, or principal employees of the predecessor organization (if so, a list of the tenants must be included, along with a copy of each lease); and (8) whether any new operating policies were initiated as a result of the transfer of assets from the for-profit organization to the nonprofit organization. Additionally, the applicant nonprofit organization must attach (1) a copy of the agreement of sale or other contract that sets forth the terms and conditions of the sale of the predecessor organization or of its assets to the nonprofit organization and (2) an appraisal[97] by an independent qualified expert showing the fair market value at the time of sale of the facilities or property interest sold.

Likewise, if a for-profit organization is endeavoring to convert to a nonprofit organization and be a tax-exempt social welfare organization[98] or a business league,[99] and is requesting a determination from the IRS as to recognition of tax-exempt status, it must reveal as part of the exemption application the name of the predecessor organization, the period during which it was in existence, and the reasons for its termination, as well as submit copies of all documents by which any transfer of assets was effected.[100]

If a for-profit organization sells assets to a nonprofit organization, the seller would be liable for taxes on any gain, just as would be the case were any other purchaser involved. There are special rules in this regard in the case of liquidations.[101]

If assets and/or income are contributed to a tax-exempt charitable organization by a for-profit organization, a charitable contribution deduction would likely result. This deduction may be limited by one or more factors, such as the percentage limitation on annual corporate charitable deductions[102] and the restrictions on the deductibility of gifts of inventory by businesses.[103]

---

[97] See *supra* note 84.
[98] See Chapter 12.
[99] See Chapter 13.
[100] Form 1024, Part II, question 4.
[101] See § 31.2(d).
[102] IRC § 170(b)(2). In general, Hopkins, *supra* note 84, Chapter 7 § 17. See, e.g., Priv. Let. Rul. 9703028.
[103] IRC § 170(e)(3). In general, Hopkins, *supra* note 84, Chapter 9 § 4.

Sources of the Law

The law as described in this book is derived from many sources. For those not familiar with these matters and wishing to understand just what the "law" regarding tax-exempt organizations is, the following explanation should be of assistance.

FEDERAL LAW

At the federal (national) level in the United States, there are three branches of government as provided for in the U.S. Constitution. Article I of the Constitution established the U.S. Congress as a bicameral legislature, consisting of the House of Representatives and the Senate. Article II of the Constitution established the Presidency. Article III of the Constitution established the federal court system.

Congress

The legal structure underlying the federal law for nonprofit organizations in the United States has been created by Congress. Most of this law is manifested in the tax law and thus appears in the Internal Revenue Code (which is officially codified in Title 26 of the United States Code and referenced throughout the book as the "IRC" (see Chapter 1, note 2)). Other laws written by Congress that can affect nonprofit organizations include the postal, employee benefits, antitrust, labor, and securities laws.

Tax laws for the United States must originate in the House of Representatives (U.S. Constitution, Article I § 7). Consequently, most of the nation's tax laws are formally initially written by the members and staff of the House Committee on Ways and Means, although much of this work is performed by the staff of the Joint Committee on Taxation, which consists of members of the House and Senate. Frequently, these laws are generated by work done at the subcommittee level, usually the Subcommittee on Oversight or the Subcommittee on Select Revenue Measures.

Committee work in this area within the Senate is undertaken by the Committee on Finance. The Joint Committee on Taxation again provides assistance in this regard. Nearly all of this legislation is finalized by a House-Senate conference committee, consisting of senior members of the House Ways and Means Committee and the Senate Finance Committee.

A considerable amount of the federal tax law for nonprofit organizations is found in the "legislative history" of these statutory laws. Most of this history is in congressional committee reports. Reports from committees in the House of Representatives are cited as "H. Rep." (see, e.g., Chapter 1, note 35); reports from committees in the Senate are cited as "S. Rep." (see, e.g., Chapter 1, note 96); conference committee reports are cited as "H. Rep." (see, e.g., Chapter 10, note 39). Transcripts of the debate on legislation, formal statements, and other items are printed in the Congressional Record ("*Cong. Rec.*"). The Congressional Record is published every day one of the houses of Congress is in session and is cited as "_____*Cong. Rec.*_____(daily ed., [date of issue])." The first number is the annual volume number; the second number is the page in the daily edition on which the item begins. Periodically, the daily editions of the Congressional Record are republished as a hardbound book and are cited as "_____ *Cong. Rec.*_____([year])" (see, e.g., Chapter 5, note 29). As before, the first number is the annual volume number and the second is the beginning page number. The bound version of the Congressional Record then becomes the publication that contains the permanent citation for the item.

A Congress sits for two years, each of which is termed a "session." Each Congress is sequentially numbered. For example, the 105th Congress met during the calendar years 1997-1998. A legislative development that took place in 1998 is referenced as occurring during the 105th Congress, 2d Session ("105th Cong., 2d Session ("105th Cong., 2d Sess. (1998)").

A bill introduced in the House of Representatives or Senate during a particular Congress is given a sequential number in each house. For example, the 1,000th bill introduced in the House of Representatives in 1998 is cited as "H.R. 1000, 105th Cong., 2d Sess. (1998)" (see, e.g., Chapter 5, note 107); the 500th bill introduced in the Senate in 1998 is cited as "S. 500, 105th Cong., 2d Sess. (1998)" (see, e.g., Chapter 18 § 20).

Executive Branch

A function of the Executive Branch in the United States is to administer and enforce the laws enacted by Congress. This "executive" function is performed by departments and agencies, and "independent" regulatory commissions (such as the Federal Trade Commission or the Securities and Exchange Commission). One of these functions is the promulgation of regulations, which are published by the U.S. government in the "Code of Federal Regulations" ("CFR"). When adopted, regulations are printed in the *Federal Register ("Fed. Reg.")* (see, e.g., Chapter 5, note 102). The federal tax laws are administered and enforced overall by the Department of the Treasury.

One of the ways in which the Department of the Treasury executes these functions is by the promulgation of regulations ("Reg."), which are designed to interpret and amplify the related statute (see, e.g., Chapter 1, note 58). These regulations (like other rules made by other departments, agencies, and commissions) have the force of law, unless they are overly broad in relation to the accompanying statute or are unconstitutional, in which case they can be rendered void by a court.

Within the Department of the Treasury is the Internal Revenue Service ("IRS"). The IRS is, among its many roles, a tax-collecting agency. The IRS, while headquartered in Washington, D.C. (its "National Office"), has regional and field offices throughout the country.

The IRS's jurisdiction over tax-exempt organizations is within the ambit of the Assistant Commissioner, Employee Plans and Exempt Organizations (EP/EO). Within that office is the Exempt Organizations Division. Within the Chief Counsel's office is an Employee Benefits and Exempt Organizations division.

The IRS (from its National Office) prepares and disseminates guidelines interpreting tax statutes and tax regulations. These guidelines have the force of law, unless they are overly broad in relation to the statute and/or Treasury regulation involved, or are unconstitutional. IRS determinations on a point of law are termed "revenue rulings" ("Rev. Rul."); those that are rules of procedure are termed "revenue procedures" ("Rev. Proc.").

Revenue rulings (which may be based on one or more court opinions) and revenue procedures are sequentially numbered every calendar year, with that number preceded by a two-digit number reflecting the year of issue. For example, the fiftieth revenue ruling issued in 1998 is cited as "Rev. Rul. 98-50." Likewise, the twenty-fifth revenue procedure issued in 1998 is cited as "Rev. Proc. 98-25."

These IRS determinations are published each week in the Internal Revenue Bulletin ("I.R.B."). In the foregoing examples, when the determinations are first published, the revenue ruling is cited as "Rev. Rul. 98-50, 1998–_____ I.R.B. _____," with the number after the hyphen being the number of the particular issue of the weekly Bulletin and the last number being the page number within that issue on which the item begins. Likewise, the revenue procedure is cited as "Rev. Proc. 98-25, 1998-_____I.R.B._____" (see, e.g., Chapter 23, note 21). Every six months, the Internal Revenue Bulletins are republished as hard-bound books, with the resulting publication termed the Cumulative Bulletin ("C.B."). The Cumulative Bulletin designation then becomes the permanent citation for the determination. Thus, the permanent citations for these two IRS determinations are "Rev. Rul. 98-50, 1998-1 C.B._____" (see, e.g., Chapter 3, note 94) and "Rev. Proc. 98-25, 1998-1 C.B._____" (see, e.g., Chapter 4, note 1), with the first number being the year of issue, the second number (after the hyphen) indicting whether the determination is published in the first six months of the year ("1" (as is the case in the example)) or the second six months of the year ("2"), and the last number being the page number within that semiannual bound volume at which the determination begins.

The IRS considers itself bound by its revenue rulings and revenue procedures. These determinations are the "law," particularly in the sense that the IRS regards them as precedential, although they are not binding on the courts.

The IRS also issues forms of "public" law in the name of "notices" and "announcements." A notice is initially published in the Internal Revenue Bulletin and then republished in the Cumulative Bulletin (see, e.g., Chapter 23, note 11). An announcement, however, although published in the Internal Revenue Bulletin, is not republished in the Cumulative Bulletin (see, e.g., Chapter 23, note 20).

By contrast to these forms of "public" law, the IRS (again from its National Office) also issues "private" or nonprecedential determinations. These documents principally are private letter rulings, technical advice memoranda, and general counsel memoranda. These determinations may not be cited as legal authority (IRC § 6110(j)(3)). Nonetheless, these pronouncements can be valuable in understanding IRS thinking on a point of law and, in practice (the statutory prohibition notwithstanding), these documents are cited as IRS positions on issues, such as in court opinions, articles, and books.

The IRS issues private letter rulings in response to written questions (termed "ruling requests") submitted to the IRS by individuals and organizations. An IRS district office may refer a case to the IRS National Office for advice (termed "technical advice"); the resulting advice is provided to the IRS district office in the form of a technical advice memorandum. In the course of preparing a revenue ruling, private letter ruling, or technical advice memorandum, the IRS National Office may seek legal advice from its Office of Chief Counsel; the resulting advice is provided in the form of a general counsel memorandum. These documents are eventually made public, albeit in redacted form.

Private letter rulings ("Priv. Ltr. Rul.") and technical advice memoranda ("Tech. Adv. Mem.") are identified by seven-digit numbers, as in "Private Letter Ruling 9826007" (see, e.g., Chapter 4, note 189). (A reference to a technical advice memorandum appears in Chapter 4, note 168.) The first two numbers are for the year involved (here, 1998), the second two numbers reflect the week of the calendar year involved (here, the twenty-sixth week of 1998), and the remaining three numbers identify the document as issued sequentially during the particular week (here, this private letter ruling was the seventh one issued during the week involved). General counsel memoranda ("Gen. Couns. Mem.") are numbered sequentially since they have been written (e.g., General Counsel Memorandum 39457 is the thirty-nine thousandth, four hundredth, fifty-seventh general counsel memorandum ever written by the IRS's Office of Chief Counsel. (A reference to a general counsel memorandum appears in Chapter 4, note 188.)

The Judiciary

The federal court system has three levels; trial courts (including those that initially hear cases where a formal trial is not involved), courts of appeal ("appellate" courts), and the U.S. Supreme Court. The trial courts include the various federal district courts (at least one in each state, the District of Columbia, and the U.S. territories), the U.S. Tax Court, and the U.S. Court of Federal Claims. There are thirteen federal appellate courts (the U.S. Courts of Appeal for the First through the Eleventh Circuits, the U.S. Courts of Appeals for the District of Columbia, and the U.S. Court of Appeals for the Federal Circuit).

Cases involving tax-exempt organization issues at the federal level can originate in any federal district court, the U.S. Tax Court, and the U.S. Court of Federal Claims. Under a special declaratory judgment procedure available only to charitable organizations (IRC § 7428), cases can originate only with the U.S. District Court for the District of Columbia, the U.S. Tax Court, and the U.S. Court of Federal Claims. Cases involving tax-exempt organizations are considered by the U.S. courts of appeal and the U.S. Supreme Court.

Most opinions emanating from a U.S. district court are published by the West Publishing Company in the "Federal Supplement" series ("Fed. Supp."). Thus, a citation to one of these opinions appears as "_____ F. Supp. _____," followed by an identification of the court and the year of the opinion. The first number is the annual volume number, the other number is the page in the book on which the opinion begins (see, e.g., Chapter 1, note 68). Some district court opinions appear sooner in Commerce Clearinghouse or Prentice Hall publications (see, e.g., Chapter 3, note 2); occasionally, these publications will contain opinions that are never published in the Federal Supplement series.

Most opinions emanating from a U.S. court of appeals are published by the West Publishing Company in the "Federal Reporter" series (usually "Fed.2d" or "Fed.3d"). Thus, a citation to one of these opinions appears as "_____ F.2d _____" or "_____ F.3d _____," followed by an identification of the court and the year of the opinion. The first number is the annual volume number; the other number is the page in the book on which the opinion begins (see, e.g., Chapter 1, note 65). Appellate court opinions appear sooner in Commerce Clearinghouse or Prentice Hall publications (see, e.g., Chapter 3, note 106); occasionally these publications contain opinions that are never published in Federal Second or Federal Third series. Opinions from the U.S. Court of Federal Claims are also published in the Federal Second or Federal Third.

Opinions from the U.S. Tax Court are published by the U.S. government and are usually cited as "_____ T.C. _____," followed by the year of the opinion (see, e.g., Chapter 2, note 67). Some Tax Court opinions that are of lesser precedential value are published as "memorandum decisions" and are cited as "_____ T.C.M. _____" followed by the year of the opinion (see, e.g., Chapter 3, note 97). As always, the first number of these citations is the annual volume number, the second number is the page in the book on which the opinion begins.

U.S. district court and Tax Court opinions may be appealed to the appropriate U.S. court of appeals. For example, cases in the states of Maryland, North Carolina, South Carolina, Virginia, and West Virginia are appealable (from either court) to the U.S. Court of Appeals for the Fourth Circuit. Cases from any federal appellate or district court, the U.S. Tax Court, and the U.S. Court of Federal Claims may be appealed to the U.S. Supreme Court.

The U.S. Supreme Court usually has discretion as to whether to accept a case. This decision is manifested as a "writ of certiorari." When the Supreme Court agrees to hear a case, it grants the writ ("cert. gr."); otherwise, it denies the writ ("cert. den.") (see, e.g., Chapter 3, note 4).

In this book, citations to Supreme Court opinions are to the "United States Reports" series, published by the U.S. government, when available ("_____ U.S. _____," followed by the year of the opinion) (see, e.g., Chapter 1, note 21). When the United States Reports series citation is not available, the "Supreme Court Reporter" series, published by the West Publishing Company, reference is used ("_____ S. Ct. _____," followed by the year of the opinion) (see, e.g., Chapter 1, note 1). As always, the first number of these citations is the annual volume number, the second number is the page in the book on which the opinion begins. There is a third way to cite Supreme Court cases, which is by means of the "United States Supreme Court Reports—Lawyers' Edition" series, published by The Lawyers Co-Operative Publishing Company and the Bancroft-Whitney Company, but that form of citation is not used in this book. Supreme Court opinions appear earlier in the Commerce Clearinghouse or Prentice Hall publications.

In most instances, court opinions are available on Westlaw and LEXIS in advance of formal publication (see, e.g., Chapter 24, note 421).

STATE LAW

The Legislative Branches

Statutory laws in the various states are created by their legislatures. There are no references to state statutory laws in this book (although most, if not all, of the states have such forms of law relating, directly or indirectly, to tax-exempt organizations).

The Executive Branches

The rules and regulations published at the state level emanate from state departments, agencies, and the like. For tax-exempt organizations, these departments are usually the office of the state's attorney general and the state's department of state. There are no references to state rules and regulations in this book (although most, if not all, of the states have such forms of law relating to tax-exempt organizations).

The Judiciary

Each of the states has a judiciary system, usually a three-tiered one modeled after the federal system. Cases involving nonprofit organizations are heard in all of these courts. There are a few references to state court opinions in this book (see, e.g., Chapter 6, note 330) although most, if not all, of the states have court opinions relating, directly or indirectly, to tax-exempt organizations.

State court opinions are published by the governments of each state and the principal ones by the West Publishing Company. The latter sets of opinions (referenced in this book) are published in "Reporters" relating to court developments in various regions throughout the country. For example, the "Atlantic Reporter" contains court opinions issued by the principal courts in the states of Connecticut, Delaware, Maine, Maryland, New Hampshire, New Jersey, Pennsylvania, Rhode Island, and Vermont, and the District of Columbia, while the "Pacific Reporter" contains court opinions issued by the principal courts of Arizona, California, Colorado, Idaho, Kansas, Montana, Nevada, New Mexico, Oklahoma, Oregon, Utah, Washington, and Wyoming.

PUBLICATIONS

Articles, of course, are not forms of the "law." However, they can be cited, particularly by courts, in the development of the law. Also, as research tools, they contain useful summaries of the applicable law. In addition to the many law school "law review" publications, the following (which is not an exclusive list) periodicals contain material that is of help in following developments concerning tax-exempt organizations.

> *The Chronicle of Philanthropy*
> *Daily Tax Report* (Bureau of National Affairs, Inc.)
> *Exempt Organization Tax Review* (Tax Analysts)
> *Foundation News* (Council on Foundations)
> *The Journal of Taxation* (Warren, Gorham & Lamont)
> *The Journal of Taxation of Exempt Organizations* (Faulkner & Gray)
> *The Nonprofit Counsel* (John Wiley & Sons, Inc.)
> *The Philanthropy Monthly* (Non-Profit Reports, Inc.)
> *Tax Law Review* (Rosenfeld Launer Publications)
> *The Tax Lawyer* (American Bar Association)
> *Tax Notes* (Tax Analysts)
> *Taxes* (Commerce Clearinghouse, Inc.)

Internal Revenue Code Sections

Following are the provisions of the Internal Revenue Code of 1986, as amended, which comprise the statutory framework for the law of tax-exempt organizations, coupled with references (by chapter or chapter section) to the portion(s) of the book where the provision is discussed:

Section 41—tax credit for increasing scientific research activities [Chap. 9 § 2, 11.1(f)].

Section 68—floor on certain income tax deductions, including charitable deduction [2.5].

Section 74(b)—rule concerning prizes and awards transferred to charitable organizations [11.4].

Section 84—tax on appreciated property gifts to political organizations [17].

Section 103—exclusion for interest on governmental obligations [6.9, 18.7].

Section 115—exclusion from gross income for revenues of political subdivisions and the like [6.9, 18.7].

Section 117—exclusion from gross income for qualified scholarships [4.5, 6.5, 11.4 (e)].

Section 120—exclusion from gross income for value of prepaid group legal services (expired) [16.6].

Section 162(e)—denial of business expense deduction for expenses of most lobbying and political campaign activities; flow-through rule relating to dues; "anti-cascading rule" that operates to ensure that lobbying expense disallowance rule results in denial of deduction at only one level [20.8].

Section 168(h)—tax-exempt entity leasing rules [29.5].

Section 170—income tax deduction for charitable contributions [2.5, 3.2(b), 5].

Section 170(b)(1)(E)(ii)—pass-through foundation rules [11.1(d)].

Section 170(b)(1)(E)(iii)—conduit foundation rules [11.1(e)].

Section 192—income tax deduction for contributions to black lung benefit trusts [16.5].

Section 274(a)(3)—denial of business expense deduction for payment of club dues [14.1].

Section 277—treatment of deductions incurred by certain nonexempt membership organizations [3.4, 13.6, 14.3].

Section 318—indirect control test for purposes of taxing revenue from controlled entities [27.1(n)(ii)].

Section 337(b)(2)—recognition of gain or loss for property distributed to tax-exempt parent in liquidation of subsidiary [31.2(d)].

Section 337(d)—recognition of gain or loss for property distributed to tax-exempt organization generally in liquidation [31.2(d)].

Section 401(a)—general rules for qualified pension, profit-sharing and like plans [4.9, 16.1, 19.4(i)].

Section 401(k)(4)(B)(i)—maintenance of 401(k) plans by tax-exempt organizations [16.1(h), 19.4(i)].

Section 403(b)—treatment of certain annuity contracts provided by charitable organizations to their employees [3.2(e), 16.1(g), 19.4(i)].

Section 419—welfare benefit fund rules [14.2, 16.3, 16.4].

Section 457—deferred compensation plans of tax-exempt organizations [3.2(e), 16.1(f), 19.4(i)].

Section 501(a)—source of tax exemption for nearly all exempt organizations [3.1].

Section 501(b)—tax-exempt organizations subject to tax on unrelated business income [28.1].

Section 501(c)(1)—tax exemption for instrumentalities of the United States [18.1].

Section 501(c)(2)—tax exemption for single-parent title-holding corporations [18.2(a)].

Section 501(c)(3)—tax exemption for charitable, educational, religious, scientific, and similar entities [5–11].

Section 501(c)(4)—tax exemption for social welfare organizations [12].

Section 501(c)(5)—tax exemption for agricultural, horticultural, and labor organizations [15].

Section 501(c)(6)—tax exemption for business leagues, including trade, business, and professional associations [13].

Section 501(c)(7)—tax exemption for social clubs [14].

Section 501(c)(8)—tax exemption for certain fraternal beneficiary societies [18.4(a)].

Section 501(c)(9)—tax exemption for voluntary employees' beneficiary associations [16.3].

Section 501(c)(10)—tax exemption for certain domestic fraternal societies [18.4(b)].

Section 501(c)(11)—tax exemption for teachers' retirement fund associations [16.6].

Section 501(c)(12)—tax exemption for benevolent or mutual organizations [18.5].

Section 501(c)(13)—tax exemption for certain cemetery companies [18.6].

Section 501(c)(14)—tax exemption for certain credit unions and mutual reserve funds [1.2, 18.7].

Section 501(c)(15)—tax exemption for certain insurance companies or associations [18.8].

Section 501(c)(16)—tax exemption for crop operations finance corporations [18.9].

Section 501(c)(17)—tax exemption for supplemental unemployment benefit trusts [16.4].

Section 501(c)(18)—tax exemption for certain pension plan trusts [16.6].

Section 501(c)(19)—tax exemption for veterans' organizations [18.10(a)].

Section 501(c)(20)—tax exemption for group legal service organizations (expired) [16.6].

Section 501(c)(21)—tax exemption for black lung benefit trusts [16.5].

Section 501(c)(22)—tax exemption for multiemployer benefit trusts [16.6].

Section 501(c)(23)—tax exemption for certain veterans' organizations [1.2, 18.10(b)].

Section 501(c)(24)—tax exemption for certain employee benefit trusts [16.6].

Section 501(c)(25)—tax exemption for multiparent title-holding corporations or trusts [18.2(b)].

Section 501(c)(26)—tax exemption for high-risk individuals health care coverage organizations [18.14].

Section 501(c)(27)—tax exemption for workers' compensation reinsurance organizations [1.2, 18.15].

Section 501(d)—rules for religious and apostolic organizations [8.7].

Section 501(e)—cooperative hospital service organizations [6.8, 10.4].

Section 501(f)—cooperative educational service organizations [6.8, 10.5].

Section 501(g)—definition of term "agricultural" [15.2].

Section 501(h)—election of expenditure test as to lobbying [20.5(a)].

Section 501(i)—prohibition of discrimination by social clubs [14.5].

Section 501(j)—rules for certain amateur sports organizations [10.2].

Section 501(k)—rules for certain child care organizations [7.7].

Section 501(l)—list of specified exempt U.S. instrumentalities [18.1].

Section 501(m)—rules concerning issuance of commercial-type insurance [1.2, 22.1, 25, 17.1(o)].

Section 501(n)—tax exemption for qualified charitable risk pools [1.2, 10.6].

Section 501(o)—treatment of hospitals participating in provider-sponsored organizations [6.2(a)].

Section 502—feeder organizations [23.7(a), 28.6].

Section 503—denial of tax exemption to certain organizations engaged in prohibited transactions [23.8].

INTERNAL REVENUE CODE SECTIONS

Section 504—rules as to status of nonexempt charity because of lobbying or political campaign activities [12.3, 20.3(b), 21.2].

Section 505—additional requirements for certain employee benefit funds [16.2].

Section 507—rules by which the private foundation status of charitable organizations is terminated [11.4].

Section 508—special rules for charitable organizations, including notice requirements [4.3(a), 11.1(a), 11.1(g), 23.3, 23.4].

Section 509—description of charitable organizations that are not private foundations [11.3].

Section 509(a)(1)—rules as to certain charitable institutions and donative publicly supported charitable organizations [11.3(a), (b)].

Section 509(a)(2)—rules as to service provider publicly supported charitable organizations [11.3(b)(iv)].

Section 509(a)(3)—rules as to supporting organizations [4.1, 11.3(c)].

Section 509(a)(4)—rules for organizations that test for public safety [11.3(d)].

Section 511—imposition of tax on unrelated business income [28.1].

Section 512—definition of unrelated business income [14.3, 26.1, 27.1, 29.1].

Section 512(b)—various modifications in computing unrelated business income [27.1].

Section 512(c)—special unrelated business rules for partnerships [28.4].

Section 512(d)—nontaxation of certain associate member dues [27.2(l)].

Section 512(e)—taxation of interests in S corporations [27.2(m), 31.1(b)].

Section 513—general unrelated business rules [26, 27].

Section 513(c)—definition of "trade or business" [26.2].

Section 513(d)—trade show and like activities rules [27.2(f)].

Section 513(e)—rules as to certain hospital services [6.8, 27.2(g)].

Section 513(f)—rules as to bingo games [27.2(h)].

Section 513(g)—rules as to certain pole rentals [27.2(i)].

Section 513(h)—rules as to rentals of lists and distribution of low-cost articles [27.2(j)].

Section 513(i)—nontaxation of qualified sponsorship payments [27.2(n)].

Section 514—rules as to unrelated debt-financed income [29.1–29.4].

Section 521—tax-exempt farmers' cooperatives [18.11].

Section 526—tax-exempt shipowners' protection and indemnity associations [18.12].

Section 527—tax-exempt political organizations and tax on political activities [17].

Section 527(f)(1)—tax on political expenditures [17.3, 21.3].

Section 4955—taxes on certain political expenditures [21.2].

Section 4958—intermediate sanctions with respect to public charities and social welfare organizations [19.11].

Section 4961—abatement of private foundation additional taxes [11.4].

Section 4962—abatement of public charity and private foundation initial taxes [11.4].

Section 4976—taxes with respect to funded welfare benefit plans [14.1, 16.3, 16.4, 16.6].

Section 5276(c)—exemption from occupational tax for U.S. instrumentalities [3.2(h)].

Section 6011—requirement of return for payment of certain excise taxes, including those imposed for excess benefit transactions [7, 11, 19.11, 20.6, 21.2].

Section 6012—requirement of income tax returns [24.3(a)(v)].

Section 6031—requirement of partnership tax returns [32.5].

Section 6033—requirement of filing of annual information returns [24.3].

Section 6033(e)(1)(A)—dues nondeductibility disclosure rule for associations; imposition of proxy tax [20.8].

Section 6050—information return concerning certain transfers of property to charity [2.5].

Section 6071—authority in IRS to prescribe time for filing a return, where filing date not set by statute [11, 19.11, 20.6, 21.2].

Section 6072(e)—time for filing returns [24.3(a)(vi)].

Section 6104—required publicity of information from certain exempt organizations and trusts [24.4].

Section 6110—rules as to public inspection of written determinations [24.2].

Section 6113—disclosure as to nondeductibility of contributions [3.3, 22.2].

Section 6154(h)—estimated unrelated income quarterly tax payments [28.1].

Section 6501(1)—limitations on assessments or collections; special rule for Chapter 42 taxes [24.3(a)(viii)].

Section 6651(a)(1)—addition to tax for failure to timely file unrelated business income tax (and other tax) return [24.3(a)(viii)].

Section 6652(c)(1)(A), (B)—penalties for failure to file annual information return [24.3(a)(viii)].

Section 6652(c)(1)(C)—penalties for failure to provide public access to annual information return [24.4].

Section 6652(c)(1)(D)—penalties for failure to provide public access to application for recognition of exemption [24.4].

Section 6652(d)(1)—rules concerning failure to file a return [6.10(d), 24.3].

Section 6653(b)—penalty for evading taxes due [8.2].

Section 6655(g)(3)—penalties for failure by a tax-exempt organization to pay estimated unrelated business income taxes [28.1].

Section 6673—use of Tax Court as delaying tactic [8.2].

Section 6684—penalties with respect to liability for Chapter 42 taxes [11.4].

Section 6710—penalties for failure to disclose that contributions are nondeductible [22.2].

Section 6711—penalties for failure to disclose that certain information or service is available from federal government [3.3, 24.5].

Section 6852—termination assessments for flagrant political expenditures by public charitable organizations [21.2].

Section 6901—rules as to transferred assets [24.2].

Section 7409—action to enjoin flagrant political expenditures by public charitable organizations [21.2].

Section 7421(a)—prohibition of restraint on assessment or collection of taxes [24.6(a)].

Section 7428—declaratory judgment provision for charitable organizations [24.6(b)].

Section 7454(b)—burden of proof in foundation manager cases [11].

Section 7611—church audit rules [24.8(b)].

Section 7701—definition of "partnership" and "corporation" [4.1, 32.1, 32.2(I), 33.1].

Section 7802(b)(1)—authorization, within IRS, of an Assistant Commissioner (Employee Plans and Exempt Organizations) [2.3, 3, 16].

Section 7805(b)—discretion in IRS to grant relief [24.1].

Section 7871—rules as to Indian tribal governments [18.18].

63 Categories
of Tax-Exempt Organizations

Agricultural organizations [IRC § 501(c)(5)]

Amateur sports, promotion of organizations [IRC § 50l(c)(3)]

Apostolic organizations [IRC § 501(d)]

Associations, membership [IRC § 501(c)(3), (6)]

Associations of churches [IRC §§ 501(c)(3), 170(b)(1)(A)(i), 509(a)(1)]

Black lung benefits trusts [IRC § 501(c)(21)]

Boards of trade [IRC § 501(c)(6)]

Benevolent organizations [IRC § 501(c)(12)]

Business leagues [IRC § 501(c)(6)]

Cemetery companies [IRC § 501(c)(13)]

Chambers of commerce [IRC § 501(c)(6)]

Charitable remainder trusts [IRC § 664]

Charitable risk pools [IRC §§ 501(n), 501(c)(3)]

Churches [IRC §§ 501(c)(3), 170 (b)(1)(A)(i), 509(a)(1)]

Conventions of churches [IRC §§ 501(c)(3), 170 (b)(1)(A)(i), 509(a)(1)]

Credit unions [IRC § 501(c)(14)]

Crop operations finance corporations [IRC § 501(c)(16)]

Cruelty, prevention of on behalf of children or animals [IRC § 501(c)(3)]

Domestic fraternal societies [IRC § 501(c)(10)]

Educational institutions [IRC §§ 501(c)(3), 170(b)(1)(A)(ii), 509(a)(1)]

Educational organizations, in general [IRC § 501(c)(3)]

Employee trusts, certain [IRC § 501(c)(24)]

Farmers' cooperatives [IRC § 521]

Foundations supporting public colleges and universities [IRC § 170 (b)(1)(A)(iv), 509 (a)(1)]

Fraternal beneficiary societies [IRC § 501(c)(8)]

Funded pension trusts, certain [IRC § 501(c)(18)]

Governmental units [IRC §§ 170(b)(1)(A)(v), 509(a)(1)]

63 CATEGORIES OF TAX-EXEMPT ORGANIZATIONS

Health care providers [IRC § 501(c)(3), 170(b)(1)(A)(iii), 509(a)(1)]

High-risk individuals health care coverage organizations [IRC § 501(c)(26)]

Homeowners' associations [IRC § 528]

Horticultural organizations [IRC § 501(c)(5)]

Indian tribes [IRC § 7871]

Instrumentalities of federal government [IRC § 501(c)(1)]

Insurance companies, certain [IRC § 501(c)(15)]

Integral parts of government [no statute]

Integrated auxiliaries of churches [IRC §§ 501(c)(3), 170(b)(1)(A)(i), 509(a)(1)]

Labor organizations [IRC § 501(c)(5)]

Literary organizations [IRC § 501(c)(3)]

Local associations of employees [IRC § 501(c)(4)]

Medical research organizations [IRC § 501(c)(3), 170(b)(1)(A)(iii), 509(a)(1)]

Multiemployer pension plan trusts [IRC § 501(c)(22)]

Mutual organizations [IRC § 501(c)(12), (14)]

Retirement and pension funds [IRC § 401]

Political organizations [IRC § 527]

Political subdivisions [no statute]

Prepaid tuition plans {IRC § 529]

Private foundations [IRC §§ 501(c)(3), 509(a)]

Professional football leagues [IRC § 501(c)(6)]

Publicly supported charitable organizations, in general [IRC §§ 501(c)(3), 170(b)(1)(A)(vi), 509(a)(1), 509(a)(2)]

Religious organizations, in general [IRC § 501(c)(3)]

Scientific organizations [IRC § 501(c)(3)]

Shipowners' protection and indemnity associations [IRC § 526]

Social clubs [IRC § 501(c)(7)]

Social welfare organizations [IRC § 501(c)(4)]

Supplemental unemployment benefit trusts [IRC § 501(c)(17)]

Supporting organizations [IRC §§ 501(c)(3), 509(a)(3)]

Teachers' retirement fund associations [IRC § 50l(c)(11)]

Testing for public safety organizations [IRC §§ 501(c)(3), 509(a)(4)]

Title-holding corporations, single parent [IRC § 501(c)(2)]

Title-holding corporations, multiparent [IRC § 501(c)(25)]

Veterans' organizations [IRC § 501(c)(19), (23)]

Voluntary employees' beneficiary associations [IRC § 501(c)(9)]

Workers' compensation organizations [IRC § 501(c)(27)]

Table of Cases

TABLE OF CASES

TABLE OF CASES

TABLE OF CASES

Table of IRS Revenue Rulings and Revenue Procedures

Revenue Rulings	Book Sections	Revenue Rulings	Book Sections	Revenue Rulings	Book Sections
51-170	§ 32.1	55-558	§ 18.11	57-449	§ 5.5(a)
53-44	§ 14.1	55-587	§§ 6.5, 7.4	57-453	§ 13.4
54-12	§ 18.11	55-611	§ 18.11	57-466	§§ 15.2,
54-73	§ 27.1(l)	55-656	§§ 6.2(h), 13.4		15.2,
54-134	§§ 24.1(b),	55-676	§ 27.2(b)		26.4(g),
	27.2(d)	55-715	§§ 13.4,		26.5(e)
54-243	§§ 4.1,		13.5	57-467	§§ 5.5(c),
	24.6(c)	55-716	§§ 12.1(a),		6.2(d)
54-282	§ 15.2		18.5	57-493	§ 12.4
54-296	§ 6.9	55-749	§ 27.2(j)	57-494	§ 18.3
54-369	§ 32.1	56-65	§§ 13.1,	57-574	§ 8.7
54-394	§ 12.1(a)		13.4	58-117	§ 12.1(b)
54-420	§ 27.1(h)	56-84	§§ 13.2,	58-143	§§ 15.1,
54-442	§ 13.1		13.4		30.2(a)
55-133	§§ 18.1,	56-138	§§ 5.5(a),	58-147	§ 6.8
	18.7		19.4(i)	58-190	§ 18.6
55-139	§ 6.9	56-152	§ 19.6	58-194	§§ 6.5,
55-156	§ 12.1(b)	56-185	§§ 6.2(a),		7.6,
55-176	§ 14.1		6.2(d)		23.7(a),
55-189	§ 18.12	56-225	§ 12.2		26.5(a)(i)
55-192	§ 30.5	56-245	§ 15.2	58-209	§ 3.4
55-230	§ 15.2	56-249	§ 16.4	58-224	§§ 13.2,
55-240	§ 18.8(b)	56-305	§ 14.1		27.2(f)
55-261	§ 6.2(h)	56-403	§ 5.5(a)	58-265	§ 6.9
55-311	§§ 12.1(a),	56-475	§ 14.1	58-293	§ 4.1
	18.3, 18.5	56-486	§ 6.5	58-294	§ 13.1
55-406	§ 6.1	56-511	§ 26.2(e)	58-328	§ 8.7
55-439	§ 12.4	57-128	§ 6.9	58-482	§§ 26.4(g),
55-444	§ 13.2	57-187	§ 6.9		27.1(h)
55-449	§ 26.4(g)	57-297	§§ 12.1(b),	58-483	§ 18.11
55-495	§§ 12.1(a),		12.4	58-501	§ 14.4
	18.4(a)	57-313	§ 26.4(g)	58-502	§§ 19.6,
55-516	§ 12.1(a)	57-420	§ 18.5		26.4(f)

TABLE OF IRS REVENUE RULINGS AND REVENUE PROCEDURES

Revenue Rulings	Book Sections	Revenue Rulings	Book Sections	Revenue Rulings	Book Sections
58-547	§ 29.2	62-23	§ 7.3	65-5	§ 18.11
58-566	§ 18.2(a)	62-66	§ 6.9	65-6	§ 18.6
58-588	§ 14.2	62-71	§ 20.4(a)	65-14	§ 13.2
58-589	§§ 14.1, 19.7, 19.4(f)	62-113	§ 30.2(d)	65-60	§ 9.2
		62-167	§§ 12.1(a), 14.1	65-61	§ 10.3
				65-63	§ 14.2
58-616	§ 18.8(b)	62-191	§§ 15.1, 26.4(g), 26.5(e)	65-64	§ 14.4
59-6	§§ 7.4, 15.1			65-99	§ 18.5
				65-164	§§ 13.1, 26.5(d)(iv)
59-41	§ 6.9	63-15	§ 6.8		
59-129	§ 8.3	63-20	§ 6.9	65-174	§ 18.5
59-151	§ 18.10(a)	63-190	§§ 12.1(a), 14.1	65-191	§ 6.5
59-152	§ 6.9			65-195	§ 12.1(a)
59-234	§ 13.4	63-208	§ 6.8	65-201	§§ 12.2, 18.5
59-310	§§ 6.3, 5.5(a)	63-209	§ 6.8		
		63-220	§§ 6.5, 7.6	65-219	§ 14.2
59-330	§§ 15.1, 26.4(g), 26.5(e)	63-234	§ 7.6	65-244	§ 13.4
		63-235	§§ 6.5, 23.7(a)	65-270	§§ 6.7, 7.4
				65-271	§ 6.7
59-391	§ 13.1	63-252	§ 30.2(d)	65-298	§§ 5.5(a), 7.4, 9.2, 9.4
60-86	§§ 15.2, 26.5(e)	64-108	§§ 4.6, 13.4		
60-143	§ 6.5	64-109	§ 18.6	65-299	§ 12.1(a)
60-193	§§ 4.3(d), 12.3, 20.4(a), 21.1(e), 21.4	64-117	§ 6.5	65-536	§§ 8.2, 27.1(m)
		64-118	§§ 6.5, 14.1	66-46	§ 6.7
		64-128	§ 7.3	66-47	§§ 26.4(g), 27.1(i)
60-206	§§ 27.1(a), 27.1(h)	64-174	§ 6.7		
		64-175	§ 6.7	66-59	§ 18.3
60-228	§ 26.4(g)	64-182	§§ 4.5(a), 4.7, 6.8, 26.4(f)	66-79	§ 30.2(d)
60-243	§ 6.9			66-102	§ 18.2(a)
60-323	§§ 14.2, 19.7	64-187	§ 12.4	66-103	§§ 6.5, 6.7
		64-192	§ 7.5	66-104	§§ 5.5(e), 7.6
60-324	§ 14.2	64-193	§ 18.5	66-105	§ 15.2
60-351	§§ 7.5, 7.6	64-194	§ 18.4(a)	66-108	§ 18.11
60-367	§ 30.5	64-195	§§ 7.4, 20.4(a)	66-146	§§ 6.3, 6.6
60-384	§§ 4.1, 6.9			66-147	§§ 7.5, 9.4
61-72	§ 6.2(d)	64-217	§ 18.6	66-148	§ 12.1(a)
61-87	§§ 6.5, 7.6	64-231	§ 6.2(d)	66-149	§ 14.2
61-137	§ 18.6	64-246	§ 18.11	66-150	§§ 12.1(b), 14.1, 18.2(a)
61-153	§ 12.1(a)	64-274	§ 6.5		
61-158	§ 12.1(b)	64-275	§ 7.4		
61-170	§§ 13.4, 19.4(g), 26.5(d)(iv)	64-286	§ 6.8	66-151	§§ 13.1, 13.2, 26.4(g), 26.5(d)(i), 26.5(d)(iv), 26.6(d)(ii)
		64-313	§ 12.1(b)		
		64-315	§ 13.5		
61-177	§§ 13.1, 20.8	65-1	§§ 5.5(e), 9.2		
62-17	§ 15.1	65-2	§§ 6.6, 7.4		

Revenue Rulings	Book Sections	Revenue Rulings	Book Sections	Revenue Rulings	Book Sections
66-152	§ 18.11	67-7	§ 15.1	67-293	§§ 12.3, 20.7
66-177	§ 4.1	67-8	§§ 14.1, 19.4(g)	67-294	§ 12.1(a)
66-178	§ 6.7,	67-71	§§ 12.3, 21.1(d), 21.4	67-295	§ 13.1
66-179	§§ 6.3, 7.5, 12.1(a), 13.1, 14.1, 15.3	67-72	§§ 6.5, 7.4, 19.10	67-296	§§ 19.6, 26.4(f), 26.5(d)(iv)
66-180	§ 18.3	67-77	§ 13.1	67-302	§ 14.2
66-212	§ 16.3	67-109	§§ 12.1(a), 26.4(a)	67-325	§§ 5.4(a), 5.5, 5.5(a)
66-219	§ 4.1	67-128	§ 18.11	67-327	§§ 7.4, 26.5(a)(iii)
66-220	§§ 6.4, 7.5, 7.6	67-138	§§ 6.1, 6.6, 7.5	67-342	§ 7.5
66-221	§ 26.1	67-139	§§ 7.5, 14.1	67-343	§ 13.1
66-222	§ 19.6	67-148	§ 7.4	67-344	§ 13.1
66-223	§ 13.1	67-149	§§ 6.5, 6.8	67-346	§ 18.11
66-225	§ 19.7	67-150	§§ 6.1, 7.4	67-367	§§ 5.5(a), 19.4(g)
66-255	§ 7.5	67-151	§ 10.1	67-368	§§ 12.3, 21.4
66-256	§§ 7.5, 21.1(e)	67-152	§ 18.11	67-390	§ 24.1(b)
66-257	§§ 5.5(a), 6.1	67-170	§§ 5.5(d), 18.6	67-391	§§ 6.3, 7.5
66-258	§§ 12.3, 20.4(a), 21.1(e), 21.4	67-175	§ 13.1	67-392	§§ 6.7, 7.4
		67-176	§§ 13.2, 26.5(d)(ii)	67-393	§ 13.1
66-259	§§ 19.3, 19.4(c)	67-182	§ 13.4	67-394	§ 13.1
		67-216	§§ 7.5, 15.2	67-422	§ 18.11
66-260	§ 13.1	67-217	§§ 6.5, 7.6	67-428	§§ 14.1, 14.2
66-273	§ 12.1(a)	67-218	§§ 27.1(a), 27.1(h)	67-429	§ 18.11
66-295	§§ 18.2(a), 28.6	67-219	§§ 26.4(f), 27.2(f)	67-430	§ 18.11
66-296	§ 28.6	67-223	§ 18.11	68-14	§§ 6.3, 7.5, 12.2, 19.10
66-323	§§ 6.2(h), 26.2(c), 26.4(g)	67-249	§ 14.1	68-15	§§ 6.3, 6.6, 7.5
66-338	§§ 13.4, 26.5(d)(i)	67-250	§§ 6.1, 6.6, 7.5	68-16	§ 7.4
		67-251	§ 19.6	68-17	§§ 6.1, 6.6, 7.5
66-354	§§ 12.1(a), 13.4, 15.1, 16.3	67-252	§§ 13.4, 15.2	68-26	§§ 4.5(a), 6.4, 8.2, 28.6
66-358	§§ 6.3, 19.9	67-253	§ 18.11	68-27	§ 6.2(e)
		67-264	§ 13.1	68-45	§ 12.1(b)
66-359	§ 10.1	67-265	§ 18.5	68-46	§§ 12.1(b), 26.4(g)
66-360	§ 12.1(b)	67-284	§ 18.18	68-70	§§ 6.6, 7.5
67-4	§§ 5.5(b), 6.5, 6.8, 7.5	67-290	§ 6.9	68-71	§§ 7.4, 7.5
		67-291	§ 6.5	68-72	§§ 6.4, 7.4
67-6	§§ 6.6, 12.2, 12.3, 20.7	67-292	§§ 6.3, 6.10(a), 7.3	68-73	§ 6.2(h)
				68-75	§ 18.5

TABLE OF IRS REVENUE RULINGS AND REVENUE PROCEDURES

Revenue Rulings	Book Sections	Revenue Rulings	Book Sections	Revenue Rulings	Book Sections
68-76	§ 18.11	68-504	§§ 5.5(a),	69-257	§ 6.5
68-104	§ 26.5(l)		7.4, 19.10	69-266	§§ 4.6,
68-117	§§ 6.1,	68-505	§§ 26.3(b),		6.2(h),
	30.2(d)		26.4(g),		19.4(j)
68-118	§ 12.1(a)		27.2(e)	69-267	§ 26.5(b)
68-119	§ 19.7	68-534	§ 15.1	69-268	§§ 26.5(b),
68-123	§§ 8.2,	68-535	§ 19.7		26.5(c),
	26.4(g)	68-538	§ 7.6		27.2(b)
68-157	§ 7.6	68-550	§ 26.4(d)	69-269	§ 26.5(b)
68-164	§ 7.5	68-563	§ 6.4	69-278	§ 18.2(a)
68-165	§§ 6.1,	68-564	§ 18.5	69-279	§§ 4.3(a),
	7.4,	68-581	§ 26.5(a)		4.3(b)
	30.2(d)	68-609	§ 33.4(b)	69-280	§ 12.2
68-166	§ 6.1	68-638	§ 14.2	69-281	§§ 12.2,
68-167	§ 6.1	68-655	§ 6.6		14.1
68-168	§ 19.7	68-656	§§ 12.3, 20.7	69-282	§ 18.7
68-175	§ 7.3	68-657	§ 13.1	69-283	§§ 18.1,
68-182	§§ 13.1,	69-16	§ 6.5		18.7
	13.2	69-51	§§ 26.4(g),	69-381	§ 18.2(a)
68-217	§ 24		26.5(e)	69-383	§ 19.3
68-222	§ 18.2(a)	69-52	§ 18.11	69-384	§ 12.1(a)
68-224	§ 12.1(a)	69-68	§ 14.1	69-385	§§ 12.1(b),
68-225	§ 26.4(f)	69-69	§§ 26.4(g),		12.4
68-263	§§ 20.4(a),		27.1(a),	69-386	§ 15.1
	21.1(e)		27.1(h)	69-387	§ 13.1
68-264	§ 13.4	69-80	§ 30.2(d)	69-400	§§ 6.5, 7.4
68-265	§§ 13.2,	69-96	§ 3.4	69-417	§ 18.11
	13.4	69-106	§ 13.2	69-430	§ 27.1(a)
68-266	§ 14.1	69-144	§ 16.3	69-441	§§ 6.1, 7.5
68-267	§ 26.4(g)	69-160	§ 10.4	69-459	§ 6.9
68-296	§ 31.1(a)	69-161	§ 6.1	69-464	§ 29.2
68-306	§ 6.4	69-162	§ 27.1(g)	69-492	§ 7.3
68-307	§ 7.5	69-174	§ 6.1	69-526	§§ 6.2(h),
68-371	§ 18.2	69-175	§ 19.4(g)		9.1, 9.2
68-372	§ 7.3	69-176	§ 19.4(c)	69-527	§ 14.1
68-373	§§ 9.2,	69-177	§ 7.6	69-528	§§ 6.8,
	10.3,	69-178	§§ 27.1(a),		28.6
	19.4(g),		27.1(h)	69-538	§ 6.5
	27.1(l)	69-179	§ 27.1(g)	69-545	§§ 6.1,
68-374	§ 26.5(b)	69-217	§ 14.2		6.2, 6.2(a),
68-375	§ 26.5(b)	69-219	§ 14.2		6.2(e),
68-376	§ 26.5(b)	69-220	§§ 14.2,		33.3(b)
68-422	§§ 5.5(a),		26.1	69-572	§§ 5.5(b),
	19.4(i)	69-222	§ 18.11		6.8,
68-438	§§ 6.6, 7.5	69-232	§§ 14.3,		21.1(f)
68-455	§ 12.1(b)		14.4	69-573	§§ 6.5,
68-489	§ 5.5(b)	69-256	§§ 4.3(a),		14.1
68-490	§ 18.2(a)		4.3(b),	69-574	§ 26.2(e)
68-496	§ 18.11		19.4(g)	69-575	§ 18.11

TABLE OF IRS REVENUE RULINGS AND REVENUE PROCEDURES

Revenue Rulings	Book Sections	Revenue Rulings	Book Sections	Revenue Rulings	Book Sections
69-632	§§ 5.5(e), 9.1, 13.1, 19.4(g)	70-535	§ 12.1(b)	71-581	§§ 26.5(g), 27.2(c), 28.6
69-633	§§ 3.4, 6.8, 10.4, 26.4(g), 27.2(g)	70-536	§ 16.4	71-614	§ 26.2(c)
		70-562	§ 6.9	72-16	§§ 6.2(h), 7.4, 26.5(b)
69-634	§ 13.1	70-566	§ 18.12		
69-635	§ 14.1	70-583	§§ 6.1, 7.4	72-17	§ 18.6
69-636	§ 19.7	70-584	§§ 6.3, 6.5, 7.4, 12.3, 21.4	72-36	§ 18.5
69-637	§ 18.6			72-37	§ 18.7
69-651	§ 18.11	70-585	§§ 6.1, 6.6	72-50	§ 18.11
69-683	§ 10.4	70-590	§§ 6.2(h), 7.5, 26.2(c)	72-101	§§ 6.5, 7.3, 19.10
70-4	§§ 6.6, 12.1(a)	70-591	§ 13.2	72-102	§§ 12.2, 18.13
70-31	§ 13.1, 13.4	70-640	§§ 4.6, 7.5	72-124	§§ 5.5(a), 5.5(c), 6.2(d), 26.2(c)
		70-641	§§ 6.2(g), 7.5, 13.1, 13.3		
70-32	§ 14.1	71-29	§ 6.3	72-147	§ 19.4(g)
70-48	§ 19.7	71-97	§ 6.5	72-209	§ 6.2(h)
70-79	§§ 6.3, 6.6, 7.5, 20.4(a)	71-99	§ 6.3	72-211	§§ 13.1, 13.4
		71-100	§ 18.11	72-228	§§ 6.6, 7.5
70-80	§ 13.2	71-131	§ 6.9	72-355	§§ 3.4, 17
70-81	§§ 13.1, 13.5, 29.2	71-132	§ 6.9		
		71-155	§§ 13.1, 13.4, 26.5(d)(ii)	72-369	§§ 4.5(a), 4.6, 6.8
70-95	§ 13.2				
70-129	§ 6.5	71-156	§ 16.4	72-391	§§ 15.1, 15.2, 19.4(g)
70-130	§ 18.5	71-175	§ 13.4		
70-132	§ 29.1	71-276	§ 24.1(b)	72-430	§ 7.3
70-186	§§ 6.3, 6.10(a), 19.4(g), 19.10	71-300	§ 18.6	72-431	§§ 26.4(g), 26.5(g), 27.2(j)
		71-311	§ 29.3		
		71-395	§§ 6.7, 19.4(g)	72-512	§ 21.1(d)
70-187	§ 13.1	71-413	§ 6.5	72-513	§§ 20.2(b), 21.1(d)
70-188	§ 16.4	71-421	§ 7.4, 14.1		
70-189	§ 16.4	71-447	§ 5.4(a)	72-542	§ 28.6
70-202	§ 18.3	71-460	§§ 4.1, 30.2(d)	72-559	§§ 4.6, 6.1, 5.5(b)
70-244	§ 13.1				
70-270	§ 11.1(g)	71-504	§ 13.3		
70-321	§§ 6.5, 7.5, 21.1(e)	71-505	§ 13.3	72-560	§§ 6.3, 7.5
		71-506	§§ 7.5, 9.4, 13.3	72-589	§ 18.11
70-372	§ 15.2	71-529	§§ 6.5, 6.8, 7.6, 26.2(c)	73-45	§§ 6.7, 26.2(c)
70-411	§ 16.3				
70-449	§ 20.4(a)	71-544	§ 18.2(a)	73-59	§ 18.11
70-533	§§ 4.5(b), 6.1, 7.3, 19.9	71-545	§ 7.3	73-93	§ 18.11
		71-553	§ 6.8	73-104	§§ 26.4(f), 26.5(c)
70-534	§§ 7.4, 26.5(a)(iii)	71-580	§§ 6.4, 19.4(g)		

TABLE OF IRS REVENUE RULINGS AND REVENUE PROCEDURES

Revenue Rulings	Book Sections	Revenue Rulings	Book Sections	Revenue Rulings	Book Sections
73-105	§ 26.5(c)	74-13	§ 18.18	74-475	§ 17
73-126	§ 19.4(i)	74-14	§ 6.9	74-488	§ 15.2
73-127	§§ 7.6, 26.4(b)	74-15	§ 6.9	74-489	§ 14.2
		74-16	§ 7.4	74-490	§ 24.1(b)
73-128	§§ 5.5(b), 6.1, 7.4, 7.6, 26.4(b)	74-17	§§ 12.2, 18.13	74-518	§ 15.2
				74-523	§ 30.2(d)
		74-18	§ 16.3	74-553	§§ 6.2(g), 9.2, 13.1
		74-21	§§ 3.4, 17		
73-148	§ 18.11	74-23	§ 17	74-563	§ 12.2
73-164	§ 28.6	74-30	§ 14.1	74-567	§ 18.11
73-165	§ 18.4(a)	74-38	§ 26.5(f)	74-572	§ 6.2(a)
73-192	§ 18.4(a)	74-81	§ 26.5(d)(i)	74-574	§§ 21.1(d), 21.1(e)
73-193	§ 27.1(g)	74-91	§ 13.4		
73-247	§ 18.11	74-99	§ 12.2	74-575	§§ 6.4, 19.9
73-248	§ 18.11	74-116	§ 13.1		
73-285	§§ 6.4, 6.6	74-117	§ 21.1(d)	74-587	§§ 6.6, 6.10(e)
73-306	§ 12.1(b)	74-118	§ 15.2		
73-307	§§ 12.2, 16.4	74-146	§§ 5.5(e), 6.5, 6.8, 19.9	74-595	§ 7.5
				74-596	§ 15.1
73-308	§ 18.11			74-604	§ 12.2
73-313	§§ 4.6, 5.5(e), 6.2(g), 6.2(h)	74-147	§ 13.1	74-614	§§ 6.5, 6.8
		74-148	§§ 14.1, 19.4(f)	74-615	§ 7.5
				75-4	§ 18.11
		74-167	§ 15.1	75-5	§ 18.11
73-349	§ 12.1(b)	74-168	§ 14.2	75-38	§§ 4.3(a), 11.1(g)
73-364	§ 24.3(b)(ii)	74-194	§ 10.1		
73-370	§ 18.4(b)	74-195	§ 15.2	75-65	§ 30.2(d)
73-386	§ 26.4(b)	74-196	§ 18.8(b)	75-74	§§ 6.1, 6.10(d)
73-411	§§ 4.6, 13.5	74-197	§ 29.3		
		74-199	§§ 3.4, 17, 18.13	75-75	§ 6.10(d)
73-422	§§ 23.4(b), 24.1(b)			75-76	§ 6.10(d)
				75-97	§ 18.11
73-424	§§ 26.3(a), 26.5(f)	74-224	§ 8.4	75-110	§ 18.11
		74-228	§ 13.4	75-145	§ 26.4(g)
73-434	§ 7.3	74-246	§ 6.3	75-196	§§ 5.5(a), 5.5(e), 7.3, 7.4, 19.10
73-439	§ 19.4(f)	74-281	§ 18.3		
73-440	§ 20.1(a)	74-287	§ 11.2(b)		
73-452	§ 13.1	74-308	§ 13.4	75-197	§ 6.2(h)
73-453	§ 18.5	74-318	§ 3.4	75-198	§§ 5.5(a), 6.1, 6.2(d), 6.2(h)
73-454	§ 18.6	74-319	§ 3.4		
73-455	§ 11.2(a)	74-327	§ 18.11		
73-504	§ 23.4(a)	74-361	§§ 6.3, 12.1(a), 12.4, 26.4(f)		
73-520	§ 14.1			75-199	§§ 12.1(a), 18.4(a)
73-543	§ 7.3				
73-567	§§ 6.2(g), 13.1			75-200	§ 26.5(f)
		74-362	§ 18.5	75-201	§§ 26.5(f), 26.5(g)
73-569	§ 7.5	74-368	§ 11.1(g)		
73-570	§ 18.11	74-399	§ 26.5(c)	75-207	§ 6.10(a)
73-587	§ 26.4(g)	74-443	§ 10.4	75-215	§ 7.3

Revenue Rulings	Book Sections	Revenue Rulings	Book Sections	Revenue Rulings	Book Sections
75-228	§ 18.11	76-22	§ 6.1	76-441	§ 33.3(b)
75-231	§ 5.4(a)	76-31	§ 15.1	76-442	§ 5.5(e)
75-252	§ 6.4	76-33	§§ 26.5(a)(iv),	76-443	§ 7.5
75-258	§§ 3.4, 6.6		26.5(b)	76-452	§ 6.2(a)
75-282	§§ 6.2(b),	76-37	§ 6.5	76-455	§ 9.2
	6.8,	76-38	§ 13.4	76-456	§ 21.1(e)
	23.7(a)	76-147	§ 6.6, 12.2	76-457	§ 18.4(b)
75-283	§ 6.1	76-152	§ 6.7	76-495	§ 18.13
75-284	§§ 6.5, 7.4	76-167	§ 7.3	76-550	§ 18.17
75-285	§ 7.5	76-204	§§ 6.5,	77-3	§ 6.1
75-286	§§ 6.3,		6.10(a),	77-4	§ 7.5
	12.2,		15.2	77-5	§ 15.1
	19.10	76-205	§§ 6.4,	77-42	§ 6.1
75-287	§§ 13.1,		6.6, 7.5	77-43	§ 16.4
	15.2	76-206	§§ 6.7,	77-46	§ 15.1
75-288	§ 15.1		19.1,	77-47	§ 29.2
75-290	§ 23.3(a)		19.10	77-68	§§ 6.2(h),
75-359	§§ 6.8, 6.9	76-207	§§ 13.1,		6.5, 7.4
75-384	§§ 5.5(f),		13.5	77-69	§ 6.2(g)
	6.3,	76-233	§ 18.11	77-70	§ 18.6
	12.1(a)	76-241	§ 15.2	77-71	§ 29.2
75-385	§§ 5.5(a),	76-244	§§ 5.5(a), 6.1	77-72	§ 29.3
	6.1	76-296	§§ 9.3,	77-111	§§ 4.6,
75-386	§ 12.2		26.4(g),		6.6,
75-387	§ 11.3(b)(iv)		27.1(l)		6.10(e)
75-388	§ 18.11	76-297	§ 27.1(g)	77-112	§ 13.1
75-434	§§ 6.4,	76-298	§ 18.11	77-114	§ 23.3(a)
	30.2(d)	76-323	§§ 8.2,	77-116	§ 23.4(b)
75-436	§ 6.9		26.4(g)	77-121	§ 28.6
75-470	§§ 6.6, 7.3	76-335	§ 18.2(a)	77-124	§ 28.6
75-471	§§ 5.5(e),	76-336	§ 6.5	77-153	§ 15.2
	6.7	76-337	§ 28.3	77-154	§ 15.1
75-472	§§ 6.2(h),	76-341	§ 26.4(g)	77-159	§ 24.1(b)
	7.4,	76-354	§ 29.3	77-162	§ 24.3(a)(vii)
	26.4(f),	76-366	§ 7.6	77-165	§§ 6.9,
	26.5(b)	76-384	§ 7.3		18.17
75-473	§ 15.1	76-388	§ 18.11	77-206	§ 19.6
75-492	§ 7.3	76-399	§ 15.2	77-207	§ 23.4(a)
75-494	§§ 12.2,	76-400	§ 13.1	77-208	§ 24.1(b)
	14.1, 19.7	76-402	§ 26.4(d)	77-214	§ 3.4
75-516	§ 27.2(f)	76-408	§ 6.6	77-232	§§ 6.9,
75-517	§ 27.2(f)	76-409	§ 13.4		13.3
75-518	§ 27.2(f)	76-410	§ 13.1	77-246	§§ 5.5(a),
75-519	§ 27.2(f)	76-417	§ 7.3		6.1
75-520	§ 27.2(f)	76-418	§ 6.3	77-258	§ 18.4(b)
76-4	§§ 7.5,	76-419	§ 6.6	77-261	§ 18.17
	19.9	76-420	§ 15.1	77-272	§§ 5.4(a),
76-5	§ 6.10(d)	76-440	§§ 11.3(b),		6.5, 7.4
76-21	§ 6.1		11.3(b)(iv)	77-278	§ 27.1(h)

TABLE OF IRS REVENUE RULINGS AND REVENUE PROCEDURES

Revenue Rulings	Book Sections	Revenue Rulings	Book Sections	Revenue Rulings	Book Sections
77-283	§ 21.1(d)	78-145	§§ 6.2(h),	79-99	§ 5.4(a)
77-290	§§ 8.3,		26.2(c),	79-122	§ 29.3
	26.4(g)		26.2(d)	79-128	§ 18.3
77-295	§ 8.7	78-160	§ 21.1(e)	79-130	§ 7.3
77-365	§§ 5.4(c),	78-188	§ 8.2	79-222	§ 28.4
	7.4, 26.4(d)	78-189	§ 8.2	79-316	§ 12.1(b)
77-366	§§ 4.4, 6.4, 7.4	78-190	§ 8.2	79-323	§ 6.9
77-367	§§ 7.3, 19.9	78-225	§ 13.5	79-349	§ 29.3
77-381	§ 8.5	78-232	§ 19.4(j)	79-358	§§ 6.1, 6.2(h)
77-384	§ 18.11	78-238	§ 18.5	79-359	§ 6.4
77-407	§ 23.4(b)	78-239	§ 18.10(a)	79-360	§§ 26.4(g),
77-416	§ 33.3(b)	78-240	§ 27.2(f)		26.5(b)
77-429	§§ 18.2,	78-248	§ 21.1(e)	79-361	§§ 26.4(g),
	18.2(a)	78-287	§ 15.1		26.5(b)
77-430	§ 6.4	78-288	§ 15.1	79-369	§§ 6.7, 7.5
77-436	§ 26.4(g)	78-289	§ 24.0	79-370	§ 26.5(f)
77-440	§ 18.11	78-305	§ 7.2	80-21	§ 7.3
77-469	§ 24.1(b)	78-309	§ 7.3	80-63	§ 12.2
78-41	§§ 6.2(b),	78-310	§§ 6.5,	80-86	§ 18.5
	23.7(a),		6.8, 7.4	80-103	§ 17.3(a)
	30.2(c)	78-315	§ 11.1(b)	80-106	§§ 19.9, 28.6
78-42	§§ 6.5, 15.1	78-316	§ 24.3(b)(iii)	80-107	§ 12.1(b)
78-43	§ 26.5(a)(iii)	78-384	§§ 6.5,	80-108	§ 23.3(a)
78-50	§ 12.1(a)		6.10(a)	80-113	§ 23.4(a)
78-51	§ 26.5(d)(i)	78-385	§§ 6.4,	80-114	§ 6.2(h)
78-52	§ 26.5(d)(i)		7.5, 8.2,	80-124	§ 16.4
78-68	§§ 6.3,		26.4(g)	80-130	§ 19.7
	12.1(a)	78-426	§§ 9.2,	80-200	§ 6.10(f)
78-69	§§ 6.3,		10.3	80-205	§ 12.1(a)
	12.1(a)	78-427	§ 6.2(h)	80-206	§ 12.1(b)
78-70	§ 13.5	78-428	§§ 6.1,	80-215	§ 6.6
78-82	§ 7.3		26.2(c)	80-259	§§ 23.3(a),
78-84	§ 6.10(b)	78-429	§ 12.2		23.3(b)
78-85	§§ 5.5(e),	78-434	§ 18.9	80-278	§§ 5.5(b),
	12.2	78-435	§ 26.5(b)		6.10(a),
78-86	§ 4.6	79-9	§ 24.2(b)		21.1(f)
78-87	§ 18.4(a)	79-11	§ 17.1(a)	80-279	§§ 5.5(b),
78-88	§§ 26.2(e),	79-12	§ 17.1(a)		6.10(a),
	29.3	79-13	§ 17.1(a)		21.1(f)
78-95	§ 11.3(b)	79-17	§§ 6.1,	80-282	§ 21.1(e)
78-98	§ 26.4(d)		26.2(c)	80-286	§§ 6.5,
78-99	§ 7.5	79-18	§§ 5.5(a),		6.10(f),
78-100	§ 8.7		6.1,		7.4,
78-129	§ 6.9		26.2(c)		30.2(d)
78-131	§§ 6.7,	79-19	§§ 6.1,	80-287	§ 13.4
	12.1(a)		26.2(c),	80-294	§§ 19.6,
78-132	§ 12.1(b)		26.5(b)		26.5(a)(ii),
78-143	§ 18.6	79-26	§§ 6.5, 7.2		26.4(f)
78-144	§ 27.2(a)	79-31	§ 26.2(d)	80-295	§ 26.5(a)(ii)

TABLE OF IRS REVENUE RULINGS AND REVENUE PROCEDURES

Revenue Rulings	Book Sections	Revenue Rulings	Book Sections	Revenue Rulings	Book Sections
80-296	§ 26.5(a)(ii)	81-117	§ 18.4(b)	84-81	§ 18.11
80-297	§ 26.4(d)	81-127	§§ 13.1,	84-140	§ 18.10(a)
80-298	§ 26.4(d)		26.4(f)	85-1	§ 6.3
80-301	§ 19.4(g)	81-138	§§ 13.1,	85-2	§ 6.3
80-302	§ 19.4(g)		13.5, 29.2	85-109	§ 27.2(b)
80-309	§ 6.2(h)	81-174	§ 13.4	85-110	§ 26.5(b)
80-316	§ 10.4	81-175	§ 13.4	85-115	§ 17.3(a)
81-19	§§ 23.7(a),	81-177	§ 23.3(b)	85-160	§ 4.3(a)
	27.2(b)	81-178	§ 27.1(g)	85-173	§ 23.3(b)
81-28	§§ 6.1, 6.2(h)	81-209	§ 6.9	85-184	§ 30.5
81-29	§§ 5.5(b),	81-276	§§ 5.5(e),	85-199	§ 16.3
	5.5(e), 6.5,		6.2(g), 6.3,	86-49	§ 6.6
	6.8, 19.9,		11.3(b)	86-75	§ 18.4(a)
	26.2(c),	81-284	§§ 6.6,	86-95	§ 21.1(e)
	26.5(b)		6.10(e)	86-98	§§ 12.1(a),
81-58	§§ 12.1(b),	81-291	§ 18.5		12.1(b),
	18.4(a)	81-295	§ 18.18		13.4
81-59	§ 15.2	82-138	§§ 13.1,	87-2	§ 6.9
81-60	§§ 15, 19.6		26.5(d)(iv)	87-119	§ 17.1(a)
81-61	§ 26.4(f)	82-139	§ 26.5(d)(i)	87-126	§ 12.1(b)
81-62	§ 26.4(g)	82-216	§ 17.0	88-56	§ 18.13
81-68	§ 16.4	83-43	§ 18.5	89-74	§ 8.2
81-69	§ 14.3	83-74	§ 18.13	89-94	§§ 18.1,
81-75	§ 26.5(d)(i)	83-104	§ 5.4(a)		24.3(b)(ii)
81-94	§§ 8.2,	83-140	§ 7.3	90-36	§ 13.6
	19.4(j)	83-153	§§ 11.3(b),	90-42	§ 18.11
81-95	§§ 12.3,		11.3(b)(iv)	90-74	§ 18.17
	17.3(b),	83-157	§ 6.2(a)	90-100	§§ 23.3(a),
	21.4	83-164	§ 13.1		23.4(a), 23.6
81-96	§ 18.11	83-166	§§ 10.4, 18.7	93-73	§ 8.2
81-101	§ 26.5(f)	83-170	§§ 12.1(a),	94-16	§ 18.18
81-108	§ 18.2(a)		14.1, 18.5	94-65	§ 18.18
81-109	§ 18.5	84-48	§ 18.4(a)	94-81	§ 18.18
81-116	§§ 4.6,	84-49	§ 18.4(a)	95-8	§ 29.3
	12.1(a)	84-55	§ 26.5(a)(iii)	97-21	§ 19.4

Revenue Procedures	Book Sections	Revenue Procedures	Book Sections	Revenue Procedures	Book Sections
59-31	§ 30.2(d)	72-5	§ 23.2	75-50	§§ 5.4(a),
62-28	§ 24.1(a)	72-16	§ 18.11		5.4(c)
67-37	§ 18.11	72-54	§ 5.4(a)	76-9	§ 24.3(a)(ix)
68-14	§ 23.2(b)	73-29	§ 24.3	78-9	§ 24.6(a)
71-17	§ 14.2	73-39	§ 18.11	79-2	§ 24.3(a)(ix)
71-39	§§ 5.5(b),	75-13	§ 6.10(d)	79-6	§ 24.3(a)(v)
	6.10(d)			79-8	§ 24.3(a)(vii)

TABLE OF IRS REVENUE RULINGS AND REVENUE PROCEDURES

Revenue Procedures	Book Sections	Revenue Procedures	Book Sections	Revenue Procedures	Book Sections
80-27	§ 23.6	90-29	§ 18.11	98-5	§§ 23.2, 23.2(c)
80-28	§ 24.6(c)	91-20	§§ 8.3, 8.6		
80-30	§ 23.2	92-58	§ 27.2(j)	98-8	§ 23.2(d)
81-7	§ 11.3(b)(iv)	92-85	§§ 18.13, 23.3(a)	98-12	§ 26.5(d)(iii)
82-2	§§ 4.1, 4.3(b)				
83-23	§ 24.3(b)(iii)	92-102	§ 27.2(j)		
83-36	§ 24.4(a)	93-28	§ 23.3(a)		
84-47	§ 23.3(a)	93-49	§ 27.2(j)		
84-86	§ 24.2	94-17	§ 24.3(b)(iii)		
85-58	§ 24.3(a)(ix)	94-72	§ 27.2(j)		
86-43	§ 7.2	95-21	§ 26.5(d)(iii)		
87-51	§ 22.1	95-35	§ 20.8(b)		
88-8	§ 23.2(d)	95-48	§ 24.3(b)(iii)		
90-27	§§ 17.3(b), 23.2, 23.2(a)-23.2(c), 23.3(a), 23.6, 23.8, 24, 24.1(a), 24.6, 24.6(b)	95-53	§ 27.2(j)		
		96-32	§ 6.1		
		96-59	§§ 20.8(a), 27.2(j)		
		97-57	§§ 27.2(j), 27.2(l)		
		98-4	§§ 23.2, 24.4(a)		

Table of IRS Private Letter Rulings, Technical Advice Memoranda, and General Counsel Memoranda

The following citations, to pronouncements from the Internal Revenue Service issued in the context of specific cases, are coordinated to the appropriate footnotes (FN) in the suitable chapters.

Citations are to IRS private letter rulings, technical advice memoranda, and general counsel memoranda, other than those specifically referenced in footnotes, directly pertinent to the material discussed in the text. Seven-number items are either private letter rulings or technical advice memoranda; five-number items are general counsel memoranda.

While these pronouncements are not to be cited as precedent (IRC § 6110(j)(3)), they are useful in illuminating the position of the IRS on the subjects involved.

FN	Private Letter Rulings, etc.	FN	Private Letter Rulings, etc.	FN	Private Letter Rulings, etc.
Chapter 3		116	8142024, 8204016,	101	7851096, 8327066,
71	39782		32689, 34682,		33752, 37462, 39082,
79	8337006		36130, 37596,		39117
			38686	126	8910001, 39792
Chapter 4		117	39684	144	37858
11	8705078, 8709069,	142	39288, 39716	153	8024109
	8810048	162	9036001	157	9307027
16	9014063, 9629020	222	9243008, 9316052	161	8736046
36	8936050, 9526033			162	8405083
57	30808			163	8827074
60	39736	**Chapter 5**		166	9631004
70	8501082	70	39800	174	9351027, 38050
111	9132005	96	35986, 37462	175	9718034

TABLE OF IRS PRIVATE LETTER RULINGS

FN	Private Letter Rulings, etc.	FN	Private Letter Rulings, etc.	FN	Private Letter Rulings, etc.
177	9214031	158	7823052	353	8432038, 8432050,
182	37257, 37787, 38459	159	9731038	cont'd	8435027, 8435028,
194	9408026	185	8629045, 9802045		8435080, 8435089,
		186	8429102, 8629045,		8435102, 8436042,
Chapter 6			9048046, 9237027		8437021, 8437038,
5	9718034	199	39562		8437040, 8437041,
6	9752064	201	9118012		8437068, 8437082,
13	8801067, 9311034,	213	9539013		8437095, 8438019,
	9411037	218	9247030		8441014, 8442081,
17	8637141	220	9025073, 9306034		8443031, 8443077,
21	9325061	221	9306034		8444019, 8444053,
32	9411037	222	39360		8445027, 8447013,
49	9204033	227	38050		8447059, 8447084,
56	9043059, 9535023	228	9407005, 9526033		8447102, 8448020,
69	8633038	230	32961, 33217		8448021, 8450009,
71	9241055, 9242002	233	9014063		8452018, 8501077,
72	8251089, 8251096,	245	8705078		8502026, 8502037,
	8736046, 8936045,	246	37518		8502071, 8503031,
	8936046, 9527035	247	37518		8505010, 8506035,
81	9307027	250	8536099, 9014063,		8506048, 8507018,
87	9412002		35936, 35966, 37180,		8507034, 8514019,
88	9246004, 38735, 39057,		38401, 38322		8516027, 8516048,
	39487, 39799, 39828,	263	9210026		8516093, 8517026,
	39829, 39830	271	8334001, 8849072		8517027, 8518072,
96	9714011, 9716021,	274	8734007		8522024, 8524111,
	9721031, 9722042,	276	8906062, 35945		8534020, 8534056,
	9738038–9738054	279	7816061, 7905129,		8536027, 8536037,
110	38686, 38894, 39120		7951134		8537014, 8537040,
112	8237052, 8509044,	280	7902019, 8920084		8541025, 8542010,
	8509073, 8511082,	290	7816061		8543014, 8544015,
	8625081, 9408026,	294	8753049, 9242002,		8544027, 8546060,
	39340		9635037, 39562		8603034, 8607010,
115	32896, 36827	315	8839024		8607040, 8609020,
116	9325061	321	8351103		8609033, 8610025,
123	9210032, 9735048	326	8448020, 8717020,		8611036, 8620036,
127	9001011		8721022, 8921061,		8621085, 8622034,
136	9411037, 9541003,		9347001		8639024, 8639039,
	9629002	327	7909026, 8347031,		8650008, 34704
137	8723052, 9243008,		8348025, 8944068	354	8342022, 8412064
	9246032, 9246033,	333	8630021	356	7823052, 9526033
	9629002, 38693, 39347,	339	8349017, 8438027,	359	39055
	39348, 39682, 39685,		8511032	378	8429051, 9240001,
	39852	351	8836056		39047, 39883
138	9047049, 39348	353	8425019, 8425031,	379	9048046, 9539015
149	9249026		8425032, 8425038,	381	39633
150	9530025, 9530026,		8425064, 8426029,		
	9537035–9537053		8429012, 8429028,	**Chapter 7**	
155	9408026		8430026, 8430044,	75	8823088
157	39733		8431024, 8431025,	78	8705078

FN	Private Letter Rulings, etc.	FN	Private Letter Rulings, etc.	FN	Private Letter Rulings, etc.
83	9325061	112 *cont'd*	8432110, 8433053,	112 *cont'd*	8453096–8453101,
94	9211002, 9211004		8433054, 8433111		8501061, 8501062,
97	8645017		8434064–843067,		8502062, 8502063,
115	8909004		8435047, 8435086,		8502076–8502078,
117	8846002		8435158–8435161,		8502085–8502090,
126	9414003		8435168,		8502096, 8502101,
132	9019046		8435171–8435174,		8503040, 8503042,
154	8751007, 8811021,		8435090–8435098,		8503071,
	9036025		8436036, 8436037,		8503078–8503082,
155	9210026		8436039, 8436040,		8504052, 8504057,
180	9048046, 9237027		8436050, 8437070,		8504081,
203	8930052		8437076, 8437090,		8505061–8505064,
205	9638001		8437101, 8437102,		8505077, 8506067,
221	9335061, 39622		8437104, 8437112,		8506078–8506080,
			8437114, 8438045,		8506084, 8506101,
Chapter 8			8438061, 8438062,		8506103, 8506119,
68	33574, 36254, 36787,		8438066, 8439014,		8508082–8508085,
	37503		8439015, 8439081,		8508100, 8508104,
96	37622, 37503, 37391,		8439097, 8439102,		8509068, 8509101,
	37247		8439103, 8440092,		8510041, 8510042,
109	8626100, 8626101,		8440093,		8510058–8510060,
	8627044, 8628077,		8440097–8440100,		8510090, 8510091,
	8629051,		8441046, 8441065,		8511051–8511053,
	8641069–8641072,		8442065–8442073,		8511069, 8511070,
	8643055		8442075, 8442093,		8512075, 8512076,
112	8422171, 8422174,		8442097–8442101,		8512080, 8512091,
	8423078, 8423079,		8442110, 8442132,		8512092,
	8424056, 8424098,		8442134–8442141,		8514056–8514059,
	8425058, 8425076,		8443049–3443051,		8514061, 8514062,
	8425115, 8425118,		8443081,		8514078, 8514083,
	8425123,		8443090–8443092,		8514084, 8514086,
	8425130–8425135,		8444085,		8514096, 8514097,
	8426022, 8426023,		8444087–8444089,		8515065, 8516059,
	8426045, 8426047,		8444095, 8444096,		8516097, 8516102,
	8426068, 8426091,		8445074–8445078,		8516108, 8516109,
	8426107–8426109,		8445080,		8516115, 8516136,
	8427096–8427099,		8445101–8445107,		8516137,
	8427103, 8427104,		8446033, 8446037,		8517059–8517061,
	8428108,		8447066, 8447067,		8517065, 8518055,
	8428110–8428113,		8447088–8447090,		8510856,
	8428115,		8448041–8448043,		8518081–8518086,
	8429065–8429068,		8448045, 8448049,		8518091, 8518092,
	8429106, 8429107,		8448055–8448058,		8519035, 8519036,
	8429110, 8430073,		8448070, 8449068,		8520047, 8520052,
	8431067–8431069,		8450072–8450074,		8520064, 8520067,
	8431075,		8451051,		8520071, 8520118,
	8431081–8431083,		8452070–8452073,		8520119, 8521013,
	8432068–8432070,		8452075,		8521100, 8521104,
	8432076–8432078		8452081–8452084,		8521105,

TABLE OF IRS PRIVATE LETTER RULINGS

FN	Private Letter Rulings, etc.	FN	Private Letter Rulings, etc.	FN	Private Letter Rulings, etc.
112 *cont'd*	8522080–8522083	112 *cont'd*	8550074–8550076,	112 *cont'd*	8624168, 8625089,
	8522085, 8523082,		8551048–8551050,		8625102–8625105,
	8523087, 8523091,		8551052–8551059,		8626100, 8626101,
	8523094, 8523095,		8551067–8551070,		8627044, 8628077,
	8523101, 8523104,		8551078–8551080,		8629051, 8631061,
	8523106–8523111,		8551081, 8552108,		8631072, 8631073,
	8524065–8524069,		8601056, 8601057,		8631080, 8631083,
	8525076,		8601059–8601062,		8631092, 8631093,
	8525088–8525090,		8601064, 8601065,		8631097–8631099,
	8526083, 8527045,		8601068–8601072,		8631107, 8631108,
	8527049, 8527067,		8602048, 8602065,		8631110, 8631111,
	8529051, 8529052,		8603089–8603095,		8631113–8631117,
	8529098, 8529105,		8603097,		8633037, 8634061,
	8530054–8530058,		8603107–8603109,		8634064, 8635056,
	8530134, 8531051,		8603122–8603124,		8635057, 8638124,
	8531066, 8531067,		8604081, 8604083,		8641069–8641072,
	8532014, 8532015,		8604084, 8604090,		8833001, 9624001,
	8532024, 8532044,		8604091, 8604094,		36078, 36993, 37116
	8532047, 8532060,		8605048, 8605050,	149	9448017, 39614
	8532069,		8606070, 8606071,	157	9518021
	8532095–8532097,		8606073, 8606076,	174	9434002
	8533020, 8533079,		8608081, 8608082,		
	8534062, 8534086,		8609070, 8609071,	**Chapter 9**	
	8534087, 8535060,		8610079, 8610080,	14	8723061–8723064
	8535061, 8535119,		8610084, 8611047,	15	9240001, 39883
	8536089,		8611049,	18	7852997, 8028004
	8536090–8536094,		8611080–8611083,	19	9627023
	8537059, 8537060,		8614045, 8615045,	29	9346006
	8537102–8537107,		8615047, 8615049,	50	8512084
	8538067, 8539090,		8615058–8615062,	51	9017052
	8540032, 8540083,		8615088–8615090,	52	9311032, 9722032
	8540089, 8541106,		8616057,		
	8541109, 8541110,		8616062–8616065,	**Chapter 10**	
	8542059, 8542066,		8616096, 8618045,	16	9211004, 39459, 39560,
	8542096, 8542097,		8618046, 8618066,		39775
	8543048,		8619048–8619050,	19	9129040, 39459,
	8543057–8543063,		8619054–8619060,		39560
	8543090, 8544087,		8619063–8619066,	32	39799
	8546100–8546106,		8620059–8620063,	60	36738, 39598
	8546113, 8546114,		8620081, 8620083,		
	8546116, 8546124,		8621102, 8621114,	**Chapter 12**	
	8546130, 8546132,		8622046–8622048,	1	9149004, 9201039,
	8546136, 8546137,		8622052–8622054,		39574, 39866
	8547059, 8547060,		8622057, 8622061,	24	8923001
	8547068–8547073,		8623045, 8623052,	34	37518
	8548081, 8549064,		8624080–8624083,	59	9044060
	8550048, 8550049,		8624091, 8624093,	103	39763
	8550052,		8624094, 8624128,	126	8829072
	8550054–8550056		8624152, 8624166	131	8828058, 8838052

TABLE OF IRS PRIVATE LETTER RULINGS

FN	Private Letter Rulings, etc.	FN	Private Letter Rulings, etc.	FN	Private Letter Rulings, etc.
328 cont'd	9233025, 9242018, 9250023, 9315020, 9348018, 9406032, 9413046, 9735021	398 cont'd	8823034, 8823035, 8824015, 8825034, 8825081, 8825087, 8825096, 8825100, 8826026, 8826037, 8826048, 8829041, 8829062, 8831047, 8832020, 8832047, 8832056, 8832066, 8832067, 8834031, 8835034, 8836056, 8836038, 8839014, 8839024, 8839039, 8839083, 8842070, 8842071, 8847032, 8849023, 8850037, 8850038, 8850063, 8920056, 8920023, 8920037, 8921024, 8921055, 8923024, 8925010, 8925014, 8925015, 8925028, 8926078, 8927058, 8928061, 8929039, 8930036, 8931008, 8931061, 8931068, 8931069, 8932031, 8933011, 8934009, 8934026, 8934052, 8935012, 8936028, 8938018, 8938044, 8939047, 8940032, 8940034, 8941052, 8942037, 8943051, 8943053, 8944008, 8944031, 8944032, 8944068, 8948057, 8948060, 8950050, 8951048, 8951057, 8951012, 8952016, 8952036, 9002016, 9004034, 9012031, 9015057, 9017052, 9025062, 9026015, 9026054, 9026055, 9027025, 9027028, 9027038, 9028033, 9032012, 9033062, 9034041, 9035013	398 cont'd	9035024, 9037019, 9037046, 9038036, 9041054, 9041070, 9042059, 9042060, 9043017, 9043035, 9043047, 9043067, 9045021, 9046039, 9046042, 9046060, 9049025, 9050052, 9050055, 9103009, 9106007, 9106023, 9106026, 9107032, 9109020, 9110004, 9110022, 9110062, 9113021, 9114055, 9115016, 9115037, 9129043, 9137019, 9140046, 9140050, 9140070, 9142019, 9143057, 9145042, 9149011, 9151026, 9201027, 9205020, 9206012, 9212010, 9217032, 9218014, 9238011, 9238024, 9240024, 9243044, 9245007, 9247014, 9247015, 9248024, 9249015, 9342029, 9347001, 9401003–9401006, 9401010, 9402028, 9403025, 9405024, 9409040, 9410034, 9411017, 9412027, 9421008, 9421009, 9423038, 9424007, 9425029, 9435031, 9436048, 9436052, 9440012, 9443032, 9443034, 9505015, 9506037, 9507019, 9522043, 9523008, 9524028, 9530017, 9530018, 9533040, 9540007, 9541030, 9544024, 9545015–9545017, 9546012, 9546014
341	8524011, 9038018				
380	9130026				
381	9130036, 9611044				
386	7821037, 8107117, 8147094, 8313060, 8314050, 8342022, 8425032, 8453038, 8603034, 8609020, 8621085, 8633034, 8650008, 8721061, 8728057, 8728058, 8728073				
387	9348021, 9515014				
388	9244003				
392	8719023, 9109030, 9149007				
398	8630021, 8639024, 8645036, 8705015, 8705038, 8705054, 8710016, 8713030, 8719023, 8721022, 8721061, 8722030, 8725010, 8725024, 8725033, 8728057, 8728058, 8729038, 8733018, 8737090, 8738036, 8740015, 8743032, 8747010, 8748017, 8748031, 8748024, 8749030, 8751017, 8752011, 8752022, 8753008, 8803020, 8803022, 8803033, 8803035, 8803057, 8804028, 8804058, 8806028, 8806062, 8809038, 8809047, 8809051, 8810060, 8810062, 8810084, 8814018, 8815009, 8815010, 8815027, 8816022, 8816040, 8819046, 8819055, 8820030, 8821030, 8821046				

FN	Private Letter Rulings, etc.
398 cont'd	9549030, 9552045, 9605006, 9609034, 9613007, 9622019 (withdrawn by 9631011), 9624013, 9627016, 9630018, 9631008, 9635017, 9637037, 9646018, 9646026, 9627016, 9706006, 9706007, 9722029, 9723042, 9725022, 9731023, 9740005, 9741002, 9742003, 9746035, 9746057, 39761
399	9627016
401	9439008

Chapter 19

FN	Private Letter Rulings, etc.
51	9525056
55	9231045, 9621035
58	9112006, 9201035
70	8731032
74	38394
76	35638
92	8838047
142	8807081, 8808070
149	9025089, 37180, 38283, 39670
150	32518, 35865
180	9428035
218	39876
227	9530024–9530026

Chapter 20

FN	Private Letter Rulings, etc.
11	39694
35	39694
38	9244003
81	9622002
101	9507020
102	9507020
104	9332042
124	9332042, 9347034
198	9510047, 9534021, 9602026, 9636016

Chapter 21

FN	Private Letter Rulings, etc.
3	9117001
30	39694

FN	Private Letter Rulings, etc.
65	8906062
109	9433001
126	9117001

Chapter 22

FN	Private Letter Rulings, etc.
2	8725056, 9201039, 39718, 39737, 39799, 39828, 39829, 39866
5	39761
7	9752023
9	9645007
10	39829
14	39655, 39764
16	9108021, 9110012, 9743054
33	9042043, 39826

Chapter 23

FN	Private Letter Rulings, etc.
99	9145001
144	8906008
146	8649001
154	9145039
165	39833
201	39830
202	39830

Chapter 24

FN	Private Letter Rulings, etc.
2	9141050
3	8935063
4	9446033, 9446034
28	8906008
34	9408066
181	8728057, 8728058, 8728073
193	8642083, 8709049, 8724057, 8738039, 8747032, 8818046, 8819037, 8819057, 8819071, 8825044, 8834010, 9040038, 9103047, 9253044, 9310045, 9510068, 9518021, 9619024
196	9803015
205	9152046
209	8710016, 8715013, 8725010, 8725024, 8738077, 8823091, 8926078, 8932031

FN	Private Letter Rulings, etc.
209 cont'd	8944068, 9029043, 9150055, 9348021, 9401010, 9409040, 9421009, 9436052, 954007
212	9411011

Chapter 25

FN	Private Letter Rulings, etc.
79	9243008, 9316052

Chapter 26

FN	Private Letter Rulings, etc.
5	9120029
16	9338043
66	8722082, 9735047, 32896, 36827
67	9217001
71	9325061
80	9401031
82	9242035
86	36827
89	9720035
91	8822057
92	8840020, 8841041
93	8806056, 9318047
100	9042038
110	9438040, 9505020, 9509041, 9510039
117	8651086, 8708052, 8841041
118	8829003, 8932004, 9309002
119	8717002, 8717063, 8733037, 8734005, 8901064, 8934050, 8936013, 9003059, 9017058, 9018049, 9240937, 9337027, 9340061, 9340062, 9349022
120	9425031
136	8922064, 9407005, 9413020
138	9417003
141	9137002, 9417003, 9509002, 9721001
147	8641001
149	9302023
155	9539005
156	8819005, 9723046

FN	Private Letter Rulings, etc.	FN	Private Letter Rulings, etc.	FN	Private Letter Rulings, etc.
160	9535023	343	9110042, 9226055	542	9250001
165	9750056	349	9750056	600	9623035
166	9641011, 9728034, 9715041	357	8809092, 8817017	603	8725058
		359	8626102,	604	9736046
168	8732029, 9041045, 9350045		8640052–8640054,	607	9315001, 9321005
			8640056, 8640057,	614	8813067
191	9014069		8645064, 8833002	616	9711002, 9718029
200	9107030, 9110012, 9137002	360	8949093	618	9752023
		361	8814001, 9138003		
204	9428035	363	8641060	**Chapter 27**	
210	8432003	380	9645027	1	9012058
211	8743081, 8743086, 8743087, 9347036	381	8815002	4	8708031, 9442035
		389	9147054, 9550001, 9527001	10	9042038
212	9349024			13	8836037
216	9110042, 9329041	396	8707003, 8842002, 9037063, 9548001, 39723	32	9030048
				39	9231045
218	8643091			45	9151001, 9309002, 9306030, 39827
224	9149002	397	9220054		
226	8643049, 9141053, 9150052, 9152039	398	9220054, 9306030, 9318005, 9535004 (withdrawn by 9542046), 9612003, 39827	50	8839016
				52	9346014
233	9107030			54	8827017
253	9321072, 9321087, 9323035			58	9316045, 9319042, 9419033, 9503024, 9552019
262	9137049	400	8841003		
268	9128003	413	8734004, 39735	62	8222066, 8645050,
282	9138003, 9145002, 9147005, 9320050, 9323035, 39864	414	9550001		8717066, 8717078,
		418	9029047		8721102, 8728060,
		439	9428035		8808002, 8808003,
		440	8852002		8810097, 8824054,
295	8025222	443	9325003		8828011, 8845073,
299	9137002, 39860	444	9128002		8846005, 8922084,
304	8641090	453	9137002, 9147054, 9205037, 39860		8941011, 8941062,
308	9231001				8948023, 9015038,
311	9521004	454	8947002, 9044071, 9234002, 9304001, 9345004, 9724006		9023091, 9024026,
312	8846002				9043039, 9108021,
314	8650083				9316052, 9404003,
315	9014069	457	9023003		9404004, 9417036,
317	39843	458	9302035		9417042, 9417043,
318	39762	460	8932004		9419033, 9436001,
321	8735004, 8815031, 8817066, 9730941, 9739042	466	8726069, 9302023		9440001, 9441001,
		475	9023001, 9023002, 9204007, 9402005		9450028, 9703025,
					9705001, 9709029,
323	8736046	478	9247001		9714016, 9723001,
327	8736046, 8817017, 9445024	479	8834006, 8835001, 9023001, 9023002, 9217002, 9402005, 9419033, 9734002		9724006, 39615
				65	9139029, 9212030,
335	8721103, 8809092, 8921091, 8941082, 9023041				9231045, 9234043,
					9551019, 35957,
					39568
340	9736047	480	8403013	66	9450045
342	9750056, 9803001	482	9248001		

FN	Private Letter Rulings, etc.	FN	Private Letter Rulings, etc.	FN	Private Letter Rulings, etc.
67	8950072, 9139029, 9141051, 9146047, 9702003	153	8641061, 8831007, 8932004, 8942070, 9033056, 9302023, 9544029, 9605001, 9704012	**Chapter 29**	
				8	8708031, 8717066
				10	8738006, 9144044
68	8445005, 8720005, 8802009, 8925029, 39825			11	8522040, 8651091, 8906003, 8935058, 9147058, 9204048, 9726005
71	9450045	159	8836037, 8922047, 9024026, 9024026, 9027051, 9043039, 9407007		
75	8713072, 8822096, 8932042			18	8748064–8748065, 9024085, 9315021
76	8822057, 9551019	167	39786	22	9246032, 9246033
86	9245036, 9246032, 9246033, 9301024, 9315021, 9703025	169	8832043, 39752	25	8950073, 9047040
		170	8736046, 9241055	28	9241052
		178	9023081	29	9651001
88	9136037	185	8915005, 9217001	32	8044023, 8104098, 8107114, 8110164, 8338138, 8738006, 8807082, 9031052, 9407023, 9703026
99	9108034, 9108043, 9127045, 9128030, 9132040, 9132061, 9144032–9144035, 9150047, 9204048, 9247038, 9252028, 9547040, 9551021	186	8728080		
		196	39734		
		203	9302035, 9303030		
		207	9232003		
		208	8920084	34	9010025, 9431001, 9533014
		215	9726030	38	9533014
101	9619068	230	9652004	42	8822057
102	9616039, 9619068, 9619069, 9630031, 9631025, 9631029, 9652028, 9704010, 9745025	232	8721005, 9029047, 9316045, 9321005, 9724006, 39638	44	9042043, 9108021, 9110012, 9527033, 9743054, 39826
				45	9012001
				51	8945038
110	9108034, 9108043, 9128030, 9132040, 9132061, 9144032, 9144035, 9150047, 9252028 (modified by 9428037), 9308040, 9316032, 9319044, 9401029, 9407005, 9411018, 9411019, 9412039, 9414002, 9432019, 9629032, 9651014	**Chapter 28**		59	8818008, 8923077, 9031052, 9047069, 9218006, 9218007
		15	9147008, 9149006, 39863		
		17	9324002	61	9450045
		26	9145003, 9328003	63	9508031
		28	9141003, 9141004, 9145031, 9145032, 9147059, 9216033, 9242014, 9247039	72	9128020
				75	9002030
				81	8721104, 8721107, 9042038
		31	9247039, 9517035		
120	8201024	32	8905002, 8943009, 9721034, 9310034, 9344028, 9628022, 39773	83	9619077
139	8729005, 8832084, 8833002, 8903083, 8922047, 9010073, 9045003, 9108016, 9308047, 9324026, 9404004, 9438029, 9506046, 9535022, 9547039, 9601047, 9642054, 9705028			84	9637053, 9642051
				86	9717004
		35	8728008, 8728009, 8925091, 9016039, 9310034, 9351042, 9410048, 9413042	113	9010011
				Chapter 30	
		44	9319044, 9750056	10	8626102, 8627056–8627060, 8627104, 8628052, 8628069, 8639089, 8642062, 8645063, 8645083, 8649081, 8650061, 8709051
		58	39778		
		73	39684, 39874		
		74	9527035		
		93	9033056		

TABLE OF IRS PRIVATE LETTER RULINGS

FN	Private Letter Rulings, etc.	FN	Private Letter Rulings, etc.	FN	Private Letter Rulings, etc.
10 *cont'd*	8710083, 8712062, 8712068, 8714053, 8715007, 8715048, 8715058, 8717045, 8717076, 8718066, 8718074, 8718075, 8719030, 8720048, 8721072–8721075, 8721087, 8722066, 8722067, 8722072, 8722081, 8722091, 8722093–8722098, 8722109, 8723037, 8723071, 8723079, 8724070, 8725049, 8725072–8725074, 8725087, 8727074, 8727075, 8727081, 8728070, 8728075, 8728076, 8729082, 8729084, 8730055–8730057, 8730068, 8732044, 8732092, 8735043, 8735044, 8735069–8735071, 8736041, 8737086, 8737101, 8741085, 8742068, 8742074, 8742082, 8744059, 8744062, 8744064, 8744065, 8745044, 8746053, 8746071, 8747033, 8747057–8747060, 8747077, 8748050, 8748061, 8749064, 8750070, 8752051, 8752056, 8752088, 8752090, 8752095, 8753044, 8753049, 8753052, 8753053, 8753056, 8802012, 8802085, 8803009, 8803072, 8803083, 8803084, 8806009, 8806055, 8806070, 8806080, 8807007, 8807010, 8807049	10 *cont'd*	8808007, 8808073, 8808082, 8809093, 8809100, 8810033, 8810077, 8811015, 8812076, 8814008, 8814046, 8814047, 8816020, 8817051, 8818005, 8818038, 8818041, 8819057, 8819069, 8819071, 8820074, 8820091, 8821062, 8822092, 8823044, 8823059, 8823087, 8824004, 8825018, 8825077, 8825104, 8827006, 8827016, 8827028, 8827059, 8827060, 8828010, 8830005, 8830005, 8830038, 8830083, 8831010, 8834089, 8807007, 8837016, 8837042, 8837053, 8837062, 8839005, 8839019, 8841004, 8841011, 8845020, 8845027, 8846004, 8846019, 8846057, 8847009, 8849080, 8850026, 8850054, 8850069, 8901051, 8901052, 8901065, 8903017, 8904038, 8904039, 8907060, 8909056, 8912042, 8913051, 8914057, 8917073, 8918079, 8920021, 8920054, 8920055, 8920085, 8921060, 8922065, 8922079, 8925049, 8925069, 8925089, 8925090, 8926083, 8926086, 8929009, 8929038, 8929050, 8932010, 8932012, 8934004, 8934030, 8934031, 8935040, 8940012	10 *cont'd*	8941007, 8941012, 8941015, 8941061, 8941073, 8941083, 8942102, 8943008, 8943049, 8944014, 8944059, 8945062, 8947041, 8948022, 8950052, 8950070, 8951071, 9001041, 9002037, 9003036, 9003060, 9008088, 9009009, 9011049, 9013049, 9014016, 9014050, 9016053, 9022055, 9024034, 9028075, 9030039, 9034073, 9104023, 9109057, 9110018, 9112025, 9128037, 9134025, 9135054, 9136031, 9138056, 9139025, 9142035, 9151041, 9151049, 9152040, 9203041, 9215047, 9216035, 9217042, 9226044, 9233042, 9234042, 9235054, 9235056, 9238041, 9243045–9243047, 9231041, 9318048, 9318049, 9326055, 9333046, 9343024, 9347031, 9347032, 9350037, 9401034, 9403029, 9404027, 9408024, 9409038, 9424027, 9425006–9425009, 9426040, 9435030, 9438039, 9438046, 9442035, 9447051–9447053, 9448027–9448029, 9450034, 9501037, 9501040, 9503021, 9511035, 9511036, 9511038, 9511046, 9513003, 9517052

TABLE OF IRS PRIVATE LETTER RULINGS

FN	Private Letter Rulings, etc.	FN	Private Letter Rulings, etc.	FN	Private Letter Rulings, etc.
10 cont'd	9519057, 9521014, 9527013, 9527043, 9531005, 9533007, 9535017, 9535018, 9538026–9538031, 9541007–9541014, 9542009, 9542039, 9542043, 9542044, 9544028, 9544033–9544036, 9551006, 9551039, 9552021, 9608006, 9608037, 9608038, 9615031, 9630013, 9635028, 9635029, 9635037, 9636026, 9646032, 9651015, 9651026, 9740001–9740002, 9747029–9747032, 9750054–9750056, 9751020, 9752062, 9804054, 9805038	11 cont'd	8749058, 8749059, 8805059, 8810082, 8811003, 8819034, 8821044, 8833002, 8840056, 8846053, 8901012, 8901050, 8903083, 8909029, 8925051, 8934064, 8952076, 9005068, 9024068, 9024026, 9024086, 9030063, 9033069, 9108016, 9119060, 9131058, 9245031, 9308047, 9311031, 9316052, 9341024, 9346013, 9402031–9402933, 9408026, 9417036, 9417042, 9417043, 9421006, 9438041, 9447043, 9523027, 9528020, 9530009, 9535022, 9539014, 9542045 (amended by 9720036), 9547039, 9626021, 9630014, 9637051, 9705028, 9721038, 9726010, 9720031, 9722032	57 cont'd	9404004, 9438029, 9535022, 9547039, 9705028
17	9740001–9740004			60	9303030, 9305026, 39866
33	9002036, 9014061				
41	9119069, 9547013			**Chapter 32**	
45	9242002			20	9230001, 9350044
46	9629020			36	8628049, 8705089, 8715039, 9715040, 8717057, 8723065, 8724060, 8727080, 8806057, 8807012, 8814047, 8817039, 8818008, 8820093, 8833009, 8901054, 8909036, 8912003, 8912041, 8915065, 8917055, 8931083, 8936047, 8936077, 8938002, 8939024, 8940039, 8941006, 8942099, 8943050, 8943064, 9021050, 9029034, 9109066, 9122061, 9122062, 9122070, 9147058, 9318033, 9319044, 9323030, 9345057, 9349032, 9352030, 9438030, 9502035 (updating 8528080), 9603839, 9642051, 9736039, 9736043, 9739001, 9709014, 9718036, 9722032, 39732,
49	9135003				
50	8714050	20	8934064, 9242038, 9408026, 9421006		
54	9031051				
74	9119069, 9242002	26	39598, 39646		
75	9246033	27	39776		
92	8810048	31	8625078, 8720048, 8732040, 8743070, 8840056, 8934064, 9027050, 9305026, 9734026, 9734027, 9734036, 9734037, 9734039, 9734040		
93	8417019, 9335022				
100	7903079, 9042004				
105	9435029, 9752062, 9752063, 9752065, 9752067				
106	9425009	35	8839002	58	8925052, 8945063
110	9623057, 9623059, 9623060, 9738055, 9738056, 9620027	36	8709051, 9305026	61	8621060, 8903060, 8912003, 8925052, 8936073, 8945063, 9029034, 9035072, 9105029, 9105031, 9215046, 9308034, 9323030 9352030,9407022, 9518014, 9517029
		52	8849072, 9136032, 9148051		
Chapter 31		57	8729005, 8832084, 8833002, 8903083, 8922047, 9010073, 9027051, 9045003, 9108016, 9308047		
3	9308047				
11	8304112, 8606056, 8705087, 8706012, 8709071, 8720048			62	9637050, 9645018, 9739036–9739039

■ 915 ■

TABLE OF IRS PRIVATE LETTER RULINGS

FN	Private Letter Rulings, etc.	FN	Private Letter Rulings, etc.	FN	Private Letter Rulings, etc.
73	8925051, 9547039	**Chapter 33**		34	8640056,
75	8921203, 8932085,	16	9451001	*cont'd*	8640057
	8941006, 8949034,	26	8944017	76	8219066,
	9001030, 9521013	34	8640054,		9538026–9538031

Table of IRS Private Determinations Cited in Text

Private Determination	Book Sections	Private Determination	Book Sections	Private Determination	Book Sections
7740009	§ 8.7	7922001	§§ 13.1, 26.4(f), 26.5(a)(ii)	8234084	§ 19.4(l)
7741004	§ 27.1(g)			8244114	§ 27.1(a)
7816061	§ 26.4(f)			8303001	§ 26.4(g)
7820007	§ 10.3	7926003	§ 27.1(g)	8303078	§ 26.5(a)(ii)
7820057	§ 32.6	7930005	§ 10.3	8306056	§ 9.5
7820058	§ 32.2(a)	7930043	§ 26.5(ii)	8317004	§ 14.5
7823048	§ 26.2(e)	7935043	§ 6.9	8326008	§ 26.5(c)
7823062	§ 26.4(e)	7936006	§ 27.1(l)	8332072	§ 26.4(f)
7826003	§ 26.4(d)	7937002	§§ 18.4(a), 26.5(d)	8337092	§ 14.4
7833055	§ 29.2			8337094	§ 23.6
7838028	§ 8.2	7944018	§ 15.1	8338127	§ 32.2(a)
7838029	§ 8.2	7946001	§ 26.5(g)	8349051	§ 26.4(f)
7838030	§ 8.2	7948113	§§ 26.5(a)(ii), 26.5(f)	8351160	§ 26.4(f)
7838031	§ 8.2			8402014	§ 8.5
7838032	§ 8.2	7951134	§§ 6.8, 19.9	8409055	§ 10.3
7838033	§ 8.2	7952002	§ 32.2(a)	8416065	§ 8.5
7838034	§ 8.2	8004011	§ 26.5(b)(i)	8417003	§ 26.4(f)
7838035	§ 8.2	8006005	§ 27.1(g)	8422168	§ 26.4(f)
7838036	§ 8.2	8020010	§ 26.3(d)	8422170	§ 13.1
7838103	§ 14.2	8024001	§ 26.4(d)	8429010	§§ 15.2, 26.5(e)
7839042	§ 26.4(g)	8025222	§ 26.5(a)(i)		
7840014	§ 26.5(d)	8037103	§ 10.2	8429049	§ 18.13
7840072	§ 26.4(d)	8107006	§ 26.4(f)	8432004	§ 26.5 (c)
7845029	§ 26.5(a)(ii)	8109002	§ 18.5	8433010	§ 26.4(g)
7847001	§ 25.5(d)	8112013	§ 26.4(f)	8433077	§ 18.13
7851003	§ 26.5(a)(ii)	8120006	§ 26.4(f)	8442064	§ 4.9
7902006	§§ 13.4, 26.5(d)	8127019	§ 26.5(g)	8442092	§ 26.4(f)
		8145011	§ 18.2(a)	8446047	§ 24.1(b)
7903079	§ 30.5	8202019	§ 17.4	8452074	§ 26.4(g)
7905129	§ 26.3(a)	8203134	§§ 26.3(b), 26.5(g)	8452099	§ 26.5(b)(vi)
7908009	§ 26.4(d)			8503103	§ 26.5(d)
7919053	§ 26.5(a)(ii)	8216009	§ 26.5(g)	8505044	§ 31.2(a)
7921018	§ 19.4(k)	8232011	§ 26.5(g)	8505047	§ 26.4(f)

TABLE OF IRS PRIVATE DETERMINATIONS CITED IN TEXT

Private Determination	Book Sections	Private Determination	Book Sections	Private Determination	Book Sections
8511082	§ 26.4(g)	8836038	§ 22.1	9246004	§ 22.1
8512058	§ 16.3	8836040	§ 30.5	9246032	§ 27.1(h)(i),
8512084	§§ 9.5,	8842025	§ 31.3		30.3
	26.4(f)	8842071	§ 18.17	9247038	§ 27.1(i)
8518067	§ 23.3(a)	8910001	§ 5.4(b)	9249001	§ 26.4(f)
8518090	§ 26.4(f)	8925092	§ 32.5	9249026	§ 32.3
8523072	§ 26.4(f)	8936002	§ 21.1(f)	9252037	§ 26.4(f)
8524006	§ 13.4	8938001	§ 32.2	9302023	§ 27.2(a)
8530043	§ 26.4(g)	8942099	§ 19.8	9303030	§ 30.6, 31.4
8539091	§ 18.10(a)	9002036	§ 6.5	9305026	§§ 31.2(a),
8541108	§ 32.2(b)	9003045	§ 13.1		31.5(b)
8604006	§ 31.4	9014061	§ 6.5	9308047	§§ 31.1(a),
8606056	§ 31.1(d)	9016072	§ 31.1(a)		31.2(d)
8606074	§ 26.4(f)	9017003	§ 30.2	9309037	§ 30.6
8621059	§ 31.4, 32.3	9019004	§ 30.2(c)	9314059	§ 30.6
8623081	§ 26.4(f)	9023081	§ 26.5(d)	9316032	§ 26.2(e)
8624127	§ 26.4(f)	9029047	§ 26.5(d)	9316052	§§ 9.5,
8626080	§§ 26.4(f),	9032005	§ 13.1		19.4(a)
	26.5(b)(v)	9036025	§ 26.5(a)	9317054	§ 30.6
8628049	§ 26.4(f)	9042038	§ 27.1(i)	9320042	§ 26.4(c)
8633034	§ 26.4(f)	9043001	§ 26.4(g)	9325062	§ 26.4(f)
8638131	§ 31.4	9050002	§ 13.1	9329041	§ 26.5(b)(iv)
8643091	§ 26.4(f)	9105029	§ 31.4	9335001	§ 32.2
8643049	§ 26.4(f)	9108021	§ 27.1(c)	9335061	§ 26.4(f)
8705041	§§ 18.2(a),	9128003	§§ 13.4,	9346015	§ 30.6
	30.5		26.4(g)	9352030	§ 31.4
8706012	§ 31.1(a)	9130002	§§ 19.4(l),	9401031	§ 26.4(f)
8708031	§ 27.1(g)		32.2	9401035	§ 18.5
8709051	§ 31.2(a)	9137002	§§ 26.3(d),	9403022	§ 26.4(f)
8709072	§ 26.4(f)		26.4(f)	9404029	§ 26.5(b)(i)
8715055	§ 32.6	9141050	§ 23.2(d)	9408002	§ 26.5(d)
8725056	§ 26.4(g)	9145002	§ 26.4(g)	9414002	§ 18.2
8730060	§ 26.4(f)	9216033	§ 16.3	9414044	§ 16.3
8736046	§ 26.5(b)(vi)	9217001	§ 6.7	9425030	§ 26.4(a)
8737090	§ 18.17	9220010	§ 12.1	9425032	§ 17.3(a)
8739055	§ 30.2(b)	9231047	§ 19.8	9428029	§ 16.5
8749085	§§ 26.4(f),	9233037	§ 19.8	9428030	§ 16.5
	26.5(b)(vi)	9237034	§ 5.5(e)	9429016	§ 20.8(a)
8802079	§ 26.4(f)	9237090	§ 26.4(f)	9434041	§ 6.2(b)
8814004	§ 26.4(g)	9241055	§§ 26.4(f),	9436002	§ 26.4(g)
8817039	§ 32.3		26.5(b)(v)	9438029	§ 31.2(d)
8818008	§ 32.3	9242002	§ 18.2(a)	9438030	§ 32.2(b)
8819034	§ 27.1(p)	9242035	§ 26.4(f)	9440001	§ 13.2
8820061	§ 26.4(f)	9242038	§ 31.2(b)	9441001	§ 26.5(d)
8820093	§ 19.8	9242039	§ 31.2(b)	9442013	§ 27.2(d)
8822065	§ 26.5(b)(vi)	9243008	§ 9.5	9448036	§ 19.6
8824018	§ 26.4(f)	9244003	§ 17.2	9450028	§ 27.1(g)
8826012	§ 30.5	9245031	§§ 31.1(d),	9451067	§ 11.4(d)
8833038	§ 32.3		31.2(a)	9506046	§ 31.3

TABLE OF IRS PRIVATE DETERMINATIONS CITED IN TEXT

Private Determination	Book Sections	Private Determination	Book Sections	Private Determination	Book Sections
9507037	§ 18.17	9550001	§§ 13.1, 26.4(g)	9651046	§ 26.4(g)
9516006	§ 17.1(a)			9651047	§§ 6.2(f), 26.5(g)
9522022	§ 30.6	9551009	§ 30.6		
9522039	§ 18.17	9603019	§ 29.2	9652026	§ 17.1(a)
9527031	§ 9.5	9608039	§§ 11.3(b), 32.2(a)	9703028	§ 30.2(d)
9527043	§ 30.1			9709014	§ 32.4
9530008	§ 30.6	9615030	§ 19.10	9710030	§ 6.2(a)
9530024	§ 6.3	9615045	§ 27.1(h)(i)	9715031	§§ 31.1(d), 32.4
9530032	§ 19.4	9619069	§ 27.1(j)(i)		
9530036	§ 30.6	9629030	§ 27.1(j)(i)	9731038	§ 6.1
9533015	§ 30.6	9631004	§ 5.5(a)	9732022	§ 15.2
9535023	§§ 26.4(b), 26.4(f), 27.2(b)	9633044	§ 26.4(g)	9732032	§ 26.5(a)
		9637050	§§ 31.1 (b), 32.3	9733015	§ 30.5
9535043	§ 11.2(b)	9637051	§ 31.5(b)	9738055	§ 30.6
9535050	§ 26.4(f)	9641011	§ 26.5(g)	9738056	§ 30.6
9539015	§ 26.4(f)	9645007	§ 22.1	9739043	§ 26.5(b)(iii)
9539016	§ 19.4(a)	9645017	§§ 31.2(d), 31.5(b)	9740032	§ 27.1(h)(i)
9548019	§ 30.6				

Index

INDEX

INDEX

INDEX